The Muslim Brotherhood and the West

The Muslim Brotherhood and the West

A History of Enmity and Engagement

MARTYN FRAMPTON

The Belknap Press of Harvard University Press

Cambridge, Massachusetts
London, England
2018

Library of Congress Cataloging-in-Publication Data

Names: Frampton, Martyn, author.
Title: The Muslim Brotherhood and the West : a history of enmity and
    engagement / Martyn Frampton.
Description: Cambridge, Massachusetts : The Belknap Press of Harvard
    University Press, 2018. | Includes bibliographical references and index.
Identifiers: LCCN 2017036659 | ISBN 9780674970700 (hardcover : alk.
    paper)
Subjects: LCSH: Ikhwåan al-Muslimåun. | Arab countries—Foreign
    relations—United States. | Arab countries—Foreign relations—Great
    Britain. | United States—Foreign relations—Arab countries. | Great
    Britain—Foreign relations—Arab countries. | Islam and politics.
Classification: LCC BP10.I385 F73 2018 | DDC 322.4 / 2—dc23
LC record available at https://lccn.loc.gov/2017036659

For Rose and Dylan

Contents

Note on Transliteration and Spelling

For Arabic terms, I have relied on a slightly modified version of the transliteration system recommended by the *International Journal of Middle East Studies*. This means that diacritics have not been used (though 'ayn and hamza have been preserved, except where hamza occurs at the start of the word).

For those names that enjoy a degree of familiarity in English (Gamal Abdel Nasser, and Hasan al-Banna), I have used the popularized versions rather than the transliterated so as to avoid confusion. Similarly, where an individual has an anglicized form of his or her name (such as Kemal el-Helbawy), I have kept their preferred version. In all cases too, where individuals were mentioned in American and British primary sources, I have reproduced the various spellings that appear in the original documents.

Introduction

I N THE SUMMER of 2013, Egyptian protestors took to the streets to voice their opposition to Muhammad Morsi, their country's first democratically elected president and a member of the Muslim Brotherhood. After massive demonstrations, the army intervened to remove Morsi from power. In the months leading up to that dramatic denouement, Egypt's president, and the movement to which he belonged, had been subject to widespread criticism. Many of the most poisonous accusations leveled against Morsi concerned the alleged relationship between the Muslim Brotherhood and the West.

One striking poster that appeared at anti-Morsi rallies, for example, referenced the title of a Hollywood movie, with the words "We know what you did last summer" superimposed over a picture of the American ambassador to Cairo, Anne Patterson, shaking hands with the leader of the Brotherhood, Muhammad Badi'e. The implication was clear: that Morsi had been elevated to power in 2012 mainly because of pressure and interference from the United States. Other, less imaginative banners included one that decried President Barack Obama for supporting a "fascist regime"; another that featured the composite image of "Obama bin Laden"; and a third, which carried Patterson's picture under the caustic headline "Kick This Bitch Out of Egypt." Such images and insults expressed the widespread belief that Washington had decisively embraced Morsi and the Brotherhood. This idea had gained widespread currency over

1

the previous two years among opponents of the Brothers. As early as July 2011, just a few months after the fall of President Hosni Mubarak, the American Embassy in Cairo reported that activists in the city's Tahrir Square believed the United States was "supporting the Muslim Brotherhood (MB) and wished to see a religious state in Egypt." Despite American protestations that this was not the case, officials remarked that the notion of a "special relationship" between the United States and the Brotherhood had become ingrained in certain quarters.[1]

Among the more voluble advocates of this idea was the vehemently anti-Brotherhood journalist-turned-politician Mustafa Bakri. In his book *The Army and the Ikhwan,* for instance, Bakri claimed that the United States had originally conspired with the Brotherhood to secure the downfall of Mubarak via secret meetings held in Qatar and Istanbul from 2002 onward. On Bakri's account, a deal was done by which the United States agreed to support the Brotherhood's ascent to power in return for a promise that the Egyptian-Israeli peace treaty would be respected. Further, Washington's decision to back the Brotherhood was said to be the first stage in a wider US plan to build a "new Middle East," in which existing states like Saudi Arabia, Syria, and of course Egypt would be broken up (Egypt into four parts). This would, it was said, allow the triumph of the Greater Israeli Zionist dream, in line with a secret plan that had been formulated by the academic Bernard Lewis and accepted by the US Congress in 1983.[2]

As conspiracies go, Bakri's ruminations painted quite a picture. But as outlandish as they may seem, such thinking was not uncommon.[3] It found parallel in the writings of people like Tawhid Magdi, whose sensationalist tome *Conspiracies of the Brotherhood: From the Files of the CIA and MI6—Top Secret* included everything from claims of a Brotherhood alliance with Adolf Hitler to the suggestion that the group was a tool of the US Central Intelligence Agency (CIA).[4] The July 2013 ouster of Morsi did nothing to lessen the pervasiveness of such theories. In December of that year, the secular liberal newspaper *al-Dustur* carried the front-page headline, "The Conspiracies of Washington with the Group of Treachery [the Brotherhood] to Assassinate al-Sissi [Morsi's successor as president]."[5] The same month, the British Embassy was forced to issue a statement denying that they were funding Brotherhood activists in the Nile Delta provinces of Menufiya and Sharqiya.[6] And at his retrial in August 2014, former Egyptian interior minister Habib el-Adly alleged that the United States had given training to the Brotherhood and other opposition groups in an effort to foment revolution as part of a "new Middle East plan."[7]

Clearly, the idea of secret ties between the Brotherhood and the Western powers has proven an enduring leitmotif of Egyptian politics. In part, this is because it taps into a vein of suspicion about Western intentions that has a long provenance within Arab nationalist discourse—although it might be added too that there is nothing exclusively Egyptian about this belief. A glance at the out-pourings of right-wing commentators like Frank Gaffney and websites like Frontpagemag and Breitbart demonstrates that similar assertions about the connection between the Muslim Brotherhood and the Obama administration enjoyed a constituency across the Atlantic.[8] It was one element within broader conspiracy theories about Obama that flourished on the alt-right and to some extent fueled the presidential campaign of Donald Trump.

The irony, meanwhile, is that Egypt's Islamists themselves adhere to a conspiracy-minded critique of US policy in the Middle East.[9] Washington's sup-port for both Israel and various authoritarian governments (not least in Cairo) has long been portrayed as part of a plot to control the region. After the overthrow of Morsi, it became an article of faith inside the Brotherhood that the United States had abandoned his "legitimate" government in favor of an accommodation with autocracy. Secretary of State John Kerry's 2013 com-ments that the Egyptian army had been "restoring democracy" when it opted to remove Morsi were seen as particularly telling in this regard.[10] In one of its weekly bulletins to supporters, the Brotherhood condemned Western "hypoc-risy" and "complicity" in the crackdown against the group.[11] In November 2013, 'Amr Darrag, one of the few leaders of the group to have avoided arrest, offered a withering assessment of Kerry and American policy more generally, declaring that it had become "absolutely clear" that Washington had "supported the coup from the first moment" and was "behind the attempts to abort the Arab Spring in all countries that have gone that route."[12] As can be seen, the US government has frequently found itself damned on all sides.

Accounts like these are invariably long on lurid assertion and somewhat shorter on hard evidence. Yet, as with many conspiracy theories, they are built on certain kernels of truth: past moments when there have been contacts between the West and the Muslim Brothers. Most of these encounters took place behind closed doors, away from public view. Inevitably, this encouraged distortion, ex-aggeration, and outright falsification. The truth of the actual relationship be-tween the Muslim Brotherhood and the West has been obscured. It is against this backdrop that this book offers the first sustained and comprehensive aca-demic analysis of that relationship, charting its evolution from the founding of the group in 1928 to the eve of the revolt against Hosni Mubarak in 2011.

To be clear, this is not an account of Egypt's experience of the Arab Spring, nor of the ties between the Brotherhood and the Western powers after 2011. Instead, the aim here is to historicize more contemporary debates: to examine the trajectory of a relationship that has existed, for the most part, in the shadows.

Not only is this story crucial for understanding recent developments in Egypt but also it sheds new light on the broader history of Western engagement with the Middle East during the second half of the twentieth century and the first decade of the twenty-first. Furthermore, this subject is crucial for understanding the history of the Brotherhood itself and the way in which the group views the world. Over the last ninety years, the West—both as a concept and as a political reality—has been a critical point of reference for the Brotherhood and its leaders. It is no exaggeration to say that absent the West, the group would not exist. As the essential Other, it has defined the Brotherhood and the way in which it has understood its sociopolitical mission. The idea of the West and a vision of what it represents sit at the very center of the group's ideology. Consequently, changes and continuities in the Brotherhood's thinking on this issue reveal much about the broader evolution of the group.

DESPITE ITS IMPORTANCE, the history of the relationship between the Muslim Brotherhood and the West has received only marginal attention from scholars. Elements have been touched on—yet they comprise only fragments and are scattered across a range of historiographical fields.[13] The foremost academic treatments of the Brotherhood by scholars like Brynjar Lia, Richard P. Mitchell, Carrie Wickham, Hazem Kandil, and Alison Pargeter reflect on the issue only in passing.[14] Others have alluded to the Brotherhood's contacts with the West within studies that consider ties between the Western governments and Islamism more broadly. In particular, there has been some focus on the extent to which the British and the Americans considered allying with the advocates of conservative Islamic ideals (including the Muslim Brotherhood), either to preserve national interests or during the Cold War.[15] Few doubt that the apotheosis of this outlook came after 1979, with the decision of the United States to offer covert support to the "mujahideen" against the Soviet Union in the wake of the latter's invasion of Afghanistan. The course of what followed is now well-known (and is a story invariably told to emphasize the dangers of shortsighted political expediency and its potential for blowback). Western policy toward Afghanistan during the 1980s is seen as symptomatic of wider efforts to promote militant forms of Islam as an alternative to communism.[16]

To imagine a grand strategic conspiracy on the part of the West to harness Islamism against the dangers of Arab nationalism and communism is to overstate the case. Still, it is evident that an impulse for engaging with a group like the Brotherhood had a long prehistory. This impulse was intertwined with attempts to secure Western influence amid "great power" and imperial competition going back to the nineteenth century. In this context, it is worth noting that the subject of the present book resonates with work by scholars of empire, such as Frances Robinson and John Ferris, who examine earlier British interactions with Islam. Fears of an Islamic "menace"—based on the underlying unity that Muslims were thought to possess—shaped British perceptions of (first) the subcontinent and (then) the Middle East.[17] To some extent, an analysis of Western relations with the Brotherhood represents an extended case study on a related theme and is consonant with calls for historians to consider the "official mind" of what policy makers thought about Islam. In this instance, the focus is on one particularly important Islamic movement.[18] British reflections on the Brotherhood reveal much about their attempt to try to preserve their position in Egypt and the Middle East in the period that straddled the Second World War during the final phase of empire.

Moreover, by extending the frame of analysis to consider the rise of American power in the region, this book identifies continuities (and some differences) in outlook between London and Washington, as the latter took on the former's mantle of self-proclaimed global hegemon. In this regard, the book's theme intersects with those works that have reflected on the Anglo-American approach to the Middle East in general, and those that have examined the United States' post-1945 relationship with Egypt in particular.[19] More broadly, it contributes to an understanding of the ideas shaping US foreign policy over the last seventy years; it follows in the vein of recent invaluable studies discussing the role and place of religion in policy formation; and it builds on the efforts of those who have analyzed how American diplomats "imagined" the Middle East in the 1950s and 1960s.[20]

Since the late 1970s, scholars have drawn attention to more contemporary Western views of Islamism amid a surge in interest driven initially by the Iranian revolution.[21] This event has rightly been seen as marking a critical caesura in the American mind-set about Islamism and Islam in general.[22] The end of the Cold War further stimulated thinking on the subject of Islamism. After 1989, much analysis of groups like the Muslim Brotherhood turned on the question of whether or not they were committed to democracy and the extent to which they were implicated in violent militancy. Events in Algeria gave a decisive fillip and focus to these discussions, which tended to polarize along "accommodationist" and "confrontationalist" axes. The debate was also influenced by the corresponding trajectory of political parties connected to the Brotherhood in countries like Jordan, Sudan, and of course Egypt.[23]

As more recent work has shown, though, Western governments failed to develop truly coherent policies for dealing with "participatory" Islamist movements of the Brotherhood's ilk. Rather, positions evolved in an ad hoc manner and varied from place to place. Moments of engagement were followed by, or even coexisted with, a preference for marginalization.[24] The following situates these latest developments within their wider historical context—to construct a fuller history of relations between the Brotherhood and the West and to do so from both sides. A core premise is that it is vital to understand not just how Western officials have viewed the Brotherhood but also to examine the Brotherhood's perception of the West. The latter has proven to be a less worn path for scholars, yet it reveals something fundamental about the nature of the group.[25]

To date there has been no effort to write a single-volume comprehensive history of the relationship between the Muslim Brotherhood and the West. This book seeks to fill that gap. The hope is that it can add something to the best histories of the Brotherhood that have been produced over the last half century, while deepening our understanding of Western foreign policy in the Middle East more generally.

THIS BOOK IS not an attempt to rewrite the organizational evolution of the Brotherhood. Nor is it an examination of the social dimensions of the group or of the role played by, say, certain conceptions of gender identity. The focus here is primarily political and geopolitical. The book also concentrates largely on the Egyptian Brotherhood. Yet, in order to understand Western views of that movement and the phenomenon of Islamism more widely, it takes a broader perspective where necessary. There is therefore some consideration of the other incarnations of the Brotherhood elsewhere in the region. The later chapters reflect, too, on the arrival of the Brothers in the West and the evolution of looser, more informal networks.[26]

It should also be made clear that in this book, the term *the West* is for the most part taken to mean the United States and the United Kingdom. This is for two reasons: first, these were the external powers that dominated Egypt during the course of the twentieth century; and second, these were the countries that the Brotherhood generally imagined when talking about the West, references to

"Europeans" notwithstanding. Of course, the Brothers did not lack for an awareness of the French role in North Africa and the eastern Mediterranean—and indeed in the period after World War II, this loomed especially large in their
minds. Nonetheless, I would argue that within the mental landscape of the
Brotherhood, the French were subsumed into an Anglocentric vision, in the same
manner as were the Soviets.

To tell this story, I have drawn on a range of sources, including almost every
British and American diplomatic or intelligence document pertaining to the
Brotherhood that has been declassified for public viewing. In addition, I utilized the Wikileaks cables, which give an insight into more contemporary US
views of the Brothers across the Middle East. This has allowed me to understand in fine detail changing Western perspectives on the group. In parallel with
this, I used Brotherhood publications in both Arabic and English—memoirs,
pamphlets, and newspaper articles—gathered in London and Cairo, to build a
thorough picture of how the movement has seen the West. This has been supple-
mented by a smattering of interviews with Brotherhood figures (such as their
London spokesman Abdullah al-Haddad) and former leaders of the group (such as
Kemal el-Helbawy).[27]

The book is divided into two parts, each with four chapters, that proceed
chronologically. Part One covers the era of British hegemony over Egypt (and
the Middle East). It begins with the origins of the Brotherhood and examines,
in particular, the importance of the West as an idea and a reality with which
the founder, Hasan al-Banna, was in dialogue. Consideration is given to the first
encounters between the Brothers and Western officials, as well as the growing
militancy of the group and its eventual confrontation with both the local authorities and the British presence in Egypt. The relationship between the Brotherhood
and the West was a critical part of the political equation in the period leading up
to and beyond the July 1952 "revolution," when the Free Officers seized power
in Cairo under the direction of Gamal Abdel Nasser. This episode marked the
beginning of the end for British influence in Egypt. In the new dispensation, it
was the United States that emerged as the major external (and Western) power
that held sway over Cairo.

Part Two of the book examines the way in which relations between the Brotherhood and the West evolved in the age of American ascendancy. Initially,
Egyptian politics continued to be dominated by the interplay of a triangle of
forces, which were themselves internally divided: the regime (split between
Nasser and the titular head of the revolution, Muhammad Naguib); the West
(with the British and Americans in uneasy collaboration); and the Brotherhood

(itself suffering from factional rivalry). By the end of 1954, each of these conflicts had been effectively resolved. The Brotherhood now entered a long recession, having been crushed by Nasser. But from 1970, it made its slow return to public life and once more became an important part of the Egyptian political landscape. In this context, Western attention focused again on the Brotherhood, and there were renewed efforts to comprehend its character. This shift occurred against the backdrop of a broader Islamic "resurgence," and new modes of analysis developed for thinking about the group. Increasingly, assessments dwell on the nature and prospects of "fundamentalism." The geopolitical revolution of 1989–1991 and then the events of 11 September 2001 gave new salience and urgency to these debates. The Brothers came to be recognized as a major force not only in Egypt but also across the region and among Muslim communities in the West. For its part, meanwhile, the Brotherhood continued to see "the West" as a crucial—almost wholly deleterious—influence on the Muslim world. It is with this interplay of considerations that the book concludes by analyzing the relationship between the Brotherhood and the West on the eve of the Arab Spring.

Relations between the Muslim Brotherhood and the West have generated countless myths. In telling this story in an empirical fashion, I hope to offer a new perspective on the history of the Brothers as well as on Western foreign policy making in the Middle East.

PART **I**

In the Shadow of Empire

One   Origins and First Encounters

1928–1939

THE SOCIETY OF the Muslim Brothers—the Muslim Brotherhood (al-Ikhwan al-Muslimun, hereafter the Ikhwan)—was created in March 1928 by Hasan al-Banna, a twenty-one-year-old Egyptian schoolteacher in the provincial city of Ismailia.[1] In his later memoirs,[2] al-Banna recalled how six men came to swear allegiance to him, declaring, "We are sick of this life: a life of shame and shackles. Here you see that the Muslim Arabs have no chance of status or respect in this country. . . . We do not see the way to work as you see it, or know the path to serve the country and the religion and the nation as you do. All we want now is to offer to you what we possess so that we are exonerated in front of God. You are in charge of it and what we do." Inspired by this reverent address, al-Banna claims that he had no choice but to accept the commission. Each man present then pledged to be a "soldier" in the service of the "Islamic *Da'wa*" and took an oath of fealty to work and struggle in the path of God. Finally, al-Banna announced with an appropriate sense of drama, "We are brothers in the service of Islam and we are, therefore, the Muslim Brothers."[3]

A World Turned Upside Down—and under British Control

Whether apocryphal or not, this quasi-official account of the Brotherhood's creation reveals much about the impulses that drove the movement from the start. It is striking that in al-Banna's narrative, his petitioners referred directly to the contemporary sociopolitical context. They expressed their anger at their "life of shame and shackles"; of the fact that Muslims had "no chance of status or respect" in their own country; of their desire to serve "the religion and the nation." Here, the sacred mingled with the problems of the temporal world. At the heart of the latter was the sense that Egyptians did not believe themselves to be in control of their own country. The words of the Ikhwan's putative founding declaration thus betrayed a strongly held desire for national self-fulfillment.

At first glance, such sentiments might seem strange. A month earlier, in February 1928, Egypt had marked six years of formal "independence." And yet, one did not need to delve deep beneath the surface to expose the emptiness of that phrase. The country had been occupied by British troops for nearly fifty years. Since 1882, various forms of Egyptian self-government had coexisted with underlying British preeminence. The late nineteenth century, for instance, had seen the continuation of the Khedival system, but within constraints set by the guiding influence and "advice" of a British consul general. This "veiled protectorate," under Lord Cromer and his successors, had served the British well down to the First World War. Then, confronted with the awkward legal fact that the Ottoman Empire—of which Egypt was still nominally a part—had taken up arms against Britain and her allies, the decision was made to drop the veil. Egypt now became a formal protectorate and Britain's local representative was transformed into a high commissioner. This naked display of British authority, however, served only to provide a focus for local discontent, which had been temporarily suppressed but also exacerbated by the war. Consequently, in 1919, the British faced a great popular uprising, and the emergence of the "Wafd," a mass nationalist party demanding Egyptian self-determination.[4]

British officials and statesmen subsequently scrambled to find a new dispensation that might once more guarantee their de facto supremacy beneath a cloak of self-rule. It was in this context that London's man in Cairo, the general turned high commissioner, Edmund Allenby, declared Egypt independent *on its behalf* (a typically British formulation) as part of a process designed to preserve London's key interests. Thereafter, despite the issuing of a constitution that provided for Egyptian self-government through a king (Fu'ad I) and parliament, there was little doubt where real authority lay. The Egyptian administrative apparatus was permeated by British officials whose first loyalty was to London rather than their nominal superiors; foreigners resident in Egypt enjoyed exemption from the local legal system; the Egyptian army, such as it was, remained under the control of a British senior officer (the sirdar); and force majeure was guaranteed by numerous detachments of the British army in situ across the country—not least in Cairo, Alexandria, and on the banks of the Suez Canal.[5]

As a result, political life in "post-independence" Egypt was dominated by an ongoing power struggle between the "three-legged stool" of competing forces: the king, the Wafd, and the British Residency.[6] In the final analysis, it was the voice of the latter that almost always proved decisive (though as James Whidden has demonstrated, this is not to deny the agency of the other parties and the intensity of their conflict over the meaning of *modernity* in Egypt).[7] The truth of this was made plain as early as 1924, when, following the assassination of the sirdar, Sir Lee Stack, Allenby effectively forced the resignation of the Wafdist prime minister and great nationalist hero, Saʿd Zaghlul. Just ten months earlier, Zaghlul had led his party to an overwhelming victory in the country's first general elections, standing on a platform that called for complete independence. His brusque treatment at the hands of the high commissioner offered categorical proof, were any needed, as to who held the whip hand in Egyptian politics. (Indeed, London seems to have been somewhat unnerved by so overt a demonstration of power and soon recalled Allenby).[8] Periodically thereafter, this truth was reemphasized by successive high commissioners. Lord Lloyd (in office 1925–1929), for instance, became notorious for his penchant for summoning gunships to Alexandria to impress his authority on the Egyptian government. Against this backdrop, it was clear that Egypt remained a critical part of Britain's "undeclared empire" in the Middle East.[9]

Hasan al-Banna seems to have been keenly aware of such political realities. In his memoirs, he claimed to have participated, while still at school, in the 1919 "revolution." As a thirteen-year-old living in the provincial city of Damanhur in the Nile delta (where he was attending a teacher training institute), his experience was surely limited. Nevertheless, this episode appears to have been a crucial formative moment for al-Banna, as for so many others of his generation. Al-Banna later asserted that despite their youth, he and his classmates joined in strikes and protests and listened to speeches about the national question. He sought to capture the spirit of the moment, reflecting, "I still see before my eyes the scene of university demonstrations and the general strike, in which the whole country was organised from the first to the last." This sense of national unity made a deep impression on al-Banna. He recalled the songs that were sung by the anti-British protestors, which spoke of a love of country; he remembered too the sight of the British soldiers who descended on their village in order to restore order. And his experiences convinced him that "national service was a jihad from which there was no evasion."[10]

In the following period, al-Banna seems to have become ever more conscious of the wider social and political picture in Egypt—especially after he arrived in Cairo for the first time in 1923, to attend the Dar al-'Ulum teacher training college. At the time, the capital was well on the way to becoming a megacity.[11] It threw into stark relief all the features of Egypt's rapidly changing society. Since the late nineteenth century, the country had been exposed to deep commercial and financial penetration, which locked Egypt into a position of dependency in this first era of globalization. Foreign ownership dominated the local economy. And the country's reliance on the cotton trade left it open to the vicissitudes of the international markets. At the same time, Egypt experienced a great wave of modernization. New roads, railways, canals, and telegraphs crisscrossed the country. Population growth exploded as a result of developments in food production as well as medical and hygiene advances. One result of this was increasing landlessness, which in turn fueled rapid urbanization. New urban and professional classes emerged and society became more complex. Old sociocultural practices were challenged and displaced.[12] This was the world that Hasan al-Banna saw around him in Cairo—an evolving melting pot and cosmopolitan environment described by the great Egyptian novelists of the era such as Tawfiq al-Hakim and Naguib Mahfuz.[13]

Evidently, the young al-Banna was profoundly struck—and disturbed—by a sense of the world turned upside down. Already in his youth, he had shown a sincere interest in questions of moral probity. While at preparatory school (aged roughly twelve to thirteen), al-Banna became president of his own "Moral Ethics Association."[14] In his memoirs, he also recounted a story in which he was shocked by the sight of a wooden statue depicting a naked man that was hanging from the mast of a boat on the Nile, in his small village of Mahmudiyya. Al-Banna was particularly worried by the thought that this image might be seen by women and young girls collecting water from the river. He therefore reported the owner to the authorities, who ordered the statue to be removed. Subsequently, the young man's burgeoning interest in public morality led him to become involved with an "Association for Preventing the Forbidden," whose members took it upon themselves to write letters to people judged lax in their Islamic observance.[15]

In short, it seems clear that al-Banna was already a committed and active moralist long before he arrived in Egypt's capital. What he found in Cairo, though, took his prudery to a new level. According to his memoirs, al-Banna was appalled by the "degeneracy and remoteness from Islamic morals" that he found "in many places." Newspapers, he observed with evident horror, were publishing things "incompatible" with religious teachings. More generally, it seemed to him that a "wave of atheism and indecency" had engulfed Egypt since the First World War. Operating under the pretext of calls for intellectual or personal freedom, this had brought a decay of opinions, principles, and morals and weakened the hold of religion, especially among the youth. Egyptians, al-Banna declared, were standing "in the darkness of ignorance"; the young and the educated were lost in the "desert of bewilderment and doubt."[16]

Such concerns were amplified by al-Banna's perception that the 1924 abolition of the caliphate by Turkish nationalist leader Mustafa Kemal had unleashed a wider intellectual-cum-moral crisis. Though this post had long been of largely symbolic, rather than direct, political importance, many reacted with dismay to the removal of the formal head of the Islamic world. In Cairo, there was a heated debate over how to respond. At one end of the spectrum were men like the scholar 'Ali 'Abd al-Raziq, who in a radical work (*Islam and the Origins of Government*) sought to challenge the whole concept of the caliphate as a governing institution. Such views, though, were very much in a minority and judged heretical by most; in 1925 al-Raziq was expelled from his post at the famous Islamic seminary, al-Azhar. An entirely different conclusion was reached by those like Rashid Rida, who called for the restoration of the caliphate under new leadership. Al-Banna, who was close to Rida (see below), was part of these debates, reflecting on the legitimacy of the religiopolitical framework under which he lived. Significantly, in his memoirs he connected the Kemalist revolution in Turkey with the moral decline he perceived around him in Cairo.[17]

Al-Banna's obvious unhappiness at that decline was exacerbated further by his belief that much of what he saw was of foreign origin. "My people," he wrote, "by virtue of political developments through which they navigate, the social influences which they face, and the effect of Western civilization, with its European characteristics and materialist philosophy and Frankish customs—are far from the purposes of their religion." Al-Banna felt that the social life of the Egyptian nation was swinging between Islam on the one hand and the cultural effects of a "violent Western invasion" on the other. In his mind, the "camp of atheism and indecency" seemed only to grow stronger, while that of Islam continued to shrink. The religious establishment centered on al-Azhar was, he concluded, failing to respond effectively to the challenges posed by "atheists and the debauched." Deeply troubled, al-Banna resolved that something had to be done.[18]

However, an answer to the question of exactly what to do seems not to have been fully formed in his mind when the time came for al-Banna to graduate from the Dar al-'Ulum in 1927. True, he had begun to give lectures and write articles about the state of the world, but the scope of this activity barely seemed commensurate with the scale of the crisis that he saw around him. At a personal level, too, al-Banna now faced a choice—between further study, possibly abroad, or entering government service. He opted for the latter, gaining a job as a teacher in a government primary school in Ismailia—an appointment he did not welcome initially given that he knew nothing about the city. After a failed attempt to have his posting changed, though, he accepted the commission and left Cairo in September 1927. It would prove a momentous decision.

Ismailia, situated on the banks of the Suez Canal, was home to the headquarters of the eponymous company that operated the waterway. In his memoirs, al-Banna recorded his immediate shock at the disparity he witnessed between the lifestyles of Ismailia's native population and the Suez Canal Company's French and British administrators. He quickly became aware that the city "was dominated by the European tendency," surrounded as it was by a British military camp to the west and the "administrative colony" of the Canal Company to the east. Most of Ismailia's inhabitants worked in one of these two places and were therefore brought into close contact with a European way of life. The "English camp," al-Banna averred, by dint of its overwhelming strength and authority, stirred "jealous grief and regret" in the soul of every citizen who was forced to consider the "hateful occupation." The Canal Company, meanwhile, was said to oppress its Egyptian workers, even as it honored the foreigners who acted as if they were the real rulers of the country. In al-Banna's view, Ismailia was defined by this stark division. The foreigners lived in luxury homes in a special neighborhood—a sight that contrasted sharply with the poor and small houses of the Egyptians. Even the street signs of the city, he observed, were written in the language of the "economic occupation," English.[19]

While in Cairo, it seems that al-Banna already had grasped the truth of Britain's neo-imperial hold over Egypt. But it was his time in Ismailia that confirmed him in his convictions. The city made manifest the reality of Britain's enduring military presence, the economic predominance of Western interests, and Egypt's growing vulnerability to European cultural penetration. Al-Banna linked all of this to the moral decline that he had diagnosed with such acuity during his time in the capital. His conclusion was that Egypt was facing a major crisis. Crucially, however, he believed all was not lost. He felt that an Islamic spirit remained among the people. What was required was someone who would foster that spirit and chart a path toward revival; it was this that drove him to establish a "general Islamic call founded on knowledge and education and jihad."[20] This was the message that al-Banna began to propagate in lectures and impromptu sermons around Ismailia. He found there a ready audience and it was this evangelism that, as described earlier, led to the creation of the Muslim Brotherhood.[21]

East versus West

In the years that immediately followed, al-Banna expanded on his initial insights to construct a distinctive ideology that framed the activity of his Brotherhood, or Ikhwan. The essence of that worldview can be gleaned from close analysis of the various "letters" that he composed, which became compulsory reading for members of the movement. What these reveal is that when al-Banna looked at the world, he conceived of it as divided between two broad civilizational currents: "East" and "West." At the heart of the former sat Islam—often used in synonymous fashion for the East, and counterpoised to a West that he identified primarily with Europe. (In so doing, al-Banna reflected the relatively limited interaction between the United States and the broader Middle East prior to the Second World War; America during the 1930s featured little on his radar. Equally, as Mitchell noted, for al-Banna "the West" also encompassed the Soviet Union.)[22]

Al-Banna believed that it was possible to identify the life cycle of these broad civilizations: they experienced periods of youth and old age, health and sickness. Moreover, he considered that the vitality of a civilization at any given moment was determined by the potency of its spirit: "The cause of the weakness of nations and the humiliations of peoples is the feebleness of their spirits," he wrote.[23] He saw the spirit, or morality, as *the* key agent of history. God, al-Banna stated, had made "changes in the affairs of the nations dependent on change in their morals and reform of their souls."[24] Or, as one of his earliest followers, Muhammad 'Abd al-Khaliq, put it, the "health" of any civilization was circumscribed not by what it produced in material terms but by its "spirit"; and that spirit was in turn defined by the ideas, values, and principles that existed within the souls of the people.[25]

Al-Banna acknowledged that the contemporary Eastern world was weak in "material" terms. Yet even more important in his view was the diminution of its "spiritual strength." He deemed the former to be the inevitable consequence of the latter. Conversely, the path to renewed Islamic strength was said to run through a process of moral rectification.[26] To al-Banna's mind, the people of the East were squandering the "amazing spiritual quality" that lay latent within their "souls."[27]

Of critical importance here was the stark juxtaposition that al-Banna and his supporters drew between a "purely materialistic West" and an inherently more "spiritual" East.[28] During the previous half century, such notions had been commonplace even among those Muslim intellectuals who sought to emulate the West.[29] Indeed, perceptions of a more "spiritual" East, as set against the more rational and materialistic West, were prominent within both European and Muslim cultures.[30] In modified form, of course, views of this kind were fundamental to "orientalist" imaginings of the East. Therein, Eastern spiritualism became identified with sensuality and decadence, and was compared unfavorably with the rational West. To some extent, al-Banna took the construction of the colonial world's "self"—as a land of order, reason, and power—and subverted it, as a means of reempowerment.[31] That imperial "self" had been deployed, particularly in Egypt, to justify the British presence after 1882, with officials emphasizing their commitment to moral regeneration, self-reliance, probity, and virtue. Against this, they "imagined" the lazy, childlike, corrupt, and degenerate natives.[32] Al-Banna effectively inverted this schema. Many of the things that made for Eastern corruption in orientalist renderings—notably their romantic spirituality and religious predisposition—were appropriated as a source of concealed strength. By contrast, the material power of the West was interpreted as masking a spiritual void. According to 'Abd al-Khaliq, Western civilization was defined by its total exclusion of religion from public life and the pervasiveness of personal, material considerations. It made no provision, he claimed, for spirituality and it was this that explained *its* moral corruption and sexual degeneracy.[33] Furthermore, it was assumed that this decadence ensured Western power was inherently brittle and might yet be overcome.

East and West, al-Banna surmised, were locked in a deep-rooted existential struggle, the contours of which explained the arc of history. Hazem Kandil has recently done much to emphasize the importance of that historical understanding in cementing the Brotherhood's ideology.[34] The first tract ever produced by al-Banna, *Between Yesterday and Today*, offered a clear example of his thinking on the issue. Therein he presented a "decline and fall" story of Islamic history, from the high point of the Prophet Muhammad and his immediate successors, down to the corrupt present day. The original Islamic state that the Prophet founded was judged to be the embodiment of divine unity made real on earth; it was this that explained its "miraculous" success. Al-Banna repeatedly highlighted the experience of the "righteous predecessors" (*al-Salaf al-Salih*, the phrase that gives rise to the Salafi phenomenon), as representing a golden age of moral and political fulfillment.[35] On this reading, it was the strength of faith shown by the first Muslims that allowed them to overcome their enemies, including "guileful Judaism," the Christians, and the polytheists. Al-Banna believed that subsequent generations had gradually abandoned a true understanding of Islam, becoming debased, divided, and weak. As a result of this decay, the Muslims had suffered major defeats. The first of these had come at the hands of the Crusaders; another was inflicted by the Mongols. The shock of these reverses had served briefly to concentrate Muslim minds and they were thus followed by a period of "revival," begun (suggestively no doubt in al-Banna's mind) in Egypt under Salah al-Din, who had been able to restore the caliphate. This, however, had proven but a short-term respite. More recently—and more seriously—the Islamic world had succumbed to a fresh assault from Western imperialist powers and Zionism.[36]

In seeking to elucidate this narrative further, al-Banna argued that Europe had been empowered by first the Renaissance (which he attributed to their "contact with the superior culture of Islam") and then the Reformation. The latter, he said, had allowed Europe to escape from the dead hand of Christianity and to excel in scientific and material development. Invention and discovery had allowed for machine production and the rise of industrial society. The pope had been "confined to the Vatican" and "Europe retained its Christianity only as a historical heirloom" (though paradoxically, as shall be seen, he was convinced that Europe retained a "Crusader-ist" impulse). As a consequence, al-Banna affirmed, the pendulum of world history had swung: where once the lands of Islam had been able to turn back and defeat the Western threat, they themselves had grown weaker and now yielded to the greater strength of their enemies; where once the "leadership of the world" had been "in the hands of the East entirely," now it had been inherited by the West—while the East had fallen "into its long sleep."[37]

In al-Banna's assessment, Europe had for centuries been "aiming with a single purpose at the dismemberment of the Islamic state," against which it had waged a "ruthless war."[38] This assumption of perpetual Western antagonism for Islam became an integral part of the Brotherhood's belief system. The senior

Brotherhood leader, Mahmud Abu al-Saʿud, for instance, later declared that the Allies had deliberately divided the Islamic world and carved up the Middle East in the aftermath of the First World War, when the British applied the terms of the secret Sykes-Picot treaty. According to al-Saʿud, under the terms of this agreement, Egypt had been handed over to the British Empire and what followed was an occupation that was both physical and psychocultural.[39] As far as the Brotherhood was concerned, Egypt and the wider East were suffering from a "disease," the "symptoms" of which could be seen across the political, economic, social, juridical, and intellectual spheres.[40] The "enemies of Islam," al-Banna insisted, had persistently tried to infect them with such germs; by his reckoning, the modern world seemed to reflect their success.[41]

Secularization was viewed as the foremost manifestation of a cultural assault, deliberately launched by the West on the East, of which the ultimate aim was the destruction of Islam. Indeed, al-Banna accredited it with being perhaps the most insidious and devastating weapon ever devised by Europeans—a potentially mortal thrust to the heart of the Islamic faith (and one, he argued, that was far more deadly than military campaigns). He saw in secularism a challenge to the core Islamic ideal of *tawhid*—the unity of life that reflected the nature of the divine.[42] Looking around him, al-Banna observed what he judged to be the results of the secularist onslaught: apostasy, licentiousness, individualism, and usury. He opined that these were the sins of Europe transported to the heart of the Muslim world. The "Europeans," he averred, had "worked assiduously to enable the tide of this materialistic life, with its corrupting traits and its murderous germs, to overwhelm all the Islamic lands." They had imported "their half-naked women into these regions, together with their liquors, their theatres, their dance halls, their amusements, their stories, their newspapers, their novels, their whims, their silly games, and their vices." According to al-Banna, the Europeans had created a "frivolous, strident world, reeking with sin and redolent with vice."[43]

Equally, though, he believed that Muslims themselves were guilty for having allowed all this to happen. Al-Banna felt that their ignorance of the true comprehensive nature of Islam had left them vulnerable to the temptations of materialism and secularism, as purveyed by a "drastic, well-organized social campaign" to undermine Islam. Muslim "ignorance of the true meaning of their religion" had exposed them to the West's siren call.[44] In particular, al-Banna excoriated the upper classes and those of "rank and authority" for their tendency to "regard as sacred anything Western." Their "imitation of the West," he said, had allowed the "viper's venom" to creep "insidiously into their affairs, poisoning their blood and sullying the purity of their well-being."[45]

Still, al-Banna thought that all was not lost. For against the backdrop of this darkly pessimistic picture, he offered a "cure"—a message of redemption. To reverse their enfeeblement, al-Banna urged Muslims to return to the "path of truth"—Islam, conceived as a "comprehensive order" and a complete guide to life, applicable in all times and places.[46] In a famous passage, he described Islam as "creed as well as worship, homeland and race, religion and state (din wa dawla), spiritualism and work, Qur'an and sword."[47] The Qur'an was said to include all the "fundamentals" that mankind required, something that had been recognized by the first Muslims. Contemporary generations, al-Banna argued, should reembrace Islam, properly understood. "This umma [the Islamic nation] will prosper," he insisted, "only through the means by which it prospered in its beginnings."[48] "We must understand Islam," he declared, "as the Companions [of the Prophet] and the followers among the righteous predecessors, understood it."[49] It was for this reason that Hasan al-Banna's brother, Gamal, later described the Ikhwan as being of "Salafi frame and Sufi passion."[50] What was required, according to Hasan, was the "reawakening" of the people, bringing them to accept the truth that Islam was "a perfect system of social organization" that encompassed "all the affairs of life."[51]

The Muslim Brotherhood was therefore created for this purpose: to engage in da'wa, the call of Muslims back to the true form of their faith, so that they might flourish in the world once again. As al-Banna told his followers, he imagined the group as "a Salafi call (da'wa salafiyya) . . . a Sunni order . . . a Sufi reality . . . a political organization . . . a sporting group . . . a cultural, scientific association . . . an economic company . . . and a social ideology."[52] He believed that only Islam could "supply the renascent nation with its needs."[53] And hence, the job of the Ikhwan was to "work so that God may restore health and youth" to the Islamic nation and the East.[54]

Al-Banna took it for granted that the "failure of the West" was imminent, given its inability to provide for mankind's essential nature. He thought humanity had "become tired of purely materialistic conditions" and desired "some spiritual comfort," proclaiming that the only place this could be found was in the "perfection" of Islam.[55] Western civilization, al-Banna stated in 1936, had achieved brilliance "by virtue of its scientific perfection," but was "now bankrupt and in decline." "Its foundations," he contended, were

crumbling, and its institutions and guiding principles are falling apart. Its political foundations are being destroyed by dictatorships, and its economic foundations are being swept away by crises. The millions of its wretched unemployed and

hungry offer their testimony against it, while its social foundations are being
undermined by deviant ideologies and revolutions. . . . Their congresses are failures,
their treaties are broken, and their covenants torn to pieces: their League of Nations
is a phantasm, possessing neither spirit nor influence, while their strong men, along
with other things, are overthrowing its covenant of peace and security.[56]

Such words underlined both al-Banna's pessimism about the West and the extent to which he was very much a man of his time, keenly aware of the problems of the mid-1930s: the global depression and mass unemployment; the rise
of authoritarianism in both fascist and communist form; and the deterioration
and collapse of international order and the undermining of the League of
Nations, as demonstrated most spectacularly by Benito Mussolini's invasion
of Abyssinia.

At the same time, al-Banna was clearly influenced by an earlier generation of
Islamic intellectuals and debates that had been under way since the late nineteenth century. As Albert Hourani described, this era saw various writers and
thinkers tackle the question of how Muslims might respond to the realities of
Western power and increasingly rapid socioeconomic change. Jamal al-Din al-
Afghani (1839–1896) is invariably identified as the critical foundational figure
in this regard. His appeals to pan-Islamic solidarity as the best means by which
to resist the seemingly inexorable encroachment of the West served as a catalyst
for others.[57] Al-Afghani's ideas were taken on and developed in different directions by his disciples. For present purposes, the most significant connection he
made was with the Egyptian scholar Muhammad 'Abduh (1849–1905). The latter,
briefly exiled by the British after their occupation of his country in 1882, gave
greater intellectual and theological substance to al-Afghani's insights. 'Abduh,
who became grand mufti of Egypt, was a firm believer in the importance of
reason, and came to focus principally on the need for religious reform and
education.[58] Like al-Afghani, he also served to inspire others, not least the aforementioned Rashid Rida (1865–1935), a Syrian-born scholar who had moved to
Cairo in 1897. Rida, who wrote a biography of 'Abduh, devoted himself to the
further clarification of what he considered to be his mentor's purposes. In particular, Rida echoed 'Abduh in calling for a return to the spirit of the first generations of Muslims. Yet whereas his teacher had taken a fairly open view of who
might be included within that frame of reference, Rida narrowed the focus,
identifying the Prophet and the first four "rightly-guided Caliphs" as the only
people to have truly followed the right path. For this reason, he is often seen as

one of the fathers of the modern Salafist movement, whose ideas were taken on by others, including, of course, al-Banna.[59]

Irrespective of their differences, however, what these thinkers shared was a perception of a world in flux in which Islam faced serious, indeed, existential problems—many of which emanated from the West. These were the debates to which al-Banna had been drawn, especially after his arrival in Cairo. It was there that he joined the Salafiyya Library and reading circle associated with men like Rida and Sayyid Muhib Khatib al-Din.[60] Moreover, through his studies at the Dar al-'Ulum, it seems probable that al-Banna was exposed (if he had not been already) to the thinking of 'Abduh. As Hilary Kalmbach has explained, the latter had briefly served as a teacher at the Dar between 1877 and 1879. Though al-Banna would not attend the institution for another forty years, 'Abduh's influence in all likelihood endured—not only because of his stature as a scholar but also because the graduates of the Dar frequently went on to become faculty, teaching the works that they themselves had been taught.[61]

In later years, al-Banna and his followers would attempt to identify themselves explicitly with the kind of intellectual lineage described above. In Brotherhood terminology, Jamal al-Din al-Afghani became known as the "caller" who had first recognized the need for Islamic reform; Muhammad 'Abduh was then the "thinker" who had begun to develop an appropriate response; and Rashid Rida was the "archivist" or "historian." Al-Banna, meanwhile, was the actual "builder" of the Renaissance (a play on the rendering of his name in Arabic). In the eyes of the Ikhwan, he was the first to find a "practical" application of what hitherto had been only a scholarly tradition.[62] To cement the connection, in 1939 al-Banna took over Rida's journal, *al-Manar,* and oversaw the publication of six issues until it was suspended in September 1940.[63]

Beyond this, it is possible to identify a broader web of influences—both Islamic *and* Western—that helped to shape the mental landscape of Hasan al-Banna. This is particularly evident in his belief that the world could be divided into discrete "civilizations," a concept that carried strong echoes not just of Ibn Khaldun but also of European writers like Francois Guizot and Herbert Spencer. With regard to the former, Robert D. Lee has even suggested that the Muslim Brothers were to Ibn Khaldun what Lenin was to Marx—in the sense that they operationalized the earlier man's concept of history, transforming it into a discourse on power and the state in the service of a political project.[64] In all of this, Muhammad 'Abduh and the Dar al-'Ulum may have again been a key link in the chain of intellectual transmission. Kalmbach has shown that

'Abduh drew on the works of Ibn Khaldun when teaching the philosophy of history at the Dar in the late nineteenth century; she also suggests that he may have utilized the writings of Guizot.[65] (Meanwhile, 'Abduh's own mentor, al-Afghani, was persuaded both by Guizot's view of "civilization" and the argument that civilizational strength or weakness was determined by moral well-being.)[66] What is more, 'Abduh knew Herbert Spencer personally and translated his *Education* into Arabic. Indeed, he called him the "chief of the philosophers on social questions" and shared his concern about the growing involvement of the state in family life and education.[67] It is therefore highly plausible that such ideas were reflected in 'Abduh's teaching at Dar al-Ulum and that al-Banna was, in turn, exposed to them during his time at that institution. Whatever the precise manner of his exposure to the writings of men like Guizot and Spencer, al-Banna certainly echoed many of their ideas in his own work. In one of his letters to his followers, for example, he even quoted directly from Spencer's tract on education in support of his arguments.[68]

More contemporaneously, al-Banna's reflections on the coming collapse of the West had much in common with the ruminations of thinkers like Arnold Toynbee and Oswald Spengler.[69] Equally, others in the Muslim world were arriving at similar conclusions; most striking in this regard was Abul A'la Mawdudi in India.[70] The extent to which al-Banna was aware of such writers and consciously sought to emulate their work is unclear. At a minimum, though, the intellectual resemblance of their collective output is suggestive of the fact they were responding to shared stimuli, at a particular moment when debates about the West and its relationship with the wider world were current.

For present purposes, the significance of all this is twofold. First, it underlines the degree to which al-Banna was a man of his time. Even as he sought to excavate an unchanging "essence" of Islam, he was in fact reflecting—however unwittingly—an inherently contemporary range of ideas and obsessions. Second, the foregoing also demonstrates the centrality of "the West" as a concept to the genesis and worldview of the Brotherhood.

Challenging the West

Al-Banna described the "two fundamental goals" of the Brotherhood as being: "that the Islamic fatherland be freed from all foreign domination," and "that a free Islamic state may arise in this free fatherland, acting according to the precepts of Islam, applying its social regulations."[71] Similarly, on another occasion he talked of two key objectives: "the first is the liberation of the nation from its political bonds so that it may obtain its freedom and regain its lost independence and sovereignty," and "the second is its reconstruction."[72]

A key pillar of the new Egypt that al-Banna wished to see was the placing of the state's constitution on an Islamic footing and the reform of the law: "Every paragraph which Islam cannot tolerate and which its prescriptions do not sanction must be expunged . . . [the] body of law must be derived from the prescriptions of the Islamic Sacred Law [the shari'a]." This was to include the implementation of "the punishments prescribed by God."[73] As al-Banna stated in the 1940s missive *The Message of the Teachings,* an "Islamic government" would ensure that the "obligations" and "rules and teachings of Islam" were properly implemented. He thought that this would facilitate the reform of social conduct along more moral lines. It would, he imagined, deliver social justice, greater equity, and national unity; it would revivify the Islamic nation (*umma*), with a view to the eventual reconstitution of the "lost Caliphate."[74]

Al-Banna was invariably vague about the precise structure of the Islamic state that should exist in the interim. Clearly, its defining characteristic was to be the implementation of the shari'a and a rejection of the separation between religion and state. To this was added a belief that the ruler should be a devout Muslim male; al-Banna also utilized the concept of *shura* or consultation, to suggest that the ruler should respect the will of the *umma* as the source of his authority.[75]

Such language has been used to impute to al-Banna a protodemocratic outlook. Certainly, he seemed ready to accept some form of constitutional system and often talked about the importance of "the people." But all of this was balanced by his insistence on the primacy of the shari'a above all else. What he did not accept was anything resembling liberal democracy or full-blown political pluralism. A key target of al-Banna's ire was the party political system in operation at that time in Egypt. To his mind, the existing parties possessed no definable programs. Instead, they were based solely on personalities whose only goal was to get into power by any means possible. He believed that what he called *hizbiyya* (political partisanship) had "corrupted the people," damaging their morals and dividing the country.[76] In this, one can perhaps detect the enduring influence on al-Banna of 1919 and his ardent hope that a spirit of national unity might be rekindled. The initial item on the first full set of political demands that he issued was for the "elimination of *hizbiyya*" and the direction of the political forces of the nation toward a "united front."[77] Al-Banna maintained that the parliamentary system could "do without the system of parties"; it would be better to merge them into "a single popular organization to work for the interests of the nation on the bases of Islam."[78]

On top of this, al-Banna suggested that only those "suitably qualified" to assess the validity of laws in shari'a terms should be permitted to run for election. The state he envisaged was to be a democracy in which the people did not have the right to override the laws prescribed by God. Moreover, the nature of the demos was in the first instance, defined by religion: "the people" were Muslims. This raised numerous questions both then and since about the place within al-Banna's schema for Egypt's large Coptic minority.

Beyond this, much else was left open-ended and opaque—deliberately so. In one pamphlet, al-Banna suggested that those pressing him and the Ikhwan for more detailed exposition were doing the work of the devil. He preferred to talk in generalities, stating that the "institutions of Islam" had "combined both great breadth and precision" and were "the most perfect and most beneficial institutions known to mankind."[79] For this reason, ambiguities would remain for much of the Brotherhood's history about its commitment to democracy, pluralism, and minority rights.[80]

What could not be doubted, however, was al-Banna's emphasis on the need for the moral and cultural reform of both the individual and society. (Indeed, it was for this reason that Richard Mitchell submitted that it was better to see the Brotherhood as aiming at an "Islamic order," rather than at an "Islamic state" per se.)[81] To this end, al-Banna placed particular importance on the question of education. In his memoirs, he spoke of his own profound love for learning, and he had clearly spent time reflecting on its purpose. In this, he claimed to have been influenced by Imam Abu Hamid al-Ghazali (the eleventh-century theologian) and his argument that man only required a level of education sufficient to make a living; knowledge for its own sake was to be avoided. (On this basis, al-Banna claimed that he himself had nearly decided against applying to the Dar al-'Ulum, distrusting his own ambitions.)[82] One of the Brotherhood's earliest pamphlets, a 1929 missive entitled *A Memorandum on Religious Education,* offered a clearer insight into his views on the subject. Education, according to al-Banna, should reshape the individual—spiritually, intellectually, physically, and morally—building a truly "Islamic personality" possessed of a "sincere faith."[83] It should be about moral instruction rather than personal success or material advance. As Roxanne Euben and Muhammad Zaman argue, he believed that the essence of education was the inculcation of the "good life" as dictated by Islam.[84]

"Learning," al-Banna maintained, "was a type of jihad."[85] Teaching was a "vocation" to be lived rather than merely performed. It was this reason that he continually stressed his own role as a "guide," while urging his followers to live exemplary lives that would serve as the core of their outreach to others.[86] In his memoirs, he drew on what became a favored Brotherhood analogy to describe educators as a "shining light" that burned like a "candle" bringing enlightenment to the people.[87] Al-Banna wanted the Ikhwan's teachers to be the "bearers of a message, preachers of an idea, and builders of a generation."[88] The raising of this new generation, he maintained, would in turn provoke a "social reformation" in which the *umma* would be cast with a "comprehensive Islamic dye in every sphere of its life."[89] It was this idea that drove his near-constant focus on efforts to win over younger Muslims.[90]

Al-Banna was deeply critical of the existing educational system, which he felt produced people devoid of a sense of either their cultural traditions or their identity. He feared the secularization of Egypt's Fu'ad I University and its adoption of "materialist thinking" imported from the West. He worried that this would further incite revolt against religion and Islamic social customs.[91] What was required, according to al-Banna, was a thoroughgoing process of reform across all education sectors to imbue them with the spirit of Islam. He called for religious instruction, including Qur'an memorization, to be made a foundation subject in all schools and in the university. In addition, he wanted Islamic history to be taught and the Arabic language to be encouraged at every stage—this at a time when English and French were the languages of the elites. Above all, al-Banna wanted an education policy that would "instill a virtuous, patriotic spirit and a proper morality."[92]

Significantly, such views again revealed the influence not just of Islamic reformers such as 'Abduh and Rida but also Western theorists of education and self-improvement. With regard to the latter, for example, Gudrun Krämer has highlighted the strong echo of ideas about self-help and moral improvement that had been current in the work of people like Samuel Smiles. His book on "self-help," Krämer points out, had been translated into Arabic in the 1880s, and been embraced by Egyptian nationalists including Mustafa Kamil. It could be that al-Banna too had become familiar with such writings, given his proclivity for reading Western texts in Arabic translation.[93] Ehud Rosen has underlined al-Banna's abiding interest in notions of holistic pedagogy, drawn from the work of educationalists like Maria Montessori and Friedrich Foebel.[94] It is telling that in his memoirs, al-Banna makes explicit reference to theorists such as the eighteenth-century Swiss educator Johann Heinrich Pestalozzi and those of the "Waldorf school" movement that began in interwar Germany, both of which advocated a comprehensive approach to education. He claimed that he adapted their methods "in a new manner, appropriate to the Islamic tendency."[95]

In addition to these intellectual influences, as Beth Baron has demonstrated in an important recent study, the urgency with which al-Banna approached the question of education was in part a response to the activities of Western Christian missionaries. The latter had flourished in Egypt under the aegis of the British, who facilitated and protected them. This was a matter of long-standing interest for al-Banna. As a young man growing up in Mahmudiyya, he had formed a "Hasafi Welfare Society" with his friend Ahmad al-Sukkari, in order to challenge the "Christian Evangelical Mission" that had settled in the town. Al-Banna later remembered his shock at discovering that this group, comprised of three women, had been preaching Christianity under the cover of welfare and education work.[96]

Al-Banna's unease with the activities of missionary institutions accompanied him into early adulthood. In places like Ismailia, Protestant evangelicals had established successful and popular schools. To al-Banna such institutions posed a threat to the very fabric of Egyptian society. Indeed, Baron suggests that perhaps the key reason why al-Banna created the Ikhwan—as distinct from Muslim organizations already in existence—was his sense that those others were not doing enough to combat missionary education. One of the first projects of the Brotherhood was the establishment of a school to teach Islamic studies and Qur'anic recitation. In pursuing this course, as Baron has emphasized, al-Banna openly imitated the activities of the foreign evangelical missions.[97]

A boys' school, the Hira' Islamic Institute, was thus established in Ismailia in 1931. A partner institution for girls—the School for Mothers of the Believers—followed the next year. (The latter served as the "launching pad" for the establishment of the affiliated "Muslim Sisters," soon to be headed by the prominent activist Labiba Ahmad.)[98] Those educated under the aegis of the Brotherhood were taught to internalize the Qur'an and the Sunna, and to apply the shari'a in everything they did. Pupils were imbued with a moral code drawn from the divine sources while they were trained practically (in writing, reading, and arithmetic), industrially (at workshops run by the Brothers), and physically (via athletics).[99] They were taught both the "practical and spiritual aspects" of the faith, so that they might go out and engage in da'wa.[100] The Ikhwan placed the creation of such schools at the center of its mission. Frequently, these were attached to a mosque, forming the core of a complex of institutions that would cater to all the needs of the pious. The hope was that this might insulate young Muslims from corrupting influences of the kind purportedly disseminated at foreign and state-run schools.

The Ikhwan positioned itself as "the vanguard of the anti-missionary movement." Its members petitioned the authorities, initiated newspaper campaigns, and even appealed directly to King Fu'ad for action.[101] The Brotherhood explored every available avenue to stress the threat posed by the missionary movement.[102] Their efforts not only brought them to national prominence but also provided the stimulus for the convening of the group's first general conference, held in Ismailia in June 1933 and dedicated to combating the missionary threat. That same year, al-Banna helped found the Committee for the Defence of Islam under the presidency of Sheikh Mustafa al-Maraghi, which continued to be active against the missionaries.[103]

In this way, the Brotherhood's initial foray into public affairs was driven by a desire to combat directly an immediate tangible threat from "the West." Not only was this a movement founded in part out of a dialogue with Western ideas but also it was the manifestation of a keenly felt need to challenge the activities of certain Westerners on the ground.

The anti-Christian campaigning of the Ikhwan, coupled to its localized activism and social welfare-cum-educational provision, helped it to expand across the Egyptian delta. The group's second conference was held in January 1934 in Port Said, a central hub of the countermissionary campaign. In attendance were representatives from over thirty Brotherhood branches—more than double the number registered just a few months earlier.[104] In the years that followed, concerns over Christian missionary schooling drew many would-be recruits into the movement's orbit.[105]

The British, it should be said, seem to have paid little attention to the Brotherhood at this point. There is scant evidence of the group in correspondence between the Cairo Embassy and London. Even during the "orphan scandal" that fueled the antimissionary campaign in Port Said (and which is the subject of Baron's book), British officials did not identify the Muslim Brotherhood by name.[106] The closest the documents came to distinguishing the group was a reference to Hasan al-Banna's attendance at the meeting to establish Sheikh al-Maraghi's aforementioned committee. There were also references to "various agitators" who were thought to be behind the "missionary agitation" in Port Said. But the Ikhwan per se was not mentioned. Figures like al-Maraghi—of genuinely national standing—loomed far larger in the British imagination.[107]

Neglect of the Brotherhood was hardly surprising. The group in the early 1930s was merely one part of a smorgasbord of Islamic associations then in existence. Indeed, a few years later, the British orientalist scholar James Heyworth-Dunne would identify some 135 different Islamic organizations as active in Egypt.[108] Amid this cacophony, the voices of the Muslim Brothers scarcely seemed louder than others around them. Indeed, when set alongside an institution such as the Young Men's Muslim Association (YMMA), which enjoyed the patronage of figures like Sheikh al-Maraghi, it seemed of limited significance. More broadly, the Ikhwan was of only minor interest to British officials, as compared to the formal political world centered on parliament and the constant interplay between the palace, the mainstream parties, and of course the embassy itself.[109] In the years that followed, however, this began to change as the Brothers forced their way onto the national political agenda.

Going Political?

In 1932, Hasan al-Banna was transferred back to Cairo, and the Brotherhood's center of gravity shifted to the Egyptian capital.[110] In the same period, the group's formal organizational structure was consolidated and then ratified at its third general conference in 1935.[111] Even sympathetic observers have noted that this marked the centralization of the movement under the absolute authority of al-Banna himself.[112] To some extent, this was perhaps inevitable given the corresponding growth in the size of the Ikhwan. A clearer, more defined structure was necessary to ensure that the group's leaders retained control; for as Krämer has described, after the move to Cairo, the Brotherhood began its evolution into a mass political movement.[113] By the middle of the decade, it had moved from being a local welfare society to a potentially national organization.[114]

In making this transition, it was one of several groups to benefit from increasing popular disillusionment with Egypt's postindependence political institutions and parties, especially the Wafd.[115] During the 1930s, Egypt experienced what might be termed a "cult of youth," which fueled support for extraparliamentary movements that spoke for, and to a younger generation.[116] Among the most prominent were the YMMA, Young Egypt (Misr al-Fattat), and of course the Muslim Brotherhood itself. Young Egypt was the 1933 creation of Ahmad Husayn and Fathi Radwan and called for the creation of a strong, patriotic Egyptian state. The group proclaimed its loyalty to "God and Fatherland" and demanded a total British evacuation from the Nile valley. In language redolent of al-Banna, Husayn was an advocate of moral reform and spoke about the need for a more martial national spirit. In line with this, he created a quasi-paramilitary wing whose members held rallies and paraded in a uniform of green shirts, coupled with the tarbush of the *effendi* class (roughly equivalent to the lower-middle and middle classes).[117]

This was just one of several shirt organizations to emerge in this period. Each of the leading sociopolitical movements possessed such a section: the Wafdist "Blue Shirts" (the League of Wafdist Youth) competed for control of the Egyptian street with Young Egypt's "Green Shirts" and the Muslim Brotherhood's own "Yellow Shirts," the latter formed by the group's Rover (*al-Jawwala*) units that engaged in physical training and marches.[118] Street clashes became commonplace and the involvement of the Ikhwan symbolized its new confidence on the national stage.

By the end of the decade, al-Banna was more openly expressing obviously political goals. In a March 1938 tract aimed at students, he declared: "I can say publicly and frankly that a Muslim will not fulfill his Islam unless it is political." This was not, al-Banna claimed, a new position: "God knows, oh dear brothers, that the Ikhwan were never non-political for a single day . . . their call never distinguished between politics and religion."[119] In a further missive, he underscored the political character of his movement, proclaiming: "We summon you to Islam, and if this smacks of 'politics' in your eyes, then it is our 'policy'! And if the one summoning you to these principles is a 'politician,' then we are the most respectable of men, God be praised, in 'politics'!"[120] In line with this, May 1938 saw the creation of *al-Nadhir* newspaper under the direction of Salih 'Ashmawi, with the first issue said to mark "the beginning" of the Ikhwan's involvement in the "external and internal political struggle."[121]

The Brotherhood, al-Banna maintained, did "not demand government for themselves." If they found "someone within the umma who [was] ready to carry this burden, implement this faith and govern according to the Qur'anic Islamic programme," then they would be content to be merely "his soldiers, supporters and agents." But he was equally clear that if they did not find such a person, then "governing" was part of their mission and they would "work to extract it from the hands of those who [did] not implement the orders of God."[122] Al-Banna insisted that the "righteous predecessors" had understood the importance of politics, and it was for this reason that they had been "monks by night, horsemen by day."[123] It was this spirit that al-Banna sought to inculcate in his followers—especially after he organized them into "Battalions" in 1938.[124]

Of course, as Brynjar Lia has underlined, the Brotherhood's call for widespread reform was inherently political from the start—even prior to any involvement in formal politics. Al-Banna believed that Islam existed to transform both individuals and society. It was, he suggested, "a great social revolution" that aimed to produce a "virtuous nation."[125] Moreover, al-Banna recognized that the kind of change he sought required action by the state. It was for this reason that the aforementioned pamphlet on education was addressed to the government. It was the first of many such memoranda by which al-Banna hoped to persuade those in power—the king, the prime minister, the cabinet—to adopt his program.[126]

The 1936 pamphlet *Toward the Light* laid out in particular detail al-Banna's vision for reform. As might be expected, this contained a number of palpably moral prescriptions, such as the demand for the prohibition of prostitution (at that time permitted) and the closing down of bars that sold alcohol as part of a "war against vice."[127] Myriad individual recommendations of this kind were underpinned by the core premise that by fostering a more pious Muslim nation, the Brothers would bring about a socioeconomic-political renaissance—a posture succinctly labeled "religious determinism" by Hazem Kandil.[128]

The desire to promote virtue thus informed al-Banna's approach to the "issue of women": he urged the government to stop the mixing of male and female students; he also demanded legislation to protect marriage and the family, as well as the publication of "guidance" to women on what to wear.[129] Beyond this, there were calls for social reform and measures to combat poverty and disease. Al-Banna affirmed that good "physical health and strength" were prerequisites for national rebirth, even asserting that the Prophet had spoken of the need for a "'preventive' approach to medicine."[130] Finally, the pamphlet also set out proposals for a more morally infused national economy. These blended "Islamic" strictures (such as the call for usury to be banned and *zakat* [alms giving] implemented) with a form of economic nationalism.[131] Al-Banna, it was clear, was not opposed to private property or commercial activity. But he did call for the "sequestration" of those businesses in the hands of foreigners and their transfer to a "purely national sector."[132] On another occasion, too, he specifically noted that there were more than 320 foreign companies in Egypt and that "all economic institutions" were "in the hands of profiteering foreigners."[133] In al-Banna's view, this situation had to be changed and the economy Egyptianized.[134] He also registered his opposition to "monopolistic companies" and emphasized the importance of "raising the production level of the peasant and the industrial worker."[135] As Ellis Goldberg has observed, the Brotherhood's vision, taken as a whole, was essentially paternalist in character, looking to the creation of a harmonious, self-reliant, and virtuous community.[136]

These sentiments were even reflected in the uniform that was required at the Brotherhood's first school. This comprised a *gallabiya* (a long, loose fitting shirt) and coat made from national textiles, to be worn with a white tarbush and sandals, also of Egyptian origin.[137] According to James Heyworth-Dunne, al-

Banna himself likewise made a point of wearing clothes manufactured in Egypt.[138] The pamphlet *Toward the Light* envisaged the gradual unification of fashion styles across the whole nation. Al-Banna's ultimate objective was "the elimination of the foreign spirit in homes, as regards language, customs and fashion."[139] What was required, he averred, was "a call for the return to the teachings of Islam and the abandonment of . . . the evils of Western civilisation."[140] In facing a world dominated by the West, the Ikhwan held that Muslims now stood at a "crossroads." Either they could embrace their conquerors and ape the ways of the Western world, or they could turn back to the thing that had made them strong in the first place: Islam.[141]

As the memoirs of Ikhwan members make clear, this did not mean a blanket rejection of all things Western. Hasan Hathut, for instance, recalled one incident when al-Banna was asked by one of his followers whether cinema was halal (permitted under Islamic law) or *haram* (forbidden by Islamic law). His simple, somewhat tautological reply was that "haram cinema is haram, halal cinema is halal"—the point being that he had no problem with modern media per se; what mattered to him was the content.[142] What al-Banna opposed was both the continued colonial occupation of Egypt and the "blind emulation" of "the West" as a culture and civilization.[143] In fact, he called on his followers to identify those elements of Western society that could safely be adopted.[144] Hence, Mitchell posited that the Ikhwan distinguished between the "internal" West on the one hand, which carried some positives (freedoms, rights, material advancement), and the "external" West on the other, which was projected into Muslim lands. Al-Banna believed that the best of the former could already be found within Islam, properly understood—and as such, it was safe for Muslims to accept those elements.[145]

On occasion, too, al-Banna sought to emphasize that he bore no ill intent toward Western countries, provided that they treated Muslims well. If they offered security to Islam, he maintained, this would be reciprocated. Such assertions, however, sat rather uncomfortably alongside the Brotherhood's narrative of history, which, as described, imagined the West as inherently hostile to Islam. Al-Banna was forthright in his condemnation of what he saw as ongoing Western aggression against Muslim countries—as practiced by the European empires. He demanded the liberation of the entire *umma*.[146] And his earliest followers saw the *foremost* objective of the Ikhwan as being to rid Egypt of British colonialism and to purify the country of its "internal ideological defilements."[147] As Lia has remarked, the Brotherhood thus became a "powerful vehicle" for anti-imperialist sentiment, articulating a distinct form of "Islamic nationalism."[148]

Al-Banna was insistent that the goals of Egyptian nationalism, Arab nation-alism, and Islamic unity were entirely compatible, seeing them as three inter-locking "circles" of concern. He argued that as Muslims they were required "to work for the good of the country and . . . to serve the nation in which they were born." Indeed, it was because of this that he stated a Muslim was inevitably "the most profound nationalist and [provided] the greatest benefit to the nation." Al-Banna declared that the Muslim Brothers loved their country and cared deeply about national unity—even as they viewed this as merely the first step toward a broader liberation. In addition to supporting Egyptian independence, al-Banna called for "Arab unity, considering it the second circle in the awak-ening." He backed the cause of the Arabs, he claimed, because of their special place within Islam (with Arabia as its birthplace and Arabic as the language of the Qur'an). Consequently, he attested, "if the Arabs are humiliated, Islam is hu-miliated." "Arab unity" was said to be "necessary to restore the glory of Islam and the establishment of its state" (the third and final "circle"). With regard to the latter, the Brotherhood stated that Islam did "not recognize geographical borders nor racial, nor blood differences." Rather, it considered "all Muslims together as one nation" and conceived of the "Islamic homeland as one country." According to al-Banna, they believed "every piece of land" in which a Muslim says "there is no God but God and Muhammad is the Prophet of God" to be "their country." For this reason, he looked toward the "total enclosure of the general Islamic nation" and, as already described, the return of the caliphate—though he did acknowledge that this would require much preparation and several interme-diate steps (he seemed to envisage it as a kind of grand alliance between Islamic nations).[149]

In all of this, it again seems clear that al-Banna was influenced by con-temporary debates about identity in an era that saw the flourishing of diverse reflections about the interrelationship between Egyptian nationalism, pan-Arabism, and pan-Islamism.[150] His conception of three overlapping and com-patible circles or spheres of interest (Egyptian, Arab, and Islamic) was echoed by others—albeit with different priorities attached to the different circles. Young Egypt, for example, tended to emphasize the Egyptian and pan-Arab aspects over the cause of Muslim unity. Years later, Gamal Abdel Nasser would also frame Egypt's place in the world by reference to three circles (this time Egyp-tian, Islamic, and African).[151] The significance of all this lies not in any effort to try and determine who influenced who; rather, this convergence of ideas offers another illustration of the extent to which al-Banna and his Brotherhood were the products of a particular historical moment.

Liberation, Jihad, and Palestine

Whatever the source of his inspiration, there was no doubting al-Banna's absolute commitment to the liberation of the "Islamic fatherland" from "all foreign domination." He predicted that the road to such liberation would pass through several stages. The first stage was to build the individual Islamic personality. On this foundation, he wished to establish the Islamic family (stage two)—and from there would emerge an Islamic nation (stage three). The fourth stage would then see the creation of an Islamic government based on the "rules and principles" of Islam. With this Islamic state in place, the fifth stage was to "regain every part" of the "Islamic nation" that had been "usurped" by the Western nations. In keeping with his support for pan-Arabic and pan-Islamic unity, al-Banna rejected the division of the wider Middle East and North Africa—from Morocco to Syria and Yemen—into nation-states. Under his vision, these were to be reunited under the banner of Islam. The analogy he chose to illustrate this point was striking; for he pointed to the Reich in which every German "believed that it was imposed upon him to support every one else." The "Islamic creed," al-Banna argued, similarly required "every strong Muslim to consider himself a protector for every person whose soul [had] absorbed the teachings of the Qur'an."[152]

With the broader Islamic fatherland thereby re-created, the sixth stage was to "make the banner of Islam rise high and wave over those lands, which were cheered, for a certain period of time with Islam." Among the countries identified in this category were Andalusia, Sicily, the Balkans, and southern Italy. Once more, al-Banna reached for a contemporary parallel of some significance, pointing to the desire of Mussolini to revive the Roman Empire. In this context, he averred, it was surely right for Muslims to restore "the Islamic empire," which was said to be "based upon Justice, equity and the spread of light and guidance among human beings."[153] After the return of that empire, the seventh and final stage of the Brotherhood's mission was to make the Islamic call "reach . . . the whole world." Ultimately, al-Banna foresaw that every unjust ruler would be subjugated to its command. He acknowledged that some would see all of this as "fantasy and an illusion"—but he dismissed such skepticism as weakness, declaring that, "every Muslim who does not have faith in this ideology and does not act towards its achievement has no salvation." The Brotherhood, he insisted, was founded on the "unshakeable" conviction that they would achieve their divine mission.[154]

To this end, al-Banna called on his followers to engage in "jihad." He maintained this was a "religious duty imposed by God on the Muslims" that should be seen as a pillar of Islam, ranked alongside the other five pillars such as prayer and fasting.[155] Jihad for the sake of God was said to be a divine commandment, the purpose of which was to ensure that His "call" would reach all of the people. In a letter to his followers, which specifically addressed the subject, al-Banna argued that Allah had imposed jihad on every Muslim as a "necessary and absolute obligation" to which there was "no alternative."[156] Abstention from, or the evasion of, jihad was said to be "one of the seven mortal sins" that guaranteed "annihilation."[157] Jihad was thus central to the Brotherhood's ethos. Indeed, Abd al-Fattah M. el-Awaisi has suggested that it was al-Banna's focus on the concept of jihad that distinguished the Ikhwan from other Islamic associations then in existence.[158] This was reflected in the famous motto of the movement: "Allah is our objective. The messenger is our leader. The Qur'an is our constitution. Jihad is our way. Dying for the sake of Allah is our highest hope."[159]

When he talked of jihad, al-Banna used the term in the broadest sense. It encapsulated the spirt of activist engagement that he sought to encourage and signified the Brotherhood's "struggle" to achieve its goals. Within this, however, al-Banna was also clear that jihad could include "fighting and soldiering." He affirmed that if the people refused to heed the message and resorted to "defiance, oppression and revolt," then the "sword" might be used to "disseminate the call."[160] In line with this, al-Banna dismissed those who sought to draw a distinction between the so-called lesser jihad ("fighting the enemy") and greater jihad ("the jihad of the soul"). According to al-Banna, this concept was used by some Muslims to avoid the true jihad, but was based on an unsound hadith (a saying of the Prophet). Moreover, he maintained that even if the hadith in question was authentic, this would not legitimate the abandonment of physical force jihad. With regard to the latter, al-Banna provided his followers with a selection of verses from the Qur'an, as well as alternative examples from the hadith and judgments issued by scholars from each of the four main schools of Islam, which stressed variously: the idea that jihad entailed "armed combat"; the need for "obedience and organisation"; the belief that someone killed in the path of jihad became a "martyr" who went straight to heaven and earned numerous rewards; that there was a "necessity to fight the People of the Book" (indeed, God allegedly doubled the reward of those who did); and the claim that jihad was superior to other devotions such as prayer.[161]

On another occasion, he resorted to a proverb to make the same point: "How wise was the man who said: 'Force is the surest way of implementing the right, and how beautiful it is that force and right should march side by side.' "[162] "Strength is the slogan of Islam," al-Banna declared, "even in prayer." He drew on another hadith, which stated that "the strong believer is better than the weak believer."[163] Likewise, he often cited the verse of the Qur'an (al-Anfal, 60), in which God commanded that the Prophet Muhammad "prepare for them what force you can, including war horses so as to terrorize the enemy of God and your enemy."[164] Unsurprisingly, al-Banna's most prominent latter-day exegetist, Yusuf al-Qaradawi, confirms that the use of force was written into the Brotherhood's program from the outset—albeit defined in a limited way.[165] To this day, the emblem of the Brotherhood includes the word "prepare" underneath an image of two crossed swords and the Qur'an.

The conclusion to al-Banna's tract on jihad left little room for doubt: "Allah bestows on the nation that excels in the industry of death, and knows how to die nobly, a rich life in this world and eternal bliss in the next." His followers were urged to prepare themselves and "be enthusiastic for a death that would bring life."[166] It was for the same reason that al-Banna's 1936 pamphlet called on the government to strengthen the army and establish "youth squads" that would be "inflamed" with an enthusiasm for "Islamic jihad."[167] It spoke further about the need for resurgent nations to have strength and a "martial" spirit, especially in the present age, when it was said the only way to peace was through preparedness for war. In a further nod to more profane influences on his thinking, al-Banna noted that the modern nations of the world such as those under Mussolini's fascism, Hitler's Nazism, or Marx's communism rested on "purely military foundations." Rather than reject this, he felt that Muslims should in part emulate such systems, while recognizing that they were inferior to the "militarism of Islam," which enjoyed divine sanction.[168]

Al-Banna invested considerable time in identifying the way in which the "communal obligation" of jihad could be transformed into an "individual obligation" akin to prayer. The former, al-Banna averred, existed to "spread the call" to Islam—and as long as some people performed this duty every year, then the remainder of the Islamic nation was released from the requirement to act. In the event that this did not happen, however, he was clear that responsibility for jihad devolved on the individual Muslim.

More significant still was the way al-Banna repeatedly emphasized that Muslims had a duty to "defend" the broad Islamic nation against an "attack of the unbelievers."[169] The logic of this for the contemporary world was spelled out in unmistakable terms: "Today the Muslims, as you know, are compelled to humble themselves before non-Muslims, and are ruled by the unbelievers. Their lands have been trampled over, and their honor besmirched. Their adversaries are in charge of their affairs, and the rites of their religion have fallen into abeyance within their own domains, to say nothing of their impotence to broadcast the summons [to Islam]. Hence it has become an individual obligation, which there is no evading, on every Muslim to prepare his equipment, to make up his mind to engage in Jihad, and to get ready for it until the opportunity is ripe."[170] With such words, al-Banna effectively invested jihad with anti-imperialist meaning. He was clear that if "aggression" fell on any part of the imagined Islamic nation, then the duty of jihad fell on all Muslims individually. Al-Banna held that "Islam does not accept for its sons anything less than freedom and independence as well as sovereignty and the announcement of jihad even if that costs them blood and money." "Death," he declared, was better than this "life of slavery, serfdom and humiliation!"[171] The consequences of this for how the Brotherhood judged the situation in Egypt and the broader Middle East—given the realities of Western and especially British imperial dominance—seemed obvious.

Nonetheless, in spite of his fierce rhetoric on jihad in the abstract, the political path charted by al-Banna was largely a pragmatic one, based on the careful accumulation of strength and a readiness to operate within legal parameters. In his speech to the Brotherhood's fifth conference in 1939, he spoke of "gradualism" and the need to advance their program in three stages. The first was the "stage of propaganda, acquaintance and preaching the ideology"; this was to be followed by the "stage of formation, choosing supporters and preparing the soldiers"; and finally, there was the "stage of implementation, work and execution." Of course, al-Banna stated, these stages could proceed side by side. But he was equally clear that the group's final objectives would not be realized "except after generalization of the propaganda and multiplication of supporters and strength of formation." In laying out this phased approach, he explicitly warned his followers to be patient and to persevere; "it might be a long path," he observed, "but there is no other." Al-Banna cautioned against those who hastened to "pick the fruit before it is ripe or pluck the flower before it has bloomed."[172] The Ikhwan, he insisted, did "not believe" in revolution but instead were focused on education and reform.[173] Time and again al-Banna demonstrated a strategic preference for pragmatism in his dealings with those who might otherwise be classed as "enemies"—both at home and abroad.[174] He did not advocate the overthrow of the state and, throughout the 1930s, eschewed confrontation with the authorities. The same, though, could not be said about his attitude to the burgeoning unrest in neighboring Palestine.

El-Awaisi has described how the Ikhwan's commitment to this issue flowed from the intertwining of religious, nationalist, and political motives.[175] The

Brothers believed that "if the Jews succeeded" in occupying Palestine, then it would "become a dangerous and permanent home to supporters of evil, and a volcano full of fire permanently upsetting the security and peace of the Arab countries."[176] The Arabs, it was claimed, faced a "conspiracy" driven by their foremost enemies: the Zionists and the British. "Imperialist English politicians" were blamed entirely for creating the problem. The 1917 Balfour Declaration, promising the Jews a national home within Palestine, was viewed as a deeply iniquitous assault on the fundamental rights of Arab Muslims and the *umma* as a whole. Merely to think of such a thing, according to the Ikhwan, was to damage the rights of the Muslim world. The awarding of a "mandate" to Britain to govern Palestine was considered a similarly grievous blow, given that it included a commitment to implementing Balfour. In so doing, the British "betrayed" the Arabs and the promises that they had made to Sharif Husayn during the First World War. Thereafter, they were said to have facilitated Jewish fundraising and immigration into Palestine, while simultaneously taking steps to impede Arab opposition. Britain's mandate administrators (the majority of whom were believed to be Jewish) were also accused of transferring land from poor Arab farmers to the Jews; and it was alleged that they had even allowed Jews to import weapons and trained them for combat.[177]

In all of this, the Brothers imagined that the British were driven by their hatred of, and opposition to, Islam. The group warned of a "British plot in the Islamic world . . . to take Muslims away from their religion and to corrupt their social life." Events in Palestine were thought to be just one manifestation of this malevolence.[178] As a consequence the country had, by the 1930s, become "a stage for bloody revolutions and violent battles between the revolutionaries and the occupation forces." The British, it was claimed, had resorted to "barbaric methods," but this had only strengthened the determination of the Arab people not to be beaten. The Brotherhood announced its commitment to fighting British and Zionist intrigues by any means possible.[179]

In 1935, a Brotherhood delegation, including al-Banna's brother 'Abd al-Rahman, was sent to Palestine as a first step toward expanding the group beyond Egypt's borders. There they met with the grand mufti, Hajj Amin al-Husayni, and, with his help, also made contacts in Syria and Lebanon.[180] Hasan al-Banna himself had already met al-Husayni back in 1927, during the latter's visit to Cairo.[181] Thereafter a relationship seems to have been sustained with the controversial al-Husayni, a noted anti-Semite who was, from the early 1930s, in contact with the Nazis.[182] It has been suggested that al-Husayni's influence worked to harden the Brotherhood's own anti-Semitism.[183] Certainly, the contacts were to prove of lasting significance, and were strengthened further after the eruption of the Arab Revolt in 1936.

From the beginning of this conflict, the Brotherhood was extremely active, campaigning for the Arab cause.[184] In May 1936, a Central Committee for Aid to Palestine was established, headed by al-Banna and the senior Brother Salih 'Ashmawi. Subcommittees were formed across the Brotherhood organization at branch level, tasked with propaganda and fund-raising activities. Al-Banna also joined the Supreme Committee for Relieving Palestinian Victims, formed on the initiative of the YMMA.[185] Throughout this period, the Brotherhood took a hard-line position. It was fiercely opposed to the 1937 Peel Report (which recommended the partition of the territory) and it supported the Arab resort to irregular warfare.[186] Indeed, as early as 1936, al-Banna seems to have concluded that physical force jihad was essential in Palestine.[187] Thereafter, the Ikhwan began sending weapons to the Arabs and cooperated closely with the mujahideen fighting against the British and the Jews, especially those in the north of the country led by 'Izz al-din al-Qassem.[188] It was in this context, too, that the Muslim Brotherhood appeared on the British radar for the first time.

The Brotherhood through British Eyes

In April 1936, the British high commissioner to Egypt, Sir Miles Lampson, sent a telegram to London that included a report from the Special Section of the Egyptian Ministry of Interior. Based on the work of an informer, this gave details of a "tea party" held by a branch of the "Moslem Brethren Society," to mark the visit of a large delegation from a Syrian charitable association.[189] Of the two hundred Muslim Brothers present, most were thought to be students drawn from either Fu'ad I University or al-Azhar. They were described as "devout young men . . . to the point of fanaticism." Some, it was claimed, had given speeches lamenting the bygone days of the Arabs and calling for the "imperialists" to be chased out of the region. There had been numerous references to the Qur'an and the Prophet Muhammad, and a strong emphasis on ideas of martyrdom and self-sacrifice for the sake of God and country. The report's author expressed his concern that the Muslim Brotherhood might "in the course of time . . . produce a reckless and heedless generation who will not abstain from selling their lives cheap[ly]."[190]

In commending this report to his superiors, the British high commissioner effectively revealed his own reservations about the character of the Brotherhood.

Furthermore, the use of words like fanaticism in connection with the group was, as Francis Robinson has shown, entirely in keeping with how many British officials viewed Islam across the empire. It was seen as a backward, irrational religion, whose adherents were prone to "holy war" and the appeals of demagoguery.[191] In the late nineteenth and early twentieth centuries, the adjective fanatical was a natural partner to references to "Mohammedans" and Islam.[192] Early British commentaries on the Ikhwan therefore operated within an established register; these first encounters did little to disabuse them of a belief in the fanatical nature of many Muslims.

Just over a month after the original 1936 memorandum, Embassy Cairo forwarded a further report to London compiled by the Egyptian director of public security and focused solely on the Brothers (a sign of their growing prominence). This offered more in-depth analysis of the Ikhwan, which was now thought to enjoy a presence across Egypt and in places as far afield as Palestine and even China (a claim that seems rather unlikely). Hasan al-Banna was identified as the group's leader and the Ikhwan was likened to the Young Men's Muslim Association, with its focus on a rigid adherence to religion. At the same time, the Brotherhood was distinguished by its "anti-foreign and particularly anti-Imperialistic views." Al-Banna and his followers, it was claimed, wished "to purge all Islamic countries of the presence and control of Europeans."[193] Needless to say, such an assessment was liable to prick the attention of British officials— so too the movement's stark criticism of events in Palestine. Al-Banna, it was noted, had used a meeting in May to call on Egyptians to "defend the Masjid Al Aqsa" and contribute money to the Arab cause. The Brotherhood also had passed a string of resolutions outlining possible future agitation. Again, such details were likely to stir British curiosity about the group, even if for the moment it was not seen as too great a threat. With a total membership estimated at eight hundred, the report concluded that the movement was "growing in strength," but was "not at present in any way dangerous."[194]

Nevertheless, as 1936 progressed, the capacity of groups like the Brotherhood, Young Egypt, and the YMMA to cause problems became increasingly clear. Diplomatic dispatches pointed to their ongoing activism, particularly in relation to Palestine.[195] To some officials, this appeared indicative of wider political trends. By the mid-1930s, British embassies across the Middle East were drawing attention to the "pan-Islamic Arab movement," which was thought to have been empowered by unrest in Palestine, Syria, and also Egypt.[196] In Cairo, for example, Sir Miles Lampson signaled his nervousness over the "new spirit of common feeling" that he saw developing within Arab countries.[197] This phenomenon, it should be said, induced varying reactions—from the near-insouciance of Sir Archibald Clark Kerr, the ambassador in Baghdad, to the alarmism of the Sudan Agency.[198] One particularly florid verdict was offered by the British consul in Damascus, Gilbert Mackereth, who judged pan-Arabism to be a product of the oriental mind. The latter, he asserted, was inherently different from that of the European: "None but those who have lived among Asiatics can understand how an oriental mind can brood over an idea. It is perhaps the most marked distinction between him and the Western man." While expressing "considerable doubt" as to its "potentialities" and lack of substance, Mackereth shared Lampson's fears that pan-Arabism might prove inimical to law and order, and become increasingly anti-European and religious in character.[199]

Conversely, it is interesting to note that there were other officials who appeared inclined to see pan-Arabism in a more positive light. One Foreign Office mandarin, for instance, minuted that if Egypt were to be included in a future "Arab State," having first made an alliance with the British, then pan-Arab sentiment could be of use to them.[200] Such unconventional speculation, though, remained very much in the minority. Far more typical was the anxiety that a vague yet growing sense of regional "solidarity" with the Arabs of Palestine was fueling ideas of "holy war." British officials worried that any attempt to partition Palestinian territory by force might lead to a general declaration of jihad and the further spread of both "pan-Arab" and "anti-British" feelings.[201] They were especially anxious lest Egyptian politics become infected with these sentiments. The embassy in Cairo reported with concern the spread of protests against British policy in Palestine.[202] The fear was that Egypt's hitherto relatively isolated stance with regard to the wider Arab world was being eroded to potentially damaging effect.[203]

In an effort to shore up the British position, an Anglo-Egyptian Treaty of Friendship had been signed in August 1936. Ever since 1922, there had been repeated attempts to arrive at an agreement that might provide a legal basis for the British presence in the country. Negotiations with various administrations had failed to deliver.[204] However, the worsening geopolitical climate of the mid-1930s—in particular following the Italian invasion of Abyssinia—had served to concentrate minds on all sides.[205] The resulting treaty put an end to some of the powers that Britain had "reserved" back in 1922–1923; it also allowed for Egyptian entry into the League of Nations and paved the way toward the cancellation of the "capitulations" (the extraterritorial legal rights enjoyed by foreigners in Egypt). In the aftermath, there was some expectation in London that this might allow the British to draw back from direct involvement in Egyptian affairs. Foreign Secretary Anthony Eden was clear that interference in the internal political matters of Cairo was to be "limited as a general rule to cases in which British interests are actually at stake."[206] Significantly, the British did not intercede in late 1937 to save the Wafdist government that had signed the treaty, when the king dismissed it from office.[207]

At the same time, of course, the continued presence of thousands of British troops guaranteed that the reality of Egyptian "independence" remained heavily qualified. The UK Foreign Office likewise insisted on the diplomatic preeminence of its Cairo ambassador (as the high commissioner now became known), and it delineated various circumstances in which his intervention in local affairs would be thoroughly justified. The reality was that the 1936 treaty was consistent with the evolving character of Britain's imperial possessions—what M. A. Fitzsimons called "empire by treaty," the "half-way house of British imperialism." Across the Middle East in the interwar period, the British sought to secure their "preponderant" position by dint of legal arrangements that established a tutelary relationship with local governments and provided for the stationing of British forces at key strategic bases.[208] The aim was to secure "a privileged position without maintaining the burden of imposing an imperial order and peace."[209] Seen from this perspective, the Egyptian treaty was, to apply John Darwin's insight, merely the latest in an "endless" series of "adjustments" to the edifice of British power, by which London sought to achieve the "classic objectives of Victorian imperialism: the creation of a compliant local regime which would preserve Britain's political and strategic interests while relieving her of the trouble and expense of ruling directly over an alien and unpredictable society."[210]

Despite their apparent success in this regard, however, an intelligence report from October 1936 painted a "very gloomy picture." It captured the fear that the British position was deteriorating in Egypt and across the region. Events in Palestine were assumed to be driving this process, which was magnified further by wider geopolitical shifts—in particular, Mussolini's success in Abyssinia. Because of the latter, "British prestige" was said to have suffered "an extremely severe set-back in the Near East."[211] The report's author also suggested that the forthcoming period would be decisive for Egypt; and the omens, he argued, were not good.[212]

During the late 1930s, Egyptian political life appeared ever more fluid, unstable, and violent. One major source of anxiety was the new king, Faruq, who had succeeded his father in 1936. After initial optimism surrounding his accession, problems had quickly begun to appear, focused variously on: the fact that Faruq did not appear "constitutionally minded," as evidenced by his 1937 dismissal of the Wafd;[213] his fractious relationship with Ambassador Lampson, who likened the king to "a schoolboy putting out his tongue at us";[214] his known sympathy for all things Italian;[215] and what officials referred to euphemistically as his scandalous "nocturnal wanderings."[216] Beyond the palace, demonstrations and strikes proliferated on Egypt's streets—many of them involving youth groups and students.[217] As occurred elsewhere, there were signs of a loss of faith in the liberal, constitutional system.[218] And in November 1937, a member of Young Egypt's Green Shirts attempted to assassinate Wafdist leader Mustafa al-Nahas.[219]

All of this was watched with a mounting sense of unease by British officials. In their judgment, the "shirt organisations" had learned the "Fascist secret of imposing an imperium in imperio by means of organised terrorism [emphasis in original]."[220] Doubtless they were relieved when the Egyptian government moved to ban all paramilitary youth movements in March 1938. (The Brotherhood's formation escaped prohibition by officially designating itself as part of the Egyptian scout movement.)[221]

In this period, Young Egypt was viewed as a particular menace. Officials held it responsible for numerous acts of violence and believed it to be fundamentally anti-British.[222] The group had made plain its pro-Palestinian position and called for the overthrow of the existing regime in Egypt.[223] Its leader, Ahmad Husayn, was considered an open admirer of fascism, which he was said to blend with a "measure of fanatical Islamic intolerance."[224]

Comments of this kind also spoke to a deeper anxiety about the growing involvement of religion in Egyptian public life. In early 1938, Ambassador Lampson declared himself "greatly perturbed" by a sermon that the rector of al-Azhar, Sheikh al-Maraghi, had delivered calling for pan-Islamic solidarity and the "fanatical observance of Islam." According to Lampson, the address, which included attacks on lay conceptions of government, missionaries, the Copts, and the British had created "a most disagreeable impression in all enlightened Egyptian circles."[225] The ambassador sought reassurance from then prime minister Muhammad Mahmud that al-Maraghi's words did not mark the "recrudescence of the anti-Christian movement in Egypt."[226] In due course, Lampson met with the sheikh himself and pressed him to keep religion out of politics.[227] His worry was that "fanaticism, once stirred up," could not "often be checked before causing serious trouble."[228] Elsewhere, in what appears to be a direct reference to the Brotherhood, Lampson noted that Egypt had seen "the multiplication of Islamic Societies with obscurantist Islamic programmes." These groups, he observed, demanded "the revival of mediaeval claims for the Islamisation of the judicial and administrative structure of the State" and indulged in "attacks against so-called modern forms of corruption."[229] In Lampson's assessment, no good could come of such movements.

British attention was likely drawn to the Brotherhood as it moved ever more clearly in the direction of formal political involvement. By this stage, al-Banna had established a good relationship with the "strong man" of Egyptian politics: Ali Maher Pasha. After 1937, Maher came to be seen as a powerful influence on the young King Faruq. He was chief of the royal cabinet and widely rumored to be seeking a return to the post of prime minister (having served briefly in that role in 1936). Described by the British as an "inveterate intriguer," he was thought to be the "evil genius" behind the king.[230] As such, a burgeoning connection between Maher and the Brotherhood was an obvious cause for concern. Maher appears to have encouraged the palace to cultivate the era's new movements—like the Ikhwan—in order to build up an anti-Wafd, pro-palace coalition that was also anti-British. James Jankowski has suggested that financial aid and political encouragement was given to Young Egypt.[231] Others have posited that a similar arrangement was made with the Brotherhood.[232] According to Lia, al-Banna met with Maher as early as 1935, and their association developed over the remainder of the decade.[233]

It may have been at Maher's instigation, for instance, that al-Banna was also now able to build a personal rapport with Sheikh al-Maraghi, with whom he had previously had dealings during the antimissionary agitation.[234] Both al-Banna and al-Maraghi looked to the king as a potential "Islamic prince"; they shared an opposition to the factionalism of parliamentary government.[235] According to Heyworth-Dunne, al-Banna approached al-Maraghi in 1938 to try to secure the placement of Brotherhood preachers in official capacities throughout the country. Though this suggestion was not implemented, the sheikh did instruct al-Azhar affiliates across Egypt to cooperate with representatives of the Ikhwan.[236]

As el-Awaisi notes, none of this meant that the Brotherhood became a mere puppet of the authorities—far from it. Al-Banna always rejected the claims of those who said that the Muslim Brothers worked for, or were in any way beholden to, others—especially members of Egypt's sociopolitical elite. The Brothers, he insisted, worked "to achieve only their own purpose" and had not "asked for help from any individual, agency or organization."[237] In his address to the Brotherhood's fifth conference in 1939, he declared that the group had "not accepted a single subsidy from the government," but instead relied solely on its own members "or those who love the Brotherhood."[238] Such denials appear rather questionable when set against the various alliances of convenience that al-Banna made throughout his public career. These dated back to the founding of the movement and famously included a readiness to accept a sizable donation from the Suez Canal Company, which helped the Brotherhood to build its first mosque in Ismailia. (The story of the donation is interesting in that al-Banna manages to present himself as a "victim" despite taking the money, complaining that the sum—£E500—was paltry relative to the £E500,000 that the company was thought to be spending on a church at that same moment.)[239] A few years later, al-Banna publicly acknowledged, too, that the Brotherhood had gained funding from the Social Affairs Ministry for their welfare work.[240] On top of this, there were strong suspicions that the Brothers had received subsidies from the palace, as well as from foreign powers.

The reality was that al-Banna was quite prepared to cooperate with, and secure support from, sociopolitical elites—both locally and at the national level. With regard to the former, he always sought to avoid antagonizing local notables whenever he visited a village or town.[241] The Brotherhood was likewise careful to stress its fealty to the king and, as described, the group established durable connections with members of the Egyptian upper class like Ali Maher.[242] In all of this, al-Banna again revealed his strategic preference for pragmatism as a mode of politics. This helped bring him nationwide influence and the Ikhwan was increasingly seen as an important anti-Wafdist force that could not be ignored.[243] By 1938, for example, al-Banna was meeting with Prime Minister Muhammad Mahmud to discuss events in Palestine.[244]

As Israel Gershoni has underscored, it was the Brotherhood's activism on Palestine that drove its expansion and won it prestige at the national level. In 1937, the group's guidance council sent a letter to the British ambassador protesting the Balfour Declaration.[245] As the Arab revolt neared its peak the following summer, al-Banna continued to press the issue. Moreover, in August 1938, Brotherhood members were involved in violent clashes with the police for the first time, when demonstrations were held in violation of banning orders.[246] Abbas al-Sissi, who had joined the Brotherhood two years earlier, later recalled being involved in those protests, which heard cries of "Palestine is Arab and Islamic," "Destroy the enemies of Islam," and "Down with Britain, ally of the Jews and down with the Balfour Declaration."[247] In addition, he remembered the circulation of pamphlets and books with titles such as "Fire and Destruction in Palestine," which described the horrors of the battles between the Muslims on the one side and the English and the Jews on the other.[248]

The circulation of such material did not escape the attention of the British. Officials noted that the Brothers were distributing anti-Jewish and anti-British pamphlets calling for "holy war" against infidels, tyrants, and colonizers.[249] They also observed that members of the group had delivered speeches that were "calculated to incite the audience to volunteer their services in aid of the Palestinian Arabs in their fight against the British and the Jews." As an example, one dispatch contained an account of a meeting held in Zagazig in early September 1938, which was attended by some six hundred students and fellahin. This gathering had sent greetings to Grand Mufti al-Husayni and all Palestinian fighters. It pledged to launch new demonstrations against both the British Embassy and the Egyptian government. There were also appeals for a boycott of British and Jewish goods, as well as for volunteers to join in the defense of al-Aqsa mosque.[250]

Subsequently, the Brotherhood welcomed the anti-Zionist World Parliamentary Congress of Arab and Muslim Countries for the Defence of Palestine, which met in Cairo in October 1938. According to al-Sissi, those attendee delegations that passed through Alexandria were received with acclamation by contingents of the Ikhwan chanting "allah akbar, allah al-hamd (God is greatest, God is praised)," by now established as the group's rallying cry. Members of the Brotherhood also helped steward the proceedings of the Congress. The following month then saw fresh rallies to mark the anniversary of the Balfour Declaration.[251] And in January 1939, at the Brotherhood's fifth conference, Hasan al-Banna declared that Palestine, "the land of Islam and cradle of the Prophets," was "a debt owed by the English to the Muslims."[252]

Closer to home, meanwhile, al-Banna was emerging as a vocal critic of British policy in Egypt, claiming that England was still harassing his country. He labeled the 1936 treaty "a shackle around the neck of Egypt and a manacle on its hands." Al-Banna called for "work and good preparation" to put an end to such fetters, noting provocatively that "the tongue of force is the most eloquent tongue," something Muslims should bear in mind if they wanted "freedom and independence."[253] Abbas al-Sissi later recounted a conversation with al-Banna during this same period, in which he spoke of the need to engage in "struggle and jihad" until they had liberated their "great country from all foreign authority."[254]

In light of such rhetoric, and with "scurrilous" anti-British articles having appeared in the Brotherhood's newspaper *al-Nadhir,* the British Embassy had already complained to the Egyptian director-general of public security, Hamdi Bey Mahbub. Nevertheless, Mahbub played down the issue, suggesting that such societies were "trivial" and "need not be taken seriously." The Brotherhood was said to comprise people who were of no importance and carried little weight with influential Egyptians. According to Mahbub, the agitation of the group was merely "a kind of 'safety-valve' which could do little if any harm."[255]

Needless to say, the British were not reassured by this response and continued to argue that "in the aggregate," groups like the Brotherhood were "making mischief" and could be a source of further trouble. There was even speculation that the Ikhwan was being "secretly financed by the Wafd to make propaganda locally against the British policy in Egypt and Palestine under the guise of religion." A promise was eventually extracted from Mahbub that he would discuss matters with the minister of interior, "with the object of putting a stop to any further anti-British manifestations on the part of religious organisations."[256] Still, the British seemed far from satisfied, and fresh complaints were taken up with the prime minister.

There was, though, little sign of any diminution in the volume of the agitation; on the contrary, this was felt to be "steadily increasing." Anti-British and anti-Jewish publications continued to circulate, many of them luridly detailing alleged "atrocities."[257] One example that drew the particular ire of British officials called for jihad and revolution against the "enemies of Islam" who were said to be destroying al-Aqsa mosque.[258] Another similar pamphlet was tellingly entitled *Palestine the Martyr*.[259]

It was in the midst of this propaganda campaign that Hasan al-Banna was arrested for the first time (for twenty-four hours) in 1938.[260] Yet this move failed to put an end to the Brotherhood's activism. New pamphlets were produced and the group even lobbied the British directly, with al-Banna sending a telegram to the embassy to protest against acts of injustice and cruelty in Palestine.[261]

As far as Ambassador Lampson was concerned, talk about "Holy War" in Palestine amounted to nothing more than "artificially provoked Islamic fervor."[262] At the same time, he was keenly aware of the fact that groups like the Brotherhood and Young Egypt could claim to be in step with mainstream public opinion on the Palestine issue. As early as mid-1937, Lampson had informed London that "it would be idle to disguise that there is universal public condemnation of the idea of partition."[263] He noted that opposition to the main lines of British policy was as discernable within the Wafdist press as it was among the smaller, mosquito press (of which the Brotherhood was a part).[264] Palestine was said to be the one subject where the otherwise fractious Egyptian media displayed "practically no divergence of opinion."[265]

In all of this, the British viewed the growth of anti-Jewish sentiment with particular apprehension. Certain newspapers were reported to be attacking the Jews in Egypt on account of their alleged support for Zionism.[266] The Brotherhood's *al-Nadhir,* for instance, ran a column entitled "The Threat of the Jews in Egypt." The newspaper encouraged a boycott of Jews and their expulsion from the Muslim world.[267] From the British perspective, such trends raised the troubling possibility that Egypt might become vulnerable to Axis propaganda. By the late 1930s, there were concerns that the Germans and Italians could utilize Arab disaffection over Palestine to undermine Britain's hold on its broader Middle Eastern empire. In the Foreign Office, mandarins expressed particular alarm at Mussolini's anti-Jewish campaign in the context of events in Palestine. If the "rot" were not stopped soon, they feared, then "the religious side of the Palestine Arab question may get such a hold on Arab countries that pogroms will begin"; if these were to start, it was suggested, they would spread "like wild fire."[268] In a similar vein, there was speculation over the possible involvement of Grand Mufti al-Husayni and agents from Nazi Germany in stirring up the Egyptian press.[269] The fact that the Jews could be depicted as the shared antagonists of both Hitler's Germany and the Arabs was thought to make the latter susceptible to Nazi propaganda. (In October 1938, it was observed too that the Germans had hosted a number of Islamic "guests" at that year's Nuremberg rally.)[270]

Embassy summaries of the Egyptian media in late 1938 and into 1939 revealed increasing nervousness about the impact of German and Italian propaganda—much of which was issued in Arabic. The output of Bari Radio was felt to be especially pernicious, with the Deutsches Nachrichten Büro (DNB) also identified as a relentless purveyor of stories about alleged British atrocities / mistreatment. The effect, it was judged, was to "undermine the confidence of the public in the strength and good faith of the democracies and to associate the latter with the sinister machinations of the Jews."[271] By autumn 1939, some officials were pointing to a growing "popular revulsion against the Jews," which ran together with criticism of the British.[272]

As has been shown, the activities of the Brotherhood seemed to bring together many of these worries. During the previous three years, the group had gained national standing, in part by dint of its voluble opposition to British policy in both Palestine and Egypt. To Western minds, it represented the recrudescence of a particularly Islamic fanaticism, with calls for jihad seen as a challenge to the British position in Cairo and across the region.

Countdown to War

As the situation in Europe deteriorated, British officials were terrified at the prospect of Middle Eastern instability. Palestine was an obvious source of anxiety given the fear that the "balloon in Europe" might go up at any moment.[273] It was this apprehension that drove renewed attempts to find a settlement to the conflict there. Some, though, viewed Palestine as an "incurable disease"—to be "treated as such," by which they meant "opiates to reduce the pain" rather than an effort to find a solution.[274] Egypt, meanwhile, remained a major cause for concern. The greatest immediate worry was that the government in Cairo might resile from its obligations under the 1936 treaty. Ambassador Lampson warned London in mid-January 1939 that the "evil seed . . . of the idea of Egyptian neutrality in the event of war [had begun] to bear poisonous flowers." The extent to which this idea developed further, he argued, would depend "in large degree on whether or not we are able to recover our former prestige and strength in the Near and Middle East." Egypt needed to be convinced, Lampson averred, that the British were sufficiently strong to protect her.[275] Ironically, in the ambassador's view, it was actually the Wafd Party—regardless of the venomous editorials appearing in its newspaper *al-Misri*—that stood most firmly on the principle that, in the event of war, Egypt must stand by Britain in accord with her treaty obligations.[276]

More broadly, in a long dispatch in early 1939, Lampson spoke at length about the problems that he saw in the country. Uppermost in his mind was the growth of an unemployed, "half-baked intelligentsia" that posed a latent "revolutionary danger." The general atmosphere was believed to be one "of anxious expectancy and of confusion of purpose and ideas." He suggested that many Egyptians had lost faith in the Wafd, but found nothing with which to replace it—on the contrary, it remained a symbol and bulwark "of their emancipation." But Lampson reckoned that affection for the party had diminished. As such, the ambassador worried for the health of Egypt's constitution: "Nearly all dislike Palace rule, but enthusiasm for the Parliamentary system has disappeared."[277]

In August 1939, Ali Maher finally achieved his goal of being reappointed Egyptian prime minister after the resignation of Muhammad Mahmud.[278] Though hardly unexpected (on account of Mahmud's ill health), the British were disappointed by the loss of the man they had come to regard as their "prop and mainstay in Egyptian affairs" at precisely the moment that events in Europe were at their most delicate.[279] Nevertheless, they were prepared to accept Maher as the best option to secure their interests. Indeed, it is striking that even prior to this there had been some suggestion that Maher was not truly anti-British and knew "better than most which side his bread is buttered."[280] Officials anticipated a relationship based on "mutual friendship and confidence," irrespective of Maher's public hostility.[281] Significantly, such thinking was indicative of an inherent British tendency to believe that business could be done with almost any group or individual, regardless of their professed antagonism for Britain and its interests. On this view, even the most vociferous opponent might prove amenable, if a mutually beneficial arrangement could be found. Though not applied to everyone in all cases, this mentality surfaced repeatedly in Egypt: here, in relation to Maher; later, with regard to the Brotherhood.

In keeping with this mind-set, the British initially viewed Maher's government in relatively benevolent fashion, as a "strong" ministry "headed by a man with great drive and energy." One official soon noted that with "the very important" exception of his failure to declare war on Germany, Maher was "cooperating very satisfactorily."[282] There were clouds on the horizon, however. Of concern, for instance, was the man appointed to the position of war minister—Muhammad Salih Harb Pasha (a "First World War deserter"). In addition to being personally objectionable, Harb was expected to make 'Aziz 'Ali al-Misri Pasha chief of the general staff of the Egyptian army (as, indeed, he did). The latter was considered to be a "Germanophil [sic]," and of questionable judgment and even sanity.[283] The prospect of such people wielding political power was scarcely to the liking of British officials. It also fed deeper suspicions about where Ali Maher's sympathies really lay and, as Charles Tripp has demonstrated, the elevation of al-Misri was consonant with Maher's politicization of the Egyptian army officer corps—a process that proved deeply destabilizing in the long term.[284]

The British were terrified lest Egypt become a haven for subversion and the activities of "fifth columnists." Among those identified as being particularly problematic in this regard were the Muslim Brotherhood. In May 1939, the embassy reported that the Brothers were continuing to gain influence "among both students and the people" and constituted the "most strenuous agitators against policy in Palestine."[285] There were also fresh signs that they enjoyed official patronage. Earlier in the year, when Ali Maher had traveled to London for the "Round Table Conference," a delegation of Brothers had been on hand to cheer both his departure and return.[286] Increasingly, too, the group seemed emboldened in opposition to the British. In May 1939, Hasan al-Banna described London's "White Paper" on Palestine as "disastrous," and called on the Egyptian government to resign in protest. The Brotherhood leader insisted that both the English and the Jews understood only one language: that of "revolution, force and blood."[287] Against this backdrop, and with Ali Maher returned to the premiership, a key question for the British was whether the Brotherhood might directly challenge Britain's hold over both Egypt and Palestine—perhaps with the covert support of the Axis.

In November 1939, military intelligence reported that the Egyptian police had uncovered various documents at the houses of German nationals who appeared to be engaged in subversive activity. Wilhelm Stellbogen, director of the DNB in Cairo, was said to be a close associate of a leading Nazi agent, Hans Beckhoff, and to be involved in the circulation of extensive anti-Jewish and anti-British propaganda (with a special focus on Palestine). To this end, he had apparently paid friendly foreign and local journalists and helped fund certain newspapers. According to the British intelligence report, "Stellbogen and Beckhoff were in close touch with the 'Moslem Brotherhood,' a fanatical and subversive anti-British association of Moslems, led by one, HASSAN EL BANNA. Proofs of this are offered by notes among Stellbogen's papers recording payments to the Moslem Brotherhood [emphasis in original]."[288]

One such note, dated 18 August 1939, confirmed that there had been multiple payments to the Brotherhood. The police also found records Stellbogen had made of a conference organized by the Ikhwan, which urged every Egyptian and Arab to participate in the "holy war" in Palestine. Little of this came as a shock to the British. The Brothers' call for jihad in support of the Palestine Arabs was obviously congruent with the German desire to cause the British maximum discomfort in the Middle East. Al-Banna, it should be said, would always deride claims that he had received funding from the Germans, Italians, and others as "false accusations."[289] Ten years later, though, a Foreign Office report on Egypt's political parties stated categorically that the Ikhwan had benefited from "assistance from Axis sources between 1934 and 1939, as a result of which Hassan al Banna became actively anti-British."[290] A similar assessment was provided by James Heyworth-Dunne: in a 1954 letter to Sir Roger Allen, he claimed that in 1936, the Nazis had paid more than £5,000 to the Muslim Brotherhood, with Grand Mufti al-Husayni acting as the intermediary between Hasan al-Banna and Berlin.[291] Whether the specifics of this claim are correct or not, it seems evident that, at a minimum, the Brothers had established a line of communication with the Germans; and it is at least plausible that some kind of financial arrangement was made. The existence of such ties merely confirmed British views as to the pernicious character of the Ikhwan.

Conclusion

On the cusp of the Second World War, therefore, the British had clearly come to see the Muslim Brotherhood as a threat. In the first years of its existence, the group had barely registered on the horizons of UK officials. A decade on, however, and there was no doubting the national importance of the Ikhwan. It had risen to prominence offering an analysis of the world that made sense of British and, indeed, Western strength by reference to Egyptian and Islamic weakness. Egyptians and Muslims generally, according to al-Banna, had fallen prey to a Western cultural invasion, which had the effect of corroding their moral fiber. On the basis of this diagnosis, he prescribed a clear remedy: a return to the "true" path of Islam.

The British orientalist James Heyworth-Dunne, writing in 1950, described Hasan al-Banna as aiming at the "rejection of all forms of Westernism." The Brotherhood was driven, he believed, by a refusal to "accept the modernistic applications of Western philosophy and scientific advancement"; he also suggested it was fiercely opposed to both constitutional democracy and the foreign presence in Egypt.[292] Other scholars have offered similarly bleak impressions of the group. American scholar Christina Harris labeled the Ikhwan "militant reactionaries" against Western *Christian* penetration.[293] Afaf Lutfi al-Sayyid al-Marsot also saw in Hasan al-Banna an "aversion toward all things western" and presumed that this reflected his lack of exposure to Western influences.[294] As explained above, however, this was not an entirely accurate picture of the Brotherhood and its founder.

The reality is that al-Banna's views were formed in dialogue with the West; he was shaped by the interplay between Islamic *and* Western influences. Consequently, historians have recognized al-Banna's ambivalence toward the West, noting that he drew on it when it suited him to do so, while rejecting its imperialism and "civilizational" values. In the eyes of the Brothers, technical and scientific expertise were benign and worthy of incorporation; the social sciences, arts, and humanities were to be avoided at all costs because they carried the imprint of "Western" thought.[295] As Krämer has underlined, al-Banna's central message was that Egyptians needed to shake off their sense of inferiority vis-à-vis the West, while embracing those aspects of Western civilization that might benefit them.[296]

This ethos was captured neatly in P. H. Newby's 1955 novel, *The Picnic at Sakkara,* which depicted a member of the group (Muawiya) as torn between a longing to emulate "the West" and a fierce desire to drive out and even kill the foreigner (the English professor, Edgar Perry).[297] Elsewhere, al-Banna himself revealed much about what drove the Ikhwan in his account of how an unnamed Muslim Brother was insulted by an engineer at the Suez Canal Company, who accused him of trying to overcharge for his services. An argument ensued in which the Brother emphasized his indignation at the behavior of a "guest" in "my country." Eventually, the foreigner apologized and even tried to tip the Brother in question—an offer that was refused because the latter only wanted his "right."[298] Though perhaps apocryphal, the story was surely illustrative of the Brotherhood's guiding spirit: the pursuit of dignity through the creation of an authentically "Islamic" society freed from any sense of subjection to the West.

What al-Banna and his movement wished to contest was not modernity per se, but a modernity constructed on a "foreign" basis in which Muslims seemed to be consigned to subordinate status. Much of what they saw around them was irretrievably tainted by its association with Western penetration and colonialism.[299] As Frances Robinson has observed, the British Empire was "the context in which many Muslims experienced the transition to modernity."[300] Groups like the Brotherhood were one kind of response (among many), with al-Banna and his followers offering an answer to the challenges of a rapidly changing world clothed in the mantle of authenticity.[301]

In this way, as Richard Mitchell suggested, it is perhaps most fruitful to see the Brotherhood as embodying a particular mood or style of politics.[302] Islam was cast as a force for solidarity and cohesion—distinct from "foreign-origin" ideas of socialism and liberalism. The Ikhwan represented a reaction not only to Western power but also to the "foreign" culture, which was identified with the indigenous elites who controlled Egypt and who were thought to have succumbed to the allure of "Westernization," even as they failed to deliver on their various political promises.[303] As Brynjar Lia has noted, the Brotherhood saw itself as a popular mass movement, struggling for cultural and national liberation and speaking in the name of a new upwardly mobile social group that wished to challenge existing elites; in short, it stood for an "Islam of the effendia."[304] Al-Banna looked to "the Islamization of modernity" by a mixture of appropriation (of many "Western" concepts) and the reinterpretation (of key elements of a more traditional discourse).[305] In line with this, he accepted many of the core parameters of modern political life, such as the nation-state.[306] Hence, as Barbara Stowasser has underlined, the creation of the Muslim Brotherhood marked something qualitatively new—and it was, in essence, unlike anything that had gone before. The Ikhwan, though laying claim to an intellectual heritage intrinsic to Islam, was fundamentally a movement born in response to Western—specifically British—power.

Consequently, "the West" as a concept was absolutely central to al-Banna's ideological framework. He developed and utilized what Andrea Mura called an "occidentalist narrative" that challenged Western hegemony.[307] In so doing, al-Banna offered a jaundiced and one-dimensional view of the West that was juxtaposed to an idealized, spiritual past to which he hoped the Muslim "community" might return, even as it acquired the tools of Western scientific and technological advance.[308] This was a romantic view par excellence, with an emphasis on recovering the "soul" of the nation.[309] Simultaneously, the Brothers held to a highly pessimistic view of a "West," which they frequently equated with the "enemies of Islam." They were convinced of Western hostility—for Islam generally and for the Brotherhood in particular. The British were thought to be "fearful" of a movement that would "contest politics in the name of religion" (as described above, there was much truth in this). According to the senior Brotherhood figure Sheikh Ahmad al-Baquri, it was for this reason that al-Banna initially avoided formal politics and gave the impression that the Brothers were purely a Sufi organization in order to distract the Western world from considering the Brothers a threat. This is perhaps too cynical a view of the Ikhwan's attachment to Sufism, but the underlying sentiment is undoubtedly correct: the Brotherhood lived in a world in which there was good and bad, heroes and enemies. It anticipated opposition and struggle; and it was therefore unsurprised when this arrived. As al-Baquri went on to state, "the West began to whisper to the leaders of the Arab world . . . alleging that the Muslim Brotherhood was a danger to them."[310]

During the 1930s, the Brotherhood had emerged as a national political movement that encapsulated the dominant cultural and intellectual trends of the era. The Brotherhood proved popular among a young, educated cohort; and the movement talked in supra-Egyptian terms about a pan-Islamic, pan-Arab vision. It was this outlook that made the Brothers so preoccupied with the fate of neighboring Palestine—and also why they were so effective in mobilizing around that issue. The Brotherhood grew initially in the shadow of the Palestinian conflict, the "incurable disease," fiercely critical of both the Jewish settlers and the British government. It was this agitation that brought the Ikhwan to the attention of the Cairo Embassy. The latter had hoped, by the mid-1930s, to restructure the British position in Egypt, conceding more of the formal trappings of independence while retaining ultimate control. Yet few were fooled. In reality, British influence was never far from the surface—in part because of the enduring volatility of Egyptian political life. In this context, embassy officials were deeply concerned about emerging new political forces, one of which was the Brotherhood.

Ambassador Lampson and his colleagues deemed the Brotherhood to be inherently antithetical to British interests. On more than one occasion, the embassy asked the Egyptian authorities to take tougher measures to suppress the movement. Such requests went unanswered, however, and the Brotherhood seemed to flourish as one element of a loose alliance of forces that were judged problematic. Alongside them were other religious groupings—particularly at al-Azhar—Young Egypt, the king, and the veteran "intriguer" Ali Maher. It was acknowledged that the latter had utilized groups like the Ikhwan to undercut the appeal of the Wafd and bolster the position of the palace. The success of this approach saw Maher reassume the premiership on the eve of war.

It might have been expected that the British would view this development with deep alarm, but many officials saw in Ali Maher a man with whom they *could* do business. Irrespective of his known antipathy for the British and his sympathy for Italy, it was assumed that he would prove amenable to their interests. Clearly, this was a gamble; the threat of sedition remained. Of crucial importance was the question of whether Maher would implement the treaty as demanded by the British and, in turn, whether he would act against those groups considered a threat—especially given that the Axis seemed intent on subversion. The Brotherhood stood at the nexus of many of these concerns and few doubted it would be a critical part of the equation in wartime Egypt.

Two Wartime Liaisons

1940–1944

I N OCTOBER 1941, Hasan al-Banna was interned by the
Egyptian government. His arrest came against a backdrop
of mounting British apprehension over the activities of the
Muslim Brotherhood. Embassy officials were delighted at the move; it was, however, to be of only temporary relief. Al-Banna's imprisonment provoked protests by Brotherhood members and well-placed supporters; those connected with
the palace made "continued interventions" on his behalf. Consequently, after
less than a month's incarceration, the Brotherhood leader was released.[1] Officials in London were furious, describing the move as "extremely unsatisfactory."[2] Ambassador Lampson declared himself ready for a "first-class row" and
called the Egyptian prime minister to give him "undiluted Hell."[3]

British consternation over the release of al-Banna stemmed from their growing
belief that the Brotherhood lay at the heart of a constellation of malevolent forces
working against them in Egypt. One intelligence agent reported that the group
was "fundamentally anti-British" and liable to be "most dangerous." "It would
be far better," he suggested, if the group's leaders "were locked up."[4] Others had
reached similar conclusions. A parallel report from November 1941 stated that
"the long term policy of secret planning and organization adopted by Hassan el
Banna has achieved for the Ikhwan el Muslimeen a predominant position among
subversive associations in Egypt."[5]

By this stage, therefore, the British were clearly convinced of the Brotherhood's malign intent. Concerns over the group and its actions had been growing throughout the latter half of the 1930s. From a British perspective, the rise of the Ikhwan was bound up with the deterioration of Egypt's sociopolitical environment. The movement was seen as a danger to their interests, and it was unsurprising that British officials should have been calling for an anti-Brotherhood crackdown. However, not everyone was convinced that repression could solve the problems posed by Egypt's subversive groups. Amid the crises of the war, some had begun to speculate about the viability of an alternative approach and the extent to which the Brotherhood and those of its ilk might be susceptible to subtler methods.

The Demands of War

During late 1939 and early 1940, the most pressing question for leading British officials in Cairo was whether the Egyptian government of the day, under Prime Minister Ali Maher, could be trusted. Maher's suggestion that Cairo might become an "open city," protected from the ravages of war, did little to alleviate British concerns about the depth of the prime minister's commitment to the Allied cause.[6] Disquiet was voiced about pro-Italian sympathies within the government and the palace—the fear being that these might push Egypt toward an ill-defined "neutrality."[7] An important political test of the government's bona fides was whether Maher was willing to suppress those groups that he had previously encouraged, which were judged to be working against the British—principally Young Egypt and the Muslim Brotherhood. The former, now styling itself the "Islamic National Party," remained deeply involved in antitreaty and antiforeign agitation.[8] Ambassador Lampson was particularly exercised by their penchant for sending him "improper communications" (mostly demanding his own dismissal).[9] Of greater concern still was the fact that British officials claimed to have "convincing evidence of this agitation having received foreign—Italian—money."[10] In their view, Ahmad Husayn and his followers needed to be "checked," lest they "threaten the maintenance of public order."[11] Consequently, Lampson called on both the king and prime minister to demand the suppression of Young Egypt.[12]

On this issue, however, the ambassador found himself rebuffed; neither was he granted satisfaction with regard to the Brotherhood. The memoirs of the Cairo-born Alfred Sansom reflect the extent to which the Ikhwan was seen as a threat by the British throughout the war. Sansom had joined the Field Security branch of the British Military Police and swiftly became aware of the "terroristically inclined . . . Moslem Brotherhood." He recalled hearing al-Banna speak once, describing him as a "a short, snub-nosed man . . . [who] looked anything but a demagogue." "But there was," Sansom claimed, "a fanatical fire in his eyes, and above all a lyrical resonance in his voice, that made him an electrifying mob-orator."[13] Such characteristics put al-Banna and his movement at the top of the British list of undesirable elements in Egypt. The fact that the Cairo government seemed reluctant to curb the Brotherhood only heightened fears about its trustworthiness.

By June 1940, Lampson had run out of patience with Ali Maher. He noted in his diary that he no longer had any doubt "whatsoever that this man is double crossing us and we simply cannot afford to go [on] with that."[14] In the ambassador's assessment, Maher was "non-coperative [sic], unreliable and indeed double faced"; his "continuance in office" posed a very real threat to "our armies in the field."[15] What followed was the first of two major wartime interventions by Lampson into Egypt's internal affairs. He went to King Faruq and insisted on both the dismissal of Ali Maher and the appointment of a government enjoying popular support—as Lampson well knew, this meant the return of Mustafa al-Nahas and the Wafd.[16]

The ambassador found, however, that the king was determined neither to accept al-Nahas, nor to bow supinely to Lampson's wishes. And rail though he might against the obstinacy of "that stupid boy," he was then confronted with a "master-stroke" from Faruq.[17] The king, while accepting that Maher would have to go, refused to call al-Nahas; instead, he asked the independent politician Hasan Sabri Pasha to form a ministry. Lampson immediately recognized that Sabri had "no political support in the country." This made him dependent entirely on the palace and allowed the king to preserve his influence. At the same time, Sabri's well-known pro-British views made it hard for the embassy to raise objections against him. Lampson felt that he had no choice but to acquiesce in this fait accompli, for the alternative might have meant dethroning the king and the imposition of martial law, which in turn would have required a major diversion of troops. For now, the British preferred to avoid such a "major crisis" and accepted the "second-best" outcome of a "rather weak but pro-British Government" at the helm in Cairo.[18]

Whatever its shortcomings, the new Sabri administration was immediately faced with renewed calls from the embassy for the curtailment of anti-British activities.[19] Of particular concern was the possibility that Ali Maher, though out of power, might retain a deleterious influence over the king—especially as Maher now argued publicly against a formal Egyptian entry into the war. From a British perspective, this amounted to unwelcome rabble-rousing. At a more practical level, meanwhile, there remained suspicions that Maher was at the center of an anti-British, pro-Axis network of individuals, which included 'Aziz 'Ali al-Misri (commander in chief of the Egyptian army, who was later dismissed for passing British defense plans to the Italians), 'Abd al-Rahman Azzam Bey (a pan-Arabist diplomat and subsequently first secretary-general of the Arab League), and Muhammad Salih Harb Pasha (the former defense minister and president of the Young Men's Muslim Association, or YMMA).[20] By this stage, the embassy believed that the king and Maher had made "some definite re-insurance arrangement with Italy." British officials were convinced that the former prime minister was at the heart of the "internal rot" within Egypt, and that more "energetic" action against him was required.[21]

Groups like the Brotherhood, Young Egypt, and the YMMA continued to be seen as key vehicles for Maher's influence and subversion. There was even speculation that he might seek to establish an "Islamic Union" to unify such forces inside Egypt and strengthen ties with like-minded organizations abroad. One British official observed that the "palace [had] always toyed with Pan-Islamic ideas in a vague way," and reports now suggested a marked escalation in these activities, which were given a distinctly anti-British coloring.[22] Doubtless, embassy misgivings were exacerbated by the worsening military situation over the course of 1940. Defeats in the Western Desert at the hands of the advancing Italians seemed to threaten Britain's physical hold over Egypt. In this context, Axis-inspired propaganda appeared all the more insidious. The Romanian legation in Cairo was thought to be especially active in stirring up unrest.[23] Equally, Lampson was again troubled by Arabic broadcasts from Rome and Berlin.[24] To British minds, Axis and palace-inspired "defeatism" was a serious drain on Egyptian confidence in their position.

Officials were also aware that the behavior of the king presented an ongoing challenge. Some had come to the conclusion that Faruq should be "ruthlessly liquidated," and "the sooner the better."[25] The ambassador tended to agree, noting that "we shall ere much longer have to grasp this Palace nettle," else "it will go on stinging us."[26] As palace obstructionism continued into the autumn of 1940, Lampson received authorization from London that in the event of another crisis, he might force the abdication of the king.[27] For the moment, the ambassador balked at issuing any ultimatum to Faruq. Exasperation with the king was balanced by a fear that precipitous action might make the situation worse.[28]

This tense status quo endured through the end of 1940, surviving the premature death of Hasan Sabri and his replacement as prime minister by another pro-British pasha, Husayn Sirri. Indeed, if anything, Sirri's accession to the premiership was seen as an "eminently encouraging" step in the right direction given his "strong character" and his apparent determination to eliminate "evil influences."[29]

An Alternative to Repression?

Throughout the first year of the war, Ambassador Lampson had pressed the Egyptian authorities to take a tougher line against all subversive movements and individuals. Others, however, took a different view. It seems clear that some British officials had begun to experiment with alternatives to repression as a way of heading off the threat posed by groups like Young Egypt and the Muslim Brotherhood. At the heart of this endeavor was the conviction that such organizations, irrespective of their ideological hostility, might be swayed by material inducements. State papers show that from the summer of 1940, British military intelligence officers initiated an attempt to reach an accommodation with Ahmad Husayn and his party. This episode is worth looking at in detail because it established a pattern of behavior that would reemerge in relation to the Brotherhood.

In a July telegram to the War Office, the commander in chief of British Forces in the Middle East, General Archibald Wavell, ordered that no pressure be applied to Husayn, with whom contact had been established. The diaries of Sir Miles Lampson indicate that Brigadier Eric Shearer, the director of British military intelligence in Cairo, had been tasked by Wavell to oversee the initiative.[30] The general appreciated the "risk of double crossing" but also believed that they had "already established [a] financial hold [on Husayn] which could be used if necessary [to] utterly discredit him." In Wavell's estimation, if it was possible to have Young Egypt "genuinely work for us" then the result "would be immeasurably better than unsuccessfully trying to stopper [the] effervescent body."[31]

Wavell's dispatch thus reveals the extent to which the military authorities were engaged in an effort to suborn Young Egypt. It was hoped that financial incentives might successfully put an end to the group's anti-British agitation. The advocates of this policy did not entirely think that Ahmad Husayn could be "bought against his own convictions," but they did believe he could be persuaded to cease activity in the short term. Furthermore, they hoped to convince him that the embarrassments he caused were helping the dictators, who he professed to see as a greater menace than the British.[32] (Though it should be said that such claims by Husayn, in his conversations with British interlocutors, rather flew in the face of his earlier public declarations of sympathy for the Axis governments, and it is interesting that they were treated credulously.)[33]

It seems evident that Ambassador Lampson was more than a little skeptical about all this. He noted that "Shearer and his merry men" supposed they could "buy" Ahmad Husayn. "With some misgiving," the ambassador had agreed to go along with the endeavor—though clearly against his better judgment. Lampson reiterated his preference that Young Egypt be "dealt with severely as being prospectively dangerous." In addition, he argued that the group was, in 1940, on a "downward grade if not actually moribund." In his view, British engagement might actually serve to resuscitate the "financial or moral sinews" of an otherwise declining force. Finally, Lampson also expressed reservations about the actions of military intelligence, noting that there were some sixty officers working in this field at no small expense. There was, he stated, "no sort of Treasury control over their expenditure . . . just the same as in the last war." Indeed, Lampson feared there was little meaningful oversight of any kind over their work. The result, he believed, was that intelligence officers could embark on ventures of dubious purpose, such as that to win over Ahmad Husayn.[34]

The ambassador did acknowledge that the policy had brought some superficially positive effects, including a short-term reduction in Husayn's openly anti-British activities. At the same time, however, Lampson's own sources suggested that Young Egypt was involved in a plot to assassinate the Egyptian prime minister and interior minister, as well as General Wavell and the ambassador himself. Though he admitted that such plots were often to be taken "with a grain of salt," Lampson maintained that they put the attempt to accommodate Young Egypt in a rather different light. He declared himself "very doubtful whether conciliation will lead anywhere with a fanatic like Ahmed Hussein [sic]."[35] Or, as he put it more pointedly in his diary, he felt it was "at least anomalous" that the military should be "dealing out funds" to someone who "up till recently was on his very last legs," even as he was "plotting to bump off the British Ambassador!"[36] Lampson claimed to have written directly to Brigadier Shearer, offering him the Arab proverb (in French) that he felt was most appropriate: "Celui qui réchauffe un serpent court plus de risqué [sic] d'en être piqué" (Those who nurse a viper to their bosom run a greater risk of being bitten).[37]

After a meeting with the military service chiefs, Lampson further noted his belief that "it was all very well" for British military intelligence "to try to win

Ahmed Hussein over to us," but he felt "there were limits as to how long that should go on when we knew as a fact that his party were actively organising a campaign of violence." It would be better, he argued, to abandon the effort to conciliate Husayn and return to a policy of pressing the Egyptian government to take "drastic action" against Young Egypt. Evidently, though, Wavell was not convinced. The general claimed that Husayn was not "personally aware of these plottings" and "could hardly accept responsibility for these acts." Lampson's rejoinder was that he was quite "content" for Wavell himself to "take responsibility for anything that might occur." And, in his diary, the ambassador declared himself to be "increasingly conscious of what strikes me as a rather alarming lack of what I can only call, for lack of a better term 'political sense' amongst our military leaders."[38] In a telegram back to London, Lampson loudly voiced his reservations, stating, "I am by instinct mistrustful of this meddling by the British military in Egyptian internal politics: they will probably end by burning their and our fingers."[39] It was a prescient warning. Just over a decade later, Ahmad Husayn's Young Egypt would be heavily implicated in the destruction by fire of much of "British Cairo" during the "Black Saturday" riots of January 1952 (see Chapter 4). Of course, officials can hardly be blamed for failing to predict the future. Nevertheless, the ambassador's words carry a certain retrospective poignancy—about the long-term dangers of artificially sustaining an anti-British organization—and Lampson's own discomfort with a policy of trying to pacify Young Egypt was clear.

In London, Foreign Office mandarins reserved judgment. They accepted that those "on the spot" were best placed to handle matters. If, as seemed to be the case, the military authorities believed there was "a real possibility that the leopard [was] changing his spots," then they were content to support efforts to secure an accommodation with Husayn. However, they also added that this initiative "could not be allowed to run indefinitely and [they] could not run risks of plots" and other threats. On balance, though perhaps less obviously alarmist, the Foreign Office tended to share its ambassador's skepticism that Ahmad Husayn could be "really responsive to a policy of appeasement."[40]

Significantly, it would appear that one of those centrally involved in this initiative was the academic turned security operative, Professor James Heyworth-Dunne.[41] According to his curriculum vitae, between 1940 and 1943, Heyworth-Dunne "ran [his] own information and propaganda centre in the Middle East with [his] own printing press and edited a number of papers, reviews and brochures."[42] Yet, alongside such relatively innocuous activities, he seems to have been an active intelligence agent. Foreign Office officials would later note that Heyworth-Dunne "worked under Brigadier [Iltyd] Clayton" (deputy head of the Cairo-based Middle East Intelligence Centre) during the Second World War.[43] Similarly, his obituary stated that during the war, "he gave his services to the British Intelligence services in the Middle East."[44] Perhaps most pertinently, Lampson's testimony confirms that Heyworth-Dunne's activities in Egypt were supported by Brigadier Clayton and Colonel Raymund Maunsell (head of Security Intelligence Middle East, the regional branch of Military Intelligence Section 5, or MI5).[45] The ambassador's diary also records Heyworth-Dunne's involvement in the "negotiations" with Ahmad Husayn—much to the ambassador's obvious chagrin: "I have warned General Wavell personally that he should not take what D[unne] says as being necessarily reliable."[46] In a further entry, Lampson referred to the "continued presence in Egypt of this wretched man Heywood Dunne [sic] who is used by our military with such disastrous results." He pressed the minister of state in the Middle East, Oliver Lyttleton, to remove someone who, to his mind, had established "a strange influence with our military, especially Brigadier Clayton who ought to know better."[47]

In spite of such warnings, the military authorities continued to defend their approach, believing it to be effective. The commander in chief telegraphed London in late September 1940 to assert: "We have evidence that our contact made at a critical period when a change of ministry was in progress and spectacular utterances if not doings were expected of [Ahmad Husayn] by his own hotheads kept the individual quiet and discredited him with his own party. This fact and his present attitude make any special measures unnecessary for the time being. He is however under such close and continual police surveillance that immediate action can be taken if necessary."[48]

Yet, even as those words were being composed, the British were receiving further reports that suggested their attempt to win over Husayn had been "only a temporary success." In mid-October, officials in London noted that since the end of August, Husayn had resumed his anti-British activities and was believed to be in receipt of funds from Ali Maher. It was also now thought that he had always maintained a line of contact with the Italians and had been trying to create an anti-British movement across several Middle Eastern states.[49] Unsurprisingly, it would seem that the policy of trying to suborn Young Egypt was abandoned soon after. Instead, at Lampson's instigation, Ahmad Husayn was arrested and the ambassador resumed his efforts to have the party as a whole suppressed. For the next three years, Lampson demanded that the Egyptian government maintain pressure on the group.[50]

Despite its apparent failure, however, this episode reveals much about the different strands of thinking that existed across British officialdom. Evidently, there were those who believed that ardently anti-British individuals and organizations could be brought to some form of understanding if only the right terms of trade could be found. As described earlier, during the 1930s, the diplomats had expressed such views with regard to Ali Maher. On this occasion, it was now the military commanders who favored an approach of this kind toward Young Egypt; by contrast, it was the Foreign Office mandarins—and, in particular, Ambassador Lampson—who took a more robust line. The significance of all this becomes apparent when considering attitudes toward that other mainstay of anti-British opinion in Egypt during this era, the Muslim Brotherhood; for it seems clear that some officials felt the moment was ripe for an accommodation with the Ikhwan.

In exploring this issue, one again encounters the enigmatic figure of James Heyworth-Dunne. His personal papers contain handwritten notes that suggest he himself became interested in the Brotherhood in early 1940. He observed that Hasan al-Banna had developed from an "unknown student to an important religious leader." According to Heyworth-Dunne, al-Banna had won over his followers by the force of "his teaching and personality." The Brotherhood leader was said to be on "friendly terms" with potential rivals including the "Wahhabis," and Heyworth-Dunne was aware that "many politicians" and the palace had approached the Ikhwan, offering support. Although he believed that al-Banna had thus far "preferred to stay out of politics," Heyworth-Dunne felt this was "all the more reason to keep an eye on him." Indeed, he remarked that the movement as a whole was "worth watching closely."[51]

There is little doubt that Heyworth-Dunne heeded his own advice—and that things quickly developed beyond a watching brief. In his 1950 book on the Brotherhood, Heyworth-Dunne acknowledged wartime discussions about trying to establish some kind of alliance with the group. On this account, it was the Ikhwan itself that initiated the process in late 1941, when Hasan al-Banna "gave out through agents, that he would be prepared to co-operate with the British and gave the impression that he would be amenable to some kind of payment." Brotherhood representatives, including al-Banna's close ally Ahmad al-Sukkari, allegedly asked for $40,000 and a car in return for their support. Apparently, al-Banna sought to convey the message that he no longer wished to take on the British. But according to Heyworth-Dunne, "nothing was farther from the truth. He had no intention of receiving the money of infidels. . . . For twelve years, the Ikhwan had been fed on anti-British propaganda, it would have been virtually impossible to have asked them to work for the British."[52] As a result, the initiative came to nothing.

In an interesting coda a few years later, Heyworth-Dunne again publicly dismissed the idea that the Brotherhood could ever work with the British. He declared such claims to be "absurd" given its "violently anti-British" out-look. The Ikhwan, Heyworth-Dunne now said, had always been against them, even while al-Banna and his agents were pestering the British for money during the war.[53] Thus, in his postwar recounting of the episode, Heyworth-Dunne presented himself as a firm skeptic. He derided the possibility of a rapproche-ment with the Brotherhood, insisting that the ideology of the group made this inconceivable. Yet, this self-confident clarity stands somewhat in contrast with his earlier, privately noted and rather more nuanced views of the Ikhwan. More-over, it certainly diverges starkly with his approach to Young Egypt—a group no less hostile to the British than was the Brotherhood. In this context, it is hard not to wonder if there was more to the discussions than Heyworth-Dunne suggests, and it is worth taking a closer look at these events.

Egyptian enemies of the Brotherhood would later use the original testimony of Heyworth-Dunne as evidence for the group's supposedly friendly relations with the British.[54] This, of course, proves nothing. Nevertheless, as Richard P. Mitchell observed, Brotherhood leaders did admit that discussions had taken place; they maintained, however, that the initiative for contact came from the British, who sought to "purchase" the Ikhwan through the exertions of Heyworth-Dunne.[55] The Brotherhood historian Muhammad al-'Adawi recorded that the British were represented in talks by an orientalist—surely, an allusion to Heyworth-Dunne—and al-Banna was offered payment in return for an al-liance. He turned this down, but was later visited by another individual, who offered him a check for £10,000. Again, al-Banna refused, allegedly replying with a smile, "You are in a state of war and in greater need of these thousands [than me]." Still the British persisted: first, they raised the amount of money on offer, and when this did not succeed, they even told al-Banna to name his price. The Brotherhood leader, though, held out against all blandishments. According to al-'Adawi, other Brothers including al-Sukkari had actually wanted to ac-cept the money, but al-Banna overruled them.[56]

An additional perspective on this matter comes from the researches of a roving American journalist, John Roy Carlson (real name Arthur Derounian), who traveled through Egypt in 1948 on his way to Palestine. He later sent the US Embassy a report on his journey and published a version entitled *From Cairo to*

Damascus (1951). Significantly, the former contains reference to accusations that the Muslim Brotherhood had previously been in receipt of British money. One source of Carlson's information was the Wafdist lawyer Aziz Fahmi. Given that the Wafd and the Brotherhood were by then fierce political rivals, Fahmi's evidence might simply be disregarded as an obvious smear. Nevertheless, Carlson noted that it was corroborated by the testimony of Ahmad al-Sukkari, al-Banna's onetime confidante and the man named by Heyworth-Dunne as having been involved in wartime negotiations.[57] He told Carlson that in 1940, Brigadier General Clayton had visited the Brotherhood's headquarters at Helmia al-Gedida Square in Cairo, at the instigation of "one Howarth-Dunn"—unmistakably a reference to Heyworth-Dunne. By al-Sukkari's account, Clayton told him and al-Banna that the British were anxious to have "friends instead of enemies among the Moslems." Thereafter, Heyworth-Dunne and a Major Goodwin "wined and dined" the Brotherhood leaders. According to al-Sukkari, the culmination of this courtship came in November 1940, when Heyworth-Dunne visited him alone at his house and—speaking in Arabic—offered £E20,000 to "assist" the Ikhwan with their work in return for the group's promotion of pro-British propaganda. Al-Sukkari said that he refused the offer, but that Hasan al-Banna subsequently accepted some £E10,000 from the British.

It should be said that al-Sukkari's evidence is itself far from unproblematic, particularly regarding al-Banna's alleged acceptance of British money. By the time of his meeting with Carlson, he had fallen out spectacularly with his erstwhile friend and had been expelled from the Brotherhood. Al-Sukkari had then written articles for the Wafdist press excoriating the group. In addition, Carlson admits that while al-Sukkari claimed to have documentary proof to support his allegations, he never produced this; he also judged him not to be a particularly strong character. And yet Carlson simultaneously described al-Sukkari as "honest and religious," and declared that, on balance, he was inclined to believe him—certainly in relation to the visit and propositions of Heyworth-Dunne.

It is noticeable too that across the accounts of Carlson, al-'Adawi, and Heyworth-Dunne there are certain points of agreement. Taken together, it seems fair to conclude: first, that talks *were* held in 1940–1941 between the Brotherhood leader and British representatives; second, that Heyworth-Dunne was heavily involved in this process; and third, that there was some discussion about a possible financial arrangement. In the context of the latter, it is striking that Carlson reckoned that the British, having tried to buy off the Ikhwan, were unlikely to have been discouraged. In his assessment, it was "more than likely that successful attempts [had] been made."[58]

Again, Carlson's verdict does not in itself definitively prove that Hasan al-Banna accepted British funding during the war. Indeed, a categorical answer to the question of whether he did or not is perhaps impossible; the evidence is circumstantial rather than watertight. Nevertheless, it is worth stating that a readiness to make such a deal would scarcely have been out of keeping with al-Banna's past and future practice. As described in Chapter 1, he operated in highly pragmatic fashion, especially when it came to building relationships and securing material support for his movement. During the formative era of the Ikhwan, al-Banna took money from the Suez Canal Company; for a period, he was likely in receipt of German funding; and he also made an alliance of convenience with Ali Maher. In the years that followed, he would obtain assistance from Egyptian governments of differing stripes, including that of the Wafd. Against this background, it would surely come as little surprise if he was open to accepting British monies. Of perhaps greater significance, then, was the fact that the British authorities were willing to offer him such financial inducements.

What this episode therefore revealed, when placed alongside the similar incident with Young Egypt, was a certain way of doing things that was current in British circles during the war and with which Heyworth-Dunne was closely identified. The essence of this approach was the belief that every organization or individual was ultimately "biddable," no matter how strident their public hostility to the British. It was this outlook that informed the attempt to entice Young Egypt into an accommodation; on the same basis, the hope was that the Brotherhood might be brought to accept a similar arrangement.

By way of addendum, it is worth noting that Muhammad Hamid Abu al-Nasr, the future general guide of the Brotherhood, recorded in his own memoirs that a further effort was made to bribe the Brotherhood toward the end of the war. According to Abu al-Nasr, a delegation that included the British minister responsible for the Middle East and the ambassador visited the Ikhwan central offices in Cairo and offered al-Banna another large monetary contribution. Once more, the Brotherhood leader refused, insisting that his movement relied only on the support of its members. It was this, said Abu al-Nasr, that led the British to conclude that al-Banna was "the most dangerous man in the Middle East."[59] It may be that Abu al-Nasr's narrative is a retelling-cum-distortion of the earlier affair—it seems unlikely, for instance, that Ambassador Lampson would have been party to such an approach. Even so, it reflects an important point: the Brothers believed that the British failure to purchase them left UK officials implacably opposed to al-Banna and the Ikhwan.[60] As was increasingly evident, this perception of British hostility was not without foundation.

Crackdown

One of the ironies of British attempts to secure an alliance with the Brotherhood was that this came at the same moment that the group was moving in a more militant direction. As explained in Chapter 1, al-Banna had been clear from the beginning on the need to revive the spirit of jihad within the Islamic world. To this end, he had established first "Excursion" groups and then "Rover" scouts to develop a martial ethos and provide physical training to the Brotherhood youth. After 1938, adult members were arranged into "Battalions" for the same purpose. In 1940–1941, this was taken a stage further with the creation of a "Special Apparatus" or "Secret Organisation," initially under the leadership of Salih 'Ashmawi.[61] The precise date of its founding remains disputed, though al-Banna would later state that the first cohort of Brothers to take the pledge of jihad did so in April 1940.[62] Similarly, Salah Shadi, a police officer and senior Brotherhood leader, claimed that the Special Apparatus (SA) was created in 1940 to wage jihad against "the English" and the Zionists, and also to defend the movement against the aggression of Egyptian governments. The most committed members of the Ikhwan were invited to join this formation, where they were given weapons training and taught to "listen and obey."[63]

In the words of another leading figure, Hasan Dawh, the SA represented "the summit of sacrifice and loyalty to the group." It was the hidden counterpart to the Brotherhood's open activities and was meant to create a "youth elite" that would protect the movement and also prosecute the jihad in Palestine and Egypt.[64] Shadi claimed that the group carried out its first operations toward the end of the Second World War, when members threw a bomb at "the British club" (though he does not specify where, presumably in Cairo). The aim, he averred, was not to kill people but rather to "terrorise" the British into realizing that they were not welcome in Egypt.[65]

It is not clear how far the British were actually aware of these underground developments. But in any case, they needed little additional persuasion that the Brotherhood was a hostile force. Ambassador Lampson and his colleagues were already convinced that the Egyptian government should take action against the movement. In part because of their pressure, the Egyptian Ministry of Education transferred Hasan al-Banna to Qena in Upper Egypt in March 1941—a move said to have caused "considerable perturbation amongst the Ikhwan." The British hoped that al-Banna's absence would "weaken" the group's influence in Cairo and Lower Egypt, though they accepted that it also ran the risk of stimulating Brotherhood activities in Upper Egypt. Officials worried too that it might give al-Banna "the popularity of martyrdom." Despite this, they felt that "on balance," the move offered "an advantage from the security aspect."[66]

As it happened, al-Banna's exile proved relatively short-lived, and by September he had returned to Cairo. Brotherhood accounts of this episode portray it as a "clear victory," with al-Banna using his time in Upper Egypt to develop the movement. On this reading, it was concern at his success that led the "enemies of Islam" to bring al-Banna back to the capital.[67] Suffice to say, most British officials would have been surprised to learn that al-Banna's return marked a triumph for them; on the contrary, it was considered a setback in the struggle against internal subversion.

Once more, the context for increasing British anxiety about the Brotherhood was framed by the deteriorating military situation in the Western Desert. Defeats in Cyrenaica and the advance of the Italian army toward the Egyptian border were believed to have bolstered anti-British forces. Similar in effect was the Iraqi coup d'état that brought the pro-Axis Rashid 'Ali al-Gaylani to power in April 1941. Although at first it was assumed that Egyptian "parochialism" would ensure that the impact of events in Baghdad was "slight," British officials feared that "if Rashid Ali gets away with it, his example might inspire hopes that Ali Maher's return to power might equally be imposed upon us."[68] Maher himself was therefore now threatened with internment unless he refrained from all political activity.[69] Beyond him, the dispatches sent by the embassy to London identified a familiar cast of characters as problematic: Ahmad Husayn, 'Abd al-Rahman Azzam, Isma'il Sidqi (another former prime minister, typically described as an inveterate purveyor of political intrigue), and of course, Hasan al-Banna.[70] Equally troubling were reports that King Faruq himself might "bolt" into exile.[71]

Alfred Sansom claims that the British were also fearful of a possible Egyptian army revolt at this time.[72] Nervousness about potential disloyalty had been aggravated by the earlier discovery of allied military plans in the possession of captured Italian commanders, an episode that led to the dismissal of the Egyptian army chief, 'Aziz 'Ali al-Misri, who was believed to be acting in league with the enemy.[73] In May 1941, al-Misri was then caught trying to flee the country to Iraq.[74] His pilot in the failed attempt was 'Abd al-Mon'im 'Abd al-Ma'ruf, an army officer who joined the Brotherhood after his release from prison the following year.[75]

It was against this disquieting background that al-Banna had been ordered out of Cairo. Concurrently, Ambassador Lampson urged Prime Minister Sirri to accept that the "time had come" when Ahmad Husayn and his supporters should be "run in." Yet he was disappointed to find that the prime minister pre-

ferred to give Husayn "a little more rope to hang himself."[76] Lampson informed
the Foreign Office that the need to move against "hostile internal elements may
easily arise at the shortest notice."[77] In London, senior officials welcomed the
prospect of "some strong arm stuff with such enemies as Sidky [*sic*] and Ali
Maher," which "might have a good effect in a wider sphere than Egypt."[78] The
head of the Egyptian Department at the Foreign Office, Charles Bateman, was
even more blunt, arguing for the "jugging" and deporting of their opponents,
including Sidqi, Ahmad Husayn, and Ali Maher. If necessary, Bateman believed
they should impose full "British military law and government without the Egyptian Parliament." While he acknowledged this would somewhat undermine the
British "fight for democracy," he felt they should do whatever it took to "keep the
Gyppies 'under.'"[79] A telegram from London to Cairo thus told Lampson that
while they did not seek a clash, "we should certainly not shrink from vigorous
action if circumstances showed it to be necessary."[80]

Ultimately, the crisis of spring-summer 1941 passed. The coup in Baghdad
was reversed; and Sirri's government maintained control over the internal situation in Egypt.[81] But more than ever, the British classified the Muslim Brotherhood as a hostile group and perhaps the foremost instigator of agitation. The
truth of this can be seen from the growing frequency with which the Ikhwan
appeared in the reports issued by military intelligence. In August 1941, a summary produced by the Middle East Intelligence Committee identified various
"agents" across the region who were said to be linked to the "extremist" Hasan
al-Banna. The list featured people from Sudan, Algeria, Amman, Beirut, Aleppo,
Saudi Arabia, the Hadhramut, and even Bombay and Hyderabad in India.[82]
Though the accuracy of the report is perhaps open to question, its significance
lay in what it said about the way in which the Brotherhood was seen. Military
intelligence had clearly reversed course. Gone now were any thoughts that the
group might be won over by the British. Instead, the focus was on containment
and repression.

Anxiety over the Ikhwan was clearly exacerbated by the fact it appeared to
have a reach beyond Egypt's borders. In addition to the foregoing, the British
were aware of the long-standing ties between the Brotherhood and the former
grand mufti of Palestine, Hajj Amin al-Husayni. What made this all the more
troubling was the mufti's infamous cooperation with Nazi Germany and his
calls for Muslims to back Berlin against their common enemies of the Jews, the
communists, and the British.[83] Domestically, too, there were signs that the
Brotherhood continued to enjoy support from figures known to be anti-
British. On 16 October 1941, Lampson referred in his diary to a report he had

received, which stated that Ali Maher had recently sent £E400 to both the National Islamic Party (Young Egypt) and the Muslim Brotherhood to encourage their "anti-British intrigue." It was further alleged that this money had originally come from the palace—though Prime Minister Sirri had rejected this assertion.[84]

Consequently, Embassy Cairo was obviously delighted when the Egyptian government decided that same month to arrest and intern Hasan al-Banna, together with his key lieutenant, Ahmad al-Sukkari, as well as Fathi Radwan, a leading figure in Young Egypt. All three were accused of being involved in "anti-British agitation." As described earlier, however, this proved to be something of a false dawn, with the Brotherhood leaders quickly released, having promised to refrain from political activity.[85] In the face of Lampson's vehement protests, Prime Minister Sirri accused the British military authorities of "employing unreliable agents who were furnishing misleading reports" about the Ikhwan. At this, Lampson did admit privately that he himself was not always convinced by the "bona fides" of the military: "Experience has shown that they are quite liable to ask for people to be run in on the basis of reports which are either exaggerated or cannot be substantiated." Nevertheless, when it came to the Brotherhood, he was sure that their judgment was accurate and he continued to complain "vigorously" at the release of the men.[86]

A further report from November 1941 described the Brotherhood as occupying a "predominant position among subversive associations in Egypt." The group was believed to have branches throughout the country and members from all social classes; it was judged to be in good financial health and to enjoy protection from the palace, as well as numerous notables, officials, and parliamentarians. Moreover, a reference to the Brotherhood's "secret planning and organisation" may well reflect British awareness of the existence of the Special Apparatus. Whether or not this was the case, there was no doubting their conclusion that the "Ikhwan el Muslimeen" was "now an important element in the body politic."[87]

Officials worried that "the weight of Egyptian influence" was by this time "in favour of anti-British propaganda," much of it driven by the Brotherhood.[88] At the turn of the year, the group was said to be spreading rumors that food shortages were the result of a British move to seize all available stocks.[89] British intelligence also claimed to have information about a secret meeting at which Hasan al-Banna had declared that an Allied victory in the war would "mean eternal slavery for Islam and would sound the death knell to Egypt's independence." According to al-Banna, it was therefore "every Moslem's duty to fight

Great Britain with all his might and to do all in his power to prevent a British victory." At the same gathering, the Brotherhood leader had apparently announced his support for the cause of Ali Maher and intimated that he enjoyed palace funding. This was said to be consistent with other reports indicating palace "benevolence" toward the Ikhwan.[90] One dispatch confirmed that the group was part of "the Palace Fifth Column organisation."[91]

Against this backdrop, Ambassador Lampson continued to press for the reinternment of the Brotherhood's leader. At a meeting on 7 January 1942, Lampson presented the prime minister with a paper detailing al-Banna's "pretty damning record." Sirri promised to study the report, but argued that his approach for dealing with al-Banna was superior to that recommended by the British. His aim, he revealed, was to avoid direct confrontation with the Ikhwan and instead foment internal unrest within the group. Sirri claimed that this had been so successful that al-Banna had even visited the Interior Ministry "to invoke protection against physical violence from some of his own inherents [sic]."[92] Such assertions are almost impossible to verify, and Ambassador Lampson was certainly not convinced. For the moment, he was not willing to force the issue lest it undermine the Egyptian government—but the question of the Brotherhood refused to go away.

The Brotherhood Conciliated

From a British perspective, the failure of Sirri to deal adequately with the threat posed by the Brotherhood was consonant with his wider inability to impose those measures deemed necessary for the war effort. Since 1940, senior British officials, including Ambassador Lampson, had believed that only a government led by the Wafd would have the strength—both within the country and against the palace—to fulfill British demands. Hitherto, King Faruq had been able to sidestep calls for a ministry headed by Mustafa al-Nahas. By late 1941, however, Lampson believed that "as and when practicable," the Wafd should be brought back to power. The ambassador recognized that this would require him to take a "high hand" with "the boy"—Faruq—but equally, he believed it was the best long-term option for Egypt's future.[93]

In early 1942, Lampson was finally presented with an opportunity to bring about the desired change in government. The immediate pretext was the crisis that arose from the decision of the Sirri government to break relations with the Vichy regime at the request of the British. The prime minister did as he was asked, but in the process failed to obtain the proper authorization from the palace. The king construed this as a violation of his prerogative powers and demanded the dismissal of Sirri's foreign affairs minister. After a brief standoff, the prime minister himself resigned. For Lampson, the episode constituted merely the latest evidence of Faruq's propensity to interfere and undermine his own government (he also believed Ali Maher's influence to be behind the king's actions).[94] The stage was thus set for the decisive events of 4 February 1942. Regarding the details of what occurred that day, for present purposes it suffices to say that Lampson opted now for "forcible action" to impose al-Nahas on Faruq. The latter was threatened with deposition if he refused to call the Wafdist leader to form a government.[95] A note of abdication was even prepared and handed to the king in theatrical fashion by the ambassador, accompanied by the general officer commanding of British troops in Egypt, General Robert Stone, and "an impressive array of specially picked stalwart military officers armed to the teeth." Faced with this, Faruq backed down, pleaded for his throne, and agreed to summon al-Nahas. Thus, 4 February 1942 became a day of infamy for all Egyptian nationalists, including members of the Muslim Brotherhood.[96] In the aftermath, one of their senior members, Ahmad al-Baquri, wrote a pamphlet criticizing the British and the Wafd—a move that led to his arrest.[97] Numerous other Brothers cited the events of that day as symptomatic of British imperialism and the shallowness of Western rhetoric about freedom.[98]

On taking office, the new Wafdist administration faced a difficult period. The party had been returned to power by a resentful and hostile king at British behest. In the months that followed, the king engaged in a kind of procedural guerrilla warfare, challenging al-Nahas's authority wherever he could.[99] The prime minister only prevailed in these struggles because of the indirect but clear backing afforded to him by the British ambassador.[100] Such support did not come cost free, however. In return, the British expected al-Nahas to make a priority of dealing with subversive elements. Lampson urged the prime minister to give public support to the Allied cause in the war and to confront "fifth columnism" decisively.[101]

The day before al-Nahas's appointment, some five thousand students had been involved in a demonstration demanding both that Ali Maher be given the premiership and that the British stay out of Egypt's internal affairs. Amid chants in support of Maher and the king, cries were heard of: "We are Axis soldiers, advance Rommel, down with Churchill." British intelligence analysts surmised that the protests were the work of the Muslim Brotherhood together with the "Ali Maher group."[102] Unsurprisingly, therefore, Lampson pressed al-Nahas to deal "more drastically" with Maher, described as the "root of all our troubles."[103] Under his influence, the palace was believed to have built up a formidable anti-British alliance, comprising "the full weight of Moslem religious influence, the majority of non-Wafdist politicians and their followers, and a very large proportion of Egyptian army officers."[104]

As reflected by the reference to religious sentiment, al-Azhar was a definite source of concern for the embassy in this period, with reports that efforts were being made "to enlist reactionary Moslem feeling in the country" against both the British and the Wafd. Sheikh Mustafa al-Maraghi continued to be seen as a troublesome character, and Lampson was thus gratified that al-Nahas warned him to stay out of politics.[105] The ambassador was similarly encouraged to see that the president of the YMMA, Salih Harb Pasha, was interned after protesting against the events of February 4.[106]

Yet it was clear from the beginning that not everything would run smoothly with the Wafd. Already on February 10, Lampson was confiding in his diary his irritation with al-Nahas, who he found "pig-headed and very difficult." The question of internees was an immediate source of disagreement, with the prime minister actually seeking British agreement for the *release* of several prisoners, including Ahmad Husayn. Needless to say, Lampson rejected this suggestion out of hand.[107] The British wanted to see more, not less, people in detention. They were dismayed when al-Nahas preferred to have Ali Maher confined to his estate rather than arrested.[108]

Of equal if not greater concern were reports of heightened disaffection within the Egyptian army after February 4. Lampson privately believed that the situation there was "very serious," with reports that an "elaborate secret association" had come into existence that aimed to "stab us in the back if we find ourselves occupied with the enemy in the Western Desert or elsewhere." There were suggestions that King Faruq himself might be involved in the affair and the matter was raised confidentially with al-Nahas.[109] The British kept an especially close watch on younger army officers, one of whom—Captain Anwar al-Sadat—was linked to the "Eppler Case," the most serious German attempt at espionage in wartime Egypt. It also did not escape the attention of security officers like Alfred Sansom that al-Sadat was in contact with Hasan al-Banna.[110]

Once again the Muslim Brotherhood seemed enmeshed with the anti-British network operating beneath the surface in Egypt. By this stage, Ambassador Lampson was firmly convinced of the "misbehaviour of the Ikwan [*sic*]" and hoped that al-Nahas would finally "play" on this front. He was keen that "some of these people at last will be re-interned."[111] Like his predecessor, though, the prime minister seemed reluctant to extend repressive action to encompass al-Banna and his organization. In March 1942, Lampson recorded that "Nahas now believes that he can amnesty Ikhwan El Muslimin to help both him and us. I have expressed extreme scepticism."[112] The ambassador's warning went unheeded. Instead, the Wafd settled on a path of trying to conciliate and co-opt the Ikhwan. Not only was al-Banna allowed to remain at liberty but also he was initially permitted to stand as a candidate for Ismailia in the March 1942 parliamentary elections.[113] (At the Brotherhood's sixth conference the previous year, the decision had been made that the movement would enter electoral politics.[114] Abbas al-Sissi explains this as a tactical decision driven by the belief that, amid wartime repression, parliament remained a "flicker of light illuminating the darkness of the oppressed," a place where debate and complaint could still be aired.)[115] Many felt that the Ikhwan had a realistic chance of capturing a seat in the town of its birth; and al-Banna was one of seventeen Brotherhood members who put themselves forward for election on a platform that called for the implementation of shari'a (Islamic law).[116]

Al-Nahas eventually prevailed on al-Banna and his followers to withdraw from the contest. Later histories of the Brotherhood attributed this move to pressure from the British Embassy, which was determined to prevent al-Banna's entry into parliamentary politics.[117] From the available evidence, the extent of direct British interference in this matter is difficult to gauge. Certainly, it is hard to imagine that they were unhappy to see the Brotherhood's candidates withdraw. Yet whatever comfort they took from that outcome soon evaporated as it became apparent that al-Nahas had, in fact, made an agreement with al-Banna. The Brotherhood leader had agreed to step back from elections in return for the government enacting a series of measures, including the banning of alcohol sales during Ramadan and the prohibition of prostitution.[118] As part of the deal, al-Banna published an open letter to al-Nahas in *al-Ahram*, declaring loyalty to both the government and the Anglo-Egyptian Treaty.[119] It seems evident, however, that the British authorities were far from persuaded by this outward show of support. Intelligence analysts noted gloomily that al-Nahas's drive against "subversive elements" seemed to be "losing its momentum"; and while al-Banna and his followers temporarily refrained from public expression of anti-British feeling, the Ikhwan was still viewed as a serious "potential danger."[120]

A history of the Brotherhood compiled by the British authorities in late 1942 observed that the settlement with al-Nahas did cause some problems for the group. For one thing, the palace briefly ended its support for them, piqued by the Brothers' apparent endorsement of the Wafd. Internally, meanwhile, al-Banna was subjected to "widespread criticism" from many Ikhwan members who considered it "an ignominious surrender." There were even suggestions that there might be a split.[121] Yet this failed to materialize, and al-Banna was soon able to reassert his authority over the Brotherhood. Palace disaffection with the group proved similarly fleeting. As early as April 1942, the British were informed that the king had resumed his patronage of the Ikhwan.[122] To this were added further reports of an agreement between al-Banna and Mahmud al-Nuqrashi (the deputy leader of the Sa'dist Party).[123] By the early summer of 1942, therefore, the Brotherhood appeared to have squared all sides of Egypt's domestic political scene. It straddled the divide, which had traditionally separated the king and the minority parties on the one hand, and the Wafd on the other. The deal with al-Nahas thus marked another triumph for al-Banna's pragmatic mode of politics. The Brotherhood could now focus on its own expansion, safe in the knowledge that it enjoyed an unprecedented degree of political protection.

It was perhaps for this reason that the Ikhwan remained a point of serious contention between the British and a government with which they were otherwise well satisfied.[124] In mid-April, Ambassador Lampson and his embassy staff met with the senior Wafdist Amin Osman to discuss the "dangerously active" Brotherhood. Osman laid out the government's approach for dealing with the group, arguing that "by far the wisest way to handle the Ikhwan was not to drive them underground but to put it straight to the leaders of the Brotherhood that if they brought politics into their organization they would have to be dealt with drastically." In this regard, Osman sought to reassure the British that the government was prepared to intern Brotherhood members *if* evidence against them was forthcoming—either from the Egyptian Intelligence Service or the British authorities. The head of British military intelligence, Brigadier Clayton, who attended the meeting, accepted this argument but warned that al-Nahas "should be on his guard against strengthening, however unintentionally the position and status of the leaders of the Brotherhood." Other British officials took an even more robust line. According to Lampson, the Oriental counselor, Walter Smart, "rather hankered after the suppression forthwith of the whole Brotherhood and produced quite good reasons, intrinsically, for doing so." For his part, the ambassador continued to evince skepticism over Wafdist policy, though this was tempered by his feeling that "as foreigners" they were less well placed to deal with a matter that touched on religion.[125]

In May there was a further meeting between Osman and representatives of the UK military authorities, together with Walter Smart. Again, the question of the Brotherhood was the main topic of conversation. The British claimed to have "more and more evidence" that the group had been carefully organized "for

Fifth Column purposes." They were thought to have "laid down the nuclei of sabotage organizations" and the British reported that a number of Brotherhood members had "for some time been engaged in espionage on behalf of the enemy."[126] They even furnished Osman with a list of those Muslim Brothers rated as the most dangerous. Yet in spite of this, the Wafdists still insisted that "no offensive action" would be taken against the Ikhwan. There were no arrests and al-Banna was not asked to remove anyone from his movement. Osman's argument was again that the government did not wish to see the Brotherhood driven underground. Instead, their objective was to "kill" the Ikhwan "by kindness." The British were told that it was unrealistic to expect an open declaration of support from al-Banna. A "far more effective" route, Osman argued, was to allow the Brothers to start a newspaper and publish a series of articles "supporting democratic principles," in the hope that this would "disintegrate the Ikhwan" or at least bring them into line. To this end, too, the government apparently intended to introduce "reliable agents" into the Brotherhood. These would gather intelligence on the group while also attempting to create a "schism" between al-Banna and his key lieutenant, Ahmad al-Sukkari. Furthermore, Osman informed the British that "subsidies from the Wafd to the Ikhwan el Muslimin would be discreetly paid by the Government and they would require some financial assistance in this matter from the Embassy."[127]

This last comment is fascinating, not least because it once more raises the prospect of de facto British subsidization of the Ikhwan (albeit with the money flowing through the Egyptian government). Were such payments actually made? There is no way of knowing for sure, but it would seem highly likely that money supplied by the British to the al-Nahas administration ended up in the Brotherhood's coffers. It is clear that if such funds ever were transferred, this now took place against the better judgment of various British diplomats and intelligence officers. They urged the Wafdist ministry to take a tougher line with the Brotherhood. But they were frustrated by al-Nahas's readiness to adopt the same approach, with which the British themselves had experimented in 1940–1941.

The exigencies of war created the space and inclination to try such unorthodox strategies. The key question was whether the conciliatory approach of the al-Nahas government might now succeed in curbing the Ikhwan. As 1942 progressed, the British saw precious little evidence to support such a proposition. In September, the Brotherhood used its newfound wealth to launch a weekly newspaper, *Al-Ikhwan al-Muslimun,* with government approval. This proclaimed the opening of a "new stage" of struggle, in which ever greater attention would be paid to formal politics.[128] The movement was also able to expand its activities more generally throughout the year.[129]

The Brotherhood Empowered

In June 1942, the British position in Egypt appeared to be on the verge of collapse with Rommel's advance toward el-Alamein some sixty miles west of Alexandria, which initiated "the flap" in Cairo.[130] British assessments were that there was "little enthusiasm" for the Germans amid the bulk of Egypt's population; but there was said to be a "small pro-Axis minority."[131] It seems clear that the Ikhwan was counted as prominent among the latter, for as Rommel advanced, Brotherhood students were involved in fresh pro-German demonstrations.[132] British intelligence analysts suspected that the group yearned for an Axis victory and was ready to assist Rommel's forces, even as al-Banna sought to convey privately that he "wished to avoid conflict with the government or ourselves."[133] There were reports that the Brotherhood leader had boasted to his followers of their plans for conducting "extensive railway sabotage"—and the Brothers were thought to be monitoring British military movements.[134] In July, the Ikhwan was described as "the most serious danger to public security" in Egypt.[135]

A few months later, the British commander of the Cairo City police force, Sir Thomas Russell Pasha, wrote to Ambassador Lampson warning that the Brotherhood might be plotting to cause trouble.[136] Others reported that the group was involved in efforts to organize a strike at the Suez Petrol Refineries.[137] In addition, the British heard about a secret meeting, said to have been held in Ismailia, at which al-Banna had raised the prospect of collaborating with al-Azhar's Sheikh al-Maraghi to incite opposition to both the government and the British.[138] In the face of all this, the embassy renewed its calls for action against the Ikhwan and, on this occasion, the diplomats were pleased to see the imposition of a temporary ban on public Brotherhood meetings and the threat of further repressive measures.[139]

This tougher line, though, did not last long. Soon afterward, al-Nahas met directly with al-Banna and a new "accommodation between them was arranged."[140] A British account of that meeting suggested that the Brotherhood leader had insisted his movement was purely religious in character and had no wish to cause political disturbances. Al-Banna promised that the Brothers would not hold meetings in Cairo and he pledged—under threat of internment—to support al-Nahas's government. All that he asked in return was that the Ikhwan be permitted to go about its business. However, as the British noted, this offer was coupled with a veiled threat: al-Banna said that even if the government rejected the deal, the Brotherhood would not be deflected from its path because its members feared neither persecution nor death. In this context, al-Nahas seemed content to accept the proposed arrangement, which unsurprisingly did little to ease British anxieties. Al-Banna was reported to have told his followers that the prime minister had given them permission to continue their anti-British agitation, provided it remained hidden—and provided they dis-avowed any contact with enemies of the Wafd (such as the palace). British in-telligence suspected that this was not true; rather, it was assumed to be a lie concocted by al-Banna to justify his latest pragmatic shift.[141] Nevertheless, his comments were taken as further evidence of the Brotherhood's intent.

Moreover, it soon became clear that the pause in the movement's activity in Egypt's capital did not prevent it from operating elsewhere. The provincial city of Tanta previously had been identified as a hub of anti-British activity in which the Ikhwan enjoyed "considerable influence."[142] In October 1942, the embassy received police reports that local members of the Brotherhood were printing and distributing subversive, pro-Axis pamphlets—allegedly with the full knowledge of Hasan al-Banna, whose house was raided during the investigation.[143] The hawkish Walter Smart subsequently raised this issue with Amin Osman and was again reassured that al-Nahas did not trust al-Banna. The prime minister was, Osman averred, ready to intern the Brotherhood leader if this was what the British wanted. Somewhat surprisingly, though, the embassy itself now hesitated at the suggestion. Smart recorded that they were "of the opinion that this was perhaps premature pending more definite evidence" against al-Banna.[144] Exactly why they took such a timid stance is difficult to determine; it seemed to cut against the grain of long-standing British efforts to have the government adopt a more forceful policy against the Brotherhood. Whatever the explanation, though, there was no doubting that the British were watching the Ikhwan carefully.

In December 1942, military intelligence produced a lengthy but revealing analysis of the group, "The Ikhwan el-Muslimeen Reconsidered." This docu-ment provides the fullest insight into wartime British understandings of the Brotherhood and its history. In many ways, it underlines the extent to which their thinking about the movement remained confused, tending to see it as containing a mass of contradictions. The founding of the Ikhwan was dated (erroneously) to 1930. Hasan al-Banna, meanwhile, was described variously as "respectable" and "a good speaker," but also "circumspect, even cowardly." The report stated that "those who have met him form an impression of cunning and ambition behind his simplicity." Ideologically, the Brothers were said to be inspired, rather incongruously, by both the Saudi Wahhabis and Gandhi. Even more confusing was the adjacent comment that members of the group were "social-democrats" in general outlook and possessed a genuine "social programme." It was for this reason that they were thought to enjoy support from "the most respectable" Muslim circles, as well as contacts abroad (in Iraq and the Hadhramut). So far, so benign. However, the report went on to state that the Brotherhood wished to "re-establish the government and institutions of Egypt on pure Koranic principles, to restore the Shari' law [sic] . . . and to exclude all the elements of Western culture, which they regard as intrusive and deleterious."[145] On this basis, the Ikhwan was labeled an "extremist organisation," with a "militant" and "anti-foreign" outlook. "Being fervently Moslem," it was said to be "implicitly anti-European, and in particular anti-British." There were also references to the "moral and material support" that the group had obtained from "the powerful anti-British clique whose leader was Ali Maher." The document noted that since October 1941, the king had given instructions to the provincial governors not to interfere with the Ikhwan, and the Brothers were assumed to have benefited significantly from palace "favour."

Furthermore, British officials compared the organizational format of the Brotherhood to that of the "Nazi-fascist" groups. The Brotherhood's "Gawala" (Rovers) were seen as analogous to the Nazi SA (Sturmabteilung, literally "Assault Division"), while the "Kata'ib" (Battalion) formations were considered the equivalent of Hitler's SS (Schutzstaffel, literally "Protection Squadron").[146] Members of the Ikhwan were thought to be involved in planning acts of sabotage on vital British communications infrastructure and installations. More worrying still were rumors that the group had developed "suicide squads." In September 1941, al-Banna had purportedly revealed that he had two thousand handpicked armed men at his disposal and ready to obey orders—a rather disconcerting prospect in British eyes. To all of this was added the Brotherhood's belligerency on the Palestine issue, which had evidently brought it to the attention of the Germans and the Italians. As described in Chapter 1, the former had sent financial assistance to the group. And while the report concluded there was "very little evidence" that contacts had continued during the war, it was inferred that the Brotherhood hoped for an Axis victory. There were even (unsubstantiated) suspicions that the Japanese legation had paid the Ikhwan.[147]

Overall, the British recognized that the threat from the Brothers had for the most part remained rhetorical, and it was reckoned that al-Banna's brief internment in 1941 had made him more cautious. The Brothers, it was argued, were unlikely to "jeopardize their future by precipitate and rash action when their prospects of attaining power by Fabian methods are considerable." However, there was no denying that as a whole, the Ikhwan was viewed as "exceedingly dangerous." The "power and influence" of this "highly-organised association" was said to be "constantly increasing." The numerical strength of the group was, by this time, estimated as being somewhere between one hundred thousand and half a million. The report quoted Amin Osman to the effect that the scale of the Brotherhood's organization was "comparable only with that of the Wafd itself" (though Osman also doubted their capacity to win more than twelve seats in parliamentary elections). In sum, while the Ikhwan was seen as neither an "*immediate* danger [emphasis added]" to the British nor a rival to the Wafd, it was judged "capable of taking a significant part in the future political development of Egypt." The "day may arrive," it was suggested, "when the Ikhwan will seriously compete with the Wafd for office and power in its own name and on its own programme."[148]

It should be noted that not everyone agreed on this last point. In the gloss that he added to the report, Ambassador Lampson offered a more skeptical view as to the long-term outlook for the Ikhwan. In his opinion, while there was no doubting the "appeal" of the group to many "simple devout Muslims," its demand for "a return to pure Islamic legislation, custom and practice" was "out of harmony with the main current of progress in modern Egypt." The main attraction of the Brotherhood, Lampson believed, lay "chiefly on the lines of xenophobia" and he judged it "unlikely that a great national party like the Wafd could be replaced by such a narrow religious and obscurantist organisation."[149]

Lampson's words were interesting in that they demonstrated something else important about British attitudes toward the Ikhwan. For while arriving at different conclusions, what the ambassador and the intelligence analysts shared was an understanding of the group as essentially reactionary and chauvinistic. Occasional references to its putative "social democratic" character aside, the Brotherhood was seen through the dominant prism of an inherently *Islamic* fanaticism and extremism. As had been the case in the 1930s, the militancy and antiforeign spirit of the Ikhwan was attributed to its Muslim nature; it was taken to embody an essential characteristic of Islam that ran counter to the ethos of the modern world. Where Lampson and the military men disagreed was over the extent of its potential. The latter feared that it could eventually take power in Egypt, whereas the ambassador supposed that the tide of human "progress" would eventually consign the Brothers to oblivion.

Of course, Lampson's confidence in the fundamentally backward nature of the Brotherhood did not prevent him from seeing it as a major threat in the here and now. Diplomatic and intelligence reports continued to convey the impression that the Ikhwan constituted a danger that needed to be watched closely.[150] A further indication of the degree to which the group was now very much on the British radar was the inclusion of Hasan al-Banna on the list of important Egyptian "personalities" that the embassy transmitted to the Foreign Office in January 1943.[151] That short biography described the Brotherhood leader as someone "strongly suspected of using his religious revivalism as a cloak for eventual subversive activities against the British."[152] He was thought to be playing a "dubious game," with his present policy of affected friendliness toward both the embassy and the Wafdist government a mere tactic to avoid "interference" while the Brotherhood strengthened its position.[153]

Such reservations about the Brotherhood were echoed by others. In February 1943, the Foreign Office received two reports on Anglo-Egyptian matters from Professor Sir Hamilton Gibb, the renowned orientalist scholar who was close to the Foreign Office's Research Department.[154] While the first of these memoranda offered analysis of the Anglo-Egyptian Treaty, the second considered the main "political forces in Egypt."[155] Therein, Gibb pointed to the emergence of certain Muslim religious organizations that enjoyed support among the working classes and displayed a "strongly pan-Islamic and xenophobic tendency." Though allied to the "intensely conservative and monarchist" Azhari establishment, these groups were said to comprise "a kind of Jacobin wing" of the movement. Gibb identified the Ikhwan as the largest of these "proletarian" religious societies, with its supporters counted in the millions. Further, he suggested that the future "lines of division" within Egyptian politics would be between advocates of "social reform" along Western lines and those wanting "social revolution on Moslem principles." He clearly identified the Brotherhood with the latter tendency, and in so doing, his analysis tended to endorse the observations of Ambassador Lampson, who juxtaposed Western modernity on the one hand, and "Islamic" principles of the kind espoused by the Ikhwan on the other.[156]

Neither was it just the British who had concerns about the Brotherhood in this period. In January 1943, al-Nahas's government reinstated its ban on all Cairo meetings of the group, with the exception of a single weekly gathering at which only religious subjects could be discussed.[157] The move apparently provoked disaffection within al-Azhar, as well as provincial religious institutes like the one at Tanta.[158] But the authorities seemed determined to press forward. The new pro-Wafdist sheikh al-Azhar, Muhammad al-Banna (no relation of Hasan), ordered the closure of provincial branches of the Ikhwan.[159]

In response, Hasan al-Banna persevered with a cautious and conciliatory posture. He opted merely to lodge a formal protest with the minister of justice over the restrictions placed on the Ikhwan. He also urged Cairo members of the movement—especially Azharis—to refrain from agitation, and he signaled that he wished to reach a new accommodation with the government. At the same time, he again deployed references to the more militant attitude of his followers as a rhetorical device by which to put pressure on al-Nahas. In mid-February, for instance, the British noted that the Brotherhood leader had "insisted that only with the greatest difficulty" was he able to "restrain the more ardent of his supporters from rash acts."[160]

Once more, this twin-faceted approach appeared to pay off. Al-Nahas subsequently indicated a readiness to lift restrictions on the Ikhwan—on condition that al-Banna offer a public apology for past criticisms of the Wafd. The Brothers were also required to engage in progovernment propaganda and submit their organization and finances to the supervision of the Ministry of Interior.[161] Such terms were clearly not what al-Banna had in mind, and he therefore sought to prevaricate, in the hope of securing a personal meeting with (and better terms from), al-Nahas.[162]

As the deadlock continued, al-Banna's efforts to strike a new bargain were hampered by the prime minister's illness in the early spring of 1943. By this time there were renewed suggestions that some Ikhwan members were "growing . . . restive at the delay."[163] British intelligence observed that the leaders of certain branches of the movement seemed ready to "take the law into their own hands" if their premises were not soon reopened. There were reports, too, of a quarrel between al-Banna and his principal lieutenant, al-Sukkari, with the latter wanting to organize demonstrations against the authorities even as al-Banna pursued a peaceful settlement.[164]

The political situation was transformed, however, with the publication of Makram 'Ubayd Pasha's "Black Book" in late March, which detailed the corruption of the Wafdist government. Since early summer of the previous year, the British had watched anxiously as relations between al-Nahas and Makram, his one-time ally and finance minister, had deteriorated, culminating in the latter's departure from government and his expulsion from the Wafd.[165] Makram's public excoriation of al-Nahas's administration now gave the king the chance to renew hostilities with his prime minister—and Faruq launched a boycott of the government. This in turn placed the British in a quandary.[166] As embassy officials put it, the British had the choice of being seen as either throwing their friends to the wolves or condoning corruption.[167] Already, officials had lamented the "familiar amateurism" of al-Nahas's government and acknowledged the prevalence of internal nepotism. Yet such failings had been explained away by typically orientalist references to the fact that Egyptians had never governed themselves and had lived under foreigners ever since the time of the Persian conquest. Moreover, the declared view of Ambassador Lampson was that al-Nahas had passed the stern tests of 1942 with "flying colours," keeping Egypt "completely quiet." He felt the British had an "obligation" to support the prime minister. To do otherwise would be an act of "betrayal" and a sign of weakness.[168] The king was therefore warned not to get any ideas about a fresh attempt to unseat the Wafd and Faruq reluctantly backed down.[169]

Nevertheless, Lampson recognized that the "Black Book" episode had proven damaging. Not only did it lead the political opposition to come out "openly" against the British but it also gave Hasan al-Banna the opportunity to repair his pact with al-Nahas. In recognition of this, the Brotherhood issued "strong criticism" of both Makram and the "Black Book," while lending its support to the embattled prime minister.[170] As far as the ambassador was concerned, this was deeply regrettable. He observed that to bolster its position, the government was again now "endeavouring to enlist the support of the reactionary and xenophobic . . . society of the Moslem Brethren, whose activities have caused so much concern in the past to our security authorities."[171] A report from 21 April 1943 noted the authorities had allowed the reopening of Ikhwan premises across the country.[172] On May 16, four cabinet ministers attended a meeting with the Brotherhood at their Cairo headquarters.[173] The British believed that a "definite bargain" had been struck and that "in return for various privileges," al-Banna had instructed local leaders of the Ikhwan to "render the greatest possible assistance to the Wafd."[174] In July came the news that al-Nahas's policy of trying to cooperate with the Brotherhood had extended to offering its deputy leader, Ahmad al-Sukkari, a senior post within the Interior Ministry (an offer that had been accepted).[175] Al-Sukkari was thus appointed to a commission to combat illiteracy.[176] There was also speculation that a post might be found for Hasan al-Banna himself within the Ministry of Education, as relations between the Brotherhood and the government grew "steadily more friendly."[177]

This latter possibility was never realized, but evidence of the Wafd-Ikhwan entente continued throughout the summer. As previously, al-Banna's approach proved uncongenial to some of his supporters, with rumors that leading members of the group in Zagazig had resigned in protest.[178] The Brotherhood leader refused to be deflected, however. At one meeting, al-Banna was said to have "bitterly reproached" those Muslim Brothers who continued to criticize the Wafd and even the British in public. By mid-August, there were reports that "the antagonism of provincial branches of the Ikhwan to this policy of collaboration with the Government [was] being slowly overcome."[179] The fact that the strategy was reaping clear dividends by this stage probably helped to convince the doubters.[180] That same month, Lampson observed that al-Banna had sent a telegram to al-Nahas wishing him success in achieving Arab unity (the prime minister was then hosting Iraqi prime minister Nuri al-Said for discussions in Cairo). This had been reproduced in full, in the official Wafdist newspaper—"another indication of the Government's policy of maintaining friendly relations with that organization."[181]

The British authorities judged that this relationship had definitely bolstered al-Nahas's administration after it had been weakened by the "Black Book" scandal. The Political Intelligence Centre Middle East (PICME) concluded that the Wafd had been "much strengthened" by its alliance with the Ikhwan. At the same time, the British were scarcely blind to the darker side of the liaison between the government and a group that was routinely referred to as "anti-Christian" and "anti-Semitic."[182] In June 1943, for instance, Lampson offered a reflection on what he saw as the long-term effects of these developments. Prolonged cooperation between the Wafd and "an anti-foreign organization" such as the Brotherhood, he argued, could "hardly fail to develop on dangerous lines, both religious and xenophobic."[183] Indeed, the period following the renewal of ties between the Wafd and the Ikhwan was alleged to have witnessed a lurch in a more "anti-foreign" direction by al-Nahas's government.[184]

Concerns of this kind were not new. Ambassador Lampson had previously made plain his belief that "politics and religion should be kept apart" (see Chapter 1)—and he reiterated this view during the war.[185] The embassy expressed disquiet about the impact of "reactionary Islamism" coupled with "nationalist xenophobia." The diplomats reckoned that such ideas served only to distort Egyptian politics. To their mind, whereas once the Wafd had been "covertly" following the example of Turkey and the "lay tendencies" of Atatürk, now it was having to compete with its rivals in "Islamic fervour."[186] Anxiety over growing levels of xenophobia became an increasing staple of diplomatic reportage in late 1943.[187] The embassy pointed to the perceived "encouragement of fanaticism," which included a great deal of "shouting [about] the glory and the future of Islam."[188]

Officials recognized that al-Nahas had hoped, by a "mixture of bribery and threats," to "utilise" the Ikhwan "in the interest of the Wafd." The prime minister, they assumed, had wished to secure "the professed adherence of this society" and even persuade it to "disown any anti-British intent." From the British perspective, however, this ambition was a chimera: "The value of this agreement is more than dubious. It is not at all unlikely that the Ikhwan Al Muslimin hope by a semblance of conciliation towards the Government and ourselves to avoid repressive measures and to be able under this cover to organise themselves more strongly for future action against us in any case if not also against the Wafd."[189]

In London, the mandarins were similarly candid in their criticism of the Wafdist government's decision to pay "subsidies" to a group like the Ikhwan.[190] The prevailing view in Whitehall was that the Brotherhood was a serious threat to the British position in Egypt—an enemy that needed to be treated as such. And yet, even then there were some within British circles—albeit very much a minority—who remained ready to argue for an alternative approach.

An Alternative to Repression—Redux?

In July 1943, a report from a Cairo-based MI5 agent proposed that, while the British should continue to support the Wafd, they should also "establish some reliable and sympathetic unofficial contact with Hassan al Banna, as leader of the second most representative group in Egypt." Such contact, it was acknowledged, would need to be explained to al-Nahas so he did not think the British were "competing with him for al Banna's hand." The aim of the initiative would be simply, in the first instance, to seek information and try to explore the Brotherhood's outlook. At the same time, though, the agent did raise the possibility of using this approach to try "to liberalise" the Ikhwan.[191]

Viewed in hindsight, this last suggestion was especially intriguing, for it raised the prospect of going beyond a purely material accommodation with the Ikhwan (of the kind attempted previously). Rather, it spoke to the idea that engagement might encourage the Brothers to become more moderate. In this way, the report provides an early example of a notion that would gain much wider traction decades later: that dialogue with the Brotherhood might lead it to change both its behavior and its values.

In making his case, the agent in question offered a more sympathetic picture than many of his colleagues of the impulses driving the Ikhwan. The group was described as a force for "moral regeneration," seeking both political and cultural independence from the West. It was said to have emerged from the impact of nineteenth-century liberalism on the Egyptian Moslem character—and to be part of a broader phenomenon in the region.[192] There was also some elision of the more pernicious aspects of the Brotherhood's character, which tended to be the focus of most diplomatic commentary on the movement. Perhaps most significant, however, was the way the Brotherhood was portrayed as the embodiment of something essential within Islamic societies—an interpretation that would also become a common feature of later arguments in favor of engagement with the Brotherhood.

At the time, those wishing for dialogue found little support for their position. Indeed, the MI5 memorandum triggered a minor interdepartmental quarrel. A minute from Edwin Chapman-Andrews at the Foreign Office described it as "well written and interesting," but judged the author "immature and shallowly informed." With palpable irritation, Chapman-Andrews went on to argue that the Ikhwan were "not to be taken so seriously" and labeled the suggestion that the British should establish contact with them as "ridiculous." Al-Nahas, he suggested, "would think we had gone mad and Sheikh Hassan el Banna would be made for life." According to Chapman-Andrews, they already had "most reliable and detailed . . . secret information about the Sheikh's organisation," and that was all they required. He further dismissed the Muslim Brothers as "ignorant" pretenders to "Islamic puritanism." Though happy to talk in an antiforeign fashion, he believed that there was not "one among them to be taken seriously"; "though they talk a lot about martyrdom," Chapman-Andrews said, "they are not too [keen] to suffer it."[193]

In response to these vehement criticisms, a follow-up telegram from MI5's man in Cairo sought to justify his original conclusions. This maintained that the membership of the Ikhwan numbered between a quarter million and half a million people, while the group's appeal to "younger 'intelligentsia'" was said to give them "an influence" far exceeding that.[194] The Brotherhood was also thought to enjoy support among respectable Muslims, including several prominent political figures. On this basis, MI5's Egypt representative stood by his earlier assertions as to the importance of the Ikhwan, stating that, after the Wafd, it was the "most formidable and well-organised society in Egypt." They could not be "disregarded," he insisted, and he again recommended the opening of contacts.

Chapman-Andrews, though, was unmoved. In the margins of this latest letter, he scribbled a note to the effect that there was "not a single heavy weight" within the Brotherhood, which he decried as "a miserable lot." In his opinion, the only real significance of the Brothers was that they would make "ready murderers"—

hence the need to watch them. Beyond that, Chapman-Andrews continued to reject the idea that the group would ever amount to a major political force: "It is dangerous to prophesy in politics but I feel sure the Ikhwan will <u>never</u> count in Egyptian politics as a <u>party</u>, like the Wafd [emphases in original]." Clearly growing somewhat frustrated with the discussion, Chapman-Andrews added a minute on July 25, which stated simply that it was "profitless" to pursue the issue further; it could perhaps, he ventured, be brought up again in ten years' time.[195]

Still, this was not the last time that the question of the Brotherhood helped generate an interagency spat within the British government. In mid-October 1943, Terence Shone at the British Embassy sent his own assessment to the Foreign Office's Patrick Scrivener. Shone's view was that the Political Intelligence Committee Middle East (PICME) had exaggerated in depicting the Brotherhood as an "immediate and actual danger." It was better understood, he suggested, as a "future and potential" threat, the realization of which would depend first on prolonged Wafdist support for the group, and second on the government losing control of the situation. "At present," Shone averred, while the Ikhwan was increasing in strength, "the Wafd seems to realise the necessity of caution." Shone claimed that the Defence Security Office (DSO)—the branch of MI5 that operated in Britain's colonial territories and dependent possessions—had always promoted the idea that the Brotherhood might one day "replace" the Wafd as the great majority party, but he felt this was "unlikely." Shone also took the opportunity to criticize what he called "uncontrolled political reporting by a military organization" that was neither qualified to do it, nor inclined to consult the embassy.[196]

As might be expected, such accusations provoked a robust response from Major General F. H. N. Davidson, the director of military intelligence at the War Office. Davidson wrote to Victor Cavendish-Bentinck, assistant undersecretary for foreign affairs, to argue that for all the embassy's complaints, the analysis of PICME actually differed little in substance from that of the diplomats: "The Embassy state that the Ikhwan <u>might</u> become a dangerous major political force: P.I.C.M.E. say that it <u>may</u> become a major political force [emphases in original]." The evident reality, he said, was that the Ikhwan was "increasing its membership" as a result of its cooperation with the Wafd. That being the case, Davidson asked pointedly whether it was not indeed correct to assume, as PICME had done, that the Ikhwan constituted "an immediate and actual danger instead of a future and potential one."[197] In reply, a somewhat chastened Cavendish-Bentinck preferred to ignore the substance and focused solely on the procedural question—PICME's lack of consultation with the embassy.[198]

Leaving aside what these exchanges reveal about the capacity for intra-Whitehall rivalry over relatively minor points of bureaucratic practice, their significance for present purposes is the extent to which they highlight burgeoning official concern about the Muslim Brotherhood. In particular, the documents confirm that the British were deeply perturbed by the Wafd government's conciliatory approach toward al-Banna's movement—a policy that was felt to be storing up problems for the future.

In this context, British diplomats likely welcomed reports at the end of October 1943 that hinted at a possible fraying of the relationship between al-Nahas and al-Banna. The prime minister was said to be "increasingly doubtful" of the good faith of the Brotherhood, which he suspected of deceiving him by means of a "simulated alliance." Al-Nahas apparently feared that the Ikhwan was once more preparing to "play an independent role based on Palace support." If the king were to move against the Wafdist government, the prime minister worried that the Brotherhood would throw its support to Faruq. He therefore ordered the group to be kept under stricter surveillance.[199]

On the other side, too, there were rumors that al-Banna had become "disillusioned" with what he saw as the "lukewarm" assistance on offer from the government.[200] When the authorities banned a procession and conference that the Ikhwan had organized to mark the opening of a new headquarters building, Brotherhood leaders lambasted the move.[201] The British observed that al-Banna seemed concerned that the Wafd might betray *him*. They wondered whether he might henceforth opt to "to turn the whole force" of the Ikhwan against the government (though they still doubted he would act precipitately).[202] For the moment, officials believed that the Brotherhood leader was being overly pessimistic; relations between the government and his movement remained good.[203] But it was clear that the political plates were shifting.

In May 1944, British intelligence reported that while al-Banna continued to preach a policy of restraint, his "moderating influence" had not been so effective among his followers in the provinces. There, they discovered mounting evidence of intolerance, with the Copts the principal targets of abuse. In addition, the Ikhwan was said to be preparing a sharp reaction to any British intervention to keep the Wafd in power.[204] In late July, intelligence analysts tracked the Brotherhood leader's tour of the Delta. One dispatch recorded how, everywhere al-Banna went, he met "scenes of enthusiasm unparalleled in the history of the Ikhwan." There were suggestions too that whilst he had largely avoided controversial topics during public speeches, he had spoken more ambitiously in private. By one account, al-Banna had talked of his desire to have some eighty thousand trained Rover scouts stationed across Egypt by the end of the year, a target the authorities did not discount. Al-Banna's impact on the group in any given area was thought to be "immense": "Hundreds of fallahin [*sic*] from the Delta provinces are said to have flocked to the nearest Ikhwan el Muslimeen premises in order to enrole [*sic*]; the strength of Gawala [Rover] bands has increased by leaps and bounds." The Brotherhood was also judged to be making progress in Upper Egypt. And as a result, the British believed that al-Banna's "ultimate objectives" were becoming clear. He had no intention, they averred, of collaborating with the Wafd or any other party; instead, he sought "political prominence" for himself. It was feared that the Wafd's "benevolent eye" had allowed him to make significant progress in that direction.[205]

Conclusion

By late 1944, the shadow of war had receded from Egypt. The previous year, Axis forces had been expelled from North Africa and, thereafter, Cairo became something of a political backwater for the remainder of the conflict. In this context, many British officials began to question whether they should continue to uphold al-Nahas's government. The rambunctious Chapman-Andrews, for instance, argued that the British should try to step back once more from any direct involvement in Egyptian domestic politics. He suggested that the king and the Wafd should be allowed to "fight it out."[206] British doubts over the wisdom of continuing to support the Wafd were bolstered by the view that al-Nahas seemed to be showing his "old colours," with the party indulging "the more extreme forms of nationalism." In particular, the British were concerned by Wafdist signals that they intended to seek the revision of the 1936 Anglo-Egyptian Treaty.[207] The last years of the war brought growing calls for negotiations, focused on a demand for the withdrawal of British troops and the extension of Egyptian control over Sudan.[208] For the most part, such rhetoric met a distinctly cool reception among the diplomats in Cairo and London alike.[209] In spite of this, Ambassador Lampson (or Lord Killearn as he now became) continued to believe that British interests were best served by preserving al-Nahas in office.[210] There was, he concluded, "no workable alternative to the present Government."[211] For a time, this outlook prevailed—primarily because Foreign Secretary Anthony Eden and Prime Minister Winston Churchill endorsed the ambassador's assessment; attempts by King Faruq to dismiss the Wafd were thwarted.[212] But by late 1944, it was clear that change was coming.

In October, the long-awaited crunch arrived. During a period in which Lord Killearn was out of the country (on holiday in South Africa), King Faruq dismissed al-Nahas and his government. A new administration was formed by the leader of the minority Sa'dist Party, Ahmad Maher (brother of Ali)—a clever move by the palace given Maher's known pro-British views (Lampson had described him as having long been his "second string in the event of al-Nahas going").[213] The absence of the British ambassador while all of this took place was symbolically significant—and doubtless encouraged the king to make his move—but, as described, the reality was that the British had moved position. The fall of the Wafdists was accepted with little dissension. The protection of al-Nahas's government was no longer seen as the sine qua non of policy. As an end to the war loomed, the British were content to see Egyptian internal politics placed on a new footing.

Over the previous four years, the strength and influence of the Muslim Brotherhood had increased—to the near-permanent consternation of the British. At the outset of the war, the Ikhwan was identified as being central to a network of anti-British forces that enjoyed the patronage of highly placed individuals, up to and including the palace. The British had hoped to see the group repressed, with officials repeatedly expressing their opposition to policies that gave the Ikhwan space to grow. They viewed the Brothers not only as a security threat but also as having a deleterious effect on Egyptian society as a whole. The growing prominence of the Ikhwan was linked to what officials saw as a worrying surge in xenophobia and antiforeign attitudes. Al-Nahas, they feared, had nurtured a "viper" to his breast.

With that said, a minority strand of opinion, identifiable particularly in military / intelligence circles, had on more than one occasion raised the question of whether it might be possible to win over the Brotherhood. Such a strategy had been attempted (unsuccessfully) with Young Egypt in 1940; some wondered whether it might not also be tried with the Ikhwan. For now, however, such views remained beyond the pale to most of those charged with the actual formulation and implementation of British policy in Egypt.

In the crisis years of 1940–1942, anxiety over the Brotherhood had led the British to intervene directly to demand restrictions on the organization. In the first instance, the effect of this was to see al-Banna transferred away from Cairo; later, the Brotherhood leader was interned. In the Ikhwan's historical memory, World War II brought the moment when the group was first subject to repression in the form of greater surveillance, arrests, and the disruption of its activities.[214] Yet the Brotherhood's difficulties proved short-lived and al-Banna showed himself

a highly adroit political tactician. Through a mixture of implied threat (of serious unrest should the government attempt to crush the Ikhwan) and an
openly conciliatory posture, the movement was able to preserve its freedom of
maneuver. This was particularly so from the spring of 1943 onward, when al-Banna
could exploit al-Nahas's weakened position (following the "Black Book" affair) to
achieve a rapprochement with the government. In return for the removal of all
restraints on Ikhwan activity, the movement provided political ballast to the
Wafd. To secure this alliance, it abjured all criticism of both the government
and even the British (at least in public).

As a result, by the time al-Nahas was dismissed from power, the Muslim
Brotherhood was more powerful than ever. The realities of all this were rue-
fully acknowledged by British diplomatic and intelligence analysts. A lengthy
July 1944 PICME assessment offered an overview of the Brotherhood's wartime
experience. Al-Banna, it was noted, had "developed into a clever and by no
means scrupulous politician." His actions since at least 1943 were said to have
been driven by a desire to "render himself so indispensable to [the government]
that they would be prepared to oppose any subsequent British demand for repressive action against his organisation." From the autumn of 1943, the Brotherhood was thought to have shown a new vibrancy—as demonstrated by the fact
that its Rover scouts had begun to parade at least once a week "and were given
elementary semi-military training." It was this new vitality that had generated
new "qualms" on the part of al-Nahas about the growing strength of the Ikhwan.
Yet the reality, in the judgment of the British authorities, was that "sheltered by
the Wafd's policy of non-intervention" al-Banna had been able "to accomplish
more in twelve months than he had previously achieved in twelve years."[215]

He had built an organization opposed to "modern Western civilization,"
which argued that the whole system of government in Egypt was rotten and
needed to be totally reorganized. And though the British felt that al-Banna
lacked "courage" and would not himself initiate an uprising, they predicted that
"in the event of another 1919," he would "undoubtedly throw his powerful following into the struggle and would endeavour to gain the leadership." For this
reason, they believed that the Ikhwan was "destined to play a prominent part
in future political development." Indeed, it was surmised that "apart from
the Wafd," the Muslim Brotherhood was "the only well organised political machine in Egypt and as such it lies a menacing shadow across the political
life of the country."[216]

As Egypt and Britain stood on the brink of the postwar era, then, the question
of how to deal with the Ikhwan remained fundamentally unresolved. Hitherto,

the diplomats—and the Cairo authorities—had alternated between repression and accommodation in the hope of halting the Brotherhood's advance. Against a backdrop in which there were suggestions that the existing "party system" in Cairo was "on its last legs," many now expected the Brothers to play a decisive role.[217] The years that followed would prove the accuracy of such expectations, as Egypt entered into a new era of instability that ended ultimately in revolution.

Three   Best of Enemies

1944–1949

O N 12 FEBRUARY 1949, Hasan al-Banna was shot dead in central Cairo. The immediate investigation into the murder declared it to be the work of an "un-known" assassin, but there were strong suspicions from the beginning that the Egyptian authorities were involved.[1] Within days, the British Embassy's security representative was able to present a fairly exhaustive account of the crime, with the perpetrators identified as police officers and Interior Ministry officials who had acted on government orders and with the "approval of the Palace."[2] Further details followed—with the Egyptian prime minister himself allegedly implicated in the plot.[3] There were even reports that King Faruq had greeted news of al-Banna's death with a "sickly grin" and all but confessed his own complicity.[4]

British reactions to the murder were mixed. On the one hand, officials registered little public objection to the killing of al-Banna. On the other, some—such as the British minister in Cairo, Edwin Chapman-Andrews—recorded their distaste for the Egyptian government's resort to "gangster methods." Such an approach, Chapman-Andrews believed, was "highly dangerous." In his view, "strong and swift court action" was "the one and only safe method of repressing terrorism and asserting government authority."[5] His sense of unease was shared by others. The British security representative in Cairo expressed concern that al-Banna would be seen as a "martyr at the hands of a reactionary Government."[6] American diplomats also worried that the assassination might generate a surge of "terrorist activities" by those seeking to avenge the Muslim Brotherhood leader.[7]

Anxieties of this kind were not without foundation. Publications produced by the Ikhwan in the immediate aftermath of the murder declared al-Banna to be the victim of an "infernal conspiracy concocted by those who are in authority." They pledged retribution against an un-Islamic "prostitute Government," declaring: "We shall dog and chase this band of iniquity; we will curb every haughty head; and we shall twist every neck that boasts in vanity. . . . No fortified citadel or well-defended palace will rescue them."[8] It became an established part of Brotherhood orthodoxy that al-Banna's murder was a "gift" to King Faruq to mark the royal birthday one day earlier.[9] Half a century later, this was how Yusuf al-Qaradawi explained the timing of the assassination. He also pointed to underlying Western culpability.[10] Secret documents were said to prove that the British, French, and American ambassadors had met beforehand at the military camp of Fayyid in the Suez Canal Zone and agreed on the necessity of destroying the Brotherhood. They had then put pressure on the Egyptian government to take action against the group.[11] Brotherhood newspapers devoted considerable energy to propagating this narrative in the years that followed al-Banna's death.[12] Famously, too, the future Brotherhood leader Sayyid Qutb, who was at a hospital in the United States at the time, later testified that the employees of the institution rejoiced at news of the killing.[13] Needless to say, the idea that New York-based hospital workers were aware of al-Banna's murder—let alone jubilant about it—seems more than a tad fanciful. Such claims were surely a projection on the part of Qutb of how he *assumed* they must feel.[14] Nevertheless, it seems clear that many Western officials found little to lament in the passing of a man who, to their mind, led a dangerous organization at a time when Egypt seemed to teeter on the brink of chaos.

The murder occurred against the backdrop of a rising tide of violence and political assassination in Egypt, responsibility for which had been lain largely at the door of the Muslim Brotherhood. Only a few weeks previously, a member of the organization had shot dead then prime minister Mahmud al-Nuqrashi—a murder itself carried out in retribution for al-Nuqrashi's decision to dissolve the Brotherhood. The killing of al-Banna was widely understood as an act of vengeance commissioned by al-Nuqrashi's own supporters. For this reason, British officials reported that there had been "singularly little expression of sympathy" for al-Banna among the general public in Egypt.[15]

More broadly, during the previous half decade, Egyptian society had appeared ever more unstable. The war had temporarily suppressed but also exacerbated many of the trends that had become apparent during the 1930s. Disillusionment with the Wafd had continued to grow, for example, given its evident failure to fulfill the country's national aspirations. The events of February 1942 left the party compromised by association with the British. To this was added the corruption and incompetence that al-Nahas then showed in office. The scandal arising from the "Black Book" episode is discussed in Chapter 2. Similarly, Nadav Safran points to the impact of the malaria epidemic of 1943–1944, which killed some two hundred thousand people and was partially blamed on government maladministration.[16] The war also generated fresh socioeconomic problems, including rising inflation and unemployment, amid greater industrialization and urbanization. As faith in the political system eroded, nationalist agitation escalated. People voiced their opposition to an overbearing British presence and demands for a revision of the 1936 Anglo-Egyptian Treaty became almost ubiquitous.[17]

All of this helped fuel the popular appetite for alternative ideologies, especially among the country's educated youth. Communism emerged as the choice of some, the Brotherhood the choice of many.[18] It offered a vehicle by which people might articulate their grievances, and it was in this era that the Ikhwan reached its historic peak in terms of size and influence. It has been suggested that as many as two million of Egypt's twenty million–strong population belonged to the Brotherhood at that time. The figures—though surely open to challenge—are hard to prove either way. But what seems undeniable is that many believed the Brothers to be on the cusp of power. It was not a prospect that Western observers welcomed. Before proceeding to examine their relationship with the Ikhwan in this crucial period, however, it is worth pausing to consider the broader context in which diplomatic officials were operating.

The Evolving Western Position

The British ended the war determined to hold on to their position in Egypt. In April 1945, Anthony Eden had gone as far as to recommend that the government retain responsibility for the defense of the Suez Canal "in perpetuity." This, he said, would allow them to play "the predominant part in the defense and political control of the Middle East."[19] It was an outlook shared by the chiefs of staff and the ambassador in Cairo.[20] Egypt continued to be viewed as the keystone of Britain's imperial system; and few policy makers were ready to abandon empire. In this respect, there was little to differentiate postwar Labour and Conservative Party administrations. It was an article of faith across the po-litical class that Britain should remain both an empire and in Egypt. Though decolonization would follow in the years and decades after 1945, this was some-thing that happened in piecemeal and reluctant fashion.[21]

With that said, statesmen and officials were scarcely oblivious to the changed postwar environment and its multiple challenges—particularly in the Middle East. For one thing, there was no doubting the growing appeal of nationalism, with many of its advocates preaching a "gospel of violent change."[22] Across the region, there was a clamor for an end to empire and for national self-determination. In trying to navigate these difficult waters, the British also had to contend with a more active and assertive United States. David Lesch has de-scribed the Second World War as marking the great divide in US policy toward the Middle East.[23] Previously, with the exception of their position in Saudi Arabia, the Americans had been prepared to "defer" to British and French pre-eminence in the region.[24] That now changed, with the Middle East elevated to an area of "vital interest" to the United States, which took a far closer interest in local affairs.[25] Egypt, in particular, was identified as a country of major "stra-tegic importance."[26] (A sign of the shifting outlook was the decision to upgrade US diplomatic representation in Cairo and other regional capitals, a move hith-erto held in abeyance in deference to British sensitivities.)[27]

The UK Foreign Office observed this American awakening in the Middle East warily. The mandarins were keen, for instance, to impress on their US counter-parts the idea that Britain should retain its "first place in Egyptian affairs."[28] In Cairo, Ambassador Lord Killearn suggested to the resident American minister that "just as America had her Munroe doctrine [sic] and Russia, I believe, hers, there seemed no good reason why we [the British] should not have ours in re-gard to the Eastern Mediterranean."[29] Killearn believed it was essential that the British keep their "special position" in the region and especially in Egypt.[30] For the most part, his colleagues eschewed such bold declarations—worried that they might do more harm than good given America's publicly stated opposition to both empire and spheres of influence.[31] Even so, they shared Killearn's desire to bind in Washington's support for the maintenance of the British position—a position that seemed further threatened by the onset of the Cold War.

Western policy makers viewed the "Near East" as potentially a "highly dan-gerous trouble-spot" in the global competition between the "western democratic, free enterprise system" and the "authoritarian, closed economic system of the Soviet Union."[32] In 1945, Egypt was seen as part of the "free world" and they were determined it should remain that way.[33] The perception in London was that Moscow had launched a "savage" propaganda campaign to destabilize the British across the region.[34] It was for this reason that an attempt was made to "modernise" the public face of empire by infusing it with a new vocabulary that spoke of "partnership" rather than domination. In particular, the Labour government that took office in July 1945 expressed a desire to work with "people not pashas."[35] More tangibly, the British Middle East Office (BMEO) was created to support socioeconomic development and the improvement of living standards.[36] The hope was that this new approach, based on cooperation rather than coercion, would allow for the renewal of Britain's "empire by treaty" across the region.[37] To the mind of Foreign Secretary Ernest Bevin, the effect of this would be to secure "the Moslems" of the Middle East "for the West" in the context of the Cold War.[38]

The British soon became aware too that the exigencies of East-West rivalry could draw the public sting of American anti-imperialism. From 1945, US officials talked with increasing clarity of their desire to keep the Soviets out of the Middle East.[39] The region came to be seen as a "main theatre" in the struggle between "humanism and totalitarianism."[40] Moscow, it was believed in Washington, wished to "sever [the] British Empire jugular at Suez."[41] Moreover, there were fears that Egypt's deep-seated socioeconomic problems, coupled to its nationalist aspirations, made it especially susceptible to the allure of communism.[42] For this reason, the United States came to favor the perpetuation of the regional status quo, including British paramountcy. The articulation of the Truman Doctrine in early 1947 was a critical moment in this regard, built as it was on the principle of containment in the Near East. It effectively resolved the "diplomatic schizophrenia" that had seen America torn between anticolonialism and anticommunism.[43] Washington accepted the British as "a partner-in-dominance."[44]

In the subsequent imagining of George McGhee, soon to become assistant secretary of state for Near Eastern, South Asian, and African Affairs, Britain would bear "primary responsibility" for the Middle East, even as the United States signaled a greater commitment to the area.[45] In London, the US ambassador, Lewis Douglas, was authorized to inform Clement Attlee's government that "the fundamental cornerstone of our thinking is the maintenance of Britain's position to the greatest possible extent."[46] Anglo-American cooperation in the Middle East was enshrined at the "Pentagon Talks" later that same year.[47] McGhee was among those who believed that British and American interests in the region were now "parallel" rather than "competitive"; their ultimate objectives, he averred, were "identical."[48] In line with this, the United States effectively endorsed British efforts to secure control of the Suez Canal and the vast military base that had grown up there, as well as their position in Egypt more broadly.[49] (Not everyone in Washington was entirely convinced, however. In this period, more than one US official lamented what were considered "characteristic British failings" in their handling of the Middle East—particularly in relation to the growing challenge from nationalism.[50] But, ultimately, the balance of opinion across America's foreign policy–making elite favored London.)[51]

As the threat of war had receded from Cairo in 1944–1945, UK diplomats had begun to contemplate a political withdrawal to "the role of interested spectators."[52] This inclination was reinforced by the conviction, current in Foreign Office circles, that the British should seek a rapprochement with King Faruq.[53] As explained above, a decision already had been made not to continue the policy of securing the Wafd in government. Not only was this a response to the party's perceived shortcomings but also a product of the belief that an alliance with the king was the best option for securing British "strategic interests." Faruq, it was suggested, was the only "available instrument" for achieving much-needed "social and political reform."[54] Paradoxically, therefore—given the Labour government's expressed desire to work with "people not pashas"— the diplomats sought now to work with the king as "the chief element of continuing stability in Egypt."[55] (One of those not convinced by such arguments was Lord Killearn, yet he was finally replaced as ambassador after ten years in the post, in February 1946.)[56]

The new British approach, it should be said, was not born of any desire to unleash "an uncontrolled King," any more than they wanted "an uncontrolled Wafd." Rather, the hope was that the familiar triangle of Egyptian politics (palace-Wafd-embassy) might be reinstated, albeit with Faruq now in the ascendant.[57] What all this failed to recognize, of course, was the extent to which Egypt, and indeed the region, had changed—socioeconomically, culturally, ideologically, and politically. The scholar Sir Hamilton Gibb was among those who perceived this at the time, pointing to the "poisons" and problems that beset the Middle East. Within Egypt, he reckoned, discontent had spread and neither the palace nor the Wafd were the forces they once were. Demands for the fulfillment of Egyptian social and nationalist objectives could not easily be sated; political life had become more turbulent and unpredictable. Gibb recorded that for the first time in his life he had heard talk of "social unrest, of revolution" in the Middle East. To his mind, there were only two serious options for those in search of an alternative: a dictatorship based on the army (which Gibb believed would be a disaster); or a "Moslem revolution." In Gibb's estimation, the latter, though likely to take anti-Western form, would enjoy the support of the masses and might yet demonstrate "a certain idealism" and emerge as a "force making for unity and social justice."[58]

These words, it can be confidently surmised, were written with one eye firmly on the burgeoning power of the Muslim Brotherhood—a group increasingly of interest not merely to the British but also now to the Americans (and it is striking that Gibb's words, delivered in London, were picked up in Washington). The Brotherhood had first come to the attention of US diplomats during the war. Prior to that point, they had paid little heed to the group. The future ambassador, John Badeau, who was in Cairo during the late 1930s as a private citizen, later claimed not to have noticed the rise of the Ikhwan, observing rather haughtily that "one did not have friends who were Muslim Brothers."[59] In 1944, however, officials at the US Legation in Cairo identified the Brotherhood as a movement involved in "subversive activities." In their view, the Brothers were inclined to "auction [their] loyalty to the highest bidder" and had taken on a "new lease of life" following their 1942 deal with al-Nahas's government, which gave them access to financial subsidies. For this reason, American officials pledged to keep a close eye on the group in the future.[60] Not long afterward, they compiled a report dedicated specifically to the "fanatical Moslem Society," the "Ikhwan el-Muslimin." The immediate spur for this assessment was the fact that the legation had received some three hundred pro forma letters in a single day, complaining about both British actions in Palestine and French policy in Algeria. To these were added a personal telegram from Hasan al-Banna, which protested "America's attitude with regard to Palestine." The legation chose to ignore the messages, but the episode did prompt an examination of what was known about the Brotherhood.

The resulting document is fascinating both for its inaccuracies and for its analysis of what drove the Ikhwan. It was believed that al-Banna, erroneously described as a graduate of al-Azhar, had founded his movement in 1938. More apposite was the suggestion that its growth had been fueled in part by "accusations against Catholic missions that they were Christianizing Moslem children"; likewise the assertion that the Brotherhood had benefited from the patronage of "highly placed personages," such as Ali Maher. As described in Chapter 1, the Ikhwan did gain early prominence because of its campaigns against Christian orphanages (though these were run mostly by evangelicals rather than Catholics); there was also no doubting the assistance afforded to the group by a range of figures from across the political spectrum, including Maher. Furthermore, the authors of the report were clear that the Ikhwan was a cause for concern.

Though it had hitherto "confined its activities to religious propaganda of a pan-Islamic nature," its "fanatical principles" and militancy were thought to make it a potential source of danger in the future.[61] A similar picture emerged from a *Washington Post* article in the same period, which referred to the Brotherhood as a "new political-religious movement" comprised of "ultra-conservative, or rather, reactionary religious fanatics." It was said to be opposed to "social progress" and in favor of eliminating "all foreign elements" from Egypt.[62] In this way, American observers tended to follow their British counterparts in deploying the language of "fanaticism" when considering the Ikhwan. It was seen in almost wholly negative terms as an inherently anti-Western and antimodern phenomenon.

Nevertheless, as the war ended, the Brotherhood remained only of marginal interest to US policy makers, for whom Egypt itself was still of secondary concern. It was the British who continued to assume the principal responsibility for upholding the Western position in Cairo and, as such, had to work out how to deal with groups like the Brotherhood.

The Brotherhood Flexes Its Muscles

The period immediately following the Second World War seems to have renewed Hasan al-Banna's sense of the world in tumult. In one of his regular "Tuesday lectures," he noted that the Islamic world was consumed "with the fire of revolution," pointing to events in India, Egypt, Palestine, Indonesia, and Iraq. "The world," he declared, "burns for its future," and he predicted that those flames could not be extinguished.[63] On another occasion, he told his followers that the war might prove to be an agent for good, as it was likely to have changed the balance of power in the world, "between Arab and Muslim countries on the one hand, and Western imperialist countries on the other." His hope was that the West might "taste despair" at the hands of its enemies and emerge from the conflict in a weakened state.[64]

As such words suggested, al-Banna's critique of the West had been little diminished over the previous years. The Brotherhood newspaper *al-Ikhwan al-Muslimun* thus declared that the "fires of war" actually had been unleashed by the material instincts of Western life.[65] Elsewhere, the group seemed ever more fearful about moral decline in Egypt as a result of cultural "invasion" from the West. Practices such as belly dancing, the drinking of alcohol, and gambling were said to be a "heinous assault on morals and virtue."[66] Muslims remained caught between "two civilizations": the "mechanical materialist life" of the West and the "spiritual" world of "higher values" that they inherited from their religion. The Ikhwan continued to argue, therefore, that they should "take from Western civilization [only] that which is useful in terms of science, knowledge, industry and methods," while calling "the nations of the West to utilize [the] great spiritual heritage" of Islam, so they might "save humanity and stabilize peace and security."[67]

Al-Banna believed that the world now stood at a crossroads: in one direction lay communism and Soviet Russia; in the other, the democracies headed by "the English" and the Americans. To his mind, both paths offered manifestations of the materialist society that defined "the West" in the broadest sense. More than ever, al-Banna was convinced that Western civilization was bankrupt, characterized by "sins, lusts, alcohol, women and noisy parties." He contended that it was incapable of satisfying mankind spiritually, and left the "soul" trapped in a "material prison." According to al-Banna, the effects of this materialism had impacted Islamic societies everywhere—"in the valley of the Hijaz, the deserts of Yemen, the jungles of Africa, the plateaus of Asia and the plains of Egypt; among the Bedouin and the settled, the villages and the cities." For this reason, he urged his followers to "confront this new wave" so that rather than choosing communism or democracy, Arabs and Muslims might embrace Islam anew. He insisted that this was the only way in which the non-Western world could attain national self-fulfillment. There would be "no glory to the east," he proclaimed, unless it relied "on itself and the blessings of Allah." The only hope for humanity as a whole, said al-Banna, was to turn to Islam.[68]

In this period, too, the Brothers were especially vociferous in their denunciation of colonialism and the way it corrupted societies. During the latter stages of the war, *al-Ikhwan al-Muslimun* advocated "sound nationalism" and underlined the group's commitment to "struggle and jihad" in pursuit of "a life of glory or . . . the death of martyrs."[69] Brotherhood propaganda highlighted the hypocrisy of the British, pointing to Winston Churchill's rhetoric about democracy and freedom, and contrasting this with his treatment of his "ally and friend, Egypt."[70] Fathi Osman, who had joined the Ikhwan in 1942 in the rural province of Minya, was at Cairo University in this period and later remembered nationalist demonstrations demanding independence and the unity of the Nile valley. The Brotherhood invested much energy in disseminating the call for "liberation" from the British.[71] Al-Banna looked to the realization of Egypt's "rights" and a future in which there would be "dignity" and "strength."[72]

Imperial "cruelty and arrogance," he claimed, brought only "poverty, humiliation and unhappiness."[73]

By 1945, according to senior Brotherhood leader Salah Shadi, the group was firmly committed to expelling the British from Egypt—not only to end the occupation there but also because of its impact on Palestine. It was in this "fraught atmosphere of hatred for the English and the Zionists" that Shadi began, at al-Banna's behest, to organize the Brotherhood inside the security forces and the army, establishing the "sections" department to that end.[74] In public, meanwhile, there were various indications over the course of 1945 that the Brotherhood was ready to flex its muscles.

At the start of the year, al-Banna served notice that the Ikhwan had every intention of participating fully in national politics. When new elections were announced for January 1945, the Brotherhood's leader declared that his movement would enter the "battle."[75] Subsequently, al-Banna and five of his colleagues stood for parliament on a platform stressing their commitment to the rights of their "beloved country," as well as a familiar program of Islamically framed socioeconomic-cultural reform.[76] The first demand on the Ikhwan's inaugural electoral bulletin was "the complete preservation of the freedom, unity and independence of the Nile Valley, and the driving out of all foreign authority."[77] The group's newspaper stated that it alone offered a "new ideology in the field of Egyptian nationalism."[78] In a "conflict between principle and programme versus *hizbiyya* [political partisanship], money and titles," voters were urged to choose righteous, capable men who could bear the "heavy burden" of service to the country.[79]

As it happened, however, not a single Brotherhood candidate was successful in what were widely recognized to have been among the most corrupt elections in Egypt's history to that point. With the Wafd boycotting the polls, government manipulation, intimidation, and forgery were directed largely at the candidates of the Ikhwan and Young Egypt.[80] Within the annals of the Brotherhood, al-Banna's own experience in Ismailia became a celebrated example of injustice: a demonstration of the authorities' decadence and their collusion with the British. Hasan Hathut thus claimed that "the English" police commander in the Canal Zone ordered his officers to surround polling stations in order to prevent Brotherhood supporters from taking part in the ballot.[81] The government was said to have issued false electoral papers to thousands of workers from Upper Egypt who then voted for al-Banna's opponent. Against this background, tensions escalated in Ismailia and there were clashes between the security forces and Brotherhood members. According to Abbas al-Sissi, when the results were announced, violence was only averted by al-Banna's appeal for calm. In a speech to assembled supporters, he decried the "inability of the nation to send one of its sons to parliament," citing this as evidence that "freedom was hypocrisy" and "imperialism was the hidden scourge" of the country. Despite this, he also asked his followers to "conceal their rage and save their blood for another day" by dispersing to their homes, which they duly did.[82]

Irrespective of such setbacks, it seemed clear that al-Banna was committed to becoming a major political player. *Al-Ikhwan al-Muslimun* posited that the electoral results actually represented a "victory" given the authentic character of the group's support.[83] Prior to the elections, al-Banna had stated that the moment had arrived for the Brotherhood to take its work to parliament and the national stage.[84] That same year, when faced once more with the prospect of being transferred away from Cairo, he resigned from his teaching job and committed himself full-time to public life.[85] The Brothers reiterated their commitment to "politics" as an integral part of their faith.[86]

The 1945 elections were won by the Sa'dist Party of Prime Minister Ahmad Maher, who had succeeded al-Nahas a few months earlier. In the wake of his triumph, Maher announced Egypt's entry into the war on the Allied side. It was little more than a symbolic gesture, given the contemporary military context with the war nearing its end. Maher's aim was to guarantee his country a place at the forthcoming San Francisco peace conference—in the hope he could use this to put pressure on the British. He paid for the move, however, with his life. On his way out of the Chamber of Deputies where he had revealed the decision, Maher was shot dead. Speculation as to the perpetrator's motives immediately saw attention focus on the Muslim Brothers as possible culprits. Al-Banna and other leading figures in the movement were arrested.[87] They were soon released, as it emerged that the assassin was actually a hard-line member of the nationalist al-Watan Party.[88] In spite of this, though, many associated the murder with the Brotherhood—a sign of the extent to which the group was becoming identified with militant methods. To many, both then and since, it was axiomatic that the Brotherhood *would* be involved.[89] The Ikhwan had condemned Ahmad Maher's policy of bringing Egypt into the war, and Hasan al-Banna publicly opposed the conflict on religious grounds.[90] In his view, there was no reason for Egypt to involve itself in a foreign war in which it had no stake.[91]

Maher's short premiership was in many ways emblematic of the new era that was dawning in Egypt. On the one hand, he had placed Egypt's nationalist demands firmly on the political agenda. On the other, the violent end to his life was "symptomatic of a growing disrespect for law and order."[92] Maher was succeeded as prime minister by the deputy leader of his party, Mahmud al-Nuqrashi, who was determined to push forward with his predecessor's policies. From the beginning, the British Embassy had expressed dissatisfaction with al-Nuqrashi, whom Ambassador Killearn labeled "a narrow, pig-headed, hair-splitting obstinate schoolmaster!"[93] The new prime minister was seen as a "Nationalist of the most extreme type," and it was feared that he would not "play ball" in the manner desired by the British.[94] This proved a prescient assessment. An Egyptian delegation was sent to the San Francisco conference and the government publicly gave notice of its intention to secure Egypt's national aspirations. Al-Nuqrashi called for the "withdrawal of all British troops" and the satisfaction of Egyptian rights in Sudan.[95]

Against this backdrop, the Brotherhood initially gave cautious support to al-Nuqrashi's premiership, endorsing his tough stance on the national question. Al-Banna insisted that there was no point in negotiations with the British, who he felt used talks only as a means of prevarication.[96] Equally, it was clear that the Brotherhood leader—ever the pragmatist—saw an opportunity here to reach out to the new government, which had itself seemed amenable to a repeat of the Wafd's wartime alliance with the Ikhwan. Hagai Erlich has suggested that al-Nuqrashi's government wished to utilize the Brotherhood's student members to combat the rising influence of left-wing Wafdists and communists on campus. To this end, the prime minister apparently reached an agreement with al-Banna, providing a fresh injection of funding (which made possible the construction of a new headquarters building) in return for Brotherhood quiescence. The effect of this was to split the student movement.[97]

In this way, it appeared as if al-Banna had opted again for the path of pragmatic accommodation with the authorities. Yet this latest covenant was short-lived. And Mitchell suggests that from the start, al-Nuqrashi did not entirely believe al-Banna's pledge of support and ordered increased surveillance of the group even as he talked about reconciliation.[98]

Skepticism over the intentions of the Ikhwan was not entirely surprising. The memoirs of various Brothers confirm that this was a period of increasingly intense nationalist agitation during which they sought to arouse the passions of the Egyptian street. Young activist orators such as Hasan Dawh, Mustafa Mu'min, and Sa'id Ramadan articulated a firebrand message that underlined the urgency of the nationalist struggle.[99] Dawh had joined the Brotherhood at Cairo University in 1944–1945, and quickly became a "revolutionary preacher" who, in his own words, delivered "violent" speeches in which he heaped "abuse on the English," as well as the political and social elites. The goal, he admitted, was to incite the people against the British and to bring down weak governments.[100]

Al-Ikhwan al-Muslimun, meanwhile, denounced the "corruption" and "weakness" of contemporary life, demanding adherence to the virtues of "faith," "jihad," and "martyrdom."[101] In May 1945, the newspaper declared that the end of the war had not brought a "day of victory for Egypt." Such a day would not arrive, it proclaimed, until the unity of the Nile valley north and south was achieved, so that Egypt and Sudan became a "single nation"; nor would it come until the British evacuated their forces so that "not a single foreign soldier" remained on Egyptian soil.[102] The Brothers were clear that the 1936 treaty had done little to end British interference: "The truth that is known by the man of politics and the man in the street is that nothing is done in Egypt without the agreement of the English." The imperialists were aided, the Brotherhood declared, by "Egyptian hands and leaders"; for this reason, the group called on all politicians to boycott the government. To "accept ministry in the shadow of occupation and foreign intervention" was said to be "a great betrayal and national crime" that could not be "forgiven."[103] The implication of such words for those in office like al-Nuqrashi—as much as for the British themselves—could hardly be ignored.

In June, British intelligence reported on a Brotherhood demonstration that featured cries of "Down with the Occupation," "Arabs are all one nation," and "Foreigners cannot be tolerated." Speeches delivered by al-Banna and Ahmad al-Sukkari allegedly struck a "xenophobic note." British observers were also struck by al-Banna's ability to control the crowd. After heading a two thousand–strong march to 'Abdin Square, where he led chants in praise of King Faruq, he had ordered the assembled group to disperse and been "immediately obeyed."[104] The following month, the Brotherhood again called its members onto the streets to hold protests against French policy in North Africa.[105] All of this seemed indicative of al-Banna's capacity to play the role of demagogue, undermining the stability the British craved in Egypt.

Of course, nothing generated as much emotional excitement among supporters of the Ikhwan as events in Palestine. British officials were dismayed to see this issue return to the forefront of public concern across the region.[106] In Egypt, it was the Brotherhood that continued to serve as the loudest voice of opposition against British policy.[107] The Ikhwan had been extremely active in fund-raising and distributing propaganda on the Palestinian question since the 1930s. As the end of the Second World War approached, the group resumed its public activism in support of the Arab cause.[108] According to *al-Ikhwan al-Muslimun,* with Hitler's defeat, there was no longer any need for the Jews to immigrate to Palestine because now they could "return to Italy, Germany, Austria and every country in Europe." For this reason, they demanded an end to both Jewish immigration and the sale of Arab land to the Jews. The Brotherhood also restated its opposition to partition and any form of "Zionist government" in Palestine.[109] In this context, too, the Brothers were alarmed by the election victory of the British Labour Party, which they deemed to be pro-Zionist. And the group condemned the comments of US president Harry Truman endorsing the entry of one hundred thousand Jews into Palestine. Truman, they said, had "opened the Zionist bottle and released it from its shackles upon the world, to direct its scourge against Palestine."[110]

In the face of the Zionist "threat," the Ikhwan was openly committed to "armed struggle," urging volunteers to come forward to participate in physical force jihad. Branches of the group around the country gathered weapons for dispatch to Palestine—often with the tacit acquiescence of the authorities.[111] A young activist such as Hasan Dawh had no doubts about the justice of their cause, believing the Jews to be "the enemies of our religion, conspiring against it since the era of the Prophet." He asserted that they had "violated the land that the Muslims own and in the heart of which, is located the al-Aqsa mosque."[112]

In early November 1945, there were major demonstrations in Cairo to mark the anniversary of the Balfour Declaration. These were followed by attacks on foreigners and Jewish-owned property. In the aftermath, the British placed much of the blame on the Egyptian government. There was a perception that al-Nuqrashi's administration had effectively encouraged the protestors while simultaneously hampering the police response, thereby creating a situation in which violence was likely.[113] Such official culpability notwithstanding, British accounts also identified the Muslim Brotherhood as having played a crucial role. Military Intelligence Section 5 (MI5) reported that spokesmen for the group (together with those of Young Egypt and the Young Men's Muslim Association, YMMA), had made "virulent and outspoken" speeches and written inflamatory articles, in the buildup to the unrest. Further, on the day that saw the greatest violence (November 2), the Ikhwan had arranged vehicles (courtesy of the recently established Ikhwan el Muslimeen Transport Company) so that their members might tour Cairo to ensure that a general strike was observed. In addition, al-Banna had led the main march through the city from Al-Azhar to the 'Abdin Palace.[114] Once there, it was acknowledged, the Brotherhood leader had called for purely peaceful protests, decrying the "evil work" of those who engaged in acts of vandalism. He also asked his followers to go home at the end of the official rally and had generally been obeyed in a "most orderly fashion." With all that said, however, it was obvious that not everyone had responded to this appeal. Instead, the gathering had served as a platform for major acts of "hooliganism" in Cairo (with parallel unrest in Alexandria). In British eyes, the Brotherhood, though repudiating any direct involvement in violence, had helped to create the atmosphere in which it occurred. Al-Banna and his colleagues had incited the passions of the crowd to the point where disturbances became inevitable. As such, the Ikhwan was attributed a large portion of the blame for the resulting violence.[115]

In the same period, the US Legation was inundated by telegrams and letters bearing the signature of various branches of the "Ikhwan el-Muslimeen."[116] One typical example (from Alexandria) condemned the "ill-omened Balfour Declaration" and international efforts to implant Zionism in the "throbbing heart of the Arab world"; another letter carried a pledge to defend Palestine and sacrifice "soul and everything else for her sake"; and a third warned the "Western world" that the Brotherhood would send "commandos to save every part of the Arab home from the claws and teeth of colonization and subjection." The letters advised the United States not to allow itself to be "used by the Jews for the satisfaction of their ambitions." "Arabs and Muslims," it was argued, wanted "to be friends of the Americans. Why then should Americans side with the Jews? . . . Arabs will be better than the Jews as friends to the Americans."[117] Needless to say, such petitions went unanswered. Yet the well-organized nature of the campaign clearly stirred the interest of some within US officialdom. Several months later, the Near East Unit of the Office of Strategic Services (OSS) compiled a long report on the episode, which was said to show much about the Brotherhood's modus operandi.[118] The fact that the letters consisted of the "unimaginative repetition of phrases deriving from a fixed and obviously dictated pattern," and had been sent to the entire diplomatic corps, was seen as evidence that they were the work of a coordinated and energetic campaign. As during the 1930s, events in Palestine were thought to be driving the "growing influence of the Moslem Brethren."[119] Moreover, the letter-writing campaign underlined the extent to which al-Banna did not rely solely on street activism but was instead prepared to lobby Western governments directly.

The truth of this had been made apparent earlier in the year. In October 1945, the Brotherhood sent the British Embassy a memorandum outlining the decisions passed at its most recent general assembly. This placed particular emphasis on the Ikhwan's support for Egyptian national rights. The Brothers called for: the immediate evacuation of British troops from the Nile valley; a solution to the Sudan question based on its unity with Egypt; the recognition that Egypt

alone should guard and administer the Suez Canal; the cancellation of all economic and financial restrictions on the country; and the release of Egypt's
frozen sterling balances. In the event that these demands were not satisfied, the
Brotherhood warned that they would act against "aggressive foreign states,"
and the "unpatriotic" governments that aided them.[120]

Unsurprisingly, rhetoric of this kind captured British attention. From London,
A. Victor Coverley-Price noted that the Brotherhood had in effect declared itself "a new political party." He observed that it would be necessary to keep
"watch" on a group that was "likely to make progress."[121] In Cairo, that same
month, Sir Walter Smart of the British Embassy met with Hasan al-Banna (apparently the second such encounter between the two—Smart's report suggests
that he had talked with al-Banna at his home eighteen months previously). On
this occasion, the Brotherhood leader again pressed Egypt's national goals. In a
reflection of his growing confidence, he also emphasized that "the religious objectives in Islam were inevitably . . . political."

Beyond this, interestingly, al-Banna reiterated what Smart called his "old
thesis," that "the Moslem Brethren were our most useful allies in a society threatened with dissolution." Al-Banna argued that the Brotherhood was "the greatest
barrier against communism and the strongest factor working for stabilisation."
"Islam," he said, "while democratic, was a force of conservatism."[122] The historian 'Abdallah Imam has claimed that this message, about the ability of the
Brotherhood to repel communism, was a common theme of al-Banna's in conversations he had with representatives of the Egyptian government during this
period.[123] Here, it was deployed as part of the effort to reach some kind of understanding with the British—similar to those previously arrived at with the
Wafd and al-Nuqrashi. Al-Banna offered a marriage of convenience that might
forestall hostilities between the two sides. He did so in such a way as to resonate with Cold War concerns about the threat posed to Egypt by communism,
the suggestion being that the religious character of the Brotherhood could serve
as an impediment to the growth of more radical and revolutionary creeds.

Clearly, some within Egyptian governing circles were convinced by this logic.
A close ally of King Faruq, Hasan Rifaat, told Smart that he believed the king
should give a "little encouragement" to the Muslim Brotherhood as the "best
instrument for the fight against communism." In Rifaat's view, the growth of
the Ikhwan was a "natural development," not something to be feared. He maintained that al-Banna was "amenable" to moderation, and while Rifaat acknowledged that the Brotherhood had in the past accepted money from the Italians
and Germans, he asserted that such funds had not been spent on personal ag-

grandizement but rather on the organization (which, to his mind, made it somehow less reprehensible). As a result, Rifaat felt that it made good sense to try and harness the Ikhwan's influence for good.[124]

British officials, it seems evident, were not persuaded. One expressed misgivings as to the democratic bona fides of the Brotherhood—albeit on the somewhat orientalist grounds that Islam in general could scarcely be called "democratic."[125] For his part, Sir Walter Smart continued to see the Ikhwan as "a xenophobic obscurantist Society" that was "anxious to replace al-Nahas and the Wafd." He judged al-Banna's offer of an alliance to be merely the latest example of his penchant for political maneuvering. Smart argued that the Brotherhood wished to "avoid clashes," both with the Egyptian authorities and with the British, so as to facilitate its own growth. On this basis, Smart set himself firmly against any accommodation, noting: "We have pointed out to successive Governments the danger of encouraging the Ikhwan el-Muslimin, who might one day get too powerful to handle easily."[126]

Increasingly, however, officials like Smart worried that they were working against the grain of Egyptian opinion. An annual political summary observed that al-Nuqrashi's administration and the palace had indeed "come to the conclusion that the Moslem Brethren could be of service in combating the evil of communism." The British believed that the authorities had therefore embarked on a policy of "leaning" on the Brotherhood. The embassy made plain its distaste for this approach: "The Moslem Brethren remain a permanent danger to friendly co-operation between not only Great Britain and Egypt, but between Egypt and Europeans generally. Strengthened by the folly of successive Governments, who have tried to use them, the Moslem Brethren have now openly become a political body and are not hiding their hope that they will eventually replace the Wafd and become the Government of the country."[127]

Though the prospect of a Brotherhood-led administration remained somewhat distant, the British were disturbed by what they took to be the consequences of the group's empowerment. They thought, for example, that the Ikhwan was again involved in stirring up "anti-Christian and anti-foreign feeling."[128] MI5 warned that the group might be planning further major protests against the British because of their refusal to concede Egyptian national demands. It was suggested that the Ikhwan and other subversive groups were displaying "their customary propensity for fishing in troubled waters."[129]

British disquiet was hardly assuaged by the fact that the rise of the Ikhwan was paralleled by, and intimately linked to, the worsening of the security situation in Egypt. According to Salah Shadi, a senior figure in the group, in late 1945, the Brothers carried out a gun and bomb attack in Cairo on a train thought to be carrying British soldiers to Palestine to help "strengthen the formation of the new Zionist state."[130] During the same period, acts of violence proliferated. In December, an attempt was made by unknown assassins to kill Wafdist leader Mustafa al-Nahas. The following month, Amin Osman Pasha—the former Wafdist finance minister who had served as an intermediary in discussions with the British—was shot dead. (One of those involved in the murder was the future president, Anwar Sadat.)[131] MI5's Cairo representative mourned the loss of this voice of "moderation," and there were fears that al-Nuqrashi's government was "incapable of handling" the burgeoning crisis.[132] The Brotherhood appears not to have been directly involved in the Osman assassination, but they later helped the perpetrator, Husayn Tawfiq, hide after he had escaped from prison.[133] More immediately, the militant posture of the Brotherhood seemed only to exacerbate a growing sense of instability.

By early 1946, there were signs that al-Nuqrashi's short-lived alliance with the Ikhwan had broken down. At the end of the previous year, the government had delivered a short note to the British, formally requesting revision of the 1936 treaty.[134] The Brothers deemed this to be a much too insufficient step; they believed Egypt should not beg for its rights from London but should instead simply take them. As far as the Ikhwan was concerned, "negotiating" meant "bargaining" and this had "no place" when "the rights of a people and the freedom of a nation" were at stake. The job of the politicians, it was suggested, was simply to assert Egypt's demands; if these were refused, then it would be necessary to launch violent jihad.[135]

As the rift between the Brotherhood and al-Nuqrashi widened, there was speculation that the former might be reconciled to the Wafd, with the two groups united in opposition to both the government and the British.[136] February 1946 brought massive demonstrations in Cairo. Government attempts to disperse the protests led to violent clashes (known locally as the "Battle of Giza / Abbas Bridge") and several days of rioting. Three people were killed and another two hundred injured.[137] Hasan Hathut later claimed that the prominent Brotherhood student leader Mustafa Mu'min had played a key role in planning the demonstrations.[138] For their part, contemporary Western officials were in no doubt as to who was to blame for the unrest. The British Embassy noted that the agitation was "mainly contrived by [the] Wafd and [the] Moslem Brothers"; and in their view, it was the latter that had proven decisive. It had only been when the Ikhwan threw its "weight" behind the disorders that these proved "pretty effective." This decision on the part of the Brotherhood was taken as evidence that it had abandoned al-Nuqrashi's government, believing it to be "on its last legs."[139] So it proved.

The Brotherhood Ascendant

The violence of early February 1946 prompted the king to secure al-Nuqrashi's resignation. Subsequent British analysis concluded that it was fear of the Brotherhood and its ability to provoke countrywide disorder that pushed Faruq to intervene. The independent politician Isma'il Sidqi now returned as prime minister (having served in the post more than a decade earlier under King Fu'ad). Popularly caricatured as the "strong man" of Egyptian politics, he was seen as the embodiment of patrician, authoritarian nationalism. The change in government, though, did not bring an immediate end to the upheavals.

On the contrary, 21 February 1946 witnessed huge rallies and a general strike to mark the "Day of Evacuation." Once more, the protests degenerated into violence, this time with attacks on British military and civilian property. At least twenty people were killed and more than one hundred fifty wounded.[140] In the aftermath, the Brotherhood blamed the British for the trouble and called on the government to declare Egypt's cities "out of bounds" to British soldiers. It demanded that all "English" officers and officials (such as the chief of the Cairo police, Thomas Russell) be discharged from Egyptian service.[141] For their part, senior British diplomats again laid responsibility for the disturbances squarely at the door of the Wafd and the Brotherhood. Hasan al-Banna, it was suggested, had "bared his fangs" and shown the "potentialities" of the Ikhwan.[142]

In addition, the British were indignant about what they saw as the complicity of the authorities. There were accusations, for instance, that the Cairo police had been prevented from exercising proper control.[143] This was made more troubling by signs of a fresh rapprochement between the Ikhwan and the Egyptian government. Salah Shadi later averred that King Faruq had even consulted al-Banna on the appointment of Sidqi. Suspicions deepened when the newly installed prime minister himself then made a courtesy call at the Brotherhood's headquarters.[144] As a result of these exchanges, Sidqi agreed to release all imprisoned students; he also removed the ban on meetings of the Brotherhood (and Young Egypt) and there was renewed speculation that the group had been provided with a government subsidy.[145] Soon afterward, the Ikhwan was granted a license for a daily newspaper and an allocation of newsprint.[146] This allowed the daily edition of *al-Ikhwan al-Muslimun* to be launched in the spring of 1946 under the editorship of Ahmad al-Sukkari. It adopted a fiercely anti-British line, proclaiming itself to be "the voice of truth, strength and freedom."[147] The unprecedented "rapidity" with which the paper had come into existence was seen as confirmation of the fact that the new government was following the policy of its predecessor and "leaning" on the Brotherhood.[148] In the assessment of the embassy, the prime minister and the palace were prepared to play "the game of national heroes and to associate themselves with the elements responsible for [the] disorders of February 21st." It was assumed that they hoped thereby to maintain their influence in the streets and put pressure on the British to offer concessions. Ambassador Killearn voiced fresh concern that they might end up relying on "the most dangerous elements" in Egyptian society, such as the Ikhwan.[149]

Further violence followed in early March, amid another general strike and clashes in Alexandria to mark "Martyrs Day." Ten people were now killed, including two British soldiers, generating another round of complaints from the embassy to the government. Brotherhood histories of the episode accused foreigners of instigating the trouble by firing on demonstrators, leading angry crowds to take revenge.[150] Yet the incident was in keeping with the wider deterioration in public security at this time, which many blamed on the Ikhwan. On March 11, a grenade attack on the Miami Cinema in Cairo—a venue known to be frequented by Europeans, which had been showing a British film—left one person dead and almost forty injured. In the aftermath, Ahmad Husayn and other members of Young Egypt were arrested. The Brothers were left conspicuously untouched, though as far as the British were concerned, this was scarcely proof of their innocence.[151] And if not responsible for this specific attack, officials believed the Ikhwan was creating the climate in which such episodes occurred. In their view, the group had been empowered by its "strongly xenophobic" and "virulently anti-British policies," and "cashed in" on popular emotions and the "strong national feeling among all sections of Egyptians."[152]

Eventually, Sidqi's government did take steps to suppress the unrest. It soon became apparent, however, that this was made possible precisely because the prime minister had secured the acquiescence of the Brotherhood and thereby split the opposition. Whereas the Ikhwan had hitherto joined the Wafd in bringing people onto the streets, it now suspended its agitation. This divided the students—perhaps the most important constituency for street politics. Already, the Brotherhood had abstained from joining the National Committee of Workers and Students (NCWS) that had been formed under Wafdist leadership in mid-February. It then formally announced that it would no longer co-operate with the NCWS and instead formed a rival organization (together with Young Egypt and the YMMA), the National Committee of Students (NCS), under Mustafa Mu'min.[153] What followed was a period of renewed competition between the Brotherhood and the Wafd, with the former challenging the latter for control of the streets and the loyalties of the country's youth.[154] This rivalry was so intense that there were physical clashes between supporters of the two groups.[155] By the summer of 1946, people were being killed in violent confrontations in Cairo that pitted Wafdists against Muslim Brethren.[156] Inevitably, Brotherhood accounts attributed these events entirely to the actions of the Wafd, insinuating that communists had successfully infiltrated the party.[157] Al-Nahas and his party, by contrast, accused the Ikhwan of selling out to the government—an allegation that was not without foundation.

Certainly, al-Banna again demonstrated his pragmatic side during this period, as the Brotherhood lent cautious support to the Sidqi government, which had entered into negotiations with the British. On the one hand, al-Banna continued to call for the total fulfillment of Egyptian demands: the evacuation of British troops; the unity of the Nile valley; and the settling of outstanding financial matters.[158] The Brotherhood leader sent a personal telegram to the UK minister of foreign affairs declaring his deep disappointment with British policy and pledging "incessant struggle" in pursuit of Egypt's "independence and unity."[159] Similarly, he expressed public regret that Brotherhood representatives had not been asked to join Sidqi's negotiating team and insisted that, in the event that dialogue failed, Egypt should take her case to the United Nations (UN). Nevertheless, alongside all this, the Brothers backed Sidqi's approach as essentially the correct one; and in return, the progovernment press lauded the Ikhwan as the most "dynamic power in this new movement of national feeling."[160]

The British negotiators, meanwhile, were conscious of the Ikhwan's importance. Lord Stansgate, who was sent to Egypt to hold talks with Sidqi in April 1946, identified the Brotherhood (and the Wafd) as likely to "seize on anything short of complete evacuation as a pretext for arousing the passions of the people."[161] By comparison, the prime minister was seen in familiar terms as a hard-liner, but as a man with whom the British might do business (somewhat as they had seen Ali Maher years earlier). Sidqi, it was noted, had spoken of his desire for an alliance "on a footing of real equality," if only the British would evacuate their troops.[162] For this reason, Stansgate recommended the withdrawal of the army and won the backing of his superiors for the proposal. In May 1946, the British government announced its readiness to remove all armed forces from Egypt within five years, provided that they retained access to the vast Suez Base under the auspices of a joint Anglo-Egyptian Defense Board. (The hope was that Egypt might also be bound to a more general scheme for the collective defense of the Middle East.)[163] The British offer, though, did not break the impasse. Ideas for reciprocal arrangements of this kind cut little ice with most Egyptian nationalists. For them, the departure of the British military was the sine qua non of any settlement; any lingering British troop presence would signify the persistence of imperialist control.

Despite the gap between the two sides, efforts to reach an agreement persisted throughout the year. As they did so, Sidqi faced pressure from his erstwhile allies to stand firm. Hasan al-Banna sent a public letter to the prime minister in June and this was accompanied by an appeal for fresh protests. There were also reports of Brotherhood involvement in anti-British (and anti-Christian) agitation.[164] As the negotiations dragged on, the Ikhwan further hardened its position. The group called for talks to be broken off and for the unilateral abrogation of the 1936 treaty.[165] As tensions mounted, al-Banna even threatened Sidqi with "revolution" if he tried to ignore the will of the people.[166] The Ikhwan stated baldly that there was "nothing after the failure of negotiations except jihad."[167]

At the end of August, the Brothers held their annual general assembly, with an estimated five thousand members from across Egypt and the wider region in attendance. Significantly, a Brotherhood representative made sure that an account of the proceedings was forwarded to the US Legation—testament to al-Banna's desire to try to influence American opinion. During the conference, Brotherhood leaders reiterated their opposition to talks that were a "British trick to waste time and disseminate the seeds of dissension among the Egyptians." What was required, they professed, was nothing less than the renunciation of the 1936 treaty. Proposals for a new accord were said to be "incompatible with Egypt's independence and sovereignty," which could only be satisfied by the "complete evacuation and unity of the Nile Valley." If the British refused to comply within a year, the Ikhwan wanted the government to submit a case to the UN Security Council. In a sign of their growing frustration with the prime minister, Brotherhood speakers raised the prospect that Sidqi would be deemed an "accomplice of the usurper" if he failed to deliver. Every political leader or party that showed a readiness to compromise was to be "considered a dissenter working in concert with the country's enemies" (and the Brothers boasted of their ability to bring down any government). This bombastic rhetoric was accompanied by various resolutions calling for the waging of "jihad" against both "occupiers and foreign usurpers in the Egyptian government." As US officials noted, this language sat rather uncomfortably alongside Brotherhood pledges to use only "legal" methods. And the tenor of the conference certainly seemed to confirm the breakdown of the Sidqi-Ikhwan relationship.[168]

Despite this, the prime minister did not allow himself to be deflected. He pushed forward with negotiations to the point where a draft treaty—the so-called Bevin-Sidqi Agreement—was initialed after talks in London in October. The Ikhwan fiercely rejected this settlement and called for immediate "jihad."[169] The Brothers were adamant that dialogue was nothing but a "new conspiracy" by which "the English" sought the right to remain militarily in Egypt. There should, they argued, be "no treaty except after evacuation."[170] In their view, Sidqi had betrayed the promises he had made to the Brotherhood earlier in the year.[171] As a result, Hasan al-Banna now took his followers back onto the streets. In November 1946, the Brothers joined with the Wafd and Young Egypt to create a new umbrella organization, the National Front of All Students of the Nile Valley, which vowed to oppose any government that failed to press for core nationalist demands (namely, evacuation and unity of the Nile valley). The Ikhwan organized the printing of several million red badges inscribed with the word "evacuation," which it distributed across the country for a specified day of protest.[172] Demonstrations were held and produced the inevitable violent clashes. On November 22, more than fifty Brotherhood members were arrested in Alexandria and charged with endangering the security and safety of the state. In response, the group charged the government with resorting "to terrorism to cow the nation." Ahmad al-Sukkari pledged firm opposition to the Bevin-Sidqi treaty, declaring: "The Moslem Brothers are caged like lions, but their faith in God will make their prison a garden of Eden. They will go down in history as Egypt's heroes. Let Sidky [sic] sign his treaty over our dead bodies. We shall struggle and avenge our nation."[173]

The Ikhwan called for noncooperation with the British and for a "cultural boycott" to "eradicate all ties" with the imperialists. They urged Egyptians to "remove the English" from their "hearts" in order to remove them from the land.[174] In line with this, the group appealed for every shop sign or advertisement written in English to be torn down or converted to Arabic. On November 25, the Ikhwan even organized a "Day of Fire," in which English-language books, magazines, and newspapers were gathered and burned in the main squares of the Egyptian capital.[175]

Beyond this, the Muslim Brothers were implicated in several bomb attacks on police stations, as well as bars frequented by British military personnel and the premises of the Anglo-Egyptian Union. They were also linked to a failed assassination bid against the life of Muhammad Husayn Heikal, the leader of the Constitutional Liberal Party. Consequently, the Sidqi government announced an inquiry into the activities of the Brotherhood, pointing to its "unpatriotic motives."[176] Its offices were searched and then closed down; Ahmad al-Sukkari, chief editor of the group's daily newspaper, was arrested and charged with publishing libelous or subversive articles.[177] Yet such moves failed to stem the tide and did little to reduce the menace of the Ikhwan from a British perspective. It was generally said to be "Suspect No. 1" whenever "outrages" occurred, like the spate of bombings that hit Cairo on Christmas Eve in 1946.[178]

It should be said that al-Banna publicly repudiated acts of terrorism, stressing his commitment to the principle of nonviolence. If individual Muslim Brothers had been involved in violence, he contended, then it was solely because of the provocation of the government.[179] However, not many were persuaded by half-hearted denials of this kind. A dispatch from the new US Embassy in the Egyptian capital described the Muslim Brotherhood and the Wafd as the "two most dangerous trouble-makers" in Egypt. The Brothers were said to be heavily involved in violence and terrorism.[180] The *Times* of London similarly pointed to the group's "xenophobic propaganda" and saw traces of fascism in its makeup. The Ikhwan's core objective, it averred, was to "create ill will, suspicion, and eventually hatred between two peoples who have many friendships and long associations"; this was said to be "unpardonable."[181] The Brothers were, on this reading, "the leading organizers of disorder" in Egypt.[182]

On 8 December 1946, Sidqi resigned. His position had been rendered untenable by differing Egyptian-British interpretations of the protocol for dealing with Sudan contained within the draft Bevin-Sidqi Agreement. The furor over this issue not only destroyed his political credibility but also ended any possibility that a treaty might be finalized. King Faruq now turned back to Mahmud al-Nuqrashi who, on becoming prime minister, affirmed his belief in the unity of Egypt and Sudan, and canceled any further negotiations.[183] His alternative strategy was to try and exert international pressure via the United Nations, and in mid-July 1947, al-Nuqrashi sent a letter to the Security Council, asking it to enforce a British withdrawal from Egypt.[184]

Somewhat surprisingly, given the breakdown of their relationship with al-Nuqrashi a year earlier, the Brotherhood was "curiously restrained" in its response to the new prime minister.[185] Inevitably, this fueled conjecture that al-

Banna had made yet another pact of mutual convenience with an Egyptian government. Unconfirmed reports suggested that the Brotherhood leader had held a positive meeting with the king, paving the way for reconciliation with al-Nuqrashi himself. One of the latter's first acts in office was to release those Ikhwan members who had been arrested for their role in fomenting disorder against Sidqi's government. Soon afterward, al-Banna publicly endorsed the prime minister's decision to bring Egypt's case to the UN (it was, after all, a step he had called for previously).[186] Simultaneously, he disavowed the rival telegram sent to the Security Council by the leader of the Wafd, Mustafa al-Nahas, who disputed al-Nuqrashi's right to speak for the nation.[187]

Of course, given Britain's permanent membership of the Security Council, this latest Egyptian initiative was always unlikely to succeed. Officials in London had been anticipating such a move since the breakdown of the Sidqi talks, believing that the king and prime minister might seek a "diversion" of this kind to bolster their standing against domestic opposition.[188] Permanent undersecretary of state at the Foreign Office, Sir Alec Cadogan, was dispatched to San Francisco to mount a ferocious defense of the British position. The Brothers, meanwhile, sent their own delegation to the United States to observe proceedings. Led by the charismatic student orator Mustafa Mu'min, this declared the group's full support for the policy of Prime Minister al-Nuqrashi. As it became clear that the UN would not deliver on Egyptian demands, Mu'min made an emotional speech from the spectators' gallery, rejecting talks and brandishing a document that he claimed was signed in the blood of students. Though he was expelled from the room, Mu'min continued his protests in the days that followed.[189] Interestingly, the ever-pragmatic Hasan al-Banna subsequently repudiated Mu'min when in conversation with US diplomats—perhaps embarrassed at the controversy he had caused. But officials noted that when applying for a visa at the US Consulate, Mu'min had stated he was the "head of the graduate section of the Moslem Brotherhood" and had been formally delegated to fight for Egypt's cause on its behalf.[190]

For their part, American diplomats still hoped that it might be possible to arrive at a "reasonable" solution to the Anglo-Egyptian dispute.[191] They backed the resolution put to the Security Council by the Brazilian delegate, which called for the resumption of direct negotiations between the two sides.[192] The British were delighted by this outcome and rather than use it as a springboard for further talks, resolved on a period of inactivity, convinced that an "acceptable settlement" was no longer possible—at least while al-Nuqrashi remained in power.[193] Conversely, the Egyptian government was bitterly disappointed and denounced both the British and the Americans for events at the UN.[194] On his return to Egypt, the prime minister received a warm reception from the Brothers, who joined with other nationalists in condemning the United Nations.[195] The British security officer, Alfred Sansom, later recalled that a mass meeting was held in central Cairo where al-Banna made a "fiery speech" to several thousand supporters, working them "up to a state of frenzy." Clashes with the police ensued, leading to violent riots and chants of "Egypt must be evacuated by blood" and "Down with America." Several people, including al-Banna himself, were wounded; three Brotherhood members were among those killed in the unrest, which was followed by the bombing of the Brazilian Legation, an act for which Sansom blamed the Ikhwan.[196]

Western anxiety about the role of the Brotherhood had grown during the first half of 1947. In April, the *Times* carried a report that a number of Coptic lawyers had appealed to King Faruq for protection from a campaign of persecution apparently being waged by the Ikhwan in connection with the YMMA.[197] Observers also noted that the group's newspaper, *al-Ikhwan al-Muslimun,* had called for the deportation of all foreigners who supported the British; it even had suggested that pro-British Egyptians should be hanged.[198] To this was added the fact that the Brotherhood openly blamed the British for the cholera epidemic that swept Egypt in 1947, saying that military camps were the source of the contagion (and hinting that it had been started deliberately).[199] Rhetoric about jihad was heard with ever-greater frequency. From the spring onward, for instance, al-Banna's "Friday Talks" regularly spoke of this as the only means by which the nation could secure its rights.[200] Such incendiary rhetoric could scarcely be ignored given that it came in parallel to a number of violent attacks. In May 1947, the Metro Cinema in Cairo was bombed, killing four people and leaving almost forty injured. Two student members of the Ikhwan were convicted for the crime.[201] The midsummer of 1947 then saw street fighting between formations of the Brotherhood's Rover Scouts and the police in Cairo.[202]

Tensions heightened still further after the conclusion to the political process at the UN. Al-Banna now called on all political leaders to unite behind a proposal for the unilateral abrogation of the 1936 treaty. Plans were laid for a mass demonstration on August 26, the anniversary of the treaty's signing, to demand its annulment. The authorities eventually banned this event, to the indignation of the Brotherhood leader.[203] But anti-British and antiforeign agitation continued.

Against this backdrop, a senior official at the US Embassy, Philip Ireland, sat down with Hasan al-Banna to discuss the political situation—the first major meeting between an American diplomat and the Brotherhood leader. Ireland's record of the encounter provides a vivid picture of "a man of less than middle height with a sallow face, slightly pockmarked and topped by curly receding hair and surrounded by a scanty frizzled beard. From his nervous and impulsive actions and his mobile face one might suspect that he was inclined to nervous disorders. He was quick in speech and agile in debate, speaking at times in common places and at other times forcefully and with energy. Notwithstanding such force and energy and his general air of self-assurance, one was never convinced that the Shaikh was speaking with veracity and accuracy."[204] Suffice it to say, Ireland's first impressions were not entirely positive. He pointed to al-Banna's "past record of opportunism," and was struck by his assertion that he could start and stop unrest at will. Ireland believed there was much truth in this, though he doubted al-Banna's "ability to put out the conflagration once started." Further, the American noted the gap between al-Banna's private declarations of peaceful intent and the public position of the Brothers. Ireland asked how al-Banna hoped to reconcile his promise that there would be no further trouble with a piece in *al-Ikhwan al-Muslimun,* which was written in "the language of blood." Apparently, the Brotherhood leader simply "smiled into his beard and changed the subject."[205]

Significantly, the embassy account states that al-Banna spent much of this meeting criticizing his rivals and seeking to win the favor of the United States. He condemned the Wafd's youth wing, for example, as comprising "light-headed youths in the pay of the Soviets." Moreover, in a clear nod to US interests, he extolled Islam as "the great barrier" to communism. On this basis, al-Banna appealed for an alliance with the United States, proposing that "America and [the] Ikhwan should become allies in fighting Communism."[206] This, of course, directly echoed the message that al-Banna had previously delivered to Sir Walter Smart at the British Embassy in 1945: namely, that the Brotherhood represented the best bulwark against the spread of radical, left-wing forces. Elsewhere, too, the group had made plain its opposition to the political Left. In May 1946, Ikhwan members had helped defeat communist agitation for a strike among textile workers in the Cairo suburb of Shubra.[207] During this period, Muslim Brothers repeatedly showed themselves to be firm opponents of communism and clashed with leftists on Egypt's streets. And the Ikhwan was also withering in its criticism of perceived Soviet support for the Zionist movement in Palestine. In this context, as Jeffrey Herf has shown, the group readily deployed anti-Semitic tropes about the synthesis between "the Jews" and communism.[208]

In 1947, the Brotherhood leader clearly sought to turn his movement's intuitive anticommunism to his advantage. In keeping with his pragmatic outlook, he wished to exploit the opportunities presented by the Cold War to bid for US support. For this reason, too, he stressed the size and capability of the Ikhwan, claiming that there were some 600,000 members of the Brotherhood in Egypt, with a further 300,000 abroad. Though he confessed that not all of these were totally committed, he pointed to a core "action group" of "between 25,000 and 30,000," composed of about 15,000 scouts with an average age of 17, who had received some "perfunctory" military training, and around "10,000 other members with an average age of 25." Evidently, al-Banna hoped to underline the strength of the Brotherhood and the extent to which it could be a real asset to the Americans if the two sides could reach some form of modus vivendi.

In return for his opposition to communism, al-Banna sought certain concessions, particularly in the realm of foreign policy. He reprimanded the Americans for their "unfriendliness" toward Egypt. This had been typified in al-Banna's mind by the refusal of the United States to endorse the Egyptian position at the UN. Of equal if not greater import was the question of Palestine, where events had further soured the Egyptian mood—and that of the Ikhwan in particular—over the previous two years.[209] Senior Brotherhood leaders firmly believed that the British and Americans were in "collusion" with the Zionists. The Egyptian and neighboring Arab governments were similarly thought to be, at best, lax in their defense of Palestine, and at worst, conspiring to deliver it to the Jews.[210] As far as the Ikhwan was concerned, whereas the Zionists enjoyed global support, the Palestinian Arabs had been left to stand "alone in the square fighting the intrigues of the Jews and the imperialists."[211] The Brothers were therefore determined to mobilize the Islamic "umma [nation]," inculcating the spirit of jihad in support of the Arabs.[212]

In 1946, the Brotherhood had joined with the YMMA and a number of other societies to present the British Embassy with a collective protest against the report of the Anglo-American Palestine Commission (which had called for increased Jewish immigration into the territory).[213] Al-Banna himself had given evidence to that commission—and complained about its refusal to hear testimony from the former grand mufti, Hajj Amin al-Husayni. (Al-Husayni had been given a rapturous welcome by the Ikhwan on his arrival in Cairo in May 1946, after he had fled from France. The group's newspaper called him "the Arab hero" and "our leader in struggle and jihad.")[214] By this time, al-Banna had become increasingly critical of the United States and its support for the Zionist position; he repeatedly urged the US and UK governments to abandon

any notion of partition.[215] Subsequently, the Ikhwan denounced the British decision to place the issue before a United Nations Special Committee on Palestine (UNSCOP)—the body that then called for the division of the territory
into Jewish and Arab states. It was with this in mind that al-Banna warned
Phillip Ireland that any attempt to damage the Arab cause in Palestine would
meet with "dire results."[216]

As the UN General Assembly moved toward acceptance of the UNSCOP
report, there were fresh signs that the Brotherhood was becoming more militant. Egyptian newspapers noted preparations for the mobilization of the group's
branches in the provinces. Ghada Osman's biography of her father, Fathi, describes how the Rover sections in Minya "came to be trained more as military
than as scouts," with an emphasis on drill, order, and discipline.[217] "Recruiting
offices" were opened to gather volunteers willing to fight for the Palestinian
cause.[218] In Cairo, a representative of the Ikhwan even approached the US military attaché's office to request manuals on weapons training.[219] Such training was
being carried out, according to Ahmad al-Baquri, in the Muqattam hills overlooking the capital, with the apparent acquiescence of the authorities.[220] Al-Banna
offered to place ten thousand men at the disposal of 'Abd al-Rahman Azzam
Pasha, the secretary general of the Arab League, as the first detachment of an
"army of salvation" for Palestine.[221] In a follow-up telegram to Azzam, he urged
the Arab states to withdraw from membership of the UN. He also called on
them to deprive Jewish citizens of their nationality if they failed to support the
Palestinian cause.[222] These demands were repeated when the actual partition resolution was passed in early December 1947. At that time, al-Banna sent an open
letter to the grand rabbi of Egypt, stating that Egypt's Jews should make clear
their support for the Arabs in the face of an "international conspiracy" led by
Zionism; the grand rabbi's reply (asserting that Egyptian Jews were a loyal part
of the nation) was judged insufficient by the Brotherhood's newspaper.[223]

The growing bellicosity and anti-Jewish nature of al-Banna's thinking on Palestine was palpable in the answer that he gave to one of his followers who asked
with concern about the growing number of Jewish immigrants resident there.
According to Abbas al-Sissi, al-Banna replied by posing his own questions:
"What disturbs you? Do you not remember the reply of Alexander—that the
skillful butcher delights in a large number of sheep?"[224] The violence of the
imagery (of Jews as lambs to the slaughter at the hands of the Arabs) was consistent with the Brotherhood's increasingly frenzied views on Palestine.

Of course, all of this was deeply troubling for the British—still in formal control of the Palestinian mandate. The only good news from their perspective was

that they did not think the Ikhwan possessed sufficient weaponry to make their men into an "efficient force." Though al-Banna might wish for government support, this was deemed "most unlikely." The Egyptian authorities were said to be wary of actively arming the Brothers, "lest they should one day turn against the Government itself."[225]

Still, the British worried about the potential for the turmoil in Palestine to rebound back on to Egypt, with the Brotherhood's militancy on the former dispute reinforcing its hard-line position on the national question in Cairo. Over the course of 1947, leaders of the Ikhwan proclaimed their conviction that Egypt would only secure its independence through "struggle." Negotiations, it was said, were mere "political manoeuvres aiming to cause dissension." The British Embassy reported that within Brotherhood circles there was "much talk of guerrilla warfare" and the possible formation of "liberation battalions."[226] The group helped to create the Nile Valley Liberation Committee, which offered paramilitary-style training to its recruits. This umbrella organization was part of a broader mobilization that drew in government figures, mainstream politicians, and members of civil society.[227] Even so, the Ikhwan was recognized as "the most active group" involved in such agitation. The British surmised that its position had been boosted by the degree of "support, or at least tolerance" that it enjoyed from the "present Government and the Palace."[228]

In October 1947, a Brotherhood member and employee of the Royal Air Force, Rifaʿt ʿAbd al-Rahman al-Naggar, bombed the King George Hotel in Ismailia.[229] According to Salah Shadi, the aim was to disrupt the activities of the British intelligence services, who were thought to be using the premises for surveillance. Al-Naggar was seriously injured in the attack, but succeeded in his objective since the British were forced to draw down their operations in the city.[230] Moreover, the episode seemed to mark a significant escalation by the Brotherhood. Not long afterward, Western diplomats observed that the group had become much more censorious of al-Nuqrashi, abandoning their earlier support for his government.[231] It was recorded, for example, that the Ikhwan newspaper had described a cabinet reshuffle as a "calamity," which was "incapable of solving our external or internal problems."[232] The British felt that the prime minister retained a belief that the Brothers might yet be "covertly suborned," but toward the end of 1947, there were indications that this policy had definitively failed.[233]

Beyond this, both British and American assessments of Egypt concluded that the country's domestic situation was increasingly "precarious." They identified serious discontent within the ranks of the police, as well as a surge of anti-al-Nuqrashi sentiment among the students.[234] The same period saw rumors circulate about the foiling of a major plot against the regime led by army officers.[235] From across the political spectrum came calls for far-reaching social and political reform, as well as action to achieve Egypt's national goals. To this, of course, the Brotherhood added its own demands for an Islamic state and the implementation of shari'a; and the group seemed to loom ever larger within the Egyptian political firmament.[236] US officials imagined that "the importance of [the] Ikhwan in any future political controversy in Egypt" could not be "overlooked."[237] The Brotherhood was described as a serious cause for concern given its "extreme antipathy to foreign interference in the Arab world."[238] Similarly, the British Foreign Office commented that the Ikhwan was becoming ever more "political and xenophobe." In their estimation, the Brothers were responsible for most of the anti-British demonstrations and acts of violence over the preceding two years.[239]

The Brotherhood International

Events in Egypt were being played out against the backdrop of instability across the whole region. For this reason, attempts were made to situate the Brotherhood within the context of wider sociopolitical trends. Western officials noted that the group was just one of a number of "xenophobic" and anti-British "youth movements" that had appeared since the 1930s, many of them inspired by fascism. In classically orientalist fashion, the British attributed the emergence of these movements to the lack of self-control exhibited by the peoples of the Middle East, coupled with the absence of "healthy" recreational outlets, which meant that youths fell "prey to the agitator and the demagogue."[240]

More generally, the British believed there was a serious problem with the "effendi" class in the region. An extended debate took place between the Foreign Office and various diplomatic residencies, exploring the challenges posed by these "educated and semi-educated products of Eastern universities and schools." Effendis were said to be the "have-nots" of Middle Eastern societies, "the poorly-paid government officials, the commercial clerics and the 'out of work' graduates," who had enjoyed only a "scrappy western-styled education" and, as a result, suffered from both an "inferiority complex" and "unjustified self-assertiveness." As "good Orientals," younger effendis were thought to crave "heroics and spectacular self-expression." Officials feared that their "restlessness" and sense of "social grievance" might leave them vulnerable to the blandishments of communism, pan-Arabism, and other anti-British influences.[241]

Reflections on the Middle East's effendis were not restricted to British foreign policy makers. In his 1949 book, for instance, Kermit "Kim" Roosevelt, the Central Intelligence Agency (CIA) operative and board member of the Institute for Arab American Affairs, identified the "young effendis" as a "progressive element" in the region. In his judgment, they formed a nascent middle class, whose members would be naturally oriented toward the West, even if they were often ardent nationalists. The effendis were, according to Roosevelt, "essentially, moderates, [and] progressive as distinct from revolutionary." Expanding on this, he defined a "moderate" in Middle Eastern terms as someone who was "working for the advancement of his country along Western liberal lines" and someone who was "not a xenophobe." Roosevelt argued it was crucial that the position of these "moderates" not be undermined; were this to happen, it would lead to increasing hatred of the West and the creation of "an isolationist, fanatically reactionary and xenophobic force."[242] To Roosevelt, significantly, the Muslim Brotherhood was the embodiment of this latter tendency—one to be rejected at all costs.[243]

Western officials were aware by this time that the influence of the Brotherhood extended beyond Egypt. Hasan al-Banna had always looked beyond the nation-state and placed a premium on Islamic unity. He took an interest in "Muslim causes" around the world and sought to build alliances abroad. As early as 1928, for example, al-Banna had met with Sheikh Hafez Wahba, an adviser to King Ibn al-Saud, when Wahba visited Cairo to try to recruit Egyptians to teach in the Hijaz. Al-Banna himself even appears briefly to have considered taking a post in Mecca. Ultimately, this proposal fell through—in part because the Egyptian government had not then recognized Saud's regime, something that al-Banna attributed to the influence of "the English," who wished to maintain divisions between Muslims. Nonetheless, the episode was symptomatic of his early interest in, and support for, the emerging Saudi state. He claimed in his memoirs that the educated classes of Egypt looked to a "new renaissance in the Hijaz as their greatest hope and security."[244] In 1934, al-Banna twice met with the governor of Medina while the latter was in Cairo and struck up a lasting friendship. Two years later, he went to Saudi Arabia to perform the Hajj and made repeat visits in the years that followed.[245] (On one such trip in 1948, he met with the US ambassador to Jeddah, Hermann Eilts.)[246] When King 'Abd al-Aziz visited Cairo and Alexandria, the Brotherhood's Rover Scouts formed processions to greet him.[247]

Also of enduring interest to al-Banna was the situation in Yemen. In 1929–1930, he had met with one of the governors of Sana'a, Sayyid Muhammad Zabara

al-Hasan. The occasion was a YMMA-organized gathering in Cairo to commemorate the Prophetic *hijra* (Muhammad's migration from Mecca to Medina).
According to al-Banna, he and al-Hasan established a rapport based on their
shared concern about the "rampant spread of atheism and debauchery" in both
Yemen and Egypt. The two men became friends, and al-Banna was again offered
a teaching position—this time in Sana'a. Al-Banna alleged that the possibility of
such a move was then discussed with the Imam of Yemen, but as with the Saudi
proposition, the idea came to nothing. Still, from that point al-Banna stayed in
contact with al-Hasan and others in Yemen.[248] The Brotherhood, for instance,
lent assistance to the Yemeni delegation that was sent to the 1939 London Conference on Palestine.[249]

Even more significant, the Brotherhood appears to have been a major influence on the Free Yemeni Movement (FYM) that developed after 1945, demanding
change and modernization within the Imamate. A. Z. al-'Abdin describes
the critical role played in that movement by Fadil al-Wartalani, an Algerian
Muslim Brother resident in Egypt. Al-Wartalani had business interests in Yemen
and helped write the FYM's "Sacred National Pact" proposing reform on Islamic
lines. In its calls for the implementation of a government based on shari'a, *shura*
(consultation), and development, the FYM was much influenced by the ideology
of the Ikhwan.[250] At a practical level, too, there were reports that the group's
Cairo headquarters served as an important meeting point for Free Yemenis living
in exile.[251] (Though the Brothers also welcomed the son of the Yemeni ruler, Sayf
al-Islam 'Abdullah, to their offices.)[252]

In February 1948, a coup in Sana'a saw the overthrow and murder of Imam
Yahya at the hands of 'Abdullah al-Wazir, who had aligned himself with the
FYM. The Ikhwan immediately lent its support to the new government (as did
the British). A Brotherhood delegation including 'Abd al-Hakim 'Abdin and al-
Wartalani traveled to Yemen and made contact with al-Wazir.[253] *Al-Ikhwan
al-Muslimun* published the full text of the FYM's "Sacred National Pact." Hasan
al-Banna, meanwhile, boasted to US officials "with much pride" about his role
in events in Sana'a. Though the diplomats noted this was "by no means conclusive," given al-Banna's penchant for "blowing his own horn," they acknowledged
that there were strong connections between the Ikhwan and the Free Yemeni
Movement. They thought al-Banna was keen to open the country to Brotherhood
influence, as well as to use the episode to bolster "the size, power and prestige of
his organization."[254] In line with this, the tumult in Yemen encouraged the
Brotherhood leader in his efforts to secure a rapprochement with the Americans. Al-Banna told Philip Ireland that he intended to fly by chartered plane to

Sana'a to help bring peace, and said that "he wished to emphasize that contrary to general belief the Brotherhood was not a reactionary organization[,] but looked forward to creating in the Arab world democratic and liberal governments combined with the purity of Islam." On this basis, al-Banna called on the United States both to recognize the new Yemeni regime and to support liberal, democratic, and modern governments across the Middle East.[255]

As it happened, the Egyptian government refused to allow the Brotherhood leader and his delegation to fly to Yemen on security grounds. But the Ikhwan had made plain its sympathy for al-Wazir's regime, and this appears to have been reciprocated.[256] Heyworth-Dunne records rumors that after the coup, al-Wazir had planned to send £E100,000 to al-Banna—before he was deposed in the countercoup of Imam Ahmad.[257] Whatever the truth of this, the group's involvement in Yemen was certainly symptomatic of the Brotherhood's desire to extend its influence beyond Egypt's borders.

Already during the Second World War, the Brotherhood had developed its international focus and one could see the evolution of a definable "foreign policy." *Al-Ikhwan al-Muslimun* encouraged its readers to think about "international relations" and events across the "Islamic world."[258] The newspaper also loudly supported the cause of Arab unity, albeit emphasizing that it was "a means and not a goal, and a step, not an end," on the path to a deeper *Islamic* unity.[259] In line with this, the Brothers welcomed the creation of the Arab League in 1945.[260] In the words of Ahmad al-Sukkari, Arabs were "one nation and one body."[261] Elsewhere, the group had initially embraced the San Francisco conference and the attempt to build a new, postwar international order.[262] That support, however, soon faded as the UN Charter came to be seen as a betrayal of "the hopes of small countries for justice and equality."[263]

To facilitate its international activism, the Brotherhood established a department dedicated to "contact with the Islamic world," with four geographically focused subcommittees to gather information and produce publicity on key issues.[264] The goal of this unit, according to al-Baquri, was both to study the unique problems of the different Arab and Muslim nations and to spread the Brotherhood's *da'wa*. It was subsequently expanded to include seven subcommittees catering for, respectively: Sudan; the fertile crescent (Syria, Lebanon, Palestine, Jordan, and Iraq); the Arabian Peninsula (Saudi Arabia, Yemen, and the Gulf principalities); North Africa (Ethiopia, Somalia, Nigeria, and Senegal); Asian Muslim countries (Indonesia, India, Ceylon, Iran, Afghanistan, and later, Pakistan); Islamic minorities in Asia (China, Malaysia, and the Philippines); and Muslims in Europe (Turkey, Russia, and beyond). These committees dispatched delegations abroad, while the Ikhwan headquarters in Cairo regularly received foreign dignitaries. It was envisaged too that the Brothers would hold conferences to which members of the different Islamic movements around the globe could be invited to discuss shared problems, such as the fight against colonialism.[265]

Al-Banna frequently denounced what he saw as the ongoing attempt to divide the world's four hundred million Muslims into "statelets," which denied them their rights and values.[266] The Brotherhood urged its followers to adopt the struggles of their coreligionists, wherever they were.[267] "The English" remained the foremost enemy. They were said to "hate" Islam and to have worked throughout history—going back to the Crusades—to weaken and divide Muslims.[268] According to al-Banna, "the English" excelled in "guile," and had sustained their occupation of Egypt by making Muslims understand their religion as the English saw theirs—a process that the Ikhwan hoped to reverse.[269] The Brothers were also especially exercised by the trajectory of Sudan and called on Egyptians to reach out to political leaders there—a task that al-Banna had begun back in the 1930s.[270] He believed the British were encouraging the independence of Egypt's southern neighbor in order to divide the Nile valley.[271]

Al-Banna's opposition to imperialism, though, was not confined to "the English." The other European powers were similarly excoriated for their colonialist policies. Prior to the war, al-Banna had claimed that the Italians wished to "eradicate and erase all trace of Arabism and Islam" in Libya.[272] After 1945, he continued to bemoan events in Tripoli, blaming not only the imperialists but also Muslims themselves for being ignorant of what was happening.[273] Throughout the 1940s, too, al-Banna expressed support for the Indonesian nationalist movement against Dutch colonial control. The Brotherhood's newspaper published telegrams that he had sent to the Dutch government and to the UN secretary general, protesting against the situation in the Far East. Al-Banna called on all Muslim leaders to back the Indonesian cause.[274]

Still more attention was placed on the actions of France. Al-Banna had always asserted that the French had a "long account" with Muslims, given their imperialist ambitions in the region.[275] After the Second World War, the Brotherhood became a particularly vocal supporter of the right of Syria and Lebanon to independence. It implored the Arab League to endorse these demands, and al-Banna publicly offered tens of thousands of volunteers to fight on Syria's behalf.[276] In his memoirs, the future leader of the Brotherhood, Muhammad Hamid Abu al-Nasr, recalled an occasion when the English manager of the local branch of Barclays Bank in Manfalut asked him for a donation for the "unknown soldier," and he refused on account of developments in Syria and Lebanon. Abu al-Nasr was convinced that the British should have pressured France to withdraw from the Levant (and as a result of this, he claims he was questioned by British intelligence).[277]

The Brotherhood was similarly indignant about French policy in North Africa. The group gave its backing to "our dear brothers—the youth of free, struggling, nationalist Morocco."[278] In the decade leading toward the country's independence, the Ikhwan repeatedly condemned the "tyrannical French" for their Moroccan policy.[279] Unsurprisingly, neighboring Algeria also became a cause célèbre for the Ikhwan—as much as for other nationalists. Veteran Brotherhood leaders such as Ibrahim Munir remember that the struggle for independence there did much to poison their view of the European nations, and the West more generally. They were appalled by rumors of French "savagery."[280] As far as the Brothers were concerned, the French had rewarded wartime Algerian loyalty with "clear aggression," revealing the duplicity of their rhetoric about democracy.[281] No sooner had the war in Europe ended, said Ahmad al-Sukkari, than "the small bird became like an eagle, and the defeated wolf turned into a tiger." He maintained that the French had reneged on their promises and repaid the "Arab East" with "iron and fire."[282] Despite this, Hasan al-Banna declared that the "struggling Maghrib"—the "left wing of Arabism"—would be "victorious with the permission of God." Though they might face a long and bitter jihad, he predicted that they would "see the dawn and . . . the onset of the morning and the rise of the light." To this end, he exhorted his followers to stand with their brethren in North Africa "for God and the religion, for country and Brotherhood."[283] And in line with this, al-Ikhwan al-Muslimun publicized the work of the self-proclaimed "Defence Front for North Africa" that had been formed by the Algerian Brother Fadil al-Wartalani.[284]

In addition to its strident anti-imperialism during this period, the Brotherhood was fiercely critical of the new state of India, which it referred to as "Hindustan." Al-Banna had previously established a correspondence with Muhammad Ali Jinnah, the leader of the Muslim League, and he sent greetings and congratulations to mark the founding of Pakistan in August 1947.[285] He described the death of Jinnah in September 1948 as a "terrible calamity to the Islamic world." That same month, he cabled Indian president Jawaharlal Nehru to protest his government's "barbaric aggression" against Hyderabad, which according to al-Banna, belonged to Islam. To this was added a critique of Indian policy toward Kashmir.[286]

Beyond such "foreign policy" positioning, meanwhile, the primary manifestation of the Brotherhood's "international" character was the drive to establish branches of the movement outside Egypt. Some histories of the Ikhwan suggest that the first international chapter was founded in Djibouti.[287] If true, this would appear to be something of an outlier given al-Banna's more obvious focus on the immediate hinterland around Egypt. To the south, the British governor general of Sudan reported in early 1946 that the Ikhwan wished to open a chapter of their society in the city of Atbara.[288] Officials in London quickly voiced opposition to this move, commenting that the Sudanese government was "laying up for themselves a heap of trouble by allowing [the Brotherhood] into the Sudan in any form [emphasis in original]."[289] As it was, the Atbara proposal was dropped in favor of the creation of a seemingly more innocuous "Islamic Virtuous Society."[290] However, the British were aware of ongoing efforts to organize the Brotherhood in Sudan from that point.[291] By the end of 1947, the group had set up a branch in the country under the leadership of Mahmud Khalifa, a schoolteacher at Gordon College in Khartoum.[292] In the following two years, though the Ikhwan continued to be denied legal recognition, it spread to other provincial towns and cities. British assessments of the Brotherhood in Sudan concluded that it was especially focused on combating "intellectual and spiritual imperialism." Spokesmen for the local movement had apparently stated that "all the English, whatever their official position, work[ed] as agents of British imperialism"; they had also claimed that the most important battle facing the world was that being waged "between the English and the Islamic countries." Alongside this, the Ikhwan *had* labeled communism, "the disease of the modern Moslem youth," and emphasized that it could only be opposed by "Islamic ideas."[293] Yet such anticommunist invective hardly eased British anxiety over the Sudanese Brotherhood, which, like its Egyptian counterpart, was active in demanding the unity of the Nile valley and agitating in favor of the Palestinian cause.

Within Palestine itself, al-Banna had sent a delegation to build ties with local Muslim leaders, including Grand Mufti al-Husayni, in the mid-1930s. Branches of the Ikhwan were then created in the decade that followed—at Jerusalem, Jaffa, Gaza, and Nablus—thanks mainly to the efforts of Sa'id Ramadan. These remained part of the Egyptian Ikhwan movement (rather than having an independent structure) and therefore took instructions directly from Cairo headquarters. At the same time, it was clear they were permitted to act autonomously at the local level—and they received encouragement from al-Husayni's

Supreme Muslim Council.[294] In October 1946, in a sign of their growing confidence, the Brothers in Palestine helped organize a major conference in Haifa, which condemned Britain for its treatment of the Arabs.[295] As the situation in Palestine worsened, the local branches of the Ikhwan inevitably became involved in irregular fighting against Jewish groups.[296]

In so doing, they were supported by other Brotherhood formations in adjoining countries, nowhere more so than in Syria, where contacts between the Egyptian Ikhwan and indigenous Islamic groups also went back to the 1930s.[297] These ties had been cemented by the agitation of the Egyptian brothers on the Syrian national issue. In 1945, for instance, al-Banna had dispatched a high-profile delegation to Damascus after French attempts to suppress the nationalist movement there. He promised that, here too, tens of thousands of Brothers were ready to serve as volunteers in the Syrian army, to "perform their obligation" and struggle against the French.[298] The following year, several existing Syrian Islamic organizations formally merged with the Ikhwan, and Mustafa al-Siba'i, a prominent scholar who had spent time studying in Cairo, was appointed controller general of the Syrian Brothers.[299] As Raphaël Lefèvre has described, in this early phase, the new group was defined by a pragmatic ethos and a commitment to peaceful participation within the Syrian political system.[300]

British views of the Syrian Ikhwan, though, were clearly mixed. On the one hand, they recognized its avowed anticommunism; on the other, they noted it was vehemently critical of the European powers in the "usual terms of Arab extremism." Officials observed that the group was an open advocate of jihad, and its youth section was imbued with a mixture of "fanatic Mohammedism, xenophobia and political intransigence." British apprehension seems to have been shared by their US counterparts. The latter were aware that the Syrian Brotherhood ran its own newspaper, *al-Manar* (the circulation of which was later estimated to be around six thousand) and wielded "considerable power."[301] According to the diplomats, that power had been demonstrated in the 1947 parliamentary elections when the Brothers—referred to as "reactionaries"—had "shown unexpected strength."[302] Subsequent analysis portrayed the Ikhwan as "tightly-knit," with a "clear-cut program" that was "intensely anti-foreign."[303] The American political attaché, Daniel Dennett, memorably described the group as comprised of emotionally unstable "typical café intellectuals" who might be inclined to engage in "irresponsible" acts.[304]

The alleged emotionalism of the Syrian Brotherhood was unmistakable when it came to the situation in Palestine. In September 1947, for example, the American Legation in Damascus reported on an Ikhwan meeting at the Umayyad Mosque that had seen "inflammatory speeches urging blood and fire" to save the Arab cause.[305] The Syrian Brotherhood proclaimed the struggle against Zionism to be a just and necessary "jihad."[306] Mustafa al-Siba'i joined with other scholars in signing a declaration that stated it was "the duty of all the Arabs and Moslems" to oppose partition "by all the force, weapons, men, and money that they possess."[307] Al-Siba'i was also part of an Interior Ministry committee tasked with collecting contributions for the "liberation of Palestine."[308] All of this inevitably made the Syrian Brotherhood an object of concern for Western officials. Their reservations were magnified at the end of November 1947 when, following the UN decision in favor of partitioning Palestine, members of the Ikhwan "predominated" among a "well organized" and "well equipped" mob that broke into the US Legation in Damascus, tore down the Star Spangled Banner, and burnt a diplomatic car.[309] The episode seemed to confirm the way in which anti-Zionism could drift quickly into anti-Western violence.

The attack on the US Legation was paralleled by the storming of the French Embassy, where, American diplomats commented wryly, the mob had wreaked havoc and "hitting where it hurts, [had] entered Minister [Jean-Charles] Serres' wine cellar and broke over 150 bottles of his best wine." Interestingly, in a discussion with the US consul general, the incandescent Serres had claimed that the Brotherhood was being financed, organized, and controlled by the British.[310] Though it seems clear that the Americans did not believe this allegation, a subsequent dispatch did note that the local British press officer, Wilfred Kirkpatrick, enjoyed wide contacts inside the Syrian Ikhwan.[311]

Elsewhere in the region, meanwhile, Western officials were conscious of the existence of smaller branches of the Brotherhood. In Iraq, the British thought that the group operated under the "cover" of the Muslim Ethical Society (the "Jamiyat al Adab al Islamiya," hereafter, MES), which had been created in August 1946 under the presidency of Amjad Zahawi.[312] A lengthy intelligence report on the MES described its policy as being "to foster Wahabism and thus to encourage xenophobia, Islamic militancy and hatred of Zionism." In addition, it was said to have ties to the anti-Hashemite, right-wing Istiqlal Party, while individual members had links to Rashid 'Ali al-Gaylani, the 1941 rebellion, the former grand mufti al-Husayni, and general anti-British activity.[313] All in all, officials were clear that the MES was a rather less than wholesome organization. Neither were they in any doubt that it was a front for the Brotherhood. One of its most prominent members, the al-Azhar graduate Muhammad Mahmud al-Sawwaf, was said to be "one of the leading promoters of the Ikhwan in Iraq" and a known member of the Egyptian movement. Al-Sawwaf had apparently applied for permission to create a branch of the Brotherhood in March 1948. When this was refused, he opted to persevere with the "thin" disguise of the MES, which was seen as an "increasingly potent influence" and "a powerful propaganda agency serving the purpose of Right Wing nationalism."[314] Once more, therefore, officials viewed the Brotherhood as a potential threat to Western interests.

A slightly different view did prevail in nearby Jordan, where British diplomats were less exercised by the emergence of the Ikhwan. There, it was again Sa'id Ramadan who had helped to establish the first branches of the Brotherhood in late 1945 and early 1946, under the leadership of Sheikh 'Abd al-Latif Abu Qura.[315] From the beginning, however, its activities appear to have been sanctioned by the authorities, and the Brothers adopted a pragmatic, reformist posture, stressing their loyalty to the Hashemite regime.[316] In May 1947, Ambassador Sir Alec Kirkbride reported from Amman that King Abdullah had shown "marked favour" to the secretary general of the Egyptian Brotherhood, 'Abd al-Hakim 'Abdin, during the latter's visit to Jordan.[317] The king was said to have described the local Ikhwan—which was only six hundred strong—as "praiseworthy" for its work in recalling the younger generation to their religious duties, which he saw as a barrier to the spread of communism. Kirkbride also commented that he knew some of the local leaders personally and did not regard them as "politically objectionable." He therefore agreed with the king and his prime minister that there were no grounds for intervention at this stage. Back in London, such views met a skeptical response. One official stated, "These people will have to be watched in spite of Sir A. Kirkbride's belief in their innocence."[318] Kirkbride's indifference was thus very much the exception to the rule. For the most part, the Ikhwan was considered a problem and a likely threat to both British interests and the stability of the region.

Descent into Conflict

The growing stature of the Ikhwan across the Middle East set the stage for what many had come to see as an inevitable clash with the Egyptian authorities.[319] By early 1948, the Brotherhood's leaders were declaring their commitment to the nationalist cause in unequivocal terms. In February, al-Banna delivered a speech, broadcast live on Egyptian radio, to mark the anniversary of the death of Mustafa Kamil, the creator of the original Nationalist Party (Hizb al-Watan). Al-Banna declared portentously that Kamil was the founder of a movement and the leader of "the umma." Forty years on, he called on Egyptians to reembrace his goals and methods, standing firm on the principle of "no negotiation except after evacuation."[320]

For some time, there had been speculation over the extent to which the Ikhwan might be willing to resort to extralegal means to achieve its objectives. This had only been intensified by the hyperactive militancy of the Brothers on Palestine and their readiness to legitimize violent jihad. As is well known, the situation there had worsened with the British announcement that the mandate would be terminated in May 1948. The formal withdrawal of the British presence led to Israel's immediate declaration of independence and the invasion of Arab armies from Egypt, Syria, Transjordan, and Iraq.[321] Long before this, however, al-Banna had wholeheartedly committed his group to the battle. Salah Shadi wrote that the first battalion of Ikhwan volunteers had traveled to Palestine as early as October 1947, and included such prominent leaders as Muhammad al-Farghali and Mahmud Labib.[322] (Al-Farghali became known in Brotherhood circles as "the terror of the Jews" because of his exploits during the conflict.)[323] These "vanguard" units were soon involved in clashes with Jewish irregulars, for example at Deir al-Balah in Gaza.[324] During the next few months, they were joined by other Ikhwan forces, many of whom arrived in Palestine via Syria, where they had linked up with local Brotherhood members. In his memoirs, Abbas al-Sissi recounted one incident in which al-Banna sent a detachment of volunteers on its way with an address that valorized their zeal for "jihad for the sake of Allah, to fight the Jews, the enemies of Islam and the nation." The Brotherhood leader also toured Palestine to review preparations for war.[325] And he begged all Egyptians and Arabs to join the jihad against their "enemies."[326]

Altogether, three "battalions" of Egyptian Muslim Brothers took part in the fighting alongside additional recruits from Syria and Jordan.[327] Kamil al-Sharif, the future minister of Awqaf in Jordan, who had crossed into Palestine in November 1947, was the overall commander of Ikhwan forces.[328] In the south, Mahmud 'Abduh led Brotherhood units that cooperated closely with the Egyptian army under General Fu'ad Sadeq, who later commended them for the bravery they had shown during the war.[329]

In subsequent years, many prominent Brotherhood members would speak proudly of their involvement in the 1947–1949 conflict.[330] Yusuf al-Qaradawi, for example, claimed to have participated in the effort to liberate the land from the "abomination of Zionism."[331] Another of those who fought in Palestine was

Abu al-Futuh 'Afifi, who went on to spend seventeen years in prison before be-coming a member of parliament for the Brotherhood in the 1990s. He entered Palestine in April 1948 and fought in battles at Kfar Darom, Bir 'Asluj, and else-where in the Gaza Strip.[332] According to Salah Shadi, the Ikhwan lost almost one hundred members who were "martyred" in Palestine, with almost the same number again injured or taken prisoner.[333] Others put the number even higher, with up to five hundred Brotherhood members allegedly killed.[334] Such figures seem fanciful, and Thomas Mayer has questioned the overall effectiveness of this military effort. He suggests that the Brotherhood was somewhat better at pro-paganda and fund-raising than actually physically waging jihad.[335] Neverthe-less, it is clear that the war came to occupy a prominent place within the collec-tive memory of the Ikhwan. In the words of 'Afifi, the blood of their fighters helped sustain "the tree of martyrdom and the struggle for liberating the lands of Muslims."[336] Brotherhood folklore recounts how the Israeli general Moshe Dayan reputedly wished to avoid confrontation with their fighters because they had "embraced" death, which made them extremely difficult to defeat.[337] Whether true or not, the story captures the Ikhwan's sense of itself as the most obdurate of those who fought for Palestine.

There is little doubt that across the region the different branches of the Broth-erhood were firmly committed to the war and fiercely opposed to any suggestion of a truce with the Israelis. Hence, the newspaper of the Syrian chapter, *al-Manar*, insisted that an "honorable death" was better than "life and submis-sion."[338] When King Abdullah of Jordan seemed poised to accept the UN's armistice proposals, the same outlet described him as a traitor who obeyed only the British, and declared provocatively that "an end should be put to King Abdullah's dreams and crimes. . . . We shall not regard him as sacrosanct . . . but shall follow the Law of God which states that false idols . . . should be smashed."[339] Later Brotherhood histories postulated that Abdullah's betrayal, in accepting a ceasefire in June 1948, robbed the Arab armies of certain victory.[340]

Inevitably, meanwhile, the escalation of the conflict in Palestine seemed to further destabilize the situation back in Egypt. Al-Banna had previously advo-cated action against "disloyal" Jews in Arab countries and *al-Ikhwan al-Muslimun* had stated that Zionism was a universal threat.[341] Now the consequences of such words became clear. In early January 1948, the renowned Cicurel department store in Cairo was bombed, as was the family home of this famous Jewish en-trepreneur. In previous months, *al-Ikhwan al-Muslimun* had accused Clement Cicurel of being one of the leaders of the Zionist movement in Egypt. On other occasions, the newspaper carried reports of "Zionist dens" operating in secret across the country. Jews were said to be hoarding gold so that it could be smuggled to foreign companies abroad, and there were suggestions that the Jews were planning to blow up Cairo's sewage works and commit other "terrible crimes."[342]

Further acts of violence followed, the impacts of which were felt beyond Egypt's Jewish community. In February, an explosion occurred at a Brotherhood branch office in the Citadel area of Cairo—apparently caused by the detonation of "cartridges" that had been stored in the building.[343] By this time, the CIA reckoned that the group had stockpiled "arms and explosives in their varying premises" across the country.[344] These supplies had been built up, many Western officials believed, with the acquiescence of the Egyptian government; but the fear was that they might now be turned against the authorities. In March 1948, Judge Ahmad al-Khazindar, who had recently issued a tough sentence against several Muslim Brothers, was shot dead in Helwan on the outskirts of Cairo.[345] Al-Banna denounced the killing, saying that Egypt had lost one of its great men.[346] Nonetheless, Salah Shadi and Hasan Dawh acknowledged in their respective memoirs that members of the Ikhwan were responsible for the attack (though Shadi claimed al-Banna knew nothing of their plans and blamed the independent-minded head of the Special Apparatus [SA], 'Abd al-Rahman al-Sanadi).[347] Subsequent incidents followed a similar pattern. In April, al-Nahas's house was bombed, with the Brothers once more identified as the most likely culprits. Again, al-Banna sent a public telegram to the Wafdist leader repudiating the crime; as previously, few people believed him.[348]

In May 1948, martial law was effectively imposed. Prime Minister al-Nuqrashi was appointed military governor and new restrictions were placed on civil liberties.[349] Even so, the onset of open warfare in Palestine was accompanied by a fresh surge in anti-Jewish rhetoric in Egypt.[350] *Al-Ikhwan al-Muslimun* resumed its agitation against the local Jewish population. Salih 'Ashmawi stated that "every Jew is a Zionist," and accused those in Egypt of financing their brethren in Palestine.[351] There was fresh talk of "secret plans" to damage the country and allegations that the Jews controlled Cairo's "financial establishments." Jewish "spies" were said to be preparing acts of espionage—and the Brotherhood pressed for Jews to be deprived of their citizenship, nationality, and property, in the event that an Israeli state was established. At one rally, al-Banna declared: "If the Jewish state becomes a fact, and this is realized by the Arab peoples, they will drive the Jews who live in their midst into the sea." Jews were described by the Brotherhood leader as dangerous "fifth columnists."[352] *Al-Ikhwan al-Muslimun* said that the Arabs had previously supported the Jews only to find themselves betrayed; the only way to respond, the newspaper proclaimed, was by "continuous jihad."[353] The Brotherhood called on Arab and Islamic states to withdraw from international bodies like the UN and form their own union, which would work to combat "international Judaism." The Ikhwan was adamant that a military solution was the only way to ensure the land of Palestine was "purified" from Zionism.[354]

By this time, King Faruq and the Wafd were issuing statements that sought to diminish sectarian tensions and hostility toward Egypt's Jews by emphasizing the distinction between Jews and Zionists. The Ikhwan, however, displayed no such reticence.[355] Furthermore, in a familiar pattern, the increase in intemperate rhetoric was paralleled by violent attacks on Egypt's Jewish community. In mid-June, the Gamaliya district of Cairo, home to many of the city's Jews, was bombed. Over forty people were killed, and more than fifty others injured. The official police investigation concluded that the "attack" was the result of the premature explosion of materials obtained by Jewish terrorists intent on subversion. Yet many were far from convinced by this explanation.[356] From the beginning, there were strong suspicions of Brotherhood involvement.[357] The US Embassy was informed by a "realistic source" that "a group within the Palace" was "making use of the more fanatical elements in the Ikhwan to carry out the bombings."[358]

The next month saw mass demonstrations in the Egyptian capital, rebuking variously, the Jews, the Americans, and the British. Among the slogans chanted by the mob were cries of "destroy the Jews, rid Egypt of Jews, Britain is our enemy and down with Truman." The protests then degenerated into attacks on cars and some shops.[359] A few days later, there was another spate of bombings in downtown Cairo, again targeting the Cicurel and Oreco department stores, as well as the Metropole Cinema. These were followed by further anti-Jewish and antiforeign riots.[360] July also brought a failed attempt to blow up the offices of the Sudan Agency in Cairo.[361] And, in the face of all this, the government seemed powerless to act.[362]

By the autumn of 1948, after the initial wave of Arab defeats in Palestine, concern about the Brotherhood reached new heights. Many of the group's volunteers—who had gained combat experience—returned home embittered, believing that the nation's politicians had betrayed them. Egypt witnessed a fresh wave of anti-Jewish violence in which the Ikhwan was implicated. On September 22, nineteen people were killed and more than sixty injured by another explosion in Cairo's Jewish quarter.[363] In addition, there were various attacks on foreigners. Alfred Sansom would later observe that while Hasan al-Banna publicly deplored these acts of violence, "he and other leaders of the Moslem Brotherhood excited the mob to the frenzy that led to them."[364] Similarly, US diplomats specifically identified the Brotherhood as inciting "religious fanaticism."[365]

In late October, the Port Said and Ismailia branches of the Ikhwan were closed down by military proclamation.[366] The move was linked to the discovery of a large quantity of arms and explosives on the estate of Sheikh al-Farghali, the senior Brotherhood figure in Ismailia who was heavily involved in the group's activities in Palestine. The cache was believed to be one of a large number distributed around the country and under the control of the Ikhwan.[367] Elsewhere, steps were taken to restrict the movement's propaganda, yet such oppression seemed only to prompt greater violence.[368] On November 3, the Cairo house of the Egyptian ambassador to London, 'Abd al-Fattah 'Amr Pasha, was bombed. Five days later, al-Nahas was again targeted for assassination—for the sixth time in ten years—by assailants using an automatic weapon and a grenade.[369] The Egyptian police strongly suspected the Brotherhood to be behind both attacks.[370]

That same month, ten more people were killed and over thirty wounded when the premises of the Société Orientale de Publicité were bombed. This publishing house, which produced the English-language newspaper the *Egyptian Gazette* among other titles, had been threatened previously for its allegedly "pro-Israeli orientation."[371] The memoirs of leading Brotherhood members effectively admit that the group's Special Apparatus was behind this and other attacks— as many contemporary observers had concluded.[372] By early December, British officials stated that it had "now been established beyond all reasonable doubt that members of the Ikhwan el Muslimin" were behind the attacks on Jewish properties.[373] The American Embassy likewise believed that the group bore "primary responsibility" for numerous bombings. They described the Brotherhood as a "Frankenstein monster," created by the king for use against the Wafd, which had now run out of control. Al-Banna, they assumed, was now intent on taking power.[374]

Most Western diplomats had come to see the Brotherhood as a serious threat to the government and the regime. Suspicions of this kind gained further traction as a result of the "jeep case" that came to light in mid-November 1948, when the police arrested thirty members of the Ikhwan and seized a jeep loaded with arms, explosives, and alleged plans for a coup. The latter apparently identified various assassination targets and properties to be destroyed, including the British, American, and French embassies, as well as the houses of al-Nahas and 'Amr Pasha (both of which had been previously targeted).[375]

At the time, Hasan al-Banna was out of the country performing the Hajj in Saudi Arabia, and some of his followers suggested it might be better (and safer) for him if he did not return. The Brotherhood leader rejected this idea, however, and on arriving back in Egypt, attempted to calm the situation. He and another senior brother, Muhammad Hamid Abu al-Nasr, visited the palace and signed the register with a note of goodwill toward the king.[376] In parallel, Salih 'Ashmawi, the editor of the Ikhwan's daily newspaper, sought to downplay the group's connection to the "jeep case."[377] The effect of such conciliatory gestures was undermined, though, by the fact that the violence continued. In early December 1948, the chief of the Cairo police, Salim Zaki Pasha, was killed by a hand grenade allegedly thrown by a Brotherhood student during demonstrations at Fu'ad I (Cairo) University.[378] As a result, the police launched a large-scale campaign of arrests and the university was closed indefinitely. Shortly thereafter, the newspaper *al-Ikhwan al-Muslimun* was forced to suspend publication.[379] By this time, British diplomats were expressing "grave anxiety about the state of public security in Egypt"; they pressed the Cairo government to take "effective action" to deal with the Muslim Brotherhood and other subversives.[380]

On 8 December 1948, Prime Minister al-Nuqrashi issued a military proclamation ordering the dissolution of the Ikhwan. The group stood accused of seeking the overthrow of "the established regime" by violent means that "aimed at revolutionising political and social principles by force and terrorism." According to the authorities, the Brotherhood had neglected the "religious and social ends for which it had been founded" and allowed itself to become embroiled in crime in the pursuit of power. The government therefore felt it had no choice but to proscribe the group.[381] Al-Banna was placed under temporary house arrest and other senior figures were taken into custody.[382] Former student leader Mustafa Mu'min and General Secretary 'Abd al-Hakim 'Abdin were among those detained.[383] The property, funds, and archives of the Ikhwan were sequestered.[384] And there were reports that the police had seized "sizable" quantities of arms and explosives.[385]

While pleased by this outcome, the British Embassy judged that Prime Minister al-Nuqrashi had, to the last, been reluctant to move against the Ikhwan—for fear both that the authorities might struggle to suppress them and that he himself might be targeted for "some form of reprisal." Apparently, it was only the determination of the king to crush the Brotherhood that had finally induced al-Nuqrashi to act. With that said, there was a feeling that once the military proclamation had been announced, the prime minister *had* committed himself to seeing the policy through.[386] Representatives of the Egyptian government now informed the embassy of their intention to "suppress" the Ikhwan "good and proper and finish them off."[387]

British diplomats welcomed the dissolution of the Brotherhood as "advantageous in all respects." In their assessment, the group had "never ceased to encourage hatred of the British" and its propaganda had blamed foreign influence for "all the evils from which their country suffered."[388] In London, officials applauded these "satisfactory" developments.[389] The *Times* voiced relief that this "most useful tool and dupe" of the Soviets had been eliminated. The newspaper's correspondent reflected on the Brothers' involvement in many outrages and concluded that they had become "a danger to the State," and were likely "penetrated and influenced by Communists."[390] Meanwhile, US diplomats surmised that "representative Egyptians" were "pleased" that the "coup de grace" had been administered to the Brotherhood.[391] This found echo in the reports of the pro-British Ikhwan al-Hurriya, which attested that the government's move had met with "almost universal relief especially in the provinces."[392]

Faced with the crackdown, Hasan al-Banna remained defiant. In an interview with the weekly newspaper *Rose al-Yusuf*, he said that the Brotherhood's work was merely on hold, not at an end. When asked about the allegation that he had abandoned religious aims and indulged in politics, he replied: "We have spent 20 full years to make people understand that Islam is a religion and a state, and that it is not a religion of worship and devotion, but one of struggle." More enigmatically, al-Banna added that "the withdrawal of a man's birth certificate does not make him lose his existence, although it makes him lose his personality from the legal point of view." The Brotherhood leader, it seemed, had no intention of meekly accepting the dissolution order.[393] In a further statement (that turned out to be the final thing he wrote), al-Banna condemned a government "in the shadow of which, the foreigner can live safe and secure in his self, money, frivolity and corruption, and whose soldiers guard alcoholic bars, brothels, houses of ill repute and the doors of discos . . . and which is completely unable to save its people from the clutches of poverty, sickness and ignorance and the obscene cost of living which burdens both the strong and the weak." He went on to highlight the danger posed by the "hidden fingers" of those who had conspired against the Brotherhood from the beginning: international Judaism, international communism, the imperialist countries, and supporters of atheism and pornography. These forces, al-Banna asserted, knew that the Ikhwan was an "impervious block" to their ambitions and therefore sought its destruction.[394] On previous occasions, he had warned his followers that they would face repression; that the message of the Brotherhood would be met with "the severest opposition and the cruellest hatred"; that they would face "numerous hardships and obstructions"; and that there would be a "stage of trial and test" in which Brothers would be "imprisoned, detained, transferred and expelled." But ultimately, al-Banna averred, God had promised them victory and he urged his followers to stay the course, confident in the knowledge that they were "the bearers of a burden" that all other people had denied.[395]

For their part, British officials were far from convinced that the authorities were actually capable of suppressing the Brotherhood—not least because of earlier revelations about the group's hidden arms caches.[396] Perhaps most troubling were reports the embassy received that the Ikhwan might seek to kill "several Egyptian personalities with Noqrashi [sic] on top of the list."[397] It did not take long for such grim prophecies to be fulfilled. Within weeks of the dissolution order, a student member of the Brotherhood, 'Abd al-Majid Ahmad Hasan, had murdered the Egyptian prime minister.[398] In the aftermath, the Ikhwan did not deny that Hasan was a Muslim Brother—but they insisted that he had acted alone, without the knowledge of the organization's leaders.[399] Al-Banna described the murder of al-Nuqrashi as an "awesome crime" and claimed that his movement had nothing to do with such acts. He denounced "lawlessness in all its forms" and condemned those involved in it.[400] The Egyptian authorities, though, were not persuaded. Al-Nuqrashi's successor, Ibrahim 'Abd al-Hadi Pasha, vowed that strong measures against the Ikhwan would continue, including the use of military courts against suspects.[401] The Egyptian ambassador in London stressed that al-Hadi's government was determined to "stamp" out the Brotherhood.[402]

Again, British observers worried that the Ikhwan was "by no means disposed of" and might have further "well organised plans for reprisal action."[403] The Cairo correspondent of the *Economist* deemed the Brothers to be "fanatical young men," who were probably responsible for some, if not all, of the "recent terrorist activities in Cairo."[404] Similarly, the *Times* believed that the group was poised to enact a "murderous campaign against any Egyptian leader" who did not accept their "reactionary views."[405] Even James Heyworth-Dunne now reappeared as a critic of the "insidious Ikhwan," which he labeled "fanatical, anti-Western" and reactionary. Heyworth-Dunne said that the Brothers aimed at nothing less than the "destruction of the constitutional form of government on western lines and the creation of a purely Islamic state." To this end, he inferred, Hasan al-Banna was ready to mount "some sort of armed coup."[406]

In January 1949, the local British Security Service representative, G J. Jenkins, characterized the Ikhwan as an ongoing threat to the stability of the Egyptian state.[407] Sources within the Cairo police provided the British with reports that were "not encouraging" about the progress made in suppressing the group.[408]

There were hints too that the Brotherhood might sustain itself by linking up with other political forces. On the one hand, there were suggestions this could mean a merger with the Watanist Party, which had publicly opposed their pro-scription.[409] On the other, US officials were privy to "disquieting" rumors that Brotherhood members might be "flocking into the ranks of the Misr al Fattat."[410] The latter possibility fed into concurrent fears about a Young Egypt revival, with that body branded a bastion of "fanaticism and extremism," which could be used as cover by the Ikhwan.[411]

Of still greater concern was the fact that acts of violence continued to occur. In mid-January, an attempt was made to bomb the office of the prosecutor general who was responsible for the investigation into the al-Nuqrashi murder and other Brotherhood-related acts. Two people were killed and more than twenty injured. The Court of Appeals and adjoining premises were damaged. The man behind the attack was quickly identified as one Ibrahim Anas, a junior official in the Agriculture Ministry and a known Muslim Brother who had previously been detained in connection with the "jeep case."[412] Salah Shadi maintained that this bombing was another attack ordered by the head of the Special Apparatus, al-Sanadi, contrary to the wishes of al-Banna—his goal being to destroy legal evidence pending against the Brotherhood.[413] Whatever its objective, Western diplomats feared that the bombing presaged a more extensive "terrorist campaign" by the Ikhwan; and there were dark whispers about caches of explosives earmarked for use on Coptic churches.[414] Elsewhere, the British military suspected that the Brotherhood was gathering intelligence on their installations in the Canal Zone in preparation for acts of sabotage.[415] There were warnings too that the Ikhwan might seek to target the British ambassador in Cairo and officials in Sudan.[416] With regard to the latter, the British received information about a possible attempt on the life of the Sudanese governor general.[417] Ultimately, a "terrorist campaign" in Sudan did not materialize, but the situation in Egypt looked deeply unsettled.[418] Against this background, the view of embassy officials was that "as long as the Ikhwan remains as active as it is, the first requirement from anyone's point of view, including ours, is that the Egyptian PM [prime minister] should be firm and determined in putting them down."[419]

Altogether, the security picture at the end of January 1949 looked fairly bleak. US officials were told of new threats to blow up, variously, the Ministry of Foreign Affairs, the auditor general's department, and the Council of State.[420] A group calling itself the Phalange of the Holy Struggle for the Liberation of Islam sent letters to certain cabinet ministers demanding the restoration of the

Brotherhood.[421] Some Western officials worried that government moves against the "terrorists" had come "too little too late."[422]

Everything changed, however, with the news in early February that Hasan al-Banna himself had been murdered.[423] Western diplomats were quickly convinced that the authorities were behind the killing. In the assessment of the British Embassy, the Egyptian government had come to see al-Banna as an "embarrassment," but had been reluctant to arrest him for fear of the unrest this might generate. They also did not trust the justice system to produce a conviction for the Brotherhood leader. A decision had therefore been taken that "a would-be martyr in his grave would prove a less effective source of inspiration than one behind the bars of a prison."[424] On similar reasoning, it was believed every attempt was made to prevent the Brotherhood from exploiting al-Banna's death to build popular support. The police insisted that he be buried quickly and without ceremony. High-profile individuals who visited the house to offer condolences were detained—with the exception of the flamboyant politician Makram 'Ubayd, who was the only public figure to attend al-Banna's funeral.[425]

In this context, officials in London pondered what the future might hold for the Brotherhood: would the movement now "disintegrate with the death of its leader" or would it endure and seek revenge?[426] By early March, the local British Security Service representative reckoned that more than nine hundred Muslim Brothers had been interned inside Tora prison near Cairo. Police sources had apparently expressed confidence that they had the "most fanatical" members of the group—those most likely to seek vengeance for al-Banna's death—"under lock and key."[427] Even now, though, the diplomats were uncertain that the authorities had "gained the upper hand in the struggle against organised terrorism" and especially against the Brotherhood.[428] Officials feared that they had not "heard or seen the last of the Ikhwan el Muslimeen."[429]

Throughout the spring of 1949, stories of arrests, gun battles, and the seizure of Brotherhood property continued to appear.[430] The very fact that such incidents were occurring seemed testament to the scale of the challenge. This was confirmed in early May, when an attack was launched on the motorcade of the president of the Chamber of Deputies, Hamid Guda Bey. Muslim Brotherhood "terrorists" threw grenades and opened fire on his car with a machine gun, in the mistaken belief that it was actually the vehicle of Prime Minister al-Hadi.[431] Though Guda escaped unhurt, the episode seemed to underline the threat posed by the Ikhwan.

As the memoirs of Hasan Dawh make clear, many within the Brotherhood *did* want revenge. Therein, he recalled his time in a prison camp (to which he and his colleagues had been sent directly from Palestine), where there was a "desire for jihad and to participate in combatting the government which had aggressed against the General Guide and our brothers." Dawh himself admitted to being "filled with [thoughts of] violent methods for confronting [our] enemies," by which he meant "the English, the Jews, the king and the parties." Because of this, an attempt was even made to build a new Special Apparatus that was to begin operating as soon as they were released—but such plans faded away as their period of incarceration lengthened.[432]

Martial law was extended for another year in May 1949.[433] Thereafter, Egyptian security sources periodically warned British officials about the ongoing dangers posed by both the Ikhwan and communism. Indeed, there was a concerted effort to link the two together. The Egyptian ambassador in London, for instance, informed the British that the Brothers had received "considerable money from Russia."[434] Arrests were said to have uncovered evidence of these financial ties.[435] And there were various claims that the Ikhwan had been "infiltrated" by communists.[436] More exotically, when Prime Minister al-Hadi told the Americans that an "outside agency" was supplying the Brotherhood with plans and money, he implied it was not the communists but the Israelis who were to blame.[437] Of course, there was nothing to support such insinuations, but al-Hadi's assertions were an early example of an allegation that would become commonplace in later years among anti-Ikhwan Egyptians: that it was a tool of the Israeli state.

As 1949 progressed, the authorities repeated that there would be no letup in the campaign of arrests until they were "satisfied that the reign of terror" had been brought to an end.[438] By the time al-Hadi left office in July, some four thousand Muslim Brothers were in prison.[439] Throughout this period, Western diplomats backed the government's drive against the Ikhwan, while expressing their unease at the broader health of the Egyptian polity. US officials were uneasy about a drift toward "royal dictatorship."[440] To this was added concern about growing popular social and economic discontent.[441] In London, the mandarins came to accept that their post-1945 gamble on the king had failed: the Anglo-Egyptian dispute remained "at a complete standstill"; the internal situation looked less promising than ever; and few could be sure that the threat from the Brotherhood had been eliminated.[442]

James Heyworth-Dunne was among those who did not expect the Egyptian government's crackdown to succeed. In his judgment, the Brotherhood was "the largest group in the whole of the Near and Middle East." He believed that a clash between the Ikhwan and the ruling classes had been all but inevitable—there being no other way that the movement could remain true to its "revolutionary" spirit. Furthermore, he thought that the "idea behind Hasan al-Banna's leadership" would likely be "of longer duration than any Egyptian Ministry."[443] Similar opinions were current within the US State Department. One undated (and anonymous) thesis on "political life in Egypt" concluded that the Ikhwan would survive the dissolution order and repression, operating "underground" if necessary. The author of the paper described the Brotherhood as "more of a Religio-Political movement than a Party" that had "distinguished itself" by its "loyalty and faith towards its principles." The expansion of the Ikhwan was said to be a consequence of "the failure of the political system in Egypt" and the gap between the people and the governing classes.[444] In this view, there was unlikely to be any quick fix to the challenge posed by the Brothers; rather, they were expected to be an enduring feature of Cairo's political landscape.

Conclusion

In early 1948, the American investigative journalist John Roy Carlson had traveled to the Middle East and sought out groups like the Brotherhood and Young Egypt. In March, he voluntarily sent the State Department a memorandum outlining his key research findings, which formed the basis of the book he later published on the same subject. Carlson's account was replete with every kind of orientalist stereotype. The "otherness" of Cairo was relentlessly conveyed in his depiction of "men in gallabiya [long, loose fitting shirts]," "copper-skinned Bedouins," "un-veiled Egyptian beauties," and "swarms of urchins."[445] He affirmed that "the mode of living" there "had changed but little in the last five thousand years," and Egypt's fellahin were said to be "among the most miserable human beings on earth."[446] As Melani McAlister has observed, such notions were a staple of early twentieth-century American depictions of the Middle East, with a focus on its dirtiness, degradation, sensuality, and backwardness.[447]

For present purposes, what was interesting about Carlson's commentary was the fact that he came away convinced that the Brotherhood was an anti-Semitic, antiforeign, and extremist organization. The Ikhwan, he said, was responsible for the spread of anti-Jewish propaganda in Cairo and actively sought jihad against both the British and the Jews in Palestine and Egypt alike. To this end, al-Banna was believed to control "espionage squads" and even a "special assassin squad." According to Carlson, the Brothers possessed a "strong militarist, terrorist aspect" and were committed to a "religious totalitarianism" that sought to "smash modernism in government and society." Here, he recorded, "were zealots of every description—ultra-nationalist, ultra-religionist, ultra-fanatic Moslems who vowed to make every day a day of Jehad [*sic*] against nonbelievers." Al-Banna was portrayed as "a man with a gift for intrigue," who reminded Carlson of "the rather hypocritical clergyman who while singing the praises of the Lord, casts ravishing eyes on the girls in the choir"; he declared himself "very unpleasantly impressed" with this "short, squat ratty-faced man with puffed cheeks and fleshy nose," who possessed a "deep hatred" of Europeans and was, in Carlson's assessment, "the most loathsome man" he had met in Cairo.[448]

It was a verdict with which few Western diplomats would have argued. In the period after the Second World War, they had watched unhappily as the power of the Brotherhood grew, seemingly unchecked. Abbas al-Sissi would later describe the period between 1942 and the end of 1948 as "the most blessed and most successful of times in the history of the da'wa."[449] The movement reached a historic peak in terms of size and influence. It expanded beyond Egypt's borders and, to Western minds, posed a grave threat to the "proper" development of the Middle East. In Cairo, al-Banna played a skillful political game, once more demonstrating his strategic preference for pragmatism and a capacity to modulate his position, so as to run with the hare of popular protest, while hunting with the hounds of the political elite. In so doing, the Brotherhood showed a capacity to make and break governments, helping to destabilize two administrations headed by Mahmud al-Nuqrashi and one under Isma'il Sidqi.

Throughout this time, too, the Ikhwan maintained a strident opposition to imperialism—though again, al-Banna's pragmatic instincts saw parallel efforts to engage with Western officials. In those meetings, he presented his movement as both a moderate democratic force and an avowed enemy of communism. He pitched for an accommodation with both the British and the Americans. The diplomats, however, struggled to reconcile al-Banna's conciliatory tone in private with his evident willingness to play the part of demagogue in public. The gap between words and action proved too great—and concerns about the Ikhwan heightened from 1947 onward, as the Brothers held to an uncompromising position on Egyptian national demands. These would only be realized, the group's leaders announced, through the evacuation of British troops and the unity of the Nile valley. In adhering to this hard-line stance, the Brothers benefited from the growing delegitimation of the existing political parties and the parliamentary system. They also won popularity on account of their relentless hostility to the Zionist movement in Palestine, playing an active part in efforts to prevent the creation of Israel by force of arms.[450]

Ultimately, this militancy rebounded on Egypt and reinforced the Brother-hood's intransigent thinking, which placed a premium on "struggle" as the only means by which Egypt might secure its objectives. Hitherto, the Brothers had offered qualified endorsement to Sidqi's negotiations and al-Nuqrashi's deci-sion to take his country's case to the United Nations. After the failure of both of these initiatives, the Ikhwan seemed ever more inclined to challenge the Egyptian authorities, as it became embroiled in anti-Jewish violence inside the country's borders. By late 1948, many suspected that the Brothers were pre-paring to try to seize power in Cairo. The "jeep case" appeared to confirm these fears. As a result, al-Nuqrashi's second ministry resolved to dismantle the move-ment. In this, it received the firm backing of the major Western governments, which had themselves come to believe that the Ikhwan should be tackled sooner rather than later.

The dissolution of the Brotherhood sparked an intense cycle of violence that saw the murder of both the prime minister and Hasan al-Banna. Hundreds, if not thousands, of Brothers were arrested and interned without charge. The Ikhwan would come to see the period that followed December 1948 as the group's "first *mihna* [ordeal]."[451] They labeled it a "stab in the back," which came at a moment when the Brotherhood was fighting for the "umma," against the "ene-mies of Islam" in Palestine.[452] In the words of Abu al-Futuh 'Afifi, Hasan al-Banna was killed by "treacherous hands, [working] with a Western-Zionist con-spiracy." His death served as "testimony to the collusion of Arab organisations and their betrayal of the issues of the umma," as well as "the machinations of enemies and their enmity for the da'wa."[453]

Out of this was born the narrative with which this chapter began: that the proscription of the Brotherhood was directly ordered by the Western powers after a meeting of the leading ambassadors at a British military base.[454] The "ene-mies of Islam," it was argued, had acted because they feared the "strong guerrilla spirit" that the Brothers had inspired in the country. Abbas al-Sissi asserted that the British had demanded the suppression of the Ikhwan, on threat that they would reoccupy Cairo if al-Nuqrashi refused.[455] Kamil al-Sharif, the commander of Brotherhood forces in Palestine, later wrote that the "reactionary parties" and the British were frightened by the success of the Ikhwan in "gathering the people around the ideology of Islam and its strong nationalist principles." They therefore resolved to "extinguish the light" of the Brotherhood's call.[456] In a similar vein, Yusuf al-Qaradawi stated that Western pressure on al-Nuqrashi was driven both by Anglo-American anxieties and their desire to assist Israel. By his account, the new government in Tel Aviv was aware that the "Islamic current" posed the greatest threat to its existence and to its dreams of expanding until it controlled land stretching "from the Euphrates to the Nile." For this reason, the Israelis and their Western allies had urged the destruction of the Brotherhood.[457] According to Salah Shadi, it was this that then made possible the Rhodes armistice agreement of February 1949, which ended the first Arab-Israeli war.[458] In this way, the Brothers linked their own "ordeal" to the Arab failure to overcome Zionism.

In subsequent years, Brotherhood narratives pointed to the malign role allegedly played by certain well-placed Jews who had worked to "blacken" their name. One such individual was reputed to be the Reuters journalist Jon Kimche, who in early 1946 had penned an article labeling the Ikhwan a "fascist group" that stood ready to initiate a campaign of violence. Kimche was said to be both confused and engaged in naked incitement against the Ikhwan.[459] Also singled out for blame was a female Jewish journalist "Ruth Kariv."[460] She apparently had written an article for the *Sunday Mirror* in early 1948, in which she called for an international force to be sent to Palestine to fight the Brotherhood. Ikhwan histories depicted this as yet another example of Jewish attempts to smear the reputation of the movement.[461]

While many Brothers thus came to see themselves as the innocent victims of a malicious conspiracy, some latter-day Brotherhood leaders such as Yusuf Nada have acknowledged that members of the Ikhwan *were* involved in violence in the 1948–1949 period—though Nada insists this was the work of a "maverick group" within the wider organization.[462] Yusuf al-Qaradawi likewise contends that, at most, the violence was the work of a few individual Brothers and was anathema to al-Banna.[463] The mainstream Brotherhood view is that the movement's Special Apparatus, though formed for the right reasons, lost its way in this era—either because of the arrogance of its leader, 'Abd al-Rahman al-Sanadi; or because it misinterpreted the religion; or because of some mixture of these two factors.[464] The result was that the SA slipped out of al-Banna's control and made fatal mistakes. While the Brothers would argue that it was entirely legitimate for the SA to wage jihad against the British and the Zionists, they accept that it went beyond its designated purposes when it targeted Egyptian judges and policemen.[465] Moreover, the effect of this, the Brotherhood believes, was to leave the movement as a whole exposed to the machinations of its "enemies." In the end, *real* responsibility for the dissolution of the Ikhwan was laid at the door of its guileful opponents—secularists, Zionists, and imperialists.

Of course, none of this is to deny that most Western officials *did* view the Ikhwan in a wholly negative light. They encouraged al-Nuqrashi and al-Hadi to take action and were more than happy to see the Brotherhood repressed. For a time in 1949, it appeared as if the very existence of the group might be in jeopardy. But as the months went by, Western observers became concerned by what they saw as the durability of the Ikhwan, fearing that this "fanatical," "extremist," and "terrorist" organization might survive underground. They worried about what this would in turn mean for the future of an increasingly fragile Egyptian polity.

Four   The War of the Canal Zone

1950–1952

O N 13 JANUARY 1952, fighters from self-declared "liberation battalions" launched an attack on the British
army base at Tel el-Kebir in the Egyptian delta prov-
ince of Sharqiya. They succeeded in blowing up a train carrying soldiers and
equipment, but at heavy cost to their own forces. Among those killed were two
student members of the Muslim Brotherhood, 'Umar Shahin and Ahmad al-
Menisa. From that time onward, these men were venerated by the Ikhwan.[1] In
the words of Abu al-Futuh 'Afifi, who was involved in planning the operation,
they were a "symbol of the struggle of the youth," who did not hesitate to go
out to jihad and embraced martyrdom.[2] According to Hasan Dawh, who was
also involved in the fighting in the Canal Zone, the subsequent funeral of Shahin
"shook the sentiments of the nation and stirred its anger against the English
and the throne."[3] Soon afterward, the Brothers at Alexandria University cooperated with members of the Wafd, Young Egypt, and other groups in a major
protest against the British, which reverberated to cries of the Brotherhood's most
famous mantra, "allah akbar, allah al-hamd [God is Greatest, God be praised]."[4]
The "battle of Tel el-Kebir," which evoked memories of the 1882 encounter of
the same name, was celebrated as a signature episode in what the Brotherhood
called "the war of the Canal Zone." Whereas seventy years earlier, Egyptian defeat had set the seal on British occupation, now events at Tel el-Kebir were said
to have advanced the cause of liberation.

151

The British, of course, looked on all this and on people like Shahin and al-Menisa in rather less celebrated fashion. In their view, the Brotherhood's fighters were terrorists, to be dealt with forcefully. It was a constant source of frustration to British minds that the Egyptian authorities seemed unwilling to take a firm enough line against the "liberation battalions." During the previous two years, they had watched as the Ikhwan regained much of the ground it had lost as a consequence of dissolution. Repeated warnings appeared to have fallen on deaf ears; and by late 1951–early 1952, the British were clear that the Brothers were at the forefront of those groups launching attacks on their forces.

The return of the Brotherhood had occurred amid a broader destabilization of Egypt. The conflict in the Canal Zone had been sparked by the unilateral decision of the government in Cairo to abrogate the 1936 Treaty of Alliance. This, in turn, came after a seemingly interminable process of negotiations that had failed to produce a settlement to the long-running Anglo-Egyptian dispute.[5] As earlier, the British remained determined to preserve their access to the "indispensable" Suez Canal Base.[6] Officials in London hoped to win firm American backing for an arragement that would see that base retained as the linchpin of a regional security system.[7] A June 1950 review of global strategy had described the Middle East as one of three key pillars of UK defense policy.[8] For their part, the Americans continued to afford their translantic allies crucial diplomatic cover—despite growing criticism of the way the British were handling the Egyptian situation. The outbreak and development of the Korean War cemented US support for the British position, and Washington called for an "amicable agreement" that would allow for Western control of the Suez Base.[9] By late 1950, London and Washington were "unanimous" in judging Egypt's maximal nationalist demands to be "impossible" and they asserted that "the cardinal principle of the defense of the Middle East should not be overlooked."[10] Inevitably, this joint Western posture produced mounting frustration within Egypt and set the stage for abrogation and conflict.

The Return of the Wafd, the Return of the Brothers

By the middle of 1949, many British officials had come to believe that the decision to back King Faruq, as against the Wafd, had been a mistake. The king and the minority governments he imposed had failed to deliver either stability or a revised treaty.[11] American observers also were increasingly concerned that the status quo in Egypt could not endure. The Central Intelligence Agency (CIA) officer Kim Roosevelt was one of those who felt that the basis of the country's "democracy" was "inadequate."[12] In October 1949, the US Embassy compiled a memorandum on Faruq, "the most important single figure" in Egyptian political life, which laid out his weaknesses in unsparing detail. Yet even now the diplomats hoped that the king might "develop into a serious, progressive and influential young monarch." The palace was said to be the one permanent tradition in Egyptian politics, which carried a "strong appeal for the Oriental mind."[13] Consequently, it was decided that Roosevelt should be sent to try to steer Faruq down a more acceptable path.

The king himself seemed aware of the need for change. It was likely for this reason that he was willing to countenance rapprochement with his erstwhile enemy, Mustafa al-Nahas, in the second half of 1949. The government of Ibrahim 'Abd al-Hadi, which had carried through the crackdown on the Muslim Brotherhood and delivered some semblance of order, was thus dismissed in July. In its place, a caretaker administration under Husayn Sirri oversaw preparations for new elections at the end of the year. Those polls brought the last great electoral victory of the Wafd, when it won more than 70 percent of the seats in parliament.[14] Al-Nahas became prime minister for the fourth (and final) time in January 1950. British reactions betrayed a degree of satisfaction at this outcome. The minister of state at the Foreign Office, Hugh McNeil, thought the elections had shown that "even the upper classes are no longer able to stomach Farouk [sic]." While McNeil felt that the British should not "cling too close" to the Wafd, he said they would "weep no tears" if al-Nahas were to "humble this squalid little monarch." In McNeil's view, the reality was that Faruq was "in recess," and he therefore recommended that the British "trim" their "sails" and work with the prime minister.[15]

Crucially for present purposes, the Wafd had smoothed the way for its return to power, not only by repairing ties with the king but also by reconciling to the Ikhwan. Relations between the two groups had been fractious over the previous three years. In the run-up to the elections, however, the Wafd had made a definite effort to heal the rift. In October 1949, the newspaper *al-Misri al-Wafd* published an interview that had been conducted with Hasan al-Banna prior to his death. US officials considered this to be a deliberate attempt to "entice" Brotherhood supporters into the Wafdist camp ahead of the ballot.[16] At that time, the Ikhwan was still struggling to come to terms with the loss of its founder and the repressive measures to which it had been subjected. It was perhaps this weakness that persuaded the Wafd that it could safely harness the Brothers' support. Other articles in pro-Wafdist newspapers followed, highlighting the alleged mistreatment of the Brotherhood by al-Hadi's government.[17] Al-Nahas pledged that on regaining the premiership, he would end martial law and allow the group to resume its activity.

Already, al-Hadi's departure from office had brought an easing of the authorities' grip on the Ikhwan. As the government of Husayn Sirri began to release interned Muslim Brothers, there were the first "signs" of renewed "life" in the group. In August 1949, for instance, the Ikhwan had issued a pamphlet blaming the Western powers for orchestrating its dissolution.[18] (As described in Chapter 3, the Brothers had concluded that it was British pressure that was primarily responsible for their suppression.)[19] Later that month, the US Embassy was informed that the Brotherhood was "not politically dead," just "quiet at the moment." It was said to retain "revolutionary possibilities" and to be reorganizing, especially in Upper Egypt.[20]

By late autumn of 1949, the Egyptian authorities were warning the British about a possible "revival" of the Ikhwan that might lead to an "inevitable" recrudescence of terrorism.[21] To officials like the British minister in Cairo, Edwin Chapman-Andrews, the possible "resuscitation and re-establishment" of the Brotherhood was far from welcome. Chapman-Andrews's earlier insouciance about the Brotherhood (see Chapter 2) had been replaced by no small amount of trepidation. In November, he minuted that "this organisation more than any other is a danger to us . . . for it is fundamentally anti-foreign, reactionary and fanatical." As a result, Chapman-Andrews urged his colleagues to do whatever they could to ensure its continued proscription.[22] (He remained critical, though, of the extrajudicial approach adopted by the Egyptian authorities. In his opinion, it was wrong simply to lock up Brotherhood members and "subject them to cruelties"; he argued that this only made them more dangerous when eventually they were released. It was far better, he affirmed, to apply the rule of law, albeit expeditiously against those accused of the most serious crimes.)[23]

American observers of Egypt shared British anxieties. In his 1949 book, Kim Roosevelt had identified the Ikhwan as one of only two groups in the country that possessed a strong organization, the other being the Wafd. Yet whereas the latter was judged corrupt and decaying, Roosevelt saw the Brotherhood as a "young, aggressive party," eager to "descendre dans les rues [take to the streets]." Roosevelt's assessment of the Ikhwan mixed a degree of fascination with obvious unease: "Fanatically religious, antiforeign and reactionary," he noted, "it is well organised and growing in strength." Roosevelt also remarked on the tendency of the other Egyptian political parties to encourage the Brotherhood in the hope of using it against their rivals. The Sa'dists were thought to be par-

ticularly culpable in this regard. Roosevelt commented that "the Saadist successors to Nokrashi [sic] must already look at the brotherhood as the inventor
of Frankenstein [sic] looked on his handiwork." In addition, he echoed earlier
fears that the Brothers were benefiting from "Soviet gold"—and this fed into
his broader thesis that Egypt was ripe for communist subversion.[24] On this last
point, the US Embassy's military attaché seemed inclined to agree, warning
that the communists might seek to cooperate with disaffected Muslim Brothers
to cause "disorders" during the 1949 election campaign.[25]

Prior to that ballot, the British Security Service representative in Cairo reported that a number of Ikhwan members—perhaps as many as thirty-five—
were planning to stand for parliament, either as independents or as members of
Makram 'Ubayd's Wafdist Bloc (Kutla) Party. The king, it was said, had given
instructions that none were to be elected; but the British had little confidence
in the ability of the authorities to deliver the desired result. The Brotherhood, it
was suggested, was not a "spent force" and "could by no means be discounted
as a future danger to security."[26]

After his reinstatement as prime minister, al-Nahas himself seemed to have
second thoughts about the wisdom of allowing the Ikhwan space to recover. In
January 1950, US officials predicted that while the Wafd might bring forward
legislation to end the state of emergency, the government would seek to preserve
measures for "controlling dangerous ideologies and organizations, including
religious ones"—an obvious reference to the Brotherhood.[27] It was imagined
that al-Nahas would do only the bare minimum to redeem his preelection
promises. The king too was thought to be opposed to any relegalization of the
Ikhwan.[28] Thus, the first two months of the Wafd's return to power passed
without throwing "any more light on the Government's intentions as regards the
Moslem Brethren Society." Martial law and the dissolution of the group remained in force.[29]

Unsurprisingly in this context, Brotherhood disillusionment with the Wafd
grew. In lieu of formal restoration, the movement was rebuilt in the semiopen.
By the end of March 1950, US diplomats were reporting small-scale demonstrations by Ikhwan members, which heard cries of "down with Nahas." A
"growing antagonism" toward the Wafd was observable in Brotherhood ranks
due to the government's failure to reinstate the organization. The Americans
expressed concern that the Ikhwan might move fully into opposition, and perhaps even become involved in terrorism once more.[30] This being so, they were
relieved that the law, which officially ended Egypt's "state of siege" in April, extended certain provisions for an additional twelve months—one of which was

the proscription of the Brotherhood. It was further announced that the group would only be allowed to reemerge when a new societies law had been passed.[31]

On other issues, meanwhile, Western diplomats were somewhat less satisfied with the trajectory of the Wafdist government. They had been hopeful that on resuming the premiership, al-Nahas might be ready to finally resolve the Anglo-Egyptian dispute. Yet relations between the new government and the British had quickly soured. The Wafd had stood on an uncompromising nationalist platform and al-Nahas publicly demanded nothing less than a full British withdrawal and Egyptian control of Sudan.[32] This stance caused consternation in London. The retiring head of the Foreign Office's African department lamented al-Nahas's "distressing" lack of "political realism."[33] By the autumn of 1950, such optimism as had surrounded the return of the Wafd had all but dissipated. In September, British officials confided to their American counterparts that recent discussions with the Egyptians had proven "almost entirely negative" and the picture was one of "complete deadlock" (for which London, naturally, blamed the Cairo government).[34] The US Embassy in Egypt worried about the effect of the impasse, given that it paralleled rising domestic discontent.[35] The Americans observed there were "occasional rumors that [a] coup d'etat [was] in [the] offing."[36] Indeed interestingly, given subsequent events, there were suggestions that the Wafdist government might be challenged by an "unholy alliance" between the Ikhwan and "Army malcontents" (this might be described as a jaundiced but not wholly inaccurate description of the movement that seized power in July 1952). For the moment, no such alliance materialized; but elsewhere there were signs that the Kutla and Nationalist opposition parties might embrace the cause of the Brotherhood. US diplomats were disturbed by the growing volume of evidence, which pointed to the revival of a group that "regardless of its stated objectives in a printed form," was "known to be an extremist organization given to terroristic actions to achieve its real ends."[37] They anticipated that the Ikhwan would try to exploit any sign of social unrest, to resurface as a "potent political factor."[38] Evidently, this was not a prospect that the embassy welcomed.

In late 1950, however, the Americans could only watch in horror as the Wafdist interior minister, Fu'ad Sirag al-Din, indicated he might now countenance the legal reinstatement of the Brotherhood—to prevent it from linking up with his political opponents. The Wafdist press, it was observed, once again embarked on a "full-scale campaign" to show that the party was the "one and only true friend" of the Ikhwan.[39] Progovernment newspapers stressed that the Brotherhood was innocent of the charges previously leveled against it, which were described as the work of the devious and disreputable Sa'dist former administration.[40]

As reports emerged of concrete negotiations between Sirag al-Din and a senior Brotherhood figure, Sheikh Ahmad al-Baquri, the US Embassy continued to pay close attention to the Ikhwan.[41] A detailed translation of the Brotherhood's constitution was thus sent back to Washington.[42] Throughout the year, too, officials had tried to divine the internal workings of the group, especially with regard to the post–al-Banna succession.[43] A long memorandum in early November, for example, identified three broad camps within the Ikhwan. The first, under the former student leader Mustafa Mu'min, allegedly favored the reconstitution of the group under a new name, "Islamic Renaissance"; a second faction, by contrast, wished to retain the title of the "Ikhwan," but was willing to forswear political activity; and finally, a hard-line camp around Salih 'Ashmawi and Mahmud Labib apparently demanded the unconditional restoration of the Brotherhood in unadulterated form. American sources suggested that the latter, "legitimate" faction, which also included both Sheikh al-Baquri and 'Abd al-Hakim 'Abdin, the group's former secretary general, had taken control of the Ikhwan's executive and expelled Mu'min for engaging in unauthorized talks with the government. Ironically, these same people had then proceeded to initiate their own contacts with Sirag al-Din, in which al-Baquri played a central role.[44]

By this time, US officials were also aware of the fact that "a certain Hassan Ismail AL HIDAIBI Bey [sic]" had been chosen as the new leader of the Brotherhood.[45] In truth, the man to whom they referred, Hasan al-Hudaybi, had been elevated to the post of general guide in May 1950—at the initiative of senior Ikhwan members. As Salah Shadi recorded in his memoirs, this followed internal disagreements over who should succeed Hasan al-Banna, in which four others competed for the position: Ahmad al-Baquri (whom al-Banna himself had chosen as his short-term replacement); 'Abd al-Rahman al-Banna (Hasan's brother); Salih 'Ashmawi; and 'Abd al-Hakim 'Abdin. Amid ongoing dispute, al-Hudaybi—a judge who had served on Egypt's highest court (the Court of Cassation)—had emerged as a compromise candidate. He had initially refused the post, and only accepted on condition that he receive the unanimous backing of the Brotherhood's founding committee.[46] This was secured via a formal election some eighteen months later, and in October 1951, al-Hudaybi was publicly confirmed as leader.[47] According to Ghada Osman, a key part of al-Hudaybi's appeal to the Brotherhood was his establishment connections, particularly with the palace and the judiciary. His new colleagues hoped that this respectability might help to safeguard the group against renewed repression.[48]

US officials described al-Hudaybi as a "conservative and moderate individual of a very different type" than most of the Ikhwan's leaders. For this reason, they considered it "highly possible" that he was "only a front man" for more radical voices.[49] It was assumed that real internal power lay more with someone like Salih 'Ashmawi.[50] British assessments concurred in seeing 'Ashmawi as now the "strongest figure" inside the Brotherhood, with al-Hudaybi merely a "respectable figurehead."[51] The diplomats felt that the elevation of al-Hudaybi made little difference to the actual behavior of the Ikhwan. When representatives of the group participated in a meeting in Alexandria to mark the anniversary of the Balfour Declaration in early November 1950, Salih 'Ashmawi reiterated the Brotherhood's hard-line stance with regard to Israel, declaring: "We will take up the struggle and will take Arab Palestine away from the Jews by force."[52] The following month, the same man gave an interview to the Associated Press in which he insisted that the group would not stand "aloof" from politics. 'Ashmawi did go on to profess loyalty to the government (provided its members acted like "true Egyptian patriots"), and he disavowed the use of violence.[53] But half-hearted disclaimers of this kind did little to alleviate Western concerns. A December 1950 policy statement, produced by the US Office of Near Eastern Affairs, listed the Muslim Brotherhood as a manifestation of the "extreme rightist or ultra-nationalist elements," which might "exercise greater influence" in Egypt and form a "greater threat to [the] maintenance of a pro-Western orientation than the communists."[54] Early the next year, an embassy officer referred to the Ikhwan as a "reactionary and fascist" group, with a potential for violence and revolution.[55]

The British, meanwhile, had lobbied Interior Minister Fu'ad Sirag al-Din, who apparently promised that he would "crush the Ikhwan" with a "velvet glove." King Faruq similarly offered assurances that the Brothers were under surveillance and would be "rendered harmless" by the authorities. Even so, British ambassador Sir Ralph Stevenson foresaw "great potential danger" ahead. He feared that the Wafd's failings would create space for "political extremism," whether in the form of communism or the Muslim Brotherhood. In Stevenson's assessment, the recent "professions of moderation" on the part of the Ikhwan could not be taken "at face value." While the ambassador acknowledged that the Brothers had repudiated terrorism, he noted that they had not abandoned those from within their ranks who stood accused of terrorist crimes.[56]

As Stevenson's comments attest, the question of the Ikhwan's relationship with the rule of law returned to prominence at that time, in part because of the trial that began in December 1950 of those Muslim Brothers linked to the "jeep case." This was the episode that had done much to convince al-Nuqrashi's government that the Ikhwan posed a revolutionary threat that required a firm response.[57] Yet the group's leaders had always maintained that the arms and explosives to which they had been linked were intended solely for use in Palestine. Significantly, the trial saw the former mufti of Palestine give evidence on their behalf.[58] Senior army commanders also testified as to the "valuable military service" performed by the Brotherhood during the 1948–1949 war. The commander in chief of Egyptian forces during that conflict, General Fu'ad Sadeq, even vouched that the group's volunteers had fought like "heroes."[59]

In addition to this, a key part of the Brotherhood's defense was the claim that its proscription was the result of British intervention. Their lawyers produced putative British army records, which were said to prove their case, and these documents quickly became "part of the Ikhwan's standard mythology."[60] The embassy publicly dismissed the authenticity of the papers in question—though, interestingly, their internal account was rather less conclusive. In a dispatch to London, Ambassador Stevenson stated that their denials had been issued at the behest of former prime minister 'Abd al-Hadi, who wished to rebut the allegation. Yet he did not actually pronounce the documents to be false.[61] It also seems clear that US diplomats were not entirely persuaded by British disclaimers. And the Egyptian press carried a healthy debate over the veracity or otherwise of the documents.[62]

Ultimately, in March 1951, only nineteen of the thirty-two accused in the "jeep trial" were found guilty and these mostly received short prison terms of one or two years. A majority of the defendants were released, having already served their time. Among the few to be more severely punished were government officials Mahmud al-Sayid Khalil al-Sabbagh and Mustafa Mashur—the latter, a future general guide of the Ikhwan—who each received sentences of three years hard labor.[63] Even these punishments seemed light, though, given the nature of the offenses. The court's lenient verdict was based in part on the belief that much of the evidence against the accused had been collected improperly and by violent methods. Of greater import still, was the fact the judgment explicitly stated that the Brothers were "not criminals by profession." While finding that they had "done wrong" and needed to be taught a "lesson," the court took into consideration "that they were filled with noble aspirations of which the first was the attainment by their helpless people of its political aims." On this basis, the judge opted to "exercise clemency."[64]

To the Brotherhood, such an outcome was a huge victory. Ghada Osman later suggested that the "euphoria" of the Brothers over the result was "indescribable."[65]

The front page of their newspaper *al-Da'wa* led with the simple headline, "Innocent!"[66] The memoirs of various Brotherhood members likewise echoed the view that the verdict was a great vindication. Salah Shadi, for example, felt the case proved that the Ikhwan was not a terrorist organization but rather a group committed merely "to the liberation of the Nile Valley and all Islamic countries." The violence to which they had been linked, Shadi said, was merely a product of the "new spirit" that the Brotherhood had inculcated in the "umma," which demanded a response to political and social injustice.[67]

British diplomats were appalled by the court's "derisory" verdicts. They too saw the judgment as, "to all intents and purposes" an exoneration of the Brotherhood and a "condemnation" of the security authorities. Ambassador Stevenson reckoned that the "prestige" of the Ikhwan had "increased considerably" as a result.[68] More soberly, US officials noted that the verdict was "scarcely" unfavorable to the Brotherhood.[69] Of particular concern from the Western perspective was the way in which animosity toward the British had been accepted as a mitigating factor by the judge. The British Embassy reflected that this was sadly "symptomatic of a malaise deep-rooted in Egyptian life and politics [emphasis in original]," by which violence was not subject to "moral disapprobation."[70] After all, the Brotherhood's defense counsel had apparently asked provocatively in court whether "British Imperialism and the foreign domination to which Moslem countries are subjected" could be fought "merely with pamphlets and speeches."[71] As far as the British could see, the legal outcome offered a resounding "no" to that question, with all that that entailed for the legitimacy of anti-British violence. (Observant diplomats later remarked wryly that the president of the court who delivered the judgments, Ahmad Kamel Bey, was chosen by the Ikhwan to lead discussions on various social issues—proof to their mind of the partiality of the judicial process. Invoking Lewis Carroll, one of them commented knowingly that "the Snark was a Boojum you see!")[72]

The courtroom drama had been paralleled by a wider surge in nationalist feeling across Egypt in late 1950–early 1951. As a result of the ongoing stalemate in negotiations, the British had suspended all arms shipments to Egypt. In retaliation, and out of broader frustration with the slow progress of talks, Prime Minister al-Nahas publicly threatened to abrogate the Anglo-Egyptian Treaty during the course of an uncompromising "speech from the throne" in November 1950.[73] At this time, both the British and the Americans still believed there was little alternative to the Wafd; but the confrontational path taken by al-Nahas's government disturbed them greatly.[74]

The first months of the new year brought a further rush of anti-British rhetoric within the Egyptian press.[75] The Brotherhood was a leading purveyor of this invective, with the group's newspaper stressing the iniquitous role played by "the English," not just in Egypt but also across the region (in Iraq, Palestine, Sudan, Jordan, Libya, India, Pakistan, and Iran).[76] A new take was provided on Britain's alleged historical animus against Islam by reference to nineteenth-century prime minister William Gladstone, who was said to have told the House of Commons, while holding up a copy of the Qur'an, that there would be "no peace for the empire . . . as long as this book exists."[77] This anecdote would become a familiar one in Brotherhood circles, offered as proof of Britain's abiding enmity toward Islam.[78] To it was added the supposed statement of General Allenby on entering Jerusalem, that "today the Crusades ended." "The English," according to the Brotherhood, were driven by a deep-seated hatred of the Muslim world generally, and Egypt in particular. They viewed the latter, it was argued, as the "leader of the Islamic world and the heart of Arabism," and for this reason, they subjugated Egypt in order to dominate Islam.[79] As far as the Brothers were concerned, the contemporary British presence in the Canal Zone was merely the latest phase in England's long war against the religion.

Increasingly, the Ikhwan seemed determined to initiate hostilities against the imperialist enemy. In February 1951, the Brotherhood joined a "national front" comprising representatives from the militant parties such as Young Egypt and al-Watan.[80] This umbrella organization advocated more concrete action to secure Egypt's demands and the effect was to narrow the options available to the government. When the British launched a fresh set of proposals that they hoped might secure a settlement in April, al-Nahas rejected them out of hand, to popular acclaim.[81]

As the deadlock dragged on in Cairo, Western observers were also troubled about the trajectory of events across the wider region. Of particular importance were developments in Tehran. In March 1951, the Iranian parliament had voted to nationalize the British-owned Anglo-Iranian Oil Company against a background of rising instability and political violence. Many felt that the episode served as a powerful fillip to other nationalist movements.[82] Certainly, the Brothers were among those watching Iran closely. They imagined British policy there to be an extension of the West's "crusader war" of religion against the Muslim East.[83] Moreover, the lesson they took from Iranian actions was the fact that "the English only respect force" and that there was therefore no point in pursuing negotiations. Instead, the Brotherhood preached the virtues of "jihad and struggle."[84]

This was also the message that the group continued to advance with regard to Palestine. In 1951, Kamil al-Sharif called on Muslims to confront the new state of Israel with a twin-pronged approach, defined by an economic boycott on the one hand, and the launching of guerrilla warfare on the other. According to al-Sharif, the great mistake that had been made in 1948–1949 was to have handed matters over to regular armies. The Arabs, he argued, needed to follow the example of partisan fighters in Yugoslavia, France, China, and Indo-China, and initiate an insurgent campaign to "exhaust Israel and destroy its resources."[85] Clearly, there could be no question of accepting the existence of Israel. The Brothers still blamed the British for the loss of Palestine and claimed there was an "English conspiracy" to try to normalize the status quo.[86] They held the Americans, too, at least partly responsible, seeing them as in cahoots with the Jews in an effort to bring a peace settlement.[87] In the years that followed, the Ikhwan remained committed to combating the "conspiracy" that had brought a "plague of Jews" to Jerusalem, where the "battle of life or death" was being waged. The Brotherhood insisted there was no solution to the conflict in Palestine "except by force, to answer arms with arms and aggression with fire."[88]

In light of this militant rhetoric, the CIA worried that the Brothers might resort once more to an "assassination-type of politics." Agency officials speculated that the group's increased "dissatisfaction" with the Cairo government could lead to a resumption of "terrorist activities" in Egypt.[89] The embassy likewise voiced reservations about the ability of the authorities to contain the Ikhwan.[90] By now, there were reports that Brotherhood propagandists were increasingly active across the country and the British had concluded that the Ikhwan had "completely abandoned the pretence" that its existence was "clandestine."[91] New publications had been developed to replace those that had fallen foul of the censor. Salih 'Ashmawi, for instance, founded and edited the weekly al-Mabahith, which served as a vehicle for the writings of figures like Sa'id Ramadan, Sheikh Muhammad al-Ghazali, and Fathi Osman, who promulgated Brotherhood ideas about Islamic socialism, social justice, and of course, national independence. In January 1951, 'Ashmawi also launched the weekly al-Da'wa newspaper. Significantly, this latest organ, which blended social and political criticism with religious insight, received an official license from the Interior Ministry, despite there being no doubt as to its affiliation.[92] Al-Da'wa wasted no time in demanding the restoration of the Brotherhood and criticizing the Wafd for having broken its promises to the group.[93] In one typical article, 'Ashmawi asked provocatively who benefited from the "Cold war" being waged on the

Ikhwan, answering his own question by reference to the "Zionists," "imperialists," "communists," and "the corrupt."[94]

The long-awaited end to martial law and the expiry of the ban on the Brotherhood finally arrived on 1 May 1951. *Al-Da'wa* issued a defiant statement of the Ikhwan's undiminished commitment to its goals.[95] Other newspapers reported that branches of the group had assembled in mosques across Egypt to mark the moment. They had then marched to their various local offices to erect posters announcing their return. In Cairo, only a heavy police presence had prevented Salih 'Ashmawi from leading a procession of Brothers to their Helmia Square headquarters. US officials remarked that the "excellent discipline" of the Brotherhood was once more in evidence, as was the "growing anxiety" with which the Wafd Party viewed "this Frankenstein monster from which it has but recently been forced by political necessity to remove the chains."[96]

At the last minute, Interior Minister Sirag al-Din apparently had contemplated an attempt to extend the ban on the Brotherhood, only to deem this unfeasible.[97] Nonetheless, he did secure the passage of a new law on societies (Law No. 66 of 26 April 1951), by which the Wafd hoped to force the group to adhere to "democratic principles."[98] Among the strictures of this legislation was a prohibition on societies recruiting felons or minors. Additional regulations required societies: to register with the authorities full details about their objectives, members, and sources of funding; to remain firmly within the limits of their declared objectives; and to refrain from any kind of paramilitary organization. All of these provisions appeared to have been written with the Brotherhood specifically in mind, to provide the authorities with greater control over the group.[99]

Unsurprisingly, the Ikhwan reacted strongly to the new law, leading British officials to comment that the "truce" between the Brothers and the Wafd was well and truly "over." The Brotherhood held a demonstration "in strength" outside the Egyptian parliament and submitted a petition decrying the injustice of the societies legislation. Its leaders averred that the whole idea of differentiating between social, religious, and political purposes was of Western origin, and incompatible with Islam. The Ikhwan proclaimed its intention to flout the regulations. Naturally, British diplomats pondered what this might mean: whether the Brotherhood would seek to circumvent the law by declaring itself a political party; or whether it would in fact return to terrorist methods.[100] Similarly, the Americans surmised that the Ikhwan had three options: to reorganize as a political party, foregoing other activities; to operate as a cultural society under the new legislation, thereby forswearing politics; or, to continue its "sub rosa" existence in defiance of the government.[101]

Sirag al-Din, meanwhile, insisted that he was "not in the least nervous" about the reemergence of the Ikhwan. He declared himself convinced that the group had truly changed its ways and argued that, even if he were proved wrong, the new societies law would stop the Brothers from becoming a "really dangerous nuisance." The British, though, still harbored doubts. In their judgment, while the Ikhwan might not now possess a leader of al-Banna's caliber (al-Hudaybi was again dismissed as a "mere figurehead"), Salih 'Ashmawi was thought "fanatical and, in many ways, irresponsible." The diplomats feared that Sirag al-Din might be "under estimating" the potential of the Brotherhood to cause trouble.[102]

The Americans took a slightly different view. They concluded that the Wafd was in fact capable of dealing with the Brotherhood should that be necessary.[103] After Senate elections in early May, it was noted that the Wafd enjoyed absolute majorities in both houses of parliament, and there was a feeling that the party was "in [the] strongest position yet to deal not only with normal opposition but also Communist and Moslem Brotherhood [groups] on [the] extremist fringe."[104] Indeed, American officials suspected that some in al-Nahas's ministry favored a tougher line and wished to crush the Ikhwan altogether.[105]

The British too recognized that the prospect of renewed confrontation was "not without its attractions" to the Egyptian authorities.[106] In the immediate term, no conflict materialized. Instead, the two sides settled down to a renewed period of "shadow boxing," the end result of which remained hard to predict. The US Embassy spoke for many, however, when it stated that the eventual outcome would be "as important to the long term orientation of Egypt both domestically and internationally as any other single political factor."[107]

Drift toward Conflict

In May 1951, a report in the *Economist* on the "undeclared deadlock" in Anglo-Egyptian negotiations conveyed alarm at the reemergence of the Muslim Brotherhood "menace," pointing to the group's "xenophobic and strongly anti-Jewish tendencies." "At present," the author wrote, "this powerful political and religious movement is uneasily controlled by the Government, but at any moment, should the Brothers disagree with the Wafd, they may pursue a policy of their own and attempt to achieve their ends by acts of violence."[108] That summer, most

Western officials presumed that Egypt was on the brink of a new bout of instability. The US Embassy recorded the existence in the country of trained and well-armed "guerrilla bands," and identified the Ikhwan as one of several groups planning acts of terrorism and sabotage against the British presence in the Suez Canal Zone.[109]

By July, the Cairo government itself appeared increasingly unsettled by the possibility of disorder.[110] That month, the authorities banned demonstrations to commemorate the 1882 bombardment of Alexandria by the British, which had been jointly organized by different opposition groups including left-wing Wafdists, nationalists, socialists, and the Ikhwan.[111] Typically, the Brothers attributed the event's cancellation to British intervention, denouncing the interior minister and other politicians as "carbon copies of [historical] lackeys of imperialism and creatures of the English." They were declared to be the "first enemy" of the "struggling nation" and its youth.[112] Despite the shrill rhetoric, American diplomats believed that, on this occasion, the Ikhwan had been anxious to avoid violence, recognizing that the government might exploit it to label them "terroristic." Yet this reserve was judged to be merely tactical: as "experienced agitators," the Brothers knew the "value" of "waiting until the right moment to introduce violence."[113] Thus, while the episode on the one hand could be seen to reveal the strength of the government (in that it successfully forestalled disturbances), on the other, it was also read as evidence of the latent power of the Brotherhood and other "discontented elements." With the treaty question unresolved, the possibility for unrest seemed ever present.

Subsequently, US diplomats reported on a conversation with Major Alfred Sansom of the British Embassy, who told them he "did not like the smell of things" which were "boiling up for trouble." In particular, Sansom said he was "very distrustful" of the rejuvenated Ikhwan and he predicted a new wave of political violence.[114] Sir Cecil Campbell, one of the "pillars of Anglo-Egypt" likewise contacted the British ambassador to express disquiet at the atmosphere of "tension" in Cairo. The Brotherhood and other groups, such as Young Egypt and the Young Men's Muslim Association (YMMA), were said to be plotting to "start a general conflagration" against the British, the monarchy, and the entire "established regime." In this endeavor, Campbell claimed, they were more coordinated and confident than previously.[115] He was not the only one to experience premonitions of impending disaster. Additional diplomatic reportage spoke of a general recrudescence of extremist organizations, many of them ultranationalist and anti-British.[116] Police summaries obtained by the US Embassy indicated a rapid expansion in Ikhwan membership.[117] The group also intensified its demands for the immediate cancellation of the 1936 treaty.[118] It decried any attempt to restart a process of negotiation as tantamount to "servile waiting."[119] The government, the Brothers asserted, should either "lead the people in their jihad" or make way for those who would.[120] It seemed as if the only thing holding them back was their uncertainty over the Wafd's likely reaction. The Brotherhood said that it wished to know the view of the government before launching "guerrilla war" against "the English." *Al-Da'wa* recalled the "stab in the back" the Ikhwan had received in 1948, when they had engaged in jihad in Palestine; they feared that al-Nahas and his colleagues might do the same "to please their masters the imperialists and occupiers." It was therefore imperative, the Brothers stated ominously, that the people "purify the internal front first."[121] By September 1951, the group was openly calling for jihad and distinguishing between the "camp of the corrupt rulers" and the "camp of the strugglers."[122]

In the context of this seemingly inexorable rhetorical escalation, US officials described Egyptian politics as being in a state of "suspended animation." The prevailing situation of calm was seen as "totally artificial," hiding the fact that "forces" beneath the surface were "building toward [an] inevitable denouement unless some entirely new factor" entered the scene.[123] A further lengthy assessment concluded that the "factors of instability in Egypt outbalance by far the factors of stability." The Ikhwan was identified as a major threat that blended violence, xenophobia, and fanaticism. At the same time, it was acknowledged that the focal point for all discontent continued to be the British presence.[124]

By this time, it seems clear that UK officials had all but lost faith in the capacity and performance of the Wafd. The prime minister himself seemed to embody the torpor of his administration. There were rumors that the seventy-year-old al-Nahas was in increasingly poor health and spent only an hour and a half per day in his office.[125] Ambassador Stevenson regretted that the "state of the country left much to be desired." Corruption and nepotism were said to be rife, while economic and social conditions worsened amid mounting concerns about public security.[126] To British minds, it was this domestic crisis that was the true cause of the instability in Egypt. Stevenson argued that the *real* issue was not a nationalist one, but rather the "ineptitude and blatant corruption" of a Wafdist government that was incapable of reversing "the deterioration of the standard of living." He postulated that the local politicians sought to escape the discontent of the masses by telling them that "their chains" were "made in England." A similar explanation was said to account for the appeal of groups like the Ikhwan: "The Moslem Brotherhood, whose fire is really directed at the moral rottenness of their own countrymen, hang a Union Jack over their target, and other extremists do the same."[127] The ambassador's analysis found echo in London, where there was a belief that "public opinion" did not really exist in Egypt. Most of the people, it was suggested, were actually "indifferent" to the presence of British troops.[128]

On another occasion, Stevenson rued the fact that the Americans seemed unable to grasp the degree of "demagogic exaggeration" in which a "minority of professional politicians" indulged in Egypt. Washington was too inclined, he averred, to "admit the thesis of those Egyptian leaders and publicists" who had "founded their careers on the simple demand for 'independence' or 'evacuation.'"[129] Assessments of this kind fueled British unhappiness with the stance of the United States. Time and again, Foreign Office officials complained about what they saw as the unhelpfulness of the Americans who, in their view, did not truly understand political realities in Cairo. To British eyes, the United States was too willing to nourish nationalist demands. In fact, throughout this period, the United States did continue to encourage a settlement on lines broadly favorable to London—even sending George McGhee to Egypt in early April 1951, to try to persuade al-Nahas to accept a new treaty. Yet it is perhaps fair to say that the Americans were often frustrated by British intransigence and their "condescension" toward the "Gippies."[130]

With Anglo-Egyptian relations at an impasse, the situation received another jolt from developments in Iran. In September, the Mossadegh government ordered troops to seize the Abadan Refinery complex. The apparent impotence of the British government in the face of the move only served to encourage those in Egypt who hoped for more dramatic action locally.[131] The same month, Ambassador Stevenson wrote to Interior Minister Sirag al-Din to complain about the Wafdist government's failure to prevent press agitation in favor of anti-British "guerrilla" or "irregular" warfare. Various articles were said to be inciting the murder of British subjects; and a member of the Royal Army Service Corps had already been attacked by a mob. Interestingly, one journalist singled out as being of special concern was a "Maitre Sayed Kotb [Sayyid Qutb]," whose articles in the Brotherhood's *al-Da'wa* newspaper were judged particularly egregious.[132]

With the atmosphere worsening, internal British discussions were held about the possibility of trying to persuade the king to dismiss the government. Ambassador Stevenson reckoned that Faruq's reluctance might be overcome by "making his flesh creep" about the likelihood of revolution. The aim would be to bring about a new administration of "moderate leaders" who would be prepared to initiate real internal reform and accept a settlement of the Anglo-Egyptian dispute.[133] Before anything might be done about this, however, the

Wafdist government acted to transform the political environment, adopting a more confrontational approach to the British question.[134]

On 8 October 1951, while speaking to the Chamber of Deputies, al-Nahas announced Egypt's unilateral abrogation of both the 1936 Treaty of Friendship and the 1899 Sudanese Condominium. The move was wildly popular. The Egyptian parliament endorsed it unanimously and US diplomats noted that even the most "westernized" sections of the population supported the decision.[135] Protestors filled Cairo's streets, chanting "Long Live Mossadegh, Long Live Nahas."[136] In spite of this, the British were unmoved. Foreign Secretary Herbert Morrison told the Americans that withdrawal was "unthinkable" and that the British would do whatever was required to hold the Suez Base.[137] In Washington, Dean Acheson demurred, but essentially backed the British stance. The United States was ready, he stated somewhat awkwardly, to provide "full political and diplomatic support to measures necessary (but which do not go beyond what is necessary) for the purposes of protecting the Suez Base and keeping the Canal open."[138] With a degree of evident cynicism, local diplomats commented that Egypt was "currently enjoying [a] xenophobic emotional jag with typical lack of thought for [the] inevitable morning-after hangover."[139]

The extent to which Western governments had failed to appreciate the significance of abrogation was reflected in the fact that, within days, they proceeded to present the Egyptian government with their latest proposals for settling the treaty quarrel. These turned on an attempt to bind Egypt into a scheme for regional collective self-defense, the "Middle East Command," which would effectively legitimate the maintenance of a British presence on the Suez Canal.[140] Al-Nahas rejected the scheme immediately. The Egyptian government insisted that only full British evacuation and the unity of the Nile valley would be acceptable. Moreover, there were suggestions from various quarters that the time for talking might now have passed.

The War of the Canal Zone

Abrogation of the treaty set the stage for the so-called War of the Canal Zone.[141] This short and oft-forgotten conflict saw attacks on British troops, acts of sabotage, and the withdrawal of civilian labor from military installations.[142] From the beginning, Western observers regarded the Muslim Brotherhood as the "main enemy" of the British.[143] Though officials considered it unlikely that the group would be able to "corral" sufficient force to present a serious

threat to entrenched military positions, they were seen as "capable and de-
sirous" of being a constant source of "irritation and menace to individuals and
property."[144] The CIA believed that the "fanatic Moslem Brotherhood" was
ready to initiate a "program of violence and terrorism," and to this end, had
acquired twenty-five machine guns. Furthermore, in an echo of earlier
analyses, the agency claimed to have "evidence" of Brotherhood contacts with
communists.[145]

Clearly, British officials shared many of these misgivings. They were aware
that the Brotherhood had called for the formation of "Liberation Armies" and
"Struggle Squads."[146] The Ikhwan headed a list of "extremist elements in Egyptian politics" compiled by the embassy at this time. On the one hand, the British
deemed the group to be weaker than three years earlier and, consequently, less
able to mount an "insurrection"; on the other, it was thought to retain "a countrywide organisation and mass support." The Brothers were also said to possess "a
cadre of trained terrorists" and "probably a fair amount of armament."[147] As
such, they were identified as "likely to be the chief perpetrators of terrorist acts
either in the Canal Zone or elsewhere." Mandarins in Whitehall viewed the
group as "the most important single extremist alternative to the Wafd."[148]

In mid-October 1951, the UK Embassy sent a note to the Egyptian government protesting against the resolutions that had been passed at a recent congress of Brotherhood students. These begged the authorities to announce a state
of war between Egypt and Britain, and brand the latter's troops "enemy forces."
The Ikhwan demanded that its members be allowed to carry firearms and be
given indemnity for attacks on the British. They also urged the government to
create a "national guard" of some sixteen thousand, drawn from veterans of the
fighting in Palestine. Finally, the Brothers wanted an end to all political, cultural, and economic contacts with the British. If the Wafd implemented these
measures, then the Ikhwan promised to stand behind them in the "struggle." If
they did not, however, then the Wafd was to be seen as "collaborating with the
British," with all that this might imply.[149]

Threats of this kind might have been dismissed as mere rhetoric but for the
fact that the Brotherhood was simultaneously involved in efforts to generate
street demonstrations around the country.[150] At the end of October, for example,
the British received reports that members of the Ikhwan had incited an anti-
British riot in Bilbeis, in the delta province of Sharqiya. In an echo of earlier
obsessions, this had targeted the employees of a school run by the "Egyptian
General Mission" organization and threatened the lives of five British people.[151]
Subsequently, "armed parties" of the Brotherhood were said to be manning

road blocks in the vicinity of Bilbeis and El-Abaseya.[152] There were rumors too that the Suez chapter of the Ikhwan was implicated in the intimidation of labor contractors working for the British.[153] As Salah Shadi later recalled, this was a key feature of the Brotherhood's approach: to prevent Egyptian workers from servicing the military bases in the Canal Zone.[154]

Perhaps most worrying from a British perspective were the growing appeals for physical-force jihad. The Ikhwan had always been skeptical about negotiations, believing that Egyptians should not bargain for that which was naturally theirs. To their minds, such dialogue was a shameful process. What was required instead was the direct assertion of clearly articulated, absolute rights. According to Yusuf al-Qaradawi, al-Banna had been prepared to give negotiations a chance, but only within a limited time frame and on the assumption that they had a realistic chance of delivering Egypt's goals. In the event that this did not happen, he felt that the process should be terminated, the treaty canceled unilaterally, and a state of war declared; the government would then have a duty to place life on a war footing—economically, socially, and politically.[155] In the eyes of the Brotherhood, this moment had now arrived and armed struggle to free Egypt from ongoing occupation was therefore entirely legitimate.[156] One imam from the group reportedly instructed his followers to "knock on [the] gates of Heaven with British skulls."[157]

The memoirs and accounts of numerous Muslim Brothers reflect the belief that the Canal Zone conflict was "their" struggle, in which they fought actively, while the rest of the population stood idly by, content to act only "symbolically."[158] Hasan Dawh, for instance, wrote: "I say with complete impartiality: the Brotherhood bore the burden of this battle and bore it with supreme bravery and courage." By Dawh's reckoning, everything that followed thereafter—including the revolution of July 1952—could not have happened without the "blows of the youth of the Ikhwan" in the Canal Zone, which reduced the throne to "rubble" and brought the "great decay of the British Empire in Egypt."[159]

Veterans of the Palestine conflict such as Kamil al-Sharif, Sheikh Muhammad al-Farghali, and Mahmud 'Abduh led the Brotherhood campaign in the Canal Zone, alongside newer faces like 'Abd al-Qadir 'Awda and Yusuf Tal'at.[160] According to Hasan Dawh, planning for conflict actually began in the Ikhwan student branch before being taken over by both the Special Apparatus (under the leadership now of Tal'at) and the "Sections Unit" (under Salah Shadi).[161] Even then, the group's younger members continued to play a critical role, with the Brotherhood enlisting and training volunteers within the Cairo and Alexandria Universities. There, Abbas al-Sissi remembered, they found many people filled with a "higher Islamic spirit."[162] The aim of the Ikhwan was to channel this spirit into "long-term guerrilla war."[163] Their success can be judged from the fact that many subsequent leaders of the Brotherhood were first drawn to the group at this time. Yusuf Nada was one of those who claimed to have received military training at Alexandria University in 1951.[164] The future general guide Muhammad Mahdi 'Akef was especially active in recruiting fighters at Ibrahim Pasha University (now Ain Shams) in Cairo.[165] One of the men who 'Akef trained, 'Adel Ghanim, became a celebrated Brotherhood "martyr" after an attack on a British checkpoint in el-Abaseya.[166] Among the others who responded to the call to jihad inside Egypt's universities, either as part of the Ikhwan or as members of the broader student movement, were Yusuf al-Qaradawi, Ahmad al-Assal, and Yasser Arafat.[167] An outside observer caustically noted the influence that the Brothers enjoyed on campuses, where they had proven formidable organizers, "in a country not notable for discipline."[168] Altogether, the Ikhwan recorded that five of its student members (including Ghanim and the aforementioned Shahin and al-Manisi) were killed during the "War of the Canal."[169]

From within the Suez Canal Zone, British military intelligence reported "increasing evidence of preparations for terrorist activity by Ikhwan and Socialist Egyptian Party [Young Egypt] extremists." Estimates suggested that around one thousand members of the Brotherhood were being given weapons training.[170] The British military authorities judged it essential that such preparations be disrupted, but expressed their lack of confidence in the Egyptian authorities. Indeed, they believed that the foreign minister, Muhammad Salah al-Din, was actively encouraging "Ikhwan extremists." They asked Whitehall for authorization to act unilaterally to arrest "ringleaders" and troublemakers.[171] In London, the head of the African department at the Foreign Office, Roger Allen, likewise advocated preemptive action, particularly against the Brothers, who were said to be "inciting the Egyptian people to acts of terrorism against the British."[172]

Consequently, the chiefs of staff were told that commanders could at "discretion arrest and detain ringleaders of I. E. M. [Ikhwan el-Muslimin] and other terrorist organisations" operating in the Canal Zone—though they were urged to utilize these powers sparingly and to be mindful of international opinion.[173] Senior military figures seemed disinclined to heed such reservations. The commander of British forces in Egypt, Lieutenant General Sir George Erskine, would later state that to label their opponents "terrorists" was actually "much too complimentary"; he preferred the term "thugs." In his assessment, the fighters were recruited "largely from the criminal classes in the delta and the Canal Zone," as well as among the students in Cairo.[174] That being the case, Erskine felt a hard-line response was entirely merited.

Erskine's analysis was echoed, to a degree, by those diplomats who presumed that the "peaceable" sections of the Egyptian population were "unanimous" in seeing the Brotherhood as a "danger to law and order."[175] Yet others clearly recognized that the Ikhwan was in step with mainstream public opinion. Richard Nolte, the future American ambassador to Egypt, then at the Institute of Current World Affairs, had arrived in the country just as the unrest began, and in a series of letters back to the United States, Nolte offered his own impression of the disorders that afflicted the canal cities of Port Said and Ismailia.[176] He observed that there was a near universal belief among literate Egyptians that "the English must go."[177] Further evidence to this effect came with the formation of a cross-party umbrella body committed to advancing the national cause, which included representatives of the Kutla and Nationalist Parties, the YMMA, the Socialist Party, the Wafd, Constitutional Liberals, and various other luminaries and government officials. Salih 'Ashmawi and Hasan al-Hudaybi participated for the Muslim Brotherhood. This "national pact" supported abrogation, opposed the resumption of negotiations, and called for "struggle" against the British.[178] Elsewhere, some religious scholars had ruled that the "murder of British imperialists" was permissible.[179] The rector of al-Azhar also published a statement recommending that Egyptians assist those working for "liberation from imperialism," on the grounds that "every nation, [and] every individual, has the right to resist aggression."[180]

The government, meanwhile, openly blamed British troops for escalating tensions by their provocative behavior in the Suez Canal Zone. The Egyptians even suspected that the British were planning to separate that region formally from the rest of the country in a "flagrant aggression against the territorial integrity, independence and sovereignty of Egypt and a juridical and political aggression under the United Nations charter."[181] The British rejected these accusations and insisted that it was the responsibility of the Egyptian government to protect all foreign lives and property, and prevent "the promulgation of . . . incitements to murder."[182] As far as the British were concerned, it was the Egyptians who were failing to meet *their* obligations, not the other way around.[183] The military, in particular, felt that transgressions by the Cairo authorities should be punished and threatened to cut off oil supplies to the capital.[184]

Such tactics, however, caused consternation in various diplomatic quarters. US ambassador Jefferson Caffery, for example, was firmly opposed to a punitive approach. He claimed that his British counterpart, Sir Ralph Stevenson,

largely agreed with him and was in "black despair" at the policies of his own
military.[185] Though perhaps overstated, Caffery's assessment carries an air of
truth; for although Stevenson wrote to Lieutenant General Erskine praising his
handling of the crisis, his telegrams back to London evinced a far more skeptical tone.[186] These made plain his dissatisfaction with what he saw as an absence of any "long term policy."[187] The ambassador also spoke of his fear that
"ineradicable bitterness" was being stored up in Anglo-Egyptian relations. The
simple truth, he said, was that the treaty had been de facto abrogated and
the "evacuation" of British troops had become "a truly national sentiment."[188]
Stevenson contended that for this reason, any settlement would have to adjust
to the new political realities.

Against this, leading British military commanders held to an intransigent
line. Erskine was unrepentant and disagreed with the subsequent decision to
relax oil restrictions on the Delta.[189] A proclamation was even prepared by which
Erskine would announce the creation of a military government to administrate
areas "in and adjacent to" the Suez Canal Zone, which envisaged the use of military courts and a dusk-to-dawn curfew.[190] Ultimately, this proclamation was
never issued. But events in the Canal Zone became "progressively more serious" as the weeks progressed, with November bringing the first British military casualties. Ismailia proved to be the flash point. Immediately after abrogation, the city had witnessed major riots that led to the deployment of British
troops. The Egyptian authorities also sent their own reinforcements in the form
of the "Bulak al-Nizam," the auxiliary police. In the words of Erskine, tension
between these rival forces constituted a "potentially explosive element in an already sufficiently inflammable situation."[191] It did not take long for the mixture
to ignite. On November 17 and 18, three soldiers were killed in a succession of
clashes between the British army and the Egyptian police (whose own casualties were more numerous).[192] In the aftermath, Erskine ordered the evacuation
of all military families from Ismailia and declared the town out-of-bounds to
his troops.[193]

By the start of December, "home-made bombs" were being used regularly in
the Canal Zone and "Liberation Battalion" attacks and sabotage became endemic. The activities of the "Bulak al-Nizam" were a particular irritation to the
British and there were again fatal clashes between the army and members of
the police.[194] The situation in key cities like Ismailia, Suez, Port Said, and even
Alexandria was said to be especially bad.[195] An attempt to bolster the army's
position at one vulnerable spot led to the notorious demolition of the village of
Kafr Ahmad Abdu near Suez, which further poisoned the atmosphere.[196] By

this stage, too, the British were struggling to cope with the near total withdrawal of Egyptian labor from the Canal Zone (only about 10 percent of the total was estimated to remain by mid-December). The region's commercial life all but ground to a halt. As Lieutenant General Erskine reflected, the "long suffering" army was forced to tolerate difficult conditions, "much longer than was reasonable."[197]

There were, as already outlined, strong suspicions in British quarters that certain Egyptian ministers such as Salah al-Din favored a "full-blown alliance" with the Brotherhood, which would give the latter "arms and a free hand" against the British.[198] Mixed signals were also emanating from Interior Minister Sirag el-Din. On occasion, he was said to be "flirting" with extremists like the Ikhwan.[199] Other reports suggested he was wary of the threat the Brotherhood might pose to the government itself. Still, there was speculation that the Wafd would supply "limited quantities of arms" to the Ikhwan so that they could let "off steam" in the Canal Zone. Pro-British Egyptian sources informed the embassy that the Brothers had already received weapons from the Cairo government (which was also said to be sending funds to Young Egypt).[200] A joint UK-US assessment concluded that the Egyptian authorities had connived in the formation of the "liberation battalions." It was believed the Wafd had settled on an approach that combined "administrative obstruction" of the British, with "incitement to terrorism." The greatest danger in this, from the perspective of Western officials, was that it might lead to a loss of government control. They imagined a scenario in which countrywide dissatisfaction—on socioeconomic as well as national issues—could "develop into an insurrectionary or even revolutionary movement if guerrilla warfare in the 'national cause' were to be seriously prosecuted or if the central government's control of security were to break down."[201]

Other Western observers reckoned the Egyptian government to be caught on the horns of a dilemma. Richard Nolte eloquently captured this when he noted that al-Nahas was "unable to 'put up,' and unwilling to 'shut up.' " Harsh rhetoric and complaints about British iniquities, he said, had been accompanied by little meaningful preparation for action.[202] With regard to the liberation battalions, there was a recognition that the Wafd could not repress organizations supporting its own anti-British policy; equally, the government was thought to appreciate the threat that "private armies" posed to public security.[203] Evidence of the potential for instability came in early December, with violent antigovernment demonstrations in Cairo.[204] Soon afterward, Interior Minister Sirag al-Din announced that the government intended to regulate the liberation battalions, bringing them under the authority of the Egyptian security forces. Yet, the effectiveness of this move was diluted by a concurrent decision to allow all Egyptians to carry arms, on notification of the Interior Ministry.[205]

Drawing on a familiar analogy, commentators believed that the Egyptian government, like its Iranian counterpart before it, now faced the "Frankenstein monster" of contemporary Middle Eastern nationalism. It was assumed that this was, at root, deeply antiforeign and propelled by "social discontent." The fear was that it might provoke a full-blown revolution.[206] US diplomats described the key challenge for the Cairo authorities as being "to take action which [would] satisfy public opinion . . . but which [would] not . . . result [in] more harm to Egyptian interests than to British."[207] In Washington, officials grew anxious that Egypt might be lost to "chaos and anarchy."[208]

A Deal with the Brotherhood?

With the situation going from bad to worse, British diplomats again pondered whether they might seek to effect a "change of Government" in Egypt. At a bare minimum, they felt some kind of "severe jolt" was needed. As things stood, officials found it "impossible" to imagine that the Wafd would ever deliver an agreement compatible with British defense desiderata (which continued to be based on a revised version of the Middle East Command scheme).[209] From the start of the crisis, the British military authorities had argued that there was no prospect of reaching a settlement with al-Nahas. In their view, the only feasible alternative was an administration based on "the King and his armed forces." To this end, British commanders urged the adoption of a policy that would bring the "complete collapse" of the Wafdist position. They even floated the idea that troops might be sent to reoccupy the Delta and thereby "facilitate" the establishment of a new government.[210] The CIA recorded that while most Whitehall officials were unwilling to contemplate so drastic a step, they too hoped for a changing of the guard in Cairo that "might bring a more moderate group of Egyptians to power."[211]

Remarkably, during December 1951 and January 1952, one possibility contemplated, albeit briefly, was that the Muslim Brotherhood, hitherto seen as an integral part of the problem, might actually be the solution. In arriving at this point, officials were in part reacting to what they saw as the trajectory of political events in Egypt. They were aware, for instance, that the Brotherhood's new general guide, Hasan al-Hudaybi, had met with King Faruq in mid-November—allegedly to discuss ways of maintaining calm outside the Canal Zone. A British report on this meeting held that al-Hudaybi had foresworn any revolutionary intent and guaranteed his support for the palace, promising Faruq that the Brotherhood would not use violence against Egyptians or "innocent" foreigners. The general guide also gave assurances that his group would never cooperate with the communists, whom he dismissed as atheists, incompatible with a "religious organization."[212] Soon afterward, the Foreign Office was told that King Faruq had definitely decided to build up the Brotherhood as an "effective counterweight" to the Wafd.[213] London sought clarification from Ambassador Stevenson, who informed them that the palace was indeed funding the Ikhwan once again and might turn to the group politically, in the "last resort." Stevenson ventured that although the Brothers would be "highly inconvenient allies" given their criticism of his private life, the king might be ready to bring them into government in order to rid himself of the Wafd.[214]

At this time, the embassy believed that the Ikhwan was itself preparing to contest elections—possibly with a view to entering a coalition administration in the future. Knowledgable Egyptian sources had indicated to the British that the Brotherhood could be transformed into a full-fledged political party. If this were to happen, it was expected that they would be "an extremely powerful" force.[215] The Ikhwan was described as "the only large organisation in the country, other than the Wafd who were discredited."[216] Proof as to the latent strength of the Brotherhood was offered when Student Union elections were held at Cairo University in late 1951, and the group's candidates swept the board across all faculties—from agriculture and science to arts and law.[217] The British anticipated that, in any national competition with the Wafd, the Brothers would have "numbers and discipline" on their side, as well as a "reputation for integrity." In a context framed by ongoing violence and instability, in which the established parties and the whole parliamentary system had been brought into contempt, officials surmised that many Egyptians could be drawn to a revolt "against Western civilisation as a whole." The result would be a triumph for the Muslim Brotherhood, with the group capitalizing on the disenchantment and despair of those people who wanted "above all, some assurance of security and stability."

Significantly, it was assumed that the *Islamic* character of the Ikhwan gave them a crucial advantage over their communist rivals: "It is natural that in this uncertainty some should turn to Moscow, but it is far more natural for the conservative Egyptian to turn to Mecca, as he was taught in childhood to do, and to find his assurance of stability in the familiar words of the Adhan which he hears five times a day: 'Come to prayer; come to safety.' " Ambassador Stevenson thus warned his colleagues not to "underestimate the power of puritanism." Provided that elections were organized with a modicum of fairness, he thought that the Brotherhood "might win a victory over the Wafd, and, a fortiori over any other party [emphasis in original]." Furthermore, if the corruption of public life went unaddressed, Stevenson expected increasingly more Egyptians to be attracted to "the idea of government by a party of comparatively well-drilled devotees whose inspiration will be religious and whose methods may approach fascism."[218] As this last remark implied, the ambassador was hardly enthused by what he saw in the Brotherhood. At the same time, however, he seemed to accept that the Ikhwan was the coming power in Egypt. This, in turn, raised the question of how a Brotherhood-led ministry might behave—especially concerning the national question—and on this front, the embassy had earlier received an interesting approach.

In December 1951, a Foreign Office official had met with Farkhani Bey, a de facto intermediary to Hasan al-Hudaybi; Farkhani was said to be a close friend and adviser to the Brotherhood's general guide. The resulting intelligence reports highlighted the apparent differences between the group's new leaders and its rank and file. Al-Hudaybi was described as being of an "entirely different type from Hasan al-Banna . . . and . . . capable of leading the Ikhwan to much better purpose." In the margins of the document, one official scribbled, "many people say this." According to Farkhani, the Brotherhood's leader—irrespective of outward demonstrations of loyalty—"despised the King," did not trust the Wafdist government, and wished to stay out of the "national struggle" because of his fear that the Ikhwan would be repressed once more. Though he wanted to see the British depart from Egypt, it was suggested that al-Hudaybi regarded "corruption and particularly the immorality of the king, the Government and the Pashas as an even higher priority target"; he was also said not to care "one small damn" about Sudan.[219]

All of this doubtless made intriguing reading for the British and generated a fresh debate about the true position of the Brotherhood and its leader. It could reasonably be assumed that Farkhani was acting under instruction from al-Hudaybi. His comments cut against the grain of previous reports that portrayed the general guide as an ally of the king. More significant still, if Farkhani was to be believed, al-Hudaybi was open to a relationship with the British and appeared ready to curtail the Brotherhood's agitation. The general guide, it would seem, sought to replicate Hanna al-Banna's much-noted pragmatism—and accounts by Ikhwan members insist that al-Hudaybi sincerely hoped the West could be persuaded to engage with the group. In line with this, he wished to impress on the British the "moderate" character of the Brotherhood's thinking.[220]

This overture certainly caught the attention of British officials desperately seeking a way out of the Anglo-Egyptian crisis. When Farkhani offered to arrange a direct meeting with al-Hudaybi, the Foreign Office authorized the embassy to pursue the initiative. It was anticipated that this might provide an opportunity to appraise further the character of the Brotherhood leader.[221] In a follow-up discussion, Farkhani Bey sought to emphasize the benefits of engagement with al-Hudaybi, drawing attention to the possibility that the Brotherhood might form the next government. According to Farkhani, the king had intimated that the Brotherhood might enter a palace-led coalition administration to replace the Wafd when he had received al-Hudaybi in November. Again, a note in the British record of the meeting confirmed that this tallied with other information in their possession, as it stated: "This idea seems to be gaining ground."[222]

Also at that second meeting, Farkhani Bey once more tried to persuade his embassy interlocutors that the Ikhwan were "not anti-British." He maintained they were merely anti-Wafd. In reply, British officials weighed the obvious discrepancy between the "commendably moderate" public utterances of al-Hudaybi and the ongoing involvement of Muslim Brothers in violence in the Canal Zone. Events on the ground, it would seem, rather belied statements of good faith emanating from the general guide. Faced with this, Farkhani "admitted that there was still a strong terrorist element" inside the Brotherhood, which would "need all Hodeibi's [sic] powers to control it." Nonetheless, he assured them that the general guide could cement his authority and steer the Ikhwan in a more peaceable direction.[223]

The British were thus presented with a fascinating prospect: that it might be possible to reach an agreement with the Ikhwan under al-Hudaybi's leadership that would help to calm the situation in Egypt. Of course, much ambiguity remained. On the one hand, officials were conscious that al-Hudaybi had made a series of statements distancing the Brotherhood from the fighting in the Canal Zone. On the other, these pronouncements were, as Mitchell later put it, an almost "inexplicable contradiction of facts."[224] They were disproved almost daily by intelligence reports, which depicted the Ikhwan as heavily involved in subversion, up to and including terrorism.[225] The Brothers were judged to possess a paramilitary organization "of long standing," which was perhaps "more formidable" than that of the "Liberation Battalions" as a whole.[226] Even more confusing was the fact that al-Hudaybi himself then gave a speech in Alexandria, which seemed to indicate the open embrace of the Canal Zone struggle and the use of violence. Therein, al-Hudaybi announced the Ikhwan's support for al-Nahas's government and its policy of abrogation. He then declared that "Our attitude from the Islamic point of view is also clear: if an enemy occupies any Islamic territory it is the duty of every Moslem to make war on him and expel him . . . it is our duty to make war on the British since they are enemies invading our territory."[227] It seemed rather hard to reconcile such words with the general guide's earlier professions of peaceful intent. And British observers now speculated that either the Wafd had "bought" al-Hudaybi "back from the King" or he had "surrendered" to the "extremer Brethren."[228]

In all of this, Western observers were evidently drawn to the notion that there was a divergence of opinion between the Brotherhood leadership and many of its followers. Even prior to the onset of conflict, the diplomats claimed to detect a split within Ikhwan ranks, in the run-up to al-Hudaybi's formal election as general guide in mid-October 1951. It had not gone unnoticed when the Brothers suddenly announced that the newspaper al-Da'wa had no formal connection with the group. That publication was known to be under the control of Salih 'Ashmawi, whose rivalry with al-Hudaybi had become increasingly apparent.[229] Many then wondered whether the strains of the Canal Zone "war" might not deepen the rift. Alfred Sansom, for instance, mused whether discontented and more "extreme" members of the Brotherhood might use the fighting to challenge the "moderate" and "mild leadership" of al-Hudaybi.[230] In a similar vein, US officials expressed "serious doubt" as to whether the "conservative" general guide would be able to restrain his more "fanatic" followers who were responsible for many of the "terrorist acts in the Canal area."[231]

Amid this uncertainty, the British Embassy decided to take a closer look at the Ikhwan. On New Year's Day 1952, Ambassador Stevenson prepared a lengthy dispatch to London on the activities of the group and its prospects for the future. This charted the reconstitution of the Brotherhood under al-Hudaybi and his efforts to demonstrate that they had become more "respectable." Again, the general guide was described as a "man of different type from the fanatical Hassan al Banna." His public pronouncements were said to be "studiously moderate"; and it was believed that during his audience with the king, he had assured Faruq he had "no intention of undertaking terrorist activity." According to Stevenson, though, doubts endured about whether al-Hudaybi was truly in control of the Ikhwan or was simply a "tool" of the Brotherhood's guidance council, who was "being used as camouflage by unrepentant terrorists" who had "learnt some subtlety through adversity." The ambassador also predicted that in the event it took office, any Brotherhood-led government would be "suspicious, uncompromising and disdainful in its dealings with [the British]."[232] Any "bargain" reached with them, he imagined, would be a "hard one." In Stevenson's estimation, the Brotherhood had been as "intransigent as anyone" on the Anglo-Egyptian dispute. He foresaw that the "lack of realism" they exhibited on Egypt's "internal troubles" would extend to their foreign policy. The ambassador assumed that the Ikhwan would continue to view the world through a religious lens and be suspicious of a "Christian power" such as Britain. He was skeptical of the idea that a government of "stern fanatics and fundamentalists" could ever accept British demands regarding the Suez base.

And yet Stevenson also suggested that, once in power, the Ikhwan would behave pragmatically and in the long term be diminished by the experience: "Such accession would almost certainly corrupt them as it has corrupted every other organization in the Middle East however firm their principles may be when in opposition." On top of this, he considered it likely that in the intervening period, the Brotherhood would be able to draw on "a certain amount of administrative talent" (among supporters in the judiciary and civil service) to support any government they formed. The ambassador contended there was "at least a chance that they could administer the country with a degree of efficiency." He felt certain they could "hardly prove worse than the Wafd." For this reason, he averred: "We might be on more solid ground with a Moslem Brotherhood Government: if they could retain power long enough, and if I am right in thinking that they could produce a fairly efficient and clean administration. We should then be spared the familiar diversion to foreign affairs of the discontent caused by Government scandals and incompetence, and it is arguable that any agreement reached with such a Government might have more chance of enduring and being honoured than one made with a clique of Pashas."[233]

A further caveat noted that such conclusions rested on the assumption that the Brotherhood's principles would be "reflected faithfully in their practice when in power," something the author admitted could not be counted on. Nonetheless, here was a striking notion: that the British might assent to—and perhaps even seek—the creation of an Ikhwan-led government in Egypt, in the belief that the organization would eventually respect British parameters for a settlement of the Anglo-Egyptian dispute. Written at a time when Brotherhood members were heavily involved in "armed struggle" against British forces, it was an arresting proposition. In this respect, the report may reflect the degree to which officials, out of desperation, were ready to contemplate almost any option, no matter how far-fetched. One corollary was a willingness to reassess even their most inveterate antagonists, the Muslim Brotherhood.

The memorandum arguably raised a tantalizing "what if" scenario: could the British have secured an accommodation with the Ikhwan? Ultimately, of course, this outcome never came close to being realized. And even as Stevenson's dispatch was being composed, the political context in Egypt was transformed by the critical events of 25–26 January 1952.

Toward the Revolution

Since the start of the year, the situation in the Canal Zone had continued to deteriorate. The night of January 12–13 saw the battle of Tel el-Kebir, with which this chapter began. Elsewhere, the "liberation battalions" launched major attacks against British positions in Port Said and Ismailia (where Muhammad al-Farghali was identified as a "the chief inspirer" of the Brotherhood's campaign).[234] In one incident, an American nun, Sister Anthony, was killed.[235] According to Salah Shadi, in a period in which the atmosphere in Egypt was "fraught with hatred for the English," the Brotherhood cooperated with sympathetic army officers (including Gamal Abdel Nasser) to acquire weapons and carry out guerrilla operations.[236] As an example of the latter, Shadi pointed to a planned assault on a British ship passing through the Suez Canal that was to be targeted with an underwater mine. Twice, he claimed, the Brotherhood prepared the attack, but twice it was abandoned for various logistical reasons. ('Afifi relates the same story, but adds that the operation was abandoned after Shadi learned that women and children were on board the ship.)[237] Other attacks, though, did go ahead. There were constant acts of sabotage on military infrastructure such as water pipes, bridges, and telephone wires; British patrols were ambushed; a major British weapons store was destroyed at Abu Sultan near Ismailia; and a train carrying weapons and ammunition was blown up at al-Qantara West, close to the Canal.[238]

Against this backdrop, the *Times* noted that the Cairo government was under ever-greater pressure from "the extremists" of the Left and the Muslim Brotherhood, to stoke the fire of the "national struggle."[239] There also was renewed speculation that the Ikhwan wished to overthrow the regime.[240] Leading members of the group frequently articulated their support for armed struggle. Secretary General 'Abd al-Hakim 'Abdin, for example, gave several speeches praising the activities of the "Liberation Battalions." At the mid-January funeral of one student "commando," both 'Abdin *and* General Guide al-Hudaybi played a "prominent" role. The Brotherhood, the diplomats concluded, remained "committed to the battle."[241]

By now, too, the British authorities were convinced that attacks on their troops enjoyed official Egyptian sanction. Statements from the Interior Ministry were said to offer "very little pretence" that such incidents were spontaneous. Rather, the government's "hostile intentions" were readily apparent—as was the role of the police in assisting the guerrillas. Anti-British attitudes were observed across a broad swath of Egyptian public life, and especially in the press.[242] One newspaper, *al-Gumhur al-Misri,* even announced a reward of £E1,000 for any "commando" who killed Lieutenant General Erskine—with a £E100 prize for the death of a more junior officer.[243] A senior scholar from al-Azhar signed a pamphlet exhorting people to participate in "jihad" against the British.[244] And more generally, it was possible to adduce the broader contraction of the British position in Egypt. Symbolic in this regard was the decision of the authorities to ban the Ikhwan al-Hurriya, the society created a decade earlier to advance pro-Western views.[245]

In the face of what appeared to be government collusion in anti-British activity, the military authorities once more opted to take matters into their own hands. On January 25, they launched "Operation Eagle" in Ismailia, an attempt to disarm the local auxiliary police who were accused of complicity in the ongoing violence.[246] The commander of the Egyptian unit, however, received a direct order from the interior minister that he should refuse to surrender. In the ensuing firefight, some fifty Egyptians were killed and a further one hundred injured (the British lost three men, with thirteen wounded).[247] US officials reckoned that the situation now approached the "point of no return."[248] In fact, the events of the next twenty-four hours perhaps indicated that this moment had come and gone.

January 26 saw an outpouring of grief and anger in Cairo. Protests turned violent and the police, rather than impede the mob, stood back and allowed destruction on a vast scale. British establishments across the city were targeted and burned. In what became known as "Black Saturday," some £E30 million of damage was caused and famous landmarks, synonymous with "British Egypt," disappeared for good, as did a number of luxury properties associated with the king and the upper classes. Among the premises destroyed were: Shepheard's Hotel, the "most famous hotel in the Near East"; the Victoria Hotel; Barclays Bank; Thomas Cook; the Turf Club; the Cicurel, Chemla, and Oreco department stores; virtually every nightclub in the city (including the [in]famous Badia

Club situated on Opera Square and those that lined the Pyramids Road); and numerous other shops, cinemas, bars, and restaurants (including Groppi's, L'Americaine, and the Cecil Bar).[249] At least thirty people were killed, ten of them British. In addition, the damage to specifically UK interests was estimated to be in the region of £5 million.[250] American losses totaled $1 million.[251] Eventually, the deluge was stopped only by the intervention of the Egyptian army and the imposition of martial law.

The question of who was responsible for the violence of Black Saturday has never been categorically resolved. The official Egyptian investigation into the disorders laid the bulk of the blame at the door of Ahmad Husayn's Young Egypt (now calling itself the Socialist Party).[252] At the time, the British fingered the Wafd, in conjunction with Husayn and his party. This was the conclusion of a lengthy embassy inquiry into the unrest, which censured al-Nahas's government on account of its inflammatory rhetoric and support for the "liberation units." It was alleged also that Interior Minister Fu'ad Sirag al-Din had been subsidizing Ahmad Husayn in the months prior to Black Saturday.[253] One British source even suggested that Sirag al-Din had wanted a "normal riot" on the day, only to see things get out of hand.[254] An alternative strand of explanation held that it was actually the king who had wished for a "bad show" in order to justify the dismissal of the Wafd—though he too had been taken aback by how far things went.[255]

The *Times* emphasized the role of "extremists" in the "orgy of destruction" that befell Cairo, commenting that the violence had "the dimensions of a popular rising," being "well organized and ruthlessly led." The newspaper reported the participation of radical left-wing elements and members of the Muslim Brotherhood.[256] In a similar vein, initial US assessments posited that events had been "carefully planned . . . on [a] selective basis," targeting places of "amusement and sin," as well as those linked to the British and pasha class.[257] A general "antiforeign slant" was said to have been discernible—a feature that perhaps pointed to the involvement of a group like the Ikhwan.[258] At the same time, there were suspicions that the violence had been communist-led.[259] One embassy report described it as a "typical underground Commie operation."[260]

Richard Nolte was another to reflect on the organized character of the violence. Cairo, he claimed, had been "divided into districts with a special destruction squad assigned to each." Under the guidance of this leadership, which was "dressed in western clothes" and carried the "appropriate tools," "the barefoot Cairo proletariate [*sic*] fell to . . . destroying, looting, and burning." Nolte was clear as to the "selective" character of the devastation that had been visited on the city—though he judged that "the basis for the selection still baffles analysis." On balance, he too was inclined to believe that Interior Minister Sirag al-Din had "connived" in the rioting, only for it to be exploited by some as-yet-unknown grouping.[261]

What of the Muslim Brotherhood? In the wake of Black Saturday, a number of the movement's members were detained in connection with the violence.[262] Several observers such as John Badeau, then president of the American University in Cairo, were convinced that the Ikhwan was culpable.[263] The *Economist*'s correspondent likewise hypothesized that the Brotherhood's anti-Westernism could be detected in the character of the violence.[264] Alfred Sansom later wrote that members of the group were definitely involved in the rioting—but thought the incendiary squads were the work of Young Egypt, possibly with input from rogue army officers.[265] Another British official was told by a palace insider that "the extremist wing" of the Brotherhood had surely joined in the disorder once it was under way.[266]

For its part, the Brotherhood always denied any responsibility for Black Saturday. Hasan Dawh, for example, described it as a "conspiracy" organized by the king, the parties, and their allies, which actually served to derail the "mighty popular revolution" that had been building on account of the struggle in the Canal Zone.[267] Similarly, other senior Brothers such as Salah Shadi and Hasan al-'Ashmawi recorded that the Ikhwan played no part in the fire—which they viewed as a disaster—beyond helping Nasser to move illegally held arms and ammunition away from the city. In a meaningful aside, al-'Ashmawi noted that the explosives they transported out of Cairo were of the same kind used to set the fires—the implication being that Nasser and his allies may well have been the guilty party. (For the Brotherhood, this episode became a celebrated example of Nasser's perfidy, as the weapons—which were relocated to the estate of Hasan al-'Ashmawi's father in Sharqiya—were later seized by Nasser's government and used as evidence that the Ikhwan had been plotting revolution.)[268]

Back in 1952, the general guide, Hasan al-Hudaybi (who was among those briefly arrested) issued a statement on January 28, in which he "condemned" the destruction of Cairo. It was preferable, he said, to boycott British goods rather than engage in such violence.[269] Still, the British Embassy was clear that "individual members" of the Ikhwan had participated in Black Saturday—especially in the attacks on bars, cinemas, cabarets, and hotels.[270] At a meeting with UK officials, al-Hudaybi's representative, Farkhani Bey, admitted that some Muslim Brothers had been involved in the disturbances. From the British per-

spective, one of the most troubling aspects of this was that it seemed to suggest al-Hudaybi was "losing his grip" on the movement and was "unable to
control many of the members."[271] This possibility caused consternation in
Whitehall, where the fear was that the Brotherhood's "terrorist bands" might
break away and act independently, or even in cooperation with the communists.[272] Again, this fit the wider perception—as expressed by the *Daily Telegraph*'s
correspondent—that although al-Hudaybi might be a "moderate leader," he
tended to give "an entirely false impression of the organisation's ramifications
and aims."[273] Thus, irrespective of the degree to which the Brothers were actually behind the events of January 26, the episode served to reinforce Western
anxieties about the true character of the Ikhwan and the threat that it posed.

Of more immediate consequence, meanwhile, was the fact that the chaos of
Black Saturday gave the king the excuse he needed to remove the Wafd from
office. There had been speculation since December 1951 that Faruq might change
the government because the Wafd had led Egypt into a "cul-de-sac."[274] On January 26, the king had ordered the army onto the streets to restore order. A
curfew was declared and martial law imposed. Al-Nahas was initially named
military governor general, but then sacked the following day.[275] In his place,
the veteran independent politician Ali Maher was recalled and asked to form a
ministry. Once the bête noire of the embassy, the new prime minister was
now the repository of British hopes in Egypt.[276] Richard Nolte observed that
Maher's administration was the "last chance" for a solution to the Anglo-
Egyptian crisis. To his mind, all parties—the Wafd, the Socialists, and the Muslim
Brotherhood—were waiting to see what would happen next.[277]

Maher took office, avowing not to conclude a deal with the British and emphasizing his commitment to both evacuation and the unity of the Nile valley.[278]
For this reason, the Brotherhood offered to work with the new prime minister
in the pursuit of Egypt's national objectives in return for a reduction in the
use, or abolition, of martial law.[279] There were rumors too that a new "national front" might be formed, including both the Wafd and the Brotherhood,
to support the government. These proposals, though, came to nothing.[280] In
the meantime, the British Embassy sought to find ways to alleviate the tension.[281]
They were encouraged that Maher seemed ready to try to bring the situation
under control.[282] Subsequently, US officials in the Suez Canal Zone testified to
a marked fall in the level of violence—while noting that a "pronounced feeling
of uneasiness" remained.[283]

It did not take long for Egypt's underlying political instability to be exposed.
The apparent readiness of Ali Maher to deal in conciliatory fashion with the

Wafd ensured that the king's confidence in him was short-lived.[284] In early March, Maher was dismissed and replaced by Neguib al-Hilali. Parliament was suspended and there was an expectation that it might be dissolved altogether. Henceforth, Egypt was in the hands of a government that maintained itself exclusively on military force and the use of martial law. The new prime minister was described by US officials as being "old" Wafd—someone critical of the corruption that surrounded figures like Sirag al-Din and al-Nahas. On this assessment, al-Hilali's government was composed of political independents and professionally competent, honest, and hardworking men.[285] The American Embassy reported (in an echo of how Maher had been seen just a few weeks earlier): "Majority informed opinion is that this is the last chance for moderate government in Egypt."[286] In a similar vein, British diplomats reacted positively to al-Hilali's elevation, anticipating that he would focus on an effort to clean up public life and would take decisive steps against the Wafd.[287] (There was an assumption that al-Nahas's party was, for the moment, unlikely to return to power.)[288]

Elsewhere, ambiguities persisted over the position of the Ikhwan. On the one hand, there were signs that the Brothers would lend "partial support" to al-Hilali.[289] In late March, al-Hudaybi sent a public letter to the prime minister (published in *al-Misri*) in which he pledged support for an anticorruption campaign. It was necessary, he said, to cleanse Egyptian society of its "moral defects and irreligious ways of entertainment." According to al-Hudaybi, there needed to be a reformation of "souls and morals," starting with those people in positions of leadership. This, he asserted, would allow the country to unify behind the goal of independence. With regard to the national question, al-Hudaybi effectively reprised Hasan al-Banna's position from a few years earlier. He thus announced his opposition, in principle, to continued dialogue with the British. At the same time, he said that he was prepared to support al-Hilali in his efforts to secure Egypt's aspirations.[290] If the prime minister felt he had no choice but to negotiate with the British, then al-Hudaybi confirmed he would accept this, providing that any talks were time limited; and providing that, if dialogue proved unsuccessful—as he expected—then the government would try other paths. "Struggle alone," al-Hudaybi stated, was "the key to evacuation and Nile Valley Unity." It had to be waged "unrelentingly . . . until unity is realized and every foreign soldier has left the land of our dear country."[291] In the weeks that followed, the Brotherhood's newspaper openly called for a renewal of armed struggle.[292]

All of this was a long way from the more emollient tone that al-Hudaybi had struck just a few weeks earlier in private representations to the British. Officials at the Foreign Office received al-Hudaybi's statement as "the most sinister single development" since Black Saturday. The head of the African department, Roger Allen, wondered whether "the more extreme wing" was gaining ground inside the Ikhwan. He feared the emergence of a "formidable" new alliance between the Muslim Brothers and the Wafd.[293]

Less-alarmist analysis, though, suggested that the Ikhwan had experienced something of an "anti-climax" after the fall of al-Nahas's government. Whereas the Brothers had previously been on an upward trajectory—and many had believed it would come to wield "decisive" political influence—their role had actually proven "much less important" than predicted. This, it was inferred, had damaged morale within the group and caused internal confusion. The embassy thought that the "official policy" of the Brothers was now one of "wait and see," while preparing for parliamentary elections.[294] Indeed, after it was announced that those elections would be held in mid-May, Stevenson interpreted the Brotherhood's more bellicose stance as the opening shot of the group's electoral campaign.[295] Yet the Brotherhood then sprang a surprise by stating that it would neither participate in the ballot as an organization, nor permit its members to stand as independents. This being so, the triumph of the Wafd was once more expected.[296] And as a result, al-Hilali opted to postpone the electoral process indefinitely.[297]

Of course, no one could be sure at the time, but Egypt was living through the final few months of monarchical governance. A report from the US Embassy in February 1952 commented that "the masses" were "ripe for almost anything." "Time" was said to be "running out." The clear view of American officials was that "reoccupation, revolt, revolution may sound like over-emphasis but they are all visible on the cards in Egypt today."[298] "The moderates," it was argued, had to "make progress on the Anglo-Egyptian dispute in order to survive."[299] US diplomats were dismayed by the continuing British unwillingness to deliver concessions that might secure the "constructive leadership" of al-Hilali.[300] If the prime minister fell, they warned, Egypt might succumb to a "romantic vision of an heroic national struggle for 'liberation,'" which had "lost none of its appeal for such groups as the University students or the Muslim Brotherhood."[301]

The *Daily Telegraph*'s Cairo correspondent, Rainald Wells, was another who supposed that a "revolutionary situation" now existed in Egypt, which might see the masses rise against the throne and the "pasha class."[302] By this time, many British officials were in agreement. In a late February letter to Michael Cresswell at the Cairo Embassy, Roger Allen had voiced his frustration with the "inertia" of the British military and those who refused to make "the minimum concessions necessary to secure an agreement." In sardonic vein, Allen remarked that "the British soldier seems willing to put up with a great deal of sniping and bomb-throwing for the sake of a few tennis-courts and amenities such as a place to have his pre-prandial drink." Such flippancy aside, Allen worried that "the deluge" might be approaching. He concluded that, "if we hold out for our full requirements and do not get an agreement at all, there may be such an explosion in Egypt that we shall be buried in the ruins."[303] Cresswell concurred with this gloomy prognosis. He anticipated "a series of 'Palace' Governments relying uneasily on the King and the Army, while the underlying resentment and discontent in the country" grew "steadily greater" and "the hands of the extremists" became "proportionately stronger." In Cresswell's judgment, they had to take seriously the prospect of a revolution, or the emergence of "an extreme Nationalist Government—possibly Ikhwan—which would take up the Wafd's terrorist cudgels." This, he thought, could well mean the "wholesale expulsion of British nationals from the Delta by an Ikhwan Government."[304]

In his late March, biweekly political summary of Egyptian affairs, Ambassador Stevenson acknowledged that "no Egyptian Government can now either hope to remain in power or get far with any internal reform unless it can first exhibit to the people a striking success in both parts of the 'National Cause' [that is, evacuation and unity of the Nile valley]."[305] Foreign Secretary Anthony Eden likewise observed that Egypt was on "the verge of anarchy"—and pleaded with Prime Minister Winston Churchill to accept the "principle of evacuation" (Churchill was famously and openly intransigent on the Egyptian question for both international and domestic reasons). Eden echoed the American verdict that time was not on their side and that the al-Hilali government represented the "best"—and perhaps last—opportunity for a deal: "If we merely seek to hold the Canal Zone by force, we must expect sooner rather than later a revolution in Egypt."[306]

In spite of this, there was no sign of any breakthrough in negotiations. By early May, US officials reported that the Egyptian government saw further talks as "futile," and while an "artificial calm" prevailed, "the road ahead" looked "rocky."[307] It was a timely assessment; the government in Cairo now changed hands between successive minority regimes, each weaker than its predecessor. Al-Hilali thus lasted less than four months before resigning, to be replaced (eventually—after an eighty-four-hour hiatus where Egypt was without a government) by Husayn Sirri.[308] The British deemed this latest administration "weak," and wholly dependent on the whims of the king.[309] So it proved. Three weeks later, Sirri resigned—largely because of a dispute with the palace over the leadership of the army officers' club.[310] This led to a fresh round of "musical chairs" until al-Hilali returned once more on July 22.[311] By this time, the provisions of martial law enacted in January had been extended indefinitely. The Chamber of Deputies had been dissolved and elections postponed for the foreseeable future.[312] Constitutional and parliamentary life in Egypt was in de facto abeyance.

While all this was happening, the Ikhwan appeared content to sit "on the fence," and act as "a dark horse." In the estimation of British intelligence, by being "committed to no party," the Brotherhood kept its reputation clean and remained in a "strong position."[313] The group's own account of this period claims that in the wake of Black Saturday, the movement reorganized its fighters in the Canal Zone to create a "secret armed movement" under the leadership of Mahmud 'Abduh, which then resumed operations against "the English."[314] The contemporary British record bears this out. In late June, the UK Joint Intelligence Committee (JIC) described the "notorious Moslem Brotherhood" as "a relatively efficient semi-underground extremist organisation with a nation-wide following and a powerful streak of politico-religious fanaticism." The JIC also noted that the Brothers had "recently shown signs of developing into a political party."[315] In line with this, the embassy was apprehensive lest the Ikhwan link up with an "extremist faction" of the Wafd to form a potent new force. Within the Brotherhood, Salih 'Ashmawi and Hassan Dawh (identified as the former head of the group's university training camps) were thought to favor such an alliance on the basis of a hard-line, militant approach to the British question.[316]

Ultimately, however, speculation of this kind was rendered redundant. Al-Hilali's putative government lasted less than twenty-four hours. On the night of July 22–23, it was swept aside by Gamal Abdel Nasser and his "Free Officers," who seized power and went on to proclaim a "revolution."[317] In the ensuing struggle for power, the Brotherhood, as well as the Anglo-Egyptian dispute, were vital elements that helped to define the new era.

Conclusion

The foregoing demonstrates the extent to which the Brotherhood was central to British thinking during the final years of Egypt's ancien régime. For much of this period, the group was a major source of anxiety. The Ikhwan was associated in Western minds with extremism and terrorism. For this reason, British diplomats—together with their American counterparts—had been deeply uncomfortable with the reemergence of the Brotherhood after Ibrahim al-Hadi's dismissal in 1949. Al-Nahas and the Wafd returned to power promising to restore the Ikhwan. Subsequently, though, they hesitated to follow through on this—to the evident satisfaction of Western officials. In an oft-repeated metaphor, the Brotherhood was seen as the political incarnation of Dr. Frankenstein's monster in Egypt. The result was that the group was left in an uneasy limbo: still officially dissolved, but playing an increasingly active and public role. It was only in May 1951 that the Brotherhood regained legal status—to the chagrin of most Western diplomats.

Thereafter, as relations between Cairo and London worsened, the Brotherhood was judged to be a pernicious influence. It remained committed to a hard-line position on the national question and encouraged al-Nahas's growing intransigence. As far as the Brothers were concerned, jihad was the only means by which to secure true liberation from the "English," who were portrayed as inveterate "enemies" of Islam. The British presence on the banks of the Suez Canal was read as merely the latest manifestation of an undying enmity between the West and the Muslim world; and as such, the Ikhwan felt that it had to be met with physical force.

When the Wafdist government opted for unilateral abrogation of the treaty in October 1951, the Brothers' rhetorical militancy was translated into action. The "War of the Canal Zone" saw the group launch a violent jihad for the second time in its history (the first being in Palestine in 1947–1949). Many Brotherhood members took part in the fighting, which produced several celebrated "martyrs." In the historical memory of the Ikhwan, this was "their" war, waged against unrepentant imperialists on behalf of the Egyptian and Muslim people. Certainly, the Brotherhood's involvement with the national cause seemed only to reinforce its popularity. As the Wafd struggled to navigate through the crisis, many observers wondered whether the moment might have arrived for the Brotherhood to take power.

In this context, the British Embassy itself began to consider what a Brotherhood-led government might look like and how it might act. All things being equal, it was clearly not a welcoming prospect. And yet there was some suggestion that the Ikhwan's assumption of office might not be all that bad and could, in fact, facilitate a compromise settlement on the question of the Suez Base. The Brotherhood leadership around Hasan al-Hudaybi sought to foster this perception, effectively reprising the posture of strategic pragmatism that al-Banna had deployed, to reach out to the British in late 1951, consciously presenting the group as "moderates" with whom the embassy could work.

Western officials, it seems evident, were never fully convinced. Though they constantly drew on a "moderate" versus "extremist" paradigm when trying to understand the Brotherhood's internal dynamics, they were not persuaded that the "moderate" al-Hudaybi could deliver his own "more extreme" followers. They never lost sight of the substantial gap between certain peaceable statements that the Ikhwan leadership made and other, manifestly pro-jihad declarations. By the same token, there was no denying the continued violence in which the Brotherhood was implicated in the Canal Zone. It was that campaign that helped to sweep the Wafd from power in late January after the destruction of Black Saturday in Cairo. Ironically, in those seminal events, the Ikhwan itself appears to have played only a limited role, yet its "armed struggle" against the British had set the stage for the unrest in the capital. Thereafter, the Brothers seemed to hesitate. In the final months of the monarchy, the group stood somewhat on the sidelines of Egyptian politics as governments came and went in quick succession. In British eyes, however, the Ikhwan remained a looming presence—one to be watched and feared. And, as Egypt entered a period of rapid, revolutionary change, debates about the nature and status of the Brotherhood proved an enduring preoccupation.

PART II

In the Age of America

Five   The Upheavals of Revolution
1952–1954

O N 15 JANUARY 1954, an Egyptian government dissolved the Muslim Brotherhood for the second time
in just over five years. Once more the group stood ac-
cused of seeking political power and having engaged in efforts to "overthrow
the regime under the cover of religion."[1] To this was added a new indictment:
that the Ikhwan had forged an alliance with the forces of "imperialism."[2] The
Egyptian government claimed to have uncovered contacts between senior
Muslim Brothers and the British, dating back to April 1953. It was alleged that
officials from the UK Embassy had opened a channel of communication to
Brotherhood sympathizers that led to meetings between the Oriental counselor,
Trefor Evans, and several Brotherhood figures—including the general guide
Hasan al-Hudaybi. The government also "revealed" that there had been secret
liaisons between Hasan al-ʿAshmawi and the British minister in Cairo, Michael
Cresswell. It was suggested that these channels had been used to discuss the
Brotherhood's attitude toward both the government and the still-unresolved
Anglo-Egyptian dispute. According to the authorities, the Ikhwan had intimated
a willingness to accept a settlement that compromised on key Egyptian demands
and had thereby undercut the official government negotiating position.[3]

The British Embassy in Cairo immediately denied meddling in internal Egyptian affairs. It described the accusation that Cresswell had ever met al-ʿAshmawi
as "completely unfounded." The British insisted that the minister had never even

heard of him, "nor had he ever met any member of the Ikhwan at any time." Alongside this, the embassy *did* acknowledge that Trefor Evans had met with al-Hudaybi, but it stressed that this had been at a moment when there was no public disagreement between the Brotherhood and the Egyptian government. Diplomatic dialogue with the Muslim Brothers was said to be aboveboard and merely a function of the normal duties performed by officials.[4] As a result, they pressed the Egyptian foreign minister to withdraw the allegations.[5]

In a subsequent encounter with then Egyptian interior minister Gamal Abdel Nasser, Evans emphasized that "he had constantly discussed with him [Nasser] the affairs of the Moslem Brotherhood, and had at the time admitted to him that there had been contacts with Hodeibi [*sic*] and the others." Evans reported that Nasser did not deny this; rather, he simply maintained that the purpose of the revelations had been "to blame the Brotherhood and not the British."[6] The government's assertions were therefore not retracted—much to the frustration of the diplomats. They came to see the episode as a classic example of the "old tactics" of "discrediting a political party in the eyes of the Egyptian public by seeking to prove some connexion [*sic*] between them and ourselves."[7]

Doubtless there was much truth in this assessment. Nevertheless, accounts by regime insiders would frequently point to the depth and duration of the relationship between the Ikhwan and the "English." General Fu'ad 'Allam, for instance, later claimed that the two sides had been in contact from the moment that the Brotherhood had come into existence, with the British seeking to harness the group as a bulwark against nationalist forces.[8]

On 20 January 1954, the government-aligned newspaper, *al-Gumhurriya*, reprinted the earlier allegations in extended form, with talks between the Brotherhood and the British now traced back to February 1953. The senior Brotherhood leader Salih Abu Ruqayak was said to have told Trefor Evans that "if Egypt searched throughout the world for a friend she would find none other than Britain."[9] Interestingly, the UK Embassy's report on the article largely confirmed the accuracy of this version. Therein, officials noted the "existence of a group" of individuals within the Brotherhood's leadership who were "prepared to co-operate with Britain, even if not with the West (they distrusted American influence), and to that extent to abandon the intransigent opposition of the extremists [to] all things Western." This outlook was attributed to the "increasing middle-class influence in the Brotherhood, compared with the predominantly popular leadership of the movement in the days of Hassan al-Banna."[10]

For present purposes, the accuracy or otherwise of such analysis was of less importance than the simple fact that the embassy clearly believed it to be true. In a subsequent reflection on the period, the ambassador, Sir Ralph Stevenson, expanded on the idea that the Ikhwan had evolved in character. It had originated, he said, "to a large extent [as] a revolt against western political influence and also western civilisation as a whole." Over time, though, according to Stevenson, it had become more middle-class in composition—and diplomatic engagement with al-Hudaybi was said to have revealed that "he and his closest supporters were by no means adverse to Anglo-Egyptian cooperation once a settlement of the Canal Zone problem was reached." In the judgment of the ambassador, al-Hudaybi's professions of friendship for the British were genuine. He was thought to be "deeply suspicious" of the Americans and to look with more favor on the United Kingdom. Other Brotherhood leaders were deemed to be similarly inclined: "Sheikh Farghali consistently gave proof of realism and moderation and even Saleh Ashmawi, Hodeibi's [sic] bitterest opponent, was at one stage anxious to establish contact with this Embassy." Given the erstwhile militant reputations of both al-Farghali and 'Ashmawi, these were fairly remarkable conclusions.

At the same time, the ambassador's evaluation—and that of his embassy—should not be misconstrued. All things being equal, Stevenson considered that in the "unlikely event" of the Brotherhood coming to power, it would not sign an agreement with the British on terms better than those available from the Egyptian government. As in 1952, it could hardly be said that British officials were enthusiastically seeking to make a deal with the Ikhwan. On the contrary, they continued to harbor serious misgivings about the organization. Nevertheless, the diplomats did reckon that the Brotherhood was changing and perhaps becoming more moderate. They also identified certain individuals within the Brotherhood's leadership who were assumed to be open to cordial relations with the British—a prospect the embassy did not dismiss out of hand. Rather, there was a presumption that, ideological hostilities notwithstanding, business might be done between the two sides. As described in part one, such an idea was consonant with a key strand of thinking inside British officialdom. During the past twenty years that mind-set had buoyed speculation about the amenability of various individuals and groups: Ali Maher, Young Egypt, Isma'il Sidqi, the Wafd, and of course, the Muslim Brotherhood.

Still, in the Egypt of the early 1950s, a relationship with the Ikhwan was the "road not taken" by British policy. There is no "smoking gun" in the archives that shows Ambassador Stevenson and his colleagues wished to empower the Muslim Brotherhood as a vehicle for securing UK interests. Nor does it seem likely they would have adopted such a policy, given that they invariably saw the group as a threat. Contrary to the conspiracy theories of the time (and since), there was no secret pact with the Ikhwan. Instead, both British and American diplomats continued to prioritize their relationships with Egypt's government.

In January 1954, that government was a revolutionary one that had come to power eighteen months earlier and abolished the monarchy. Its leading light, as had become increasingly apparent, was Nasser. It was his "Free Officers" movement that had carried out the coup of July 1952, and in the years that followed, the new regime oversaw a dramatic transformation of Egypt, both domestically and in terms of its place in the world. With regard to the latter, perhaps the most crucial element was Egypt's relationship with the West. Not only did this pass through a period of flux, but also the face of "the West," as viewed from Cairo, changed. Nasser's rise to power coincided with—and further exacerbated—the collapse of British influence in Egypt, as Washington replaced London as the dominant external force across the Middle East.

The two years after the July 1952 coup-cum-revolution saw the playing out of several key issues, among them the questions of who ran Egypt; whether it was Britain or the United States that spoke for the West in Cairo; and the nature of the connection between Egypt and the outside world. The Muslim Brotherhood was intimately involved in each of these debates. In many ways, this era saw a new "three-legged stool" operating in Egyptian politics, comprised of the West, the regime, and the Ikhwan. After initially welcoming the Free Officers' ascent, the Brotherhood evolved from being uneasy ally to fierce antagonist of Nasser. Ultimately, the group faced defeat—and a crisis that put its very survival at risk. In this context, an examination of the Brotherhood's relationship with the West does much to illuminate both the movement's own history and the wider trajectory of Egypt during this critical period.

The Revolution

Western diplomats had long forecast the overthrow of Egypt's constitutional monarchy. As far back as 1949, American officials had suggested that a "rising sea of discontent, hunger and despair" made some form of upheaval "inevitable."[11] The fear of many was that the growth of extreme nationalism and the prospect of revolution might provide an opening for communism—in Cairo, as elsewhere in the region.[12] The diplomats worried too about the vogue for "neutralism" in some countries, believing that such a posture worked to the advantage of the Soviets (and was itself being fostered by a "highly organized and intensive Communist campaign").[13] For this reason, they remained anxious to find "moderate" nationalists and rulers who would implement reform "without forcing too rapid change of the existing order."[14] The hope was that the slow introduction of liberal ideas and the greater provision of social justice would inoculate Middle Eastern societies against the allure of more revolutionary creeds.

By the early 1950s, however, the prevailing trends were thought to be "inimical to Western interests," with the "prestige and position" of the British and Americans in terminal decline. US policy makers envisaged that the Middle East would soon be "lost to the West."[15] In Egypt, the diplomats became increasingly convinced that the continuation of the status quo seemed only to be driving the country ever closer to the abyss. It was with this in mind that covert operatives such as Kim Roosevelt had been sent to the country in late 1951, in the first instance to try to persuade King Faruq to "forestall a revolution by conducting one himself."[16] As they lost faith in the king's capacity to deliver, though, the Americans began exploring various alternative options.[17] The (not unproblematic) memoirs of former Central Intelligence Agency (CIA) agent Miles Copeland describe how he and his colleagues wished to find a "charismatic leader," a "chosen one," who might serve US interests—a "Moslem Billy Graham."[18]

It was at this time that Copeland encountered Hasan al-Hudaybi, the "newly appointed head of the dread *ikhwan el-muslimin* [emphasis in original]," making a "fiery speech . . . intoning a philippic against America's corruptive influence in the world." As might be expected, the CIA man was less than impressed (and this verdict of course matched that of Roosevelt himself—see Chapter 3). Copeland believed the Brotherhood had been close to the Nazis during the Second World War, before then being penetrated by the Soviet (and British and French) intelligence services. Despite this, he claimed that Roosevelt at one stage urged the king to give funds to the Brothers, on the premise that they would bring about a coup dominated by "a 'return to God' movement of Egypt's fundamentalist Moslems." Copeland himself had similarly imagined that the only effective revolution possible in Cairo would be one based on "a combination of the army and the Ikhwan." He even makes the intriguing suggestion that al-Hudaybi may well have been a CIA "asset." There is, however, little to substantiate this latter contention. And in the end, American operatives seem to have backed away from any idea of utilizing the Brotherhood, preferring instead to make contact with the Free Officers. Copeland stated that he and Roosevelt first met Nasser in March 1952. "We had sought a Moslem

Billy Graham," he recalled, "and in Gamal Abdel Nasser we thought we had a reasonable approximation of one. . . . Nasser was the most satisfactory—or least unsatisfactory—leader we could possibly have in Egypt at that time." Thereafter, various lines of communication were established with his Free Officers movement.[19]

The existence of such contacts has inevitably fueled speculation over the extent of American involvement in the coup that followed. Certainly, for the Brotherhood, it became an article of faith that Nasser enjoyed close, collusive relations with the United States. Mahmud 'Abd al-Halim's long history of the Ikhwan, for example, devoted much space to analyzing Copeland's testimony—drawing extensively on his book *Game of Nations*—to highlight Nasser's ties to the CIA and his purported readiness to safeguard Western interests.[20] 'Abd al-Halim also noted how the Free Officers, once in power, built their repressive apparatus with US assistance—especially the expertise provided by "the American Jew," James Eichelberger.[21] The CIA, it was alleged, played a critical role in helping the Egyptian government defame and then eliminate its rivals—including the Ikhwan.[22]

Similarly, in their accounts of the revolutionary era, Brotherhood members like Hasan al-'Ashmawi portray Nasser as liaising closely with American interlocutors and deferential to their wishes.[23] Indeed, in these narratives Nasser emerges as someone obsessed with the reactions of the West and keen to reach an understanding with the United States.[24] Salah Shadi testified that from the spring of 1952, Nasser refused to talk about "Anglo-US imperialism"—focusing instead solely on the British—because he had won the support of American officials. Shadi further contended that the United States agreed to support Nasser's coup on the condition that he exclude the Ikhwan and communists from office.[25]

It would be a mistake, however, to overstate the role of the United States in the events of July 1952. The most plausible interpretation is that the American intelligence services, having engaged Nasser previously, were aware that something was likely to happen—but unclear as to precisely what and when. The Free Officers were not brought to power "on a CIA train."[26] The future Egyptian president Anwar Sadat claimed that the Americans were only informed about the coup (by Ali Sabri) in the early morning of July 23.[27] Certainly, diplomats at the US Embassy seemed as surprised as anyone by news that the army had seized power in Cairo. The first official US knowledge of the coup came when the king cabled Ambassador Jefferson Caffery to tell him that "Cairo is in the hands of the insurgents." Caffery, who would become increasingly prominent during these years, in turn reported to Washington that General Mu-hammad Naguib, the Egyptian army's chief of staff, was now in "undisputed command" of the situation, while Faruq was clearly seeking British military intervention to save his throne.[28] Such external interference was clearly some-thing that the Free Officers wished to avoid. Messages were therefore relayed to the British, both directly and via the US Embassy, stressing that Egypt's new rulers were focused solely on domestic corruption and "not concerned with any foreign issue."[29] US secretary of state Dean Acheson effectively endorsed this line and emphasized that any outside meddling would be "disastrous."[30]

Hitherto, the British had worried that a military "rising" might be exploited by "extremists" and degenerate into "anarchy."[31] Nonetheless, while they put their troops in Egypt on greater alert, they reassured the Free Officers that they had no desire to get involved.[32] The British believed a unilateral intervention that did not enjoy "active moral or political support" from the United States risked "a major cleavage" between London and Washington, which they were unwilling to countenance.[33] Foreign Secretary Anthony Eden thus told the House of Commons that the government viewed the coup as a purely "internal affair."[34] The same point was relayed directly to General Naguib. As Michael Thornhill notes, this marked a "momentous shift" in Britain's Egypt policy: London effectively signaled that it would no longer defend the system it had helped to create and preserve in Cairo.[35]

Even so, the British were clearly concerned about the direction of travel—especially given the confusion that surrounded the coup. In the days—and indeed weeks—that followed, it was far from clear who exactly was in charge in Egypt. Initial reports spoke of a "young air force officer" leading the army movement that had seized power (Nasser, it should be remembered, was in the infantry).[36] British informants suggested that "dissident officers . . . under Kamel Sidki" (himself in the air force) were behind the coup, and General Naguib was la-beled a "mere figurehead."[37] Another source told Minister Michael Cresswell that the "real leader" was a "young officer Bimbashi Anwar Sedat [sic]."[38] Com-bining these ideas, a subsequent—and rather confusing—British Embassy overview described the "Free Officers' Movement" as a subversive force within the army, under the leadership of "Major Kamel Sidki"; actual planning for the coup was attributed to "a group of ten officers led by Lieutenant Colonel Anwar al Sadati"; but the diplomats seemed uncertain as to the precise relationship be-tween these factions.[39] Other Western officials highlighted the figure of "Capt. Kamal Salem," who was said to exert "paramount influence on Naguib."[40] A senior Egyptian army officer, Major General Fu'ad Sadeq, offered a different version again. He told the British that Colonel Rashed Mehanna, a "coura-geous and intelligent" officer, was the chief organizer of the coup.[41] According to Sadeq, Mehanna had been joined in his plotting by certain army officers who were also members of the Ikhwan: the aforementioned Gamal Salim, Anwar Sadat, and Gamal Abdel Nasser. Interestingly, the embassy's covering dispatch concluded that Sadeq, as an "old-line" officer, was not in a position to know the "real inner workings" of the coup and certainly tended to exaggerate the role played by both Mehanna and Nasser—the irony being of course that Sadeq's opinion was far nearer the truth than the diplomats' own estimations.[42]

Amid all this confusion, it seems clear that British officials were especially disturbed by the notion that Egypt's new rulers might be "anti-capitalist" and under the sway of "commies and Moslem Brethren."[43] During meetings with US representatives in London, Foreign Office mandarins claimed to detect evi-dence of "Ikhwan influence." A number of the leading army officers, including Naguib himself, were believed to be members of the group. British anxiety fo-cused on the "puritanical concepts" and nationalism espoused by the Brothers, which they expected to generate "anti-West, anti-Israel manifestations."[44] They worried that the empowerment of the Ikhwan would lead to the resumption of "a terrorist campaign of far greater ruthlessness and efficiency" than that which had been waged the previous winter.[45] Furthermore, Michael Cresswell voiced fears that they were witnessing the creation of a "classic Kerensky-type regime" that would later be "swamped by extremists."[46] With this in mind, the British were keen to strengthen "moderate elements" in the new dispensation.[47] As in the early part of the year (see Chapter 4), their hopes again rested on Ali Maher, who was appointed prime minister on the insistence of the Free Offi-cers, prior to the forced abdication of the king.[48] The Foreign Office wished to "give Ali Maher every encouragement to keep the military under con-trol," as he governed in uneasy collaboration with a Command Council of the Revolution (CCR).[49]

American officials betrayed less apprehension than their British counterparts about the overall character of the new government—a reflection maybe of their greater inside knowledge.[50] The embassy described those behind the coup as "an amorphous group of middle grade army off[icer]s bound together by common disgust with their superiors."[51] The US consul to Alexandria likewise suggested that "20 'idealistic' officers including several members [of the] Moslem Brother-hood" were responsible for the "core planning" behind the coup. (The highest-ranked member of this group was said to be a lieutenant colonel, possibly in reference to Nasser, though no names were given.)[52] Initially, US diplomats were reassured that there was no communist influence over Egypt's military-led government. However, they too were concerned by the prospect that the Brotherhood might come to play an "increased role." It was noted that Hasan al-Hudaybi had already been mentioned as a possible minister of justice in the emergent regime.[53] Caffery reported that Naguib himself had a "pro-Ikhwan history" that was far from encouraging.[54] On a slightly different reading, he was said to be entirely "in [the] hands of his subordinates," who included Ikhwan "extremists."[55] Back in Washington, the CIA commented that an "alliance between Nagib [sic] and the Moslem Brotherhood or the Wafd Party would offer a new threat to moderate government and to Western interests."[56]

At this juncture, it is perhaps worth pausing to consider what is known about the role of the Brotherhood in the July "revolution." 'Abdallah Imam has pointed to the complexity of the Ikhwan-Free Officer relationship, with views diverging on the extent of ties between the two groups.[57] Husayn al-Shafi'i, for instance, was one of those on the military side who later denied that anyone in a position of leadership (himself included) had previously been a member of the Ikhwan—though he accepted that many officers had been *sympathetic* to the group at one time, and that the Brothers had assisted with making the revolution.[58] Others, such as former security chief Fu'ad 'Allam, admitted that the Free Officers movement included Muslim Brothers, though he insisted that the Ikhwan leadership played little role in the coup (which they were slow to support).[59] Different again was the account of Anwar Sadat, who was more forthcoming about his own connection to the Brotherhood. Sadat claimed to have met Hasan al-Banna in 1940, and to have been deeply impressed by the general guide, for whom his "admiration was unbounded." They agreed, Sadat said, to cooperate in making a revolution in Egypt—and to this end, the Brotherhood recruited additional Free Officers to their movement, such as 'Abd al-Mun'im 'Abd al-Ra'uf (who became the liaison between the two sides).[60] An indication of the groups' closeness was the fact that when Sadat was imprisoned for his part in the assassination of Amin Osman in 1946, al-Banna helped support his family.[61]

Brotherhood histories go further and assert that the Free Officers were actually created as a branch of the Ikhwan within the army. Salah Shadi, for example, maintained that Nasser and others such as Kamal al-Din Husayn, 'Abd al-Hakim 'Amer, Salah Salim, and Husayn al-Shafi'i were all formerly members of the Brotherhood's Special Apparatus (SA). On this account, Nasser was first introduced to the Ikhwan by 'Abd al-Mun'im 'Abd al-Ra'uf and then swore the oath of loyalty to the group under the aegis of 'Abd al-Rahman al-Sanadi, the head of the SA. Subsequently, according to Shadi, Nasser grew close to Mahmud Labib, the man whom al-Banna had put in charge of Brotherhood activities inside the army. From an early stage, though, Nasser apparently demonstrated an independent streak and this intensified—first, after the dissolution of the Brotherhood in 1948, and second, after the death of Labib in 1951. The name of the "Free Officers," Shadi averred, was initially just an alias used as cover by military-based Ikhwan members; later, Nasser used it for his own purposes, creating an organization bound by loyalty to himself rather than to the Brotherhood.[62] A similar story was told by Hasan al-ʿAshmawi, who attested that Nasser was originally a sworn and active member of the SA, involved in the March 1948 killing of Judge Ahmad Khazindar, before leaving the organization to operate alone.[63] Whatever the truth of this, there seems no doubting Nasser's one-time affinity for the Ikhwan. Ahmad al-Baquri recounted that when Nasser visited the tomb of Hasan al-Banna after the revolution (see below), he declared: "Do not think, Oh Ikhwan, that I am a foreigner to you, for I am one of you."[64] More broadly, Brotherhood members have also referred to their cooperation with Nasser and other senior officers during the conflicts in both Palestine and the Suez Canal Zone.[65]

In many ways, collaboration of this kind was unsurprising. Scholars including James Jankowski and Joel Gordon have identified the degree to which the Free Officers took much ideological inspiration from groups like Young Egypt and the Brotherhood. Each of these movements owed a great deal to the intellectual ferment of the 1930s and 1940s, and the search for socio-political alternatives. They were responding to similar impulses and tended to express themselves in a common vocabulary that spoke of unity, strength, liberation, and, perhaps above all, dignity.[66]

With regard to the specific events of July 1952, al-ʿAshmawi's dramatized yet plausible account of those "critical days" suggests that the Brotherhood *was* heavily involved in preparations for the coup. By his reckoning, the Free Officers hoped that the Brotherhood could provide reassurance against "English" intervention— either by showing a readiness to fight, or by establishing contact with the British in advance (even though the Brothers maintained they had no such privileged access).[67] According to al-ʿAshmawi, Nasser insisted on meeting with senior Brotherhood figures like himself and Salah Shadi rather than going through the group's formal army liaison figures Abu al-Mukarim ʿAbd al-Hayy and ʿAbd al-Raʿuf, whom he did not trust.[68] (Indeed, al-ʿAshmawi claims that Nasser wanted to appoint Shadi interior minister—though the latter refused.)[69] As a result, on the night of July 22–23, the Brotherhood's "fedayeen," operating in civilian uniform, were tasked with guarding key institutions (such as foreign embassies) in Cairo and other cities, as well as the road running from the Suez Canal Zone to the capital. Their mission was to keep order and also to intercept any attempt by British troops to abort the coup.[70]

'Abd al-Halim thus recorded that prominent Brotherhood leaders were forewarned about the coup. Indeed, he stated that Nasser delayed proceeding until he knew the opinion of General Guide al-Hudaybi (who offered support, while arguing it would be best if there was no obvious tie to the Ikhwan, so as not to provoke Western intervention).[71] Similarly, Salah Shadi certified that the Brotherhood had reached an agreement with Nasser that the goal of the revolution would be reform and the creation of a government based on "Islamic principles." The two sides decided "not to be frank" about this because they feared that the "enemies of Islam" might attack the movement in its infancy. But it was agreed, Shadi asserted, that the Brotherhood would act as the "popular base" of the new regime, even as it stayed hidden from public view.[72] No sooner had victory been won, though, than tensions began to emerge. Brotherhood sources claim that Nasser resented what he felt was the reluctance of the Ikhwan's leaders to pledge unconditional support to the new dispensation.[73] Equally, the Brothers were convinced that Nasser had reneged on his promises, as he now insisted that nothing had previously been agreed.[74]

Needless to say, the true extent of these contacts and arrangements across secretive, conspiratorial organizations can never truly be verified. The origins of the Free Officers movement, as well as the 1952 revolution, remain shrouded in ambiguity. The picture is also complicated by the fact that the Brotherhood was far from united internally. As Barbara Zollner has described, Hasan al-Hudaybi's hold over much of the organization was tenuous at best—especially with regard to the Special Apparatus, which was the section closest to Nasser.[75] Nevertheless, the weight of evidence seems to confirm that several Free Officers were formerly Brotherhood members and that the group itself had advance knowledge of the July coup and was involved in it at some level.[76] At the time, al-Hudaybi denied that he had received any prior warning of the Free Officers' intentions. Such disavowals, however, surely need to be seen within the context of the above-noted fears about a possible British intervention.[77] Furthermore, on July 28, al-Hudaybi met with Naguib and then distributed a circular that instructed the Brothers to support the army movement "in order to permit it to attain the ends towards which the country aspires."[78] This was followed by the release of a thirteen-page statement on August 1, praising the "heroic" leaders of the "revolution" and their "blessed movement."[79] Soon afterward, the Brotherhood-aligned *al-Da'wa* newspaper published its first open attack on the royal family as a whole—rather than on just King Faruq—a move that appeared to intimate their public embrace of the military regime.[80]

The Ikhwan, of course, entered the postcoup era with its own reform agenda. In an interview with the *Observer,* al-Hudaybi backed calls for a purge of Egyptian politics and urged the establishment of an "Islamic democracy." The Brotherhood, he said, was not itself a political party and would not contest elections, but it would continue its efforts "to bring about good government."[81] For this reason, the group complied with Naguib's demand that existing parties issue an official platform. What emerged was an "authoritative" statement of the Brothers' social and political doctrine. This stressed their commitment to the ideals developed by Hasan al-Banna during the previous two decades: support for the nationalist cause and the strengthening of the army; calls for political reform so as to implement "Islamic principles"; proposals for the "Egyptianization" of the economy, industrial development, and increased social welfare expenditure; and, inevitably, the appeal for moral reform to combat "vice and oppression."[82]

British and American officials scrutinized all of this with some misgiving. As William Morris remarked from London, "the possibility that they are approaching the responsibility of office does not appear to have mellowed the Moslem Brethren or modified their programme."[83] It was noted in particular that al-Hudaybi had given press interviews restating his opposition to any resumption of negotiations, prior to the withdrawal of British troops from Sudan and Suez.[84] Other observers suggested that Christians and foreigners were especially "fearful of the potential fanaticism" of the Ikhwan.[85] Taken together, reservations of this kind captured the sense of disquiet in Western circles about the perceived influence of the Brotherhood in the aftermath of the coup.

With the "dust settling," Ambassador Caffery foresaw three possibilities for Egypt's future: a "more or less 'benevolent' " military dictatorship, likely under Muslim Brotherhood control; a Wafd-dominated republic; or the continuation of the existing alliance between Ali Maher and the Free Officers. Though he offered no firm prediction as to which scenario would prevail, the ambassador did comment that the Officers already appeared "jealous of [the] role they have played." He surmised they were not keen to relinquish power, and it seemed clear that Caffery was comfortable with this outcome.[86] In the weeks that followed, his support for the Free Officers hardened—a shift that coincided with his embassy's recognition of the fact that Brotherhood influence was more limited than some had feared. The US military attaché, Lieutenant Colonel David Evans III, now reported that General Naguib was "definitely not" a member of the Ikhwan, which the new government claimed to find "too extremist."[87] Caffery likewise concluded that the Egyptian army's desire for Western military equipment, and possibly even an alliance with the United States, was evidence that the Brotherhood was not in the ascendancy, for the group was believed to be "implacably opposed" to such steps.[88] The "young officers," the ambassador declared, were "almost too good to be true," albeit with the caveat that it was "much too early to say what [the] end will be."[89] The army was said to have emerged from the coup "with Kudos, but no program," while the prime minister, Ali Maher, had "a program, but little Kudos." "The combination of the two," Caffery reckoned, was "potentially potent" and might "provide [a] channel for [the] achievement of long-sought stability in [the] political realm."[90] In mid-August, the ambassador characterized the initial performance of the CCR-led regime as "good," pointing out that it had avoided extremes, maintained law and order, and made a start in dealing with the corruption and social injustice that had spread like a "malignant cancer" through the Egyptian body politic. In Caffery's assessment, the "fondest hopes of the West for stability in Egypt and the Middle East" had been given "a new possibility of realization."[91]

As Geoffrey Aronson has illuminated, such a verdict was, in many ways, unsurprising. The US diplomatic community was almost predisposed to see Egypt's military rulers as a significant improvement on the "old gang" elite. There was a tendency in this era to look benignly on "enlightened dictators" who, it was assumed, might bring discipline, reform, and more constructive forms of nationalism to the Middle East.[92] *Time* magazine captured this spirit when it described Naguib as a "good man" who had given Egypt "hope." He was heralded as "the most promising figure to appear in the Middle East since Turkey's late great Kemal Ataturk." (Tellingly, the same piece spoke of the Muslim Brotherhood as "a fanatic, powerful secret society.")[93] As Matthew Jacobs has demonstrated, the Atatürk exemplar exercised a powerful appeal over the official American mind—appearing as a model by which otherwise "backward" countries might progress toward modernity.[94] US officials sought out replicas of the Turkish leader across the region and often ended up looking to local militaries. In September 1951, for instance, a dispatch from Embassy Damascus had argued that while the influence of the army in politics would normally "be deplored," in a country like Syria, it could be seen as a positive. Significantly for present purposes, it was suggested that "the sort of movement it is most against is represented by the Moslem Brothers." It was assumed that "religious fanaticism, puritanism, [and] thorough anti-Westernism" were "not congenial to the Syrian military." The United States was therefore said to have a "community of interest" with the army—as against a group like the Ikhwan.[95] According to Copeland, it was this outlook that had led the United States to get involved in Syria's first coup in the postwar era, which brought to power Lieutenant Colonel Husni al-Za'im in 1949.[96] In subsequent years, the United States backed other "strong man" military dictators in the country—notably, Lieutenant Colonel 'Adib al-Shishakli—on the basis that they too were better than any conceivable alternative.[97]

With regard to Egypt, it was the same sentiment that solidified the State Department's judgment that the United States should "cooperate" with the Free Officers. American officials wished to avoid an unseemly rush to embrace the regime, but equally, they did not want to appear aloof. If Naguib's government was able to maintain law and order, remained "well disposed" to the West, and showed an inclination to settle the Anglo-Egyptian dispute, then the diplomats were ready to establish friendly relations.[98] This preference for working with Cairo's new rulers was doubtless strengthened by the fact that the army-backed government set itself firmly against any hint of social disturbance and communist agitation. The rapid and severe response to the riot that took place at a factory in the Delta town of Kafr al-Dawar on August 12 offered firm testimony to this effect.[99] The US Embassy reported soon afterward that it was helping the regime to establish "effective security measures to combat Communist subversion."[100]

The British, by contrast, continued to evince more skepticism. The embassy still perceived a "strong affinity" between the Ikhwan and leading army officers.[101] In addition, trans-Atlantic differences on the sway of the Brotherhood overlapped with a broader divergence on the question of how to engage Cairo. At Caffery's urging, Secretary of State Dean Acheson signaled Washington's support for the officers' government in early September, with a public statement that praised recent "encouraging developments" in Egypt.[102] Acheson's words were received warmly in Cairo and formed the backdrop to the dismissal of Prime Minister Ali Maher. Naguib now became prime minister himself and numerous old-regime politicians were simultaneously arrested.[103] Ambassador Caffery surveyed all of this with equanimity, suggesting that it might inaugurate a "period of relative governmental stability."[104]

The British, however, were furious. They had set much store in trying to shore up Ali Maher's position as the necessary "moderate" force within the postcoup dispensation. For this reason, they questioned the value of Acheson being seen to praise Egypt's military rulers. The danger, in their view, was that "extremist elements" inside the regime might interpret this as providing them with "carte blanche from the United States Government [emphasis in original]."[105] As far as officials in London were concerned, the dismissal of Maher proved the prescience of their earlier predictions. James Bowker, the assistant undersecretary for foreign affairs, observed that Maher had been "pushed off the knife edge on which he was balancing," as the "military junta" had been "freed from restraint."[106] It was anticipated that this would lead to "a greater degree of control by the extremist elements"; and in this regard, special attention was given to the appointment of the Muslim Brother Sheikh Ahmad al-Baquri as minister of *awqaf* (religious endowments).[107] A biographical profile of the new minister stated that al-Baquri, though not a radical himself, was "inclined to side with the extremists" inside the Brotherhood against the leader, Hasan al-Hudaybi.[108] British unease was only partly allayed by Egyptian assurances that al-Baquri had only joined the government in a private capacity, having resigned from the Ikhwan.[109] The fear remained that Naguib was looking to the Brothers, together with the hard-line Watanists, as a core base of support, and might yet move in a more militant direction.[110]

In fact, it would later emerge that the government reshuffle was actually a cause of major disagreement between the Ikhwan and the ruling CCR. According to Hasan al-'Ashmawi, Nasser had wanted three Brothers to join the new ministry, but reserved the right to choose two of them himself (he wanted al-'Ashmawi and al-Baquri). General Guide al-Hudaybi had refused to accept this, both on the grounds that he preferred to remain independent of the government and because he rejected the idea that Nasser should make selections on the Brothers' behalf. Despite this, al-Baquri went ahead and resigned from the Brotherhood to take up his post.[111] Frictions of this kind were obviously not evident to contemporaries, who tended to focus on the actual presence in the cabinet of al-Baquri and other "extremists."

British distress over the fall of Maher was exacerbated by the feeling that the Americans had helped bring it about. Foreign Office concern about the approach of the US Embassy in Egypt—and, in particular, Ambassador Caffery—had been growing over the course of 1952.[112] Now, in an ill-tempered minute of September 10, the head of the African department, Roger Allen, commented that American "friendliness" toward the military government had caused serious "embarrassment" to the British.[113] In a further note, he pointed to the "real difference of opinion" between London and Washington. Allen argued that the Americans were "busy trying to build up their influence with the military junta," in the erroneous belief that they would be able "to use this influence in the direction of moderation."[114] The effect of this, he said, had been only to embolden more radical voices. James Bowker agreed, stating that by their "assiduous wooing" of the Egyptians, the Americans had "created the impression that [the] U.S. Government will back the new regime whatever it does (so long as it does not introduce suspected Communists into the Government)." Bowker's tersely expressed view was that it was "a pity that the universal American desire for popularity should in practice result in encouraging the more extreme elements in Egypt."[115] In British eyes, anything that smacked of "appeasement" was likely to have such an effect. Caffery, they maintained, had taken "entirely [the] wrong line."[116]

For their part, US diplomats vigorously defended the "efficacy" of their approach and argued that the "new regime and reform program" brought with it the "greatest hope for stability [in] Egypt." It made sense, they maintained, to seek "close and friendly working relations" with the CCR-led government.[117] In a meeting with Ambassador Stevenson, Caffery expressed his surprise at the "medieval thinking" of the British. He asserted that London had completely misread the Egyptian revolution and their mistakes had brought them to the "nadir" of British influence in Cairo.[118] Privately, the American ambassador went even further. On being informed of British criticism, he telegraphed Washington to declare: "As record will show, over and over again during past two years London [Foreign Office] tactics have been wrong and over and over again I have predicted consequences. They are wrong again." Moreover, the ambassador claimed, "it is fact that at this juncture Brit have practically not (rpt not) a friend in Egypt." The reality, he insisted, was that if the Americans and the British wished to get Egyptian agreement on Middle Eastern defense, then this would have to be done through the American Embassy. According to Caffery, the only viable way forward was his own preferred policy of seeking to build confidence with the regime.[119] The ambassador acknowledged, with reference to Hasan al-Baquri, that it was not "pleasant to have men long on extremism and short on admin[istrative] experience" in the government, but he felt that al-Baquri was at least from the "more moderate section of [the] brotherhood." In addition, Caffery said that he had prevented even more unappealing individuals from obtaining cabinet portfolios. He contrasted this influence with the ever-worsening position of the British, who were now "literally out in [the] cold here in Egypt."[120]

It was perhaps their own awareness of this shift that led the British gradually to modify their position in the last months of 1952. A mid-September article in the *Times* appeared broadly favorable to the officers' regime, which was described as vastly preferable to the "extreme Moslem Brotherhood."[121] Similarly, the *Economist* in this period described Naguib as "maturing swiftly in the role of leader."[122] Embassy officials like Michael Cresswell were also coming to the view that the Free Officers might be "more practical and realistic" in their attitude toward the defense question than their recent predecessors. (Cresswell, significantly, was also less inclined to take "an utterly black view of the present role of the Americans.")[123] The ruling CCR, it was assumed, preferred an "empirical approach"—a "typically British way of dealing with problems"—over a dogmatic attachment to any particular program. Ambassador Stevenson suggested that the officers were pro-Western by inclination and as such, he felt the "omens" for future relations were "not unfavourable."[124]

This argument slowly gained ground back in Whitehall, where the mandarins came to accept that "moderate elements" were in control and ready to cooperate with the West. One revealing assessment posited that Egyptian politics were once more exhibiting a familiar "moderate-extremist" divide.[125] Within this schema, Naguib was identified as the leader of the "moderates," while more intransigent nationalists and groups like the Brotherhood were seen as the "extremists." Against this background, the focus for the British, as always, was to strengthen the former against the latter and to ensure that the regime did not embrace "extremist elements particularly the Moslem Brotherhood."[126] As a result, UK officials effectively moved closer to the US position and announced themselves ready to pursue "more forthcoming policies," including the provision of "material assistance" to Egypt, which might allow Naguib to maintain stability and develop a "more reasonable attitude" in foreign affairs.[127]

In coming to this conclusion, as can be seen, fear of the Brotherhood—and the broader forces of extremism with which it was associated—played a critical role in shaping Western views of Egypt's emergent military regime. The dominant paradigm of "moderate" versus "extremist" ensured that even the British came to see the Free Officers as the best option, as against the seemingly "anti-Western" Brotherhood. Ambassador Stevenson now suggested that putative divisions *within* the CCR between extremists and moderates were "a good deal less real than has commonly been supposed." He postulated that it instead made sense to see the officers as united by a shared set of "basic political ideas" that were "first nationalist and secondly middle-class socialist."[128] Michael Cresswell echoed this analysis, explicitly dismissing the attempt to divine moderates and extremists on the basis that "who takes the extreme line seems to depend in each case on the subject under discussion." Cresswell, it should be said, was less optimistic than Stevenson about what this meant for Anglo-Egyptian relations. On the question of negotiations, he felt that "few, if any" of the leading officers could be counted on to take a "moderate line."[129] Even so, Cairo's military rulers were clearly judged to be preferable, from a British perspective, to the unquestionably "extremist" Ikhwan.

In the same period, it is worth noting, Western officials continued to apply the moderate-extremism paradigm to the Brotherhood itself. In late September, the US Embassy compiled a memorandum on the "considerable internal dissension" inside the group between "moderate leaders" such as al-Hudaybi and al-Baquri, and extremists who were said to sympathize with Salih 'Ashmawi. Ambassador Caffery reported that while it had "always been" difficult to gather precise information about the Brotherhood, he believed the moderate faction to be in control. For this reason, he sent Washington an account of a conversation that an embassy official had previously held with al-Baquri—albeit adding the caveat that it did not necessarily reflect the "dangerously extremist type of thinking or action normally associated with the Brotherhood."[130] In that discussion, al-Baquri had emphasized that the Ikhwan did not wish to govern Egypt, nor impose its ideas by force. He also drew attention to the group's firm opposition to communism and, though critical of US policy in both Egypt and Israel, expressed his hope that better bilateral relations might be possible.[131] Al-Baquri, in other words, reprised Hasan al-Banna's earlier appeal for an alliance of mutual convenience between the Brothers and the United States (see Chapter 3).

Manifestly, the overture fell on deaf ears. That notwithstanding, it seems clear that the diplomats remained fascinated by the vagaries of the Ikhwan's internal politics. They watched with palpable interest when further evidence of rifts inside the Brotherhood surfaced in October, when the group submitted an application to the Interior Ministry to register as a political party. There were strong rumors that al-Hudaybi had been fiercely opposed to the move, which was driven by rivals such as Salih 'Ashmawi; there was even speculation that the general guide might have resigned. Al-Hudaybi and his colleagues subsequently refuted these reports, but there were unmistakable signs of division within the Brotherhood.[132] When the Interior Ministry announced in mid-November that it had decided the Ikhwan was not a political party, this was read as a victory for al-Hudaybi's faction and the "more moderate elements" who opposed the Brotherhood's formal entry into politics.[133]

Diplomatic fascination with the balance of power inside the Ikhwan overlapped with concerns that the group might already be growing discontented with the army-led regime. The US Embassy, for instance, pondered whether the Wafd might make a "deliberate bid for Brotherhood support." It was anticipated that a rupture between the Brothers and the military could cause serious problems for the government.[134] Conjecture about an incipient split was encouraged in mid-October by the dismissal of Rashed Mehanna from his position on the Regency Council.[135] Among his sins, according to the US military attaché, was the contact Mehanna had allegedly maintained with the Ikhwan.[136] As such, his departure seemed to portend a worsening of relations between the two sides. Richard Mitchell would later pinpoint this episode as marking the beginning of the Brotherhood's doubts about Nasser.[137] (As it happened, both US and UK officials concluded that even though he favored some kind of Islamic Republic, Mehanna was in fact closer to the Wafd and had "less definite" ties to the Brotherhood.)[138]

It was in this context that a significant encounter took place in November 1952 between a US diplomat and Mahmud Makhluf, a prominent businessman with "very close connections" to the Brotherhood. The son of the grand mufti of Cairo and the brother-in-law of al-Hudaybi, Makhluf was thought to reflect the views of the "more conservative faction" within the Ikhwan, which supported the general guide.[139] Crucially, Makhluf now openly expressed reservations about the military regime, noting that the living conditions of the masses had not improved since July. In his assessment, the government had lost support and would come to rely increasingly on dictatorship and repression.[140] Such comments seemed to confirm the Brotherhood's growing unhappiness. In a further meeting, this time attended also by al-Hudaybi himself and his assistant, Sa'id Ramadan, the Brotherhood's leaders voiced support for the idea of a parliamentary republic—a proposition that carried an implicit challenge to continued army rule.[141] Furthermore, in a tour d'horizon designed to appeal to American sensitivities, al-Hudaybi again appeared to bid for Western support. He rejected the notion that the Ikhwan wished to renew guerrilla war against the British and claimed that "the principles of his movement had been basically misunderstood in the western world" (a theme he also stressed in an article for the Brotherhood-aligned magazine, al-Muslimun, in this period). Al-Hudaybi reiterated his opposition to communism and said that the aim of the Ikhwan was simply to attain a government "founded on Koranic lines."[142]

In this way, the general guide perhaps hoped to reassure the Americans about Brotherhood intentions—and even secure their support—as a precursor to any break with the government. If that was the objective, though, there were few hints of any US interest in an alliance with the Ikhwan. A November 1952 report for the National Security Council referred to it as an "extreme nationalist" movement. The government in Cairo, by comparison, was said to be of moderate reformist bent.[143] There seemed little doubt as to where American sympathies would lie in the event of a confrontation between the Brothers and the Free Officers.

For the moment, this prospect did not materialize. Evidence of Brotherhood disillusionment with the regime was balanced by signs of continuing collaboration. The Ikhwan, for example, lent its organizational power to General Naguib's triumphal tour of the Delta in October, helping to "stimulate the enthusiasms of the masses" in favor of the CCR. Three senior members of the group were then appointed to a Constitution Drafting Committee.[144] In December, the diplomats noted that while most of the people arrested three months earlier had been released, those directly implicated in the murder of Hasan al-Banna were among the minority still being held on criminal charges.[145] This followed a decision to amnesty several individuals convicted of high-profile "political murders" under the old regime. Those released included the Brotherhood members responsible for killing Judge Khazindar and Prime Minister Mahmud al-Nuqrashi.[146] Moves of this kind seemed to confirm an enduring congruence of interest between the Ikhwan and the army.[147] A lengthy dispatch from Ambassador Stevenson stated that, even as Naguib might wish to curb its "excesses," the Brotherhood remained a "valuable" source of support to the Free Officers.[148] Hasan al-'Ashmawi's memoirs also suggest that at this stage, relations were still reasonably positive. He records that in December 1952, Nasser asked him and the Algerian Brotherhood member Fadil al-Wartalani to go to Kuwait to try to secure a £20 million loan (at a time when the country's finances were in a perilous state due to the freezing of their sterling balances). The mission proved to be a failure, but was nevertheless an indication that leading Brothers like al-'Ashmawi enjoyed the confidence of the regime.[149]

As 1952 drew to a close, therefore, there was much that remained unresolved in Egypt. As if to underline this, on December 10, the 1923 constitution was formally annulled. Amid talk of a longer transition process during which the military would retain "absolute control," there seemed little prospect of the officers leaving power.[150] At the same time, some observers felt that the regime had "lost much of its popular support." Ambassador Stevenson described the internal Egyptian situation as "essentially brittle" and worried about the "increased boldness and influence of the Moslem Brotherhood."[151] American diplomats claimed to detect a "noticeable but not yet alarming deterioration" in the internal position of the CCR-led government.[152] Against this backdrop, key questions thrown up by the revolution had yet to be answered: Where exactly did power lie within the new regime? How would the government deal with the Anglo-Egyptian dispute? What would be the relationship between the Free Officers and the United States? What did all of this mean for the position of the Ikhwan? And how would this affect relations between the Brothers and the West?

1953, Year of Division

The sense of uncertainty that bedeviled Egypt in late 1952 was scarcely allevi-ated by the turn of the year; 1953 began with the exposure of an alleged plot involving former Regency Council member Rashed Mehanna. As described, there had previously been speculation over Mehanna's connection with the Ikhwan. Little was made of this, though, after his January arrest. Instead, atten-tion focused on his links to the communists and the Wafd. Ambassador Caffery reported that the Egyptian government believed the latter to be involved, pos-sibly with British support, in an effort to force the army to return to barracks.[153] Fears of covert British-Wafd scheming to overthrow the regime would remain current throughout the year.[154] However, there is no evidence from British state papers to corroborate such theories. On the contrary, the UK Embassy tended to see the detention of Wafdists and communists as a "distinct advantage" and welcomed their arrest as "reassuring."[155]

The extent of Mehanna's actual plotting is far from clear. Hasan al-'Ashmawi later posited that Nasser moved to destroy Mehanna because of the threat he posed on account of his popularity within the army.[156] Whatever the truth of this, the episode was symptomatic of the prevailing climate of instability. It was followed by an official announcement abolishing all political parties and de-claring the beginning of a three-year transition period. The US Embassy saw this shift as a preemptive response to an emboldening of the regime's enemies. It was assumed that the government's "inability thus far to produce substantial benefits either in foreign affairs or [the] economic sphere" had led it to adopt more "dictatorial methods."[157]

The Brotherhood escaped dissolution, having been designated as a non-political party a few months earlier. Nevertheless, leaders of the Ikhwan were evidently perturbed by the drift of events, and especially by the January 1953 founding of the "Liberation Rally," an entity meant to serve as the "organized expression of Egyptian national aspirations."[158] From the beginning, the Rally was considered a potential rival to the Brotherhood, which had positioned it-self as the main civilian prop to the regime. Nasser, who was secretary general of the Rally, subsequently confirmed to US Embassy officers that he wished to build up the organization as a mass political party (modeled, he claimed, on Atatürk's Republican People's Party). Nasser envisaged that this would free the government to eliminate all other groups.[159] The diplomats believed that the Brothers had "seen the hand-writing on the wall" and this reinforced the "increasing coolness" between the Ikhwan and the government.[160] Indeed, the British identified the creation of the Liberation Rally as a "turning point in the Brotherhood's attitude towards the regime."[161]

Ikhwan accounts likewise tend to agree that this was a crucial moment—the second occasion (after the argument about ministers the previous September) on which the Brothers said "no" to Nasser, who wanted them to merge into the Liberation Rally.[162] From the other side, Sadat commented that it was "then that the Muslim Brotherhood openly declared war on us, with the obvious intention of overthrowing us and taking over the rule of Egypt."[163] Leaving aside the accuracy of Sadat's narrative, his words were indicative of the growing rift between the Free Officers and the Ikhwan at this time. For the moment, a façade of unity was maintained. In February 1953, for instance, both Naguib and Nasser visited the grave of Hasan al-Banna on the anniversary of his death.[164] Nonetheless, as the year progressed, intimations of discord became increasingly hard to ignore.

The first half of 1953 also witnessed the growing prominence of Nasser on the political stage. During celebrations to mark the launch of the Liberation Rally, Naguib had been driven through cheering crowds in an open-top car, with Nasser standing to his left.[165] The significance of this was not lost on the diplomats, who recognized that the latter was now clearly the "second most powerful man in Egypt."[166] Even prior to this point, officials had concluded that Nasser was "dominant" within the CCR.[167] Caffery noted that it had become "increasingly apparent" that the "real locus of power" within the regime lay with Nasser as opposed to Naguib.[168] Nasser, the ambassador averred, was not an "absolute behind-the-scenes dictator," but he was the foremost individual inside the CCR—the "ringleader" who could usually expect to get his way.[169] On this reading, while Naguib remained the "darling of the masses," "real" authority lay with the CCR, in which Nasser was by far the "strongest" figure.[170] The British were arriving at similar conclusions.[171] What is more, some senior figures such as Foreign Secretary Selwyn Lloyd had obviously decided that the "anti-communist" Nasser was intelligent, friendly, and rather "reasonable" in his views.[172]

As words of this kind attest, most Western officials were happy to see Nasser in the ascendant. Their hope was that the consolidation of his power might facilitate progress toward the resolution of the Anglo-Egyptian dispute. In this regard, they were encouraged by the fact that the resumption of negotiations in January 1953 led with surprising speed to a settlement on Sudan—the issue that had derailed earlier talks. The two sides agreed on a process of "Sudanization," leading toward a plebiscite on independence three years later. A deal to this effect was signed on February 12.[173] There was an expectation that the Sudan accord would in turn provide a platform for efforts to secure a treaty on the Suez Canal Base question—certainly, this was what British foreign secretary Anthony Eden imagined.[174] US National Intelligence Estimates agreed that the "opportunistic" and pragmatic government in Cairo was ready for an alliance with the West.[175] The recently elected administration of Dwight D. Eisenhower urged the British to come to an understanding with Nasser.[176] Yet a settlement proved elusive; the breakthrough on Sudan did not yield a convergence between the two sides on Suez.

Instead, in late February, Nasser delivered an "ominous" speech in which he underlined his government's commitment to the "unconditional evacuation" of UK forces. He avowed that Egypt would not "bargain" for its liberty and he spoke of their readiness to fight for freedom.[177] In the assessment of the Americans, Nasser remained "profoundly distrustful" of British intentions and was disinclined to compromise.[178] Equally, too, London's position hardened appreciably during the spring of 1953. In part, this was a product of mischance: the illness of Eden left policy in the hands of the ailing yet stubborn prime minister, Winston Churchill. The latter had taken an increasingly inflexible view of the Egyptian situation. As Thornhill explains, the events of Black Saturday in 1952 had convinced Churchill that the country was run by little better than "savages," undeserving of any concession. Famously, the prime minister had rebuked Eden for seeking a settlement with the Egyptians, remarking acerbically that he did not know "Munich was situated on the Nile." For Churchill, anything that smacked of "appeasement" was to be repudiated. He preferred to stand on the Canal, "sit on the Gippies" and, if necessary, "have a 'whiff of grapeshot.'"[179] In this unpropitious atmosphere, fresh attempts to arrive at an agreement in March, and again in May, collapsed.[180] Thereafter, Churchill sent Robin Hankey to Egypt as his envoy, with the famous instruction that he should be a "patient, sulky pig." The prime minister said he would be "very content" if nothing happened—negotiation-wise—for six months.[181] Almost inevitably, Churchill got his wish.

British intransigence may have been fueled by the perception that the Egyptian regime faced greater opposition domestically, with "considerable sections of the people" said to be "growing tired of the Army Revolution."[182] The American Embassy was similarly aware of trouble "beneath the surface," with the CCR under pressure from students, leftists, and also the Brotherhood.[183]

Hasan al-'Ashmawi would later claim that Nasser told him in May 1953 that he no longer needed either the Ikhwan or Naguib and was ready to do away with them. According to al-'Ashmawi, Nasser even talked about liquidating the Brothers, declaring that if 30 percent of the country were with the Ikhwan, then he was ready to sacrifice that 30 percent to save the other 70 percent.[184] Though there is no way of confirming this account, there were reports at the time that relations between the government and the Brotherhood were becoming "markedly more critical and bitter."

The British assigned particular importance to the worsening of Brotherhood-regime ties, given that the "active participation" of the Brothers was thought to be "essential" if the government wished to relaunch conflict in the Canal Zone.[185] Even so, Ambassador Stevenson reckoned that if the struggle there did turn "hot," then the Ikhwan would likely still support the authorities. He feared that this might yet allow the group to gain real influence over the government (though again he deemed the Brothers to be divided between extremists who would "gladly pull Egypt down and preach among the ruins," and more moderate members who feared a descent into chaos).[186]

Certainly the Ikhwan was to the fore in demanding "government-sponsored action against the British" in the wake of "any breakdown in the talks."[187] It had affirmed that only a return to "armed struggle" could liberate the Canal Zone.[188] US diplomats noted that Hasan al-Hudaybi was once more speaking publicly about the need for "holy Jihad."[189] Caffery perceived that "some elements" in the group were "anxious" to force a showdown with the British, and were becoming increasingly cavillous with the regime for its refusal to initiate a conflict.[190] Other observers pointed to evidence of Brotherhood incitement to violence against the British.[191] At a minimum, it seemed clear that this pressure would stymie any prospect of the regime moving away from its own "uncompromising nationalism."[192]

More generally, US officials worried that the Free Officers had failed to develop a "body of doctrine" to justify their position. The result was an "unconscious drift to fascist techniques," with the regime reliant on two symbolic causes to secure support and national unity: the Canal and Israel. "Both drums" were being "pounded," it was said, "in direct ratio to the Army's failures in other spheres."[193] British intelligence had previously expressed concern that a "deadlock" in negotiations might lead to a resumption of violence and guerrilla warfare in the Canal Zone.[194] They reported that units of the Egyptian army were being redeployed, perhaps in readiness for clashes that might follow a complete collapse of talks.[195] There were fears that the Egyptian leadership, contrary to earlier expectations, was in fact now "fundamentally opposed" to a settlement.[196] And subsequent American-backed attempts to restart negotiations went nowhere.[197]

Rather, from the spring of 1953 there was a marked increase in violence targeting British military positions in the Canal Zone.[198] Significantly, members of the Muslim Brotherhood were reported to be participating—either independently, or as part of the government's revived "Liberation Battalions." Churchill informed his cabinet of intelligence assessments, which stated that a thousand members of the Ikhwan were operating "under German leadership" to carry out "sabotage and guerrilla activities."[199] The British and Americans were aware that senior ex-Nazis were involved in the training of both the regular Egyptian army and would-be insurgents.[200] (The Cairo government did not deny the German presence, claiming that they had already done more to develop Egypt's military than the British had achieved in thirty years.)[201] The role of Major Gerhard Mertens was a particular irritation, as he had allegedly provided assistance to the Brotherhood's "sabotage squads."[202] It was reckoned that Muslim Brothers accounted for the majority of those who had received instruction in government-run camps. As a result, the group was estimated to possess "kateiba [sic—battalion]" formations of some five thousand "comparatively well trained" men, in addition to a further eight thousand recruits who had been given the military basics at the Brotherhood's own centers. British intelligence concluded that Ikhwan volunteers, most of whom were based at the main universities, were of a "higher morale" and standard than those loyal primarily to the government. The organization as a whole was thought to be relatively well equipped; and there was talk about the possible development of Brotherhood "suicide squads."[203]

Despite this, UK diplomats believed that the "fanaticism" of the Ikhwan and its willingness to engage the British were tempered by "political caution." It was assumed that the Brothers still feared a repeat of their experiences during the Palestine war, when they had "sent their best men and fighting squads" into combat, only to be "proscribed and smashed" at home. With this in mind, it was judged unlikely that the group would commit to a new conflagration, other than on its own terms.[204] Officials noted too that al-Hudaybi continued to pledge his "full support" to the government, even as he also underlined the Ikhwan's dedication to achieving British withdrawal, and their readiness for action in the Canal Zone.[205]

It was against the background of this enduring ambiguity over the position of the Brothers that the British initiated dialogue with them—the talks that were then used by the regime to malign the group.[206] The accounts of various Ikhwan members are adamant that it was the British who broached the contact. Hasan al-'Ashmawi claimed that the embassy's Oriental counselor, Trefor Evans, had approached them seeking a meeting as early as December 1952.[207] According to Salah Shadi, the intermediary was Muhammad Salim, a legal adviser within the civil service who had ties to both the embassy and the senior Brothers Munir al-Dilla and Salih Abu Ruqayk. In February 1953, Salim got in touch with Abu Ruqayk and told him that British officials wanted to talk to the Ikhwan to explore their views on the Anglo-Egyptian dispute. This request was relayed to Hasan al-Hudaybi, who then asked Abu Ruqayk and al-Dilla to meet with Evans on a purely listening brief. Shadi insisted that contrary to the regime's subsequent disclosures, the general guide was careful to seek approval from Interior Minister Nasser before proceeding.

The same source provides a summary of the Brotherhood's narrative on what transpired next. At the meeting, Evans allegedly intimated that the British would agree to evacuate their forces within two years, on condition that Egypt sign up to a collective regional defense pact; he also asked to talk with al-Hudaybi personally. These comments were passed back to the general guide, who in turn passed them on, in writing, to Nasser. After the latter again gave consent, al-Hudaybi himself sat down with Evans, and he was presented with the same terms. Shadi's memoir states that the Brotherhood leader stressed his group's commitment to unconditional evacuation and neutrality. The most he would concede was the possibility of some kind of secret deal, by which Egypt would ask for Western help and allow the British to reenter the country in the event that it was attacked by Russia—on the proviso that the government of the day agreed such a step was necessary. Al-Hudaybi, though, would countenance no formal treaty, nor the continuation of a British presence at the Suez base in peacetime. Once more an account of all this was forwarded to Nasser.[208]

Hasan al-'Ashmawi averred that al-Hudaybi then met with Nasser to discuss everything that had happened. During this conversation, the general guide underlined his belief that there should be no new treaty with Britain. Egypt, he said, should stick to the cancellation of the 1936 agreement, demand unconditional evacuation, and commit to "neutrality."[209] Al-Hudaybi argued that if the British persisted on a "right of return," then this should only happen with the assent of both sides—or by adjudication from the UN Security Council (the assumption being that this body would never give such approval). In al-'Ashmawi's telling, it was actually Nasser who deemed al-Hudaybi's stance to be too hard-line. In addition, the interior minister apparently alluded to his own preference for an alliance with the West versus communism, as opposed to "neutrality."[210] That notwithstanding, al-'Ashmawi recorded that Nasser expressed his appreciation for al-Hudaybi's position, because he said that it would allow the government to push for the best possible terms from the British.[211]

Needless to say, the story offered by the government a few months later presented a very different picture.[212] This made no mention of the fact that Nasser had been given advance notice of the dialogue. It insinuated too that the Brothers had shown a readiness to compromise on key Egyptian demands. The Ikhwan saw the discrepancies between the two versions as flowing entirely from Nasser's dishonesty. In their view, it was a result of deliberate distortion, the purpose of which was to smear the Brotherhood and justify the dissolution of the group.

And yet, it may be that regime disquiet over contacts between the Brothers and the British was real—and had been exacerbated by an awareness of the fact the talks were part of a broader diplomatic effort on the part of the Ikhwan. The memoirs of security officer Fu'ad 'Allam make clear the government's unhappiness over simultaneous Brotherhood efforts to strengthen relations with the United States.[213] In April, American officials again met with al-Hudaybi's spokesman, Mahmud Makhluf, who disclosed that the Ikhwan was "concerned" about the trajectory of events in Egypt. The group's leaders predicted that the regime was preparing for their "eventual elimination." In the assessment of the diplomats, Brotherhood-government relations were, by then, in a delicate state of "uneasy truce."[214]

It was perhaps with this in mind that the Brothers sent Makhluf to the United States in the early summer of 1953, in order to acquaint the American people with the "true nature" of the movement. The trip was facilitated by the embassy in Cairo, which provided a letter of introduction allowing Makhluf to meet with State Department representatives. Initially, the visit proved less than successful: on arriving in the United States, Makhluf was abused as "a Negro" and contemplated cutting his tour short.[215] Officials, though, persuaded him to reconsider and several meetings were held. Significantly, during one encounter, Makhluf "made a special point of emphasizing the importance of the Moslem Brotherhood and the advisability of increasing United States contacts with this organization." Further, he insisted that the Ikhwan was "not a fanatical" group. It was, Makhluf said, fiercely opposed to communism and even ready to help bring about a settlement with Israel.[216]

It seems evident, therefore, that Makhluf's mission marked another attempt by the Brothers to improve their image in American eyes as a stepping-stone toward better relations with the United States. As previously, it may be that a key aim was to garner American support ahead of any potential move against the group by the Egyptian authorities (Makhluf was once more noted to be noncommittal on the situation between the Brotherhood and the regime). If this was indeed the objective, then the Ikhwan was not alone in adopting such an approach. The US Embassy in Cairo reported similar overtures from the Wafd (which were rebuffed).[217] But the Brotherhood appeared to invest considerable energy in reaching out to the United States throughout 1953.

Later that year, Sa'id Ramadan traveled to the United States to attend a conference organized by the State Department's newly formed propaganda arm, the International Information Administration (IIA), in collaboration with the Library of Congress and Princeton University.[218] As the former personal secretary and son-in-law of Hasan al-Banna, Ramadan was by this time one of the most influential members of the Ikhwan. The memoirs of other Brothers make clear that he had established himself very much as "his master's voice" and was a leading figure in several media ventures.[219] Ramadan had served as editor of the Brotherhood's monthly magazine al-Shihab and then occupied the same role at al-Muslimun. In addition, he had built up an international profile, helping to found branches of the Ikhwan in Palestine (where he was active during the 1948–1949 war), and becoming secretary general of the World Islamic Conference based in Karachi.[220]

Ramadan used his address to the 1953 Princeton colloquium to present the ideology and outlook of the Brotherhood in as favorable a light as possible. Islam, according to Ramadan, was "in essence a great liberation movement" that was opposed to the "spiritual, intellectual and social chains which had encumbered human life." Freedom of opinion and freedom of belief were said to be central to Islamic belief; and he pointedly contrasted this with the approach taken in the "Communist domain." After outlining the Brotherhood's demand for the implementation of "divine law," Ramadan stressed their adherence to a conservative social vision in which morality, the family, and "motherhood" would be protected. In his description of the rights and obligations that an individual held vis-à-vis state and society, Ramadan suggested that the vision of the Ikhwan was "similar" to that provided by modern forms of "social security" and "social insurance." Such words appear to have been framed with his audience very much in mind. Ramadan sought to make the principles of the Brotherhood intelligible—and even appealing—to his American listeners. For this reason, he also attempted to alleviate the degree of "confusion" that surrounded many people's understanding of the shari'a (notably regarding the application of the punishments for crimes like theft and adultery)—though on this front, one might imagine he was rather less successful.[221]

Irrespective of how persuasive or otherwise he was, the significance of Ramadan's Princeton speech lay in the fact that it was delivered at all. It is clear that *he* asked to go to the colloquium; he was not initially among the invitees selected by the US Embassy (see Chapter 6). His determination to attend was in many ways symptomatic of the Brotherhood's desire to engage with the United States at this time. Ramadan's mission, like that of Makhluf before it, was part of a diplomatic charm offensive toward the West—and undertaken with at least half an eye on the group's worsening relations with the government in Cairo.

While in America, Ramadan sought to exploit additional opportunities to articulate the ideas of the Ikhwan. In October, for instance, he addressed a meeting of the Washington Cooperative Group. A staff member of the British Embassy reported that Ramadan was "sweet reasonableness itself," and "drew a picture of the Moslem Brotherhood as a religious society working for the uplift of moral standards."[222] Elsewhere, he gave a long interview to *Middle East Report,* in which he underscored the moral focus of the Brotherhood's message and renounced extremism.[223] Ramadan testified that the Ikhwan rejected the use of violence to achieve its goals. He positioned it as a conservative, moderate (though he did not use the word) religious group enjoying wide popular support (he claimed a membership of some two million in Egypt and across the region). Again, while not stated explicitly, this was a message obviously designed to cater to conservative American sensibilities.

Back in Egypt, Brotherhood leaders increasingly seemed ready to voice their grievances to US diplomats. In a meeting with an embassy official at the end of June 1953, al-Hudaybi was openly critical of the Cairo government, which he said was wasting its time with gimmick policies while failing to deal with "important things," such as the removal of the British. On this occasion, too, the Brotherhood leader appeared to hint at a more belligerent posture, asserting that the military regime did not have the power to abolish the Ikhwan. The Brothers, he affirmed, would simply ignore any law aimed at their disbandment.[224] During a further conversation, the US Embassy reported that Brotherhood representatives (though not the general guide, nor his assistant Sa'id Ramadan) were inclined to make "hostile remarks" about Nasser. They were thought to be increasingly confident that the regime would soon be "out of power."[225] (Brotherhood members, though, also denied having any interest in a "counter-coup" from within the army.)[226]

Toward the end of July, the embassy's political officer, Howard Elting Jr., sat down with Makhluf and al-Hudaybi in Alexandria to discuss the situation.[227] The Brotherhood had recently taken part in a scout-commando parade organized by the authorities—the first time since the revolution that the Brothers had marched in a public rally. This had prompted speculation about an improvement in their relationship with the government. However, in this latest encounter with Elting, al-Hudaybi stressed that the Brotherhood's participation in the parade had been purely expedient: to have done otherwise, he averred, would have been interpreted as a show of support for the dethroned king.[228] The reality, according to the general guide, was that the Ikhwan did not approve of the way in which the CCR was attempting to implement its program. Asked his views on the future, al-Hudaybi prophesied the collapse of the regime, due to its inability to improve social conditions. What is more, he now actively expressed a preference for the withdrawal of the military from government and their replacement by a coalition of "good men" (but he denied this meant the Muslim Brothers themselves). Al-Hudaybi also hinted that the Ikhwan wished to see "certain members" of the CCR "eliminated." Though not named, US officials took this to be a reference to Nasser. On the subject of the Canal Zone, the general guide told the Americans that he felt the government had made a "great mistake" in publicly advocating for military action there. He argued that it would have been better if they had allowed "others" to take the lead on that issue. As to who exactly he had in mind, the diplomats formed the "distinct impression" that al-Hudaybi favored a leading role for the Brotherhood and wished to launch "guerrilla action" to dislodge the British from Egypt.

US diplomats were clearly unimpressed by all this. They described al-Hudaybi's thinking on the Suez Base as "completely muddled" and felt that he had little understanding of its importance.[229] With that said, Elting's somewhat quixotic conclusion was that al-Hudaybi was "only moderately fanatical on the subject of Islam." His views on the use of violence in the Canal Zone were said to reflect merely that he had imbibed the "full measure of the average Egyptian's hatred for the British" and was "equally emotional about it." More encouraging from the US perspective was the general guide's strident opposition to communism. Al-Hudaybi had asserted both that this was making "great advances" in Egypt and that only the Brotherhood's "moral approach" was capable of stopping it—a blatant appeal once more to US sympathies.[230]

Interestingly, the British Oriental counselor, Trefor Evans, observed at this time that the Americans *did* consider "cultivating" the general guide through the efforts of Elting—before deciding that he was at heart "an extremist and a born opportunist." The British themselves were taking stock of al-Hudaybi at the same moment. They saw him within the context of the Brotherhood as "more of a moderate than an extremist." In August, Evans met again with the general guide in Alexandria. At that gathering, as earlier, al-Hudaybi seemed anxious to try and improve contacts with his western interlocutor. He spoke "frankly" about relations between the Ikhwan and the regime, acknowledging that "all was not well." In particular, the Brotherhood leader complained that the government was not keeping him informed about the progress of the Anglo-Egyptian talks. The British found this dissatisfaction "a little surprising," given that the Ikhwan had apparently been granted notable concessions, including the right to train and maintain their own "para-military formations." Overall, British assessments of al-Hudaybi were mixed. On the one hand, they were encouraged by the fact that, on this occasion at least, he appeared ready to support the *principle* of negotiation and disavowed Brotherhood responsibility for recent attacks in the Suez Canal Zone. On the other hand, the diplomats noted that he refused to answer with clarity when asked about the sort of agreement that would be acceptable to the Ikhwan.[231] As a result, UK officials tended to arrive at a similar verdict as their American counterparts, finding al-Hudaybi's words confusing and rather unconvincing. There was a suspicion that the general guide's more conciliatory remarks were not a "genuine expression of Ikhwan policy." Roger Allen labeled them a "bit of soft soap," which did not mask the fact that al-Hudaybi would not allow the regime to be "too forthcoming" in dialogue with the British. The Whitehall view was that al-Hudaybi's emollient tone was belied by ongoing Brotherhood military preparations.[232] By this time, British military intelligence had concluded there was a "real threat" that the Ikhwan "khateibah [*sic*—battalion]" units would launch guerrilla attacks against their forces.[233]

Hence, while some UK diplomats might have seen al-Hudaybi as more "moderate" than many of his colleagues, there was little confidence that he could deliver the Ikhwan as an organization. The Brothers were too openly identified with calls for jihad against the British presence in Egypt for much stock to be placed in professions of friendship.[234] Throughout 1953, the group had continued to press for the expulsion of "imperialists" from Muslim lands.[235] In one interview with the French newspaper *Le Monde,* for instance, Hasan al-Hudaybi admitted that some Brothers had received weapons training and stood ready to "fight for the liberation of Egypt."[236] Western officials naturally weighed comments of this kind against private professions of good will and, in this context, it was hardly surprising that they remained skeptical about the Brotherhood and its leader.

To this can be added the fact that the British were scarcely oblivious of the political backdrop to their conversations with al-Hudaybi. By the late summer–early autumn, various indicators of underlying friction between the regime and the Ikhwan had become visible. The diplomats recorded a marked deterioration in relations and reported that Nasser had ordered all branches of the Brotherhood to be placed under surveillance. Conversely, it was observed that the Brothers had begun to remove their members from government-run training camps.[237] Ikhwan-regime differences, especially on the question of what to do about the Canal Zone, were thought to be undermining the already "fragile" truce between the two sides. The British and Americans surmised that, public statements of solidarity notwithstanding, the Brotherhood was now "fundamentally opposed" to the CCR.[238] Trefor Evans believed the Ikhwan had abandoned its early backing for the revolution and moved to a position that was "equivocal and potentially hostile."[239] At the same time, the diplomats thought that the worsening atmosphere was clearly making General Guide al-Hudaybi "uneasy."[240] Seen in this light, his efforts to engage the British (and indeed, the Americans) could be read as a purely expedient step—a strategic gambit to try to strengthen the Brotherhood's hand against the regime.

For the moment, tensions between the Ikhwan and the government simmered but did not boil over, and there were still occasional signs of a willingness to improve relations. For instance, a member of the Brotherhood's guidance council, al-Bahi al-Khuli, was appointed as religious adviser to the Liberation Rally.[241] In addition, the CCR's "Revolutionary Tribunal" prosecuted former prime minister Ibrahim 'Abd al-Hadi and various other individuals on charges of murdering Hasan al-Banna and torturing members of the Muslim Brotherhood during the 1948–1949 suppression on the group.[242] The subsequent death sentence issued against al-Hadi (which was commuted) was interpreted by many as "an act of political revenge" designed to appease the Ikhwan.[243]

Elsewhere, the diplomats noted placatory rhetoric from regime figures such as Husayn al-Shafi'i, who on a visit to Ismailia told his audience that those who had died fighting the British in 1951 (including Brotherhood members) were martyrs. In a further hint of possible rapprochement, al-Shafi'i delivered an address at a Muslim Brotherhood center, where he spoke of the government's readiness to introduce the kind of spiritual and educational reforms desired by the group.[244]

US sources also suggested that a meeting between Brotherhood emissaries and Nasser's close ally, Hakim 'Amer, had produced an "amicable understanding."[245] Nasser informed the Americans that a subcommittee had been created, comprising two representatives each from the Ikhwan and the CCR, which was tasked with developing plans for future cooperation.[246] There were even reports that the CCR had held "consultations" directly with al-Hudaybi.[247] The drawing together of the two groups seemed to be confirmed when the general guide publicly pledged his followers' support for the government in the "forthcoming battle" to drive the British out of Egypt.[248]

By this time, however, Western officials were aware that al-Hudaybi's position had been weakened by serious internal unrest within the Brotherhood. As outlined above, there had long been a perception that al-Hudaybi differed in outlook from most other Brothers. In March 1953, the British Embassy described how the senior Brotherhood figure Salih 'Ashmawi had openly censured the general guide for having forced Ahmad al-Baquri to resign the previous September; he claimed too that under al-Hudaybi, the Ikhwan was stagnating. The Brotherhood, 'Ashmawi declared, should "play an active role . . . and exploit their influence as the most powerful organisation in the Middle East in the interest of the people." They could not do this, he argued, as long as al-Hudaybi remained leader.[249] Though attempts were then made to deny that 'Ashmawi had said any of this, British officials believed his words had been reported accurately. One mandarin commented that if the Brothers continued to "wash their dirty linen in public like this, the resulting open split may decrease their political power and their ability to bully the Government." This, he said, would be a "welcome" outcome for the British.[250]

The Americans were likewise mindful of problems inside the Ikhwan. At their meeting in July, Makhluf had divulged to Elting that there had been efforts to dislodge the general guide from his post. Makhluf maintained that these would not succeed because al-Hudaybi enjoyed the support of the majority of Brotherhood members. Still, US officials had taken this as evidence of renewed tensions within the group—and they suspected that Nasser was involved behind the scenes.[251] Egyptian sources had told them that a "strong faction" inside the Brotherhood led by 'Abd al-Rahman al-Banna—the brother of Hasan—was being encouraged to oppose al-Hudaybi. There was a suggestion that the government might try to replace the general guide with al-Baquri. Even if such "intriguing" with anti–al-Hudaybi factions failed, American diplomats believed the CCR was determined that the Ikhwan should be "dealt with," one way or another.[252]

During the same period, Trefor Evans sought out Nasser himself in an effort to better understand the situation. At dinner in mid-September, Nasser acknowledged that he was "on personally bad terms" with al-Hudaybi and his closest supporters. He also said that he was in contact with opponents of the general guide inside the Ikhwan. Nasser told Evans that he expected this anti–al-Hudaybi faction to take control of the Brotherhood's guidance council at elections in October. The British, though, were worried that Nasser might be courting danger by relying on the "more extreme elements" in the Ikhwan.[253]

That autumn, the crisis within the Brotherhood reached a climax. The aforementioned guidance council elections were held and, in the judgment of the diplomats, weakened al-Hudaybi "to a considerable extent." Nine members of the new council were deemed to be pro-CCR, with the general guide left in a minority of four. In particular, Khamis Humayda, installed now as deputy general guide, was thought to be "hand in glove" with the government. Yet it was not all bad for al-Hudaybi. He did defeat attempts to limit his term to just three years and was instead confirmed in office for life. Further, his ally 'Abd al-Hakim 'Abdin was retained as the Brotherhood's secretary general; and two of his fiercer opponents, Salih 'Ashmawi and Ahmad al-Baquri, were not reelected to the council.[254] Nevertheless, Nasser was surely justified in subsequently boasting to the Americans that al-Hudaybi's internal authority had been "curtailed."[255] The British were similarly convinced that the CCR had "strengthened" its hold over the Brotherhood.[256] And officials in London welcomed this "encouraging" outcome.[257]

It quickly became apparent, however, that the Brotherhood's internal situation was far from resolved. The truth of this emerged in mid-November, in what remains a murky episode. It began with the murder of a Brotherhood member, Sayyid Fayiz, who was killed by a bomb concealed in a dessert tray that was sent to his home. Brotherhood accounts suggest that the man behind the assassination was 'Abd al-Rahman al-Sanadi, who had been resisting al-Hudaybi's attempts to take control of the Special Apparatus, over which he had been the dominant influence since the time of al-Banna. When the general guide discovered what had happened, he ordered an inquiry that recommended the expulsion of al-Sanadi and three others from the Brotherhood. Rather than accept this, al-Sanadi's supporters joined with other opponents of al-Hudaybi (such as Salih 'Ashmawi) and took over the group's headquarters. They then announced that the guidance council had been "sacked" and a delegation visited the general guide at his home to try to pressure him to resign. Al-Hudaybi, though, refused—and his partisans were then able to reoccupy the headquarters building.

In a final act, the general guide moved quickly to have the leading coup plotters (including his rival 'Ashmawi and the prominent cleric, Sheikh Muhammad al-Ghazali) expelled from the Ikhwan.[258]

The memoirs of senior Brotherhood leaders identified Nasser as the man really behind these events. The interior minister was said to be in close touch with, and urging on, al-Hudaybi's enemies.[259] At the time, too, British officials concluded that the affair revealed much about the ability of the CCR to manipulate "serious divergences" inside the Ikhwan. Nasser, it was said, seemed content to "play the role of 'tertius gaudens.'"[260] In conversation with Trefor Evans, Nasser offered his own analysis of the Brotherhood's internal troubles. Despite having previously admitted to being in contact with al-Hudaybi's opponents, in a display of some chutzpah, he now complained about the general guide's inability to control his followers. He stated that the Brotherhood's leaders were "a poor lot," engaged in a struggle for power over the organization. The government, he insisted, "could not tolerate a State within a State." Though intrigued by Nasser's version of events, it seems clear that British diplomats were not entirely persuaded. In their assessment, Nasser had definitely supported Brotherhood dissidents in order to "clip Hodeibi's [sic] wings." With the damage done, he had then withdrawn his support for the rebels, as they were expelled from the group.[261] Throughout it all, the British judged, Nasser's policy had been to "ensure" that the Ikhwan was "a divided organisation."[262]

Whatever they thought of his methods, there is little doubt that they were content to see the Brotherhood diminished; for the Ikhwan continued to be seen as a decisive—and unhealthy—presence in Egyptian politics. It was perhaps for this reason that in late autumn 1953, a Captain Hardie inside the British War Office produced a remarkable twenty-nine-page review of the Ikhwan, which was duly passed on to the Foreign Office.[263] Therein, Hardie described the Brothers as being "in many ways" the embodiment of Egyptian nationalism, noting that some experts believed them to be "the most influential" political force in the country. Beyond this, Hardie provided a detailed account of the Brotherhood's outlook and history, drawing on the first scholarly works on the movement, such as that composed by Ishaq al-Hussaini.[264] It was suggested that the Ikhwan was driven by a "hatred of European influence in Egypt" and was able to mobilize the "latent fanaticism" of the Muslim masses for a range of activities: from preaching the "Islamic renaissance" to social welfare projects; from political agitation to preparations for armed jihad. Hardie ventured that if all other methods failed, the Brotherhood would support an "insurrection" to "take over the state." On this reading, the group had contemplated a "violent coup d'état" in 1948–1949, but had failed to see it through; the murder of al-Banna had then dealt the Ikhwan a "stunning blow" from which it had struggled to recover. Hardie affirmed that the Brothers had experienced a "recession" of influence, which persisted after the July 1952 revolution. Even so, he was clear as to their enduring significance, given their mass popular appeal. Hardie gave a conservative estimate of perhaps half a million group members, drawn mainly from "the working and student classes." In his opinion, the Brotherhood remained "well disciplined and active." He assumed that its advocacy of "religious nationalism," coupled with demands for "social reformation," made it a powerful organization, critical of both the existing Egyptian elite and any residual imperialist presence.[265]

In light of such assessments, it was unsurprising that Western officials continued to favor an accomodation with the Egyptian government, rather than with a group like the Brotherhood. The considered view of someone like Trefor Evans was that the British should endeavor to strengthen the "better elements" in the CCR—by which he meant Nasser—so as to increase their control over the country. Robin Hankey tended to agree. He reckoned that "no better Government than the present one" could be foreseen in Egypt. He felt the alternatives were likely to be "either an obscurantist Moslem Brotherhood Government or a demagogic Wafdist Government." Neither of these, observed Hankey, would be "at all conducive" to British interests.[266]

Over the course of 1953, there had been further confirmation as to Nasser's leading position within the Egyptian power structure. In June, it had been announced that Egypt was to become a republic, with Naguib elevated to the presidency (as well as being prime minister). Despite this apparent promotion for the general, US officials judged that, in reality, this "placed actual control even more firmly" in the hands of Nasser and his CCR colleagues. Naguib had been "moved upstairs" and separated from the army, while Nasser held the "strategic" posts of interior minister and deputy prime minister. Simultaneously, his "most trusted lieutenant," Hakim 'Amer, had been made commander in chief of the military.[267] The CIA thus noted the "concentration of power" within the CCR "in a small clique headed by Colonel Nasr."[268]

With all that said, however, Naguib could not be ignored entirely; many felt that he enjoyed a wider popularity that Nasser lacked. The potential for an intraregime power struggle could not be discounted. This picture was complicated further, of course, by the persistent ambiguities that surrounded the Brotherhood. Egyptian politics retained an air of instability and discord. And neither was this sense of disharmony confined to Egypt. Throughout 1953, the West had also been split—and doubly so. On the one hand, it was clear that the United States was unconvinced by Britain's handling of the Anglo-Egyptian dispute, frustrated at London's refusal to make the concessions necessary for a settlement. The British government, meanwhile, was itself riven by disagreement on how to proceed. The difference in approach between Prime Minister Churchill and Foreign Secretary Eden was all too evident.[269] Hence, as the year drew to a close, Egypt remained beset by uncertainty: over Western policy toward Cairo; over the balance of internal power; and, of course, over the position of the Brotherhood. The subsequent twelve months would see the resolution of each of these issues.

1954, Year of Decision

The long-anticipated break between the Ikhwan and the regime came on 12 January 1954. The immediate cause was a clash at Cairo University between students belonging to the Liberation Rally and the Brotherhood, respectively. The Ikhwan had organized a commemorative gathering for its "martyrs" from the Canal Zone struggle against the British, which was addressed by the Iranian radical Nawab Safavi.[270] Hasan Dawh recalled in his memoirs that he had doubted the wisdom of giving Safavi a platform, fearing that he would be too extreme. Yet Dawh himself seems to have delivered an incendiary speech on the day, which included calls for a return to democracy. According to Dawh, even before he had finished speaking, members of the Liberation Rally had attacked the assembled Brothers—the suggestion being that the episode was entirely contrived, to provide a pretext for their suppression.[271] Brotherhood leaders would later assert that Nasser targeted them in order to remove the one force that could oppose an agreement with the British, thereby proving to both London and Washington the scope of his power.[272] Certainly, given the scale of the crackdown that followed, it would appear that events at the university were merely the trigger for a long-planned move (a view that was shared by both the British and American embassies). Within twenty-four hours, several hundred Brotherhood members—including al-Hudaybi—had been arrested. Among them was the young Yusuf al-Qaradawi.[273] Three days later, it was announced that the Brotherhood was a political party and therefore subject to the 1953 law of dissolution.[274] As described at the outset of this chapter, the government published a lengthy communiqué explaining its actions, highlighting the various infractions of the Brothers, including their contacts with the British.[275]

Several days into the clampdown, it was reported that the security forces had uncovered radio transmitters and explosives at Brotherhood premises around the country.[276] Attention was drawn, in particular, to a substantial cache of arms that had been found in the cellar of an estate in Sharqiya province belonging to the family of Hasan al-'Ashmawi.[277] The Brothers would always insist that these revelations were spurious (see Chapter 4). For Western observers, though, the discovery of such weapons seemed merely to validate the CCR's contention that it had no choice but to dissolve the Ikhwan. The *Times*, for instance, commented that "no government" had "been able to work with the Brotherhood" and the attempt to suppress the organization was seen as an important moment for Egypt.[278]

President Neguib told British ambassador Stevenson that he believed repressive measures "should really have been taken earlier." In spite of this, Neguib declared himself confident that all "influential and dangerous" members of the Ikhwan had been detained and the group dismantled "completely."[279] The ambassador observed that the CCR had "almost certainly won the first round in their bold move against the Brotherhood." This was, he felt, "all to the good," given that the "ineffective" leaders of the Ikhwan seemed unable to control their "terrorist organisation."[280]

By this point, the settled view of UK officials was that there was "no alternative" to the military regime. They feared anything that seemed to portend "mob rule" and the empowerment of either the Brotherhood, or the Wafd.[281] Indeed, the principal worry in British circles was that the government might not be able to maintain its "initial advantage" against the Ikhwan. Ambassador Stevenson expressed misgivings about the increased threat of assassination.[282] British military intelligence noted that the regime's move against the Brotherhood had been well-planned and was likely to be "a very different thing and far more effective than the proscription of the IEM [Ikhwan el-Muslimeen] by the Wafd [*sic*] in 1948."[283] Even so, they harbored doubts about how far the authorities had captured the Brotherhood's "secret funds and weapons"; and they too were apprehensive lest retaliation come in the form of violence.[284]

Unsurprisingly, US officials joined the British in offering a cautious welcome to the crackdown on the Brotherhood. The CIA recorded that the Egyptian government was seeking to remove its "only remaining opponent," a "fanatical religio-nationalist organization." The suppression of the Ikhwan was described as a "necessary" step, if the regime was "to achieve a settlement of [the] Suez dispute." The assumption was that this would give the CCR "greater freedom of action in its relations with [the] West"; and the decision to dissolve the

Brotherhood was said to prove that the Egyptians were "not yet ready to turn to anti-Western neutralism."[285] Still, American diplomats also echoed British anxieties that the government might fall short in its objectives. The Brothers, they acknowledged, appealed to a "large body" of the Egyptian public. They anticipated that it might endure in a "more or less clandestine form."[286]

Beyond this, American analysts had, from the beginning, expected that repression would be confined to the Brotherhood leadership around Hasan al-Hudaybi.[287] This prognosis quickly seemed borne out by events. Within days of the initial round of arrests, more than fifty members of the Brotherhood had been released. The Egyptian state press appeared at pains to draw a distinction between the "faithful and patriotic rank and file" and their "intriguing and ambitious" leaders.[288] Even at senior levels, meanwhile, only half of the Brotherhood's guidance council was detained.[289] The CCR's campaign was aimed specifically at al-Hudaybi and his closest supporters, with propaganda focused on the alleged crimes of the general guide. He was accused of failing to support the revolution, indulging in dictatorial tendencies, and operating through a clique. Under al-Hudaybi, the Brotherhood was said to have lost its sense of purpose and to have betrayed the memory and traditions of Hasan al-Banna.[290] This theme was underscored in February, when Nasser again visited the grave of al-Banna on the anniversary of his death (at which time, as mentioned, he pitched to the sympathies of the assembled Brothers—see above).[291] The message he sought to convey was that the Ikhwan had been led astray by al-Hudaybi—and Nasser even advanced this line in discussion with the US ambassador. He told Caffery that he had worked with the Brotherhood since 1946 and known all the principal figures within the group. Only latterly, he averred, had he come "reluctantly" to the "conclusion they were up to no good."[292] On another occasion, Nasser alluded to his personal links with a number of Brotherhood members, and American diplomats speculated that he might allow the Ikhwan to reform at some point in the future, provided it agreed to abide by certain conditions.[293] In line with this, there was a suspicion that the government might try to empower the anti–al-Hudaybi faction linked to the recently expelled Salih 'Ashmawi. As far as the British were concerned, this strategy carried its own risks. 'Ashmawi was judged to be "more extreme" than al-Hudaybi, and the fear was that he too might eventually turn against the regime.[294] It would be far better, they believed, for the Brotherhood to be destroyed permanently.

In the event, the government's attempts to eliminate the Ikhwan proved abortive at this stage. The group was rescued by the crisis that hit the regime in

February–March 1954.[295] The roots of this unrest had little to do with the Brotherhood directly and arose instead out of the long-simmering tension between Naguib and Nasser. On February 25, the former resigned as president, prime minister, and chairman of the CCR. In a statement, the government claimed that relations had become impossible and accused Naguib of disavowing decisions that he himself had approved (including the dissolution of the Ikhwan). More generally, the CCR charged that Naguib had attempted to aggrandize his personal political power and when thwarted, had resigned. Nasser now acceded to the vacant posts of prime minister and CCR chairman; the position of president was left empty.[296]

British officials were clearly disconcerted by these developments—less because of any affection for Naguib and more from a fear that it might lead to instability. Ambassador Stevenson judged the removal of Naguib to have "weakened" the CCR both at home and abroad.[297] Back in London, Robin Mackworth-Young warned that the Ikhwan might "take courage" from intraregime disunity and perhaps even turn to assassination.[298] Similarly, the *Times* pondered whether the regime would now face "domestic difficulties" stemming from either the old political parties or the Brotherhood. The latter was thought to be "still a formidable force despite its recent proscription."[299]

A similar reaction was in evidence among American diplomats. Ambassador Caffery described Naguib's resignation as a "serious loss."[300] Again, though, this was not so much a product of sympathy or support for the general (indeed, Caffery felt that the crisis was a product of Naguib's "injured vanity"). Rather, it flowed from disquiet about the potential for unrest. The ambassador saw Naguib as a fundamentally good, honest, and sincere man, but also someone who was "weak." Neither the Egyptian public nor the wider world, he attested, were aware of the extent to which Nasser had "from [the] beginning planned and guided [the] movement." For this reason, Caffery's principal concern was that it would "be extremely difficult . . . to convince [the] public of what is obvious to anyone meeting him in more intimate circumstances; i.e., that at 36 Nasir is already head and shoulders above Naguib in ability and strength of character."[301] US officials worried that the removal of the man previously built up as the leader of the revolution would leave the regime in an "extremely delicate position."

The truth of this was made manifest sooner than anyone anticipated. Almost immediately, Nasser faced a challenge from within the army. On the night of February 26–27, a group of young cavalry officers mutinied, demanding the reinstatement of Naguib and the restoration of constitutional government.[302] The next two days saw student demonstrations and popular protests in the streets of Cairo and Alexandria. Cries of "back to the barracks" filled the air. At a rally at the 'Abdin Palace, cheers in favor of Naguib were coupled with shouts of "down with [the CCR]—we want Nasir's head—Islam is behind bars." Though the government kept control of the situation, there were clashes between rioters and the police, and there was a discernable groundswell of opposition to the Free Officers' regime.[303]

Confronted by the toxic blend of popular unrest and intra-army revolt, Nasser and the CCR decided that discretion was the better part of valor and opted for conciliation, albeit laced with deception. At an early meeting with the rebellious cavalry officers, Nasser assured the dissidents that a well-known leftist Free Officer, Khalid Muhi al-Din, would be appointed prime minister and that Naguib would be restored. With the situation thereby defused (and having called up loyalist units), he then had the mutineers arrested. Nasser would later admit to US officials that he had only offered to make Muhi al-Din prime minister because he "knew the Army would never accept it"; he claimed to have "planned the whole maneuver to bring Khalid out in [the] open" and was "only surprised at how quickly the officers reacted."[304]

A similar, albeit more drawn-out approach was applied to the wider populace, with Nasser again appearing to retreat before moving to reestablish firm control. During the February 28 disturbances, Nasser met with Naguib and agreed that the latter would indeed return as president. In addition, plans were announced for a Constituent Assembly to pave the way for a parliamentary republic.[305] Subsequently, the two leaders stood together on the balcony of the 'Abdin Palace, where Naguib addressed, pacified, and dispersed the crowds.[306] Alongside them on the balcony were several senior Muslim Brothers, including Salih 'Ashmawi and 'Abd al-Qadir 'Awda—a clear sign that Nasser had also sought to conciliate the Ikhwan.[307]

From the outset, the US Embassy had been inclined to believe that the Brotherhood and the communists were responsible for the antigovernment protests. One diplomatic dispatch reported that armed Ikhwan members had been involved in the distribution of inflammatory pamphlets and acts of violence.[308] Whatever the truth of these allegations, there seems little doubt that the Brotherhood was prominently involved, as evinced by the slogans voiced during the demonstrations. Nasser now sought to turn this to his advantage. The government depicted the upheavals as the work of the Ikhwan and other allegedly dangerous influences. In the first days of March, 'Awda and more than forty other Muslim Brothers were arrested, along with Ahmad Husayn, members of the defunct Socialist Party, Wafdists, and communists.[309] During the next several days, state newspapers disclosed that "reactionaries and subversive elements" were behind a "serious plot" to foment chaos in Egypt.[310]

Western officials watched all this with mounting unease. The US Embassy judged that public sympathy for the CCR had been brought to an "all-time low," while the CIA forecast further "deterioration" and "struggle." It was reckoned that Nasser had "lost face" and perhaps also "lost some of his nerve," even as Naguib remained "basically weak" and "indecisive." The analysts again wondered, in this new atmosphere of uncertainty, whether the CCR might drift into either "more extremist military dictatorship," or toward disintegration, allowing the old-line politicians, communists, or the Muslim Brotherhood to take power. None of this was thought to be to the benefit of the United States and its allies.[311] The British likewise intimated that "it may be to the advantage of all concerned," if the CCR did not "relax their grip too completely or too soon."[312]

Despite this, on March 5, the CCR issued a series of resolutions ending press censorship and announcing that elections would be held within three months so that a Constituent Assembly could be convened in mid-July. The US Embassy observed that if elections were held on a party basis, the Ikhwan would win.[313] Needless to say, this was not a gratifying prospect. Caffery supposed that the Brothers were preparing for a "prolonged struggle" against Nasser, who they now made the focus of their opposition.[314] Such conclusions were based in part on insights gleaned from a remarkable interview between American officials and an unnamed yet "reliable" member of the Ikhwan. This source affirmed the Brotherhood's commitment to a nonviolent approach, but spoke of their desire to "isolate" Nasser and "kill" him politically. The informant was also defiant on the position of al-Hudaybi, stressing that any attempt by the government to impose proregime leaders on the Ikhwan would end in "failure." Moreover, real control of the group was said not to lie at the "centre," but rather with "virtually unknown secondary" leaders spread throughout Egypt. The cohesion of this hidden leadership, it was claimed, was based on shared "beliefs" and secured by a dispersed structure of rural centers that continued to operate freely; this structure would ensure that the Brotherhood remained "an ever present force of which any Egyptian Government will be aware and with which it will have to deal."[315]

With such words, the interviewee provided a fascinating glimpse into the restive mind-set of the Ikhwan. In the early spring of 1954, the group seemed newly emboldened. There were reports, for example, that it was cooperating with the communists to organize demonstrations on university campuses.[316] On March 12, the still-imprisoned al-Hudaybi formally appealed to the State Council to rescind the order dissolving the Brotherhood.[317] In addition, he wrote a public letter to Naguib that was published in *al-Misri,* calling for national unity, the restitution of political freedoms, and the release of imprisoned Muslim Brothers.[318]

In mid-March, Nasser informed the Americans that a fresh collision between the CCR and its opponents was "probably inevitable." He promised that the government would not yield "tamely" to those—such as Wafdists, communists, and Muslim Brothers—who wished for "freedom and democracy." In the wake of these comments, Ambassador Caffery anticipated that Nasser would shortly reassert his position, for he was a "man of boldness and cunning and not one to be easily discouraged by a set-back."[319] For the moment, a visit to Egypt by King Saud was said to have imposed a temporary lull, but serious trouble was expected to follow his departure.[320]

On March 25, both the Wafd and the Ikhwan issued statements in the press outlining their respective positions. The former declared that, while it accepted the achievements of the revolution, it believed it was time for a return to parliamentary government.[321] The Brotherhood, by contrast, focused on its own status, demanding an end to the group's proscription—which was said to have been a "serious mistake" desired by "imperialists and their agents." The revolution was described as the product of "a hard and bloody fight on the part of the Muslim Brothers against a Royal tyranny and against prevailing conditions." The Ikhwan presented itself as the only real safeguard for the new regime against the machinations of the British, the Jews, and the "old politicians."[322] If relegalized, the group pledged to "stand watch" against any "reactionary measure" that sought a return to the past. Crucially, the Brotherhood also emphasized its internal unity. The seven individuals who had been expelled the previous year signed the statement and swore their fealty to al-Hudaybi's leadership. As the US Embassy inferred, by making their case in these terms, the Brothers as a single bloc both asserted their ownership of the revolution and appeared ready to accept a rapprochement with the regime—if only they were restored to their former position.[323] This implicit "offer" was backed by a threat, as the Ikhwan stated: "Let those who think that the Muslim Brothers have discarded their weapons, patience and the continuous struggle until God intervenes with his wishes, beware."[324] The challenge to, and possible opportunity for, the regime was unmistakable.

In response, Nasser and the CCR sought to reclaim the initiative, utilizing the tactics that had proven so effective earlier: namely, an ostensible withdrawal coupled with the strategic deployment of loyal forces so as to overcome all opposition. Thus, the government at first appeared to concede key demands. A date was set for an official end to the revolution and political parties were allowed to resume their organizing at once. All political detainees—including al-Hudaybi, 'Abd al-Qadir 'Awda, and Reshad Mehanna—were freed. Press restrictions were lifted and individual political rights restored. It was announced that martial law as a whole would soon be brought to an end.[325] Evidently, the US ambassador was less than pleased by all this. He attributed the decisions to the ongoing "political maneuvering" of Naguib, who in Caffery's estimation had shown he was willing "to play along with [the] worst elements in [the] country, including Wafdists, Muslim Brotherhood, and Communists to stay in power."[326]

It was obvious from the beginning, though, that the CCR was not quietly retiring from the political scene. Nasser made this abundantly clear to US officials, telling them that his goal was merely to remove the ambiguity from the situation.[327] In addition, the CCR acted quickly to split the opposition. As Caffery recognized, the regime had effectively met the most significant requests set forth in the Brotherhood's statement of March 25, thereby removing the group's formal grievances. Indeed, by releasing Mehanna, for which the Ikhwan had been calling since July 1953, the government seemed to have gone a step further—a sure signal of their desire to conciliate the Brothers. This was underlined further by the visits that Nasser and his colleague Salah Salim paid to al-Hudaybi and other top Brotherhood leaders immediately after their release from prison. The diplomats presumed such meetings marked an attempt to reach a "formal understanding" between the two sides.[328]

Though there is no known official record of any deal, the circumstantial evidence would strongly suggest that some kind of accommodation was achieved. The Ikhwan once more showed its pragmatic flexibility; for as the embassy subsequently remarked, the group effectively opted for neutrality, neither backing nor opposing the CCR.[329] Instead, al-Hudaybi issued a new statement calling simply for national unity. The Ikhwan pledged not to enter partisan politics and publicly re-embraced the revolution, saying it was just "one phase of a wider and more far-reaching revolution—[that of] the Muslim Brothers' movement." Though al-Hudaybi pronounced his support for various freedoms, he also repeated his deep opposition to corruption of the kind that had preceded July 1952. In the judgment of US officials, comments of this kind represented an effort to return the Ikhwan to the status quo ante of 1953. The Brotherhood held out "a certain identity with the Army movement," so as to reserve for itself the position of "social conscience for Egypt's public life."[330]

All of this was entirely compatible, of course, with the continued rule of the CCR, and as such, it bespoke the Brotherhood's de facto endorsement of the government.[331]

Furthermore, the practical effect of their revised stance was that the Brothers now abandoned the streets and their tentative alliance with other opposition forces. As the US Embassy reported, the Wafdist newspaper *al-Misri* had called for a joint Wafd-Communist-Ikhwan front, yet there was little response from the latter. Pointedly, al-Hudaybi instead held further meetings with Nasser. In consequence, antigovernment demonstrations became markedly smaller in number. And this gave Nasser the opportunity to deploy his own partisans. His first step in this regard had been to secure the allegiance of the army— especially the Free Officers—and fresh declarations of loyalty were obtained from all the service branches.[332] With the regime thereby sure of its foundations, it moved to reassert control of the streets. Organized labor was "deliberately and effectively" mobilized via the Liberation Rally and official trade unions, in a fashion that, to the minds of some US diplomats, had "definite 'Peronist' over-tones."[333] Pro-CCR marches and labor strikes rejected the return of the po-litical parties. These protests were allowed to continue over several days until the army was at last called in to restore order. With the "will of the people" thus established, the CCR reversed its earlier concessions. The decisions of March 5 and 25 were suspended; plans to convene a constituent assembly were abandoned in favor of a purely consultative body. The revolution, it was pro-claimed, would press forward with the CCR now resuming full powers.[334]

As the CIA put it, Nasser and his colleagues were "again back in top posi-tion."[335] In the shared assessment of the British and American Embassies, the events of March had "severely" shaken the CCR, but the regime had perhaps emerged stronger than ever.[336] There had always been a belief that the reunion between Nasser and Naguib was "bogus" and it was soon clear that the latter was being marginalized.[337] A further dispatch from Ambassador Caffery at the end of March made plain his own feelings about this outcome: "While I do not (repeat not) approve all methods Nasir used during recent week and events, I point out that the results from our point of view can be called satisfactory . . . in my opinion, Nasir is [the] only man in Egypt with strength enough and guts enough to put over an agreement with [the] British."[338] Caffery was not alone in his analysis. The British ambassador likewise noted that Nasser had proven himself to be "an astute, if unscrupulous, politician."[339] All things considered, the CCR was seen as "anti-Communist and relatively pro-western" and there-fore worthy of support. Of equal if not greater significance was the verdict that there was "no alternative government in sight which would be as satisfactory from [the] point of view of the West."[340]

As calm returned to Cairo, there were fresh indications that the regime was growing in confidence. In the wake of the March crisis, Nasser published his *Philosophy of the Revolution,* a document that in British eyes threw a "not un-favourable light" on his beliefs. The work was praised (faintly) for displaying a "certain breadth of vision, humanity and idealism which one might be excused for not expecting from a man of his background."[341] By May 1954, the embassy was reporting that the CCR's internal position had "gradually improved," with Naguib "virtually isolated and powerless." The previous month, Nasser had re-turned as prime minister (having briefly relinquished the post following the March crisis). Opposition elements such as the students or the press had been "cowed," while the Brotherhood was said to be "quiescent."[342]

In this context, there was an expectation on both sides of the Atlantic that it might finally be possible to resolve the Anglo-Egyptian dispute.[343] The Americans thought that such a settlement would "do more than any other single thing to stabilize the situation and consolidate the regime."[344] Optimism that this could be achieved was strengthened by shifts within the British government. For one thing, the proagreement Eden was restored to health and to work; for another, the hitherto-intransigent Churchill seemed more open to a deal. In part, this was a function of changes within British strategic thinking, linked to reassessments of "global strategy" and the creation of the hydrogen bomb.[345] As a contemporary Foreign Office minute put it, the "developments of modern warfare" had rendered irrelevant the question of whether the Egyptian army could maintain the liberty and security of navigation through the Suez Canal.[346] This logic was reinforced by the fact that the situation in the Canal Zone itself remained deeply unsettled. Though there had been no return to the levels of violence seen in late 1951–early 1952, attacks against British troops had persisted during the first two years of Free Officer rule. Eleven soldiers were killed during 1953.[347] In January 1954, five more died in a series of attacks, and others were killed as the year progressed—all of which generated criticism in the British media and the House of Commons.[348]

Against this backdrop, the UK government at last appeared ready to accept a settlement. In early June, the minister of state at the Foreign Office, Selwyn Lloyd, prepared a memorandum for his cabinet colleagues, which described the latest treaty proposals as "probably as satisfactory from our point of view as any possible alternative." British economic problems, Lloyd said, made an agreement and military drawdown "essential." It was also recognized that the Americans were unlikely to go on withholding aid from the Egyptian regime—as they had done hitherto at British request.[349] In early July, therefore, Churchill's cabinet formally authorized the resumption of talks. The prime minister himself even declared in favor of troop withdrawals.[350]

Nasser too seemed ready to forge ahead.[351] In June he had given an interview to the *Sunday Times* in which he proclaimed his openness to a new approach from Britain.[352] The following month it was reported that he had read the "riot act" to Naguib after the latter attempted to make an inflammatory speech against the British, belittling prospects for an accord. According to the US Embassy, the episode reflected both Nasser's determination to secure a deal and the fact that Naguib truly had been reduced to a mere "figurehead role."[353] By the end of July, an Anglo-Egyptian "Heads of Agreement" document had been signed, which would open the way to a full-blown treaty.[354] It was seen as a triumph for Western—and in particular US— foreign policy.[355] In the immediate aftermath, discussions were held about the transfer of sizable tranches of American aid to Cairo. Though this funding fell short of what Nasser had hoped (he had sought some $100 million worth of assistance, but was initially offered just $40 million, divided equally between economic and military aid), it seemed a promising start. Before the year was out, Washington had restated its commitment to sending substantial funds to Egypt.[356]

The settlement at last of the Anglo-Egyptian dispute, by a government under the increasing control of Nasser, served to highlight the one major unresolved issue in Egyptian domestic politics: the position of the Ikhwan. CIA analysts noted with concern that the "fanatic Brotherhood," with its estimated half million members, was still "capable of initiating serious activities against the regime."[357] Caffery informed Washington that Nasser faced probably the "toughest political fight of his career" in order to sell his agreement with the British in the face of criticism from the Wafd, communists, and the Ikhwan.[358]

Prior to this point, the Brotherhood had appeared largely to abide by the terms of its informal March compact with the regime. Al-Hudaybi, for instance, had reiterated his opposition to both the revival of the old parties and corruption— effectively endorsing the revolution.[359] In spite of this, antagonism between the Ikhwan and the CCR was never far from the surface. Al-Hudaybi had made manifest his preference for the return of some kind of parliamentary system, as well as for the restoration of civil liberties such as freedom of opinion and of the press. He had also renewed his demand for a constitution based on Islam, rather than on the European models favored by the regime's constitutional committee. Inevitably, these differences created friction. To this were added the Brotherhood's ongoing calls for jihad against the British, even as Nasser looked toward a political settlement.[360] In his March 1954 press statement, for example, al-Hudaybi had declared categorically that with regard to the Suez Base, "we never accepted negotiations as a means of achieving our independence. There is only one course which we shall follow—JIHAD."[361] At a time when Nasser was in peacemaking mode, this could only be embarrassing. There was thus no denying the likelihood of further conflict.

In early May, al-Hudaybi sent Nasser a semiopen letter lambasting the regime and demanding reforms. Though not published in the newspapers, the document was reprinted and circulated widely. In it, al-Hudaybi publicly accused Nasser of breaking his promises to the Brotherhood.[362] American officials observed that the Ikhwan knew the danger of antagonizing the government and had anticipated "reprisals"—perhaps even involving "bloodshed"—but this had not deterred it from acting.[363] Increasingly, it seemed only a matter of time before a new clash occurred. This was the prism through which the diplomats viewed al-Hudaybi's decision to leave on a tour of the Middle East in early summer. His first stop was Saudi Arabia, where he went ostensibly to perform the Hajj, but also to meet King Saud. US officials thought this significant given the king's support for reconciliation between the CCR and the Brotherhood earlier in the year. Al-Hudaybi's latest engagement with Saud was seen as a bid to win his support ahead of any fresh conflict with the regime. It was, in other words, a return to the policy of using overseas diplomacy to bolster the Ikhwan domestically—"a continuation of the 'war of nerves'" between the government and the Brothers. The assumption was that the Ikhwan, faced with Nasser's overwhelming strength within Egypt, was trying to build up its regional hinterland.[364] Hence, after leaving Saudi Arabia, al-Hudaybi moved on to Syria and Jordan in a further effort to consolidate external backing.[365]

Within Egypt, meanwhile, the US Embassy reported that the "armed truce" in place since March was "disintegrating" rapidly.[366] Inevitably, the Anglo-Egyptian Agreement had raised tensions to a new level.[367] On July 29, the Brotherhood's guidance council met and formally rejected the accord. In an interview with *al-Manar Damascus,* the organ of the Syrian Ikhwan, al-Hudaybi condemned the deal as an extension of the 1936 treaty, which he said had already been canceled and was, in any case, due to expire in 1956. He complained that the "cunning and wily" English had now been given a reason to stay in the Suez Base, and Egypt had been tied indelibly to the "Western camp." In addition, he declared that Britain had gained a new vehicle with which to encircle "the Arab countries with treaties and military alliances." For this reason, al-Hudaybi was adamant that any settlement could only be ratified by a freely elected parliament that truly represented the Egyptian people. Until this happened, he was pledged to oppose it.[368]

As these words indicated, al-Hudaybi's stance was symptomatic of the Brotherhood's deeply ingrained suspicion of the British. In autumn 1953, the senior Brotherhood leader Sa'id Ramadan had offered an unequivocal if rather unusual example of this in an article for *al-Muslimun,* in which he drew heavily on a Mass at All Souls Church in London, which he had heard courtesy of the British Broadcasting Corporation (BBC). Ramadan recounted how he had been struck by the words of the hymn, "Let the song go around the earth," in which the composer looked to the "Lands where Islam's sway, Darkly broods o'er home and hearth" and urged them to "Cast their bonds away." This was, Ramadan believed, a classic restatement of London's unceasing "policy of aggression toward Islam and Muslims," which revealed the English "spirit of hatred" for Islam. This sentiment was said to be the "black reality" behind British colonialism, past and present, which had driven the "conspiracy of England and its allies against the Caliphate of the Ottomans."[369] Convinced in this way of British badmindedness, it was only natural that the Brothers should have been ideologically opposed to any Anglo-Egyptian agreement. To their minds, this was merely the latest manifestation of London's nefarious imperial practice.

Soon afterward, the Brotherhood issued a new statement demanding that negotiations be abandoned until such time as a British evacuation was complete. The group called on the government to provide military education and spread the "spirit of jihad" so that the people might seize their rights and expel their oppressors.[370] In the same period, the Brothers were also thought to be behind the circulation of a pamphlet entitled *Muhammad Neguib . . . President of the Republic: Criticises the Anglo-Egyptian Agreement,* which complained about the way Naguib had been excluded from the talks. What had emerged, according to the pamphlet, was a settlement that was even worse than the 1936 treaty. Much focus was placed on the base reactivation clauses in the deal. It was claimed that these compelled Egypt to participate in a regional defensive pact and made "enemies of those who are not our enemies." Nasser was accused of having "harnessed" Egypt to "the chariot wheel of the West."[371]

An additional Brotherhood tract discussed the role of the Americans in pushing the Egyptian government toward dialogue rather than "armed struggle." The Ikhwan contended that preparations had been made for a violent campaign against the British, but that the US ambassador had intervened to thwart this and advance a negotiated settlement. On this interpretation, the United States and the United

Kingdom had together worked to exploit the rift between Nasser and Naguib, so as to weaken the CCR and secure a treaty that was detrimental to Egyptian interests. The agreement, it was averred, was "evil" and "should be eradicated."[372]

In response to all of this, state media launched a series of attacks on the "bearded charlatans" who used religious ideas for personal gain.[373] In *al-Gumhuriyya*, Sadat attacked those "Islamic reactionaries" who distorted the face of religion.[374] This rhetorical escalation paralleled and further contributed to the steady deterioration in the atmosphere between the Ikhwan and the regime.[375] The authorities soon moved to suspend the Brotherhood's publication, *al-Ikhwan al-Muslimun*.[376] And when al-Hudaybi tried to publish another open letter criticizing the government and denouncing the Anglo-Egyptian agreement, the newspapers were prevented from carrying it.[377]

Against this background, the US State Department wrote to its embassy in Cairo in mid-August, seeking clarification on a number of points: Was the Brotherhood's dissolution order still in place? Had it been recognized and sanctioned as a "socio-religious society"? Was the Ikhwan engaging in activities in defiance of the regime?[378] The very fact that such questions could still be posed was testament to the degree to which, even at this stage, some uncertainty remained over the position of the Brotherhood. It was not long, however, before all such ambiguity was removed.

Destroying the Brotherhood

In late August 1954, antigovernment protests by worshippers at the Sharif Mosque on Roda Island in Cairo led to clashes with the security forces and a number of people were injured. It was alleged that one of the Brotherhood's most prominent university leaders, Hassan Dawh, had made a speech calling for violent opposition to the regime.[379] Dawh's own account confirms that he criticized the government for following the path of Atatürk and demanded a foreign policy based on neutrality between East and West. He also urged the people to wrap themselves around the Brotherhood and begged the police to "save their bullets for our real enemy, the English." By his own admission, he finished his address with rousing expressions that inflamed the zeal of the crowd and, as a result, there was a confrontation that led to several people being arrested, Dawh among them.[380] According to US officials, many Brothers feared that the episode presaged a wider repressive campaign.[381] A couple of weeks later, there were reports that Ikhwan members had been involved in fighting at a mosque in Tanta. The unrest had been sparked by objections to a political sermon delivered in the mosque, during which the preacher described the ruling officers as "heretics." Between fourteen and seventeen people were detained, most of whom were Brotherhood members.[382] As the memoirs of Hasan al-'Ashmawi make clear, the Ikhwan now concluded that the government had indeed initiated a crackdown against it, and by September, some five hundred Brothers had been imprisoned.[383] Likewise, in his history of the Brotherhood, Yusuf al-Qaradawi dates the group's "third ordeal" as having begun in this period.[384]

Supporters of the regime lined up to attack the Ikhwan and its leaders. Sadat's *Al-Gumhurriya* continued to be particularly vehement in its criticism of al-Hudaybi, labeling him a reactionary feudalist who was against reform. The general guide's opposition to the Anglo-Egyptian settlement was denounced as an act of treachery.[385] Other state media compared al-Hudaybi to Rasputin—someone who exploited religion to deceive people and secure power for himself. There were also accusations that the Brothers were linked to communism.[386] Even Hasan al-Banna's brother, 'Abd al-Rahman, joined in, publishing a stinging critique of al-Hudaybi in the pages of *al-Ahram*.[387] US officials judged all of this to be part of a "conditioning" exercise, as a prelude to further government action against the Ikhwan.[388] Furthermore, as relations worsened, it became known that Hasan al-Hudaybi had gone into hiding, perhaps even fled the country. There were rumors too that the Brotherhood had finally decided that "peaceful co-existence" with the regime was no longer possible and had opted to take the "strongest measures." Some wondered whether this might include the attempted assassination of Nasser.[389]

Despite this, interestingly, American officials retained a channel of communication to the Ikhwan. Toward the end of September, an embassy official met with a Muslim Brother described as "very intelligent and certainly [someone who] cannot be considered a fanatic." In a wide-ranging discussion, which again saw a focus on the decentralized and durable character of the Ikhwan, the group's representative admitted that there was no unified view within the movement on the Anglo-Egyptian Agreement, though he insisted that most were opposed to it. At the same time, the informant underscored the Brotherhood's rejection of violence and its adherence to open and peaceful propaganda methods. The Brothers' underground structures, he averred, would become active only if "the entire machinery of the overt organization [came] to a standstill due to government persecution [emphasis in original]."[390]

By that time, though, such persecution was increasingly evident. In late September, the CCR enacted measures to deprive five Muslim Brothers (and one

Wafdist) of their nationality. These individuals, including 'Abd al-Hakim 'Abdin and Sa'id Ramadan, were collectively accused of engaging in acts of treason abroad.[391] 'Abdin and Ramadan were in Damascus at the time and, in response, the Syrian Brotherhood organized a conference in their honor that saw "more or less violent attacks" on the Egyptian government, which was said to comprise "evil-doers and heretics."[392]

Little by little, it seemed as if both sides were girding themselves for a fight. In early October, the Egyptian Council of Ministers revised the provisions of martial law that had been in force since January 1952, tightening legal powers of repression.[393] The CIA reported that Nasser had decided definitively to suppress the Brotherhood and that some leaders of the group had been arrested already.[394] On October 19, the long-awaited Treaty of Friendship was signed between British and Egyptian representatives.[395] That same day, Caffery informed Washington that an embassy officer had been told "in strictest confidence" that Nasser intended to "take steps [to] liquidate [the] Muslim Brotherhood in [the] near future."[396]

It seems scarcely a coincidence that at precisely this moment, there were renewed signs of discord *within* the Ikhwan. Already, the early autumn had seen fresh whispers about internal unrest.[397] Then, on October 20, a statement appeared in the press, allegedly signed by a majority of the group's constituent assembly, which said that in light of the ongoing "state of dissension," they had decided to place al-Hudaybi on administrative leave. The existing guidance council was also to be relieved of its duties, replaced by a new "provisional" council composed almost entirely of al-Hudaybi's enemies. All decisions relating to expulsions, suspensions, and the dissolution of local branches during the previous three years were to be annulled. British officials were not alone in seeing this démarche as a well-timed maneuver instigated by those who favored cooperation with the CCR. Doubtless, too, it was a move coordinated with Nasser—his latest effort to overcome al-Hudaybi and split the Ikhwan.[398] If this was the plan, however, it was quickly overtaken by the events of October 26, which dramatically transformed the political environment.

That evening, the regime organized a rally to celebrate the new treaty at Manshiyya Square in Alexandria, where Nasser himself gave a major speech. In the middle of his address, a man suddenly fired eight shots at the podium. Remarkably, Nasser was unhurt and, as noted by the US Embassy, he was immediately able to wring "political capital" from the incident, delivering a "highly emotional harangue" to the crowd. The whole affair was recorded and rebroadcast on the radio thereafter, and a "hero's welcome" was prepared for Nasser on his return to Cairo.[399] For "the first time," according to the CIA, Nasser "achieved genuine popularity and admiration."[400] Of equal significance was the fact that the culprit, Mahmud 'Abd al-Latif, was soon identified as a Muslim Brother from Cairo. The attempted assassination thus provided the regime with the casus belli with which to tackle the Ikhwan. Whereas hitherto it seemed to have avoided "extreme methods," it now tilted decisively toward a policy of "rigorous suppression."[401]

On October 27, a pro-Nasser mob broke through a police cordon surrounding the Brotherhood's Cairo headquarters and set fire to it, destroying the premises as well as an adjacent building that housed the group's printing press.[402] Other Ikhwan properties around the country were attacked.[403] Simultaneously, the authorities launched a "full fledged propaganda campaign" against the Brothers.[404] Senior regime figures such as Sadat and Nasser declared that the government had reluctantly accepted the need to "destroy reactionaries" of the Brotherhood's ilk.[405] The government, the Americans assumed, was "preparing for [the] liquidation of Hudaibi [sic] and [the] destruction [of the] Brotherhood as [an] effective organization."[406]

Mass arrests followed, and arms caches were seized. By the end of the month, al-Hudaybi and some five hundred of his supporters had been detained and charged with conspiracy to commit acts of terrorism.[407] Over the ensuing weeks, the pace of detentions did not drop.[408] US officials detected that in contrast to the January 1954 crackdown, which had been focused mainly on the Brotherhood's Cairo and Alexandria chapters, the rural branches of the movement were being systematically targeted. This shift was symptomatic of the degree to which the regime was "seriously going about the business of destroying the entire Brotherhood."[409]

Western observers of all this tended to sound a note of guarded approval. Previously, the *Economist* had described the Brotherhood as "both an offensive anachronism and a very serious problem."[410] The struggle between the CCR and the Ikhwan was portrayed as one that pitted those wishing to advance by "modern and western means" against those who looked to "ancient and reactionary ones."[411] There was scarcely any doubt where the newspaper's sympathies lay. In a similar vein, immediately after the failed assassination bid, the *Christian Science Monitor* stated with undisguised relief that "at long last the Moslem Brotherhood in Egypt has overplayed its hand." It welcomed the attendant "setback for extremism."[412] Meanwhile, British officials affirmed that within "moderate and sensible quarters" in Egypt, there was a "certain feeling of satisfaction" at the government's decision to "deal firmly" with the

Ikhwan. A few months earlier, their biggest concern had been that the authorities would fail to make a "clean sweep" of the group and might instead face a violent backlash.[413] Post-Manshiyya, such anxieties faded as the scale of repression became evident.

On November 1, the CCR established a special tribunal under the direction of regime "wild man" Gamal Salim, together with Anwar Sadat and Husayn al-Shafiʻi, to combat "treason against the Motherland."[414] This paved the way for a succession of public trials, the aim of which, the diplomats recognized, was to convict the Muslim Brothers en masse, "irrespective of their connection" with the Manshiyya "plot." Among the cases brought before the tribunal were several that predated the assassination attempt: ʻAbd al-Qadir ʻAwda was charged in relation to the March riots; Hasan Dawh was indicted for his part in the Roda Mosque incident of August. When legal proceedings got under way on November 9, Egyptian State Broadcasting provided live coverage. Events in court were also followed closely by the Egyptian press and, in turn, by the US Embassy.[415] Senior Brotherhood figures stood accused of having formed and commanded an "armed secret organization," namely the Special Apparatus. It was alleged that the SA had actively conspired to overthrow the regime by means of assassination and destruction.[416] The prosecutors built their case, based in large part on confessions extracted from the leading defendants (many of which had already been leaked into the public domain).[417] Much time was spent outlining the organizational dynamics of the SA, plainly with a view to connecting this unit to the wider leadership of the Brotherhood.[418] In particular, the prosecution sought to demonstrate that the SA had operated under the direct control of al-Hudaybi—something he vigorously denied.[419] As the trials continued, though, it was clear that the general guide was being implicated by the testimony of others. (One such confession came from Sayyid Qutb, then known as the editor of the defunct Brotherhood daily newspaper.)[420]

With regard to the actual murder plot, it was claimed that the Brotherhood had discussed various plans to kill members of the CCR: from the use of a "dynamite belt," to the deployment of an assassination squad wearing military uniforms.[421] To this were added allegations of a Brotherhood conspiracy to infiltrate the armed forces and police, and secret liaisons with the British Embassy.[422] With regard to the latter, the familiar charge was that al-Hudaybi was willing to reach an agreement more favorable to the British than the one signed by Nasser.[423]

An important substrand of the prosecutors' case focused on the purported role played by President Naguib. He was attacked for having arrived at an "understanding" with the Brotherhood to oppose the Anglo-Egyptian Agreement (with attention drawn to Naguib's appearance on the 'Abdin Palace balcony alongside senior Brothers such as 'Abd al-Qadir 'Awda back in February; the fact that Nasser had also been on that platform was quietly overlooked).[424] This provided the setting for the CCR, on November 14, to finally remove Naguib from his posts as president of the republic and chair of the council.[425] This step, taken with little public fanfare, was linked "semi-officially" to the accusations being made against Naguib.[426] In reality, the British considered it the result of "long and careful planning," with the tribunal's proceedings merely offering a pretext.[427] Interestingly, US intelligence agent Wilbur Eveland Crane would later speculate as to whether the CIA itself—through the person of Miles Copeland—might have "plotted with Nasser to get rid of Naguib."[428]

Without question, the People's Court functioned as a political vehicle for Nasser to destroy his remaining opponents, principally Naguib and the Brotherhood. Recognition of this has inevitably led many to question the veracity of the assassination bid itself—suspicions heighted by the rapid and comprehensive nature of the authorities' suppression of the Ikhwan.[429] Even at the time, some thought it altogether too convenient that 'Abd al-Latif had been arrested carrying his Brotherhood membership card.[430] Inevitably within Ikhwan circles, where Nasser had already become a hate figure, a narrative took hold that stressed the fictitious character of the event. The accounts of Brotherhood figures almost invariably refer to the "performance," or "play" of Manshiyya.[431] Hasan al-'Ashmawi, for instance, recalled that the group's leaders were completely surprised and confused by news of an attempt to kill Nasser. He asserted that not a single senior member of the Brotherhood, and certainly no one on the guidance council, favored such an act.[432]

Al-'Ashmawi also recounted conversations with Yusuf Tal'at, the head of the Brotherhood's Special Apparatus in 1954, who was adamant that neither he nor his subordinates had ordered the attack, which he believed to have been "fabricated."[433] A similar story was told by Abu al-Futuh 'Afifi; and Yusuf al-Qaradawi always maintained that the incident at Manshiyya was surrounded by "many doubts and suspicions."[434] Mahmud 'Abd al-Halim was another who called attention to inconsistencies in the evidence used to prosecute the Brothers (such as the fact that the empty cartridges found at the scene did not match the gun taken from the accused, but rather a second gun that was produced a few days later).[435] Most striking was al-'Ashmawi's contention that the Ikhwan had obtained a secret nine-page report, prepared by the intelligence services and dated 11 August 1954, which raised the possibility of "fabricating events" and attributing them to the Brotherhood—as a platform for a wide campaign of arrests, rapid trials, and life sentences. He inferred that this was the plan then implemented after Manshiyya.[436]

Others, by contrast, have dismissed the notion that the assassination attempt was counterfeit, pointing to the history of the Brotherhood's involvement in violence.[437] CCR member Husayn al-Shafi'i, for example, was later contemptuous of the idea that something of this nature could have been staged.[438] At the time, too, Western officials seem to have been convinced by the truth of the plot. One American dispatch stated that while the "benefits" to Nasser from the episode had been so great as to encourage rumors that it was faked, they discounted this idea: "On [the] basis of all evidence avail[able] Embassy rejects staging theory."[439]

All things considered, it seems reasonable to assume that there was a genuine attempt on the life of Nasser. The recording of his speech at Manshiyya, which reveals his hysterical reaction to the shooting, certainly carries an air of authenticity.[440] Either the Egyptian president was a truly remarkable actor, or someone who really did fear for his life in that moment. The fact that Nasser's public persona was normally so calm and assured surely makes it all the more unlikely that the event was a spoof. Indeed, this point might be broadened for the regime as a whole. The CCR was invariably at pains to present an image of control and authority. To have so public a failure of security was scarcely congruent with this central legitimating idea. The most probable explanation, therefore, is that someone did try to kill Nasser—and it seems equally clear that that person was a member of the Brotherhood's Special Apparatus. What is far less certain is the extent to which the would-be assassin was acting on the orders of the Ikhwan leadership—or even that of the SA. On this issue, the diplomats themselves had their doubts. They contemplated the "amateurish" nature of a murder bid in which the chances of success had been distinctly limited: firing from inside a dense crowd at a distance of some sixty-five feet; and the fact that the shooter missed eight times. They contrasted this with the earlier, much more proficient killing of Prime Minister al-Nuqrashi, as well as the attempted murder of his successor, al-Hadi (see Chapter 3). Seen from this perspective, what had transpired at Manshiyya looked less the product of an elaborate conspiracy and more like the work of a lone actor—albeit one who was unquestionably part of the Brotherhood's SA.[441]

Subsequently, a US diplomat talked to a member of the Brotherhood about the existence or otherwise of a plot. The latter acknowledged that some Brothers had been involved in the affair, but also said that he "seriously doubted" whether the whole SA was behind it. Instead, the attack was attributed to a single would-be assassin—an explanation that appears entirely plausible.[442] Further evidence to this effect emerged at the People's Tribunal and, in particular, from the testimony of Yusuf Tal'at. He proved to be, in the words of American officials, an "extremely effective" speaker and a "spectacular" witness, who stood up to the court with unusual spirit and courage, and moved spectators to the point of tears.[443] Crucially, in articulating his own defense, Tal'at offered perhaps the clearest indication of what lay behind Manshiyya. For while he pled guilty to being the head of a secret armed organization, he denied being part of a criminal conspiracy that aimed to carry out assassinations and destroy property in an attempt to foment an insurrection. The distinction that he sought to draw is arguably persuasive. On the one hand, there was no denying the existence of the SA, nor that this was an armed formation of Brotherhood members committed to the use of physical force. Brotherhood histories of this period do not question any of these facts. Indeed, some acknowledge that Hasan al-Hudaybi, who had once sought to eliminate the SA, restored it in mid-1954 for self-defense purposes, as relations with the regime soured.[444] At the same time, it seems doubtful that the SA, as an entity, initiated a specific plot to kill Nasser; rather, individuals within the organization launched this on their own initiative.

The distinction, of course, may seem a fine one. It certainly did not remove all responsibility from the Ikhwan, which had, after all, created a secret armed organization. The fact that one of its members should engage in a violent attack on the state was hardly a surprise and not unprecedented, though this is not to say that he was acting on orders. Broadly speaking, this was the conclusion arrived at by British intelligence. They saw events at Manshiyya as reflecting "the seriousness of the threat presented by a fanatical religious organisation trained and experienced in terrorist activities and in living 'underground.'"[445] Ultimately, it was hard to disagree that the Brotherhood bore a significant degree of culpability for what had occurred.

On December 4, the principal Brotherhood defendants—Mahmud 'Abd al-Latif, Hasan al-Hudaybi, Yusuf Tal'at, Hindawi Duwayr, Ibrahim al-Tayyib, 'Abd al-Qadir 'Awda, and Sheikh Muhammad al-Farghali—were all found guilty and condemned to death. The same day, the CCR ratified the sentences—with the exception of that given to al-Hudaybi. The general guide's punishment was commuted to penal servitude for life, on the basis of his age (sixty-three), ill health, and the fact that he had supposedly fallen under the malign influence of others. The real reason for this "astute" move, according to the US Embassy, was that the regime did not wish to create a "martyr" who might then emerge as a "focal point for Ikhwan propaganda."[446] On the morning of December 7, the remaining six Muslim Brothers were hanged.[447] Reports said that the vengeful final words of 'Awda were: "My blood will be a curse on the revolution leaders. Allah be praised! I die as a Muslim and a martyr. I committed no crime."[448]

For all their desire to see the Brotherhood dissolved, British officials voiced some "misgivings" about these "very severe" punishments. They feared that the use of the death penalty "for obviously political reasons" created a dangerous precedent. It was also thought likely to generate "great hate and bitterness" toward the CCR and Nasser. As one Foreign Office mandarin pithily commented, "no grass grows beneath the gallows."[449] Similarly, CIA analysts worried that the executions would "further alienate the Egyptian masses" from the regime. They suggested, too, that Nasser's government had "probably lost some of the prestige and influence it [had] recently gained in the Moslem world."[450]

Irrespective of this, the regime was not to be deterred in its repression of the Ikhwan. Fresh death sentences and lengthy prison terms were issued to other Muslim Brothers found guilty (including the future general guide, 'Umar al-Tilmisani). However, there were no further hangings, as the CCR now commuted these penalties.[451] Caffery surmised that this was partly to secure public opinion, which had been "repelled" by the hangings. The government, he felt, had managed to garner "the support, or at least the acquiescence, of the overwhelming majority of the people in its attempt to destroy the Brotherhood"; a display now of "magnanimity" was deemed a judicious step to prevent the rise of a new opposition that might exploit popular resentment.[452]

Again, the embassy perceived that the authorities were intent on targeting the Ikhwan as an organization. The objective appeared to be to show "that membership in the Brotherhood itself [was] a crime against the nation." All members of the group's guidance council were therefore brought before the People's Tribunal and found guilty. Their convictions were in effect based on the leadership positions they held within the Ikhwan, rather than because of their involvement in particular crimes. The trials themselves seemed to be increasingly "more an implement of internal propaganda than a legal proceeding."[453] Beyond the courtroom, the Egyptian press was ready to entertain ever-more "sensational disclosures" about Brotherhood plots in the army, plans to blow up Nasser's plane, and the discovery of secret arms caches.[454] The CCR appeared committed to what US officials described as a "methodical attempt to destroy the basic strength of the Brotherhood," especially in rural areas.[455]

At the end of November, in an effort to speed things up, three new military courts had been formed as sub-branches of the main tribunal to deal with more junior members of the Ikhwan.[456] This quasi-judicial process continued until, on 27 December 1954, *al-Gumhurriya* reported that the trials of those Muslim Brothers accused of plotting against the regime would be wrapped up early in the new year.[457] The ensuing weeks brought a wave of mass convictions that included prominent Brothers such as Hasan al-'Ashmawi (in absentia), Salah Shadi, and Hasan Dawh.[458] Indeed, there was a sense in which this final phase marked the tying up of loose ends. Many of those brought before the court were lesser Ikhwan figures, and there was a notable increase in the proportion receiving suspended sentences, or even being acquitted entirely.[459] By February, it was clear that the People's Tribunal had run its course. In total, it had heard cases against some nine hundred people; many thousands more had been interned without trial in concentration camps in the desert.[460] In the judgment of British officials, the effect was to leave the CCR in a "reasonably strong position," though the risk of assassination remained. They reckoned the authorities had "succeeded to a very large measure in disrupting and paralysing the Brotherhood as an organized political force." For the most part, Egyptian public opinion seemed "favourable" to the "determined course" adopted by the government. "The removal of the Brotherhood from the immediate political scene," officials concluded, was "an event over which few tears will be shed."[461]

In late December 1954, a US diplomat had met with a member of the Ikhwan to discuss the situation. The latter confirmed the considerable "internal confusion" within the Brotherhood following the incapacitation of the group's higher echelons. Despite this, perhaps unsurprisingly, the Brother in question struck a recalcitrant note, insisting that the group had not been completely suppressed. As before, there was talk of "unknown secondary 'real' leaders of the Brotherhood" who had avoided the attention of the authorities and would keep the organization alive. And yet there was no denying the damage that had been done; and the Americans' informant admitted that only time would show whether the Brotherhood truly had the "recuperative power" to reemerge.[462]

Conclusion

In the two and a half years since the Free Officers had taken power in Cairo, the Muslim Brothers had been central players on Egypt's political stage. Western relations with the country's new rulers had in part been framed by changing understandings of the role of the Ikhwan. Initially, many diplomats, especially at the British Embassy, had feared that the Brotherhood was the dominant influence behind the regime. Such anxiety reinforced their natural tendency to look askance at the self-avowed revolutionaries who had destroyed the political constitution that the British had built in Egypt. By comparison, the Americans were much better informed about the true nature of the army movement and lent early support to the CCR as a modernizing, essentially pro-Western force. In particular, the CIA and Ambassador Caffery were ardent advocates of building a close relationship with Nasser, who they looked at as potentially a new Atatürk.[463] The British took far longer to be convinced about Egypt's military rulers. What united London and Washington, however, was their shared conviction that the Brotherhood and other "extremists" should be kept away from the exercise of power. By the end of 1952, British officials had come to accept the US contention that the CCR was the best means by which to achieve this objective. They therefore endorsed Nasser and his colleagues as the "moderate" partners with whom they might do business.

The Brotherhood at various points hoped to change the way it was seen by the West. The group invested time and energy in trying to win over the Americans—in particular by emphasizing the Brotherhood's opposition to communism and its avowed "moderation." Similar messages were relayed to the British, who for their own reasons were ready to engage with the Ikhwan in this period. London sought insight into the Brothers' position regarding the Suez Canal question—so as to strengthen the hand of its negotiators during the official talks process. Though Nasser permitted Ikhwan leaders to pursue this dialogue, it was later used as a stick with which to beat the group when he decided to move against them.

The uproar created by the subsequent public disclosure of contacts between the British and the Brotherhood was significant. It reflected the extent to which relationships with an external power like the British or the Americans comprised a form of political capital to be deployed in different ways. The Egyptian authorities used the revelations to intimate that the Brothers were disloyal to the nation. For this reason, it is tempting to assume that the government was entirely cynical in its outrage over Ikhwan behavior. However, government sensitivity on the issue was itself proof of the fact that the contacts—which no one denied to have occurred in some form—possessed a certain worth. The truth of this can also be seen in the complaints made to the British by one CCR representative, that Hasan al-Hudaybi had "bragged" of his dialogue with the embassy "in order to increase his importance among his followers in the provinces."[464] Rather than simply dismiss such words as part of the after-the-fact justification for the Brotherhood's repression, they can be taken as evidence that talks of this kind *did* matter. Evidently too, Ikhwan leaders engaged with the British (and the Americans) precisely because they considered this process to be of intrinsic value. That value stemmed from the importance of foreign actors as a dynamic feature of the Egyptian political equation. It was also a function of the Brotherhood's belief about the power of "the West" and its capacity to impact events in Cairo. Viewed from this perspective, the attempt to try to win influence with British and American actors was a logical—if high-risk—political gambit.

Ultimately, the relationship between the Ikhwan and its western interlocutors never developed—largely because neither side committed wholeheartedly to it. For the Brotherhood, a willingness to talk to the British did not equate to a desire to conspire actively with them against the regime. On the contrary, according to future general guide 'Umar al-Tilmisani, if the Ikhwan wished to seek help from someone in their struggle with Nasser, then the "English" were "the last people they would think to ask" given their history of shared antagonism.[465] Equally for the British and Americans, perceptions of the Ikhwan remained focused on the group's "extremism." This image was reinforced by the fact that the Brotherhood was publicly committed to the forcible evacuation of British troops from the Suez Canal Zone—calling, at various points, for negotiations to be abandoned in favor of jihad. This hard-line stance served to poison relations, not only between the Brothers and the West but also between the Brothers and the regime.

After July 1952, it soon became clear that the Ikhwan enjoyed only a faltering relationship with the Free Officers. Ideologically, there were points of convergence and leading members of the CCR, not least Nasser himself, had previously been part of the Brotherhood. Nonetheless, ambiguities surrounded the postrevolutionary dispensation. Many of these flowed from the difficult personal relationship that prevailed between Hasan al-Hudaybi and Nasser. Tensions were made worse by the internal instability that al-Hudaybi faced within the Ikhwan and in which Nasser was inclined to meddle.

Between July 1952 and the end of 1953, the situation had remained fluid. Key questions—either left over from the old regime or thrown up by the revolution—went unanswered. Many of these turned on the critical triangle of relations between the Brotherhood, the regime, and the British (with the Americans closely bound in, as well). However, 1954 proved decisive. The long-standing Anglo-Egyptian dispute, which had served to destabilize Egyptian politics for a decade (and arguably far longer) was finally resolved. That settlement resulted from crucial shifts in both the British and Egyptian political arenas. With regard to the former, Eden returned from illness and proved victorious in his quarrel with Churchill. More significant, Nasser had emerged as the foremost figure in Cairo—exerting himself first against Naguib and eventually against the Brotherhood. Events at Manshiyya in October dramatically accelerated a conflict that was already incipient between the Ikhwan and the regime. Earlier in the year, the CCR had made it plain that it would brook no rival. The move to suppress the Ikhwan that began in January had been suspended amid the February–March crisis and the struggle for power between Nasser and Naguib; but the clash was merely deferred, not abandoned. For much of 1954, there was, at best, an uneasy "truce." The Anglo-Egyptian agreement of July was the signal for the revival of antagonism. By the late summer, both sides were maneuvering for advantage and the first arrests of Brotherhood members were made. Against this backdrop, the attempt to kill Nasser provided the regime with an excuse to pursue a course of action on which it was already set—although it doubtless served to increase the scale, speed, and severity of the authorities' repression.

Western officials saw few reasons to object to the dissolution of the Brotherhood. Almost unanimously, they understood the group to be a pernicious, extremist, and threatening force, without which Egypt would be better off. Conversely, policy makers and scholars were, for the most part, very positive about the revolutionary regime. The academic Christina Harris spoke for many when she described it as being led by "realistic and forward-looking . . . young military men." There was an expectation that the CCR would lead Egypt down the path of modernization and social reform, and initiate changes that had hitherto been blocked by "reactionary forces" (among whom Harris listed the Muslim Brotherhood).[466] The destruction of the Ikhwan was thus seen as a necessary, if somewhat unpleasant, evil through which Egypt needed to pass. In the era that followed, the assumption was that the Brothers belonged to history, while Nasser embodied the future.

Six   The Age of Nasser

1955–1970

I N THE LATE summer of 1965, the Egyptian government
announced that it had foiled a major Muslim Brotherhood
conspiracy. Ten years after the apparent liquidation of the
group, many Western observers were surprised to learn of its existence—let alone
that it appeared capable of threatening Nasser's regime. In the intervening
period, it had been assumed that the Brothers were all but extinct in Egypt. It
was recognized that they retained a presence elsewhere in the region, but rarely
did the Ikhwan figure prominently on the horizons of policy makers.

As details of the 1965 plot filtered into the public domain, these proved yet
more startling, for it emerged that while several of those involved in the conspiracy were Brotherhood veterans, many others were drawn from a younger
generation—either students or those recently graduated. Most of the latter were
occupied in professions that had previously been thought "immune" to the appeals
of a "traditionalist" group like the Ikhwan.[1] US officials repeatedly commented
on the fact that the accused included a number of engineers, scientists, doctors, and
technicians. As one mandarin remarked, these were "more than effervescent un-
dergraduates or brooding lawyers. They were theoretically mature members of
the intellectual establishment, educated in the scientific tradition." As such, it
had been imagined they would be impervious to "Ikhwan doctrines."[2] The connection of these people with the Brotherhood appeared to show that Nasser's
new order did not satisfy everyone: an "uncomfortable number" of Egyptians

adhered to an alternative vision based on the creation of a more "Islamic" society.[3]

American diplomats reported that the regime had been "taken aback by the extent of the plotting that had been going on under its nose." The Brotherhood, they felt, had shown that its "emotional-political appeal" and "revolutionary credo" could endure.[4] Consequently, the exposure of the 1965 conspiracy raised difficult questions in many quarters about both the character and allure of the Ikhwan: Why did this "obscurantist" organization appeal to so many qualified and educated young men? What did the staying power of the Brotherhood say about the nature of mid-1960s Egypt? And might the group yet pose a threat to Nasser's regime? Unsurprisingly, therefore, new attention was paid to the Brotherhood in the wake of the 1965 conspiracy revelations, as attempts were made to understand these issues, reflect on the survival of the group, and situate it within the prevailing trends of the age.

The Brotherhood Endures

At the end of 1954, there had been many who imagined that the Brotherhood had been definitively broken by the intense bout of suppression to which it had been subjected. The wave of arrests, imprisonments, and executions had left the group traumatized. Even at this moment, however, some Western officials unearthed evidence of ongoing activity. Indeed, at one level, the fact that the first months of 1955 saw Brotherhood members still being detained spoke to the durability of the organization, especially on university campuses.[5] In February, US diplomats observed that people were being brought before the People's Tribunal, accused of trying to revive the Ikhwan—tacit recognition that the group had survived the post-Manshiyya repressive blitz.[6] British intelligence noted that in the Canal Zone, and in Ismailia in particular, the Ikhwan continued to enjoy some support.[7] Added to this, even at the worst of times, American officials were able to meet with Brotherhood informants who struck a defiant posture.[8]

Meanwhile, the Egyptian government itself seemed to acknowledge that the struggle with the Brotherhood was not over. In late January 1955, Nasser gave an interview to an Indian journalist, in which he heralded the destruction of the Brotherhood's underground organization and the weakening of its public presence. At the same time, he cautioned that if the regime were to relax its grip, "within two years" the Ikhwan would be as strong as ever. US officials interpreted the comments as a sign that the government did not believe the "menace" of the Brotherhood had been beaten. The embassy went on to suggest that, ultimately, "repressive methods" were unlikely to overcome an "indigenous nationalistic movement such as the Ikhwan," which was "based essentially on a reaction among young Egyptians to the corruption of Islamic values in modern Egyptian life," a corruption that many Brothers attributed to "Western cultural pressure and domination."[9]

In coming to such a view, American diplomats unwittingly echoed their British forbears. The Ikhwan was thus seen as an almost inevitable reaction to the process of modernization. On this reading, any attempt that Nasser made to develop Egypt—which was understood to mean the steady adoption of Western ways—was thought likely to generate fresh opposition from the Brotherhood.[10] Though the group might have been "neutralized at least temporarily" by the jailing or execution of its leaders, it was anticipated that its ideas would continue to command "wide popular support" among those who rejected either the "secularism" of the Command Council of the Revolution (CCR) or close relations with the West. In early 1955, the diplomats did not dismiss entirely the possibility that the Ikhwan might resurface.[11]

These conclusions were buttressed in March 1955 when the legal adviser to the Egyptian cabinet admitted to US officials that the government had not destroyed the Brotherhood. The authorities now said that this had never been their intention; rather, they had wished to render the Ikhwan "temporarily immobile" while leaving it "bodily intact."[12] Of course, as the embassy realized, such reasoning bore all the hallmarks of a "face saving device," designed to cover up the failure to eradicate the Brotherhood altogether. Equally, though, the diplomats perceived that the destruction of the Ikhwan perhaps required deeper cleavages in Egyptian society than the regime had ever been prepared to risk. They also debated whether a "revived Brotherhood" might actually be "quite useful" to the government in helping to manage domestic problems. In the past, it was observed, Nasser had been inclined to try to win over a faction of the Brotherhood's leadership (in 1953, and again the following year); it was evidently not implausible that he could attempt a revised version of this approach. Speculation of this kind had appeared in the *Economist* back in November, with the suggestion that Nasser might try to separate the "apostles of violence" in the Ikhwan from those committed to "peaceful but wholly nebulous means."[13]

For the same reason, the US Embassy watched with interest the reappearance of Salih 'Ashmawi's *al-Da'wa* newspaper in early March 1955. 'Ashmawi was a known critic of Hasan al-Hudaybi, who had previously been expelled from the Ikhwan because of his opposition to the general guide. In spite of this, he was thought to be still a "fervent believer" in Brotherhood principles, and *al-Da'wa* reflected this. The newspaper had been discontinued after the attempted assassination of Nasser (though as a critic of al-Hudaybi who had been useful to the regime, no action was taken against 'Ashmawi personally). Now it reemerged—though without making any reference to the Brotherhood by name. Instead, it focused on discussing the teachings of Islam, made attacks on Western culture, and reported on current affairs as they impinged on the "Muslim world." The diplomats wondered whether the regime hoped to use 'Ashmawi and his newspaper as a safe outlet for those of a Brotherhood persuasion—a sanitized version of the original movement.[14] (In a similar vein, Sheikh Ahmad al-Baquri was expected to retain a public role on account of his earlier split with the Ikhwan and his proven loyalty to the CCR.)[15]

During this period, the embassy was informed by Brotherhood sources that the government had even contacted senior figures in the group—including al-Hudaybi and his deputy Khamis Humayda—to see if they could work out some kind of cooperative arrangement. In response, Ikhwan leaders had apparently taken an uncompromising line, with al-Hudaybi saying that Nasser should take it up with 'Abd al-Qadir 'Awda (one of those hanged the previous December). Simultaneously, US officials recorded that one hundred people (including about fifty students and several junior army officers) had been arrested for their alleged involvement in Brotherhood activity.[16] The two sets of developments were presumed to be related, with Nasser resorting to carrot-and-stick tactics with the Ikhwan. On the one hand, he kept up the pressure on what remained of the formal organization. On the other, he wished to appear "sufficiently conciliatory" that some Brothers would work under him to help restore domestic peace and "prevent any group of . . . Ikhwanis who [were] still at liberty from feeling that the situation [was] so unbearable that desperate action against the regime [was] necessary."

Overall, the diplomats judged reconciliation to be unlikely and expected no fundamental change in policy: "It is believed that the regime will continue to take all necessary measures to prevent the Brotherhood from growing strong enough to cause it any difficulty."[17] By the same token, the Ikhwan itself seemed in little mood for rapprochement. There were reports that many Muslim Brothers thought the regime's days were "numbered" and, consequently, saw little point in bolstering a government they hated.[18]

Sa'id Ramadan's *al-Muslimun* magazine, by this time published from Damascus, offered an interesting insight into how the Brothers saw their own position vis-à-vis the Egyptian authorities. In 1955, an obviously allegorical article referred readers to the story of Moses and the pharaoh, described as an "archetype" in Islamic history. The battle between them, it was stated, had not been one between equals in material terms. Pharaoh had used his "monopoly" over the "consciences of the people" to try and turn them against Moses; he had, Ramadan suggested, accused the Israelites of "disturbing the peace and stirring terrorism." Undeterred, Moses had embarked on his struggle, "revolting against tyranny," and, through God's help, had vanquished his seemingly powerful enemy. Ramadan's message for his fellow Muslim Brothers was self-evident: there could be no concession to the modern day pharaoh in Cairo.[19]

Against this background, the Ikhwan maybe worried less about the political threat of the West in the years immediately after 1954 than it did about domestic rivals such as Nasser. In another article, Ramadan opined that they were "in the habit of blaming the Western powers for the ruthlessness with which they exploited" Muslims, yet he urged them not to "shirk" their "own responsibility." In a direct echo of Hasan al-Banna, he argued that it was Muslim weakness—their "perpetual laziness, and disgraceful preoccupation"—that left them vulnerable to the blandishments of the West.[20] As far as Ramadan was concerned, Muslims had fallen "asleep," and it was this that allowed the "conspiracies of the many enemies of Islam" to triumph.[21] Of course, this did not mean that the Brothers had set aside their belief in the essential antipathy of the West toward Islam. They still imagined that the "enemies of the umma [Islamic nation]" were active—especially in Palestine, where they supported Zionism to unleash "subversion and destruction" on the house of the Arabs.[22] Ramadan restated his firm conviction that throughout its history, the Islamic *umma* had faced "terrible conspiracies"—most recently from "colonialism, Zionism and tyranny." He declared, as per al-Banna, that alongside the "armed invasion"—as had occurred during the Crusades and, more recently, with European imperialism (which itself showed the "survival of that spirit of the Crusades")—there had been a "cultural invasion" that was "always more dangerous." According to Ramadan, Muslims had been deliberately drawn away from their religion by missionaries and "anti-Islamic systems of education," because the imperialists knew that Islam stood as an immovable impediment to their political control.[23]

Nonetheless, Ramadan's undiminished anti-imperialism was balanced by his insistence that the great challenge they faced in the contemporary world was the "painful ignorance" of "the overwhelming majority of generations of Muslims." What was required, he stated, was "to liberate the educated" in society from "external ideas and currents." In particular, he called on Muslims to "treat those who held the reins of power," rescuing them from the disease with which they were afflicted. For this reason, Ramadan concluded: "If the battle of yesterday was an armed battle between Muslims and their imperialist enemies, today it has become a battle amongst themselves: between those who based their lives upon Islam—as God intended—and those whose minds have been formed as the imperialists wanted."[24] Again, Ramadan was fairly transparent as to which side of this divide Nasser belonged. This was not to say, he maintained, that the Brothers had abandoned the battle against colonialism—indeed, the "goal of eliminating Western imperialism" was said to be the one thing on which they and their rivals agreed. However, Ramadan announced that the internal battle was now under way, fought principally between nationalists, communists, and the "preachers of Islam."[25]

It was, in part, this elevated sense of purpose that helped sustain the Brotherhood in Egypt. By the middle of 1955, the group was said to be maintaining a quiet level of underground activity—principally collecting funds for prisoners' families. According to American assessments, much of this money came from abroad and was smuggled into the country on a weekly basis.[26] The diplomats considered such fund-raising to be the minimum required to ensure the survival of an "activist militant organization" like the Brotherhood. They believed the group could not afford to remain "totally inactive"; to do so would lead to "virtual dissolution" and the drifting away of its members. In this way, the Ikhwan was deemed to be different from conventional political parties like the Wafd, which relied on popular support given to nationally recognized leaders in the form of electoral votes. Interestingly, there was an assumption that these characteristics gave the older parties more durability than the Ikhwan because they could tolerate periods of torpor, while the Brothers were "compelled to continue a minimum of activity in spite of the risks incurred."[27] In reality, of course, the exact reverse proved to be true. The fact that parties like the Wafd were limited to electoral competition meant that in the absence of a parliamentary context, they were condemned to wither away.[28] By comparison, it was the "militant" activism of the Ikhwan that kept it alive through years of repression.

In June 1955, Brotherhood sources told US officials that they had now decided to avoid any direct confrontation with the regime. A "military dictatorship," they argued, could only be removed via a mass uprising and, while they were convinced such an insurrection would occur eventually, they conceded it was unlikely for the present. For the moment, therefore, the Brothers were resolved on a more "passive" approach, focused on reestablishing the Ikhwan as "a completely underground organization."[29] This was complemented by a low-level anti-Nasser propaganda campaign. During a conference of Arab prime ministers held in Cairo, for instance, the Ikhwan was reported to be distributing a letter to delegates that criticized the "brutal and undemocratic" nature of the regime.[30] In July, the American Embassy was informed that the group also planned to hand out anti-Nasser leaflets in Mecca during the Hajj (the major Islamic pilgrimage). Despite the fact that King Saud was then on good terms with the Egyptian government, there were suggestions that he might be facilitating this agitation. It was alleged that on two occasions since November 1954, Saud had contributed large sums to the Ikhwan, with Sa'id Ramadan acting as a key conduit for the money.[31] US analysts judged this entirely plausible in light of other information they had received. In March 1955, *Newsweek*'s Middle East correspondent recounted to Ambassador Henry Byroade (who had just replaced Jefferson Caffery in Cairo) how Ramadan had sat next to King Saud at a recent dinner in Riyadh. Byroade conjectured that Ramadan's presence in the kingdom was further evidence he was benefiting from some kind of financial sponsorship from the Saudis.[32]

Alongside the emphasis on fund-raising and propaganda, there were still occasional hints that the Brothers might yet revert to a more violent path. In July 1955, they were said to be "once again speaking of assassination," and US officials reckoned that "with the individual cells of the Brotherhood virtually uncontrolled by any high authority," it was "possible" that "one or more cells" might decide "to plot Nasser's death." While the government's security apparatus was thought capable of coping with any threat, it was also anticipated that a renewal of militant Ikhwan activity would definitely add to the "internal tension existing in Egypt."[33] In this context, the fresh wave of arrests that took place in August gained added significance. The diplomats explained that these latest moves in the "running battle" between the regime and the Ikhwan came after a warning from the Saudis that the Brotherhood planned to agitate against Nasser during his visit to the kingdom (contra the expectations of the Brotherhood, raison d'état plainly trumped Islamic solidarity as far as Riyadh was concerned). There had also been rumors of a fresh attempt to assassinate Nasser—and equally, intimations that the regime might target leading members of the Ikhwan in Syria.[34]

By late 1955, though, many Western observers saw these exchanges as the dying embers of the conflict between the Brotherhood and the Egyptian authorities. In October, the outgoing British ambassador, Sir Ralph Stevenson, pointed to the "eclipse" of the Ikhwan in his farewell dispatch.[35] His successor, Humphrey Trevelyan, subsequently reported that the Brotherhood had been reduced to a "low level" and was "unlikely" to "reorganise itself in the near future."[36] Similarly, a US memorandum on "communism in Egypt" noted in passing that the regime had "succeeded in suppressing its most dangerous opponent," the Brotherhood, at least "for the present."[37]

By this time, most Egyptian Brothers not in prison had fled into exile. As described earlier (see Chapters 3 and 4), the Ikhwan had spread throughout the Middle East in the years after 1945, and the group had shown a readiness to utilize international support networks to bolster its position in Egypt.[38] Now those same networks acted as a crucial lifeline. The fugitives had made for various destinations around the Arab world. Unsurprisingly given the apparent sympathies of the king, Saudi Arabia proved to be a particularly important haven.[39] Kuwait also became a primary destination for Brotherhood émigrés. In January 1955, the American consul there, Harrison Symes, reported the presence of several "terrorist members of [the] Moslem Brothers Society." Most of them were said to be lying low, fearing extradition back to Cairo; they were not participating in the activities of the Islamic Guidance Society—the local "affiliate" of the Brotherhood. In truth, Symes felt they had little to fear because they enjoyed the protection of Sheikh Abdulla al-Jabir al-Sabah, the minister of justice and education.[40] Thereafter, US officials kept track of the Brotherhood's presence in Kuwait.[41] By early 1956, the "score or so" Egyptian Brothers who had taken refuge in the country were said to be increasingly "acrimonious and disunited," and suffering the effects of prolonged exile.[42]

Elsewhere, escapee Muslim Brothers were rather more vibrant as they mingled with local chapters of the movement. In the summer of 1954, it will be remembered, with tensions between the Ikhwan and the Egyptian government mounting, Hasan al-Hudaybi had embarked upon a tour of the Middle East. One of his stops was Bhamdun in Lebanon, where he chaired a conference attended by numerous regional leaders of the Brotherhood—Mustafa al-Siba'i of Syria, Muhammad Mahmud al-Sawwaf from Iraq, and Muhammad 'Abd al-Rahman Khalifa, the new head of the Jordanian branch.[43] The purpose of the gathering was, in part, "to establish a central office for the wider propagation of the Brotherhood's principles and for the coordination of their efforts."[44] Clearly, this was a move taken with one eye on developments in Cairo. After the suppression of the group in October, several prominent Brothers sought sanctuary with their regional counterparts.[45]

Syria emerged as perhaps the most important location for Brotherhood activism in this period. The February 1954 overthrow of President Adib al-Shishakli, who had repressed the Brothers during his time in power (with al-Siba'i briefly imprisoned), created new opportunities in the country.[46] As the pressure on the Ikhwan in Egypt intensified, there were even whispers that the group might move its headquarters to Damascus, where the Brothers had been "emboldened" by the weakness of the government and become increasingly prominent.[47] There was speculation too that Mustafa al-Siba'i might replace al-Hudaybi as the main administrator of Brotherhood affairs outside Egypt.[48] In November 1954, the US chargé d'affaires in the Syrian capital, Robert Strong, noticed that the four Brothers who had been stripped of their Egyptian nationalities—'Abd al-Hakim 'Abdin, Kamil al-Sharif, Sa'id Ramadan, and Sa'd al-Din al-Walili—were all now resident in the city. Though the authorities in Cairo had asked for the men's passports to be confiscated, the government in Damascus ignored the request.[49]

Western officials followed all of this anxiously, seeing the Brothers in Syria as "anti-west and neutralistic."[50] Earlier in the year, al-Siba'i had given a speech in which he declared that an "armed attack" was the only way to liberate the Suez Canal Zone, and that the Brothers were publicly opposed to any Arab participation in a pro-Western military pact. He also said that US-provided "Point Four" aid was the work of a "Jewish spy ring" and labeled its directors the "envoys of American colonisation in the Arab world."[51] As one mandarin in London commented, all of this was "typical of the Brotherhood."[52] Slightly more positive from a Western perspective was the fact that the group was recognized to be avowedly anticommunist—a useful characteristic given the anxieties that surrounded Syria at the time.[53] That notwithstanding, though, the Syrian Ikhwan was identified as one of the "extremist elements" in the country, and "a potential threat to the orderly development of democratic civilian government."[54]

In December 1954, the Syrian Brothers mobilized large demonstrations after the execution of their comrades in Egypt.[55] UK diplomats estimated that some fifteen thousand people took to the streets of Damascus to protest against both Nasser and the West. "Wild talk" was heard about jihad against the Cairo regime.[56] In the wake of all this, the Central Intelligence Agency (CIA) warned that "the activity of the Brotherhood leaders in Syria threatens both the security of the Nasr [sic] regime in Egypt and the stability of the weak Syrian coalition government." The situation was said to be "made to order" for extremists such as the Brotherhood, as well as communists, and radical Arab socialists.[57] Officials in Whitehall agreed, noting that in a comparatively short span of time, the Ikhwan had successfully established for itself an "influential position in Syria," the effects of which were likely to be pernicious and to exacerbate "existing tendencies to nationalism and anti Western feeling."[58]

A similar appraisal of the Brotherhood also now prevailed in nearby Jordan. In early 1954, American diplomats in Amman had reported that the Ikhwan there was becoming "somewhat more active than previously." Though described as still being "essentially a religious and not a political force," it was thought to be "flexing its muscles a bit."[59] As the year progressed, there were various signs of Brotherhood agitation, much of it anti-Western in tone.[60] The group organized rallies against the enduring prominence of British officers within the Jordanian army, for example. It was critical, too, of Western cultural influence and the apparent failure of the government to implement Islamic laws (like the prohibition of alcohol). In December, 'Abd al-Rahman Khalifa, the leader of the Jordanian Ikhwan, led protests against the treatment of the Brotherhood in Egypt. Though these proved much smaller than the parallel events in Damascus, they were seen as further evidence of the Brothers' growing confidence.[61] In early 1955, the US Embassy in Amman compiled a long memorandum on the Ikhwan, which characterized it as possessing "fascist inclinations." Though perhaps "willing to bide their time," it was assumed that the Brothers expected "ultimately to take over the state."[62] US observers further suggested that even though the Brotherhood's constitution made no reference to the use of force, this was merely "a matter of caution," rather than an indication that violence had been "foresworn." It was for this reason that the government of Jordan was said to view the Ikhwan as a "threat to political stability."[63]

In reality, things were somewhat more complicated; for whatever their differences, the Jordanian Brothers and the regime were united by their shared antipathy to both Nasserism and communism. During this era, the Ikhwan backed the king against his challengers and, as Ziad Abu-Amr argues, effectively functioned as a "loyal opposition."[64] They hewed to a nonviolent, "accommodationist" path and benefited from what Mansour Moaddel calls King Hussein's "authoritarian pluralism."[65] Hence, the Brothers were granted a license to operate as a "comprehensive and general Islamic Committee." When the king proscribed all political parties in April 1957, the Ikhwan was permitted to continue its activities—and Controller General 'Abd al-Rahman Khalifa himself was later allowed to enter parliament as an independent.[66] Kamil al-Sharif, the exiled Egyptian Brother who had earlier played so prominent a role in Palestine, even went on to serve as the Jordanian minister of *awqaf* (religious endowments). A couple of decades later, another locally based Brother, Ishaq Farhan, was appointed minister of education.[67]

The ambiguities of the relationship between the Ikhwan and the Jordanian government were mirrored in the way that the diplomats looked at the group.

As above, it was clearly seen as a potentially "subversive" movement.[68] There was also no doubting the Brothers' hostility to US foreign policy in the region: they had vigorously denounced American Point Four aid and the pro-Western Baghdad Pact as tools of "imperialism."[69] Like their Egyptian counterparts, the group saw the infusion of "Western" cultural practices as part of a deliberate "Christian-imperialist plot" to undermine Islam.[70] In January 1956, Jordan witnessed a spate of attacks on American and other foreign-owned property, in which the Brotherhood was heavily implicated (significantly, the targets included missionary institutions).[71] Against this backdrop, the British Embassy was not alone in seeing the growing strength of these "parochially-minded local fanatics" as a "disturbing development."[72] And yet, simultaneously, Western officials recognized that the Brotherhood *was* a pillar of support for the Jordanian regime and a prominent anticommunist voice.[73] They thus saw the benefits of its existence and the role it played within the political system.

Across the region as a whole, then, American and British diplomats were conscious that the Brothers had not disappeared. The local chapters of the movement enjoyed varying degrees of prominence and continued to feature at least somewhere on the Western radar. For the most part, they were seen in the same way as they always had been: as extremist forces, hostile to Anglo-American interests. Yet in Jordan—and to a much lesser extent in Syria—there was some acknowledgment that the Brotherhood and the West were on the same side when it came to opposing communism. The practical consequences of this, however, appear to have been limited. And more generally, in the period after 1954, the question of the Ikhwan tended to slip down the political agenda, which was dominated by the man the Brothers viewed as their nemesis: Nasser.

The Challenge of Nasser

As far as most outsiders could discern, by the end of 1955, the civilian opposition to Nasser in Egypt—from the Brotherhood to the Wafd and the communists—had been nullified. The reality seemed to be that there was little alternative to the military-led government, which appeared more secure than ever. Already, at the end of the previous year, British officials had noted a transformation in Nasser: "A considerable development seems to have taken place in him since his escape from assassination and his triumph over both General Naguib and the Moslem Brotherhood: he is more sure of himself . . . perhaps over-confident and even a little inflated."[74] Nasser's participation in the famous Bandung conference of March 1955 underlined that growing sense of self-confidence.[75] As the year progressed, he consolidated his position as an international statesman and carried off the major strategic-diplomatic coup of the "Czech" arms deal in September.[76] In the view of the CIA, the latter brought Nasser "prestige and a position of leadership" in the Arab world.[77] Domestically, too, it was in this period that the government made new attempts to normalize the political framework, after the rather transient existence of the previous two years. In June 1956, this led to the abolition of the CCR and the issuing of a constitution under which Nasser was confirmed as president by referendum.[78]

Concurrently, Western diplomats expended significant energy in trying to build good relations with the Egyptian government. The British had hoped that the 1954 treaty might allow for a new era in Anglo-Egyptian affairs.[79] The architect of the deal on the UK side, Anthony Eden, replaced Winston Churchill as prime minister in early 1955, and many expected him to build on his diplomatic triumph. That July, the valedictory dispatch of outgoing ambassador Sir Ralph Stevenson voiced the ambition that "real friendliness" might blossom between London and Cairo. Nasser's regime, Stevenson opined, was "as good as any previous Egyptian Government since 1922 and in one respect better than any, in that it is trying to do something for the people of Egypt rather than merely talking about it." As such, the ambassador said that it deserved "all the help that Great Britain can properly give them."[80] Officials in London were inclined to agree, preferring to support Nasser's government on the basis that "any probable successor would be infinitely worse."[81] The man who inherited Stevenson's post, Humphrey Trevelyan, endorsed this line. In his judgment, Nasser recognized that his "interests" lay with the West and, as a result, Trevelyan felt they should "be able to do business with him."[82]

As highlighted already, this outlook was entirely in keeping with earlier British approaches toward Egypt, which placed a premium on the idea that most people were biddable, irrespective of apparent ideological differences (see Chapters 1 and 2). A willingness to work with Nasser was also very much in line with US thinking. The American Embassy had long championed a relationship with the Free Officers' regime and, in the wake of the Anglo-Egyptian Treaty, the diplomats urged Washington to push ahead with military assistance to Cairo. A key sticking point, though, was Nasser's refusal to allow US military advisers into the country. According to former CIA operative Wilbur Eveland Crane, one of the ways the Egyptian president justified his stance was by reference to the Ikhwan: "Nasser explained that the Moslem Brotherhood had tried to murder him for agreeing [in the treaty] that the British might return under certain conditions. There was no way [he said] . . . that he could survive politically if he were to permit American officers and soldiers to take up posts on Egyptian soil."[83] The extent to which Nasser was simply using the Brotherhood as a convenient excuse to reject terms that he himself judged unacceptable is not clear. That notwithstanding, US officials remained upbeat that Cairo could be brought into some kind of alignment with the West.

As it happened, however, this was to be a turbulent period in relations between the Western powers and Egypt. On a succession of issues, Washington and Cairo found themselves at loggerheads. Nasser, for instance, was deeply opposed to the anti-Soviet "Baghdad Pact" that was created in 1955, seeing it as a vehicle to divide the Arab states, build up his Iraqi rivals, and prolong the imperial presence in the Middle East.[84] His fierce criticism of the pact—and those regional governments that had signed it—did much to poison the atmosphere between Nasser and the West.[85]

Even prior to this, there had been growing hints from Cairo that the regime desired a truly independent—"neutral"—foreign policy and American officials were aware of the "widespread mistrust" of their motives in Egypt.[86] In July 1955, Nasser had delivered a series of speeches in which he firmly rejected any involvement in alliances and denounced the "big powers" for their attempts to dominate the Middle East.[87] Rhetoric of this sort struck a nervous chord among US diplomats who worried about the degree to which "Arab nationalism [had] gained widespread acceptance" throughout the region and into North Africa.[88] There was an apprehension that such nationalism, which was vehemently opposed to the "vestiges of imperialism," might in turn fuel the "rapid growth of a neutralist sentiment" within the Arab states—especially Syria and Egypt.[89] It was assumed that neutralism of the kind "openly espoused by Egypt" worked in favor of the Soviet bloc because it was "directed against established Western positions."[90]

In spite of this, for much of 1955, a majority of American officials had been optimistic that Nasser had "not yet fully made up his mind" and might yet be won over—if US policy proved agreeable. They argued that every effort should be made to try to halt his drift away from the West. In the assessment of the Cairo Embassy, Nasser's government was still the "best hope" for Egypt.[91] The arms deal of September 1955 did little to alter this shared Anglo-American calculus. At a minimum, a deal with Nasser was seen as the least worst option.[92] The diplomats felt the Egyptian leader remained well disposed toward the West in the Cold War struggle for dominance. They also surmised that he might accept a peace settlement to the Arab-Israeli conflict (and, consequently, he was the focus of President Eisenhower's "Alpha" initiative).[93] It was with all this in mind that the British and the Americans came forward with an offer to support the construction of the Aswan Dam. A key fear was that if they did not provide funding, then the Soviets would fill the gap and thereby strengthen their own hold over Cairo.[94]

In the winter of 1955–1956, State Department officials pondered ways in which the United States might associate itself with "the principal philosophic and political goals of the people of Africa and Asia." To this end, they recommended an embrace of the "Arab Renaissance" and an acceptance of the "spirit of Bandung." The United States, it was averred, needed to act "as revolutionaries," so as to avoid driving the Arabs into the arms of the Soviets. Egypt figured centrally in these debates. It was suggested that the United States might exploit its own status as an "anti-colonial power" to foster moderation in Cairo.[95] Similarly, the British continued to believe that "reasonable" levels of cooperation could be achieved with an Egyptian government that was "as good a bet as any."[96] Nonetheless, there were unmistakable signs that relations were worsening. In particular, Whitehall was frustrated by what it saw as Nasser's relentless propaganda campaign against their interests across the Middle East.[97] Increasingly, the British reckoned both that the Egyptian president wished to expel them from the region and that he was a pawn (perhaps unwittingly) of the Soviets.

London's discomfort reached a new level when John Glubb Pasha was dismissed as commander of the Arab Legion in Jordan on 1 March 1956. The British immediately suspected that Nasser was behind the move. A Foreign Office memorandum from later that month, which received cabinet approval, compared Nasser to Mussolini—the point being not merely that his regime was akin to fascist dictatorship but also that he was "beholden to a ruthless power." Just as Mussolini had been in thrall to Hitler, so was Nasser presumed bound to the Soviet Union.[98] To be sure, most British officials did not think the Egyptian president was an actual communist, but they did consider him blind to the dangers of working with Moscow. They thought his "neutralism" served as a vehicle for Soviet influence across the Middle East.[99] Moreover, Nasser was portrayed as aggressive, "double dealing," anti-Western, obsessed with destroying Israel, and anti-British. On this basis, he was seen as a force to be contained and challenged, not appeased.[100]

At the same moment, the Americans were reluctantly arriving at the same opinion. The Egyptian leader's capacity to irritate US sensibilities had been demonstrated when he opted to recognize communist China in the spring of 1956.

Of even greater significance was the fact that Washington had lost faith in Nasser's willingness to make peace with Israel. As a result, US officials had also come to view him as part of the problem, rather than part of the solution.[101]

It was this shared outlook that led the British and Americans to agree on "Project Omega." Until today, the exact details of this policy are enveloped in secrecy. Despite this, historians have been able to piece together a broad outline of what it entailed from those state papers that have been released. A report by a secretive US-UK joint working group, for instance, called for a "coordinated political, economic, and psychological program," utilizing "overt and covert means," to place "maximum pressure" on Nasser, in order to weaken his "internal and external position" over the long term.[102] President Eisenhower referred to a "high class Machiavellian plan to achieve a situation in the Middle East favourable to our interests." Under this scheme, there would be "no open break with Nasser," but the ultimate goal was manifestly his removal from power.[103] To this end, the Americans and the British hoped to "mobilize the necessary internal political opposition" against the regime. Though Nasser's domestic enemies were judged to be "neither sufficiently strong nor well-placed" to overthrow the government in the near future, it was assumed that many would-be opponents were held back by the prestige of Nasser. Hence, a core aim of the joint US-UK program was to diminish the stature of the Egyptian president. If this were to happen, it was expected that many of those who had lost out under Nasser would come forward: businessmen, purged officers, monarchists, Wafdists, and, of course, Muslim Brothers.[104]

It remains far from clear whether meaningful contacts were established with such opposition forces during this period. With regard to the Muslim Brotherhood in particular, there is precious little evidence of any serious consideration being given to the group. In his memoirs, British ambassador Humphrey Trevelyan labeled the Ikhwan "an extreme religious organisation"—a characterization that hardly bespoke a readiness to work with them. In addition, he recorded his perception that Nasser had suppressed the Brothers thoroughly after late 1954—again suggesting that he did not really consider them a viable option.[105] American analysts of the domestic Egyptian scene were apt to agree. Miles Copeland, for example, deemed the Ikhwan as being of little further import after 1954, certainly as compared to Nasser (in whom he at least continued to place much faith).[106]

Nonetheless, the journalist Said Aburish alleged that the British reactivated a channel of communication with the Brotherhood in late 1955 and sought to enlist it in a regional alliance against both Nasser and communism.[107] He even contended that Muslim Brothers in exile were entrusted with planning the assassination of Nasser; "Operation Sipony," according to Aburish, was only aborted at the last minute.[108] Similarly, Mark Curtis has asserted that the "Suez Group" of parliamentarians and Military Intelligence Section 6 (MI6) operatives made contact with Brotherhood émigrés in Switzerland, with encouragement from the Saudis, in the hope of organizing against Nasser.[109]

There is little to back up the claims of either Aburish or Curtis. The Suez Group was a loose coalition of MPs, which included Julian Amery (the son-in-law of Harold Macmillan), Captain Charles Waterhouse, Fitzroy Maclean, and Enoch Powell, as well as Lords Hankey and Killearn from the Upper House. It had come together in 1953 to oppose the "sell-out" on Sudan. Subsequently, it became fiercely critical of Eden's policy of seeking a negotiated settlement to the Suez Base dispute.[110] After the 1954 treaty was signed, it continued to censure British policy toward Egypt, demanding a hard line against Nasser. For this reason, there is some logic to the idea that the Suez Group might have been willing to work with the Egyptian opposition, including the Brotherhood. But as far as can be ascertained, there is no proof that they actually did so.

Moreover, even if Curtis is right to say that an approach was made to the Brotherhood, it does not seem to have progressed particularly far—not least because of the Suez crisis, which overwhelmed more subtle plans for dealing with Nasser, whether of the Suez Group or Project Omega. There is not the space here to examine this episode at any length and the narrative is well known. In July 1956, the Egyptians were abruptly informed that the Americans were withdrawing funding for the Aswan Dam. Nasser responded by nationalizing the Suez Canal Company—to the fury of the British and the French.[111] Prime Minister Eden, in particular, seemed intent on punishing Nasser and, as a recent history of British intelligence makes clear, various schemes for his assassination were again floated (though, as above, there is no evidence that the Brotherhood figured in any of these plans).[112] Publicly, attempts were made to find a solution to the Suez crisis that might satisfy all parties. But at the end of October, British and French forces invaded Egypt in collusion with the Israelis. The reaction in Washington was one of shock. President Eisenhower and his secretary of state, John Foster Dulles, condemned the attack (about which they had no prior knowledge) and applied critical political and financial pressure to their allies. This proved decisive for the British, who had no choice but to withdraw, effectively collapsing the operation.[113]

A future US ambassador to Cairo, John Badeau, later described the Suez war as "the most disastrous piece of postwar Western diplomacy in the Middle

East."[114] It led to the final disintegration of "British Egypt," with many people who had spent most, if not all, of their lives in the country, either forced to flee or expelled.[115] In London, Eden resigned the premiership in the wake of the debacle, to be replaced (with American approval) by Harold MacMillan. The star of Nasser, meanwhile, burned brighter than ever, with the Egyptian president able to convert his country's military defeat into a major political triumph.[116] In the face of the "tripartite aggression," even his erstwhile enemies—including many Brotherhood leaders around the region (such as Mustafa al-Siba'i and 'Abd al-Rahman Khalifa)—had offered public support to the Cairo regime.[117]

One of the great ironies of the Suez war was the fact that in the aftermath, the Eisenhower administration came to share many of the same fears that had propelled the British into action. US officials quickly recognized that the result had empowered the "opportunistic and nationalistic Nasser government" across the region.[118] In January 1957, Eisenhower launched his eponymous "Doctrine" by which he pledged to support any country threatened by "international communism."[119] Regardless of the rhetoric, few doubted the real target of the initiative: Nasser. Salim Yaqub has described how US officials feared a post-Suez vacuum that would be filled by the iconic Egyptian leader and they therefore sought to interpose American power directly into the Middle East.[120] More than ever now, Western diplomats were concerned at Nasser's capacity to damage Western interests and wondered how he might be stopped.

Islam as a Bulwark?

Miles Copeland has detailed the way in which, during the early years of the Cold War, the CIA hoped to find a "Moslem Billy Graham" (see Chapter 5). Such a figure, it was imagined, might stand as a powerful bulwark to the growth of communist influence across the Middle East.[121] As Matthew Jacobs has shown, at a moment when there were serious misgivings that disillusioned and half-educated Muslim and Arab radicals might turn to the Soviets, conceptions of a "timeless Islam" fueled the belief that religion could be used to block the advance of more revolutionary creeds.[122]

Of course, ideas about the potential pliability of Islam were nothing new. During the previous century, numerous British officials had speculated on the latent power of Muslim sentiment and its capacity for mobilization.[123] To some, this posed a threat to the stability of the British Empire, especially in India; others, though, saw only opportunities.[124] During World War I, for instance, there had been discussion about trying to harness Islamic forces as a means by which to undermine the Ottoman Empire.[125] Similarly, during the Second World War, a few officials—most notably Lord Linlithgow, the secretary of state for India—had wondered whether Muslim opinion might be channeled against the Axis (though others opposed the suggestion, which, in any case, failed to gain momentum).[126]

In the postwar period too, there had been a proposal for an "Islamic Alliance," centered on King Abdullah of Jordan, which would also include Iran, Iraq, and Turkey.[127] The hope was that such a grouping might stand against the "aggression" of the Soviets on the basis of "their common religion."[128] Elsewhere, diplomats pondered whether "pan-Islamism" might "form a bulwark against the spread of communism."[129] (A comparable strand of thinking would also later lead some to advocate "pan-Africanism" as constituting a strong, "indigenous, natural defence" against more revolutionary influences.)[130] One official observed that "in so far as a modern Panislamic [sic] movement is designed to create a common front against Communism it is evident that we should do everything in our power to assist it."[131]

Views of this kind flowed from a belief that it was the decline of religion, coupled with the poor living standards of many peoples in the Middle East, that lay behind the rise of communism. As one diplomat remarked: "It is in the loss of the hold of Islam on the younger generation and in the creation of an urban proletariat which is abandoning the Islamic way of life that the danger lies, rather than in reactionary tendencies of the ulama . . . the conditions of the majority in town and country are such as to favour the spread of communist propaganda. . . . To some extent the fellahin are immunised by the brand of near-fatalism which their reading of religion induces, but the relaxation of the hold of religion on the poor of the towns has largely removed this form of protection."[132] Once more, at the heart of this analysis lay the perception that Islam was inherently opposed to modernity, whether in a Western or communist mold. That being the case, it was held to be better for Muslim societies to retain their faith (and, implicitly, remain backward), rather than risk infection from dangerous modern ideas. For this reason, it was argued that a pan-Islamic movement could be a boon if channeled away from politics and into social reform.[133] Some mandarins felt that a purely "religious movement" could be of real benefit to the British.[134]

Such thinking was not confined to the corridors of power. As potent a scholar as the historian Bernard Lewis sounded a similar note when he argued that "pious Muslims—and most Muslims are pious—will not long tolerate an atheist creed." The "present revolt of the Muslims," Lewis expounded in 1954, though it "may temporarily favour the Communists," would ultimately "work against Communism."[135] The obvious corollary of this logic was that the West could usefully encourage an adherence to Islam for Cold War advantage.

Few diplomats, however, were convinced. Sir John Troutbeck of the Middle East Office, for example, cautioned that pan-Islamists were likely to "train" their "biggest guns against Western imperialism," and especially the British.[136] By Troutbeck's reckoning, pan-Islamism was fueled by a desire to "eliminate all trace of western influence." Groups like the Muslim Brotherhood, he stated, were "virulently xenophobe" and of the sort that he would not "wish to give encouragement."[137] By the same token, British analysts in Iraq dismissed the idea that the local branch of the Ikhwan might serve as "an effective barrier." Though communism was said to be "anathema" to the Brotherhood and its local front organization, the Muslim Ethical Society (see Chapter 3), it was thought "hardly conceivable . . . that even in a country as politically backward as Iraq," a movement "built on the precepts of a theological autocracy could find enough stable support to be effective against a 'Progressive Democracy.' "[138] (Brotherhood histories agree that the group had struggled to build a presence in Iraq, which proved an inhospitable domain for their *da'wa*.)[139]

Beyond this, British officials continued to express deep reservations about various "extremist" Islamic groups that were invariably described as "fanatical" and anti-Western.[140] There was a recognition too that pan-Islamist international activism could manifest itself in ways that ran counter to UK interests. In February 1951, for instance, the Foreign Office had been sent a resolution issued by a "World Muslim Conference" that had been hosted in Karachi under the chairmanship of the former grand mufti of Palestine, Hajj Amin al-Husayni. This condemned the presence of British troops in the Suez Canal Zone, calling for their evacuation from Egypt, as well as for the unity of the Nile valley.[141] Two years later, officials watched uneasily as a Brotherhood-sponsored "Islamic Congress" met in Jerusalem.[142] They expressed concern, not only that the Jordanians had allowed the gathering to go ahead, but also that the prime minister had received some of the delegates for a private audience. The conference—the latest in a series of attempts by forces considered hostile to British interests to organize "Islam" internationally—blamed the "imperialist powers" for the partition of Palestine and insisted that the struggle against Israel was the "the inescapable and immediate duty" of "every Muslim."[143] Among the seven-man permanent committee established at the congress were several prominent Ikhwan members: Sa'id Ramadan, Kamil al-Sharif, Sayyid Qutb, the Algerian Fadil al-Wartalani, and 'Abd al-Rahman Khalifa of the Jordanian Brotherhood.[144] In the months that followed, this committee moved between the capitals of the Arab world, espousing a militant hard line.[145] Such activity was unlikely to persuade the British that conferences of this kind were worthy of support— regardless of the avowed anticommunism of their participants.

In 1954, the Joint Intelligence Committee (JIC) added its voice to those questioning the feasibility of using Islam as a bulwark against communism. In the Committee's estimation, while the religion appeared "superficially" as an "effective barrier," its influence tended to be "over-rated." The impact of Islam, the JIC surmised, was "largely negative": it kept Muslim societies "static," but where "modern civilization" had broken through, Islam was "powerless to prevent a rapid demoralisation in the face of materialism." On this basis, the JIC maintained that while Muslim leaders should "be encouraged to preach a strenuous resistance to Communism," they doubted whether Islam could "adapt itself to modern conditions and remain a stabilising influence."[146] It is interesting to note that these conclusions demonstrated a similar logic to that recorded earlier, albeit arriving at an opposite verdict. Once more, Islam and modernity were held to be fundamentally incompatible; but here, the assumption was that the former could scarcely hope to stand in the way of the latter. The JIC therefore argued that there was little to be gained from trying to bind the forces of religion to the Western cause. Islam was seen as inherently reactionary, antiquated, and unlikely to survive in the modern world.

This notion, of course, was one that had a long pedigree within UK thinking about the Middle East generally, and Egypt in particular. The man who had done much to build the edifice of British power in Cairo, Lord Cromer, had believed Islam to be a degenerate and failed religion. Part of the mission he foresaw for himself and his colleagues was to prepare the way for the onset (eventually) of a post-Islamic modernity (what they called "civilization") in Egypt. Again, the underlying premise was that the religion was incompatible with progress.[147] Scholars like Arnold Toynbee presented a similar thesis. In a 1948 reflection on "Islam and the West," he deduced that "pan-Islamism" was "losing such hold as it may ever have obtained over the minds of Muslims." To Toynbee, it was a manifestation of reactionary "zealotism," engendered by the spread of Western civilization. He imagined that it was destined to fail, being superseded by the forces of nationalism (though he did posit that the sleeping power of pan-Islamism might yet "awake if ever the cosmopolitan proletariat of a 'Westernized' world revolts against Western domination and cries out for anti-Western leadership").[148]

The itinerant James Heyworth-Dunne offered a slightly different take. In his 1950 book on the Brotherhood, he had attested that the "one power . . . equipped to serve as a barrier" to communism was "Islam, as taught and represented by Hasan al-Banna to the classes mostly affected by communistic ideas."[149] And yet even Heyworth-Dunne doubted whether the Brotherhood could really "hold out" against communism—especially with al-Banna gone. In his judgment, extensive and meaningful progressive social reform was ultimately required if countries like Egypt were not to succumb to the allure of Moscow.[150]

In the same period, however, there were some American observers who remained drawn to the idea that Islam could be a vital asset in the Cold War ideological battle.[151] For example, William A. Eddy, a former special assistant to the secretary of state for research and intelligence, advocated the building of a "moral alliance" between Christianity and Islam to combat atheistic communism. He urged the United States to "extend the hand of friendship to the Near East" and exploit the "common ground" between the monotheistic religions.[152] G. Lewis Jones, the director of Near Eastern affairs at the State Department, was another who seemed intrigued by the possibility that Islam could form an "obstacle" to communism, both in theory and practice.[153] And Loy Henderson likewise contemplated whether "religious fanaticism" could be used to block communism, at least in the short term (though he shared the conviction that it lacked the positive content to endure over a longer time frame).[154]

Under the Truman administration, the balance of opinion evidently came down against any effort to stimulate pan-Islamism. Most American officials were inclined to see this phenomenon as reactionary, inherently anti-Western, and likely to damage US interests.[155] Nevertheless, State Department documents reveal that by the early 1950s, US officials were considering ways to appeal to Muslim countries, *as* Muslim countries. Internal memoranda spoke of "countering [the] mistrust" of American motives in the Middle East by developing "specialized materials" that would reflect "Islamic" culture.[156] The mandarins aspired to create a program that would demonstrate "sympathetic United States interest in the Arabs and Islam."[157]

In line with this, one signature initiative was the aforementioned "colloquium on Islamic Culture," that the State Department's International Information Administration (IIA) organized in collaboration with the Library of Congress and Princeton University. This was the event that brought the Ikhwan's Sa'id Ramadan to the United States in 1953 (see Chapter 5). The purpose of the conference was to assemble "distinguished scholars," in order to "impress the Muslim world with [the] United States' interest in Islamic culture," and also to "stimulate interest about, and understanding of, the Islamic world in the United States."[158] State Department planning documents make it clear that this was to be more than "an exercise in pure learning." It was hoped that the colloquium would contribute to "both short term and long term United States political objectives in the Moslem area."[159] For this reason, each "Islamic" government was invited to send one representative; local US diplomatic missions were given the task of nominating and vetting potential attendees.[160] During the conference, delegates had a fifteen-minute audience with President Eisenhower at the White House, and State Department circulars heralded it as "probably the outstanding event of the decade in United States cultural relations with the Islamic world."[161]

Based on Ramadan's involvement, Ian Johnson has highlighted the gathering as symptomatic of an incipient alliance between the United States and the Brotherhood.[162] Yet this interpretation rather overlooks the fact that the organizers were less than keen to have Ramadan present. Those embassies tasked with selecting conference participants largely opted for members of the establishment in their respective countries: judges, senior academics, and politicians.[163] The initial Egyptian invitees included a cultural officer at al-Azhar, the director general of antiquities and the rector of Fu'ad (Cairo) University.[164] It was actually Sa'id Ramadan who came to the American Embassy asking whether he might attend as an independent observer.[165] In response, the State Department was unenthusiastic. A telegram to Cairo stated that they had not planned to allow observers, and the key criterion for choosing delegates was that they should be of high scholarly repute, which was far from established in this instance.[166] It thus fell to the embassy to press Ramadan's case, which it did by describing him as "among the most learned scholars of Islamic culture in the Ikhwan el Muslimin"—though, perhaps more important, their recommendation that Ramadan be invited was driven mainly by a fear of "offending this important body."[167] As a result, the State Department relented and allowed Ramadan to attend—and not merely as an observer but as a "regular member" of the conference. But even then, a line was drawn at paying for him. Beyond his living expenses while at the colloquium, Ramadan was expected to fund his own visit to the United States. In addition, he was not issued with a formal invitation. Rather, the Cairo Embassy was tasked simply with doing what was "necessary" to facilitate his travel. And Washington officials seemed anxious to stress that Ramadan was being accredited not as a representative of the Muslim Brotherhood, but as an "individual selected because of intellectual merit."[168]

All of this hardly suggested a rush on the part of US diplomats to join hands with Ramadan and, through him, the Ikhwan. Furthermore, the conference itself seems to have done little to change their minds about the group. A CIA spectator at the colloquium recorded being "deeply impressed" with everyone who participated, "with the exception of the Muslim Brotherhood's Said Ramadhan [*sic*]." The latter was described as a "political reactionary [and] . . . Phalangist or Fascist type," who had been concerned solely "with political pressure rather than with cultural problems." Ramadan was said to be interested solely in "the grouping of individuals for power" and offered little to discussion beyond the ideas of the Ikhwan. Despite being present at a lively intellectual session, he "took no part and did not seem interested in academic matters."[169] All in all, it seems fair to conclude that Ramadan did not make a good impression on American officials. Their caustic perception of him was, in turn, wholly in keeping with US assessments of the Brotherhood during the early 1950s— the period when American diplomatic support for Nasser was nearing its peak.

Even so, the Eisenhower administration did give consideration more broadly to the possibility that religion could be used to thwart communism. The head of the Psychological Strategy Board, C. D. Jackson, was a particular exponent of this line of thinking. In 1954, National Security Council (NSC) Paper 162/2 was produced, which called for the mobilization of spiritual and moral forces against the Soviets. Likewise, a close adviser to the president, Edward P. Lilly, wrote a memorandum entitled "The Religious Factor," which made a similar case.[170] Eisenhower himself seems to have felt there was some merit in the notion. As early as March 1956, he pondered whether King Saud might be able to exploit his position as a "spiritual leader" to impede more radical forces.[171] Two years previously, the king had shown a readiness to deploy his religious credentials in the service of a more active international role when, on a tour of Egypt, Pakistan, and Jordan, Saud had spoken of his desire to strengthen "the spirit of true Islamic brotherhood."[172] Subsequently, the king had drifted into Nasser's orbit, joining with Egypt and Syria in opposition to the Baghdad Pact. After the Suez conflict, however, as misgivings about the Egyptian president grew, the Americans appeared desperate to "win" Saud over to the West.

In February 1957, the king visited Washington at the invitation of the White House and a lucrative arms deal was signed. It was the beginning of a more concerted effort to build up the Saudi monarch as a counterfoil to Nasser. The US press soon carried talk about the "titanic rivalry for leadership of the Arab world"; "Saud vs. Nasser" was said to be a "study in contrasts."[173] Other pro-Western governments followed the American lead in seeking to foster this division. In August, for example, the Iraqi foreign minister told Ambassador Robert Strong that he had attended a dinner hosted by King Saud when performing the Hajj, and urged the king to utilize the power of religion in the fight against communism.[174] (The Iraqis themselves were particularly strident in their opposition to Nasser. Prime Minister Nuri al-Said told US diplomats that the Egyptian president was the "source of all the disturbances in the Middle East." The objective of the West, Nuri stated, should be to try and maneuver Nasser into revealing his true "communist face.")[175]

American officials sought to cultivate closer ties with King Saud, "as the Arab par excellence, as custodian of the Holy Places, and as the beneficiary of huge oil royalties." The king was deemed to be "the best qualified to challenge President Nasser's claim to speak on behalf of the Arabs."[176] An NSC staff study recommended that the United States maintain the "friendliest relations" with Saud, and push him "to use his influence" to realize American objectives in the region.[177] For their part, the Saudis were thought to be anxious to bolster "the prestige of the House of Saud among the Arab and Muslim nations" by stressing the king's religious responsibilities and his position as "an Islamic leader."[178]

After the failure of a US-backed coup in Damascus in 1957, American diplomats spoke with ever more urgency about the necessity of building up the "moderate" Arab states like Saudi Arabia and Jordan, to present Nasser with a stark "choice between moderation and extremism."[179] In this context, they set some store in the idea that Saud might exploit the "political and moral authority" he enjoyed to rally opposition against the leftist Syrian government.[180] Indeed, the US Embassy in Amman remarked that the one "redeeming aspect" of an otherwise bad situation in Syria was the prospect that it might illustrate conclusively the "great threat to Islam posed by Communist control" of Damascus. It was argued that every effort should be made to rebuild relations with the Arabs by accentuating communism's atheistic character. It was further proposed that the United States try to recruit the "top religious leaders of Islam" to denounce the Soviets. American officials contemplated asking King Saud to host an anticommunist conference that "might even end with [a] call for Jihad against Syrian Communists."[181]

The attempt to bolster the Saudi monarchy was just one feature of a wider effort to engage "Islam" in this era. In the summer of 1957, for instance, President Eisenhower officially dedicated the Washington Islamic Center. Within the State Department, this ceremony was viewed as yet another "excellent opportunity for a demonstration of American cultural interest and solidarity with the Moslem world."[182] That same year, a joint circular was issued to US missions in the Middle East, which called for a stepping up of the "psychological campaign" against communism. Among the themes to be promoted was an emphasis

on American support for Arab unity, freedom, and the forces of "genuine nationalism" (by which they meant the movements in Libya, Morocco, Tunisia,
and Sudan). On the other side, communism was to be portrayed as a threat to
peace and the "enemy of religion."[183] Simultaneously, too, US officials sought
ways to improve their "psychological warfare program in the Middle East"
by placing greater focus on the "mutuality of religious interest between the
United States and Moslem countries." Diplomats were encouraged to draw
attention to the degree to which "Atheistic communism" was "not compatible
with Islam."[184]

As Ian Johnson has underscored, 1957 also saw the creation of an "Ad Hoc
Working Group on Islam," bringing together representatives from the United
States Information Agency (USIA), the State Department, and the CIA.[185] The
group produced a long report for the Operations Coordinating Board (OCB)
that oversaw US national security policy, which identified possible areas for increased activity in the Islamic world. The document was notable, not least
because of the way it framed Islam in a fashion congruent with the vision of
the Ikhwan. The "nature of Islam," it was claimed, was to color "every aspect of
life"—an echo of the Brotherhood's core message about comprehensiveness. In
addition, Islam was said to be opposed to "foreign influences" and favor "neutralism" in foreign affairs. Muslim "historical reactions against the west," it was
argued, made cooperation difficult because of the conflict and domination to
which Muslims had been subjected by "Western civilization." All of this was
very much in keeping with the ideology of the Ikhwan.

Moreover, the same report observed that the United States was missing a trick:
neither government agencies nor private American organizations were maintaining "extensive contacts with the Islamic world" that could "affect these
peoples as Muslims." The State Department especially was criticized for "doing
little with Islamic organizations as such." The authors insisted that Muslims
held values "compatible" with the United States, particularly their spirituality,
which cut against Soviet atheism. They advised that Islam "should be defined
as a constructive force" that could play a "stabilizing" role in comparison to
pan-Arabism and extreme nationalism. The working group advocated "additional U.S. Government activity regarding Islamic organizations which exert
political influence." Crucially, various theological, cultural, and political
organizations were then identified in the appendix to the report as potential
targets for American outreach. The first entry under the category of "political"
groups read: "The Muslim Brothers: Syria, Pakistan, Jordan, Sudan, Egypt,
and other countries."[186]

This document thus raises an interesting question: were contacts with the Ikhwan pursued in the late 1950s as part of US efforts to combat communism? At one level, such a move would have made sense. As outlined earlier, the idea that Islam might constitute the best antidote to communism was one that the Brotherhood had itself sought to foster in the years after the Second World War. Both Hasan al-Banna and Hasan al-Hudaybi had made claims to this effect in conversations with British and American officials (none of whom were persuaded).[187] In March 1951, *al-Da'wa* had argued that "only ideas" could "combat ideas" and hence "only true Islam" was able to "eliminate communism."[188] Likewise, Sa'id Ramadan was an ardent exponent of the notion that Islam could inhibit communism, which was held to be a product of "materialism."[189] This had been one of his primary talking points at the 1953 Princeton colloquium. On other occasions, too, Ramadan asserted that Islam offered a third way between "the vices of capitalism," which allowed "the greedy few to control the destinies of the many," and the "vices of communism," which destroyed "the individuality of man and transform[ed] him into a machine."[190] In September 1956, US diplomats recounted a conversation with Wilton Wynn, the former Beirut chief of the Associated Press then based in Cairo, who was said to be an "old friend" of Ramadan. Wynn had informed them that Ramadan wanted "to use his influence among the Moslem Brethren to carry out a broad scale anti-communist (though not anti-Soviet) campaign."[191] Throughout this period, the itinerant Ramadan sought out Western officials around the region in order to impress his views on them.[192] He continued to call for an end to the "blind imitation of the West" within Muslim societies, and inveighed against the "cultural invasion" to which they had been subjected; but equally, Ramadan was adamant that the greatest threat facing Islam was communism, described as "a totalitarian way of life which stems from an exclusive faith in materialism."[193] It was against this backdrop, according to Ian Johnson, that the CIA recruited Ramadan to help contain Soviet influence.[194]

Across the Middle East, meanwhile, the local branches of the Ikhwan had established themselves as avowed enemies of their communist rivals.[195] Neither was there any doubting their opposition to Nasser and his brand of Arab nationalism. In Jordan, for example, the Brotherhood was known for being both a "faithful" friend to the king and "fanatically anti-Communist."[196] This was why, when the authorities banned all other political parties, the Ikhwan was exempted on the grounds it was a religious organization. Soon afterward, US officials seem to have made a specific effort to reach out to the local Brothers, and the consul general in Jerusalem met with a Brotherhood parliamentarian. Though perhaps not "the most desirable ally imaginable," the Ikhwani was judged to be "better than some of the possible alternatives," given his anticommunism and support for the Jordanian king.[197]

Similarly within Syria, US officials now identified the Ikhwan as a potentially useful force for stemming the advance of communism at a time when the diplomats were "particularly concerned" about growing Soviet influence.[198] In late 1956, the Brotherhood's Muhammad al-Mubarak had publicly excoriated Prime Minister Sabri al-Asali for being soft on Syria's communists.[199] By the spring of the following year, the Ikhwan had joined an anticommunist coalition in Damascus to fight forthcoming by-elections.[200] During those contests, Brotherhood leader Mustafa al-Siba'i stood as a candidate in Damascus, and it was assumed that pro-Western voters, despite seeing al-Siba'i as a "fanatic demagogue," considered him the "lesser of two evils."[201] There were also rumors of US financial support for the Ikhwan and the wider anticommunist coalition. The truth of this is impossible to determine from the available sources. If it did occur, though, it proved unsuccessful, as al-Siba'i and his allies were defeated.[202] Still, the antagonism between the Ikhwan and the Ba'th Party was clear, with the former accusing the latter of being in league with communism.[203] US diplomats deemed it unlikely that the Brotherhood in Damascus would cease its opposition to either the Syrian or the Egyptian governments.[204]

In both Jordan and Syria, therefore, American readings of the Brotherhood remained equivocal. Officials harbored no illusions as to the fact that the Ikhwan was often deeply critical of the West. The group was regularly described as an "extreme right-wing" force.[205] At the same time, there was a perception that it could diminish the appeal of communism. The diplomats welcomed the fact that Brotherhood leaders were prepared to be critical of the Soviet Union.[206] And there did seem to be some form of low-level engagement with local chapters of the Ikhwan.

In Egypt itself, of course, the Brothers were still reeling from Nasser's ferocious repression. Nonetheless, in the wake of the Suez war there were some reports that the Brotherhood had "gained ground" and might even be in a position to challenge Nasser (the short-lived truce between the two sides over Suez having come to an end).[207] US officials heard rumors that former prime minister Ali Maher was in "indirect contact" with Ikhwan elements and desired a "successful rightist counter-coup" that would return him to power. Needless to say, this vista proved to be a mirage.[208] While officials noted that the Brothers, together with the Wafd and the communists, had "renewed their political activity," amid the electoral campaign for Egypt's first postrevolutionary parliament in 1957, government restrictions ensured that this was tightly constrained. According to "virtually all observers," the reality was that there was "no imminent threat to the stability of the present regime."[209] In July, one British mandarin recorded that the Brotherhood was "active against Nasser both inside and outside Egypt" (especially in Jordan, where the Brothers were waging a "vigorous" propaganda campaign). However, it was judged that the group posed no danger to the Egyptian president, whose authority was nearly absolute.[210] Indeed, in the words of the US consul in Port Said, the Brotherhood had been reduced "from a movement to a police problem." By this account, little had really been heard of the group since its suppression in 1954.[211]

Even so, the American Embassy in Cairo did detect a "growing conviction" *within* the regime that the United States was in fact "actively promoting subversive activity" against Nasser. Such fears were said to be the impulse for a new wave of arrests, targeted against former politicians and ex-army officers.[212] There were also fresh allegations of an assassination plot targeting Nasser and his cabinet.[213] And when the trial of the purported conspirators opened in August 1957, in front of the Supreme Military Court, there was much focus on what was dubbed the "Eisenhower plan" and supposed US efforts to engineer the downfall of the government. American imperialism was said to be colluding with local reactionaries, in an effort to remove Nasser.[214]

Senior State Department officials dismissed these accusations as "patently absurd."[215] Diplomats in Cairo reported that the whole trial had been "staged."[216] Yet these fervent denials were complicated somewhat by the later testimony of Kim Roosevelt. He affirmed that in this period, the CIA *did* endorse the principle of removing the Egyptian leader—though Roosevelt added that at no stage were they "satisfied that the appropriate conditions existed to carry it out successfully." The Americans, stated Roosevelt, had been unable to identify "the palace revolutionaries" who might undertake a coup "with any chance of success."[217] Irrespective of such caveats, it might be said that these words do not entirely exclude the possibility of US involvement in anti-Nasser conspiracies, and it could be that there was more truth to the Egyptian allegations than was admitted at the time. At a minimum, the episode reflected both the sensitivities of the regime and the depth of antagonism that then existed between Washington and Cairo.

In December 1957, another putative plot against the Egyptian government was uncovered—the so-called monarchy conspiracy case. The resultant trial saw the prosecution of former interior minister Murtada al-Maraghi and other ancien régime politicians, as well as a "propaganda exposition" against the "imperialist countries." In addition, the court heard "revelations" about the purported involvement of King Saud in intrigues against Nasser—an indication perhaps of the shifting stance of the Saudi kingdom during 1957, and the faith that had been placed in it by some Western officials.[218] If this was the case, it is ironic that at the same moment the United States was once more reassessing its approach to the Middle East. In part, this was driven by the disappointment that American diplomats had felt over the performance of King Saud, especially in Syria.[219] Saud's reluctance-cum-inability to intervene and check the growth of leftist influence in Damascus led to something of a volte-face with regard to US views on Nasser.

The Challenge of Nasser—Revisited

As far back as the middle of 1956, some within the State Department had argued that the United States should "accept the facts of Arab hostility and [the] resultant anti-Western neutralism." On this view, rather than "play the aggrieved suitor or the carping critic," Washington should seek an accommodation with leaders like Nasser.[220] Egypt was judged to be "in no sense a Soviet satellite."[221] Though under the spell of an Arab nationalism that was "hypersensitive and xenophobic," it was not seen as a "Trojan horse" for communism. That being so, advocates of this standpoint urged the pursuit of cordial relations with nationalists of Nasser's ilk.[222] By late 1957, arguments of this kind seemed to have gained ascendancy within US foreign policy-making circles. The idea that the Egyptian president could be won over to the West was voiced with renewed vigour.[223] The American ambassador to Damascus, for example, advised that the United States withhold criticism of Nasser and instead encourage him to "concentrate [his] fire" on Syria, where he enjoyed "prestige and influence."[224] By December, it was being reported that some in Damascus saw a union between Syria and Egypt as the only means by which to reduce communist influence there. In the assessment of the embassy, too, "rightist opposition" to the Soviets was "no longer effective" and in this context, Arab nationalists, including even the Ba'th Party, could be counted as a "moderate (relatively speaking) element."[225] Soon afterward, the United States appeared to give a green light to the merger of Syria and Egypt under the Nasser-controlled "United Arab Republic [UAR]."[226]

Inevitably, this U-turn in the American position caused consternation in London, where officials continued to believe that the "disappearance of the

Nasser regime" should be the "main objective" of UK policy.[227] To men like Foreign Secretary Selwyn Lloyd, Nasser remained "public enemy No. 1 in the Middle East."[228] For Washington, though, the ends justified the means: if the forces of religion could not stand as an effective barrier to the advance of communism, then they were prepared to reengage with Arab nationalists. Seen from this perspective, Nasser's broad popular appeal, the very thing that made him so threatening to the regional status quo, was precisely what made him so attractive as a potential partner to the United States. If Nasser could be harnessed—and brought into alignment with Western objectives—it was assumed that *he* might yet serve as the perfect bulwark to communism. In the final years of Eisenhower's presidency, this outlook gained increased traction within the administration.[229]

There were, it should be said, still moments of crisis. In mid-1958, for instance, Iraq's July revolution delivered a major shock to the regional order and raised fresh questions about the wisdom of embracing Nasser. The man who emerged as leader in Baghdad, Brigadier Abd al-Karim Qasim, initially declared his allegiance to pan-Arab ideals and many expected Iraq to be absorbed into the UAR. American officials worried that a "tidal wave" of revolution would engulf the Middle East, sweeping away conservative and Western-backed regimes.[230] It was to prevent this nightmare scenario from being realized that US marines were temporarily dispatched to Lebanon (itself already in a state of near civil war) to bolster the pro-Western government. The British undertook a parallel mission to reinforce King Hussein in Jordan.[231]

It was not long, however, before US diplomats recovered their balance. As the tremors unleashed by the Iraqi upheaval subsided, many quickly came to the conclusion that little had changed in terms of policy options. As one official had commented even at the height of the crisis, the only alternative to direct US intervention in the region was an attempt to build "cooperative" relations with Nasser.[232] Consequently, efforts to establish warmer ties with Cairo resumed. In late 1958, NSC Strategy Paper 5820 elevated this to the level of doctrine, stating that the "most dangerous challenge to Western interests" arose "not from Arab nationalism per se but from the coincidence of many of its objectives with many of those of the USSR and the resultant way in which it [could] be manipulated to serve Soviet ends."[233] To counter this possibility, the paper said that the US government ought to make it known that its objectives were "fundamentally compatible with the goals of Arab nationalism." While not abandoning pro-Western alliances in the Middle East, it was argued that the United States should accept neutralist policies "where necessary." There was no mistaking what this meant in terms of Nasser, "the foremost current spokesman of radical pan-Arab nationalism." Without appearing to accept "the inevitability of Nasser's undisputed hegemony over the whole of the Arab world," policy makers were urged to pursue a policy of "accommodation," to secure an "effective working relationship" with the Egyptian leader.[234]

The new willingness of the United States to seek a rapprochement with Nasser was underpinned by the supposition that his government embodied the ascendant forces in the region. Conservative and pro-Western governments were thought to be on the decline. There was enduring speculation that the Lebanese, Jordanian, and Saudi regimes might fall.[235] To many observers, therefore, it made sense that the United States should try and build bridges with Cairo. The allure of such an approach was strengthened further by the rivalry that soon emerged between the Egyptian and Iraqi governments as President Qasim moved closer to Moscow.[236] As far as the United States was concerned, this merely confirmed that Nasserism was the true face of an authentic Arab anticommunism and potentially a crucial ally of the West.

As a result, this era saw the implementation of various measures designed to improve US-Egyptian relations.[237] The most important of these was the decision to supply American wheat to Cairo under the terms of Public Law 480 (PL-480)—a concession for which Nasser's government had long been pressing.[238] In the two years that followed the resumption of aid in November 1958, Washington authorized some $290 million worth of assistance for the UAR. Of this total, $180 million was accounted for by PL-480 wheat aid.[239]

The process of US-Egyptian "normalisation" was pushed forward during Eisenhower's last year in office. In February 1960, analysis by the OCB noted with satisfaction the "deep and widening gulf" between the Soviets and Arab nationalists. It was argued the latter had "shown that against communism they can muster ideological weapons far more powerful than anything the US or its allies could bring to bear."[240] Furthermore, American officials felt that they had successfully improved ties with "the enfant terrible of Arab nationalism," Nasser.[241] Of course, they claimed to be under no illusions about the reliability of the Egyptian leader, and there were evidently points of friction. Periodically, for instance, Nasser launched fierce attacks on "imperialism and Zionism," identifying the United States with both.[242] At the same time, though, the diplomats believed that Cairo wanted to cooperate on matters of "mutual interest," and they saw Nasser as a force for "moderation," especially in Syria.[243]

The broad picture, then, as Eisenhower's administration gave way to that of John F. Kennedy, was of a steadily improving relationship. The new president came to office, having pledged to take a "new look" at US policy in the Middle East. With regard to Egypt, however, Kennedy's arrival in the White House brought only a change of style rather than substance; the underlying strategy was retained. In an effort to take forward the rapprochement with Cairo, the president opened a personal correspondence with Nasser. He also asked John Badeau, the former head of the American University in Cairo, to return to Egypt as ambassador. Badeau later remembered how his focus was on building areas for cooperation with the Egyptians while keeping points of disagreement "in the icebox." The settled view of the Kennedy administration (inherited from Eisenhower) was that Nasser was "not an ideologue" but rather a "highly pragmatic man." The Egyptian president's "pragmatic state socialism" was seen as wholly preferable to communism and as a "kind of vaccination . . . against a real onslaught of a worse disease." The overall verdict was that "a stable developing Egypt, even in a revolutionary pattern," was very much to the American interest.[244]

Whatever his shortcomings, Nasser was held to be the most powerful "opponent of Communism in the Arab Near East."[245] To this was added the sense that in Egypt there were few meaningful alternatives.[246] One assessment concluded that, while the atmosphere in Cairo was "less exciting and less excited" than it had been in earlier periods, the regime was "by far the most solid and entrenched in the Middle East."[247] Not only was Nasser thought to be secure, but also it was imagined that any successor government would likely be "less stable and more troublesome." As a consequence, officials remained supportive of a "step by careful step approach" designed to improve relations.[248] Consideration was thus given to whether Nasser might be invited to the White House.[249] More importantly, the State Department backed the signing of a multiyear PL-480 agreement to provide substantial food assistance to Cairo—a deal finalized in the late summer of 1962.[250]

Needless to say, these developments left little room for an alliance between the United States and a group like the Muslim Brotherhood. By this time, at least in Egypt, there was scant evidence of life in the Ikhwan, despite the odd meeting between American officials and Brothers in exile.[251] Elsewhere in the region, the various chapters of the Brotherhood enjoyed mixed fortunes. In Jordan, for example, the diplomats acknowledged that the group continued to buttress King Hussein and oppose communism, even as it caused some concern to the local authorities and was fiercely critical of US foreign policy.[252] By contrast, in Iraq, the Iraqi Islamic Party (IIP)—which had superseded the Muslim Ethical Society as the local branch of the Brotherhood in 1958—was repressed following the revolution that same year, and the leadership of the party froze its activities in 1961–1962.[253] The IIP was only revived as a functioning body thirty years later—and by then it was operating from exile in Britain.[254]

The Ikhwan in Syria fared only marginally better. First, it had to contend with the Nasser-controlled UAR, which forced the dissolution of the group's executive. Despite this, the Brothers retained a presence and several members had participated in the short-lived National Union.[255] After Syrian secession from the UAR in 1961, the US Embassy in Damascus observed a "mild resurgence in the influence of . . . the Muslim Brethren," and, in elections that December, the group won a number of seats.[256] For a brief period, the Ikhwan even appeared to have some influence over the government, but this soon dissipated as the country drifted to the left during 1962.[257] American diplomats did identify the Brothers as an important opposition force that was "outspokenly anti-Commie."[258] But they doubted whether the movement could ever wield meaningful and lasting power: "The process of modernization and secularization," they concluded, had "gone too far."[259]

This latter sentiment was a common one. In a similar vein, a UK Foreign Office memorandum discussed the "general tendency in the more advanced Muslim countries . . . towards secularisation and a modernist interpretation of Islam." It was presumed that this process undercut groups like the Brotherhood, who were defined by a "fanatical and unrealistic advocacy of an Islamic theocracy."[260] In the eyes of many Western analysts, the Ikhwan was an outmoded vestige of a former time and rather peripheral to the contemporary political scene. Certainly, compared to the power of Arab nationalism and the rulers of the various "officers' republics," the Brothers appeared to be of only limited significance.[261]

By the spring of 1962, the bilateral US-Egyptian relationship seemed in a better condition than at any time since the "low point" of 1957. As one official commented, "a new cordiality and a degree of cooperation exists which has not been experienced for some time."[262] Various memoranda and telegrams pointed to the "new normalcy" inside the UAR, arising out of regime stability and confidence. In foreign policy, too, Nasser was thought to be behaving in a "more genuinely neutral or non-aligned" fashion, and with a "greater degree of moderation." Diplomats reported a "greater steadiness and maturity," with less violent swings of the pendulum between East and West.[263]

Yet even as such words were being drafted, darker clouds were gathering. The outbreak of civil war in Yemen in the autumn of 1962 proved to be a critical moment. Nasser's decision to support the republican side, while the Saudis backed the royalists, complicated the regional environment. The United States found itself pulled between the exigencies of its alliance with Riyadh and its desire for conciliation with Cairo.[264] Already, some within the State Department had begun to question the administration's "softly-softly" approach toward Nasser and the failure to establish reciprocity between economic aid and political performance. On this reading, the "record of getting Nasser to respect [American] interests in the Near East" had not been particularly impressive.[265] Egyptian policies in Yemen generated fresh misgivings. And concerns were exacerbated further by the Ba'thist coups that occurred in Iraq and Syria in early 1963. Many anticipated that a fresh wave of revolutionary energy would break across the Middle East.[266] To some American observers, Nasser once more appeared as a "compulsive 'Arab Socialist' revolutionary, bent on the overthrow of old political and economic orders and the eradication of foreign influence throughout the Arab world."[267]

Almost inevitably, US dealings with Cairo now became more cautious. This, in turn, prompted a further cooling of the atmosphere; and this was aggravated too by the assassination of President Kennedy. Thereafter, the Lyndon B. Johnson administration, at least initially, attempted to replicate the Middle Eastern policies of its predecessor. But irrespective of this, the Egyptians perceived the new president to be a far less sympathetic figure, given his apparent ties to US oil interests and support for Israel.[268] This all made for a less harmonious relationship between Washington and Cairo.

Of course, there were still prominent advocates of the policy of rapprochement, such as Ambassador Badeau.[269] And even those unenthusiastic about Nasser were inclined to believe that the United States could neither "destroy" nor "replace him with a viable and more moderate government." As such, there remained support for an accommodation with the Egyptian leader as the only realistic policy option.[270] Nevertheless, as 1964 progressed, there were unmistakable signs of a steady deterioration in the bilateral relationship. In his annual May Day speech, for example, Nasser struck a "fighting" tone and inveighed against the British and Americans for "plundering" Arab oil and backing Tel Aviv.[271] A few weeks later, the Egyptian president welcomed Soviet premier Nikita Khrushchev to Cairo and stressed their shared "bonds of friendship."[272] A key symbolic moment then came in June, when John Badeau left Egypt having tendered his resignation. As described, the ambassador had been a firm exponent of the effort to establish closer ties with Nasser, but even Badeau had to admit that a tranquil, mutually beneficial relationship had been "not really discoverable."[273]

The Cairo Embassy continued to make the case that the United States should avoid oversimplistic, one-dimensional forms of analysis: "US-UAR relations are neither [a] football game nor [a] western movie with 'bad guys chasing good guys.'"[274] A review of policy "alternatives" again concluded that "tactical cooperation" with Nasser offered the best prospects for success.[275] By the end of 1964, however, it was hard to ignore the worsening situation. Thanksgiving Day had been marked by the burning down of the United States Information Service (USIS) library in Cairo by students protesting against American actions in the Congo. The diplomats were "indignant" at what they saw as the tacit condoning of the episode by Egyptian officials.[276] Things were complicated yet further by the shooting down of an American cargo plane flying over Alexandria and the subsequent political fallout.[277] This culminated on 23 December 1964, when Nasser delivered a "breast-beating" speech, attacking the United States for allegedly using economic aid as a means by which to exert control over foreign countries.[278] He vowed that the Egyptians would embrace a new period of austerity rather than trade their dignity and submit to the will of the Americans. "If anyone reproaches us," Nasser proclaimed, "we'll cut out his tongue." Famously, he followed this with a personal message for recently arrived ambassador Lucius Battle: "If he does not like our behavior, he can drink the salt water of the Mediterranean. And if that isn't enough, he can drink the water of the Red Sea."[279]

In Washington, officials hypothesized that Nasser was reaching for confrontation with the United States in order to head off domestic problems.[280] Even now, though, senior figures in the White House reckoned that any split with Cairo would cost the United States more than it could gain.[281] To this was added the enduring belief that there was no real alternative in Egypt. A mid-January 1965 assessment by the Cairo Embassy examined potential scenarios arising out of Nasser's "sudden disappearance." The likelihood of a "bourbon restoration" of the old regime was dismissed out of hand. Nor was it envisaged that a "new junta" could emerge from within the military. Crucially for present purposes, there was no discussion whatsoever of the possibility that an opposition movement such as the Muslim Brotherhood might capture power. Instead, the most plausible vehicle for change was deemed to be a "palace revolution" that would alter the balance internally within the regime. Moreover, the diplomats feared that any successor government might either be riven by instability or espouse politics farther to the left than the incumbent. For this reason, they considered that the United States had little choice but to work with Nasser.[282] And to this end, they were prepared to set the bar fairly low for the Egyptian president in terms of his behavior. They did not expect him to agree with the United States on all issues: "We can tolerate deterioration in a few . . . categories if the over-all US-UAR relationship is evolving to our advantage."[283] The bottom line, as articulated by National Security Adviser Robert Komer, was relatively simple: "At a time when we have enough trouble in Vietnam and elsewhere we have got to keep the Middle East reasonably quiet."[284]

Washington was encouraged by the fact that, by the summer of 1965, Nasser seemed ready for a peace settlement in Yemen. In September, the Jidda Agreement was signed, which looked to regularize ties between Cairo and Riyadh. The following month, King Faisal (who had succeeded Saud at the end of the previous year) stopped off in Cairo on his way to the third Arab Summit—a further harbinger of the thaw in Saudi-Egyptian tensions.[285] In addition, US officials hoped to use the June 1965 expiry of Kennedy's three-year PL-480 food arrangement to reset the US-Egyptian relationship.[286] To their satisfaction, a new deal was reached in November—albeit only for six months.[287] By that time, however, the mood had soured considerably once more. In large part, this latest decline was driven by fresh "revelations" about secret conspiracies involving Nasser's opponents both home and abroad; at the heart of these sat the Muslim Brotherhood.

The "1965 Organisation": The Return of the Brotherhood

Since the turn of the decade, US diplomats had been aware of murmurings of discontent in Egypt. One report, for instance, commented that Nasser faced a "crisis in morality" due to popular perceptions of corruption and extravagance.[288] Officials recorded growing disillusionment among the middle classes.[289] Egypt was seen as a country ill at ease with itself amid a pervasive atmosphere of "drabness and uncertainty." The dominant outlook was thought to be one of apathy. According to the US Embassy, Nasser's effort to cultivate both popular enthusiasm for the regime and a genuine sense of "national consciousness" had proven unsuccessful.[290] CIA National Intelligence Estimates offered a picture of a government that had lost its "revolutionary elan."[291] Nasser himself was said to bear witness to his country's "remarkable political, social and economic deterioration": "Today he looks like any middle class Egyptian businessman with a poor tailor. . . . Middle age has overtaken him as well as his revolution."[292] Naguib Mahfuz evocatively captured the stifling, cheerless ambience of mid-1960s Cairo in his piercing novellas, *Adrift on the Nile* and *Karnak Café*.[293] It was a society in which suspicion hung in the air, and the newspapers and courts intermittently exposed sensational conspiracies against the state, often involving foreign powers.[294]

In 1965, a slew of such revelations dominated the headlines. Initially, there was little hint of any connection to the Ikhwan. The first "plot" to be exposed involved Mustafa Amin, a press tycoon and editor of the daily newspaper *al-Akhbar,* who was detained while lunching with Bruce Odell, an embassy attaché in Alexandria, who was alleged to be a CIA "intelligence officer."[295] The United States was quick to deny any wrongdoing, but it seems likely that Odell was indeed working for the CIA. Wilbur Eveland Crane later wrote that Mustafa Amin and his brother Ali were "constant CIA sources," having been recruited by Kim Roosevelt back in the 1950s.[296] Elsewhere, it has been suggested that Nasser was fully aware of Amin's contacts and had even used them to pass messages to the United States. The decision to collapse this conduit could thus be read as proof of his displeasure with the Americans at a time when relations were worsening. Whatever the truth of this, Amin was indicted and then convicted on twin charges of passing UAR state secrets to a foreign power and engaging in an illicit foreign currency transaction.[297] In August 1966, he was sentenced to life imprisonment with hard labor.[298]

The Egyptian media followed the Amin case closely, publishing transcripts of his conversations with Odell, which had been recorded by State Security. Among the questions apparently put to Amin by Odell was one about whether the Muslim Brotherhood was looking to Kamal al-Din Husayn, the former Free Officer and vice president who had resigned in 1964, as a "prospective leader." The local press seized on this detail as being of particular significance given that in the wake of the Amin arrest, the Egyptian security services said they had foiled another major plot, this one linked to the Ikhwan.[299]

With regard to the latter, the first official recognition that anything had happened came during a state visit to Moscow when Nasser told a meeting of students that they had uncovered a Brotherhood conspiracy to overthrow the regime.[300] In addition, on August 30, the US Embassy noted reports of a violent clash between the military police and Ikhwan members in the Cairo suburb of Kerdassa. This had led to the area being placed under martial law. Wild rumors circulated about what had transpired. Some said that up to one thousand people had been killed.[301] American officials were skeptical of such claims, but soon afterward, they became aware that large numbers of alleged Muslim Brothers were being detained across Egypt. There were also vague allusions to arrests having been made inside the army officer corps and the confiscation of weapons caches.[302] Equally, there was talk of far-flung intrigues, even involving exiled Muslim Brothers in Switzerland.[303]

On September 7, the Egyptian state media began to release information about the "secret terrorist organisation" that had been "discovered" under the control of the Ikhwan.[304] Large quantities of arms and ammunition had apparently been seized alongside plans for assassination and sabotage (the blowing up of bridges, power stations, and the airport).[305] The conspirators were said to have harbored ambitions to kill Nasser, as well as other top UAR officials and the American ambassador; this was to be followed by the murder of the Soviet, British, and French representatives. US ambassador Lucius Battle observed wryly that this "flattering disregard" for diplomatic precedence was entirely "unsolicited."[306]

Subsequently, the authorities initiated a major propaganda campaign against the "despicable reactionaries" said to be behind the "sinister plot." On September 24, the now government-run daily *al-Akhbar* carried an eight-page supplement on the Brotherhood and this was accompanied by numerous editorials in both the same newspaper and *al-Gumhurriya* attacking the conspiracy. Much emphasis was placed on the idea that the Ikhwan had violated the precepts of religion. Cartoons depicted the Brothers as terrorists standing outside "orthodox Islam."[307] Posters appeared in Tahrir Square and other prominent public spaces, denouncing the group as anti-Islamic.[308] The Sheikh al-Azhar, Hasan Ma'mun, accused the Brotherhood of serving imperialist interests and distorting the faith "in the minds of a handful of young men," so as to make them into "allies of the enemies of Islam."[309] The religious magazine *Minbar al-Islam* devoted an entire edition to statements from numerous other sheikhs and religious leaders condemning the Ikhwan.[310]

This deluge of anti-Brotherhood material was echoed on television and radio. In the last days of September, state media began broadcasting nightly "confessions" of arrested Ikhwan members (with transcripts appearing in the following day's newspapers). Audiences were shown pictures of captured matériel.[311] Nasser, meanwhile, spoke publicly about his sense of betrayal at the hands of the Brotherhood. In an address to youth leaders in Helwan, for example, he attested to his "strong friendship" with Hasan al-Banna and acknowledged the early cooperation between the Brothers and the Free Officers. According to Nasser, they had parted ways because the government "refused to become subject" to the Ikhwan.[312] Similarly, in his Victory Day speech of December 1965, the president reflected at length on the 1952–1954 period and the reasons why the government had fallen out with the Brotherhood, citing both their "backward-looking demands" and their ties to the British Embassy. He alleged that the group sought the reinstitution of the caliphate and what amounted to "real Fascist rule." In indignant fashion, Nasser noted that ten years after the October 1954 attempt to kill him, the last of the Ikhwan detainees had been released—only for them to "reward" him with a new assassination plot.[313]

In trying to excavate the facts of this putative conspiracy, the historian faces a difficult challenge—even more so than with regard to events in 1954. A decade later, Nasser's regime was entrenched and skilled in its ability to manipulate the press. It was also unquestionably paranoid and inclined to blame its difficulties on the machinations of enemies, both domestic and foreign. In later years, the Muslim Brotherhood and its supporters would again emphasize the fabricated nature of what had transpired in 1965.[314] Interestingly, too, even Anwar Sadat would posit in his autobiography that the latter Brotherhood plot was "purely imaginary."[315] By contrast, other regime sources maintained that there was a genuine threat, and they insisted that the Ikhwan opted to ally itself with "outside opposition forces" to try to topple Nasser by violence.[316]

In all of this, much remains hard to decipher. Contemporary Western observers were deeply aware of their own ignorance. For instance, one official in London commented that, if anything, the episode had revealed "how little" they knew about the internal affairs of Egypt. The same mandarin doubted whether the Brotherhood did constitute a "really serious threat to the regime," but admitted "the fact that we have been taken by surprise must give us pause."[317]

Other close followers of the Egyptian scene seemed convinced that the conspiracy was real. Israeli intelligence experts, for example, informed US officials in this period that they believed Nasser *could* be overthrown given the "surprisingly large scope of the recent Ikhwan plot," which had included "army elements."[318] For their part, both American and British diplomats appear to have been persuaded that there was some substance to the government's allegations. The former had assumed initially that the rumors were "confection or greatly exaggerated" by the authorities in order to frighten would-be dissidents. Nevertheless, the details that emerged were said to have the "ring of authenticity." Increasingly, the US Embassy viewed Egyptian propaganda as an effort to put the conspiracy "in perspective," rather than one of outright fabrication. "On balance," officials concluded, "we think [the] plot real."[319] By the middle of 1966, they had "no doubt" that the Ikhwan was a "subversive organization," planning the "assassination and overthrow" of the regime. The charges against the Brothers were described as "real and based on pretty firm evidence"; the people in jail were presumed "to be guilty of very serious plotting against [the] state"; and their crimes "seemed clearly established."[320]

In arriving at this assessment, the Americans expressed surprise that the Ikhwan had "managed to build up [a] clandestine organization in spite of omnipresent police surveillance." Yet this was taken to be indicative of the group's "determination and skill."[321] The British Embassy similarly saw "no reason to doubt that the Brotherhood were planning some kind of a coup including the assassination of the President." Moreover, they reckoned that the Egyptian government had been unnerved by what the plot seemed to reveal about both "popular resentment" and the poor performance of the security forces.[322] The latter was said to explain the appointment of Zakariyya Muhi al-Din as prime minister in October 1965. Zakariyya had previously played a central role in creating the Egyptian intelligence apparatus after July 1952; he had also served as interior minister. Now he resumed that position alongside the premiership, and US officials inferred that he had been tasked with reorganizing the security services, giving them the "new broom treatment," because of their "failure to discover the Ikhwan plot sooner." There were reports of wholesale retirements and new appointments being made at senior levels.[323] In light of such changes, it seemed hard to avoid the conclusion that Nasser felt there had been serious intelligence deficiencies. More than one embassy source suggested that the regime had been "surprised and appalled" to discover the extent of the plotting against it.[324]

Embassy records, when placed alongside press coverage of the legal process and the confessions of the defendants, provide a wealth of data about the case built by the authorities against the Ikhwan. On this basis, it is possible to build a fairly extensive picture of the conspiracy *as seen and portrayed by* the Egyptian regime. Obviously, that depiction has to be treated with a degree of caution. US officials observed that several of the "confessions" had a "hollow ring" about them and were full of vague references to "certain persons."[325] The readiness of the security forces to extract testimony by coercive means— including torture—was attested to by various sources. The diplomats also acknowledged that the authorities were not beyond inventing "evidence" altogether.[326] In spite of this, given the anxieties of the regime, it seems likely that the details of the plot were grounded in some essential truths. What follows is an effort to piece together the most plausible account of what had occurred.

To begin with, it is worth clarifying that State Security actually exposed at least two discrete conspiracies in the autumn of 1965. The first of these— and by far the more amateur—centered on Husayn Tawfiq. As discussed in Chapter 3, Tawfiq had previous connections to violence, having been responsible for the murder of Amin Osman Pasha in 1946, a crime committed with the assistance of Anwar Sadat.[327] In his 1965 confession, Tawfiq admitted to having created a new terrorist group two years earlier. His plan had been simply to murder Nasser, using the Kennedy assassination as inspiration. American officials were far from impressed. In their estimation, Tawfiq was "merely a disgruntled bourgeois with a terrorist past."[328] His scheming appeared crude and underdeveloped, and there were just fourteen people in his "organisation." What gave them added import, though, was the fact that in attempting to secure weapons and money, Tawfiq had contacted the Muslim Brotherhood. In so doing, he helped to expose their more elaborate plans to the security services.[329] Thereafter, the authorities seemed determined to tie Tawfiq to the Brotherhood, contending that they had joined forces against the government.[330] But embassy diplomats were deeply skeptical of this. In their judgment, Tawfiq and his accomplices were a "separate, lunatic fringe group" under the control of someone who was himself "mentally unbalanced." They were thought to have little real connection to the Ikhwan, which it was assumed "wouldn't touch the Tawfiq group with a ten-foot pole."[331]

The mainstream Brotherhood conspiracy, by comparison, appeared an altogether different proposition. In total, more than two hundred people were indicted for membership of a "terrorist organization," and the government sought the death penalty for the seven who allegedly made up its "command council": Sayyid Qutb, the purported leader; Muhammad Yusuf Hawwash, said to be second in command; 'Ali Ahmad 'Ashmawi; 'Abd al-Fattah Abdu Isma'il; Ahmad 'Abd al-Magid al-Sami'e; Sabri Arafa; and Magdi 'Abd al-Aziz Mitwalli. These men, together with their subordinates, were charged with rebuilding the Brotherhood's Special Apparatus (SA) with a view to overthrowing the Egyptian government.[332] Of course, one person conspicuous by his absence here was the general guide, Hasan al-Hudaybi—an indication perhaps that he had been effectively sidelined. At his trial, Ali 'Ashmawi did testify that al-Hudaybi had been told about, and given his blessing to, the new group's existence. 'Ashmawi, though, was accused by his codefendants of lying. In due course, al-Hudaybi was prosecuted by the authorities—but this seemed more of an afterthought than the product of any serious conviction that he was involved in the conspiracy.[333] To some extent, this was borne out too in the charges brought against him. He was accused of trying to revive the old Ikhwan, rather than for his part in any assassination plot.

The origins of what came to be known as the "1965 Organisation" lay in the second half of the 1950s. As Nasser's government had slowly relaxed its repression of the Ikhwan, groups of Brothers had emerged either from prison or from hiding, and gradually reestablished contact with one other.[334] They had also used trips to Saudi Arabia (to perform the Hajj) to liaise with exiled Ikhwan leaders, including Kamil al-Sharif, 'Ashmawi Sulayman, Mahmud Abu al-Sa'ud, and Sa'id Ramadan. In 1963–1964, most of these hitherto independent groupings amalgamated to form a new leadership council under the direction of Sayyid Qutb.[335] Qutb had spent much of the previous decade in jail, having been convicted in 1954 of conspiring to overthrow the government. During this time, he had been in touch with key individuals seeking to restore the Brotherhood on the outside. A line of communication ran through Qutb's sister Hamida and Zaynab al-Ghazali, a longtime devotee of the Ikhwan who had previously served as head of the "Moslem Women's Society."[336] In May 1964, Sayyid Qutb was released from prison and promptly informed by the Brothers that a secret, cell-based "commandos organization" had been created with the aim of assassinating senior figures and toppling the regime. He was asked to head this group and agreed.[337]

With a leadership structure in place inside Egypt, the new Brotherhood organization made plans for a coup and held several paramilitary training camps. Both Ali 'Ashmawi and 'Abd al-Fattah Abdu Isma'il testified that Qutb was fully apprised of these military preparations. By May 1965, it would appear that the revived Ikhwan, fearing the government was becoming aware of their scheming, decided to accelerate their timetable for action. Even as they prepared to strike, however, the police began to make arrests. Sayyid Qutb was himself detained on August 9 in the Cairo suburb of Imbaba, at which point leadership of the organization passed to Muhammad Yusuf Hawwash. Within days, he too had been captured. In parallel, the authorities recovered various kinds of explosives and weaponry (including Molotov cocktails, pistols, daggers, and machine guns). Ali 'Ashmawi and the remaining leaders sought to press ahead, but the group was too small and disorganized to carry through any kind of violent campaign. Many of the lower ranks appear to have known little, if anything, about an actual plot. 'Ashmawi was arrested on August 20 and, thereafter, almost the entire Brotherhood network was rolled up.[338]

What followed was the aforementioned deluge of anti-Ikhwan propaganda, coupled with another specially constructed legal process, which ran over several months. It was not until August 1966 that Egypt's State Security court issued its first verdicts, when Husayn Tawfiq and his main accomplices were each given life sentences. Soon afterward, the seven members of the Brotherhood's command council were condemned to death; twenty-five others received life sentences; and a further eleven, prison terms of between ten and fifteen years.

Altogether, some 195 people were convicted of crimes in relation to the Qutb conspiracy.[339] Many thousands more were interned without trial.

Four of the death sentences were commuted to life imprisonment with hard labor (the younger Brotherhood members were spared). But on August 29, Qutb, Hawwash, and Isma'il were hanged.[340] As in 1954, the severity of the punishments and the executions immediately generated some protests abroad.[341] The Ikhwan's exile network and regional chapters were inevitably to the forefront of these. In Sudan, for example, the local branch of the Brotherhood mobilized large demonstrations attacking Nasser that clashed with police.[342] Similarly, US officials in Pakistan observed a "surprisingly vigorous" reaction there to the hangings, which they attributed to the efforts of the Islamist group Jamaat-i-Islami.[343] Elsewhere, though, reactions were more muted. An editorial in the Jordanian Brotherhood's *al-Manar* newspaper declared that "the blood of the Muslim Brothers cannot be shed with the approval of the Arab and Islamic conscience."[344] Yet, when the group attempted to hold a rally outside the Egyptian Embassy in Amman, diplomats noted that only seventy-five people turned up; and anti-Nasser placards drew a hostile response from his supporters within the kingdom.[345] The Iraqi Brotherhood likewise struggled to organize protests, hamstrung by what the local embassy described as its "general unpopularity." As emotions over the executions faded, it was forecast that the Brothers in Baghdad would "probably revert to their semi-dormant status."[346]

Within Egypt, as outlined at the start of this chapter, American officials surmised that the government had been particularly unnerved by the involvement in the conspiracy of "young, modern-educated" people, who were the supposed beneficiaries of the Free Officers' revolution and "the mainstay of the regime."[347] The trials of the accused had apparently demonstrated that "most of the defendants" were motivated by "high-minded, ultra-Moslem" idealism.[348] They could not be dismissed merely as some kind of holdover from the Ikhwan organization that had been repressed a decade earlier. The fact that "qualified" and educated young men should still find something appealing in the "obscurantist" message of the Brotherhood was taken as evidence of Nasser's enduring problems.[349] The diplomats affirmed that those convicted enjoyed sympathy "from all strata of the population."[350]

The US Embassy admitted that it had no "good estimate" of the strength of the Ikhwan. The Egyptian Interior Ministry's 1948 figure of two million Brothers was said to be the "nearest thing" they had to a "reliable point of reference." Ten thousand was offered as a "conservative maximum."[351] Other American sources suggested that as many as thirty-eight thousand people, drawn from "all segments of Egyptian life," had been detained during the latest crack-down.[352] It is not clear whether or not such figures were deemed credible. Yet what cannot be doubted is that Western officials believed the Ikhwan to command substantial support. As British ambassador Sir George Middleton commented, one "obvious" conclusion from the conspiracy revelations was that the Brotherhood was "something more than the lunatic band it is now represented to be."[353] The US Embassy's counselor for political affairs, Richard Parker, arrived at a similar verdict. In his assessment, while the actual terrorists represented a "lunatic fringe," the Ikhwan as a whole had won the backing of "conservative rural and urban elements" that were resistant to "social modernization." (This was thought to be distinct from the modernization of production, or a desire to increase living standards—goals with which the Brotherhood was said to agree.) "Just how big the submerged portion of the traditionalist iceberg is," Parker acknowledged, "we do not know, nor does anyone else for that matter." His assumption was that peasant "docility" would ensure that it remained hidden; however, he also felt it was "just possible" that "Islamic conservatism" would prove to "be the nemesis of the present regime."[354] The ferocity of Nasser's drive against the Brotherhood was thought to be a reaction, at least in part, to this perceived threat.

In addition to this, the other aspect of the conspiracy that seemed to cause particular consternation to the Egyptian authorities was the alleged involvement of external actors. From the mid-1950s, Nasser had become increasingly suspicious that the Western powers were intriguing against him. Throughout 1965 and 1966, there was much conjecture about foreign funding and arms supplies to the Brotherhood.[355] Connections were drawn between the Ikhwan and the arrest of the CIA "spy" Mustafa Amin. The state press declared "colonialism" to be the "architect of all conspiracies."[356] According to American observers, nearly every news item about the Brotherhood plot was determined to mention the Central Treaty Organization (CENTO), or the West, no matter how irrelevant or strained the reference, and despite the fact that the defendants' confessions did not really support such claims.[357] The Egyptian government was especially exercised by the putative role played by émigrés like Sa'id Ramadan and Kamal al-Sharif. Both had been deprived of their nationality back in 1954 and been in exile ever since. Now they were charged, tried, and convicted in absentia. When Nasser had first spoken of the conspiracy during his trip to Moscow, he had specifically mentioned Ramadan by name.[358] The security services labeled him "a western agent" who had cooperated with foreign "intelligence organs" and CENTO in "implementing imperialist plans."[359]

Interestingly, the Egyptians were not the only ones to have reached such a conclusion. As Ian Johnson has elucidated, at that time the Swiss police believed Ramadan to be an "information agent" of the British and Americans.[360] Whatever the truth of this, there was no mistaking that Ramadan remained very active, traveling widely to promote the cause of the Brotherhood and critique the Nasser regime.[361] On a September 1966 trip to London, for instance, he again appeared to bid explicitly for Western support when he announced: "Only Moslem ideology can save the Middle East. It is either Islam or Communism. It's time the West became alive to that."[362]

Statements of this kind were grist to the Nasserite mill. The authorities in Cairo highlighted Ramadan's purported links to the 1965 conspiracy as proof of foreign meddling. From January 1966, the Egyptian media focused too on the supposedly nefarious conduct of the Saudis, who were thought to be receiving encouragement from the United States. The trials of the conspirators heard repeated allegations to this effect.[363] In a February speech, Nasser publicly accused King Faisal of having financed opposition to the regime, in league with CENTO. The Egyptian president talked at length about an "Islamic Pact" that was said to link the Saudis, the Shah of Iran, and President Habib Bourguiba of Tunisia under "joint British-American sponsorship," in order to control the Middle East and destroy Arab nationalism.[364] Throughout 1966, Nasser returned to the subject of this "Islamic Pact" and attacked the Saudis for colluding with imperialism.[365] In May, for example, in a thinly veiled reference to King Faisal, he condemned the "man with [the] long beard who embezzled the people's money but who wants them to call him prince of believers." In the end, Nasser declared, the people would "pluck his beard," just as the Egyptians had "plucked the beards of our bearded ones in 1952."[366]

This rhetoric was given added salience by the fact that, at the time, King Faisal *was* loudly talking up the possibility of Islamic "solidarity" to combat the forces of atheism.[367] In February 1966, he had proposed a conference to discuss the social and cultural problems facing the "Muslim world," and spoken of his desire to foster "Islamic Brotherhood." The venture was seen by many in the West as the beginning of an effort to create a rival organization to the Arab League, the latter being dominated by Nasser.[368] Crucially in this regard, the king did seek to utilize the Brotherhood for his own ends. Ikhwan members who had fled to the kingdom featured prominently in the Muslim World League that had been established in 1962 to promote Islam as an alternative to Arab nationalism and socialism.[369] They also helped to develop Saudi Arabia's educational infrastructure, being involved in the founding of the Islamic University of

Medina (established in 1961) and King 'Abd al-Aziz University (established in 1967).[370]

Across the region, Brotherhood chapters were firm backers of Faisal's call for Islamic solidarity. The Jordanian Ikhwan stated that the Muslim world was the natural supporter of the Arabs in the battle against imperialism and Zionism. In a transparent swipe at Nasser, it added that "all attacks [on] endeavors for Islamic solidarity are aimed at Islam rather than any individuals."[371] The Egyptian president was censured for trying to divide the Arabs and thereby bolstering Israel.[372] In adopting such a stance, the Jordanian Brothers once again followed the lead provided by King Hussein, as 1966 brought a strengthening of ties between Amman and Riyadh. The Ta'if Accord was signed between the two countries and Hussein emphasized Islamic cooperation of the kind championed by Faisal.[373] US diplomats observed the "growing ideological and political rapport" between the two kings. In their opinion, it helped fuel an escalating "propaganda battle" between Jordan and Egypt, in which Nasser was labeled a "dictator," "butcher," and the "killer of real Moslems."[374]

More broadly, this was the era in which commentators and scholars began to speak of an "Arab Cold War" pitting Nasser against King Faisal.[375] CIA intelligence assessments described this as a "struggle" between, on the one hand, "the dynamic, politically-appealing, revolution-exporting government" of Egypt, and on the other, the "conservative Arab governments" that opposed Cairo.[376] US officials wrote in plain terms about a regional divide between "moderate and progressive" states—or between the "revolutionaries led by Nasser and supported by the Soviets" and the "evolutionaries, with Faisal the symbolic head, supported by the West."[377]

In this context, the Johnson administration, which had grown ever more disillusioned with the Egyptians, made it evident that King Faisal was a "friend," to be treated as such. US interests were said to "depend heavily on [the] gradual modernization" of the Middle East "under moderate leaders like Faisal."[378] Consequently, American-Saudi relations showed a marked strengthening. In June 1966, King Faisal visited Washington and in a meeting with the president, described communism as being "like a germ which, if allowed to grow, ultimately destroyed the whole body."[379] This was surely music to Johnson's ears. For their part, US officials wished to reassure the king that he had American support, while avoiding too close an identification with his "Islamic solidarity" concept.[380] Given the increasingly entrenched divisions within the region, however, it seemed obvious to most that the Americans were lining up behind the Saudis and against Egypt.

In many ways, therefore, it was hardly surprising that Nasser tended to suspect that Washington and Riyadh were implicated in the Brotherhood plot. Yet, it is important to note that there is nothing within the available documents to confirm US involvement. American diplomats seemed as taken aback as anyone by the revival of the Ikhwan. Of course, neither of these points necessarily proves the case either way. Covert operations are rarely exposed by a paper trail—certainly not one made available to researchers working only half a century later; and as alluded to earlier, CIA operatives often worked without the knowledge of their colleagues in the State Department. Said Aburish was among those who concluded that Faisal, with the backing of the United States, was indeed hoping to use the Brotherhood against Nasser.[381] But his grounds for arriving at this verdict were somewhat opaque.

Moreover, in the mid-1960s, the American foreign policy community appeared convinced that, for all the problems Nasser caused, there were few better alternatives to him. For one thing, they continued to distrust the capacity of any opposition force—Brotherhood or otherwise—to overthrow the regime.[382] Beyond this, one official commented that there seemed to be "a sort of Gresham's Law of Arab politics" that "more extreme leadership" generally drove out "less extreme." Even if this did not prove to be the case in Egypt, it was imagined that any successor to Nasser would probably be weaker, a situation that would bring its own difficulties. The dominant assumption appears to have been that it was better to stick with the devil they knew.

Washington thus sought to mend its fences with Cairo. But the reality was that relations between the United States and Egypt seemed locked in a downward spiral.[383] In December 1965, Nasser broke off ties with the British because of the Rhodesian crisis.[384] In the months that followed, US officials grew ever more frustrated at "incorrigible" Egyptian subversion of the British and Saudi positions in Yemen and south Arabia, respectively.[385] Against this backdrop, the decision was taken not to renew the six-month PL-480 agreement with the UAR that expired in June 1966.[386] Remarkably, even now officials still clung to the hope that a "climate of continuing negotiation" might encourage Nasser to behave more "moderately." State Department analysts reckoned that "of the theoretically available policy alternatives, neither extreme of 'chosen instrument' nor 'enduring hostility' seem[ed] warranted." What they wanted was a policy based on "limited liability-limited expectations," with modest efforts to achieve equally modest returns over the next three to five years. What they actually got, though, was another surge in Nasser's invective against imperialism and the reactionary states.[387] In addition, in September 1966, the Zakariyya government that had been viewed with a degree of promise by Washington was dismissed.[388]

Subsequently, the State Department judged that the regime had taken a "definite leftward trend."[389] The year 1966 brought fresh signals that the Egyptians and the Soviets were moving back toward "closer cooperation" in pursuit of common objectives.[390] This came in the wake of a deal that had been struck the previous year between the regime and the Egyptian Communist Party, in which the latter agreed to give its full support to Nasser's Arab Socialist Union (ASU).[391] The Egyptian president also aligned himself with the radical Ba'thists who took power in Syria's ninth coup inside seventeen years in February 1966. A few months later, he signed a treaty of mutual defense with the new rulers of Damascus, in what was to prove a fateful decision.[392] Simultaneously, in an otherwise low-key State of the Union address, Nasser accused King Faisal of collaborating with imperialism and Zionism to divide the Arab world. Interestingly, he also referenced Eisenhower's recently released autobiography, which was said to prove that America had endorsed an "Islamic pact" centered on Riyadh. The Saudi army, Nasser asserted, was under direct "Anglo-American supervision and served 'imperialist'" interests across the Middle East.[393]

The impact of all this on the US-Egyptian relationship was predictable. Officials accepted that the periodically oscillating "pendulum" that defined their experiences with Nasser had swung decisively toward confrontation.[394] A State Department memorandum from 1 December 1966 noted starkly: "The Kennedy Experiment is over." US efforts to make an ally of Egypt based on a multiyear aid agreement, personal correspondence, and a certain amount of "human respect" had failed.[395] During the first five months of 1967, relations between Washington and Cairo continued to deteriorate, as Nasser publicly castigated the United States and its allies.[396] A favored theme of the Egyptian president was the alleged desire of the CIA to unseat him in cooperation with the Saudis.[397] By this time, American diplomats felt Nasser was "neurotically suspicious" of the United States, using them as a scapegoat for all his problems, and seeing the "CIA's hand behind everything" that went wrong.[398] Ambassador Battle recounted several conversations with leading regime figures, which indicated that Egyptian officials genuinely believed the United States had changed its policy in the Middle East and was "supporting conservative against more progressive regimes." Some even thought, Battle recorded, that the Americans were "attempting [to] undermine [the] regime or overthrow it."[399] Frequently, the Brotherhood was identified as the mechanism for bringing about this putative coup—a mark of the enduring legacy of the 1965 conspiracies.

The irony, meanwhile, was that the Ikhwan itself was persuaded that outside forces were conspiring to determine the fate of Egypt and the wider region. And at this point, it is worth pausing to consider how the Brothers had interpreted the events of 1965 and how they understood the world around them.

The Brothers between East and West

To understand the outlook of the Brotherhood during this era, it is necessary to examine the views of the man who Hazem Kandil calls the "second founder" of the group, the aforementioned Sayyid Qutb.[400] After the destruction of the Egyptian Ikhwan in 1954, it was Qutb who rebuilt the organization at an intellectual level. Though a relatively late convert to the cause—only becoming a Muslim Brother in 1953—he proved himself the movement's most prolific ideologue. Qutb reinforced, and in places expanded upon, many of the concepts first propagated by Hasan al-Banna. What emerged was a famously caustic image of the world, encapsulated in his seminal tract *Milestones on the Road*.

Crucially, this short book was part of the evidence used against Qutb at his own trial. It offered a dystopian vision of humanity as staring into an abyss, facing the "danger of complete annihilation." Islam, he averred, had vanished from the world. According to Qutb, modern life was steeped in an "all-encompassing Jahiliyyah"—an ignorance equal to and perhaps greater than that which had prevailed during the pre-Islamic era—based on a rebellion against God's sovereignty on earth.[401] He claimed it was this that humiliated the common man and stripped him of his dignity. What was required, Qutb argued, was for a vanguard to keep itself "somewhat aloof" from the *jahiliyyah* and work for the revival of Islam, liberating humankind through submission to God. This was the role, as he saw it, for a rejuvenated Muslim Brotherhood.[402]

Like al-Banna, Qutb believed that the group's mission would be long and gradual. It would pass through several stages, the first of which was focused on "preaching and persuasion." But he was unequivocal in stating that it would eventually have to use "physical power and jihad for abolishing the organizations and authorities of the Jahili system." Qutb maintained that oppressive political regimes had to be destroyed and he was certain that "those who have usurped the authority of God" would not give up their power "merely through preaching."[403] It was this that made violence and revolution essential and, in the words of US officials, ensured that Qutb's work was infused with an ethos of "militancy and martyrdom."[404]

These were the ideas, too, that inspired Qutb, by his own admission, to support the creation of the Brotherhood's revived "1965 organisation" as "a base for establishing the Islamic system." In his last testament, he stressed that his goal had been to restore a proper understanding of the meaning of Islam—in the broadest and deepest sense—rather than simply to push for the implementation of Islamic laws or the establishment of an Islamic governing system. He claimed that the Brothers were not interested in taking power. Yet he equally insisted that they had to take steps to protect themselves from aggression. This included paramilitary training and an effort to import weapons from abroad. Qutb also admitted that plans had been laid for acts of sabotage and the assassination of key regime figures (including Nasser), with a view to paralyzing the government. Qutb said that he had in fact tried to abort these schemes at the last minute, as he realized they were futile, but by then it was too late.[405]

Integral to Qutb's worldview was a searing critique of "the West," which to his mind had failed to provide mankind with "high ideals and values," and was now bankrupt as a civilization.[406] Like al-Banna, he saw "materialism" as the defining characteristic of the Western world. The truth of this was revealed, Qutb suggested, by the degeneracy and immorality of the West. In a striking example to prove his point, he cited the 1961 John Profumo scandal, when the eponymous British secretary of state for war had resigned after revelations of an affair with a woman who was simultaneously involved with the Soviet naval attaché. What struck Qutb about this episode was that it had not been "considered serious to British society because of its sexual aspect," but rather solely because of the perceived damage to national security. In this way, he concluded, it demonstrated the "backwardness" and moral corruption of Western life.[407]

This impression was one that Qutb had developed over many years. From the mid-1940s, he had become increasingly critical of Western imperialism—especially because of what he saw as its complicity with Zionism.[408] As is well known, his views of the West hardened during a period spent in the United States between November 1948 and August 1950.[409] While there, interestingly, Lawrence Wright claims that Qutb was offered ten thousand dollars for the rights to translate one of his books into English, in what was a transparent attempt by the CIA to recruit him. The intermediary was allegedly none other than James Heyworth-Dunne (see Chapter 2). By this account, Qutb was appalled and refused indignantly.[410]

After his return to Egypt, Qutb wrote a missive entitled "The America That I Have Seen: In the Scale of Human Values," which condemned US society as fast-living and shallow, defined by inanity and an attachment to "material riches." American art, for instance, was held to be crude; jazz music, according to Qutb, had been invented by "negroes . . . to satisfy their primitive inclinations" and "to excite bestial tendencies."[411] The United States, he said, had abandoned religion and "erected in its place a three-headed God (mass production, money and pleasure)." Consequently, their world was a "mad rush" and "nothing but an ever turning windmill, which grinds all in its way: men, things, places and time."[412] As mentioned, Qutb was especially repelled by Western moral laxity and sexual libertinism. And as one Brotherhood profile of Qutb later put it, his time in the United States exposed him to the "big American fib."[413]

In much of this, as John Calvert and Malise Ruthven have underlined, Qutb's observations confirmed preexisting biases. He approached the United States with a "closed mind, determined to see only its most negative aspects."[414] It is worth noting that the book *Social Justice in Islam,* which Qutb had written prior to his departure for America (but which was only published in 1949—and reissued repeatedly thereafter), already contained a withering assessment of Western society. He characterized this as an intrinsically materialist civilization; it had separated "religion and worldly affairs," unlike Islam, which was an "indivisible whole."[415] The result, Qutb felt, was the Western abnegation of all standards of decency and morality. In its treatment of women, for example, he posited that the West preferred exploitation to genuine equality, sacrificing female chastity and allowing "hungry passions and treacherous eyes" to "flicker" about a woman's body.[416] Qutb's own experience of the "rubbish heap of the West" then confirmed him in his belief that the "free mixing of the sexes" and what he called the "vulgarity" of female emancipation were mere manifestations of an underlying spiritual void.[417]

Against this decadent West, Qutb counterpoised a comprehensive, self-sufficient Islam. The two civilizations were said to be fundamentally incompatible.[418] What was required, he reasoned, was the removal from Muslim societies of alien "cultural influences" and a return to the original and pure sources of the faith.[419] Qutb imagined that the United States acted to prevent such an Islamic revival, precisely because it recognized that it would challenge imperialism and tyranny; instead, Washington wished only to see a supine form of "American Islam," denuded its social and political content. True Islam, Qutb stated, was the "greatest liberating revolution" in the world, and he pledged to confront imperialism—in all its forms—with a relentless "holy hatred."[420] Ibrahim

Abu-Rabi' has highlighted how, in his condemnation of "Americanized Islam" and the "dark English"—those Egyptians who aped the ways of the "white English"—Qutb's thinking paralleled Frantz Fanon's call for total cultural liberation.[421] More broadly, as Shahrough Akhavi has described, it can be seen that Qutb's philosophy, like that of al-Banna before him, betrayed the deep influence of Western concepts and intellectuals, even as he overtly rejected them.[422] Further evidence of this can be seen from his references to various disillusioned Western writers, such as George Bernard Shaw, Julian Huxley, Alexis Carrel, and T. W. Arnold, whom he read in translation. John Calvert argues that he was particularly influenced by Oswald Spengler's prophecy of an inevitable decline of the decadent, materialist West and the rise of a more wholesome, spiritual East.[423]

In Qutb's hands, however, such ideas drew close to the concept of *takfir*: the practice of labeling someone a non-Muslim. Though he himself denied any such intention and he never dealt directly with the question of individual apostasy, his writings certainly suggested a direction of travel.[424] Qutb declared that what he saw around him in the world was "not Islam," and if people insisted on living the "life of Jahiliyyah," then they were "not Muslims."[425] As William Shepard has observed, it was Qutb's original contribution to the notion of *jahiliyyah*—which had previously gained prominence in the hands of South Asian writers Abu a'la Mawdudi and Abu Hasan al-Nadvi—that he used the term about ostensibly Islamic societies. Whereas Mawdudi and al-Nadvi had identified *jahiliyyah* solely with the Western and communist worlds, Qutb (and his brother Muhammad) held that it could be applied to the whole world.[426] The implication of this was hard to miss: that those claiming to be Muslim were, in fact, nothing of the sort—they had been infected with the "jahili" disease that had its origins in the West.[427] In making this case, Qutb clearly included the communist countries within the bracket of "the West." At one point, he wrote that communism was "the natural completion of the materialistic Western spirit," which lacked the "spiritual values in human life." He presumed that the Western nations would, in time, themselves succumb to communism (though he later modified this prediction). The only real escape from *jahiliyyah*, Qutb averred, lay in the path of Islam.[428]

This binary view predisposed him to believe that the Western-backed *jahiliyyah* was locked in existential struggle with the Muslim world. "The enemies of this religion [Islam]," Qutb proclaimed, had "over many centuries put forth enormous, deceitful and wicked efforts, and continue to do so." Despite the obvious materialism of the West, he reckoned that "the Crusader hostility toward

Islam" was "latent in the European soul"; in later years, too, he referred to the American "crusaderist" imperialists. Indeed, it was Qutb who popularized the notion of "crusaderist imperialism," using it to denigrate a West that was judged inveterately hostile to Islam, and especially to the Ikhwan.[429]

The reality of all this, Qutb contended, had become apparent to him when he was in the United States. In his final testimony, he wrote that American and British newspapers had gloated over the death of Hasan al-Banna.[430] (As described, a different version said that while receiving treatment in a southern California hospital, Qutb witnessed nurses celebrating and drinking champagne at news of al-Banna's murder.)[431] After going back to Egypt, Qutb became increasingly paranoid about the activities of Christians and Jews, who were deemed to be agents of Westernization, seeking to undermine the faith and lead Muslims astray. He fulminated against Zionists and modern-day "crusaders"; and he seemed inclined to see Western enemies everywhere.[432] Salah Shadi, for instance, later recalled a conversation with Qutb in autumn 1953, amid the internal upheavals the Brotherhood was then experiencing, in which Qutb pointed to the machinations of the Jews as contributing to their problems.[433] In the same period, he produced a vitriolic tract under the revealing title *Our Struggle with the Jews,* which outlined in lurid terms the Jewish "conspiracy" to destroy Islam.[434] Revised editions of Qutb's book *Social Justice in Islam* included references to "the role of worldwide Zionism" that was thought to have joined with the "Crusader imperialist" and "materialist communist" worlds in a grand "plot against Islam."[435]

After the Free Officers had come to power, Qutb initially worked with them. Indeed, he may have been offered a position within the government. By February 1953, however, disagreements had emerged over both the role of the Liberation Rally and the program to which Nasser was committed. According to Qutb, tensions were deliberately fostered by (of all things) the US-backed "farmers association." Differences between the two sides culminated in the events at Manshiyya (see Chapter 5), which he, like many other Brothers, saw as a "performance" directed by "foreign fingers." The Ikhwan, Qutb said, had been targeted because it was the only organization able to "stand in the way of the Imperialist Crusader and Zionist plans." After its dissolution, he believed Egypt and the region had fallen victim to the spread of atheistic ideas and moral decline, the purpose of which was to smooth the path for those same imperialist crusaders and Zionists.[436] The conspiracies, though, did not stop there. Qutb also imagined that the infamous prison massacre of 1957, in which twenty-one Muslim Brothers were killed by their Egyptian guards, was the result of a plot that was underpinned by foreign involvement (and, typically, his account asserted that one of the prison wardens most hostile to the Ikhwan was friendly with Jewish inmates).[437]

Furthermore, Qutb later stated that, as he and his supporters reconstituted the Ikhwan in 1964–1965, they were aware that the Zionists and imperialist crusaders were among those most opposed to them. He recorded that some senior Brotherhood figures such as Munir al-Dilla were convinced both that Zaynab al-Ghazali was a CIA informant, and that the United States was deliberately provoking some of the more reckless Brothers to act precipitously. In addition, Qutb suggested that the collision with the regime in 1965 came partly at the instigation of communists and Christians (again, these blurred into one single menace in his eyes). "Our enemies," Qutb concluded, "and the enemies of this religion and the enemies of the movements of Islamic renaissance from outside, were greater than those from inside."[438]

Brotherhood accounts have taken up these ideas to infer that Nasser suppressed the Ikhwan in 1965–1966 (and executed Qutb) in order to appease the communists.[439] According to Yusuf al-Qaradawi, this "fourth ordeal" in the history of the Brotherhood was a product of the regime's links with the Soviets. Others charged that Nasser "bent the knee" to Moscow by targeting the Ikhwan.[440] In the scathing verdict of Salah Shadi, Nasser opted for the "Russian swamp," having previously stained himself with "the sludge of America."[441] In his own memoirs, meanwhile, Hasan Dawh said that he had received word some five months prior to the crackdown that the government was planning to deliver a "violent blow" to the Ikhwan. As soon as he heard this, he tried to escape Egypt, but was refused permission to travel. Dawh contended that the origins of the subsequent repression lay in the regime's foreign policy shift to the East. The domestic effect of this, he said, was to empower the country's communists, who were nothing more than "a parrot pronouncing the words of the Soviet Union." They were, according to Dawh, fiercely opposed to Islam and determined to destroy those whom they labeled "supporters of reaction." Dawh wrote that when Nasser returned from Moscow in autumn 1965, the communists met him at the airport with cries of "Kill Kill ya Gamal . . . no reaction and no Ikhwan"—and, in response, Nasser "prepared to enter the battle of liquidation against the Muslim Brotherhood."[442] In this way, Dawh appeared to attribute primary responsibility for the 1965 ordeal to the intrigues of the communists. He did balance this, though, with the suggestion that the underlying reason for the hostility of leftists toward Islam was because they had fallen under the influence of "Zionist and Western Imperialist agents."[443]

Such caveats notwithstanding, as the foregoing seems to indicate, by the mid-1960s, the danger of communism loomed especially large in the minds of Dawh and his fellow Brothers. Of course, the old enemies remained—particularly the Zionists. But in any hierarchy of importance, the Soviet Union appeared to have risen to the top, while the West—in a traditional sense—had fallen back (although, as has been explained, in the Brothers' eyes, these actually comprised a single materialist menace). Hence, exiled Brothers like Saʿid Ramadan argued that the only beneficiaries of the crackdown on the Ikhwan were "international communism and Zionism."[444] To a limited extent, therefore, the United States and the Brotherhood could be said to be on the same side, at least insofar as they shared a deep hostility to communism.

Added to this, was their mutual antipathy for Nasser. This period witnessed a manifest decline in relations between Cairo and Washington, which predated and was then exacerbated by the events of June 1967. To the Brothers, Egypt's defeat in the Six-Day War was a punishment from God, directed against their Nasserite nemesis.[445] Likewise, many Americans felt that the troublesome Egyptian president had finally got his comeuppance. As a result of the conflict, Ambassador Richard Nolte (who had only replaced Lucius Battle in April) was expelled from Cairo, as the authorities there insisted on repeating what American officials called the "big lie": the allegation that US and British warplanes had participated in attacks on Egyptian forces. In the years that followed, Washington would push for a retraction of this accusation, without success.[446]

Against the background of this fresh deterioration in the American-Egyptian relationship, there were obvious grounds for thinking that the enemy of Washington might also be the enemy of the Ikhwan—and it is striking that there was renewed American interest in the group at this time.

Limited Reassessments

An analysis of the Six-Day War lies well beyond the scope of this study. Suffice it to say, this proved one of the most pivotal moments in the history of the modern Middle East. Almost overnight, the geopolitical environment was transformed. Israel emerged as a regional "superpower" and its Arab rivals reeled from their second great defeat inside two decades. As Malcolm Kerr observed, the old political divisions were rendered redundant, to be replaced by new ideas and debates.[447] For Egypt, the *naksa* (setback) was a mortal blow to the heart of the Nasserite project. The president tendered his resignation just days after the

fighting ceased. Huge crowds then took to the streets demanding that he reverse course—which he duly did. The degree to which this was all choreographed
by the regime in an effort to head off wider discontent can only be guessed at
(it is worth noting that it does very much fit with Nasser's modus operandi, as
described earlier: a tactical retreat to draw out opponents before the rallying of
those loyal to the cause). The government was soon felt to have "weathered the
immediate storm" and to be back in "reasonably firm control."[448] Yet there was
no doubting that Nasser's position had been shaken as never before.[449] In the
ensuing months, confusion reigned. Cairo was, in the words of one US official,
a city "full of rumor," with persistent whispers that the president might be deposed.[450] In September, Nasser faced arguably his greatest internal challenge
with the apparent coup attempt made by his right-hand man and longtime best
friend, Hakim 'Amer (which ended with 'Amer's "suicide" while under house
arrest).[451]

Moreover, in early 1968, the military trials of those officers held responsible
for the previous year's defeat stirred popular discontent in Egypt. In February,
after relatively lenient sentences had been imposed on the country's "guilty men,"
there were disturbances among workers at a factory in Helwan on the outskirts
of Cairo. This led, in turn, to major student demonstrations and clashes with
police.[452] In response, Nasser accused "reactionary and imperialist elements" of
inciting trouble and also promised change.[453] He reshuffled his cabinet and
dismissed various familiar figures such as Zakariyya Muhi al-Din.[454] The government then produced a "national action plan" for reform that was put to a
referendum (and passed with no less than 99.989 percent support!).[455] Nonetheless, US officials felt that the public reaction to all this was "rather sour."[456]
Egypt as a whole was said to be "in the doldrums."[457] As 1968 wore on, there
were further protests—this time focused on Mansura and Alexandria.[458] And
the diplomats again detected signs of a "deepening malaise."[459]

It was in this context that there was fresh speculation in Western circles about
the potential for opposition to the regime, and this time, the Brotherhood
featured prominently. Ever since the 1965 conspiracy revelations, American
officials had portrayed Nasser as preoccupied with the latent menace of the
Ikhwan. In their judgment, this "threat" was overstated, but they did not discount
the possibility of the group reemerging as a "rallying point" for conservative
opposition.[460] In the wake of the June 1967 conflict, a CIA national intelligence estimate surmised that the Brotherhood had demonstrated its capacity
to survive repression. Given the problems now faced by Nasser's government,
it was thought that the group's "appeal to certain discontented and disillu-

sioned elements could be considerable."[461] The unrest of 1968 appeared to provide further evidence in support of this supposition. As Haggai Erlich recorded, there were reports that Brotherhood students were heavily involved in the Mansura protests, in which four people were killed.[462]

It was perhaps as a consequence of all this that the final years of Nasser's rule witnessed a new level of Western interest in the Ikhwan. The British archives show that the US State Department asked its UK counterpart for information about the Brotherhood in the spring of 1968. Lucius Battle, now assistant secretary of state for the Near East and North Africa, was said to be especially interested in the subject, about which London was forced to admit it knew little by this time. Even so, the Foreign Office's Research Department did produce a short brief on "recent Muslim Brotherhood activity in the United Arab Republic [Egypt]." On the one hand, this reiterated that government repression had done "much to disorganise the movement," depriving it of both cohesion and leadership. Some of the "more influential" Muslim Brothers were known to be in exile abroad, notably in Jordan, Kuwait, Saudi Arabia, Iraq, and Sudan, while it was estimated that around one thousand members remained in prison in Egypt. In spite of this, though, the British stated that the Ikhwan was still "a force" to be reckoned with, enjoying widespread influence across society. Officials concluded there had been a "recrudescence" of Brotherhood propaganda since the 1967 war. According to the British, the group had resumed its criticism of Nasser and sought to exploit the "underlying resentment" of the people. In the spring of 1968, there were even fresh rumors of a new Brotherhood plot against the regime. Whether true or not, the Ikhwan was said to be well placed to "take advantage of any expression of discontent"—as had occurred with the February protests.[463]

In May 1968, the State Department circulated a lengthy memorandum of its own on the Brotherhood, at the request of Assistant Secretary Battle, which reviewed both its history and current strength. This described the Ikhwan as "a tenacious enemy of Nasser" and "virtually the only popular-base movement outside the structure of the regime." Brotherhood elements were noted to have participated in the recent riots in Cairo—and on this basis, the State Department's analysts arrived at the "irresistible conclusion" that the movement was "alive and functioning." At the same time, however, the contemporary Ikhwan was considered to be "a feeble remnant of the powerful organization" of the 1940s, comprised of loosely connected cells and individuals. With regard to its prospects, the report suggested that it was "all but inconceivable" that the Brotherhood could seize, or hold, power in the "foreseeable future." US

officials found it hard to imagine a situation in which a critical portion of the
Egyptian people would lend their support to the Ikhwan. They reckoned that
such a development could *only* occur if the "trauma of defeat were to produce a
mood of self-abasement and religious revival." In May 1968, the diplomats saw
no sign of this; and while there was undoubtedly "considerable disillusionment"
with the regime across Egyptian society, they did not anticipate that the disaffected would turn to the Brotherhood in large numbers. For this reason, it was
assumed that the group's greatest potential role lay in the realm of assassination,
or as partners in a new military coup. "An alliance of [the] Brethren with ex-
officers," it was argued, "would join the outermost extremes of the Egyptian
philosophical spectrum." But again, this was deemed unlikely.

What is more, in the unlikely event that the Brotherhood did reach power,
US officials felt that this would bring Washington "only marginal benefits." In
their view, the only advantages of a Brotherhood-led government lay in the discomfort it would cause to their "inveterate enemies," the communists; for
while the Brotherhood's opinion of the United States was "not high," it was
thought to be "relatively less negative than their view of the USSR." With that
said, officials recognized that the Brotherhood saw the United States as "materialistic and sinful" domestically and "inconstant" abroad, especially because
of alleged US support for Nasser. Added to this was the group's "extremely hostile" attitude toward Israel (which also fed its antagonism toward the United
States).[464] Overall, the assessment of the diplomats was that there was little to
be gained from the empowerment of the Brotherhood.

Perhaps more important, meanwhile, was the fact that US officials evidently
believed prospects for a Brotherhood resurgence to be slim. The mandarins
stated that "the social and psychological climate in the UAR in the last twenty
years [had] turned away from the methods of the Ikhwan." The Brotherhood,
in their minds, was indelibly associated with "old-fogeyism, backwardness or
worse, dangerous fanaticism." The group was said to be under the control of
"intellectually sterile" leaders, and its attachment to "anachronistic religious
rules" was thought to cut against the grain of twentieth-century life.[465] Once
again, one can see in this analysis the juxtaposition between modernity on the
one hand, and "Islam" on the other. As a manifestation of the latter, the Ikhwan
was seen as an organization out of its time, destined to be swept away by the
process of modernization and social change.

More generally, the diplomats were still unpersuaded that there was any credible alternative to Nasser. The way that the regime overcame the upheavals of
1968 seemed to prove the point. By the summer of the following year, formal

US assessments were referring to "the change that wasn't" on the UAR "domestic front." Officials concluded that despite some cosmetic adjustments, there had been little meaningful alteration to the "power structure" in Cairo, which remained centered on Nasser.[466]

This apparent continuity within Egypt was mirrored in the US-UAR relationship. At the time President Johnson left office, mutual hostility was barely concealed. In January 1969, Nasser sent a letter to incoming US president Richard Nixon, calling for a resumption of relations, but the initiative went nowhere.[467] US officials perceived that Nasser was as paranoid as ever about the United States, suspecting that Washington wished to "do him in and rub Egyptian noses in it."[468] In September, Donald Bergus, who served as the principal officer for the US interests section of the Spanish Embassy, composed an extended analysis of the state of Egypt, pointing to widespread discontent, especially among the young. Striking a distinctly orientalist note, Bergus averred that, by any "western criteria," Nasser should have fallen—whether because of the 1967 defeat or because of endemic socioeconomic problems. Obviously, this had not happened—in large part, Bergus felt, because a majority of Egyptians continued to see Nasser as personifying "their most important aspiration—dignity." Indeed, Bergus argued that by the "more exotic criteria of this area . . . [the] Nasser regime is doing quite well." With regard to the future, he rated the odds to be "probably better than even" that Nasser would be around for some time.[469]

The following month, the State Department produced its own reflection, largely endorsing Bergus's appraisal, under the revealing title "And Quiet Flows the Nile—The Internal Scene." This examined how, in the face of unrest in 1968, the regime had responded with both a "velveteen glove"—being willing to tackle some grievances—and a "cast iron fist," the latter based on "an extensive and effective intelligence and security apparatus" that reached into "almost every corner of Egyptian society." For this reason, despite occasional rumors of anti-regime plotting or arrests, no group was thought capable of posing a serious danger to Nasser. The Ikhwan, it was acknowledged, *could* strike a "responsive chord" among the conservative masses and may even have some support in the armed forces. Yet ultimately, US officials judged it "highly unlikely" that the Brotherhood "could present a credible threat to the status quo in its own name."[470]

As the end of the decade approached, therefore, State Department officials had little doubt that Nasser was firmly in control of Egypt. They conceded there was disaffection among intellectuals, students, and other civilians, but believed these lacked any organization, or leader to rival Nasser.[471] In September

1970, US diplomats commented that the Egyptian president's internal position was "probably as strong as at any time since the June 1967 war."[472] That same month, however, things were suddenly and irrevocably transformed by perhaps the only thing that could have brought real change to Egypt: Nasser's death.

Conclusion

In the wake of the 1954–1955 suppression of the Muslim Brotherhood, there were many who had assumed that the group had been consigned to oblivion. Some Western officials were aware that the Ikhwan had not been entirely destroyed, but they mostly deemed its best days to be behind it. The Brothers found themselves overawed and overshadowed by Nasser, who dominated the politics of the era, both in Cairo and internationally. As Western images of Nasser oscillated— from hero to villain, from villain to essential ally, from ally to bitter antago- nist—the question of the Ikhwan often appeared to be of only secondary importance.[473]

As Peter Hahn has noted, US officials ultimately "found it impossible to rec- oncile Nasser's nationalism to their security interests."[474] Unfortunately for the Brothers, however, their dissolution at the hands of the Egyptian security ap- paratus meant that they missed maybe their best opportunity to pitch for an alliance with the Western powers. As American—and especially British— concern with Nasser grew in the mid-1950s, there was clearly some consider- ation of whether it might be possible to build a conservative, religious coalition to stand as a bulwark against radicalism, whether of an Arab nationalist or com- munist stripe. In another world, it is perhaps plausible that the Ikhwan could have been a partner to the West—though it equally seems evident that most US and UK diplomats continued to see the group as an extremist and pernicious force. In any case, such a debate was rendered moot by the fact that there were few signs of life from the Brotherhood in Egypt at that crucial stage. In addition, while the Brothers in Jordan and Syria were known to be active—and there did seem to be some kind of low-level engagement with US officials— this never proved decisive. There was no strategic decision to pursue an alliance with the Brotherhood.

In seeking to understand why there was not more Western interest in the Ikhwan, the most important factor was surely intellectual. The prevailing view within diplomatic and scholarly circles was that the forces of religion in the Middle East were in retreat, as compared to their modernizing, secularizing rivals. Egypt seemed the embodiment of this reality. The historian Christina Harris captured this outlook when she described the Brotherhood as "an ideological throwback to the eighteenth century," which "rejected progress along Western rationalist lines." "Intensely xenophobic," it had been categorically destroyed, she stated, by Nasser's government.[475] In similar fashion, John Marlowe's history of Anglo-Egyptian relations between 1800 and 1956 concluded that after 1954, the Brotherhood had "ceased to count as a significant factor in the Egyptian scheme of things."[476] As far as most academics and commentators were concerned, the future belonged to others—not least the Egyptian president himself.

Toward the end of the 1950s, as British power in the Middle East waned, US officials had moved to a more positive assessment of Nasser. They were prepared now to accept that he was not a puppet of Moscow, and they also recognized his enduring appeal internationally. On this reading, it was Nasser—not religion—that could serve as the most effective bulwark against communism. For a period of around five years after 1958, therefore, Washington sought a cordial relationship with the "enfant terrible" of Arab nationalism. In the end, though, this effort foundered on the fundamental incompatibility of American-Egyptian interests, given the way in which both sides conceived of those interests in that period. As relations then deteriorated under the Johnson administration, many US officials hoped that a rapprochement could be salvaged. Almost invariably they worked on the assumption that there was no meaningful alternative to Nasser. There is little evidence that they were actively trying to unseat him—even though it is clear that the authorities in Cairo sincerely believed this to be the case.

Against this background, the revelations of a new Muslim Brotherhood conspiracy against the Egyptian government caught most Western observers by surprise. Both then and now, the "1965 organisation" has been mired in secrecy and uncertainty. Many saw the conspiracy as at best exaggerated, at worst entirely fabricated—certainly this was the contention of the Muslim Brotherhood itself. And yet, both British and American officials concluded that there had been a tangible and militant revival of the Brotherhood under the aegis of Sayyid Qutb and that this posed a real threat. They also recognized that three aspects of the alleged plot generated serious concern within the Egyptian government: first, the scale of their apparent intelligence failure; second, the fact that the Ikhwan seemed to have successfully recruited from a new generation that had grown up under and benefited from the revolution; and third, the suspicion of foreign involvement. The latter issue reinforced Nasser's fears about

US intentions and intertwined with the broader division of the region into "conservatives" and "progressives." The Egyptian president became convinced that American allies in the former camp, particularly King Faisal, were sponsoring domestic opposition to his regime. Anxieties about an "Islamic Pact" were a reflection of Nasser's conviction that external forces were conspiring against him, and it was this that made the Brotherhood a natural object of suspicion.

Ironically, the Brothers too assumed that external forces were plotting against them. The ideas of Sayyid Qutb, which powered the reconstitution of the Ikhwan, were founded on his stark worldview, in which the West appeared as a spiritual wasteland with an ineradicable hostility toward Islam. Western civilization was held to be the fountainhead for the *jahiliyyah* that had swept across the world and erased the true Muslim society. Qutb maintained that Zionists and imperialist crusaders had worked assiduously to deform and destroy Islam. Communism, he said, was merely an extension of the malignant Western conspiracy. Increasingly, though, the Brotherhood would come to focus on the communists as the most inveterate of their enemies—and the specific cause of their downfall in 1965.

In the aftermath of that episode, many Western officials were forced to acknowledge that, in the words of the *Guardian*'s David Hirst, the Brotherhood was "still a force to be reckoned with." Equally, however, they continued to imagine that nothing could "possibly halt the secular trend in the long run."[477] As Jacobs has argued, speculation about either the long-term viability of a group like the Ikhwan, or the possible utility of Islam as a barrier against communism and pan-Arabism, was eclipsed by the more engrained belief that traditional religion was doomed to extinction. As a faith, Islam was deemed to be incompatible with modernity and thus a diminishing factor in the Middle East as the region developed.[478]

By the late 1960s, there were occasional hints that conclusions of this kind might be subject to challenge. Writing in the *Times,* for instance, Professor W. Montgomery Watt identified an increased religiosity in the Middle East, and predicted that "if the right leader could appear and speak the right word . . . Islam might become one of the great political forces in the world."[479] In addition, developments such as the formation of the Organisation of the Islamic Conference (OIC) in Ribat in 1969 could be seen as proof that religion retained a political relevance. At this stage, though, such arguments remained at the margins.

Moreover, the Muslim Brotherhood itself was judged to be very much a relic of the past. An article in the *Times* from November 1970 suggested that the group had been decisively "crushed" in Egypt; and though the author acknowledged that the Brothers still existed in "underground cells," he did not believe that its message could possibly stand in the way of the inevitable advance of the state and the modern world. The same article went on to assert that there had "never been any reason to suppose that, if it had a taste of power, the Brotherhood would be able to preserve any of its absolute principles intact."[480] Even more stark was the assessment offered a couple of years later by the renowned scholar L. Carl Brown, who observed, in a review of Richard P. Mitchell's book on the Muslim Brothers, that the "organizational strength" of the group seemed to have "crested long ago." There was, Brown said, "little prospect for a new round of religious fundamentalism as a political movement."[481] Of course, by the time these words were published, they themselves were beginning to appear out of date.

Seven Reassessments amid the
"Fundamentalist" Revival

1970–1989

I N LATE 1979, emissaries of US president Jimmy Carter
made contact with the third general guide of the Muslim
Brotherhood, 'Umar al-Tilmisani. The move had little to
do with the situation in Egypt, but rather was a response to events in distant
Tehran. There, following the Iranian revolution and amid Ayatollah Khomeini's
drive toward an Islamic state, more than sixty Americans had been taken hostage.
The Carter administration hoped that the Muslim Brotherhood might be willing
to mediate for their release. Al-Tilmisani, it would seem, was initially prepared to
help. A broadcast by the Tehran International Service in April 1980 noted that
the Muslim Brotherhood had informed the Iranians of an approach from the
political attaché at the US Embassy in Cairo, who wished them to intercede on
behalf of the prisoners.[1] The memoirs of Youssef Nada, who describes himself
as having been the "de facto foreign minister" of the Brotherhood in this era,
provide further confirmation that al-Tilmisani was open to US entreaties.[2]
Nada claims that the Brotherhood leader actually came to see him at his home in
Campione (the Italian enclave in Switzerland) to oversee the dialogue. However,
al-Tilmisani wanted assurances from the United States that Carter himself had
directly authorized contacts with Tehran. According to Nada, these never
materialized and, consequently, the initiative fell apart.[3]

A different version is offered by the scholar Walid Abdelnasser, who contends
that a tentative attempt was actually made to negotiate the release of the

hostages—but that the Ikhwan backed away from the talks as it became clear, not only that the Iranian government was disinclined to make a deal, but also that Tehran viewed anyone intervening on the Americans' behalf as a servant of imperialism.[4] On this point too, it is striking that al-Tilmisani stated in his own memoirs that Tehran accused the Brotherhood, and him in particular, of being an American agent.[5] Whatever the specific reason, the result was that the undertaking failed and the hostages were not released.

Despite this, the episode was significant in that it revealed much about US estimations of the Brotherhood by the late 1970s. During the previous decade, American diplomats had followed the reemergence of the Ikhwan and its renewed influence, both in Egypt and across the region. The return of the Muslim Brothers was set against a backdrop of a broader Islamic revival that had proven the lie of many expectations about the advance of secular modernity in the Middle East. After 1967, the nationalist (usually pan-Arabist) model of postcolonial governance experienced a structural "crisis" that lent new credibility to alternative ideologies such as those of the Islamists.[6] In this context, the Brotherhood no longer appeared as an anachronism, in fact quite the opposite. Many people were forced to reexamine their assumptions about the sustainability and character of a group like the Ikhwan. A new language arose for thinking about these matters, and this blended with older debates and obsessions, as Western officials sought to understand both the survival of the Brotherhood and its prospects for the future.

The Muslim Brothers and Sadat as Allies

When Gamal Abdel Nasser died in September 1970, many were unsure as to what would come next. In November, the Central Intelligence Agency (CIA) admitted that it knew little about what was happening "behind the scenes" in the "struggle for power and position" in Cairo. The analysts did not, however, rule out the possibility of serious upheaval. Among the groups thought likely to cause unrest was the Ikhwan—at that stage submerged, but as the events of the previous two years had shown, still active.[7] The *New York Times* observed anxiously that the "extremist" Muslim Brotherhood was "stirring again," describing it as "a force for conservatism—and often violence" that had shown a "penchant for assassination" throughout its history.[8] In the months and years that followed, it became increasingly obvious that the Ikhwan would play an important role in determining Egypt's path.

In the early summer of 1971, as Nasser's little-fancied successor, Anwar Sadat, consolidated his position and enacted his "corrective revolution," British diplomats suggested that the Muslim Brotherhood was "again becoming a force to be reckoned with."[9] The new president's earlier association with the Ikhwan was well known—after all, he had acknowledged it publicly himself.[10] Sadat, the British reported, made no secret of his admiration for this "most nebulous" group, which had permeated Egyptian society "to an extent which no other organisation with voluntary membership has ever achieved." In Cairo, Ambassador Richard Beaumont picked up rumors that the new president might be "trying to encourage the Muslim Brethren to recruit again, as a possible antidote to Communist infiltration."[11] It was also recognized that an amnesty issued to all those convicted of political offences prior to May 1971 had worked predominantly to the benefit of both the communists and the Muslim Brothers.[12] In analyzing these developments, officials assumed that Sadat would not allow the Ikhwan to become a threat to the regime and *would* act to prevent any upsurge in "xenophobia." In London, the future ambassador to Iran, Anthony Parsons, was among those who surmised that Sadat was "unlikely to foster the growth of any political movement of this sort . . . unless he could be sure of keeping them well under control." Though aware of the president's past connection with the Brothers, Parsons thought Sadat had become disillusioned with the movement after it had abandoned its "earlier high principles" and adopted "terrorist tactics for their own sake." "On the whole," he concluded, "we are doubtful whether the Moslem Brotherhood will become a factor of any importance in Egyptian politics in the near future."[13]

Not everyone, however, was convinced. Other Whitehall mandarins soon felt they had been too quick to discount the possibility of an Ikhwan "renaissance."[14] They worried that Sadat might underestimate the difficulty of restraining this "potentially handy weapon," and they watched uneasily as known Muslim Brothers were released from prison. In their assessment, this included "some of the 'hard core' fanatics" and was "part of a policy designed to balance Leftist influence."[15] By this time, it had become evident that Sadat wished to harness the forces of religion to strengthen his position. A new constitution stipulated that Islam was the official religion of the state and proclaimed shari'a a source of legislation. Religious instruction was made mandatory in schools.[16] And attempts were made to develop an Islamic banking sector. Changes of this kind were paralleled by the growing prominence of religious symbols and discourse in public life (not that Islam had ever disappeared under Nasser— his regime had likewise sought to exploit official Islam for its own purposes).

Sadat styled himself the "believer president," and a new government-led emphasis on piety and moral values was matched by greater popular devotion. All of this helped to create an environment more favorable to the growth of Islamist movements like the Ikhwan.[17]

A key site for the social transformation that Egypt experienced in this period was higher education. Sadat oversaw a massive growth of the sector, with the number of students quadrupling in the first five years he was in office. Much of this came through the establishment of new provincial institutes and the opening of the system to the urban lower classes and rural populace, so that almost all secondary school graduates attended a university. The effect of this rapid expansion was to impoverish the quality of the education, putting an unmanageable burden on infrastructure and staff. Amid the resulting pressures and shortages, Islamist activists stepped in to help students and fill the gaps left by the state.[18] As scholars have demonstrated, these Islamists received crucial encouragement—at least initially—from the authorities. Sadat and his close advisers, such as Muhammad Uthman Isma'il, deemed them preferable to the Nasserists and leftists who had previously dominated Egypt's campuses.[19] In an important study, Abdullah al-Arian has explored the impact of this approach in detail. He recorded, for instance, how Sadat appointed Ahmad Kamal Abu Magd, a lawyer known for his Brotherhood sympathies, as general secretary of the Socialist Union Youth Organization in August 1971. Alongside this, attempts were made to co-opt new Islamic groups like Shabab al-Islam and al-Gama'a al-Islamiyya, which became active in this period.[20]

Tacit support for the growth of Islamism was coupled with a liberalization of campus life. From late 1971, genuine elections were held for student unions, which were subsequently allowed to operate with greater freedom. Sadat hoped the reinvigoration of these bodies under Islamist control might generate a support base that would back him in his struggles against leftist and Nasserist "centres of power." As it happened, however, he was frequently disappointed. January 1972, for example, brought a serious outburst of student protest, expressing resentment against Sadat and the "no war, no peace" situation in the country (a legacy of the 1967 defeat to Israel and Nasser's later "war of attrition"). CIA analysts noted that among those involved in the demonstrations were, as expected, leftists of various hues, but also "members of the outlawed Muslim Brotherhood."[21]

Despite this, the Egyptian government continued to court the Islamists, and particularly the Ikhwan, during the early 1970s. 'Umar al-Tilmisani recalled in his memoirs that the authorities reached out to him in 1972–1973, offering a

meeting with Sadat to resolve their differences. Al-Tilmisani said that he welcomed the overture and, having obtained approval from then general guide
Hasan al-Hudaybi, agreed to the talks. According to al-Tilmisani, negotiations
advanced to the point where the government asked the Brotherhood to form a
committee to meet with Sadat to put the finishing touches on an agreement;
but the process was then abruptly terminated. That notwithstanding, further
engagement saw al-Tilmisani and other senior Brothers—notably Ahmad Malt
and Mustafa Mashhur—meet government representatives, including Hosni
Mubarak.[22] As a result of this dialogue, the Ikhwan was quietly allowed to resume activity. Al-Arian speculates that this occurred, in part, because Sadat was
keen to build ties with Brotherhood exiles resident in the Gulf. He wished to
persuade them to return to Egypt, bringing their capital with them (many of
them having become successful businessmen), and he imagined that this
might also create opportunities for cooperation with their Saudi, Qatari, and
Kuwaiti benefactors.[23]

For its part, the Brotherhood underwent a period of internal introspection
and debate after the release of its senior leaders from prison. This ended with
the decision, by no means guaranteed, to rebuild the structures of the movement. In attempting to do this, though, the Brothers still faced huge problems.
The reconstituted Ikhwan was small in size and lacked legitimacy. In the wake
of al-Hudaybi's death in late 1973, a "hidden" general guide was appointed in
secret—an expedient that caused much unrest within the movement.[24] Thereafter, 'Umar al-Tilmisani cemented his position as a unifying figure around
whom the Brothers could gather.[25] And by late 1974, the British were conscious
of the fact that the Ikhwan was "back in business."[26] Nonetheless, even two years
later, US officials appeared not to know al-Tilmisani's identity as general guide
(and also believed that al-Hudaybi had only recently died).[27]

In the meantime, the Brotherhood's attitude toward Sadat—and its outlook
more broadly in this period—was shaped fundamentally by its critique of the
Nasser era. This echoed many of the ideas put forward by Sayyid Qutb (see
Chapter 6). Al-Tilmisani opined that Nasser had created a "jahili age," defined
by corruption and a lack of freedom. Under his "dictatorship," prisons had "swal-
lowed" all opposition, while the people's property was stolen, citizens were left
without recourse to the law, blood was spilled, lies spread, and morals declined.[28]
Nasser stood accused of delivering Egypt into the "palm" of Moscow, with the
country receiving little in return except for some old, damaged factories.
Al-Tilmisani argued that Nasser had debased education and the media, replacing all mention of religion with "communist principles," which opened the

door to "apostasy from Islam." Various Brotherhood members explained the suppression they had experienced in 1965 by reference to the machinations of the communists; al-Tilmisani was no exception. Added to this was the suggestion that Nasser had embroiled Egypt in futile conflicts in Congo and Yemen that were damaging to Islam and proved financially ruinous: "We destroyed our economy and bankrupted our treasury, and took on God knows how much debt and all for nothing but to spread communism in the Islamic countries." Al-Tilmisani insisted that by turning to Russia to build the High Dam (itself condemned as an environmental disaster), Nasser had facilitated the entry of communism into Egypt, thereby opening the "floodgates" so that it could engulf the whole Islamic world. Far from being an unintended consequence, this was alleged to have been Nasser's real aim: to make Egypt communist in order to eliminate Islam and secure his personal rule.[29]

The latter was a recurrent theme of Brotherhood commentaries on their great antagonist—the belief that Nasser was driven, above all, by his lust for power.[30] Salah Shadi, for instance, asserted that the key to understanding the former president, and the thing that had led to his many defeats and betrayals was his "self-worship and vast desire for influence and power."[31] Similarly, Hasan Dawh hypothesized that Nasser sought absolute control and that "the enemies of the nation, the enemies of the revolution and the enemies of the Ikhwan" helped him to achieve it.[32] In line with this, the Brothers liked to relate the story of Nasser saying that he wished to have two buttons on his desk: if he pushed one, then the country would mobilize; if he pushed the other, it would stop. As far as the Brotherhood was concerned, this mindset was symptomatic of Nasser's dictatorial tendencies (set against their own supposed preferences for freedom and democracy).[33] As previously, Ikhwan accounts compared Nasser to the figure of Pharaoh found in religious scriptures—indeed Nasser was said to be even worse than the ancient tyrant—with the Brothers collectively cast in the role of Moses, leading an oppressed people toward eventual emancipation.[34]

Brotherhood members further reinforced these ideas by questioning the extent to which Nasser was in any way committed to his purported principles. Hasan al-'Ashmawi relayed how during their conversations together, Nasser—the great hero of pan-Arabism—had been dismissive of both Islamic and Arab unity other than as a means to acquire power.[35] Before the revolution, according to al-'Ashmawi, Nasser had often expressed his contempt for the Arabs; in office, he was said to have willfully ignored opportunities to establish closer relations with neighboring countries.[36] In a similar vein, the Brothers described Nasser as a "false hero" to the cause of neutrality. His attacks on the Baghdad Pact during the 1950s were attributed to his personal ambition, rather than any serious commitment to the ideals of Arab nationalism and nonalignment (unlike the Brothers themselves, who of course stressed their adherence to these principles).[37] Ikhwani memoirs depicted Nasser as someone who actually favored an alliance with the West.[38] They suggested that only when this failed to eventuate, had he then opted "to walk side by side with the Soviet Union."[39] This shift was made possible, the Brothers affirmed, by Nasser's fundamental cynicism, and it proved disastrous for Egypt. Socialism, they argued, had "failed 100%"—an outcome that was inevitable because "every application of socialism in a Muslim country must fail."[40]

The Ikhwan considered the 1967 war to be the "scandalous conclusion" to Nasser's policies, as Egypt suffered ignominious defeat.[41] The military debacle was, the Brothers maintained, the inexorable result of dictatorship. They also felt that the Soviets had shown themselves to be poor friends to Egypt. Al-Tilmisani said that by warning the Israelis not to cross the Suez Canal, Moscow had effectively given a "green light" to the occupation of Sinai and other Muslim lands. Afterward, rather than help the Arabs to regain lost territory, the Soviets had called for peace and refused to supply them with the weapons they needed.[42] Through it all, Salah Shadi intimated, all Nasser had cared about was remaining in power. This was assumed to be the motivation behind his decision to move ever closer to the Soviets after 1967, allegedly offering Moscow an alliance and even the right to negotiate on Egypt's behalf.[43] (Scholars would agree that, in the wake of the defeat, Nasser did align himself more with the communist bloc as he sought to rebuild his shattered armies.)[44] The effect of all this, al-Tilmisani stated, was that Nasser, having "thrown out the English from Egypt finally," invited a "new Soviet occupation."[45] Similarly, Dawh's verdict was that, at his death, Nasser left Egypt divided: one part occupied by the United States (embodied by Israel); the other occupied by Russian soldiers (in the form of military advisers).[46]

Against this backdrop, it was hardly surprising that senior Brotherhood figures should have looked with favor on Sadat's attempt to reduce the influence of the left in Egypt. They welcomed his move to expel all Soviet military personnel in July 1972. Internally, too, they were happy to see a reduction in the influence of Nasserists and communists. Moreover, the Ikhwan's support for Sadat reached new heights when he launched the October War against Israel in 1973. This campaign, which the regime clothed in religious rhetoric (code-naming the attack "Badr" and using the declaration "allahu akbar"—God is greatest—as a rallying cry), enjoyed the support of most Egyptians, but especially the Islamists.

It was widely seen as a triumph, with the famous "crossing of the Canal" said to have restored Egyptian dignity after the calamity of 1967.[47]

In retrospect, it seems evident that the period immediately following the October War constituted the high point of Sadat's tenure. By this time, he was firmly established in office after seeing off all potential rivals. Sadat also now enjoyed the prestige of having challenged the Israelis on the battlefield and—if hardly delivering the victory portrayed—his armies had avoided the kind of defeat that proved so devastating to Nasser. In so doing, Sadat was judged to have repaired Egyptian credibility on the international stage. From this position of relative strength, he was able to press forward in new directions. Abroad, the president sought to leverage his qualified military advance into lasting political gains, beginning the process of disengagement and looking toward peace negotiations. Domestically, meanwhile, Sadat felt secure enough to extend the process of "liberalisation" in various spheres. The year 1974 thus saw the proclamation of the "infitah"—the start of Egypt's economic opening both to the West and private Arab capital.[48] At the political level, there was space for limited electoral competition, with the ruling party, the Arab Socialist Union (ASU), divided into three platforms: left, right, and center. Eventually, this led to the return of more recognizable political parties. Sadat also gave new freedom to civil society actors and relaxed restrictions on the press.[49]

In 1975, the British ambassador to Cairo, Sir Philip Adams, spoke of a "quiet counter-revolution," by which Egypt was being turned into a "constitutional, if qualified, democracy." Sadat, in this estimate, resembled a "Tudor monarch in a benevolent mood." He was "autocratic and all powerful," but used this power "discreetly" and in a way that was "responsive to public feelings." Among those to benefit most from the new dispensation were the Muslim Brothers. Adams reported that the Ikhwan was "again being talked about" in Cairo and predicted that a "Brotherhood-type organisation" might be able to "cultivate" the social and political opportunities afforded by Sadat.[50] Neither did it escape the attention of American officials that the "politburo" for the center platform of the ASU included Salih Abu Ruqayk, who was identified as a "leading member of [the] Muslim Brotherhood 'secretariat.'" (Abu Ruqayk had been a senior Ikhwan figure close to Hasan al-Hudaybi, and one of those involved in dialogue with the British in the early 1950s; see Chapter 5.) This was read as evidence that the Brothers had opted "unofficially to endorse" Sadat's constitution.[51] Though Abu Ruqayk subsequently stepped down, six other Brothers entered parliament in the 1976 elections, a development further suggestive of their revival and reconciliation to the regime.[52]

There were, however, clear limits to the government's benevolence vis-à-vis the Ikhwan. The following year, al-Tilmisani initiated a court case by which he sought to reverse the formal dissolution of the Brotherhood and thereby attain legal status. His efforts proved fruitless: the case was repeatedly delayed and never delivered a formal verdict.[53] In addition, the authorities were careful to ensure that neither the communists nor the Muslim Brothers could establish their own independent parties (whereas the Wafd was permitted to return, albeit briefly).[54] The Political Parties Law of 1977 prohibited the creation of any party based on "religious lines."[55] At the same moment, the Egyptian government assured the Americans that the Brotherhood would "not be allowed to re-emerge as [a] discrete political organization."[56]

Such impediments aside, the Brotherhood signaled its return to public life by launching a new media outlet. One of three weekly papers to appear in 1976 was *al-Da'wa,* the unofficial (but generally accepted) organ of the Muslim Brotherhood, and the lineal successor of Salih 'Ashmawi's earlier publication of the same name. Indeed, 'Ashmawi remained editor in chief, and he was joined on the editorial board by Brotherhood veteran Salah Shadi and general guide 'Umar al-Tilmisani. The latter became both president and managing editor. A later CIA memorandum on the state of the Egyptian press commented on the high production values of the newspaper-cum-magazine, which mixed pieces on theology and morality with "current news," updates on Brotherhood activities, and articles about the place of Islam in society. Its circulation was estimated to be between seventy and eighty thousand, and the paper was thought to be in good health financially, in part because of sponsorship from abroad, including from Saudi Arabia. Above all, the success of *al-Da'wa* was said to demonstrate the "Brotherhood's appeal to the emotions of many Egyptians."[57]

The rejuvenation of the Brotherhood was further consolidated by its absorption of many of the most active members of the campus-based al-Gama'a al-Islamiyya. Geneive Abdo has postulated that the writings of Qutb served as a common point of reference for the two groups that helped bring them together.[58] As the most detailed history of this period shows, meanwhile, the decision of many within the Gama'a to join the Ikhwan infused the latter with the energy and dynamism of a younger generation. In return, the student activists were provided with national leadership and an organizational structure that transcended their university years. Those who remained within the Gama'a moved in a more militant and Salafist direction. The Brotherhood, by contrast, seemed increasingly ready to reenter the social and political mainstream.[59]

US officials watched all of this with unease. The embassy in Cairo described Sadat's policy of encouraging "religious cells" and a revived Muslim Brotherhood, in order to take on Nasserists and Marxists, as "potential dynamite." The diplomats believed that the "religious right" had "vastly more potential disruptive power in Egypt" than did the left. For the government "to connive deliberately at [a] Muslim Brotherhood renaissance" was judged tantamount to "playing with fire."[60] In late 1976, Sadat himself divulged to the British that he was "now 'cooperating' with [the] Ikhwan . . . for his own purposes." The Brothers, the mandarins reckoned, were more than happy to be "used" by the regime as "weapons against the left," but UK officials directly echoed their American counterparts in seeing this as akin to "playing with fire."[61]

Western observers took some comfort in the fact that the regime at least stopped short of any reform that might threaten Sadat's overall control. Indeed, the only real fear for the president, British ambassador Adams remarked rather presciently, was "the unexpected: assassination or a conspiracy of fanatics."[62] Ultimately, of course, it was the combination of the two that cost Sadat his life. Such comments were also significant at the time, for the extent to which they reflected the diplomats' awareness of a growing militant Islamist threat. In 1974, the existence of a violent underground was confirmed by the April assault on the Cairo Military Technical Academy that killed eleven people. Sadat's government blamed Libyan-backed "Muslim fanatics" for the attack, which was carried out by the Islamic Liberation Party. In the aftermath, the US Embassy wondered whether the Brotherhood might also be implicated in the attack, yet local informants told them that the plotters were more akin to a "new Muslim left."[63] Other Western officials worried that the episode might be only "the tip of the iceberg of religious fanaticism."[64] And this found echo in CIA speculation that events of this kind illustrated the "susceptibility among Egyptian youth to the appeal of a religious fanaticism reminiscent of the old Muslim Brotherhood."[65]

The notion here that contemporary "religious fanaticism" bore resemblance to the *old* Ikhwan was especially noteworthy, for it raised once more the question of the group's attitude to the use of force. Ever since the suppression of the 1965 organization, the surviving leaders of the Brotherhood had tried to emphasize that they did not endorse revolutionary violence. As Barbara Zollner has shown, general guide Hasan al-Hudaybi put together his seminal work *Preachers Not Judges*—in which he tackled some of the controversies raised by Sayyid Qutb— in the final months of Nasser's rule. Al-Hudaybi insisted that the Brothers were best served by methods of argument and persuasion, rather than Qutbist ideas about the modern *jahiliyyah* (state of ignorance) that, in turn, raised the prospect of takfirism (the process of excommunicating fellow Muslims) and violent jihad.[66] In similar fashion, 'Umar al-Tilmisani explicitly rejected the use of physical force against *Muslim* governments—even if they were unjust or corrupt. Like al-Hudaybi, he said that the Brothers were "preachers," not "revolutionaries or rebels," affirming that ever since the 1930s, the Ikhwan had embraced political struggle but not criminal or terrorist approaches—despite what the "opponents of Islam" might claim.[67]

The prominence of Islamist-inspired militancy during the 1970s made such declarations all the more important. Though never large in number, violent radicals became a permanent feature of Egyptian sociopolitical life. In 1976–1977, for instance, a new group was uncovered: the Society of Muslims, or "takfir wa-l-hijra" as it was dubbed by the press. Led by Shukri Mustafa, a former Muslim Brother and self-proclaimed disciple of Qutb, it gained notoriety for its cultlike practices and absolute rejection of Egyptian society (its members even lived for a time in caves in the desert). In June 1977, the group kidnapped and then murdered the former minister of religious affairs, Muhammad al-Dhahabi. This provoked a major security crackdown with the arrest of virtually the entire organization, followed by the trial and execution of its leaders in March 1978.[68] Fearing that the Brothers might be tarnished by association, 'Umar al-Tilmisani publicly denounced the resort to abduction and killing, saying that the kidnapping of al-Dhahabi was "against religion."[69] Moreover, as Zollner has highlighted, it is telling that al-Hudaybi's refutation of key Qutbist ideas, *Preachers Not Judges,* was published openly for the first time in 1977—some eight years after its completion (and four years after al-Hudaybi himself had died). Its release appears to have been driven by the desire to distance the Brotherhood from the activities of groups like the Society of Muslims.[70]

Elsewhere, the senior Brotherhood leader Mustafa Mashhur stated plainly that what he called the "the turn to takfir" was an intellectual mistake that was in keeping with neither the original message of the Prophet nor the vision of Hasan al-Banna.[71] Mashhur produced regular columns for the Ikhwan newspaper under the heading "The Path of Da'wa" (later gathered in a collected work), in which he maintained that to wrongly pronounce a Muslim a "Kafir" (unbeliever) was the greatest sin. For this reason, Mashhur argued, as long as someone made the declaration of faith, then he or she should be accepted as part of the religion. It was perfectly possible, he attested, to be a "disloyal" or "bad" Muslim, while remaining within the boundaries of the faith.

In addition, both Mashhur and al-Tilmisani denied that the Brotherhood believed it *alone* constituted the only "society of Muslims" and was in any way inclined to disparage others as un-Islamic. They vowed that the Ikhwan saw themselves merely as preachers to Islam. As such, they talked of approaching like-minded groups in a spirit of "love, brotherliness and loyalty," hoping to be Muslim brothers together rather than *the* Muslim Brotherhood.[72]

In spite of all this, as Zollner has elucidated, Qutb was never repudiated tout court by the Brothers and a certain ambiguity was observable in the way they related to their most charismatic ideologue. Al-Hudaybi's oft-cited "anti-Qutbist" work, for instance, never mentioned him by name.[73] Instead, it refuted the concepts to which self-appointed guardians of Qutb's ideological legacy adhered. Similarly, senior figures such as al-Tilmisani and Mashhur tended to ignore or sidestep Qutb—rather than challenge his views head-on. And among ordinary Brothers, Qutb continued to be revered as a pious and faithful member of the group—a martyr who had sacrificed his life in the struggle with the impious Nasserite regime.[74]

Qutb left a palpable ideological imprint on the Ikhwan. As noted earlier, leaders such as al-Tilmisani themselves described Nasser's Egypt as a "jahili" society. Mashhur likewise stated that the Brotherhood faced an era akin to that which the Prophet had encountered: "Islam is alien [to the people], the jahili-yyah prevails and the preachers of Islam are oppressed." More broadly, Mashhur maintained that just as the original "enemies of the call" were "the polytheists of the [Arabian] peninsula, the Zoroastrians in Persia, the Romans and the Jews," so contemporary Muslims faced their "enemies represented by the communists, crusaders and Zionists, and those Muslims with worldly interests."

Once again, therefore, it was notable that the Brotherhood still talked in binary terms of a world divided between believing Muslims on the one hand, and the "enemies of Islam," or the "enemies of God," on the other. The West evidently belonged in the latter category. There was little hint of any revisionism in how the Ikhwan looked at countries like the United States and the United Kingdom. The principal opponents of the Brotherhood, Mashhur declared, were "those who had occupied Muslim countries for a long time" and who had well-established plans to "eliminate the essence of Islam" from the lives of Muslims. These forces were said to be strong in material terms and to have worked assiduously to divide the *umma* (Islamic nation) and separate the faithful from their religion, "sometimes with carrots and lures, other times by terrorism and torture." In this fashion, the "enemies of Islam" imagined by the Brotherhood traversed the domestic and the foreign; they included the Western powers abroad, and Egypt's military and secularists at home. To confront them, according to Mashhur, the mission of the Brotherhood was to raise a new generation imbued with the proper Islamic spirit.[75]

The core message of the Brotherhood thus differed little from that which it had always been: to promote a comprehensive understanding of Islam. Mashhur averred that it was not possible to leave one aspect of life outside the purview of religion. Consequently, the political imperative of the Ikhwan remained as strong as ever.[76] As Jeffery Halverson concluded, al-Tilmisani's vision of politics had not abandoned a focus on the establishment of an Islamic state.[77] And while Mashhur reiterated the Brotherhood's commitment to "gradualism" (and drew on al-Banna to warn against those who would act rashly), he also stressed that the ultimate goal was "Islamic government" and the creation of an "international Islamic state," resting on a "broad wide coherent base," in which the shari'a would be implemented.[78] Indeed, Mashhur went as far as to assert that in the modern age, the single most important goal was that of restoring "the state of Islam" and the rightly guided Islamic caliphate. This state, he said, would then work to reclaim every sliver of territory torn from Muslim hands, at the forefront of which was Palestine. Muslims "sinned," Mashhur proclaimed, if they did not "work to establish the state of Islam."[79]

Beyond this, it is arresting that in laying out their arguments, Mashhur and al-Tilmisani came close to engaging in apologetics for the more violent groups—even as they repudiated their actions. They described militants as "victims" who were motivated to use force by society's "departure from [the] teachings of God" and the government's failure to properly implement the laws of religion.[80] With regard to those who had killed Sheikh al-Dhahabi, al-Tilmisani quoted the journalist Mustafa Amin to suggest that they were people who had grown up in, and been impacted by, an age of repression: "They were born echoing the songs calling them to violence and force . . . they opened their eyes in an age that celebrated the birth of Lenin more than it celebrated the birth of the Prophet . . . years when atheism was nationalism and faith in God was reactionary and treachery."[81] Takfiri ideas, the general guide said, were the product solely of the brutality and torture that had occurred inside Nasser's prisons.[82] And Mashhur seemed willing to accept that those practicing takfirism were inspired by only the best of intentions.[83]

What is more, Brotherhood leaders were clear that physical-force jihad—in some form—remained an eternal obligation for Muslims, prescribed in the Qur'an.[84] Without it, Mashhur stated, Muslims faced "conquest, humiliation and extermination," whereas jihad secured their dignity and empowered Islam.

Hasan al-Banna, he pointed out, had been unequivocal on this—as were they—though he again warned against being reckless and rushing too quickly into jihad.[85] As such assertions made manifest, the Brotherhood of the 1970s imagined itself as returning to, or reasserting, the authentic character of the movement as defined by al-Banna (somewhat ignoring the extent to which the Ikhwan, in the first phase of its existence, had been implicated in the use of violence).

In passing, it is worth noting that this narrative rather cut against the grain of those external analyses that contrasted the "old" and "new" Brotherhood. Leaders of the Ikhwan did not conceive of their history as showing the reform or linear evolution of the movement, but rather the effort to restore the group's original, sound principles. It is interesting to consider the degree to which, in adopting this outlook, the Brothers effectively held to a "salafist" interpretation of their own past. In other words, later generations idealized the era of al-Banna as one in which the group had adhered to the "right path"; the assumption was that after his death, they had gone astray (no doubt unintentionally); and it thus remained for the contemporary generation to return to the original, pure form of the mission.

All of that aside, it was perhaps no surprise that American officials in the 1970s were unsure of where to place the Brotherhood in relation to more militant groups. On the one hand, they saw an ideological resemblance based on a shared attachment to "fundamentalist" ideas that rejected "westernization" and "all modern innovations." It was said the Brotherhood "sympathized to some extent with the ideology of the terrorists and may have provided support." Against this, there was an acknowledgment that the Ikhwan had been quick to denounce Shukri Mustafa's Society of Muslims. Yet such condemnation was assumed to have been, in part, a merely practical response, fueled by a desire to preserve the Brotherhood's "semilegitimate status and freedom of operation."[86] In the eyes of many, the jury was still out on the question of whether the Brotherhood had renounced violence in principle.

In November 1977, an American Embassy officer visited al-Tilmisani in his capacity as managing editor of al-Da'wa. During a long conversation, in which al-Tilmisani declared that the Ikhwan was "as healthy now as it ever ha[d] been," the general guide once more distanced the Brotherhood from the takfiris, while simultaneously intimating that their resort to violence was a consequence of the Ikhwan's "suppression." The government would have avoided such problems, he said, if it had allowed the Brothers to fulfill their "proper role" in society. In familiar fashion, too, al-Tilmisani sought to appeal to American sensibilities, avowing that the Ikhwan saw its main goal as being to combat communism and atheism. In line with this, he said that "despite U.S. aid for Israel," the Brothers far preferred America to Russia. Al-Tilmisani maintained that they would have no dealing with the "atheistic" Soviets; the Americans, by contrast, he praised as "people of the book" who were "acceptable despite foreign policy failings." The general guide claimed to have been impressed by the "openness" of US society, during a tour there at the invitation of various Islamic groups in 1975. Finally, he spoke of toleration and a desire to work with Christians and Jews.

The American Embassy was far from persuaded. A subsequent report on the encounter noted: "Talmasani's [sic] description of [the] Ikhwan as a benign, even benevolent, society is at variance with [the] historical record and is obviously self-serving. Arab governments, including Egypt, have opposed [the] organization since its inception because of its clandestine activities, including [the] use of violence."[87] Such caustic judgments notwithstanding, the one area where the diplomats did accept the veracity of al-Tilmisani's words concerned the "health" of the revitalized Ikhwan. They observed that the organization was "flourishing" in the wake of Sadat's liberalizing reforms. Doubtless, this was an accurate assessment, though by this stage there were signs that the Brotherhood's relationship with Sadat was not entirely cordial.

The Rising "Fundamentalist" Challenge

In the second half of the 1970s, the atmosphere between Sadat and his opponents worsened markedly and the process of "controlled liberalisation" ground to a halt. The events of 1977 proved crucial. The start of the year witnessed major food riots sparked by an attempt to raise the price of basic commodities. Seventy-nine people were killed and the army had to be called onto the streets to restore order.[88] Not only was this destabilizing in itself but also these domestic difficulties seemed to make Sadat more determined to define his presidency by foreign policy accomplishments. In particular, it became increasingly obvious that he wanted to make peace with Israel. November 1977 thus saw him make his dramatic trip to speak in front of the Israeli Knesset. The following year then brought the hard-won Camp David peace accords, which paved the way for a full treaty with the Israelis in 1979.[89] In pursuing this course, Sadat enjoyed the support of many within Egypt who wished for an end to the long war with Israel. Alongside this, however, he faced vehement criticism from both the left and from the various Islamist groups who were deeply hostile to any peace process with the "Zionists." As early as October 1975, the US Embassy recorded that "leftists and Nasserites" were "trying to make common cause with right-wing Muslim Brotherhood elements to oppose Sadat and [the Sinai Interim] agreement."[90] At the time of Sadat's visit to Jerusalem, American officials wondered whether the Ikhwan might be willing to give the president's peace initiative the "benefit of [the] doubt."[91] But subsequently, the group's criticism grew more trenchant.

To a large extent, of course, the Brotherhood's rejection of the Camp David process was to be expected. 'Umar al-Tilmisani made it plain that the Brothers were against a settlement on ideological grounds. Israel, he said, was an implacable and existential threat to Islam, which had no right to exist. The general guide decried any "normalization with the Jews," arguing that this would lead to the subversion or destruction of the entire Muslim *umma*. It was impossible to make an agreement, al-Tilmisani insisted, on the basis that the "thief" retained control of what he had "stolen." He therefore called on the leaders of the Islamic and Arab world to understand the reality of the "abyss" that the crusaders, communists, and Zionists had prepared for them and their people. Al-Tilmisani declared that "it was necessary" to unite the peoples and rulers of the region "to save them from this octopus that absorbs [their] blood little by little, [and] to eliminate this cancer that threatens their existence." He urged Sadat to strengthen the army and fight the Israelis, not make peace with them.[92]

In line with this, the Brotherhood's *al-Da'wa* newspaper demanded jihad against Israel and the recovery of "every inch of Islamic territory usurped by non-Muslims."[93] In opting to sign a treaty, the Ikhwan portrayed Sadat as emulating Nasser, who they claimed had always been ready to make peace with Israel (another example of what they saw as his lack of ideological principle).[94] Moreover, senior Brothers contended that Egypt was wasting the victory that it had won by the crossing of the canal in 1973. That conflict was reimagined as a great missed opportunity, with Sadat having wanted only a "television battle" rather than a real jihad based on faith.[95]

In this context, US diplomats were taken aback when al-Tilmisani told them in a face-to-face meeting that he would "not make trouble for Sadat over Camp David," even though he considered the accords to be "morally unacceptable." On that occasion, the Brotherhood leader also made "repeated disavowals of violent intent." Embassy officials noted, with evident surprise, that, in person, al-Tilmisani was "substantially more moderate" than he had previously appeared and they found his position on the peace process to be "most encouraging."[96]

Furthermore, in October 1978, officials observed that the "religious right" in general had been "extraordinarily muted" in its initial response to Camp David. This verdict was balanced, though, by the parallel assertion that Islamists remained the "greatest potential source of trouble" in the country.[97] The Brotherhood's al-Da'wa was judged to have offered the "harshest criticism" of the accords of any of Egypt's Islamic groups.[98] Its commentary included arguments that were clearly anti-Semitic. Such sentiments had always been a part of the Ikhwan worldview, but they seemed to grow sharper in this period. In one article, for example, al-Da'wa explored the "Jewish mentality" throughout history, defining it as infused with "fanaticism, selfishness, treason, rigidity, greed and treachery." Irked US officials promised to bring this "offensive article" to the attention of the Egyptian authorities, yet it was very much in keeping with the thinking of senior Brothers.[99] In making his case against Camp David, for instance, al-Tilmisani cited the Qur'anic verse that implied the Jews were the bitterest enemies of the Muslims.[100] Similarly, in a piece discussing the "enemies of Islam," Mustafa Mashhur quoted the Qur'an to the effect that "the Jews and Christians will never be pleased with you until you follow their ways."[101] In analyzing the fate of the Muslim umma since the fall of the caliphate, Mashhur asserted that Jewish-inspired "waves of darkness" had spread over Muslim lands: "darkness from the crusader West, paid for and planned by the Jews, and also darkness from the atheist east, created at the hands of the Jews." He surmised that as a result of this Jewish conspiracy, many Muslims had fallen for the allure of materialist civilization.[102] Al-Tilmisani likewise argued that Marxism was the "daughter" of Zionism, created to ruin the world so as to render it susceptible to Jewish domination and control.[103] It was for this reason, the general guide said, that the Zionists "did not hate anyone in the world" the way they "hated the Muslim Brotherhood"—for the Ikhwan was the most effective barrier to their plans.[104]

Statements of this kind underscored the extent to which Brotherhood reactions to Camp David were informed by their perception of a world divided between, on the one hand, "forces opposed to Islam" and on the other, the Muslims led by the Ikhwan.[105] As Gilles Kepel has stressed, al-Da'wa's output was framed by four key themes: anti-Semitism, anti-Crusaderism, anticommunism, and antisecularism. The underlying premise was that Islam faced a constant and extreme threat.[106] In line with this, al-Tilmisani named the three great enemies of the Islamic "call" as "the communists, the crusaders and the Zionists," all of whom were said to be seeking the destruction of the Brotherhood, precisely because it formed an "insurmountable obstacle" to their designs.[107] Often, these enemies were assumed to be operating in collusion. Hence, *al-Da'wa* claimed that Israel was "supplied with arms by America and men by Russia," so that it could "wipe out Islam and Muslims." The general guide likewise described the United States and the Soviets as together constituting the "severest opponents of Islam."[108] And the Islamic East was said to be still under a "Western colonial yoke," from which it needed liberation.[109]

Al-Da'wa offered a fierce critique of the evils of Western imperialism, which were thought to be both physical and ideological in character. Criticism of the "sex-ridden and degenerate" culture of the United States served as a regular refrain.[110] True, the prevalence of this kind of material should not be exaggerated. As al-Arian observes, articles dedicated to "foreign affairs" were relatively few in number. Even so, the Brothers' critique of the West occupied a prominent place in their mental landscape.[111] US officials therefore took note of *al-Da'wa*'s "substantial criticism of U.S. Mid-East policies" and the accusations of hypocrisy that the newspaper leveled at President Carter for raising human rights concerns while ignoring Israel's "plundering and looting" of the Palestinians. "Basic to this" stance, the diplomats believed, was the "Ikhwani fear that [the] West, most particularly [the] Christian West," was inveterately anti-Islam.[112] As Jeffrey Halverson has shown, this motif was also at the forefront of the message propagated by scholars identified with the Brotherhood, such as Yusuf al-Qaradawi and Muhammad al-Ghazali. Al-Ghazali had been a Brotherhood member in his youth before being expelled in 1953 (see Chapter 5). Despite this, he had remained close to many within the movement, particularly the newer generation of Brothers such as 'Abd al-Mon'im Abu al-Futuh.[113] Al-Ghazali counseled Egyptians to free themselves from "educational, legislative, and intellectual colonialism."[114] He argued that the country's political elite had "deserted" their religion and made themselves the willing instruments of imperialism and exploitation; he proposed that only the revitalization of the true faith would allow Muslims to turn back the "cultural invasion" and overcome the "enemies of Islam."[115]

In January 1979, *al-Da'wa* published what was said to be a CIA report, allegedly authored by the academic Richard P. Mitchell, which urged the Egyptian government to repress Islamic organizations, including the Brotherhood. The authorities confiscated the issue—because of its implicit suggestion that Sadat took orders from Washington—and al-Tilmisani was reprimanded.[116] Given that Sadat was, by this time, overtly repositioning Egypt within the Western orbit, the episode seemed to highlight the potential for tension between the authorities and the Ikhwan. Previously, the US Embassy had expressed disquiet over the growing criticism faced by Sadat domestically, pointing to both the economic problems facing Egypt and the emergence of an oppositional "Muslim right" that featured the Brotherhood.[117] The latter's denigration of Sadat's peace initiative was coupled to an ongoing reproach for the government's "infitah" policy, which, according to the Ikhwan, risked importing foreign "ideas and philosophies."[118] American officials presumed that the readiness of the Egyptian government to allow *al-Da'wa* to appear in spite of such "broadsides" did not reflect "sympathy" for the Ikhwan as much as a "desire to avoid confrontation with this potentially powerful element."[119]

The year 1978 had brought further evidence of just how strong the Islamists had become, when the university-based al-Gama'a al-Islamiyya won major victories in campus elections in Cairo and Alexandria. This was also followed by landslide success in the nationwide student union polls.[120] In the aftermath, British officials did wonder whether the Islamists had won simply because of their better organization and determination, as opposed to their depth of support. "A small but active group," it was noted, could have "a disproportionate effect on an election in which the majority is apathetic." Yet at the same time, the mandarins recognized that the Islamists had emerged as a bastion of "anti-establishment opinion" in Egypt.[121] In this period, too, the US Embassy referred to the "latent" strength of the "religious right" and labeled it "potentially the most powerful political force" in the country, outside the military. Though there was thought to be "no immediate threat to Sadat or the peace process"—and the Brotherhood was described as "fragmented" and lacking in "dynamic leadership"—the group was identified as a possible source of trouble for the authorities.[122]

Many observers viewed what was happening in Egypt through a regionwide lens. The UK Foreign Office was already reflecting on the challenge posed by "fundamentalists" whose influence had grown because of the "set-backs" suffered by Nasserism across the Middle East.[123] In similar fashion, the State Department drew attention to the "general resurgence of Islamic fundamentalism throughout the Muslim world," and especially in Egypt.[124] Western officials offered different analyses of what lay behind this phenomenon. Some saw it as the latest effort to find a "synthesis" between Islam and the "modern world" that had been ongoing since the days of the Ottoman Empire.[125] Others talked more in terms of a "hostile reaction" to the effects of a modernization process that had brought little economic benefit to the population as a whole. Sadat's "more liberal attitude toward the religious right" was also thought to have been decisive. That "religious right" was deemed to possess a "reactionary" ideology and to be rooted in "the urban middle and lower middle classes."[126] Another version again put more emphasis on the "alienated urban poor" who were assumed to be particularly susceptible to the appeal of the Ikhwan and "other radical Islamic movements."[127] In short, there were plenty of grand theories to explain the Islamic resurgence of the 1970s, but little confidence about how to deal with this phenomenon.

These debates were given fresh impetus by the events of 1979, arguably the most important single year in the recent history of the broad Islamist movement. It began with the deposition of the shah, as the Iranian revolution reached a crescendo. For the United States, this meant the loss of a key pillar of the "client state" strategy that had informed policy toward the Middle East since the 1960s.[128] To Islamists, by contrast (and to others, especially on the left), the shah had been a hate figure, reviled because of his alleged subservience to the United States and for the repressive apparatus he had constructed at home (the infamous SAVAK, the Organisation of National Intelligence and Security). The shah's overthrow by popular revolt was thus heralded by groups like the Brotherhood as the dawn of a new age in the region. The fact that the revolution bore an Islamic mantle—with the dominant role of Ayatollah Khomeini—merely amplified its significance. Here was proof that an Islamist movement, albeit of a Shi'a variety, could seize power. As Emmanuel Sivan has shown, the extent of cross-sectarian cooperation among Islamists should not be overstated. Many Sunnis found it hard to look past the distinctly Shi'a character of the Iranian Islamic Republic.[129] Still, despite deep reservations born of both religious difference and practical politics, Khomeini's proclamation of an Islamic state gave a major fillip to Islamist movements of all stripes. It evoked sympathy and inspiration, not least because Shi'a and Sunni Islamists shared a common set of enemies: namely, secular authoritarian regimes, Western "imperialists," and Zionists. Some imagined that it was a harbinger of things to come, foreshadowing the collapse of other repressive governments and the emergence of a "true" Sunni Islamic state.[130]

Such dreams were given added piquancy in the last months of 1979 by two additional developments of critical significance. The first was the seizure of the Grand Mosque in Mecca by Saudi Islamist militants under Juhayman al-'Utaybi. This attack on the authority and legitimacy of another "pro-Western" monarch in the Middle East inflamed the passions of Islamists everywhere, especially since the House of Saud had to enlist foreign support (French special forces) to defeat al-'Utaybi's movement. Moreover, in the wake of this incident, the Saudi government sought to bolster its religious credentials by unleashing a new wave of proselytization both at home and abroad—in an effort to counter the perceived dangers from revolutionary Shi'ism and Sunni militancy alike.[131] The effects of this campaign reinforced the broader Islamic revival already under way across the region. It also proved a boon to many Islamist movements, with groups such as the Muslim Brotherhood profiting from Saudi largesse, either directly or indirectly.

This "forward" policy on the part of Riyadh was intensified still further amid the fallout from the third crucial moment of 1979—the Soviet military intervention in Afghanistan. As is well known, resistance to the Red Army manifested itself principally in calls to jihad. The Afghan mujahideen won the backing of not only the Saudis and their American allies, but also an empowered and increasingly global Islamist support network. In this atmosphere, the influence of the latter seemed only to grow.

In each case, then, the nature of what had occurred in Iran, Saudi Arabia, and Afghanistan confirmed the return of "Islam" as a factor of major geopolitical relevance. From the perspective of Western officials, the prominence of "Islamic fundamentalism" in this period served to deepen their interest in a movement like the Brotherhood. At a superficial level, the Ikhwan appeared to have been somewhat bypassed by the events of 1979, overtaken by more dynamic modes of Islamist thought and practice. In truth, however, these developments combined to lend new meaning and purpose to their activities.

Brotherhood reactions to the Iranian revolution, for example, were initially positive. As 'Abd al-Mon'im Abu al-Futuh relates, to many young Brothers, the shah was the embodiment of those authoritarian regimes in the region that were servile to the United States. Consequently, they felt huge sympathy for what was seen as a "popular Islamic revolution." It nourished their ambitions—as leaders of Islamic groups who themselves faced repression.[132] When Ayatollah Khomeini returned to Tehran from his French exile, the Ikhwan sent him a message of fraternal solidarity. And it was against this backdrop of Brotherhood affection for the new Iranian government that the American authorities, as described at the outset of this chapter, approached al-Tilmisani in an abortive attempt to secure a negotiated end to the hostage crisis.

Thereafter, it should be said, Brotherhood assessments of the Islamic Republic soured. Events in Syria, where the Iranians lent assistance to the government of Hafez al-Assad, played an important role in this shift. The leader of the Syrian Ikhwan, for instance, recounted that he had initially "sympathized" with the Iranian revolutionaries and aimed to build relations with Tehran. This sympathy had turned to disappointment, though, because of Khomeini's decision to move in a "sectarian direction" by drawing closer to Assad. On this reading, the Iranians were neither serious about wanting to liberate Palestine, nor about building a state that adhered to "the traditions of Islamic morality."[133] In similar fashion, 'Umar al-Tilmisani became increasingly critical of the calls for jihad and revolution that were emanating from Tehran.[134]

Their disillusionment with Iran notwithstanding, the Brothers did at least take heart from the fact that Khomeini and his followers had been able to overturn the pro-Western shah. In addition, they applauded Khomeini for being "steadfast" in the face of American threats during the hostage crisis. To Brotherhood minds, this made him a hero to Muslims (and they contrasted his approach sharply with what was seen as the supine behavior of Sadat).[135] When Khomeini's regime was then attacked by Iraq, al-Tilmisani denounced Saddam Hussein for his aggression and urged all Islamic countries to work toward a peaceful resolution. The conflict, he argued, was merely the latest attempt by the "enemies of Islam" to stir Shi'a-Sunni division, and was the product of an international Zionist conspiracy.[136] In this way, Brotherhood attitudes to what had transpired in Iran betrayed the kind of ambiguity that was typical of many other Sunni Islamists.

Elsewhere, the Brothers were scarcely disinterested spectators with regard to events in Saudi Arabia. They had been closely involved in the kingdom's attempts to promote its version of Islam as an alternative to Arab nationalism and socialism. This effort had been carried forward over several decades, and particularly after the vast financial windfall that came the way of the Saudis as a result of oil price surges in the 1970s. Members of the Egyptian Ikhwan in exile like Kemal el-Helbawy played a vital role in the creation of new institutions dedicated to this objective, such as the World Assembly of Muslim Youth (WAMY).[137] Numerous private and semiofficial bodies (including the Islamic Development Bank, the Muslim World League, the al-Haramain Foundation, and the International Islamic Relief Organization) dispersed funds globally as part of a campaign that saw the building of Islamic centers, mosques, and schools. As was observed at the time, much of this financial support was funneled toward groups such as the Brotherhood and the south Asian Islamist party, the Jamaat-i-Islami (JI).[138] Just as the Iranian revolution served to galvanize the Ikhwan intellectually, so the consequences of the unrest in Saudi Arabia were of practical benefit to the group.

Finally, too, the onset of conflict in Afghanistan had a considerable impact on the Brothers. They quickly became leading advocates of the notion that the fight against the Soviets was a legitimate jihad that should be backed by Muslims around the world. To those familiar with the Brotherhood this hardly came as a shock. US officials had suspected that what they termed Afghan-based adherents of the Ikhwan had been behind attempts to overthrow successive governments of Afghanistan, going back several years.[139] After the Communist Party coup in 1978, these "Brotherhood" elements were identified as one of the "main threats" to the new leftist regime.[140] Whatever the truth of this assessment (and it seems to have been based on the conflation of indigenous groups like the Hizb-e-Islami with the actual Ikhwan), there was no doubting the depth of Brotherhood support for the anti-Soviet insurgency after 1979.[141] Al-Tilmisani, for instance, was happy to acknowledge that "the Ikhwan called for volunteers for jihad in the cause of saving Afghanistan."[142] From across the region, members of the Brotherhood emigrated to participate in the conflict (one of the most famous Arab mujahideen was Abdullah Azzam, a former devotee of the Jordanian Ikhwan).

Yet of perhaps greater significance was the fact that the Brotherhood mobilized its burgeoning international network (see below) to provide financial and political assistance to the jihad. Again here, Kemal el-Helbawy figured prominently. He claims to have been in charge of Brotherhood activities in Afghanistan between 1988 and 1994, by means of a Peshawar-based coordination center. This sought to facilitate the travel of Brothers from all over the world into Afghanistan. According to el-Helbawy, the Egyptian Ikhwan sent a large number of doctors, engineers, and teachers who helped build and run schools and hospitals across the country. He also says that the Ikhwan worked to harmonize the efforts of the mujahideen fighting for different groups.[143] In so doing, the Brotherhood cooperated closely with the Jamaat-i-Islami. El-Helbawy, for example, spent much time at Peshawar's Institute of Policy Studies (a body headed by the JI's Khurshid Ahmad), the Arabic department of which he had helped to establish. From this vantage point, he edited the Brotherhood's weekly magazine on Afghanistan, *International Issues*.[144] More broadly, the Ikhwan remained closely engaged in Afghan developments throughout the 1980s and 1990s.

The Brotherhood's firm stance on the conflict in Afghanistan did not just bring it into contact with other Islamist groups, of course. Rather, it provided another context in which the Brothers effectively found themselves aligned with Western and especially US policy. Soon after the Soviet invasion, American commentators began to argue that the United States should show support for the "traditional Islamic forces" fighting against communism.[145] The United States, it was suggested, should foster a "rising Islamic consciousness" and "reinforce it against the threat to the region posed by the Soviet Union."[146] As various scholars have shown, first the Carter and then the Ronald Reagan administrations embraced this logic.[147] What followed was the largest program of covert aid in the CIA's history, amounting to some $3 billion channeled to the anti-Soviet insurgency via Pakistan (with the Saudis matching US aid, dollar for dollar). In 1984, President Reagan hosted mujahideen commanders in the White House, praising them as "freedom fighters" and endorsing their struggle against communism. As Andrew Preston has described, Reagan was happy to use religious imagery to frame all this as a necessary part of the battle against the forces of atheism.[148] US policy in Afghanistan thus represented the actualization of ideas that had been circulating since the 1950s about utilizing Islam as a bulwark against the Soviets (see Chapter 6).

Despite this, American support for the mujahideen appears to have made little impression on the way Brotherhood leaders looked at the United States. Indeed, 'Umar al-Tilmisani remarked in his memoirs that Afghanistan was a "victim of the conspiracies of the United States and the Soviets against the Islamic world." He dismissed American criticism of Soviet actions in 1979 as "specks of dust in the eyes," designed to distract attention from their "real" support for Moscow. Al-Tilmisani attached particular significance to President Carter's comments that the United States would not tolerate the movement of Soviet armies outside Afghanistan—a statement said to reflect the fact he had no objection to the actual invasion itself.[149] In this way, the general guide contrived to ignore US support for the mujahideen, in preference for a narrative that stressed ongoing American hostility toward Islam.

It is hard to ascertain whether US officials were aware that this was al-Tilmisani's view; but it is unlikely it would have come as much of a surprise. They certainly did know of the Brotherhood's opposition to American foreign policy in the broader Middle East, as well as the inherently conspiratorial vision of international affairs to which the group adhered. Of far greater concern to American diplomats in any case was the question of whether the events of 1979 made it more or less likely that the Ikhwan might come to power in Egypt. The CIA noted the "obvious parallels between the devout Muslim fundamentalism exhibited by the Brotherhood . . . and the emotional following commanded by the Ayatollah Khomeini in Iran." The great anxiety for many policy makers post-1979 was that an "Iranian-style revolution" might similarly coalesce to bring down the regime in Cairo.

Against this background, the Americans were troubled by reports that the Brotherhood enjoyed "fairly strong" support within the Egyptian army. The fear was that the Ikhwan, maybe in alliance with leftists, might be emboldened to take on Sadat. Moreover, the president himself was said to be "somewhat at a loss to figure out an effective way to deal with the religious right." There was, diplomats observed, "considerable evidence" that Sadat increasingly regarded the Brotherhood as a danger, but held back from launching a campaign against it for "fear of arousing a storm of protest from the conservative, deeply religious Egyptian masses—Sadat's own natural constituency."[150] Scholars like Hamid Algar agreed in seeing the Brotherhood as an important part of a growing Islamic threat to the Egyptian government.[151]

At the turn of the decade, there was little doubting the antagonism between Sadat and the Ikhwan. This was only exacerbated by his decision to push ahead with policies that aroused Islamist anger, such as a new Personal Status Law, which broadened women's rights (Law 44, often known as "Jehan's Law" because it had been championed by the president's wife).[152] In addition, Sadat announced that political activity would no longer be tolerated on university campuses, and he accused the Islamist student societies of fomenting sectarian unrest, linking them to attacks on Egypt's Coptic Christian minority.

There have been suggestions that, even at this point, Sadat remained ready to try to conciliate the Brotherhood. Al-Tilmisani later averred that he was in contact with Interior Minister Nabawi Isma'il during 1978–1979, to discuss ways the Ikhwan might cooperate with the authorities to tackle both sectarianism and the more radical challenge posed by groups like al-Gama'a al-Islamiya.[153] Yet dialogue of this kind failed to alter the trajectory of a relationship that was in palpable decline. The truth of this became apparent in an extraordinary tele-vised confrontation between al-Tilmisani and Sadat that took place in August 1979. On that occasion, Sadat condemned the Brotherhood for its alleged attempt to build a "broad national front" with leftists in order to oppose the government. He warned them against interfering in politics and threatened the Ikhwan and its newspaper *al-Da'wa* with complete dissolution. In the process, Sadat made reference to a favorite theme of Nasser's: that the Brothers had moved away from the original teachings of Hasan al-Banna, whom Sadat claimed as a friend and ally, and betrayed their founder's legacy. In reply, al-Tilmisani the-atrically professed his loyalty to the president and repudiated any association with the far left. The Brotherhood leader alluded to the "antagonism between Islam and communism" and stated that the two could "never stand together."[154] But this obvious appeal for a truce did not convince Sadat, and the president seemed increasingly set on repression.

Western diplomats, meanwhile, sought to gain an insight into the thinking of the Ikhwan. In his memoirs, al-Tilmisani asserted that between 1979 and 1981 he was contacted multiple times by Joseph Lawrence, the press adviser at the US Embassy in Cairo, who visited him at his office at the newspaper. Al-Tilmisani recorded that he was always careful to make sure that the Interior Ministry was kept fully informed and did not object. He did this, he said, because he had "not forgotten Mr. Evans" (see Chapter 5).[155] In the same period, the general guide also claimed to have been contacted by the British Embassy, which wanted to arrange a meeting between him and a high-ranking Foreign Office representative due to visit Cairo. Al-Tilmisani said that he turned this request down because he did not want to discuss politics with a "foreigner"—except with the prior permission of the government.[156] The very fact that approaches of this sort were being made, however, was itself noteworthy; for it demonstrated the consensus among diplomats that the Brothers were actors who could not be ignored on the Egyptian political stage.

For the same reason, American officials closely watched internal developments inside the Ikhwan. In April 1980, the Foreign Broadcast Information Service (FBIS) relayed a long article that had originally appeared in the Lebanese weekly *al-Watan al-Arabi,* which described the Brotherhood as divided between three factions: a "semi-official current" associated with al-Tilmisani and *al-Da'wa* that sought to regain legal status for the Ikhwan; the "puritanical" "Banna-ites" who were thought to be more starkly opposed to Sadat, even as they preferred proselytism and education to politics; and finally, the "Qutbiyyun" group, which, as the name implied, followed the ideas of Sayyid Qutb and took an uncompromising stance toward the government and society.[157] Assessments of this kind were indicative of the enduring ambiguity over the Brotherhood's "real" position. The interest in trying to identify different internal factions—which would return as a regular feature of diplomatic reportage on the group in the decades that followed—was a product of the secrecy and mystery that surrounded the Ikhwan. Reports of this kind made interesting reading for those analysts charged with following the Egyptian scene, not least because by 1980, there was an awareness that Cairo was in the midst of a political vacuum. Opposition to Sadat seemed only to be growing and was expressed principally in an Islamic idiom. This rhetoric, in turn, raised the prospect of more sectarian forms of politics—and it escaped no one's attention that incidents of Muslim-Coptic violence were on the rise, especially in Upper Egypt.[158]

As the situation deteriorated, Sadat equivocated on the best way forward. On the one hand, he made what seemed to be a new effort to win over "moderate" strands of the Islamist movement. In early 1981, for example, Sheikh Muhammad al-Ghazali was appointed deputy minister of *awqaf*. Some interpreted this as a signal that Sadat still wished to find common ground with the Ikhwan. And yet, no sooner was al-Ghazali in post than the authorities again swung toward more hard-line methods, launching a crackdown on the media and other critics of the president. This culminated in the infamous mass arrests of September 1981, in which large swathes of the opposition were detained. Almost all the leading figures of the Brotherhood—whether from the older generation like Al-Tilmisani or younger members like Abu al-Futuh—were imprisoned.[159] The scale of the repression, though, was not enough to save Sadat. In early October 1981, he was assassinated by members of the small Islamist militant group al-Jihad.[160]

The Brothers and Mubarak

As might be anticipated, the murder of Sadat deepened American interest in the character of Islamism, particularly in Egypt. Already in 1981, a CIA intelligence assessment had concluded that what it called "resurgent Islamic Nationalism" was usually "destabilizing for the societies concerned and detrimental to the strategic and economic interests of the United States." In an echo of earlier analyses, it was argued that Islam had emerged as a "potent political force" in diverse national contexts as a response to "widespread psychological and social displacement" caused by "rapid modernization." On this reading, religion offered people "a sense of psychological and social authenticity" after they had been "uprooted . . . from their traditional milieu." The problem faced by the United States, according to the CIA, was that it was typically associated with both the modernization process *and* neocolonialism. It was this that made it a target for "vituperative anti-American rhetoric." The "root cause" of this hostility was held to be the "dissatisfaction and humiliation" that the "Muslim peoples" experienced in their daily lives—though the CIA did also acknowledge that US "global strategies" (particularly its support for Israel and the oil-rich states) played a role as well. The result of all this, it was said, was that there were "no totally reliable allies in the Islamic world for the United States." Furthermore, the CIA felt that there was little Washington could do to alter this situation: "No matter how helpful the United States is to these societies in transition, the outlook is for continuing hostility over the next few years."[161]

This striking pessimism regarding the regional position of the United States was paralleled by a fatalistic view of the power of religion across the Middle East. CIA officials reckoned that the question of whether "religious forces"—by which they meant Islam—destabilized or strengthened a particular government was determined by that government's relationship with the local "religious hierarchy." Where these were in harmony, as in Saudi Arabia, the state was thought to be strong; but where the government attempted to contest the hierarchy, as had occurred in Iran, it was judged vulnerable to religious agitation. Leaving aside the fact that this constituted a rather one-dimensional reading of the Iranian revolution, what was implicit here was the notion that Middle Eastern societies were inherently pious. This character, it was assumed, made Islam especially powerful and a potential menace to the authorities. From this perspective, governments had a choice when it came to religious forces: appease, co-opt, and succeed; or confront, repress, and fail. Moreover, this outlook was itself predicated on the idea that groups like the Brotherhood embodied certain essential characteristics latent within Muslim societies as a whole.[162]

The assassination of Sadat seemed to confirm the validity of such theories about the enduring power of Islam. An intelligence assessment produced shortly afterward predicted that the "Islamic fundamentalist movement" was likely to be a "violent opposition force" to the Egyptian government throughout the 1980s. It was said that the ability of Sadat's successor, Hosni Mubarak, to overcome the challenges he faced was contingent on his approach to that movement. As above, it was imagined that "repression" would merely extend the influence of the Islamists. Similar in effect would be a "continued close association with [the] United States" and "government endorsement of [a] birth control program." By contrast, the "Islamization of government policy along [the] model advocated by extremists" was deemed likely to reduce the danger of militancy. A "more Islamic Egypt," it was proposed, "would probably remain linked to the United States," albeit with the "intensity of the bond" diminished.

This latest report thus again betrayed an inherent fatalism with regard to Islamism. The presumption was that there was little the Egyptian authorities could do to halt the rise of "fundamentalist" groups beyond implementing policies designed to appease them. As the executive summary stated: "The Mubarak regime . . . can reduce the risk of violent confrontation with extremist groups by normalizing relations with the Arab world, putting greater distance between itself and the United States and Israel, and resisting excessive Westernization and corruption."[163]

The same document was also interesting for what it said specifically about the Ikhwan. This was held to be a typical example of what were labeled "crisis cults," which had "sprung up around the world in reaction to political, economic and social stress." These movements, it was asserted, followed a clear and "predictable" life cycle, evolving "from early militancy to later moderation." By this time, the Brotherhood was thought to be moving very much in the latter direction. This is not to say that the CIA was oblivious to more troubling aspects of the group's behavior; reference was made to its penchant for clandestine activity, its history of violence, and rumors that it retained a "small, secret militia." Added to this was a recognition that the Brothers were inclined to see the "enemies of Islam" everywhere, and perceived things like women's liberation and birth control to be "part of a Western Conspiracy to destroy Islamic society." Overall, though, the Ikhwan was judged to hold a "politically moderate position" and to reflect "middle class values." While committed to its goal of a "truly Islamic society," it was considered supportive of Mubarak and critical of the "extremists." "We expect the Muslim Brotherhood," the report concluded, "to continue to move toward the center of the Egyptian political spectrum as it evolves through the culturally and politically acceptable phase of the cult cycle."[164]

Commentary of this sort revealed the way in which the potential threat emanating from jihadist groups effectively encouraged a reassessment of the Brotherhood. The Ikhwan was now placed on a spectrum of "Islamic fundamentalist" groups that ran from "moderate" on the one hand to "extreme" on the other; an emphasis was placed on the Brothers' relative moderation.[165] Such analysis reinforced earlier appraisals in which it had been argued that the Brotherhood's "demand for the integration of a fundamentalist type of Islam with a traditional Islamic political system and a modern social welfare system" was "ultimately not immoderate."[166]

It was this kind of logic that led US officials to commend President Mubarak's decision to replicate the "accommodation" that Sadat had reached with the Brotherhood during his first years in office. These policies were said to have been "generally effective," as indicated by the "moderating influence" allegedly exerted by the group during disturbances in Cairo, Asyut, and Minya in 1981. The American understanding was that it was Sadat's attempt to *crack down* on the Brotherhood (and others) in September 1981 that had been the real mistake. Mubarak, the CIA hoped, would learn the lesson of this and instead co-opt "moderate" forces like the Ikhwan.[167] As a result, many Western officials probably welcomed reports that the new president had released most of those arrested in the final months of Sadat's life. Leading Muslim Brothers such as 'Umar al-

Tilmisani were prominent among them.[168] In subsequent years, Mubarak basically reinstated the unofficial covenant that had existed under Sadat: the Ikhwan was permitted to operate in semiopen fashion; and, in return, the group refrained from any direct challenge to the regime.[169] In opting for this approach, Mubarak was aided by the fact that, with the passage of time, the Egyptian-Israeli peace treaty somewhat receded from view. Of course, the Brotherhood and others remained ideologically opposed to the agreement, but as relations settled down (and notably after Israel completed its withdrawal from the Sinai in 1982), the issue generated less friction. Egyptian-Israeli peace became normalized as a fact of political life and no longer stood as an insuperable irritant between the government and the opposition.[170]

Beyond this, Mubarak initiated his own period of liberalization and "controlled democracy." Newspapers were once more afforded greater leeway in what they could print (albeit while required to stay within certain "red lines" that prohibited, say, criticism of the president or the army). There was also an expansion of the space available to civil society institutions, such as the professional syndicates and trades unions. Finally, parliamentary elections were held, in which authorized political parties were allowed to participate.[171]

As under Sadat, the Brotherhood was among the groups to benefit from this era of renewed openness.[172] In particular, the Ikhwan set about developing its presence within the professional syndicates, with prominent members running for positions on the national boards.[173] The breakthrough came in 1984, when seven Brothers were elected to the twenty-five-person governing body of the doctors' syndicate. From there, success followed success. In 1987, for instance, Ikhwan-affiliated candidates won forty-five out of sixty-one seats on the engineering syndicate board and a Brotherhood veteran, Murad al-Zayyat, was chosen as secretary general.[174]

In parallel with this, the Ikhwan formed political alliances that enabled it to sit, unofficially, in parliament. In the 1984 elections the group lent its backing to the "New Wafd," which had been permitted to reorganize. According to 'Umar al-Tilmisani, it was actually the Wafd that first approached the Ikhwan about some kind of tactical cooperation, and an agreement was reached on forming a unified political opposition, combining "the Wafd [as] the legal channel and the Ikhwan [as] the popular base."[175] Twelve Muslim Brothers were among the fifty-eight candidates then elected under the Wafdist banner.[176] The Brotherhood won support, in part, for its provision of social and religious services, which encompassed the funding, building, and managing of hospitals, schools, charities, and mosques across Egypt. Such activities were made possible, in turn, by the involvement of senior figures in Islamic financial and commercial businesses, which endowed the movement with the resources necessary to establish what Robert Springborg has called "para-state" facilities.[177]

The Brothers justified their participation in parliament on the grounds that it allowed them both to publicize their message and to work for legal change.[178] Ikhwan-affiliated MPs thus strongly welcomed a government-sponsored initiative to bring all legislation into line with the shari'a. During the ensuing debates, al-Tilmisani appeared before the Religious Affairs Committee of the People's Assembly, despite not being a parliamentary deputy himself—a sign of the Brotherhood's burgeoning influence. As ever, there were limits beyond which the Brotherhood was not permitted to proceed, and Mubarak made sure that the review of Egypt's laws to make them shari'a-compliant dragged on interminably.[179]

Nevertheless, in April 1984, the CIA observed that a "truce" appeared to have been put in place between the regime and the "relatively moderate fundamentalist Muslim Brotherhood." As could be inferred from terminology of this kind, the Americans were relaxed about the arrangement. It was affirmed that the Ikhwan had perhaps earned a "more sinister reputation" than it deserved; it was clearly identified now with a moderate approach; and in so being, it was juxtaposed to more "extreme" movements that advocated the "violent overthrow of the government."[180] In a similar vein two years later, the CIA posited that the Brotherhood could act as a "counterweight" to "more revolutionary Islamic groups."[181]

American officials *did* also continue to see the Ikhwan as a "potential anti-US force." They noted, for instance, its opposition to both Camp David and the US Agency for International Development (USAID), which the Brothers saw as a tool of Western "cultural penetration." Yet such concerns were balanced by the belief that the Brotherhood, as a group committed to a "gradualist strategy" and "moderate tactics," was vastly preferable to more extreme alternatives. The fact that Ikhwan tactics were thought to include the "infiltration of the Egyptian education system," so as to influence the next generation, received little in the way of comment. Of far greater interest was the Brotherhood's "marriage of convenience" with the authorities, which saw it "cooperating with the government to wrest leadership of the Muslim fundamentalist movement from more radical groups." Hence, while it was expected that a stronger Ikhwan would "tend to make Egypt less sympathetic to US goals in the Middle East," it was feared that a "weakened Brotherhood" would "strengthen Islamic extremists" who would be "even less accommodating to the United States" and thereby damage American interests.[182]

Again, such reasoning evinces a remarkable pessimism-cum-fatalism about the likely trajectory of Egypt and the Islamic "fundamentalist" movement. The overriding assumption seemed to be that predominantly Muslim countries must necessarily tend toward some kind of Islamic polity. The CIA was convinced that "time" favored the Brotherhood, with Egypt "steadily becoming a more religiously conservative society."[183] This perception led US officials to two key conclusions: first, that President Mubarak was (as he himself claimed) holding back a "fundamentalist" tide and it therefore made sense to give him full support; and, second, that in the face of that inevitable tide, the Brotherhood was, from a US perspective, the least worst option. The Americans were thus entirely comfortable with Mubarak's accommodation with the Ikhwan, effectively overlooking the long-term implications of this (as might arise from, say, the group's acknowledged attempts to "infiltrate" the Egyptian education system). Conciliation of the Brotherhood, under the aegis of the autocratic Mubarak, was seen as the best way to diminish the appeal of more "extreme" Islamist forces.

In keeping with this, American diplomats themselves took steps to build bridges to the Ikhwan. As described, the 1970s had seen a revival of direct dialogue between senior Muslim Brothers and US Embassy staff. This engagement was carried forward under Mubarak, presumably after something of a hiatus during the more repressive period either side of the Sadat assassination. Cables published by Wikileaks show that diplomats in Cairo established contact with the Muslim Brotherhood in the context of its post-1981 rehabilitation. A dispatch from September 1986, for example, reporting on the death earlier that year of general guide 'Umar al-Tilmisani stated that embassy officers had held "periodic talks with Talmasani [sic] in the two years preceding his death."[184] If this was indeed an accurate statement of the time frame involved, it would mean that discussions of some kind were under way, at least from the first months of 1984—and that these featured meetings between American officials and the most prominent members of the Ikhwan. Further missives likewise make clear that dialogue was ongoing from around that point. A cable dated March 1985 proves that al-Tilmisani was, by then, in conversation with US representatives; the manner of its reportage also implies this was not a new occurrence. An additional dispatch from the same period refers to other private diplomatic channels that existed with Brotherhood members.[185] Evidently, therefore, by 1984–1985, multiple lines of communication had been established.

The death of al-Tilmisani in May 1986 did not bring these contacts to an end. Rather, the embassy sent one of its officers to make an introductory call on the

new (and fourth) general guide, Muhammad Hamid Abu al-Nasr. On that occasion, the Americans seemed eager to smooth the path for further talks—in
the face of a more cautious approach from the Ikhwan. The embassy expressed
a desire to avoid setting the precedent of requesting permission for meetings
from the Egyptian government. By contrast, it was the Muslim Brothers who
reiterated the importance of gaining such written consent from the authorities.
Henceforth, while the Americans judged the group "keen to establish a dialogue
with the U.S. Embassy" (on the basis that it would "add to the MB's [Muslim
Brotherhood's] legitimacy"), it was also thought to be "very worried about
avoiding problems with the Ministry of the Interior."[186]

As such, this episode provided a window into both the dynamics of the US-
Ikhwan relationship and the Muslim Brothers' acute sense of their own vulnerability. The diplomats reckoned that Ikhwan leaders were distinctly lacking in
"self confidence and cohesion."[187] The shadow of the 1950s experience seemed
to hang over the Brothers and impacted their behavior. As in the previous decade, they were anxious to prevent a repeat of the "Evans" incident. Senior members of the Ikhwan were reluctant to do anything that might jeopardize the
space afforded to them by Mubarak.

Earlier in 1986, the regime had been shaken by major riots led by conscripts
of the Central Security Forces. During that unrest, in an echo of Black Saturday in 1952, there had been suggestions of Brotherhood involvement in
violence that targeted symbols of luxury and "foreign" influence.[188] In the
end, the government had been forced to call the regular army onto the streets
to restore law and order (just as had happened thirty-four years earlier)—an
exigency that plainly disturbed Mubarak. It was perhaps with this in mind
that the Brotherhood wished to stay out of anything that could further antagonize the regime. By contrast, it was the diplomats who were keen to preserve
channels to the Ikhwan. The aforementioned cable from September 1986 contained the assertion that, while the embassy had no desire to get caught in the
middle of a conflict between the Brotherhood and the government, it would
"continue to pursue contacts with the MB."[189]

Thereafter, there is a gap within the sources, but a cable from almost two
years later indicates that some form of communication was maintained. A
dispatch from Ambassador Frank Wisner in August 1988, for instance, recounted discussions with a "spokesman" from the Brotherhood. Once more,
the group was said to be "wary of any official contacts or involvement" with the US
government.[190] But this caution evidently did not prevent informal talks, which
persisted in a low-key fashion.[191]

For American officials, engagement of this kind was part of the ongoing effort to gain a better insight into the Brotherhood, its "bases of support," and its inner dynamics. Throughout this period, considerable energy was invested in attempts to understand the group. In May 1986, for example, a CIA research paper examined the "fundamentalist network" (comprising businesses, factories, hotels, and charities) that underpinned Brotherhood activities.[192] There was also analysis of the "increased factionalism" inside the Ikhwan. As mentioned earlier, this was something in which the diplomats routinely took an interest. Now there was a perception that the Brotherhood had become more fissiparous, principally because of the "moderate tactics" pursued by the leadership, which had generated opposition from more radical members. The "moderates" under 'Umar al-Tilmisani and Ma'mun al-Hudaybi (the son of the former general guide, Hasan), who favored an accommodation with the government, were thought to be the largest faction. Yet, it was reported that they had to contend with more militant voices like those of Mustafa Mashhur and Abbas al-Sissi. US officials believed that Brothers advocating a more confrontational approach had "defied the leadership's instructions and . . . maintained a covert military capability." Ultimately, the group was expected to cleave to the pragmatic and "moderate" path. Nevertheless, amid an escalating "power struggle," it was anticipated that Mashhur might succeed al-Tilmisani as leader.[193] As described, this did not happen, with Abu al-Nasr taking over instead, but American diplomats still speculated over the true locus of internal Brotherhood authority. One subsequent cable suggested that the new general guide was "more a figurehead than the real power."[194] The latter was thought to reside with his deputy, the influential Mashhur—an interpretation endorsed by scholarly accounts of the Ikhwan during this period.[195]

In mid-1987, US officials identified no fewer than "five distinct factions" within the Brotherhood. The most serious divide was said to pit the "wealthy old guard, represented by the current leadership," against "younger radical members," who accused their leaders of collaborating with the government in order to gain political power. If the Brotherhood's strategy failed to bring concrete benefits, the Americans predicted that the "radicals" would press their leaders to take "a harder line." "Although unlikely," it was not thought impossible that "impatient radicals" could target "old guard deputies for assassination."[196] Of course, such drastic prophecies were not realized; and in any case, the approach pursued by the Brotherhood's leaders did seem to deliver progress. The Ikhwan emerged even stronger from the April 1987 parliamentary elections, considered by US observers to have been "the most fairly conducted since the

1952 revolution." As they had done three years previously, Brotherhood candidates participated in the ballot unofficially, though this time as part of an alliance with the Socialist Labor and Liberal Parties.[197] Of the fifty-nine seats won by this coalition, some thirty-six were occupied by Ikhwan members.

In the parliament that followed, the Brothers showed themselves to be the most important segment of an otherwise divided and weak political opposition.[198] US officials guessed that all of this would encourage the Ikhwan to "pursue diligently but patiently their agenda to bring about an Islamic society." They also received reassurances from Brotherhood deputies that they wanted only gradual reform and to "employ Islam to bolster development, increase production, and provide people with adequate food, housing, and other necessities." On this basis, the diplomats concluded that the Ikhwan had decisively left behind its "history of unrelenting and sometimes violent opposition to the government."[199]

Even now, though, the occasional note of caution was sounded. The CIA warned that if the Brothers became frustrated, they might yet revert to a more aggressive strategy. Intelligence analysts recorded, too, the "strong misgivings" that "many in Egypt's ruling establishment" had expressed about the return of the Ikhwan. Mubarak himself, for instance, had apparently been surprised by their "strong showing" and was therefore anxious to find ways to prevent them and other opposition forces from "interfering with his exercise of power."[200] In addition, from a Western perspective, the mandarins were aware that many senior Muslim Brothers continued to articulate "extremely anti-American" views. There was a recognition that the group's outlook on the world was little altered, with "the West" still imagined to be inherently inimical to Islam.[201]

That notwithstanding, the diplomats *were* convinced of the clear distinction that should be drawn between the Brotherhood and openly militant Islamist groups such as al-Gamaʿa al-Islamiyya. Over the course of the 1980s, al-Gamaʿa had developed a presence within certain marginalized urban communities (including several in Cairo, such as Imbaba and Ain Shams). The movement had become increasingly assertive in its attempts to police public morality.[202] Further south, in rural provinces like Asyut, its activities had helped to stir sectarian tensions and violence. By the end of the decade, whether intentionally or not, al-Gamaʿa was set on a path of confrontation and jihad against the state.[203] As might be expected, American observers deemed movements of this ilk to be a far less appealing prospect than the Brotherhood. They were aware that tensions existed between the Gamaʿa and the Ikhwan based on "mutually hostile perceptions": the Brotherhood saw "the 'jihadists' as errant and ignorant youth at best"; while the latter charged the Brothers with "cowardice and 'forbidden' collaboration with the secular state."[204] Officials were also alert to the fact that Mubarak at that stage continued to differentiate between "radical or violent Islamic political activity" on the one hand and the Brotherhood on the other. While not entirely sanguine about the latter, the Egyptian president reportedly preferred "that the Brotherhood be permitted to operate openly," to "give the public an opportunity to hear—and reject—its agenda" and to "avoid driving the group underground" where it would be harder to monitor. Likewise, the Americans had inferred that the Ikhwan wanted to work "within the system" and deliberately eschewed "disruptive tactics" inside Egypt's parliament.[205] Again, much of this corresponds to established accounts of the Brotherhood's evolution in Egypt during the 1980s.[206] At the time, such analyses seemed to confirm the relatively benign nature of the Ikhwan and its project.

By July 1989, the underlying assumption of US diplomats was that the Brotherhood had been co-opted by the state and made more "manageable." Indeed, the threat posed by "revolutionary Islam in general" was said to have diminished—a striking (if understandable) misapprehension. The Ikhwan, they surmised, was targeting the Egyptian "political center" through moderate-sounding policies and an improved image. The manifesto produced by its candidates for elections to the Egyptian Shura Council (the upper house of Parliament) in 1989 was described as being "notably short on Islamic cant and long on . . . everyday, liberal, centrist bromides." The Brothers were even thought to be "by Egyptian standards . . . a model of both rhetorical and substantive moderation." Consequently, it was accepted that the Ikhwan had entered the "mainstream political arena [while] forswearing underground activity."[207] According to one embassy cable, the group was "defanged but rehabilitated"; it was seen as posing little threat to the Mubarak government (a "far more influential force"), despite comprising the "largest . . . and certainly the most cohesive bloc of opposition deputies in the [People's] Assembly."[208]

In arriving at such an assessment, there was a perception that the Ikhwan had been normalized to some degree within Egypt. As far as many officials were concerned, this outcome had to be set within a regional context that had seen Islam become a potent political factor over the previous two decades. Viewed from this perspective, the trajectory of the Egyptian Brotherhood appeared far more congenial than that of many other Islamist movements, including other branches of the Ikhwan.

The Brothers beyond Egypt

In 1982, a lengthy CIA research paper had described the Brotherhood as "the most important fundamentalist Islamic organization in the Arab World" and noted that the popularity of the group had soared amid the broader Islamic resurgence.[209] The memorandum observed further that the various chapters of the Brotherhood, while sharing a "basic ideology" and narrative of history, operated independently. As discussed in Chapter 6, these different branches had been founded during the 1940s and enjoyed divergent fortunes thereafter. In the 1960s, Sayyid Qutb had acknowledged the lack of coordination between members of the Ikhwan family, seeing this as an asset insofar as it allowed them to modulate their behavior according to local conditions.[210] Others, though, appear to have felt a more structured approach was required. The early 1980s saw attempts to harmonize the work of these autonomous branches—an endeavor to which Mustafa Mashhur was central. Mashhur was a firm believer in the internationalist character of the Brotherhood's *da'wa* (call), stressing that Muslims comprised "one community, one group and one nation." With this in mind, he urged his fellow Brothers to work for the "universality" of their message by cooperating in a framework of unity.[211]

As various scholars have identified, it was Mashhur who drove the creation of the Brotherhood's International Organisation (IO).[212] In July 1982, the "internal statute" of the IO was issued, establishing a "general guidance council" and "general shura council." The Egyptian general guide sat atop this new structure, which was committed to producing a long-term "Global Strategy for Islamic Politics."[213] The senior Brotherhood figure Ibrahim Munir has said that the goal was to facilitate shared work on the basis of "one goal, one ideology," while recognizing the "different policies and contexts" that existed. In addition, Kemal el-Helbawy has pointed out that the Brotherhood's IO operated alongside another "coordination council of Islamic movements" that was formed in the 1980s to reconcile the educational and political programs of the Brotherhood with those of like-minded Islamist groups such as the Jamaat-i-Islami and their Turkish counterparts. El-Helbawy served as secretary general of this second council, which also included Necmettin Erbakan, Khurshid Ahmad, and Hasan al-Turabi. The hope was that cooperation might foster a higher level of "intellectual unity."[214]

Despite such lofty ambitions, the reality proved rather disappointing. Coordination remained ad hoc and limited, and the Brotherhood's own IO was mostly a paper organization. In later years, according to Anas Altikriti, it functioned as little more than a "contact list," with annual or biannual meetings, but scarcely much activity in between times.[215] As a result, the national branches of the Brotherhood retained—and guarded—their independence.

The truth of this was only too apparent to American observers. In Syria, for example, the diplomats had watched the evolution of the local Ikhwan, which had moved in a more militant direction since the 1960s. After the Ba'th Party seized power in 1963, the Brothers had been repressed and their leader, Issam al-'Attar (who had succeeded Mustafa al-Siba'i), was forced into exile. As a result of this, the group had struggled to contain those demanding a more bellicose stance toward the authorities—many of whom, like Marwan Hadid, were inspired by the writings of Sayyid Qutb.[216] It was Hadid who led an abortive revolt in Hama in 1964; he then led a breakaway faction that styled itself the "Fighting Vanguard."[217] Inside the Ikhwan, disagreements over strategy intertwined with factional rivalry to divide the organization.[218] After a split in the early 1970s, and in the face of pressure for more direct action, the militant-minded 'Adnan Sa'd al-Din emerged as leader of the Syrian Brothers in 1975, and plans were laid for an armed campaign.[219] This was launched the following year with a series of attacks on Alawite targets tied to the regime of Hafez al-Assad, particularly in Hama and Damascus.[220] In 1979, a major assault on the Artillery School in Aleppo killed more than eighty military cadets and signaled a new upsurge in violence. A jihad was formally proclaimed and there were numerous further attacks.[221] The Jordanian Brotherhood lent critical cross-border logistical support to their Syrian counterparts.[222] In June 1980, the attempted assassination of Assad led to a retaliatory massacre in Tadmur prison in which more than a thousand Brothers may have been killed. The Damascus government also passed Law No. 49, which made membership of the Ikhwan punishable by death.[223] In this context, the Brotherhood's leaders opted to amalgamate with the Fighting Vanguard (now under 'Adnan 'Uqlah), forming an "Islamic Front"; the group then published a manifesto that called for "Islamic revolution."[224] In 1981, Brotherhood leader Sa'd al-Din declared that the regime was "not Muslim in any sense," but rather "blatant kufr [unbelief]." He averred that jihad had become "obligatory" on every individual Muslim, and advocated for a "general and comprehensive attack on the regime," to be led by the "Islamic Front" of Syria.[225]

In a familiar pattern, each side in this conflict accused the Western powers of supporting their opponents. Thus, Sa'd al-Din claimed that the Assad regime enjoyed the backing of the "enemies of Islam" and especially "all the major powers, the USA, the Soviet Union, France and China."[226] Washington, he stated, favored Assad because his regime prevented Syria from playing its "traditional role" as a "snake pit for American imperialism."[227] In addition, he argued that Assad effectively "played with Camp David" (that is, supported the Egyptian-Israeli peace process), even as he pretended to be against it. Like his Brotherhood counterparts in Cairo, Sa'd al-Din maintained that "Nothing disturbs Zionism as much as our movement" (and he went on to offer implicit endorsement of the assassination of Sadat, the man who had signed the "treacherous agreements").[228] The real struggle of the Islamic Front was said to be with Israel; the fight against the Assad regime was portrayed as a necessary step on the road to that more important jihad.[229]

The Syrian government itself, meanwhile, accused the United States and its allies of assisting the Brotherhood.[230] In an echo of Nasser's rhetoric from the 1960s, Assad labeled the Ikhwan an instrument of the "imperialist-Zionist conspiracy" to undermine Syrian "steadfastness" so as to facilitate American plans for Middle East peace.[231] The marked congruence of Washington's opposition to the Damascus regime with that of the Brotherhood spawned rumors of an alliance of convenience—yet as Raphaël Lefèvre affirms, the allegation that Sa'd al-Din had met US officials in Amman in 1982 has never been proven.[232]

Ultimately, the Brotherhood's Syrian jihad was crushed in 1982, after a large-scale uprising was attempted in Hama. On that occasion, the response of the Assad regime was unforgiving: the city was subjected to unrelenting artillery bombardment and perhaps as many as forty thousand people were killed. The scale of the violence was sufficient to break the rebellion. In the immediate aftermath, the Brotherhood's leaders pledged to escalate their "armed struggle" and proclaimed that Assad was "all but finished."[233] The reality was to prove somewhat different, however, as it was the Syrian Ikhwan that was effectively destroyed amid the "ashes of Hama."[234] In later years, US diplomats acknowledged that the Brotherhood had abandoned "armed struggle" and shifted to purely "political and organizational activity." While Assad continued to see the Ikhwan as a "significant threat," the Americans judged that the group now lacked a meaningful "organized political base" inside Syria. In their assessment, it was "irreconcilably split" and no longer capable of overturning the regime.[235]

While the Syrian branch of the Ikhwan therefore met a distinctly unhappy fate, the fortunes of their Sudanese counterparts fluctuated more wildly down to the end of the 1980s. Formed four decades previously, the Brotherhood in Sudan had struggled to establish itself at the popular level, with politics dominated by two parties that themselves deployed an Islamic discourse. Faced with these more powerful rivals, the local Ikhwan leader, Hasan al-Turabi, had openly admitted that theirs was an "elitist" movement.[236] Nonetheless, in 1965, al-Turabi created the Islamic Charter Front (ICF) in order to contest elections, and managed to win several seats in the Sudanese parliament.

After General Jaafar Nimeiri seized power in a 1969 coup, the ICF was dissolved and al-Turabi imprisoned. For the next eight years, the Brotherhood worked with the communists and other opposition activists against Nimeiri's regime.[237] The group was suspected of involvement in more than one attempted coup.[238] Yet the Sudanese Ikhwan then shifted position, in response to Nimeiri's 1977 "national reconciliation" initiative. By this time, the president had himself moved to the right politically and become a firm ally of Egypt's president Sadat. In many ways, Nimeiri sought to emulate the approach of his neighbor in trying to accommodate the Ikhwan. Hence, the group was allowed to resume activity; al-Turabi was released from prison; and in July 1978, he was given a senior position within the government. Al-Turabi was also appointed to a committee for Islamization and between 1979 and 1983 served as the country's attorney general. The Ikhwan leader justified this volte-face in his relations with Nimeiri by claiming that the Brotherhood would now "work from within" to achieve its aims. Though progress on "Islamisation" was initially slow, al-Turabi displayed a familiar Ikhwani pragmatism, as he insisted that the existing regime was better than any likely alternative.[239]

US diplomats, meanwhile, viewed the Nimeiri-Brotherhood alliance as one born of expediency, and they anticipated that the president stood ready to crackdown on the Brothers if they stepped out of line or resorted to terrorism in their "attempt to promote reactionary Islam."[240] Al-Turabi's support for the regime was understood to be similarly contingent—on a visible process of "Islamisation." Nimeiri's September 1983 decree to implement shari'a law was seen through this latter prism: as a move taken to placate the Brothers, who had begun to show signs of disaffection. For this reason alone, news of the initiative was received with some misgiving—even setting aside the upheavals it generated. American officials also worried that the more power that flowed to the Brotherhood, the more likely it was that Sudan would keep a "greater distance from the United States." Though not "openly hostile" to Washington, the Ikhwan was thought to be less inclined to uphold American interests, particularly in terms of military cooperation.[241]

In April 1985, Nimeiri was ousted in a bloodless coup led by his defense minister, who set up a transitional military council to oversee a return to democracy. The Brotherhood had backed Nimeiri's regime almost to the end.[242] Only in the last few months did relations between the two parties sour, leading al-Turabi to endorse the coup. In spite of this late shift of position, CIA analysts remarked that the Brothers had been damaged by their close association with Nimeiri. The Americans also felt that such transparent opportunism exposed the promiscuous nature of the Ikhwan's politics. US officials forecast that al-Turabi, who had created a new party called the National Islamic Front (NIF), would "seek support from almost any country likely to give him aid," tailoring his message according to the audience: "He will probably stress Islamic issues with Iran and Libya while underscoring the Front's moderate stance with Egypt, Saudi Arabia, and the United States." The Brotherhood leader was thought to favor "cordial relations" with the United States, even as he was convinced that Washington was "biased against Islamic fundamentalist groups." At the same time, he was said to be "anti-Communist," but someone who wanted a normalization of relations with the Soviet Union as part of a "nonaligned foreign policy."[243] In short, it seemed evident that American diplomats—conscious of these ambiguities—did not trust al-Turabi.

That skepticism hardened after parliamentary elections were held in April 1986 and the Brotherhood's NIF came in only third (with al-Turabi himself failing to win a seat). In the wake of these results, the CIA designated the group a "serious threat" to the stability of Sudan's new coalition government. The Ikhwan was said to retain a capacity to "stir up trouble on the streets" and it was also reckoned to be building an "armed militia." According to the CIA, the Brotherhood represented "the extreme religious right" in Sudanese politics and, while officially opposed to violence, its democratic bona fides were judged suspect.[244] This proved to be a discerning assessment. In 1989, General Omar al-Bashir overthrew the government in Khartoum, with support from Hasan al-Turabi and the NIF. Subsequently, the Brotherhood reprised its earlier policy of collaborating with a Sudanese military ruler.[245]

Elsewhere, the Jordanian brothers pursued a more stable course as they maintained the "accommodationist" strategy that they had followed since the 1950s. After King Hussein suspended parliament in 1967, the Ikhwan was permitted to remain active, albeit under more straitened conditions.[246] Its newspaper, al-Manar, was suspended in compliance with revised press laws (along with all other publications), and the Brothers had to be more careful than previously in their criticism of the government. Despite this, the Ikhwan soon adapted to the new environment.[247] US officials commented that it was "closer to a real political party than any other grouping" and it was believed that Prime Minister Wasfi al-Tell had encouraged the Ikhwan to participate in politics, "presumably because of its strong anti-Nasser sentiments."[248] As a consequence of its support for the monarchy, the king allowed the Brotherhood to operate in order to "counter leftist influence," even as he recognized that "fundamentalist Islam could pose a threat to his survival."[249] A tacit alliance thus endured. In September 1970, when King Hussein's position was challenged by the Palestine Liberation Organization (PLO), the Ikhwan counseled restraint on both sides, but ultimately stayed loyal to the regime. It was rewarded with the appointment of Ishaq al-Farhan—a known Brotherhood sympathizer—as minister of education and later, as minister of *awqaf*.[250] In 1980, the local leader of the group, ʿAbd al-Rahman Khalifa, told a journalist for the *Times* of London that the Brothers considered the Amman regime to be "an Islamic Government," albeit "not wholly Islamic." In Khalifa's opinion, they still had some way to go until the shariʿa was enforced properly, but he felt that this could only be achieved by working within the system.[251] Given Western backing for the kingdom, this stance was obviously to be welcomed in London and Washington.

In the years that followed, several observers did warn that the Jordanian Brotherhood was undergoing a slow process of both radicalization and "Palestinian-ization." In 1984, the Brotherhood took many unwares with its strong performance in by-elections held after the king decided to recall parliament (in abeyance since 1967). It also became more outspoken in its criticism of the government, demanding political reform within Jordan, to the obvious chagrin of the authorities.[252] King Hussein's decision to initiate a rapprochement with the Assad regime in 1985—and his attendant crackdown on Syrian Brothers resident in Amman—further stoked tensions.[253] The effect of all this was that friendly cooperation gave way to "uneasy coexistence."[254] And American diplomats began to worry about the capacity of the Ikhwan to destabilize their Jordanian allies.

Such concern was exacerbated by the fact that this evolution in Jordan paralleled the more obvious transformation of the Muslim Brothers in neighboring Palestine. Previously, the branch of the Ikhwan there had insisted that Israel could only be defeated and Muslim lands liberated *after* society had returned to Islam. With this in mind, the Brothers were inclined to shy away from violence and even politics more broadly, focusing instead on missionary work. As a result, the group had benefited from the de facto toleration extended toward it by the Israeli occupation authorities in the Gaza Strip and West Bank, who saw it as less pernicious than the PLO because of its noninvolvement in armed struggle. In this permissive environment, the Brotherhood was able to build a welfare and educational network that rooted it within Palestinian society. By the 1980s, though, certain leaders of the Ikhwan had come to the conclusion that the group needed to move beyond its politically quietist posture. This faction was strengthened by the growing unrest within the occupied territories, which exploded in 1987 with the outbreak of the first intifada. The response of the Brotherhood was to create a distinct organizational vehicle to pursue a policy of "jihad now" against the Israelis: the Islamic Resistance Movement, which became known simply as Hamas.[255]

Article 2 of the new group's charter stated clearly that it was "the branch of the Muslim Brotherhood in Palestine." Numerous other provisions emphasized Hamas's commitment to physical-force jihad as an inviolable principle. Article 13, for instance, stated that "the so-called peaceful solutions and international conferences to find a solution to the Palestinian problem" contradicted "the Islamic Resistance Movement's ideological position." The group was adamant that Palestine was "a religious Islamic endowment [waqf] for all Muslims until Resurrection Day." For this reason, Hamas avowed that it was "forbidden to relinquish it or any part of it or give it up or any part of it." There was said to be "no solution to the Palestinian problem except jihad," which was proclaimed an individual obligation on all Muslims to defeat the "Zionist enemy."[256] Beyond this, too, Hamas followed its "parent" movement in seeing Zionism as linked umbilically to a hostile "West," which was led by the United States and sought to control the Muslim world.[257] Inevitably, therefore, American officials were deeply perturbed by the character of Hamas and its politics. Though the movement was still small as the 1980s drew to a close, there was a fear that this kind of "Islamic fundamentalism" could play the role of "spoiler" in any attempt to achieve Israeli-Palestinian peace.[258]

It can be seen, then, that across the Arab world, the United States tended to be wary of the Brotherhood. It was noticeable that throughout the 1970s and 1980s, the Ikhwan and the United States often found themselves on the same side: in Syria, they were both opposed to the Assad regime; this was also true in Jordan, in Sudan during the later Nimeiri years, and of course, in Egypt, where both the Brothers and the Americans were (for the most part) supportive of the respective governments. Yet this shared outlook did not translate into especially warm bilateral relations. US diplomats never lost sight of the fact that the Brothers held to an ideological agenda that was, at its root, deeply problematic. They looked askance at the spread of "fundamentalism" and viewed the Ikhwan through that lens. Equally, most Brothers persisted in seeing "the West" as the embodiment of forces hostile to Islam—this, despite the emergence now of Ikhwan offshoots within a Western setting.

The New Muslim Brothers in the West

By the 1970s, the Brotherhood's international presence was not confined to the Middle East. Rather, the Ikhwan had followed those Muslim communities who had migrated to Europe and North America. Brigitte Marechal has emphasized that the arrival of the Brotherhood in the West was "above all the result of individual trajectories." There was, she contends, no specific strategic decision to relocate there.[259] Instead, the Ikhwan developed organically and, at least initially, informally, in parallel with new diasporic, transnational networks.[260] Yet, while this is broadly true, it is worth noting that since the mid-1940s, the Egyptian Brotherhood had become increasingly interested in Europe, with a subcommittee of its outreach section dedicated to that region.[261] Within the pages of the group's *al-Ikhwan al-Muslimun* newspaper, it was possible to read about the different manifestations of Islam in Europe—even about Poland's tiny Muslim community.[262] Moreover, in 1945, the Brotherhood had spoken of sending preachers to America to work within local Muslim communities "to bring [the people] to religion . . . to defend their existence and counter their enemies—especially as the Jews in America [had] a wide propaganda operation."[263]

Thereafter, Sa'id Ramadan's *al-Muslimun* magazine had carried pieces from Muslims based in Western countries, like the director of the London Islamic Centre. One such contribution discussed the "strong attraction" that the modern West exerted on students, given its science and power. Unsurprisingly, this was coupled to a searing critique of Western "egotism" and "stark materialism."[264] It was interesting, though, that Ramadan did occasionally offer a more nuanced picture. In a mid-1957 article, he recounted his own experiences of seeing a "side of America very different from [the] usual impression" that was associated with New York and "the tyranny of materialism and its bustle and disorder." In small-town Virginia, Ramadan said that he found a "humble and quiet" life in which religion played a major role and there was "a strong spiritual thirst." This world was itself thought to be under threat from the society of New York and other large cities.

From all this, Ramadan drew two main conclusions: first, that to understand the United States, it was important to look more closely at Christian activities; and, second, that there was an American public opinion distinct from the actions of "the West." He believed that this hidden America was covered by an "Iron Zionist Curtain." To counter this, Ramadan echoed the earlier call for Brotherhood preachers to emigrate to the United States. The job of these missionaries, he asserted, would be both to ensure that Muslims stayed true to their religion and also to challenge the Zionist narrative. At present, he surmised that the "dominant logic of American public opinion" was influenced by "strong Zionist propaganda" and the "activities of the Zionist network." However, Ramadan claimed to detect a "current of opposition" to this from non-Jewish Americans, which the Brotherhood should seek to exploit. Furthermore, he suggested that the only reason why many Americans had supported Israel in the past was out of the hope that this would "solve the Jewish problem" in the United States (by leading them to leave the country). Indeed, according to Ramadan, the American people were themselves among "the victims of Zionism." He argued they were not "the fundamental enemy that established Israel to destroy the Arabs . . . rather Zionism [was] the real enemy." On this basis, Ramadan felt that it might be possible to persuade Americans to set aside their backing for Israel (and he was much encouraged on this front by the 1956 victory of Eisenhower over Adlai Stevenson, as he deemed the latter an advocate for Zionism). What was required, Ramadan stated, was "sound leadership" and a "strong daʿwa" that would allow those Muslims resident in the United States to confront the "octopus of Zionism."[265] Clearly, he aspired for the Brotherhood to fill this gap.

Of course, none of this is to say that the subsequent arrival of the Ikhwan in Western countries on either side of the Atlantic was driven by some kind of over-arching master plan. Manifestly, it was not. Students and exiles served as the primary instruments of ad hoc Brotherhood expansion. Members of the group who went to study at British, European, and American universities simply took their beliefs and attachments with them, as well as their commitment to an activist mode of the faith. The result was the formation of new organizations that could serve as vehicles for the Brotherhood mission in a Western context.[266] Out of this emerged what Lorenzo Vidino has termed "the new Western Brothers." They subscribed to the gradualist, nonviolent strategy adopted by the Egyptian Ikhwan from the 1970s onward and founded an array of interwoven groups and alliances. Invariably, they eschewed any open or formal declaration of allegiance to the Brotherhood, but those involved possessed "historical, financial, personal, organisational and ideological ties to the Muslim Brotherhood and other Islamic revivalist movements."[267]

Certain figures from the Egyptian Ikhwan seem to have played a conspicuous role in this process. One such individual was the ever-busy Saʿid Ramadan. According to Ian Johnson, Ramadan first went to Europe in the mid-1950s, while acting as a Jordanian "ambassador at large."[268] (Though as Sayyid

Qutb's testament reveals, his behavior was a source of dissatisfaction to the Jordanian Ikhwan.)[269] In 1958, Ramadan settled in Geneva and from there completed a doctoral thesis at the University of Cologne under the title "Islamic Law: Its Scope and Equity."[270] Of perhaps greater significance was the fact that he worked hard to encourage Saudi proselytization, playing an important part in the aforementioned Muslim World League after 1962 (see above), and helping to establish connections between friendly governments, Brotherhood exiles, and "sister" groups like the Jamaat-i-Islami.[271] In particular, Ramadan persuaded the Saudi government and the country's wealthy elite to invest in numerous European Islamic centers, including his own at Geneva.[272]

Similarly, as Ian Johnson has detailed, Ramadan lent critical support to efforts to build a large mosque in Munich—quickly becoming the chairman of the project. Though he resigned from that post within a year, this was not before he had used it to make key contacts with a new generation of would-be Muslim leaders. Through this venture, for example, he became close friends with a young Syrian, Ali Ghaleb Himmat.[273] Together, these men ensured that the Munich mosque became, in the words of Johnson, a "beach-head" for the western expansion of the Ikhwan. In 1973, Himmat himself became chairman of that mosque—a position he held for the next three decades.[274] Throughout that period, the strong affinity between the institution and the Muslim Brotherhood was unmistakable. Between 1984 and 1987, for instance, Muhammad 'Akef, the future general guide of the Ikhwan, was employed as head imam at the mosque.[275] In the meantime, too, the governing committee of the Munich organization aspired to represent a wider community of Muslims. In 1963, it was renamed the Islamic Commission of South Germany. In 1982, it dropped the word "South," so as to claim the mantle of being a truly national body. By that time, it was at the center of a network of institutions and associations that shared its outlook. The Islamic Centre in Aachen, for example, was one such body—an establishment that included among its members the former head of the Syrian Ikhwan, Issam al-'Attar; and Kurshid Ahmad, a senior figure in the Jamaat-i-Islami.[276]

Beyond Germany, an array of institutions were created in other European countries under the guiding hand of men drawn from, or profoundly shaped by, the Muslim Brotherhood. In France, the Association of Islamic Students was formed in 1963, before evolving into the Union of Islamic Organisations of France (UOIF) two decades later.[277] Key leaders of the group were known adherents of the Brotherhood. In the United Kingdom, the Association of Muslim Students (AMS) that was founded in the late 1950s marked the first organizational presence there of the Ikhwan.[278] Its mission was to safeguard Arab and Muslim students from being "lost in the furnace of the lewd, materialist West," and also to spread the "Islamic da'wa" among the community.[279] The AMS was initially led by various individuals who had escaped from persecution in the Middle East—and especially from Egypt itself. During the "first mihna (ordeal)" of 1948–1949, a number of Brothers had fled to London via Libya.[280] Subsequent bouts of repression brought others to Britain. Hasan Dawh later recalled visiting the United Kingdom in 1963 and being surprised to find a fellow Brother there who had been arrested alongside him at the Roda Mosque in August 1954 (see Chapter 5). Dawh recorded that "many of the leaders of the Islamic movements in Europe and America had belonged at one time" to the Ikhwan.[281]

Within the UK, a qualitative shift in terms of Brotherhood structures came with the establishment of the Muslim Welfare House (MWH) in 1970.[282] This new body aimed to cater broadly to the social, educational, and welfare needs of the growing Muslim community in Britain.[283] Its founder, Dr. Ahmad al-Assal, was an Egyptian Muslim Brother and close associate of both Sheikh Ahmad al-Baquri and Sheikh Yusuf al-Qaradawi. He had studied with the latter at al-Azhar before moving to the United Kingdom, where he obtained his PhD in Islamic philosophy at Cambridge in 1968.[284] As he revealed in a later interview, al-Assal's activism rested on the firm conviction that the Muslim world was under threat from a plot to "Westernize" the *umma*. Typically, this plot was said to be both political—as demonstrated by the "conspiracy of Sykes-Picot" and "the implanting of the Zionist entity" in the region—and cultural-intellectual. Al-Assal suspected that the United States wished to separate Muslims from their religion (and, as an example, he pointed to the "true Furqan" project that attempted to reconcile Islam with Christianity). To combat this perceived threat, al-Assal committed himself to the *da'wa* and helped set up the MWH in order to inoculate the Muslim community in the UK against the lure of Western culture.[285]

In time, the MWH sought to fulfill two different functions: the first centered on preaching, as well as social, cultural, and educational activities; the second was to provide a place where Muslim students could live in an Islamic atmosphere.[286] With regard to the former, the MWH published a number of translations of eminent Islamist thinkers and also launched a media company (News and Media Ltd.), which then produced *Impact International: The Independent Muslim News Magazine* from 1971.[287] The magazine aimed to provide "the only comprehensive, stable and reliable source of news and commentary about the Muslim world" in English.[288] During the 1980s, it carried advertisements urging donations to the "Islamic struggle for the liberation of Afghanistan."[289] Within its pages, too, readers were encouraged to buy the literature available from a range of Islamist-influenced institutions such as the Muslim Educational Trust and the Islamic Foundation.[290]

As these advertisements reflected, the Brotherhood in the United Kingdom played an important role in nurturing links between the Ikhwan and their South Asian equivalents, the Jamaat-i-Islami of Abu a'la Mawdudi. To some extent, this was a marriage of necessity. The Brotherhood had always been a predominantly Arab organization, yet the vast majority of Muslims in Britain were from the Indian subcontinent. It therefore made sense to collaborate with an aligned movement like the JI, which already had a presence within the UK's diaspora communities. As Gilles Kepel has highlighted, groups like the above-mentioned Muslim Educational Trust and the Islamic Foundation were inspired by Mawdudism and sought "to perpetuate a specific Islamic cultural identity and to prevent the assimilation of Muslim children into British society."[291] To this end, they joined with other JI-influenced organizations such as the UK Islamic Mission (UKIM) that were involved in an array of community-based activities (in particular, running mosques and schools and engaging in social welfare). In 1963, UKIM leaders had also pushed forward the formation of the Federation of Student Islamic Societies (FOSIS).[292] From the beginning, this body served as an arena for the "cross-fertilisation" of ideas between Brotherhood and JI activists. FOSIS held a range of events, including an annual conference that regularly featured prominent Islamist speakers like Ghulam Azzam, Khurshid Ahmad, and Abu Hasan al-Nadvi.[293] Sa'id Ramadan was himself a regular visitor to FOSIS gatherings during the 1970s.[294]

By this time, London had emerged as a critical hub for international Islamist coordination and cooperation. In the summer of 1973, for instance, the city played host to "the first ever conference of Islamic Cultural Centres and Bodies," the aim of which was to "discuss the problems and prospects of the Islamic Da'wah [sic] in Europe." The Saudis played a decisive part in facilitating this gathering, which focused on education, training, and Islamic propagation in a European setting. At the close of proceedings, a seven-member Islamic Council for Europe (ICE) was established, including Khurshid Ahmad, Ghaleb Himmat, and Salem Azzam, who took the role of secretary general.[295] Azzam was another important figure active in this period—someone who personified the drawing together of different strands of the international Islamist movement. Born into a wealthy Egyptian family from just outside Cairo, he had become immersed in anti-British politics and seems to have enlisted in the Ikhwan in the 1940s. After being exiled from the country following the Free Officers' ascent to power, he joined the Saudi foreign service. According to his obituarist, he then "used his diplomatic position to bring together various members of the Islamist movement and mobilise support." In 1964, he moved to the United Kingdom and began to build contacts in the fledgling Muslim community there, all while working at the Saudi Embassy. From this vantage point, he helped drive the creation of the ICE in 1973.[296] (Subsequently, he was elevated to the rank of Saudi ambassador as "Minister Plenipotentiary and Envoy Extraordinary, Class I.")[297]

In 1976, Azzam was reelected unanimously for a second term as secretary general of the ICE. Among those also elevated to the board at that time was Sa'id Ramadan. At the organization's 1976 conference, Azzam provided a clear vision for future ICE activity. The purpose of the council, he said, was to act as the "supreme co-ordinating body of Muslim organisations in Europe." It was committed to working for the "proper projection of Islam in the West as well as for the welfare of the European Muslim communities." With this in mind, Azzam spoke of his desire to build "mosques and Islamic cultural centres in every city in Europe with a sizeable population." He also referred to the ICE's plans for an "extensive programme" of book publication. Finally, he announced the appointment of three commissions to deal with specific issues: the status of human rights in Islam; the problems faced by Muslim migrant workers; and Islamic education (the latter headed by Khurshid Ahmad).[298] Over the ensuing years, the ICE became a leading advocate of Islamic educational needs, calling for the founding of a network of Muslim schools (citing Catholic educational provision as a model to be emulated).[299] In addition, the ICE continued to work for the "causes of the Ummah," agitating against corruption, tyranny, and persecution in the Arab and Muslim world in places like Palestine, Kashmir, and Sudan. The overriding goal of this work, Azzam said, was "to protect and preserve their Islamic identity."[300]

The ICE was just one manifestation of a broader international network of institutions that flourished during this period, with the aim of spreading the "call" of the Ikhwan among the new Muslim communities developing *within* the West.[301] In keeping with their original focus, Western-based Brothers placed a premium on welfare and education, with a view to safeguarding the "true" form of the Islamic faith against the dangers posed by a secular civilization to which ever-greater numbers of Muslims were being exposed. To combat this menace, they engaged in *da'wa* to spread the ideas of men like Hasan al-Banna, Abu a'la Mawdudi, and other Islamist thinkers.

Among those most animated by the intellectual and cultural threat facing Muslims in the West was the Brotherhood exile, Yusuf al-Qaradawi, who was seen by many as the most important single custodian of the Brotherhood's ideology in the world.[302] Born in 1926, al-Qaradawi had joined the Ikhwan when just fourteen and quickly become an active member of the group.[303] He took part in the "war of the Canal Zone" against the British. He was also imprisoned in 1949 and twice more during Nasser's repression of the Ikhwan (between 1954 and 1956, and again in 1962). After the latter occasion, al-Qaradawi emigrated to Qatar, where he built a close relationship with Emir Sheikh Khalifa bin Hamad al-Thani. Along with other émigré Muslim Brothers, al-Qaradawi helped to develop the country's education system. At the same time, he cultivated his profile as a public intellectual of significant weight, propagating the message of the Brotherhood: that Islam was comprehensive and applicable to all spheres of life.[304] This was the theme of his first and most popular work, *The Lawful and the Prohibited in Islam*. The book gathered jurisprudence (*fiqh*) on a range of (mostly quotidian) issues, offering the reader a guide to living a truly Islamic life.[305] This emphasis on the all-encompassing character of Islam was to prove an enduring obsession for al-Qaradawi.

Simultaneously, he also positioned himself as the voice of a centrist, moderate Islam, emphasizing gradualism and his adherence to a "middle way" (*wasatiyya*) between the putative extremes of jihadism and secularism. In al-Qaradawi's rendering, this "middle way" captured the true essential purpose of the Brotherhood.[306] The group's *da'wa*, he contended, represented the "right path" and he urged an Islamic awakening, led by religiously informed scholars.[307] As might be anticipated, he warmly praised Islamist thinkers, both from within and external to the Brotherhood: al-Banna, al-Hudaybi, Ramadan, Mawdudi, al-Nadvi, and even Qutb. His tributes to the latter, however, were qualified by his criticism of the way that Qutb had drifted into extremism and made serious mistakes on the subject of jihad.[308]

Al-Qaradawi has asserted that he was thrice approached by the Egyptian Ikhwan and invited to become the group's general guide, the first such offer coming in the mid-1970s after the death of Hasan al-Hudaybi.[309] Each time, though, he declined, preferring to remain an autonomous figure, aligned with but distinct from the Ikhwan as an organization.[310] On one account, in 1988 al-Qaradawi officially asked the international organization of the Brotherhood to grant him exemption from formal membership (but he did not formally resign)—so he could secure his status as an independent symbol of the *umma* as a whole.[311]

From the early 1960s, al-Qaradawi became ever more interested in the experience of Muslim communities resident in the West.[312] He strongly endorsed the new wave of transnational Islamist activism that sought to connect with those communities. In 1977, for example, he was involved in the Lugano Conference, which as Lorenzo Vidino has described led to the creation of the International Institute of Islamic Thought (IIIT), a body that brought together leading Islamists and which was dedicated to the "Islamization of Social Sciences." The IIIT received major Saudi financial support, but in 1978 it relocated to the United States where its president, Professor Ismail al-Faruqi, was based.[313]

The United States was, by this time, home to its own network of Brotherhood-inspired organizations that had developed over the previous two decades.[314] Among documents that came to light during a 2007 court case was a history of the Ikhwan in North America written under the name of Zeid al-Noman, who was said to be an "official" inside the US branch of the Brotherhood.[315] According to this account, the message of the Ikhwan was carried to America by activists from individual Arab countries (such as Egypt, Jordan, and Iraq). These initially formed their own autonomous sub-groups, while also operating under the aegis of a Coordination Council. Eventually, however, a unified leadership structure emerged. Both Steve Merley and a *Chicago Tribune* investigation have identified this with the establishment of the Chicago-based "Cultural Society" in 1962. The choice of this seemingly innocuous name appears to have been part of a deliberate strategy—maintained in later years—to obscure the organization's connection to the Ikhwan.[316]

This was then followed by the formation in 1962–1963 of the Muslim Students Association of North America (MSA), based at the University of Illinois. Among the key founders of this group were three Iraqi Kurds: Ahmad al-Haj Totonji, previously educated in the United Kingdom, who went on to serve as MSA Chairman; Jamal al-Din Barzinji, another future MSA president; and Hisham Yahya al-Talib.[317] An additional figure of note was Ahmad al-Qadi—the son of one Egyptian Ikhwan leader, who was married to the daughter of another (Mahmud Abu al-Sa'ud was his father-in-law). A biography on an official Brotherhood website states that al-Qadi—a surgeon and formerly private doctor to King Faisal—joined the Brotherhood in the United States in 1968 and became treasurer of the movement there. In 1974, he and colleagues in the Cultural Society created the Missouri Benevolent Corporation in order to take forward the *da'wa*.[318] The efforts of al-Qadi, who was himself later president of the MSA, were praised by the subsequent general guide, Muhammad

'Akef, who said that he had "saved several generations of Muslim children from dissolving into the American life style, which elevates material values."[319]

More broadly, as the British magazine *Impact International* has outlined, the MSA was the creation of "young Muslim students" who came from an Ikhwan and Jamaat-i-Islami background.[320] The group publicly affirmed its commitment to three aims: to foster the individual "Islamic personality"; to develop "community level institutions"; and to promulgate a "common intellectual base at the international level." To this end, MSA activists were involved in a range of supplementary organizations, like the North American Investment Trust (NAIT).[321] This was registered in Indiana in the early 1970s under the control of al-Talib and Barzinji as a nonprofit company that would hold "investment property" on behalf of the MSA. It also helped to coordinate fund-raising from abroad, much of which came from Saudi Arabia and the Gulf.[322]

On top of this, graduating MSA activists helped to construct an array of professional-based bodies catering to their Islamic sensibilities: the Islamic Medical Association (IMA, 1967); the Association of Muslim Scientists and Engineers (AMSE, 1969); the Association of Muslim Social Scientists (AMSS, 1972); and the Muslim Arab Youths Association (MAYA, 1976). Again, many of the same faces featured among the founders of these groups. Barzinji, for example, was an initial member of both the AMSE and AMSS. The first president of the AMSS, meanwhile, was the aforementioned Ismail al-Faruqi of the IIIT, who spent eight years in the role.

This was the era that al-Noman's history called the "period of codification," which brought into being a more defined framework for Brotherhood activity across the United States. It was followed by a phase of growth and recruitment, but also controversies and disagreements. Out of this emerged a new leadership in 1978 that sought a more centralized structure and developed a slew of new organizational vehicles. Of particular importance among the latter was the Islamic Society of North America (ISNA), which was formed in 1982 as an umbrella body for all Muslim groups. It came to occupy a huge compound site purchased by NAIT at Plainfield, Indiana, and was home to a 500-person mosque, an 80,000-volume library, and a research facility.[323] *Impact International*'s report on ISNA's second annual convention in 1983 described the group's lineage in the following terms:

> A time soon came [for the MSA] when non-students outnumbered students; and permanent secretariat and permanent headquarters were also established. But those who were once part of MSA were now living *as* a community, or *in* a community.

Hence they needed centres and mosques; also educational centres. . . . So, such centres also began to spring up. Professionals felt the need of directing their knowledge to Islamic purposes: the results appeared in the form of the Association of Muslim Social Scientists (AMSS), Association of Muslim Scientists and Engineers (AMSE), and Islamic Medical Association (IMA). The anomalies in running such a loose, multi-dimensional set up under the banner of MSA were not difficult to see. After long deliberations it was decided to create a supra-organisation, an umbrella, for all single-purpose ventures: the Islamic Society of North America (ISNA), constituted of MSA, AMSS, AMIE, IMA and the newly created MCA (Muslim Communities Association).[324]

Dr. Ilyas Baynunus was elected president of ISNA at that second annual convention, an event judged to be something less than a success, with participation lower than expected. Nonetheless, the gathering did underline the international ties of the US Brotherhood network. Hence, Khurram Murad, the director general of the British-based Islamic Foundation and the vice president of the Pakistani Jamaat-i-Islami, delivered both the Friday sermon and a keynote address entitled "An Islamic Movement in Contemporary Times."[325]

Thereafter, the MSA held its own annual conference in parallel with the yearly ISNA convention. The former kept up its student-focused activities on a North American–wide basis—organizing events such as "Islam Awareness Week," which were designed to provide a regular focus for *da'wa* work.[326] In addition, the MSA mirrored the work of European groups like the ICE in putting much emphasis on translation projects, with the writings of Qutb, al-Banna, and Mawdudi published in English and distributed widely, often free of charge. This outpouring of Islamist literature dwarfed the production of more traditional or more modernist interpretations of the faith, ensuring that the views of the Brotherhood and likeminded movements were by far the most accessible.[327]

In line with this, too, the US-based Islamist movement was particularly active in efforts to promote the "Islamisation" of knowledge. Ismail al-Faruqi was a prominent advocate of this concept over several years. At the AMSS's second national seminar in 1973, for example, he urged the "Islamizing" of the social sciences as part of a drive to build an Islamic society based on proper values and ethics. At that same seminar, there was a strong focus on the importance of education. In a typical intervention, one of the speakers stressed the necessity of "de-educating the youth of the Western influences and re-educating them in Islamic tradition." It was suggested that this would facilitate the "Islamization of personality and [the] development of [a] practical attitude towards religion."[328] Such objectives were pursued both nationally and at the international level. As explained, the IIIT had been created in 1977, and after its move to the United States in 1978, it was to the forefront of this endeavor.[329] Its fourth international conference on the "Islamization of Knowledge," for instance, was held in August 1986, and focused on the behavioral sciences (anthropology, psychology, and sociology), as well as education.[330]

Beyond educative and intellectual work of this kind, perhaps the most important sphere of activity for the Brotherhood's US affiliates was the attempt to agitate around and raise funds for "Islamic" causes—especially Palestine. The Islamic Association of Palestine (IAP) was established in 1981 to improve this political and media lobbying effort.[331] According to analysts, the IAP was but one element in a chain of interlinked bodies overseen by the Brotherhood's "Central Committee for Palestinian Activism" in the United States.[332] Other important groups within this network were the United Association for Studies and Research (UASR) and the Occupied Land Fund (OLF, later the Holy Land Foundation).[333] Meanwhile, the future head of Hamas's political bureau, Musa Abu Marzook, was integral to the coordination of Palestinian support activities (until he was arrested and deported to Jordan in 1997).[334]

There is not the space here to explore the activities of each of these groups in detail, yet what the foregoing hopefully demonstrates is the extent to which the period from the 1960s onward saw the development of a network of Brotherhood-inspired institutions *within* the West. This "new" Brotherhood operated differently from the organization in the Middle East. Another of the most preeminent émigré figures, the Swiss-based Egyptian Brother Youssef Nada, recognized this when he stated that there was no "official registration" for becoming a member of the Ikhwan in the West. The movement there, he revealed, did not operate in the "classic way." Rather than being required to submit to an organizational hierarchy, a "Brother" in Europe and America was, said Nada, merely someone who adopted "our way" and accepted the ideas of the Ikhwan.[335] The Brotherhood in the West was thus "not a membership," it was "a way of thinking."[336]

To some degree, the absence of more openly acknowledged structures—and the attendant inclination for secrecy—was an inevitable consequence of the fact that many Brotherhood activists came to the West in exile, fleeing repression in their countries of birth. Many continued to fear the security services of Arab governments; it was therefore natural that they preferred to conceal their affiliations. Nevertheless, the reluctance of Brotherhood-inspired groups to concede their intellectual and organizational associations has been a cause of controversy for the movement. Perceptions of the conspiratorial and hidden nature of their activities have bred suspicion as to their methods and ultimate goals.[337] For this reason, some leaders, such as el-Helbawy, claim to have advocated for a more open declaration of allegiance to the Brotherhood.[338] Yet to date this has not been forthcoming.

The Ikhwan in the West focused on a range of objectives, of which the most pressing was the preservation of an explicitly Islamic form of identity, in order to secure the boundaries of the "Muslim community."[339] Crucially, as Lorenzo Vidino and others have highlighted, the evolution of the Brotherhood presence in Europe and North America also brought an intellectual shift, centered on a limited reinterpretation of "the West." In the past, this had been seen (to varying degrees of intensity), as "dar al-kufr (the house of unbelief)" or "dar al-jihad (the house of jihad)," juxtaposed to "dar al-Islam (the house of Islam)." The traditional opinion of Muslim scholars had been that any believing Muslim who found himself in the former should, as soon as possible, seek to return to the "dar al-Islam." In an era that saw the permanent settlement of Muslim communities in the West, such an outlook no longer seemed tenable. Scholars like al-Qaradawi, Faisal al-Mawlawi, and Sheikh Taha Jaber al-Alwani therefore led the way in reframing the West as "dar al-daʿwa (the house of mission)," "dar al-ʿahd (the house of treaty)," or even as part of "dar al-Islam" itself.[340] According to one senior leader, this meant that an entry visa could be construed as a "contract" by which Muslims were, for the first time, permitted to practice their faith—and enjoy indefinite terms of residence—in Western countries.[341] Arguments of this nature may seem rather rarefied, yet they were indicative of the fact that some Brothers had begun to ponder the challenges faced by Islam *within* the West; and this was the same process that helped generate the aforementioned network dedicated to advancing the mission of the Ikhwan.

Of course, the establishment of Brotherhood offshoots (and those of other Islamists) internal to the West posed new questions for governments. Previously, the Ikhwan had been a matter purely of foreign policy concern. To this was now added a set of issues that impinged squarely on the domestic affairs of countries like the United Kingdom and the United States. American officials were, to some degree, aware of these developments. They acknowledged the existence of a "network of Islamic centers in Europe, the United States," and beyond, which helped sustain the Ikhwan. "The foremost of these," it was noted, was "the center in Geneva, Switzerland, headed by Saʿid Ramadan."[342] In spite of this, as the 1980s drew to a close, it seemed evident that Western thinking about such matters remained in its infancy. It was only with the end of the Cold War that new intellectual space opened up in which to consider anew the role of Islam and the Islamists.

Conclusion

The two decades after 1970 were an era of change for the Muslim Brotherhood. In Egypt, the group resumed its activities, encouraged to do so by President Sadat, who sought to harness the forces of religion against his leftist and Nasserite rivals. The leaders of the Ikhwan were only too willing to play along, believing as they did that communism posed a major threat to Islam, while also recognizing the strategic benefits to be had from an alliance with the Egyptian state. When Sadat repositioned Egypt as an ally of the West, this led to a situation in which the Brothers again found themselves de facto on the same side as the United States in the Cold War. Events in Afghanistan seemed to confirm this convergence. Yet the potential implications of all this for Ikhwan-Western relations were never realized—not least because the Egyptian Brotherhood's views of "the West" remained largely unreconstructed. Moreover, Sadat's moves to make peace with Israel quickly served to poison the atmosphere and the Brothers were then caught up in the president's final repressive months.

At this time, American officials were increasingly conscious of the danger posed by "fundamentalism," given the broader Islamic revival in the Middle East. Groups like the Ikhwan were now considered analogous to other "fundamentalisms" around the world. Such perspectives were not confined merely to diplomats and officials; rather, they also permeated scholarly work. A classic example in this regard was the six-year study of the phenomenon directed by Martin E. Marty and R. Scott Appleby that was launched by the American Academy of Arts and Sciences in 1987.[343]

With regard to the Brotherhood specifically, the Western focus on "fundamentalism" cut two ways. On the one hand, it stimulated fears about "crisis cults" and anti-Western attitudes; on the other, the Brotherhood could be seen as the "moderate" manifestation of the wider fundamentalist wave. The latter assessment fostered the notion that this was a movement to be accommodated, so as to help contain more "extreme" elements. It was with this in mind that US officials were content to see Hosni Mubarak replicate Sadat's bargain with the Brotherhood after he took power in 1981. To many diplomats, the Ikhwan appeared to be the least worst option. Middle Eastern societies were believed to be inherently religious and conservative, and increasingly so. For this reason, the mandarins felt that the United States should engage the Brotherhood as a movement immeasurably preferable to more militant voices.

As the 1980s progressed, the Brotherhood appeared, in American eyes, to have been "defanged" and co-opted by the Mubarak government. Even so, US attitudes toward and diplomatic access to the Ikhwan in this period remained profoundly dependent on the course of the group's relationship with the Egyptian state. The Brothers were themselves anxious not to upset the authorities for fear of a renewed bout of repression. American officials, while keen for dialogue with the Ikhwan, did not want this to come at the expense of their strategic relationship with Cairo. Mubarak had shown his commitment to strengthening US-Egyptian ties, following the path set by Sadat to transform Egypt into a loyal ally of Washington. Consequently, the diplomats were quite prepared to defer to the wishes of the regime on the question of the Brotherhood.[344]

Beyond Egypt, policy makers were aware that local branches of the Ikhwan enjoyed some influence across the region, especially in Syria, Jordan, Palestine, and Sudan. However, their analysis of these various national Brotherhoods reflected the enduring ambiguity that surrounded the group as a whole. American diplomats were certainly troubled, for instance, by the character of the Ikhwan in Syria and Sudan. In Jordan, by contrast, it was recognized that the local Brotherhood had helped to sustain the ruling monarchy—though even there, doubts endured. The emergence of a newly militant vehicle for the Brothers in neighboring Palestine was an even greater cause for concern, and on the whole, it seems clear that the Ikhwan continued to be seen as a pernicious and problematic entity.

Finally, during the same period, Muslim Brothers developed a network of institutions within Europe and North America. Typically, these began life as bodies catering to a transient population of students and exiles; but as Muslims set down more permanent roots, the Brothers sought to give leadership to these communities, founding dedicated organizations to this end. The result was that the Ikhwan could now be seen as a genuinely global phenomenon with a presence inside the West, even as its center of gravity remained in the Middle East. Western reflections as to what this might mean had barely begun when the end of the Cold War ushered in a new era in which much greater focus would be placed on the question of Islam generally, and that of the Brotherhood in particular.

Eight   Blurred Lines and
New Debates

1989–2010

I N 2006, the political editor of the *New Statesman*, Martin
Bright, revealed that the British Foreign Office was considering whether to engage with the Egyptian Muslim
Brotherhood.[1] Bright's exposé was based on evidence leaked to him by a civil
service whistle-blower, which offered a fascinating glimpse into a debate then
under way inside Whitehall. That debate had begun a couple of years earlier,
when some officials had begun to argue that the United Kingdom should initiate dialogue with "moderate Islamist tendencies," so as to confront them "with
the realities of power and responsibilities."[2] To reflect on the matter further, a
roundtable on the subject of Islamism had then been held in Paris in June 2005,
where, according to Foreign Office records, the French scholar Olivier Roy had
made the case that attempts to contain and marginalize Islamist groups in the
Middle East had failed. Consequently, Roy asserted, "if the West was now interested in [political] reform . . . it had to consider how to integrate Islamists
into the political system." It was a line of reasoning that British mandarins found
persuasive. As one official commented subsequently, given that Islamists were
"often less corrupt than the generality of the societies in which they operate," it
might be worth "channelling aid resources through them, so long as sufficient
transparency" was "achievable."[3]

These ideas were expanded upon in a specially commissioned paper prepared
by Basil Eastwood, previously ambassador to Damascus, and Richard Murphy,

a former US assistant secretary of state for Near Eastern affairs. Eastwood and Murphy contended that the West should "talk to political Islamists in the Middle East," because they enjoyed substantial "popular support." They drew a parallel between Islamists and Europe's Christian Democrats to make the case for engagement with the former. In addition, Eastwood and Murphy suggested that "perhaps the best evidence" in favor of dialogue with groups like the Ikhwan was the fact they were "criticized bitterly by those Muslim extremists who do advocate violence to bring in authoritarian clerical rule."[4] Seen in this context, members of the Brotherhood were deemed "moderate" allies with whom Western governments could work, so as to defeat the threat from more radical voices.

It seems evident that such arguments were gaining traction in the summer of 2005. At that time, the Foreign Office paid new attention to the Brotherhood, examining its history and ideology. In one substantial memorandum, officials acknowledged that "the intellectual, political and geographical milieu" the Ikhwan inhabited meant there would "always be members who move[d] to more violent activity, even terrorism, in other organisations." Against this, though, the mandarins believed that the Brotherhood itself had abandoned violence and placed a "reduced emphasis on a quick route to power." In their judgment, the Ikhwan was an organization that favored "grassroots activism and preaching"; it was also described as "the largest and most effective opposition grouping in Egypt."[5] Overall, the conclusions appeared to reinforce the thesis that the British should develop ties with the Brothers.

However, there were voices raised against this proposition—among them the ambassador to Egypt, Sir Derek Plumbly, who advised against talking to Islamists "as a matter of principle." Plumbly warned there was "a tendency for us to be drawn towards engagement for its own sake; to confuse 'engaging with the Islamic world' with 'engaging with Islamism'; and to play down the very real downsides for us in terms of the Islamists' likely foreign and social policies."[6] In Plumbly's estimation, there were "relatively few contexts" in which the British would be able "significantly to influence the Islamists' agenda." Moreover, he feared the impact of any engagement on relations with the Egyptian government, and cautioned that it could actually make the task of achieving democratic reform more difficult: "The Brothers are the regime's red line. Mubarak has it is true been dragged over other red lines. But this one is existential, not just for the leadership but for the class from which they are drawn and for the vision of society to which they subscribe. They can be encouraged to accommodation on it. . . . But we need to judge the message very carefully. Pressing for legalisation of the Brothers as a political party, or dealing with them ourselves directly . . . will panic the horses . . . I am not keen actually to encourage the Brothers."[7]

Plumbly's views, however, did not carry the day—at least not in 2005. After the Muslim Brothers performed well in Egyptian parliamentary elections that year, the decision seems to have been taken to pursue a policy of deliberate engagement. The UK Embassy in Cairo now sought to "increase the frequency of working-level contacts with Muslim Brotherhood parliamentarians." The Foreign Office, too, undertook to urge others, including the European Union (EU) and the United States (who were already thought to be reviewing their position), to follow a similar policy. It was envisaged that this would not only improve their understanding of "political Islam," but also might help with "discouraging radicalisation."[8] It was against this backdrop of renewed contact with the Ikhwan that Bright published his account of internal Foreign Office discussions, which in fact echoed a wider debate that had been ongoing during the previous decade and a half.

The Islamist Dilemma

At the end of the Cold War, many observers of the Middle East had hoped that the region would benefit from the "third wave" of democratization.[9] Some talked about the "end of history" and envisaged an end to the ideological struggles that had overshadowed the twentieth century.[10] Others proclaimed a "new world order," in which liberal internationalist values would become dominant.[11] A less benign outlook posited that humanity might now witness a "clash of civilizations." Samuel Huntington's famous exposition on this theme imagined future conflicts along the "bloody borders" between Islam and the West.[12] There were suggestions too that parts of the Islamic world had rejected and were hostile to "western civilization."[13] In their most extreme form, such arguments were used to conjure up the notion of a "green peril" that had replaced Soviet communism as the new security threat.[14] Concerns of this kind were fed by the legacy of the Iranian revolution and fears about "Islamic fundamentalism," as well as various acts of terrorism that seemed, to many, to bear an Islamic imprint.[15]

Of critical importance to debates about prospects for democracy in the Middle East and the relationship between Islam and the West were questions about the future role of Islamist groups—and especially the degree to which they had embraced democracy.[16] Events in Algeria after 1989 were cited as a key "test case."

There, an attempt had been made to open up the political system after two decades of authoritarian postcolonial governance. Yet when elections were held, the group that seemed likely to triumph was the Islamist umbrella body, the Islamic Salvation Front (FIS). At municipal polls in 1990, the FIS was victorious and set about implementing its vision for a more pious nation at a local level—to the consternation of secular-minded Algerians. Anxieties peaked after the FIS won the first round of national parliamentary elections in December 1991. With the movement poised to confirm its political supremacy, the Algerian military intervened in January 1992 to annul the ballot and outlaw the FIS. What followed was a brutal civil war that lasted for much of the next decade and devastated Algerian society. Forced underground, the FIS split and many of its members broke away to form the Armed Islamic Group (GIA), an organization committed to violent jihad in pursuit of an Islamic state, which was responsible for some of the worst atrocities of the conflict.[17]

According to Fawaz Gerges, in the face of this turmoil, the George H. W. Bush administration initially mirrored the policy of the French government, adopting a "neutral" stance and refusing to condemn the Algerian generals. Of course, to many, this reluctance to criticize equated to tacit endorsement. In Gerges's assessment, this posture revealed underlying fears about Islamism and the concern that Algeria might become the "new Iran."[18] The FIS was openly anti-American, and apparently some within the first Bush administration felt that democracy should be sacrificed in order to prevent the Islamists from gaining power. Secretary of State James Baker, for example, later admitted that they preferred "a policy of excluding the radical fundamentalists in Algeria, even as we recognized that this was somewhat at odds with our support of democracy . . . because we felt that the radical fundamentalists' views were so adverse to what we believe in and what we support, and to what we understood the national interests of the United States to be."[19]

Thereafter, the Clinton administration developed a more balanced approach, seeking to bring about an accommodation that would secure the military-based regime, while simultaneously drawing in more "moderate" sections of the Islamist opposition. Assistant Secretary of State Robert Pelletreau was among those to propose that a solution to the Algerian crisis lay "not in a strategy of repression, but [in] one of inclusion and reconciliation."[20] There was, Pelletreau stated in 1994, "an urgent need for real political dialogue" in Algiers and a "broadening of political participation to encompass all political forces in the country, including Islamist leaders who reject terrorism."[21] Beyond this, some officials clearly worried that the existing government in Algeria was doomed to collapse and, remembering events in Tehran in 1979, were anxious not to be caught on the "wrong side of history." For all these reasons, back-channel communications were established between American representatives and the FIS. The group's spokesman, Anwar Haddam, was even permitted to reside in Washington.[22]

After Algeria's 1995 presidential elections, however, the United States shifted position again, as talks with the FIS were suspended and calls for reform shelved. The Clinton administration now publicly backed Liamine Zeroual's new government—and many concluded that Washington had reverted to a familiar policy of acquiescing to authoritarianism. Yet the situation was more complex than might appear at first glance. Though very much the creation of the military, Zeroual did also enjoy the support of Algeria's branch of the Muslim Brotherhood: the Movement of Society for Peace (Hamas) of Mahfoud Nahnah.[23] This has often been overlooked, with attention tending to focus instead on the FIS—but it is evident that US diplomats saw Nahnah and his party as the voice of "moderate Islamism" and a welcome alternative to more radical voices.[24] In this way, American policy toward Algeria was in part informed by an evolving perception of which Islamists might be suitable for inclusion within the political system.

More generally, meanwhile, the Algerian civil war helped galvanize a debate within both foreign policy making and academic circles about how to foster liberalization and democratization in an authoritarian regional context, in which "Islamic fundamentalists" (or advocates of "political Islam," as they were often called)[25] seemed likely to reap the benefits. Discussions about this "Islamist dilemma" were, in the words of one former official, polarized between "apostles of conciliation and of confrontation, between strategies of détente and containment."[26] "Confrontationists" were inclined to see all Islamist groups as inherently undemocratic and linked to terrorism. They disputed the notion that there were "moderate" Islamists. Martin Kramer, for example, underscored the "militant" ideological character of this creed and its "pursuit of power." He maintained that violence had been "the inescapable shadow of fundamentalist Islam from the outset." Furthermore, Kramer insisted that the "supposed line between 'revivalist' and 'extremist' [had] been difficult to draw." Instead, he identified a "common reservoir for ideas, strategies and support" that included a "resolute anti-Westernism, a vision of an authoritarian Islamic state, a propensity to violence, and a pan-Islamic urge."[27] In a similar vein, Daniel Pipes attested that there was no distinction between "good and bad fundamentalists." In his opinion, "while fundamentalist groups and ideologies" might differ in numerous ways, all of them were "inherently extremist and all despise[d] our civilization." Pipes thus argued that "the U.S. government ought in principle not to cooperate with fundamentalists, not encourage them, and not engage in dialogue with them." Rather than trying to "work with fundamentalists," he urged the United States to "stand up against them." Pipes favored policies that would support those governments fighting "fundamentalists" in places like Algeria.[28] And other advocates of this standpoint could be found at conservative think tanks such as the Washington Institute for Near East Peace (WINEP) and the Heritage Foundation.[29]

An entirely different view, by contrast, was advanced by "accommodationists" like John Esposito, who said it was a "knee-jerk reaction" to equate all Islamic fundamentalists with extremism or radicalism.[30] "A significant number, if not a majority" of such people, Esposito contended, were ready to "participate within the system," whereas only a "small minority" were extremist—by which he meant ready to use violence. He therefore counseled officials to draw "the critical distinction . . . between extremists and those that are more moderate or realistic or pragmatic." On the same basis, Esposito stated that the United States should distinguish between those movements that were "irreconcilably anti-American" and those that were not. The failure to do this, he suggested, led to "indiscriminate state repression" and this, in turn, risked radicalization and the transformation of "reformers into violent revolutionaries." Conversely, Esposito reckoned that liberalization drove a "wedge between the moderate mainstream and the radical fringe." The United States, he said, "should not in principle object to the implementation of Islamic law or involvement of Islamic activists in government."[31]

Esposito's arguments found echo in the writings of other scholars. Graham Fuller and Ian Lesser, for instance, agreed on the need for the United States to differentiate between Islamists, and advocated for the inclusion of moderates within the region's political systems. They believed, too, that such inclusion was likely to foster further moderation, whereas exclusion would produce radicalization.[32] By the same token, Geneive Abdo described the "moderate Islamists" as Egypt's "only hope for a brighter future."[33] In this way, as Gerges and Maria do Céu Pinto have explained, accommodationists were ready to accept the legitimacy of nonviolent Islamists and see them as authentic mainstream actors. To a greater or lesser extent, they considered Islamism to be a natural response to the socioeconomic and political grievances of the Middle East.[34] Consequently, they concluded that the United States should attempt to reach a modus vivendi with "moderate" Islamism rather than automatically seeking to exclude it across the region.

At the policy level, an accommodationist ethos was prevalent among officials such as Edward Djerejian, who served as assistant secretary of state
for Near Eastern affairs under both George H. W. Bush and Bill Clinton (and
who went on to become ambassador to Syria). In his memoirs, Djerejian commented that engagement with nonviolent Islamism was the best way to bolster
the forces of moderation against those of extremism and terrorism in the Middle
East.[35] Back in the early 1990s, Djerejian was somewhat less explicit in public,
but the underlying impulse was the same. In a famous Meridian House speech
in June 1992, he sought to highlight that the US government did "not view
Islam as the next 'ism' confronting the West or threatening world peace." The
Cold War was "not being replaced," Djerejian said, "with a new competition
between Islam and the West." In a section of his address under that same heading,
he discussed the rise of "a phenomenon variously labeled *political Islam*, the
Islamic revival, or *Islamic fundamentalism* [emphases in original]." Djerejian
observed that there were various "groups or movements seeking to reform their
societies in keeping with Islamic ideals," but he denied that these were controlled by any "monolithic or coordinated international effort." Moreover, he
pointedly acknowledged that some governments tolerated "Islamist political
activity." The United States, Djerejian intimated, did not oppose this. On the
contrary, he maintained that they wished to see an end to conflict, as well as
the attainment of social justice in the region and the broadening of political
participation. Implicit here was the idea that moderate Islamists could be part
of the equation, though Djerejian did qualify this by warning against "those
who would use the democratic process to come to power, only to destroy that
very process in order to retain power and political dominance." The United
States, he affirmed (borrowing Bernard Lewis's well-known aphorism), did "not
support 'one person, one vote, one time.'"[36]

On another occasion, Djerejian rejected "the notion that a renewed emphasis
on traditional values in many parts of the Islamic world must lead inevitably to
conflict with the West."[37] Again, this was balanced by the assertion that the
United States would have nothing to do with those who sought to "advance their
agenda through violence, through terror, through intolerance, through coercion"; Djerejian reiterated their firm opposition to "extremism." Crucially,
though, it was evident that he and his State Department colleagues defined that
extremism solely by reference to the use, or not, of violence. Assistant Secretary
of State Robert Pelletreau thus stated that only "groups or individuals" who
acted "outside the law" and espoused "violence to achieve their aims" were
"properly called extremists." He quoted John Esposito to make the point that it

was a mistake to imagine that "Islam equals Islamic fundamentalism equals extremism." The United States, Pelletreau averred, had no problem with Islam. He also stressed that "Islamic political groups" were "not monolithic": some chose to participate electorally, others resorted to violence. While he admitted that there were difficulties in "defining exactly where one category starts and another stops," Pelletreau went on to say that the United States should be discriminating in its approach, recognizing that not every Islamist was a terrorist. Moreover, he asserted that the growth in support for fundamentalism was attributable to the "lack of economic, educational and political opportunities" in the Middle East. That being the case, Pelletreau posited that the best way to defeat extremism was to address the conditions in which it thrived, while simultaneously seeking to draw in moderate Islamist voices.[38]

The arguments of Djerejian and Pelletreau stand as good exemplars of the accommodationist argument as it developed within officialdom. It is worth underlining the equivocal—and at times muddled—character of all this. Often, policy makers appeared to conflate "Islam" and "Islamism" (even as they talked about the need to delineate the two). Discussions about "fundamentalism" were invariably bound up with repeated assertions of the fact that the United States bore no ill will for Islam in general.[39] Though well intentioned, one effect of this was actually to help sustain the very confusion they wished to avoid. That aside, a recognizably accommodationist message could be identified: first, the mandarins were predisposed to see certain socioeconomic and political "root causes" as driving the success of Islamist groups; second, they drew a distinction between moderate and extremist forms of fundamentalism and were willing to engage with the former; and third, their definition of extremism centered primarily on the use of violence. Moderate groups were characterized by their abstinence from physical-force methods and their participation in the political process.

While such views unquestionably gained greater traction during the early 1990s, it would be a mistake to exaggerate the extent to which they drove policy. For one thing, other senior officials like National Security Adviser Anthony Lake continued to focus on the wider geopolitical picture and were less interested in the specific question of Islamism. In Lake's mind, the real challenge to the United States came from what he called the "reactionary backlash states" (Iran, Iraq, Sudan, and Libya). This being so, he favored giving support to "moderate" allied governments in the region, such as those of Saudi Arabia and Egypt.[40] These governments were often the ones most engaged in repressing the Islamist groups with whom accommodationists wished to work. But to "realists" such as Lake, this was a matter of only secondary importance. And even someone like Djerejian was clear that the United States appreciated the "friendship and cooperative relationship" that it had enjoyed with Cairo "for many years," praising President Mubarak for his "invaluable leadership" in the search for peace in the region.[41]

Fawaz Gerges is therefore correct to observe that while the Clinton administration made a "conscious attempt to accommodate and reach out to moderate Islamists" and set aside a "confrontationalist posture," it also stood by its authoritarian allies.[42] It is a verdict with which Robert Satloff would tend to agree, albeit from an entirely different perspective. In his assessment, US policy on Islamism remained sound during the 1990s, despite being articulated poorly. The effect of this, in Satloff's estimation, was that policy regularly appeared ambiguous. On the one hand, this reflected the very real disagreements that existed about how best to balance the desire for democratization with enduring concerns about the agenda of the Islamists. On the other, it also revealed a gap between abstract rhetoric that was accommodationist in tone, and a more complex picture that was often confrontationalist in practice, when it came to looking at particular Islamist groups.[43]

There is much to commend in this analysis. As will be demonstrated, the Islamist question was indeed tackled on a case-by-case basis and with a view to wider US interests. There was no comprehensive policy for how to deal with Islamism per se; neither was there any unified approach toward the different manifestations of the Ikhwan throughout the Arab world. It is therefore necessary to look at the detail of US-Brotherhood relations across the region.

The Muslim Brothers in the Arab World

During the 1980s, American officials had tracked the divergent paths taken by the various national chapters of the Brotherhood; this continued into the following decade. In Sudan, they watched as the Ikhwan effectively returned to power after Omar al-Bashir's military coup in 1989. The group's leader, Hasan al-Turabi, gained a prominent position as an adviser to Bashir and became speaker of the national assembly. Many saw him as the dominant influence over an unmistakably authoritarian government that reflected Brotherhood thinking. Non-Islamists were dismissed from public-sector posts and shari'a law was entrenched.[44] A program of "Islamization" was targeted at southern Sudan—a move that helped precipitate civil war.[45] And in the face of this, al-Turabi spoke openly of the need for jihad to secure the unity of the country and create an "Islamic state."[46]

Needless to say, US diplomats found little to cheer in all of this, especially as al-Turabi seemed determined to exert international influence in a way that stood starkly opposed to American interests. In April 1991, the Popular Arab Islamic Conference (PAIC) was held in Khartoum, attended by leading Islamists from around the world. The focus for this gathering, according to Martin Kramer, was the "repudiation of Western hegemony" after the Gulf War of 1990–1991. Resolutions were passed demanding that the West leave Iraq, end sanctions against Saddam Hussein, and abjure any further intervention in the Middle East. The conference also saw a fresh attempt to create an enduring secretariat for transnational Muslim organization, with al-Turabi now as secretary general.[47]

In subsequent years, too, the Sudanese government gave succor to more militant forces. As is well known, Khartoum played host to Osama bin Laden (even then singled out as an extremist and financier of terrorism) and built a network of alliances with other radical Islamists.[48] The United States labeled Sudan a leading state sponsor of terrorism and thought that its influence was "uniformly negative in terms of U.S. values and interests"—despite attempts by al-Turabi and his followers to present themselves, in conversations with US officials, as moderate Islamists. In the judgment of the diplomats, nowhere was the extremism of al-Turabi "more apparent" than in his "treatment of the West." The latter was routinely depicted as "ungodly, decadent, and hostile." The United States was portrayed as a "malevolent power bent on combating Islam."[49] Al-Turabi publicly exhorted Muslims to use religion "as a shield against the power of the West," which was accused of seeking to impose a "new world order." He was fiercely critical of the United States and Europe, pointing to the hypocrisy of their rhetoric about democracy and justice. Al-Turabi claimed that international law was "applied by the West only when it serve[d] western advantage." As American officials in Khartoum remarked, al-Turabi's overall message was certainly "not benign" and the "devil" he invariably attacked was the United States.[50] In addition, the Sudanese government was thought to be "indoctrinating its people" in a "radical, anti-western version of Islam" that it also wished to promote abroad.[51] Suffice it to say, this made for grim reading from Washington's perspective.

Elsewhere, the trajectory of the Jordanian Brotherhood, though perhaps not quite as startling as that of its Sudanese counterpart, was also a cause for Western disquiet. In 1989, after King Hussein had initiated his own process of liberalization, the Ikhwan won twenty-two seats in parliament, to which they could add the support of twelve independent Islamists (in an assembly of eighty). The result confirmed the emergence of the Brotherhood as a powerful and more assertive voice in Jordanian politics. Other successes followed in local and municipal council elections, as well as in contests for professional syndicates.[52] A senior Ikhwan leader, 'Abd al-Latif 'Arabiyyat, was chosen as speaker of parliament in November 1990. Soon afterward, five Brothers (and two independent Islamists) joined the government, taking ministerial portfolios that included health, justice, and education. As it happened, though, this political triumph proved short-lived. King Hussein dismissed the Ikhwan ministers in the wake of the Gulf War (in which they took a pro-Saddam stance) and then introduced new electoral laws designed to curtail Brotherhood influence. At fresh polls in 1993, the movement's recently formed political party, the Islamic Action Front (IAF), saw its representation reduced to sixteen seats. The group then opted to boycott the 1997 elections, as it struggled to cope with the "containment" strategy adopted by the regime vis-à-vis Islamism.[53] This did not, however, mean the abandonment of the Brothers' historic posture of seeking reform, rather than revolution; nor did they seek to dispute the legitimacy of the Hashemite monarchy.[54]

During this period, interestingly, US diplomats in Amman engaged directly with leaders of the Ikhwan to better understand the character of a movement that they still found frustratingly hard to decode. By one assessment, the Brothers were described in the usual fashion as divided between "hawks" and "doves."[55] An alternative reading posited three competing camps: "moderates," "political activists," and "religious conservatives." The same memorandum went on to express unease about a "rising tide of extremism within the MB [Muslim Brotherhood] rank and file."[56] Such internal pressures were thought, in part, to explain the group's more militant posture. It had been noted, for example, that the group's longtime leader, 'Abd al-Rahman Khalifa, had travelled to al-Turabi's PAIC in 1991. The outbreak of the first intifada in Palestine was assumed to have been a further agent of radicalization, with the Brotherhood a vociferous critic of the later Israeli-Palestinian peace process. As might be expected, its leaders were equally opposed to the 1994 peace treaty that the government in Amman signed with Israel. 'Abd al-Majid al-Dhunaybat, who succeeded Khalifa as controller general of the Jordanian Ikhwan, condemned the concessions made by King Hussein and pledged comprehensive resistance to the normalization of ties with Tel Aviv. Though he insisted that the Brotherhood had no desire for a clash with any Arab government, he simultaneously declared that they would refuse to allow their rulers to "play the role of guards watching over Zionist dreams."[57] This kind of threatening language made it almost inevitable that the relationship between the Brothers and the authorities would become more confrontational.

In parallel with this, the Jordanian Ikhwan appeared to move closer to the organizational vehicle of the Palestinian Brothers, Hamas.[58] There is not the space here to explore at length the history of that group, but its rejection of the US-led peace process was made manifest in the 1990s by a campaign of violence that included the use of suicide bombing against Israeli targets.[59] Against this background, US officials came to see Hamas as one of the major obstacles to the realization of American objectives in the Middle East. As far as many in Washington were concerned, it was the Islamist "terrorist" organization par excellence in this era.

With regard to Palestine, Jordan, and Sudan, then, the Brotherhood seemed to stand firmly against the thrust of US policy. The Syrian branch of the Ikhwan, by contrast, was in a somewhat different place politically. After the immolation of the movement in the early 1980s, the Brothers had slowly regrouped in exile and shown signs of a readiness to reevaluate their position.[60] Already prior to this, amid the armed struggle, there had been suggestions that the group could be open to a process of ideological revision, so as to incorporate elements of democratic discourse. One of its senior figures, Saʿid Hawwa for instance, had written a book on the Ikhwan in 1979 (*Introduction to the Preaching of the Muslim Brotherhood on the Occasion of the Fiftieth Anniversary of Its Foundation*), which appeared to embrace concepts like equal citizenship, freedom of expression, and the exercise of power based on consultation. The Brothers also spoke out against political repression and declared themselves to be in favor of civil liberties.[61] At the same time, spokesmen like Hawwa certainly did not disavow the message of al-Banna (nor that of Sayyid Qutb, which was seen as entirely complementary to the thinking of the Brotherhood's founder). In familiar fashion, Hawwa pictured a world divided between Islam and an aspiritual West; and he urged Muslims to "sacrifice their lives and properties" in the effort to build an "Islamic state" in which the shariʿa would be applied—and from there to "restore the international position of the Muslim Ummah" and, ultimately, revive the caliphate.[62] Hawwa stated too that while he preferred "the peaceful method" of practising *daʿwa,* if this route was blocked, then Muslims had the right to "think of other means"—words consonant with the fact that he had backed the revolt against Hafez al-Assad.[63]

It was only in the aftermath of their defeat that the process of reassessment seems to have accelerated within the Syrian Ikhwan. After the catastrophe of Hama, the Islamic Front dissolved and the Brotherhood distanced itself from the hard-line militants of the Fighting Vanguard. The Brothers gave notice that they would defer demands for the implementation of an Islamic state, and they sought a rapprochement with the secular and nationalist opposition to the Assad regime.[64] Countervailing tendencies remained; a prominent leader of the Syrian Ikhwan, 'Adnan Sa'd al-Din, was another of those present at the aforementioned Khartoum conference in 1991, for example. But increasingly, the evidence seemed to indicate that the Syrian Brothers were prepared to move beyond a traditional Islamist agenda. After 'Ali Sadr al-Din al-Bayanuni became their controller general in 1996 (moving to London in 2000 when he was exiled from Jordan), the Ikhwan went further in repudiating the use of violence, reiterating its commitment to a civil state, pluralism, and human rights. The Syrian Brothers also expressed a willingness to revisit their thinking about "the West"—to consider it in a less negative light.[65]

This apparent openness to self-critical reflection was paralleled by other groups and individuals associated with the Ikhwan. In Tunisia, the local branch of the Islamist movement was dominated by Rashid al-Ghannouchi, who rose to wider prominence at this time. Al-Ghannouchi's relationship with the Brotherhood might best be characterized as that of "independent affiliate." In the early 1980s, he had founded an organization called the "Islamic Movement Tendency" (MTI), which had struggled to establish itself under Tunisia's authoritarian regime. In 1989, after President Zine el-Abidine Ben Ali launched a tentative process of liberalization, the MTI renamed itself al-Nahda (Renaissance) and took part unofficially in elections. It surprised many by coming in second (to the ruling Democratic Constitutional Rally) and as a result, the authorities moved to suppress the party. This prompted al-Ghannouchi to flee into exile where he became a vocal exponent of "democracy" and "human rights." In his book *Civil Liberties in Islam* al-Ghannouchi announced his support for democratic reform and political pluralism, albeit within the overarching framework of shari'a.[66] In various public statements, meanwhile, he specifically criticized the theories of Samuel Huntington, saying that those who hoped to manufacture a "new threat" after the end of the Cold War were deliberately stirring fears of a "conflict between the West and Islam." The reality, al-Ghannouchi stated, was that Islam was "not a religion of aggression but a religion of peace and pluralism."

From a Western perspective, there seemed much here to admire. It should be noted, though, that in making his critique of Huntington, al-Ghannouchi offered his own civilization-based analysis, which juxtaposed "Islam" and "the West." Countries like Tunisia, he said, had been subjected to a Western-inspired "secular brand of theocracy." This had led to a "political conflict" between "oppressor" and "oppressed"—between "the people" and a "Mafia style oligarchy." Westernized elites, al-Ghannouchi argued, had failed to build successful modern states, and instead opted to repress the masses. Consequently, he asked governments in the West to change their policies and support those who were "victims" (including the Islamists) rather than staying "silent," as they had done in Algeria. This appeal to conscience was coupled with a pointed reference to Western self-interest. "Sooner or later," al-Ghannouchi opined, "the Islamists are coming." In Tunisia and elsewhere in the Arab world, he insisted, the atmosphere was boiling, "waiting for the right moment to explode." Al-Ghannouchi predicted that groups like al-Nahda would triumph eventually; he therefore urged Western governments to embrace the inevitable. He warned that if they remained indifferent or even dared to play a more "malicious role," then the "volcano" would erupt and "western democracies would find themselves incapable of anything to preserve their interests."[67] On this rather ominous basis, al-Ghannouchi called explicitly for "dialogue between Islam and the West."[68]

In itself, that plea for engagement was enough to satisfy many accommodationists, for whom al-Ghannouchi became the archetypal "moderate" Islamist.[69] On other issues, however, his outlook appeared rather unreconstructed. He too, for example, had traveled to al-Turabi's Popular Arab Islamic Conference. In addition, he was convinced that the "Zionist project" wanted to "inherit" the "umma" and also "the West itself." Zionism was labeled "an atheist movement" and the "continuation of colonialism;" confronting this threat was said to be the "main battle" facing contemporary Muslims. In al-Ghannouchi's judgment, the difficulty was that the Zionists were successfully "mobilizing the West" against Islam, distorting its image to secure Western aid for themselves. It was partly for this reason that he believed dialogue was so important, in order to draw Western countries away from the allure of Zionism.[70] And in this respect, al-Ghannouchi's talk about engagement was, to some degree, a function of his largely unreformed, conspiracy-laden perspective on the world.

This blend of progressive rhetoric with more traditional ideological positions was one that was typical of the Ikhwan and its affiliates in this period—and nowhere more so than in Egypt itself. The Brothers had reestablished themselves there over the course of the 1980s as a vibrant sociocultural presence with latent political strength. The success they had in rebuilding their organization was such that by the start of the new decade, the government of Hosni Mubarak seemed increasingly worried by the esteem in which the group was held. Anxieties over the ambitions of the Ikhwan were fueled by the "Salsabil affair" of 1992, when raids by the government's intelligence services on a computer company owned by the senior Brotherhood figure Khayrat al-Shater reportedly uncovered documents showing the extent of the movement's reach and planning.[71] In the wake of the episode, several leading Brothers (including al-Shater) were imprisoned.[72]

Regime nervousness about Islamism was doubtless exacerbated by the broader wave of radical militancy that swept Egypt in the early 1990s. This saw the waging of a bloody insurgency by the acolytes of al-Gamaʿa al-Islamiyya and al-Jihad.[73] Between 1990 and 1997, thousands of lives were lost and there were several high-profile attacks. In 1990, gunmen shot dead the speaker of parliament, Rifaʿt al-Mahgub; two years later, the high-profile secularist Farag Foda was assassinated in Cairo; in 1994, Naguib Mahfuz was seriously injured in a knife attack; and Mubarak himself was targeted for assassination in Addis Ababa in 1995. Against this background, the government clamped down on all forms of Islamism, including the Ikhwan.[74] New measures, for instance, were enacted to roll back the space that the Brothers had carved out for themselves within the professional syndicates. In 1993, Associations Law 100 was passed, giving the authorities the right to take over the syndicate boards. Subsequently, both the engineers' and lawyers' associations—that had become Brotherhood strongholds—were placed under state custodianship.[75] In the 1995 parliamentary elections, meanwhile, pressure from the security forces ensured that the Ikhwan won only a single seat (Essam al-Erian, who was soon expelled from the assembly).[76] That same year, a swath of Brotherhood activists were arrested. In the ensuing military trials, fifty-four leading members of the group were sentenced to prison terms of varying lengths.

In keeping with all of this, Mubarak openly renounced his earlier stance of trying to co-opt the Ikhwan as a bulwark against more radical forces. In one interview with the *New Yorker,* he declared Middle Eastern terrorism to be "a by-product of our own, illegal Muslim Brotherhood."[77] Moreover, he accused American officials of being "in contact with these terrorists from the Muslim Brotherhood."[78]

Within Western media, several voices were raised in opposition to Mubarak's shift in policy. The *Economist,* for example, urged the Egyptian president to "turn back." Mubarak would be better served, it was argued, by resuming the "well-tried strategy of isolating the militants by winning over the moderate majority of Islamists." On this interpretation, it was a mistake to adopt a policy by which "moderates and extremists . . . [were] lumped together." According to the *Economist,* it was not possible to "defeat a mass movement, rooted in disillusion with a corrupt governing class, by using undiscriminating force."[79] Elsewhere, Mary Ann Weaver, writing in the *New Yorker,* outlined an Islamist "revolution by stealth" and the loss of the "old multi-cultural, cosmopolitan, secular Egypt." In Weaver's assessment, the Mubarak regime was itself complicit in this social transformation—doing little to counter, and at times encouraging, the Islamization of the public sphere.[80] The truth of this, as far as Weaver was concerned, made repressive policies redundant. Needless to say, though, such criticism made little impact on the Egyptian authorities, who carried through the harder-line approach.

Faced with this, the Brotherhood's leaders attempted once more to distance themselves from the militants, condemning attacks on Western tourists and the state. The group publicly rejected "any form of violence and coercion."[81] Yet as earlier, the force of these words was undermined by the readiness of Ikhwan spokesmen to engage in de facto apologetics for the militants, as they accused the state of being "primarily responsible for the violence."[82]

During this same era, the Brotherhood also sought to burnish its own reformist credentials, making various pronouncements replete with references to democracy and pluralism.[83] In 1994, the group produced a document that for the first time talked explicitly about citizenship and freedom of expression.[84] Other position papers certified that the "legitimacy of any government in a Muslim country" rested fundamentally on "the people's choice, their consensus and their contentment with that government's performance." The Brothers asserted that the Islamic notion of "shura" was entirely compatible "with the democratic system in essence" and they upheld the validity of the electoral process. Again, however, closer inspection of those same statements raised questions as to how far the group had truly modified its views. Democracy, according to the Brotherhood, still had to function "within the framework" of the Islamic shari'a.[85] As Gudrun Krämer has pointed out, this left no room for "the enemies of Islam—the hypocrite, the skeptic and the atheist, the libertarian and the subversive." Manifestly, the Brothers were not ready to accommodate full-blown political pluralism.[86]

By the same token, a pamphlet on the "role of Muslim women in Islamic society" presented a vision of gender relations that might be summarized as "separate but equal." While at pains to emphasize the "equality" between men and women, this publication stressed that they had "different functions": the former had the "directing role" in the family, as the husband and provider; a woman, by contrast, was told to preserve her modesty, dignity, and virtue, by acting as a wife and mother.[87] In line with this, in 2000, the Brothers opposed modifications to Egypt's Personal Status Law, which were meant to increase the ability of women to attain a divorce.[88] On another occasion, Sheikh Muhammad al-Ghazali, the former Muslim Brother who remained close to the group, denounced the United Nations Population Conference, which sought to promote ideas about family planning and women's rights, as a conspiracy launched by "the enemies of Islam . . . to bring down [the faith] and destroy Islamic countries economically and morally."[89] Later, Brotherhood MPs also condemned changes to the Child Law, arguing that the US Agency for International Development (USAID) was behind the proposals in order to undermine "Islamic civilization" and replace it with a "western one that issues legislation in conflict with our culture and permits freedom in all things to children and homosexuals and makes women equal . . . in all things."[90]

Other incidents served to heighten doubts about the depth of the Brotherhood's ideological revisionism on a range of issues. In arguably the most famous example, in April 1997, the recently elevated general guide, Mustafa Mashhur, stated that Copts, rather than being seen as equal citizens, should pay the "jizya" (poll tax) required of them as "dhimmis" (protected non-Muslims). The comments brought down a wave of criticism, and while the Brotherhood tried to roll back Mashhur's position, the damage was done.[91] (It should be said too that Mashhur's conception of an Islamic state had long envisaged the attribution of distinct religious status, such as that of "dhimmi," and "apostate," to those who merited it; his public statements, in other words, were entirely consistent with his established views.)[92]

Moreover, it was telling that those who went furthest in their efforts to "modernize" the political discourse of the Ikhwan found themselves forced out of the group. In 1996, a cohort of Brotherhood activists led by Abu al-'Ala Madi and Essam Sultan announced the creation of the Wasat (Centre) Party, and made known their acceptance of popular sovereignty, political pluralism, equal citizenship, and human rights. They then attempted to obtain official permission to contest elections. To some, the initiative was suggestive of a new "post-Islamist" alternative, emerging from within the Brotherhood. Yet, the Wasat Party was caught between the hammer of Mubarak and the anvil of the Ikhwan leadership. The former refused to grant it a license to operate; the latter showed itself deeply hostile to the endeavor, which was seen as a serious breach of organizational discipline. Brotherhood members involved in the Wasat were ordered to withdraw or face expulsion. Madi and Sultan were among those who chose to resign and, thereafter, their fledgling party struggled to survive.[93]

Perhaps unsurprisingly, US diplomats trying to make sense of these developments appear to have grown more skeptical as to the extent of the Brotherhood's professed moderation. A 1997 dispatch, for instance, concluded that the group's articulation of the language of pluralism and human rights was merely "a tactical maneouver rather than a sincere conversion to democratic practices."[94] Two years later, the assessment from the Cairo Embassy was even more stark: "We should have no illusions. . . . In the MB ideology, God's law trumps democracy, and God's law as they interpret it does not favour heretical views, women's participation in government, or equal rights for non-Muslims in an Islamic society."[95]

Be that as it may, the diplomats were also aware of the Brotherhood's enduring relevance. Indeed, they claimed to detect a renewed "upsurge in [the] popularity" of the group, which was seen as the "antithesis of [a] corrupt, wealthy, secular ruling elite."[96] This was thought to explain the relative success of the Ikhwan in the 2000 parliamentary elections, when it saw seventeen of its members returned (as independents) to the People's Assembly.[97]

Against this backdrop, American officials continued to indulge in what might be called "kremlinology." Efforts were made to identify the most important figures and factions within the Brotherhood and the likely significance of their ascendancy or demotion. In 1991, for example, Mustafa Mashhur had been singled out as the representative of those Brothers who retained "at least a theoretical attachment" to militancy, due to both his background in the Special Apparatus and his attendance at radical Islamic conferences abroad in Pakistan and Sudan.[98] Ma'mun al-Hudaybi, by contrast—who had been the head of the Brotherhood's assembly delegation in the 1987–1990 parliament—was described as the "chief advocate of participation in Egypt's political game." The two men were said to be aspirants to the post of general guide and, in 1991, the embassy anticipated that "the battle for leadership" would soon be joined.[99] (In 1996, Mashhur succeeded Abu al-Nasr as the fifth general guide of the Ikhwan.)

Beyond this, a belief in the existence of definable factions inside the Brotherhood was the prism through which regime repression of the movement was analyzed. It was thus assumed that the mid-1990s crackdown had been targeted deliberately against the "mid-range cadre of the MB," while "leaving the septuagenarians in the leadership untouched." The effect of this, it was argued, had been to exacerbate generational tensions within the Ikhwan and to influence the internal debate over the future policy of the movement.

Subsequently, the Brothers were deemed to be struggling with serious internal divisions. As in Jordan, diplomats in Cairo perceived a split between "hawks" and "doves." In 2001, the hawks were said to be drawn more from the older generation and to include Mashhur *and* Ma'mun al-Hudaybi—the latter recategorized now, as compared to the earlier period, when he had been labelled a moderate. Younger figures placed amongst the hawks included 'Abd al-Mon'im Abu al-Futuh, Muhammad Habib and Muhammad Mahdi 'Akef (the future general guide). Given their subsequent histories, the labeling of people like Abu al-Futuh and Habib as "hawks" is especially striking, as many would come to see them as leading "reformists" within the Ikhwan, rather than hard-liners.[100] In 2001, though, the key "doves" were instead identified as Sayf al-Islam al-Banna, Essam al-Erian, Ibrahim al-Za'farani, and Salah 'Abd al-Maqsud—all of whom were classified as "politicians" rather than "revolutionaries." As had been the case a decade earlier, officials again imagined that the selection of the next general guide, to replace the then incumbent Mashhur, would "likely represent a struggle between the hawks and the doves."[101]

In arriving at such conclusions, it is evident that the embassy drew in part on the channels of communication that it had kept open with the Brotherhood. As mentioned, this had become a matter of some sensitivity for the Mubarak regime; and given the contemporary climate, it can fairly be surmised that interaction in the 1990s proved less easy and occurred less frequently than before. Nevertheless, as an "in-depth" investigation by the newspaper *Asharq al-Awsat* later revealed, American officials did continue to talk to the Ikhwan throughout the decade. Daniel Kurtzer, for example, who served as US ambassador to Egypt between 1997 and 2001 (and who had previously been deputy assistant secretary of state to Edward Djerejian), acknowledged meeting individuals affiliated with the Brotherhood while in office—albeit not in an official Brotherhood capacity.[102] The Wikileaks cables confirm his account. A 1997 dispatch from Cairo records meetings that had been held with Ikhwan figures who were also on the board of the journalists' syndicate. Officials remarked that the Brothers had been pushed on to the "defensive" by government repression, but equally that they retained support at all levels of society. In the assessment of the embassy, the Ikhwan was "down but not out."[103] A similar analysis was offered two years later, in a cable that described the Brotherhood as having been at a "low ebb" since 1995, even as it remained "Egypt's largest and best organized opposition movement." Furthermore, that same dispatch verified that the embassy was in contact with the Brotherhood via "influential MB members" who were "also active in the professional syndicates." In an undoubted reflection of the atmosphere at the time, the memorandum stated: "We call on them in their capacities as syndicate leaders, not as members of a banned group."[104]

Clearly, therefore, the embassy—as intimated by Kurtzer—no longer felt able to engage openly with Brotherhood members *as* Muslim Brothers. Whereas the 1980s had seen the existence of various channels for dialogue with senior Ikhwan leaders, up to and including the general guide, these were effectively now put on hold. In their place, the embassy was forced to rely on unofficial access to those known to be in the Brotherhood, but with diplomats meeting them solely on other pretexts. Such an arrangement appeared to suit both parties—with neither wishing to antagonize a Mubarak government that was obviously hostile to international engagement with the Ikhwan. In May 2001, an embassy dispatch stated that the Brotherhood was keen for dialogue, though often "hesitant" to speak with embassy officers. The explanation given for this was both "the MB code of secrecy concerning its deliberations and plans as well as Egyptian government angst with MB electoral activities and recent gains [a reference to the 2000 parliamentary election results]."[105] As a result, it can be seen that contacts between American officials and the Brotherhood, though enduring, were also tentative and overshadowed by fears over the possible reaction of the Cairo authorities.

For the United States, there is little doubt that its alliance with the Egyptian government trumped other concerns. As Jason Brownlee has highlighted, the rise of radical Islamist militancy in the post–Cold War period underlined the importance of Washington's strategic relationship with Mubarak. Under the Clinton administration in particular, bilateral ties had been reinforced by intelligence cooperation with 'Umar Sulayman, the head of the Egyptian General Intelligence Service (EGIS), a firm advocate in Cairo of partnership with the West. Under Sulayman's aegis, Egypt became an important hub for the rendition of suspected terrorists by the CIA. In the background too, the United States kept up its provision of large quantities of military aid to the Egyptian army.[106] And as a consequence, as the domestic tide in Egypt turned against the Ikhwan in the 1990s, US diplomats naturally sought to avoid any perception that they were violating Egyptian sovereignty by dealing too closely with a group deemed to be a threat to the country's national security.

Furthermore, from the US perspective, it did not go unnoticed that the Brotherhood remained ardently opposed to American policy across the Middle East.

The Salsabil documents, for instance, had shown that the outlook of the Ikhwan on international affairs was unchanged: the United States and "the West" were imagined to be hostile forces, conspiring against the embattled Muslim "umma."[107] Brotherhood leaders, such as the exiled Youssef Nada, accused the United States of having inherited the colonial mantle of the British in the region (though he did balance this by stating that Britain's Military Intelligence Section 6 [MI6] was the manipulating hand behind Ayatollah Khomeini's infamous 1989 fatwa against Salman Rushdie).[108] In a similar vein, the US-based Egyptian émigré Hasan Hathut argued that the Crusades had "evoked a religious furor" that still lingered over "the Western mind." "Ever since the Crusades," he said, "the relation between Europe and the Muslim world" had been "distorted by the colonialist agenda of the European countries." The most recent manifestation of this was held to be "neo-colonialism, led by the United States."[109] Hasan Dawh was another to echo these ideas, urging Muslims to "confront the new imperialism" in the world, which was reckoned to be under the control of international Zionism. (Nada offered a slightly different take, implying that it was, in fact, Washington that used Israel to maintain its control of the Middle East, rather than vice versa.)[110]

All of this was tied to an extremely negative view of globalization, which the Brotherhood tended to equate with Americanization and Western imperialism.[111] It was seen as indistinguishable from the "unbridled capitalism" that worked to the advantage of the West. According to Hathut, globalization threatened to destroy the "twin golden-egged geese of the world's resources and peoples of the Third World."[112] The democracies, he posited, were determined to "suck the blood of the third world and all the Muslims in it."[113] Likewise, in the judgment of Hasan Dawh, the present day goals of the imperialists in the Middle East were the same as they had always been: to divide the Arabs, cleanse the Palestinians (from their land), and steal the riches of the region.[114]

Many Brothers attached particular importance to the 1991 Gulf War. They had preferred that the Arabs solve the crisis generated by Iraq's invasion of Kuwait themselves. Western involvement was seen as an example of neo-imperialism driven by a desire to control and exploit the Middle East.[115] As the US-led coalition launched its campaign to dislodge Saddam Hussein's forces from Kuwait, various branches of the Ikhwan called for violent jihad against Western troops.[116] Though not endorsing Hussein's actions, they vehemently opposed any external intervention and instead spoke of the need for Muslim and Arab unity. In so doing, they made the war an issue of domestic contention in Egypt, implicitly critiquing Mubarak's decision to act as a full partner to the United

States—though the Brothers balked at challenging the regime head-on.[117] The senior Ikhwan leader, Ma'mun al-Hudaybi, declared that it would be "better that we struggle for 20 years to free Kuwait, than for America to intervene or for a foreign foot to be set on Arab soil."[118] Indeed, to some Brothers, the situation had been manufactured for precisely that reason, with Saddam said to be in "the clutches of American intelligence," who wished to engineer an excuse for US intervention.[119] The general guide, Abu al-Nasr, described the war as a "malicious plot" to destroy Iraq's military capabilities, with the United States accused of playing a "sly, destructive role in our Arab region."[120] (The irony, as Hossam Tammam observed, was that rather than being a driver of unity, this conflict provoked the first great schism in the International Organisation of the Brotherhood itself, as the Gulf-based branches of the Ikhwan and especially the Kuwaiti chapter were content to see Iraqi forces defeated, whereas their comrades across the wider region were not.)[121]

As Maha Azzam has explained, the Ikhwan took President Bush at his word when he linked the Gulf War to the emergence of a "new world order." To the Brothers, this meant the United States was intent on reshaping the Middle East to ensure that Muslims were kept weak and subject to Western, and Israeli, hegemony. (The destruction of Iraq's military was seen as merely the latest effort to "neutralize" Israel's enemies.)[122] Ma'mun al-Hudaybi thus condemned American "arrogance" in the region and claimed that the United States was engaged in aggression against Islam and Muslims.[123] As a symbol of their rejection of the "new world order," the Egyptian Brothers sent al-Hudaybi, together with Mustafa Mashhur, to represent them at al-Turabi's Popular Arab Islamic Conference.

Moreover, as might have been anticipated, the Brotherhood was also staunchly opposed to the Israeli-Palestinian peace process that gathered momentum in this period. In October 1991, members of the Egyptian Ikhwan joined with other Islamists from across the Sunni-Shi'a divide (Palestinian Islamic Jihad, Hizballah, Hamas, the Jordanian Brothers, the Afghan Jamaat-i-Islami) for the International Conference to Support the Islamic Revolution of the People of Palestine in Tehran. This event demanded a renewal of jihad in order to combat all peace initiatives.[124] In line with this, Kemal el-Helbawy, the Brotherhood's representative in the West, wrote an open letter to Yasser Arafat, asking him to abandon the Oslo accords, which gave the "enemy . . . powers it did not deserve" while leaving the "dreams and hopes of the Palestinian people badly bruised and unfulfilled." In the name of the Ikhwan, el-Helbawy begged Arafat to "resume" a "programme of active struggle . . . based on strength, sacrifice, wisdom and affiliation to the Arab nation." "We believe," el-Helbawy declared, "it is the legitimate right of Hamas and Al-Jihad al-Islami, and all other Palestinian forces to engage in the struggle for freedom with all lawful means at their disposal."[125] Ma'mun al-Hudaybi was similarly adamant that the Brotherhood did not think negotiations could deliver anything positive for the Palestinians, but would instead lead only to "surrender." For this reason, he said the Palestine Liberation Organization (PLO) should stand "in one rank with Hamas" and wage jihad. Al-Hudaybi also voiced support for Hamas's "martyrdom operations," saying that all religious scholars agreed they were legitimate.[126] His colleague Hasan Dawh even expressed hope that in the coming years they would see "a huge grave filled with Jews, upon which would be written 'here was Israel, which was buried by the hands of the Israelis themselves.'"[127]

Other Brotherhood-affiliated ideologues such as Yusuf al-Qaradawi echoed the condemnation of the peace process and urged active "resistance" to Israeli occupation. The Oslo agreement was repudiated as a product of iniquitous Western—particularly American—power in the "new world order."[128] And all branches of the Ikhwan lent their support to Hamas's violent campaign to undermine the peace process.

Elsewhere, too, the Brothers sought to promote other "Muslim" causes such as the wars in Bosnia, Kosovo, and Kashmir. Ikhwan leaders lamented the relative lack of activism within the Islamic world on these issues (a failing that was blamed on the "shackles" that governments had imposed on their people).[129] Each conflict was, in its own way, seen as symptomatic of a world in which Islam was under attack from its "enemies," especially "the West." And yet this uncompromising, dualistic vision sat rather awkwardly alongside the fact that the Brotherhood itself was, by this time, very much present in a Western setting.

The Brotherhood in the West

In the same way that the end of the Cold War had provoked much deliberation about what would come next internationally, so it also encouraged fresh ideas about the challenges facing Western societies domestically. This reinforced a change already under way, by which concepts like multiculturalism were subject to criticism and reassessment. An important moment in this regard was the "Rushdie Affair" of 1988–1989, which Kenan Malik labeled the "first major cultural conflict" that called into question previously accepted notions of "social integration."[130] The episode put the issue of "Islam" on the British political

agenda in an unprecedented way. What is more, events in the United Kingdom
were paralleled elsewhere in Europe—for example by the debate that erupted
in France over whether Muslim schoolgirls might be permitted to wear the
veil.[131] Controversies of this kind fostered an increased interest in Islam
among governments and publics alike, and simultaneously mobilized Islamist
groups, allowing them to gain greater traction than previously within Muslim
communities.[132]

Subsequently, the 1990s was an era of change for the Brotherhood-aligned
movements in the West, with the creation of an array of new organizational
structures. In the United Kingdom, this was signaled at the very start of the
decade with the formation of the Islamic Society of Britain (ISB). Brigitte
Marechal has described this as emerging from a rather "chaotic partnership"
between the Muslim Brotherhood and former members of the Jamaat-i-Islami.
The British government's 2015 review of the Ikhwan offered a similar evaluation,
stating that the ISB was decisively "shaped" by the Brothers.[133] Drawing on
this heritage, the group sought to articulate the needs of a younger generation,
born and raised entirely in Britain. It had an active youth wing, Young Muslims UK (YMUK), and also published its own magazine, *Trends*.[134] Set in context, the ISB was the product of a particular moment in the evolution of Muslim
communities within the West. Analogous organizations were established across
Europe, such as the Young Muslims of France (*Jeunes Musulmans de France*,
or JMF).

In Britain, the exiled Egyptian Brother Kemal el-Helbawy again proved to
be a seminal figure in the process of institutional innovation.[135] After coming
to the United Kingdom, el-Helbawy had acted for a time as public relations
officer to the Brotherhood-inspired Muslim Welfare House (MWH), while
also being designated as the official spokesperson of the Ikhwan in the West.
Under his influence, London became a critical base for Brotherhood activity
outside Egypt. According to Marechal, their newspaper, *al-Da'wa*, was published
in the British capital from the 1980s down to 2002. In the 1990s, an additional London-based organ entered circulation: *Risalat al-Ikhwan*, a weekly
bulletin issued by the Brotherhood's guidance council.[136] After el-Helbawy resigned as spokesperson in 1997, he was succeeded by Ibrahim Munir, a member
of the Brotherhood's guidance council and secretary general of the group's
International Organization, who was also resident in London.[137]

Despite stepping down from his post, el-Helbawy remained a member of
the Ikhwan and became more focused on trying to build up a network of
Brotherhood-inspired institutions in the West.[138] Perhaps the most important

of these, from the Ikhwan perspective, was the Muslim Association of Britain (MAB). The government's 2015 review asserted that the Brotherhood "dominated" the MAB, which was seen by many as the de facto branch of the movement within the United Kingdom.[139] El-Helbawy was among the founders and served as the first president of the group until 1999. The MAB brought together Muslim Brotherhood members and sympathizers from a range of ethnic backgrounds. The former head of the Iraqi Brotherhood, Osama al-Tikriti (in exile in Britain since 1970), was a member of the group, as was his son Anas. Also involved was another prominent Iraqi émigré, Ahmad al-Rawi, who later became president of the MAB.

Two other individuals of note within the MAB were the Palestinian activists Azzam al-Tamimi and Muhammad Sawalha.[140] Al-Tamimi had lived previously in Jordan, where he was close to the local Ikhwan in the 1990s. He has publicly stated that he belongs to the "affiliates of the Muslim Brotherhood school of thought."[141] A self-described "Islamist," al-Tamimi gained notoriety in 2004, when he told the British Broadcasting Corporation (BBC) that he would be prepared to carry out a suicide bombing against Israel if the opportunity arose.[142] More generally, he was an outspoken critic of the Israeli-Palestinian peace process, referring to the Oslo accords as "an aberration or deviation from what hitherto had been a unified Palestinian position vis-à-vis the Israeli occupation of Palestine."[143]

In holding to such views, al-Tamimi had much in common with Muhammad Sawalha. A resident of the United Kingdom since the 1990s, Sawalha was said by the BBC to be a "fugitive Hamas commander" and perhaps "the most influential Muslim Brother in Britain today."[144] Sawalha himself has denied having ever been a "military commander of Hamas," but confirmed that he was "proud" of his "service to the oppressed people of Palestine" and supported their "legitimate struggle."[145] Furthermore, one of his colleagues has stated that he was formerly a "leading figure" in Hamas.[146] A grand jury indictment in the United States in 2003, which focused on Hamas fund-raising activities, identified Sawalha as a coconspirator.[147] Similarly, during the Holy Land Foundation trial of 2007, he was listed as an unindicted coconspirator and labeled a "member of the US Muslim Brotherhood's Palestine Committee."[148]

Within the United Kingdom, Sawalha acted in a number of roles within the Brotherhood-aligned firmament. In 2005, for instance, he was simultaneously a trustee of the Muslim Welfare House, a trustee of the reopened North London Central Mosque (see below), and a Director of the Muslim Association of Britain (a post he had held since 1999).[149] Islam Online also described him as an "official to the political committee of the international organization of the Ikhwan in Britain."[150]

The fact that the MAB was created and run by men such as Sawalha revealed much about the group's ideological center of gravity. One of the original members of the MAB, Anas Altikriti, has acknowledged that "most, if not the majority of founders" were either members of the Brotherhood, or sympathizers.[151] The declared aim of the MAB was to "fill in the gap" in terms of Islamic *da'wa* work in Britain, "where the call for a comprehensive Islam that encompasses all aspects of life" was said to be lacking. Intellectually, the group publicly traced its origins to the "pioneering work of Imam ash-Shaheed Hassan al Banna" and his efforts to "call people back to the true teachings of Islam." Abul A'la Mawdudi of the Jamaat-i-Islami was also singled out for praise: "His efforts were at the peak of Islamic intellectualism, calling for the widespread implementation of Islam as a way of life." The MAB presented itself as an organization committed to carrying forward the legacy of groups like the Ikhwan and the Jamaat.[152] Altikriti freely recognized his support for the "fundamental ideals of the Muslim Brotherhood," which he described as providing a "coherent set of values" and guide for "modern life."[153]

The MAB listed its practical goals as: spreading Islamic teachings and culture; strengthening the integrity of the Muslim community; promoting Islamic education; making Muslims aware of their duty toward society; encouraging Muslims to take an active role in efforts to solve their problems; building connections with other faiths; and improving relations between the Muslim community and British institutions, as well as with the broader Muslim world.[154] In line with this last objective, leaders of the MAB were closely involved in the formation—also in 1997—of the Muslim Council of Britain (MCB). This umbrella body aimed to speak as *the* voice of the British Muslim community and brought together different strands of Islamist and non-Islamist activity within the United Kingdom. As the British government later observed, the Muslim Brotherhood "played an important role in establishing and then running the Muslim Council of Britain," once more operating alongside individuals associated with the Jamaat-i-Islami.[155]

The MAB, meanwhile, devoted much of its energy to arranging conferences, seminars, study circles, and summer camps.[156] In addition, it published a monthly newsletter, the *New Dawn*. A typical edition from late 2000 was illustrative of the ideological universe that the group inhabited. It contained articles about Islamic history (the capture of Jerusalem by Omar bin al-Khattab); Palestine (where the "occupying power" was said to be destroying mosques); the obligatory character of *da'wa;* and news on recent Islamic legal rulings. There was also a short piece that, without context or explanation, cited the purported comments of Benjamin Franklin on "the Jewish Threat" to American society. Those comments were in fact an infamous anti-Semitic hoax, thought to have been forged by an American Nazi outfit in the 1930s. Despite this, the MAB quoted Franklin to the effect that "we must protect this young nation from an insidious influence and impenetration [*sic*]. That menace, gentlemen, is the Jew. In whatever country Jews have settled in great numbers, they have lowered its moral tone, depreciated its commercial integrity, have segregated themselves, and have not been assimilated, have sneered at and tried to undermine the Christian religion . . . they are Vampires and Vampires do not live on Vampires. . . . They must sub-sit [*sic*] on Christians and other peoples not of their race."[157] Naturally, the appearance of such an article raised questions about the extent to which the MAB was facilitating the spread of anti-Semitic tropes—though perhaps this would not be entirely surprising given the well-established views of the Muslim Brotherhood. The British government's 2015 review drew attention to this, when it noted that senior members of the Ikhwan have "routinely" used "virulent, anti-Semitic language."[158]

More broadly, the issues covered by the *New Dawn* newsletter and the worldview it articulated clearly identified the MAB as a tributary of the Brotherhood. At this point, it should be acknowledged that the group's leaders have categorically denied either being an Islamist organization or promoting Islamist ideology. They are more vague on their relationship with the Muslim Brotherhood specifically. On the one hand, the MAB stresses its independent character and UK focus. Altikriti has stated that it is an "exclusively British organisation."[159] Yet, he and his colleagues also admit to sharing "some of the main principles that the Muslim Brotherhood stands for; like upholding democracy, freedom of the individual, social justice and the creation of a civil society."[160] In 2004, the MAB claimed "the right to be proud of the humane notions and principles of the Muslim Brotherhood." Equally, it reserved "the right to disagree with or divert from the opinion and line of the Muslim Brotherhood, or any other organization, Muslim or otherwise on any issue at hand."[161]

Beyond this, it is notable that both the MAB and the Muslim Welfare House are members of the Federation of Islamic Organisations in Europe (FIOE), an umbrella group that was established in 1989 to coordinate a range of Brotherhood-linked movements. Among its other affiliates are the aforementioned Union of French Islamic Organisations (UOIF) and the Islamic Community of Germany (*Islamische Gemeinschaft in Deutschland*, or IGD).[162] Initially situated in the

United Kingdom at Markfield just outside Leicester, on premises provided by the Islamic Foundation, the FIOE subsequently relocated to Brussels.[163] It is described by Ikhwanwiki, an online portal operated by the Egyptian Brothers, as the "European wing" of "the international Muslim Brotherhood." The same website traces the heritage of the FIOE to the 1950s, the journey to Europe of both students and exiled Brotherhood figures (like Sa'id Ramadan), and the development of various Islamist groups on a country-by-country basis.[164] As Sara Silvestri has shown, though not proclaimed openly the intertwined relationship between the FIOE and the Ikhwan is confirmed by its past history, its emphasis on certain Islamist themes, and the personal histories of its most conspicuous members.[165]

One of the founders and later president of FIOE was the MAB leader, Ahmad al-Rawi. In an interview with the *Wall Street Journal,* al-Rawi did not deny a close association with the Muslim Brotherhood, but asserted simply that many within the West unfairly traduced the Ikhwan. He said that the Brothers were to be admired for their opposition to authoritarianism in the Middle East. "We are interlinked with them," he admitted, "with a common point of view . . . [and] a good close relationship."[166] Several other senior FIOE figures were drawn from the various Brotherhood-inspired organizations across Europe: Ahmed Jaballah, Fouad Alaoui, and Abdallah ben Mansour from the UOIF (of which Jaballah was president at the time of the FIOE's creation); Ibrahim el-Zayat of the IGD; and Ahmad Sheikh Muhammad of the MAB.[167]

The function of the FIOE was to unify the efforts of these national branches and to act as a pan-European lobby group on a range of "Islamic issues," such as the debate over the hijab.[168] According to Ikhwanwiki, it adopted a twenty-year plan of work and sought to build relationships with government officials and with the European Union. Amid its declared aims was the "settlement" of Islam in the West and the "positive integration" of Muslims into European societies—albeit in a way that preserved an "Islamic identity."[169] Ahmad al-Rawi has emphasized that the FIOE hoped to change the European "understanding" of Islam and to challenge more extreme voices—while also providing a legal framework that would allow Muslims themselves to live as faith-abiding minorities within the West. A key related goal, al-Rawi has explained, was to safeguard the Muslim community from the "materialist values" of Western society.[170]

Many of these concepts were reflected in a later "Muslims of Europe Charter" that the FIOE produced, which laid out their vision in greater detail. This repudiated "all inclinations of extremism and exclusion" and claimed that the "true spirit of Islam" was "based on moderation," avoiding "both laxity and excessiveness." Various paragraphs affirmed respect for human rights, equality, democracy, and pluralism. At the same time, in speaking of the need for "rapprochement" between Islam and the West, the document effectively reinforced the idea that these were two distinct civilizations. Muslims were to be seen as a discrete communal faith bloc: "Muslims of Europe constitute one religious entity within the framework of Islamic principles, united by fraternity." They were "urged to come together, co-operate and co-ordinate"—and to defend their rights as distinct "religious communities." The FIOE called on Muslims "to integrate positively [emphasis in original]" and to participate in politics and society. But again, the basis for this was to be a "harmonious balance between the preservation of Muslim identity and the duties of citizenship." Integration, it was said, had to be carried out in such a fashion as to "preserve their Islamic personality."[171] The self-ascribed mission of the FIOE was to advance this notion. As Silvestri has commented, it was created to be "primarily a public relations and political organisation," working to "raise awareness" of Islam and showing Muslims how to "live Islamically while also abiding by European rules."[172]

In pursuit of its goals, the FIOE oversaw a range of purpose-specific institutions, such as the Institut Européen de Sciences Humaines (European Institute for Human Science, EIHS) that was inaugurated in the early 1990s, at a site near Château-Chinon in Burgundy. Further campuses were then added in Paris, Wales, Birmingham, and, from 2009, London (the latter, based at the MWH headquarters in Finsbury Park).[173] The EIHS offered education and instruction to would-be imams and, as Silvestri has elucidated, was actually comprised of four separate departments: the European College for Islamic Studies, the Arabic Language Institute, the Institute for the Training of Imams, and the Institute for Learning the Holy Qur'an.[174] The first director of the EIHS was a French-based Iraqi asylum seeker, Zuhair Mahmoud, who had been heavily involved in the creation of the UOIF. At the time of writing, the current head of the Welsh branch of the institute was Kazem al-Rawi, brother to Ahmad (formerly president of both the MAB and the FIOE), who was himself a director of the EIHS in Birmingham.[175]

Another significant organization within the FIOE network was the European (later, Europe) Trust, set up in 1994, "in order to support and promote" the work of the parent group by "providing stable financial reserves." Similar to the US-based North American Investment Trust (NAIT), this ran a property portfolio that could furnish a steady income stream. In addition, it drew in donations from around the world, but especially from the Gulf, to help sustain FIOE-endorsed activity.[176] For a time, Ahmad al-Rawi headed both the Trust and the FIOE (being chairman of the former until 2006, and president of the latter until 2007). However, after concern was raised that this partnership might breach charity law in the United Kingdom (where it was based), the two entities were formally separated.[177] Nonetheless, the close connection between the FIOE and the Europe Trust remained apparent.

On top of this, the FIOE helped found the Forum of European Muslim Youth and Student Organisations (FEMYSO) in 1996, to work toward "increasing the awareness of Muslim youth and preserving their identity." The Young Muslims UK—the youth section of the ISB—was also to the fore in the creation of FEMYSO, alongside their French equivalents (the JMF) and the Swedish Muslim Youth Organisation. Thereafter, FEMYSO developed a network of almost forty Islamic youth groups across Europe and cemented ties with international Islamist bodies including the Saudi-run World Assembly of Muslim Youth (WAMY). Once more, the commonality of personnel was readily observable, with eminent FIOE members, such as the German-based Ibrahim el-Zayat one of the architects of FEMYSO.[178] Men like el-Zayat were crucial to the genesis of this new cohort of Islamist-inspired organizations, which both drew on and sought to supplement the work of existing institutions in the West.

A final body worth mentioning is the European Council for Fatwa and Research (ECFR), which the FIOE established in March 1997, with Sheikh Yusuf al-Qaradawi as chairman. Al-Qaradawi had continued to grow in international prominence throughout the 1990s, in large part because of his ready embrace of the media. When Qatar launched the satellite news channel *al-Jazeera* in 1996, he became one of its foremost contributors by virtue of his weekly program *Shari'a and Life*. In the years that followed, he was also quick to exploit the Internet, with popular websites such as Islam Online. The ECFR was an important part of al-Qaradawi's own expanding network, linking him with other leading scholars, many of whom likewise came from an Islamist background. Notable fellow members included Faisal Mawlawi (vice chair), the Bosnian grand mufti Mustafa Ceric, Ahmad al-Rawi, and Rashid al-Ghannouchi—men all very much associated with the ideology of the Ikhwan.[179] The objective of the ECFR was to produce religious rulings for those Muslims living as minorities within European countries. Through this council—and through the International Union of Muslim Scholars (IUMS), which al-Qaradawi also formed in 2004—the aim was to provide "an international Islamic reference for all Muslims" that reached beyond "local juristic assemblies."[180] In a world in which traditional forms of Islamic leadership appeared to be losing their hold on the masses, al-Qaradawi wanted to offer authoritative interpretation of the shariʻa to the worldwide Muslim *umma*—with himself acting as a kind of "global mufti" for a "virtual Caliphate."[181]

The transatlantic counterpart to the ECFR was the Fiqh Council of North America (FCNA), which had commenced its work in 1994 under the care of Sheikh Taha Jaber al-Alwani (an associate of al-Qaradawi and a onetime president of the International Institute of Islamic Thought, IIIT).[182] It was al-Alwani who first proposed the idea of "fiqh al-aqaliyat" (jurisprudence of the minorities) as a new Islamic legal concept, to try to build a framework of shariʻa law that might cater for those communities living in majority non-Muslim societies (such as in the West).[183]

More generally, meanwhile, just as the late 1980s and early 1990s saw a fresh wave of institution building by the Brothers in Europe and the United Kingdom, so this also occurred in the United States. As outlined in Chapter 7, over the previous three decades, an alphabet soup of organizations had been established that together comprised the Muslim Brotherhood "universe" in North America: the Muslim Students Association (MSA), NAIT, the Islamic Society of North America (ISNA), the Association of Muslim Social Scientists (AMSS), the Association of Muslim Scientists and Engineers (AMSE), the Muslim Arab Youths Association (MAYA), the Islamic Association of Palestine (IAP), the Islamic Medical Association (IMA), and the International Institute of Islamic Thought (IIIT). Now, there was an attempt to expand on these bodies, to make them more cohesive and, where necessary, to create new groups. Outsiders were given a unique insight into this process by the remarkable "explanatory memorandum" on the "general strategic goal" of the Brotherhood, which surfaced during the 2007 Holy Land Foundation trial. This document was apparently written back in 1991 by "Muhammad Akram" (thought to be Mohammed Adlouni). It described the "long-term plan" that had been approved by the Brotherhood's US Shura Council and Organizational Conference in 1987.[184]

Therein, Akram examined the "historical stages" through which "Islamic Ikhwani activism" in the United States had passed. This had evolved, he said, from an initial stage of "searching for self and determining the identity," through to the creation of "mosques and Islamic centers" and the building of "Islamic organizations." In particular, Akram underlined the importance of the various Islamic centers that had been established "in every city." These, he argued, formed the "axis" of the movement on which everything else stood; the individual center was a "seed" for a "small Islamic society" in each community.

Above it, according to Akram, were a range of other groups—from those focused on *da'wa* and education to those engaged in media production. The problem, he maintained though, was that these were all "scattered" elements. For this reason, Akram called for a new phase of activity based on the "reviving and establishing [of] the Islamic organizations." What was required, he insisted, was the transformation of these otherwise disparate bodies into "comprehensive, stable, 'settled' organizations" that were "connected with our Movement and which fly in our orbit and take orders from our guidance." In Akram's judgment, the United States was "a country which understands no language other than the language of the organizations." This was no problem for the Brotherhood, he surmised, because it was entirely compatible with the history of Islam as practiced by the Prophet and revived by Hasan al-Banna. Akram therefore identified their goal as being "to build a country of organizations" across North America.[185]

The report ended by listing those groups said to belong either to the Ikhwan movement or their "friends." It included all the aforementioned US-based Islamic institutions. Next to them, Akram commented: "Imagine if they all march according to one plan!!!"[186] A united, "observant Islamic base" in the United States and Canada, he declared, would "be the best support and aid to the global Movement project." Indeed, Akram set the objectives of the Brothers as being to establish "an effective and stable Islamic Movement led by the Muslim Brotherhood which adopts Muslims' causes domestically and globally, and which works to expand the observant Muslim base; aims at unifying and directing Muslims' efforts; presents Islam as a civilization alternative; and supports the global Islamic state, wherever it is."

These multilayered goals were bracketed under the heading of "settlement"—the same phrase, incidentally, used by the Muslim Brotherhood to describe the mission of the FIOE in Europe. Here, the concept was defined as the process by which "Islam and its Movement become a part of the homeland it lives in." It was placed alongside other core ideas such as "establishment" (meaning the creation of "firmly-rooted organizations"), "stability," "enablement," and "rooting." As the terminology implies, all of these turned on the desire to ensure that the Brotherhood was firmly implanted within Muslim communities living in Western societies.

With these foundations in place, Akram believed that the Brotherhood would be able to pursue a "civilization-jihad process." The Ikhwan, he said, "must understand that their work in America is a kind of grand Jihad in eliminating and destroying the Western civilization from within and 'sabotaging' its miserable house by their hands and the hands of the believers so that it is eliminated and God's religion is made victorious over all other religions."[187]

Needless to say, such language appears somewhat fantastical, and spokesmen for many of the organizations listed by Akram sought to downplay the significance of both the memorandum and the author. Yet what Akram's report seemed to capture was the long-term, idealistic, and in many respects, quite unreconstructed views of many Brotherhood members.

Moreover, there *were* grounds for concluding that a new "phase" of Islamist activism—of the kind discussed in the memorandum—was indeed initiated in the United States during this period. In 1987, ISNA had formed a Public Affairs Committee, the ISNA-PAC—an indication perhaps of its desire to play a more advanced political role. This was followed in 1990 by the establishment of the American Muslim Council (AMC), explicitly focused on efforts to encourage political activism and civic participation. Among the founders of this group were the Egyptian exile Mahmud Abu al-Sa'ud and Abdurahman al-Amoudi (previously a senior figure in ISNA and a former president of the MSA). In subsequent years, al-Amoudi enjoyed high-level access to both the Clinton and George W. Bush administrations. For instance, he was appointed as a State Department "good-will" ambassador to the Middle East in 1997, and in the wake of the 11 September 2001 (9/11) attacks, he stood alongside President Bush during a ceremony at the Islamic Center of Washington. Thereafter, al-Amoudi became mired in controversy because of his support for Hamas and other militant groups.[188] The AMC itself shut down in 2003.[189]

In the meantime, other more enduring groups had emerged from the Brotherhood firmament. In 1993, the Muslim American Society (MAS) was founded under Esam Omeish, with headquarters initially in Illinois and then Alexandria, Virginia, and more than fifty chapters nationwide. The creators of this body included Jamal Badawi (a longtime senior leader in ISNA and NAIT), Omar Soubani, the aforementioned Ahmad al-Qadi, and Mahdi 'Akef, the future general guide of the Egyptian Ikhwan.[190] The purposes of the MAS echoed those of their ISNA and AMC forerunners. It was active on a range of "Islamic" issues both domestically and abroad, as it sought to present itself as the authoritative voice of the Muslim community in the United States.

Similar in character was the Council on American Islamic Relations (CAIR), which was launched in September 1994 by individuals who had previously been involved with the Islamic Association of Palestine: Nihad Awad, Omar Ahmad, and Rafiq Jaber.[191] (The previous year, Ahmad and Awad were among those who had participated in a meeting in Philadelphia—a gathering, it later turned out, that had been bugged by the FBI—at which a strategy was discussed to "defeat the Israeli-Palestinian peace accord.")[192] CAIR, which denied any formal link to the Muslim Brotherhood, was based in Washington, DC, and was committed to tackling "anti-Muslim discrimination nationwide." In addition, it sought to build political influence, working alongside the federal government, advising and lobbying on Muslim matters. CAIR, for example, secured a niche for itself as the definitive provider of "diversity" and "sensitivity" training to various federal and state agencies. This, in turn, afforded its leaders high-level political access, including to presidents Clinton and Bush.[193]

The *Chicago Tribune* has reported that organizations like the MAS and CAIR made a deliberate decision to conceal their affiliation with the Ikhwan.[194] Whenever ties with the Brotherhood were acknowledged, these were said to be purely historical and no longer of contemporary relevance. Hence, Shaker Elsayed, an official with the MAS, admitted that "Ikhwan members" had "founded" the group, but insisted that it had then developed "way beyond that point of conception." As with British-based bodies like the MAB, however, there was more than a hint of ambiguity. Even as he denied any association with the Brotherhood, Elsayed alluded to his admiration for the ideas of Hasan al-Banna, and said that his teachings comprised "the closest reflection of how Islam should be." To confuse the matter further, he added: "We are Ikhwan . . . [but] we are not your typical Ikhwan."[195] In this way, many Brotherhood-inspired groups seem to have imbibed an ethos of "constructive ambiguity" when talking about their relationship with the Ikhwan.

In so doing, they benefited from the fact that the Brotherhood as a whole has embraced what the former deputy general guide Muhammad Habib called "decentralization in action" at the international level. In 2007, Habib stated that there were "entities that exist in many countries all over the world," which had the "same ideology, principle and objectives [as the Ikhwan] but . . . work in different circumstances and different contexts." It made sense, Habib averred, for "every entity" to work "according to its circumstances and according to the problems it is facing." This, in Habib's estimation, achieved two things: first, it gave "flexibility" to the movement; second, it led to a focus on "action."[196] It was partially on the basis of such testimony that Brigitte Marechal suggested that the contemporary Muslim Brotherhood should be understood as "literally a 'movement,' an ideological reference point, and not so much an organisational structure."[197]

Certainly, the influence of the Brotherhood's putative "International Organisation" appears to have declined further during the 1990s, before being abandoned altogether in the aftermath of 9/11, when increased US attention to "terrorism financing" rendered its operations ever more difficult and it was split by fresh divisions over how to respond to the 2003 invasion of Iraq.[198]

Within Western countries, the slackening of formal ties linking Brotherhood-origin groups to their ideological founders was also encouraged by the new agenda that they adopted. As mentioned, organizations like the ISB and the MAB in the United Kingdom, or the MAS and CAIR in the United States, came to focus increasingly on questions about citizenship, discrimination, accommodation, and integration—subjects that were of critical importance to a younger generation that was culturally different from their immigrant elders. Of course, groups both old and new continued to promote "Islamic" causes such as those of Kashmir, Iraq, and Chechnya.[199] But this sat alongside a discourse that appealed more to Muslims born and raised in a Western context.[200] Particular emphasis, for instance, was placed on the battle against "Islamophobia," the term that entered popular usage after a 1997 report on the subject by the Runnymede Trust.[201] Under this banner, the challenge of combating anti-Muslim prejudice was taken up enthusiastically by the Brotherhood network. To activists permanently resident in the United Kingdom or the United States, it loomed at least as large as more traditional matters of concern, such as American policy in the Middle East.

Marechal has argued that this evolution in the priorities of Western-based Islamists has been accompanied by further ideological changes in the way that the Brotherhood sees "the West." In her assessment, it was not possible for the group's European affiliates to regard Western civilization in monolithic fashion as an aspiritual, amoral wasteland committed to the colonial occupation of "Muslim lands." Marechal quotes Ahmad al-Rawi, who claims to have become more aware of the diversity of the West, no longer seeing it as the binary opposite of Islam. Al-Rawi described his own role—in groups like the FIOE and the MAB—as being akin to a "bridge," trying to bring the two worlds together. He was sure Islam could offer something to the West—helping to save it from its otherwise inevitable decline. At one level, this did perhaps represent a less acerbic vision of the Western world; on another, al-Rawi's outlook still presupposed a view of the West as in need of saving. And as Marechal has acknowledged, more caustic judgments on Western civilization still abounded within the ranks of the Brotherhood.[202]

Yusuf al-Qaradawi was someone who, in his public pronouncements, typified the Brotherhood's mixed messages regarding the West. On the one hand,
he spoke about the need for an "opening to the West," but on the other, he reminded his audience of the "many tragedies" that had been inflicted on Islam by
Westerners—from the Crusades, with their bloodshed and atrocities, to the
"bitter and brutal experience of 'modern Western imperialism' that had injured
all Muslim countries." Even now, al-Qaradawi insisted (writing in 1999), the West
sought to impose its will on Islamic nations. "Wherever an Islamic issue arises,"
he stated, "we find the West standing against it"—and especially, in Palestine. In
spite of this, though, he declared himself in favor of "coexistence"—provided
that the West ended its "aggression" against Muslims and treated them as equals.[203]

Elsewhere, some Ikhwan leaders did accept that a distinction could be drawn
between Western people and their governments. This in itself was no real surprise; the proposition, after all, was one that Sa'id Ramadan had raised back in
the 1950s. More recently, Hasan Hathut stressed that ordinary Westerners were
"very different from the foreign policy of their politicians and statesmen."[204]
There were myriad other examples of senior Ikhwan members making a similar
case. Sa'd al-Katatni, while critical of Western policy in the Middle East, urged
Islamists to distinguish between "different 'Wests'": between the European Union
and the United States; between governments and societies; and between different
political parties. With regard to the former of these couplets, al-Katatni expressed the belief that the United States tended "to take a more radical stance
regarding Muslims . . . based on its short term interests in the region." The European Union, by contrast, was deemed to be less biased toward Israel and more
concerned with ethical issues. That aside, al-Katatni maintained that the
Muslim Brotherhood did "not have an ideological stance against the West."[205]

The general guide Mahdi 'Akef, meanwhile, once stated that when he talked
about "the West's enmity [toward] Islam," he did not mean "all people of the
West," but rather "governments, centers of influence, and those hateful imperialist interests." Yet at other moments, he referred to the "fierce war" being waged
by the West "on different levels, against our Muslim identity, culture, civilization, and curricula."[206] In this way, 'Akef's words demonstrated with particular
clarity the limits of the Brotherhood's ideological revisionism. Though certain
prominent Brothers occasionally spoke about the need for nuance, "the West," as
an organizing category of analysis, remained the crucial "other" to the Ikhwan.
Furthermore, in the early twenty-first century, this sense of a world divided between Islam and "the West" if anything grew stronger in Brotherhood circles
rather than diminishing—especially in the context of "the war on terror."

The War on Terror and the Freedom Agenda

To say that 9/11 was a transformative moment is to state the obvious. Not only did it radically alter the nature of George W. Bush's presidency and the orientation of American foreign policy, it also ensured that the issue of the Muslim Brotherhood took on new salience. In the wake of the attacks, many now wondered how to locate groups like the Ikhwan in relation to al-Qaeda and "salafi-jihadism" generally.[207] What is more, the launching of the "war on terror"—to be followed closely by Washington's pursuit of a "freedom agenda"—profoundly altered the immediate context in which the various branches of the Brotherhood operated. The enormity of al-Qaeda's assault on the United States encouraged the Bush administration to see the world in binary fashion: America and its allies on the one side; their enemies on the other.[208] Such an ethos carried major implications for those organizations like the Brotherhood, whose attitude to the United States was ambiguous at best.

According to the Egyptian Brothers, Muhammad Morsi (then leader of the group's parliamentary bloc) visited the American Embassy in Cairo in the aftermath of 9/11 to reiterate their rejection of terrorism.[209] Brotherhood-aligned scholars such as Yusuf al-Qaradawi also denounced the al-Qaeda attacks.[210] Despite this, it would seem that almost all lines of communication between US officials and the Brotherhood were soon cut. In trying to determine the precise point of caesura, it is worth noting a diplomatic dispatch from July 2007, which stated that, by that time, there had been a lack of contact for "several years."[211] A further cable from the same month referred to a meeting between a congressional delegation and members of the Egyptian parliament as the first "contacts *in six years* with the full range of Parliamentary membership [emphasis added]," including the leader of the Brotherhood's "independent" MPs.[212] In light of the fact that throughout the preceding period, US officials had routinely met with other parliamentarians, it seems reasonable to conclude that the novelty here was the presence of Ikhwan members. This would tend to confirm that there had been no high level, face-to-face dialogue with the Brothers since 2001. Moreover, given that meetings with the Ikhwan—of various kinds—had been standard diplomatic practice during the previous thirty years, it seems likely that such a shutdown was the product of presidential edict. Even then, though, if the Brotherhood is to be believed, there was still the occasional encounter. The group has stated that some of its MPs attended a reception hosted by the deputy US ambassador to Cairo in August 2003.[213]

US policy, therefore, was not entirely free of ambiguity. This was doubly so when the regional picture was taken into account. Relations with the different Brotherhood branches remained dependent on the local context; there was no universal policy on this issue; and certainly, there was no comprehensive breaking of contact with the Ikhwan after 9/11. Relations with the Jordanian Brothers, for instance, had already been complicated by a visa dispute in 2000, which led to a hiatus in communications. In 2002, though, the US special coordinator for public diplomacy, Ambassador Christopher Ross, met repeatedly with leaders of the Islamic Action Front, the political party attached to the Jordanian Brotherhood. At the same moment, the US Embassy in Amman sought dialogue with "moderate leaders" of the Ikhwan.[214] Thereafter, it was actually the IAF that signaled an unwillingness to meet with the Americans—because of *their* opposition to the US-led war in Iraq.[215] Interestingly, this pattern appears to have been paralleled elsewhere. *Asharq al-Awsat* recorded that the Brotherhood's affiliates in Morocco likewise took a step back from contacts with the United States in protest at the Iraq War.[216]

It thus seems evident that the US invasion of Iraq introduced a new level of friction into relations between the United States and various Islamist groups. Equally, however, it should be acknowledged that the legacy of the war cut both ways. Alongside the obvious difficulties that it caused, the conflict also created significant opportunities for the Ikhwan because of Washington's decision to proclaim a "freedom agenda" in the Middle East. After Saddam Hussein's regime had been toppled, the Bush administration came to place greater emphasis on the importance of democratic change, not only in Iraq but also across the wider region. This "freedom agenda" would become a core element in the "Bush doctrine."[217] It led to renewed demands for political reform in countries like Egypt where, previously, the United States had prioritized economic, as opposed to political, liberalization.[218]

To some extent, this new emphasis on democratization rested on the assumption that liberal forces existed beneath the surface of many Middle Eastern societies and could be strengthened by outside encouragement. It seems clear that initially the various Islamist movements in the region were seen as far from ideal partners in the effort to promote democratic change. Hence, when the State Department launched its Middle East Partnership Initiative (MEPI) in 2004, there was an effort to ensure that none of these funds flowed to the Brotherhood.[219] A preference for liberals, though, was balanced by the American insistence that they *would* accept Islamist electoral success in more open and competitive environments. In 2003, for example, the director of policy planning at the State Department, Richard Haas, promised that the United States would "support democratic processes even if those empowered [did] not choose policies strategically in line with US interests." To underline the point, Haas stressed that they were "not opposed to parties with an Islamic character [holding] . . . positions of responsibility."[220] President Bush himself was anxious to convey the same message. And in his memoir, he affirmed that the United States should not only back elections when it "liked the projected outcome."[221]

In truth, the American posture remained more equivocal. A range of localized variables affected the way in which the "freedom agenda" impacted ties between the United States and the different branches of the Brotherhood—as well as other Islamist movements. Washington adjusted its approach on a country-by-country basis.[222] Unsurprisingly, the United States regarded groups like Hizballah and Hamas as terrorist organizations beyond the pale of contact. At the other end of the spectrum, by comparison, American officials were prepared to work with Islamist parties such as the Justice and Development Party (PJD) in Morocco, al-Watha'iq in Bahrain, and al-Islah in Yemen.[223] Advocates of dialogue were again adamant that it was important to distinguish between "moderate" and "extremist" Islamists, in order to encourage the pragmatism of the former.[224] The PJD, in particular, was a long-term interlocutor for US diplomats. In May 2006, for instance, the State Department invited Sa'd Eddin el-Othmani, then secretary general of the party, to Washington.[225]

In Iraq, meanwhile, the local chapter of the Brotherhood emerged from its long suppression under the Ba'th to give political support to the new democratic dispensation in the country. The Iraqi Islamic Party was one of the few bodies representing the Sunni Muslim community to engage with the post-Saddam, American-backed authorities. With that said, this picture of tacit cooperation was complicated by the fact that the Brotherhood simultaneously lent support to the Association of Muslim Scholars, which was part of the "resistance" waging an insurgency against the US military presence in Iraq.[226] To some degree, the Ikhwan seemed to have a foot in each camp—of war and politics—and this situation inevitably generated confusion as to where it really stood.

Post-2003, another group that proved difficult to read was the Jordanian Brotherhood.[227] Throughout this era, officials again tracked the alleged split between "doves" and hawks" within the movement, as they struggled to map its internal contours. While the leadership of the Ikhwan was thought to be "dominated by moderates," there was a perception that many grassroots members wished to see "a more radical public line."[228] In August 2003, American diplomats in Amman described the Ikhwan as inclined to accept political pluralism and a "comparatively moderate" entity, but they were still reluctant to see its members participate in US-sponsored "assistance programs." The embassy was aware of statements attributed to the group that "appeared to favor terrorist acts against Israel and/or resistance to the US in Iraq."[229] As ever, the Brothers were noted to be vocal opponents of the "American-Zionist project" in the region; and the group labeled the "war on terror" a fresh "Crusader-Jewish assault" on the Muslim world.[230]

Against this backdrop, relations between Washington and the Jordanian Ikhwan were always likely to be fractious at best. They were undermined further by the fact that the Brothers came under increased pressure from the authorities in this period. In the 2003 parliamentary elections, the Islamic Action Front performed disappointingly, winning only sixteen seats. The Brothers blamed this setback on government repression. Soon afterward, the authorities decided to take control of the Islamic Center Association—the Brotherhood's main social welfare and charitable arm (created in 1953), which had previously been left untouched. Fresh parliamentary elections in 2007 then brought a further reduction in the IAF's share of the seats (as it fell to a rump of six) and American diplomats pointed to the "most serious confrontation between the regime and the MB since [King] Abdullah came to power."[231]

Faced with this, the Brotherhood in Jordan seemed to harden its position. In 2005, IAF parliamentarians offered formal condolences to the family of the dead al-Qaeda leader, Abu Mus'ab al-Zarqawi, one of them eulogizing him as a holy warrior and martyr. The comments provoked an outcry in Amman and led to the MP in question being stripped of his parliamentary immunity and sentenced to a short prison term. Despite this, the Ikhwan appeared set on a more confrontational path with the government. It renewed its criticism of the kingdom's alliance with the United States, as well as the peace treaty with Israel. In the summer 2006 war between the latter and Hizballah, the Brothers gave their full support to the anti-Israeli axis.[232] Subsequently, American diplomats reported that Hamas's 2006 electoral victory within the Palestinian Authority had "energized" the "zealots" inside the Jordanian Ikhwan, who were "emboldened" to pursue a more aggressive strategy toward the Amman government. By that time, officials reckoned a "long-term struggle for control" was under way within the Brotherhood.[233]

In 2006, the IAF had elected Zaki Sa'd Bani Irshad, a Jordanian considered close to Hamas, as its new secretary general.[234] Two years later, Sheikh Hammam

Sa'id, a man of Palestinian origin who was generally thought to be among the group's "hawks," was elected as controller general, replacing the seemingly more "moderate" Salim al-Fallahat.[235] These events intensified concerns that the Jordanian Ikhwan was being both radicalized and "Hamas-ized." Diplomatic assessments now theorized that there were four internal groupings within the Brotherhood divided by attitude and generation: traditional camps of "hawks" and "doves" sat alongside younger factions of "Centrists" and "Fourth Trend" radicals. Amid the ongoing debate over the movement's tactics, US officials anticipated that the new leadership would "take a more confrontational position," a prospect that was clearly far from welcome.[236]

Elsewhere, American diplomats were content to see the declining influence of the Sudanese Brotherhood. In late 1999, Hasan al-Turabi had been displaced by his erstwhile protégé, Omar al-Bashir. The president dissolved the already-pliant parliament, sacked al-Turabi as secretary general of the governing National Congress Party (NCP), and placed him under house arrest. In the aftermath of these upheavals, US officials recorded that the removal of al-Turabi had a "much more profound effect than could be generally imagined." The diplomats felt it had led the government to reverse course and promote a "less intolerant" version of Islam. After al-Turabi's fall, too, Khartoum seemed less intent on maintaining its "maleficent influence throughout the Arab world." As a result, "down with America and spread the gospel, jihad, victory and martyrdom" had "given way to the more traditional stuff of looking after your own soul and doing good to others."[237] Bashir was deemed to be essentially a pragmatist, who, while influenced by Islamism, especially in domestic policy, was concerned first and foremost with retaining power.[238] His regime, of course, continued to be seen as deeply problematic—and Washington accused Bashir of carrying out a genocide in Darfur—but the dismissal of al-Turabi does appear to have been interpreted as one small step in the right direction. (It is worth stating, however, that US officials still met with the Brotherhood leader, who now reinvented himself as an advocate of "political freedom.")[239]

Wth regard to other regional branches of the Brotherhood, it was perhaps with the Syrian Ikhwan that Western governments established the closest connection. In the first decade of the twenty-first century, this group seemed set on a trajectory away from violence and toward an acceptance of democratic, more pluralistic forms of politics. This evolution was encapsulated by the "National Honour Charter" that the Brothers produced in 2001, as well as the December 2004 "Cultural Project for Syria of the Future." While calling for the implementation of the shari'a and expounding a familiar, comprehensive vision of Islam, these documents stressed a commitment to equal citizenship, democracy, and human rights; physical force was explicitly renounced. The Syrian Ikhwan talked of its desire for a civic rather than Islamic state.[240] In addition, it showed its readiness to collaborate with secular opposition forces, contributing to the 2004 "Damascus Declaration for Democratic National Change" and then joining the National Salvation Front (NSF) with former Syrian vice president Abdul Halim Khaddam in 2006. In a 2007 interview with the magazine *Islamism Digest,* the leader of the Syrian Brotherhood, Mohammed Walid, stated that the strategy of the Ikhwan was "non-violent opposition and coordination with other opposition forces" against the "totalitarian regime" of Bashar al-Assad. He justified cooperation with Khaddam on the grounds of "political realism" and called on the United States to maintain pressure on the Syrian government.[241] (The alliance with Khaddam drew criticism from those who saw it as "opportunistic," and the initiative later collapsed after the Brotherhood suspended its opposition to the Assad regime during the 2008–2009 Israel-Gaza War.)[242]

Suggestively, in that same article, Walid categorically denied that there had been "contacts with, or [an] approach from, the US government to the Syrian Muslim Brotherhood."[243] His comments came in response to various rumors of dialogue between Western diplomats and the Syrian Ikhwan.[244] Two years earlier, the *New York Times* had reported that the Bush administration wished to engage the enemies of Assad, including the National Salvation Front.[245] Furthermore, within days of Walid's interview being published, the NSF admitted that it had held meetings with officials from the US National Security Council and the State Department, as well as with congressional staffers. The NSF also announced that it was opening an office in Washington to be headed by Hussam al-Dairi, their North American representative.[246] In this instance, therefore, it does seem likely that a shared antipathy for the Assad regime did foster limited cooperation between Western officials and the Syrian branch of the Ikhwan. The extent—and import—of this, however, should not be overstated. On balance, US diplomats thought that "the potential political influence of the Muslim Brotherhood in Syria" had been "exaggerated," given its complete destruction two decades previously.[247] This verdict surely undercut any countervailing inclination to invest heavily in the Ikhwan as a serious alternative to the Assad regime.

Overall, then, in reflecting on US policy toward regional affiliates of the Brotherhood, there is much to be said for the five criteria identified by *Asharq al-Awsat* as determining American attitudes. The newspaper posited that

Washington's approach to a given Brotherhood chapter was governed by its reading of several key characteristics of the body in question: (1) its legitimacy in its home country; (2) whether or not it had appeared on the US list of terrorist organizations; (3) its agenda and ideology; (4) its practice; and (5) the likely effect of dialogue on American interests. The first of these, predicated on the relationship between the Brothers and the local government, was judged to be by far the most important.[248] Though not infallible, this schema does seem to capture the essence of the US position, including in Egypt.

In Cairo, the Brotherhood had appeared increasingly keen to assert its reformist credentials. In March 2004, the group produced a policy platform, "On the General Principles of Reform in Egypt," which underscored a respect for freedom of belief and demanded political change and an end to the long-standing Emergency Law.[249] The document pledged support for a "republican, parliamentary, constitutional and democratic political order." Alongside this, it did also stress the importance of adhering to the "principles of Islam" and implementing the shari'a.[250] As an April 2004 report by the International Crisis Group remarked, therefore, the group remained shrouded in uncertainty. While seeming to embrace democracy, the Brothers had not acknowledged, still less repudiated, "the illiberal and anti-democratic strand" of their ideological heritage.[251]

By this time, much academic scholarship tended to emphasize the evolution of the Ikhwan. Mona el-Ghobashy, for example, argued that it had "morphed from a highly secretive, hierarchical, antidemocratic organization led by anointed elders into a modern, multivocal political association steered by educated, savvy professionals."[252] Close attention was paid to the younger generation of Brothers, often seen as reformists—men such as Essam al-Erian, Muhammad Habib, Ibrahim al-Za'farani, and 'Abd al-Mon'im Abu al-Futuh. Under the influence of this "new guard," the Brotherhood was thought to have moved toward "secular politics."[253] The group was reckoned to be more open to the possibility of an alliance with antiregime leftists.[254] It was noted too that the Ikhwan had become an increasingly vocal opponent of the idea that Gamal Mubarak might inherit power from his father. To this end, it was involved in the formation of the "Popular Movement for Change" and built an alliance with the small but influential "Kefayah" movement.[255]

In this period, the United States was nudging the Cairo government in the direction of reform.[256] Partly as a result of this, in September 2005, Egypt saw its first-ever multicandidacy presidential elections. In the past, Egyptians had only been permitted a referendum on whether to accept or reject a single candidate (in the 1999 "contest," some 94 percent said "yes" to Mubarak). Now they were given something that looked more recognizably like an election. Even though, as expected, Mubarak won a fifth term by a handsome margin (taking 89 percent of the vote), it seemed to portend a greater openness. The presidential election was followed a few months later by fresh parliamentary polls. The Ikhwan was allowed to participate on an unofficial basis and ran a large number of candidates as independents. The group's campaign literature reiterated its reformist stance and sought to allay fears about the Brotherhood's intentions; at the same time, it pledged that the Ikhwan would liberate the nation from foreign political, cultural, and economic dominance and provide greater support to the Palestinians.[257]

The election results proved shocking to many, both within Egypt and beyond. Eighty-eight Muslim Brothers were returned to the People's Assembly—still very much a minority of the 454-member house (of whom 311 belonged to the ruling NDP), but an increase in their representation of over 500 percent.[258] (It later came to light that the regime was perhaps not as "shocked" by these results as it made out; it had made a secret deal with the Brotherhood's leadership to coordinate the outcome.)[259] In the wake of the ballot, the US Embassy pointed to the growing confidence of the Brotherhood. The group used its newfound position, holding a fifth of the parliamentary seats, to challenge and scrutinize the government in an unprecedented manner.[260]

The effect of these events in Egypt—as well as those elsewhere in the region—was to reinvigorate the discussion about Western policy toward Islamists. Debates between "accommodationists" and "confrontationists" had rumbled on during the previous decade. They were now given added purpose by the post-9/11 and "freedom agenda" context. As already mentioned, John Esposito was a long-established proponent of dialogue with "mainstream" Islamists as part of a strategy to foster meaningful democratic change across the Middle East.[261] Others too endorsed this position, arguing that the "moderation" of groups like the Muslim Brotherhood made them "viable interlocutors."[262] Former CIA analyst Emile Nakhleh, for instance, agreed that the Brothers should be seen as part of the "mainstream" in countries like Egypt. They were, he said, committed to gradual peaceful change and had disavowed terrorism and violence. The democratization of the region, according to Nakhleh, required the involvement of parties like the Brotherhood.[263]

In his 2008 autobiography, former Syrian ambassador and assistant secretary of state Edward Djerejian put forth a similar case, urging "differentiation, engagement and dialogue." It was crucial, Djerejian stated, to appreciate "the difference between moderate Islamists and Islamic radicals." Placed in the former category were "the Muslim Brotherhood in Egypt and Jordan." Djerejian called on the United States to accept the fact that "Islamist parties and movements" would "play an important political role in the electoral process." For this reason, he felt Washington should talk to the Ikhwan. An effort had to be made, Djerejian insisted, to draw them into the "political mainstream" where they might be subject to a process of "moderation."[264]

Views of this kind were echoed by scholars like Ahmad Moussalli and Shadi Hamid, who also made the case for engagement. Moussalli attested that nonviolent, moderate Islamists should not be seen as a threat to US interests. He contended they were movements that supported democracy and human rights, and sought merely to empower people.[265] Hamid, meanwhile, said that the United States should engage with the Brothers, on the basis that they had moderated their position since the mid-1990s.[266] From another perspective, Marc Lynch opined that the Brotherhood could "serve as an important 'firewall' against al-Qaeda style radicalization in Arab countries," even as he took seriously the prospect that it might act as a "transmission belt" to jihadism in some circumstances. The key thing, Lynch concluded, was for the United States to have an open mind, and act pragmatically.[267]

Perhaps the most notable contribution to the discussion was the article penned by Steven Brooke and Robert Leiken, researchers at the Nixon Center in Washington, DC, for *Foreign Affairs* in 2007 under the revealing title "The Moderate Muslim Brotherhood." This presented the thesis that when it came to the Ikhwan, the "beginning of wisdom" lay in recognizing the differences between the various branches. Brooke and Leiken counseled a "case-by-case approach" that would see the US government engage with the Brotherhood where appropriate, given that the group as a whole had rejected "global jihad" and might therefore serve as a bulwark against al-Qaeda and other violent Islamists.[268]

Significantly, the Brotherhood was itself very much aware of this whole debate and keen to bolster the accommodationist argument. Kemal el-Helbawy claims to have liaised closely with Leiken and Brooke when they were working on their article.[269] Other Brotherhood leaders sought variously to stress their nonrevolutionary intent, their commitment to reform and civil liberties, and their rejection of "violence in all its forms."[270] 'Abd al-Mon'im Abu al-Futuh, for instance, restated the Brotherhood's commitment to "reform" and its opposition to al-Qaeda–style terrorism (though he was equally adamant that he supported "resistance in occupied Palestine and Iraq").[271] More arresting still was the assertion of Essam al-Erian that "without us most of the youth of this age would have chosen the path of violence. . . . The Brotherhood has become a safety valve for moderate Islam."[272]

Many such comments were obviously framed with one eye on Western opinion. Brothers like Abu al-Futuh and al-Erian were regular participants in conferences and seminars hosted by American and European research institutes during this period.[273] Furthermore, al-Erian was part of a Brotherhood delegation that met with EU officials in 2004, and repeated calls for dialogue.[274] The following year, prior to Egypt's parliamentary elections, the Ikhwan made a concerted effort to improve its image before an international audience. In a famous *Guardian* editorial, Khayrat al-Shater wrote of the Ikhwan's adherence to a gradualist approach and reassured readers that their success "should not frighten anybody." The Brothers were, al-Shater affirmed, "committed to democracy" and would "respect fair elections, whatever the outcome." Their aim, he said, was simply "to win a limited number of seats in parliament" that could contribute to an "inclusive debate about the priorities of reform and development."[275] Language of this kind, in one of the leading Western journals of left-wing thinking, seemed designed to appeal to those who wanted to see democratic change in Egypt. Also noteworthy at that time was the creation of an English-language Internet portal, "ikhwanweb.com." According to Ibrahim el-Houdaiby (grandson and great-grandson of former general guides), the website was the initiative of al-Shater, who hoped it might act as "a bridge between the Brotherhood members and Western intellectuals and policymakers."[276]

This outreach was sustained in the wake of the Brotherhood's 2005 electoral success. Early the next year, amid speculation that the Brothers were talking to the British (see below), al-Shater insisted there was "no dialogue or contact between the Muslim Brotherhood and any western government in any form or shape." However, he went on to state that "dialogue with the west" was the "ideal method to bridge the dividing gaps and resolve all grievances." The Brotherhood, he contended, did "not promote an anti-western agenda" and would welcome a "constructive dialogue that promotes rapprochement among civilizations."[277] By the same token, in late 2006, the leader of the Brotherhood's parliamentary bloc, Saʿd al-Katatni, declared that dialogue between Islamists and the West was "a necessity." He implored foreign policy makers to "recognize the clear ideological difference between moderate and radical Islamists." Al-Katatni argued that a failure to do this, in conjunction with the West's preference for "propping up oppressing regimes," risked reinforcing the popularity of the radicals. Furthermore, he echoed the earlier arguments of Rashid al-

Ghannouchi by suggesting that "sooner or later, the will of the people will be victorious . . . and Islamists will eventually come to power." Al-Katatni advised the West to prepare for this future by establishing good relations with the Brotherhood.[278]

The Ikhwan evidently aspired to be seen as indispensable moderate partners in the push for democratization and in the battle against more extreme forms of Islamism in the Middle East and North Africa. And yet, not everyone within the group was entirely persuaded by the importance of dialogue with the West. The group's former official spokesman, Kemal el-Helbawy, told *Al-Sharq al-Awsat* that he did not think the Brotherhood was enamored by the prospect of talks with the United States, given "American injustices in the Arab and Muslim world and other places." El-Helbawy said that he personally favored engagement on matters of shared interest. He hoped the Ikhwan would be given the opportunity to impress its views on Western governments.[279] Nevertheless, this position was not held unanimously. Israel Altman deduced that Brotherhood "reformists," who wanted talks with the United States, were opposed by a faction around general guide Mahdi 'Akef, which believed conflict with the West to be inevitable and total. In truth, the stance of 'Akef himself was rather hard to pin down. Sometimes, he too evinced a preference for engagement, provided this occurred via the Egyptian Foreign Ministry.[280] At other times, 'Akef dismissed the possibility of dialogue with a "satanic" and "imperialist" United States that was supposedly trying to construct a new world order for the benefit of the "Sons of Zion." He instead advocated an economic and cultural boycott of the Americans and their allies.[281] In one letter to his followers, 'Akef spoke of the "American cancer" and the West's "war on Islam." The "alleged September attacks," he averred, had given President Bush the platform to advance the American "dream" of controlling the world. The Americans, 'Akef intimated, were waging a "crusade" against terrorism that was really aimed at Muslims.[282]

The depth of 'Akef's feelings on this subject had been illustrated in April 2005, when the newspaper *Al-Sharq al-Awsat* published an exposé of purported US plans to reestablish a channel of communication with the Ikhwan. As the US Embassy reported, the story was "baseless." Yet, the reaction of the general guide was striking, for 'Akef quickly rejected the idea out of hand, pointing to "fundamental and not just political differences" between the Brothers and the Americans.[283] On further occasions, too, 'Akef claimed that the United States was intent on spreading "destructive chaos" in the region, and he urged all Muslims to focus their efforts against "the real enemy of the Umma, the enemy which occupies, kills, desecrates and plunders . . . in al-Quds [Jerusalem], in Baghdad and in Kabul."[284] He condemned the United States for its "colonialism," arguing that Washington did "not wish well" to the Islamic world.[285] According to 'Akef, "the new international system" led by the United States was merely the "old imperial system using new tools." To his mind, those tools included support for authoritarian governments and a total bias in favor of Israel.[286]

All of this was very much in keeping with the outlook of many of his fellow Brothers, whose views about the United States and its role in the Middle East had changed little. Even a putative "reformist" such as Abu al-Futuh attacked the United States during this period, accusing Washington of having "abandoned the principles of the American revolution" by its "unconditional support for the Zionist regime, the occupation of Iraq and other areas."[287] Abu al-Futuh asserted that the United States backed "the worst dictatorships in the Muslim world" and had reduced Egypt to being "a satellite state of America."[288] Likewise, Essam al-Erian inferred that the United States had a "package deal" with the Mubarak regime: "The regime works for US interests in the region, and the US remains silent on its abuses." Those abuses, al-Erian argued, were targeted primarily against Islamists—and this made it all the more galling to the Brotherhood that American officials ignored them. El-Erian thus complained that Ambassador Francis Ricciardone Jr.—who he claimed to have known for eighteen years, going back to the diplomat's earlier posting in Cairo— "didn't say a word" when he was in jail, nor congratulate him on his release.[289] There was, it should be said, some truth in this: the United States and its European allies did pay greater attention to the travails of more secular and liberal figures, like Saad Eddin Ibrahim and Ayman Nour.[290] Manifestly, this was a source of discontent among the Brothers, and it led many of them to assume the worst about Western intentions.

In 2007, 'Akef actually blamed the Americans for the ongoing repression of the Ikhwan in Egypt. Such repression, he assumed, was carried out "upon Zionist-US orders," because of "the Muslim Brotherhood's support to the Palestinian Cause, Palestinians, Hamas and the Lebanese people." The Ikhwan, said 'Akef, was known for its opposition to a US policy "that launched wars and committed genocides in several countries starting from Palestine across Iraq, Afghanistan and Sudan."[291] Another Brotherhood author, Muhammad Abdallah al-Saman, agreed, arguing that the Egyptian government and other Arab regimes were loyal servants of Washington. Al-Saman regretted the fact that the Arabs had "bowed before" the United States after 9/11. In his assessment, the Egyptian security forces did the bidding of the CIA and pursued Islamists; and al-Saman believed American military bases had been implanted across Muslim countries so that they could control the wealth of the *umma*.[292]

To some extent, Brotherhood attitudes on these issues were in tune with a broader anti-Americanism that seemed ever more entrenched across the Middle East at that time—as reflected in successive Pew Research Global Attitudes Project surveys.[293] The United States was widely perceived to be a hostile, aggressive power that failed to live up to the values that it so loudly proclaimed.[294] And yet, the Ikhwan's conception of the forces at work in the region was especially elaborate and driven by fears about the machinations of the "enemies of Islam." The Brothers, for instance, gave credence to the notion that the British scholar Bernard Lewis—himself labeled one of the "worst enemies" of Muslims—had developed a complex plot to "fracture the Islamic world."[295] The future general guide, Muhammad Badi'e, claimed that the US Congress had, in 1983, secretly committed itself to implementing the "Lewis plan" and thereafter, America had sought to build a "new Middle East" that would safeguard their hegemony and Israeli power.[296] The "colonial plan drafted by the international Crusader Zionists," it was said, envisaged the transformation of the Islamic world, from Pakistan to Morocco, into a "mosaic" that could easily be controlled.[297] This was thought to explain events like the 2003 Iraq War, as well as unrest in Yemen and the Horn of Africa, the crisis in Darfur, and the subsequent division of Sudan. The purported aim was the fragmentation of all the states in the region. By this account, Egypt was to be divided between Sunni, Christian, Nubian, Bedu, and Palestinian statelets.[298] Moreover, Brotherhood members reckoned there was an active plan to create a "Greater Israel" that would spread to both banks of the Jordan River and stretch from the Nile to the Euphrates in line with "Zionist-American interests."[299] There was much conjecture too about the extent to which the Zionist (or Jewish) lobby controlled US policy.[300]

Interestingly, this grand vision appears to have been generated by the cross-fertilization of several conspiracy theories, each of which carried its own unique anti-Semitic emphasis. The former Brotherhood member Sameh 'Eid, for instance, has revealed how the group drew on well-established and notorious anti-Semitic tracts such as the *Protocols of the Elders of Zion* and *Pawns in the Game* by William Guy Carr.[301] Famously, the charter of the Brotherhood's Palestinian offshoot, Hamas, contained numerous references to the *Protocols*. Elsewhere, Brotherhood members often resorted to crude anti-Semitic imagery. For example, in his 2003 book, Muhammad Abdallah al-Saman lamented the ongoing weakness of the Muslim world and its failure to "liberate," in particular, those of its lands that were "defiled by the feet of the children of the killers of the Prophets, the most evil of Allah's creation and the descendants of monkeys and pigs" (that is to say, Palestine).[302]

To these older tropes were added newer theories that foregrounded malign Jewish intent and power. Arab opponents of Zionism made much of the article written by the Israeli journalist Odel Yinon in 1982, setting out "a strategy for Israel in the Nineteen Eighties." This also raised the idea of "breaking Egypt down territorially into distinct geographical regions," as well as the dissolution of the other Arab states. Yinon's article was translated and distributed by anti-Zionists who heralded it as an "accurate representation of the 'vision' for the entire Middle East of the presently ruling Zionist regime of Begin, Sharon and Eitan."[303]

Meanwhile, it is intriguing to note that the aforementioned allegations about Bernard Lewis (himself, of course, Jewish) seem to have originated with *Executive Intelligence Review* (*EIR*), the organ of the US-based Lyndon La-Rouche movement. In 1979, *EIR* had published an article claiming that the "Bernard Lewis Plan" was a "blueprint for the deliberate destruction of the Arab world by British and Israeli intelligence."[304] Ironically, *EIR* described the Muslim Brothers as "London's shock troops for the new dark ages," involved in everything from the overthrow of the shah to the insurgency in Afghanistan and the assassination of King Faisal.[305] Needless to say, this last piece of the story dropped out of the version of the conspiracy that was subsequently imbibed and recirculated by the Ikhwan (and not just by them—as made clear in the introduction to this study, these fantasies were also picked up by those most opposed to the Brothers).[306]

Whatever its inspiration, there was little doubting that the Brotherhood remained deeply suspicious of US policy in the Middle East in the years after 2003. Despite protestations to the contrary, they were unconvinced by the depth of American commitment to the "freedom agenda" and the extent to which the United States was willing to accept Islamist success at the polls. Such fears crystallized around Western reactions to developments in Palestine, where Hamas won a shock victory in the January 2006 legislative elections. The decision to impose sanctions on the Palestinian Authority was seen by many Islamists as indicative of American (and European) double standards and hypocrisy.[307] One of the leaders of the Jordanian Ikhwan thus stated that Washington only wanted "democracy according to American standards." The United States was castigated for trying to avoid genuinely "free and clean elections" because it knew this would produce a "parliament that hated America."[308] In Egypt, Essam al-

Erian suggested that the Americans were among those "opposing the participation in power of moderate Islamist movements."[309] Sa'd al-Katatni likewise
voiced "skepticism" about "the West's genuine belief in democracy," commenting that there was "a huge gap" between its "political discourse and its
political action."[310]

Again, such views were not entirely unjustified. Under the impact of what
Jason Brownlee termed the "annus horribilis" of US policy in the Middle East,
with crises in Palestine, Iraq, Lebanon, Gaza, and Egypt, Washington did seem
to back away from a focus on democracy promotion after 2006. It looked the
other way as authoritarian allies such as Mubarak opted for repression.[311] And
yet, the paradox was that this posture was accompanied by a reassessment of
the Egyptian Ikhwan, which led to the first contacts between US officials and
the Brothers in several years.

Before considering the character and scope of that reassessment, though, it is
worth examining the British position; for by taking the decision to look again at
the Brotherhood question, American officials were, to some extent, following
in the footsteps of their UK counterparts. The British Foreign Office was, by
this time, much further down the road toward a policy of engagement with the
Ikhwan and other Islamist groups.

The British Debate, Home and Abroad

It seems clear that among British officials there was a longer-running predisposition in favor of dialogue with known Islamists. In 2001, for example, the Foreign Office cosponsored a conference (with Exeter University) that featured
"new Islamist" thinkers like the Egyptian Fahmi Huwaydi.[312] Such "new Islamists" were not members of the Ikhwan, but they articulated many of its
ideas, echoing Hasan al-Banna's call for a revived and renewed Islam to deal
with the social, cultural, and political crisis that they felt was in train across the
Middle East.[313] It was thus not without significance that UK officials were keen
to hear what Huwaydi and others had to say.

More generally, Kemal el-Helbawy has contrasted the tentative character of
US-Brotherhood dialogue in the early twenty-first century with the approach
adopted by London. He has attested that contacts between the Ikhwan and UK
representatives never stopped. El-Helbawy has even claimed that the British government offered him personal protection during the 1990s, when the Mubarak
regime stepped up its repression of the Brotherhood.[314] Whatever the truth of

this assertion, there was no doubting that certain departments of the UK government were inclined to pursue engagement.

According to a leaked document, prior to 2002 British officials in Cairo maintained "infrequent working-level (Second Secretary) contact with Muslim Brotherhood members of parliament." This was scaled back when the Egyptian authorities "made clear their displeasure." Thereafter, "only occasional contacts with MB members" were kept up, "including one or two contacts with parliamentarians and random unplanned encounters."[315] Correspondence released under the Freedom of Information Act reveals that this situation continued at least "up until June 2003." At the same time, it also shows that "contacts were not restricted to elected PA [People's Assembly] members." Instead, British diplomats also "met the Supreme Guide of the time, Ma'moun al-Hodeibi [sic], and other prominent MB activists, such as Essam al-Aryan [sic], none of whom were in the PA."[316] Lines of communication were thus preserved between the British and the Brotherhood that reached to the most senior levels of the group.

For the United Kingdom much more than for the Americans, debates about the character of the Brotherhood and Islamism carried a strong domestic dimension. After 9/11, and especially following the suicide bombings in London in July 2005 (7/7), fears grew about the "radicalization" of the British Muslim population and the potential threat posed by "home-grown" extremism. Many now accepted that it was no longer possible to draw a line between the "domestic" and the "foreign"; there was a recognition that policies pursued abroad could impact at home. It was partly for this reason that in 2004, the Foreign Office established the Engaging with the Islamic World Group (EIWG) under the former ambassador to Yemen, Frances Guy. The purpose of this unit was both to "increase understanding of and engagement with Muslim countries and communities" and to "counter the ideological, and theological underpinnings of the terrorist narrative, in order to prevent radicalisation." To this end, the EIWG sought to initiate "constructive engagement with a wide range of groups and opinion."[317]

From 2005, this effort took on new salience as part of the Foreign Office's departmental contribution to the government's "Prevent" program.[318] Prevent was one of the four prongs making up the wider "Contest" strategy for counterterrorism in the UK.[319] The other three strands, "pursue," "protect," and "prepare" were more concerned with what might be termed "hard power" responses to immediate security threats.[320] Prevent, by contrast, marked an attempt by the government to deploy "soft power" in the struggle against violent extremism.

As such, it was from the start concerned primarily with engaging Muslim communities, groups, and individuals—both within Britain and abroad.

In this context, a fundamental question was whether Islamists should be seen as appropriate partners for government. In the wake of the 7/7 attacks, when the security imperative appeared especially urgent, there were signs that the authorities were ready to work closely with groups bearing an Islamist imprimatur. For example, the government engaged with the Muslim Council of Britain (MCB) to produce the "Preventing Extremism Together" report—the first substantive policy response to the London bombings.[321] Among the initiatives to emerge from that report was what became known as the Radical Middle Way (RMW) program, a traveling road show of Islamic scholars that toured Britain's Muslim communities with the aim of "empowering the voices of mainstream Islam," to counter "extremist misinterpretations."[322] This project enjoyed the financial backing of several government departments (including the Foreign Office), and was also supported by the Islamist-influenced Young Muslim Organisation (YMO) and the Federation of Student Islamic Societies (FOSIS; see Chapter 7).[323] One of those invited to participate in the RMW was Kemal el-Helbawy, the former Muslim Brotherhood spokesman. As such, the road show seemed indicative of an eagerness on the part of some UK officials to work with reputedly "moderate" Islamists, in the battle against violent extremism.

This ethos was in evidence across government and was captured by one Foreign Office memorandum, which stated: "Not only does HMG [Her Majesty's Government] now recognise that engagement with Islamic countries is of high strategic importance, but it acknowledges that work with Islamists—those who base politics on Islamic principles—is a key element to this engagement. . . . We must first identify who we are talking about: it is easy to point to the self-proclaimed Islamist parties which operate in the more open political systems . . . but what about the Islamist media . . . intellectuals (e.g. Qatar-based Yusuf al-Qaradawi) and religious institutions? . . . These too play a political role."[324] As these words reflect, a central aim for the Foreign Office in this period was to determine those "leading personalities in the Muslim world," including "figures with transnational religious influence," who might be of assistance.[325] This being the case, the above reference to Yusuf al-Qaradawi was especially telling.

In August 2004, a visit by al-Qaradawi to London at the invitation of then mayor Ken Livingstone had stirred controversy. Critics pointed to al-Qaradawi's well-known, illiberal views on a range of matters: homosexuality, women's rights, and the permissibility of suicide bombing in Palestine and Iraq.[326] For a group of officials, however, his "objectionable" beliefs were precisely what made al-Qaradawi a potentially crucial ally who should be cultivated. Earlier in the year, William Ehrman, director general for defense and intelligence at the Foreign Office, had talked about the challenge of reaching out to "radicalised constituencies" who were "potential recruits to terrorism." Such people, Ehrman averred, "might . . . listen to religious arguments about the nature of jihad, that, while anti-Western, eschew terrorism"; they might, in other words, listen to al-Qaradawi.[327] Certainly, this was the opinion of Ehrman's colleague, Mockbul Ali—an "Islamic Issues" adviser at the Foreign Office—who proposed that al-Qaradawi should be seen as an important voice in "promoting mainstream Islam and countering the AQ [al-Qaeda] narrative."[328] According to Ali, al-Qaradawi was "the leading mainstream and influential Islamic authority in the Middle East and increasingly in Europe" who had "repeatedly and authoritatively condemned terrorist attacks." On this basis, Ali urged engagement with the scholar and warned that any attempt to exclude al-Qaradawi from the United Kingdom (as had been demanded by the critics) risked giving "grist to AQ propaganda of a Western vendetta against Muslims" and was also likely to alienate "significant and influential members of the global Muslim community."[329]

The counsel of Ehrman and Ali was reinforced by the Metropolitan Police's Muslim Contact Unit (MCU), a body set up in 2002 under Detective Inspector Robert Lambert to facilitate dialogue with British Muslims. In the assessment of the MCU, al-Qaradawi made "a positive Muslim community impact in the fight against Al Qaida propaganda in the UK." In particular, it was felt that his "support for Palestinian suicide bombers" added "credibility to his condemnation of Al Qaida."[330] As Lambert later put it, people like al-Qaradawi were useful precisely because they espoused ideas that might be deemed "radical" or "subversive to democracy."[331]

A slightly different thesis again was that provided by Ken Livingstone in testimony to the Home Affairs Select Committee in September 2005. On that occasion, Livingstone compared al-Qaradawi to Pope John XXIII, describing him as "the most powerful, progressive force for change and engaging Islam with Western values." "If we cannot talk to Qaradawi," said Livingstone provocatively, "[we] will not really be talking to anybody from the Muslim community."[332]

Irrespective of the precise logic, it would appear that the Foreign Office did come to accept the benefits of working with al-Qaradawi. In June 2006, the British flew him and his wife to Istanbul to attend a high-profile "Muslims in Europe" conference, which had been sponsored by the "Engaging with the Islamic World Group." This gathering brought together various Muslim thinkers and scholars to produce a theological declaration rejecting terrorism and extremism.[333] At other times too, delegations of British Muslims were sent abroad to meet with al-Qaradawi and others—the aim being both to showcase the (good) conditions enjoyed by Muslims in the United Kingdom and also to cement contacts with "moderate" voices.[334] In Sudan, for example, one such delegation was introduced to Hasan al-Turabi.[335]

As outlined at the start of this chapter, the attempt to build a connection with Islamists like al-Qaradawi and al-Turabi paralleled a shift in approach with regard to the Egyptian Muslim Brotherhood itself. By 2006, the dominant assumption within the Foreign Office was that interacting with "political Islam" was "an important element" of the "Engaging with the Islamic World strategy." Officials pledged to try to "influence" those groups enjoying "significant reach with the 'grass roots'" of Egyptian society.[336] Consequently, the policy of talking to the Ikhwan was taken forward—albeit cautiously, for fear of damaging relations with Mubarak. The home secretary Charles Clarke, for instance, sought to play down the change in position during a meeting with his Egyptian counterpart, Interior Minister General Habib el-Adly. In an effort to reassure el-Adly, Clarke told him that "the British Government was not seeking to encourage the MB." Rather, he insisted, it was simply their "standard policy to have contact, when appropriate, with all elements of a Parliament."[337] To guard further against accusations of impropriety, diplomats were instructed "to engage only with MB parliamentarians, in their parliamentary capacity."[338]

In keeping with this posture, in May 2006, a British official attended a hearing of the Egyptian Parliament's Foreign Relations Committee, whose members included Youssri Ta'lib, a member of the Ikhwan. Although the session featured criticism of UK foreign policy, it was reported that "the vibes—even from the MB . . . were welcoming and friendly."[339] There were other encounters, too, between British representatives and Brotherhood MPs, both before and after. The truth of this was confirmed in the House of Commons, when the Middle East minister Kim Howells acknowledged that diplomats had met "with members of the Egyptian parliament, including occasional contact with members of the Muslim Brotherhood since September 2001." Howells also stated that meetings had been held with emissaries of the Ikhwan in Jordan, Kuwait, and Lebanon, as well as "members of the Syrian Muslim Brotherhood," whose leadership was in exile in London.[340]

This burgeoning relationship was put to the test during Hizballah's war with Israel during the summer of 2006. While the UK government effectively gave diplomatic cover to Tel Aviv, the Brothers enthusiastically backed the Lebanese organization, labeling its initial capture of Israeli soldiers a "heroic act." They called on all Muslims to rally behind Hizballah, and promised the movement their full support.[341] Despite this, the notion that the Brotherhood was a group with which the British could—and indeed should—do business continued to gather momentum. Think tanks like Conflicts Forum and the Institute for Public Policy Research came out strongly in favor of engagement with the Ikhwan. The former was, in part, the creation of ex-MI6 officer Alistair Crooke, who was a particularly outspoken advocate of dialogue with Islamists.[342] Similarly, in 2007, a report from the House of Commons Select Committee on Foreign Affairs concluded that "as long as the Muslim Brotherhood expresses a commitment to the democratic process and non-violence, we recommend that the British Government should engage with it and seek to influence its members."[343] Ikhwan leaders in Egypt hailed the report and said they would "welcome serious dialogue" in the sake of the "national interest."[344]

Meanwhile, a disposition that favored engagement with the Brotherhood abroad was, for a time, mirrored domestically. Islamist-inspired groups found that they were able to garner increased traction with the authorities. The Muslim Welfare House, for instance, had worked hard to position itself as a valued intermediary to the British "Muslim community" and a reliable partner to government. Its success in this regard could be gauged from the significant levels of funding that it was able to obtain from the Home Office, the European Social Fund, the local council, and the London Development Agency.[345] The MWH was clearly seen by various officials as a viable and useful vehicle for engagement with British Muslims.

In a different way, the Muslim Association of Britain also developed a prominent public profile in the first years of the new century. In response to the outbreak of the Second Intifada in 2000, the group worked to heighten "awareness amongst the British public regarding the issue of Palestine and the Zionist agenda in general." To this end, it formed alliances, both with other Muslim groups and with "non-Muslim organizations over issues of common interest." In April 2002, the first flowering of this effort came with the holding of a large rally in the aftermath of "the Jenin atrocity."[346] The MAB asserted that nearly one hundred thousand people marched from Hyde Park Corner to Trafalgar Square, where speakers including Kemal el-Helbawy, Iqbal Sacranie (the secretary general of the MCB), Rashid al-Ghannouchi, Azzam al-Tamimi, and several left-wing politicians (Tony Benn, George Galloway, and Jeremy Corbyn) condemned "Israeli aggression of epic proportions," and accused Ariel Sharon's government of committing "crimes against humanity." There were calls for the British government to sever trade links and suspend weapons sales to Israel.[347] The gathering marked the beginning of a period in which the MAB cooperated closely with a range of other parties and individuals. In the wake of the Jenin demonstration, for example, the Palestine Solidarity Committee invited the MAB to help organize its annual rally in support of Palestine.[348]

Furthermore, on 28 September 2002, the MAB formed a pact with the "Stop the War Coalition" (itself the creation of the Socialist Workers Party and a number of small leftist groups).[349] According to Richard Phillips, the MAB was careful to preserve its independence. The coalition was to be a partnership of equals rather than a merger. The two sides agreed to place equal focus on events in Palestine and Iraq (where war then appeared likely); their joint slogan was "No war in Iraq, justice for Palestine."[350] The MAB was thus able to put itself at the heart of one of the largest antigovernment protest movements in modern history. It has been estimated that up to one million people took to the streets in February 2003, to march against the impending attack on Iraq.[351] The leaders of the MAB were among the most outspoken opponents of the war.

Despite this readiness to challenge UK government policy, the newfound status of the MAB was confirmed in 2005, when it was embraced as a partner by the authorities and given a critical role in the transformation of the "Finsbury Park" (North London Central) Mosque. This institution had previously become notorious as a home for the overtly pro-jihadist preacher Abu Hamza al-Masri. Under Abu Hamza's auspices, the mosque, in the words of one account, had been turned into "a suicide factory," with the would-be "shoe bomber" Richard Reid, and the so-called twentieth hijacker Zacarias Moussaoui having passed through its doors.[352] In 2003, the mosque was closed down after a police raid had uncovered, inter alia, weapons, ammunition, and even biochemical clothing. Two years later, members of the MAB and MWH were approached by a combination of people who included "the old trustees, the police, the Home Office [and] MPs" and they were invited to take over the running of the mosque.[353] In February 2005, the building reopened—dedicated to "serving the local Muslim community" and "working with everyone to promote dialogue and understanding in our multi-cultural society."[354] The first Friday sermon at the restored mosque was delivered by Kemal el-Helbawy.[355] Kim Howells, the junior Foreign Office minister, subsequently commented that the MWH had been "instrumental in helping the Metropolitan Police hand control of Finsbury Park Mosque back to mainstream Muslims."[356]

The mosque was thereby transformed into a core hub for the MAB-MWH network in the United Kingdom; this was confirmed by the profile of those involved in the post-2005 governance of the institution. The new trustees were identical to those registered as owners of the MWH at that time: Mohammed Kozbar, Muhammad Sawalha, Ahmad Sheikh Muhammad, Abdel Shaheed el-Eshaal, and Hafez al-Karmi. Four of these men were also previous or existing directors of the MAB (al-Karmi being the exception).[357] The chairman of the trustees, Abdel Shaheed el-Ashaal, was described as a "senior MAB member."[358] Until 2000, he had been the secretary of the "Hassan el-Banna Foundation," the aim of which was to "give a correct image of the thoughts, ideology, and life of Imam Shaheed Hassan el-Banna." Moreover, in an interview with *Islamism Digest,* a magazine produced by Kamal el-Helbawy's "Centre for the Study of Terrorism," el-Ashaal was referred to as a senior member of the Muslim Brotherhood.[359] All of this reflects the close and overlapping ties that cut across these different institutions, as well as the extent to which they belonged, intellectually at least, to the Ikhwan.

During this era, however, the authorities saw affiliations of this kind as being no impediment to working with the MAB. On the contrary, the connection with the Brotherhood was evidently seen as an asset. Among the brokers of the deal to hand over the Finsbury Park Mosque to the MAB-MWH was the aforementioned Robert Lambert, who continued to promote the view that the authorities should work with hard-line Salafists and Islamists.[360] Lambert, though, was far from alone in believing that groups whose origins lay with the Brotherhood could play an important role in tackling extremism. Soon after the takeover of the Finsbury Park Mosque, the government asked the MAB to be one of four founding organizations behind the Mosques and Imams National Advisory Board (MINAB)—another initiative that was meant to help combat violent radicalism.[361]

Nonetheless, the creation of MINAB in some ways marked the high-water mark of the MAB's influence; for if the British government had led the way in terms of being ready to engage with the Brotherhood post-9/11, it was also the first to seriously reconsider this approach. From late 2006, there were signs that the pendulum was beginning to swing back the other way, with the authorities looking at the Ikhwan through a less benign lens. To a significant degree, this seems to have been a function of governmental unhappiness with what was seen as the complicity of groups like the MAB and the MCB with the "grievance culture" that underpinned extremist ideology.[362] Already in 2005, some had begun to analyze the MCB with a critical eye, pointing to links between leading figures in the group and the Jamaat-i-Islami. Martin Bright for the *New Statesman* and Policy Exchange and John Ware for the BBC's *Panorama* were at the forefront of this shift.[363] Concerns were then raised over the role played by those identified with the Brotherhood during the "Danish cartoons" crisis of February 2006.[364] Yusuf al-Qaradawi, for instance, was conspicuous in demanding a boycott of all Danish goods until the government in Copenhagen apologized for the publication of the drawings.[365] Within the United Kingdom, the MAB organized a large protest against the cartoons under the slogan "United against Islamophobia and United against Extremism"; the demonstrators there included several people carrying banners inciting violence ("behead those who insult Islam" being one especially virulent example).[366] The episode surely prompted some reconsideration of whether the MAB was truly a suitable partner for government.

A more decisive moment, however, seems to have been the "airline plot" of August 2006, when the police thwarted a conspiracy to blow up multiple transatlantic airliners simultaneously. In the aftermath, the MCB and its allies issued a statement that appeared to blame British foreign policy in the Middle East for driving the terrorist threat. To key ministers like Ruth Kelly, the secretary of state for communities and local government, as well as to Prime Minister Tony Blair himself, this was unacceptable.[367] What followed was a revision of the government's Prevent strategy in order to strengthen the focus on ideology. Henceforth, the government promised to place more emphasis on the problems of "non-violent" as well as "violent" extremism. In that context, those formerly described as "moderate" Islamists, such as the Brotherhood, were examined more critically and groups like the MAB found it harder to gain funds and recognition.[368]

At this moment, too, the MAB appears to have experienced some internal problems that resulted in an undeclared split and the creation of a new entity, the British Muslim Initiative (BMI). This laid bare the extent to which the post-2000 politicization of the MAB and its overt and at times confrontational strategy had proven controversial to many of its own members.[369] On the one hand, the alliance with "Stop the War" had been crucial in developing the organization. As Richard Phillips has explained, it had furnished a hitherto "relatively obscure" body with a national profile. Membership of the MAB had increased from around four hundred people to somewhere between eight hundred and a thousand. But many within the group feared the abandonment of its original educational-cultural focus. They were also concerned about the adoption of too forceful a position vis-à-vis the authorities. As Azzam al-Tamimi told Phillips, the ensuing "crisis" was fueled by objections that "the leaders of MAB . . . had over-politicised MAB and put [it] on a crash-course with the government."[370]

A rival faction succeeded in overturning the group's leadership in December 2005, electing a new president and executive board.[371] Anas Altikriti has described this as a kind of "coup" within the organization—with the result that "all of a sudden," the leadership of the MAB was filled by people who were, in Altikriti's eyes, "non-entities." The new leaders then allowed the formal alliance with "Stop the War" to lapse. It was in response to this that those in favor of maintaining an openly political profile, such as Altikriti, formed the British Muslim Initiative (BMI) in February 2006.[372]

Subsequently, the exact nature of the relationship between the MAB and the BMI was difficult to determine. As revealed by Phillips, some members saw it as a "wholly new organisation, not warmly regarded by MAB's leadership." Others, by contrast, believed the BMI was "effectively—though not officially—a branch of [the] MAB, its principal members drawn from the membership and former leadership of that organisation."[373] In 2008, Altikriti summarized the situation in the following terms: "The MAB is a grassroots organisation established almost 11 years ago, and I had the honour of being amongst its founding members. I am a member of MAB and was its president in 2004, although I no longer hold a leading post within it. BMI is a political organisation founded by a group of activists in 2006. It does not have a membership, nor does it cover aspects of a British Muslim's life beyond politics (such as MAB does). I am one of the founding members, and currently spokesman for BMI."[374] Altikriti was joined in the BMI by other senior activists like Azzam al-Tamimi and Muhammad Sawalha. They persisted with efforts to engage at a political level—lending their support, for example, to the Respect Party that was created to contest the 2005 general elections.[375] In addition, Altikriti was a key organizer behind the "Muslims 4 Ken" movement prior to the 2008 London mayoralty elections.[376] By such cooperation, BMI members sought to extend their earlier concordat with sections of the political left. The group served, too, as a useful "holding" exercise until the aforementioned "coup" was reversed in 2009, when Altikriti and his allies reexerted control over the MAB.[377]

A further venture launched by Altikriti in this era was the Cordoba Foundation (of which he was the CEO).[378] This was to be an "independent strategic think tank" that sought dialogue with a range of partners, not least government.[379] It mixed research with advocacy, training, and the hosting of a variety of events.[380] In 2015, for instance, it held a national conference on the theme of "Islam and Democracy: Exploring the Strategies of Political Islam and the Muslim Brotherhood's Contribution."[381] Alongside this, the Cordoba Foundation produced a number of publications, including the *Arches Quarterly* journal and several policy reports. Most recently, it launched *The MENA Report: Analysis and Insights from the Arab World*.[382] The ambition of the Cordoba Foundation to build a public profile, though, was hampered by controversy. In 2008, David Cameron, while still leader of the opposition, publicly identified the group as a "front" for the Muslim Brotherhood and questioned whether it was a deserved recipient of government counterextremism funding.[383] Later, the government's 2015 review of the Brotherhood remarked on the links between the Foundation and the MAB and described it as "associated with the Brotherhood (though claiming to be neither affiliated to the Muslim Brotherhood nor a lobby organization for it)."[384]

The difficulties experienced by the Cordoba Foundation were symptomatic of changing official attitudes toward groups identified with the Ikhwan. It had been partly in order to mitigate the impact of this worsening atmosphere that in 2006, Kemal el-Helbawy had founded yet another new body, the aforementioned Centre for the Study of Terrorism (CFSOT). This, in turn, published the *Islamism Digest* magazine that was devoted to studying Islamist movements around the world. The inaugural issue, for example, contained an article on the Association of Muslim Scholars in Iraq, as well as interviews with, variously, 'Abd al-Mon'im Abu al-Futuh of the Egyptian Ikhwan, a former member of the Iraqi Islamic Party, and Khurshid Ahmad of Pakistan's Jamaat-i-Islami.[385] The main purpose of the magazine and the CFSOT was to produce a definition of "terrorism" that excluded "legitimate" forms of "resistance."[386] In a piece to mark the first anniversary of the CFSOT's creation, el-Helbawy stated that the center examined terrorism from a "Muslim" perspective, in order to "present a more balanced view . . . and to identify the 'real' terrorists." El-Helbawy criticized the conflation of Islamism with terrorism and specifically rejected the idea that Hizballah and Hamas should be considered terrorist groups. He also declared his opposition to the US-led "War on Terror," portraying this solely as a vehicle for American "global hegemony."[387] On another occasion, *Islamism Digest* similarly took aim at British counterterrorism policies—an indication, perhaps, of their sense that the tide of the debate was, within the UK at least, running against them.[388]

By late 2007, organizations like the MAB, BMI, CFSOT, and the MCB were clearly aware of the shifting outlook of the British government. A sign of the changing environment was the 2008 decision of Home Office Minister Jacqui Smith to ban Yusuf al-Qaradawi from coming to the UK for medical treatment. Another individual excluded from Britain at this time was Wagdy Ghoneim, a preacher associated with the Egyptian Brotherhood. Ghoneim, who had previously taken part in MWH-sponsored seminars, was prevented from entering the country because he had engaged in unacceptable behavior linked to the justification or glorification of terrorist violence.[389] He had long been a controversial figure. Earlier, on a 1998 visit to the United States, Ghoneim was recorded singing a song, "No to the Jews, Descendants of the Apes" at a mosque in Brooklyn. That same year, he was denied entry to Canada, and in 2004, he was arrested and accepted voluntary departure from the United States rather than risk deportation, after he had been accused of fund-raising "that could have helped terrorist organizations" (namely, Hamas).[390] In a statement that appeared on his website in 2006, Ghoneim openly advocated jihad against "the oppressive and usurping enemy." Muslims, he averred, should pray for the protection of their brothers "in beloved Palestine, Lebanon, Iraq, Afghanistan, and Chechnya, and all the Muslims."[391] It was against this backdrop that Ghoneim was stopped at the airport and denied entrance to the United Kingdom.

In the face of such developments, the MAB and BMI remained defiant in their views and, if anything, became even more fierce in their criticism of British counterterrorism policy. In October 2009, the BMI stated that it was the victim of "a dark political undercurrent of hostility engineered by the Zionist, Islamophobe and Neo-Con alliance (ZINC)." The group also called on the government to scrap the "discredited and wasteful" Prevent strategy.[392] Senior figures in the MAB such as Muhammad Kozbar likewise asserted that Prevent was toxic and part of an effort to "silence Muslims."[393]

As the foregoing suggests, the accusation that organizations like the MAB and MWH were the victims of "Islamophobia" became a central element in their attempts to reverse the post-2006 trajectory of government policy. More broadly, the battle against Islamophobia became a core, mobilizing theme.[394] In March 2008, for instance, the MAB condemned the film *Fitna,* produced by right-wing Dutch politician Geert Wilders, which attacked Islam. In a statement, Ahmad al-Rawi said that European Muslims were being "victimised twice"—first, by being targeted, along with everybody else, in terrorist attacks and, second, "by far right and fascist groups." The MAB urged political leaders to "promote community cohesion rather than hate and evil."[395] The following year, the BMI arranged for a demonstration in front of the German Embassy to protest the murder of Marwa al-Sherbini in Dresden. Among the banners on display were those that read: "Stop the culture of hatred toward Muslims" and "The Muslims are not second-class citizens."[396]

Without question, of course, there was a problem during this period with a rise in anti-Muslim bigotry and hate crimes.[397] Yet some challenged the appropriateness of the term "Islamophobia" and the way in which certain groups seemed to use it to impugn the motives of their critics.[398] Suffice it to say for present purposes that the campaign against Islamophobia, which itself seemed rooted in a "grievance narrative," did not heal the rift between the government and organisations like the MAB.

Other initiatives led by the MAB and its allies served only to harden the authorities' caution in dealing with them. A good example in this regard was their activism on Palestine. After the Gaza Strip was subject to an international blockade following Hamas's 2006 electoral victory, the MAB and BMI spearheaded a campaign to promote the Palestinian cause. One of those most prominently involved was Muhammad Sawalha.[399] In February 2009, he signed a document applauding the "principled stand" of the Turkish people and government during a crisis over Gaza.[400] The same month, he attended a conference of Islamic scholars held in Istanbul under the banner of the "Global anti-aggression campaign," which culminated in the issuing of a statement that demanded the opening of a "third jihadist front" in Palestine (alongside those in Iraq and Afghanistan). The "Islamic Nation" was urged to "carry on with the jihad and resistance against the occupier until the liberation of all Palestine," and to resist "by all means and ways" any incursion of "foreign warships" seeking to stop smuggling into Gaza.[401] Given that British prime minister Gordon Brown had offered to send the Royal Navy to help police the eastern Mediterranean, this so-called Istanbul Declaration generated a fresh storm of controversy around its UK-based signatories such as Sawalha and the MCB's Daud Abdullah.[402]

Within Britain, meanwhile, leaders like Sawalha and Anas Altikriti organized numerous rallies in which they took center stage alongside known Islamists. At one gathering in March 2010, for instance, Altikriti appeared on a platform together with al-Ghannouchi and el-Helbawy. The latter declared that "resistance" was "the only language that the occupation [that is, Israel]" understood. He therefore pleaded with those present to act, according to their capacity, "to liberate Palestine—all Palestine." It was essential, el-Helbawy said, that the Islamic nation was "prepared for jihad in all its forms," until the occupier was expelled from its land.[403]

Needless to say, such strident rhetoric did not sit well with the British government and strengthened the hand of those opposed to engagement with groups like the MAB and MWH. The election of a conservative-led government in 2010 further reinforced the perception that suspected Islamists were now personae non gratae in official circles. A key focus for David Cameron's administration was a fresh review of the Prevent strategy, which led to an even greater emphasis on the need to tackle extremism all told, in both its violent *and* nonviolent formats. The prime minister and other senior ministers highlighted this shift in a succession of speeches.[404] And this process culminated in the launching of a new "Counter-Extremism Strategy" in 2015, which specifically identified Islamism as part of the problem. Brotherhood ideologues Hasan al-Banna and Sayyid Qutb were mentioned by name; and there was a pledge to avoid "engaging with extremists."[405]

In coming to such a position domestically, it is worth noting that the British government now held to a line that was markedly more stringent than the one pursued by Washington. Initial US conceptions of the War on Terror had imagined it as a conflict to be fought "over there," rather than on the home front. For this reason, there was no immediate American equivalent to the United Kingdom's Prevent strategy. It was only in 2011 that President Barack Obama's administration produced a formal Countering Violent Extremism (CVE) program.[406] Prior to this point, thinking about issues like engagement had been rather "ad hoc." Within that context, the US authorities showed a general inclination to work with groups that had their origins in the Brotherhood network, such as the MAS, CAIR, and ISNA.[407] That picture, though, did change somewhat in the wake of the 2007 Holy Land Foundation trial, which prompted a definite cooling of relations.[408] In 2009, the FBI banned all contact with CAIR, saying that it did not view it as "an appropriate liaison partner."[409]

Nonetheless, there appears to have been no government-wide injunction against cooperation with organizations of this kind. Instead, the picture continued to be mixed, with different departments and institutions following their own policies. Moreover, under the Obama administration it seems clear that officials—especially those tasked with "public engagement" and outreach—*were* prepared to meet with representatives of groups like CAIR.[410] Almost inevitably, this stance encouraged a cottage industry of writers who made sensationalist and wildly overblown claims about Brotherhood infiltration of the administration (or the even more egregious suggestion that Obama himself was a Muslim). The more prosaic reality was that it was simply a function of the president's self-declared willingness, particularly during his first term, to talk to anyone: his government was prepared to engage with a range of actors who might otherwise be considered "undesirable." Administration officials therefore appeared at ISNA conferences in 2009 and 2012. The president himself met with the leaders of ISNA and the MAS at the White House.[411]

In this way, the Obama administration demonstrated a preference for engagement at home, of the kind it also applied with the Brotherhood abroad, albeit in circumspect fashion; for it was possible to discern a cautious openness to talks with the Ikhwan in the Middle East in the period after 2009. Some heralded this as a major change. Yet it actually represented an element of continuity between Obama and the last years of the Bush administration. Somewhat surprisingly, it was the latter that had initiated the process of reassessment that led to a resumption of contacts with the Brothers.

Engagement and Its Limits

The Mubarak regime was deeply suspicious of anything that, from its perspective, seemed to imply a drawing together of the United States and the Ikhwan. The great fear in Cairo was that Washington might seek to insure itself against the day when Mubarak fell by building a relationship with his opponents. As a result, Secretary of State Condoleezza Rice had tried to reassure the Egyptian government, in the wake of her June 2005 Cairo speech (at the height of the Bush administration's zeal for the "freedom agenda"), that "we have not engaged the Muslim Brotherhood and we don't—we won't."[412] This stance was buttressed by the fact that American officials were still unconvinced by the Ikhwan's vocal commitment to democracy and human rights. Its adoption of such rhetoric was reckoned in 2005 to be more of a "tactical shift rather than an indication of [an] evolving ideology." The organization was thought to remain "decidedly Islamist in its outlook and agenda," with the rank and file deemed especially unrepentant.[413]

In spite of this, and regardless of the prohibition on diplomatic dialogue with the Brotherhood, various international and US-based nongovernmental organizations (NGOs), working to promote democratic reform and the growth of civil society in Egypt, had maintained some contact with offshoots of the broad Islamist movement.[414] More significant, from 2006, there appeared to be a definite turn toward official, government-led engagement. In October of that year, the US Embassy in Cairo sent Washington a dispatch outlining the organizational structure and internal dynamics of the Brotherhood. It did so in response to "INR queries" (INR being the US Bureau of Intelligence and Research within the State Department).[415] The very fact that such requests were being made implies that the Ikhwan—as an issue for foreign policy makers—was now back on the agenda in Washington. This would correspond with the assertion of Ian Johnson, that from 2006, certain arms of the American state (including the CIA) began to reappraise the character of the Brotherhood, seeing it in a somewhat more positive fashion.[416]

In March 2007, the Brothers' parliamentary leader Sa'd al-Katatni visited the consular section of the Cairo Embassy. A subsequent memorandum recounted that a warm and friendly encounter had taken place and that US officials had stressed to al-Katatni their willingness to meet with any parliamentarians. The Brotherhood leader had apparently "noted that it was unfortunate that there had been no USG-MB [United States Government-Muslim Brotherhood] contact for so long," as he regularly talked to staff from other embassies.[417] Thereafter, a faltering and tentative set of exchanges took place. In April, for example, al-Katatni was permitted to attend an academic conference at Georgetown University in Washington, where he renewed in general terms his call for dialogue with the United States (while still expressing "several reservations" about the Bush administration).[418] That same month saw the aforementioned visit of a congressional delegation under Democratic House majority leader Steny Hoyer to Egypt, which met with Brotherhood members of parliament—both at the People's Assembly and then again at a reception hosted by Ambassador Ricciardone.[419] The Ikhwan's al-Katatni later stated that at these gatherings they had avoided discussion of domestic Egyptian matters, with conversation instead focused on regional issues such as Palestine and Iraq.[420] For his part, Ricciardone merely confirmed that talks had taken place "in the full light of day."[421]

In the months that followed, contacts with the Brotherhood continued, but these were kept at a low level and there was no fundamental reorientation in the US outlook of a kind that might have threatened the strategic relationship with the Egyptian government. The Wikileaks cables show that US diplomats maintained "telephone contact" with al-Katatni. But this did not lead to additional face-to-face meetings until the first half of 2009.[422] Ikhwan leaders themselves tended to play down the significance of these exchanges. In June 2008, the deputy chairman of the Brotherhood acknowledged that some of their members in the People's Assembly had met US congressmen, but he insisted that this was "not a negotiation." It was, he said, "a dialogue with civil society organizations, researchers and academics."[423] This stance was reiterated the next month by the general guide, Mahdi 'Akef, who stated that the Brothers were willing to speak to civil organizations, media outlets, universities, and research institutes, but took a different line when it came to the American government. 'Akef was adamant that "no dialogue with foreign governments [could] take place in the absence of an Egyptian government representative."[424]

On the other side, meanwhile, US officials evidently held mixed views about the Ikhwan. They were aware, for example, of the Brotherhood's support for "resistance" against the "Zionist Anglo-American occupiers" in Palestine and Iraq.[425] Within Egypt, the diplomats cast a critical eye over the Brothers' attempts to write a draft political program in August 2007. The document that emerged, they noted, was replete with the language of pluralism, human rights, equal citizenship, and democratic reform. In the judgment of the embassy, it contained "unprecedented" detail about the group's positions and spoke about the "full range of political and religious freedoms." And yet, the diplomats simultaneously expressed concern that the manifesto both signaled "a potentially contradictory commitment to more robustly implementing shari'a," and took a "hard line on Israel."[426] In fact, the platform caused major controversy because of proposals for the creation of a council of Islamic scholars (who would vet all legislation), as well as the prohibition on women or Christians becoming head of state. These stipulations generated a "firestorm" of external criticism that led general guide 'Akef to announce that work on the manifesto had been suspended. In addition, the episode appeared to expose internal Ikhwan differences. Nathan Brown and 'Amr Hamzawy identified an "ideological division" that "pitted a conservative or reactionary wing against a reformist wing," alongside a "generational struggle" that saw an "old guard" take on a "new guard."[427]

This notion of factional splits proved of enduring fascination to the diplomats. Confusions over the "true" position of the Ikhwan encouraged attempts to understand the group's internal dynamics. In 2005, for instance, the embassy passed on rumors that general guide 'Akef had been sidelined by those who thought him "excessively pragmatic." This move had been accompanied, it was said, by the "temporary suspension" from the organization's guidance council of 'Abd al-Mon'im Abu al-Futuh—now, unlike earlier, described as a "reformer" and "liberal." "More rigid" members of the group, such as Muhammad Habib and Khayrat al-Shater were reputed to have taken over from a leader who was "unpopular" among the grass roots.[428]

Leaving aside the accuracy or otherwise of such reports, their significance for present purposes lay in the extent to which they were symptomatic of ongoing US efforts to uncover and interpret the "real" politics of the Ikhwan.[429] By the start of 2008, embassy officials were referring to the "schizophrenia" of the Brotherhood. They perceived the movement as divided between a "religiously-oriented conservative wing" and a "politically-oriented moderate wing." The former were estimated to be numerically stronger, comprising around 55–60 percent of the group, and bolstered by a "worrisome Salafi tendency among some younger MB members." Conversely, just 30–35 percent of Brothers were considered moderates.[430] Throughout 2009, the embassy portrayed the Ikhwan as riven by "an inter-generational and ideological battle."[431]

In trying to read the runes of the Brotherhood's "internal clashes" during this era, much attention again focused on the question of who would succeed Mahdi 'Akef as general guide. In 2008, it was assumed that his successor would be drawn from the conservative wing of the group—a reflection of the aforementioned factional balance of strength.[432] Toward the end of the following year, by contrast, there were whispers that the Ikhwan's next leader would be Muhammad Habib—'Akef's deputy (and the man around whom there had been speculation of an internal coup in 2005).[433] As it was, however, Muhammad Badi'e was elected as the group's new general guide in January 2010. A subsequent dispatch from the American Embassy admitted that Badi'e was an "administrative insider and relative unknown"; and while one of their informers allegedly described him as a moderate, others labeled him variously as a compromise candidate, or indeed a conservative. (The latter assessment was the one favored by most commentators, with Badi'e said to belong to the "Qutbiyyun" faction within the Ikhwan.)[434] In the end, the diplomats concluded somewhat plaintively: "The verdict is still out on what recent internal elections mean."[435]

Once more, then, "kremlinology" of this kind seemed only to highlight the ambiguous and undetermined character of the Brotherhood and its trajectory, as US officials struggled to decode its internal currents. The failure to anticipate the emergence of Badi'e was but one illustration of this. By the same token, it is arresting to note that someone like 'Abd al-Mon'im Abu al-Futuh could at one stage be classified as a "hawk," and later be portrayed (perhaps more accurately) as a "reformer"; the same had been true in an earlier period of Ma'mun al-Hudaybi. Others such as Muhammad Habib seemed to defy repeated attempts at categorization. All of this highlights the problematic and artificial nature of the endeavor. As Ambassador Margaret Scobey presciently remarked, labels like "'Conservative' and 'reformer' are shorthand terms used by outside observers to describe MB members in Arabic, but not necessarily used by MB actors to describe themselves."[436] What Scobey thereby recognized was the extent to which embassy officials, in trying to identify "moderates" as opposed to "extremists," tended to project a framework of their own creation onto the Brotherhood.

Elsewhere, US diplomats had acknowledged the difficulty of trying to identify "moderates" and "hardliners" within Sudan's ruling National Congress Party (itself, of course, an offshoot of the Brotherhood). Often, they stated, the only real difference between factions was the role that people were asked to play: "the seemingly moderate and polished negotiators" were those tasked with talking to the Americans; whereas the "hardliners" were those whose job was to ensure the movement remained in office. In the end, the officials averred, it perhaps made more sense to see the NCP "not as a regime with hardliners and moderates, but merely as a regime with powerful and less powerful actors."[437] Similarly in Jordan, officials confirmed that it was "sometimes quite hard to distinguish between the policy stances of so-called moderates and hawks."[438] Insofar as there was a distinction, it was said to be born of "demographics and [their] relationship with the [government of Jordan]."[439] Evidently, the same observations could be made, mutatis mutandis, with regard to the Egyptian Ikhwan. There, too, as Abdullah al-Arian has commented, internal conflicts were mostly not "ideological in nature," but rather about the structure of the organization.[440] In this context, the delineation of hawks and doves, or extremists and moderates, brought little analytical clarity.

Moreover, it is clear that the Brotherhood and its allies had long wished to assert their own moderation, albeit using that term in a particular way. Yusuf al-Qaradawi had developed and expounded the concept of the "wasatiyya" (middle way) as a way of summarizing the ideology of the Ikhwan. He said the Brothers constituted a "middle nation," and adhered to centrist views. What he meant by this was that, on the one hand, they rejected secular and materialist culture; on the other, they were critical of what al-Qaradawi called "conservative traditionalism," literalism, and intellectual stagnation.[441] In addition, he claimed that the Brotherhood bore no sectarian animus against Christians, arguing that they should enjoy a special status as "People of the Book." (On the Jews, al-Qaradawi's views were less benign, as he accused them of showing hostility toward, and fighting, the Islamic da'wa.)[442]

As this suggests, when people like al-Qaradawi or Mustafa Mashhur defined the Brotherhood as "moderate," they were saying something quite specific: namely, that it held to a comprehensive vision of Islam without "exaggeration and embellishment" and without "neglect and concession."[443] The Brothers thus used the term "moderate" quite differently from Western observers. Their "moderation" was not part of a process of evolution; rather, it was deemed to be inherent in the character of the Ikhwan as established by Hasan al-Banna. Their self-ascribed "moderation" lay in their attachment to the parameters of the *da'wa,* as practised by the Brotherhood.

For the same reason, al-Qaradawi insisted that secularism was something they could not accept, for it meant the "abandonment of Shari'ah, a denial of the divine guidance and a rejection of Allah's injunctions." He argued that "the call for secularism among Muslims is atheism and a rejection of Islam." Indeed, according to al-Qaradawi, the acceptance of secularism "as a basis for rule in place of Shari'ah" was "downright riddah [apostasy]."[444] What such comments reveal is the way a supposedly "moderate" outlook could actually end up being very close to de facto takfirism—with secularized Muslims being placed outside the boundaries of the faith.

In the hands of the Brothers, therefore, the word "moderate" could not be used as a synonym for "free-thinking" or "open-minded," and certainly not for "liberal." American officials perhaps had it right when they noted in 2005 that the term "moderate" was "a label embraced by a wide range of Muslim views and agendas in the region, and . . . even the extremists think they are moderates."[445] This being so, it was no surprise that the diplomats continued to highlight the ambiguity surrounding Brotherhood positions on a range of subjects, including the use of violence.

When Barack Obama came to office in 2009, there had been much conjecture that he would initiate a more forward policy with the Brotherhood. In June of that year, he delivered a much-heralded speech in Cairo, promising to rebuild US ties with the Islamic world. The president declared forcefully: "America respects the right of all peaceful and law-abiding voices to be heard . . . even if we disagree with them. And we will welcome all elected, peaceful governments— provided they govern with respect for all their people."[446] The *Washington Post* inferred that this message was aimed directly at the Muslim Brothers—several of whom attended the speech in their capacity as parliamentarians.[447]

Beyond Egypt, too, there were hints that more energy was being invested in the effort to reestablish communication with other chapters of the Ikhwan at that time. There were reports, for example, that President Obama had met with Western-based members and sympathizers of the Brotherhood; and that at those gatherings, the latter had underlined their commitment to democracy and their opposition to terrorism.[448] In September 2009, the US Embassy in Amman recorded that it had begun a "quiet yet deliberate process" of mending relationships with the Jordanian Brotherhood and the Islamic Action Front.[449] The move came in response to a letter sent by Zaki Bani Irshad, the head of the IAF, to President Obama, in which he appealed for dialogue. One of Irshad's deputies had also traveled to the United States for an academic seminar in Washington; and American officials in Amman were invited to meet with "moderate" members of the Ikhwan.[450] At one such encounter, Brotherhood representatives had offered a critique of US foreign policy (and its alleged hypocrisy when it came to democracy promotion), while stating that they "would welcome the resumption of political dialogue, albeit in a careful, methodical, behind-the-scenes manner."[451] As a result, US diplomats had opted to break the "taboo" that had grown up in the wake of 9/11 and decided to "reach out to known moderates" in the first instance, with the eventual aim of maintaining "a broader range of contacts."[452]

And yet, for all the speculation (and at times, hysteria) occasioned by these policy adjustments, the reality was that relations with all branches of the Brotherhood changed relatively little. In Jordan, engagement was still strained by doubts over where the Brotherhood stood. As Mansoor Moaddel has pointed out, it *was* possible to find evidence that the Ikhwan had abandoned a binary vision of the world in favor of a more nuanced outlook. The post-2009 head of the IAF, Ishaq Farhan, for instance, declared that their aim was "not replacing Western civilization with Islam" and he spoke of "a duty to cooperate with the West and learn from it." Yet equally, it was repeatedly made apparent that not everyone shared this viewpoint. Other Brothers such as former controller general 'Abd al-Majid al-Dhunaybat—ironically, someone frequently identified as a moderate—never ceased to hope for the collapse of both American civilization and the "Zionist enemy," and he railed against the decadence of Western society.[453]

In Egypt, meanwhile, the stumbling block throughout this period was once more the attitude of the Mubarak regime. From the spring of 2006 onward, the Egyptian authorities had launched a new "unrelenting crackdown" against the activities of the Brotherhood, targeting senior leaders and rank-and-file members alike. Over the course of the year, there was a steady drumbeat of arrests and the process accelerated after the "al-Azhar militia" controversy in December—when masked Ikhwani students performed a martial arts demonstration.[454] At a minimum, this seemed an especially foolhardy move, and it provided the government with the opportunity to escalate its repressive campaign.[455] Moreover, this was set within a wider context that saw the "renewal" of autocracy within Egypt, as the Mubarak regime signaled its decisive rejection of any democratizing process.[456]

Rumors that Western governments were considering engagement with the Brotherhood only encouraged the Egyptian authorities to toughen their stance against the group. In the late summer of 2007, the US Embassy reported that the regime had reacted particularly "testily" to foreign governmental outreach to the Ikhwan.[457] A few months later, the first military trials of Brotherhood figures since the mid-1990s saw more than twenty senior leaders, including Khayrat al-Shater, given lengthy prison sentences. In parallel, a sustained campaign of obstruction, harassment, and detentions prompted the Ikhwan to call for a boycott of the country's local elections.[458] From the middle of 2009, the regime engineered a further "ramping up" of pressure on the Brothers, arresting various high-profile members and accusing them of belonging to an "international MB conspiracy" involving revolutionary activity and money laundering.[459]

The effect of all this, as Sa'd al-Katatni admitted to his US interlocutors, was to create a "difficult" environment for the Brotherhood.[460] This being the case, it is perhaps remarkable that contacts of any kind continued to take place—as indeed they did. At the same time, it is possible to discern the reasons why a posture of "limited dialogue" made sense for both sides. Washington, as described, had come to accept that pressure for democratization in the Middle East seemed likely to empower Islamists of the Brotherhood's ilk. The results of the "freedom agenda" had convinced many that there was no liberal option in the region. This perception underscored earlier judgments about the *inevitability* of Islamist success in the event that the region's authoritarian systems experienced change. This, in turn, led to a belief in many quarters that Western countries needed to build relations with the Ikhwan. For their part, the Brothers sought links with external actors like the United States as a means of garnering legitimacy. This was part of a long-running strategy by which Ikhwan leaders hoped to bolster their position within Egypt through appeals to an international audience.[461]

By late 2009–early 2010, as one former Brotherhood member told the US Embassy in Cairo, the reality was that "both the MB and the GOE [government of Egypt]" were "anxiously awaiting signals from the new U.S. administration on its policy towards dialogue with the group."[462] Subsequently, intermittent communication—of the kind conducted during the previous two years—persisted.[463] But there was no fundamental transformation in US policy. The senior Ikhwan leader, Gamal Heshmat, later attested that the opposition of the Egyptian government had proven an insuperable "obstacle" to better relations and helped distort views "of Islam and the Islamists in the Western mind."[464]

Ultimately, Washington prioritized bilateral relations with the Mubarak regime. In the decade after 9/11, new importance had been attached to security and intelligence cooperation with Cairo. Irrespective of occasional moments of tension with the Egyptians (such as over the Iraq War, US democracy promotion, or the Brotherhood), the Bush administration wished to preserve that strategic relationship and did not pursue regime change.[465] Furthermore, after 2006, Washington effectively soft-pedaled the "freedom agenda" and raised few objections, either to Mubarak's crackdown on the Ikhwan or to his efforts to secure the succession of his son, Gamal.[466] As secretary of state, Condoleezza Rice ignored congressional attempts to make economic aid to Egypt conditional and instead sought rapprochement with Cairo. This was carried through in the first years of the Obama administration, which had little interest in the "freedom agenda" and seemed content to follow the trajectory established in the final phase of the Bush presidency.[467]

In this context, both the United States and the Brotherhood remained wary of more extensive engagement—for fear of the potential reaction from the Mubarak government. It was not until the collapse of the regime in the first months of 2011 that the situation altered decisively—and it was only then that the United States and other Western countries felt able (and indeed compelled) to look at the Brotherhood in fresh light. At this point, the evolution of Western views about the "inevitability" of the Brotherhood as the force of the future became crucial, and it was then that what Youssef Nada called a "historic shift in foreign policy" took place.[468]

Conclusion

The period after 1989 saw a blurring of the boundaries in Western approaches toward Islamism, and especially the Muslim Brotherhood. Discussion of these subjects was often bound up with and affected by numerous other issues: debates about multiculturalism, integration, and the place of Islam within Western societies; debates about how best to encourage democratization in the broader Middle East and whether Islamists could be partners in a project of liberal reform; and debates about how best to "prevent" and diminish the violent threat posed by jihadist terrorists.

Against that background, what was once of concern solely to the Foreign Office and the State Department, respectively, now became a subject of interest to those arms of government with a domestic remit. In part, such developments reflected the evolution of the Ikhwan itself. During the previous half century, it had evolved from being an organization that mattered solely to Western policy in Egypt to become an international movement with a region-wide presence, as well as active branches and adherents among Muslim communities in the West. Thus, the Brotherhood itself now straddled the line between "within" and "without." In 2010, the group's spokesman in the West, Ibrahim Munir, told the BBC that in "every European country you can find [the] Muslim Brotherhood"; he might have added North America too.[469]

As scholars like Lorenzo Vidino and Brigitte Marechal have highlighted, the transfer of the Ikhwan's activities into the West involved a shift in the group's modus operandi. The Brothers produced new organizational forms and exploited changes in communication technology. Simultaneously, the international structures originally created by the Egyptian Ikhwan appeared to wither. The separate national branches were allowed to operate more or less autonomously, albeit while maintaining a preference for cooperation where possible. It seems clear too that "membership" of one of the Brotherhood's offshoot groups in Europe increasingly meant something quite different from the experience of belonging to the Ikhwan back in Egypt or elsewhere in the Middle East.

With that said, what continued to unite the Brotherhood—across the globe—was a particular vision of Islam. There was a shared commitment to what Marechal called a broad "corpus" of ideas, each of which could be encapsulated in a key term: *shumuliyya* (the comprehensiveness of Islam), *wasatiyya* (their adherence to the middle path), and jihad.[470] The latter, in particular, symbolized the Ikhwan's conception of Islam as praxis. The Brothers believed that to be a Muslim required the public performance of specific "norms" of morality and an activist mentality. As Vidino has described, this manifested itself in a commitment to "struggle" on behalf of Muslim causes, both abroad—notably in Palestine—and closer to home. Within Western societies, the goal of the Ikhwan, as defined by al-Qaradawi, was "a conservatism without isolation, and an openness without melting"; and he himself played a critical role in attempts to "draw boundaries" around the community, determining what it meant to be a "true" Muslim.[471]

To achieve their aims, the Brothers invariably presented themselves and their institutions as "moderate" yet authoritative voices of the Muslim community—the necessary interlocutors to whom the authorities should turn in order to understand "Islamic" issues. In the process, they embraced a new discourse centered on "rights" and "accommodation." The same might be said, to a lesser degree, about their counterparts in the Arab world.[472] The latter too appropriated the language of democracy, pluralism, human rights, and reform. But whereas the Ikhwan in Egypt and other Muslim countries still looked to attain power, the Brothers in the West focused solely on a form of identity politics. In so doing, they helped to drive what Gilles Kepel has labeled the "new communalism." Even as they talked about the virtues of "integration," they sought to foster an autonomous space within Western societies for a distinct Muslim community to which they would act as gatekeeper.[473] Despite their relative numerical weakness, their capacity for organization and the energy of their activism enabled them to exert a "totally disproportionate" influence within Muslim communities.[474]

Across the Middle East, meanwhile, many Western officials had identified the Ikhwan as the most important opposition force in otherwise authoritarian societies. By the end of the first decade of the twenty-first century, a consensus seemed to prevail that the group was an essential component of any region-wide process of democratization. After 2003, American officials had been forced to confront the reality of liberal weakness, as opposed to Islamist strength. It was for this reason that the Bush administration had, in hesitant fashion, restarted a process of dialogue with the Brothers. To be clear, there was no rush to embrace the Ikhwan. Throughout the two decades examined in this chapter, engagement with Islamist groups took second place to the safeguarding of bilateral relations with established pro-Western governments—and when those governments, such as that of Mubarak, objected to contacts, talks were abandoned.[475]

Officials also retained a number of concerns about the character of the Ikhwan and its politics. One result of this was the frequent penchant for "kremlinology" and attempts to square the circle between the apparent contradictions in Brotherhood ideology. Significant diplomatic energy was likewise invested in efforts to pick out moderate as opposed to more extreme factions. To many officials, though, the Ikhwan remained wrapped in ambiguity.

For its part, the Egyptian Brotherhood showed the same cautious pragmatism that had defined its existence during the previous eighty years. On the one hand, it clearly hoped to establish contact with Western governments; such ties were thought to afford it useful cover against regime repression. On the other hand, "the West" remained what it always had been for the Ikhwan: a hostile civilization, forever implicated in the Zionist project and committed to the destruction of Islam. Consequently, accommodation with the West could only ever be a tactical maneuver, driven in part by fear of that same Western power that the Brothers despised. Even then, they were reluctant to pursue dialogue wholeheartedly, lest it provoke the Mubarak regime. Thus, on the eve of the Arab Spring, a kind of stasis prevailed. Over the past four years, a policy of tentative engagement had been tried, but this had made little progress in the face of fierce resistance from the Egyptian government. It was only with the transformation of the broader sociopolitical context, with the eruption of the Arab Spring in 2011, that new possibilities truly emerged.

Conclusion

D URING THE LAST ninety years, the relationship between the Muslim Brotherhood and the West has
followed a winding and at times difficult path. The
Brotherhood was established in a context indelibly imprinted by Western power.
The movement's founder, Hasan al-Banna, held the West responsible for the defeat and abolition of the Ottoman empire and caliphate, seeing this as the
latest—and most pernicious—assault on Islam by an alien civilization that had
long been intent on destroying the faith. This was an "occidentalist" vision par
excellence, with history read as a battle between, on the one hand, a spiritual,
Islamic "East" and, on the other, a monolithic "West" that was imagined to be
simultaneously secularist-materialist and yet also the bearer of a Christian "cru-
sading" spirit.[1] As Jacques Waardenburg has observed, in this kind of thinking,
the occident was defined as the absolute negation of Islam.[2]

Al-Banna's worldview was a reflection of what he saw around him in Egypt,
where he was deeply conscious of the socioeconomic, cultural, and political influence enjoyed by foreigners—most obviously the British, whose military
presence served as a permanent reminder of their dominance. He associated that
tangible physical power with the profound social transformation taking place
in Egypt at the time. Al-Banna feared that the youth of the country were being
lost to Islam and succumbing to the allure of materialism. He watched, too,
the proselytizing activities of Christian missionaries and worried for the future

452

of Muslim society. He therefore formed the Brotherhood to combat what he saw as the many-headed beast of Western hegemony. The group aimed at the liberation of Egypt and other Muslim lands from European colonialism in all its forms. The Brothers looked to the restoration of a specifically *Islamic* civilization, via the (re-)construction of an *Islamic* social order, to be overseen by an *Islamic* state and, ultimately, a revived caliphate.

In this way, al-Banna effectively offered an "Islamic nationalist" alternative to the secular (and sometimes liberal) version of nationalism that was ascendant in contemporary anti-imperialist discourse. The message of the Brotherhood was framed as a more authentic form of national identity.[3] Religion constituted the one frontier that the colonial occupier could not cross: the British were not, nor ever could be, Muslim (or so it was imagined).[4] The Brothers' emphasis on the cultural-religious "otherness" of the West confirmed their own purity, as compared to their secular rivals who were accused of having been seduced by European ways. Hence, the Brotherhood also represented a powerful critique of the Egyptian elites of the 1920s and 1930s, who were seen as politically and culturally compromised. To someone like al-Banna, most members of the "pasha" class that controlled Egypt's government in this period were as remote as any foreigner. By their wealth, by their education, and by their sociocultural norms, they inhabited a different world to him. According to al-Banna, their "imitation of the West" was part of the problem, to be tackled by a return to Islam—not as a rejection of modernity, but to uncover its properly Islamic face.[5]

It makes sense, therefore, to view the Brotherhood as having emerged in a "liminal space" between East and West.[6] As far as al-Banna was concerned, he was not anti-Western per se; rather, he wished to harness the best elements of "the West" (which he himself often conflated with modernity) and reconcile this with an Islamic spirit. Yet the ideology of the Brotherhood invariably meant it was diametrically opposed to British interests: on the Egyptian national question; in the Brotherhood's broader aversion to European imperialism in the Middle East and North Africa; and in particular on the subject of Palestine. The latter helped bring the group to the attention of the British, when the Brothers sought to mobilize support for the Arab Revolt of 1936–1939.

From the outset, Western officials viewed the Brotherhood not only as a direct security threat but also as a challenge to their own self-understanding. They could not countenance the idea that the Brotherhood was trying to postulate an alternative Islamic *modernity*, shorn of its Western *accoutrements*. To their minds, "the West" and "modernity" were one and the same, an elision usually encapsulated in the rhetoric of "civilization." Since the late nineteenth century, British officials had embraced, to varying degrees, the notion that they carried a civilizing mission within countries like Egypt. From this perspective, a rejection of Western tutelage was a rejection of civilization itself. The Brotherhood thus tended to be seen in one-dimensional fashion, as reactionary, fanatical, and extremist.

Of course, this was reinforced by the fact that the Brothers were indeed hostile to the British presence in Egypt and the wider region. On the eve of the Second World War, officials were unnerved to uncover evidence of financial ties between agents of the Nazi regime and the Brotherhood. Al-Banna was believed to be part of a pro-palace, anti-British coalition of political forces connected with Prime Minister Ali Maher. The embassy also seemed aware that the Brothers were moving in a more militant direction as, in the early 1940s, they created a Special Apparatus, a paramilitary section dedicated to the virtues of physical-force jihad. For these reasons, the suppression of the Brotherhood was one of the first items on the wartime agenda of British diplomats. After pressuring King Faruq to dismiss Maher in 1940, they asked successive prime ministers to take action against al-Banna. In 1941, this led to the Brotherhood leader first being exiled (briefly) from Cairo, and then interned. The British were dismayed when the Egyptian government failed to follow through on this hard-line policy.

Against the backdrop of faltering efforts to crack down on the Brotherhood, some British officials—particularly within the military—appear to have flirted with more unorthodox options. A precedent had been set in 1940, when efforts were made to "buy off" Ahmad Husayn, the leader of the nationalist Young Egypt movement. Soon afterward, Hasan al-Banna and his deputies were subject to similar overtures. Negotiations were initiated by the academic-turned-intelligence operative James Heyworth-Dunne, who hoped to bribe al-Banna into softening his opposition to the British. The attempt failed—but thereafter, there were those who argued that a conciliatory approach to the Brotherhood might help to "liberalise" the movement. This was in keeping with a broader mind-set, current within sections of British officialdom, which imagined that otherwise unfriendly political forces might ultimately be "biddable." With regard to the Brotherhood, it would be a mistake to overstate the influence of this outlook; the weight of opinion continued to favor more "assertive" methods. Nevertheless, this debate would be revisited in the years—and decades—that followed.

In 1942, the British made their most direct intervention into Egyptian domestic affairs in twenty years when they insisted—almost literally at gunpoint—that the king appoint a ministry of their choosing. The result was the return to office of Mustafa al-Nahas and the Wafd Party, who were urged to deal decisively with all forms of subversion. Again, though, the British were to be disappointed with the new government's unwillingness to repress the Ikhwan. Al-Nahas instead opted for reconciliation and hoped to "kill" the Brothers with "kindness." Senior UK diplomats such as the ambassador, Sir Miles Lampson, were deeply skeptical about the likely effectiveness of these methods in dealing with an organization they had come to see as the "most serious danger to public security" in Egypt. Moreover, they expressed misgivings about the impact the Brotherhood was having on the fabric of society, pointing to a creeping intolerance that officials linked to the rise in "obscurantist" religious groups. There was, however, little they could do to reverse this trend. Sheltered by its accommodation with the authorities, the Brotherhood had grown to new proportions by 1945.

As Egypt entered the postwar period, the Brotherhood seemed ready to flex its political muscles on the national stage, amid growing instability and a sense of crisis. The group now approached the peak of its influence, offering a distinct vision of sociopolitical reform and articulating an uncompromising stand on the Egyptian national question. In common with mainstream nationalist opinion, the Brothers demanded the total evacuation of British troops and unity with Sudan. They exhorted successive governments to fulfill these goals, and showed their capacity to make—and break—administrations. In early 1946, it was Brotherhood-instigated unrest that helped bring down the first government of Mahmud al-Nuqrashi; within a year, they had effectively returned al-Nuqrashi to office after turning against Prime Minister Isma'il Sidqi (who they had initially supported).

This era also saw an escalation in rhetoric about jihad, and observers began to question the attitude of the Brothers toward violence. Hasan al-Banna regularly repudiated such acts—and in personal encounters with both British and American officials, was keen to present a reasonable face and stress his openness to accommodation. But as nationalist pressure grew, these denials appeared less convincing. Developments in Palestine were a critical part of the equation. As the Western powers and the United Nations came to embrace a partitionist settlement, al-Banna called for action and sent volunteers to participate in the Brotherhood's first physical-force jihad between 1947 and 1949.

The Brotherhood's commitment to Palestine was consonant with the widening horizons of the group. Branches of the movement spread across the Arab world and the Brothers became ardent campaigners for a range of "Islamic" causes. In Sanaʿa, for example, they had connections to the Free Yemeni Movement. Elsewhere, they were fierce in their condemnation of French policy in North Africa and the eastern Mediterranean, and there too they prescribed violent jihad against colonialism. British officials were among those who worried that such militant activism might rebound into Egypt. Certainly, by 1948 the Brotherhood's belligerence on Palestine appeared to have spilled across the border, with the group's Special Apparatus involved in attacks on Jewish targets in Cairo. These were coupled with acts of violence against the Egyptian authorities, and eventually, Prime Minister al-Nuqrashi ordered the dissolution of the Brotherhood in November 1948. He did so with the support of British (and other foreign) diplomats. To the Brotherhood, this endorsement confirmed the fact that their subsequent "ordeal" was the result of foreign intrigues. Perceptions of betrayal fueled the resultant cycle of violence. In retaliation for the proscription order, a member of the Special Apparatus killed the prime minister. Security agents then shot dead Hasan al-Banna in early 1949.

With the murder of their founder and leader, the Brotherhood faced its first great crisis. There were even suggestions that the group might be consigned to oblivion as it was forced to operate underground. Before the end of 1949, however, there were signs not only that it would survive, but also return to public prominence. After King Faruq decided to hold elections—a move that all but guaranteed a Wafdist return to power—the Brothers regrouped and made an alliance with al-Nahas's party. Throughout 1950, there was a steady growth in Brotherhood activity, despite the fact that the organization remained officially dissolved. A new leader was chosen to replace Hasan al-Banna: the former judge Hasan al-Hudaybi, who strove to regain the Brothers' legal status. Finally, in April 1951, the banning order was lifted and the movement re-entered political life. It did so amid a fresh surge of nationalist agitation, in which the Brothers were heavily involved. Demands for the cancellation of the Anglo-Egyptian Treaty of 1936 had been articulated—with increasing vehemence—over the previous two years. Prior to the elections, the Wafd had pledged to secure complete independence, whatever the cost. In late 1951, Prime Minister al-Nahas abrogated the treaty that he himself had signed fifteen years earlier. The Brotherhood took this as a cue to launch violent jihad against British forces located on the banks of the Suez Canal.

The "War of the Canal Zone" saw relatively few casualties—certainly on the British side—but it did produce the Brotherhood's first "martyrs" in an Egyptian context and consolidated the impression that the group was at the forefront of the struggle for independence. The conflict also proved to be the final straw for Egypt's ancien régime. In January 1952, after serious rioting in Cairo (provoked by the death of some fifty Egyptian policemen fighting the British in Ismailia), martial law was introduced and the Wafdist government dismissed. During the next six months, Egypt was ruled by consecutive minority governments. The Brotherhood cast a looming shadow across these events, with Western officials blaming the group for much of the ongoing violence in the Canal Zone. Remarkably, though, even as their troops were tasked with fighting the Brotherhood's "fedayeen," some British diplomats pondered whether the movement's more "moderate" leaders might be open to some kind of accommodation. Talks were held between embassy officials and representatives of general guide al-Hudaybi. The British ambassador wondered if a Brotherhood-led government might prove more amenable to a settlement. Such speculation, however, yielded no tangible results—and in some ways, said more about British desperation than the prospects for an actual alliance. In July 1952, in any case, all of this was rendered redundant by the coup that swept away Egypt's constitutional monarchy.

In the wake of the Free Officers' seizure of power, the British were tormented by fears that the Brotherhood wielded real authority behind the scenes. The group was seen as the epitome of the dark "extremist" forces that threatened to dislodge Western influence from the Middle East. Amid the uncertainties of revolutionary upheaval, the British desperately searched for "moderates" who might consent to them retaining a presence in Egypt. US diplomats, by contrast, showed little reticence in embracing the Free Officers (indeed, there were suspicions that the Central Intelligence Agency [CIA] had forewarning of the coup). In part because of this, the Americans slowly supplanted the British as the principal Western voice in the country. US Ambassador Jefferson Caffery and his colleagues regarded Gamal Abdel Nasser and the other army officers as mostly pragmatic modernizers—akin to the secularizing Atatürk—who could deliver progressive change. One issue on which they did agree with the British, though, was that the Brothers were "extremists" to be kept as far away from government as possible, especially given their intransigence on the national question.

The Brotherhood, meanwhile, continued to call for a resumption of jihad against the British. These demands helped poison the atmosphere between the group and the ruling junta. Initially close relations gave way to friction as the

Brothers struggled to navigate the challenges of the new era. From late 1952 and into 1953, tensions mounted, a process exacerbated by the unresolved nature of the power dynamics on all sides. In an effort to bolster their position, the Brothers engaged in dialogue with both the Americans and the British. Representatives like Mahmud Makhluf and Sa'id Ramadan sat down with US officials in Egypt and also traveled to Washington to promote the Brotherhood. In Cairo, the group's leaders held meetings with Trefor Evans of the British Embassy. In the end, this dialogue went nowhere, floundering on the Brotherhood's opposition to an Anglo-Egyptian settlement on terms acceptable to London. And the Cairo authorities then used the talks as evidence of Brotherhood treachery and double-dealing.

By early 1954, Nasser—who had consolidated his status as the dominant figure in the regime—decided to suppress the Brotherhood. An abortive attempt to achieve this goal in January was followed by a period of "uneasy truce." Nasser took this opportunity to finally reach an agreement with the British. Yet the Brothers vociferously rejected this settlement, and also now demanded a return to constitutional life. In response, the authorities began to arrest leaders of the group. This phase of "phony war" gave way to all-out conflict after a member of the Brotherhood's Special Apparatus tried to assassinate Nasser in October. Thousands of Brothers were detained and brought before a People's Tribunal. Many were sentenced to lengthy prison terms; six leaders were executed. Though not entirely comfortable with these methods, most Western diplomats expressed satisfaction with the outcome and welcomed the apparent destruction of the Brotherhood as a meaningful force in Egyptian political life.

The eclipse of the Brotherhood was paralleled by the ascent of Nasser. The Egyptian leader seemed to personify the modernizing future of the Middle East, far removed from the backward-looking and "fanatical" Brothers. As reflected in the work of scholars like Christina Harris and Manfred Halpern, such conclusions were informed by a particular view of what the modernization process entailed. Halpern, writing in 1963 for instance, described the far-reaching "revolution" he thought was in train across the region, which was "shattering the traditional community of Islam." Both "orthodox" and "reformist" versions of the faith were said to be doomed and giving way to "secular leadership." Groups like the Brotherhood—referred to variously as "antimodern," "extremist," "fascist" and "neo-Islamic totalitarian"—were seen as antediluvian movements of reaction.[7] In this view, a modern Middle East, like its Western counterpart, would be a secular place—and the hope was that Cairo's military regime might foster a positive social transformation in this direction.

As is well known, relations between Nasser and the West soon soured. Consequently, the United States sought to contain the Egyptian leader, worried that he would act as a "stalking horse" to communism. This was the thinking that lay behind successive measures such as the Omega Plan and the Eisenhower Doctrine (though the Americans balked at British, French, and Israeli actions over Suez in late 1956). Beyond this, consideration was given to ways in which the United States might bolster religious forces as a bulwark against revolutionary ideologies in the Middle East. This willingness to contemplate harnessing the "power" of Islam might, in theory, have worked to the benefit of the Brotherhood. Certainly, since the 1940s, senior leaders of the group had routinely portrayed themselves as "the greatest barrier against communism" in Egypt; on this basis, they advocated for an alliance with both the British and the Americans. Yet these appeals had fallen on deaf ears, overpowered by the prevailing Western reading of the Brotherhood as "xenophobic" and "extremist." Moreover, by the mid-1950s, despite evidence that the Brothers had survived Nasser's repression and were active across the region, the United States seemed little interested in making them an instrument of policy. To the extent that Washington did seek to mobilize "religion" for its own ends, this focused on attempts to "build up" King Saud and later King Faisal. The United States put its faith in the conservative and "moderate" *states* of Saudi Arabia and Jordan, rather than in *movements* like the Brotherhood—and even this policy was not maintained with any consistency. Instead, for a six-year period from late 1957, Washington mostly sought a rapprochement with Nasser, accepting him to be the most influential actor in the Middle East. At an intellectual level, officials were unpersuaded by the capacity of Islam to survive in the face of advancing modernity. Its role was deemed to be purely negative, perhaps staving off communism in the short-term, but only by retarding the inevitable forces of progress.

Against this background, it is striking that even as relations with Nasser deteriorated once more in the mid-1960s, and the United States further strengthened its ties with the Saudis and Jordanians, officials reckoned that this left them on the "wrong side" of history. They habitually believed that there was no real alternative to Nasser and the Arab nationalism-cum-socialism that embodied the future. Groups of the Brotherhood's ilk were seen as outmoded relics of a world that would soon disappear.

US diplomats were therefore as surprised as anyone by the revelations of the 1965 "conspiracy," which led to the arrest and execution of Sayyid Qutb and other Brotherhood leaders. Though aware of speculation that the Egyptian authorities had fabricated this episode, Western officials concluded that the plot was genuine and they were taken aback, in particular, by the youth and "modernity" of the alleged conspirators. The involvement of well-educated members of Egypt's aspirant middle classes—the "children of the revolution"— gave pause for thought about the character and durability of the Brotherhood. What followed was a limited process of reassessment that was encouraged by the problems Nasser's regime experienced, both before and after the June 1967 war. The diplomats now recognized that the Brotherhood *did* retain an appeal, though this still tended to be seen as residual—the dying embers of an anachronistic movement that was contrary to the "spirit of the age." Judgments of this kind informed even the best academic accounts of the Brotherhood in this period, such as that of Richard P. Mitchell.[8] The perception held that there was no lasting, viable alternative to Cairo's military rulers.

It was only during the 1970s that a more thoroughgoing reappraisal occurred. This came amid a broader Islamic revival across the region—and, relatedly, Anwar Sadat's decision to permit the Brothers to reorganize. Western onlookers now began to consider the group through the lens of an "Islamic fundamentalism," which had prompted many to revise their assumptions about the link between secularism and modernization. Furthermore, many were inclined to see the Brotherhood as a "moderate" form of this phenomenon, juxtaposed to more violent "extremists." CIA analysts imagined that fundamentalist "crisis cults"—brought into existence by the failures of the postcolonial state—passed through a life cycle. As an example of such a cult, the Brotherhood was thought to have evolved out of its more militant phase and to be subject to a process of moderation. Interestingly, this narrative ran counter to the Brotherhood's own understanding of its history. The men who oversaw its activities at this time, such as 'Umar al-Tilmisani and Mustafa Mashhur, saw their mission as being to restore the group to what it had been under Hasan al-Banna. This was reflected in the ideologically unreconstructed nature of the Brothers. During the previous two decades, they had held the West responsible for their misfortunes and blamed the United States for its "support" of Nasser.[9] Though the Brothers condemned the Egyptian president for his alleged communism and were vitriolic about the Soviets—especially after 1965—they often subsumed this within a wider critique of "the West." The Brotherhood's belief in the essential antagonism between that civilizational monolith and "Islam" was undiminished.

The movement's second great ideologue, Sayyid Qutb, sharpened the binary character of their thinking on many of these issues. And while the "neo-Muslim

Brethren" of the 1970s rejected Qutb's resort to conspiracy and his more radical views about Islamic society (which approached a doctrine of "takfir"), they
absorbed his bleak vision of the West, which was seen as an all-encompassing
political and cultural threat.[10] It is striking too that this pessimistic assessment
was barely altered by the emergence of Brotherhood-inspired institutions in a
Western setting. As these latter organizations matured, they developed an agenda
that was attuned to life in non-Muslim-majority societies. Less concerned with
questions of national power and statecraft, they focused instead on "communal"
politics, seeking to preserve Islamic identity and prevent the assimilation of
Muslim communities into European and American societies. In the process,
though, they devoted little energy to modifying the core principles of the
Brotherhood canon.

In the Middle East, as Sadat moved toward peace with Israel, the Brotherhood's condemnation of the United States intensified. Even the Soviet invasion
of Afghanistan was attributed by some senior Brothers to the machinations of
"the West." American officials were scarcely oblivious to this criticism. Nonetheless, they were prepared to meet with Brotherhood leaders as part of their
drive to understand the mind-set of "Islamic fundamentalism." The importance
attached to this endeavor was boosted by the Iranian revolution of 1978–1979,
which impacted the Brotherhood in different ways. On the one hand, it inevitably heightened fears about the dangers of "fundamentalism," and the
Brotherhood was tarnished by association. On the other hand, the group could
be seen—and actively sought to present itself—as a "moderate" alternative to
the Ayatollahs. As with the other seminal events of this era—in Saudi Arabia
and Afghanistan—the revolution in Tehran served to galvanize the Brotherhood and made its message appear all the more resonant.

As the 1980s progressed, US diplomats became increasingly interested in
the Brotherhood and even began to reflect on the likelihood that it might—at
some point in the future—attain power in Egypt. Again, it would be a mistake
to exaggerate the effect of such assessments. After the assassination of Sadat,
Hosni Mubarak strengthened his country's alliance with Washington and ensured that American thinking about Egypt and the region was framed by
reference to regime interests. US relations with the Brotherhood continued
to play second fiddle to broader strategic considerations. Even so, it was not
insignificant that a belief took hold among certain officials that Islamic "fundamentalists" would, at some point, win office. Time was thought to favor
groups like the Brotherhood, and there was a fatalism about the trajectory of
many societies in the Middle East. As a result, there was a view that the most

governments like that of Mubarak could do was delay the inevitable and appease the Islamists.

After 1989, discussion of the Brotherhood—and Islamism generally—was energized further by predictions that the region would witness a process of democratization. The Algerian situation in particular exercised a powerful influence on US officials. A new debate took place over whether it made sense to "accommodate" or "confront" Islamic fundamentalism (at times now renamed "political Islam"). Again, many drew a distinction between putative "moderates" and "extremists." But scholars and policy makers disagreed on where to locate the Brotherhood on this spectrum. Others, meanwhile, engaged in a kind of "kremlinology" to try to differentiate between internal Brotherhood factions, distinguishing between "hawks" and "doves," or "conservatives and "reformers." The events of 11 September 2001, and the broader rise of salafi-jihadist violence, reinforced the salience of many of these issues.

In the wake of 9/11, the United States appears to have severed ties with the Brotherhood, at least in Egypt. Subsequently, however, Western officials contemplated reaching out to the group, or sections of it, in the hope that it could act as a "firewall" against more extreme forces. This debate carried both foreign and domestic significance—given the development of Brotherhood branches in the West—and it was the British who led the way toward a policy of engagement. This, though, proved short-lived. And while the United States also initiated a reassessment of the Brotherhood in 2006–2007, this remained hamstrung by Washington's commitment to the bilateral relationship with Cairo. In the run-up to the Arab Spring, relations between the West and the Brotherhood were in much the same state as they had been during the previous eight decades: fragmented and surrounded by ambiguities and mutual suspicion.

THROUGHOUT THIS PERIOD, according to the Brothers themselves, Palestine stood as a "fundamental obstacle" to a good relationship with the West. Hasan al-Banna and his successors blamed the British for the foundation of Israel.[11] This issue likewise soured the Brotherhood's view of the United States. In 1944–1947, there had been some evidence that al-Banna was open-minded about the Americans, but such goodwill as existed dissipated amid US support for the nascent Israeli state. Of course, given the global position of the United States, it was always likely that the Brotherhood would have come to regard it in pernicious light—in the same way as it did the British. But events in Palestine accelerated and embittered this process. Israel was judged to be a Western artifice, implanted into the heart of the Arab and Islamic world, for the express purpose of dominating the region. On occasion, there was some divergence on whether Israel was the tool of the West, or whether it was Zionism that was manipulating the Western powers (as suggested by Sa'id Ramadan in the 1950s). Yet anti-Semitic conspiracy theories were never far away—such as the notion that Atatürk was a Jew, or the belief that groups like the Masons had been "established by the Jews to draw Muslims away from their religion and destroy their faith in themselves."[12] Moreover, what was not in dispute among the Brothers was the image of "the West" as a materialist civilization antithetical to Islam, peopled by those who were determined to destroy the religion. This perception was integral to the worldview of the Brotherhood, which changed little across the decades.[13] As Hazem Kandil has underlined, the Brothers lived mentally in a permanent "state of war." They saw themselves, and Muslims more generally, as the victims of a ceaseless, worldwide conspiracy, drawing in "crusaders," Zionists, and other "enemies of Islam." Within this vista, Western political and cultural power, writ large, was seen as an existential threat.[14]

This was why the group had originally been vociferously opposed to the British and other European empires. By the same token, American rhetoric about a "new world order" after 1989 aggravated the suspicions of Brotherhood members that they were suffering at the hands of a neocolonial project. This was seen as merely the latest manifestation of the West's undying enmity toward the Muslim world, an extension of the earlier imperial era.

It was for this reason that historical events continued to resonate with latter-day Brotherhood leaders. It is telling, for instance, that in 2015, the Brotherhood's spokesman in the United Kingdom felt it necessary to repeat a fanciful story that "demonstrated" nineteenth-century British prime minister William Gladstone's hatred for Islam. As described in Chapter 4, this tale had been circulating in Brotherhood circles since at least the 1950s, though Abdullah al-Haddad's version contained the added twist of Gladstone tearing up a copy of the Qur'an on the floor of the House of Commons.[15] To the Brothers, such "incidents" remained relevant because of what they revealed about Western ill will toward Islam. (In lending credence to these myths, the Brothers were not unique in Egypt or the wider region. This kind of conspiracy theorizing has long been a staple of political and journalistic discourse in Egypt and the Middle East. For example, the former Free Officer Husayn al-Shafi'i similarly stated in his memoirs that Atatürk was a foreign agent and also recounted the story of Gladstone's animus against Islam.[16] Even so, the Brotherhood's imagining of conspiracies proved especially grandiose and potent.)

With all of this in mind, it is perhaps surprising that there *were* moments when Brotherhood leaders seemed open to some kind of accommodation with either the British or the Americans. Yet this inclination toward dialogue is explicable in two ways. First, it was a reflection of the deeply pragmatic nature of Hasan al-Banna and many of his successors. From the beginning, the Brotherhood displayed a capacity to act so as to advance its own interests as an organization, rather than as might be expected according to its ideology. This pragmatism was engrained within the mentality of the Brotherhood and may well be a consequence of the premium that was placed on loyalty inside the group. To many Brothers, especially at leadership level, what mattered above all else was the health and prospects of the movement. In the service of that objective, much that might otherwise have been precluded was deemed permissible.

In this context, too, it is worth drawing a distinction between pragmatism and moderation. The former has little to do with the latter. Indeed, the most ideologically committed can often be the most ruthlessly pragmatic, ready to do whatever it takes to advance their cause. Recognition of this leads on to the second reason why the Brotherhood may have been ready to balance public denunciation of the West, with private appeals for reconciliation: namely, that there was a logic to this from an ideological standpoint. Given that the Brothers had always seen the West as a powerful force scheming against them and the wider Muslim world, it made sense that they would try to temper Western antipathy in any way possible. The Brotherhood hoped that a mollifying approach might shield them from the repression of local governments, who were invariably seen as little more than puppets of outside forces. (Simultaneously, somewhat contradictorily, repression was also considered part of God's plan for the Brotherhood—akin to the "ordeal" experienced by the Prophet and the first generation of Muslims in Mecca.)[17]

Based on all of this, one can begin to explain what Marechal labels the "chaotic" relationship between the Brotherhood and the West.[18] Offers of dialogue have coexisted with fiery condemnations of European and American governments. The Brotherhood's critique of the West has been little altered by the fact that individual Brothers have, since at least the 1950s, accepted that there is no Western monolith. Leaders such as Sa'id Ramadan and Ahmad al-Rawi have acknowledged that there were different currents of opinion within Western societies. But this did not dilute their enmity toward "the West" as an intellectual "construct."[19] This was preserved as an indispensable organizing category of thought for the Brotherhood. The group inhabited a world in which its "enemies" pressed in on all sides.[20] "The West," as an ideal, continued to be imagined as an inveterately hostile force. Just as had been the case under al-Banna, it was defined primarily by its materialism and moral degeneracy, though again, it was also said to carry an abiding "Crusader" ethos. Hence, someone like Yusuf al-Qaradawi could argue that the West was secular in character, even as it evinced a "Christian, Jewish or Sabean" mind-set.[21]

FACED WITH THIS, Western officials have certainly been conscious of the Brotherhood's ideological outlook. In the first decades of the group's existence, this ensured that the feelings of antagonism were mostly mutual, with the Brothers seen as a threat to British or American interests. Nonetheless, there were moments when a policy of engagement was considered. This readiness to pursue dialogue revealed a distinctive strand of Anglo-American foreign policy making: what Robert Holland has called the "characteristic search for malleable local partners to reduce the pressures and embarrassments of overseas rule."[22] This impulse has defined what one scholar called the "pax Anglo-Saxonica."[23] It was made manifest by a particular language of diplomacy: the constant reversion to a paradigm of trying to identify "moderates," and the desire to foster "moderation," as against the forces of "extremism." As demonstrated, this has been a critical prism through which both British and American officials have judged not only the Muslim Brotherhood but also other actors in the Middle East.

In seeking to excavate the origins of this inclination, it is useful to borrow Harold MacKinder's concept of the "world island"—the Eurasian land mass—to understand the United States and the United Kingdom as peripheral states, with liberal constitutions, seeking to project influence and manage global systems of power without the direct commitment of vast military resources, and especially without the resort to large armies (British strength was built on naval prowess; its American successor combined naval and aerial dominance).[24] Throughout history, UK policy makers had often favored mechanisms of "informal empire" over overt control (as was the case in Egypt, which was never formally incorporated into the imperial edifice). As their global power waned, empire "on the cheap" became essential.[25] In the period after World War I—and again after 1945—officials sought to accommodate nationalism and "rally the moderates" in such a way as to marginalize "extremist" voices and preserve British influence.[26] The demarcation of allies was therefore a critical part of the "information order" constructed by the British to uphold their position and target relatively limited resources more effectively against their enemies.[27] Similarly, the United States always eschewed formal empire, preferring instead to maintain an informal "preponderance" of power that nonetheless secured the international order under US hegemony.[28]

To both the British and the Americans, then, local allies were vital in order to compensate for what John Darwin labeled a "coercive deficit."[29] The search for "moderate" native partners was a defining feature of the Anglo-American method of power projection (even as the United States did not self-consciously model itself on its British predecessor).[30] This approach proved enduring despite the fact that the process of choosing and anointing allies was often self-defeating; for those willing to serve as "moderate" voices were frequently compromised by the experience. This was the fate of the Wafd in Egypt after 1936, and especially post-1942. The party's association with the imperialist occupier crippled the intellectual and moral legitimacy of its liberal nationalist project— and, as described, this helped create the space into which the Brotherhood could move, offering a critique of seemingly tarnished elites.[31]

Over the last nine decades, Western officials have attempted to locate the Brotherhood on the "moderate-versus-extremist" spectrum. For much of its existence, the group was placed unquestioningly in the latter category, but from the 1970s, there were those who were ready to validate its "moderate" credentials. Of course, to some extent, this was a reflection of the steps taken by senior Brothers to distance themselves from the use of violence, at least against Arab governments. They wanted no repetition of the events of the late 1940s and early 1950s; and to avoid any renewed bout of repression, the Brotherhood disavowed any revolutionary intent. This being so, it made sense to many outside observers to see the Brothers as a moderate force in contrast to those committed to physical force jihad.

At the same time, though, it is worth noting that discussions of the Brotherhood have tended to be driven by external preoccupations and perspectives. Often, Western officials have "read" the Brotherhood against other concerns: the exigencies of imperialism; the challenges of communism and the Cold War; and the presumed threat from Islamic fundamentalism and jihadism. Frédéric Volpi has helpfully set out four key grand narratives that, in his assessment, have shaped views of Islamism generally: initial fears about the political backwardness of the Middle East in a modernizing and secularizing world; apprehensions over the revolutionary potential of "fundamentalism" in the 1980s; debates in the 1990s about the democratic compatibility of Islamism; and finally, questions about the relationship between violent and nonviolent forms of Islamist politics.[32] At various points, each of these have been applied to the Brotherhood.

In all of this, as Joel Beinin and Joe Stark suggest, Western policies on Islamism have been mostly a mixture of "benign neglect" and "instrumentalism."[33] The relationship between Western officials and different chapters of the Brotherhood has always been shaped by the broader national, regional, and global context. The former of these was by far the most important. US (and British) attitudes toward the Brotherhood were determined primarily by the matrix of relationships *inside* any given country—between the group, the local government, and the outside powers. In this respect, Jason Brownlee is right to state that Western influence on a country like Egypt operated "less like an external force and more like a local participant in the ruling coalition."[34] The precise configuration of the "three-legged stool"—the regime, the Brotherhood and the West—has been an important determinant of the power structure in Cairo. With that said, after 1952, it was Egypt's military rulers who set the rules of the game when it came to relations between the Brotherhood and the West. The British and the Americans largely preferred to work with the grain of state power, and from the late 1970s in particular, stood by their authoritarian allies. There was, therefore, no grand conspiracy to align the West with the Brotherhood— no secret deal to deliver Cairo and other capitals into the group's hands.

And yet, what does seem to have occurred in the late twentieth century was a slow process by which many Western observers concluded that the Brotherhood was *the* coming force in politics across the Middle East, and especially in Egypt. To be clear, this did not mean an abandonment of Hosni Mubarak and a readiness to gamble on revolution; the strategic relationship with the Egyptian military was held dear. Alongside this, however, there was a supposition that, in the event that authoritarian rulers in places like Cairo were overturned, then the Brotherhood would inevitably emerge triumphant. Khaled Fahmy drew attention to this when commenting on the dissonance between Western and Egyptian readings of the Brotherhood: "Among the most significant differences in the perception of Western media and that of many Egyptian citizens was the belief . . . that our region is deeply conservative and religious by nature; that the Muslim Brotherhood is the best representation of this conservative and pious essence; and that while it would have been better, in the interest of achieving stability, to have an 'enlightened' secular elite lead the countries of the region, these elites, unlike the Brotherhood, are alienated from their societies, far removed from their people and unconcerned with their real problems."[35] As Fahmy was implying, the result of this outlook was a kind of fatalism about the Brothers and their position within Egyptian and Arab society. From the 1980s onward, a strand of thinking in Western officialdom presumed that countries like Egypt must necessarily drift toward the empowerment of religion at a social, cultural, and political level. In that context, there was an assumption that, ultimately, the Brotherhood held the keys to the future. Added to this was the belief that the Brothers, though not ideal, were perhaps the best that could be expected—and were certainly preferable to more "extreme" alternatives. Crucially, it was this fatalism that informed Western responses to the Arab Spring. An analysis of the difficulties confronting policy makers as they attempted to deal with the upheavals that swept the Middle East after 2011 lies beyond the scope of this study. But in this new era, all actors carried with them the baggage of the past—and nowhere more so than with regard to the long-running and much-tangled relationship between the West and the Muslim Brothers.

Notes

Abbreviations

ASSNESA, SF	Office of Assistant Secretary of State for Near Eastern and South Asian Affairs, Subject Files
BDDE	*British Documents on the End of Empire, Series A,* Institute of Commonwealth Studies, School of Advanced Study, University of London (https://bdeep.org/volumes/series-a/)
CDF	Central Decimal Files
CFPF	Central Foreign Policy Files
FRUS	*Foreign Relations of the United States,* Office of the Historian, United States Department of State
HIA	Hoover Institution Archives
Lampson Diaries	Sir Miles Lampson diaries, held at the Middle East Centre, St. Antony's College, Oxford, Private Papers Collection, GB165–0176
LBJPL	Lyndon B. Johnson Presidential Library, Austin, Texas
NEA	Near Eastern Affairs
RG59	Record Group 59
RG273	Record Group 273
UKNA	United Kingdom National Archives
USNRA	United States National Register of Archives
Wikileaks	Public Library of US Diplomacy, Wikileaks (https://wikileaks.org/plusd/)

471

Introduction

1. Mattew H. Tueller (Deputy Chief of Mission), Embassy Cairo, to State Department, Washington, DC, 11 October 2011, http://www.investigativeproject.org/documents/misc /738.pdf#page=2.

2. Mustafa Bakri, *Al-Jaysh wa-l-Ikhwan: Asrar khalf al-sittar* (Cairo: Dar al-Misriyya wa-l-Lubnaniyya, 2013), especially 53–65.

3. Author experience of numerous conversations in Cairo, 2014–2015. See also Bassem Sabry, "Why Egyptians Don't Like America," *Al-Monitor,* 5 August 2013, http://www.al-monitor.com /pulse/originals/2013/08/love-hate-egyptian-american-relationship.html##ixzz3XBeP3Vsv; and Khaled Mansour, "Dances on Quicksand: The US and the Arab Spring (Part 1)," *Ahram Online,* 23 November 2013, http://english.ahram.org.eg/News/87025.aspx.

4. Tawhid Magdi, *Mu'amarat al-Ikhwan: Min waqi' malafat CIA wa malafat MI6— muntaha al-siriya* (Cairo: Dar Akhbar al-youm, 2014).

5. "Mu'amarat Washington ma' gama'at al-khiyana li-l-ightiyal al-Sissi," *al-Dustur,* 4 December 2013.

6. "British Embassy Denies Financing Brotherhood Activists," *Egypt Independent,* 20 December 2013.

7. "Mubarak's Interior Minister Says US Orchestrated 2011 Revolution," *Ahram Online,* 9 August 2014, http://english.ahram.org.eg/NewsContent/1/64/108082/Egypt/Politics -/UPDATED-Mubarak%E2%80%99s-interior-minister-says-US-orches.aspx.

8. See, for example, Frank Gaffney, "The Muslim Brotherhood and the Obama Administration," *Frontpagemag,* 13 September 2012, http://www.frontpagemag.com/fpm /143836/muslim-brotherhood-obama-administration-frank-gaffney; "Obama Bypasses Congress, Gives $1.5 Billion to Muslim Brotherhood," *Breitbart,* 21 March 2012, http://www .breitbart.com/national-security/2012/03/21/obama-bypasses-congress-gives-1-5-billion -to-muslim-brotherhood/.

9. In this study, I use the terms *Islamism* and *Islamists* not as pejoratives, but simply to denote those movements that seek to bring about a renewal of Islam throughout society, as an essential step toward instituting an Islamic State. It is taken as the translation of the Arabic term *Islamiyyun,* used by many members of the disparate Islamic political movements to describe their outlook. For a comprehensive introduction to this subject, see Peter Mandaville, *Global Political Islam* (London: Routledge, 2007); John Calvert, *Islamism: A Documentary and Reference Guide* (Westport, CT: Greenwood, 2008); and Frederic Volpi, ed., *Political Islam: A Critical Reader* (London: Routledge, 2011).

10. Michael Birnbaum, "Egypt Warns Morsi Supporters to Clear Protest Encampments in Cairo," *Washington Post,* 1 August 2013.

11. Basil el-Dabh, "Brotherhood Criticises West's 'Hypocrisy,'" *Daily News Egypt,* 20 October 2013.

12. "Amr Darrag: Kerry's Remarks Reprehensible, Fundamentally Wrong," *Ikhwanweb,* 21 November 2013, http://ikhwanweb.com/article.php?id=31429.

13. To give but one example, the former Central Intelligence Agency (CIA) operative Miles Copeland mentions the Brotherhood in passing in his memoir, *The Game Player: Confessions of the CIA's Original Political Operative* (London: Aurum, 1989).

14. Brynjar Lia, *The Society of the Muslim Brothers in Egypt: The Rise of an Islamic Movement 1928–1942* (Reading, UK: Ithaca, 1998); Richard P. Mitchell, *The Society of the Muslim*

Brothers, 2nd ed. (Oxford: Oxford University Press, 1993); Carrie Rosefsky Wickham, *The Muslim Brotherhood: Evolution of an Islamist Movement* (Princeton, NJ: Princeton University Press, 2013); Hazem Kandil, *Inside the Brotherhood* (Cambridge, UK: Polity, 2015); Alison Pargeter, *The Muslim Brotherhood: From Opposition to Power,* 2nd ed. (London: Saqi Books, 2010).

15. Ian Johnson, *A Mosque in Munich: Nazis, the CIA and the Rise of the Muslim Brotherhood in the West* (Boston: Houghton Mifflin Harcourt, 2010); Robert Dreyfuss, *Devil's Game: How the United States Helped Unleash Fundamentalist Islam* (New York: Metropolitan, 2005); Mark Curtis, *Secret Affairs: Britain's Collusion with Radical Islam* (London: Serpent's Tail, 2010).

16. Curtis, *Secret Affairs,* 131–149; Dreyfuss, *Devil's Game,* 256–291. See also Ahmed Rashid, *Taliban: The Story of Afghan Warlords* (London: Pan, 2001); Chalmers Johnson, "American Militarism and Blowback: The Costs of Letting the Pentagon Dominate Foreign Policy," *New Political Science* 24 (March 2002), 21–38; Steve Coll, *Ghost Wars: The Secret History of the CIA, Afghanistan and Bin Laden, from the Soviet Invasion to September 10, 2001* (London: Turnaround, 2004).

17. Francis Robinson, "The British Empire and Muslim Identity in South Asia," *Transactions of the Royal Historical Society* 8 (1998), 271–289; John Ferris, " 'The Internationalism of Islam': The British Perception of a Muslim Menace, 1840–1951," *Intelligence and National Security* 24, no. 1 (2009), 57–77. On the question of the colonial state's role in constructing ideas of Muslim identity, see also Farzana Shaikh, *Community and Consensus in Islam: Muslim Representation in Colonial India, 1860–1947* (Cambridge: Cambridge University Press, 1989); Alex Padamsee, *Representations of Indian Muslims in British Colonial Discourse* (Basingstoke, UK: Palgrave Macmillan, 2005).

18. David Motadel, "Islam and the European Empires," *Historical Journal* 55, no. 3 (2012), 856; Ronald Robinson and John Gallagher with Alice Denny, *Africa and the Victorians: The Official Mind of Imperialism* (London: Macmillan, 1961).

19. See, for example, Geoffrey Aronson, *From Sideshow to Centre Stage: US Policy toward Egypt, 1946–1956* (Boulder, CO: L. Rienner, 1986); Peter L. Hahn, *The United States, Great Britain, and Egypt, 1945–1956: Strategy and Diplomacy in the Early Cold War* (Chapel Hill: University of North Carolina Press, 1991); Ray Takeyh, *The Origins of the Eisenhower Doctrine: The US, Britain and Nasser's Egypt* (Basingstoke, UK: Macmillan, 2000).

20. William Inboden, *Religion and American Foreign Policy, 1945–1960: The Soul of Containment* (Cambridge: Cambridge University Press, 2008); Andrew Preston, *Sword of the Spirit, Shield of Faith: Religion in American War and Diplomacy* (New York: Alfred Knopf, 2012); Matthew F. Jacobs, *Imagining the Middle East: The Building of an American Foreign Policy, 1918–1967* (Chapel Hill: University of North Carolina Press, 2011), especially 55–94.

21. Though the revolution brought the empowerment of Shi'a Islamists who differed in many respects from Sunni groups like the Muslim Brotherhood, the revolution inevitably kindled reflections on the nature of political Islam.

22. For two very different perspectives on these issues, see Robert Satloff, *U.S. Policy toward Islamism: A Theoretical and Operational Overview* (New York: Council on Foreign Relations, 2000); Edward W. Said, *Covering Islam,* 2nd ed. (New York: Vintage Books, 1997).

23. Fawaz Gerges, *American and Political Islam: Clash of Cultures or Clash of Interests?* (Cambridge: Cambridge University Press, 1999); Maria do Céu Pinto, *Political Islam and the United States* (Reading, UK: Ithaca, 1999). See also Graham E. Fuller and Ian O. Lesser, *A Sense of Siege: The Geopolitics of Islam and the West* (Boulder, CO: Westview, 1995).

24. Lorenzo Vidino, introduction to *The West and the Muslim Brotherhood after the Arab Spring,* ed. Lorenzo Vidino (Philadelphia: Al Mesbar Studies & Research Centre and the Foreign Policy Research Institute, 2013), 3–4. And in the same volume, Steven Brooke, "U.S. Policy and the Muslim Brotherhood," 6–31.

25. For a rare analysis of Islamist views on the West, see Walid Mahmoud Abdelnasser, *The Islamic Movement in Egypt: Perceptions of International Relations, 1967–81* (London: Kegan Paul International, 1994).

26. Brigitte Marechal, *The Muslim Brothers in Europe: Roots and Discourse* (Leiden, Netherlands: Brill, 2008); Lorenzo Vidino, *The New Muslim Brotherhood in the West* (New York: Columbia University Press, 2010); and Johnson, *A Mosque in Munich.* See also Roel Meijer and Edwin Bakker, eds., *The Muslim Brotherhood in Europe* (London: Hurst, 2012).

27. The project, as originally conceived, was envisaged as including more oral history, but events in Egypt and the imprisonment and dispersal of the Brotherhood there created severe obstacles to this aspect of the research.

1. Origins and First Encounters, 1928–1939

1. There is some confusion surrounding the date of the Brotherhood's founding. Most scholars have used March 1928, but Yusuf al-Qaradawi suggests that the group was actually created sometime in April–May 1929. See Yusuf al-Qaradawi, *Al-Ikhwan al-Muslimun: 70 'aman fi al-da'wa wa-l-tarbiya wa-l-jihad,* 2nd ed. (Beirut: Mu'assasat al-Risala, 2001), 5–9. The confusion seems to stem from the fact that al-Banna, in his memoir, gives the date as March 1928, but then gives the equivalent *hijri* date (Islamic calendar) as 1347—which, in fact, only began in June 1928. Again, in his message to the Brotherhood's fifth conference in 1939, al-Banna dates the foundation to Dhu al-Qi'da 1347, which would place it in April–May 1929. See Hasan al-Banna, "Risala ila al-mu'atamar al-khamis," in Hasan al-Banna, *Majmu'at al-rasa'il* (Cairo: Dar al-Sahoh, 2012), 254. In spite of this, I judge the Gregorian calendar date to be more plausible, as it corresponds to other date markers provided by the Brotherhood.

2. In an important article, Brynjar Lia has warned against too ready an acceptance of the authenticity of this memoir, arguing for its "fictionalized nature." While recognizing the fact that this work is in many ways a document of its time (the mid-1940s), the assumption here is that there is still much we can learn from it about the founding of the Ikhwan. See Brynjar Lia, "Autobiography or Fiction? Hasan al-Banna's Memoirs Revisited," *Journal of Arabic and Islamic Studies* 15 (2015), 199–226.

3. Hasan al-Banna, *Mudhakirat al-da'wa wa-l-da'iya* (Cairo: Mu'assasat Iqra, 2011), 70–71.

4. The Wafd Party took its name from the "delegation" that nationalists hoped to send to the Paris Peace talks to make Egypt's case for full national self-determination. On this, see Marius Deeb, *Party Politics in Egypt: The Wafd and Its Rivals* (London: Ithaca, 1979);

Zaheer Quraishi, *Liberal Nationalism in Egypt: Rise and Fall of the Wafd Party* (Allahabad, India: Kitab Mahal, 1967).

5. For the most vivid literary representation of Egypt in this period and the domineering British presence, see Naguib Mahfuz, *Palace Walk,* trans. William M. Hutchins and Olive E. Kenny (Cairo: American University in Cairo Press, 1999).

6. Gabriel R. Warburg, "'The Three-Legged Stool': Lampson, Faruq and Nahhas, 1936–1944," in Gabriel R. Warburg, *Egypt and the Sudan: Studies in History and Politics* (London: Cass, 1985), 116–157.

7. James Whidden, *Monarchy and Modernity in Egypt: Politics, Islam and Neo-colonialism between the Wars* (London: I. B. Tauris, 2013).

8. Janice J. Terry, *The Wafd, 1919–1952: Cornerstone of Egyptian Political Power* (London: Third World Centre for Research and Publishing, 1982), 165–185.

9. John Darwin, "An Undeclared Empire: The British in the Middle East," *Journal of Imperial and Commonwealth History* 27, no. 2 (2008), 159–176. For fuller treatment, see John Darwin, *Britain, Egypt and the Middle East: Imperial Policy in the Aftermath of War, 1918–1922* (London: Macmillan, 1981), especially 141–242, 266–278.

10. Al-Banna, *Mudhakirat al-da'wa,* 26–27.

11. Cairo's population rose from 791,000 in 1917 to 1.3 million (out of a total Egyptian populace of 15.9 million) by 1932. See Afaf Lutfi al-Sayyid al-Marsot, *Egypt's Liberal Experiment, 1922–1936* (London: University of California Press, 1977), 23.

12. David Commins, "Hasan al-Banna," in *Pioneers of the Islamic Revival,* ed. Ali Rahnema (London: Zed Books, 1994), 125–153 (125–128). On Egypt's economic development over the previous century, see Charles Issawi, *Egypt in Revolution: An Economic Analysis* (Westport, CT: Greenwood, 1963), 18–31.

13. See Naguib Mahfuz's essential "Cairo Trilogy" (comprising the aforementioned *Palace Walk,* as well as *Palace of Desire* and *Sugar Street,* all of which are available in translation from the American University of Cairo Press); Tawfiq Al-Hakim, *Return of the Spirit,* trans. William M. Hutchins (Cairo: American University in Cairo Press, 2012).

14. Al-Banna, *Mudhakirat al-da'wa,* 12.

15. Ibid., 13–14.

16. Ibid., 45–48, 54.

17. Ibid., 48. On the impact of the caliphate's abolition, see also al-Qaradawi, *Al-Ikhwan al-Muslimun,* 16–17, 49–50.

18. Al-Banna, *Mudhakirat al-da'wa,* 49–52. See also Richard P. Mitchell, *The Society of the Muslim Brothers* (Oxford: Oxford University Press, 1993), 211–214.

19. Al-Banna, *Mudhakirat al-da'wa,* 69–70.

20. Ibid., 66. See also al-Banna, "Risala ila al-mu'atamar al-khamis," 270.

21. Al-Banna, *Mudhakirat al-da'wa,* 18–19, 37–38.

22. Mitchell, *Society of the Muslim Brothers,* 224–227.

23. Hasan al-Banna, "To What Do We Summon Mankind?," in *Five Tracts of Hasan al-Banna (1906–1949): A Selection from the Majmu'at Rasa'il al-Imam al-Shahid Hasan al-Banna,* trans. Charles Wendell (Berkeley: University of California Press, 1978), 69–102 (85).

24. Hasan al-Banna, "Risala nahwa al-nur," in al-Banna, *Majmu'at al-rasa'il,* 97–124.

25. Muhammad Farid 'Abd al-Khaliq, *Lamaha tarikhiya 'an al-marahil alati marrat bi-ha jama'at al-ikhwan al-muslimin* (n.d.), available online at Ikhwanwiki, http://bit.ly/2tszUJW. A spokesman for the Brotherhood has confirmed that this website is operated by the group

and can be read as "authoritative." Abdullah el-Haddad, interview with the author, London, 6 May 2015.

26. Al-Banna, "To What Do We Summon Mankind?"

27. Hasan al-Banna, "Our Mission," in Wendell, *Five Tracts of Hasan al-Banna,* 40–68 (44).

28. Hasan al-Banna, "Between Yesterday and Today," in Wendell, *Five Tracts of Hasan al-Banna,* 13–39 (26–31); see also Hasan al-Banna, *What Is Our Message?,* trans. Aziz Ahmad Bilyameeni (New Delhi: Markazi Maktaba Islami, 1974), 8–10, 31–32, 35.

29. Charles D. Smith, *Islam and the Search for Social Order in Modern Egypt: A Biography of Muhammad Husayn Haykal* (Albany: State University of New York Press, 1983), 53–59.

30. Jacques Waardenburg, "Reflections on the West," in Suha Taji-Farouki and Basheer M. Nafi, *Islamic Thought in the Twentieth Century* (London: I. B. Tauris, 2004), 260–295.

31. Timothy Mitchell, *Colonising Egypt* (Oxford: University of California Press, 1988), 161–171.

32. Peter Mansfield, *The British in Egypt* (London: Weidenfeld and Nicolson, 1971), 96–105; Phillip Darby, *Three Faces of Imperialism: British and American Approaches to Asia and Africa, 1870–1970* (London: Yale University Press), 223.

33. 'Abd al-Khaliq, *Lamaha tarikhiya.* See also Hasan al-Banna, "Da'watuna fi tawr jadid," in al-Banna, *Majmu'at al-rasa'il,* 357–374.

34. Hazem Kandil, *Inside the Brotherhood* (Cambridge: Polity Press, 2015), especially 53–58, 87–115.

35. Kenneth Cragg, *Counsels in Contemporary Islam* (Edinburgh: Edinburgh University Press, 1965), 111.

36. Mitchell, *Society of the Muslim Brothers,* 209–211.

37. Al-Banna, "Toward the Light," in Wendell, *Five Tracts of Hasan al-Banna,* 103–132 (107).

38. Al-Banna, "Between Yesterday and Today," 22–24, 30.

39. Mahmud Abu al-Sa'ud, *Idiulujiat al-ikhwan al-muslimin waqi' al-mujtama' al-misri qabla zuhur al-ikhwan,* cited at "al-Ikhwan al-muslimun wa nazratuhum ila al-gharb," Ikhwanwiki, http://bit.ly/1ylPhn5.

40. Franz Rosenthal, "The Muslim Brethren," *muslim world* 37, no. 4 (1947), 289–290; al-Banna, "Our Mission."

41. Al-Banna, "Our Mission," 60–62.

42. Barbara Freyer Stowasser, introduction to *The Islamic Impulse,* ed. Barbara Freyer Stowasser (Washington, DC: Center for Contemporary Arab Studies, Georgetown University, 1987), 1–11; and, in the same volume, Richard P. Mitchell, "The Islamic Movement: Its Current Condition and Future Prospect," 75–86.

43. Al-Banna, "Between Yesterday and Today," 27–29.

44. Ibid., 29. See also al-Banna, "Risala ila al-mu'atamar al-khamis," 254–255; and 'Abd al-Khaliq, *Lamaha tarikhiyya.*

45. Al-Banna, "Our Mission," 61–62.

46. Ibid., 46–47; al-Banna, "Toward the Light," 105–106, 124–125.

47. Al-Banna, "Risala ila al-mu'atamar al-khamis," 255. The same formulation can also be found in Hasan al-Banna, "Risala ila al-talab," in al-Banna, *Majmu'at al-rasa'il,* 171.

48. Al-Banna, "Between Yesterday and Today," 13.

49. A-Banna, "Risala ila al-mu'atamar al-khamis," 257.

50. Gamal al-Banna, *Khitabat Hasan al-Banna al-Shab ila Abih* (Cairo: Dar al-Fikr al-Islami, 1990), 90.

51. Al-Banna, "Between Yesterday and Today," 30.

52. Al-Banna, "Risala ila al-mu'atamar al-khamis," 258–259.

53. Al-Banna, "Toward the Light," 107.

54. Al-Banna, "Our Mission," 55–56, 62–64.

55. Cited in John L. Donohue and John L. Esposito, eds., *Islam in Transition: Muslim Perspectives* (Oxford: Oxford University Press, 2007), 79.

56. Al-Banna, "Toward the Light," 106.

57. Albert Hourani, *Arabic Thought in the Liberal Age, 1798–1939* (Cambridge: Cambridge University Press, 1962), 103–129.

58. Muhammad Abduh, *The Theology of Unity*, trans. Ishaq Musa'ad and Kenneth Cragg (London: George Allen & Unwin, 1966). See also Hourani, *Arabic Thought*, 130–160; M. A. Zaki Badawi, *The Reformers of Egypt* (London: Croom Helm for the Muslim Institute, 1978), 35–95; Mansoor Moaddel, *Islamic Modernism, Nationalism, and Fundamentalism: Episode and Discourse* (Chicago: University of Chicago Press, 2005), 86–92.

59. Hourani, *Arabic Thought*, 222–244.

60. Al-Banna, *Mudhakirat al-da'wa*, 49.

61. Hilary Kalmbach, "From Turban to Tarboush: Dar al-'Ulum and Social, Linguistic, and Religious Change in Interwar Egypt" (PhD thesis, St. Antony's College, Oxford, 2011).

62. Mitchell, *Society of the Muslim Brothers*, 321. See also "Haqa'iq thalath," *Al-Muslimun* 3, no. 8 (June 1954).

63. Gudrun Krämer, *Hasan al-Banna* (Oxford: Oneworld, 2010), 50–54.

64. Robert D. Lee, *Overcoming Tradition and Modernity: The Search for Islamic Authenticity* (Boulder, CO: Westview, 1997), 106. Lee actually made the comment with reference to Sayyid Qutb, not al-Banna, but I think the analogy is equally relevant for the latter.

65. Kalmbach, "From Turban to Tarboush," 167–168. On this issue, see also Mitchell, *Colonising Egypt*, 128–137.

66. Bassam Tibi, *Arab Nationalism: A Critical Enquiry,* ed. and trans. Marion Farouk-Sluglett and Peter Sluglett, 2nd ed. (London: Macmillan, 1990), 90–94; Smith, *Islam and the Search for Social Order,* 14–18.

67. Gregory Starrett, *Putting Islam to Work: Education, Politics and Religious Transformation in Egypt* (London: University of California Press, 1998), 24–26; Nadav Safran, *Egypt in Search of Political Community: An Analysis of the Intellectual and Political Evolution of Egypt, 1804–1952* (Cambridge, MA: Harvard University Press, 1961), 62–63.

68. Hasan al-Banna, "Risalat al-'aqa'id," in al-Banna, *Majmu'at al-rasa'il,* 472.

69. Oswald Spengler, *The Decline of the West* (London: Allen & Unwin, 1922).

70. Mawdudi took a similar view of the threat posed to Islam by "Western civilization" and, like al-Banna, created a sociopolitical movement designed to counter that challenge, the Jama'at-e-Islami. For more on this, see Seyyed Vali Nasr, *Mawdudi and the Making of Islamic Revivalism* (Oxford: Oxford University Press, 1996). For an example of Mawdudi's thinking, see Sayyid Abul A'la Mawdudi, *The Islamic Movement: Dynamics of Values, Power and Change,* trans. Khurram Murad (Leicester, UK: Islamic Foundation, 1994).

71. Al-Banna, "Between Yesterday and Today," 31–32; al-Qaradawi, *Al-Ikhwan al-Muslimun* 100–102.

72. Al-Banna, "Toward the Light," 104.

73. Al-Banna, "To What Do We Summon?," 88–89; see also al-Banna, "Toward the Light," 126.

74. Hasan al-Banna, "Risalat al-ta'alim," in al-Banna, *Majmu'at al-rasa'il,* 212–213. See also Andrea Mura, "A Genealogical Inquiry into Early Islamism: The Discourse of Hasan al-Banna," *Journal of Political Ideologies* 17, no. 1 (2012), 61–85.

75. For discussion of these issues, see A. Z. al-'Abdin, "The Political Thought of Hasan al-Banna," *Hamdard Islamicus* 11, no. 3 (1988), 59–60; Israel Elad Altman, *Strategies of the Muslim Brotherhood Movement 1928–2007,* Research Monographs on the Muslim World, Series No. 2, Paper No. 2 (Washington, DC: Hudson Institute, 2009), 10.

76. Al-Banna, "Risala ila al-mu'atamar al-khamis," 277, 287.

77. Al-Banna, "Risala nahwa al-nur." I am grateful to Hussein Omar Hussein for drawing my attention to this point.

78. Al-Banna, "Risala ila al-mu'atamar al-khamis," 287–288.

79. Al-Banna, "Toward the Light," 118.

80. On this point, see especially Mariz Tadros, *The Muslim Brotherhood in Contemporary Egypt: Democracy Redefined or Confined?* (London: Routledge, 2012).

81. Mitchell, *Society of the Muslim Brothers,* 234–241.

82. Al-Banna, *Mudhakirat al-da'wa,* 32–35.

83. Ehud Rosen, "The Muslim Brotherhood's Concept of Education," *Current Trends in Islamist Ideology* 7 (2008); al-Qaradawi, *Al-Ikhwan al-Muslimun,* 329–330.

84. Roxanne L. Euben and Muhammad Qasim Zaman, eds., *Princeton Readings in Islamist Thought: Texts and Contexts from al-Banna to Bin Laden* (Princeton, NJ: Princeton University Press, 2009), 49–55.

85. Al-Banna, *Mudhakirat al-da'wa,* 39.

86. Euben and Zaman, *Princeton Readings,* 49–55. See also Commins, "Hasan al-Banna," 146–148.

87. Al-Banna, *Mudhakirat al-da'wa,* 54–55.

88. Ibid., 91. See also Beth Baron, *The Orphan Scandal: Christian Missionaries and the Rise of the Muslim Brotherhood* (Stanford, CA: Stanford University Press, 2014), 124.

89. Al-Banna, "Between Yesterday and Today," 14–15; al-Banna, "Risala ila al-Mu'atamar al-Khamis," 273.

90. For al-Banna's focus on education, see also Maryam Jameelah, *Sheikh Hasan al-Banna and al-Ikhwan al-Muslimun* (Lahore, Pakistan: Mohammad Yusuf Khan, 1976), 11.

91. Al-Banna, *Mudhakirat al-da'wa,* 48.

92. Al-Banna, "Risala nahwa al-nur," 121–123.

93. Krämer, *Hasan al-Banna,* 104–112.

94. Rosen, "Muslim Brotherhood's Concept of Education."

95. Al-Banna, *Mudhakirat al-da'wa,* 90.

96. Baron, *Orphan Scandal,* 36, 118–119; al-Banna, *Mudhakirat al-da'wa,* 20, 46. On all of this, see also Mitchell, *Society of the Muslim Brothers,* 2–6.

97. Baron, *Orphan Scandal,* 121ff. Al-Banna's stark views on the missionary threat also challenge Lia's suggestion that the Brotherhood's antiwesternism was a later invention. See Lia, "Autobiography or Fiction?," 207–208.

98. Baron, *Orphan Scandal*, 124, 138. See also Brynjar Lia, *The Society of the Muslim Brothers in Egypt: The Rise of an Islamic Movement, 1928–1942* (Reading, UK: Ithaca, 1998), 40–43.

99. Rosen, "Muslim Brotherhood's Concept of Education." See also al-Banna, *Mudhakirat al-da'wa*, 90–91.

100. Al-Banna, *Mudhakirat al-da'wa*, 71.

101. Baron, *Orphan Scandal*, 6, 20, and especially 117–150. See also Mitchell, *Society of the Muslim Brothers*, 13.

102. "Al-ikhwan al-muslimun wa nazrathum ila al-gharb," Ikhwanwiki, http://bit.ly /1ylPhn5.

103. Baron, *Orphan Scandal*, 140–144; Krämer, *Hasan al-Banna*, 42–46.

104. Baron, *Orphan Scandal*, 196.

105. Ahmad al-Baquri speaks of this in his memoir. See Ahmad H. al-Baquri, *Baqaya dhikriyat* (Cairo: Markaz al-Ahram lil-Tarjamah wa-l-Nashr, 1988), 103. Similarly, Muhammad 'Abdullah al-Samman, who joined the Brotherhood in 1944 in Sohag Province, states that this was an issue for him. See Muhammad 'Abdullah al-Samman, *Ayam ma' al-shahid Hasan al-Bana* (Cairo: Dar al-Fadila, 2003), 62.

106. See, for example, UKNA FO [Foreign Office] 141/760/19, Letter from Ablitt [Suez Canal Police] to Keown-Boyd [Interior Ministry], 13 June 1933; and in the same file, Memorandum by Keown-Boyd, "Case of Turkia of the Salaam School, Port Said," 13 June 1933.

107. UKNA FO 141/760/19, AS to Keown-Boyd, 23 June 1933; in the same file, see also "Note on the Case of Martha Bouloss," 22 June 1933; Ablitt to Keown-Boyd, 24 June 1933.

108. James Heyworth-Dunne, *Religious and Political Trends in Modern Egypt* (Washington, DC: James Heyworth-Dunne, 1950), 30.

109. Deeb, *Party Politics in Egypt*, 126.

110. Al-Banna, *Mudhakirat al-da'wa*, 100–102, 124.

111. For further detail on this hierarchy, see Mitchell, *Society of the Muslim Brothers*, 13–14, 31, 163–184, 195; Lia, *Society of the Muslim Brothers*, 93–115. For the founding of the Muslim Sisters, see al-Banna, *Mudhakirat al-da'wa*, 102.

112. Jameelah, *Sheikh Hasan al-Banna*, 9–10. See also Lia, *Society of the Muslim Brothers*, 186–191; Mitchell, *Society of the Muslim Brothers*, 14.

113. Krämer, *Hasan al-Banna*, 36. See also Deeb, *Party Politics in Egypt*, 379–388.

114. Lia, *Society of the Muslim Brothers*, 53, 94–96.

115. See Moaddel, *Islamic Modernism*, 201–206; Selma Botman, "The Liberal Age, 1923–1952," in *Modern Egypt, from 1517 to the End of the Twentieth Century*, ed. M. W. Daly (Cambridge: Cambridge University Press, 1998), 285–298.

116. James P. Jankowski, *Egypt's Young Rebels: "Young Egypt," 1933–1952* (Stanford, CA: Hoover Institution Press, 1975), 44; Deeb, *Party Politics in Egypt*, 344–356.

117. Jankowski, *Egypt's Young Rebels*, 9–20. See also Deeb, *Party Politics in Egypt*, 72–78, 311. For more on the "effendi" class see Lucie Ryzova, "Egyptianizing Modernity through the 'New Effendiya': Social and Cultural Constructions of the Middle Class in Egypt under the Monarchy," in *Re-Envisioning Egypt, 1919–1952*, ed. Arthur Goldschmitt et al. (New York: American University of Cairo Press, 2005), 124–163.

118. On the Wafdist Blue Shirts, see James P. Jankowski, "The Egyptian Blue Shirts and the Egyptian Wafd, 1935–1938," *Middle Eastern Studies* 6, no. 1 (1970), 77–95; Deeb, *Party Politics in Egypt*, 350–356; On the Green Shirts, see Jankowski, *Egypt's Young Rebels*,

55–64. Relations between the Brotherhood and Young Egypt were mixed. Al-Banna spoke of his desire for unity and cooperation, but was clear that there were differences between them and that this had occasioned moments of antagonism. See al-Banna, "Risala ila al-mu'atamar al-khamis," 277, 289–290.

119. Al-Banna, "Risala ila al-talab," 171–172.

120. Al-Banna, "To What Do We Summon?," 79.

121. Mitchell, *Society of Muslim Brothers*, 16; Krämer, *Hasan al-Banna*, 50–54.

122. Al-Banna, "Risala ila al-mu'atamar al-khamis," 275–276.

123. Al-Banna, "Risala ila al-talab," 174. See also al-Banna, "To What Do We Summon?," 81–82.

124. Abbas Hasan al-Sissi, *Fi qafilat al-Ikhwan al-Muslimin: al-juz' al-awal*, 2nd ed. (Alexandria, Egypt: Dar al-Taba'a wa-l-Nashr wa-l-Sutiyat, 1987), 260; Hasan Hathut, *Al-'aqd al-farid, 1942–1952: Ashr Sanawat ma' al-Imam Hasan al-Bana* (Cairo: Dar al-Shuruq, 2000), 21–22; Hasan Dawh, *25 'aman fi jama'at al-ikhwan* (Cairo: Dar al-'Itisam, 1983), 26–27. On the battalions, see also Mitchell, *Society of the Muslim Brothers*, 196–198.

125. Ahmad 'Isa 'Ashur, *Hadith al-thulutha' li-Imam Hasan al-Banna: Sajjalaha wa-'addaha li-l-nashr* (Cairo: Maktabat al-Qur'an, 1985), 119–128, 356–361.

126. Lia, *Society of the Muslim Brothers*, 58–60, 67–69, 137–138.

127. Al-Banna, "To What Do We Summon?," 90.

128. Kandil, *Inside the Brotherhood*, 81–86, 107–118.

129. Al-Banna, "Risala nahwa al-nur," 121. For more on al-Banna's emphasis on the importance of "separation" between men and women, as well as his views on gender and the family, see Ashur, *Hadith al-thulutha*, 27–33; and Salah Shadi, *Safahat min al-tarikh: Hisad al-'amr* (Kuwait: Sharikat al-Shu'a, 1981), 9.

130. Al-Banna, "Risala nahwa al-nur," 109.

131. Al-'Abdin, "Political Thought of Hasan al-Banna," 62–63.

132. Al-Banna, "Risala nahwa al-nur," 124.

133. Al-Banna, "Between Yesterday and Today," 32. See also Heyworth-Dunne, *Religious and Political Trends*, 15.

134. On this aspect of the Brotherhood's message, see also Ellis Goldberg, "Muslim Union Politics in Egypt: Two Cases," in *Islam, Politics, and Social Movements*, ed. Edmund Burke III and Ira M. Lapidus (London: Tauris, 1988), 228–243; Mitchell, *Society of the Muslim Brothers*, 250–253.

135. Al-Banna, "Risala nahwa al-nur," 124.

136. Goldberg, "Muslim Union Politics in Egypt."

137. Al-Banna, *Mudhakirat al-da'wa*, 90.

138. Heyworth-Dunne, *Religious and Political Trends*, 15.

139. Al-Banna, "Risala nahwa al-nur," 123.

140. Al-Banna, *Mudhakirat al-da'wa*, 57.

141. Al-Banna, "Toward the Light," 105.

142. Hathut, *Al-'aqd al-farid*, 5.

143. See the address of al-Banna provided in the extended footnote in Abbas Hasan al-Sissi, *Hasan al-Banna: Mawaqif fi al-da'wa wa-l-tarbiya* (Alexandria, Egypt: Dar al-Da'wa, 1982), 226–228.

144. On this modulated position, see Lia, "Autobiography or Fiction?," 208. See also Lia, *Society of the Muslim Brothers*, 31.

145. Mitchell, *Society of the Muslim Brothers*, 224–227.

146. Al-Qaradawi, *Al-Ikhwan al-Muslimun*, 149–150, 233–234.

147. Hathut, *Al-'aqd al-farid*, 5.

148. Lia, *Society of the Muslim Brothers*, 79–81.

149. Al-Banna, "Risala ila al-mu'atamar al-khamis," 281–285.

150. Israel Gershoni and James P. Jankowski, *Redefining the Egyptian Nation, 1930–1945* (Cambridge: Cambridge University Press, 1995).

151. Gamal Abdel Nasser, *Philosophy of the Revolution* (Cairo: Dar al-Maaref, 1955), 69–72.

152. Hasan al-Banna, "Oh Youth!," in *The Complete Works of Hasan al-Banna,* available at https://thequranblog.wordpress.com/2008/06/07/the-complete-works-of-imam-hasan-al -banna-9/.

153. Ibid; Al-Banna, "To What Do We Summon?," 71, 93.

154. Al-Banna, "Oh Youth!"

155. Al-Banna, "To What Do We Summon?," 80. See also al-Banna, "Between Yesterday and Today," 16.

156. Hasan al-Banna, "Risalat al-jihad," in al-Banna, *Majmu'at al-rasa'il,* 423.

157. Hasan al-Banna, "On Jihad," in Wendell, *Five Tracts of Hasan al-Banna,* 133.

158. Abd al-Fattah Muhammad El-Awaisi, *The Muslim Brothers and the Palestine Question, 1928–1947* (London: Tauris Academic Studies, 1998), 119, 124–127.

159. Hasan al-Banna, *The Concept of Allah in the Islamic Creed* (New Delhi: Adam Publishers, 2008), 63.

160. Al-Banna, *What Is Our Message?,* 21. On al-Banna's articulation of a militant concept of jihad, see also Richard Bonney, *Jihad: From Qur'an to bin Laden* (Basingstoke, UK: Palgrave Macmillan, 2004), 211–215.

161. Al-Banna, "On Jihad."

162. Al-Banna, "To What Do We Summon?," 80.

163. A-Banna, "Risala ila al-mu'atamar al-khamis," 273.

164. See, for example, al-Banna, "Risalat al-jihad," 425.

165. Al-Qaradawi, *Al-Ikhwan al-Muslimun*, 132–134.

166. Al-Banna, "Risalat al-jihad," 440.

167. Al-Banna, "Risala nahwa al-nur," 120.

168. Al-Banna, "Toward the Light," 110–113. On this point more broadly, see A. B. Soage, "Hasan al-Banna or the Politicisation of Islam," *Totalitarian Movements and Political Religions* 9, no. 1 (March 2008), 21–42.

169. Al-Banna, "Risalat al-jihad," 435–436.

170. Al-Banna, "On Jihad," 150.

171. Al-Banna, "Risala ila al-mu'atamar al-khamis," 290–292. On the importance of preserving the "independence," "freedom," "dignity," and "sovereignty" of the Islamic nation, see also al-Banna, "Risala ila al-talab," 174–176.

172. Al-Banna, "Risala ila al-mu'atamar al-khamis," 263–266.

173. Ibid., 273–274; Mitchell, *Society of the Muslim Brothers*, 260–262.

174. This caution helped provoke the first major split within the group. At the end of the decade, a faction anxious to carry forward jihad broke away to create the Youth of Our Lord Muhammad group; the editor and owner of *al-Nadhir* also departed the Brotherhood, taking his newspaper with him. See Krämer, *Hasan al-Banna,* 50–54.

175. El-Awaisi, *Muslim Brothers,* 1–18.

176. Kamil al-Sharif, *Al-Ikhwan al-Muslimun wa-l-Harb fi Filistin,* 3rd ed. (Amman, Jordan: Maktabat al-Manar, 1984), 31.

177. Ibid., 17–22.

178. El-Awaisi, *Muslim Brothers,* 51–53.

179. Al-Sharif, *Al-Ikhwan al-Muslimun,* 22–24.

180. Lia, *Society of the Muslim Brothers,* 154, 237; Krämer, *Hasan al-Banna,* 35–36, 47–50; El-Awaisi, *Muslim Brothers,* 31–32; Israel Gershoni, "The Muslim Brothers and the Arab Revolt in Palestine, 1936–39," *Middle Eastern Studies* 22, no. 3 (1986), 367–397.

181. Shmuel Bar, *The Muslim Brotherhood in Jordan* (Tel Aviv: Moshe Dayan Center for Middle Eastern and African Studies, 1998), 9.

182. On al-Husayni, see Jeffrey Herf, *Nazi Propaganda for the Arab World* (London: Yale University Press, 2009), 8, 16, 29–30, 236; David Motadel, *Islam and Nazi Germany's War* (Cambridge, MA: Belknap, 2014), 41–47.

183. Ian Johnson, *A Mosque in Munich: Nazis, the CIA and the Rise of the Muslim Brotherhood in the West* (Boston: Houghton Mifflin Harcourt, 2010), 111–112.

184. Kemal el-Helbawy, "The Muslim Brotherhood in Egypt: Historical Evolution and Future Prospects," in Khaled Hroub, *Political Islam: Context versus Ideology* (London: Saqi Books, 2010), 70.

185. El-Awaisi, *Muslim Brothers,* 35–38.

186. Lia, *Society of the Muslim Brothers,* 235–247; Gershoni, "Muslim Brothers," 371–379.

187. El-Awaisi, *Muslim Brothers,* 14.

188. Al-Sharif, *Al-Ikhwan al-Muslimun,* 31–33. See also Abu al-Futuh 'Afifi, *Rihalati ma' al-Ikhwan al-Muslimin* (Cairo: Dar al-Tawfiq wa-l-Nashr al-Islami, 2003), 17; al-Baquri, *Baqaya,* 45.

189. UKNA FO 371/19980, E 2120/381/65, Telegram No. 382, Sir Miles Lampson (Ambassador), Embassy Cairo to FO, 8 April 1936.

190. Ibid.

191. Francis Robinson, "The British Empire in the Muslim World," in *The Oxford History of the British Empire: Volume IV: The Twentieth Century,* ed. Judith Brown and W. Roger Louis (Oxford: Oxford University Press), 405–407; Francis Robinson, "The British Empire and Muslim Identity in South Asia," *Transactions of the Royal Historical Society* 8 (1998), 271–289. See also John Ferris, " 'The Internationalism of Islam': The British Perception of a Muslim Menace, 1840–1951," *Intelligence and National Security* 24, no. 1 (2009), 57–77.

192. Mansfield, *British in Egypt,* 31.

193. UKNA FO 371/19980, E 31530/381/65, Telegram No. 616, Lampson, Cairo to Anthony Eden (Foreign Secretary), FO, 28 May 1936; also, FO 141/536, 403/12/36, "Note: Moslem Brotherhood."

194. UKNA FO 371/19980, Lampson to Eden, FO, 28 May 1936. See also FO 141/536, 403/12/36, "Special Section: Ministry of Interior," 17 May 1936.

195. UKNA FO 371/20035, E 4415/3216/31, Telegram No. 71, Lampson to FO, 3 July 1936. For the Young Men's Muslim Association (YMMA), see, for example, FO 371/21881, Telegram No. 559, David V. Kelly (Minister), Cairo to FO, No. 559, 17 June 1936, on the group's attempt to send a delegation to Palestine; FO 141/676, 52/244/37, No. 1284, Lampson to Eden, FO, 12 November 1937.

196. See, for example, UKNA FO 406/74, E 1173/381/65, Telegram 101, Sir Archibald C. Clark-Kerr (Ambassador), Embassy Baghdad, to Eden, FO 24 February 1936.

197. UKNA FO 371/19980, No. 362, Memorandum from Lampson to Eden, FO, 2 April 1936.

198. UKNA FO 371/19980, E 3284/381/65, Telegram No. 260 Clark-Kerr, Bagdad, to Eden, FO, 28 May 1936. For the Sudan Agency's views, see report enclosed with E 1326/381/65, Telegram No. 223, Lampson, Cairo to Eden, FO, 24 February 1936.

199. UKNA, FO 371/19980, E 3039/381/65, Telegram No. 46, Gilbert Mackereth (Consul), Embassy Damascus to Eden, FO, 15 May 1936.

200. Ibid. Document minutes include note to this effect from "RIC" dated 13 March 1936.

201. UKNA FO 141/676, 52/255/37, Alan C. Trott (Chargé d'Affaires), Embassy Jedda to Lampson, Cairo, 19 November 1937.

202. See, for example, the protests of the Union of Azharites contained within UKNA FO 141/536, 403/19/36.

203. UKNA FO 371/19980, E 5831/381/65, Telegram No. 1039, Kelly, Cairo to Eden, FO, 4 September 1936.

204. Oded Eran, "Negotiating the Anglo-Egyptian Relationship between the Wars," in *Imperialism and Nationalism in the Middle East: The Anglo-Egyptian Experience, 1882–1982,* ed. Keith M. Wilson (London: Mansell, 1983), 56–75.

205. UKNA FO 371/19980, No. 362, Memorandum from Lampson, Cairo to Eden, FO, 2 April 1936.

206. UKNA FO 407/222, J 394/6/16, No. 166, Eden to Lampson, Cairo, 10 February 1938.

207. UKNA FO 371/20888, J 5009/20/16, Minute by Campbell, 3 December 1937; in the same file, J 5223/20/16, No. 712, Lampson, Cairo to FO, 16 December 1937; J 5301/20/16, No. 725, Lampson, Cairo to FO, 20 December 1937; J 5304/20/16, No. 726, Lampson, Cairo to FO, 20 December 1937; J 5405/20/16, 30 December 1937.

208. Matthew A. Fitzsimons, *Empire by Treaty: Britain and the Middle East in the Twentieth Century* (Notre Dame, IN: University of Notre Dame Press, 1964), ix, 1–3.

209. Ibid., 31.

210. Darwin, *Britain, Egypt and the Middle East,* 221, 276. Moreover, as James Whidden has noted, the treaty transformed the Wafd into a "collaborating instrument" of British "neo-colonial" power. See Whidden, *Monarchy and Modernity,* 7.

211. UKNA FO 371/19980, Appendix to SMIS No. 34, "Note by the Intelligence Officer Dated 31st October, 1936, on impressions and information gathered during his visits to Egypt, Syria and Palestine in summer of 1936."

212. Ibid.

213. UKNA FO 371/23304, J 803/1/16, Minute by Montgomery, 28 February 1939, on Telegram No. 191, Lampson, Cairo to FO, 21 February 1939; FO 371/20888, J 5412/20/16, Minute by Victor Cavendish-Bentinck, 30 December 1937.

214. UKNA FO 371/23229, J 1293/1/16, Telegram No. 72 (S), Lampson, Cairo to FO, 22 March 1939.

215. Artemis Cooper, *Cairo in the War, 1939–1935* (London: John Murray, 1989), 22–23.

216. UKNA FO 371/23304, J 796/1/16, Letter, Lampson, Cairo to Lancelot Oliphant, FO, 22 February 1939; FO 371/23306, Telegram No. 402, Lampson, Cairo to FO, 3 July 1939. See also, for example, the stories of the king contained in FO 371/23229,

J 1274/1/16, Lampson to Oliphant, 12 March 1939; and also Lampson Diaries, Killearn Box 3, 1 November 1939.

217. See, for example, UKNA FO 371/20888, J 5327/20/16, No. 739 Lampson, Cairo to FO, 23 December 1937.

218. Al-Sayyid al-Marsot, *Egypt's Liberal Experiment,* 156–170, 189–195, 229.

219. Deeb, *Party Politics in Egypt,* 372–378.

220. Appendix to SMIS No. 34.

221. Al-Sissi, *Fi qafilat al-Ikhwan,* 64.

222. Lampson Diaries, Killearn Box 3, 19 July 1939. See also UKNA FO 371/23306, No. 200 (S), 22 July 1939; and various files in FO 371/23364.

223. UKNA FO 371/23304, J288/1/16, Telegram No. 30, Lampson, Cairo to FO, 13 January 1939; FO 371/23229, J 1980/1/16, Telegram No. 535, Lampson, Cairo to Viscount Halifax (Foreign Secretary), FO, 5 May 1939; FO 371/21881, E 5898/10/31, Telegram No. 1077, Embassy Alexandria to Halifax, FO, 26 September 1938. For Young Egypt's activism on Palestine, see, for example, numerous files in FO 371/20811.

224. UKNA FO 371/23229, J 1980/1/16, Telegram No. 535, Lampson, Cairo to Halifax, FO, 5 May 1939; FO 371/22000, J 32–7/264/16, Telegram No. 923, Charles Bateman (Minister), Alexandria to FO, 4 August 1938.

225. UKNA FO 407/222, J 893/6/16, Telegram No. 172, Lampson, Cairo to Eden, FO, 17 February 1938. For more on al-Maraghi, see also, in the same file, J 2086/6/16, Telegram No. 560, Lampson, Cairo to Halifax, FO, 14 May 1938.

226. Lampson Diaries, Killearn Box 3, 8 March 1938.

227. Lampson Diaries, Killearn Box 3, 10 March 1938.

228. UKNA FO 407/222, J 1079/6/16, Telegram No. 268, Lampson, Cairo to Halifax, FO, 2 March 1938.

229. UKNA FO 371/23304, J 377/1/16, Telegram No. 41, Lampson, Cairo to FO, 16 January 1939.

230. UKNA FO 371/23304, Foreign Office Minute by Cavendish-Bentinck, 31 January 1939. See also FO 371/23304, J 437/1/16, Letter, Lampson, Cairo to Oliphant, FO, 24 January 1939; and various files in FO 371/20888.

231. Jankowski, *Egypt's Young Rebels,* 22–36.

232. Mitchell, *Society of the Muslim Brothers,* 16–17.

233. Lia, *Society of the Muslim Brothers,* 137–138, 179.

234. Mitchell, *Society of the Muslim Brothers,* 211–214.

235. Smith, *Islam and the Search for Social Order,* 109–113; 145–157.

236. Heyworth-Dunne, *Religious and Political Trends,* 26–27, 33–34, 36–37.

237. Al-Banna, "Oh Youth!"

238. Al-Banna, "Risala ila al-mu'atamar al-khamis," 272.

239. Al-Banna, *Mudhakirat al-da'wa,* 89–90. This was not the last mosque that the Suez Canal Company helped the Brotherhood to build; rather, it also assisted with the construction of a building at al-Jabasat al-Fadla' near Ismailia. See the same volume, 102–104.

240. "Kalimat fadilat al-murshid al-a'am," *al-Ikhwan al-Muslimun,* 20 September 1945.

241. Lia, *Society of the Muslim Brothers,* 131–132.

242. For Brotherhood professions of loyalty to the king, which continued through the 1940s, see, for example, the 14 February 1945 issue of their newspaper *al-Ikhwan al-*

Muslimun, the front page of which was dedicated to the king and included an article wishing him happy birthday.

243. See also Gershoni, "Muslim Brothers," 387.

244. El-Awaisi, *Muslim Brothers,* 60–61.

245. "Al-ikhwan al-muslimun wa nazratuhum ila al-gharb," Ikhwanwiki.

246. Gershoni, "Muslim Brothers," 382–385.

247. Al-Sissi, *Fi qafilat al-Ikhwan,* 33–37.

248. Ibid., 45.

249. For examples of this kind of material and its circulation, see UKNA FO 141/678, E 5820/22/31, Letter No. 193, Kelly, Cairo to HE Mustapha el Nahas Pasha, 11 September 1937; in the same file, Letter from Trott, Jedda to Lacy Baggallay, FO, 14 September 1937; Telegram No. 1219, Kelly, Cairo to Eden, FO, 27 October 1937. Also, FO 371/21876, E 3013/10/31, Telegram No. 41, Consul Jenkins, Jibuti to FO, 5 May 1938.

250. UKNA FO 371/21881, E 5898/10/31, Telegram No. 1077, Embassy Alexandria to Halifax, FO, 26 September 1938.

251. Al-Sissi, *Fi qafilat al-Ikhwan,* 51–53. On the World Parliamentary Congress, see also Gershoni and Jankowski, *Redefining the Egyptian Nation,* 184.

252. Al-Banna, "Risala ila al-mu'atamar al-khamis," 291.

253. Ibid.

254. Al-Sissi, *Fi qafilat al-Ikhwan,* 51.

255. UKNA FO 371/21881, E 5898/10/31, Telegram No. 1077, Embassy Alexandria to Halifax, FO, 26 September 1938.

256. Ibid.

257. UKNA FO 371/21883, E 6494/10/31, Telegram No. 1174, Lampson, Cairo to FO, 1 November 1938.

258. UKNA FO 371/21883, E 6509/10/31, Telegram No. 1167, Lampson, Cairo to FO, 29 October 1938.

259. UKNA FO 371/23221, E 765/6/31, Telegram No. 75900/39, Colonial Office (CO), to FO, 30 January 1939.

260. El-Awaisi, *Muslim Brothers,* 65.

261. UKNA FO 371/21883, E 30/6/31, Telegram No. 1341, Lampson, Cairo to FO, 19 December 1938.

262. UKNA FO 371/23304, J 377/1/16, Telegram No. 41, Lampson, Cairo to FO, 16 January 1939.

263. UKNA FO 371/20809, E 4194/22/31, Telegram No. 411, Lampson, Cairo to FO, 21 July 1937. For further discussion of pressures on the Egyptian government, see FO 371/20816, E 5903/22/31, Telegram No. 1129, Kelly, Cairo to Eden, FO, 28 September 1937; and in the same, E 5964/22/31, FO Memorandum and Minutes on Palestine.

264. UKNA FO 371/21876, E 2575/10/31, Telegram No. 301, Lampson, Cairo to FO, 3 May 1938. See also, in the same, Telegram No. 302, Lampson, Cairo to FO, 4 May 1938.

265. UKNA FO 371/22000, J 2711/264/16, Telegram No. 764, Lampson, Cairo to FO, 29 June 1938. See also, in the same, J 3978/264/16, Telegram No. 1108, Lampson, Alexandria, to FO, 13 October 1938. On the evolution of Egyptian attitudes to events in Palestine, see Thomas Mayer, "Egypt and the 1936 Arab Revolt in Palestine," *Journal of Contemporary History* 19 (1984), 275–287.

266. UKNA FO 371/22000, J 2254/264/16, Telegram No. 611, Lampson, Cairo to FO, 24 May 1938.

267. El-Awaisi, *Muslim Brothers*, 68–76.

268. UKNA FO 371/21880, E 5615/10/31, No. 7/50/38, Letter, Bateman to Oliphant, FO, 13 September 1938.

269. UKNA FO 371/21877, E 3172/10/31, Telegram No. 547, Lampson, Cairo to FO, 17 May 1938. See, particularly, the minute by R. Elvington-Smith.

270. UKNA FO 371/21881, E 5828, Telegram No. 446, Major Cawthorn (MI2), War Office, to FO, 4 October 1938.

271. UKNA FO 371/23364, J 1973/774/16, Telegram No. 527, Lampson, Cairo to FO, 5 May 1939. For more on the content and impact of Axis radio propaganda in the Middle East, see Herf, *Nazi Propaganda;* Motadel, *Islam and Nazi Germany's War,* 82–114.

272. UKNA FO 371/23364, J 3399/774/16, Telegram No. 1006, John Sterndale Bennett, Embassy Cairo to FO, 9 August 1939. For Egyptian criticism of the White Paper, see various files in FO 371/23236.

273. UKNA FO 371/21881, E 5726, Telegram 8/253/38, Bateman, Alexandria to Oliphant, FO, 30 August 1938.

274. Ibid. For further discussion of this issue, see also FO 371 21880, E 5238/10/31, Telegram No. 450, Bateman, Alexandria to FO, 7 September 1938; in the same, Letter, Sir Alec Cadogan, FO to Evelyn Shuckburgh, CO, 16 September 1938; E 5556/10/31, Letter, Shuckburgh, CO to Cadogan FO, 22 September 1938; E 6489/10/31, Telegram No. 588, Lampson, Cairo to FO, 5 November 1938; Telegram No. 556, FO to Lampson, Cairo (also Baghdad and Jerusalem), 4 November 1938. For Lampson's views on Palestine, see in the same, Telegram No. 1108, Lampson, Alexandria to FO, 13 October 1938; J 2177/1/16, Letter, Lampson, Cairo to Oliphant, FO, 22 February 1939; Lampson Diaries, Killearn Box 3, 7 January 1939, 1 November 1939.

275. UKNA FO 371/23304, J 377/1/16, Telegram No. 41, Lampson, Cairo to FO, 16 January 1939.

276. UKNA FO 371/23229, J 1358/1/16, Minute by Cavendish-Bentinck, 4 April 1939, on Telegram No. 233, Lampson, Cairo to FO, 31 March 1939.

277. UKNA FO 371/23304, J 377/1/16, Telegram No. 41, Lampson, Cairo to FO, 16 January 1939.

278. UKNA FO 371/23306, Letter No. 1066, Bateman, Alexandria to Halifax, FO, 25 August 1939.

279. UKNA FO 371/23306, J 2616/1/16, Minute by Cavendish Bentinck, 5 July 1939, on Telegram No. 402, Lampson, Cairo to FO, 3 July 1939. For discussion of all this, see various in FO 371/23306.

280. UKNA FO 371/23306, J 437/1/16, Letter, Lampson, Cairo to Oliphant, FO, 24 January 1939.

281. UKNA FO371/23306, J 2902/1/16, Telegram No. 205, Lampson, Cairo to FO, 21 July 1939.

282. UKNA FO371/23306, J 3525/1/16, Minute by I. Wilson Young, 7 September 1939, on Letter No. 1066, Bateman, Alexandria to Halifax, FO, 25 August 1939.

283. UKNA FO371/23306, J 3525/1/16, Letter No. 1066, Bateman, Alexandria to Halifax, FO, 25 August 1939.

284. Charles Tripp, "Ali Mahir and the Politics of the Egyptian Army, 1936–1942," in *Contemporary Egypt, through Egyptian Eyes: Essays in Honour of Professor P. J. Vatikiotis,* ed. Charles Tripp (London: Routledge, 1993), 45–71.

285. UKNA FO 371/23232, E 2444/6/31, Telegram No. 234, Lampson, Cairo to FO, 2 April 1939.

286. El-Awaisi, *Muslim Brothers,* 83–86.

287. Muhammad Hamid Abu al-Nasr, *Al-Imam al-Shahid Hasan al-Bana wa-l-qadiya al-filistiniyya,* full copy available at Ikhwanwiki, http://bit.ly/2sZNUxK.

288. UKNA WO (War Office) 208/502, "Copies of translations of documents found in homes of German nationals in Cairo: War Office, Directorate of Military Operations and Intelligence and Directorate of Military Intelligence." See especially in the same file, Telegram No. 6068, MICE, Cairo, to War Office, 3 November 1939; and "Note on Wilhelm Stellbogen," 23 October 1939.

289. 'Ashur, *Hadith al-thulutha,* 478–484.

290. UKNA FO 371/69210, J 110/68/16, Foreign Office Research Department Minute, 30 December 1947.

291. UKNA FO 371/108327, JE 1018/49, Letter, James Heyworth-Dunne to Sir Roger Allen (FO), 1 May 1954. See also Lia, *Society of the Muslim Brothers,* 179–180.

292. Heyworth-Dunne, *Religious and Political Trends,* 54, 69–73.

293. Christina Phelps Harris, *Nationalism and Revolution in Egypt: The Role of the Muslim Brotherhood in Egypt* (The Hague, Netherlands: Mouton, 1964), 14, 137–138.

294. Al-Sayyid al-Marsot, *Egypt's Liberal Experiment,* 232–237.

295. Kandil, *Inside the Brotherhood,* 38–40.

296. Krämer, *Hasan al-Banna,* 94–96.

297. P. H. Newby, *The Picnic at Sakkara* (London: Jonathan Cape, 1955).

298. Al-Banna, *Mudhakirat al-da'wa,* 72–73. It is worth noting that a very similar story appeared in the Muslim Brotherhood newspaper in 1944, albeit without any reference to the Suez Canal Company and with some minor differences of detail; this could have been a parable that al-Banna used, which may or may not be grounded in truth. See A. al-Mon'im Khilaf, "Al-'alan 'an al-Ikhwan," *al-Ikhwan al-Muslimun,* 19 December 1944.

299. Roel Meijer, "The Problem of the Political in Islamist Movements," in *Whatever Happened to the Islamists? Salafis, Heavy Metal Muslims and the Lure of Consumerist Islam,* ed. Olivier Roy and Amel Boubekeur (London: Hurst, 2012), 27–60.

300. Robinson, "The British Empire in the Muslim World," 398, 414–416. On this point, too, see Stowasser, introduction to *Islamic Impulse;* Fazlur Rahman, "Roots of Islamic Neo-Fundamentalism," in *Change in the Muslim World,* ed. Phillip H. Stoddard et al. (Syracuse, NY: Syracuse University Press, 1981), 34–35.

301. Olivier Roy, "Is 'Islamism' a Neo-Orientalist Plot?," in Roy and Boubekeur, *Whatever Happened to the Islamists?,* 17–26; R. Stephen Humphreys, "The Contemporary Resurgence in the Context of Modern Islam," in *Islamic Resurgence in the Arab World,* ed. Ali E. Hillal Dessouki (New York: Praeger, 1982), 67–83.

302. Mitchell, "Islamic Movement."

303. Mandaville, *Global Political Islam,* 72–75; Krämer, *Hasan al-Banna,* 93.

304. Lia, *Society of the Muslim Brothers,* 8–13, 181–185.

305. Mura, "A Genealogical Inquiry," 71.

306. Tibi, *Arab Nationalism,* 14–17.

307. Mura, "A Genealogical Inquiry, 76.

308. Ian Buruma and Avishai Margalit, *Occidentalism: A Short History of Anti-Westernism* (London: Atlantic, 2004), 1–7, 35–52.

309. Ibid., 70–90.

310. Al-Baquri, *Baqaya,* 43–45.

2. Wartime Liaisons, 1940–1944

1. Abbas Hasan al-Sissi, *Fi qafilat al-Ikhwan al-Muslimun, al-Juz' al-Awal,* 2nd ed. (Alexandria, Egypt: Dar al-Taba'a wa-l-Nashr wa-l-Sutiyat, 1987), 86–87; UKNA Foreign Office (FO) 371/27434, J 3601/18/16, Telegram No. 3570, Sir Miles Lampson (Ambassador), Embassy Cairo to FO, 14 November 1941; and in the same, Telegram No. 143, Lampson, Cairo to FO, 15 December 1941.

2. UKNA FO 371/27434, J 3601/18/16, Minute by D. S. Laskey, 15 November 1941, on Telegram No. 3570, Lampson, Cairo to FO, 14 November 1941. See also, in the same file, J 3664/18/16, Telegram No. 3628, Lampson, Cairo to FO, 19 November 1941.

3. Lampson Diaries, Killearn Box 4, 13 November 1941.

4. UKNA FO 371/27434, J 3664/18/16, Minute by D. S. Laskey, 20 November 1941, on Telegram No. 3628, Lampson, Cairo to FO, 19 November 1941.

5. UKNA War Office (WO) 208/1560, Appendix to Middle East Intelligence Centre (MEIC), Summary No. 642, 21 November 1941.

6. Lampson Diaries, Killearn Box 4, 22 May 1940.

7. On the embassy fears about the palace's pro-Italian sympathies, see Lampson Diaries, Killearn Box 4, 9 January 1940.

8. UKNA FO 371/24628, J 928/92/16, Telegram No. 59, Lampson, Cairo to FO, 21 March 1940. For the sake of clarity, I refer to the group by its original name, Young Egypt, as this was the practice of British officials at the time.

9. Lampson Diaries, Killearn Box 4, 5 March 1940.

10. UKNA FO 371/24628, J 1020/92/16, Minute on Telegram No. 179, Lampson, Cairo to FO, 3 April 1940.

11. UKNA FO 371/24628, J 1033/92/16, Minute by Thompson on Telegram No. 182, Lampson, Cairo to FO, 5 April 1940.

12. UKNA FO 371/24628, J 929/92/16, Telegram No. 62 (S), Lampson, Cairo to FO, 21 March 1940; J 1020/92/16, Telegram No. 179, Lampson, Cairo to FO, 3 April 1940.

13. Alfred Sansom, *I Spied Spies* (London: George C. Harrap, 1965), 28–29.

14. Lampson Diaries, Killearn Box 4, 14 June 1940.

15. Ibid. See also UKNA FO 371/24626, J 2227/1/186/40, Telegram No. 938, Lampson, Cairo to FO, 8 October 1940.

16. Lampson Diaries, Killearn Box 4, 17 June, 23 June, 26–28 June 1940.

17. Lampson Diaries, Killearn Box 4, 27 June 1940.

18. Ibid.; UKNA FO 371/24626, J 1647/92/16, Minute by Clifford J. Norton (Head of Egyptian Department), FO, 8 July 1940, on Telegram No. 655, Lampson, Cairo to FO, 3 July 1940.

19. UKNA FO 371/24626, J 1647/92/16, Telegram No. 655, Lampson, Cairo to FO, 3 July 1940.

20. UKNA FO 371/24627, J 2231/92/16, Telegram No. 933, Lampson, Cairo to FO, 7 October 1940.

21. UKNA FO 371/24628, J 2227/1/186/40, Telegram No. 938, Lampson, Cairo to FO, 8 October 1940.

22. UKNA FO 371/24627, J 2231/92/16, Minute on Telegram No. 933, Lampson, Cairo to FO, 7 October 1940. See also, in the same file, J 2231/92/16, Telegram No. 935, Lampson, Cairo to FO, 7 October 1940.

23. See, for example, UKNA WO 208/1560, Appendix to MEIC, Summary No. 433, 10 February 1941.

24. UKNA FO 371/24628, J 2050/92/16, Telegram No. 1232, Lampson, Cairo to FO, 4 October 1940.

25. UKNA FO 371/24626, J 1694/G/92/16, Note by Sir Robert Vansittart (Chief Diplomatic Adviser to the Government), to Secretary of State, 26 July 1940.

26. UKNA FO 371/24626, J 1647/92/16, Telegram No. 698, Lampson, Cairo to FO, 24 July 1940.

27. Lampson Diaries, Killearn Box 4, 4 October 1940; UKNA FO 371/24626, J 2131/92/16, Minutes by Norton and Vansittart, 30 October 1940, on Telegram No. 1393, Lampson, Cairo to FO, 27 October 1940; and in the same, Extract from War Cabinet Conclusions, 281 (40); Telegram No. 1249, FO to Lampson, Cairo, 2 November 1940.

28. UKNA FO 371/24626, J 2131/92/16, Telegram No. 1502, Lampson, Cairo to FO, 12 November 1940, and on the same, the handwritten minute by Norton, 14 November 1940. See also, in the same file, Minute by Norton, 12 November 1940, on Telegram No. 1492, Lampson, Cairo to FO, 9 November 1940; Telegram No. 1330, FO to Lampson, Cairo, 16 November 1940; Telegram No. 1331 FO to Lampson, Cairo, 16 November 1940.

29. Lampson Diaries, Killearn Box 4, 14 November 1940. For the immediate aftermath of Sabri's death, see also UKNA FO 371/24627, J 2179/92/16, Telegram No. 1414, Lampson, Cairo to FO, 14 November 1940; J 2180/92/16, Telegram No. 1530, Lampson, Cairo to FO, 15 November 1940; J 2194/92/16, Telegram No. 1546, Lampson, Cairo to FO, 16 November 1940.

30. Lampson Diaries, Killearn Box 4, 21 July 1940.

31. UKNA FO 371/24626, J 1679/G, Telegram from Commander in Chief Middle East to WO, 1/13768 Cipher 15/7, 15 July 1940. The issue of who exactly had initiated such contact remains unclear. The commander in chief's telegram implies the British initiated the process; yet a later telegram from Sir Miles Lampson suggests that Ahmad Husayn had approached them. Compare the foregoing with UKNA FO 371/24626, J1679/G, Telegram No. 844, Lampson, Cairo to FO, 2 August 1940.

32. UKNA FO 371/24626, J 1679/G/92/16, Telegram No. 737, Lampson, Cairo to FO, 16 July 1940.

33. On Husayn's admiration for Hitler, see UKNA FO 371/22000, J 32–7/264/16, Telegram No. 923, Charles Bateman (Minister), Alexandria to FO, 4 August 1938.

34. Lampson Diaries, Killearn Box 4, 21 July 1940.

35. UKNA FO 371/24626, J 1679/G/92/16, Telegram No. 844, Lampson, Cairo to FO, 2 August 1940. Lampson Diaries, Killearn Box 4, 21 July 1940.

36. Lampson Diaries, Killearn Box 4, 21 July 1940.

37. Ibid.

38. Lampson Diaries, Killearn Box 4, 24 July 1940.

39. UKNA FO 371/24626, J 1679/G/92/16, Telegram No. 845, Lampson, Cairo to FO, 2 August 1940.

40. UKNA FO 371/24626, J 1679/G/92/16, Telegram No. 744, FO to Lampson, Cairo, 5 August 1940.

41. See marginalia comment on UKNA FO 371/24626, J 1679/G/92/16, Telegram No. 737, Lampson, Cairo to FO, 16 July 1940.

42. FO 371/108327, JE 1018/49, Note, "James Heyworth-Dunne, D. Lit.," undated.

43. FO 371/108327, JE 1018/49, Minute by Sir Roger Allen (Head of the Africa Department), FO, 30 April 1954.

44. "Obituary: Prof. J. Heyworth-Dunne," Times, 13 June 1974.

45. Lampson Diaries, Killearn Box 5, 20 May 1942.

46. UKNA FO 371/24626, J 1679/G/92/16, Telegram No. 745, FO to Lampson, Cairo, 5 August 1940; in the same, Telegram No. 865, Lampson, Cairo to FO, 6 August 1940.

47. Lampson Diaries, Killearn Box 5, 16 January 1942.

48. UKNA FO 371/24626, J 1679/G/92/16, C-in-C ME to WO, I/20454 Cipher 24/9, 24 September 1940.

49. UKNA FO 371/24626, J 1679/G/92/16, Undated Minute from E. Baring.

50. James P. Jankowski, Egypt's Young Rebels: "Young Egypt," 1933–1952 (Stanford, CA: Hoover Institution Press, 1975), 79–87.

51. HIA, James Heyworth-Dunne Archives, Accession No. 49005–9.37, Box No. 7, Envelope No. 4444, Handwritten note, Various notes written in 1939, 3 January 1940.

52. James Heyworth-Dunne, Religious and Political Trends in Modern Egypt (Washington, DC: James Heyworth-Dunne, 1950), 38–39.

53. James Heyworth-Dunne, "Junta v. Brotherhood: Egypt's Dilemma," Daily Mail, 5 February 1954.

54. See, for example, Fu'ad 'Allam, Al-Ikhwan wa ana: Min al-manshiya ila al-minasa (Cairo: Akhbar al-Yom, 1996), 78–79.

55. Richard P. Mitchell, The Society of the Muslim Brothers (Oxford: Oxford University Press, 1993), 28–29.

56. Muhammad al-'Adawi, Haqa'iq wa 'Asrar: Al-Ikhwan al-Muslimun, Ahdath Sana'at al-Tarikh, full copy available at http://bit.ly/2sBNlJg.

57. For evidence of al-Banna's affection toward al-Sukkari, see Hasan al-Banna, Mudhakirat al-da'wa wa-l-da'iya (Cairo: Mu'assasat Iqra, 2011).

58. USNRA, RG59, Central Decimal Files (CDF), Box 7150, 883.00/3–2948, Enclosure No. 1 to Despatch No. 259—Memorandum report voluntarily submitted by "John Roy Carlson" in Despatch No. 259, Pinkney Tuck (Ambassador), Embassy Cairo to State Department, 29 March 1948.

59. Muhammad Hamid Abu al-Nasr, Haqiqat al-Khilaf bayna al-Ikhwan al-Muslimin wa 'Abd al-Nasir (Cairo: al-Mu'allif, 1987), 31.

60. On this view, too, see Mitchell, Society of the Muslim Brothers, 28–29. See Salih 'Ashmawi, "Al-Ikhwan al-Muslimun wa-l-ingliz," al-Da'wa, 29 May 1951.

61. Abd al-Fattah Muhammad El-Awaisi, The Muslim Brothers and the Palestine Question, 1928–1947 (London: Tauris Academic Studies, 1998), 105–119. On the Special Appa-

ratus, see also *Mahmud al-Sabbagh, Haqiqat al-tanzim al-khass wa dawruhu fi da'wat al-ikhwan al-muslimin,* full copy available at http://bit.ly/2t6730O.

62. Hasan al-Banna, "Risalat al-ta'alim," in Hasan al-Banna, *Majmu'at al-rasa'il* (Cairo: Dar al-Sahoh, 2012), 215.

63. Salah Shadi, *Safahat min al-tarikh: Hisad al-'amr* (Kuwait: Sharikat al-Shu'a', 1981), 31–32.

64. Hasan Dawh, *25 'aman fi jama'at al-ikhwan* (Cairo: Dar al-'Itisam, 1983), 30, 33. See also Alison Pargeter, *The Muslim Brotherhood: The Burden of Tradition* (London: Saqi Books, 2010), 29–30; Christine Sixta Rinehart, "Volatile Breeding Grounds: The Radicalization of the Egyptian Muslim Brotherhood," *Studies in Conflict and Terrorism* 32 (2009), 953–988, especially 965–972.

65. Shadi, *Safahat min al-tarikh,* 32–33; 84–87.

66. UKNA WO 208/1560, Appendix to MEIC Summary No. 456, 10 March 1941.

67. Al-Sissi, *Fi qafilat al-Ikhwan,* 85–86.

68. UKNA FO 371/27429, J 899/18/16, Telegram No. 862, Lampson, Cairo to FO, 7 April 1941; and in the same, J 965/18/16, Telegram No. 932, Lampson, Cairo to FO, 12 April 1941.

69. UKNA FO 371/27429, J 951/18/16, Telegram No. 920, Lampson, Cairo to FO, 11 April 1941.

70. UKNA FO 371/27429, J 853/18/16, Telegram No. 198 Lampson, Cairo to Anthony Eden (Foreign Secretary), FO, 6 March 1941.

71. Lampson Diaries, Killearn Box 4, 17 April 1941.

72. Sansom, *I Spied Spies* 63–76. For another view on British concerns arising from the Iraq coup, see Oliver Lyttelton, *The Memoirs of Lord Chandos* (London: Bodley Head, 1962), 220–221.

73. Lampson Diaries, Killearn Box 4, 13 February 1941.

74. UKNA WO 208/1560, Appendix to MEIC Summary No. 513, 22 May 1941.

75. Al-Sissi, *Fi qafilat al-Ikhwan* 83–84. For a short biography of 'Abd al-Mon'im 'Abd al-Ra'uf, see "Al-ustadh al-mujahid 'Abd al-Mon'im 'Abd al-Ra'uf Basim Abu al-Fadl," Ikhwanwiki, http://bit.ly/2s6M5Ks.

76. Lampson Diaries, Killearn Box 4, 17 April 1941.

77. UKNA FO 371/27429, J 994/18/16, Telegram No. 971, Lampson, Cairo to FO, 15 April 1941.

78. Minute by Vansittart to the Secretary of State, 17 April 1941, on Ibid.

79. Minute by Bateman, 22 April 1941, on Ibid.

80. UKNA FO 371/27429, J 994/18/16, Telegram No. 1155, FO to Cairo, 17 April 1941.

81. For the improved situation in autumn of 1941, see Lyttelton, *Memoirs,* 261–265.

82. UKNA WO 208/1560, Appendix to MEIC Summary No. 594, 30 August 1941; and also Appendix to MEIC Summary No. 642, 25 October 1941.

83. Martin Kramer, *Islam Assembled: The Advent of the Muslim Congresses* (Guildford, UK: Columbia University Press), 158–162.

84. Lampson Diaries, Killearn Box 4, 16 October 1941.

85. UKNA FO 371/27434, J 3601/18/16, Telegram, No. 3570, Lampson, Cairo to FO, 14 November 1941.

86. UKNA FO 371/27434, J 3664/18/16, Telegram No. 3628, Lampson, Cairo to FO 19 November 1941; Lampson Diaries, Killearn Box 4, 13 November 1941.

87. UKNA WO 208/1560, Appendix to MEIC Summary No. 665, 21 November 1941.

88. Ibid.

89. UKNA WO 208/1561, Security Intelligence Middle East (SIME) Cairo, Security Summary Middle East, No. 11, 5 January 1942.

90. UKNA WO 208/1561, SIME Cairo, Security Summary Middle East, No. 13, 17 January 1942.

91. UKNA WO 208/1561, SIME Cairo, Security Summary Middle East, No. 19, 9 February 1942.

92. Lampson Diaries, Killearn Box 5, 7 January 1942.

93. FO 371/27434, J 3459/18/16, Telegram No. 3418, Lampson, Cairo to FO, 30 October 1941; Lampson Diaries, 22 September, 24 September, and 30 October 1941.

94. Lampson Diaries, Killearn Box 5, 21–22 January, 26–27 January, 29 January, and 1–2 February 1942.

95. For a lengthy British retrospective analysis of the move, see UKNA FO 371/41326, J 79/31/16, Telegram No. 1190, Lord Killearn [Lampson] to FO, 22 December 1943. See also Lyttleton, *Memoirs*, 276–279; Lampson Diaries, Killearn Box 5, 2–5 February 1942.

96. Hasan Hathut, *Al-'aqd al-farid, 1942–1952: 'Ashr Sanawat ma' al-Imam Hasan al-Bana* (Cairo: Dar al-Shuruq, 2000), 29.

97. Ahmad H. al-Baquri, *Baqaya dhikriyat* (Cairo: Markaz al-Ahram lil-Tarjamah wa-l-Nashr, 1988), 59–60.

98. "Hamasat wa sihat," *al-Ikhwan al-Muslimun,* 31 January 1945; "Faransa al-taghiya: taqtul ikhwanana al-musharikin wa tadmur al-masajid," *al-Da'wa,* 6 March 1951.

99. For example, over the position of the army chief of staff who was loyal to the king, and over the disciplining of three officers who had protested the events of 4 February 1942.

100. See details in UKNA FO 371/31574. For example, J 3592/38/16, Telegram No. 2040, Lampson, Cairo to FO, 18 August 1942; J 4050/38/16, Telegram No. 2298, Lampson, Cairo to FO, 29 September 1942; J 4183/38/16, Telegram No. 2369, Lampson, Cairo to FO, 11 October 1942; J 4211/38/16, Telegram No. 2379, Lampson, Cairo to FO, 13 October 1942. See also Lampson Diaries, Killearn Box 5, 23 February 1942.

101. UKNA FO 371/31574, J 4332/38/16, Telegram No. 939, Lampson, Cairo to Eden, 28 September 1942.

102. UKNA WO 208/1561, SIME Cairo, Security Summary Middle East, No. 22, 20 February 1942.

103. UKNA FO 371/31569, J 1190/38/16, Telegram No. 793, Lampson, Cairo to FO, 12 March 1942.

104. UKNA WO 208/1561, SIME Cairo, Security Summary Middle East, No. 24, 26 February 1942.

105. UKNA FO 371/31569, J 1343/38/16, Telegram No. 876, Lampson, Cairo to FO, 22 March 1942.

106. UKNA FO 371/31569, J 1144/38/16, Telegram No. 176, Lampson, Cairo to FO, 20 February 1942.

107. Lampson Diaries, Killearn Box 5, 10 February 1942.

108. UKNA FO 371/31569, J 1190/38/16, Telegram No. 793, Lampson, Cairo to FO, 12 March 1942; Lampson Diaries, Killearn Box 5, 17 March 1942.

109. Lampson Diaries, Killearn Box 5, 19 and 21 May 1942.

110. Sansom, *I Spied Spies*, 102–132. For Sadat's account of all this, in which he admits his desire for cooperation with the Germans and his liaison with Eppler, see Anwar El-Sadat, *In Search of Identity: An Autobiography* (New York: Harper & Row, 1978), 32–40.

111. Lampson Diaries, Killearn Box 5, 18 February 1942. See also UKNA WO 208/1561, SIME Cairo, Security Summary Middle East, No. 20, 12 February 1942.

112. UKNA FO 371/31569, J 1190/38/16, Telegram No. 793, Lampson, Cairo to FO, 12 March 1942.

113. Lampson Diaries, Killearn Box 5, 17 March 1942.

114. A. Z. al-'Abdin, "The Political Thought of Hasan al-Banna," *Hamdard Islamicus* 11, no. 3 (1988), 65.

115. Abbas Hasan al-Sissi, *Hasan al-Banna: Mawaqif fi al-da'wa wa-l-tarbiya* (Alexandria, Egypt: Dar al-Da'wa, 1982), 208.

116. UKNA FO 141/838, General Headquarters Middle East (GHQ, ME), "The Ikhwan al Muslimin Reconsidered" (Appendix A to Security Summary Middle East, No. 103, 10 December 1942).

117. Hathut, *Al-'aqd al-farid*, 29–30; al-Sissi, *Fi qafilat al-Ikhwan*, 92–95; Kemal el-Helbawy, "The Muslim Brotherhood in Egypt: Historical Evolution and Future Prospects," in Khaled Hroub, *Political Islam: Context versus Ideology* (London: Saqi Books, 2010), 68.

118. UKNA WO 208/1561, SIME Cairo, Security Summary Middle East, No. 32, 30 March 1942. For more on the concessions that al-Banna extracted, see Mitchell, *Society of the Muslim Brothers*, 27; Hathut, *Al-'aqd al-farid*, 29–30.

119. UKNA FO 141/838, GHQ, ME, "The Ikhwan al Muslimin Reconsidered."

120. UKNA WO 208/1561, SIME Cairo, Security Summary Middle East, No. 30, 23 March 1942.

121. UKNA FO 141/838, GHQ, ME, "The Ikhwan al Muslimin Reconsidered." On the internal criticism that al-Banna faced because of the deal with al-Nahas and the fact that he overcame it, see also al-Sissi, *Hasan al-Banna*, 208–210.

122. UKNA WO 208/1561, SIME Cairo, Security Summary Middle East, No. 40, 27 April 1942; FO 141/838, GHQ, ME, "The Ikhwan al Muslimin Reconsidered."

123. UKNA WO 208/1561, SIME Cairo, Security Summary Middle East, No. 42, 5 May 1942; FO 141/838, GHQ, ME, "The Ikhwan al Muslimin Reconsidered."

124. For a positive British view of al-Nahas's ministry, see UKNA WO 208/1561, SIME Cairo, Security Summary Middle East, No. 36, 13 April 1942.

125. Lampson Diaries, Killearn Box 5, 20 April 1942.

126. UKNA FO 141/838, Telegram from GHQ ME, D. S. (E)/200/42 "Reporting First Fortnightly Meeting with Amin Osman Pasha, at Embassy, 25 May 1942"; Lt. Colonel Maunsell, "First Fortnightly Meeting with Amin Osman Pasha Held at the Embassy on 18 May 1942."

127. Ibid.

128. "Taheya wa 'ahd wa aml," *al-Ikhwan al-Muslimun*, 26 September 1942, and from the same edition, "Da'watuna fi tawr jadid." See also "Da'watuna fi tawr jadid," *al-Ikhwan al-Muslimun*, 21 November 1942.

129. UKNA WO 208/1561, SIME Cairo, Security Summary Middle East, No. 42, 5 May 1942; FO 141/838, GHQ, ME, "The Ikhwan al Muslimin Reconsidered."

130. Sansom, *I Spied Spies*, 96–97; Artemis Cooper, *Cairo in the War, 1939–1945* (London: John Murray, 1989), 196–208.

131. UKNA WO 208/1561, SIME Cairo, Security Summary Middle East, No. 65, 27 July 1942.

132. Heyworth-Dunne, *Religious and Political Trends,* 41.

133. UKNA FO 141/838, GHQ, ME, "The Ikhwan al Muslimin Reconsidered."

134. UKNA WO 208/1561, SIME Cairo, Security Summary Middle East, No. 54, 15 June 1942; WO 208/1561, SIME Cairo, Security Summary Middle East, No. 55, 18 June 1942.

135. UKNA WO 208/1561, SIME Cairo, Security Summary Middle East, No. 66, 30 July 1942.

136. UKNA FO 141/838, Copy of Letter from Thomas Russell Pasha, at Cairo City Police, Office of Commandant, 23 September 1942.

137. UKNA WO 208/1561, SIME Cairo, Security Summary Middle East, No. 81, 19 September 1942; WO 208/1561, SIME Cairo, Security Summary Middle East, No. 82, 24 September 1942. The latter document identified Ahmed Mohammed Sahlul, an Ikhwan member who worked for Shell Co., as one of those involved.

138. UKNA FO 141/838, Lt. Col. R. J. Maunsell, "Report on the Activities of the Ikhwan," to Sir Walter Smart (Oriental Counselor), Embassy Cairo, 10 October 1942.

139. UKNA FO 141/838, GHQ, ME, "The Ikhwan al Muslimin Reconsidered."

140. Ibid.

141. UKNA FO 141/838, Lt. Col. R. J. Maunsell, "Report on the Activities of the Ikhwan."

142. UKNA WO 208/1561, SIME Cairo, Security Summary Middle East, No. 65, 27 July 1942.

143. UKNA FO 141/838, Jays Bey [G. Naldrett-Jays, Assistant Commandant, Alexandria City Police], "Supplementary Report on the Moslem Brethren Association," 31 October 1942. On this, see also GHQ, ME, "The Ikhwan al Muslimin Reconsidered"; WO 208/1561, SIME Cairo, Security Summary Middle East, No. 93, 5 November 1942.

144. UKNA FO 141/838, Draft Letter, Sir Walter Smart, 5 November 1942; also note of 11 November 1942.

145. UKNA FO 141/838, GHQ, ME, "The Ikhwan al Muslimin Reconsidered."

146. Ibid. See also WO 208/1561, SIME Cairo, Security Summary Middle East, No. 81, 19 September 1942—for al-Banna's alleged regard for Mussolini on this issue.

147. UKNA FO 141/838, GHQ, ME, "The Ikhwan al Muslimin Reconsidered."

148. Ibid.

149. UKNA FO 141/838, Letter, Lampson, Cairo to FO, 24 December 1942; FO 371/35578, J 245/158/16, Telegram No. 1237, Lampson, Cairo to FO, 24 December 1942.

150. UKNA FO 371/35528, J 283/2/16, Telegram No. 1196, Lampson, Cairo to FO, 14 December 1942; FO 371/35530, J 1203/2/16, Letter from Major WD Shaw, MI2, War Office to Sir Patrick Scrivener (Head of Egyptian Department), FO, DO/6388/MI2a, 16 March 1943.

151. Such lists were transmitted on a semiregular basis; as far as I have been able to determine, this is one of the earliest—if not the earliest—to mention al-Banna.

152. UKNA FO 371/35528, J 546/2/16, Telegram No. 19, Lampson, Cairo to FO, 5 January 1943.

153. Ibid. See also FO 371/35530, J993/2/16, Telegram No. 168, Lampson, Cairo to FO, 15 February 1943, for a similar view.

154. For this view of him, see USNRA, RG59, Bureau of Near Eastern South Asian and African Affairs: Office of Near Eastern Affairs: Subject Files, 1920–1954, Box 3, Memo-

randum by Alling transmits paper, "Middle East Perplexities" by HAR Gibb, 19 January 1945.

155. UKNA FO 371/35530, J 1407/2/16, Professor Gibb and Press Service to Baxter, 26 March 1943. The first drafts of the reports are dated 25 February 1943; they were continuously revised until final versions were confirmed on 7 September 1944.

156. Ibid.

157. UKNA WO 208/1562, Security Summary Middle East No. 116, SIME, Cairo, 30 January 1943.

158. UKNA WO 208/1562, Security Summary Middle East, No. 119, SIME, Cairo, 19 February 1943.

159. UKNA FO 371/35530, J 1155/2/16, Telegram No. 223, Sir Terence Shone (Minister), Embassy Cairo to FO, 1 March 1943. See also Brynjar Lia, *The Society of the Muslim Brothers in Egypt: The Rise of an Islamic Movement 1928–1942* (Reading, UK: Ithaca, 1998), 224–227.

160. UKNA WO 208/1562, Security Summary Middle East No. 120, SIME, Cairo, 24 February 1943.

161. Ibid.

162. UKNA WO 208/1562, Security Summary Middle East No. 122, SIME, Cairo, 8 March 1943. See also Security Summary Middle East No. 126, SIME, Cairo, 5 April 1943, which refers to al-Banna's "exemplary discretion."

163. UKNA FO 371/35530, J 1445/2/16, Telegram No. 279, Lampson, Cairo to FO, 19 March 1943; WO 208/1562, Security Summary Middle East No. 122, SIME, Cairo, 8 March 1943.

164. UKNA WO 208/1562, Security Summary Middle East No. 127, SIME, Cairo, 16 April 1943.

165. See, for example, Lampson Diaries, Killearn Box 5, 20 and 23–24 May 1942.

166. For a full translation of this document, see UKNA FO 141/855 (Part 2). For British commentary on it, see FO 371/35536, J 2855/2/16, Telegram No. 574, Killearn to FO, 16 June 1943; and in the same, No. S.E.75/Egypt/2/B.I.B/AJK, J 2928/2/16, Note from Alex Kellar (MI5), to Scrivener, "Note on Implications of the 'Black Book,'" 2 July 1943.

167. UKNA FO 141/855 (Part 1), Memorandum, 3 May 1943.

168. UKNA FO 371/31574, J 4332, Telegram No. 939, Lampson, Cairo to Eden, FO, 28 September 1942.

169. UKNA FO 141/855 (Part 2), Telegram No. 620, State Department FO to Lampson, Cairo, 12 April 1943; FO 371/35536, J 2855/2/16, Telegram No. 574, Killearn to FO, 16 June 1943. For an overview of the "Black Book" affair, see FO 371/41327, J 828/31/16, Telegram No. 207, Killearn, Cairo to FO, 25 February 1944.

170. UKNA FO 141/855 (Part 2), Telegram No. 620 from FO to Embassy Cairo, 12 April 1943.

171. UKNA FO 371/35536, J 2855/2/16, Telegram No. 574, Killearn, Cairo to FO, 16 June 1943.

172. UKNA WO 208/1562, Security Summary Middle East No. 128, SIME, Cairo, 21 April 1943.

173. "Al-wuzara' yazurun dar al-ikhwan al-muslimun," *Al-Ikhwan al-Muslimun*, 12 June 1943.

174. UKNA FO 371/41334, J 3812/34/43, "PIC Paper No. 49 (Revised): Ikhwan el Muslimeen," 25 July 1944.

175. UKNA FO 371/35536, J 3118/16/34/43, Telegram No. 655, Killearn, Cairo to FO, 9 July 1943.

176. UKNA FO 371/35536, J 3731/16/40/43, Telegram No. 781, Killearn, Cairo to FO, 19 August 1943.

177. UKNA WO 208/1562, Security Summary Middle East No. 139, SIME, Cairo, 6 July 1943.

178. UKNA WO 208/1562, Security Summary Middle East No. 137, SIME, Cairo, 19 June 1943.

179. UKNA WO 208/1562, Security Summary Middle East No. 143, SIME, Cairo, 10 August 1943.

180. UKNA WO 208/1562, Security Summary Middle East No. 138, SIME, Cairo, 28 June 1943.

181. UKNA FO 371/35536, J3628/16/39/43, Telegram No. 758, Killearn, Cairo to FO, 13 August 1943. On the Brotherhood's support for Arab unity, see Chapter 1 of this volume.

182. UKNA FO 371/35536, J3778/2/16, Telegram No. 5304, Commander-in-Chief, Middle East, from War Office to FO, 28 August 1943; WO 208/1562, Security Summary Middle East No. 138, SIME, Cairo, 28 June 1943. It was not just the British who saw the Brotherhood in these terms. See also A. Visson, "Egyptian Paradoxes: On the United Nations' Inside Front," *Washington Post,* 28 May 1944.

183. UKNA FO 371/35536, J 2855/2/16, Telegram No. 574, Killearn, Cairo to FO, 16 June 1943.

184. UKNA FO 371/35536, J 2995/2/16, Telegram No. 615, Killearn, Cairo to FO, 26 June 1943.

185. Lampson Diaries, Killearn Box 4, 24 September 1941.

186. UKNA FO 371/31574, J 4332, Telegram No. 939, Lampson, Cairo to Eden, 28 September 1942.

187. UKNA FO 371/35536, J 4152/2/16, Telegram No. 325 (S), Shone, Cairo to FO, 27 September 1943.

188. UKNA FO 371/35539, J 4607/2/16, Telegram Charvet to Scrivener, 3 November 1943.

189. UKNA FO 371/31574, J 4332, Telegram No. 939, Lampson, Cairo to Eden, 28 September 1942. On this point, see also FO 371/41326, J 79/31/16, Telegram No. 1190, Killearn, Cairo to FO, 22 December 1943. See also FO 371/35536, J 2855/2/16, Telegram No. 574, Killearn, Cairo to FO, 16 June 1943.

190. UKNA FO 371/35536, J 3026/2/16, Minute by Edwin A. Chapman-Andrews, 12 July 1943, on Telegram No. 1389, Killearn, Cairo to FO, 10 July 1943.

191. UKNA FO 371/35536, No. S.E.75/Egypt/2/B.I.B/AJK, J2928/2/16, Note from Kellar to Scrivener.

192. Ibid.

193. Minute by Chapman-Andrews, 7 July 1943, on ibid.

194. UKNA FO 371/35536, J 3177/2/16, Telegram No. S.F. 75/Egypt/2/B.I.B, Kellar, Box No. 500 (MI5), to Loxley, 19 July 1943.

195. Ibid.

196. UKNA FO 371/35536, J 4362/2/16, Telegram No. 600, Shone, Cairo to Scrivener, 10 October 1943, "Political Situation in Egypt: Influence of the Ikhwan el Muslimin." For further FO criticism of the Defence Security Office (DSO), see in the same file, Minute

by Victor Cavendish-Bentinck, 27 October 1943; Letter, Cavendish-Bentinck to Major-General F. H. N. Davidson, DSO, MC, 27 October 1943. For responses, see FO 371/35539, J 4579/2/16, Letter, Col. Vickers of Ministry of Economic Warfare to Cavendish-Bentinck, 28 October 1943; J 4580/2/16, Letter No. C/2/41/43, Major General Davidson, Director of Military Intelligence (War Office) to Cavendish-Bentinck, 2 November 1943. For more on the DSO, see https://www.mi5.gov.uk/home/mi5-history/world-war-ii/the-battle-for -gibraltar.html.

197. UKNA FO 371/35539, J 4580/2/16, Letter No. C/2/41/43, Major General Davidson, to Cavendish-Bentinck, 2 November 1943.

198. UKNA FO 371/35539, J 4580/2/16, Letter No. D/W/164, Cavendish-Bentinck to Davidson, 3 November 1943.

199. WO 208/1562, Security Summary Middle East No. 152, SIME, Cairo, 18 October 1943.

200. UKNA FO 371/35539, J 4630/2/16, Telegram No. 998, Shone, Cairo to FO, 5 November 1943.

201. Al-Sissi, *Fi qafilat al-Ikhwan,* 112–113.

202. UKNA WO 208/1562, Security Summary Middle East No. 185, SIME, Cairo, 7 June 1944. For more on this, see in the same file, Security Summary Middle East No. 186, SIME, Cairo, 15 June 1944.

203. UKNA WO 208/1562, Security Summary Middle East No. 187, SIME, Cairo, 22 June 1944.

204. UKNA WO 208/1562, Security Summary Middle East No. 184, SIME, Cairo, 31 May 1944.

205. UKNA WO 208/1580, MI 2/1763, "Extract from Defence Security Summary of Egyptian Affairs, 27th July—2nd August 1944."

206. UKNA FO 371/35536, J 4152/2/16, Minute by Chapman-Andrews, 4 October 1943, on Telegram No. 325 (S), Shone, Cairo to FO, 27 September 1943.

207. UKNA FO 371/35541, J 4045/2/16, Telegram No. 1077, Killearn, Cairo to FO, 25 November 1943; and J 5113/2/16, Telegram No. 1088, Killearn, Cairo to FO, 29 November 1943. See also FO 371/41327, J 828/31/16, Telegram No. 207, Killearn, Cairo to FO, 25 February 1944.

208. UKNA FO 371/41326, J 414/31/16, Telegram No. 75, Killearn, Cairo to FO, 23 January 1944. For a succinct analysis of the treaty question, see HIA, Jacob C. Hurewitz Collection, Accession No. 88012–16.317/319, Box No. 49, Jacob C. Hurewitz, "The Anglo-Egyptian Agreement on the Suez Canal Base: Political and Strategic Implications."

209. UKNA FO 371/41326, J 414/31/16, Telegram No. 75, Killearn, Cairo to FO, 23 January 1944; and in the same file, Minute by Scrivener, 4 February 1944. See also FO 371/41326, J 499, Telegram No. 24 (S), Killearn, Cairo to FO, 30 January 1944; Lampson Diaries, Killearn Box 5, 5 September 1944.

210. UKNA FO 371/35541, J 5056/2/16, Telegram No. 1108, Killearn, Cairo to FO, 3 December 1943; FO 371/41326, J 38/31/16, Telegram No. 2471, Killearn, Cairo to FO, 31 December 1943; FO 371/41327, J 828/31/16, Telegram No. 207, Killearn, Cairo to FO, 25 February 1944.

211. UKNA FO 371/35541, J 5078/2/16, Telegram No. 411 (S), Killearn, Cairo to FO, 15 December 1943. For further on the embassy's readiness to back al-Nahas and press the

king to comply, see FO 371/41326, J 31/31/16, Telegram No. 424 (S), Killearn, Cairo to FO, 24 December 1943; and J 38/31/16, Telegram No. 2471, Killearn, Cairo to FO, 31 December 1943; Lampson Diaries, Killearn Box 5, 18 April 1944.

212. See various files contained in UKNA FO 371/41327 and FO 371/41328. See also Lampson Diaries, Killearn Box 5, 19–24 April 1944.

213. Lampson Diaries, Killearn Box 5, 14 November 1944.

214. Al-Sissi, *Hasan al-Banna,* 207–208.

215. UKNA FO 371/41334, J 3812/16/44, "PIC Paper No. 49 (Revised): Ikhwan el Muslimeen, 25 July 1944."

216. Ibid.

217. UKNA FO 371/35539, J 4741/2/16, Report from James Heyworth-Dunne, "New Political Elements in Egypt," 18 November 1943.

3. Best of Enemies, 1944–1949

1. USNRA, RG59, CDF, Box 7150, 883.00/3–949, Airgram A-296, Jefferson Patterson (Chargé d'Affaires), Embassy Cairo to Secretary of State [State Department], 9 March 1949.

2. UKNA Foreign Office (FO) 371/73463, J 1633/1015/16, G. J. Jenkins, Embassy Cairo, to Head of Security Intelligence Middle East (SIME), General Headquarters Middle East Land Forces (GHQ MELF), and J. G. Tomlinson, Cairo Embassy, 17 February 1949. See also FO 141/1370, 517/3/39a, Jenkins (SSR) to Head of SIME, DS (E) DS/P/62, 15 February 1949; and FO 141/1370, 517/2/49a, Minutes by Tomlinson, 16 February 1949.

3. UKNA FO 141/1370, 517/16/49g, "The Murder of Sheikh Hassan el Banna," 18 November 1949. For references to the responsibility of Prime Minister Ibrahim al-Hadi, see in the same file, Minute by Sir Edwin A. Chapman-Andrews (Minister), 10 November 1949; and also Alfred Sansom, *I Spied Spies* (London: George C. Harrap, 1965), 226–228.

4. UKNA FO 371/73463, J 1633/1015/16, Jenkins, Cairo to Head of SIME, GHQ MEL and Tomlinson, Cairo Embassy, 14 February 1949; and in the same file, Minute on "Moslem Brethren," 27 February 1949 (signed by the ambassador, Sir Ronald Campbell), 108/15/499. See also FO 371/73463, J 1792/1015/16, Telegram No. 46 (S), Campbell, Cairo to FO, 2 March 1949.

5. UKNA FO 141/1370, 517/4/49a, Minute by Chapman-Andrews, 10 March 1949.

6. UKNA FO 371/73463, J 1633/1015/16, Jenkins, Cairo to Head of SIME, GHQ MELF and Tomlinson, Cairo Embassy, 14 February 1949.

7. USNRA, RG59, CDF, Box 7150, 883.00/2–1449, Airgram A-189, Patterson, Cairo to State Department, 14 February 1949. See also Box 7151, RG59, 883.00 (W)/2–1949, Joint Weekly A No. 12, Embassy Cairo to State Department, 19 February 1949.

8. USNRA, RG59, CDF, Box 7150, 883.00/2–2149, "Enclosure No. 1 to Despatch No. 170: A Prostitute Government Assassinates a Moslem Leader."

9. UKNA FO 371/73463, J 1862/1015/16, Telegram No. 127, from Sir Ronald Campbell (Ambassador), Cairo, to Ernest Bevin (Secretary of State), FO, 1 March 1949, which contains translation of Arabic pamphlet received in the post from the Muslim Brotherhood: "The Government kills Hassan el Banna on the occasion of the Royal Birthday."

10. Yusuf al-Qaradawi, *Al-Ikhwan al-Muslimun: 70 'aman fi al-da'wa wa-l-tarbiya wa-l-jihad,* 2nd ed. (Beirut: Mu'assasat al-Risala, 2001), 5–9, 242–243.

11. Ibid., 242. See also Mahmud 'Abd al-Halim, *Al-Ikhwan al-Muslimun I: Ahdath sana'at al-tarikh: ru'yah min al-dakhil, al-juz' al-awal* (Alexandria, Egypt: Dar al-Da'wa, 1981), 35–43; Kemal el-Helbawy, "The Muslim Brotherhood in Egypt: Historical Evolution and Future Prospects," in Khaled Hroub, *Political Islam: Context versus Ideology* (London: Saqi Books, 2010), 71–73.

12. See, for example, "Al-safir al-ingliz y'amur . . . wa-l-Nuqrashi yuti'a . . . wa-l-ikhwan tuhal!," *al-Da'wa,* 30 January 1951.

13. John Calvert, *Sayyid Qutb and the Origins of Radical Islamism* (New York: Columbia University Press, 2010), 144.

14. This would be in keeping with Qutb's wider impressions of the United States. See discussion in Chapter 6.

15. UKNA FO 141/1370, 517/16/49g, "The Story of the Assassination of Sheikh Banna," undated.

16. Nadav Safran, *Egypt in Search of Political Community: An Analysis of the Intellectual and Political Evolution of Egypt, 1804–1952* (Cambridge, MA: Harvard University Press, 1961), 201–206, 231–244.

17. Janice J. Terry, *The Wafd, 1919–1952: Cornerstone of Egyptian Political Power* (London: Third World Centre for Research and Publishing, 1982), 265–276. For a sense of the overweening nature of the British presence, see Naguib Mahfouz, *Midaq Alley,* trans. Trevor Le Gassick (London: Doubleday, 1992); or Olivia Manning's Cairo Trilogy: *The Danger Tree* (1977), *The Battle Lost and Won* (1978), and *The Sum of Things* (1980), all published by Penguin, Harmondsworth, UK.

18. Zaheer Quraishi, *Liberal Nationalism in Egypt: Rise and Fall of the Wafd Party* (Allahabad, India: Kitab Mahal, 1967), 152–158.

19. CAB 66/65, WP (45) 256, "Defence of the Middle East: War Cabinet Memorandum by Mr. Eden," 13 April 1945, in *BDDE,* vol. 1, 6–9.

20. For the view of the chiefs, see "'Future Defence Policy in the Suez Canal Area': Draft Aide Memoire by the Post Hostilities Planning Staff for the COS," in *BDDE,* vol. 1, 12–15. See also Richard J. Aldrich and John Zametica, "The Rise and Decline of a Strategic Concept: The Middle East, 1945–51," in *British Intelligence, Strategy and the Cold War, 1945–51,* ed. Richard J. Aldrich (Abingdon, UK: Routledge, 1992), 236–274; David R. Devereux, *The Formulation of British Defence Policy towards the Middle East, 1948–56* (Basingstoke, UK: Macmillan, 1990).

21. For an excellent overview, see Robert F. Holland, "The Imperial Factor in British State Strategies from Attlee to Macmillan, 1945–63," *Journal of Imperial and Commonwealth History* 12, no. 2 (1984), 165–186. Clement Attlee's government—and Foreign Secretary Ernest Bevin, in particular, believed that the Middle East could serve as the fulcrum of a new, "fourth" British Empire extending from the Gulf to Africa. See also Martin Lynn, introduction to *The British Empire in the 1950s: Retreat or Revival?,* ed. Martin Lynn (Basingstoke, UK: Palgrave Macmillan, 2006), 1–3.

22. Elizabeth Monroe, "British Interests in the Middle East," *Middle East Journal* 2, no. 2 (1948), 129–146 (136–140).

23. David W. Lesch, introduction to *The Middle East and the United States: A Historical and Political Reassessment,* 3rd ed. (Oxford: Westview, 2003), 1–9.

24. "Reply from Hull to Bucknell," Washington, 12 June 1944, in *FRUS* 1944, vol. V; "Memorandum by the Chief of the Division of Near Eastern Affairs (Merriam)," Washington, 29 October 1945, *FRUS* 1945, vol. VIII. On the relationship with Saudi Arabia, see Robert Lacey, *Inside the Kingdom: Kings, Clerics, Modernists, Terrorists, and the Struggle for Saudi Arabia* (New York: Viking, 2009).

25. "Letter from President Roosevelt to James M. Landis, American Director of Economic Operations in the Middle East," Washington, 6 March 1944, *FRUS* 1944, vol. V.

26. USNRA, CREST Database, "The Current Situation in Egypt," CIA Intelligence Report, 16 October 1947.

27. "Letter from Chargé in UK (Bucknell) to Secretary of State," London, 26 May 1944, *FRUS* 1944, vol. V.

28. UKNA FO 371/41327, J 1350/31/16, "Memorandum for Use with Mr. Stettinius and Mr. Wallace Murray: Egypt and the Sudan: British and American Interests," 17 April 1944.

29. UKNA FO 371/45927, J 2231/3/16, Telegram No. 206 (S), Lord Killearn (Ambassador), Cairo to FO, 4 July 1945. For a further exposition of the ambassador's views, see "Telegam from Killearn to Foreign Office," in *BDDE*, vol. 1, 15–16.

30. UKNA FO 371/45927, J 2279/3/16, Telegram No. 1563, Killearn, Cairo to FO, 11 July 1945.

31. UKNA FO 371/45927, Minute by A. Victor Coverley-Price, 13 July 1945; and in the same file, further Minutes dated 13 and 14 July 1945, as well as Sir Orme Sargent (Deputy Under-Secretary), FO, Memorandum to State Department, 23 July 1945.

32. "Draft Memorandum to President Truman, compiled by Merriam, Chief of the Near East Division," undated—but c. August 1945, *FRUS* 1945, vol. VIII.

33. Geoffrey Aronson, *From Sideshow to Centre Stage: US Policy toward Egypt, 1946–1956* (Boulder, CO: L. Rienner, 1986), 9–14. See also Gail E. Meyer, *Egypt and the United States: The Formative Years* (Rutherford, NJ: Fairleigh Dickinson University Press, 1980), 36–38.

34. UKNA FO 953/61, PME 1499/1499/939/G, Foreign Office Minute, "Russia in the Middle East: Publicity Directive," 17 October 1946; see also "The Soviet and Islam," *Times*, 28 January 1949; Percy Cradock, *Know Your Enemy: How the Joint Intelligence Committee Saw the World* (London: J. Murray, 2002), 39–40.

35. L. J. Butler, *Britain and Empire: Adjusting to a Post-Imperial World* (London: I. B. Tauris, 2001), 75.

36. UKNA FO 957/132, British Information Services, "The British Middle East Office," ID 1114, December 1951.

37. Matthew A. Fitzsimons, *Empire by Treaty: Britain and the Middle East in the Twentieth Century* (Notre Dame, IN: University of Notre Dame Press, 1964), 1–3; Ritchie Ovendale, *Britain, the United States and the Transfer of Power in the Middle East, 1945–1962* (London: Leicester University Press, 1996), 15; Devereux, *Formulation of British Defence Policy*, 8–9.

38. "Memorandum of Conversation, by the Secretary of State," Washington, 4 April 1949, *FRUS* 1949, vol. VI.

39. William Stivers, *America's Confrontation with Revolutionary Change in the Middle East, 1948–83* (New York: St. Martin's Press, 1986), 2–8, 19–22; see also Henry William

Brands Jr., "What Eisenhower and Dulles Saw in Nasser: Personalities and Interests in U.S.-Egyptian Relations," *American-Arab Affairs* 17 (1986), 44–54.

40. Kermit Roosevelt, *Arabs, Oil and History* (New York: Harper, 1949), 4–11.

41. "The Ambassador in the Soviet Union (Smith) to the Secretary of State," Moscow, 8 January 1947, *FRUS* 1947, vol. V.

42. USNRA CREST Database, "The Current Situation in Egypt," CIA Intelligence Report, 16 October 1947.

43. Douglas Little, "Gideon's Band: America and the Middle East since 1945," *Diplomatic History* 18, no. 4 (1994), 513–540 (514). See also Laila Ann Morsy, "American Support for the 1952 Egyptian Coup: Why?," *Middle Eastern Studies* 31, no. 2 (1995), 307–316 (308); Melvyn P. Leffler, *A Preponderance of Power: National Security, the Truman Administration, and the Cold War* (Stanford, CA: Stanford University Press, 1992), 15–19.

44. Holland, "Imperial Factor," 169.

45. Secretary of State (Acheson) to Secretary of Defense (Marshall), Washington, 27 January 1951, *FRUS* 1951, vol. V. See also "Paper Prepared in the State Department: Outline of Proposed NSC Paper on US Policy toward the Arab States and Israel," Washington, 10 February 1951, *FRUS* 1951, vol. V.

46. Annex II to "Memorandum Prepared in the State Department," undated, Washington, 8 September 1947, *FRUS* 1947, vol. V.

47. "Summary Memorandum of Informal Conversations held in October 1947 between Greenhill of British Foreign Office and Officers of the State Department, on Social and Economic Affairs in the Middle East," *FRUS* 1948, vol. V; UKNA FO 371/61559, especially E 10018/5764/G, Telegram No. 5928, Lord Inverchapel (Ambassador), Washington to FO, 24 October 1947; E 10239/5764/G, Telegram No. 6127, Inverchapel, Washington to FO, 1 November 1947. For a useful overview of these talks, see Devereux, *Formulation of British Defence Policy,* 12.

48. "Annex 1: Statement by the United States and the United Kingdom Groups," Washington, 14 November 1949, enclosed with "Memorandum of Conversation by the Deputy Director of the Office of African and Near Eastern Affairs," Washington, 18 November 1949, *FRUS* 1949, vol. VI. See also Ovendale, *Britain, the United States,* 25–29.

49. For US thinking on the Suez Canal Base, see Leffler, *Preponderance of Power,* 121–122, 237–246; Peter L. Hahn, *The United States, Great Britain, and Egypt, 1945–1956: Strategy and Diplomacy in the Early Cold War* (Chapel Hill: University of North Carolina Press, 1991), 38–130; Peter L. Hahn, "National Security Concerns in US Policy toward Egypt, 1949–1956," in Lesch, *The Middle East and the United States,* 75–82.

50. "Draft Memorandum to President Truman, compiled by Merriam, Chief of the Near East Division," undated—but c. August 1945, *FRUS* 1945, vol. VIII. A particularly vocal skeptic was Loy Henderson, the director of the Office of Near Eastern Affairs (ONEA) at the State Department. See, in the same volume, "Memorandum by Director of ONEA Affairs (Henderson) to Under Secretary of State (Lovett)," Washington, 28 August 1947. See also Muhammad Abd el-Wahab Sayed-Ahmed, *Nasser and American Foreign Policy 1952–1956* (London: Laam, 1989), 18–19; Aronson, *From Sideshow to Center Stage,* 25–76; Little, "Gideon's Band," 518; H. W. Brands, "The Cairo-Tehran Connection in Anglo-American Rivalry in the Middle East, 1951–1953," *International History Review* 11, no. 3 (1989), 434–456; Ovendale, *Britain, the United States,* 66–67. On the British tendency to underestimate nationalism, see also Cradock, *Know Your Enemy,* 111–113, 132.

51. W. Scott Lucas and Ray Takeyh, "Alliance and Balance: The Anglo-American Relationship and Egyptian Nationalism, 1950–57," *Diplomacy and Statecraft* 7, no. 3 (1996), 631–651.

52. UKNA FO 371/45928, J 3526/3/G/6, "Egypt," Minute by Secretary of State, 17 October 1945, on Telegram from Commander-in-Chief (C-in-C) India to War Office, 5 November 1945.

53. UKNA FO 371/45928, J 3947/3/16, Telegram No. 761, R. James Bowker (Minister), Embassy Cairo to Howe, 10 November 1945.

54. UKNA FO 371/45928, J 3526/3/G/6, "Egypt," Minute by Secretary of State, 17 October 1945, on Telegram from C-in-C India to War Office, 5 November 1945; "Memorandum by Sir E Grigg," 23 May 1945, in *BDDE*, vol. 1, 16–17.

55. UKNA FO 371/53304, J 2955/39/G16, Telegram No. 1, 183, Campbell, Cairo to FO, 2 July 1946.

56. For Killearn's skepticism, see his "swan song" telegram, UKNA FO 371/53288, J 1135/39/16, Telegram No. 101 (S), Bowker, Cairo to FO, 6 March 1946.

57. "Letter from Sir R Campbell to Killearn," 5 May 1945, in *BDDE*, vol. 1, 14–15.

58. USNRA, RG59, Bureau of Near Eastern, South Asian and African Affairs: Office of NEA: Subject Files, 1920–1954, Box 3, Memorandum by Alling transmits paper, "Middle East Perplexities," by HAR Gibb, 19 January 1945.

59. John S. Badeau, *The Middle East Remembered* (Washington, DC: Middle East Institute, 2009), 69–70.

60. USNRA, RG59, CDF, Box 5778, 883.00/3–1344, Airgram A-142, Alexander Kirk (Ambassador), Cairo to Washington, 13 March 1944; see also in the same box, for reference to the Wafd's alliance with the Brotherhood, 883.00/6–244, Memorandum by Jacobs, 2 June 1944.

61. USNRA, RG59, CDF, Box 5781, 883.00/4–2944, Despatch No. 1785, Jacobs, Cairo to Washington, 29 April 1944.

62. A. Visson, "Egyptian Paradoxes," *Washington Post*, 28 May 1944.

63. Ahmad 'Isa 'Ashur, *Hadith al-thulutha' li-Imam Hasan al-Banna: Sajjalaha wa-'addaha li-l-nashr* (Cairo: Maktabat al-Qur'an, 1985), 466–469.

64. Abbas Hasan al-Sissi, *Hasan al-Banna: Mawaqif fi al-da'wa wa-l-tarbiya* (Alexandria, Egypt: Dar al-Da'wa, 1982), 210–211.

65. "Al-umma al-'arabiyya bayna hadaratayn," *al-Ikhwan al-Muslimun*, 17 March 1945.

66. Salih 'Ashmawi, "Hal natma'a fi islah shamil?," *al-Ikhwan al-Muslimun*, 4 April 1945; "'Aridat al-Ikhwan al-Muslimin ila . . . jalalat al-malik," *al-Ikhwan al-Muslimun*, 28 June 1945. See also A. al-Tantawy, "Ila men yughadab li-l-'arad," *al-Ikhwan al-Muslimun*, 2 May 1945; Salih 'Ashmawi, "Mushkilat al-'arad haqq b-il-ihtimam," *al-Ikhwan al-Muslimun*, 31 May 1945.

67. "Al-umma al-'arabiyya bayna hadaratayn," *al-Ikhwan al-Muslimun*, 17 March 1945. On similar themes, see Ahmad A. al-Banna, "Al-Islam huwa al-khatima," *al-Ikhwan al-Muslimun*, 17 May 1945; "Al-Islam wa-l-salam," *al-Ikhwan al-Muslimun*, 31 May 1945.

68. The quotes in this paragraph are taken from both 'Ashur, *Hadith al-thulutha*, 459–462; and Hasan al-Banna, "Al-Salam fi al-Islam," *Shihab*, 1948, available at Ikhwanwiki, http://bit.ly/2u1Ea2r.

69. Hasan al-Banna, "Da'watuna fi tawr jadid," *al-Ikhwan al-Muslimun*, 12 December 1942; M. Muhammad al-Tarbaji, "Nurid al-Islam dinan wa dawlatan," *al-Ikhwan*

al-Muslimun, 20 February 1943; Hasan al-Banna, "Min quwa'id al-bana': Nufus wa mabadi' wa mashru'at," *al-Ikhwan al-Muslimun*, 18 April 1945.

70. "Hamasat wa sihat," *al-Ikhwan al-Muslimun*, 31 January 1945. On the promises of the Allies, see also "'Aridat al-Ikhwan al-Muslimin ila . . . jalalat al-malik," *al-Ikhwan al-Muslimun*, 28 June 1945.

71. Osman's account is available in the official biography written of him by his daughter, Ghada. See Ghada Osman, *A Journey in Islamic Thought: The Life of Fathi Osman* (New York: I. B. Tauris, 2011), 29, 34–40, 42–44, 52–53, 104.

72. Hasan al-Banna, "Daqa'iq al-ghalia," *al-Ikhwan al-Muslimun*, 28 June 1945.

73. 'Ashur, *Hadith al-thulutha*, 463–465.

74. Salah Shadi, *Safahat min al-tarikh: Hisad al-'amr* (Kuwait: Sharikat al-Shu'a', 1981), 29, 31–32. Shadi was a police officer who had joined the Brotherhood in 1943.

75. Hasan al-Banna, "Limatha yashtarik al-ikhwan fi intakhabat," *al-Ikhwan al-Muslimun*, 4 November 1944.

76. For an example of an election pamphlet, see al-Sissi, *Hasan al-Banna*, 213–215.

77. "Ila al-umma al-misriyya al-karima," *al-Ikhwan al-Muslimun*, 19 December 1944.

78. Muhammad U. Nijati, "Limatha indamt ila al-Ikhwan al-Muslimin," *al-Ikhwan al-Muslimun*, 19 December 1944.

79. Salih 'Ashmawi, "Al-ma'raka al-intikhabiya fi da'irat misr al-qadima," and "Sawt al-Da'wa," *al-Ikhwan al-Muslimun*, 2 January 1945.

80. A. Z. al-'Abdin, "The Political Thought of Hasan al-Banna," *Hamdard Islamicus* 11, no. 3 (1988), 65; Terry, *Wafd*, 276–289.

81. Hasan Hathut, *Al-'aqd al-farid, 1942–1952: 'Ashr Sanawat ma' al-Imam Hasan al-Bana* (Cairo: Dar al-Shuruq, 2000), 34–36.

82. Al-Sissi, *Hasan al-Banna*, 215–218. See also Ahmad H. al-Baquri, *Baqaya dhikriyat* (Cairo: Markaz al-Ahram lil-Tarjamah wa-l-Nashr, 1988), 48–49, 65–66. For another view on the Brotherhood's attempt to participate in the elections, see Muhammad Abu al-Nasr's account of trying to stand in Manfalut: Muhammad Hamid Abu al-Nasr, *Haqiqat al-Khilaf bayna al-Ikhwan al-Muslimin wa 'Abd al-Nasir* (Cairo: al-Mu'allif, 1987), 42.

83. Salih 'Ashmawi, "Intisar . . . !," *al-Ikhwan al-Muslimun*, 16 January 1945.

84. Al-Sissi, *Hasan al-Banna*, 215.

85. Gudrun Krämer, *Hasan al-Banna* (Oxford: Oneworld, 2010), 64–70; Osman, *Journey in Islamic Thought*, 66.

86. "Al-din wa-l-siyasa," *al-Ikhwan al-Muslimun*, 18 April 1945.

87. Richard P. Mitchell, *The Society of the Muslim Brothers* (Oxford: Oxford University Press, 1993), 33–34, 43–45.

88. Lois A. Aroian and Richard P. Mitchell, *The Modern Middle East and North Africa* (London: Collier Macmillan, 1984).

89. Peter Mansfield's book on Egypt identified the Brotherhood as the culprits of the Maher murder; see Peter Mansfield, *The British in Egypt* (London: Weidenfeld and Nicolson, 1971), 282. For an even more recent example, see *al-Masry al-Yawm*, August 2015. The former senior Brotherhood figure, Ahmad al-Baquri, claimed that Issawi assassinated Maher on instruction from the Brotherhood's Special Apparatus. See Al-Baquri, *Baqaya*, 49.

90. UKNA FO 371/45927, J 2403/3/16, Telegram No. 1661, Killearn, Cairo to FO, 23 July 1945.

91. Abbas Hasan al-Sissi, *Fi qafilat al-Ikhwan al-Muslimun, al-Juz' al-Awal,* 2nd ed. (Alexandria, Egypt: Dar al-Taba'a wa-l-Nashr wa-l-Sutiyat, 1987), 114.

92. UKNA FO 371/53289, J 1330/39/16, Telegram No. 380, Bowker, Cairo to FO, 27 March 1946.

93. "Killearn to Campbell," 14 April 1945, in *BDDE,* vol. 1, 9–12.

94. Lampson Diaries, Killearn Box 6, 31 August 1945; FO 371/45928, J 3526/3/G/6, Minute by Coverley-Price, 7 November 1945, on Telegram from C-in-C India to War Office, 5 November 1945.

95. Lampson Diaries, Killearn Box 6, 31 August 1945.

96. Al-Sissi, *Hasan al-Banna,* 218.

97. Hagai Erlich, *Students and University in Twentieth Century Egyptian Politics* (London: Cass, 1989), 151–154.

98. Mitchell, *Society of the Muslim Brothers,* 33–34.

99. Hathut, *Al-'aqd al-farid,* 18.

100. Hasan Dawh, *25 'aman fi jama'at al-ikhwan* (Cairo: Dar al-'Itisam, 1983), 21–24.

101. "Taqriuna ila al-nasr . . . Iman wa jihad," *al-Ikhwan al-Muslimun,* 14 February 1945.

102. Salih 'Ashmawi, "Khawatir Hurra . . . fi al-siyasa al-dawliya," *al-Ikhwan al-Muslimun,* 17 May 1945.

103. Salih 'Ashmawi, "Intahat al-harb . . . f-matha n'amal?," *al-Ikhwan al-Muslimun,* 30 August 1945.

104. UKNA FO 371/45922, J 2096/3/16, Telegram No. 836, Harold Farquhar (Acting Ambassador), Embassy Cairo to FO, 12 June 1945. And, especially, in the same file, "Report: Ikhwan el Muslimeen Demonstration, 4th June 1945." See also J 2263/3/16, Telegram No. 918, Farquhar, Cairo to FO, 29 June 1945.

105. UKNA FO 371/45922, J 2297/3/16, Telegram No. 939, Farquhar, Cairo to FO, 4 July 1945.

106. UKNA FO 371/45394, E 8506/119/31, Telegram from D. H. A. Agboatwala Sagi, Bombay to FO, 26 October 1945; E 8502/119/31, Telegram Major Crichton, Kabul to FO, 27 October 1945; E 8537/119/31, Telegram No. 10, Burke to Henderson, FO, 4 November 1945; J 3957/3/16, Telegram No. 1502, Bowker, Cairo to FO, 9 November 1945; E 8610/119/31, Telegram from War Office to FO, 10 November 1945.

107. Erlich, *Students and University,* 151–154.

108. "Filistin al-'arabiyya," *al-Ikhwan al-Muslimun,* 25 March 1944; "Filistin," *al-Ikhwan al-Muslimun,* 31 May 1945; UKNA FO 371/53331, J 1953/57/16, Telegram No. 175, Campbell, Cairo to Ernest Bevin (Foreign Secretary), FO, 7 April 1946.

109. "Filistin," *al-Ikhwan al-Muslimun,* 9 August 1945.

110. "Al-a'alam fi usbu'a," *al-Ikhwan al-Muslimun,* 30 August 1945. See also "Unqith Filistin," *al-Ikhwan al-Muslimun,* 30 August 1945.

111. See, for example, Abu al-Nasr, *Haqiqat al-Khilaf,* 45–47.

112. Dawh, *25 'aman,* 38–40. See also numerous articles in *al-Ikhwan al-Muslimun,* 3 November 1945.

113. UKNA FO 371/45394, E 8348/119/31, Telegram No. 2343, Bowker, Cairo to FO, 2 November 1945; and in the same file, E 8354/119/31, Telegram No. 2348, Bowker, Cairo to FO, 2 November 1945; E 8418/119/31, Telegram No. 2359, Bowker, Cairo to FO, 3 November 1945.

114. UKNA FO 371/45928, J 4006/3/16, Telegram No. S.F. 75/Egypt/2, Alex Kellar, MI5 to Sir Patrick Scrivener (Head of Egyptian Department), FO, 20 November 1945. For an example of the kind of propaganda circulated in connection with the events of November 2, see in the same file, "Circular No. 1"—by "The Anti-Zionism Front of Arabic and Islamic Organisations."

115. UKNA FO 371/45928, J 4006/3/16, Telegram No. S.F. 75/Egypt/2, Alex Kellar, MI5 to Sir Patrick Scrivener (Head of Egyptian Department), FO, 20 November 1945. See also UKNA FO 371/45928, J 4078/3/16, Telegram No. 1542, Killearn, Cairo to FO, 18 November 1945, which contains reports from Russell Pasha and Fitzpatrick Pasha on events in Cairo and Baker Pasha on the situation in Alexandria; also, Erlich, *Students and University,* 151–154.

116. USNRA, RG59, CDF, Box 7149, 883.00/11–1445, Telegram No. 1164, Cecil B. Lyon (Chargé d'affaires), Cairo to State Department, 14 November 1945.

117. "Enclosure: Sample Letter in Translation from Abdel Aziz Amer, Deputy, El-Labban Branch of the Moslem Brethren, Alexandria," contained with ibid. See also USNRA, RG59, CDF, Box 7149, 883.00/2–2746, Despatch No. 1364, Pinkney Tuck (Ambassador), Cairo to State Department, 27 February 1946, including "Enclosure: 'The Egyptian Protests of 2 November 1945, 4 February 1946.'"

118. This tallies with Brotherhood assessments of where they were strongest in this era. See Osman, *Journey in Islamic Thought,* 50.

119. UKNA FO 371/45928, J 3526/3/G/6, Minute by Coverley-Price, 7 November 1945, on Telegram from C-in-C India to War Office, 5 November 1945.

120. UKNA FO 371/45926, J 3402/3/16, Telegram No. 1332, Bowker, Cairo to FO, 3 October 1945. For a full translation of the Ikhwan's regulations, see FO 371/53251, J 1324/24/16, Enclosure "B," "Rules of the Moslem Brothers' Society, as Amended at General Meeting on 3.9.1945."

121. UKNA FO 371/45926, J 3402/3/16, Minute by Coverley-Price, 30 October 1945, on Telegram No. 1332, Bowker, Cairo to FO, 3 October 1945.

122. UKNA FO 371/45926, J 3694/3/16, Telegram No. 1441, Bowker, Cairo to FO, 27 October 1945.

123. 'Abdullah Imam, *'Abd al-Nasir wa-l-Ikhwan al-Muslimun* (Cairo: Dar al-Khayyal, 1997), 9.

124. UKNA FO 371/45928, J 3955/3/16, Telegram No. 1500, Bowker, Cairo to Bevin, FO, 9 November 1945.

125. Minute, 8 November 1945, on ibid.

126. See UKNA FO 371/45928, J 3955/3/16, Walter Smart, "Ikwan el Muslimin," 1 November 1945, enclosed with Telegram No. 1500, Bowker, Cairo to FO, 9 November 1945.

127. UKNA FO 371/53289, J 1330/39/16, Telegram No. 380, Bowker, Cairo to FO, 27 March 1946.

128. UKNA FO 371/53330, J 487/57/16, Telegram No. 155, Killearn, Cairo to FO, 2 February 1946; see also, in the same, J 721/57/6, Telegram No. 165, Killearn, Cairo to FO, 30 January 1946; J 750/57/6, Telegram No. 166, Killearn, Cairo to FO, 7 February 1946.

129. UKNA FO 371/53286, J 941 139/G/6, Letter from Kellar, Box No. 500 (MI5), to Scrivener, FO, 27 February 1946, transmitting "Report from Representative in Cairo: 6 February 1946."

130. Shadi, *Safahat min al-tarikh,* 33.

131. Anwar El-Sadat, *In Search of Identity: An Autobiography* (New York: Harper & Row, 1978), 57–61; Muhammad Ibrahim Kamel, *The Camp David Accords: A Testimony* (Abingdon, UK: Routledge, 2011), 1–4.

132. UKNA FO 371/53286, J 941 139/G/6, Letter from Kellar, Box No. 500 (MI5), to Scrivener, FO, 27 February 1946, transmitting Report from Representative in Cairo, 6 February 1946; FO 371/53282, Telegram No. 22 (S), Killearn, Cairo to FO, 12 January 1946.

133. Shadi, *Safahat min al-tarikh*, 37.

134. Jacob C. Hurewitz, *Diplomacy in the Near and Middle East: A Documentary Record, 1914–1956* (London: Yale University Press, 1956), 259–260.

135. Salih 'Ashmawi, "Intahat al-Harb . . . f-matha n'amal ?," *al-Ikhwan al-Muslimun*, 30 August 1945.

136. UKNA FO 371/53283, J 539/39/16, Telegram No. 178, Killearn, Cairo to FO, 5 February 1946; J 574/39/16, Telegram No. 192, Killearn, Cairo to FO, 9 February 1946.

137. For an Arabic account of this episode, see "Ma'arak damawiya bayna jamu' al-shabab wa-rijal al-jaysh wa-l-bulees," *al-Wafd al-Misri*, 10 February 1946.

138. Hathut, *Al-'aqd al-farid*, 40–43.

139. UKNA FO 371/53284, J 668/39/16, Telegram No. 244, Bowker, Cairo to FO, 14 February 1946; FO 371/53330, J 670/57/16, Telegram No. 264, Bowker, Cairo to Bevin, FO, 16 February 1946. See also USNRA, RG59, CDF, Box 7149, 883.00/2–1346, Telegram No. 289, Tuck, Cairo to State Department, 13 February 1946.

140. UKNA FO 371/53284, J 761/39/16, Telegram No. 307, Bowker, Cairo to FO, 21 February 1946; J 763/39/16, Cipher Telegram from C-in-C Middle East to War Office, 21 February 1946.

141. "Disorders in Cairo," *Times*, 26 February 1946.

142. UKNA FO 371/53289, J 1416/39/16, Letter, Thistlethwaite to Scrivener, 27 March 1946. For the press view, see "Protests to Egypt," *Times*, 25 February 1946.

143. For a flavor of the official British response as communicated to the Egyptian prime minister and king, see UKNA FO 371/53285, J 771/39/16, Telegram No. 312, Bowker, Cairo to FO, 22 February 1946; J 794/39/16, Telegram No. 321, Bowker, Cairo to FO, 23 February 1946.

144. Shadi, *Safahat min al-tarikh*, 44–46; Dawh, *25 'aman*, 19–20.

145. UKNA FO 371/53284, J 689/39/16, Telegram No. 288, Bowker, Cairo to FO, 18 February 1946; J 698/39/16, Telegram No. 284, Bowker, Cairo to FO, 18 February 1946; FO 371/53330, J 802/2/57/16, Telegram No. 316, Bowker, Cairo to FO, 23 February 1946.

146. UKNA FO 371/53286, J 925/39/16, Telegram No. 361, Bowker, Cairo to FO, 1 March 1946.

147. Al-Sissi, *Fi qafilat al-Ikhwan*, 115; Christina Phelps Harris, *Nationalism and Revolution in Egypt: The Role of the Muslim Brotherhood in Egypt* (The Hague, Netherlands: Mouton, 1964), 174–176.

148. UKNA FO 371/53331, J 1299/57/16, Telegram No. 171, Bowker, Cairo to FO, 14 March 1946.

149. UKNA FO 371/53286, J 946/39/16, Telegram No. 377, Killearn, Cairo to FO, 3 March 1946.

150. Al-Sissi, *Fi qafilat al-Ikhwan*, 118–119.

151. UKNA FO 371/53287, J 1101/39/16, FO Minute, "Egyptian Political Parties," 11 March 1946. For a journalistic assessment of the Brotherhood as a growing force in this

period, see F. G. H. Salisbury, "What's Cooking in Egypt—The Country Which Wants Us to Quit," *Daily Herald,* 20 February 1946.

152. UKNA FO 371/53287, J 1121/39/16, Letter, C-in-C Middle East to War Office, 9 March 1946.

153. UKNA FO 371/53331, J 1435/57/16, Telegram No. 172, Campbell Cairo to FO, 20 March 1946. See also Erlich, *Students and University,* 154–159; Ahmed Abdalla, *The Student Movement and National Politics in Egypt, 1923–1973* (London: Saqi Books, 1985), 64–69.

154. See, for example, UKNA FO 371/53288, J 1256/39/16, "Memorandum" by Sir Walter Smart (Oriental Counselor), 7 March 1946, enclosed in Telegram No. 352, Bowker, Cairo to FO, 11 March 1946.

155. UKNA FO 371/53331, J 1737/57/16, Telegram No. 707, Campbell, Cairo to Bevin, FO, 20 April 1946.

156. UKNA FO 371/53332, J 3080/57/16, Telegram No. 1233, Campbell, Cairo to Bevin, FO, 12 July 1946; J 3453/57/16, Telegram No. 1351, Campbell, Cairo to Bevin, FO, 9 August 1946.

157. Hathut, *Al-'aqd al-farid,* 44–47.

158. UKNA FO 371/53288, J 1254/39/16, Telegram No. 345, Bowker, Cairo to FO, 9 March 1946. See also enclosure, "Que Pensant les Freres Musulmans ?," *La Bourse Egyptienne,* 2 March 1946.

159. UKNA FO 371/53286, J 908/39/16, Telegram from "The Moslem Brethren Association in Kingdom of Nile Valley, Hassan el-Banna, President of Association," 1 March 1946.

160. UKNA FO 371/53331, J 1435/57/16, Telegram No. 172, Campbell, Cairo to FO, 20 March 1946. On the Brotherhood's conditional support for Sidqi with regard to negotiations, see also Hathut, *Al-'aqd al-farid,* 44–47.

161. "Telegram No. 713 Lord Stansgate to Bevin," 22 April 1946, *BDDE,* vol. 1, 109–111.

162. "Record of Personal Conversation with Ismail Sidky Pasha," 25 March 1946, *BDDE,* vol. 1, 83–85.

163. "Memorandum of Conversation, by the Acting Secretary of State," Washington, 7 May 1946, *FRUS* 1946, vol. VIII; "The Ambassador in the United Kingdom (Harriman) to the Secretary of State, London," 3 May 1946, *FRUS* 1946, vol. VIII. See also "Memorandum of Conversation (with British Ambassador Lord Halifax), by the Under Secretary of State (Acheson)," Washington, 20 April 1946, *FRUS* 1946, vol. VIII. For discussion of a "general defence scheme," see UKNA FO 371/53288, J 1151/39/16, FO Minute, "Anglo-Egyptian Treaty," 12 March 1946. The idea was not for a regional defense structure, but rather for a series of bilateral arrangements between the United Kingdom and the respective local governments under the umbrella of a shared agreement on general policy. See, for example, FO 371/61558, E 9559/5764/G, "Joint Defence on the Middle East," undated, 1947.

164. UKNA FO 371/53330, J 487/57/16, Telegram No. 155, Killearn, Cairo to FO, 2 February 1946; FO 371/53286, J 925/39/16, Telegram No. 361, Bowker, Cairo to FO, 1 March 1946; FO 371/53304, J 2876/39/16, Telegram No. 761, Campbell, Cairo to Bevin, FO, 24 June 1946; FO 371/53332, J 4450/57/16, Telegram No. 1595, Bowker, Cairo to Bevin, FO, 25 October 1946; FO 371/53315, J 4372/39/16, Telegram No. 1574, Bowker, Cairo to FO, 21 October 1946; USNRA, RG59, Box 883.00/10–2446, Despatch No. 1923, Tuck, Cairo to State Department, 24 October 1946.

165. UKNA FO 371/53283, J 539/39/16, Telegram No. 178, Killearn, Cairo to FO, 5 February 1946; and in the same file, J 574/39/16, Telegram No. 192, Killearn, Cairo to FO, 9 February 1946.

166. "Threat in Egypt: 'Bloody Revolt,'" *Baltimore Sun,* 30 August 1946.

167. "Laysa b'ada fashal al-mufawadat ila al-jihad," *al-Ikhwan al-Muslimun,* 10 August 1946.

168. USNRA, RG59, CDF, Box 7149, 883.00/10–2446, Telegram No. 1923, Tuck, Cairo to State Department, 24 October 1946; for a description of the conference and its resolutions, see also al-Sissi, *Fi qafilat al-Ikhwan,* 121–123.

169. UKNA FO 371/53332, J 4263/57/16, Telegram No. 1525, Bowker, Cairo to FO, 11 October 1946; J 4351/57/16, Telegram No. 1563, Bowker Cairo to Bevin, FO, 18 October 1946; FO 371/53315, J 4314/39/16, Telegram No. 1556, Bowker, Cairo to FO, 16 October 1946.

170. Al-Sissi, *Fi qafilat al-Ikhwan,* 117–118.

171. Hathut, *Al-'aqd al-farid,* 44–47.

172. Al-Sissi, *Fi qafilat al-Ikhwan,* 126–128.

173. USNRA, RG59, CDF, Box 7149, 883.00/11–2346, Airgram A-522, Tuck, Cairo to State Department, 23 November 1946.

174. "Ikhraju al-ingliz min qalubikum, yughadiru 'ardikum," *al-Ikhwan al-Muslimun,* 5 March 1946.

175. Al-Sissi, *Fi qafilat al-Ikhwan,* 126–128. On the "Day of Fire" see also UKNA FO 371/53332, J 5075/57/16, Telegram No. 1791, Bowker, Cairo to Bevin, FO, 30 November 1946; J5201/57/16, Telegram No. 1829, Bowker, Cairo to Bevin, FO, 6 December 1946; Erlich, *Students and University,* 159–161.

176. "Sidky Pasha and the Wafd," *Times,* 2 December 1946.

177. UKNA FO 371/62990, J 722/13/G16, "Defence Security Summary of Egyptian Affairs," December 1946. For the arrest of al-Sukkari, see also Harris, *Nationalism and Revolution in Egypt,* 176.

178. UKNA FO 371/62990, J 722/13/G16, "Defence Security Summary of Egyptian Affairs," December 1946. Fathi Osman was among those briefly arrested by police investigating the attacks, and his daughter biographer accepts that the Ikhwan was behind them, though she suggests they were "simple bombs . . . not devised to hurt anyone," but rather to make a point about the Brotherhood's "potential prowess." See Osman, *Journey in Islamic Thought,* 61–62.

179. "Non-Violence in Egypt: Muslim Brotherhood's Declaration," *Times,* 28 December 1946.

180. USNRA, RG59, Bureau of Near Eastern, South Asian and African Affairs: Office of NEA: Subject Files, 1920–1954, Box 2, Memorandum W. L. Jenkins to Harry N. Howard, 5 December 1946.

181. "Nationalism in Egypt: The Muslim Brotherhood's Campaign," *Times,* 28 November 1946. See also "Groupings in Egypt," *Times,* 23 December 1946.

182. "Bomb-Throwing in Cairo," *Times,* 5 December 1946.

183. For an overview of this period, see UKNA FO 371/62990, J 722/13/G16, "Defence Security Summary of Egyptian Affairs," December 1946.

184. UKNA FO 371/73458, J 3728/1011/16, Telegram No. 229, Campbell, Cairo to FO, "General Political Review, 1947," 20 April 1949.

185. USNRA, RG59, CDF, Box 7151, 883.002/12–1246, Airgram A-574, Tuck, Cairo to State Department, 12 December 1946.

186. UKNA FO 371/73458, J 3728/1011/16, Telegram No. 229, Campbell, Cairo to FO, "General Political Review, 1947," 20 April 1949; FO 371/63021, J 3550/79/16, Telegram No. 1614, Campbell, Cairo to FO, 25 July 1947.

187. Al-Sissi, *Fi qafilat al-Ikhwan,* 172–173.

188. "Minute by Sir O Sargent to Bevin," 1 January 1947, *BDDE,* vol. 1, 216–218.

189. Mitchell, *Society of the Muslim Brothers,* 50–51. See also Hathut, *Al-'aqd al-farid,* 48.

190. USNRA, RG59, CDF, Box 7149, 883.00/8–2946, Telegram No. 2866, Tuck, Cairo to State Department, 29 August 1947.

191. See, for example, "Secretary of State to Embassy in the United Kingdom," Washington, 14 July 1947, *FRUS* 1947, vol. V.

192. "Telegram: Secretary of State to the Acting United States Representative at the United Nations (Johnson)," Washington, 8 August 1947, *FRUS* 1947, vol. V.

193. "Memorandum of Conversation by the Director of Near East and African Affairs (Henderson), Annex 1," London, 9 September 1947, *FRUS* 1947, vol. V; UKNA FO 371/61558, E 9559/5764/G, "Egypt—Future Policy," undated, 1947. In March–April 1947, British frustrations with the Egyptian prime minister already had led to a debate within the Foreign Office over whether or not to seek his removal. See various folders in FO 371/62969.

194. Ironically, the British were themselves critical of their US counterparts for failing, in their view, to support them "as we should wish." On all this, see "Telegram: Ambassador in Egypt (Tuck) to Secretary of State," Cairo, 1 October 1947, *FRUS* 1947, vol. V; UKNA FO 371/61558, E 9559/5764/G, "Draft Steering Brief for Washington Conversations on the Middle East," 2 October 1947; see also, in the same, E 9559/5764/G, "Egypt," undated, 1947.

195. Mitchell, *Society of the Muslim Brothers,* 51.

196. Sansom, *I Spied Spies,* 208–219; "1 Dead, 75 Hurt in Anti-British Riots in Egypt," *Chicago Daily Tribune,* 23 August 1947; "Moslem Mob Fights Police," *Washington Post,* 24 August 1947. According to Brotherhood accounts, al-Banna was shot in the hand during the Cairo riot; see, for example, Shadi, *Safahat min al-tarikh,* 47.

197. "Copts Appeal to King Farouk," *Times,* 9 April 1947.

198. USNRA, RG59, CDF, Box 7149, 883.00/5–247, Airgram A-281, Tuck, Cairo to State Department, 2 May 1947. See also "Moderate Voice in Egypt," *Times,* 16 August 1947.

199. Al-Sissi, *Fi qafilat al-Ikhwan,* 180; Al-Sissi, *Hasan al-Banna,* 235. James Heyworth-Dunne, *Religious and Political Trends in Modern Egypt* (Washington, DC: James Heyworth-Dunne, 1950), 44.

200. Krämer, *Hasan al-Banna,* 76–81.

201. Sansom, *I Spied Spies,* 206–207.

202. UKNA FO 371/63021, J 3165/79/16, Telegram No. 1495, Campbell, Cairo to FO, 4 July 1947.

203. UKNA FO 371/63021, J 4242/79/16, Telegram No. 113 (S), Bowker, Cairo to FO, 29 August 1947.

204. USNRA, RG59, CDF, Box 7149, 883.00/8–2947, Telegram No. 2866, Tuck, Cairo to State Department, 29 August 1947, and especially Enclosure No. 1: "Memorandum of Conversation, August 27, 1947."

205. Ibid.

206. Ibid.

207. UKNA FO 371/63021, J 3550/79/16, Telegram No. 1614, Campbell, Cairo to FO, 25 July 1947.

208. Jeffrey Herf, *Nazi Propaganda for the Arab World* (London: Yale University Press, 2009), 248–249.

209. USNRA, RG59, CDF, Box 7149, 883.00/8–2947, Telegram No. 2866, Tuck, Cairo to State Department, 29 August 1947, and especially Enclosure No. 1: "Memorandum of Conversation, August 27, 1947."

210. Shadi, *Safahat min al-tarikh,* 84. See also Hathut, *Al-'aqd al-farid,* 50–62.

211. Kamil al-Sharif, *Al-Ikhwan al-Muslimun wa-l-Harb fi Filistin,* 3rd ed. (Amman, Jordon: Maktabat al-Manar, 1984), 25–27.

212. Ibid. 33–34.

213. UKNA FO 371/53331, J 1992/57/16, Telegram No. 800, Campbell, Cairo to Bevin, FO, 5 May 1946.

214. Herf, *Nazi Propaganda,* 241–245.

215. El-Awaisi, *Muslim Brothers,* 172–199.

216. USNRA, RG59, CDF, Box 7149, 883.00/8–2947, Telegram No. 2866, Tuck, Cairo to State Department, 29 August 1947, and especially Enclosure No. 1: "Memorandum of Conversation, August 27, 1947."

217. Osman, *Journey in Islamic Thought,* 32.

218. UKNA FO 141/1182, 386/9/47, Richard L. Speaight (Counselor), Embassy Cairo to the Secretariat, Jerusalem, 24 October 1947. On the Brotherhood's recruitment offices, see also FO 386/10/47, No. 1001, Arabic Press Summaries.

219. USNRA, RG59, CDF, Box 7149, 883.00/8–2947, Telegram No. 2866, Tuck, Cairo to State Department, 29 August 1947.

220. Al-Baquri, *Baqaya,* 70–71.

221. UKNA FO 386/10/47, Arabic Press Summaries, No. 988, Minute by Embassy Official, 16 October 1947. See also FO 371/61881, E 9442/951/31, Telegram No. 1990, Bowker, Cairo to FO, 9 October 1947. See also Thomas Mayer, "The Military Force of Islam: The Society of the Muslim Brethren and the Palestine Question, 1945–48," in *Zionism and Arabism in Palestine and Israel,* ed. Elie Kedourie and Sylvia Haim (London: Frank Cass, 1982), 100–117 (106–108).

222. UKNA FO 371/63021, J 5178/79/16, Telegram No. 144 (S), Bowker, Cairo to FO, 18 October 1947.

223. Al-Sissi, *Fi qafilat al-Ikhwan,* 194–195; UKNA FO 371/63021, J 6107/79/16, Telegram No. 172 (S), Campbell, Cairo to FO, 9 December 1947.

224. Al-Sissi, *Hasan al-Banna,* 218–219.

225. UKNA FO 141/1182, 386/9/47, Speaight, Cairo to the Secretariat, Jerusalem, 24 October 1947.

226. UKNA FO 371/63021, J 4014/79/16, Telegram No. 111 (S) Bowker, Cairo to FO, 23 August 1947; FO 371/62993, J 4351/13/16, Telegram No. 773, Bowker, Cairo to FO, 6 September 1947; and in the same, J 4430/13/16, Telegram No. 121 (S), Bowker, Cairo to FO, 15 September 1947. See also "'Liberation Battalions' for Egypt: Muslim Brotherhood Plan," *Times,* 26 September 1947.

227. USNRA, RG59, CDF, Box 7150, 883.00/1–3148, Airgram A-83, Tuck, Cairo to State Department, 31 January 1948; Charles Tripp, "Egypt 1945–52: The Uses of Disorder," in *Demise of the British Empire in the Middle East: Britain's Responses to Nationalist Movements*, ed. Martin J. Cohen and Martin Kolinsky (London: Frank Cass, 1998), 112–141 (123–124); Heyworth-Dunne, *Religious and Political Trends*, 46–47; Harris, *Nationalism and Revolution in Egypt*, 184.

228. UKNA FO 371/63021, J 4014/79/16, Telegram No. 111 (S) Bowker, Cairo to FO, 23 August 1947; FO 371/62993, J 4351/13/16, Telegram No. 773, Bowker, Cairo to FO, 6 September 1947; and in the same, J 4430/13/16, Telegram No. 121 (S), Bowker, Cairo to FO, 15 September 1947.

229. Al-Sissi, *Fi qafilat al-Ikhwan*, 173; Imam, *'Abd al-Nasir*, 14–18.

230. Shadi, *Safahat min al-tarikh*, 49–53.

231. USNRA, RG59, CDF, Box 7151, 883.02/11–1147, Despatch No. 3020, Tuck, Cairo to State Department, 11 November 1947.

232. Quoted in USNRA, RG59, CDF, Box 7151, 883.002/11–2847, Despatch No. 3059, Tuck, Cairo to State Department, 28 November 1947.

233. UKNA FO 371/73458, J 3728/1011/16, Telegram No. 229, Campbell, Cairo to FO, "General Political Review, 1947," 20 April 1949.

234. UKNA FO 371/63021, J 5945/79/16, Telegram No. 169 (S), Campbell, Cairo to FO, 28 November 1947.

235. UKNA FO 371/63021, J 6107/79/16, Telegram No. 172 (S), Campbell, Cairo to FO, 9 December 1947.

236. "Radicalism of Youth Leaders Stirs Egyptian Politics," *Christian Science Monitor*, 17 June 1948.

237. USNRA, RG59, CDF, Box 7149, 883.00/8–2947, Despatch No. 2866, Tuck, Cairo to State Department, 29 August 1947.

238. USNRA, CREST Database, "The Current Situation in Egypt," CIA Intelligence Report, 16 October 1947.

239. UKNA FO 371/69210, J 110/68/16, FO Minute, Research Department, 30 December 1947.

240. UKNA FO 371/61542, E 2130/2130/65, Memorandum by Foreign Office Research Department, "Youth Movements in the Middle East," 12 February 1947.

241. The preceding quotes are taken variously from the following Foreign Office reports on the problems of the "effendis" in the Middle East, which are located in UKNA FO 141/1223: Confidential Despatch No. 32, C. W. Baxter (for the Secretary of State), FO to Campbell, Cairo, 5 January 1947; Despatch No. 30, Lawrence B. Grafftey-Smith (Ambassador), Jedda to FO, 17 February 1947; Report by Mr. P. G. D. Adams (Second Secretary) Legation Saudi Arabia; Despatch No. 36, H. M. Eyres (Chargé d'affaires), Damascus, to FO, 1 April 1947; Despatch No. 86, W. E. Houstaun-Boswall (Minister), Beirut to FO, 15 May 1947; Despatch No. 80, Hugh Stonehewer-Bird (Ambassador), Bagdad, to FO, 10 March 1947; Memorandum by W. F. Crawford (Scientific Officer, British Middle East Office), Cairo, to FO, 9 June 1947; Despatch No. 344, Campbell, Cairo to FO, 23 April 1947; Letter from Ronald Fay to Mr. Bailey, 23 February 1947.

242. Kermit Roosevelt, *Arabs, Oil and History* (New York: Harper, 1949), 41–45, 80–84.

243. Hugh Wilford, *America's Great Game: The CIA's Secret Arabists and the Shaping of the Modern Middle East* (New York: Basic Books, 2013), 82.

244. Hasan al-Banna, *Mudhakirat al-da'wa wa-l-da'iya* (Cairo: Mu'assasat Iqra, 2011), 75–76.

245. Krämer, *Hasan al-Banna*, 47–50; Brynjar Lia, *The Society of the Muslim Brothers in Egypt: The Rise of an Islamic Movement, 1928–1942* (Reading, UK: Ithaca, 1998), 140–144; Al-Sissi, *Fi qafilat al-Ikhwan*, 54–56.

246. Robert Dreyfuss, *Devil's Game: How the United States Helped Unleash Fundamentalist Islam* (New York: Metropolitan, 2005), 65–66.

247. Al-Sissi, *Fi qafilat al-Ikhwan*, 111.

248. Al-Banna, *Mudhakirat al-da'wa*, 110.

249. El-Helbawy, "The Muslim Brotherhood in Egypt," 69–70.

250. A. Z. al-'Abdin, "The Free Yemeni Movement (1940–48) and Its Ideas of Reform," *Middle Eastern Studies* 15, no. 1 (1979), 36–48.

251. USNRA, RG59, CDF, Box 7231, 890J.001/2–2148, Despatch 146, Tuck, Cairo to State Department, 21 February 1948.

252. "Abtal al-'aruba fi dar: al-ikhwan al-muslimin," *Al-Ikhwan al-Muslimun*, 28 June 1945.

253. El-Helbawy, "The Muslim Brotherhood in Egypt," 69–70.

254. USNRA, RG59, CDF, Box 7231, 890J.001/2–2848, Despatch No. 168, Tuck, Cairo to State Department, 28 February 1948, and Enclosure No. 1: "Memorandum of Conv, Philip W. Ireland."

255. Ibid. Al-Banna did not ultimately travel to Yemen. US diplomats speculated that the Cairo government may well have intervened to prevent him from traveling. See USNRA, RG59, CDF, Box 7231, 890J.001/3–548, Telegram No. 224, Tuck, Cairo to State Department, 5 March 1948.

256. Al-Sissi, *Fi qafilat al-Ikhwan*, 204–206.

257. Heyworth-Dunne, *Religious and Political Trends*, 18.

258. See, for example, "Al-Islam wa-l-'alaqat al-dawliya," *al-Ikhwan al-Muslimun*, 20 March 1943; "Al-Islam fi andunisiya," *al-Ikhwan al-Muslimun*, 15 May 1943; "Anba' al-a'alam al-islami," *al-Ikhwan al-Muslimun*, 11 March 1944; "Al-ta'awun al-a'alami," *al-Ikhwan al-Muslimun*, 17 June 1944.

259. Salih 'Ashmawi, "Al-wahda al-'arabiya," *al-Ikhwan al-Muslimun*, 9 January 1943.

260. "Al-mawqif al-siyasiya," *al-Ikhwan al-Muslimun*, 16 January 1945; "Yawm min ayam," *al-Ikhwan al-Muslimun*, 4 April 1945.

261. Ahmad al-Sukkari, "Daqq nafus al-aml," *al-Ikhwan al-Muslimun*, 28 June 1945.

262. "Mu'atamar san fransisku," *al-Ikhwan al-Muslimun*, 17 March 1945; "Siyasat al-a'alam," *al-Ikhwan al-Muslimun*, 2 May 1945.

263. M. S. al-Jawhiri, "al-a'alam fi usbu'ayn," *al-Ikhwan al-Muslimun*, 12 July 1945.

264. "Fi muhit al-ikhwan al-muslimin," *al-Ikhwan al-Muslimun*, 31 January 1945.

265. Al-Baquri, *Baqaya*, 97–99. For a slightly different categorization of these committees' respective remits, see Mitchell, *Society of the Muslim Brothers*, 170–175.

266. 'Ashur, *Hadith al-thulutha*, 470–473.

267. Osman, *Journey in Islamic Thought*, 104; UKNA FO 371/63021, J 2969/79/16, Telegram No. 1424, Campbell, Cairo to FO, 22 June 1947; J 3550/79/16, Telegram No. 1614, Campbell, Cairo to FO, 25 July 1947; J 3630/79/16, Telegram No. 90 (S), Campbell, Cairo to FO, 2 August 1947.

268. "Al-ingliz wa-l-Islam," *al-Ikhwan al-Muslimun,* 23 June 1946. See also "Al-ingliz wa-l-'arab," *al-Ikhwan al-Muslimun,* 30 June 1946.

269. 'Ashur, *Hadith al-thulutha,* 474–477.

270. Al-Sissi, *Fi qafilat al-Ikhwan,* 259.

271. "Al-sudan fi khatar," *al-Ikhwan al-Muslimun,* 13 September 1945.

272. Hasan al-Banna, "Risala ila al-mu'atamar al-khamis," in Hasan al-Banna, *Majmu'at al-rasa'il* (Cairo: Dar al-Sahoh, 2012), 292.

273. 'Ashur, *Hadith al-thulutha,* 466–469.

274. "Unqudh andunisia," *al-Ikhwan al-Muslimun,* 5 January 1946; UKNA FO 371/63021, J 3630/79/16, Telegram No. 90 (S), Campbell, Cairo to FO, 2 August 1947.

275. Al-Banna, "Risala ila al-mu'atamar al-khamis," 292.

276. "Suriya wa Lubnan," *al-Ikhwan al-Muslimun,* 31 May 1945; "Juhud al-Ikhwan al-Muslimin fi qadiyat suriya wa lubnan," *al-Ikhwan al-Muslimun,* 28 June 1945; and in the same edition, Hasan al-Banna, "'Ashrun alf mutatawa'a."

277. Abu al-Nasr, *Haqiqat al-Khilaf,* 29.

278. Al-Banna, "Risala ila al-mu'atamar al-khamis," 292. See also the 8 April 1944 special edition of *al-Ikhwan al-Muslimun,* which contains a plethora of articles on the subject; Al-Sissi, *Fi qafilat al-Ikhwan,* 96.

279. "Faransa al-taghiya: Taqtul ikhwanana al-musharikin wa-tadmur al-masajid," *al-Da'wa,* 6 March 1951; Salih 'Ashmawi, "Al-shiyu'aiya tataharak fi Iran wa misr wa bakistan," *al-Da'wa,* 13 March 1951; "Nahnu wa qadiyat marakash," *al-Da'wa,* 27 March 1951.

280. Ibrahim Munir, interview with the author, London, 23 February 2016.

281. "Al-Jaza'ir," *al-Ikhwan al-Muslimun,* 31 May 1945. See also "Al-Jaza'ir tashad . . . thawra kubra," *al-Ikhwan al-Muslimun,* 26 July 1945.

282. Ahmad al-Sukkari, "Daq nafus al-aml," *al-Ikhwan al-Muslimun,* 28 June 1945.

283. Hasan al-Banna, "Al-maghrib al-mujahid muntasir bi-ithn allah," *al-Ikhwn al-Muslimun,* 26 July 1945; and in the same edition, "Al-janah al-aysar l-il-aruba."

284. See, for example, "'Jubhat al-dafa': 'An afriqiya al-shamaliya," *al-Ikhwan al-Muslimun,* 18 April 1945; "al-a'alam," *al-Ikhwan al-Muslimun,* 2 May 1945.

285. Mahomed Ali Jinnah, *Quaid-e-Azam Jinnah's Correspondence* (Karachi, Pakistan: Guild, 1966); Al-Sissi, *Fi qafilat al-Ikhwan,* 177.

286. USNRA, RG59, CDF Box 7150, 883.00/9–1848, Despatch No. 799, Stanton Griffis (Ambassador), Embassy Cairo to State Department, 18 September 1948. See also in same box, "Manifesto in AIAM, 8 August 1948" enclosed in 883.00/8–1348, Despatch No. 703, Patterson, Cairo to State Department, 13 August 1948.

287. "Muslim Brotherhood—Historic Overview," *Cordoba Foundation: MENA Report* 1, no. 11 (November 2013).

288. UKNA FO 371/53251, J 1324/24/16, Enclosure "A," "The Moslem Brothers' Society—Atbara," undated.

289. Minute by Lambert, 27 March 1946, in ibid.

290. "Extract from Letter dated 18th April, 1946 from J. W. R. to R. C. M.," in ibid.

291. UKNA FO 141/1342, 108/7/49G, Jenkins, Cairo to Head of SIME, GHQ MELF, DS(E) 140/1, 9 February 1949.

292. UKNA FO 371/69210, J 110/68/16, Minute by Foreign Office Research Department, 30 December 1947.

293. UKNA FO 141/1342, 108/7/49G, Jenkins, Cairo to Head of SIME, GHQ MELF, DS(E) 140/1, 9 February 1949. See also in the same, Jenkins, Cairo to Chapman-Andrews, 24 February 1949.

294. Amir Cohen, *Political Parties in the West Bank under the Jordanian Regime, 1949–1967* (London: Cornell University Press, 1982), 145; El-Awaisi, *Muslim Brothers,* 150–164; and al-Sharif, *al-Ikhwan al-Muslimun,* 31–33.

295. Al-Sissi, *Fi qafilat al-Ikhwan,* 124.

296. Ibid., 164–171.

297. Itzchak Weismann, "Sa'id Hawwa: The Making of a Radical Muslim Thinker in Modern Syria," *Middle Eastern Studies* 29, no. 4 (1993), 601–623.

298. Al-Sissi, *Hasan al-Banna,* 231–235.

299. UKNA FO 371/61542, E 2130/2130/65, Memorandum from Foreign Office, Research Department, "Youth Movements in the Middle East," 12 February 1947. Al-Siba'i's title of controller general reflected his deference to al-Banna as the overarching leader of the Brotherhood as a whole. For the origins and evolution of the Brotherhood, see Raphaël Lefèvre, *Ashes of Hama: The Muslim Brotherhood in Syria* (London: Hurst, 2013), 3–27. For al-Siba'i specifically, see 'Umar F. 'Abd-Allah, *The Islamic Struggle in Syria* (Berkeley, CA: Mizan Press, 1983), 96–101.

300. Lefèvre, *Ashes of Hama,* 19–40.

301. UKNA FO 371/61542, E 2130/2130/65, Memorandum from Foreign Office, Research Department, "Youth Movements in the Middle East," 12 February 1947.

302. For speculation prior to the elections (which expected the Brothers to do badly), see USNRA, RG59, CDF, Box 7193, 890D.00/6–2847, Despatch James Moose Jr. (Ambassador), Embassy Damascus, to State Department, 28 June 1947, and 890D.00/7–847, Airgram, A-276, Monthly Political Review, Embassy Damascus to State Department, 8 July 1947. For the Brotherhood's performance at the polls, see in same box, 890D.00/7–947, Despatch No. 230, Embassy Damascus to State Department, 9 July 1947; and "Report on Elections," H. L. McGrath (Military Attache), Embassy Damascus, 28 July 1947, sent as enclosure to 890D.00/7–2947, Despatch No. 714, Robert B. Memminger (Chargé d'affaires), Embassy Damascus to State Department, 29 July 1947; 890D.00/7–2947, "Memorandum of Conversation between Memminger and Brigadier I. N. Clayton," 29 July 1947; 890D.00/8–1347, Airgram A-320, Embassy Damascus to State Department, 13 August 1947.

303. USNRA, RG59, CDF, Box 7194, 890D.00/12–1947, "Memorandum: Principal Political Parties of Syria," enclosed with Despatch No. 884, Memminger to State Department, 19 December 1947.

304. USNRA, RG59, CDF, Box 7193, 890D.00/10–2846, Telegram No. 1378, Bertel E. Kuniholk (Chargé d'affaires), Embassy Beirut to State Department, 28 October 1946, and especially, "Enclosure No. 10: The Moslem Brethren (Ikhwan al-Muslimin) in Aleppo."

305. USNRA, RG59, CDF, Box 7193, 890D.00/9–1547, Telegram No. 190, Memminger, Damascus to State Department, 15 September 1947.

306. USNRA, RG59, CDF, Box 7194, 890D.00/12–1947, "Memorandum: Principal Political Parties of Syria," enclosed with Despatch No. 884, Memminger, Damascus to State Department, 19 December 1947.

307. USNRA, RG59, CDF, Box 7194, 890D.00/12–1947, Despatch No. 885, Memminger, Damascus to State Department, 19 December 1947.

308. USNRA, RG59, CDF, Box 7194, 890D.00/12–2247, Despatch No. 889, Legation Damascus to State Department, 22 December 1947.

309. USNRA, RG59, CDF, Box 7194, 890D.00/11–3047, Unnumbered, Memminger, Damascus to State Department, received 30 November 1947. See also despatches from Memminger, Damascus to State Department: 890D.00/11–3047, Despatch No. NIACT 391, 30 November 1947; 890D.00/11–3047, Despatch No. NIACT 392; and 890D.00/12–147, Telegram No. 394, 1 December 1947.

310. USNRA, RG59, CDF, Box 7194, 890D.00/12–447, Telegram, No. 853, Memminger, Damascus to State Department, 4 December 1947; 890D.00/12–847, Memminger, Damascus to State Department, Airgram A-438, 8 December 1947.

311. USNRA, RG59,CDF, Box 7194, 890D.00/8–3048, Airgram A-299, James Hugh Keeley (Ambassador), Embassy Damascus to State Department, 30 August 1948.

312. UKNA KV5/65, SIME/OF.2301/B1, Richardson SIME to Box No. 357, London, 8 December 1948.

313. Ibid. See individual biographies in appendix F, "Personality Notes." On the Brotherhood in Iraq, see also "Al-Ikhwan al-Muslimun fi al-'iraq," al-Ikhwan al-Muslimun, 12 July 1945.

314. UKNA KV5/65, OF.524/18/B3A, SIME, Box No. 500, "Jamiyat al Adab al Islamiya—The Moslem Ethical Society," 25 January 1949.

315. El-Awaisi, Muslim Brothers, 148–149; Shmuel Bar, The Muslim Brotherhood in Jordan (Tel Aviv: Moshe Dayan Center for Middle Eastern and African Studies, 1998), 10.

316. Marion Boulby, The Muslim Brotherhood and the Kings of Jordan, 1945–1993 (Atlanta, GA: Scholars Press, 1999), 37–72; Cohen, Political Parties in the West Bank, 146–154.

317. UKNA FO 371/62231, E 4677, Despatch No. 54, Sir Alec Kirkbride (Ambassador), Embassy Amman to Bevin, FO, 20 May 1947.

318. Minute by D. Greenhill, 2 June 1947, on ibid.

319. Muhammad Abu al-Nasr is one of the few to suggest that an alternative path may have been possible. He claims that the king was so impressed by the Brotherhood's role in Palestine that he asked them to join al-Nuqrashi's ministry—on condition they set aside the name of the Ikhwan. The secretary general of the Arab League apparently put this proposal to al-Banna, but the Brotherhood's leaders decided to refuse the offer. See Abu al-Nasr, Haqiqat al-Khilaf, 49.

320. Al-Sissi, Fi qafilat al-Ikhwan, 187.

321. On the disastrous Egyptian experience, see Fawaz Gerges, "Egypt and the 1948 War: Internal Conflict and Regional Ambition," in The War for Palestine: Rewriting the History of 1948, ed. Eugene Rogan and Avi Shlaim, 2nd ed. (Cambridge: Cambridge University Press, 2007), 150–175.

322. Shadi, Safahat min al-tarikh, 56.

323. Hathut, Al-'aqd al-farid, 9.

324. Ibid., 50–62.

325. Al-Sissi, Fi qafilat al-Ikhwan, 195–197.

326. "Fi al-maydan ma' al-murshid al-a'am," al-Ikhwan al-Muslimun, 15 May 1948.

327. El-Awaisi, Muslim Brothers, 207–210; Ziad Abu-Amr, Islamic Fundamentalism in the West Bank and Gaza: Muslim Brotherhood and Islamic Jihad (Bloomington: Indiana University Press, 1994), 2–3; 'Abd-Allah, Islamic Struggle in Syria, 172–177.

328. Al-Sharif, Al-Ikhwan al-Muslimun, 38ff; Dawh, 25 'aman, 41–43.

329. Hathut, *Al-'aqd al-farid,* 64–66; Dawh, *25 'aman,* 43–45.

330. See, for example, Al-Sissi, *Fi qafilat al-Ikhwan,* 207–221.

331. Al-Qaradawi, *Al-Ikhwan al-Muslimun,* 235.

332. Abu al-Futuh 'Afifi, *Rihalati ma' al-Ikhwan al-Muslimin* (Cairo: Dar al-Tawfiq wa-l-Nashr al-Islami, 2003), 22–29, 35, 38–40.

333. Shadi, *Safahat min al-tarikh,* 61–63.

334. Muhammad 'Abdallah al-Samman, *Ayam ma' al-shahid Hasan al-Bana* (Cairo: Dar al-Fadila, 2003), 19–20, 84.

335. Mayer, "Military Force of Islam."

336. 'Afifi, *Rihalati,* 9.

337. Ibid., 31, 80.

338. USNRA, RG59, CDF, Box 7194, 890D.00/8–2548, Airgram A-295, Keeley, Damascus to State Department, 25 August 1948. See also 890D.00/6–2348, Despatch No. 387, Memminger, Damascus to State Department, 23 June 1948.

339. USNRA, RG59, CDF, Box 7196, 890D.002/11–2348, Airgram A-366, Keeley, Damascus to State Department, 23 November 1948. Similar anti-Abdullah rhetoric emanated from the Brotherhood in Lebanon in this period. See, for instance, CREST Database, CIA Despatch from Lebanon, "Activities of the Ikhwan al-Muslimin (Moslem Brotherhood)," 22 March 1949.

340. Shadi, *Safahat min al-tarikh,* 36; Hathut, *Al-'aqd al-farid,* 64–66.

341. "Al-Sahyuniya fi misr aydun," *al-Ikhwan al-Muslimun,* 30 April 1946.

342. USNRA, RG59, CDF, Box 7150, 883.00/1–1348, Letter No. 34, Tuck, Cairo to State Department, 13 January 1948.

343. USNRA, RG59, CDF, Box 7150, 883.00/3–148, Letter No. 173, Tuck, Cairo to State Department, 1 March 1948.

344. USNRA, CREST Database, CIA, "Arab World Affairs: Weekly Survey," 24 February 1948, 5.

345. Sansom, *I Spied Spies,* 220–222; Osman, *Journey in Islamic Thought,* 67.

346. Al-Sissi, *Fi qafilat al-Ikhwan,* 258–259.

347. Shadi, *Safahat min al-tarikh,* 54–55; Dawh, *25 'aman,* 30–31. Slightly different is the account of Hasan al-'Ashmawi, who suggests Nasser was involved in this and the subsequent attempt to kill Nasser. See Hasan al-'Ashmawi, *Al-ayam al-hasima wa hisaduha* (Cairo: Dar al-Tawqi'a wa-l-Nashr al-Islami), 30.

348. USNRA, RG59, CDF, Box 7150, 883.00/4–2548, Despatch No. 419, Tuck, Cairo to State Department, 25 April 1948; Al-Sissi, *Fi qafilat al-Ikhwan,* 202–203.

349. USNRA, RG59, CDF, Box 7150, 883.00/5–1648, Despatch No. 526, Tuck, Cairo to State Department, 16 May 1948.

350. USNRA, RG59, CDF, Box 7150, 883.00/5–2848, Despatch No. 620, Tuck, Cairo to State Department, 28 May 1948.

351. Salih 'Ashmawi, "Ayuha al-yahud: len ta'ishu ila fi kanf al-'arab," *al-Ikhwan al-Muslimun,* 29 May 1948. See also El-Awaisi, *Muslim Brothers,* 8.

352. "Aim to Oust Jews Pledged by Sheikh," *New York Times,* 2 August 1948.

353. "Ila al-akh al-da'iya," *al-Ikhwan al-Muslimun,* 17 July 1948.

354. USNRA, RG59, CDF, Box 7150, "Manifesto in AIAM, 8 August 1948," enclosed with 883.00/8–1348, Despatch No. 703, Patterson, Cairo to State Department, 13 August 1948.

355. USNRA, RG59, CDF, Box 7150, 883.00/5–1548, Despatch No. 402, Tuck, Cairo to State Department, 15 May 1948.

356. USNRA, RG59, CDF, Box 7150, 883.00/6–2048, Despatch No. 809, Patterson, Cairo to State Department, 20 June 1948; 883.00/7–248, Despatch No. 570, Patterson, Cairo to State Department, 2 July 1948.

357. UKNA FO 371/69210, J 4305/68/16, Telegram No. 893, Chapman-Andrews, Cairo to FO, 20 June 1948. Salah Shadi does not explicitly accept responsibility for the attack, but he appears to justify it as a reaction to events at Deir Yassin in Palestine. See Shadi, *Safahat min al-tarikh*, 55–56.

358. USNRA, RG59, CDF, Box 7150, 883.00/8–21348, Despatch No. 703, Patterson, Cairo to State Department, 13 August 1948.

359. USNRA, RG59, CDF, Box 7150, 883.00/7–1648, Despatch, No. 1003, Patterson, Cairo to State Department, 16 July 1948.

360. USNRA, RG59, CDF, Box 7150, 883.00/7–2048, Despatch No. 1015, Patterson, Cairo to State Department, 20 July 1948.

361. UKNA FO 371/69212, J 7886/58/16, Telegram No. 588, Campbell, Cairo to FO, 3 December 1948.

362. "Egyptian Attacks on Foreigners," *Times,* 17 August 1948.

363. USNRA, RG59, CDF, Box 7150, 883.00/9–2248, Despatch No. 1371, Griffis, Cairo to State Department, 23 September 1948. See also Imam, *'Abd al-Nasir,* 13.

364. Sansom, *I Spied Spies,* 223–224.

365. USNRA, RG59, CDF, Box 7150, 883.00/9–2348, Despatch No. 1379, Griffis, Cairo to State Department, 23 September 1948.

366. UKNA FO 371/69212, J 7886/58/16, Telegram No. 588, Campbell, Cairo to FO, 3 December 1948.

367. UKNA FO 141/1271, V/3/10/48, British Consulate Port Said to Tomlinson, Embassy Cairo, 7 December 1948.

368. For an overview of this wave of violence, see Heyworth-Dunne, *Religious and Political Trends,* 74–76.

369. UKNA FO 371/69211, J 7212/68/16, Telegram No. 1539, Campbell, Cairo to FO, 9 November 1948.

370. UKNA FO 371/69212, J 7886/58/16, Telegram No. 588, Campbell, Cairo to FO, 3 December 1948.

371. UKNA FO 371/90115, JE 10110/15, Telegram No. 167, Stevenson, Cairo to FO, 2 May 1951.

372. See, for instance, Dawh, *25 'aman,* 33.

373. UKNA FO 371/69212, J 7886/58/16, Telegram No. 588, Campbell, Cairo to FO, 3 December 1948.

374. USNRA, RG59, CDF, Box 7150, 883.00/11–1948, Despatch No. 944, Patterson, Cairo to State Department, 19 November 1948, and especially "Memorandum of Conversation between H. E. Abdul Rahman Bey, Under Secretary of State for the Interior and Philip W. Ireland, First Secretary of Embassy: Enclosure No. 1 to Despatch No. 944." For another view on the alleged responsibility of the palace and government for building up the Ikhwan, see 883.00/12–1448, Despatch No. 1011, Patterson, Cairo to State Department, 14 December 1948, and "Enclosure No. 2 to Despatch No. 1011, 14 December: Memorandum of Conversation."

375. UKNA FO 371/69212, J 7886/58/16, Telegram No. 588, Campbell, Cairo to FO, 3 December 1948; USNRA, RG59, CDF, Box 7150, 883.00/11–1748, Despatch, No. 1613, Patterson, Cairo to State Department, 17 November 1948. See also Al-Sissi, *Fi qafilat al-Ikhwan,* 269–275.

376. Al-Sissi, *Fi qafilat al-Ikhwan,* 275–276.

377. "Terrorist Group Arrested in Cairo," *New York Times,* 21 November 1948.

378. UKNA FO 371/69211, J 7749/68/16, Telegram No. 1676, Campbell, Cairo to FO, 4 December 1948; J 7782/68/16, No. 1679, Campbell, Cairo to FO, 5 December 1948; J 7827/68/16, Campbell, Cairo to FO, No. 1686, 7 December 1948; "Students Riot in Cairo," *Times,* 6 December 1948; "Grenade-Throwing in Cairo," *Times,* 7 December 1948; Sansom, *I Spied Spies,* 226–228.

379. USNRA, RG59, CDF, Box 7150, 883.00/12–848, Despatch No. 989, Patterson, Cairo to State Department, 8 December 1948.

380. UKNA FO 371/69211, J 7782/68/16, Telegram No. 1679, Campbell, Cairo to FO, 5 December 1948. See also FO 141/1271, 172/71/48, Embassy Cairo to Jenkins, British Middle East Office (BMEO), 18 December 1948; FO 371/69211, J 7782/68/16, Minute by Michael Wright (Under-Secretary), FO, 10 December 1948; George Clutton, African Department, FO to Donald Maclean (Counselor), Embassy Cairo, 18 December 1948.

381. UKNA FO 141/1271, 172/73/48, "Summary of a Report Submitted by Abdel Rahman Ammar Bey, Under Secretary of State, Ministry of the Interior, to the Prime Minister, Which Led to the Publication of Military Proclamation No. 63 Dissolving the Ikhwan el Muslimin," undated.

382. UKNA FO 371/69212, J 7874/68/16, Telegram No. 1695, Campbell, Cairo to FO, 9 December 1948; USNRA, RG59, CDF, Box 7150, Despatch, No. 1699, Patterson, Cairo to State Department, 9 December 1948. See also "Banning of Muslim Brotherhood," *Times,* 10 December 1948. For the full text of the dissolution order, see "Gouvernement Dissout Les 'Freres Musulmans,'" *Le Journal d'Egypte,* 9 December 1948.

383. UKNA FO 141/1271, 172/61/43, "The Ikhwan al Muslimun," 10 December 1948.

384. USNRA, RG59, CDF, Box 7150, 883.00/12–1348, Airgram A-2316, Lewis Douglas (Ambassador), Embassy London to State Department, 13 December 1948. See also 883.00/12–2748, Despatch No. 1043, Patterson, Cairo to State Department, 27 December 1948.

385. USNRA, RG59, CDF, Box 7150, 883.00/12–1648, Airgram A-1002, Patterson, Cairo to State Department, 16 December 1948; 883.00/12–2248, Despatch No. 1032, Patterson, Cairo to State Department, 22 December 1948; UKNA FO 141/1271, 172/73/48, "List of Arms and Explosives Seized from the 'Ikhwan el Muslimin,' since the 22nd October."

386. UKNA FO 141/1271, 172/73/48, Draft Despatch Embassy Cairo to FO, 29 December 1948.

387. UKNA FO 371/69212, J 8096/68/16, Telegram No. 172/65/48, Maclean, Cairo to Clutton, 13 December 1948. The Egyptian interlocutor here was Ibrahim 'Abd al-Hadi, who was shortly to become prime minister. See also FO 141/1271, 172/75/48.

388. UKNA FO 141/1271, 172/73/48, Draft Despatch Embassy Cairo to FO, 29 December 1948.

389. UKNA FO 371/69212, J 7874/68/16, Minute by D. W. Maitland, 10 December 1948.

390. "The Soviet and Islam," *Times,* 28 January 1949.

391. USNRA, RG59, CDF, Box 7151, 883.00 (W)/12–1048, Joint Week A No. 2, Embassy Cairo to State Department, 10 December 1948.

392. UKNA FO 953/385, PME 803/40/965, Ronald Fay, Ikhwan al-Hurriya, "Monthly Return for December 1948."

393. UKNA FO 141/1271, 172/73/48, Handwritten Analysis of Rose el-Youssef, 15 December 1948.

394. Shadi, *Safahat min al-tarikh,* 66.

395. HIA, Richard Paul Mitchell Collection, Accession No. 77076–8M.50, Box 3, Translation of Hasan al-Banna, "The Obstacles in our Way."

396. UKNA FO 141/1271, V/3/10/48, Minute by Embassy Official, 10 December 1948.

397. UKNA FO 141/1271, 172/68/48, "Al-Ikhwan al-Muslimun," 15 December 1948. For Watanist protest to the Brotherhood's dissolution, see FO 141/1271, 172/74/48.

398. On the assassination and US assessments of al-Nuqrashi, see USNRA, RG59, CDF, Box 7151, 883.00 (W)/12–3148, Joint Week A No. 5, Embassy Cairo to State Department, 31 December 1948; 883.002/12–2848, Telegram No. 5375, Embassy London to State Department, 28 December 1948; 883.002/12–2848, Telegram No. 1767, Patterson, Cairo to State Department, 28 December 1948; D. Schmidt, "Egyptian Premier Is Slain by Cairo Student Terrorist," *New York Times,* 29 December 1948. In October 1949, Ahmad Hasan was sentenced to death for the murder; he was executed in April 1950. Four others were condemned to life sentences with hard labor for their parts in the plot. They were: Muhammad Malik, 'Atef Attiya Hilmi, Shafiq Ibrahim Anas, and Mahmud Kamil al-Sa'id. See USNRA, RG59, CDF, Box 7150, 883.00/10–1548, Despatch No. 910, Embassy Cairo to State Department, 15 October 1949.

399. Al-Sissi, *Fi qafilat al-Ikhwan,* 287.

400. USNRA, RG59, CDF, Box 7150, 883.00/1–2249, "Enclosure No. 1 to Despatch No. 78: A Manifesto by Sheikh Hassan al Banna Published 11 January 1949," with Despatch No. 78, Patterson, Cairo to State Department, 22 January 1949.

401. USNRA, RG59, CDF, Box 7150, 883.00/1–349, Despatch No. 3, Embassy Cairo to State Department, 3 January 1949; Box 7151, 883.00 (W)/1–749, Joint Week A No. 6, Embassy Cairo to State Department, 7 January 1949.

402. UKNA FO 371/69212, J 8308/68/16G, FO to Ambassador Cairo, 29 December 1948. See also FO 371/73463, J 533/1015/16, Telegram No. 35, Chapman-Andrews, Cairo to FO, 18 January 1949.

403. UKNA FO 371/73463, J 464/1015/16G. The words are those of a British national who wrote to the embassy giving his views. See Letter from H. J., Turf Club, to Cairo Embassy, 5 January 1949. The embassy said that such analysis, though going slightly further than their own assessment, tallied "pretty closely with our own." See, in the same, Letter, Maclean, Cairo, to Clutton, FO, 13 January 1949.

404. "Rudderless Egypt," *Economist,* 1 January 1949.

405. "Changing Views in Egypt," *Times,* 25 January 1949.

406. James Heyworth-Dunne, "The Insidious Ikhwan Strikes Again," *Washington Post,* 2 January 1949.

407. UKNA FO 141/1342 (Arab Societies: Ikhwan el Muslimeen), 108/2/49G, Jenkins, Cairo to Head of SIME, GHQ MELF, DS (E) DS/P/62, 6 January 1949.

408. UKNA FO 141/1342, Letter Cairo Embassy to FO, 108/2/49G, 15 January 1949. See also FO 141/1342 (Arab Societies: Ikhwan el Muslimeen), 108/2/49G, Jenkins, Cairo to Head of SIME, GHQ MELF, DS (E) DS/P/62, 6 January 1949.

409. UKNA FO 141/1271, 172/68/48, "Al-Ikhwan al-Muslimun," 15 December 1948. For Watanist protest to the Brotherhood's dissolution, see in the same file, 172/74/48.

410. USNRA, RG59, CDF, Box 7150, 883.00/1–1749, Airgram A-60, Patterson, Cairo to State Department, 17 January 1949.

411. UKNA FO 371/73463, J 1063/1015/16, Memorandum from G. J. C. C. Jenkins, Cairo to Tomlinson, Cairo, No. DS (E) 140/2, 17 January 1949. In 1949, Young Egypt reemerged under the name of the "Socialist Party of Egypt"; see James P. Jankowski, *Egypt's Young Rebels: "Young Egypt," 1933–1952* (Stanford, CA: Hoover Institution Press, 1975), 92–106.

412. USNRA, RG59, CDF, Box 7150, 883.00/1–1349, Despatch No. 49, Patterson, Cairo to State Department, 13 January 1949; UKNA FO 371/73463, J 382/1015/16, Telegram No. 74, Campbell, Cairo to FO, 14 January 1949; "2 Killed in Cairo by Fanatic's Bomb," *New York Times,* 14 January 1949. Anas was sentenced to life imprisonment for the crime in March 1949; see USNRA, RG59, CDF, Box 7150, 883.00/3–1149, Airgram A-311, Patterson, Cairo to State Department, 11 March 1949.

413. Shadi, *Safahat min al-tarikh,* 94–96.

414. USNRA, RG59, CDF, Box 7151, 883.00 (W)/1–1449, Joint Week A No. 7, Embassy Cairo to State Department, 14 January 1949; Box 7150, 883.00/1–1749, Airgram A-60, Patterson, Cairo to State Department, 17 January 1949.

415. UKNA FO 141/1342 (Arab Societies: Ikhwan el Muslimeen), 108/2/49G, Jenkins, Cairo to Head of SIME, GHQ MELF, DS (E) DS/P/62, 6 January 1949.

416. UKNA FO 141/1342, 108/3/49G, Jenkins, Cairo to Head of SIME, GHQ MELF, DS (E) DS/P/62, 20 January 1949.

417. UKNA FO 141/1342, 108/4/49G, Jenkins, Cairo to Head of SIME, GHQ MELF, DS (E) DS/P/62, 28 January 1949; Telegram No. 35 Campbell, Cairo to Khartoum, 28 January 1949.

418. UKNA FO 141/1342, 108/4/49G, Jenkins, Cairo to Head of SIME, GHQ MELF, DS (E) DS/P/62, 28 January 1949; Minutes from 11 February 1949 on 108/7/49G. See also in the same file, 108/4/49G, Letter, CS/JWR, the Secretariat Khartoum to Chapman-Andrews, Cairo, 29 January 1949, which concluded that "Our information at this end is that the local Moslem Brothers are particularly inactive at the moment, but we are of course watching them closely."

419. UKNA FO 141/1342, Minute on 108/4/49G, Jenkins, Cairo to Head of SIME, GHQ MELF, DS (E) DS/P/62, 28 January 1949.

420. USNRA, RG59, CDF, Box 7150, 883.00/1–2549, Airgram A-89, Embassy Cairo to State Department, 25 January 1949.

421. USNRA, RG59, CDF, Box 7150, 883.00/1–2849, "Enclosure No. 1 to Despatch No. 96: Phalange of the Holy Struggle for the Liberation of Islam," in Despatch No. 96, Patterson, Cairo to State Department, 28 January 1949.

422. USNRA, RG59, CDF, Box 7151, 883.00 (W)/1–3049, Joint Week A No. 9, Embassy Cairo to State Department, 30 January 1949.

423. UKNA FO 371/73463, J 1122/1015/16, Telegram No. 244, Campbell, Cairo to FO, 13 February 1949; Telegram No. 164, Patterson, Cairo to State Department, 13 February 1949. See also "Muslim Brotherhood Leader Killed," *Times,* 14 February 1949.

424. UKNA FO 371/73463, J 1633/1015/16, Telegram No. 114 (108/8/49G) Campbell, Cairo to Bevin, FO, 23 February 1949.

425. UKNA FO 141/1370, 517/16/49g, "The Story of the Assassination of Sheikh Banna," undated. On Makram's attendance, see also Hathut, *Al-'aqd al-farid,* 27.

426. UKNA FO 371/73463, J 1633/1015/16, Minute by G. H. Stein, 7 March 1949, on Telegram No. 114 (108/8/49G) Campbell, Cairo to Bevin, FO, 23 February 1949.

427. UKNA FO 141/1370, 517/4/49a, Jenkins, Cairo to Head of SIME, 5 March 1949.

428. UKNA FO 141/1340, 517/4/49a, Draft Despatch No. 170, Embassy Cairo to FO, 21 March 1949.

429. UKNA FO 141/1370, 517/4/49a, Jenkins, Cairo to Head of SIME, 16 April 1949.

430. USNRA, RG59, CDF, Box 7150, 883.00/2–2849, Airgram A-252, Patterson, Cairo to State Department, 28 February 1949; 883.00/3–749, Aigram, A-286, Patterson, Cairo to State Department, 7 March 1949; 883.00/3–3049, Despatch No. 16, Ellis Johnson (American Consul) American Consulate, Port Said to State Department, 30 March 1949; 883.00/4–449, Despatch No. 334, Patterson, Cairo to State Department, 4 April 1949; 883.00/4–749, Despatch No. 351, Patterson, Cairo to State Department, 7 April 1949; 883.00/4–1149, Airgram A-420, Patterson, Cairo to State Department, 11 April 1949; 883.00/4–3049, Airgram A-507, Patterson, Cairo to State Department, 30 April 1949. See also: Box 7151, 883.00 (W)/4–849, Joint Week A 19, Embassy Cairo to Washington, DC, 8 April 1949; UKNA FO 141/1370, 517/7/49a, W. B. Emery SSR, to Head of SIME, DS (E) DS/P/62, 6 May 1949.

431. USNRA, RG59, CDF, Box 7150, 883.00/5–1149, Despatch No. 464, Embassy Cairo to State Department, 11 May 1949. Both Shadi and Baquri acknowledge Brotherhood responsibility for the attack. See Shadi, *Safahat min al-tarikh,* 72–73; Al-Baquri, *Baqaya,* 86–87.

432. Dawh, *25 'aman,* 45, 49.

433. USNRA, RG59, CDF, Box 7150, 883.00/5–2749, Airgram, State Department to Embassy Cairo, 27 May 1949.

434. UKNA FO 371/69212, J 8308/68/16G, Letter, FO to Embassy Cairo, 29 December 1948.

435. UKNA FO 141/1370, 517/8/49a, W. B. Emery SSR, to Head of SIME, DS (E) DS/P/62, 23 May 1949, including "Appendix 'A.'"

436. UKNA FO 371/73463, J 600/1015/16G, Memorandum by Chapman-Andrews, 19 January 1949.

437. USNRA, RG59, CDF, Box 7150, 883.00/5–1649, Airgram A-568, Embassy Cairo to State Department, 16 May 1949.

438. UKNA FO 141/1370, 517/9/49a, W. B. Emery SSR, to Head of SIME, DS (E) DS/P/62, 7 June 1949. A draft letter from Morris at the embassy to Emery, dated 26 July 1949, and in the same file, refers to "almost daily" reports of "fresh arrests," reflecting the fact that the repression continued.

439. Mitchell, *Society of the Muslim Brothers,* 72; Imam, *'Abd al-Nasir,* 15–24.

440. USNRA, RG59, CDF, Box 7150, 883.00/6–1349, Despatch No. 586, Patterson, Cairo to State Department, 13 June 1949, and "Enclosure No. 1 to Despatch No. 586: Memorandum of Conversation."

441. USNRA, RG59, CDF, Box 7150, 883.00/10–2949, Despatch No. 960, Embassy Cairo to State Department, 29 October 1949.

442. UKNA FO 371/69211, J 5843/68/G 16, Chapman-Andrews, Cairo to Wright, FO, 12 August 1948.

443. Heyworth-Dunne, *Religious and Political Trends,* 68–69.

444. USNRA, RG59, Bureau of Near Eastern, South Asian and African Affairs: Office of NEA: Subject Files, 1920–1954, Box 7, "Political Life in Egypt" (unpublished and anonymous thesis; undated but within files for 1945–1949 period).

445. John Roy Carlson, *Cairo to Damascus* (New York: Alfred A. Knopf, 1951), 52.

446. Ibid., 74. For more of the same, see 102–103, 146–147.

447. Melani McAlister, *Epic Encounters: Culture, Media and U.S. Interests in the Middle East, 1945–2000,* 2nd ed. (Berkeley: University of California Press, 2005), 13–29.

448. Carlson, *Cairo to Damascus,* 82–92; USNRA, RG59, CDF, Box 7150, 883.00/3–2949, Despatch No. 259, Tuck, Cairo to State Department, 29 March 1948.

449. Al-Sissi, *Hasan al-Banna,* 212.

450. Ziad Munson, "Islamic Mobilization: Social Movement Theory and the Egyptian Muslim Brotherhood," *Sociological Quarterly* 42, no. 4 (Autumn 2001), 487–510 (494–496).

451. Al-Qaradawi, *Al-Ikhwan al-Muslimun,* 241.

452. Al-Sissi, *Fi qafilat al-Ikhwan,* 230–254. See also al-Samman, *Ayam,* 20–21.

453. 'Afifi, *Rihalati,* 48.

454. El-Helbawy, "The Muslim Brotherhood in Egypt," 71–73. See also Osman, *Journey in Islamic Thought,* 86.

455. Al-Sissi, *Fi qafilat al-Ikhwan,* 284–285. See also 'Abd al-Halim, *Al-Ikhwan al-Muslimun I,* 35–43; and Shadi, *Safahat min al-tarikh,* 64; Hathut, *Al-'aqd al-farid,* 71–72.

456. Al-Sharif, *Al-Ikhwan al-Muslimun,* 37–38.

457. Al-Qaradawi, *Al-Ikhwan al-Muslimun,* 242–243.

458. Shadi, *Safahat min al-tarikh,* 61.

459. Al-Sissi, *Hasan al-Banna,* 225–226.

460. I have been unable to confirm the identity of the person, nor locate the article in question. The spelling given here is an approximation based on the Arabic original.

461. Al-Sharif, *Al-Ikhwan al-Muslimun,* 31–33.

462. Youssef Nada, with Douglas Thompson, *Inside the Muslim Brotherhood: The Truth about the World's Most Powerful Political Movement* (London: Metro, 2012), 15.

463. Al-Qaradawi, *Al-Ikhwan al-Muslimun,* 195, 255.

464. For various combinations of this, see Shadi, *Safahat min al-tarikh,* 94–96; Osman, *Journey in Islamic Thought,* 68–76; Al-Baquri, *Baqaya,* 73–76; Dawh, *25 'aman,* 34–35; Abu al-Nasr, *Haqiqat al-Khilaf,* 87–89.

465. For an alternative view, which holds that al-Banna was directly in control of the Special Apparatus, see Imam, *'Abd al-Nasir,* 10.

4. The War of the Canal Zone, 1950–1952

1. For an account of this episode, see "Ma'arakat al-tal al-kabir," Ikhwanwiki, http://bit .ly/2tPvzUG.

2. Abu al-Futuh 'Afifi, *Rihalati ma' al-Ikhwan al-Muslimin* (Cairo: Dar al-Tawfiq wa-l-Nashr al-Islami, 2003), 52–53.

3. Hasan Dawh, *25 'aman fi jama'at al-ikhwan* (Cairo: Dar al-'Itisam, 1983), 51.

4. Abbas Hasan al-Sissi, *Fi qafilat al-Ikhwan al-Muslimun II: al-juz' al-thani* (Alexandria, Egypt: Dar al-Taba'a wa-l-Nashr wa-l-Sutiyat, 1987), 44.

5. For the best single-volume account of this conflict and its origins, see Michael T. Thornhill, *Road to Suez: The Battle of the Canal Zone* (Stroud, UK: Sutton, 2006).

6. "Record of Informal United States-United Kingdom Discussions," London, 18 September 1950, *FRUS 1950*, vol. V.

7. "Agreed United States-United Kingdom Memorandum of Discussions on the Present World Situation: US / UK Discussions on Present World Situation," Washington, 25 July 1950, *FRUS 1950*, vol. V.

8. See "Review of Middle East Strategy: COS Committee Memorandum," 15 September 1950, *BDDE*, vol. 2, 77–87. See also Ritchie Ovendale, *Britain, the United States and the Transfer of Power in the Middle East, 1945–1962* (London: Leicester University Press, 1996), 31–32.

9. Geoffery Aronson, *From Sideshow to Centre Stage: US Policy toward Egypt, 1946–1956* (Boulder, CO: L. Rienner, 1986), 17–22.

10. USNRA, RG59, Bureau of NE, SA and A Affairs: Office of NEA (Near Eastern Affairs): Subject Files, 1920–1954, Box 6, "Summary of Developments Regarding Egypt and the Anglo-Egyptian Sudan, November 13–20 1950."

11. See, for example, UKNA FO (Foreign Office) 371/69211, J 5843/68/G 16, Letter, Sir Edwin Chapman-Andrews (Minister), Embassy Cairo to Michael Wright (Under-Secretary), FO, 12 August 1948.

12. Kermit Roosevelt, *Arabs, Oil and History* (New York: Harper, 1949), 94–95.

13. USNRA, RG59, CDF, Box 7151, 883.001 Farouk/10–2849, Memorandum No. 952, Jefferson Caffery (Ambassador), Embassy Cairo to State Department, 28 October 1949.

14. Zaheer Quraishi, *Liberal Nationalism in Egypt: Rise and Fall of the Wafd Party* (Allahabad, India: Kitab Mahal, 1967), 158–167.

15. UKNA FO 371/80347, JE 1016/17/G, Minute by Hector McNeil (Minister of State), FO, 25 January 1950.

16. USNRA, RG59, CDF, Box 7150, 883.00/10–1349, Despatch No. 900, Caffery, Cairo to State Department, 13 October 1949, and "Enclosure No. 1."

17. UKNA FO 371/80343, JE 1013/3, Telegram No. 1 (S), Sir Ronald Campbell (Ambassador), Embassy Cairo to FO, 2 January 1950.

18. USNRA, RG59, CDF, Box 7151, 883.00 (W)/8–2649, Military Attache, Embassy Cairo to Washington, DC, Joint Week A 39, 26 August 1949.

19. Kemal el-Helbawy, "The Muslim Brotherhood in Egypt: Historical Evolution and Future Prospects," in Khaled Hroub, *Political Islam: Context versus Ideology* (London: Saqi Books, 2010), 75.

20. USNRA, RG59, CDF, Box 7150, 883.00/8–2649, Despatch No. 795, Embassy Cairo to State Department, 26 August 1949, and "Enclosure No. 1 to Despatch No. 795: Memorandum of Conversation."

21. UKNA FO 141/1370, 517/16/49g, "Memorandum," 8 November 1949.

22. UKNA FO 141/1370, 517/16/49g, Minute by Chapman-Andrews, Cairo, 10 November 1949; Campbell agreed that the British should work to prevent the rehabilitation of the Ikhwan. See, on the same, the handwritten minute of RC, 21 November 1949.

23. UKNA FO 141/1370, 517/16/49g, Minute by Chapman-Andrews, Cairo, 10 November 1949.

24. Roosevelt, *Arabs,* 94–96.

25. USNRA, RG59, CDF, Box 7151, 883.00 (W)/11–2549, Military Attaché, Cairo to Washington, DC, Joint Week A 52, 25 November 1949. See also 883.00 (W)/12–249, Military Attaché, Cairo to Washington, DC, Joint Week A 53, 2 December 1949.

26. UKNA FO 141/1370, 517/19/49g, "Notes on Meeting Held on 16th December 1949." For analysis of the forthcoming elections, see FO 371/80347, JE 1016/1, Telegram No. 643, Campbell, Cairo to McNeil, FO, 28 December 1949.

27. USNRA, RG59, CDF, Box 4017, 774.00 (W)/1–2050, Joint Weekly A No. 3, Military Attaché, Cairo to Washington, DC, 20 January 1950.

28. USNRA, RG59, CDF, Box 4017, 774.00 (W)/2–1050, Joint Weekly A No. 6, Military Attaché, Cairo to Washington, DC, 10 February 1950.

29. UKNA FO 371/80343, JE 1013/14, Telegram No. 62 (S), Campbell, Cairo to FO, 4 March 1950.

30. USNRA, RG59, CDF, Box 4017, 774.00 (W)/3–3150, Joint Weekly A No. 13, Military Attaché, Cairo to Washington, DC, 31 March 1950.

31. UKNA FO 371/90115, JE 10110/17, Telegram No. 186, Sir Ralph Stevenson (Ambassador), Embassy Cairo to FO, 18 May 1951.

32. For analysis of Wafdist policy in this period, see Janice J. Terry, *The Wafd, 1919–1952: Cornerstone of Egyptian Political Power* (London: Third World Centre for Research and Publishing, 1982), 299–304; Quraishi, *Liberal Nationalism in Egypt,* 168–196.

33. "Memorandum by G. L. Clutton," 23 March 1950, *BDDE,* vol. 2, 11–17.

34. "Memorandum of Informal United States-United Kingdom Discussion," London, 19 September 1950, *FRUS* 1950, vol. V.

35. USNRA, RG59, CDF, Box 4014, 774.00/5–950, Despatch No. 1037, George C. Howard (Chargé d'affaires), Embassy Cairo to State Department, 9 May 1950. See also 774.00/8–2450, Despatch No. 467, Caffery, Cairo to State Department, 24 August 1950.

36. USNRA, RG59, CDF, Box 4017, RG59, 774.00 (W)/10–750, Joint Weekly A No. 40, Military Attaché, Cairo to Washington, DC, 7 October 1950.

37. USNRA, RG59, CDF, Box 4014, 774.00/10–2750, Despatch No. 1000, Caffery, Cairo to State Department, 27 October 1950.

38. USNRA, RG59, CDF, Box 4017, RG59, 774.00 (W)/10–750, Joint Weekly A No. 40, Military Attaché, Cairo to Washington, DC, 7 October 1950. For more on Brotherhood activity, see 774.00 (W)/10–2750, Joint Weekly A No. 43, Military Attaché, Cairo to Washington, DC, 27 October 1950.

39. USNRA, RG59, CDF, Box 4014, 774.00/11–650, Despatch No. 1066, Caffery, Cairo to State Department, 6 November 1950.

40. UKNA FO 371/90115, JE 10110/6, Telegram No. 53, Stevenson, Cairo to FO, 2 February 1951.

41. USNRA, RG59, CDF, Box 4014, 774.00/11–650, Despatch No. 1066, from Caffery, Embassy Cairo to State Department, 6 November 1950. See also on the negotiations between Sirag al-Din and al-Baquri, Box 4017, 774.00 (w)/2–1050, Joint Weekly A No. 6, Military Attaché, Cairo to Washington, DC, 10 February 1950.

42. USNRA, RG59, CDF, Box 4014, 774.00/12–750, Despatch No. 1330, Caffery, Cairo to State Department, 7 December 1950, and "Enclosure No. 1: Constitution of the Moslem Brotherhood Organization."

43. USNRA, RG59, CDF, Box 4017, 774.00 (W)/4–2850, Joint Weekly A No. 17, Military Attaché, Cairo to Washington, DC, 28 April 1950. For British views on the leadership, see UKNA FO 371/80343, JE 1013/18, Telegram No. 82 (S), Campbell, Cairo to FO, 3 April 1950.

44. USNRA, RG59, CDF, Box 4017, 774.00 (W)/4–2850, Joint Weekly A No. 17, Military Attaché, Cairo to Washington, DC, 28 April 1950. For corroborative British analysis of this, see UKNA FO 371/90115, JE 10110/6, Telegram No. 53, Stevenson, Cairo to FO, 2 February 1951. Stevenson reported that Mu'min had reached a deal with Fu'ad Sirag al-Din in July 1950 for the revival of the Brotherhood under the banner of the "Islamic Union," or the "Islamic Movement," but was expelled in September. He and his followers had then created a rival faction under the banner of the "Islamic Renaissance Association." See also Ghada Osman, *A Journey in Islamic Thought: The Life of Fathi Osman* (New York: I. B. Tauris, 2011), 90–91, which blames Salih 'Ashmawi for Mu'min's dismissal.

45. USNRA, RG59, CDF, Box 4014, 774.00/11–650, Despatch No. 1066, Caffery, Cairo to State Department, 6 November 1950.

46. Salah Shadi, *Safahat min al-tarikh: Hisad al-'amr* (Kuwait: Sharikat al-Shu'a, 1981), 79–83. For al-Baquri's own account of this, in which he too asserts that al-Banna wanted him to take his place temporarily, see al-Baquri, *Baqaya*, 82. And for another, more critical account of this process, see Hasan al-'Ashmawi, *Al-ayam al-hasima wa hisaduha* (Cairo: Dar al-Tawqi'a wa-l-Nashr al-Islami, n.d.), 146–147.

47. On this process, see UKNA FO 141/1450 "The Ikhwan el Muslimin" [II], D. L. Stewart, 4 December 1951, in Foreign Office Intelligence Reports, "The Ikhwan el Muslimin," 11 December 1951.

48. Osman, *Journey in Islamic Thought*, 93–103. On this issue, see also Abdullah Imam, *'Abd al-Nasir wa-l-Ikhwan al-Muslimun* (Cairo: Dar al-Khayyal, 1997), 29–30.

49. USNRA, RG59, CDF, Box 4014, 774.00/11–650, Despatch No. 1066, Caffery, Cairo to State Department, 6 November 1950.

50. USNRA, RG59, CDF, Box 4017, 774.00 (W)/11–650, Joint Weekly A No. 42, Military Attaché Cairo to Washington, DC, 19 October 1951. For US analysis of ten potential candidates for the leadership, see Box 4014, 774.00/9–751, Despatch No. 610, Caffery, Cairo to State Department, 7 September 1951.

51. UKNA FO 371/90115, JE 10110/6, Telegram No. 53, Stevenson, Cairo to FO, 2 February 1951.

52. USNRA, RG59, CDF, Box 4014, 774.00/11–650, Despatch No. 1069, Caffery, Cairo to State Department, 6 November 1950.

53. USNRA, RG59, CDF, Box 4014, 774.00/12–1450, Despatch No. 1396, Caffery, Cairo to State Department, 14 December 1950.

54. "Regional Policy Statement: Near East—Prepared in the Office of Near Eastern Affairs," Washington, DC, 28 December 1950, *FRUS* 1950, vol. V.

55. USNRA, RG59, CDF, Box 4014, 774.00/3–1451, Despatch No. 2173, Caffery, Cairo to State Department, 14 March 1951.

56. UKNA FO 371/90115, JE 10110/6, Telegram No. 53, Stevenson, Cairo to FO, 2 February 1951.

57. See "Descent into Conflict" in Chapter 3.

58. UKNA FO 371/90115, JE 10110/6, Telegram No. 53, Stevenson, Cairo to FO, 2 February 1951.

59. USNRA, RG59, CDF, Box 4014, 774.00/12–2050, Despatch No. 1463, Caffery, Cairo to State Department, 20 December 1950.

60. UKNA FO 371/90115, JE 10110/15, Telegram No. 167, Stevenson, Cairo to FO, 2 May 1951. See also "Al-safir al-ingliz ya'mur . . . wa-l-Nuqrashi yuti'a . . . wa-l-ikhwan tuhal!," al-Da'wa, 30 January 1951.

61. UKNA FO 371/90115, JE 10110/15, Telegram No. 167, Stevenson, Cairo to FO, 2 May 1951.

62. USNRA, RG59, CDF, Box 4014, 774.00/2–2151, Despatch No. 2006, Caffery, Cairo to State Department, 21 February 1951; 774.00/2–2751, Despatch No. 2038, Caffery, Cairo to State Department, 27 February 1951. See also "Cairo Gang Forge British Documents," Glasgow Herald, 16 February 1951.

63. USNRA, RG59, CDF, Box 4014, 774.00/3–1951, Despatch No. 2201, Caffery, Cairo to State Department, 21 February and 19 March 1951.

64. UKNA FO 371/90115, JE 10110/15, Telegram No. 167, Stevenson, Cairo to FO, 2 May 1951.

65. Osman, Journey in Islamic Thought, 89–90.

66. Salih 'Ashmawi, "Bara'!," al-Da'wa, 17 April 1951.

67. Shadi, Safahat min al-tarikh, 58–61.

68. Ibid.

69. USNRA, RG59, CDF, Box 4014, 774.00/3–1951, Despatch No. 2201, Caffery, Cairo to State Department, 19 March 1951. On the trial and its significance, see also Richard P. Mitchell, The Society of the Muslim Brothers (Oxford: Oxford University Press, 1993), 75–78.

70. UKNA FO 371/90115, JE 10110/15, Telegram No. 167, Stevenson, Cairo to FO, 2 May 1951.

71. UKNA FO 371/90115, JE 10110/6, Telegram No. 53, Stevenson, Cairo to FO, 2 February 1951.

72. UKNA FO 371/96879, JE 1018/294, John Wilton, Alexandria to FO, 24 July 1952.

73. Joel Gordon, "The False Hopes of 1950: The Wafd's Last Hurrah and the Demise of Egypt's Old Order," International Journal of Middle East Studies 21, no. 2 (1989), 193–214 (208–209).

74. For the idea that there was no alternative to the Wafd, see UKNA FO 371/90115, JE 10110/2, Telegram No. 7, Stevenson, Cairo to FO, 5 January 1951. See also in the same file, JE 10110/11, Letter, 1011/13/51G, John Wardle-Smith (Counselor), Embassy Cairo to Sir Roger Allen (Head of Africa Department), FO, 2 April 1951. For US views, see USNRA, RG59, CDF, Box 4014, 774.00/4–2851, Despatch No. 2566, Caffery, Cairo to State Department, 28 April 1951.

75. UKNA FO 371/90130, JE 1051/40, Telegram No. 231, Chapman-Andrews, Cairo to FO, 29 March 1951.

76. Salih 'Ashmawi, "Saf'a qatila l-hakumat al-irhab wa-l-bulis al-siyasi," al-Da'wa, 20 March 1951.

77. "Na'm . . . hiya harb salibiya thinaha al-isti'amar ala al-muslimin!," al-Da'wa, 27 March 1951.

78. See the Conclusion of this volume.

79. "Na'm . . . hiya harb dalibiya thinaha al-isti'amar ala al-muslimin!," *al-Da'wa*, 27 March 1951.

80. "Al-Ikhwan al-Muslimun wa-l-jubha al-qawmiya," *al-Da'wa*, 27 February 1951.

81. David R. Devereux, *The Formulation of British Defence Policy towards the Middle East, 1948–56* (Basingstoke, UK: Macmillan, 1990), 51.

82. On the interplay between events in Iran and Egypt, see H. W. Brands, "The Cairo-Tehran Connection in Anglo-American Rivalry in the Middle East, 1951–1953," *International History Review* 11, no. 3 (1989), 434–456.

83. "Na'm . . . hiya harb salibiya thinaha al-isti'amar ala al-muslimin!," *al-Da'wa*, 27 March 1951.

84. Salih 'Ashmawi, "Hawla al-qadiya al-qataniya," *al-Da'wa*, 3 April 1951; " 'Al-Asad al-britani' fi misr yusbih 'na'ama' fi Iran," *al-Da'wa*, 24 April 1951; Salih 'Ashmawi, "Al-watha'iq alati yuqadimuha al-ikhwan sahiha mi'a fi al-mi'a 9. 8," *al-Da'wa*, 12 June 1951.

85. Kamil al-Sharif, *Al-Ikhwan al-Muslimun wa-l-Harb fi Filistin*, 3rd ed. (Amman, Jordon: Maktabat al-Manar, 1984), 11–12.

86. Salih 'Ashmawi, "Al-Ikhwan al-Muslimun wa-l-ingliz," *al-Da'wa*, 29 May 1951; Salih 'Ashmawi, "Mu'amara ingliziyya tamhad li-l-i'atiraf al-duwal al-'arabiyya bi-isra'il," *al-Da'wa*, 5 June 1951.

87. Sa'id Ramadan, "Fi bayt al-Maqdis," *al-Muslimun* 2, no. 6 (April 1953); "Fi afaq al-a'alam al-islami," *al-Muslimun* 3, no. 2 (December 1953).

88. "Ma' al-haraka al-islamiya," *al-Muslimun* 3, no. 4 (February 1954).

89. USNRA, CREST Database, Office of Current Intelligence, "Daily Digest of Significant Traffic, Copy No. 39," 23 March 1951.

90. USNRA, RG59, CDF, Box 4014, 774.00/4–1151, Despatch No. 2439, Caffery, Cairo to State Department, 11 April 1951. See also 774.00/4–1951, Despatch No. 2504, Gordon Mattison (Chargé d'affaires), Embassy Cairo to State Department, 19 April 1951.

91. UKNA, FO 371/90115, JE 10110/6, Telegram No. 53, Stevenson, Cairo to FO, 2 February 1951.

92. Osman, *Journey in Islamic Thought*, 82–88; see also Mitchell, *Society of the Muslim Brothers*, 186–187.

93. "Al-Ikhwan al-Muslimun," *al-Da'wa*, 27 February 1951; "Hal t'alan al-hakuma al-harb 'ala al-ikhwan al-muslimin?," *al-Da'wa*, 10 April 1951.

94. Salih 'Ashmawi, "Li-hisab men taharibun al-ikhwan al-muslimin?," *al-Da'wa*, 30 January 1951.

95. "Ijtima'a maktab al-irshad al-a'am li-l-ikhwan al-muslimin," *al-Da'wa*, 1 May 1951.

96. USNRA, RG59, CDF, Box 4014, 774.00/5–451, Despatch No. 2606, Caffery, Cairo to State Department, 4 May 1951; Box 4017, 774.00 (W)/5–451, Joint Weekly A No. 18, Military Attaché, Cairo to Washington, DC, 4 May 1951.

97. UKNA FO 371/90115, JE 10110/17, Telegram No. 186, Stevenson, Cairo to FO, 18 May 1951.

98. USNRA, RG59, CDF, Box 4014, 774.00/4–1151, Despatch No. 2439, Caffery, Cairo to State Department, 11 April 1951.

99. UKNA FO 371/90115, JE 10110/17, Telegram No. 186, Stevenson, Cairo to FO, 18 May 1951.

100. Ibid. See also "Wa' awfu bi-l-'ahd . . . inna al-'ahd kana masa'ulan," *al-Da'wa,* 1 May 1951.

101. USNRA, RG59, CDF, Box 4017, 774.00 (W)/5–1851, Joint Weekly A No. 20, Military Attaché, Cairo to Washington, DC, 18 May 1951.

102. UKNA FO 371/90115, JE 10110/18, Letter 1011/16/51G, Wardle-Smith, Cairo to Allen, FO, 17 May 1951.

103. USNRA, RG59, CDF, Box 4017, 774.00 (W)/5–1851, Joint Weekly A No. 20 Military Attaché, Cairo to Washington, DC, 18 May 1951.

104. USNRA, RG59, Box 4017, 774.00 (W)/5–1151, Joint Weekly A No. 19, Military Attaché, Cairo to Washington, DC, 11 May 1951.

105. Ibid.

106. UKNA FO 371/90115, Telegram No. 186, JE 10110/17, Stevenson, Cairo to FO, 18 May 1951.

107. USNRA, RG59, CDF, Box 4014, 774.00/5–451, Despatch No. 2606, Caffery, Cairo to State Department, 4 May 1951.

108. "The World Overseas: Egypt's Uncertain Future," *Economist,* 19 May 1951.

109. USNRA, RG59, CDF, Box 4014, 774.00/5–2251, Airgram A-515 from Dean Acheson (Secretary of State), State Department to Embassy Cairo, 22 May 1951.

110. USNRA, RG59, CDF, Box 4017, 774.00 (W)/7–651, Joint Weekly A No. 27, Military Attaché, Cairo to Washington, DC, 6 July 1951.

111. USNRA, RG59, CDF, Box 4017, 774.00 (W)/7–1451, Joint Weekly A No. 28, Military Attaché, Cairo to Washington, DC, 14 July 1951; "State of Emergency in Cairo," *Times,* 12 July 1951.

112. "Must'amar wahid wa athnab mut'adida," *al-Da'wa,* 17 July 1951.

113. USNRA, RG59, CDF, Box 4014, 774.00/7–1751, Despatch No. 94, Caffery, Cairo to State Department, 17 July 1951.

114. USNRA, RG59, CDF, Box 4014, 774.00/7–2351, Airgram A-145, Caffery, Cairo to State Department, 23 July 1951.

115. UKNA FO 141/1433, 1011/25/51G, Letter, Campbell to Stevenson, 1 September 1951.

116. See, for example, the report on the revived Young Men's Muslim Association (YMMA), USNRA, RG59, CDF, Box 4014, 774.00/9–751, Despatch No. 600, Caffery, Cairo to State Department, 7 September 1951.

117. USNRA, RG59, CDF, Box 4014, 774.00/8–1551, Despatch No. 378, Caffery, Cairo to State Department, 15 August 1951.

118. "Ijma'a al-umma 'ala qata' al-mufawidat . . . wa ilga' ma'ahadat 36," *al-Da'wa,* 8 May 1951; USNRA, RG59, CDF, Box 4014, 774.00/8–3051, Despatch No. 526, Caffery, Cairo to State Department, 30 August 1951.

119. Salih 'Ashmawi, "Al-watha'iq alati yuqadimuha al-ikhwan dahiha mi'a fi al-mi'a 9. 8," *al-Da'wa,* 12 June 1951.

120. Salih 'Ashmawi, "Kafa mutaliba wa taswifan!," *al-Da'wa,* 21 August 1951.

121. Salih 'Ashmawi, "Nurid an n'amun zahurana min al-hikam al-misriyyin," *al-Da'wa,* 28 August 1951.

122. "Al-Ikhwan la yu'ayidun al-hakuma fi mawqifiha al-dhalil" and "Al-ikhwan wa-l-da'wa ila al-ithad," *al-Da'wa,* 25 September 1951.

123. USNRA, RG59, CDF, Box 4017, 774.00 (W)/9–2951, Joint Weekly A No. 39, Military Attaché, Cairo to Washington, DC, 29 September 1951.

124. USNRA, RG59, CDF, Box 4014, 774.00/8–1351, Despatch No. 355, Caffery, Cairo to State Department, 13 August 1951. For a similarly pessimistic report, see 774.00/9–2751, "State Department Memorandum of Conversation," 27 September 1951.

125. USNRA, RG59, CDF, Box 4014, 774.00/5–950 Despatch No. 1037, Howard, Embassy Cairo to State Department, 9 May 1950. See also Gordon, "False Hopes."

126. UKNA FO 371/90115, JE 10110/2, Telegram No. 7, Stevenson, Cairo to FO, 5 January 1951. See also in the same file, JE 10110/11, Letter 1011/13/51G, Wardle-Smith, Cairo to Allen, FO, 2 April 1951.

127. "Inward Despatch No. 244 from Stevenson to Morrison," 6 July 1951, *BDDE,* vol. 2, 194–197. Officials in London largely agreed with this analysis. See "Minutes by R. Allen and R. J. Bowker," 25–30 July 1951, *BDDE,* vol. 2, 197–198.

128. UKNA FO 371/90136, JE 1051/177, Minute by Allen, "United States Interest in Egypt," 10 August 1951.

129. "Inward Despatch No. 244 from Stevenson to Morrison," 6 July 1951, *BDDE,* vol. 2, 194–197.

130. On all this, see George McGhee, *Envoy to the Middle World: Adventures in Diplomacy* (New York: Harper & Row, 1983), 370–374; "Memorandum of Informal United States-United Kingdom Discussions, in Connection with the Visit to London of the Honourable George C. McGhee, 2–3 April 1951," London, 2 April 1951, *FRUS* 1951, vol. V; "Ambassador in Egypt (Caffery) to the State Department," Cairo, 1 April 1951, *FRUS* 1951, vol. V; UKNA FO 371/90130, JE 1051/44, Telegram No. 244, Chapman-Andrews, Cairo to FO, 2 April 1951; JE 1051/45, Telegram No. 246, Chapman-Andrews, Cairo to FO, 2 April 1951; JE 1051/47, Telegram No. 248, Chapman-Andrews, Cairo to FO, 2 April 1951; FO 371/90136, JE 1051/174, No. CAS 1529, "Draft Telegram to Sir William Elliot," 14 August 1951; JE 1051/177, Minute by Herbert Morrison (Foreign Secretary) to the Prime Minister, PM/51/59, "United States Interest in Anglo-Egyptian Relations," 14 August 1951. See also Muhammad Abd el-Wahab Sayed-Ahmed, *Nasser and American Foreign Policy 1952–1956* (London: Laam, 1989), 32–37.

131. Brands, "Cairo-Tehran Connection."

132. UKNA FO 371/90117, JE 10110/71, Letter No. 1657/2/51, Stevenson, Alexandria to His Excellency, Fu'ad Sirag el-Din Pasha, Minister of the Interior, 26 September 1951. For further British concerns regarding the press, see FO 371/90124, JE 10114/7, Telegram No. 309, Stevenson, Alexandria to Morrison FO, 8 September 1951.

133. UKNA FO 371/90115, JE 10110/29, Telegram No. 10121/1/51G, Stevenson, Alexandria to Sir R. James Bowker (Under-Secretary), FO, 5 October 1951.

134. Terry, *Wafd,* 299–304; Quraishi, *Liberal Nationalism in Egypt,* 168–196.

135. "Telegram from Caffery to State Department," Cairo, 9 October 1951, *FRUS* 1951, vol. V; USNRA, RG59, CDF, Box 4017, 774.00 (W)/10–1951, Joint Weekly A No. 42, Military Attaché, Cairo to Washington, DC, 19 October 1951.

136. Peter L. Hahn, *The United States, Great Britain, and Egypt, 1945–1956: Strategy and Diplomacy in the Early Cold War* (London: University of North Carolina Press, 1991), 126.

137. "Letter from British Secretary of State for Foreign Affairs (Morrison) to the Secretary of State," London, 12 October 1951, *FRUS* 1951, vol. V.

138. "Message from Acheson to Morrison," Washington, 17 October 1951, *FRUS* 1951, vol. V.

139. USNRA, RG59, CDF, Box 4017, 774.00 (W)/10–1951, Joint Weekly A No. 42, Military Attaché, Cairo to Washington, DC, 19 October 1951.

140. For shifts in this direction, see "Memorandum of Conversation by the Officer in Charge, Egypt and Anglo-Egyptian-Sudan Affairs (Stabler)," Washington, 19 June 1951, *FRUS* 1951, vol. V. See also Robert W. Stookey, *America and the Arab States: An Uneasy Encounter* (London: Wiley, 1975), 133–138; Ovendale, *Britain, the United States,* 33–41; Peter L. Hahn, "Containment and Egyptian Nationalism: The Unsuccessful Effort to Establish the Middle East Command, 1950–1953," *Diplomatic History* 11, no. 1 (1987), 23–40; Hahn, *United States, Great Britain,* 122–128.

141. "Al-Ikhwan al-Muslimun wa harb al-qanal aʿam 1951," Ikhwanwiki, available at http://bit.ly/2tPqVG1.

142. For a British overview of this low-intensity conflict, see UKNA WO 236/15, Lt. Gen. Sir George WEJ Erskine, "Narrative of Events in the Canal Zone, October 1951–April 1952." See also Thornhill, *Road to Suez,* 38–82.

143. "Moslem Brotherhood Believed Main British Enemy in Egypt," *Baltimore Sun,* 2 September 1951.

144. USNRA, RG59, CDF, Box 4017, 774.00 (W)/10–1951, Joint Weekly A No. 42, Military Attaché, Cairo to Washington, DC, 19 October 1951.

145. USNRA, CREST Database, CIA, Office of Current Intelligence, "Current Intelligence Bulletin," Copy No. 47, 20 October 1951.

146. UKNA FO 371/90117, JE 10110/60, Minute by Howen, 31 October 1951, on Telegram No. 349, Stevenson, Alexandria, to FO, 16 October 1951.

147. UKNA FO 371/90119, JE 10110/106, Memorandum by Willie Morris (First Secretary), FO, "Extremist Groups in Egypt," 7 November 1951.

148. Minute by R. Parsons, 16 November 1951, in ibid.

149. UKNA FO 371/90117, JE 10110/60, Telegram No. 349, Stevenson, Alexandria, to FO, 16 October 1951, and especially enclosed, "Al-Ahram: 12th October, 1951, Congress of Moslem Brethren Students."

150. See, for example, UKNA FO 371/90119, JE 10110/102, Telegram No. 8, Oliver Kemp, British Consulate General, Alexandria to Stevenson, Cairo, 23 October 1951.

151. UKNA FO 371/90118, JE 10110/87, Telegram No. 284, 1011/4/42/51, Stevenson, Cairo to Muhammad Salah-ed-din, Egyptian Minister for Foreign Affairs, 31 October 1951.

152. UKNA FO 371/90118, JE 10110/91, No. 15, Sir Thomas Rapp, British Middle East Office (BMEO), Fayid to FO, 6 November 1951.

153. UKNA FO 371/90116, JE 10110/45, Telegram No. 773, Stevenson, Cairo to FO, 19 October 1951; JE 10110/49, SBNOME to TF52, BNLO Suez, 19 October 1951; On the Brotherhood's involvement in intimidation, see "Notes of the Week," *Economist,* 27 October 1951; "Al-ikhwan al-muslimun wa-l-jihad did al-ingliz fi al-qanal 1951," Ikhwanwiki, http://bit.ly/2tKTVOG.

154. Shadi, *Safahat min al-tarikh,* 161.

155. Yusuf al-Qaradawi, *Al-Ikhwan al-Muslimun: 70 ʿaman fi al-daʿwa wa-l-tarbiya wa-l-jihad,* 2nd ed. (Beirut: Muʾassasat al-Risala, 2001), 336.

156. Ibid., 295–296.

157. USNRA, RG59, CDF, Box 4017, 774.00 (W)/10–1951, Joint Weekly A No. 42, Military Attaché, Cairo to Washington, DC, 19 October 1951.

158. Hasan Hathut, *Al-'aqd al-farid, 1942–1952: 'Ashr Sanawat ma' al-Imam Hasan al-Bana* (Cairo: Dar al-Shuruq, 2000), 20.

159. Dawh, *25 'aman*, 50.

160. Ibid., 51; 'Afifi, *Rihalati*, 51–55; "Al-ikhwan al-muslimun wa nazratuhum ila al-gharb," Ikhwanwiki, http://bit.ly/2sqaFei; and from the same website, "Al-ikhwan al-muslimun wa-l-jihad did al-ingliz fi al-qanal 1951," http://bit.ly/2u7AlcZ.

161. Dawh, *25 'aman*, 51.

162. Al-Sisi, *Fi qafilat al-Ikhwan II*, 43–44.

163. 'Afifi, *Rihalati*, 51.

164. Youssef Nada, with Douglas Thompson, *Inside the Muslim Brotherhood: The Truth about the World's Most Powerful Political Movement* (London: Metro, 2012), 6.

165. Shadi, *Safahat min al-tarikh*, 150–151.

166. Hathut, *Al-'aqd al-farid*, 20. For a full biography of him, see "'Adel Ghanim," Ikhwanwiki, http://bit.ly/2tL2SHp.

167. Dawh, *25 'aman*, 51.

168. HIA, Jacob C. Hurewitz Collection, Accession No. 88012–16.317/319, Box 32, Richard H. Nolte, "Undergraduate Affairs," *Institute of Current World Affairs Newsletter*, RHN-43, American Legation Beirut, 21 April 1952.

169. "Ma'arakat al-tal al-kabir," Ikhwanwiki, http://bit.ly/2tPvzUG.

170. UKNA FO 141/1440, 1041/2/135/51G, Secret Telegram from (GHQ) Middle East Land Forces to Ministry of Defence, London, 537/CCL, 27 October 1951. The CIA agreed that the Muslim Brotherhood was centrally involved in training the "Liberation Battalions." See, for example, USNRA, CREST Database, CIA Information Report, "Egypt: Training of the 'Liberation Battalions,'" 6 November 1951.

171. UKNA FO 141/1440, 1041/2/135/51G, Secret Telegram from (GHQ) Middle East Land Forces to Ministry of Defence, London, 537/CCL, 27 October 1951. For US assessments, see USNRA, RG59, CDF, Box 4014, 774.00/11–151, Despatch No. 626, Caffery, Cairo to State Department, 1 November 1951.

172. UKNA FO 371/90117, JE 10110/74, Memorandum by Allen, FO, 29 October 1951. On the Brotherhood, see also in the same file, Memorandum by Bowker, FO, 30 October 1951.

173. UKNA FO 141/1440, 1041/2/155/51G, Telegram No. 1228, FO to Cairo, 30 October 1951, copy of Telegram from Ministry of Defence, London to GHQ Middle East Land Forces, COS (ME) 578, 30 October 1951.

174. UKNA WO 236/15, Lt. Gen. Sir George WEJ Erskine, "Narrative of Events in the Canal Zone, October 1951–April 1952."

175. UKNA FO 141/1433, 1011/35/51G, Minute by Morris, 6 November 1951.

176. HIA, Christina Harris Papers, Accession No. 79085 10.03, Box 6, Richard H. Nolte to Walter S. Rogers, Institute of Current World Affairs, RHN-31, "We Arrive in Egypt," 18 October 1951.

177. HIA, Christina Harris Papers, Accession No. 79085 10.03, Box 6, Richard H. Nolte to Walter S. Rogers, Institute of Current World Affairs, RHN-32, "Long Live Nahas!," 7 November 1951.

178. See the entries on "The National Pact" and "Liberation Regiments," in UKNA FO 371/90119, JE 10110/106, Memorandum by Morris, "Extremist Groups in Egypt," 7

November 1951. See also USNRA, RG59, CDF, Box 4014, 774.00/11–851, Despatch No. 1133, Caffery, Cairo to State Department, 8 November 1951.

179. UKNA FO 371/90117, JE 10110/60, Telegram No. 349, Stevenson, Alexandria to FO, 16 October 1951, and especially enclosed, "Al Gomhour al Misri: 15th October, 1951."

180. "Muslim Resistance to Britain," *Times,* 13 November 1951.

181. UKNA FO 371/90117, JE 10110/73, Telegram No. 866, Stevenson, Cairo to FO, 29 October 1951.

182. UKNA FO 371/90117, JE 10110/60, Telegram No. 349, Stevenson, Alexandria to FO, 16 October 1951.

183. UKNA FO 371/90117, JE 10110/60, "Note: No. 6, Teleprinted to Agencies," 19 October 1951.

184. UKNA FO 371/90120, JE 10110/144, GHQ MELF to Ministry of Defence, London, 22 November 1951.

185. "Telegram from Caffery to Department of State," Cairo, 24 November 1951, *FRUS* 1951, vol. V. For more on the positions of Caffery and Stevenson, see "Telegram from Caffery to the State Department," Cairo, 23 October 1951; and "Telegram from Caffery to the State Department," Cairo, 24 October 1951, also available in *FRUS* 1951, vol. V.

186. UKNA FO 371/90118, JE 10110/7, Letter, Stevenson, Cairo to Erskine, British Troops in Egypt (BTE) HQ, 19 October 1951. In this letter, Stevenson declared himself "full of admiration" for the way in which Erskine had "handled the situation," though he also acknowledged that there had been a "difference of opinion" between them.

187. UKNA FO 141/1440, 1041/2/172/51G, Draft Telegram No. 894, Stevenson, Cairo to FO, 1 November 1951.

188. "Inward Telegram, No. 1167, Stevenson to FO," *BDDE,* vol. 2, 286–287.

189. UKNA WO 236/15, Lt. Gen. Sir George WEJ Erskine, "Narrative of Events in the Canal Zone, October 1951–April 1952."

190. UKNA FO 371/90120, JE 10110/129, Annex: "Proclamation by Lieutenant General Sir George Erskine."

191. UKNA WO 236/15, Lt. Gen. Sir George WEJ Erskine, "Narrative of Events in the Canal Zone, October 1951–April 1952." For a firsthand view on the turbulent situation in Ismailia, see Henry W. Harrison, *A Squaddie in the Suez Canal Zone, 1950–1951: A Summary of Events in the Military Life of a Reluctant National Serviceman in the Royal Lincolns* (St. Albans: Henry Walter Harrison, 2011), 65.

192. UKNA FO 371/90120, JE 10110/143, Telegram No. 86, Rapp, BMEO, Fayid to FO, 30 November 1951.

193. UKNA WO 236/15, Lt. Gen. Sir George WEJ Erskine, "Narrative of Events in the Canal Zone, October 1951–April 1952." See also Thornhill, *Road to Suez,* 47–48.

194. On December 3 in Suez, for example, between four and nine Egyptians were killed in such clashes. See UKNA FO 371/90120, JE 10110/147, Telegram No. 1124, Stevenson, Cairo to FO, 3 December 1951; and JE 10110/149, Telegram No. 1125, Stevenson, Cairo to FO, 3 December 1951; as well as, "Train Derailed in Canal Zone," *Times,* 17 December 1951. For a US assessment of overall casualty levels, see USNRA, RG59, CDF, Box 4014, 774.00/12–1051, Memorandum by Wells Stabler (NEA) to G. Lewis Jones (NEA), "Weekly Summary of Egyptian and Anglo-Egyptian Sudan Affairs, December 4–10, 1951," 10 December 1951.

195. USNRA, RG59, CDF, Box 4017, 774.00 (W)/12–151, Joint Weekly A No. 48, Military Attaché, Cairo to Washington, DC, 1 December 1951. See also Box 4015, 774.00/1–1452, Memorandum from Nestor Ortiz (NEA) to Samuel Kopper (NEA), "Weekly Summary of Egypt and Anglo-Egyptian Affairs, January 8–14, 1952," 14 January 1952.

196. For the British justification of this episode, see UKNA FO 371/90122, JE 10110/201, Telegram No. 128, by Rapp, BMEO, 15 December 1951; and FO 371/90123, JE 10110/242, G. Erskine, "Statement to Al-Misri Correspondent," undated. See also Thornhill, *Road to Suez,* 50–51.

197. UKNA WO 236/15, Lt. Gen. Sir George WEJ Erskine, "Narrative of Events in the Canal Zone, October 1951–April 1952."

198. UKNA FO 141/1433, 1011/35/51G, Minute by Morris, 6 November 1951.

199. UKNA FO 141/1440, 1041/2/108/51G, Minutes by Stevenson, 25 October 1951.

200. UKNA FO 141/1433, 1011/35/51G, Minute by Morris, 6 November 1951.

201. USNRA, RG59, CDF, Box 4014, Despatch No. 1279, Caffery, Cairo to State Department, Despatch No. 1279, undated.

202. HIA, Christina Harris Papers, Accession No. 79085 10.03, Box 6, Richard H. Nolte to Walter S. Rogers, Institute of Current World Affairs, RHN-32, "Long Live Nahas!," 7 November 1951.

203. UKNA FO 371/90121, JE 10110/167, Telegram No. 416, Stevenson, Cairo to FO, 3 December 1951.

204. UKNA FO 371/90122, JE 10110/195, Telegram No. 1011/4/60/51, Embassy Cairo to FO, 6 December 1951.

205. UKNA FO 371/90121, JE 10110/167, Minute by Allen, 17 December 1951, on Telegram No. 416, Stevenson, Cairo to FO, 3 December 1951.

206. "Mob without Masters," *Economist,* 15 December 1951.

207. USNRA, RG59, CDF, Box 4017, 774.00 (W)/12–2251, Joint Weekly A No. 51, Military Attaché, Cairo to Washington, DC, 22 December 1951.

208. "Telegram: Secretary of State to Embassy in the United Kingdom," Washington, 14 December 1951, *FRUS* 1951, vol. V.

209. "Minute by M. J. Cresswell to Sir R Stevenson," 5 November 1951, *BDDE,* vol., 2, 253–254. On the Middle East Command see "Telegram No. 582 from British Defence Co-ordination Committee, Middle East to COS," 16 December 1951, *BDDE,* vol. 2, 286–288; "Telegram from Eden to Stevenson," 16 December 1951, *BDDE,* vol. 2, 288–289. See also Hahn, "Containment and Egyptian Nationalism."

210. UKNA FO 141/1440, 1041/2/128/51G, Telegram No. 539/CCL from Mideast to Cairo, 27 October 1951. See also Thornhill, *Road to Suez,* 40–41.

211. USNRA, CREST Database, CIA Office of Current Intelligence, "Current Intelligence Review: The Anglo-Egyptian Crisis," 19 December 1951. For tangible examples of this kind of Foreign Office thinking, see "Letter from Bowker to Stevenson," 5 January 1952, *BDDE,* vol. 2, 312–314; USNRA, RG59, CDF, Box 4015, 774.00/1–752, Memorandum from Leonard Meeker to Ambassador Philip Jessup, 7 January 1952.

212. UKNA FO 141/1433, 1011/41/51G, Minute by Stevenson, 28 November 1951. On this, see also Mitchell, *Society of the Muslim Brothers,* 88–91.

213. UKNA FO 371/96870, JE 1018/1, Bowker, FO to Stevenson, Cairo, 15 January 1952.

214. UKNA FO 371/96872, JE1018/55, Telegram No. 1012/12/52, Stevenson, Cairo to Bowker, 26 January 1952.

215. UKNA FO 141/1433, 1011/39/51G, Minute by Stevenson, 24 November 1951.

216. UKNA FO 141/1450, "The Ikhwan el Muslimin" (II), D. L. Stewart, 4 December 1951, in Foreign Office Intelligence Reports, "The Ikhwan el Muslimin," 11 December 1951.

217. Ahmed Abdalla, *The Student Movement and National Politics in Egypt, 1923–1973* (London: Saqi Books, 1985), 48–49. Among the most prominent student leaders to be elected were Mustafa Mu'min, Hassan Hathut, and 'Izz al-Din Ibrahim.

218. UKNA FO 371/96870, JE 1018/1, Telegram No. 1, Stevenson, Cairo to FO, 1 January 1952.

219. UKNA FO 141/1450, "The Ikhwan el Muslimin" (I), 4 December 1951, in Foreign Office Intelligence Reports, "The Ikhwan el Muslimin," 11 December 1951.

220. "Al-ikhwan al-muslimun wa nazrathum ila al-gharb," Ikhwanwiki, http://bit.ly /1ylPhn5.

221. UKNA FO 141/1450, "The Ikhwan el Muslimin" (I).

222. UKNA FO 141/1450, D. L. Stewart, "The Ikhwan el Muslimin" (II).

223. Ibid.

224. Mitchell, *Society of the Muslim Brothers*, 90–91. On these statements, see also Imam, *'Abd al-Nasir*, 30–31; Fu'ad 'Allam, *Al-Ikhwan wa ana: min al-manshiya ila al-minasa* (Cairo: Akhbar al-Yom, 1996), 77.

225. UKNA WO 208/3956, BTE Weekly Intelligence Summary, No. 1, undated [yet clearly mid-November 1951].

226. UKNA FO 371/90121, JE 10110/167, Telegram No. 416, Stevenson, Cairo to FO, 3 December 1951.

227. UKNA FO 371/96870, JE 1018/1, Telegram No. 1, Stevenson, Cairo to FO, 1 January 1952. See also Al-Sisi, *Fi qafilat al-Ikhwan II*, 47.

228. UKNA FO 141/1433, 1011/44/51G, Memorandum by Sir Cecil Campbell, 16 December 1951.

229. USNRA, RG59, CDF, Box 4014, 774.00/10–351, Despatch No. 860, Caffery, Cairo to State Department, 3 October 1951; see also Imam, *'Abd al-Nasir*, 29–30.

230. Alfred Sansom, *I Spied Spies* (London: George C. Harrap, 1965), 243–249.

231. USNRA, RG59, CDF, Box 4017, 774.00 (W)/11–2351, Joint Weekly A No. 47, Military Attaché, Cairo to Washington, DC, 23 November 1951; CREST Database, CIA Office of Current Intelligence, "Current Intelligence Bulletin," 28 November 1951.

232. UKNA FO 371/96870, JE 1018/1, Telegram No. 1, Stevenson, Cairo to FO, 1 January 1952.

233. UKNA FO 371/96872, JE1018/55, Letter No. 1012/12/52, Stevenson, Cairo to Bowker, 26 January 1952.

234. USNRA, RG59, CDF, Box 4015, 774.00/1–2952, Despatch No. 139, Ellis Johnson, Consulate Port Said to State Department, 29 January 1952. On al-Farghali, see UKNA FO 371/96870, JE 1018/1, Telegram No. 1, Stevenson, Cairo to FO, 1 January 1952.

235. UKNA WO 236/15, Lt. Gen. Sir George WEJ Erskine, "Narrative of Events in the Canal Zone, October 1951–April 1952."

236. Hasan al-'Ashmawi also claims that Nasser and the Free Officers cooperated with the Brotherhood in the battle of the Canal Zone—and that this was how he first came to

know the future president. See Hasan al-'Ashmawi, *Al-Ikhwan wa-l-thawra: al-juz' al-awal* (Cairo: Al-Maktab al-Misri al-Hadith, 1973), 13–15.

237. Al-'Ashmawi tells a variant of this story, in which he insists that the Interior Ministry of Sirag al-Din was complicit and had given permission for the mine to be moved to the attack site—and also that Nasser's people wanted to attack an innocent Dutch ship but were prevented by the Brotherhood. See al-'Ashmawi, *Al-Ikhwan wa-l-thawra*, 16–17.

238. Shadi, *Safahat min al-tarikh*, 150–159; 'Afifi, *Rihalati*. 51–58; "Al-ikhwan al-muslimun wa-l-jihad did al-ingliz fi al-qanal 1951," Ikhwanwiki, http://bit.ly/2u7AlcZ.

239. "Organization of Terrorists," *Times*, 18 January 1952; "Student Riots in Cairo," *Times*, 22 January 1952.

240. "British Warning to Cairo Government," *Times*, 25 January 1952.

241. UKNA FO 371/96870, JE 1018/7, Telegram No. 1012/6/52, Stevenson, Cairo to FO, 18 January 1952.

242. UKNA FO 371/96846, JE 1013/2, Telegram No. 11 (S), Stevenson, Cairo to FO, 23 January 1952.

243. USNRA, RG59, CDF, Box 4015, 774.00/1–152, Despatch No. 115, Johnson, Port Said to State Department, 1 January 1952; "Organization of Terrorists," *Times*, 18 January 1952.

244. UKNA FO 371/96870, JE 1018/28, Wardle-Smith, Cairo to FO, No. 17415/1/52, 22 January 1952.

245. UKNA FO 371/96870, JE 1018/4, Telegram No. 87, Stevenson, Cairo to FO, 17 January 1952.

246. The move was prompted by a spate of fedayeen attacks and shooting incidents in which the auxiliary police participated. Several British soldiers had been killed and injured, while an American nun, Sister Anthony, had also died. See Thornhill, *Road to Suez*, 55–59.

247. UKNA FO 371/96846, JE 1013/5, Telegram No. 14 (S), Stevenson, Cairo to FO, 6 February 1952. For the military account of this, see WO 236/13, Brigadier R. K. Exham, "Report on Operation EAGLE—25 Jan 52, the Disarming of the Civil Police in ISMAILIA."

248. USNRA, RG59, CDF, Box 4017, 774.00 (W)/1–2552, Joint Weekly A No. 4, Military Attaché, Cairo to Washington, DC, 25 January 1952.

249. For "real-time" British coverage of the violence, see numerous files in UKNA FO 371/96870. For a retrospective American account, particularly of the attack on the Turf Club, see HIA, Jacob C. Hurewitz Collection, Accession No. 88012–16.317/319, Box 32, Richard H. Nolte, "Black Saturday," Institute of Current World Affairs Newsletter, RHN-38, Cairo, 12 February 1952.

250. UKNA FO 371/96870, JE 1018/31, Telegram No. 243, Stevenson, Cairo to FO, 29 January 1952. See also P. J. Vatikiotis, *The History of Egypt: From Muhammad Ali to Mubarak*, 3rd ed. (Baltimore, MD: Johns Hopkins University Press, 1985), 370.

251. USNRA, RG59, CDF, Box 4015, 774.00/1–2952, Despatch No. 1192, Caffery, Cairo to State Department, 29 January 1952; 774.00/1–3052, Despatch No. 1647, J. Wesley Adams Jr. (Second Secretary), Embassy Cairo to State Department, 31 January 1952.

252. UKNA FO 371/96846, JE 1013/18, Telegram No. 53 (S), Stevenson, Cairo to FO, 24 May 1952.

253. UKNA FO 371/96873, JE 1018/86, Telegram No. 48, Stevenson, Cairo to Anthony Eden (Foreign Secretary), FO, 25 February 1952.

254. UKNA FO 141/1453, 1011/21/52G, Minute by James Murray, "Conversation with Gallad Pasha," 7 February 1952.

255. UKNA FO 141/1453, 1011/19/52G, J. de C. Hamilton, "Talk with 'Former Interior Person,'" 13 February 1952.

256. "Unanimous Vote for Aly Maher Pasha," *Times,* 29 January 1952.

257. USNRA, RG59, CDF, Box 4015, 774.00/1–2952, Despatch No. 1192, Caffery, Cairo to State Department, 29 January 1952.

258. USNRA, RG59, CDF, Box 4015, 774.00/1–3152, Despatch No. 1647, Adams Jr., Cairo to State Department, 31 January 1952.

259. USNRA, RG59, CDF, Box 4017, 774.00 (W)/1–3152, Joint Weekly A No. 5, Military Attaché, Cairo to Washington, DC, 31 January 1952.

260. USNRA, RG59, CDF, Box 4015, 774.00/1–2952, Despatch No. 1240, Caffery, Cairo to State Department, 1 February 1952.

261. HIA, Jacob C. Hurewitz Collection, Accession No. 88012–16.317/319, Box 32, Richard H. Nolte, "Saturday Blitz," Institute of Current World Affairs Newsletter, RHN-37, Cairo, 31 January 1952.

262. USNRA, RG59, CDF, Box 4015, 774.00/1–3052, Despatch No. 1217, Caffery, Cairo to State Department, 30 January 1952.

263. John S. Badeau, *The Middle East Remembered* (Washington, DC: Middle East Institute, 2009), 132–134.

264. "Darkness of Egypt," *Economist,* 2 February 1952.

265. Sansom, *I Spied Spies,* 257–258.

266. UKNA FO 141/1453, 1011/21/52G, Minute by James Murray, "Conversation with Gallad Pasha," 7 February 1952.

267. Dawh, *25 'aman,* 52.

268. Shadi, *Safahat min al-tarikh,* 163–165. On this, see also al-'Ashmawi, *Al-ayam al-hasima* 30; al-'Ashmawi, *Al-Ikhwan wa-l-thawra,* 19–22, 53; Mahmud 'Abd al-Halim, *Al-Ikhwan al-Muslimun III: Ahdath sana'at al-tarikh: ru'yah min al-dakhil, al-juz' al-thalith* (Alexandria, Egypt: Dar al-Da'wa, 1981), 22ff.

269. USNRA, RG59, CDF, Box 4015, 774.00/1–2952, Despatch No. 1191, Caffery, Cairo to State Department, 29 January 1952.

270. UKNA FO 371/96846, JE 1013/5, Telegram No. 14 (S), Stevenson, Cairo to FO, 6 February 1952; FO 371/96873, JE 1018/86, Telegram No. 48, Stevenson, Cairo to Eden, FO, 25 February 1952.

271. UKNA FO 371/96872, JE 1018/78, Letter 1012/15/52, Embassy Cairo to FO, 18 February 1952. For a similar view on the role of Brotherhood members in attacks on bars, see the views of Hafiz 'Afifi Pasha, in conversation with Sir Cecil Campbell, recorded in FO 141/1453, 1011/13/52G, "Conversation with Hafez Afifi Pasha on 29.1.52," 29 January 1952. For his part, Campbell was more convinced of the Brotherhood's role as an organization and criticized efforts to "whitewash" the group.

272. UKNA FO 371/96872, JE 1018/78, Minute by R. Parsons, 22 February 1952, on Letter 1012/15/52, Embassy Cairo to FO, 18 February 1952.

273. "Egypt under Martial Law," *Daily Telegraph,* 12 March 1952.

274. UKNA FO 371/96846, JE 1013/1, Telegram No. 1 (S), Stevenson Cairo to FO, 5 January 1952; USNRA, RG59, CDF, Box 4017, 774.00 (W)/12–2251, Joint Weekly A No. 51, Military Attaché, Cairo to Washington, DC, 22 December 1951.

275. USNRA, RG59, CDF, Box 4017, 774.00 (W)/1–3152, Joint Weekly A No. 5, Military Attaché, Cairo to Washington, DC, 31 January 1952.

276. For Lampson, see Lampson Diaries, Killearn Box 6, 13 March 1945.

277. HIA, Jacob C. Hurewitz Collection, Accession No. 88012–16.317/319, Box 32, Richard H. Nolte, "Last Chance in Egypt," Institute of Current World Affairs Newsletter, RHN–40, Cairo, 28 February 1952. For the Brotherhood's "wait and see" approach, see also UKNA FO 371/96872, JE 1018/78, 1012/15/52, Embassy Cairo to FO, 18 February 1952.

278. "Unanimous Vote for Aly Maher Pasha," *Times,* 29 January 1952.

279. USNRA, RG59, CDF, Box 4015, 774.00/1–3052, Despatch No. 1214, Caffery, Cairo to State Department, 30 January 1952.

280. For reference to the Brotherhood, see UKNA FO 371/96872, JE1018/58, Telegram No. 314, Stevenson, Cairo to FO, 5 February 1952.

281. UKNA FO 371/96872, JE 1018/72, Telegram No. 101 (11/125/52), Embassy Cairo to FO, 7 February 1952. See also FO 371/96846, JE 1013/6, Telegram No. 24 (S), Stevenson, Cairo to FO, 19 February 1952.

282. UKNA FO 371/96846, JE 1013/7, Telegram No. 28 (S), Stevenson, Cairo to FO, 3 March 1952.

283. USNRA, RG59, CDF, Box 4015, 774.00/2–1152, Despatch No. 162, Johnson, Port Said to State Department, 11 February 1952. For similar analysis, see also in the same box, 774.00/2–2152, Despatch No. 1395, Caffery, Cairo to State Department, 21 February 1952; and 774.00/2–2152, Despatch No. 171, Johnson, Port Said to State Department, 22 February 1952.

284. UKNA FO 371/96874, JE 1018/108, Telegram No. 66, Stevenson, Cairo to Eden, FO, 10 March 1952.

285. USNRA, RG59, CDF, Box 4015, 774.00/3–352, Memorandum Ortiz (NEA) to Kopper (NEA), 3 March 1952.

286. USNRA, RG59, CDF, Box 4017, 774.00 (W)/3–752, Joint Weekly A No.10, Military Attaché, Cairo to Washington, DC, 7 March 1952.

287. UKNA FO 371/96846, JE 1013/9, Telegram No. 35 (S), Stevenson, Cairo to FO, 25 March 1952.

288. UKNA FO 371/96874, JE 1018/104, Telegram No. 54, Stevenson, Cairo to Eden, FO, 4 March 1952.

289. USNRA, RG59, CDF, Box 4015, 774.00/3–2452, Memorandum Ortiz (NEA) to Stabler (NEA), 24 March 1952. See also 774.00/3–1452, Despatch No. 1571, Caffery, Cairo to State Department, 14 March 1952; and Box 4017, 774.00 (W)/3–2052, Joint Weekly A No. 12, Military Attaché, Cairo to Washington, DC, 20 March 1952. On Brotherhood support for Neguib al-Hilali, see too UKNA FO 371/96846, JE 1013/16, Telegram No. 47 (S), Stevenson, Cairo to FO, 10 May 1952.

290. USNRA, RG59, CDF, Box 4015, 774.00/4–252, "Enclosure No. 1: Translation of a Letter from Supreme Guide of the Moslem Brotherhood to the Egyptian Prime Minister," with Despatch No. 2028, Caffery, Cairo to State Department, 2 April 1952; UKNA

FO 371/96874, JE 1018/124, Telegram No. 608, Stevenson, Cairo to FO, 26 March 1952.

291. USNRA, RG59, CDF, Box 4015, 774.00/4–252, "Enclosure No. 1: Translation of a Letter from Supreme Guide of the Moslem Brotherhood to the Egyptian Prime Minister."

292. UKNA FO 371/96846, JE 1013/18, Telegram No. 53 (S), Stevenson, Cairo to FO, 24 May 1952.

293. UKNA FO 371/96874, JE 1018/125, Minute by Parsons, 27 March 1952; and Minute by Allen, 29 March 1952.

294. UKNA FO 371/96874, JE 1018/117, Telegram No. 75, Stevenson, Cairo to FO, 15 March 1952.

295. UKNA FO 371/96874, JE 1018/126, "Reuter Communique," 26 March 1952.

296. UKNA FO 371/96874, JE 1018/128, Telegram No. 623, Stevenson, Cairo to FO, 28 March 1952; USNRA, RG59, CDF, Box 4015, 774.00/3–2852, Despatch No. 1675, Caffery, Cairo to State Department, 28 March 1952. See also 774.00/3–2452, Memorandum Ortiz (NEA) to Stabler (NEA), 24 March 1952.

297. "The Egyptian Scene," *Economist,* 19 April 1952. See also USNRA, RG59, CDF, Box 4015, 774.00/4–1352, Despatch No. 1804, Caffery, Cairo to State Department, 13 April 1952; 774.00/4–1352, Despatch No. 2092, Caffery, Cairo to State Department, 13 April 1952.

298. USNRA, RG59, CDF, Box 4015, 774.00/2–2152, Despatch No. 1395, Caffery, Cairo to State Department, 21 February 1952.

299. USNRA, RG59, CDF, Box 4015, 774.00/4–2852, Memorandum Stabler (NEA) to Jones, 28 April 1952.

300. USNRA, RG59, CDF, Box 4015, 774.00/3–752, Despatch No. 1491, Caffery, Cairo to State Department, 7 March 1952.

301. USNRA, RG59, CDF, Box 4015, 774.00/4–1352, Despatch No. 2092, Caffery, Cairo to State Department, 13 April 1952.

302. USNRA, RG59, CDF, Box 4015, 774.00/3–1852, Article: "Egypt under Martial Law," *Daily Telegraph,* 12 March 1952, enclosed with Despatch No. 4207, Robert B. Houghton (Second Secretary), Embassy London to State Department, 18 March 1952.

303. "Letter from R. Allen to M. J. Cresswell," 26 February 1952, *BDDE,* vol. 2, 348–349. For more on this internal divide, see Thornhill, *Road to Suez,* 66–67.

304. "Letter (Reply) from M. J. Cresswell to R. Allen," 4 March 1952, *BDDE,* vol. 2, 349–351.

305. UKNA FO 371/96846, JE 1013/9, Telegram No. 35 (S), Stevenson, Cairo to FO, 25 March 1952.

306. "Minute by Eden (Reply) to Churchill," 10 March 1952, *BDDE,* vol. 2, 355–356; for Churchill's views, see "Minute by Churchill to Eden," 9 March 1952, *BDDE,* vol. 2, 354–355. For further on Eden's desire for an agreement, see "Cabinet Memorandum by Eden, Annexes," 10 March 1952, *BDDE,* vol. 2, 356–357.

307. USNRA, RG59, CDF, Box 4015, 774.00/5–552, Memorandum Stabler (NEA) to Jones, 5 May 1952; 774.00/5–1952, Memorandum Stabler (NEA) to Kopper, 19 May 1952; 774.00/6–252, Memorandum Oritz (NEA) to Kopper, 2 June 1952.

308. USNRA, RG59, CDF, Box 4015, 774.00/6–3052, Memorandum Fowler (NEA) to Stabler, 30 June 1952; 774.00/7–752, Memorandum Fowler (NEA) to Stabler, 7 July 1952.

309. UKNA FO 141/1453, 1011/65/52G, Telegram No. 166, Embassy Cairo to FO, 13 July 1952.

310. USNRA, RG59, CDF, Box 4015, 774.00/7–2152, Memorandum Fowler (NEA) to Stabler, 21 July 1952.

311. USNRA, RG59, CDF, Box 4015, 774.00/7–2152, Despatch No. 126, Caffery, Cairo to State Department, 21 July 1952.

312. UKNA FO 371/96846, JE 1013/12, Telegram No. 39 (S), Stevenson, Cairo to FO, 10 April 1952; and JE 1013/13, Telegram No. 42 (S), Stevenson, Cairo to FO, 25 April 1952.

313. UKNA WO 208/3956, BTE Weekly Intelligence Summary, No. 26, "For Fortnight Ending 18 June 1952."

314. "Al-ikhwan al-muslimun wa-l-jihad did al-ingliz fi al-qanal 1951," Ikhwanwiki, http://bit.ly/2u7AlcZ.

315. UKNA CAB 158/13, Joint Intelligence Committee, "Review of the Middle East and North Africa," JIC (51) 88 (Final), 27 June 1952.

316. UKNA FO 371/96877, JE 1018/223, Telegram No. 10112/3/52, Embassy Alexandria to FO, 17 July 1952.

317. For an overview of the final days, see USNRA, RG59, CDF, Box 4017, 774.00 (W)/7–2452, Joint Weekly A No. 30, Caffery, Cairo to State Department, 24 July 1952.

5. The Upheavals of Revolution, 1952–1954

1. "Religion Said to Veil Plot," *Baltimore Sun,* 15 January 1954.

2. USNRA, RG59, CDF, Box 4016a, 774.00/1–1554, Despatch No. 1658, Jefferson Caffery (Ambassador), Embassy Cairo to State Department, 15 January 1954. See, especially, with the same, "Enclosure: Moslem Brotherhood Dissolved: Command Council Reveals Efforts to Usurp Power, *Egyptian Gazette,* 15 January 1954." See also UKNA FO (Foreign Office) 371/108319, JE 1016/4, Telegram No. 61, Sir Ralph Stevenson (Ambassador), Cairo to FO, 16 January 1954, and in the same, JE 1016/7, Telegram No. 11 (S), Stevenson, Cairo to FO, 18 January 1954; Hasan al-'Ashmawi, *Al-Ikhwan wa-l-thawra: al-juz' al-awal* (Cairo: Al-Maktab al-Misri al-Hadith, 1973), 41–51.

3. USNRA, RG59, CDF, Box 4016a, 774.00/1–1554, Despatch No. 1658, Caffery, Cairo to State Department, 15 January 1954. See also UKNA FO 371/108373, JE 1054/2, Telegram No. 68, Stevenson, Cairo to FO, 16 January 1954.

4. UKNA FO 371/108373, JE 1054/1, Telegram No. 62, Stevenson, Cairo to FO, 15 January 1954. For the text of the public denial, see in same file, JE 1054/3, Telegram No. 69, Stevenson, Cairo to FO, 16 January 1954. See also "British Repudiate Cairo Allegations," *Times,* 16 January 1954; and "Britons Deny Links to Moslem Fanatics," *New York Times,* 16 January 1954.

5. UKNA FO 371/108373, JE 1054/2, Telegram No. 68, Stevenson, Cairo to FO, 16 January 1954.

6. UKNA FO 371/108373, JE 1054/7, Telegram No. 15(S), Stevenson, Cairo to FO, 19 January 1954.

7. UKNA FO 371/108373, JE 1054/6, Telegram No. 81, Stevenson, Cairo to FO, 19 January 1954.

8. Fu'ad 'Allam, *Al-Ikhwan wa ana: min al-manshiya ila al-minasa* (Cairo: Akhbar al-Yom, 1996), 75–76.

9. UKNA FO 371/108373, JE 1054/8, Telegram No. 1012/26/54, Embassy Cairo to FO, 19 February 1954. For this accusation, see also 'Allam, *Al-Ikhwan wa ana,* 80–81.

10. UKNA FO 371/108373, JE 1054/8, Telegram No. 1012/26/54, Embassy Cairo to FO, 19 February 1954.

11. "Agrarian Charge in the UK (Holmes) to Secretary of State," London, 7 January 1949, *FRUS* 1949, vol. VI.

12. See Chapter 3.

13. "Communist Press Campaign in Egypt," *Times,* 27 June 1951.

14. "Regional Policy Statement: Near East—Prepared in the Office of Near Eastern Affairs," Washington, 28 December 1950, *FRUS* 1950, vol. V; "Report of the Near East Regional Conference in Cairo: Summary of Conclusions," Cairo, 16 March 1950, *FRUS* 1950, vol. V.

15. HIA, Jacob C. Hurewitz Collection, Accession No. 88012–16.317/319, Box 88, "A Report to the National Security Council on United States Objectives and Policies with Respect to the Near East," National Security Council (NSC) 155/1, 14 July 1953.

16. Kermit Roosevelt, *Arabs, Oil and History* (New York: Harper, 1949), 252–256.

17. Douglas Little, "Mission Impossible: The CIA and the Cult of Covert Action in the Middle East," *Diplomatic History* 28, no. 5 (2004), 663–701 (678); Richard J. Aldrich, *The Hidden Hand: Britain, America and Cold War Secret Intelligence* (London: John Murray, 2001), 12; W. Scott Lucas and Alistair Morey, "The Hidden 'Alliance': The CIA and MI6 before and after Suez," *Intelligence and National Security* 15, no. 2 (2000), 95–121 (97).

18. Miles Copeland, *The Game Player: Confessions of the CIA's Original Political Operative* (London: Aurum, 1989), 132–133, 142–157.

19. Ibid., 144–171, 198–199. See also Muhammad Abd el-Wahab Sayed-Ahmed, *Nasser and American Foreign Policy, 1952–1956* (London: Laam, 1989), 39–49.

20. Mahmud 'Abd al-Halim, *Al-Ikhwan al-Muslimun III: Ahdath sana'at al-tarikh: ru'yah min al-dakhil, al-juz' al-thalith* (Alexandria, Egypt: Dar al-Da'wa, 1981), 593ff. On the Brotherhood's interest in Copeland, see also Salah Shadi, *Safahat min al-tarikh: Hisad al-amr* (Kuwait: Sharikat al-Shu'a, 1981), 94–95.

21. 'Abd al-Halim, *Al-Ikhwan al-Muslimun III,* 610–611.

22. Ibid., 619–621. Al-Halim identifies US propaganda expert Paul Lineberger as a key figure behind a strategy that allegedly saw the Americans and the Nasserists work together, alongside the Israelis and the Soviets in order to undermine the image of the Brotherhood.

23. Hasan al-'Ashmawi, *Al-ayam al-hasima wa hisaduha* (Cairo: Dar al-Tawqi' wa-l-Nashr al-Islami, n.d.), 29–31.

24. Ibid., 34.

25. Shadi, *Safahat min al-tarikh,* 172, 179–180.

26. The phrase is that of an Iraqi Ba'thist referring to the 1963 coup in that country. See Little, "Mission Impossible," 684–701. By contrast, the memoir of Wilbur Crane Eveland suggests that the Central Intelligence Agency (CIA) was surprised by events in Egypt. On this issue, see also Said K. Aburish, *Nasser: The Last Arab* (London: Duckworth, 2005), 38–43.

27. Anwar el-Sadat, *In Search of Identity: An Autobiography* (New York: Harper & Row, 1978), 108.

28. USNRA, RG59, CDF, Box 4015, 774.00/7–2352, Despatch No. 144, Caffery, Cairo to State Department, 23 July 1952, 12 p.m.

29. UKNA FO 371/96879, JE 1018/301, Telegram No. 179, Stevenson, Cairo to FO, 2 August 1952. On the initially limited agenda of the Free Officers, see Joel Gordon, *Nasser's Blessed Movement: Egypt's Free Officers and the July Revolution* (Oxford: Oxford University Press, 1992).

30. USNRA, RG59, CDF, Box 4015, 774.00/7–2352, Despatch No. 494, Dean Acheson (Secretary of State), State Department to Embassies London and Cairo, 23 July 1952.

31. UKNA FO 371/96877, JE 1018/198, Telegram No. 1046, Michael Cresswell (Minister), Embassy Alexandria to FO, 20 July 1952.

32. USNRA, RG59, CDF, Box 4015, 774.00/7–2452, Despatch No. 458, Julius Holmes (Ambassador), Embassy London to State Department, 24 July 1952, 7 p.m. See also UKNA FO 141/1453, 1011/138/52G, Telegram No. 1191, FO to Alexandria, 28 July 1952. Operation Rodeo, the British army's contingency plan to send troops into Cairo and the Egyptian Delta, was put on a forty-eight-hour alert.

33. UKNA FO 141/1453, 1011/119/52G, Minute by R. A. Burroughs, 29 July 1952.

34. Anthony Eden, Hansard Online, HC Deb, 28 July 1952, vol. 504, cc1095–7.

35. Michael T. Thornhill, *Road to Suez: The Battle of the Canal Zone* (Stroud, UK: Sutton, 2006), 92.

36. UKNA FO 371/96877, JE 1018/204, Telegram No. 1060, Cresswell, Alexandria to FO, 23 July 1952; see also USNRA, RG59, CDF, Box 4015, 774.00/7–2352, Despatch No. 408, Embassy London to State Department, 23 July 1952, 6 p.m.

37. UKNA FO 141/1453, 1011/85/52G, Telegram No. 1074, Cresswell, Alexandria to FO, 23 July 1952; FO 371/96878, JE 1018/231, Telegram No. 1083, Cresswell, Alexandria to FO, 24 July 1952. This view was relayed to the United States; see USNRA, RG59, CDF, Box 4015, 774.00/7–2452, Despatch No. 456, Holmes, London to State Department, 24 July 1952, 7 p.m. For another view on Naguib's supposed "figurehead" status, see UKNA FO 371/96878, JE 1018/247, Telegram No. 1092, Cresswell, Alexandria to FO, 25 July 1952.

38. UKNA FO 371/96878, JE 1018/238, Telegram No. 1090, Cresswell, Alexandria to FO, 25 July 1952. See also USNRA, RG59, CDF, Box 4015, 774.00/7–2552, Despatch No. 183, Caffery, Cairo to State Department, 25 July 1952, 8 p.m. For more on British concerns about Sadat's role, see UKNA FO 141/1453, 1011/144/52G, Telegram No. 1145, Stevenson, Cairo to FO, 29 July 1952; and USNRA, RG59, CDF, Box 4015, 774.00/7–2652, Despatch No. 503, Holmes, London to State Department, 26 July 1952, 2 p.m., and 774.00/7–2352, Despatch No. 839, Joseph Palmer 2nd (First Secretary), Embassy London to State Department, 14 August 1952.

39. UKNA FO 371/96879, JE 1018/301, Telegram No. 179, Stevenson, Cairo to FO, 2 August 1952.

40. USNRA, RG59, CDF, Box 4015, 774.00/8–452, Despatch No. 256, Caffery, Cairo to State Department, 4 August 1952.

41. USNRA, RG59, CDF, Box 4015, 774.00/8–1552, "Enclosure: Conversation between Lewa Fu'ad Sadek (Pasha) and M. A., 11 Aug. 52," with Despatch No. 266, Caffery, Cairo to State Department, 15 August 1952. Mehanna was one of three men, alongside independent politician Bahi al-Din Barakat and Prince 'Abd al-Mon'im, chosen to sit on the

Regency Council when King Faruq was forced to abdicate on July 26. For more on this, see UKNA FO 141/1453, 1011/125/52G, Telegram No. 1122, Alexandria to FO, 26 July 1952; USNRA, RG59, CDF, Box 4015, 774.00/8–1852, Despatch No. 282, Caffery, Cairo to State Department, 18 August 1952.

42. The Americans, by contrast, to whom the British forwarded their report, considered that Sadeq "might well know what he is talking about on this matter"—perhaps a sign of their closeness to and greater familiarity with the internal dynamics of the army movement. See USNRA, RG59, CDF, Box 4015, 774.00/8–1552, Despatch No. 266, Caffery, Cairo to State Department, 15 August 1952.

43. USNRA, RG59, CDF, Box 4015, 774.00/7–2452, Despatch No. 456, Holmes, London to State Department, 24 July 1952, 7 p.m.

44. USNRA, RG59, CDF, Box 4015, 774.00/7–2552, Despatch No. 493, Holmes, London to State Department, 25 July 1952, 6 p.m.

45. UKNA FO 371/96879, JE 1018/289, FO Minute, "Statement on Egypt," 1 August 1952.

46. UKNA FO 141/1453, 1011/86/52G, Telegram No. 1077, Cresswell, Alexandria to FO, 23 July 1952.

47. USNRA, RG59, CDF, Box 4015, 774.00/7–2452, Despatch No. 456, Holmes, London to State Department, 24 July 1952, 7 p.m.; UKNA FO 371/96877, JE 1018/221, Telegram No. 1077, Cresswell, Alexandria to FO, 23 July 1952. As before, the military preferred not to go too far. The notice period for RODEO BERNARD was reduced to forty-eight hours, but that for RODEO FLAIL remained at ninety-six hours. See FO 371/96877, JE 1018/221, Despatch from Ministry of Defence, London to GHQMELF, COS (ME) 693, 24 July 1952.

48. USNRA, RG59, CDF, Box 4015, 774.00/7–2852, Despatch No. 526, Holmes, London to State Department, 28 July 1952, 6 p.m. See also Michael T. Thornhill, "Britain, the United States and the Rise of an Egyptian Leader: The Politics and Diplomacy of Nasser's Consolidation of Power, 1952–4," *English Historical Review* 119, no. 483 (September 2004), 893–901.

49. UKNA FO 371/96878, JE 1018/268, Telegram No. 1140, Cresswell, Alexandria to FO, 28 July 1952. For the best account of the emergence of the Command Council of the Revolution (CCR), see Gordon, *Nasser's Blessed Movement.*

50. UKNA FO 371/96878, JE 1018/233, Telegram No. 1088, Cresswell, Alexandria to FO, 25 July 1952.

51. USNRA, RG59, CDF, Box 4015, 774.00/7–2452, Despatch No. 163, Caffery, Cairo to State Department, 24 July 1952, 8 p.m.

52. USNRA, RG59, CDF, Box 4015, 774.00/7–2552, Despatch No. 29, Wright, Alexandria to State Department, 25 July 1952, 4 p.m.

53. USNRA, RG59, CDF, Box 4015, 774.00/7–2352, Despatch No. 163, Caffery, Cairo to State Department, 24 July 1952, 8 p.m.

54. USNRA, RG59, CDF, Box 4015, 774.00/7–2852, Despatch No. 197, Caffery, Cairo to State Department, 28 July 1952, 8 p.m.

55. USNRA, RG59, CDF, Box 4015, 774.00/7–3052, Despatch No. 216, Caffery, Cairo to State Department, 30 July 1952, 8 p.m.

56. See USNRA, CREST Database, CIA, "Current Intelligence Digest," 28 July 1952.

57. 'Abdullah Imam, *'Abd al-Nasir wa-l-Ikhwan al-Muslimun* (Cairo: Dar al-Khayyal, 1997), 34–46.

58. Husayn al-Shafi'i, *Shahid 'ala thulathat 'asur,* 2nd ed. (Cairo: Maktabat Madbula al-Shaghir, 2000), 47–62.

59. 'Allam, *Al-Ikhwan wa ana,* 107.

60. El-Sadat, *In Search of Identity,* 22–24, 100. For more on al-Ra'uf, see Hasan al-'Ashmawi, *Hisad al-ayam aw mudhakirat harib* (Cairo: Dar al-Tawzi' wa-l-Nashr al-Islami, 1991) 113–114; and Imam, *'Abd al-Nasir,* 43–46.

61. El-Sadat, *In Search of Identity,* 69–70.

62. Shadi, *Safahat min al-tarikh,* 32–33, 97, 116–149, 169–174. For a slightly different version, see 'Abd al-Halim, *Al-Ikhwan al-Muslimun III,* 21. For a more contemporary rendition of this narrative, see Kemal el-Helbawy, "The Muslim Brotherhood in Egypt: Historical Evolution and Future Prospects," in Khaled Hroub, *Political Islam: Context versus Ideology* (London: Saqi Books, 2010), 76.

63. Al-'Ashmawi, *Al-ayam al-hasima,* 48, 74, 130–135. See also al-'Ashmawi, *Al-Ikhwan wa-l-thawra,* 14; and Ghada Osman, *A Journey in Islamic Thought: The Life of Fathi Osman* (New York: I. B. Tauris, 2011), 110–111.

64. Ahmad H. al-Baquri, *Baqaya dhikriyat* (Cairo: Markaz al-Ahram lil-Tarjamah wa-l-Nashr, 1988), 71–73.

65. See Chapter 4. See also 'Umar al-Tilmisani, *Dhikriyat la Mudhakirat* (Cairo: Dar al-Taba'a wa-l-Nashr al-Islami, 1985), 138–139.

66. James Jankowski, *Egypt's Young Rebels: "Young Egypt" 1933–1952* (Stanford, CA: Hoover Institution Press, 1975); Gordon, *Nasser's Blessed Movement,* 12–13, 42–49. On this point, too, see Aburish, *Nasser,* 14–21.

67. Al-'Ashmawi, *Al-ayam al-hasima,* 17–61.

68. Ibid., 21–23, 49.

69. Ibid., 37.

70. Al-'Ashmawi, *Hisad al-ayam,* 48. See also 'Abd al-Halim, *Al-Ikhwan al-Muslimun III,* 23–24; Yusuf al-Qaradawi, *Al-Ikhwan al-Muslimun: 70 'aman fi al-da'wa wa-l-tarbiya wa-l-jihad,* 2nd ed. (Beirut: Mu'assasat al-Risala, 2001), 245–246; Hasan Hathut, *Al-'aqd al-farid, 1942–1952: 'Ashr sanawat ma' al-Imam Hasan al-Bana* (Cairo: Dar al-Shuruq, 2000), 108; and al-Baquri, *Baqaya,* 108.

71. 'Abd al-Halim, *Al-Ikhwan al-Muslimun III,* 22–23. Hasan al-'Ashmawi suggests that al-Hudaybi had reservations about the move on the basis that he did not believe in military coups and did not trust Nasser. See al-'Ashmawi, *Al-ayam al-hasima,* 46–50.

72. Shadi, *Safahat min al-tarikh,* 169–174. On this point, see also al-'Ashmawi, *Al-ayam al-hasima,* 35.

73. Al-'Ashmawi, *Al-ayam al-hasima,* 77–82.

74. 'Abd al-Halim, *Al-Ikhwan al-Muslimun III,* 24.

75. Barbara H. E. Zollner, *The Muslim Brotherhood: Hasan al-Hudaybi and Ideology* (London: Routledge, 2009), 22–27.

76. This is, for example, the verdict of Mitchell. See Richard P. Mitchell, *The Society of the Muslim Brothers* (Oxford: Oxford University Press, 1993), 95–104. See also Gordon, *Nasser's Blessed Movement,* 53–54.

77. HIA, Christina Harris Papers, Accession No. 79085 10.03, Box 2, "Hasan an-Hudeibi 'Denied to "al-Misri" on Aug. 9,'" *Mideast Mirror,* 16 August 1952.

78. USNRA, RG59, CDF, Box 4015, 774.00/8–1852, Despatch No. 282, Caffery, Cairo to State Department, 18 August 1952.

79. Shadi, *Safahat min al-tarikh,* 186–188; Osman, *Journey in Islamic Thought,* 112–113.

80. USNRA, RG59, CDF, Box 4015, 774.00/8–2052, Despatch No. 412, Caffery, Cairo to State Department, 20 August 1952.

81. USNRA, RG59, CDF, Box 4015, 774.00/8–1852, Despatch No. 282, Caffery, Cairo to State Department, 18 August 1952.

82. UKNA FO 371/96879, JE 1018/292, Telegram No. 1162, Stevenson, Cairo to FO, 2 August 1952; USNRA, RG59, CDF, Box 4015, 774.00/8–952, "Enclosure: Program of Muslim Brotherhood" (taken from the *Egyptian Mail,* 2 August 1952), included with Despatch No. 171, Caffery, Cairo to State Department, 9 August 1952; HIA, Christina Harris Papers, Accession No. 79085 10.03, Box 1, "III. Political Parties, 2. Moslem Brotherhood," *Mideast Mirror,* 2 August 1952.

83. UKNA FO 371/96879, JE 1018/292, Minute by Willie Morris (First Secretary), FO, 6 August 1952, on Telegram No. 1162, Stevenson, Cairo to FO, 2 August 1952.

84. USNRA, RG59, CDF, Box 4015, 774.00/8–1352, Despatch No. 347, Caffery, Cairo to State Department, 13 August 1952.

85. HIA, Christina Harris Collection, Accession No. 79085 10.03, Box 12, Richard H. Nolte, "Middle East: Background Information," American Universities Field Staff, Lebanon, 14 August 1952.

86. USNRA, RG59, CDF, Box 4015, 774.00/7–3152, Despatch No. 219, Caffery, Cairo to State Department, 31 July 1952, 11 a.m.

87. USNRA, RG59, CDF, Box 4015, 774.00/7–2952, Despatch No. 205, Caffery, Cairo to State Department, 29 July 1952, 8 p.m. On this, see also USNRA, RG59, CDF, Box 4015, 774.00/8–552, Despatch No. 629, Holmes, London to State Department, 5 August 1952.

88. USNRA, RG59, CDF, Box 4015, 774.00/8–752, Despatch No. 295, Caffery, Cairo to State Department, 7 August 1952.

89. Ibid. See also USNRA, RG59, CDF, Box 4015, 774.00/8–552, Despatch No. 271, Caffery, Cairo to State Department, 5 August 1952.

90. USNRA, RG59, CDF, Box 4017, 774.00 (W)/8–852, Joint Weekly A, No. 32, Caffery, Cairo to State Department, 8 August 1952.

91. USNRA, RG59, CDF, Box 4015, 774.00/8–1852, Despatch No. 282, Caffery, Cairo to State Department, 18 August 1952. On Caffery's endorsement of the new regime, see also Laila Amin Morsy, "American Support for the 1952 Egyptian Coup: Why?" *Middle Eastern Studies* 31, no. 2 (1995), 307–316 (310–311).

92. Geoffery Aronson, *From Sideshow to Centre Stage: US Policy toward Egypt, 1946–1956* (Boulder, CO: L. Rienner, 1986), 30–46; 60–62. See also Gail E. Meyer, *Egypt and the United States: The Formative Years* (Rutherford, NJ: Fairleigh Dickinson University Press, 1980), 40–46; Barry Rubin, "America and the Egyptian Revolution, 1950–1957," *Political Science Quarterly* 97, no. 1 (1982), 73–90.

93. "A Good Man," *Time,* 8 September 1952.

94. Matthew F. Jacobs, *Imagining the Middle East: The Building of an American Foreign Policy, 1918–1967* (Chapel Hill: University of North Carolina Press, 2011), 8–9, 59–63, 68–70.

95. USNRA, RG59, CDF, Box 4071, 783.00/9–2051, Despatch No. 156, James Leonard (Junior Officer), Embassy Damascus to State Department, 20 September 1951.

96. Little, "Mission Impossible," 670–672.

97. US officials hoped that leaders like Za'im and al-Shishakli might emulate Mustafa Kemal. See USNRA, RG59, CDF, Box 7195, 890D.00/6–1449, Box 7195, Memorandum, "Report on Mr. Alan Dulles' Recent Tour of the Near East," 14 June 1949. See also Box 7194, 890D.00/4–2949, Airgram-123, James Keeley (Ambassador), Embassy Damascus to State Department, 29 April 1949; Box 4072, 783.00/5–552, Despatch No. 650, Cavendish Cannon (Envoy and Minister), Embassy Damascus to State Department, 5 May 1952. See also 783.00/5–2652, Despatch No. 711, William L. Eagleton (Third Secretary), Embassy Damascus to State Department, 26 May 1952.

98. USNRA, RG59, CDF, Box 4015, 774.00/8–152, Despatch No. 217, David K. E. Bruce (Acting Secretary of State, signed also by Acheson), State Department to Cairo, 1 August 1952.

99. Hazem Kandil, *Inside the Brotherhood* (Cambridge, UK: Polity Press, 2015).

100. USNRA, RG59, CDF, Box 4015, 774.00/8–1852, Despatch No. 282, Caffery, Cairo to State Department, 18 August 1952.

101. USNRA, RG59, CDF, Box 4015, 774.00/8–1252, Despatch No. 330, Caffery, Cairo to State Department, 12 August 1952. For similar, see in the same, 774.00/8–1452, Despatch No. 852, Holmes, London to State Department, 14 August 1952.

102. "Acheson to Caffery," 8 September 1952, *FRUS* 1952, vol. IX, pt. 2.

103. For the reaction of leading Free Officers to Acheson's statement, see USNRA, RG59, CDF, Box 4015, 774.00/9–552, Despatch No. 560, Caffery, Cairo to State Department, 5 September 1952.

104. "Telegram from Caffery to US State Department," 11 September 1952, in *BDDE,* vol. 2, 453–455.

105. UKNA FO 371/96896, JE 10345/8, Telegram No. 1370, FO to Stevenson, Cairo, 27 August 1952.

106. UKNA FO 371/96881, JE 1018/362, Minute by Morris, 10 September 1952; "Letter from Sir J. Bowker to Sir R. Stevenson," 11 September 1952, *BDDE,* vol. 2, 450–451.

107. See also USNRA, RG59, CDF, Box 4015, 774.00/9–752, Despatch No. 515, Acheson, State Department to Embassy Cairo, 7 September 1952. The *Times* similarly described the appointment of al-Baquri and the Nationalist Party's Fathi Radwan as "not very encouraging." See "General Naguib Displaces Aly Maher," *Times,* 8 September 1952.

108. UKNA FO 371/96881, JE 1018/380, Telegram No. 10116/24/52, Cairo to FO, 11 September 1952.

109. UKNA FO 371/96881, JE 1018/362, Minute by Sir Roger Allen (Head of Africa Department), FO, 11 September 1952.

110. See, for example, "Minute by Trefor Evans," 13 November 1952, on "Letter from Sir W. Smart (Retired) to Sir J. Bowker on Anglo-American Relations," 11 October 1952. Bowker expressed the same assessment as to the Brotherhood's role. Both in *BDDE,* vol. 2, 467–473.

111. Al-'Ashmawi, *Al-ayam al-hasima,* 85–101; Al-'Ashmawi, *Hisad al-ayam,* 44–47. For slightly different accounts of the same episode (with disagreements on who each side wanted to nominate), see also 'Abd al-Halim, *Al-Ikhwan al-Muslimun III,* 24–26; al-Tilmisani, *Dhikriyat,* 122; 'Allam, *Al-Ikhwan wa ana,* 108; Osman, *Journey in Islamic Thought,* 115.

112. UKNA FO 371/96896, JE 10345/2, No. 1041/2/152/52G, Cresswell, Alexandria to Allen, FO, 27 June 1952; in the same file, JE 10345/16, Telegram No. 1341, Stevenson,

Cairo to FO, 9 September 1952; and "Letter from Sir J. Bowker to Sir R. Stevenson," 11 September 1952, *BDDE,* vol. 2, 450–451.

113. UKNA FO 371/96896, JE 10345/16, Minute by Allen, 10 September 1952, on Telegram No. 1341, Stevenson, Cairo to FO, 9 September 1952.

114. UKNA FO 371/96881, JE 1018/372, Minute by Allen, 12 September 1952. For a similar analysis from Ambassador Stevenson, see FO 371/96896, JE 10345/17, Telegram No. 1345, Stevenson, Cairo to FO, 10 September 1952.

115. "Letter from Sir J. Bowker to Sir R. Stevenson," 11 September 1952, *BDDE,* vol. 2, 450–451.

116. USNRA, RG59, CDF, Box 4015, 774.00/9–752, Despatch No. 515, Acheson, State Department to Embassy Cairo, 7 September 1952.

117. USNRA, RG59, CDF, Box 4015, 774.00/9–852, Despatch No. 1334, Gifford, London to State Department, Despatch No. 1334 from Walter Gifford (Ambassador), Embassy London to State Department, 8 September 1952.

118. USNRA, RG59, CDF, Box 4015, 774.00/9–952, Despatch No. 619, Caffery, Cairo to State Department, 9 September 1952.

119. USNRA, RG59, CDF, Box 4015, 774.00/9–1052, Despatch No. 632, Caffery, Cairo to State Department, 10 September 1952.

120. USNRA, RG59, CDF, Box 4015, 774.00/9–852, Despatch No. 605, Caffery, Cairo to State Department, 8 September 1952.

121. USNRA, RG59, CDF, Box 4015, 774.00/9–1552, Despatch No. 1326, Robert B. Houghton (Second Secretary), Embassy London to State Department, 15 September 1952.

122. "The World Overseas: Power Factors in Egyptian Politics," *Economist,* 20 September 1952.

123. UKNA FO 371/96883, JE 1018/433, Letter 1011/168/52G, Cresswell, Cairo to Allen, FO, 25 October 1952.

124. UKNA FO 371/96883, JE 1018/450, Telegram No. 261, Stevenson, Cairo to FO, 2 December 1952; see also in the same file, Minute by Richard Parsons (FO), 12 December 1952.

125. UKNA FO 371/96883, JE 1018/433, Minute by Morris, 31 October 1952.

126. USNRA, RG59, Box 4015, 774.00/10–752, Despatch No. 164, Houghton, London to State Department, 7 October 1952.

127. UKNA FO 371/96892, JE 1024/1, Telegram No. 1400, Stevenson, Cairo to FO, 19 September 1952; and in the same file, JE 1024/3, Telegram No. 211, Stevenson, Cairo to FO, 20 September 1952. For further evidence of shifting British attitudes, see in the same, JE 1024/3, Minute by Robin C. Mackworth-Young, 27 September 1952, and Minute by Allen, 30 September 1952.

128. UKNA FO 371/96883, JE 1018/450, Telegram No. 261, Stevenson, Cairo to FO, 2 December 1952; see also on the same file, Minute by Parsons, 12 December 1952.

129. UKNA FO 371/102703, JE 1015/35/G, Letter, Cresswell, Cairo to FO, 24 January 1953.

130. USNRA, RG59, CDF, Box 4015, 774.00/9–2752, Despatch No. 544, Caffery, Cairo to State Department, 27 September 1952. See also Box 4017, 774.00 (W)/9–2652, Joint Weekly A, No. 39, Caffery, Cairo to State Department, 26 September 1952.

131. USNRA, RG59, CDF, Box 4015, 774.00/9–2752, "Enclosure: Standish to Sparks, Conversation with Sheikh Al Baquri, Executive Council, Moslem Brotherhood,

26 January 1952," with Despatch No. 544, Caffery, Cairo to State Department, 27 September 1952.

132. USNRA, RG59, CDF, Box 4015, 774.00/10–1052, Despatch No. 651, Caffery, Cairo to State Department, 10 October 1952. For British views of this, see UKNA FO 371/108319, JE 1016/12, "The Moslem Brotherhood (Ikhwan el Muslimin) under the Naguib Regime," February 1954.

133. USNRA, RG59, CDF, Box 4015, 774.00/11–1852, Despatch No. 944, Caffery, Cairo to State Department, 18 November 1952. See also FO 371/96883, JE 1018/442, Chancery Cairo to FO, (10112/26/52), 15 November 1952.

134. USNRA, RG59, CDF, Box 4015, 774.00/9–2752, Despatch No. 544, Caffery, Cairo to State Department, 27 September 1952.

135. USNRA, RG59, CDF, Box 4015, 774.00/10–1552, Despatch No. 685, Robert Mc-Clintock (Counselor of Embassy), Embassy Cairo to State Department, 15 October 1952; HIA, Christina Harris Papers, Accession No. 79085 10.03, Box 2, "Prince Abdel Moneim Sworn in Alone," *Mideast Mirror,* ANA, 18 October 1952. See also al-'Ashmawi, *Al-Ikhwan wa-l-thawra,* 33.

136. USNRA, RG59, CDF, Box 4017, 774.00 (W)/10–1752, Joint Weekly A, No. 42, US Military Attache, Embassy Cairo to State Department, 17 October 1952. See also CREST Database, CIA, "Current Intelligence Bulletin," 16 October 1952.

137. Mitchell, *Society of the Muslim Brothers,* 109.

138. USNRA, RG59, CDF, Box 3681, 774.00/9–952, Despatch No. 141, Henry A. Byroade (Ambassador), Embassy Cairo to State Department, 2 August 1955; UKNA FO 371/108319, JE 1016/12, Memorandum, "The Moslem Brotherhood (Ikhwan el Muslimin) under the Naguib Regime," February 1954.

139. USNRA, RG59, CDF, Box 4015, 774.00/11–1552, Despatch No. 922, Caffery, Cairo to State Department, 15 November 1952.

140. "Enclosure: Memorandum of Conversation, 14 November 1952" with ibid. Ghada Osman's biography of her father Fathi suggests that al-Hudaybi had reservations about the military regime from the start. See Osman, *Journey in Islamic Thought,* 112–113.

141. USNRA, RG59, CDF, Box 4015, 774.00/12–2452, Despatch No. 1248, McClintock, Cairo to State Department, 24 December 1952.

142. "Enclosure: 'Memorandum of Conversation, December 23, 1952," with ibid. See also Hasan al-Hudaybi, "Hatha al-Qur'an," *al-Muslimun* 10 (August 1952).

143. USNRA, CREST Database, CIA, "National Intelligence Digest," 1 November 1952.

144. UKNA FO 371/108319, JE 1016/12, "The Moslem Brotherhood (Ikhwan el Muslimin) under the Naguib Regime," February 1954. See also al-'Ashmawi, *Hisad al-ayam,* 48, 117.

145. UKNA FO 371/96883, JE 1018/447, Telegram No. 1800, Stevenson, Cairo to FO, 6 December 1952.

146. UKNA FO 371/96883, JE 1018/437, Telegram No. 114 (S), Stevenson, Cairo to FO, 4 November 1952; "Muslim Brotherhood Members Freed," *Times,* 14 October 1952; "Amnesty Decree in Egypt," *Times,* 17 October 1952.

147. UKNA FO 371/96883, JE 1018/453, Telegram No. 1833, Stevenson, Cairo to FO, 11 December 1952.

148. UKNA FO 371/96883, JE 1018/463, Telegram No. 265, Stevenson, Cairo to FO, 17 December 1952.

149. Al-'Ashmawi, *Hisad al-ayam,* 52–54.

150. USNRA, RG59, CDF, Box 4015, 774.00/12–1352, Despatch No. 1140, Caffery, Cairo to State Department, 13 December 1952.

151. UKNA FO 371/102703, JE 1018/36, "Memorandum on Recent Developments in the Internal Political Situation Up to January 15th, 1953," Embassy Cairo to FO, 16 January 1953; FO 371/96883, JE 1018/448, Telegram No. 1804, Stevenson, Cairo to FO, 6 December 1952.

152. USNRA, RG59, CDF, Box 4015, 774.00/11–2152, Despatch No. 1268, Caffery, Cairo to State Department, 21 November 1952.

153. USNRA, RG59, CDF, Box 4016, 774.00/1–1553, Despatch No. 1645, Caffery, Cairo to State Department, 15 January 1953.

154. USNRA, RG59, CDF, Box 4016, 774.00/5–2353, Despatch No. 2534, G. Lewis Jones (Charge d'Affaires), Embassy Cairo to State Department, 23 May 1953.

155. UKNA FO 371/102703, JE 1015/18, Telegram No. 103, Stevenson, Cairo to FO, 17 January 1953.

156. Al-'Ashmawi, *Al-Ikhwan wa-l-thawra,* 33–34.

157. USNRA, RG59, CDF, Box 4016, 774.00/1–1753, Despatch No. 1686, Caffery, Cairo to State Department, 17 January 1953.

158. USNRA, RG59, CDF, Box 4016, 774.00/1–2753, Memorandum by Nestor Ortiz (NEA) to Stephen Dorsey (NEA), 27 January 1953.

159. USNRA, RG59, CDF, Box 4016, 774.00/7–653, Despatch No. 45, Caffery, Cairo to State Department, 6 July 1953.

160. USNRA, RG59, CDF, Box 4016, 774.00/3–353, Despatch No. 1773, Caffery, Cairo to State Department, 3 March 1953; FO 371/102703, JE 1015/36, "Memorandum on Recent Developments in the Internal Political Situation Up to January 15th, 1953," Embassy Cairo to FO, 16 January 1953.

161. FO 371/108319, JE 1016/12, "The Moslem Brotherhood (Ikhwan el Muslimin) under the Naguib Regime," February 1954.

162. 'Abd al-Halim, *Al-Ikhwan al-Muslimun III,* 26–27.

163. El-Sadat, *In Search of Identity,* 124.

164. Mitchell, *Society of the Muslim Brothers,* 109–112.

165. USNRA, RG59, CDF, Box 4016, 774.00/1–2653, Despatch No. 1488, Caffery, Cairo to State Department, 26 January 1953.

166. USNRA, RG59, CDF, Box 4016, 774.00/2–2453, Despatch No. 1708, Caffery, Cairo to State Department, 24 February 1953. This document also contains further details on the organization of the Liberation Rally.

167. UKNA FO 371/102703, JE 1015/35/G, Letter, Cresswell, Cairo to FO, 24 January 1953. See also FO 371/96883, JE 1018/448, Telegram No. 1804, Stevenson, Cairo to FO, 6 December 1952; and for the US view, USNRA, RG59, CDF, Box 4015, 774.00/11–1852, Despatch No. 954, Caffery, Cairo to State Department, 18 November 1952; and 774.00/12–1152, Despatch No. 1414, Caffery, Cairo to State Department, 11 December 1952.

168. USNRA, RG59, CDF, Box 4016, 774.00/3–2653, Despatch No. 1959, Caffery, Cairo to State Department, 26 March 1953.

169. Ibid. For a slightly different view, see 774.00/4–1753, Despatch No. 2176, Caffery, Cairo to State Department, 17 April 1953, which described Nasser as "Naguib's principal lieutenant" and tended to stress the popularity of the latter. Naguib was said to enjoy a

position akin to Mustafa al-Nahas or Sa'd Zaghlul, with his name on "on every tongue." The regime as a whole was thought to be "firmly entrenched."

170. USNRA, RG59, CDF, Box 4016, 774.00/5–1853, Despatch No. 2471, Caffery, Cairo to State Department, 18 May 1953.

171. UKNA FO 371/102845, JE 11913/11, Minute by Selwyn Lloyd (Minister), FO, 15 June 1953.

172. UKNA FO 371/102803, JE 1192/160, Minute by S. Lloyd, FO, 30 March 1953. A few months earlier, by contrast, the British had believed that Nasser led a faction opposed to Naguib "in his desire to reach a general settlement." See FO 371/96883, JE 1018/448, Telegram No. 1804, Stevenson, Cairo to FO, 6 December 1952.

173. USNRA, RG59, CDF, Box 4016, 774.00/1–2753, Memorandum by Ortiz to Dorsey, 27 January 1953; 774.00/2–1053, Memorandum by Ortiz to Dorsey, 10 February 1953; Raymond Daniell, "Eden to Press U.S. for Unity on Egypt," *New York Times*, 21 February 1953.

174. Thornhill, *Road to Suez*, 131.

175. USNRA, CREST Database, CIA, "Summary of National Intelligence Estimate 76," 25 March 1953.

176. UKNA FO 371/102803, JE 1192/135/G, Letter, President Eisenhower, Washington to Eden, London, 16 March 1953. As previously, US pressure on the British was not well received, with officials complaining bitterly about the "flagrant . . . lack of Anglo-American solidarity." See in the same file, JE 1192/155/G, Letter, Cresswell, Cairo to Allen, FO, 19 March 1953; and also "Minute by Roger Allen," 23 March 1953, in *BDDE*, vol. 3, 23.

177. USNRA, RG59, CDF, Box 4016, 774.00/2–2553, Despatch No. 1725, Caffery, Cairo to State Department, 25 February 1953.

178. USNRA, RG59, CDF, Box 4016, 774.00/2–353, Despatch No. 1773, Caffery, Cairo to State Department, 3 March 1953.

179. Thornhill, *Road to Suez*, 66, 125–127; Peter L. Hahn, *The United States, Great Britain, and Egypt, 1945–1956: Strategy and Diplomacy in the Early Cold War* (London: University of North Carolina Press, 1991), 161–162; William Roger Louis, *Ends of British Imperialism: The Scramble for Empire, Suez and Decolonization* (London: I. B. Tauris, 2006), 609–617. For an example of Churchill's uncompromising stance, see "Telegram No. 12 from Churchill to Eden," 15 January 1953, *BDDE*, vol. 3, 549.

180. Robert Doty, "London-Cairo Talks on Suez Broken Off," *New York Times*, 7 May 1953. See also UKNA FO 371/102810, JE 1192/345, Marginal Note by WSC (Winston Churchill), 31 May 1953, written on the covering brief, PM/WS/53/186, W. Strang to Prime Minister, 30 May 1956; and Aronson, *From Sideshow to Centre Stage*, 63–64.

181. "Note by RMA Hankey," 22 May 1953, *BDDE*, vol. 3, 53–54.

182. UKNA FO 371/102704, JE 1015/77, Telegram No. 121 (1011/41/53), Stevenson, Cairo, to Churchill, FO, 21 May 1953.

183. USNRA, RG59, CDF, Box 4016, 774.00/5–2353, Letter from Jones, Cairo, to Parker Hart, Director of Office of Near-Eastern Affairs, State Department, 23 May 1953. See also CREST Database, CIA, "NSC Briefing, 'The Situation in Egypt,'" 20 May 1953.

184. Al-'Ashmawi, *Al-ayam al-hasima*, 116–126. See also al-'Ashmawi, *Al-Ikhwan wa-l-thawra*, 26–27.

185. "The Egyptian Situation: Report by the JIC, Middle East to the Commanders-in-Chief Committee, Middle East," 1 and 10 June 1953, *BDDE*, vol. 3, 54–56.

186. UKNA FO 371/102704, JE 1015/77, Telegram No. 121 (1011/41/53), Stevenson, Cairo, to Churchill, FO, 21 May 1953. See also in the same file, JE 1015/76, FO Minute by Mackworth-Young to the Prime Minister, 21 May 1953.

187. UKNA FO 371/102810, JE 1192/345, Joint Intelligence Committee, Middle East, "The Egyptian Situation," JIC (ME 53)–38 (Final), 18 May 1953.

188. Shadi, *Safahat min al-tarikh,* 262–264.

189. USNRA, RG59, CDF, Box 4017, 774.00 (W)/5-1553, Joint Weekly A, No. 20, US Military Attaché, Cairo to State Department, 15 May 1953.

190. USNRA, RG59, CDF, Box 4016, 774.00/8–853, Despatch No. 2711, Caffery, Cairo to State Department, 8 June 1953.

191. "Cairo Fears Rising over British Acts," *New York Times,* 15 July 1953.

192. USNRA, CREST Database, CIA, "NSC Briefing, 'The Situation in Egypt,'" 20 May 1953.

193. USNRA, RG59, CDF, Box 4016, 774.00/5–2353, Letter from Jones, Cairo to Hart, State Department, 23 May 1953.

194. "Memorandum by Cresswell to Allen at FO," 26 March 1953, *BDDE,* vol. 3, 28–30; UKNA FO 371/102803, JE 1192/137G, No. JIC (ME) (53)—23 (Final), BMEO [British Middle East Office], Fayid to Allen, FO, 21 March 1953.

195. UKNA FO 371/102869, JE 1202/7, War Office, Orbat/MI.4 (b)/13, "Redeployment of Egyptian Army," 14 May 1953.

196. USNRA, RG59, CDF, Box 4016, 774.00/6–1953, Despatch No. 2602, Caffery, Cairo to State Department, 19 June 1953.

197. Robert Doty, "Hope of Suez Pact Is Rising in Egypt," *New York Times,* 8 June 1953; "Concession by Britain May Solve Suez Dispute," *New York Times,* 20 July 1953; UKNA FO 371/102732, JE 10345/18, Telegram No. 1473, Sir Roger Makins (Ambassador), Embassy Washington to FO, 11 July 1953.

198. Clifton Daniel, "British Commandos Embark as Egyptian Tension Mounts," *New York Times,* 13 May 1953; Kennett Love, "British Marines Reach Suez Zone," *New York Times,* 15 May 1953.

199. "Cabinet Conclusions: Egypt," 14 May 1953, *BDDE,* vol. 3., 48. For the JIC report, see UKNA FO 371/102810, JE 1192/345, Joint Intelligence Committee, Middle East, "The Egyptian Situation," JIC (ME 53)–38 (Final), 18 May 1953.

200. See, for example, the material in UKNA FO 371/102869, JE 1202/4 on Wilhelm Voss from February 1953; and USNRA, RG59, CDF, Box 4016, 774.00/7–2153, Despatch No. 215, Embassy Paris to State Department, 21 July 1953, on the role of former SS Chief Otto Skorzeny, who was said to be helping train Egyptian commando units.

201. Robert Doty, "Naguib Backs Use of German Aides," *New York Times,* 20 May 1953.

202. UKNA FO 371/102810, JE 1192/345, Joint Intelligence Committee, Middle East, "The Egyptian Situation," JIC (ME 53)–38 (Final), 18 May 1953; and FO 371/102869, JE 1202/15/G, Minute by Bowker, 5 August 1953.

203. UKNA FO 371/102869, JE 1202/15/G, Telegram No. 163, Robin Hankey, Cairo to the Marquess of Salisbury (Acting Foreign Secretary), FO, 20 July 1953, and Enclosure Report on "Para-mil Organisations," EA/36 G (Int), May 1953. The numbers are confusing. Hankey's telegram gives the figures mentioned here; the military report speaks only of six thousand Brotherhood fighters. For more on the difficulty of estimating precise numbers,

see FO 371/102869, JE 1202/26/G, Despatch No. 10121/3/53G, Embassy Cairo to FO, 16 September 1953.

204. UKNA FO 371/102810, JE 1192/345, Joint Intelligence Committee, Middle East, "The Egyptian Situation," JIC (ME 53)–38 (Final), 18 May 1953; FO 371/102869, JE 1202/15/G, Telegram No. 163, Hankey, Cairo to Salisbury, FO, 20 July 1953, and Enclosure Report on "Para-mil Organisations," EA/36 G (Int), May 1953.

205. UKNA FO 371/102810, JE 1192/342, Telegram No. 136 (S), Stevenson, Cairo to FO, 5 June 1953.

206. According to Joel Gordon, Evans's assistant, Sir John Wilton, later told him that it was now possible, for the first time, to meet the Brotherhood openly. See Gordon, *Nasser's Blessed Movement*, 216, n36.

207. Al-'Ashmawi, *Al-ayam al-hasima*, 107; al-Tilmisani, *Dhikriyat*, 130–131, 140.

208. Shadi, *Safahat min al-tarikh*, 258–260. See also 'Abd al-Halim, *Al-Ikhwan al-Muslimun III*, 28–29.

209. Al-'Ashmawi, *Al-Ikhwan wa-l-thawra*, 36–37. A more hostile account of these meetings is offered in 'Allam, *Al-Ikhwan wa ana*, 81–85, where it is claimed that the meetings were held behind the backs of the CCR—and even without the knowledge of most other senior Brotherhood members.

210. Al-'Ashmawi, *Al-ayam al-hasima*, 108–109.

211. Al-'Ashmawi, *Al-Ikhwan wa-l-thawra*, 37.

212. Zollner, *Muslim Brotherhood*, 31; Mitchell, *Society of the Muslim Brothers*, 112–114; 'Abdallah Imam takes the view that the Brothers did indeed undercut the government position on the question of the British retaining use of the base. See Imam, *'Abd al-Nasir*, 55.

213. 'Allam, *Al-Ikhwan wa ana*, 89–90.

214. USNRA, RG59, CDF, Box 4016, 774.00/4–2953, Despatch No. 2290, Caffery, Cairo to State Department, 29 April 1953.

215. USNRA, RG59, CDF, Box 4016, 774.00/5–2753, Memorandum of Conversation, State Department, 27 May 1953.

216. USNRA, RG59, CDF, Box 4016, 774.00/5–2853, Memorandum of Conversation, State Department, 28 May 1953; 774.00/6–453, Memorandum of Conversation, State Department, 4 June 1953. Again, this meeting was cited as evidence of Brotherhood duplicity and betrayal of Egypt's national cause, in 'Allam, *Al-Ikhwan wa ana*, 90–91.

217. USNRA, RG59, CDF, Box 4016, 774.00/6–553, Despatch No. 2687, Caffery, Cairo to State Department, 5 June 1953.

218. For more on this conference, see Chapter 6.

219. For Ramadan, see Hasan Dawh, *25 'aman fi jama'at al-ikhwan* (Cairo: Dar al-'Itisam, 1983), 19–20; Hathut, *Al-'aqd al-farid*, 18.

220. USNRA, RG59, CDF, Box 2485, 511.80/7–2753, Despatch No. 237, Caffery, Cairo to State Department, 27 July 1953; Ian Johnson, *A Mosque in Munich: Nazis, the CIA and the Rise of the Muslim Brotherhood in the West* (Boston: Houghton Mifflin Harcourt, 2010), 113–116.

221. HIA, Richard Paul Mitchell Collection, Accession No. 77076–8M.50, Box 3, "Said Ramadhan: 'Facts about the Muslim Brotherhood,'" submitted to the Colloquium on Islamic Culture Held in the United States between September 8–19, 1953." The full text of

Ramadan's remarks is also available in successive editions of *al-Muslimun,* February–May 1954.

222. UKNA FO 371/108319, JE 1016/19, No. 1781/8/54, Embassy Washington to FO, 26 October 1954. As a London official wryly noted (see minutes of same file), the Washington Embassy had sent in this dispatch "just a year late!"

223. "Muslim Brotherhood Leader Explains Its Aims and Activities," *Middle East Report* 6, no. 3 (2 October 1953), copy in UKNA FO 371/108319, JE 1016/19.

224. USNRA, RG59, CDF, Box 4016, 774.00/6–2353, Despatch No. 2849, Caffery, Cairo to State Department, 23 June 1953.

225. USNRA, RG59, CDF, Box 4016, 774.00/7–2953, Despatch No. 271, Caffery, Cairo to State Department, 29 July 1953.

226. USNRA, RG59, CDF, Box 4016, 774.00/7–2053, Despatch No. 173, Caffery, Cairo to State Department, 20 July 1953.

227. USNRA, RG59, CDF, Box 4016, 774.00/8–553, Despatch No. 318, Caffery, Cairo to State Department, 5 August 1953.

228. For more on the parade in question, see USNRA, RG59, CDF, Box 4016, 774.00/7–2453, Despatch No. 127, Caffery, Cairo to State Department, 24 July 1953, and 774.00/7–2553, Despatch No. 233, Caffery, Cairo to State Department, 25 July 1953.

229. USNRA, RG59, CDF, Box 4016, 774.00/8–553, Despatch No. 318, Caffery, Cairo to State Department, 5 August 1953, and especially "Enclosure: Memorandum of Conversation, July 27, 1953." This meeting is another that is used by 'Allam to highlight Brotherhood perfidy—especially given al-Hudaybi's comments regarding Nasser. See 'Allam, *Al-Ikhwan wa ana,* 94–97.

230. USNRA, RG59, CDF, Box 4016, 774.00/8–853, Despatch No. 318, Caffery, Cairo to State Department, 5 August 1953, especially "Enclosure: Memorandum of Conversation, July 27, 1953."

231. UKNA FO 371/102706, JE 1015/123, Telegram No. 1012/18/53, Hankey, Cairo, to Allen, FO, 31 August 1953.

232. UKNA FO 371/102706, JE 1015/123, Minute by Mackworth-Young, 15 September 1953; and Minute by Allen, 17 September 1953.

233. UKNA FO 371/102869, JE 1202/24, Letter, Captain M. Maude, War Office, to Mackworth-Young, FO, MI4 (G)/510, 4 September 1953, including "Enclosure: Egyptian Para-Military Forces," EA/36 G(INT), 24 August 1953.

234. For an example of their hard-line stance, see USNRA, RG59, CDF, Box 4016, 774.00/7–2453, Despatch No. 223, Caffery, Cairo to State Department, 24 July 1953.

235. USNRA, RG59, CDF, Box 4016, 774.00/10–3153, Despatch No. 1090, Caffery, Cairo to State Department, 31 October 1953.

236. HIA, Richard Paul Mitchell Collection, Accession No. 77076–8M.50, Box 3, "Les Frères musulmans sont prêts à se battre pour la liberation de l'Egypte," *Le Monde,* 4 November 1953.

237. UKNA FO 371/102706, JE 1015/123, Telegram No. 1012/18/53, Hankey, Cairo, to Allen, FO, 31 August 1953; FO 371/108319, JE 1016/12, "The Moslem Brotherhood (Ikhwan el Muslimin) under the Naguib Regime," February 1954.

238. USNRA, RG59, CDF, Box 4016, 774.00/6–1953, Despatch No. 2602, from Embassy Cairo to State Department, 19 June 1953; 774.00/9–1253, Despatch No. 720, Caffery, Cairo to State Department, 12 September 1953.

239. UKNA FO 371/102706, JE 1015/133, Telegram No. 210, Hankey, Cairo to Salisbury, FO, 3 October 1953, and especially, Minute by Trefor E. Evans, "Internal Politics in Egypt," 29 September 1953.

240. UKNA FO 371/102706, JE 1015/123, Telegram No. 1012/18/53, Hankey, Cairo, to Allen, FO, 31 August 1953.

241. USNRA, RG59, CDF, Box 4016, 774.00/8–1153, Despatch No. 386, Caffery, Cairo to State Department, 11 August 1953.

242. USNRA, RG59, CDF, Box 4016, 774.00/8–2253, Despatch No. 487, Caffery, Cairo to State Department, 22 August 1953; 774.00/9–1953, Despatch No. 770, Caffery, Cairo to State Department, 19 September 1953. See also 774.00/9–2153, Despatch No. 345, Caffery, Cairo to State Department, 21 September 1953, and 774.00/9–2553, Despatch No. 821, Caffery, Cairo to State Department, 25 September 1953; 774.00/11–1353, Despatch No. 1190, Caffery, Cairo to State Department, 13 November 1953; 774.00/11–2553, Despatch No. 1296, Caffery, Cairo to State Department, 25 November 1953.

243. "Death Sentence on Abdel Hadi," *Times,* 2 October 1953; USNRA, RG59, CDF, Box 4017, 774.00 (W)/10–353, Joint Weekly A, No. 40, Military Attaché, Cairo to State Department, 3 October 1953. Al-Hadi's sentence was later commuted to fifteen years in prison.

244. USNRA, RG59, CDF, Box 4016, 774.00/11–1453, Despatch No. 1191, Caffery, Cairo to State Department, 14 November 1953.

245. USNRA, RG59, CDF, Box 4016, 774.00/11–353, Despatch No. 1097, Caffery, Cairo to State Department, 3 November 1953.

246. USNRA, RG59, CDF, Box 4016, 774.00/10–2653, Despatch No. 1047, Caffery, Cairo to State Department, 26 October 1953.

247. USNRA, RG59, CDF, Box 4016, 774.00/11–2353, Despatch No. 1281, Caffery, Cairo to State Department, 23 November 1953.

248. USNRA, RG59, CDF, Box 4016, 774.00 (W)/11–2853, Joint Weekly A, No. 48, Military Attaché, Cairo to State Department, 28 November 1953.

249. UKNA, FO 371/102704, JE 1015/51, Telegram No. 67 (S), Stevenson, Cairo to FO, 17 March 1953.

250. UKNA, FO 371/102704, JE 1015/51, Telegram No. 68 (S), Stevenson, Cairo to FO, 19 March 1953; and in the same file, Minute by Parsons, 21 March 1953.

251. USNRA, RG59, CDF, Box 4016, 774.00/8–1753, Despatch No. 442, Caffery, Cairo to State Department, 17 August 1953.

252. USNRA, RG59, CDF, Box 4016, 774.00/9–1953, Despatch No. 769, Caffery, Cairo to State Department, 19 September 1953.

253. UKNA FO 371/102706, JE 1015/129, Telegram No. 1012/22/53, Charles Duke, Embassy Cairo to Allen, FO, 17 September 1953. See also in same file, JE 1015/132, Telegram No. 1011/96/53, Duke, Cairo to Richard Ledward, FO, 28 September 1953.

254. UKNA FO 371/108319, JE 1016/12, "The Moslem Brotherhood (Ikhwan el Muslimin) under the Naguib Regime," February 1954. See also Mitchell, *Society of the Muslim Brothers,* 120.

255. USNRA, RG59, CDF, Box 4016, 774.00/10–2653, Despatch No. 1047, Caffery, Cairo to State Department, 26 October 1953.

256. UKNA FO 371/102706, JE 1015/146, Telegram No. 1012/34/53, Embassy Cairo to FO, 5 November 1953.

257. Minute by Mackworth-Young, 19 November 1953, in ibid. The same file also contains the relevant Arab News Agency reports dated 28 November 1953.

258. Shadi, *Safahat min al-tarikh*, 99–111. For contemporary accounts of this episode, see the report by the Arab News Agency in UKNA FO 371/102706, JE 1015/146, Telegram No. 1012/34/53, Embassy Cairo to FO, 5 November 1953; in the same file, JE 1015/150, Telegram No. 1012/3/53G, Embassy Cairo to FO, 14 December 1953; and FO 371/108319, JE 1016/12, "The Moslem Brotherhood (Ikhwan el Muslimin) under the Naguib Regime," February 1954. See also USNRA, CREST Database, CIA Information Report, "Crisis in the Moslem Brotherhood," Undated; RG59, CDF, Box 4017, 774.00 (W)/12–453, Joint Weekly A, No. 49, Military Attaché, Cairo to State Department, 4 December 1953; 774.00 (W)/12–1853, Joint Weekly A, No. 51, Military Attaché, Cairo to State Department, 18 December 1953. For scholarly accounts, see Zollner, *Muslim Brotherhood*, 32–33; Mitchell, *Society of the Muslim Brothers*, 116–125.

259. Shadi, *Safahat min al-tarikh*, 99–111. See also 'Abd al-Halim, *Al-Ikhwan al-Muslimun III*, 30; Osman, *Journey in Islamic Thought*, 122–124; al-Tilmisani, *Dhikriyat*, 135–136.

260. Tertius gaudens literally means "the rejoicing third," that is, the beneficiary of a conflict between two other parties. UKNA FO 371/102706, JE 1015/150, Telegram No. 1012/3/53G, Embassy Cairo to FO, 14 December 1953.

261. UKNA FO 371/108319, JE 1016/1, Telegram No. 1012/5/53G, Embassy Cairo to FO, 30 December 1953.

262. Minute by Morris, 4 January 1954, in ibid. On this, see also Gordon, *Nasser's Blessed Movement*, 103–105.

263. UKNA FO 371/102706, JE 1015/140, Memorandum by Capt. Hardie, "The Muslim Brotherhood," included with Despatch No. M14B/416/53, Major Maude, War Office to Mackworth-Young, FO, 13 October 1953.

264. Ishaq Musa Husayni, *The Moslem Brethren: The Greatest of Modern Islamic Movements* (Beirut: Khayat, 1956).

265. UKNA FO 371/102706, JE 1015/140, Memorandum by Hardie, "The Muslim Brotherhood," included with Despatch No. M14B/416/53, Maude, War Office to Mackworth-Young, FO, 13 October 1953.

266. UKNA FO 371/102706, JE 1015/133, Telegram No. 210, Hankey, Cairo, to Salisbury, FO, 3 October 1953.

267. USNRA, RG59, CDF, Box 4016, 774.00/6–1953, Despatch No. 2603, Caffery, Cairo to State Department, 19 June 1953. For more on the changes, see 774.00/6–2453, Despatch No. 2630, Caffery, Cairo to State Department, 24 June 1953.

268. USNRA, CREST Database, CIA, "Current Intelligence Weekly, 'Egyptian Army Discontent with Military Regime's Leadership,'" 31 July 1954. For a similar verdict on the growing dominance of Nasser, see RG59, CDF, Box 4016, 774.00/6–2653, Despatch No. 2642, Caffery, Cairo to State Department, 26 June 1953.

269. See the exchange of views reflected in the following: "Minute by Churchill to Eden," 28 December 1953, *BDDE*, vol. 3, 166–167; "Draft Minute (Reply) by Eden to Churchill," 28 December 1953, *BDDE*, vol. 3, 167; "Egypt Cabinet Conclusions," 22 March 1954, *BDDE*, vol. 3, 242–243.

270. Ahmed Abdalla, *The Student Movement and National Politics in Egypt, 1923–1973* (London: Saqi Books, 1985), 119–123. For contemporary accounts also mentioning the role

of Safavi, see "Egypt Bans Fanatic Unit," *Baltimore Sun,* 14 January 1954, and UKNA FO 371/108319, JE 1016/2, Telegram No. 54, Stevenson, Cairo to FO, 13 January 1954.

271. Dawh, *25 'aman,* 57–58. See also Abbas Hasan al-Sisi, *Fi qafilat al-Ikhwan al-Muslimun: al-juz' al-thani* (Alexandria, Egypt: Dar al-Taba'a wa-l-Nashr wa-l-Sutiyat, 1987), 159–160; al-Tilmisani, *Dhikriyat,* 131.

272. Shadi, *Safahat min al-tarikh,* 164–165.

273. Al-Qaradawi, *al-Ikhwan al-Muslimun,* 245–246.

274. For a lengthy overview, see UKNA WO (War Office) 208/3961, "HQ BTE Intelligence Summary, No. 3/54, For Week Ending 16 January, 1954." See also "Many Arrests in Egypt," *Times,* 14 January 1954; Mitchell, *Society of the Muslim Brothers,* 126–127.

275. USNRA, RG59, CDF, Box 4016a, 774.00/1–1554, Despatch No. 1658, Caffery, Cairo to State Department, 15 January 1954, and especially, "Enclosure: 'Moslem Brotherhood Dissolved: Command Council Reveals Efforts to Usurp Power,' *Egyptian Gazette,* 15 January 1954." See also UKNA FO 371/108319, JE 1016/4, Telegram No. 61, Stevenson, Cairo to FO, 16 January 1954; Imam, *'Abd al-Nasir,* 64–73.

276. USNRA, RG59, CDF, Box 4016a, 774.00/1–1854, Despatch No. 1676, Caffery, Cairo to State Department, 18 January 1954, and especially, "Enclosure: 'Ministry of National Guidance Statement.'" For more on the al-'Ashmawi arms case, see also 774.00/1–1954, Despatch No. 1700, Caffery, Cairo to State Department, 19 January 1954.

277. USNRA, RG59, CDF, Box 4016a, 774.00/1–1954, Despatch No. 1700, Caffery, Cairo to State Department, 19 January 1954; "Arms Dump Found in Egypt," *Times,* 18 January 1954.

278. "Many Arrests in Egypt," *Times,* 14 January 1954.

279. UKNA FO 371/108319, JE 1016/3, Telegram No. 58, Stevenson, Cairo to FO, 14 January 1954.

280. UKNA FO 371/108319, JE 1016/5, Telegram No. 67, Stevenson, Cairo to FO, 16 January 1954.

281. UKNA FO 371/108375, JE1056/1G, Letter, Paul Mason, FO to Stevenson, Cairo, 23 January 1954; and in the same file, JE1056/4G, Telegram No. 1011/3/54G, Stevenson, Cairo, to Allen, FO, 10 February 1954.

282. UKNA FO 371/108319, JE 1016/5, Telegram No. 67, Stevenson, Cairo to FO, 16 January 1954.

283. UKNA WO 208/3961, "HQ BTE Intelligence Summary, No. 3/54, for Week Ending 16 January, 1954." It was al-Nuqrashi's government, not that of the Wafd, which proscribed the Ikhwan in 1948. See Chapter 3.

284. UKNA WO 208/3961, "HQ BTE Intelligence Summary, No. 3/54, for Week Ending 16 January, 1954"; and also in same, "HQ BTE Intelligence Summary, No. 4/54, for Week Ending 23 January, 1954"; "HQ BTE Intelligence Summary, No. 6/54, for Week Ending 6 February, 1954"; and "HQ BTE Intelligence Summary, No. 7/54, for Week Ending 13 February, 1954."

285. USNRA, CREST Database, CIA, "NSC Briefing, 'Moslem Brotherhood Threat in Egypt,'" 21 January 1954; CIA, Office of Current Intelligence, "Current Intelligence Bulletin," 17 January 1954. See also CIA, Office of Current Intelligence, "Current Intelligence Bulletin," 15 January 1954.

286. USNRA, RG59, CDF, Box 4016a, 774.00/1–1554, Despatch No. 1658, Caffery, Cairo to State Department, 15 January 1954.

287. USNRA, CREST Database, CIA, "NSC Briefing, 'Moslem Brotherhood Threat in Egypt,'" 21 January 1954; CIA, Office of Current Intelligence, "Current Intelligence Bulletin," 17 January 1954. See also CIA Office of Current Intelligence, "Current Intelligence Bulletin," 15 January 1954.

288. UKNA FO 371/108319, JE 1016/10, Telegram No. 23 (S), Stevenson, Cairo to FO, 25 January 1954.

289. UKNA FO 371/108319, JE 1016/8, Telegram No. 13 (S), Stevenson, Cairo to FO, 19 January 1954. Those arrested were: al-Hudaybi, 'Abdin, Husayn Kamal al-Din, 'Abd al-Aziz Attiya, al-Farghali, and Khamis Humayda.

290. USNRA, RG59, CDF, Box 4016a, 774.00/1–1654, "Enclosure: 'Summary from MENA re: Hudaibi,'" with Despatch No. 1672, Caffery, Cairo to State Department, 16 January 1954.

291. The same "pilgrimmage" also had been made in 1953. See Mitchell, *Society of the Muslim Brothers,* 111, 127.

292. USNRA, RG59, CDF, Box 4016a, 774.00/1–2654, Despatch No. 837, Caffery, Cairo to State Department, 26 January 1954.

293. USNRA, RG59, CDF, Box 4016a, 774.00/1–3054, Despatch No. 1804, Caffery, Cairo to State Department, 30 January 1954.

294. UKNA FO 371/108319, JE 1016/11, Despatch No. 1011/5/54, Embassy Cairo to FO, 15 February 1954.

295. For a detailed overview of this crisis, see Gordon, *Nasser's Blessed Movement,* 118–137.

296. UKNA FO 371/108327, JE 1018/3, Telegram No. 261, Stevenson, Cairo to FO, 25 February 1954; JE 1018/5, Telegram No. 272, Stevenson, Cairo to FO, 26 February 1954; and JE 1018/9, Telegram No. 284, Stevenson, Cairo to FO, 26 February 1954. See also USNRA, RG59, CDF, Box 4016a, 774.00/2–2654, Despatch No. 2053, Caffery, Cairo to State Department, 26 February 1954.

297. UKNA FO 371/108327, JE 1018/3, Telegram No. 261, Stevenson, Cairo to FO, 25 February 1954.

298. UKNA FO 371/108327, JE 1018/16, Minute by Mackworth-Young, 25 February 1954.

299. "The Colonel Emerges," *Times,* 26 February 1954.

300. USNRA, RG59, CDF, Box 4017, 774.00 (W)/2–2654, Joint Weekly A, No. 8, Military Attaché, Cairo to State Department, 26 February 1954.

301. USNRA, RG59, CDF, Box 4016a, 774.00/2–2654, Despatch No. 963, Caffery, Cairo to State Department, 26 February 1954. For more on the breach with Naguib, see also, in the same, 774.00/2–2754, Despatch No. 2066, Caffery, Cairo to State Department, 27 February 1954.

302. UKNA FO 371/108327, JE 1018/10, Telegram No. 287, Stevenson, Cairo to FO, 27 February 1954, and JE 1018/11, Telegram No. 288, Stevenson, Cairo to FO, 27 February 1954; USNRA, RG59, CDF, Box 4016a, 774.00/2–2754, Despatch No. 986, Caffery, Cairo to State Department, 27 February 1954.

303. USNRA, RG59, CDF, Box 4016a, 774.00/2–2854, Despatch No. 996, Caffery, Cairo to State Department, 28 February 1954, and 774.00/2–2854, Despatch No. 1001, Caffery, Cairo to State Department, 28 February 1954.

304. USNRA, RG59, CDF, Box 4016a, 774.00/3–254, Despatch No. 1022, Caffery, Cairo to State Department, 2 March 1954.

305. UKNA FO 371/108327, JE 1018/18, Telegram No. 297, Stevenson, Cairo to FO, 1 March 1954.

306. USNRA, RG59, CDF, Box 4016a, 774.00/2–2854, Despatch No. 1001, Caffery, Cairo to State Department, 28 February 1954; and 774.00/2–2854, Despatch No. 1002, Caffery, Cairo to State Department, 28 February 1954, 8 p.m.

307. USNRA, RG59, CDF, Box 4016a, 774.00/2–2854, Despatch No. 1002, Caffery, Cairo to State Department, 28 February 1954, 8 p.m.; CREST Database, CIA Office of Current Intelligence, "Current Intelligence Bulletin," 2 March 1954.

308. USNRA, RG59, CDF, Box 4016a, 774.00/3–154, Despatch No. 1003, Caffery, Cairo to State Department, 1 March 1954.

309. USNRA, RG59, CDF, Box 4016a, 774.00/3–154, Despatch No. 1010, Caffery, Cairo to State Department, 1 March 1954; 774.00/3–154, Despatch No. 2075, Caffery, Cairo to State Department, 1 March 1954; UKNA FO 371/108327, JE 1018/22, Telegram No. 307, Stevenson, Cairo to FO, 3 March 1954; 'Abd al-Halim, *Al-Ikhwan al-Muslimun III*, 31.

310. USNRA, RG59, CDF, Box 4016a, 774.00/3–354, Despatch No. 1025, Caffery, Cairo to State Department, 3 March 1954; see also UKNA FO 371/108327, JE 1018/21, Telegram No. 44 (S), Stevenson, Cairo to FO, 1 March 1954.

311. USNRA, RG59, CDF, Box 4017, 774.00 (W)/3–954, Joint Weekly A, No. 9, Military Attaché, Cairo to State Department, 9 March 1954; CREST Database, CIA, "NSC Briefing, 'The Egyptian Situation,'" 2 March 1954. See also in the CREST Database, CIA, "Current Intelligence Weekly, 'Egyptian Regime Shaken by Crisis over Nagib,'" 5 March 1954; CIA, "NSC Briefing, 'The Egyptian Situation,'" 10 March 1954.

312. UKNA FO 371/108316, JE 1015/12, Telegram No. 68, Stevenson, Cairo to FO, 15 March 1954.

313. USNRA, RG59, CDF, Box 4016a, 774.00/3–654, Despatch No. 1055, Caffery, Cairo to State Department, 6 March 1954.

314. USNRA, RG59, CDF, Box 4016a, 774.00/3–1354, Despatch No. 2180, Caffery, Cairo to State Department, 13 March 1954.

315. "Enclosure: 'Memorandum of Conversation, March 10, 1954,'" in ibid.

316. USNRA, RG59, CDF, Box 4016a, 774.00/3–1454, Despatch No. 1098, Caffery, Cairo to State Department, 14 March 1954. See also in the same box, 774.00/3–2554, Despatch No. 2291, C. Robert Payne, Embassy Cairo to State Department, 25 March 1954, and especially, "Enclosure: 'Memorandum of Conversation, March 16, 1954.'"

317. UKNA FO 371/108316, JE 1015/29, "Enclosure: Summary of Events, March 11–April 15," included with Telegram No. 90, Stevenson, Cairo to FO, 15 April 1954.

318. Hasan al-'Ashmawi, *Al-Ikhwan wa-l-thawra*, 55–57; Shadi, *Safahat min al-tarikh*, 367–368.

319. USNRA, RG59, CDF, Box 4016a, 774.00/3–2354, Despatch No. 2262, Caffery, Cairo to State Department, 23 March 1954.

320. USNRA, RG59, CDF, Box 4016a, 774.00/3–2554, Despatch No. 2290, Caffery, Cairo to State Department, 25 March 1954; "King Saud in Cairo," *Times*, 22 March 1954. Ikhwan accounts suggest that the king urged the CCR to release imprisoned Brothers

and also sought to facilitate a reconciliation between the two sides. See, for example, Muhammad Hamid Abu al-Nasr, *Haqiqat al-khilaf bayna al-ikhwan al-muslimin wa 'Abd al-Nasir* (Cairo: al-Mu'allif, 1987), 116–124.

321. USNRA, RG59, CDF, Box 4016a, 774.00/3–2554, Despatch No. 2293, Caffery, Cairo to State Department, 25 March 1954.

322. "Enclosure: 'Statement of Muslim Brothers, March 25, 1954,'" in ibid.

323. USNRA, RG59, CDF, Box 4016a, 774.00/3–2554, Despatch No. 2293, Caffery, Cairo to State Department, 25 March 1954.

324. "Enclosure: 'Statement of Muslim Brothers, March 25, 1954,'" in ibid.

325. UKNA FO 371/108327, JE 1018/35, Telegram No. 411, Stevenson, Cairo to FO, 25 March 1954; USNRA, RG59, CDF, Box 4016a, 774.00/3–2654, Despatch No. 2300, Caffery, Cairo to State Department, 26 March 1954.

326. USNRA, RG59, CDF, Box 4016a, 774.00/3–2654, Despatch No. 1168, Caffery, Cairo to State Department, 26 March 1954.

327. USNRA, RG59, CDF, Box 4016a, 774.00/3–2654, Despatch No. 1178, Caffery, Cairo to State Department, 26 March 1954. The British also believed that Nasser's faction was merely "biding its time"; see UKNA FO 371/108327, JE 1018/38, Telegram No. 426, Stevenson, Cairo to FO, 27 March 1954.

328. USNRA, RG59, CDF, Box 4016a, 774.00/3–2654, Despatch No. 2300, Caffery, Cairo to State Department, 26 March 1954. On the meetings between Nasser and al-Hudaybi and his colleagues, see 'Abd al-Halim, *Al-Ikhwan al-Muslimun III,* 33–34; and al-Tilmisani, *Dhikriyat,* 131–132.

329. USNRA, RG59, CDF, Box 4016a, 774.00/4–354, Despatch No. 2373, Caffery, Cairo to State Department, 3 April 1954.

330. USNRA, RG59, CDF, Box 4016a, 774.00/3–2754, Despatch No. 2305, Caffery, Cairo to State Department, 27 March 1954.

331. Mitchell, *Society of the Muslim Brothers,* 128–133.

332. USNRA, RG59, CDF, Box 4016a, 774.00/3–2854, Despatch No. 1189, Caffery, Cairo to State Department, 28 March 1954.

333. USNRA, RG59, CDF, Box 4016a, 774.00/3–3054, Despatch No. 1213, Caffery, Cairo to State Department, 30 March 1954, 6 p.m.

334. USNRA, RG59, CDF, Box 4016a, 774.00/3–2954, Despatch No. 1208, Caffery, Cairo to State Department, 29 March 1954; UKNA FO 371/108316, JE 1015/17, Telegram No. 435, Stevenson, Cairo to FO, 29 March 1954; FO 371/108327, JE 1018/41, Telegram No. 437, Stevenson, Cairo to FO, 29 March 1954; USNRA, RG59, CDF, Box 4016a, 774.00/3–3054, Despatch No. 1209, Caffery, Cairo to State Department, 30 March 1954. For a useful chronological overview, see Box 4017, 774.00 (W)/4–254, Joint Weekly A, No. 13, Military Attaché, Cairo to State Department, 2 April 1954.

335. USNRA, CREST Database, CIA, "NSC Briefing, 'The Developments in Egypt,'" 1 April 1954. See also CIA, "Current Intelligence Weekly, 'The Struggle for Power in Egypt,'" 2 April 1954.

336. USNRA, RG59, CDF, Box 4016a, 774.00/4–554, Despatch No. 1258, Caffery, Cairo to State Department, 5 April 1954.

337. For US skepticism about the initial rapprochement, see UKNA FO 371/108327, JE 1018/19, Telegram No. 304, Stevenson, Cairo to FO, 2 March 1954; and in the same, JE 1018/28, Telegram No. 310, Stevenson, Cairo to FO, 3 March 1954.

338. USNRA, RG59, CDF, Box 4016a, 774.00/3–3154, Despatch No. 1218, Caffery, Cairo to State Department, 31 March 1954. Caffery was not alone in his analysis. Other American observers of Egypt appear to have decisively embraced Nasser during 1954. See, for example, HIA, Jacob C. Hurewitz Collection, Accession No. 88012–16.317/319, Box 32, Richard H. Nolte, "The Philosophy of the Revolution," *Institute of Current World Affairs Newsletter,* RHN-54, Oxford, 8 March 1954; Robert Doty, "Egypt's Strong Man," *New York Times,* 19 September 1954.

339. UKNA FO 371/108316, JE 1015/29, Telegram No. 90, Stevenson, Cairo to FO, 15 April 1954. See also FO 371/108327, JE 1018/43, Telegram No. 449, Stevenson, Cairo to FO, 30 March 1954. For similar views back in London, see FO 371/108327, JE 1018/41, Minute by John E. D. Street (FO), 30 March 1954, on Telegram No. 437, Stevenson, Cairo to FO, 29 March 1954.

340. USNRA, RG59, CDF, Box 4016a, 774.00/4–554, Despatch No. 1258, Caffery, Cairo to State Department, 5 April 1954; see also "Telegram No. 471 from Stevenson to FO," 5 April 1954, *BDDE,* vol. 3, 244–245.

341. UKNA FO 371/108317, JE 1015/54, Telegram No. 183, Stevenson, Cairo to FO, 14 September 1954. See also USNRA, RG59, CDF, Box 4016a, 774.00/5–1854, Despatch No. 2714, Caffery, Cairo to State Department, 18 May 1954. For a similar appraisal of Nasser, see "Col. Nasser in Full Power in Egypt," *Times,* 26 February 1954; "The Colonel Emerges," *Times,* 26 February 1954.

342. UKNA FO 371/108317, JE 1015/37, Telegram No. 602, Stevenson, Cairo to FO, 10 May 1954.

343. See, for example, the views of the British ambassador in UKNA FO 371/108327, JE 1018/43, Telegram No. 449, Stevenson, Cairo to FO, 30 March 1954.

344. USNRA, RG59, CDF, Box 4016a, 774.00/3–2554, Despatch No. 2290, Caffery, Cairo to State Department, 25 March 1954.

345. On the evolution of British strategic thinking, see Thornhill, *Road to Suez,* 131–154; Louis, *Ends of British Imperialism,* 621–626.

346. UKNA FO 371/108454, JE 1193/37, Undated Minute, "Notes for Supplementaries," and Minute by Guy E. Millard (FO), 14 July 1954. It should be noted that some officials had long been reflecting on the strategic implications of atomic warfare. As early as spring 1946, the assistant under-secretary at the Foreign Office, Robert Howe, had suggested that such weaponry, allied to long-range aerial bombing, might make it "undesirable" to station troops at what "had hitherto been considered essentially strategic points of defence, such as the Suez Canal." Clearly, it took a long time for such thinking to percolate through to the country's political leaders. See FO 371/53287, J 1025/39/16, Minute by Howe, 8 March 1946, on Telegram No. 425, from Bowker, Cairo to FO, 6 March 1946.

347. Selwyn Lloyd, Hansard Online, HC Deb, 25 January 1954, vol. 522, cc1443–4.

348. UKNA FO 371/108447, JE 1193/14, Telegram No. 95, Stevenson, Cairo to FO, 22 January 1954; in the same, JE 1193/16, Telegram No. 107, Stevenson, Cairo to FO, 23 January 1954; FO 371/108454, JE 1195/30, Minute by Street, 1 June 1954; "Incidents in the Canal Zone," *Times,* 23 January 1954; Eric Downton, "Cairo Directing Zone Terror," *Daily Telegraph,* 2 February 1954.

349. "Cabinet Memorandum by Selwyn Lloyd," 3 June 1954, *BDDE,* vol. 3, 258–259.

350. "Egypt: Cabinet Conclusions," 7 July 1954, *BDDE,* vol. 3, 287–288.

351. UKNA FO 371/108317, Telegram No. 602, Stevenson, Cairo to FO, 10 May 1954.

352. John B. Slade-Baker, "Nasser 'Would Welcome Approach by Britain,'" *Sunday Times,* 13 June 1954.

353. USNRA, RG59, CDF, Box 4016a, 774.00/7–2654, Despatch No. 147, Caffery, Cairo to State Department, 26 July 1954.

354. See "Draft Heads of Agreement: Memorandum Presented to Colonel Nasser by Sir R. Stevenson," 10 July 1954, *BDDE,* vol. 3, 288–289.

355. Ray Takeyh, *The Origins of the Eisenhower Doctrine: The US, Britain and Nasser's Egypt* (Basingstoke, UK: Macmillan, 2000), xii.

356. Aronson, *From Sideshow to Centre Stage,* 91–107. See also Meyer, *Egypt and the United States,* 61–63. The obstacle to weapons transfers remained the US legal requirement to have a Military Assistance Advisory Group (MAAG).

357. USNRA, CREST Database, CIA, "Current Intelligence Bulletin," 31 July 1954.

358. USNRA, CREST Database, CIA, "Current Intelligence Bulletin," 5 August 1954.

359. USNRA, RG59, CDF, Box 4016a, 774.00/4–254, Despatch No. 2368, Caffery, Cairo to State Department, 2 April 1954.

360. USNRA, RG59, CDF, Box 4016a, 774.00/4–354, Despatch No. 2373, Caffery, Cairo to State Department, 3 April 1954.

361. USNRA, RG59, CDF, Box 4016a, 774.00/3–2754, Despatch No. 2305, Caffery, Cairo to State Department, 27 March 1954. On the Brotherhood's opposition to the emerging lines of a settlement, see 'Abd al-Halim, *Al-Ikhwan al-Muslimun III,* 356.

362. HIA, Richard Paul Mitchell Collection, Accession No. 77076–8M.50, Box 3, "Letter Sent by Hassan al-Hudaibi, Supreme Guide of the Moslem Brotherhood to Premier Lt. Col. Gamal Abd Al Nasir on May 4, 1954." The Arabic original of the letter is also there; the quotes used here are taken from the translation, checked against the original.

363. USNRA, RG59, CDF, Box 4016a, 774.00/5–2954, Despatch No. 2802, Caffery, Cairo to State Department, 29 May 1954, and especially, "Enclosure: 'Letter Sent by Hassan al Hudaibi, Supreme Guide of the Moslem Brotherhood to Premier Lt. Col. Gamal Abd Al Nasir on May 4, 1954.'"

364. USNRA, RG59, CDF, Box 4016a, 774.00/6–154, Despatch No. 2808, Caffery, Cairo to State Department, 1 June 1954; 774.00/6–454, Despatch No. 2832, Caffery, Cairo to State Department, 4 June 1954, and "Enclosure: 'Memorandum of Conversation, June 2, 1954.'" For a Brotherhood account of this tour, see Abu al-Nasr, *Haqiqat al-khilaf,* 126–127.

365. UKNA FO 371/110840, V 1781/6, Telegram No. 10601/73/54, Embassy Damascus to FO, 10 July 1954, including "Enclosure, 'Report from ALEF BA Damascus Daily Paper of Hudeibi's Speech at the Denkiz Mosque on June 9.'"

366. USNRA, RG59, CDF, Box 4016a, 774.00/7–1254, Despatch No. 177, Caffery, Cairo to State Department, 12 July 1954.

367. "Work on Canal Zone Agreement," *Times,* 12 August 1954. See also Abu al-Nasr, *Haqiqat al-khilaf,* 127–130.

368. Shadi, *Safahat min al-tarikh,* 266–267.

369. Sa'id Ramadan, "Qadas kanisat l-arwah," *al-Muslimun* 3, no. 10 (August 1954).

370. Shadi, *Safahat min al-tarikh,* 268. For the full text, see same volume, 372–381.

371. HIA, Richard Paul Mitchell Collection, Accession No. 77076–8M.50, Box 3, "Muhammad Neguib . . . ra'is al-jumhuriya: yanqud al-itifaq al-misriyya al-ingliziyya." The

folder also contains an English translation, presumably by Mitchell, from which the quotes here are drawn (checked against the original).

372. HIA, Richard Paul Mitchell Collection, Accession No. 77076–8M.50, Box 3, "The Story of the Anglo-Egyptian Agreement" (English translation of Arabic pamphlet). For more on the Brotherhood's critique of the agreement, see Shadi, *Safahat min al-tarikh,* 258–261, 265–266.

373. USNRA, RG59, CDF, Box 4018, 774.00 (w)/8–1254, Joint Weekly A, No. 32, Military Attaché, Cairo to State Department, 12 August 1954.

374. USNRA, RG59, CDF, Box 4018, 774.00 (w)/8–2754, Joint Weekly A, No. 34, Military Attaché, Cairo to State Department, 27 August 1954.

375. USNRA, RG59, CDF, Box 4016a, 774.00/8–1854, Despatch No. 278, Caffery, Cairo to State Department, 18 August 1954.

376. USNRA, RG59, CDF, Box 4018, 774.00 (w)/8–2054, Joint Weekly A, No. 33, Military Attaché, Cairo to State Department, 20 August 1954.

377. Shadi, *Safahat min al-tarikh,* 269–271.

378. USNRA, RG59, CDF, Box 4016a, 774.00/8–1354, Airgram A-45, John Foster Dulles (Secretary of State), State Department to Embassy Cairo, 13 August 1954.

379. UKNA FO 371/108319, JE 1016/13, Telegram No. 187 (S) Stevenson, Cairo to FO, 30 August 1954.

380. Dawh, *25 'aman,* 63–65.

381. USNRA, RG59, CDF, Box 4016a, 774.00/8–2854, Despatch No. 345, Caffery, Cairo to State Department, 28 August 1954.

382. USNRA, RG59, CDF, Box 4016a, 774.00/9–1354, Despatch No. 440, Caffery, Cairo to State Department, 13 September 1954; UKNA FO 371/108319, JE 1016/14, Telegram No. 198(S), Stevenson, Cairo to FO, 14 September 1954; WO 208/3965, CZLIC [Canal Zone Local Intelligence Committee] ISUM [Intelligence Summary] No. 7/54—14/54, Volume IX, ISUM 7/54, "Part 1—Political Activity" and "Security Addendum to ISUM 7/54," 16 September 1954. For a slightly different view of the Tanta disturbances, see USNRA CREST Database, CIA, "Current Intelligence Bulletin," 16 September 1954.

383. Al-'Ashmawi, *Al-Ikhwan wa-l-thawra,* 59–60.

384. Al-Qaradawi, *al-Ikhwan al-Muslimun,* 245–246.

385. USNRA, RG59, CDF, Box 4016a, 774.00/9–1354, Despatch No. 440, Caffery, Cairo to State Department, 13 September 1954; 774.00/9–1654, Despatch No. 477, Caffery, Cairo to State Department, 16 September 1954; USNRA, RG59, CDF, Box 4018, 774.00 (w)/9–1054, Joint Weekly A, No. 36, Military Attaché, Cairo to State Department, 10 September 1954.

386. USNRA, RG59, CDF, Box 4016a, 774.00/9–2154, Despatch No. 517, Caffery, Cairo to State Department, 21 September 1954.

387. USNRA, RG59, CDF, Box 4018, 774.00 (w)/10–154, Joint Weekly A, No. 39, Military Attaché, Cairo to State Department, 1 October 1954.

388. USNRA, RG59, CDF, Box 4018, 774.00 (w)/9–1754, Joint Weekly A, No. 37, Military Attaché, Cairo to State Department, 17 September 1954; "Cairo Muslims' Disunity," *Times,* 24 September 1954.

389. UKNA FO 371/108319, JE 1016/14, Telegram No. 19(S), Stevenson, Cairo to FO, 14 September 1954.

390. USNRA, RG59, CDF, Box 4016a, 774.00/9–2954, Despatch No. 564, Caffery, Cairo to State Department, 29 September 1954, and "Enclosure: 'Memorandum of Conversation, September 23, 1954.'"

391. USNRA, RG59, CDF, Box 4016a, 774.00/9–2454, Despatch No. 533, Caffery, Cairo to State Department, 24 September 1954, and "Enclosure: 'Text of RCC Statement.'" See also UKNA FO 371/108319, JE 1016/15, Telegram No. 1375, Stevenson, Cairo to FO, 25 September 1954. The five Brothers were identified by the British as 'Abd al-Hakim 'Adawi 'Abdin; Sa'id Ramadan (described as "Chief Liaison officer" of the Brotherhood), Sa'd al-Din al-Wilali (the leader of the Brotherhood's Rover Scouts), Muhammad Nagib Guwaifil (a Brother implicated in the attempted assassination of former parliamentary speaker Muhammad Guda), and Kamil Isma'il al-Sharif.

392. UKNA FO 371/110840, V 1781/9, Despatch No. 17806/11/54, Embassy Damascus to FO, 28 September 1954.

393. USNRA, RG59, CDF, Box 4016a, 774.00/10–1954, Despatch No. 731, Caffery, Cairo to State Department, 19 October 1954.

394. USNRA, CREST Database, CIA "Current Intelligence Bulletin," 12 October 1954.

395. For text of the treaty, see "Anglo-Egyptian Agreement regarding the Suez Canal Base," 19 October 1954, *BDDE,* vol. 3, 320–324. For reactions to the treaty, see "Despatch No. 206, from FRH Murray to FO," 1 November 1954, *BDDE,* vol. 3, 329–332.

396. USNRA, RG59, CDF, Box 4016a, 774.00/10–1954, Despatch No. 2523, Caffery, Cairo to State Department, 19 October 1954.

397. UKNA FO 371/108319, JE 1016/16, Telegram No. 1379, Stevenson, Cairo to FO, 25 September 1954; "The Moslem Brothers," *Economist,* 2 October 1954.

398. UKNA FO 371/108319, JE 1016/18, Telegram No. 221 (S), F. Ralph Murray (Minister), Embassy Cairo to FO, 22 October 1954; "Moslem Unit Split on Suez Zone Pact," *New York Times,* 22 October 1954.

399. USNRA, RG59, CDF, Box 4016a, 774.00/10–2754, Despatch No. 555, Caffery, Cairo to State Department, 27 October 1954; UKNA FO 371/108318, JE 1015/57, Telegram No. 1608, Murray, Cairo to FO, 27 October 1954; USNRA, RG59, CDF, Box 4018, 774.00 (w)/10–2954, Joint Weekly A, No. 43, Military Attaché, Cairo to State Department, 29 October 1954.

400. USNRA, CREST Database, CIA, "Current Intelligence Bulletin," 30 October 1954.

401. USNRA, RG59, CDF, Box 4016a, 774.00/10–3054, Despatch No. 825, Caffery, Cairo to State Department, 30 October 1954.

402. UKNA FO 371/108318, JE 1015/58, Telegram No. 1611, Murray, Cairo to FO, 27 October 1954.

403. USNRA, RG59, CDF, Box 4016a, 774.00/11–654, Despatch No. 864, Caffery, Cairo to State Department, 6 November 1954.

404. USNRA, RG59, CDF, Box 4016a, 774.00/11–554, Despatch No. 859, Caffery, Cairo to State Department, 5 November 1954; Box 4018, 774.00 (w)/10–2954, Joint Weekly A, No. 43, Military Attaché, Cairo to State Department, 29 October 1954. For examples of the press campaign against the Brotherhood, see Box 4016a, 774.00/11–1854, Despatch No. 944, Caffery, Cairo to State Department, 18 November 1954; see also UKNA FO 371/108319, JE 1016/20, Telegram No. 23(S), Murray, Cairo to FO, 18 November 1954.

405. USNRA, RG59, CDF, Box 4016a, 774.00/10–3054, Despatch No. 825, Caffery, Cairo to State Department, 30 October 1954.

406. USNRA, RG59, CDF, Box 4018, 774.00 (w)/11–554, Joint Weekly A, No. 44, Military Attaché, Cairo to State Department, 5 November 1954; Box 4016a, 774.00/11–454, Despatch No. 855, Caffery, Cairo to State Department, 4 November 1954. For a similar British view, see UKNA FO 371/108319, JE 1016/24, Telegram No. 226, Murray, Cairo to FO, 13 December 1954.

407. USNRA, RG59, CDF, Box 4016a, 774.00/10–3054, Despatch No. 825, Caffery, Cairo to State Department, 30 October 1954; UKNA FO 371/108318, JE 1015/63, Telegram No. 225(S), Murray, Cairo to FO, 1 November 1954.

408. USNRA, RG59, CDF, Box 4016a, 774.00/11–654, Despatch No. 864, Caffery, Cairo to State Department, 6 November 1954. For further on arrests and weapons seizures, see, in the same box 774.00/11–1954, Despatch No. 962, Caffery, Cairo to State Department, 19 November 1954.

409. USNRA, RG59, CDF, Box 4016a, 774.00/11–2054, Despatch No. 973, Caffery, Cairo to State Department, 20 November 1954.

410. "The Moslem Brothers," *Economist,* 2 October 1954.

411. "Nasser versus the Brotherhood," *Economist,* 20 November 1954.

412. "A Setback for Extremism," *Christian Science Monitor,* 30 October 1954.

413. UKNA FO 371/108318, JE 1015/65, Telegram No. 1650, Murray, Cairo to FO, 4 November 1954. For similar US concerns, see USNRA, RG59, CDF, Box 4016a, 774.00/ 10–3054, Despatch No. 825, Caffery, Cairo to State Department, 30 October 1954.

414. USNRA, RG59, CDF, Box 4016a, 774.00/11–254, Despatch No. 845, Caffery, Cairo to State Department, 2 November 1954.

415. USNRA, RG59, CDF, Box 4016a, 774.00/11–2454, Despatch No. 1002, Caffery, Cairo to State Department, 24 November 1954, and "Enclosure: MENA Article."

416. Such were the charges leveled at the general guide. See USNRA, RG59, CDF, Box 4016a, 774.00/11–2254, Despatch No. 980, Caffery, Cairo to State Department, 22 November 1954.

417. USNRA, RG59, CDF, Box 4016a, 774.00/11–1754, Despatch No. 934, Caffery, Cairo to State Department, 17 November 1954, including "Enclosure: 'Confessions of Deputy Supreme Guide of Moslem Brotherhood before People's Tribunal'"; UKNA FO 371/108319, JE 1016/24, Telegram No. 226, Murray, Cairo to FO, 13 December 1954.

418. USNRA, RG59, CDF, Box 4016a, 774.00/11–554, Despatch No. 859, Caffery, Cairo to State Department, 5 November 1954; 774.00/11–1054, Despatch No. 880, Caffery, Cairo to State Department, 10 November 1954; 774.00/11–1754, Despatch No. 934, Caffery, Cairo to State Department, 17 November 1954, including "Enclosure: 'Confessions of Deputy Supreme Guide of Moslem Brotherhood before People's Tribunal.'" See also Box 4016a, 774.00/11–2454, Despatch No. 1002, Caffery, Cairo to State Department, 24 November 1954, including "Enclosure: MENA Article."

419. USNRA, RG59, CDF, Box 4016a, 774.00/11–154, Despatch No. 833, Caffery, Cairo to State Department, 1 November 1954; 774.00/11–2454, Despatch No. 1002, Caffery, Cairo to State Department, 24 November 1954; 774.00/11–1954, Despatch No. 966, Caffery, Cairo to State Department, 19 November 1954; 774.00/11–2354, Despatch No. 996, Caffery, Cairo to State Department, 23 November 1954, including "Enclosure: 'Witnesses Say Hodeiby Head of Secret Group,'" *Egyptian Gazette,* 23 November

1954; UKNA FO 371/108319, JE 1016/24, Telegram No. 226, Murray, Cairo to FO, 13 December 1954.

420. USNRA, RG59, CDF, Box 4016a, 774.00/11–2054, Despatch No. 973, Caffery, Cairo to State Department, 20 November 1954; UKNA FO 371/108319, JE 1016/24, Telegram No. 226, Murray, Cairo to FO, 13 December 1954. Ghada Osman suggests that it was Qutb's testimony that "nailed" al-Hudaybi. Osman, *Journey in Islamic Thought,* 140.

421. USNRA, RG59, CDF, Box 4016a, 774.00/11–1254, Despatch No. 903, Caffery, Cairo to State Department, 12 November 1954 and especially, "Enclosure: 'Five Witnesses Give Evidence in Abdul Latif Trial,'" *Egyptian Gazette,* 12 November 1954; 774.00/11–2454, Despatch No. 1002, Caffery, Cairo to State Department, 24 November 1954, including "Enclosure: MENA Article." See also Box 4016a, 774.00/11–3054, Despatch No. 1040, Caffery, Cairo to State Department, 30 November 1954; UKNA WO 208/3965, CZLIC ISUM No. 7/54—14/54, Volume IX, ISUM 12/54, "Covering the Period 11th November to 24th November 1954."

422. UKNA FO 371/108319, JE 1016/24, Telegram No. 226, Murray, Cairo to FO, 13 December 1954.

423. Ibid.; USNRA, RG59, CDF, Box 4016a, 774.00/11–1754, Despatch No. 934, Caffery, Cairo to State Department, 17 November 1954, especially, "Enclosure: 'Confessions of Deputy Supreme Guide of Moslem Brotherhood before People's Tribunal.'"

424. UKNA FO 371/108319, JE 1016/24, Telegram No. 226, Murray, Cairo to FO, 13 December 1954; USNRA, RG59, CDF, Box 4016a, 774.00/11–2254, Despatch No. 922, Caffery, Cairo to State Department, 22 November 1954; and 774.00/11–554, Despatch No. 934, Caffery, Cairo to State Department, 17 November 1954, including "Enclosure: 'Confessions of Deputy Supreme Guide of Moslem Brotherhood before People's Tribunal.'"

425. USNRA, RG59, CDF, Box 4018, 774.00 (w)/11–1854, Joint Weekly A, No. 46, Military Attaché, Cairo to State Department, 18 November 1954.

426. UKNA FO 371/108318, JE 1015/68, Telegram No. 1691, Murray, Cairo to FO, 14 November 1954.

427. UKNA FO 371/108318, JE 1015/70, Telegram No. 1695, Murray, Cairo to FO, 15 November 1954.

428. HIA, Wilbur Crane Eveland Collection, Accession No. 80118 14.30, Box 2, Wilbur Eveland and Thomas Faber, "Manuscript for Innocents Abroad: The American Presence in the Near East, 1948–1975," 181.

429. Zollner, *Muslim Brotherhood,* 36–37.

430. USNRA, RG59, CDF, Box 4016a, 774.00/10–3054, Despatch No. 825, Caffery, Cairo to State Department, 30 October 1954.

431. The word "tamthiliya" is frequently used. See, for example, Shadi, *Safahat min al-tarikh,* 272; 'Umar al-Tilmisani, *Qala al-nas, wa lam aqul fi hukm 'Abd al-Nasir* (Cairo: Dar al-'Itisam, 1985), 186.

432. Al-'Ashmawi, *Al-Ikhwan wa-l-thawra,* 62.

433. Al-'Ashmawi, *Hisad al-ayam,* 98; al-'Ashmawi, *Al-Ikhwan wa-l-thawra,* 83–86.

434. Abu al-Futuh 'Afifi, *Rihalati ma' al-Ikhwan al-Muslimin* (Cairo: Dar al-Tawfiq wa-l-Nashr al-Islami, 2003), 61; Al-Qaradawi, *al-Ikhwan al-Muslimun,* 245–246, 296–297.

435. 'Abd al-Halim, *Al-Ikhwan al-Muslimun III,* 36–41. For a similar approach, see al-Tilmisani, *Dhikriyat,* 167–171.

436. Al-'Ashmawi, *Al-Ikhwan wa-l-thawra,* 66–68.

437. Imam, *'Abd al-Nasir,* 3–6.

438. Al-Shafi'i, *Shahid,* 61.

439. USNRA, RG59, CDF, Box 4018, 774.00 (w)/10–2954, Joint Weekly A, No. 43, Military Attaché, Cairo to State Department, 29 October 1954. For the British assessment, see various written Minutes on UKNA FO 371/108319, JE 1016/24, Telegram No. 226, Murray, Cairo to FO, 13 December 1954.

440. *Nasser at El Mansheya* (CD recording, Cairo, n.d.).

441. USNRA, RG59, CDF, Box 4016a, 774.00/11–454, Despatch No. 855, Caffery, Cairo to State Department, 4 November 1954.

442. USNRA, RG59, CDF, Box 3681, 774.00/1–655, Despatch No. 1319, Caffery, Cairo to State Department, 6 January 1955, including "Enclosure: 'Memorandum of Conversation, January 3, 1955: The Views of an Ikhwani.'"

443. USNRA, RG59, CDF, Box 4016a, 774.00/11–3054, Despatch No. 1040, Caffery, Cairo to State Department, 30 November 1954; UKNA FO 371/108319, JE 1016/24, Telegram No. 226, Murray, Cairo to FO, 13 December 1954.

444. Dawh, *25 'aman,* 63.

445. UKNA WO 208/3965, CZLIC ISUM No. 7/54—14/54, Volume IX, ISUM 10/54, "Covering the Period 13th October to 27th October 1954."

446. USNRA, RG59, CDF, Box 4016a, 774.00/12–654, Despatch No. 1099, Caffery, Cairo to State Department, 6 December 1954.

447. USNRA, RG59, CDF, Box 4016a, 774.00/12–754, Despatch No. 1111, Caffery, Cairo to State Department, 7 December 1954.

448. "Executions in Cairo," *Times,* 8 December 1954.

449. USNRA, RG59, CDF, Box 4016a, 774.00/11–554, Despatch No. 1636, Dayton S. Mak (Second Secretary), Embassy London to State Department, 7 December 1954.

450. USNRA, CREST Database, CIA, "Current Intelligence Bulletin," 8 December 1954.

451. UKNA FO 371/108319, JE 1016/22, Telegram No. 256(S), Murray, Cairo to FO, 5 December 1954; and in same file, JE 1016/23, Telegram No. 263(S) Murray, Cairo to FO, 13 December 1954; JE 1016/23(A), Telegram No. 264(S), Murray, Cairo to FO, 14 December 1954.

452. USNRA, RG59, CDF, Box 4016a, 774.00/12–1454, Despatch No. 1165, Caffery, Cairo to State Department, 14 December 1954.

453. USNRA, RG59, CDF, Box 4016a, 774.00/12–154, Despatch No. 1055, Caffery, Cairo to State Department, 1 December 1954; 774.00/12–354, Despatch No. 1072, Caffery, Cairo to State Department, 3 December 1954. The remaining three members of the guidance council—'Abd al-Moez 'Abd al-Sattar, 'Abd al-Rahman al Banna (Hasan's brother), and al-Bahi al-Khuli—were tried on 2 December. See Box 4016a, 774.00/12–454, Despatch No. 1087, Caffery, Cairo to State Department, 4 December 1954.

454. USNRA, RG59, CDF, Box 4016a, 774.00/12–454, Despatch No. 1090, Caffery, Cairo to State Department, 4 December 1954; and 774.00/12–854, Despatch No. 1116, Caffery, Cairo to State Department, 8 December 1954.

455. USNRA, RG59, CDF, Box 4016a, 774.00/12–1354, Despatch No. 1156, Caffery, Cairo to State Department, 13 December 1954.

456. USNRA, RG59, CDF, Box 4016a, 774.00/11–3054, Despatch No. 1046, Caffery, Cairo to State Department, 30 November 1954; and 774.00/12–654, Despatch No. 1096, Caffery, Cairo to State Department, 6 December 1954.

457. USNRA, RG59, CDF, Box 4016a, 774.00/12–2754, Despatch No. 1252, Jones, Cairo to State Department, 27 December 1954.

458. USNRA, RG59, CDF, Box 4016a, 774.00/12–2954, Despatch No. 1260, Jones, Cairo to State Department, 29 December 1954; 774.00/12–3154, Despatch No. 1280, Caffery, Cairo to State Department, 31 December 1954. See also Box 3681, 774.00/1–455, Despatch No. 1296, Caffery, Cairo to State Department, 4 January 1955; 774.00/1–455, Despatch No. 1341, Howard Elting Jr. (First Secretary), Embassy Cairo to State Department, 11 January 1955; 774.00/1–1555, Despatch No. 1374, Jones, Cairo to State Department, 15 January 1955; 774.00/1–2255, Despatch No. 1430, Jones, Cairo to State Department, 22 January 1955; Box 3682, 774.00 (W)/1–2855, Joint Weekly A, No. 4, Military Attaché, Cairo to State Department, 28 January 1955; 774.00 (W)/2–1155, Joint Weekly A, No. 6, Military Attaché, Cairo to State Department, 11 February 1955.

459. See, for example, USNRA, RG59, CDF, Box 3681, 774.00/2–1455, Despatch No. 1588, Jones, Cairo to State Department, 14 February 1955, which recorded that 136 out of 187 recent judgments had been either suspended sentences or acquittals (73 percent).

460. P. J. Vatikiotis, *The History of Egypt: From Muhammad Ali to Mubarak*, 3rd ed. (Baltimore, MD: Johns Hopkins University Press, 1985), 384; Hazem Kandil, *Soldiers, Spies, and Statesmen: Egypt's Road to Revolt* (London: Verso, 2012), 40.

461. UKNA FO 371/108319, JE 1016/24, Telegram No. 226, Murray, Cairo to FO, 13 December 1954. See also WO 208/3965, CZLIC ISUM No. 7/54—14/54, Volume IX, ISUM 13/54, "Covering the Period 24th November to 7th December 1954."

462. USNRA, RG59, CDF, Box 3681, 774.00/1–655, Despatch No. 1319, Caffery, Cairo to State Department, 6 January 1955, including "Enclosure: 'Memorandum of Conversation, January 3, 1955: The Views of an Ikhwani.'"

463. Gordon, *Nasser's Blessed Movement*, 157–174.

464. UKNA FO 371/108373, JE 1054/6, Telegram No. 81, Stevenson, Cairo to FO, 19 January 1954.

465. Al-Tilmisani, *Dhikriyat*, 171.

466. HIA, Christina Harris Collection, Accession No. 79085 10.03, Box 11, Christina P. Harris, "Egyptian Nationalism and the Revolution of 1952," paper prepared for Arab World Seminar, World Affairs Council of Northern California, June 1954.

6. The Age of Nasser, 1955–1970

1. LBJPL, National Security File (National Intelligence Estimates), Box 6, National Intelligence Estimate No. 36.1–66: "The Outlook for the United Arab Republic," 19 May 1966; USNRA, RG59, CFPF, Box 2760, POL 23–9, Despatch No. 690, Lucius Battle (Ambassador), Embassy Cairo to State Department, 9 September 1965; on this point, see also, in Box 2760, POL 13–6, Airgram No. A-279, Joint Weekly A, No. 37, Richard B. Parker (Counselor for Political Affairs), Embassy Cairo to State Department, 6 October 1965; POL 23–9, Telegram No. 1979, Battle, Cairo to State Department, 4 February 1966; Airgram A-761, Embassy Cairo to State Department, 15 March 1966;

POL 2–1, Joint Weekly A, Nos. 5 and 6, Airgram No. A-708, Wilbur I. Wright (Labor Attaché), Embassy Cairo to State Department, 24 February 1966.

2. USNRA, RG59, CFPF, Box 2765, POL 23–9, Airgram A-351, Parker, Cairo to State Department, 27 October 1965.

3. USNRA, RG59, CFPF, Box 2765, POL 23–9, Telegram No. 707, Battle, Cairo to State Department, 10 September 1965.

4. USNRA, RG59, ASSNESA, SF, Box 3, "National Policy Paper: United Arab Republic [UAR], Part Two, Factors Bearing on US Policy," 1 August 1966.

5. USNRA, RG59, CDF, Box 4016a, 774.00/12–2054, Despatch No. 1208, Jefferson Caffery (Ambassador), Embassy Cairo to State Department, 20 December 1954.

6. USNRA, RG59, CDF, Box 3681, 774.00/2–155, Despatch No. 1494, G. Lewis Jones (Counselor), Embassy Cairo to State Department, 1 February 1955.

7. UKNA WO (War Office) 208/3965, CZLIC [Canal Zone Local Intelligence Committe] ISUM [Intelligence Summary] No. 7/54—14/54, Volume IX, ISUM 14/54, "Covering the Period 8th December to 23rd December 1954."

8. See Chapter 6.

9. USNRA, RG59, CDF, Box 3681, 774.00/1–2555, Despatch No. 1448, Jones, Cairo to State Department, 25 January 1955.

10. Ibid.

11. USNRA, RG59, CDF, Box 3681, 774.00/4–2955, Despatch No. 2040, Henry A. Byroade (Ambassador), Embassy Cairo to State Department, 29 April 1955.

12. USNRA, RG59, CDF, Box 3681, 774.00/3–455, Despatch No. 1705, Byroade, Cairo to State Department, 4 March 1955.

13. Ibid.; "Nasser and Islam," Economist, 20 November 1954.

14. USNRA, RG59, CDF, Box 3681, 774.00/3–455, Despatch No. 1705, Byroade, Cairo to State Department, 4 March 1955.

15. USNRA, RG59, CDF, Box 3681, 774.00/4–755, Despatch No. 1913, Byroade, Cairo to State Department, 7 April 1955.

16. USNRA, RG59, CDF, Box 3681, 774.00/3–2555, Despatch No. 1843, Byroade, Cairo to State Department, 25 March 1955.

17. USNRA, RG59, CDF, Box 3681, 774.00/4–2555, Despatch No. 2014, Byroade, Cairo to State Department, 25 April 1955.

18. USNRA, RG59, CDF, Box 3681, 774.00/3–2555, Despatch No. 1843, Byroade, Cairo to State Department, 25 March 1955.

19. Abu Ayman [Sa'id Ramadan], "Fir'aun," al-Muslimun 4, no. 8 (December 1955).

20. Sa'id Ramadan, "What Are You? (8)," al-Muslimun 3, no. 9 (July 1954).

21. Sa'id Ramadan, "Qadas kanisat l-arwa," al-Muslimun 3, no. 10 (August 1954).

22. Mustafa al-Siba'i, "Durus min thikra al-Isra," al-Muslimun 3, no. 6 (April 1954); "Fi afaq al-a'alam al-islami," al-Muslimun 3, no. 7 (May 1954).

23. Sa'id Ramadan, "Ma'alam al-tariq," al-Muslimun 4, no. 5 (July 1955); Abu Ayman, "What We Stand For," al-Muslimun 4, no. 6 (October 1955); Abu Ayman, "What We Stand For (2)," al-Muslimun 4, no. 7 (November 1955).

24. Abu Ayman, "Fi sabil al-wuduh," al-Muslimun 4, no. 9 (January 1956).

25. Abu Ayman, "???" al-Muslimun 5, no. 6 (October 1956).

26. USNRA, RG59, CDF, Box 3681, 774.00/6–2555, Despatch No. 2321, Byroade, Cairo to State Department, 25 June 1955.

27. Ibid.

28. On the anemic nature of the Wafd organization—local committees tended to hibernate between elections; see Marius Deeb, *Party Politics in Egypt: The Wafd and Its Rivals* (London: Ithaca, 1979), 164–172.

29. USNRA, RG59, CDF, Box 3681, 774.00/6–2555, Despatch No. 2321, Byroade, Cairo to State Department, 25 June 1955.

30. USNRA, RG59, CDF, Box 3681, 774.00/3–455, Despatch No. 1705, Byroade, Cairo to State Department, 4 March 1955.

31. USNRA, RG59, CDF, Box 3681, 774.00/7–1955, Despatch No. 92, Byroade, Cairo to State Department, 19 July 1955. See also Box 3682, 774.00 (W)/7–2155, Joint Weekly A, No. 29, Military Attaché, Cairo to State Department, 21 July 1955.

32. USNRA, RG59, CDF, Box 3681, 774.00/3–755, Despatch No. 1717, Byroade, Cairo to State Department, 7 March 1955.

33. USNRA, RG59, CDF, Box 3681, 774.00/7–1955, Despatch No. 92, Byroade, Cairo to State Department, 19 July 1955.

34. USNRA, RG59, CDF, Box 3681, 774.00/9–655, Despatch No. 261, Alexander Schnee (First Secretary), Embassy Cairo to State Department, 6 September 1955.

35. "Despatch No. 111, Stevenson to Macmillan," 11 July 1955, *BDDE*, vol. 3, 421–425.

36. "Telegram No. 1437, Trevelyan to FO [Foreign Office]," 13 October 1955, *BDDE*, vol. 3, 455–456.

37. USNRA, CREST Database, "Communism in Egypt," 20 October 1955.

38. See above, Chapter 3, and Chapter 5.

39. Brigitte Marechal, *The Muslim Brothers in Europe: Roots and Discourse* (Leiden, Netherlands: Brill, 2008), 29; Stephane Lacroix, *Awakening Islam: The Politics of Religious Dissent in Contemporary Saudi Arabia,* trans. George Holoch (London: Harvard University Press, 2011).

40. USNRA, RG59, CDF, Box 3681, 774.00/1–1055, Despatch No. 140, Harrison M. Symes (Consul) American Consulate, Kuwait to State Department, 10 January 1955, which includes "Enclosure: 'Information on Moslem Brothers Residing in Kuwait.' "

41. USNRA, RG59, CDF, Box 3681, 774.00/1–2455, Despatch No. 155, Symes, Kuwait to State Department, 24 January 1955.

42. USNRA, RG59, CDF, Box 3682, 774.00/3–455, Despatch No. 123, William D. Brewer (Consul), Consulate Kuwait to State Department, 10 January 1956.

43. Khalifa had been appointed controller general of the Jordanian Ikhwan the previous year. See Shmuel Bar, *The Muslim Brotherhood in Jordan* (Tel Aviv, Israel: Moshe Dayan Center for Middle Eastern and African Studies, 1998), 12–14.

44. UKNA FO 371/110841, Research Department, Foreign Office, "Quarterly Review of Islamic Affairs: Third Quarter of 1954," 5 October 1954.

45. USNRA, RG59, CDF, Box 3681, 774.00/1–1555, Despatch No. 1374, Jones, Cairo to State Department, 15 January 1955. This refers to fugitive Brothers in Lebanon.

46. Raphaël Lefèvre, *Ashes of Hama: The Muslim Brotherhood in Syria* (London, UK: Hurst, 2013), 38–39.

47. USNRA, RG59, CDF, Box 4074, 783.00 (W)/9–2454, Joint Weekly A, No. 38, Military Attaché, Damascus to State Department, 24 September 1954. See also UKNA FO 371/110840, V 1781/10, Despatch No. 17806/15/54, Embassy Damascus to FO, 16 October 1954; USNRA, RG59, CDF, Box 4074, 783.00 (W)/10–2254, Joint Weekly A, No. 42,

Military Attaché, Damascus to State Department, 22 October 1954; Box 4016a, 774.00/11–1654, Despatch No. 202, James S. Moose (Ambassador), Embassy Damascus to State Department, 16 November 1954.

48. USNRA, RG59, CDF, Box 4016a, 774.00/11–1654, Despatch No. 202, Moose, Damascus to State Department, 16 November 1954.

49. USNRA, RG59, CDF, Box 4016a, 774.00/11–254, Despatch No. 180, Robert C. Strong (Charge d'Affaires), Embassy Damascus to State Department, 2 November 1954.

50. USNRA, RG59, CDF, Box 4072, 783.00/7–653, Despatch No. 13, Moose, Damascus to State Department, 6 July 1953; 783.00/7–853, Despatch No. 23, Moose, Damascus to State Department; 783.00/10–1353, Despatch No. 234, Paul F. Geren (Charge d'Affaires), Embassy Damascus to State Department, 13 October 1953; 783.00/3–2354, Airgram A-97, John Foster Dulles (Secretary of State), Washington, DC, to Embassy Damascus, 23 March 1954.

51. UKNA FO 371/110841, Research Department, Foreign Office, "Quarterly Review of Islamic Affairs: First Quarter of 1954," 6 April 1954; FO 371/110840, V 1781/4, Despatch No. 17806/3/54, Embassy Damascus to FO, 6 April 1954.

52. UKNA FO 371/110840, V 1781/4, Minute by John E. Powell-Jones (FO), 13 April 1954.

53. David W. Lesch, "The 1957 American-Syrian Crisis: Globalist Policy in a Regional Reality," in David W. Lesch, *The Middle East and the United States: A Historical and Political Reassessment,* 3rd ed. (Oxford: Westview, 2003), 106–121.

54. UKNA FO 371/110840, V 1781/3, Despatch No. 17806/1/54, Embassy Damascus to FO, 24 March 1954; USNRA, RG59, CDF, Box 4072, 783.00/4–554, Despatch No. 568, Moose, Damascus to State Department, 5 April 1954. For an example of Mustafa al-Siba'i's ongoing attack on the Western powers, see Box 4074, 783.00 (W)/4–954, Joint Weekly A, No. 14, Military Attaché, Damascus to State Department, 9 April 1954.

55. See, for example, "Protests in Pakistan," *Times,* 6 December 1954; USNRA, RG59, CDF, Box 4073, 783.00/12–654, Despatch No. 231, Moose, Damascus to State Department, 6 December 1954; 783.00/12–1454, Despatch No. 231, Moose, Damascus to State Department, 14 December 1954; Box 4074, 783.00 (W)/12–1054, Joint Weekly A, No. 49, Military Attaché, Cairo to State Department, 10 December 1954.

56. UKNA FO 371/110840, V 1781/12, Despatch No. 189, Sir John Gardener (Ambassador), Embassy Damascus to Anthony Eden (Foreign Secretary), FO, 9 December 1954; see, on the same, Minute by Powell-Jones, 20 December 1954.

57. USNRA, CREST Database, CIA, "Current Intelligence Bulletin," 7 December 1954.

58. UKNA, FO 371/110840, V 1781/12, Minutes by Powell-Jones on Despatch No. 189, Gardener, Damascus to Eden, FO, 9 December 1954.

59. USNRA, RG59, CDF, Box 4088, 785.00/3–1154, Despatch No. 319, Talcott W. Seelye (Third Secretary), Embassy Amman to State Department, 11 March 1954. On the evolution of the Brotherhood's politics in this era, see also Marion Boulby, *The Muslim Brotherhood and the Kings of Jordan 1945–1993* (Atlanta, GA: Scholars Press, 1999), 50ff.

60. USNRA, RG59, CDF, Box 4088, 785.00 (W)/4–1654, Despatch No. 358, Embassy Amman to State Department, 16 April 1954; 785.00/5–1554, Despatch No. 393, Seelye, Amman to State Department, 15 May 1954; 785.00/6–1754, Despatch No. 441, Embassy Amman to State Department, 17 June 1954; 785.00 (W)/6–954, Despatch No. 443, Embassy Amman to State Department, 19 June 1954; 785.00 (W)/6–2654, Despatch No. 450, Embassy Amman to State Department, 26 June 1954; 785.00 (W)/8–2154,

Despatch No. 71, Embassy Amman to State Department, 21 August 1954; 785.00 (W)/8–2854, Despatch No. 78, Embassy Amman to State Department, 28 August 1954; 785.00 (W)/9–454, Despatch No. 88, Embassy Amman to State Department, 4 September 1954; "King Saud in Amman," *Times,* 14 June 1954.

61. USNRA, RG59, CDF, Box 4016a, 774.00/12–1454, Despatch No. 201, Geren, Amman to State Department, 14 December 1954. See also Box 4088, 785.00 (W)/12–1454, Despatch No. 202, Embassy Amman to State Department, 16 April 1954; UKNA FO 371/110840, V 1781/13, Telegram No. 17887/8/54, Embassy Amman to FO, 8 December 1954.

62. USNRA, RG59, CDF, Box 3770, 785.00/1–355, Despatch No. 216, Geren, Amman to State Department, 3 January 1955. On the "fascist odor" of the Brotherhood, see also 785.00/2–555, Despatch No. 253, Amman to State Department, 5 February 1955.

63. USNRA, RG59, CDF, Box 3770, 785.00/1–355, Despatch No. 216, Geren, Amman to State Department, 3 January 1955.

64. Ziyad Abu-Amr, *Islamic Fundamentalism in the West Bank and Gaza: Muslim Brotherhood and Islamic Jihad* (Bloomington: Indiana University Press, 1994), 4–6; Amir Cohen, *Political Parties in the West Bank under the Jordanian Regime, 1949–1967* (Ithaca, NY: Cornell University Press, 1982), 148–150. On the Brotherhood's support for the king during the 1956–1957 crisis in particular, see Bar, *Muslim Brotherhood in Jordan,* 25–29; Boulby, *The Muslim Brotherhood,* 20.

65. Mansoor Moaddel, *Islamic Modernism, Nationalism, and Fundamentalism: Episode and Discourse* (Chicago: University of Chicago Press, 2005), 292–319.

66. Bar, *Muslim Brotherhood in Jordan,* 15, 19, 27–29.

67. Moaddel, *Islamic Modernism,* 292–319.

68. USNRA, RG59, CDF, Box 3770, 785.00/3–1555, Despatch No. 298, Amman to State Department, 15 March 1955.

69. USNRA, RG59, CDF, Box 3773, 785.00 (W)/1–356, Despatch No. 223, Lester Mallory (Ambassador), Embassy Amman to State Department, 3 January 1956; 785.00 (W)/3–2756, Despatch No. 33, Embassy Amman to State Department, 27 March 1956; 785.00 (W)/5–1757, Despatch No. 292, Embassy Amman to State Department, 17 May 1957; Boulby, *Muslim Brotherhood,* 62–69; Cohen, *Political Parties in the West Bank,* 170–173.

70. Cohen, *Political Parties in the West Bank,* 181–182, 198.

71. USNRA, RG59, CDF, Box 3770, 785.00/1–1656, Despatch No. 235, Richard B. Parker (Political Officer), Embassy Amman to State Department, 16 January 1956; 785.00/1–2356, Despatch No. 242, Parker, Amman to State Department, 23 January 1956; 785.00/1–2456, Despatch No. 246, Parker, Amman to State Department, 24 January 1956.

72. UKNA FO 371/127878, VJ 1015/7, Telegram No. 288, Charles Johnston (Ambassador), Embassy Amman to FO, 15 February 1957; and in same, VJ 1015/5, Telegram No. 1013/13/57, R. Heath Mason (Counselor), Embassy Amman to R. Michael Hadow, FO, 23 January 1957.

73. For Brotherhood support for the king and anticommunism, see USNRA, RG59, CDF, Box 3770, 785.00/2–457, Despatch No. 875, Mallory, Amman to State Department, 4 February 1957; 785.00/2–857, Despatch No. 200, Milton Carl Walstrom (Chief Political Officer), Embassy Amman to State Department, 8 February 1957.

74. "Despatch No. 228 from F. R. H. Murray to Eden, Recording a Conversation between Shuckburgh and Egyptian Leaders," 11 December 1954, *BDDE,* vol. 3, 336–339.

75. USNRA, RG59, CDF, Box 3682, 774.00 (W)/4–2955, Joint Weekly A, No. 17, Military Attaché, Cairo to State Deparment, 29 April 1955. For a British assessment of Nasser's growing "self-assurance," see UKNA FO 371/113579, JE 1015/35, Telegram No. 118, F. Ralph Murray (Minister), Embassy Cairo to FO, 18 July 1955.

76. Geoffrey Aronson, *From Sideshow to Centre Stage: US Policy toward Egypt, 1946–1956* (Boulder, CO: L. Rienner, 1986), 136–149; Gail E. Meyer, *Egypt and the United States: The Formative Years* (Rutherford, NJ: Fairleigh Dickinson University Press, 1980), 115–126.

77. USNRA, RG59, CDF, Box 3681, 774.00/10–2955, Alan Dulles (Director of Central Intelligence) to Herbert Hoover (Under-Secretary of State), "Intelligence Assessment," 29 October 1955.

78. USNRA, RG59, CDF, Box 3682, 774.00/6–956, Despatch No. 1268, Embassy Cairo to State Department, 9 June 1956. For more on the constitutional changes, see Joel Gordon, *Nasser's Blessed Movement: Egypt's Free Officers and the July Revolution* (Oxford: Oxford University Press, 1992).

79. UKNA FO 371/113579, JE 1015/27, Minute by Thomas E. Bromley, FO, 16 June 1955.

80. UKNA FO 371/113579, JE 1015/33, Telegram No. 111, Stevenson, London to Harold MacMillan (Foreign Secretary), FO, 11 July 1955.

81. Minute by Sir John Wilton, FO, 22 July 1955, on ibid.

82. "Telegram No. 1625 from Trevelyan to FO," 4 November 1955, *BDDE,* vol. 3, 468–469. See also Humphrey Trevelyan, *The Middle East in Revolution* (London: MacMillan, 1970), ix, 15–69.

83. Wilbur Crane Eveland provides an account of this whole episode; he was tasked with meeting Nasser, even though he opposed the CIA's move. See HIA, Wilbur Crane Eveland Collection, Accession No. 80118 14.30, Box 2, Wilbur Eveland and Thomas Faber, "Manuscript for Innocents Abroad: The American Presence in the Near East, 1948–1975," 173–203, 311–312, especially 194 on the Ikhwan.

84. For Nasser's opposition to the pact, see USNRA, RG59, CDF, Box 3682, 774.00 (W)/2–2555, Joint Weekly A, No. 8, Military Attaché, Cairo to State Department, 25 February 1955; 774.00 (W)/3–355, Joint Weekly A, No. 9, Military Attaché, Cairo to State Department; "Telegram No. 389, Stevenson to FO," 14 March 1955, *BDDE,* vol. 3, 401–402. See also Meyer, *Egypt and the United States,* 87–104.

85. USNRA, RG59, CDF, Box 3682, 774.00 (W)/3–355, Joint Weekly A, No. 9, Military Attaché, Cairo to State Department; UKNA FO 371/113579, JE 1015/35, Telegram No. 118, Murray, Cairo to FO, 18 July 1955.

86. USNRA, RG59, CDF, Box 4016a, 774.00/1–1254, Despatch No. 1635, Caffery, Cairo to State Department, 12 January 1954; 774.00/8–1354, Despatch No. 246, Caffery, Cairo to State Department, 13 August 1954; Box 3682, 774.00 (W)/3–355, Joint Weekly A, No. 32, Military Attaché, Cairo to State Department, 12 August 1955.

87. USNRA, RG59, CDF, Box 3681, 774.00/7–1555, Despatch No. 73, Byroade, Cairo to State Department, 15 July 1955. On a similar theme, see 774.00/8–3155, Despatch No. 256, Byroade, Cairo to State Department, 31 August 1955.

88. USNRA, CREST Database, CIA, "National Intelligence Digest," 1 April 1955.

89. Ibid.; see also CIA, "Developments in the Arab World Leading to Neutralism," undated, spring 1955.

90. USNRA, RG273, Records of the National Security Council (NSC), Policy Papers 5423–5428, Box 32, "National Security Council Progress Report on United States

Objectives and Policies with Respect to the Near East, by the Operations Coordinating Board, 17 March 1956."

91. USNRA, RG59, CDF, Box 3681, 774.00/7–1555, Despatch No. 73, Byroade, Cairo to State Department 15 July 1955.

92. USNRA, RG59, CDF, Box 3681, 774.00/10–2955, Dulles to Hoover, "Intelligence Assessment," 29 October 1955.

93. Lesch, "1957 American-Syrian Crisis."

94. Aronson, *From Sideshow to Centre Stage,* 154–162; USNRA, RG273, Records of the NSC, Policy Papers 5423–5428, Box 32, "National Security Council Progress Report on United States Objectives and Policies with Respect to the Near East, by the Operations Coordinating Board, 17 March 1956."

95. USNRA, RG59, Policy Planning Staff / Council Area Files, 1947–1962, Box 11, Dispatch No. 748, Parker T. Hart (Charge d'Affaires), Embassy Cairo to State Department, 11 January 1956, including "Recommendations as to United States Policy in the Middle East."

96. UKNA, FO 371/118861, JE 1053/1, Draft Brief for Shuckburgh, 7 January 1956.

97. "Egypt: Cabinet Conclusions," 22 February 1956; "Minute by J. H. A. Watson," 23 February 1956. Both available in *BDDE,* vol. 3, 496–497.

98. UKNA FO 371/118862, JE 1053/20, J. H. Adam Watson (Head of Africa Department), FO to Trevelyan, Cairo, 22 March 1956.

99. USNRA, RG59, CDF, Box 3682, 774.00/5–1656, Despatch No. 5313, Winthrop Aldrich (Ambassador), Embassy London to State Department, 16 May 1956.

100. UKNA FO 371/118862, JE 1053/20, Watson, FO to Trevelyan, Cairo, 22 March 1956. On the shift in British views, see also Richard J. Aldrich, *The Hidden Hand: Britain, America and Cold War Secret Intelligence* (London: John Murray, 2001), 476–491.

101. Muhammad Abd el-Wahab Sayed-Ahmed, *Nasser and American Foreign Policy, 1952–1956* (London: Laam, 1989), 116–117.

102. UKNRA, RG59, CDF, Box 3682, 774.00/10–356, "Report of the United States–United Kingdom Working Group on Egypt," 3 October 1956. See also Douglas Little, "Mission Impossible: The CIA and the Cult of Covert Action in the Middle East," *Diplomatic History* 28, no. 5 (2004), 663–701 (674–677); W. Scott Lucas and Ray Takeyh, "Alliance and Balance: The Anglo-American Relationship and Egyptian Nationalism, 1950–57," *Diplomacy and Statecraft* 7, no. 3 (1996), 631–651 (644).

103. UKNA, FO 371/118862, JE 1053/20, Watson, FO to Trevelyan, Cairo, 6 April 1956.

104. UKNRA, RG59, CDF, Box 3682, 774.00/10–356, "Report of the United States–United Kingdom Working Group on Egypt," 3 October 1956.

105. Trevelyan, *Middle East,* 3, 93.

106. See Miles Copeland, *The Game Player: Confessions of the CIA's Original Political Operative* (London: Aurum, 1989).

107. Said K. Aburish, *Nasser: The Last Arab* (London: Duckworth, 2005), 88–89, 95.

108. Ibid., 128. See also Nigel West, *The Friends: Britain's Post-War Secret Intelligence Operations* (London: Weidenfeld & Nicolson, 1988), 97–117. Douglas Little offers a different view on Operation Sipony, suggesting it had nothing to do with the Ikhwan and instead aimed at a "palace revolution." See Little, "Mission Impossible," 678–683.

109. Mark Curtis, *Secret Affairs: Britain's Collusion with Radical Islam* (London: Serpent's Tail, 2010), 62–44. See also André Gerolymatos, *Castles Made of Sand: A Century of*

Anglo-American Espionage and Intervention in the Middle East (New York: Thomas Dunne Books, 2010), 13–15.

110. Michael T. Thornhill, *Road to Suez: The Battle of the Canal Zone* (Stroud, UK: Sutton, 2006), 121–122.

111. Meyer, *Egypt and the United States,* 130–146.

112. Calder Walton, *Empire of Secrets: British Intelligence, the Cold War and the Twilight of Empire* (London: HarperPress, 2013), 295–296.

113. Meyer, *Egypt and the United States,* 167–171; Lucas, *Divided We Stand*; Ritchie Ovendale, *Britain, the United States and the Transfer of Power in the Middle East, 1945–1962* (London: Leicester University Press, 1996), 155–166; Keith Kyle, *Suez* (London: Weidenfeld & Nicolson, 1991).

114. John S. Badeau, *The American Approach to the Arab World* (New York: Council for Foreign Relations, 1968), 7.

115. See, for example, the material in UKNA FO 371/118836, JE 1015/119 and JE 1015/121.

116. It is often forgotten that in purely military terms, Suez was a resounding victory for the Anglo-French forces.

117. Cohen, *Political Parties in the West Bank,* 193–194.

118. USNA, RG273, Records of the NSC, Policy Papers 5423–5428, Box 32, "National Security Council Progress Report on United States Objectives and Policies with Respect to the Near East, by the Operations Coordinating Board," 22 December 1956.

119. Meyer, *Egypt and the United States,* 181–184.

120. Salim Yaqub, *Containing Arab Nationalism: The Eisenhower Doctrine in the Middle East* (Chapel Hill: University of North Carolina Press, 2004), 1–2; see also Elie Podeh, "The Perils of Ambiguity: The United States and the Baghdad Pact," in Lesch, *Middle East and the United States,* 86–105 (97–101).

121. See Chapter 5. For discussion over the possible use of Islam as a bulwark against communism, see also Chapter 3. For a different perspective that emphasizes the centrality of Nasser (and is deeply critical of the CIA), see Wilbur C. Eveland, *Ropes of Sand: America's Failure in the Middle East* (London: Norton, 1980).

122. Matthew F. Jacobs, *Imagining the Middle East: The Building of an American Foreign Policy, 1918–1967* (Chapel Hill: University of North Carolina Press, 2011), 77ff.

123. "The Pan-Islamic Movement," *Times,* 13 June 1907.

124. John Ferris, " 'The Internationalism of Islam': The British Perception of a Muslim Menace, 1840–1951," *Intelligence and National Security* 24, no. 1 (2009), 57–77. See also references to the debate on pan-Islamism in Joseph Heller, *British Policy towards the Ottoman Empire 1908–14* (London: Cass, 1983), 33–39, 54–55, 161–162; Francis Robinson, "The British Empire in the Muslim World," in *The Oxford History of the British Empire: Volume IV—The Twentieth Century,* ed. Judith Brown and William Roger Louis (Oxford: Oxford University Press), 405–407; and David Motadel, "Islam and the European Empires," *Historical Journal* 55, no. 3 (2012), 835–839.

125. David Fromkin, *A Peace to End All Peace: The Fall of the Ottoman Empire and the Creation of the Modern Middle East* (New York: Henry Holt, 1989), 96–105.

126. Martin Kramer, *Islam Assembled: The Advent of the Muslim Congresses* (Guildford, UK: Columbia University Press), 163–164.

127. UKNA FO 371/75120, E11745/1781/65, Telegram No. 491, Christopher Pirie-Gordon (Deputy resident), Embassy Amman to FO, 28 September 1949. See also Curtis, *Secret Affairs*, 42–44.

128. UKNA FO 371/75120, E11791/1781/65, Telegram No. 464, Sir Noel Charles (Ambassador), Embassy Angora [Ankara], to FO, 27 September 1949.

129. UKNA FO 371/75120, E 11188/1781/65, Telegram No. 407, Sir John Troutbeck, British Middle East Office (BMEO), Cairo to FO, 13 September 1949. For this kind of reasoning in a different context, see "Largest Muslim State: The Shaping of Policies in Pakistan," *Times,* 10 January 1949.

130. UKNA FO 371/137972, J 1079/24, FO Print, "Africa: The Next Ten Years," 2 December 1959.

131. UKNA FO 371/75120, E12225/1781/65, Despatch No. 37 (31/2/818), BMEO, Cairo to FO, 4 October 1949.

132. Ibid.

133. Ibid.

134. UKNA FO 371/75120, E 12225/1781/65, Draft British Minute, "Pan-Islam," undated.

135. Bernard Lewis, "Communism and Islam," *International Affairs* 30, no. 1 (January 1954), 1–12.

136. UKNA FO 371/75120, E 11188/1781/65, Telegram No. 407, Troutbeck, Cairo to FO, 13 September 1949.

137. UKNA FO 371/75120, E 12225/1781/65, Telegram No. 37, Troutbeck, Cairo, 4 October 1949. Troutbeck's critics felt he "overstated" his case and was alarmist in his analysis. See, for example, in the same file, Minute by L. G. Thirkell, FO, 14 October 1949, and Minute by K. C. Buss, FO, 14 October 1949. On all of this, see also Curtis, *Secret Affairs*, 42–43.

138. UKNA KV5/65, Box No. 500, OF.524/18/B3A, SIME (Security Intelligence Middle East), "Jamiyat al Adab al Islamiya—The Moslem Ethical Society," 25 January 1949.

139. Fareed Sabri, "The Caliphate and the Political Ideology of the Iraqi and Egyptian Muslim Brotherhood," *Arches Quarterly* 6, no. 10 (Winter 2012).

140. See, for example, the description of the Dar-ul-Islam movement of Indonesia in "Government in Indonesia," *Times,* 10 April 1952; "Insurgents in West Java," *Times,* 14 March 1950; "The Impulse of Islam," *Times,* 28 May 1953.

141. UKNA FO 371/90130, JE 1051/26, Letter, Inamullah Khan, Secretary Muslim World Conference to Ministry of Foreign Affairs London, 28 February 1951. On the same, see "Al-Ikhwan al-Muslimun," *Al-Da'wa,* 28 February 1951.

142. On the composition of this body and its ties to the Brotherhood, see UKNA FO 371/110841, Research Department, Foreign Office, "Quarterly Review of Islamic Affairs: Third Quarter of 1954," 5 October 1954; FO 371/110840, V 1781/1, Dispatch No. 1781/1/54, Sir John C. B. Richmond (Counselor), Embassy Amman, to Sir C. Martin Le Quesne (First Secretary), Bahrain, and FO, 4 January 1954; V 1781/1, Despatch No. 17820/3/54, Embassy Beirut to FO, 13 January 1954; USNRA, RG59, Box 3770, 785.00/1–355, Despatch No. 216, Geren, Amman to State Department, 3 January 1955.

143. UKNA FO 371/110841, Research Department, Foreign Office, "Quarterly Review of Islamic Affairs: Fourth Quarter of 1953," 19 January 1954; FO 371/110840, V 1781/1, Dispatch No. 1781/1/54, Richmond, Amman, to Le Quesne, Bahrain, and FO, 4 January 1954, and especially enclosure, "Resolutions." For earlier gatherings, which were also a source of concern to the British, see Kramer, *Islam Assembled,* 123–141.

144. UKNA FO 371/110840, V 1781/1, Despatch No. 17820/3/54, Embassy Beirut to FO, 13 January 1954; FO 371/110841, Research Department, Foreign Office, "Quarterly Review of Islamic Affairs: Fourth Quarter of 1953," 19 January 1954.

145. UKNA FO 371/110841, Research Department, Foreign Office, "Quarterly Review of Islamic Affairs: First Quarter of 1954," 6 April 1954; FO 371/110840, V 1781/7, Despatch No. 17806/8/54, Embassy Damascus to FO, 15 September 1954. On the same, see especially the Minute by Powell-Jones, 24 September 1954. For more discussion of the Congress, see Cohen, *Political Parties in the West Bank,* 174–178.

146. UKNA CAB 158/18, Joint Intelligence Committee, "Political Developments in the Middle East," JIC (54) 72, 19 August 1954.

147. Peter Mansfield, *The British in Egypt* (London: Weidenfeld & Nicolson, 1971), 63–64, 92–95.

148. Arnold Toynbee, "Islam, the West, and the Future," in Arnold Toynbee, *Civilization on Trial* (New York: Oxford University Press, 1948), 184–212.

149. James Heyworth-Dunne, *Religious and Political Trends in Modern Egypt* (Washington, DC: the author, 1950), 50.

150. Ibid., 78–81.

151. William Inboden, *Religion and American Foreign Policy, 1945–1960: The Soul of Containment* (Cambridge: Cambridge University Press, 2008), 1–22.

152. HIA, Christina Harris Papers, Accession No. 79085 10.03, Box 6, William A. Eddy, "How Arabs See the West Today" (transcript of a recording of an address made informally and from abbreviated notes at the Middle East Institute), 19 December 1950.

153. See, for example, the views expressed in USNRA, RG59, CDF, Box 4014, 774.00/ 4–2051, Letter, G. Lewis Jones, Director of Near Eastern Affairs (NEA) to Mr. Robert Lake of New York, replying to queries put to Congressman Riehlman, 20 April 1951.

154. Cited in Henry William Brands, *Into the Labyrinth: The United States and the Middle East, 1945–93* (New York: McGraw-Hill, 1994), 35–44.

155. Jacobs, *Imagining the Middle East,* 82–87. On the question of official views toward the region, see also Hugh Wilford, "America's Great Game: The CIA and the Middle East, 1947–1967," in Bevan Sewell and Scott Lucas, *Challenging US Foreign Policy: America and the World in the Long Twentieth Century* (Basingstoke, UK: Palgrave Macmillan, 2011), 99–112.

156. USNRA, RG59, CDF, Box 2485, 511.80/3–1452, Memorandum, "Working Group on Special Materials for Arab and Other Moslem Countries," 14 March 1952, including "Enclosure: 'Program Proposal for the Arab and Other Moslem States.'" See also, in the same, 511.80/3–1752, Memorandum, O.C. Anderson (Program Planning and Evaluation Staff, PRS) to S. Shephard Jones (NEA), 17 March 1952.

157. USNRA, RG59, CDF, Box 2485, "Transcript of Proceedings: Working Group on Special Materials for Arab and other Moslem Countries," 1 April 1952; and in the same box, 511.80/4–2852, Memorandum Helga Wall to Casler, 28 April 1952; and "Progress Report No. 1 for Working Group on Islamic Countries." For a dissenting view on all this, see 511.80/10–152, Despatch No. 255, Burton Y. Berry (Ambassador), Embassy Baghdad to State Department, 1 October 1952.

158. USNRA, RG59, CDF, Box 2485, Bruce, Circular Airgram, "Colloquium on Islamic Culture under the Auspices of the Library of Congress and Princeton University, September 1953," 1 August 1952. For debates about the structure of the colloquium, see in the same, "Minutes of Meeting September 20, 1952 on Colloquium on Islamic Culture,"

1 October 1952; and "Enclosure: Colloquium on Islamic Culture, September, 1953, Summary of Salient Facts."

159. USNRA, RG59, CDF, Box 2485, Memorandum, Wilson Compton to Bruce, 13 January 1953.

160. USNRA, RG59, CDF, Box 2485, Bruce, Circular Airgram, "Colloquium on Islamic Culture under the Auspices of the Library of Congress and Princeton University, September 1953," 1 August 1952.

161. USNRA, RG59, CDF, Box 2485, State Department Instruction CA-3066, to all NEA posts and London, Paris, Rome, Madrid and Djakarta, "Colloquium on Islamic Culture in Its Relation to the Contemporary World" and "Enclosure: Summary of the Proceedings of the Colloquium on Islamic Culture in Its Relation to the Contemporary World," 7 December 1953.

162. Ian Johnson, *A Mosque in Munich: Nazis, the CIA and the Rise of the Muslim Brotherhood in the West* (Boston: Houghton Mifflin Harcourt, 2010).

163. For an example, see the Pakistan nominees: USNRA, RG59, CDF, Box 2485, 511.80/1–1453, Despatch No. 668, Ray Lee (Public Affairs Officer), Embassy Karachi to State Department, 14 January 1953.

164. USNRA, RG59, Box 2485, CDF, Memorandum, "Participants Expected at Colloquium on Islamic Culture," 30 April 1953.

165. USNRA, RG59, CDF, Box 2485, 511.80/6–2353, Despatch No. 2849, Embassy Cairo to State Department, 23 June 1953.

166. USNRA, RG59, CDF, Box 2485, 511.80/7–153, Airgram A-1, Dulles, State Department to Embassy Cairo, 1 July 1953.

167. USNRA, RG59, CDF, Box 2485, 511.80/7–2753, Despatch No. 237, Caffery, Cairo to State Department, 27 July 1953.

168. USNRA, RG59, CDF, Box 2485, 511.80/8–1753, Theodore Streibert (Director, US Information Agency), State Department to Embassy Cairo, 17 August 1953.

169. USNRA, CREST Database, CIA, "Comments on the Islamic Colloquium, Princeton, 8–17 Sep 53."

170. Cited in Johnson, *Mosque in Munich*, 69.

171. Dwight D. Eisenhower, *The Eisenhower Diaries*, ed. Robert H. Ferrell (London: Norton, 1981), see entry for 28 March 1956. See also Yaqub, *Containing Arab Nationalism*, 43–44, 101–106.

172. "King Saud Leaves for Home," *Times*, 26 April 1954. See also "King Saud in Cairo," *Times*, 22 March 1954; "King Saud in Amman," *Times*, 14 June 1954.

173. Osgood Caruthers, "Saud vs. Nasser: A Study in Contrasts," *New York Times*, 10 November 1957.

174. USNRA, RG59, CDF, Box 3748, 783.001/8–757, Despatch No. 60, Strong, Damascus to State Department, 7 August 1957.

175. USNRA, RG59, CDF, Box 3771, 785.00/4–2657, Despatch No. 1788, Embassy Baghdad to State Department, 26 April 1957.

176. USNRA, RG59, Policy Planning Staff / Council Area Files, 1947–1962, Box 18, "United States Psychological Warfare Program in the Middle East Study and Recommendations for Improvement," 10 December 1957.

177. USNRA, RG273, Records of the NSC, Policy Papers 5813–5820, Box 48, "Staff Study: United States Objectives and Policies with Respect to the Near East."

178. USNRA, RG59, State Department Bureau of NE and SA Affairs, Lot File #A1 3129, Box 7, Letter, Parker T. Hart (Ambassador), Embassy Jidda, to Robert Strong (Director), NEA, State Department, 27 January 1962.

179. USNRA, RG59, CDF, Box 3746, 783.00/8–2157, Despatch No. 541, Strong, Damascus to State Department, 21 August 1957. On the failure of this coup, code-named "Operation Wappen," see John Prados, *Presidents' Secret Wars: CIA and Pentagon Covert Operations from World War II through the Persian Gulf* (Chicago: I. R. Dee, 1996), 128–130; Anthony Gorst and W. Scott Lucas, "The Other Collusion: Operation Straggle and Anglo-American Intervention in Syria, 1955–56," *Intelligence and National Security* 4, no. 3 (1989), 576–595.

180. USNRA, RG59, CDF, Box 3746, 783.00/8–2757, Despatch No. 326, Dulles, State Department, to Embassy Jidda, 27 August 1957.

181. USNRA, RG59, CDF, Box 3746, 783.00/8–2057, Despatch No. 321, Mallory, Amman to State Department, 20 August 1957.

182. USNRA, RG59, CDF, Box 4893, 880.413/4–1157, "Memorandum of Conversation," 11 April 1957. For further details of this episode, see also in the same file, 880.413/5–1657, "Memorandum, William M. Rountree [Assistant Secretary of State] to Secretary of State," 16 May 1957.

183. USNRA, RG59, CDF, Box 3746, 783.00/9–2557, Despatch No. 278, Dulles, Circular to Region—Joint State-USIA Message, 25 September 1957.

184. USNRA, RG59, Policy Planning Staff/Council Area Files, 1947–1962, Box 18, "United States Psychological Warfare Program in the Middle East Study and Recommendations for Improvement," 10 December 1957.

185. Johnson, *Mosque in Munich*, 127–128.

186. USNRA, CREST Database, Operations Coordinating Board, Washington, DC, "Inventory of U.S. Government and Private Organization Activity regarding Islamic Organizations as an Aspect of Overseas Operations," 3 May 1957. A further point of note is that a "list of relevant Islamic studies" in Annex B of the document featured among its twelve recommended works, James Heyworth-Dunne's *Religious and Political Trends in Modern Egypt*.

187. See Chapters 3-5.

188. Salih ʿAshmawi, "Al-shiyuʿaiya tataharrak fi Iran wa misr wa bakistan," *al-Daʿwa*, 13 March 1951.

189. Abu Ayman, "Fi Amrika," *al-Muslimun* 5, no. 9 (June 1957).

190. Abu Ayman, "What We Stand For," *al-Muslimun* 5, no. 2 (May 1956).

191. USNRA, RG59, CDF, Box 3745, 783.00/9–2456, "Memorandum of Conversation," R. A. Lincoln to Strong, Damascus, 24 September 1956.

192. USNRA, RG59, CDF, Box 4893, 880.413/2–856, Despatch No. 121, William J. Porter (Consul-General), Embassy Rabat to State Department, 8 February 1956; Box 2070, 786B.00/1–160, Telegram G-131, Howard P. Jones (Ambassador), Embassy Djakarta to State Department, 1 January 1960.

193. Saʿid Ramadan, *Three Major Problems Confronting the World of Islam* (Islamic Centre of Geneva, 1960), especially 6–11; Saʿid Ramadan, *Islam and Nationalism* (Takoma Park, MD: Crescent Publications, 1963), especially 1–6.

194. Johnson, *Mosque in Munich*, 131–133.

195. See, for instance, on the anticommunism of the Sudanese Brotherhood, UKNA FO 141/1342, G. J. Jenkins (Security Representative), Embassy Cairo to Head of SIME; GHQ MELF (General Headquarters, Middle East Land Forces), 9 February 1949.

196. UKNA FO 371/127878, VJ 1015/16, No. 594, Johnston, Amman to FO, 4 April 1957. See also VJ 1015/24, No. 883, Sir Harold Caccia (Ambassador), Embassy Washington to FO, 12 April 1957; VJ 1015/25, No. 647, Johnston, Amman to FO, 13 April 1957; USNRA, RG59, CDF, Box 3771, 785.00/4–2557, Despatch No. 2536 Embassy Damascus to State Department, 25 April 1957. See also Cohen, *Political Parties in the West Bank,* 189.

197. USNRA, RG59, CDF, Box 3771, 785.00/7–2257, Despatch No. 9, William E. Cole (Consul-General), Jerusalem to State Department, 22 July 1957.

198. USNRA, RG59, CDF, Box 3745, 783.00/5–1756, Despatch No. 2270, Dulles, State Department to Damascus, 28 May 1957. See also in the same, 783.00/5–1757, Despatch No. 2779, Moose, Damascus to State Department, 17 May 1957.

199. USNRA, RG59, CDF, Box 3745, 783.00/10–256, Despatch No. 157, Strong, Damascus to State Department, 2 October 1956. For other views of resumed Brotherhood activity, see in the same, 783.00/10–2856, Despatch No. 945, Embassy Damascus to State Department, 28 October 1956; and 783.00/10–3156, Despatch No. 990, Embassy Damascus to State Department, 31 October 1956.

200. UKNA FO 371/125415, JE 1015/132, No. 10217/22/57"S," Ian D. Scott (First Secretary), Embassy Beirut to Watson, FO, 11 April 1957; and JE 1015/138, No. 10217/24/57"S," Scott, Beirut to Watson, FO, 18 April 1957.

201. UKNA FO 371/125415, JE 1015/132, No. 10217/22/57(S), Scott, Beirut to Watson, FO, 11 April 1957, including "Annexure"; also, USNRA, RG59, Box 3745, 783.00/5–357, Despatch No. 2640, Moose, Damascus to State Department, 3 May 1957.

202. USNRA, RG59, CDF, Box 3745, 783.00/5–557, Despatch No. 2664, Embassy Damascus to State Department, 5 May 1957; 783.00/5–757, Despatch No. 2670, Embassy Damascus to State Department, 7 May 1957.

203. USNRA, RG59, CDF, Box 3745, 783.00/4–957, Despatch No. 2357, Moose, Damascus to State Department, 9 April 1957. On the split between the Brotherhood and the Ba'th, see also UKNA, FO 371/125416, JE 1015/159, No. 10217/31/57(S), Scott, Beirut to Watson, FO, 15 May 1957.

204. USNRA, RG59, CDF, Box 3745, 783.00/7–1357, Despatch No. 13, Strong, Damascus to State Department, 13 July 1957.

205. UKNA FO 371/127882, VJ 1015/180, No. 44 (S), Johnston, Amman to FO, 26 October 1957; for Brotherhood opposition to the government, see in the same file, VJ 1015/181, No. 1013/389/57, Johnston, Amman to E. Michael Rose, FO, 23 October 1957.

206. USNRA, RG59, CDF, Box 3748, 783.00 (W)/8–357, Joint Weekly A, No. 18, Richard Funkhouser (First Secretary), Embassy Damascus to State Department, 3 August 1957.

207. UKNA FO 371/125416, JE 1015/155, Foreign Office Minute, 30 December 1956.

208. USNRA, RG59, CDF, Box 3682, 774.00/2–557, Despatch No. 542, Peter Chase (First Secretary), Embassy Cairo to State Department, 5 February 1957.

209. USNRA, RG59, CDF, Box 3682, 774.00/5–2957, Telegram Unnumbered, Embassy Cairo to State Department, 29 May 1957.

210. UKNA FO 371/125444, JE 1052/20, Minute by Watson to Archibald D. M. Ross (Assistant Under-Secretary), FO, 9 July 1957.

211. USNRA, RG59, CDF, Box 3682, 774.00/12–2857, Despatch No. 115, Anthony Cuomo (Consul), Port Said to State Department, 28 December 1957.

212. USNRA, RG59, CDF, Box 3682, 774.00/5–357, Despatch No. 3416, Raymond Hare (Ambassador), Embassy Cairo to State Department, 3 May 1957.

213. USNRA, RG59, CDF, Box 3682, 774.00/7–1957, Despatch No. 180, Hare, Cairo to State Department, 19 July 1957; and in the same, 774.00/7–1957, Despatch No. 558, John Whitney (Ambassdaor), Embassy London to State Department, 19 July 1957.

214. USNRA, RG59, CDF, Box 3682, 774.00/8–1457, Despatch No. 441, Hare, Cairo to State Department, 14 August 1957.

215. USNRA, RG59, CDF, Box 3682, 774.00/9–1257, Letter, Stuart W. Rockwell, Director of Office of Near Eastern Affairs, to Roger Baldwin, Chairman of International League for the Rights of Man, 12 September 1957.

216. USNRA, RG59, CDF, Box 3682, 774.00/10–2157, Despatch No. 1024, Embassy Cairo to State Department, 21 October 1957.

217. John Ranelagh, *The Agency: The Rise and Decline of the CIA* (London: Weidenfeld & Nicolson, 1986), 298.

218. USNRA, RG59, CDF, Box 3682, 774.00/5–1057, Despatch No. 1108, Claude G. Ross (Political Counselor), Embassy Cairo to State Department, 10 May 1958.

219. USNRA, RG59, CDF, Box 3476, 783.00/8–2757, Despatch No. 326, Dulles, State Department to Embassy Jidda, 27 August 1957; Box 3477, 783.00/10–1657, Letter, Strong, Damascus to Rountree, State Department, 16 October 1957.

220. USNRA, RG59, Policy Planning Staff/Council, Country Files, 1947–62, Box 18, E. G. Matthews, Memorandum, "US Policy in the Middle East," 18 July 1956.

221. USNRA, RG59, Policy Planning Staff/Council, Country Files, 1947–62, Box 18, Intelligence Report No. 7292, "The Evolution of Egyptian Neutralism," 9 July 1956.

222. USNRA, RG59, Policy Planning Staff/Council, Country Files, 1947–62, Box 18, E. G. Matthews, Memorandum, "US Policy in the Middle East," 18 July 1956.

223. USNRA, RG59, CDF, Box 3746, 783.00/8–2657, Despatch No. 559, Dulles, State Department to Embassy Cairo, 26 August 1957.

224. USNRA, RG59, CDF, Box 3746, 783.00/9–557, Despatch No. 703, Strong, Damascus to State Department, 5 September 1957.

225. USNRA, RG59, CDF, Box 3746, 783.00/12–1057, Despatch No. 1622, Strong, Damascus to State Department, 10 December 1957. With regard to the Baʿth Party, meanwhile, it is striking that it too now expressed "sincere interest" in "improving relations with the US." See Box 3747, 783.00/1–458, Despatch No. 1839, Strong, Damascus to State Department, 4 January 1958.

226. USNRA, RG59, CDF, Box 3683, 774.00/2–2658, Despatch No. 843, Embassy Cairo to State Department, 26 February 1958.

227. UKNA FO 371/125444, JE 1052/8, Minute by Trefor E. Evans, FO, "Relations with Egypt," 11 March 1957. See also, in the same, JE 1052/11, Minute by Evans, "Egypt," 18 March 1957; JE 1052/11, Minute by Watson, "Anglo-Egyptian Relations," 8 May 1957.

228. UKNA FO 371/125444, JE 1052/21, Minute by Lloyd, "Record of a Conversation," 31 July 1957.

229. Yaqub, *Containing Arab Nationalism,* 147–270.

230. USNRA, RG273, Records of the NSC, Box 4, G. Huntington Damon (Chief), Information and Education Projects Staff, Memorandum for the Executive Officer, "The Near East," 16 July 1958.

231. Ritchie Ovendale and Nigel Ashton, respectively, have shown that these events were not quite as coordinated as was once assumed: the Americans committed to an intervention in Lebanon unilaterally; the British scrambled to follow with their own operation in Amman, perhaps exaggerating or even inventing altogether a threat that justified the move, which was scarcely welcomed in Washington. See Ritchie Ovendale, "Great Britain and the Anglo-American Invasion of Jordan and Lebanon in 1958," *International History Review* 16, no. 2 (May 1994), 284–303; Nigel Ashton, *Eisenhower, Macmillan and the Problem of Nasser: Anglo-American Relations and Arab Nationalism, 1955–59* (Basingstoke, UK: Macmillan, 1996), 168–169. See also William Roger Louis, *Ends of British Imperialism: The Scramble for Empire, Suez and Decolonization* (London: I. B. Tauris, 2006), 817–843.

232. USNRA, RG273, Records of the NSC, Box 4, Damon, Information and Education Projects Staff, Memorandum for the Executive Officer, "The Near East," 16 July 1958.

233. USNRA, RG273, Records of the NSC, Policy Papers 5813–5820, Box 48, "Draft Statement of US Policy toward the Near East: NSC 5820."

234. Ibid.; and in the same file, National Security Council 5820/1, "U.S. Policy toward the Near East," 4 November 1958. See also David W. Lesch, "'Abd al-Nasser and the United States: Enemy or Friend?" in *Rethinking Nasserism: Revolution and Historical Memory in Modern Egypt*, ed. Elie Podeh and Onn Winckler (Gainesville: University of Florida Press, 2004), 212–223; Malik Mufti, "The United States and Nasserist Pan-Arabism," in Lesch, *Middle East and the United States*, 141–160.

235. USNRA, RG59, Policy Planning Staff/Council Area Files, 1947–1962, Box 18, Special NIE No. 30-3-58, "Arab Nationalism as a Factor in the Middle East Situation," 12 August 1958.

236. USNRA, RG59, CDF, Box 3789, 786B.00/3-2159, Despatch No. 2736, Hare, Cairo to State Department, 21 March 1959; RG273, Records of the NSC, Box 5, Operations Coordinating Board: Report on the Near East (NSC 5820/1), February 3 1960; Malcolm Kerr, *The Arab Cold War: Gamal 'Abd al-Nasir and His Rivals, 1958–70*, 3rd ed. (Oxford: Oxford University Press, 1971), 16–18.

237. USNRA, RG59, Lot File No. 61 D 43, Office Files Relating to Middle Eastern Affairs, 1958–9, Box 14, "Steps We Have Taken to Improve US-UAR Relations."

238. Under this law, surplus commodities could be sold to target countries, with the proceeds used to create low-interest loans in the local currency that could be fed back into development projects. For a discussion of the policy, see Badeau, *American Approach*, 67–75. See also USNRA, RG59, Lot File No. 61 D 43, Office Files Relating to Middle Eastern Affairs, 1958–9, Box 14, Memorandum by Armin H. Meyer (Deputy Director, NEA) to Rountree, State Department, 28 April 1959.

239. USNRA, RG59, State Department Bureau of NE and SA Affairs, Lot File #A1 3129, Box 2, Memorandum, Nicholas Thacher (Deputy Director, NEA) to G. Lewis Jones (Assistant Secretary of State), State Department, 15 August 1960.

240. USNRA, RG273, Records of the NSC, Box 5, Operations Coordinating Board: Report on the Near East (NSC 5820/1), 3 February 1960.

241. USNRA, RG59, CDF, Box 2072, 786B.11/3-2160, Letter, Jones, State Department to Ambassador Ellsworth Bunker, New Delhi, 21 March 1960.

242. USNRA, RG59, CDF, Box 2071, 786B.00/6-2860, Memorandum "Comments on Nasser's Alexandria Speech," William D. Brewer (Officer in Charge of UAR), State Department to Meyer, 28 June 1960. For more on tensions with Nasser, see also 786B.00/9-960,

Despatch No. 156, Curtis C. Strong, Embassy Cairo to State Department, 9 September 1960; 786B.11/5–860, Despatch No. 3369, Embassy Cairo to State Department, 8 May 1960; RG273, Records of the NSC, Box 5, Operations Coordinating Board: Operations Plan for the United Arab Republic, 15 July 1960.

243. USNRA RG59, CDF, Box 2071, 786B.00/3–1160, Intelligence Report No. 8235, "Outlook for the United Arab Republic," 11 March 1960.

244. John S. Badeau, *The Middle East Remembered* (Washington, DC: Middle East Institute, 2009), 170–179, 191–192. See also Douglas Little, "The New Frontier on the Nile: JFK, Nasser, and Arab Nationalism," *Journal of American History* 75, no. 2 (1988), 501–527; Douglas Little, "From Even-Handed to Empty-Handed: Seeking Order in the Middle East," in *Kennedy's Quest for Victory; American Foreign Policy, 1961–1963*, ed. Thomas G. Patterson (New York: Oxford University Press, 1989), 156–177 (159–163).

245. USNRA, RG59, Bureau of NE and SA Affairs, Records of the UAR Affairs Desk, 1956–1962, Box 3, Memorandum from Roger Hilsman (Bureau of Intelligence and Research, INR) to Phillips Talbot (Assistant Secretary of State for NEA), 18 December 1961.

246. USNRA, RG59, Bureau of NE and SA Affairs, Records of the UAR Affairs Desk, 1956–1962, Box 3, Memorandum from Thacher to Jones, 7 March 1961.

247. USNRA, RG59, State Department Lot File #A1 3129, Bureau of NE and SA Affairs, Box 4, "Cumulative Report—The United Arab Republic—1961," Dr. Robert Neumann of University of California, Director of Institute of International Studies to Armin Meyer (Deputy Assistant Secretary of NE and SA Affairs), 2 October 1961.

248. USNRA, RG59, State Department, Bureau of NE and SA Affairs, Lot File #A1 3129, Box 7, Lucius Battle, Memorandum for McGeorge Bundy (Special Assistant for National Security Affairs) on US Policy toward UAR and SAR [Syrian Arab Republic] following National Security Action Memorandum No. 105 of 16 October 1961, 2 November 1961; see also RG59, Office of the Country Director for the United Arab Republic (NEA/UAR), 1961–66, Box 3, Memorandum "Action Program for the UAR," Talbot to George C. McGhee (Under Secretary of State for Political Affairs), 3 January 1962.

249. USNRA, RG59, Box 2072, Memorandum, "Advantages to Be Gained from a State Visit by President Nasser in April," Acting Secretary, January 1962. The issue remained on the agenda throughout the year—see, in the same box, Memorandum, Talbot to Dean Rusk (Secretary of State), 17 December; Rusk, Memorandum for the President, 17 December 1962.

250. USNRA, RG59, CDF, Box 2072, 786B.00/1–662, Despatch No. 346, Embassy Cairo to State Department, 6 January 1962.

251. USNRA, RG59, CDF, Box 3789, 786B.00/6–1559, "Memorandum of Conversation in State Department," 15 June 1959.

252. For a sample of the various positions of the Jordanian Ikhwan, see numerous files in USNRA, RG59, CDF, Box 2061, including 785.00 (W), Joint Weekly A, No. 29, Sheldon T. Mills (Ambassador), Embassy Amman to State Department, 20 July 1960; 785.00 (W)/2–1661, Joint Weekly A, No. 7, Mills, Amman to State Department, 16 February 1961; 785.00 (W)/10–362, Joint Weekly A, No. 14, Geoffrey W. Lewis (Charge d'Affaires), Embassy Amman to State Department, 3 October 1962; 785.00 (W)/5–1361, Joint Weekly A, No. 46, Lewis, Amman to State Department, 13 May 1964. See also Cohen, *Political Parties in the West Bank*, 151–154.

253. Marechal, *Muslim Brothers in Europe*, 26–28. For a short overview of the history of the Iraqi Islamic Party (IIP) written by a former member, see Fareed Sabri, "The Caliphate

and the Political Ideology of the Iraqi and Egyptian Muslim Brotherhood," *Arches Quarterly* 6, no. 10 (Winter 2012), 97–108.

254. "Case Study: The Iraqi Islamic Party and Its British Connection," *Cordoba Foundation: MENA Report* 1, no. 11 (November 2013).

255. USNRA, RG59, CDF, Box 3789, 786B.00/7–1359, Despatch No. 33, Robert Reams (Consul-General), Embassy Damascus to State Department, 13 July 1959; 786B.00/7–1759, Despatch No. 55, Reams to State Department, 17 July 1959.

256. USNRA, RG59, CDF, Box 2048, 783.00/3–1762, Despatch No. 235, Ridgway B. Knight (Ambassador), Embassy Damascus to State Department, 17 March 1962.

257. USNRA, RG59, CDF, Box 2048, 783.00/1–1562, Despatch No. 407, Knight, Damascus to State Department, 15 January 1962; 783.00/3–2862, Despatch No. 612, Knight, Damascus to State Department, 28 March 1962; 783.00/3–3062, Memorandum from Talbot to Secretary of State, 30 March 1962; CREST Database, CIA, "Current Intelligence Weekly Summary: Syria," 21 September 1962.

258. USNRA, RG59, CDF, Box 2049, 783.00/1–1463, Despatch No. 430, Embassy Damascus to State Department, 14 January 1963.

259. USNRA, RG59, CDF, Box 2048, 783.00/3–1762, Despatch No. 235, Knight, Damascus to State Department, 17 March 1962.

260. HIA, Richard P. Mitchell Collection, Accession No. 77076–54.05, Box No. 24, LR 6/8, Memorandum, "The Political Influence of Islam To-day," Middle East Section Research Department, Foreign Office, 11 May 1962.

261. For this concept, see Yezid Sayigh, *Above the State: The Officers' Republic in Egypt* (Washington, DC: Carnegie Endowment for International Peace, August 2012).

262. USNRA, RG59, CDF, Box 2072, 786B.00/4–2162, Despatch No. 564, Edwin G. Moline (Counselor for Economic Affairs), Embassy Cairo to State Department, 21 April 1962. See also in the same box, 786B.00/4–862, Airgram A-350, Embassy Cairo to State Department, 8 April 1962.

263. These quotes are from Donald Bergus, Counsellor of Embassy for Political Affairs; see USNRA, RG59, CDF, Box 2072, 786B.00/7–362, Airgram A-3, 3 July 1962. But they offer a fair reflection of the broader trend of diplomatic reportage.

264. Ethan A. Nadelmann, "Setting the Stage: American Policy toward the Middle East, 1961–1966," *International Journal of Middle East Studies* 14 (1982), 435–457; Little, "New Frontier on the Nile"; Douglas Little, "A Fool's Errand: America and the Middle East, 1961–1969," in *The Diplomacy of the Crucial Decade*, ed. Diane Kunz (New York: Columbia University Press, 1994), 282–319.

265. USNRA, RG59, State Department Bureau of NE and SA Affairs, Lot File #A1 3129, Box 7, Memorandum "Rationale for UAR Policy," Robert B. Elwood (INR/RNA/OD) to Talbot, 7 January 1963.

266. USNRA, CREST Database, CIA, "Special Report: The Baathist Regimes in Syria and Iraq," 27 September 1963. For a discussion of the split between the Ba'th and Nasser, see CIA, "Current Intelligence Memorandum: The Baathist-Nasir Struggle in Syria," 10 May 1963; and CIA, "Current Intelligence Weekly Special Report: Syria under the Baath," 20 May 1966; and also Kerr, *Arab Cold War*, 41–95.

267. USNRA, CREST Database, CIA, "Memorandum: The Arab World, the USSR, and the West," 12 March 1963.

268. USNRA, RG59, CDF, Box 2768, 786B.00/12–954, Despatch No. 2016, Battle, Cairo to State Department, 9 December 1964.

269. LBJPL, National Security File (Country File), Turkey, United Arab Republic, Box 158 Letter, Ambassador John Badeau to the President, 3 January 1964 (included with Dean Rusk's Memorandum to the President, 14 January 1964). See also USNRA, RG59, CFPF, Box 2767, POL UAR-UK, Despatch No. 2585, Badeau, Embassy Cairo to State Department, 3 May 1964.

270. LBJPL, National Security File (Country File), Turkey, United Arab Republic, Box 158, Memorandum for the President: "Our Policy toward the UAR," William R. Polk, Policy Planning Council to Walt W. Rostow (Chair of the Policy Planning Council), State Department, 7 April 1964. For similar analysis of Nasser's enduring strength and calls for policy continuity, see also National Security File (National Intelligence Estimates), Box 6, "National Intelligence Estimate No. 36–64: 'Main Trends in the Arab World,'" 8 April 1964; USNRA, RG59, CFPF, Box 2760, POL 2–3, Airgram A-806, Moline, Cairo to State Department, 8 May 1964; POL 2–3, Airgram A-10, Embassy Cairo to State Department, 8 July 1964; CREST Database, CIA Special Report SC No. 00634/64A: "Nasir's Arab Policy—The Latest Phase," 28 August 1964.

271. LBJPL, National Security File (Country File), Turkey, United Arab Republic, Box 158, Despatch No. 2583, Badeau, Cairo to State Department, 2 May 1964. See also in the same, Despatch No. 2585, Badeau, Cairo to State Department, 3 May 1964.

272. LBJPL, National Security File (Country File), Turkey, United Arab Republic, Box 158, Despatch No. 2836, Badeau, Cairo to State Department, 25 May 1964; and in the same, Unnumbered Despatch, Military Attaché, Cairo to State Department, 29 May 1964. Nasser enjoyed a good relationship with Khrushchev, with Egypt receiving more aid than any other noncommunist country from the Soviet Union in this period (see also in Box 158, CIA, "Special Report: 'The Soviet Union and Egypt,'" 8 May 1964).

273. Badeau, *Middle East Remembered*, 216–245.

274. USNRA, RG59, CFPF, Box 2767, POL UAR-UK, Despatch No. 1758, Battle, Cairo to State Department, 19 November 1964.

275. USNRA, RG59, CFPF, Box 2768, POL, Despatch No. 2016, Battle, Cairo to State Department, 9 December 1964.

276. USNRA, RG59, CFPF, Box 2765, POL 23–8, Despatch No. 1945, Battle, Cairo to State Department, 3 December 1964.

277. USNRA, RG59, CFPF, Box 2760, POL 2–1, Airgram No. A-455, Bergus, Cairo to State Department, Joint Weekly A, No. 51, 2 January 1965.

278. LBJPL, National Security File (Country File), Middle East—United Arab Republic, Box 159 [1 of 2], Telegram 2202, Battle, Embassy Cairo to State Department, 24 December 1964.

279. Ibid., and USNRA, RG59, CFPF, Box 2760, POL 15–1 UAR, Airgram A-56, Edward H. Springer (Consul), Port Said, to State Department, 24 December 1964.

280. USNRA, RG59, CFPF, Box 2767, UAR-UK, Memorandum, NEA, 24 December 1964.

281. LBJPL, National Security File (Country File), Middle East—United Arab Republic, Box 159 [1 of 2], Memorandum for the President, Robert W. Komer (National Security Council Staff), 31 December 1964.

282. USNRA, RG59, CFPF, Box 2768, POL 1 UAR-US, Despatch No. 2473, William Boswell (Deputy Chief of Mission), Embassy Cairo to State Department, 18 January 1965. For a similar view from Washington, see Box 2764, POL 15–1, Benjamin A. Read, Executive Secretary, Memorandum for McGeorge Bundy, The White House, 9 April 1965; also, LBJPL, National Security File (Country File), Middle East—United Arab Republic, Box 159 [1 of 2], Dean Rusk, "Memorandum for the President," 22 January 1965.

283. USNRA, RG59, CFPF, Box 2764, POL 15–1, Read, Memorandum for Bundy, The White House, 9 April 1965.

284. LBJPL, National Security File (Country File), Middle East—United Arab Republic, Box 159 [1 of 2], Memorandum by Komer, 20 April 1965.

285. USNRA, RG59, CFPF, Box 2760, POL 2–1, Airgram No. A-279, Parker, Cairo to State Department, Joint Weekly A, No. 37, 6 October 1965.

286. LBJPL, National Security File (Country File): Middle East—United Arab Republic: Box 159 [2 of 2], Despatch No. 980, Battle, Cairo to State Department, 9 October 1965; in the same box, Despatch No. 1018, Battle, Cairo to State Department, 14 October 1965.

287. LBJPL, National Security File (Country File): Middle East—United Arab Republic: Box 159 [2 of 2], Dean Rusk, Memorandum for the President, 8 November 1965; in the same box, Despatch No. 1311, Battle, Cairo to State Department, 24 November 1965.

288. USNRA, RG59, CDF, 786B.00/3–1059, Box 3789, Despatch No. 675, Ross, Cairo to State Department, 10 March 1959.

289. USNRA, RG59, CDF, Box 2072, 786B.00/2–2161, Despatch No. 195, Harlan B. Clark (Consul-General), Alexandria to State Department, 21 February 1961.

290. USNRA, RG59, CDF, Box 2072, 786B.00/3–362, Airgram A-304, Badeau, Cairo to State Department, 3 March 1962.

291. LBJPL, National Security File (National Intelligence Estimates), Box 6, "National Intelligence Estimate No. 36.1–65: 'Problems and Prospects for the United Arab Republic,'" 31 March 1965. For a similar picture, see also National Security File (Country File): Middle East—United Arab Republic: Box 159 [2 of 2], CIA, "Special Report, "Nasir's Political Dilemma: 'How to Foster Democracy in a Totalitarian Environment,'" 17 September 1965; USNRA, RG59, Records of Bureau of NE and SA Affairs (NEA), Office of the Country Director for the United Arab Republic (NEA/UAR), 1961–66, Box 2, "NEA Memorandum on Situation in UAR, 30 April 1965."

292. USNRA, RG59, CFPF, Box 2765, POL 23–9, Airgram A-351, Parker, Cairo to State Department, 27 October 1965.

293. Naguib Mahfuz, Adrift on the Nile, trans. F. Liardet (New York: Doubleday, 1993); Naguib Mahfuz, Karnak Café, trans. Roger Allen (New York: Anchor Books, 2008).

294. See, for example, USNRA, RG59, CFPF, Box 2765, POL 23 UAR, Airgram A-670, Embassy Cairo to State Department, 10 March 1965; and in the same, Despatch No. 3083, Embassy Cairo to State Department, 6 March 1965, for the case of a German couple alleged to be spying for Israel.

295. USNRA, RG59, CFPF, Box 2760, POL 2–1, Airgram No. A-113, Embassy Cairo to State Department, Joint Weekly A, No. 30, 11 August 1965.

296. HIA, Wilbur Crane Eveland Collection, Accession No. 80118 14.30, Box 3, Wilbur Eveland, "Summary of the Balance of the Book," 1–18.

297. USNRA, RG59, CFPF, Box 2760, POL 2–1, Airgram No. A-511, Parker, Cairo to State Department, Joint Weekly A, Nos. 48 and 49, 14 December 1965.

298. USNRA, RG59, CFPF, Box 2760, POL 2–1, Airgram No. A-157, Embassy Cairo to State Department, Joint Weekly A, No. 34, 27 August 1966.

299. UKNA FO 371/190250, VG 1691/7, "CIA Work in UAR Revealed," *Egyptian Gazette,* 21 August 1965, enclosed with W. H. G. Fletcher (British Interests Section), Canadian Embassy Cairo, to Peter Unwin, FO, 25 August 1966. Kamal al-Din Husayn was long rumored to have been close to the Brotherhood.

300. USNRA, RG59, CFPF, Box 2760, POL 2–1, Airgram No. A-266, Rogers B. Horgan (First Secretary), Embassy Cairo to State Department, Joint Weekly A, No. 35, 29 September 1965; "Egypt Claims Muslim Plot Crushed," *Times,* 31 August 1965.

301. USNRA, RG59, CFPF, Box 2765, POL 23–9, Despatch No. 607, Battle, Cairo to State Department, 30 August 1965. On Kerdassa, see also in the same box, POL 23–9, Despatch No. 657, Battle, Cairo to State Department, 7 September 1965.

302. USNRA, RG59, CFPF, Box 2765, POL 23–9, Despatch No. 617, Battle, Cairo to State Department, 1 September 1965. For the British perspective, see UKNA FO 371/183884, VG 1015/21, Telegram No. 011/65, John Wilton (Counselor), Embassy Cairo to FO, 1 September 1965.

303. USNRA, RG59, CFPF, Box 2766, POL 29 UAR, Despatch No. 172, Embassy Khartoum to State Department, 30 August 1965; Box 2765, POL 23–9, Despatch No. 1957, Charles Bohlen (Ambassador), Embassy Paris to State Department, 11 October 1965; POL 23–9, Despatch No. 1007, Battle, Cairo to State Department, 13 October 1965; UKNA FO 371/183884, VG 1015/21, No. 011/65, Wilton, Cairo to FO, 1 September 1965.

304. USNRA, RG59, CFPF, Box 2765, POL 23–9, Despatch No. 657, Battle, Cairo to State Department, 7 September 1965; Box 2760, POL 2–1, Airgram No. A-279, Parker, Cairo to State Department, Joint Weekly A, No. 37, 6 October 1965; UKNA FO 371/183884, VG 1015/21, No. 55 (S), Wilton, Cairo to FO, 8 September 1965. See also "Asrar mu'amarat al-ikhwan," *al-Akhbar,* 7 September 1965; "Tafasil mu'amarat al-ikhwan al-muslimin," *al-Gumhuriyya,* 7 September 1965.

305. USNRA, RG59, CFPF, Box 2765, POL 23–9, Despatch No. 657, Battle, Cairo to State Department, 7 September 1965; see also Box 2760, POL 2–1, Airgram No. A-275, Parker, Cairo to State Department, Joint Weekly A, No. 36, 2 October 1965.

306. USNRA, RG59, CFPF, Box 2765, POL 23–9, Despatch No. 674, Battle, Cairo to State Department, 8 September 1965.

307. USNRA, RG59, CFPF, Box 2763, POL 13–6, UAR, "Enclosure No. 2: Cartoons of MB," in Airgram A-289, Parker, Cairo to State Department, 6 October 1965. See also, for example, "Qisat al-irhab kamila," *al-Akhbar,* 24 September 1965; "Kayfa dabatat khilayat al-ikhwan," *al-Gumhurriya,* 9 September 1965. Both newspapers carry numerous daily articles on the subject throughout this period.

308. USNRA, RG59, CFPF, Box 2763, POL 13–6 UAR, Airgram A-289, Parker, Cairo to State Department, 6 October 1965.

309. USNRA, RG59, CFPF, Box 2763, POL 13–6 UAR, Airgram A-234, Parker, Cairo to State Department, 15 September 1965. See also Box 2760, POL 2–1, Airgram No. A-279, Parker, Cairo to State, Joint Weekly A, No. 37, 6 October 1965.

310. USNRA, RG59, CFPF, Box 2763, POL 13–6, UAR, Airgram A-289, Parker, Cairo to State Department, 6 October 1965.

311. Ibid.; "Enclosure No. 1: 'Serious Confessions by Hussain Tawfiq,' *al-Gumhuriya,* 29 September 1965." See also UKNA FO 371/183884, VG 1015/23; and "Sinister Brotherhood," *Times,* 30 September 1965.

312. USNRA, RG59, CFPF, Box 2764, POL 15–1, Airgram A-447, Parker, Cairo to State Department, 26 November 1965.

313. USNRA, RG59, CFPF, Box 2760, POL 2–1, Airgram No. A-581, Embassy Cairo to State Department, Joint Weekly A, Nos. 52 and 53, 11 January 1966; Box 2764, POL 15–1, Despatch No. 1550, Battle, Cairo to State Department, 22 December 1965.

314. See, for example, Abu al-Futuh 'Afifi, *Rihalati ma' al-Ikhwan al-Muslimin* (Cairo: Dar al-Tawfiq wa-l-Nashr al-Islami, 2003), 64–71. See also below.

315. Anwar El-Sadat, *In Search of Identity: An Autobiography* (New York: Harper & Row, 1978), 49.

316. Fu'ad 'Allam, *Al-Ikhwan wa ana: Min al-manshiya ila al-minasa* (Cairo: Akhbar al-Yom, 1996), 106, 113–130.

317. UKNA FO 371/183884, VG 1015/21, Minute by R. T. Higgins, FO, 16 September 1965.

318. USNRA, RG59, CFPF, Box 2764, POL 15–1, Airgram A-397, Stephen E. Palmer Jr. (First Secretary), Embassy Tel Aviv to State Department, 9 November 1965.

319. USNRA, RG59, CFPF, Box 2765, POL 23–9, Despatch No. 707, Battle, Cairo to State Department, 10 September 1965. For a similar verdict, see "Mideast Ferment," *Wall Street Journal,* 23 March 1966.

320. USNRA, RG59, CFPF, Box 2766, POL 29 UAR, Despatch No. 3149, Battle, Cairo to State Department, 8 June 1966; see also in the same, Despatch No. 943, David Nes (Charge d'Affaires), Embassy Cairo to State Department, 21 August 1966; "Seven Death Sentences on Anti-Nasser Plotters," *Times,* 22 August 1966.

321. USNRA, RG59, CFPF, Box 2765, POL 15–1, Despatch No. 662, Battle, Cairo to State Department, 7 September 1965. For the initial assessment of the CIA, see CREST Database, CIA, "Weekly Summary," 3 September 1965.

322. UKNA FO 371/183884, VG 1015/29, Telegram No. 28, Sir George Middleton (Ambassador), Embassy Cairo to Michael Stewart (Foreign Secretary), FO, 13 October 1965.

323. USNRA, RG59, CFPF, Box 2760, POL 2–1, Airgram No. A-312, Parker, Cairo to State Department, Joint Weekly A, No. 40, 13 October 1965; Box 2764, POL 15–1, Despatch No. 918, Battle, Cairo to State Department, 2 October 1965. See also in Box 2764, POL 15–1, Airgram A-299, Parker, Cairo to State Department, 6 October 1965; Despatch No. 950 Battle, Cairo to State Department, 6 October 1965; and also "Egypt Tightens Security," *Times,* 1 October 1965; UKNA FO 371/183884, VG 1015/29, Telegram No. 28, Middleton, Cairo to Stewart, FO, 13 October 1965.

324. USNRA, RG59, CFPF, Box 2765, POL 23–9, Despatch No. 707, Battle, Cairo to State Department, 10 September 1965. For a similar verdict, see "Mideast Ferment," *Wall Street Journal,* 23 March 1966.

325. USNRA, RG59, CFPF, Box 2765, POL 23 UAR, Airgram A-340, Parker, Cairo to State Department, 22 October 1965.

326. USNRA, RG59, CFPF, Box 2763, POL 13–6, UAR, Airgram A-289, Parker, Cairo to State Department, 6 October 1965.

327. UKNA FO 371/183884, VG 1015/32, Minute by Middle East Section, Joint Research Department Foreign Office, 22 October 1965.

328. USNRA, RG59, CFPF, Box 2765, POL 23–9, Despatch No. 674, Battle, Cairo to State Department, 8 September 1965; Box 2763, POL 13–6, UAR, "Enclosure No. 1: 'Serious Confessions by Hussain Tawfiq,' *al-Gumhuriya,* 29 September 1965," with Airgram A-289, Parker, Cairo to State Department, 6 October 1965. See also Box 2765, POL 23 UAR, Airgram A-340, Parker, Cairo to State Department, 22 October 1965; Box 2765, POL 23–9, Despatch No. 1416, Battle, Cairo to State Department, 8 December 1965; Box 2760, POL 2–1, Airgram No. A-511, Parker, Cairo to State Department, Joint Weekly A, Nos. 48 and 49, 14 December 1965; UKNA FO 371/183884, VG 1015/23; and "Sinister Brotherhood," *Times,* 30 September 1965.

329. USNRA, RG59, CFPF, Box 2765, POL 23–9, Despatch No. 674, Battle, Cairo to State Department, 8 September 1965; POL 23–9, Airgram A-503, Pierce K. Bullen (Second Secretary), Embassy Cairo to State Department, 11 December 1965.

330. USNRA, RG59, CFPF, Box 2763, POL 13–6, UAR, "Enclosure No. 1: 'Serious Confessions by Hussain Tawfiq,' *al-Gumhuriya,* 29 September 1965" with Airgram A-289, Parker, Cairo to State Department, 6 October 1965. See also Box 2765, POL 23 UAR, Airgram A-340, Parker, Cairo to State Department, 22 October 1965; UKNA FO 371/183884, VG 1015/23; and "Sinister Brotherhood," *Times,* 30 September 1965.

331. USNRA, RG59, CFPF, Box 2765, POL 23–9, Airgram A-685, Parker, Cairo to State Department, 15 February 1966; Box 2760, POL 2–1, Airgram No. A-708, Wright, Cairo to State Department, Joint Weekly A, Nos. 5 and 6, 24 February 1966.

332. USNRA, RG59, CFPF, Box 2763, POL 23–9, Airgram A-761, Embassy Cairo to State Department, 15 March 1966; Box 2760, POL 2–1, Airgram No. A-708, Wright, Cairo to State Department, Joint Weekly A, Nos. 5 and 6, 24 February 1966. See also Box 2765, POL 23–9, Despatch No. 1979, Battle, Cairo to State Department, 4 February 1966; POL 23–9, Despatch No. 2088, Battle, Cairo to State Department, 16 February 1966.

333. For the al-Hudaybi indictment, see USNRA, RG59, CFPF, Box 2766, POL 29 UAR, Despatch No. 2465, Battle, Cairo to State Department, 7 April 1966.

334. USNRA, RG59, CFPF, Box 2765, POL 23–9, Airgram A-761, Embassy Cairo to State Department, 15 March 1966, contains in-depth reports from *al-Ahram* of 5 February 1966—see document entitled "Confessions of Ikhwan Leadership." For a summary, see also Barbara H. E. Zollner, *The Muslim Brotherhood: Hasan al-Hudaybi and Ideology* (London: Routledge, 2009), 40–41.

335. USNRA, RG59, CFPF, Box 2765, POL 23–9, Telegram No. 674, Battle, Embassy Cairo to State Department, 8 September 1965; POL 23–9, Airgram A-761, Embassy Cairo to State Department, 15 March 1966; Box 2760, POL 2–1, Airgram No. A-708, Wright, Cairo to State Department, Joint Weekly A, Nos. 5 and 6, 24 February 1966; UKNA FO 371/183884, VG 1015/21, No. 58 (S), Wilton, Cairo to FO, 10 September 1965.

336. USNRA, RG59, CFPF, Box 2765, POL 23–9, "Confessions of Ikhwan Leadership," in Airgram A-761, Embassy Cairo to State Department, 15 March 1966. For more on al-Ghazali, see in the same box, POL 23–9, Despatch No. 657, Battle, Cairo to State Department, 7 September 1965.

337. USNRA, RG59, CFPF, Box 2765, POL 23–9, "Confessions of Ikhwan Leadership," in Airgram A-761, Embassy Cairo to State Department, 15 March 1966.

338. All of the foregoing is based on the extensive newspaper reports contained in USNRA, RG59, CFPF, Box 2765, POL 23–9, "Confessions of Ikhwan Leadership," in

Airgram A-761, Embassy Cairo to State Department, 15 March 1966. See also "Enclosure #2: Data on Defendants"; and POL 23–9, Airgram A-833, Clifford J. Quinlan (First Secretary), Embassy Cairo to State Department, 8 April 1966, including "Enclosure: Data on Defendants," and "Enclosure: Some Persons Implicated Who Are Not Defendants in This Case." In addition, see 'Allam, *Al-Ikhwan wa ana,* 117–130.

339. USNRA, RG59, CFPF, Box 2766, POL 29 UAR, Despatch No. 943, Nes, Cairo to State Department, 21 August 1966. See also "Seven Death Sentences on Anti-Nasser Plotters," *Times,* 22 August 1966.

340. "Cairo Plotters Hanged," *Times,* 30 August 1966.

341. See, for example, USNRA, RG59, CFPF, Box 2765, POL 23–9, Despatch No. 691, James O'Sullivan (Charge d'Affaires), Embassy Tunis to State Department, 25 August 1966; POL 23–9, Despatch No. 783, O'Sullivan, Tunis to State Department, 31 August 1966; Box 2760, POL 2–1, Airgram No. A-175, Embassy Cairo to State Department, Joint Weekly A, No. 35, 3 September 1966; "Arab World Beset by Ills on Every Side," *Times,* 25 August 1966.

342. USNRA, RG59, Box 2766, POL 29 UAR, Despatch No. 548, Thomas M. Recknagel (Charge d'Affaires), Embassy Khartoum to State Department, 23 August 1966; POL 29 UAR, Despatch No. 641, Recknagel, Khartoum to State Department, 31 August 1966; POL 29 UAR, Despatch No. 216, Embassy Khartoum to State Department, 16 September 1966.

343. USNRA, RG59, CFPF, Box 2766, POL 29 UAR, Despatch No. 712, Eugene M. Locke (Ambassador), Embassy Rawalpindi to State Department, 26 August 1966. For more on the reaction in Pakistan, see in the same box, POL 29 UAR, Airgram A-129, John Bowling (Consul-General), Dacca to State Department, 6 September 1966.

344. USNRA, RG59, CFPF, Box 2387, POL 2–1 Jordan, Airgram A-81, Embassy Amman to Washington, DC, Joint Weekly A, No. 9, 29 August 1966.

345. USNRA, RG59, CFPF, Box 2387, POL 2–1 Jordan, Airgram A-89, Embassy Amman to Washington, DC, Joint Weekly A, No. 10, 3 September 1966.

346. USNRA, RG59, CFPF, Box 2766, POL 29, UAR, Airgram A-214, Robert C. Strong (Ambassador), Embassy Baghdad to State Department, 13 September 1966.

347. USNRA, RG59, CFPF, Box 2765, POL 23–9, Airgram A-761, Embassy Cairo to State Department, 15 March 1966; UKNA FO 371/183884, VG 1015/38, Minute by Denis J. Speares (Head of North and East Africa Department), FO, 1 December 1965.

348. USNRA, RG59, CFPF, Box 2765, POL 23–9, Airgram A-992, Battle, Cairo to State Department, 26 May 1966.

349. "Harsh Decisions," *Economist,* 26 November 1966.

350. USNRA, RG59, CFPF, Box 2765, POL 23–9, Airgram A-995, Battle, Cairo to State Department, 26 May 1966. For an anecdotal example of such sympathy, see with the same file, "Enclosure: Memorandum from R. A. Bauer, Cultural Attaché to Political Section," 11 May 1966.

351. USNRA, RG59, CFPF, Box 2765, POL 23 UAR, Letter, Parker, Cairo, to Harrison M. Symmes (Director NEA/NE), State Department, 3 January 1966.

352. USNRA, RG59, CFPF, Box 2766, POL 29 UAR, Airgram A-122, David Fritzlan (Consul), Alexandria to State Department, 11 May 1966, including "Memorandum of Conversation: 'UAR Government Anti-Ikhwan Campaign.'"

353. UKNA FO 371/183884, VG 1015/29, Telegram No. 28, Middleton, Cairo, to Stewart, FO, 13 October 1965.

354. USNRA, RG59, CFPF, Box 2765, POL 23–9, Airgram A-351, Parker, Cairo to State Department, 27 October 1965. See also POL 23–9, Memorandum by Raymond A. Hare of NEA to the Secretary, "The UAR in 1965: Revolutionary Malaise. Information Memorandum," 12 November 1965.

355. USNRA, RG59, CFPF, Box 2760, POL 2–1, Airgram No. A-339, Embassy Cairo to State Department, Joint Weekly A, No. 41, 15 October 1966.

356. USNRA, RG59, CFPF, Box 2765, POL 23–9, Despatch No. 657, Battle, Cairo to State Department, 7 September 1965; Box 2760, POL 2–1, Airgram No. A-275, Parker, Cairo to State Department, Joint Weekly A, No. 36, 2 October 1965.

357. USNRA, RG59, CFPF, Box 2763, POL 13–6, UAR, Airgram A-289, Parker, Cairo to State Department, 6 October 1965.

358. USNRA, RG59, CFPF, Box 2760, POL 2–1, Airgram No. A-266, Rogers B. Horgan (First Secretary), Embassy Cairo to State Department, Joint Weekly A, No. 35, 29 September 1965; see also "Egypt Claims Muslim Plot Crushed," Times, 31 August 1965.

359. On Ramadan, see USNRA, RG59, CFPF, Box 2765, POL 23–9, Despatch No. 690, Battle, Cairo to State Department, 9 September 1965; POL 23–9, Despatch No. 702, Battle, Embassy Cairo to State Department, 10 September 1965; POL 23–9, Airgram A-516, Bullen, Cairo to State Department, 15 December 1965; Box 2760, POL 2–1, Airgram No. A-275, Parker, Cairo to State Department, Joint Weekly A, No. 36, 2 October 1965; UKNA FO 371/183884, VG 1015/45, Telegram No. 1032, Middleton, Cairo to FO, 22 December 1965.

360. Johnson, Mosque in Munich, 238.

361. USNRA, RG59, CFPF, Box 2763, POL 13–6, UAR, Despatch No. 63, Francis Henry Russell (Ambassador), Embassy Tunis to State Department, 7 July 1966.

362. "Nasser "Soon Out of Power," Daily Telegraph, 23 September 1966. On this trip to London, see USNRA, RG59, CFPF, Box 2764, POL 15–1, Airgram A-741, Embassy London to State Department, 27 September 1966.

363. USNRA, RG59, CFPF, Box 2760, POL 2–1, Airgram No. A-639, Embassy Cairo to State Department, Joint Weekly A, No. 4, 29 January 1966; POL 2–1, Airgram No. A-928, Quinlan, Cairo to State Department, Joint Weekly A, Nos. 15 and 16, 10 May 1966; Box 2766, POL 29 UAR, Despatch No. 2599, Battle, Cairo to State Department, 12 April 1966; POL 29 UAR, Despatch No. 2612, Battle, Cairo to State Department, 13 April 1966; Box 2765, POL 23–9, Airgram A-992, Battle, Cairo to State Department, 26 May 1966.

364. USNRA, RG59, CFPF, Box 2764, POL 15–1, Despatch No. 2154, Battle, Cairo to State Department, 23 February 1966.

365. USNRA, RG59, CFPF, Box 2764, POL 15–1, Airgram A-1364, Davis E. Boster (Counselor for Political Affairs), Embassy Cairo to State Department, 21 February 1966.

366. USNRA, RG59, CFPF, Box 2765, POL 15–1, Despatch No. 2815, Embassy Cairo to State Department, 2 May 1966; Box 2769, POL 1–2 UAR-US, Airgram A-1025, Battle, Cairo to State Department, 3 June 1966.

367. David Hirst, "King Faisal's Diplomacy Unfurls the Banner of Islamic Unity," Guardian, 19 February 1966.

368. "Islamic Conference to Tackle Social Problems," *Times,* 11 February 1966; LBJPL, National Security File (National Intelligence Estimates), Box 6, "National Intelligence Estimate No. 36.6–66: 'The Role of Saudi Arabia,'" 8 December 1966.

369. On the Muslim World League (MWL), see Reinhard Schulzer, *Islamischer Internationalismus im 20. Jahrhundert* (Leiden, Netherlands: Brill, 1990), 259–265. The US branch of the MWL was created in 1974, while a London office was established in 1983.

370. Gilles Kepel, *Jihad: The Trial of Political Islam* (London: I. B. Tauris, 2004), 51.

371. USNRA, RG59, CFPF, Box 2387, POL 2–1 Jordan, A-332, J. Wesley Adams, Jr. (Counselor), Embassy Amman to State Department, Joint Weekly A, No. 31, 1 February 1966.

372. USNRA, RG59, CFPF, Box 2357, POL 2–1 Jordan, A-43, Findley Burns Jr. (Ambassador), Embassy Amman to State Department, Joint Weekly A, No. 5, 1 August 1966.

373. USNRA, RG59, CFPF, Box 2389, POL Jordan-UAR, Airgram A-418, Embassy Amman to State Department, 8 April 1966. On the Brotherhood's generally positive view of Saudi Arabia, see Cohen, *Political Parties in the West Bank,* 196–197.

374. USNRA, RG59, CFPF, Box 2389, POL Jordan-UAR, Despatch No. 1535, Burns, Amman to State Department, 20 December 1966; Box 2388, POL 15–1 Jordan, Despatch No. 1324, Talcott W. Seelye (Counselor), Embassy Jidda to State Department, 21 June 1966.

375. Hendrick Smith, "The Arab Cold War—Nasser vs. Faisal," *New York Times,* 22 May 1966; Kerr, *Arab Cold War,* especially 106–117 for this period.

376. USNRA, CREST Database, CIA, "Memorandum: The Arab World, the USSR, and the West," 12 March 1963.

377. USNRA, RG59, CFPF, Box 2389, POL 32–1 ISR-Jordan, Despatch No. 477, Consulate Jerusalem to State Department, 12 December 1966; see also Box 2684, POL 12-SYR, Airgram A-27, Embassy Damascus to State Department, 19 July 1966; LBJPL, National Security File (Files of Robert W. Komer), Box 51, "State Department Strategy Paper: 'Visit of King Faisal of Saudi Arabia, June 21–23, 1966.'"

378. LBJPL, National Security File (Files of Robert W. Komer), Box 51, Walt W. Rostow (Special Assistant to the President), "Memorandum for the President," 18 June 1966. For the Johnson administration's approach to the Middle East, see Douglas Little, "Choosing Sides: Lyndon Johnson and the Middle East," in *The Johnson Years, Volume Three: LBJ at Home and Abroad,* ed. Robert Divine (Lawrence: University Press of Kansas, 1990), 150–197.

379. LBJPL, National Security File (Country File), Saudi Arabia, Box 155, "Memorandum of Conversation: 'President's Meeting with King Faisal,'" Part I, 21 June 1966.

380. Ibid.; see also National Security File (Files of Robert W. Komer), Box 51, "State Department Strategy Paper: 'Visit of King Faisal of Saudi Arabia, June 21–23, 1966.'"

381. Aburish, *Nasser,* 155–162, 230, 256–257.

382. USNRA, RG59, ASSNESA, SF, 1965–6, Box 3, "National Policy Paper: United Arab Republic, Part Two, Factors Bearing on US Policy, 1 August 1966"; Box 2763, POL 23–9, Airgram A-559, Battle, Cairo to State Department, 23 December 1966.

383. USNRA, RG59, CFPF, Box 2765, POL 15–2, "Memorandum for the President 2830: 'Visit of Anwar al-Sadat, President of the UAR National Assembly,'" 21 February 1966. See also LBJPL, National Security File (Country File), Middle East—United Arab Republic, Box 159 [2 of 2], R. W. Komer, Memorandum for the President, 23 February 1966.

384. USNRA, RG59, CFPF, Box 2767, POL UAR-UK, Despatch No. 1498, Battle, Cairo to State Department, 17 December 1965; Box 2760, POL 2–1, Airgram No. A-542, Parker, Cairo to State Department, Joint Weekly A, Nos. 50 and 51, 23 December 1965.

385. USNRA, RG59, CFPF, Box 2769, POL 1 UAR-US, Airgram A-1124, Battle, Cairo to State Department, 1 July 1966. For more on US analysis of the Egyptian role in southern Arabia, see LBJPL, National Security File (National Intelligence Estimates), Box 6, "National Intelligence Estimate No. 30–1–66: 'The Outlook for South Arabia,'" 8 September 1966.

386. LBJPL, National Security File (Country File): Middle East—United Arab Republic: Box 159 [2 of 2], Rusk, Memorandum for the President, 16 June 1966; and in the same, Rostow, Memorandum for the President, 18 June 1966.

387. USNRA, RG59, ASSNESA, SF, 1965–6, Box 3, "National Policy Paper: United Arab Republic, Part One, U.S. Policy," 28 September 1966. For anti-imperialist attacks, see the speech Nasser delivered at Alexandria University, as reported in USNRA, RG59, CFPF, Box 2765, POL 15–1, Despatch No. 483, Embassy Cairo to State Department, 29 July 1966.

388. USNRA, RG59, CFPF, Box 2764, POL 15–1, Memorandum 13790, Rodger P. Davies (Director, NEA) to the Secretary of State, 12 September 1966.

389. USNRA, RG59, CFPF, Box 2764, POL 15–1, Memorandum by NEA on United Arab Republic, October 1966.

390. LBJPL, National Security File (Country File), Middle East—United Arab Republic, Box 159 [2 of 2], CIA, Directorate of Intelligence, "Intelligence Memorandum: 'Egyptian-Soviet Relations,'" 28 May 1966. See also USNRA, RG59, Box 2760, POL 2–1, Airgram No. A-905, Quinlan, Cairo to State Department, Joint Weekly A, Nos. 13 and 14, 3 May 1966.

391. USNRA, RG59, CFPF, Box 2763, POL 12, Airgram A-839, Embassy Cairo to State Department, 10 May 1965.

392. Kerr, *Arab Cold War,* 117–122.

393. USNRA, RG59, CFPF, Box 2764, POL 15–1, Memorandum 17639, William J. Handley (Deputy Assistant Secretary of State, NEA) to the Secretary of State, 26 November 1966; LBJPL, National Security File (Country File): Middle East—United Arab Republic: Box 159 [2 of 2], Despatch No. 2999, Battle, Cairo to State Department, 28 November 1966.

394. USNRA, RG59, CFPF, Box 2764, POL 15–1, Airgram A-453, Battle, Cairo to State Department, 24 November 1966.

395. LBJPL, National Security File (Country File), United Arab Republic, Box 160, National Security File (Country File), United Arab Republic, Howard Wriggins and Harold Saunders (NSC Staff), Memorandum for Rostow, 1 December 1966.

396. USNRA, RG59, Bureau of NE and SA Affairs, Office of Egypt Affairs, Records Relating to Egypt, 1966–1975, Box 3, POL-1, "US-UAR Relations."

397. LBJPL, National Security File (Country File), United Arab Republic, Box 160, Despatch No. 5031, Battle, Cairo to State Department, 4 March 1967; USNRA, RG59, CFPF, Box 2554, POL 15–1, Despatch No. 5496, Arthur J. Goldberg (Representative to the United Nations), US Mission to the UN to State Department, 27 May 1967.

398. LBJPL, National Security File (Country File), United Arab Republic, Box 160, Rostow, "Memorandum for the President," 10 May 1967; USNRA, RG59, Bureau of NE and SA Affairs, Office of Egypt Affairs, Records Relating to Egypt, 1966–1975, Box 3, POL

1–2, "The Secretary's Appearance before the Senate Foreign Relations Committee, May 16, 1967."

399. LBJPL, National Security File (Country File), United Arab Republic, Box 160, Despatch No. 5036, Battle, Cairo to State Department, 5 March 1967.

400. Hazem Kandil, *Inside the Brotherhood* (Cambridge, UK: Polity Press, 2015), 6.

401. As Ernest Dawn has pointed out, others—from a non-Islamist background—were also using the term *jahiliyyah* in this period to critique contemporary society. See C. Ernest Dawn, "The Formation of Pan-Arab Ideology in the Interwar Years," *International Journal of Middle East Studies* 20, no. 1 (1988), 67–91.

402. Sayyid Qutb, *Milestones* (New Delhi: Islamic Book Service, 2001), 7–22; Sayyid Qutb, *Limatha a'damuni?* (Cairo: Dar 'Ashbiliya l-il-Nashr wa-l-Tawzi', 2011), 17–21. It is worth noting too that references to the *jahiliyyah* had also appeared in Brotherhood literature before, though Qutb gave this term new force and application. See, for example, "Bayna al-jahiliya wa-l-islam," *al-Ikhwan al-Muslimun,* 23 October 1943.

403. Qutb, *Milestones,* 36–76.

404. USNRA, RG59, CFPF, Box 2765, POL 23–9, "Confessions of Ikhwan Leadership," in Airgram A-761, Embassy Cairo to State Department, 15 March 1966.

405. Qutb, *Limatha,* 5, 18–20, 23–24, 28–29, 32–40.

406. Qutb, *Milestones,* 7–8.

407. Ibid., 96–99.

408. William E. Shepard, "Sayyid Qutb's Doctrine of 'Jahiliyya,' " *International Journal of Middle East Studies* 35, no. 4 (2003), 521–545 (532).

409. John Calvert, "An Islamist's View of America," in Vincent Burns and Kate D. Peterson, *Terrorism: A Documentary and Reference Guide* (Westport, CT: Greenwood, 2005).

410. Lawrence Wright, *Looming Tower: Al-Qaeda's Road to 9/11* (London: Allen Lane, 2006).

411. Daniel Burns, "Said Qutb on the Arts in America," *Current Trends in Islamist Ideology* 9 (2009), 151–157.

412. Sayid Kutb, "Humanity Needs Us," trans. M. Hafez, *al-Muslimun* 3, no. 2 (December 1953).

413. Hisham Sabrin, "Qutb: Between Terror and Tragedy," *Ikhwanweb,* 20 January 2010, http://www.ikhwanweb.com/article.php?id=22709.

414. Malise Ruthven, "Rebel with a Cause," *Literary Review* 386 (April 2011); John Calvert, *Sayyid Qutb and the Origins of Radical Islamism* (New York: Columbia University Press, 2010).

415. William E. Shepard, *Sayyid Qutb and Islamic Activism: A Translation and Critical Analysis of Social Justice in Islam* (Leiden, Netherlands: Brill, 1996), 2–11, 291, 349–351.

416. Ibid., 61–66.

417. Qutb, *Milestones,* 138–139.

418. William E. Shepard, "The Development of the Thought of Sayyid Qutb as Reflected in Earlier and Later Editions of 'Social Justice in Islam,' " *Die Welt des Islams* 32 (1992), 196–236 (209–210).

419. Qutb, *Milestones,* 94.

420. Sayyid Qutb, *Dirasat Islamiyyah,* 8th ed. (Cairo: Dar al-Shuruk, 1992), 119–121, 169–174.

421. Ibrahim Abu-Rabiʿ, "Sayyid Qutb: From Religious Realism to Radical Social Criticism," *Islamic Quarterly* 28 (1984), 103–126, (112). See also Shepard, *Sayyid Qutb,* 283.

422. Shahrough Akhavi, "Sayyid Qutb: The Poverty of Philosophy and the Vindication of Islamic Tradition," in *Cultural Transitions in the Middle East,* ed. Serif Mardin (Leiden, Netherlands: Brill, 1994), 130–152.

423. Max Rodenbeck, "The Father of Violent Islamism," *New York Review of Books,* 9 May 2013.

424. For Qutb's denial that he was engaged in takirism, see Qutb, *Limatha,* 23.

425. Qutb, *Milestones,* 137.

426. Shepard, "Sayyid Qutb's Doctrine." For more on the influence of Mawdudi, see Fathi Osman, "Mawdudi's Contribution to the Development of Modern Islamic Thinking in the Arabic-Speaking World," *Muslim World* 93, no. 3 (July–October 2003), 465ff.

427. Qutb, *Milestones,* 93.

428. Shepard, *Sayyid Qutb and Islamic Activism,* 61–66, 349–355; Shepard, "The Development of the Thought of Sayyid Qutb," 209–210.

429. Shepard, *Sayyid Qutb and Islamic Activism,*17, 279–286. References to "crusader imperialists" would later become a staple of Osama bin Laden and al-Qaeda statements.

430. Qutb, *Limatha,* 7.

431. Sabrin, "Qutb."

432. Yvonne Y. Haddad, "The Qur'anic Justification for an Islamic Revolution: The View of Sayyid Qutb," *Middle East Journal* 37, no. 1 (Winter 1983), 14–29. See also Shepard, "The Development of the Thought of Sayyid Qutb"; Ahmad Moussalli, "Sayyid Qutb: Founder of Radical Islamic Political Ideology," in *Routledge Handbook of Political Islam,* ed. Shahram Akbarzadeh (Abingdon, UK: Routledge, 2012), 9–26.

433. Salah Shadi, *Safahat min al-tarikh: Hisad al-amr* (Kuwait: Sharikat al-Shuʿa, 1981), 108.

434. Jeffrey Herf, *Nazi Propaganda for the Arab World* (London: Yale University Press, 2009), 255–259.

435. Shepard, *Sayyid Qutb and Islamic Activism,* 288. See also 304.

436. Qutb, *Limatha,* 8–12, 17.

437. Ibid., 15–16, 62–63.

438. Ibid., 28, 37–38, 46–48.

439. Sabrin, "Qutb."

440. Al-Qaradawi, *Al-Ikhwan al-Muslimun,* 247; Muhammad Abdallah al-Samman, *Ayam maʿ al-shahid Hasan al-Banna* (Cairo: Dar al-Fadila, 2003), 22–23.

441. Shadi, *Safahat min al-tarikh,* 274–275.

442. Hasan Dawh, *25 ʿaman fi jamaʾat al-ikhwan* (Cairo: Dar al-ʿItisam, 1983), 109–110, 117–118.

443. Ibid., 114.

444. USNRA, RG59, CFPF, Box 2763, POL 13–6 UAR, Despatch No. 63, Russell, Tunis to State Department, 7 July 1966.

445. Paul Salem, "Islamic Fundamentalism," in *The Bitter Legacy: Ideology and Politics in the Arab World* (Syracuse, NY: Syracuse University Press, 1994), 104; Kandil, *Inside the Brotherhood,* 104.

446. LBJPL, National Security File (Country File), United Arab Republic, Box 160, Despatch No. 6083, Rusk, State Department to Embassy Cairo, 28 January 1968. See also

Fawaz Gerges, "The 1967 Arab-Israeli War: US Actions and Arab Perceptions," in Lesch, *Middle East and the United States,* 163–181.

447. Kerr, *Arab Cold War,* 126–140.

448. USNRA, RG59, Bureau of NE and SA Affairs, Office of Egypt Affairs, Records Relating to Egypt, 1966–1975, Box 3, POL–1, "Memorandum on United Arab Republic," undated. For a similar analysis, see RG59, General Records of the State Department, Lot #80D234, Top Secret Records of the Assistant Secretary of State for the Bureau of Near Eastern and South Asian Affairs, 1965–73, Box 1, "Memorandum by Thomas L. Hughes (INR) to Secretary," 3 July 1967.

449. For US analysis of Nasser's weakened position, see USNRA, CREST Database, CIA Directorate of Intelligence, "Intelligence Memorandum: 'Nasir's Current Status within Egypt,'" No. 1392/67, 12 October 1967.

450. USNRA, RG59, Records of the State Department, Lot #80D234, Top Secret Records of the Assistant Secretary of State for the Bureau of Near Eastern and South Asian Affairs, 1965–73, Box 1, "Memorandum of Conversation, John. P. Walsh (S/S) and Lucius Battle (NEA) with Walter McDonald of Standard Oil of Indiana," 2 August 1967; RG59, CFPF, Box 2555, POL 15–1 UAR, Despatch No. 620, William Bromell (Political Officer), Embassy Cairo to State Department, 27 September 1967; POL 15 UAR, Hughes, INR Intelligence Note 812 to State Department, 12 October 1967.

451. Hazem Kandil, *Soldiers, Spies, and Statesmen: Egypt's Road to Revolt* (London: Verso, 2012), 90.

452. USNRA, RG59, CFPF, Box 2553, POL 2 UAR, Despatch No. 4470, Bergus, Cairo to State Department, 2 March 1968. See also Abdullah al-Arian, *Answering the Call: Popular Islamic Activism in Egypt* (New York: Oxford University Press, 2014), 43–45.

453. USNRA, RG59, CFPF, Box 2555, POL 2 UAR, Despatch No. 4496, Bergus, Cairo to State Department, 8 March 1968; Bureau of NE and SA Affairs, Office of Egypt Affairs, Records Relating to Egypt, 1966–1975, Box 4, POL 1–2, Memorandum "Nasser Comments on the UAR's Internal Situation," Parker to Battle, 4 March 1968.

454. USNRA, RG59, CFPF, Box 2554, POL 15–1, Memorandum, Parker (NEA/UAR) to Battle, 20 March 1968; and in the same box, POL 15–1, Despatch No. 4532, Bergus, Cairo to State Department, 21 March 1968.

455. USNRA, RG59, CFPF, Box 2553, POL 2 UAR, Despatch No. 4541, Bergus, Cairo to State Department, 23 March 1968; On the program and referendum, see Box 2554, POL 12–6 UAR, Hughes, INR Intelligence Note 327 to State Department, 3 May 1968.

456. USNRA, RG59, CFPF, Box 2553, POL 2 UAR, Despatch No. 4498, Bergus, Cairo to State Department, 10 March 1968.

457. USNRA, CREST Database, CIA, "Special Memorandum: Nasser's Limited Options," 15 April 1968.

458. USNRA, RG59, CFPF, Box 2553, POL 2 UAR, Despatch No. 5420, Bergus, Cairo to State Department, 29 November 1968.

459. USNRA, RG59, CFPF, Box 2553, POL 2 UAR, Hughes, INR Research Memorandum RNA-37 to State Department, 29 November 1968.

460. LBJPL, National Security File (Country File), United Arab Republic, Box 160, CIA Directorate of Intelligence, "Special Report Weekly Review No. 1: 'Growing Dissatisfaction in Egypt,'" 10 March 1967.

461. LBJPL, National Security File (Country File), United Arab Republic, Box 160, "National Intelligence Estimate No. 36.1–67: 'The Situation and Prospects in Egypt,'" 17 August 1967; USNRA, CREST Database, CIA, "Special Memorandum: Nasser's Limited Options," 15 April 1968.

462. Hagai Erlich, *Students and University in Twentieth Century Egyptian Politics* (London: Cas, 1989), 190–195.

463. UKNA FCO 17/224, "Recent Muslim Brotherhood Activity in the United Arab Republic," undated (spring 1968).

464. USNRA, RG59, CFPF, Box 2554, POL 13–6 UAR, Hughes, INR Research Memorandum RNA-20 to State Department, 15 May 1968.

465. Ibid.

466. USNRA, RG59, CFPF, Box 2554, POL 12 UAR, Airgram A-61, US Interests Section, Cairo, to State Department, 24 June 1969.

467. USNRA, RG59, CFPF, Box 2555, POL 15–1 UAR, "Memorandum for the President," 25 January 1969; Box 2553, POL 2 UAR, Despatch No. 6627, Bergus, Cairo to State Department, 4 October 1969.

468. USNRA, RG59, CFPF, Box 2553, POL 2 UAR, Despatch No. 6588, Bergus, Cairo to State Department, 24 September 1969.

469. Ibid.

470. USNRA, RG59, CFPF, Box 2554, POL 15 UAR, George C. Denney Jr. (US State Department Director of Intelligence and Research, INR) to Secretary of State, Research Memorandum RNA-52, 20 October 1969.

471. USNRA, RG59, Bureau of NE and SA Affairs, Office of Egypt Affairs, Records Relating to Egypt, 1966–1975, Box 7, POL 23, L. Dean Brown (NEA), Memorandum on "Internal Situation," 30 March 1970.

472. USNRA, RG59, Bureau of NE and SA Affairs, Office of Egypt Affairs, Records Relating to Egypt, 1966–1975, Box 7, "Situation in UAR," 25 September 1970.

473. On the oscillating Nasser-US relationship, see Mufti, "United States and Nasserist Pan-Arabism"; Jon B. Alterman, *Egypt and American Foreign Assistance, 1952–1956: Hopes Dashed* (Basingstoke, UK: Palgrave, 2002), xix–xxiv, 131–134; Henry William Brands Jr., "What Eisenhower and Dulles Saw in Nasser: Personalities and Interests in U.S.-Egyptian Relations," *American-Arab Affairs* 17 (1986), 44–54.

474. Peter Hahn, "National Security Concerns in US Policy toward Egypt, 1949–1956," in Lesch, *Middle East and the United States,* 75.

475. HIA, Christina Harris Papers, Accession No. 79085 10.03, Box 3, Christina P. Harris, "The First Decade of the Egyptian Revolution: 1952–1962" (paper read at the American Historical Association in October 1963). See in the same box, Christina P. Harris, "Islam in Modern Egypt," December 1955, which described the Brotherhood as the embodiment of "obscurantist, extremist forces." And also, Christina Phelps Harris, *Nationalism and Revolution in Egypt: The Role of the Muslim Brotherhood in Egypt* (The Hague, Netherlands: Mouton, 1964), 14, 138.

476. John Marlowe, *Anglo-Egyptian Relations, 1800–1956* (London: Frank Cass, 1965), 411.

477. David Hirst, "King Faisal's Diplomacy Unfurls the Banner of Islamic Unity," *Guardian,* 19 February 1966.

478. Jacobs, *Imagining the Middle East,* 87–94.

479. W. Montgomery Watt, "Islam's Power Awaits World," *Times,* 8 March 1968.

480. "Politics and Islam," *Times,* 30 November 1970.

481. Leon Carl Brown, "The Society of the Muslim Brothers (Review)," *Journal of Interdisciplinary History* 2, no. 3 (Winter 1972), 342–346.

7. Reassessments amid the "Fundamentalist" Revival, 1970–1989

1. "Muslim Brotherhood on Mediation," Tehran International Service, 20 April 1980, in Foreign Broadcast Information Service (FBIS) Daily Reports.

2. Youssef Nada, with Douglas Thompson, *Inside the Muslim Brotherhood: The Truth about the World's Most Powerful Political Movement* (London: Metro, 2012), xiv.

3. Ibid., 56–57. The incident is also touched on in Khalil el-Anani's book, which states that al-Tilmisani had sent a letter to Iran requesting permission to visit, which was granted, albeit with the proviso that they would not discuss the American hostage crisis with him. See Khalil el-Anani, *Al-Ikhwan al-Muslimun fi Misr: Shaykhukha tusari' al-zaman?* (Cairo: Maktabat al-Shuruq al-Duwaliyya, 2007), 184. In his memoirs, meanwhile, al-Tilmisani does not mention contacts with the United States, but does note that the Iranians at one point accused the Brotherhood of being agents for the United States. See 'Umar al-Tilmisani, *Dhikriyat la Mudhakirat* (Cairo: Dar al-Taba'a wa-l-Nashr al-Islami, 1985), 228.

4. Walid Mahmoud Abdelnasser, *The Islamic Movement in Egypt: Perceptions of International Relations, 1967–81* (London: Kegan Paul International, 1994), 68–71.

5. Al-Tilmisani, *Dhikriyat,* 228.

6. Bassam Tibi, *Arab Nationalism: A Critical Enquiry,* ed. and trans., Marion Farouk-Sluglett and Peter Sluglett, 2nd ed. (London: Macmillan, 1990), 5; Bassam Tibi, "Islam and Arab Nationalism," in *The Islamic Impulse,* ed. Barbara Freyer Stowasser (Washington, DC: Center for Contemporary Arab Studies, Georgetown University, 1987), 68–70; Philip S. Khoury, "Islamic Revivalism and the Crisis of the Secular State in the Arab World: An Historical Appraisal," in *Arab Resources: The Transformation of a Society,* ed. I. Ibrahim (Washington, DC: Center for Contemporary Arab Studies, 1983), 213–234; R. Hrair Dekmejian, "The Anatomy of Islamic Revival: Legitimacy Crisis, Ethnic Conflict and the Search for Islamic Alternatives," *Middle East Journal* 34, no. 1 (1980), 1–12; Nikki R. Keddie, "The Revolt of Islam, 1700 to 1993: Comparative Considerations and Relations to Imperialism," *Comparative Studies in Society and History* 36, no. 3 (1994), 463–486 (486). For a challenge to the "crisis" paradigm, see Salwa Ismail, *Rethinking Islamist Politics: Culture, the State and Islamism* (London: I. B. Tauris, 2006), 22ff; Mohamed Mosaad Abdel Aziz, "The New Trend of the Muslim Brotherhood in Egypt," in *Whatever Happened to the Islamists? Salafis, Heavy Metal Muslims and the Lure of Consumerist Islam,* ed. Olivier Roy and Amel Boubekeur (London: Hurst, 2012), 79–104; also, for the earlier period, see Ziad Munson, "Islamic Mobilization: Social Movement Theory and the Egyptian Muslim Brotherhood," *Sociological Quarterly* 42, no. 4 (Autumn 2001), 487–510.

7. USNRA, CREST Database, CIA Office of National Estimates, Memorandum, "Prospects for Egypt without Nasser," 16 November 1970.

8. Eric Pace, "Extremist Moslem Brotherhood Is Stirring Again," *New York Times,* 28 November 1970.

9. UKNA, FCO (Foreign and Commonwealth Office) 39/970, Letter, Sir Richard A. Beaumont (Ambassador), Embassy Cairo to Anthony D. Parsons (Under-Secretary), FCO, 11 June 1971. See also FCO 39/970, Letter, Sir Ernest J. W. Barnes (Ambassador), Embassy Tel Aviv, to Parsons, FCO, 25 May 1971. On the "corrective revolution," see Kirk J. Beattie, *Egypt during the Sadat Years* (New York: Palgrave, 2000), 59–73.

10. See Chapter 5.

11. UKNA FCO 39/970, Letter, Beaumont, Cairo, to Parsons, FCO, 11 June 1971.

12. Ibid.; and UKNA FCO 93/635, Telegram No. 739, Embassy Cairo to FCO, 7 July 1975.

13. UKNA FCO 39/970, Letter, Parsons, FCO to Barnes, Tel Aviv, 10 June 1971.

14. UKNA FCO 39/970, Memorandum "Moslem Brotherhood in Egypt," by Malcolm A. Holding, North African Department, FCO, 24 June 1971.

15. UKNA FCO 39/970, Confidential Minute, "Release of Muslim Brethren in UAR," 24 June 1971. See note by Kay for the cautionary words.

16. It would be a mistake to overstate the impact of this: by 1981, only 8 percent of time in the school week was set aside for such instruction. Nevertheless, what mattered was the tone set by the state. See Gregory Starrett, *Putting Islam to Work: Education, Politics and Religious Transformation in Egypt* (London: University of California Press, 1998), 80–83, 92.

17. Ibid., 126–128, 191–219, 220–230; Abdullah al-Arian, *Answering the Call: Popular Islamic Activism in Egypt* (New York: Oxford University Press, 2014), 86–90; 'Abd al-Moneim Said Aly and Manfred W. Wenner, "Modern Islamic Reform Movements: The Muslim Brotherhood in Contemporary Egypt," *Middle East Journal* 36, no. 3 (Summer 1982), 336–373 (344–348).

18. Al-Arian, *Answering the Call,* 109–111.

19. Hagai Erlich, *Students and University in Twentieth Century Egyptian Politics* (London: Cass, 1989), 201–212; Al-Arian, *Answering the Call,* 117–134; Geneive Abdo, *No God but God: Egypt and the Triumph of Islam* (Oxford: Oxford University Press, 2000), 124–126.

20. Al-Arian, *Answering the Call,* 49–74. See also Ahmed Abdalla, *The Student Movement and National Politics in Egypt, 1923–1973* (London: Saqi Books, 1985), 226–228; Abdo, *No God but God,* 117–123.

21. USNRA, CREST Database, CIA "Intelligence Memorandum, 'Egypt: Sadat's Dilemma Deepens,' " 3 May 1972.

22. Al-Tilmisani, *Dhikriyat,* 113–115. There is some confusion over when the approach was made. Al-Tilmisani states it was in 1973, but then adds that it was "shortly before" the expulsion of the Soviet advisers, which occurred in July 1972.

23. Al-Arian, *Answering the Call,* 93–95. On this point, see also Denis J. Sullivan and Sana Abed-Kotob, *Islam in Contemporary Egypt: Civil Society vs. the State* (Boulder, CO: Lynne Rienner, 1999), 44.

24. On the episode of the "hidden guide," see Samer 'Eid, *Qisati ma' al-ikhwan* (Cairo: Al-Mahrusa, 2014), 30; Ella Landau-Tasseron, *Leadership and Allegiance in the Society of the Muslim Brothers,* Research Monographs on the Muslim World, No. 2 (Washington, DC: Hudson Institute, 2010), 20.

25. Al-Arian, *Answering the Call,* 95–104.

26. UKNA FCO 93/380, Letter, F. Gallagher, Embassy Beirut to Peter Ford, Embassy Cairo, 9 November 1974.

27. Hermann Eilts (Ambassador), Embassy Cairo to State Department, "Muslim Brotherhood—New Supreme Guide?" 17 March 1976, Wikileaks. All cables are rendered here into normal typeface for ease of reading—though many appear within the Wikileaks cache entirely in capitals.

28. See, for example, 'Umar al-Tilmisani, *Qala al-nas, wa lam aqul fi hukm 'abd al-nasir* (Cairo: Dar al-'Itisam, 1985), 73–78, 108–109.

29. Ibid., 39, 55–63, 68, 108–128, 233–237.

30. Muhammad Abdallah al-Samman, *Ayam ma' al-shahid Hasan al-Bana* (Cairo: Dar al-Fadila, 2003), 22.

31. Salah Shadi, *Safahat min al-tarikh: Hisad al-amr* (Kuwait: Sharikat al-Shu'a, 1981), 316.

32. Hasan Dawh, *25 'aman fi jama'at al-ikhwan* (Cairo: Dar al-'Itisam, 1983), 63.

33. Mahmud 'Abd al-Halim, *Al-Ikhwan al-Muslimun III: Ahdath sana'at al-tarikh: ru'yah min al-dakhil, al-juz' al-thalith* (Alexandria, Egypt: Dar al-Da'wa, 1981), 27–28. According to Brotherhood leaders, Nasser expressed this idea in conversation with them. Muhammad Hassanein Heikal also relates a similar anecdote.

34. Dawh, *25 'aman*, 98–101.

35. Hasan al-'Ashmawi, *Al-ayam al-hasima wa hisaduha* (Cairo: Dar al-Tawqi' wa-l-Nashr al-Islami, n.d.), 40–42.

36. Hasan al-'Ashmawi, *Al-Ikhwan wa-l-thawra: Al-juz' al-awal* (Cairo: Al-Maktab al-Misri al-Dadith, 1973), 36.

37. Shadi, *Safahat min al-tarikh*, 273–274; Dawh, *25 'aman*, 54; al-'Ashmawi, *Al-ayam al-hasima*, 34.

38. Shadi, *Safahat min al-tarikh*, 258–261, 265–266.

39. Ibid., 275.

40. Al-Tilmisani, *Qala al-nas*, 107.

41. Ibid., 108–128, 233–237.

42. Ibid., 129–130, 160–164, 191.

43. Shadi, *Safahat min al-tarikh*, 301–302.

44. See, for example, Adeed Dawisha, "Egypt," in *The Cold War and the Middle East*, ed. Yezid Sayigh and Avi Shlaim (Oxford: Clarendon, 1997), 27–47 (35–37).

45. Al-Tilmisani, *Qala al-nas*, 191–192, 214.

46. Dawh, *25 'aman*, 137–138.

47. See, for example, Shadi, *Safahat min al-tarikh*, 303–305. In reality, of course, the war was far from a military victory. At best, it could be portrayed as a stalemate, and many would argue the Egyptians were on the brink of collapse when the superpowers stepped in to force a cease-fire.

48. Ibrahim G. Aoude, "From National Bourgeois Development to Infitah: Egypt 1952–1992," *Arab Studies Quarterly* 16, no. 1 (Winter 1994).

49. Beattie, *Egypt*, 180–200.

50. UKNA, FCO 93/625, NFE 1/1, Diplomatic Report No. 295/75, "Egypt: The Dawn of Democracy," Sir Philip Adams (Ambassador), Embassy Cairo to Secretary of State for Foreign and Commonwealth Affairs, 28 July 1975.

51. Eilts, Embassy Cairo to State Department, "ASU Center Group Gets Organized," 22 July 1976, Wikileaks.

52. Abdel Azim Ramadan, "Fundamentalist Influence in Egypt: The Strategies of the Muslim Brotherhood and the Takfir Groups," in *Fundamentalisms and the State: Remaking*

Polities, Economies, and Militance, ed. Martin E. Marty and R. Scott Appleby (Chicago: University of Chicago Press, 1993), 152–183 (166–167).

53. Jeffry R. Halverson, *Theology and Creed in Sunni Islam: The Muslim Brotherhood, Ash'arism, and Political Sunnis* (New York: Palgrave Macmillan, 2010), 106.

54. "President Sadat Legalizes Some Political Parties," *Times,* 1 July 1977. On the return of the Wafd, see Marius Deeb, "Continuity in Modern Egyptian History: The Wafd and the Muslim Brothers," in AAVV, *Problems of the Modern Middle East in Historical Perspective: Essays in Honour of Albert Hourani* (London: Ithaca, 1992), 49–61.

55. Eilts, Embassy Cairo to State Department, "Human Rights Evaluation Plan—Egypt," 22 June 1977, Wikileaks.

56. Eilts, Embassy Cairo to State Department, "Left-Right Coalition," 19 May 1976, Wikileaks.

57. USNRA, CREST Database, CIA, "The Egyptian Press: A Research Paper," redacted author, January 1979; Al-Arian, *Answering the Call,* 176–184.

58. Abdo, *No God but God,* 126.

59. Al-Arian, *Answering the Call,* 156–175. For a view on the split from the perspective of al-Gama'a al-Islamiyya, see "What Does the Gama'a Islamiyya Want?" in *Political Islam: Essays from Middle East Report,* ed. Joel Beinin and Joe Stork (London: I. B. Tauris, 1997), 314–326.

60. Eilts, Embassy Cairo to State Department, "Trouble at Universities Expected," 15 October 1975, Wikileaks.

61. Eilts, Embassy Cairo to State Department, "Muslim Resurgence: Fanatic and Mainstream," 26 November 1976, Wikileaks.

62. UKNA, FCO 93/625, NFE 1/1, Diplomatic Report No. 295/75, "Egypt: The Dawn of Democracy," Adams, Cairo to FCO, 28 July 1975.

63. Eilts, Embassy Cairo to State Department, "Academy Ploy and Possible Fedayeen Activities," 24 April 1974, Wikileaks. Subsequent analysis seemed to confirm the lack of connection between the Brotherhood and the Military Technical Academy (MTA) group. See also Frank Maestrone (Charge d'Affaires), Embassy Cairo to State Department, "Youth of Muhammad," 5 March 1976, Wikileaks.

64. UKNA FCO 93/625, NFE 1/1, Despatch from D. A. S. Gladstone, HM Consulate-General, Alexandria to Patrick Wogan, Near East and North Africa Department, FCO, 2 June 1975.

65. USNRA, CREST Database, CIA, "Weekly Review," 3 May 1974.

66. Barbara H. E. Zollner, *The Muslim Brotherhood: Hasan al-Hudaybi and Ideology* (London: Routledge, 2009). Therein, Zollner discusses the question of who exactly authored *Preachers,* concluding that various actors, including al-Azhar and the authorities had an input; See 64–71. See also Barbara Zollner, "Prison Talk: The Muslim Brotherhood's Internal Struggle during Gamal Abdel Nasser's Persecution, 1954 to 1971," *International Journal of Middle East Studies* 39, no. 3 (2007), 411–433; al-Arian, *Answering the Call,* 29–35.

67. Al-Tilmisani, *Dhikriyat,* 70–73, 91.

68. For reporting of this episode, see Cyrus Vance, Bureau of Intelligence and Research, State Department, "Intsum 356," 12 July 1977, Wikileaks. For more on this, see Barry Rubin, ed., *Islamic Fundamentalism in Egyptian Politics* (Basingstoke, UK: Palgrave Macmillan, 2002).

69. Eilts, Embassy Cairo to State Department, "Takfir Arrests Continue," 12 July 1977, Wikileaks; Eilts, Embassy Cairo, to State Department, "Takfir: Libyan Connection 'Confirmed,' " 18 July 1977, Wikileaks; see also Aly and Wenner, "Modern Islamic Reform Movements," 357–358.

70. Zollner, "Prison Talk," 425.

71. Mustafa Mashhur, *Tariq al-Da'wa* (Cairo: Dar al-Tawzi' wa-l-Nashr, 1995), 44–45.

72. Ibid., 46–47, 307–309, 316–317, 367–368; al-Tilmisani, *Dhikriyat*, 70–73, 91.

73. Zollner, "Prison Talk"; John Calvert, "Wayward Son: The Muslim Brothers' Reception of Sayyid Qutb," in *The Muslim Brotherhood in Europe,* ed. Roel Meijer and Edwin Bakker (London: Hurst, 2012), 249–271.

74. The truth of this was confirmed in an interview with contemporary Brotherhood spokesman Abdullah al-Haddad, interview with author, London, 6 May 2015.

75. Mashhur, *Tariq,* 13–14, 48, 95–98, 235–236.

76. Ibid., 22–23.

77. Halverson, *Theology and Creed,* 68–73.

78. Mashhur, *Tariq,* 14–16, 44–45, 197.

79. Ibid., 149, 161–163, 268, 350–351.

80. Eilts, Embassy Cairo to State Department, "Takfir Arrests Continue," 12 July 1977, Wikileaks.

81. Al-Tilmisani, *Qala al-nas,* 108.

82. Al-Tilmisani, *Dhikriyat,* 113. Qutb himself had made a similar argument, claiming that the inclination of certain Brothers to use force was a response to the violence they experienced. See Sayyid Qutb, *Limatha A'damuni?* (Cairo: Dar 'Ashbilia l-il-Nashr wa-l-Tawzi', 2011), 62.

83. Mashhur, *Tariq,* 44–45.

84. In this context, they often cited the verse from the Qur'an that read: "Fighting has been ordained for you, though it is hard for you" (Surat al-Baqra, "The Cow," 216). See Muhammad A. S. Abdel Haleem, *The Qur'an* (Oxford: Oxford University Press, 2010).

85. Mashhur, *Tariq,* 191–195.

86. USNRA, CREST Database, CIA, "Sadat's Liberalization Policy: A Research Paper," redacted author, June 1979. See also Eilts, Embassy Cairo, "Takfir Arrests Continue."

87. Eilts, Embassy Cairo to State Department, "State of Muslim Brotherhood/the Ikhwan Today," 4 November 1977, Wikileaks.

88. Beattie, *Egypt,* 206–211.

89. For more on declining relations, see Aly and Wenner, "Modern Islamic Reform Movements," 354–356.

90. Eilts, Embassy Cairo to State Department, "Israeli Cargo through Suez Canal," 26 September 1975, Wikileaks.

91. Eilts, Embassy Cairo to State Department, "Ikhwan Prayers Peaceful," 20 November 1977, Wikileaks.

92. Al-Tilmisani, *Dhikriyat,* 51–53, 68.

93. H. Freeman Matthews (Deputy Chief of Mission), Embassy Cairo to State Department, "More Ad Hominem Attacks on Begin, Israel, and 'Jewish Mentality,' " 10 February 1978, Wikileaks.

94. Al-Tilmisani, *Qala al-nas,* 155–157, 223–224.

95. Shadi, *Safahat min al-tarikh,* 303–307; al-Tilmisani, *Dhikriyat,* 157–158.

96. Eilts, Embassy Cairo to State Department, "Muslim Brotherhood Leader Says Ikhwan Will Not Oppose Sadat on Camp David," 16 October 1978, Wikileaks; and also Cooper, Bureau of Intelligence and Research, State Department, "Intsum 672," 19 October 1978, Wikileaks.

97. Eilts, Embassy Cairo to State Department, "Evolution of Egyptian Views about Camp David," 28 December 1978, Wikileaks.

98. Eilts, Embassy Cairo to State Department, "Right Wing Religious Views on Camp David Accords," 4 October 1978, Wikileaks.

99. Matthews, Embassy Cairo, "More Ad Hominem Attacks on Begin, Israel, and 'Jewish Mentality,'" 10 February 1978, Wikileaks.

100. Al-Tilmisani, *Dhikriyat,* 51–53. The verse is from Surat al-Ma'ida (82). See Haleem, *Qur'an.*

101. Mashhur, *Tariq,* 70; see Surat al-Baqra, 120, the Qur'an; for accuracy of translation, I have drawn on Haleem, *Qur'an.*

102. Mashhur, *Tariq,* 146–147.

103. Al-Tilmisani, *Qala al-nas,* 168.

104. Al-Tilmisani, *Dhikriyat,* 195.

105. Ibid., 5.

106. Gilles Kepel, *The Roots of Radical Islam* (London: Saqi Books, 2005), 112–127. See also Ian Johnson, "The Brotherhood's Westward Expansion," *Current Trends in Islamist Ideology* 6 (2008), 71–84, (77); Mariz Tadros, *The Muslim Brotherhood in Contemporary Egypt: Democracy Redefined or Confined?* (London: Routledge, 2012), 91–93.

107. Al-Tilmisani, *Dhikriyat.* 50, 161–163; al-Tilmisani, *Qala al-nas,* 18. The phrase "enemies of Islam" is used repeatedly.

108. Matthews, Embassy Cairo to State Department, "More Ad Hominem Attacks on Begin, Israel, and 'Jewish Mentality,'" 10 February 1978, Wikileaks; al-Tilmisani, *Dhikriyat,* 71.

109. Al-Tilmisani, *Dhikriyat.* 74–75.

110. Eilts, Embassy Cairo to State Department, "Al Dawa (Again) on Israel, U.S., USSR and Much Else," 11 July 1978, Wikileaks.

111. Al-Arian, *Answering the Call,* 184–214.

112. Eilts, Embassy Cairo to State Department, "Ikhwan Raps U.S., Russia, and GOE," 10 May 1978, Wikileaks. See also Eilts, Embassy Cairo to State Department, "Muslim Brotherhood al-Da'wa Flays Practically Everybody," 8 June 1978, Wikileaks.

113. Henry Tanner, "Sadat Learns to Compromise with His Religious Militants," *New York Times,* 5 April 1981.

114. Halverson, *Theology and Creed,* 74–78.

115. Ibrahim M. Abu-Rabi', *Contemporary Arab Thought: Studies in Post-1967 Arab Intellectual History* (London: Pluto Press, 2003), 223–245. Abu-Rabi' notes that al-Ghazali, despite his 1953 expulsion from the Brotherhood, "remained committed to the broad outlines of Banna's thought."

116. Ramadan, "Fundamentalist Influence in Egypt," 152–183 (169–170); Gabriel R. Warburg, "Islam and Politics in Egypt: 1952–80," *Middle Eastern Studies* 18, no. 2 (1982), 131–157.

117. Vance, Bureau of Intelligence and Research, State Department, "Intsum 540," 11 April 1978, Wikileaks.

118. Eilts, Embassy Cairo to State Department, "Al Dawa (Again) on Israel, U.S., USSR and Much Else," 11 July 1978, Wikileaks; USNRA, CREST Database, CIA, "The Egyptian Press: A Research Paper," redacted author, January 1979.

119. Eilts, Embassy Cairo to State Department, "Muslim Brotherhood al-Da'wa Flays Practically Everybody," 8 June 1978, Wikileaks.

120. Matthews, Embassy Cairo to State Department, "Islamic Societies in Strong Position on University Campuses," 7 February 1978, Wikileaks; Abdalla, *The Student Movement and National Politics*, 226–228; al-Arian, *Answering the Call*, 124.

121. UKNA FCO 93/1430, Kevin J. Passmore (Second Secretary), Embassy Cairo to P. J. Torry, NENAD (Near East and North Africa Department), FCO, 23 January 1978.

122. Eilts, Embassy Cairo to State Department, "Islamic Fundamentalism in Egypt: Political Attitudes, Structure and Influence," 21 November 1978, Wikileaks. See also on this issue Vance, Bureau of Intelligence and Research, State Department, "Intsum 698," 27 November 1978, Wikileaks.

123. UKNA FCO 93/1430, Memorandum, "Religion in Egypt," R. D. Lamb, Research Dept. to Torry, NENAD, FCO, 7 December 1977.

124. Warren Christopher (Deputy Secretary of State), State Department, "Intsum 709," 12 December 1978, Wikileaks.

125. UKNA FCO 93/1430, Memorandum, "Religion in Egypt," R. D. Lamb, Research Dept. to Torry, NENAD FCO, 7 December 1977.

126. Christopher, State Department, "Intsum 709," 12 December 1978, Wikileaks.

127. Christopher, State Department, "Intsum 708," 12 December 1978, Wikileaks.

128. This strategy, as first developed by the Johnson administration and then augmented by the Nixon White House, looked to "proxies" to secure US interests in the region against more "radical" forces. See Douglas Little, "Gideon's Band: America and the Middle East since 1945," *Diplomatic History* 18, no. 4 (1994), 513–540 (514); Gary Sick, "The United States in the Persian Gulf: From Twin Pillars to Dual Containment," in David W. Lesch, *The Middle East and the United States: A Historical and Political Reassessment,* 3rd ed. (Oxford: Westview, 2003), 315–331 (316); William Stivers, *America's Confrontation with Revolutionary Change in the Middle East, 1948–83* (New York: St. Martin's, 1986), 62–68; Henry William Brands, *Into the Labyrinth: The United States and the Middle East, 1945–93* (New York: McGraw-Hill, 1994), 124–125.

129. Emmanuel Sivan, "Sunni Radicalism in the Middle East and the Iranian Revolution," *International Journal of Middle East Studies* 21 (1989), 1–30.

130. Walid Muhammad Abdelnasser, "Islamic Organizations in Egypt and the Iranian Revolution of 1979: The Experience of the First Few Years," *Arab Studies Quarterly* 19, no. 2 (Spring 1997), 25–39.

131. Robert Lacey, *Inside the Kingdom: Kings, Clerics, Modernists, Terrorists, and the Struggle for Saudi Arabia* (New York: Viking, 2009), 46–53, 114–123.

132. 'Abd al-Mon'im Abu al-Futuh, *Shahid 'ala tarikh al-haraka al-islamiya fi misr, 1970–1984,* 2nd ed. (Cairo: Dar al-Shuruq, 2012), 103–104.

133. "Muslim Brotherhood Leader on Hamah, Country's Armed Forces," *Al-Watan al-Arabi,* 16–22 April 1982, trans., FBIS Near East/North Africa Report (FOUO 28/82), 30 July 1982.

134. Halverson, *Theology and Creed,* 110.

135. Shadi, *Safahat min al-tarikh,* 308–309.

136. Al-Tilmisani, *Dhikriyat,* 229, 250; Halverson, *Theology and Creed,* 111.

137. Kemal el-Helbawy, interview with author. Cairo, 4 December 2014. On Helbawy's role as the first executive director of the World Assembly of Muslim Youth (WAMY), see "First Anniversary—An Interview with Dr. Kemal Helbawy," *Islamism Digest* 2, no. 4 (April 2007).

138. Edward Mortimer, "Foreign Policy: The Impact of Islam," *Times,* 20 May 1983.

139. Henry Kissinger (Secretary of State), State Department, "Coup Rumors: Contingency Study," 11 September 1975, Wikileaks; Eliot, Embassy Kabul to State Department, "Year-End Afghan Internal Assessment," 31 December 1975, Wikileaks; Robert F. Goheen (Ambassador), Embassy New Delhi to State Department, "MEA Views of Pakistan and Afghanistan," 13 September 1977, Wikileaks; Theodore L. Eliot (Ambassador), Embassy Kabul to State Department, "Killing of Planning Minister Khurram: Political Assassination or Personal Feud?," 22 November 1977, Wikileaks.

140. Christopher, State Department, "CENTO Council of Deputies Meeting," 3 June 1978, Wikileaks. See also Adolph Dubs (Ambassador), Embassy Kabul to State Department, "Assessment of Afghan Developments and US-Afghan Relations," 14 September 1978, Wikileaks; Dubs, Embassy Kabul to State Department, "Foreign Minister Amin Sees Afghanistan Moving towards a 'Fully Socialist Society,'" 16 October 1978, Wikileaks.

141. Youssef Nada claims that he was in contact with Burhannudin Rabbani, the leader of the Jamaat-i-Islami in Afghanistan, who told him that his group "considered themselves part of the Muslim Brotherhood." See Nada, *Inside the Muslim Brotherhood,* 73.

142. Al-Tilmisani, *Dhikriyat,* 196. See also Abu al-Futuh, *Shahid 'ala tarikh,* 106–109.

143. Kemal el-Helbawy, interview with author, London, 29 December 2014.

144. Kemal el-Helbawy, "The Muslim Brotherhood in Egypt: Historical Evolution and Future Prospects," in Khaled Hroub, *Political Islam: Context versus Ideology* (London: Saqi Books, 2010), 80–81; al-Tilmisani, *Dhikriyat,* 196, 225.

145. John Heinz, "Helping the Afghan Rebels—Carefully," *Christian Science Monitor,* 16 December 1980.

146. Bill Bradley, "Arming Afghan Rebels," *New York Times,* 10 January 1980.

147. For arguably the most readable single-volume treatment of the subject, see Steve Coll, *Ghost Wars: The Secret History of the CIA, Afghanistan and Bin Laden, from the Soviet Invasion to September 10, 2001* (London: Penguin, 2004).

148. Andrew Preston, *Sword of the Spirit, Shield of Faith: Religion in American War and Diplomacy* (New York: Alfred Knopf, 2012), 579–587.

149. Al-Tilmisani, *Dhikriyat,* 196, 225.

150. USNRA, CREST Database, CIA, "Sadat's Liberalization Policy: A Research Paper," redacted author, June 1979. See also CIA, "National Intelligence Daily," 18 April 1979.

151. "A Growing Moslem Resistance," *Boston Globe,* 24 March 1979.

152. Al-Arian, *Answering the Call,* 137–138.

153. Al-Tilmisani, *Dhikriyat,* 116, 218–220; Abdalla, *The Student Movement,* 280n9.

154. "Al-Sadat Enraged at Left, Censures Muslim Brotherhood Leader on Television," *al-Watan al-Arabi,* 6–12 September 1979, trans. in FBIS, Near East / North Africa Report (FOUO 43/79), 2 November 1979; al-Arian, *Answering the Call,* 146–147.

155. Al-Tilmisani, *Dhikriyat,* 194. For Evans, see Chapter 5.

156. By one account, the approach was made in June 1979; see "Al-Sadat Enraged at Left, Censures Muslim Brotherhood Leader on Television," *al-Watan al-Arabi,* 6–12 September 1979, trans. in FBIS, Near East / North Africa Report (FOUO 43/79), 2 November 1979. Alternatively, in his memoirs, Tilmisani relates a very similar incident in which the British ambassador contacted him to say that a former foreign secretary wished to visit *al-Da'wa.* The general guide replied to the effect that this was fine, provided his visitor wished only to see the offices of *al-Da'wa,* but not if he wanted politics. As a result, the visit never occurred. Here, he dates the episode June 1980, though it seems likely he is describing the same event and got the dates wrong. See al-Tilmisani, *Dhikriyat,* 194.

157. "Sectarianism Stalks across Egypt," *al-Watan al-Arabi,* 11–17 April 1980, trans. in FBIS, Near East / North Africa Report (FOUO 22/80), 19 June 1980.

158. Ibid.

159. Al-Tilmisani insisted that the accusations against them were "pure fantasy." For his account of this period, see 'Umar al-Tilmisani, *Ayam ma' al-Sadat* (Cairo: Dar al-'Itisam, 1984).

160. "Obituary: President Sadat," *Times,* 7 October 1981.

161. USNRA, CREST Database, CIA, "Resurgent Islamic Nationalism in the Middle East: An Intelligence Assessment," March 1981.

162. Ibid.

163. USNRA, CREST Database, CIA, "Egypt: Islamic Cults, Crisis, and Politics: A Research Paper," August 1982.

164. Ibid.

165. Ibid.

166. USNRA, CREST Database, CIA, "The Egyptian Press: A Research Paper," redacted author, January 1979.

167. USNRA, CREST Database, CIA, "The Muslim Brotherhood and Arab Politics: A Research Paper," October 1982, especially the annex.

168. Al-Tilmisani, *Dhikriyat,* 196–197.

169. Halverson, *Theology and Creed,* 91.

170. Interestingly, this had always been Sadat's prognosis. He reportedly expressed the view, prior to his death, that he just needed to survive through to 1982 and the Sinai withdrawal, after which time he expected things to get easier.

171. Robert Springborg, *Mubarak's Egypt: Fragmentation of the Political Order* (Boulder, CO: Westview, 1989), 136–216.

172. Ray Takeyh and Nikolas K. Gvosdev, *The Receding Shadow of the Prophet: The Rise and Fall of Radical Political Islam* (London: Praeger, 2004), 62–65.

173. For cable analysis of the Muslim Brotherhood (MB) role in the syndicates, see Daniel Kurtzer (Ambassador), Embassy Cairo to State Department, "Egypt's Muslim Brotherhood at Low Ebb," 16 March 1999, Wikileaks. For discussion of the Brotherhood's role in the syndicates, see Carrie Rosefsky Wickham, "Islamic Mobilization and Political Change: The Islamist Trend in Egypt's Professional Associations," in Beinin and Stork, *Political Islam,* 120–135; Ninette Fahmy, "The Performance of the Muslim Brotherhood in the Egyptian Syndicates: An Alternative Formula for Reform?" *Middle East Journal* 52 (Autumn 1998), 551–562; Carrie R. Wickham, *Mobilizing Islam: Religion, Activism, and Political Change in Egypt* (New York: Columbia University Press, 2002); Mona El-Ghobashy, "The Metamorphosis of the Egyptian Muslim Brothers," *International Journal*

of Middle East Studies 37 (2005), 373–395 (379–380); Mohammed Zahid, *The Muslim Brotherhood and Egypt's Succession Crisis: The Politics of Liberalisation and Reform in the Middle East* (London: I. B. Tauris, 2010), 105–128.

174. Abdo, *No God but God*, 89–90.

175. Al-Tilmisani, *Dhikriyat*, 184.

176. El-Ghobashy, "Metamorphosis," 377–378.

177. Springborg, *Mubarak's Egypt*, 48–49, 224–226.

178. Mashhur, *Tariq*, 200–201.

179. Henry Precht (Deputy Ambassador), Embassy Cairo to State Department, "Growing Debate on Sharia Law," 8 March 1985, Wikileaks; Precht, Embassy Cairo to State Department, "Islamic Sharia Debate—Words Followed by Another Stall," 11 April 1985, Wikileaks.

180. USNRA, CREST Database, CIA, "Islam and Politics: A Compendium—A Reference Aid," April 1984.

181. USNRA, CREST Database, CIA, "The Egyptian Muslim Brotherhood: Building Bases of Support—A Research Paper," May 1986.

182. Ibid.

183. Ibid.

184. Frank Wisner (Ambassador), Embassy Cairo to State Department, "Muslim Brotherhood: Eager for U.S. Contacts, Fearful of GOE," 16 September 1986, Wikileaks.

185. Precht, Embassy Cairo to State Department, "Growing Debate on Sharia Law," 8 March 1985, Wikileaks; Nicholas Veliotes (Ambassador), Embassy Cairo to State Department, "Islamic Sharia Debate—Words Followed by Another Stall," 11 April 1985, Wikileaks.

186. Wisner, Embassy Cairo to State Department, "Muslim Brotherhood: Eager for U.S. Contacts, Fearful of GOE," 16 September 1986, Wikileaks.

187. Ibid.

188. "Egypt's Youth, Searching for Ideals, Turn to Extremists," *Washington Post,* 11 March 1986.

189. Wisner, Embassy Cairo to State Department, "Muslim Brotherhood: Eager for U.S. Contacts, Fearful of GOE," 16 September 1986, Wikileaks.

190. Wisner, Embassy Cairo to State Department, "Muslim Brotherhood Developments and Personalities," 18 August 1988, Wikileaks.

191. See, for example, Wisner, Embassy Cairo to State Department, "Muslim Brotherhood—Jihad 'Frictions,'" 6 September 1988, Wikileaks.

192. USNRA, CREST Database, CIA, "The Egyptian Muslim Brotherhood: Building Bases of Support—A Research Paper," May 1986. Among the businesses listed as being owned or operated by the Brotherhood were: Arab Contractors; Faisal Islamic Bank of Cairo (managed by active Brotherhood member Ahmad Ali Kamal); Al-Sharif Group (that owned factories); Al-Salam Group (hoteliers); and Hilal Group (the owner of fourteen diverse companies). "Islamic Charities," a Brotherhood front organization based in Kuwait, was also described as a major vehicle for the management of an investment portfolio.

193. USNRA, CREST Database, CIA, "The Egyptian Muslim Brotherhood: Building Bases of Support—A Research Paper," May 1986. Also on the factions within the Brotherhood at that time, see Springborg, *Mubarak's Egypt*, 233–238.

194. Wisner, Embassy Cairo to State Department, "Muslim Brotherhood: Eager for U.S. Contacts, Fearful of GOE," 16 September 1986, Wikileaks.

195. Alison Pargeter, *The Muslim Brotherhood: The Burden of Tradition* (London: Saqi Books, 2010), 46–50.

196. USNRA, CREST Database, CIA, "Near East and South Asia Review," 11 September 1987.

197. The alliance with the former was a long time in the making. Almost a decade earlier, US officials had noticed that the Socialist Labor Party seemed keen to attract the support of the Brotherhood. See Matthews, Embassy Cairo to State Department, "Political Party Developments," 15 September 1978, Wikileaks.

198. Springborg, *Mubarak's Egypt,* 183–186. For the Brotherhood's record of its performance in parliament after 1987, see Muhsin Rada, *Al-Ikhwan al-Muslimun taht qubbat al-barlaman vol 2: Haqa'iq . . . wa mawaqif* (Cairo: Dar al-Tawzi' wa-l-Nashr al-Islami, 1991).

199. USNRA, CREST Database, CIA, "Near East and South Asia Review," 11 September 1987.

200. Ibid.

201. Wisner, Embassy Cairo to State Department, "Muslim Brotherhood Developments and Personalities," 18 August 1988, Wikileaks.

202. Ismail, *Rethinking Islamist Politics,* 98–113.

203. Springborg, *Mubarak's Egypt,* 217–223. On the development of al-Gama'a al-Islamiyya and the factors that fueled its shift into insurgency in Upper Egypt during the 1990s, see James Toth, "Islamism in Southern Egypt: A Case Study of a Radical Religious Movement," *International Journal of Middle East Studies* 35 (2003), 547–572; Ramadan, "Fundamentalist Influence in Egypt," 161–164.

204. Wisner, Embassy Cairo to State Department, "Muslim Brotherhood—Jihad 'Frictions,'" 6 September 1988, Wikileaks. For a local-level view of the two groups, see also Mark Hambley (Consul-General), Consulate Alexandria to State Department, "Islamic Trilogy, Part I: An Overview of the Islamic Right in Alexandria," 25 February 1987, Wikileaks.

205. USNRA, CREST Database, CIA, "Near East and South Asia Review," 18 December 1987.

206. See, for example, Carrie Rosefsky Wickham, *The Muslim Brotherhood: Evolution of an Islamist Movement* (Oxford: Princeton University Press, 2013), especially 46–75.

207. Wisner, Embassy Cairo to State Department, "Muslim Brotherhood: Defanged but Rehabilitated," 20 July 1989, Wikileaks.

208. Ibid.

209. USNRA, CREST Database, CIA, "The Muslim Brotherhood and Arab Politics: A Research Paper," October 1982.

210. Qutb, *Limatha,* 41–47.

211. Mashhur, *Tariq,* 196–197.

212. Hossam Tammam, "The International Organisation of the Muslim Brotherhood," in *Islamic Movements of Europe: Public Religion and Islamophobia in the Modern World,* ed. Frank Peter and Rafael Ortega (London: I. B. Tauris, 2014), 89–94; Pargeter, *Muslim Brotherhood,* 99–132; Brigitte Marechal, *The Muslim Brothers in Europe: Roots and Discourse* (Leiden, Netherlands: Brill, 2008), 49.

213. Israel Elad Altman, *Strategies of the Muslim Brotherhood Movement, 1928–2007,* Research Monographs on the Muslim World, Series No. 2, Paper No. 2 (Washington, DC: Hudson Institute, 2009), 1, 5–6.

214. Kemal el-Helbawy, interview with author, Cairo, 4 December 2014.

215. Anas Altikriti, interview with author, London, 3 May 2017.

216. Pargeter, *Muslim Brotherhood,* 61–69; Robert G. Rabil, "The Syrian Muslim Brotherhood," in *The Muslim Brotherhood: The Organization and Policies of a Global Islamist Movement,* ed. Barry Rubin (New York: Palgrave Macmillan, 2010), 73–88 (74–79); Itzchak Weismann, "Sa'id Hawwa: The Making of a Radical Muslim Thinker in Modern Syria," *Middle Eastern Studies* 29, no. 4 (1993), 601–623 (615–616); Umar F. Abd-Allah, *The Islamic Struggle in Syria* (Berkeley: Mizan, 1983), 103–107.

217. USNRA, RG59, CFPF, Box 2686, POL 23–8 SYR, Despatch No. 715, Ridgway B. Knight (Ambassador), Embassy Damascus to State Department, 19 April 1964. See also in same box, POL 23–8 SYR, Despatch No. CX-33, Knight, Damascus to State Department, 19 April 1964; POL 23–8 SYR, Despatch No. 755, Knight, Damascus to State Department, 4 May 1964; "Development of Muslim Brotherhood in Syria Described," *Al-Watan al-Arabi,* 26 September–2 October 1980, trans. in FBIS Near East / North Africa Report (FOUO 42/80), 2 December 1980.

218. Raphaël Lefèvre, *Ashes of Hama: The Muslim Brotherhood in Syria* (London, UK: Hurst, 2013), 88–96; Abd-Allah, *Islamic Struggle,* 107–108.

219. "Muslim Brotherhood Leader on Hamah, Country's Armed Forces," *Al-Watan al-Arabi,* 16–22 April 1982, trans. in FBIS Near East / North Africa Report (FOUO 28/82), 30 July 1982.

220. Richard W. Murphy (Ambassador), Embassy Damascus, to State Department, "Indications of More Incidents Planned by Muslim Brotherhood against Authorities," 4 March 1976, Wikileaks; Murphy, Damascus to State Department, "More Explosions in Damascus," 10 August 1976, Wikileaks; USNRA, CREST Database, CIA, Weekly Summary, "Syria: Asad's Domestic Position," 16 April 1976. In a recent book, Raphaël Lefèvre argues that these attacks—and the June 1979 massacre in Aleppo—were the work of the Fighting Vanguard and not the Brotherhood, which was only dragged slowly and reluctantly into "armed struggle." See Lefèvre, *Ashes of Hama,* 72–73, 102–116.

221. "Shaikhs Shot in Syrian Mosque," *Times,* 4 February 1980; Pargeter, *Muslim Brotherhood,* 69–81.

222. Shmuel Bar, *The Muslim Brotherhood in Jordan* (Tel Aviv: Moshe Dayan Center for Middle Eastern and African Studies, 1998), 37.

223. "Syria Outlaws Muslim Brotherhood," *Times,* 9 July 1980; Robert Fisk, "Hunting of Brotherhood Reveals Its Strength," *Times,* 25 October 1980. See also Abd-Allah, *Islamic Struggle,* 84–87.

224. Weismann, "Sa'id Hawwa," 618. The manifesto was signed by key Brotherhood leaders Adnan Sa'ad al-Din, Said Hawwa, and Ali al-Bayanuni. For the full text, see Abd-Allah, *Islamic Struggle,* 201–267. For analysis of the same, see idem., 128–187.

225. "Interview: Muslim Revolt in Syria: 'The Last and the Only Resort,' " *Impact International Fortnightly* 11, no. 4 (27 February–12 March 1981); Liad Porat, "The Syrian Muslim Brotherhood and the Asad Regime," *Middle East Brief: Crown Center for Middle East Studies* 47 (December 2010).

226. "Interview: Muslim Revolt in Syria: 'The Last and the Only Resort,' " *Impact International Fortnightly* 11, no. 4, (27 February–12 March 1981).

227. "Muslim Brotherhood Leader on Hamah, Country's Armed Forces," *Al-Watan al-Arabi,* 16–22 April 1982, trans. in FBIS Near East / North Africa Report (FOUO 28/82), 30 July 1982.

228. Ibid.

229. Abd-Allah, *Islamic Struggle,* 177–179.

230. "Assad Charges US Role in Rebellion," *Boston Globe,* 8 March 1982. See also Robert Fisk, "Syrian Minister Hints at Foreign Influence behind Muslim Brotherhood Disturbances," *Times,* 21 March 1980.

231. Robert Fisk, "64 Killed by Car Bomb in Damascus," *Times,* 30 November 1981.

232. Lefèvre, *Ashes of Hama,* 132.

233. "Muslim Brotherhood Leader on Hamah, Country's Armed Forces," *Al-Watan al-Arabi,* 16–22 April 1982, trans. in FBIS Near East / North Africa Report (FOUO 28/82), 30 July 1982.

234. Lefèvre, *Ashes of Hama,* 122–128.

235. William Eagleton (Ambassador), Embassy Damascus to State Department, "The Syrian Muslim Brotherhood," 26 February 1985, Wikileaks; USNRA, CREST Database, CIA, "Syria: Sunni Opposition to the Minority Alawite Regime—A Research Paper," NESA 85–10102, June 1985. For similar analysis (as to it being "unlikely" that there would be any renewed threat from the Brotherhood), see CIA, Foreign Subversion and Instability Center, Office of Global Issues, "Syria: Scenarios of Dramatic Political Change," 28 July 1986.

236. "Interview with Sudanese Attorney General," *The Middle East* (London), September 1979, in FBIS Near East / North Africa Report, 26 September 1979. See also "Politics Only an Aspect of Islam, says Dr. Torabi," *Impact International Fortnightly* 2, no. 24, (11–24 May 1973). And Mohammed Zaid and Michael Medley, "Muslim Brotherhood in Egypt and Sudan," *Review of African Political Economy* 33, no. 110 (2006), 693–708.

237. See, for instance, Robert E. Fritts (Deputy Chief of Mission), Embassy Khartoum to State Department, "Anti-Nimairi Demonstration," 30 August 1973, Wikileaks; William D. Brewer (Ambassador), Embassy Khartoum to State Department, "Political Detainees Released," 15 March 1974, Wikileaks; USNRA, CREST Database, CIA, "Central Intelligence Bulletin," 7 September 1973.

238. Berlind (Charge d'Affaires), Embassy Khartoum to State Department, "Attempted Sudanese Coup Fails," 5 September 1975, Wikileaks; Eilts, Embassy Cairo, to State Department, "Sadat Blames Tripoli and Moscow for Abortive Coup in Sudan," 10 July 1976, Wikileaks; USNRA, CREST Database, CIA, Weekly Summary, "Sudan: Coup Quashed," 12 September 1975; and CIA, Weekly Summary, "Sudan: Beleaguered Strong Man," 13 August 1976.

239. "Interview with Sudanese Attorney General," *The Middle East* (London), September 1979, in FBIS Near East / North Africa Report, 26 September 1979.

240. USNRA, CREST Database, CIA National Foreign Assessment Center Intelligence Memorandum, "Sudan: The Numayri Regime—Orientation and Prospects," 6 September 1978. See also CIA, "The Muslim Brotherhood and Arab Politics: A Research Paper," October 1982.

241. USNRA, CREST Database, CIA, "Sudan: Islam as a Political Force—An Intelligence Assessment," NESA 84–10144, April 1984.

242. As late as February, the group was still identified as a supporter of Nimeiri. See "Africa Hit by Wave of Student Unrest," *Times,* 19 February 1985.

243. USNRA, CREST Database, CIA, Near East and South Asia Review, "Sudan: Hassan el Turabi and the Muslim Brotherhood," 2 August 1985.

244. USNRA, CREST Database, CIA, "Sudan's Political Parties: A Research Paper," NESA 87–10040, August 1987.

245. Gilles Kepel, *Jihad: The Trial of Political Islam* (London: I. B. Tauris, 2004), 177–184.

246. In the April 1967 parliamentary elections, the Brotherhood saw two candidates win seats to an institution that was largely compliant with the monarch's wishes. See USNRA, RG59, CFPF, Box 2252, POL 2–1 Jordan, Airgram A-375, Joint Weekly No. 40, Embassy Amman to State Department, 19 April 1967.

247. See USNRA, RG59, CFPF, Box 2252, POL 2–1 Jordan, Airgram A-347, Joint Weekly No. 36, Embassy Amman to State Department, 23 March 1967.

248. USNRA, RG59, CFPF, Box 2253, POL 14 Jordan, Airgram A-377, Findley Burns Jr. (Ambassador), Embassy Amman to State Department, 19 April 1967.

249. USNRA, CREST Database, CIA, "The Muslim Brotherhood and Arab Politics: A Research Paper," October 1982.

250. Bar, *Muslim Brotherhood in Jordan,* 32.

251. Christopher Walker, "Muslim Brotherhood Call for Syrian Revolt," *Times,* 8 December 1980.

252. Marion Boulby, *The Muslim Brotherhood and the Kings of Jordan, 1945–1993* (Atlanta, GA: Scholars Press, 1999), 98–101.

253. Bar, *Muslim Brotherhood in Jordan,* 39.

254. Altman, *Strategies of the Muslim Brotherhood,* 31.

255. Ziyad Abu-Amr, *Islamic Fundamentalism in the West Bank and Gaza: Muslim Brotherhood and Islamic Jihad* (Bloomington: Indiana University Press, 1994), 14–22, 35–36, 59–89.

256. "The Charter of the Islamic Resistance Movement (Hamas)," available in Shaul Mishal and Avraham Sela, *The Palestinian Hamas: Vision, Violence, and Coexistence* (New York: Columbia University Press, 2000), 175–199.

257. Andrea Nüsse, *Muslim Palestine: The Ideology of Hamas* (Abingdon, UK: Routledge-Curzon, 1998), 57–62, 105–107.

258. Philip C. Wilcox (Consul-General), Consulate-General Jerusalem to State Department, "Fundamentalism and the Intifada: Defining the Issues," 23 September 1988, Wikileaks.

259. Marechal, *Muslim Brothers in Europe,* 56.

260. On this, see also Jorgen Nielsen, "Transnational Islam and the Integration of Islam in Europe," in *Muslim Networks and Transnational Communities in and across Europe,* ed. Stefan Allevi and Jorgen Nielsen (Leiden, Netherlands: E. J. Brill, 2003).

261. See Chapter 3.

262. "Islam al-Europiyyin," *Al-Ikhwan al-Muslimun,* 29 July 1944; "Al-Watan al-islami . . . al-islam fi bulanda," *Al-Ikhwan al-Muslimun,* 17 March 1945.

263. "Ikhwanuna fi amrika," *Al-Ikhwan al-Muslimun,* 13 September 1945.

264. A. Abdul-Kadir, "Islam and the West," *Al-Muslimun* 4, no. 3 (May 1955).

265. Abu Ayman, "Fi Amrika," *Al-Muslimun* 5, no. 9 (June 1957).

266. For a useful short overview of this, see Lorenzo Vidino, *The Muslim Brotherhood in the West: Evolution and Western Policies* (London: ISCR, February 2011).

267. Ibid., 8–9. See also Pargeter, *Muslim Brotherhood,* 133–175.

268. Ian Johnson, *A Mosque in Munich: Nazis, the CIA and the Rise of the Muslim Brotherhood in the West* (Boston: Houghton Mifflin Harcourt, 2010) 186–187. On the role of

Ramadan, see also Lorenzo Vidino, *The New Muslim Brotherhood in the West* (New York: Columbia University Press, 2010), 28–30.

269. Qutb, *Limatha,* 48.

270. Johnson, *Mosque in Munich,* 120–121; Marechal, *Muslim Brothers in Europe,* 59, 135–137. The decision to go to Geneva was itself interesting. It had formerly been the home of Shakib Arslan, a Lebanese exile and strong exponent of pan-Islam and anti-imperialism.

271. Johnson, "The Brotherhood's Westward Expansion," 73; Caroline Fourest, *Brother Tariq: The Doublespeak of Tariq Ramadan,* trans., Ioana Wieder and John Atherton (New York: Encounter Books, 2008), 68–72. On the Jamaat-i-Islami, see Brigitte Marechal, "Mosques, Organisations and Leadership," in *Muslims in the Enlarged Europe: Religion and Society,* ed. Brigitte Marechal et al. (Boston: Brill, 2003), 139–141.

272. Today, the Islamic Center of Geneva is run by Sa'id's son, Hani Ramadan. See http://www.cige.org/cige/index.html.

273. Johnson, *Mosque in Munich,* 122–123, 134–135.

274. In 2002, Himmat resigned from the commission after allegations he was connected to terrorism financing (specifically, the Banque el-Taqwa); the charges against Himmat were later dropped. He was replaced on the commission by Ibrahim el-Zayat.

275. Johnson, "Brotherhood's Westward Expansion," 77.

276. Johnson, *Mosque in Munich,* 160–178, 197; Johnson, "Brotherhood's Westward Expansion," 76; Marechal, *Muslim Brothers in Europe,* 62; Melanie Kemp and Jorn Thielmann, "Germany: Islamische Gemeinschaft in Deutschland and Islamische Zentren," in Peter and Ortega, *Islamic Movements of Europe,* 99–103; Stefan Meining, "The Islamic Community in Germany: An Organisation under Observation," in Meijer and Bakker, *Muslim Brotherhood in Europe,* 209–233.

277. Gilles Kepel, *Allah in the West: Islamic Movements in America and Europe,* trans. Susan Milner (Stanford, CA: Stanford University Press, 1997), 195–203; Tammam, "International Organisation," 89–94.

278. "Muslim Brotherhood in the West," *Cordoba Foundation: MENA Report* 1, no. 11 (November 2013); Marechal, *Muslim Brothers in Europe,* 60, 70–71.

279. "Muqadima" in *Risalat al-muslimin fi bilad al-gharb,* ed. Mustafa Tahan (Irbid, Jordan: Dar al-Amal, 1999), 1–2.

280. Abbas Hasan al-Sissi, *Fi qafilat al-Ikhwan al-Muslimun, al-juz' al-awal* (Alexandria, Egypt: Dar al-Taba'a wa-l-Nashr wa-l-Sutiyat, 1987), 285.

281. Dawh, *25 'aman,* 112.

282. Innes Bowen, *Medina in Birmingham, Najaf in Brent: Inside British Islam* (London: Hurst, 2014), 103.

283. Muslim Welfare House, *Annual Review 2001–2002* (copy in possession of the author).

284. From there, al-Assal moved to Saudi Arabia, where he became chair of the department of Islamic Culture at the University of Imam Muhammad bin Saud between 1970 and 1984. Thereafter, he moved to the International Islamic University in Islamabad, Pakistan, where he remained from 1986 until 2002, during which time he also became a member of both the European Council for Fatwa and Research and the International Union of Muslim Scholars.

285. 'Abd al-Baqi Khalifa, "D. Ahmad al-'Assal: ada' al-Islam tharfiyun 'amam da'wa 'umruha 14 qarnan," Al-Moslem.net, 18 July 2010, http://bit.ly/2urjYbk; "Al-Duktur Ahmad al-'Assal," Ikhwanwiki, http://bit.ly/2srgzYA.

286. See, for example, "Hiwar ma' mudir duwar al-ra'aya al-islamiya fi britaniya," Islamweb.net, 7 March 2002, http://bit.ly/2tKcbrB.

287. Marechal, *Muslim Brothers in Europe*, 70–74.

288. See, for example, *Impact International* subscription form, undated (copy in possession of author).

289. "Islamic Unity of Afghan Mujihideen" [advertisement], *Impact International Fortnightly* (26 October–8 November 1984).

290. "Books and Teaching Aids on Islam" [advertisement], *Impact International Fortnightly* (26 October–8 November 1984); "New Publications—The Islamic Foundation Publications Unit," *Impact International Fortnightly* (8–21 November 1985).

291. Kepel, *Allah in the West*, 110–111, 121–132. For more on the Muslim Educational Trust (MET), see "MET's Third Primer on Salah," *Impact International Fortnightly* 3, no. 6 (10–23 August 1973); "Appeal to Start New Muslim School in London," *Times*, 5 July 1976. For the Islamic Foundation (IF), see "Founded on Ideals: The Islamic Foundation," *Emel*, November–December 2004; "Towards a Greater Understanding of Islam," *Impact International Fortnightly* 3, no. 12 (9–22 November 1973).

292. "The Founding Mission," *Emel* 99 (December 2012). See also Philip Lewis, *Islamic Britain: Religion, Politics and Identity among British Muslims*, 2nd ed. (London: I. B. Tauris, 2002), 102–112; Nielsen, "Transnational Islam and the Integration of Islam in Europe," 28–51 (36).

293. See, for example, A. Ally, "FOSIS Tenth Annual Conference," *Impact International Fortnightly* 3, no. 6 (10–23 August 1973); Kalim Siddiqui, "Now that the Conference Is Over," *Impact International Fortnightly* 3, no. 11 (26 October–8 November 1973).

294. David Rich, "The Very Model of a British Muslim Brotherhood," in Rubin, *Muslim Brotherhood*, 117–136 (118).

295. Ziauddin Sardar, "London Conference of Islamic Centres and Bodies in Europe," *Impact International Fortnightly* 3, no. 1 (25 May–7 June 1973).

296. "Obituary: Salem Azzam (1924–2008)," *Muslim Weekly*, 22 February 2008.

297. "People," *Impact International Fortnightly* 7, no. 20 (28 October–10 November 1977).

298. "Islamic Council of Europe: Progress and Plans," *Impact International Fortnightly* 6, no. 16 (10–23 September 1976).

299. "Council Unites Muslim Religious Activities in Britain," *Times*, 10 January 1977.

300. "Islamic Council of Europe: 'Foundation Well Laid,'" *Impact International Fortnightly* 8, no. 10 (26 May–8 June 1978); "Obituary: Salem Azzam (1924–2008)," *Muslim Weekly*, 22 February 2008.

301. For other components of that network, see Steve Merley, *The Muslim Brotherhood in the United States* (Washington, DC: Hudson Institute, 2009), 16, 25–26; Vidino, *New Muslim Brotherhood*, 34.

302. For al-Qaradawi, see *Global Mufti: The Phenomenon of Yusuf al-Qaradawi*, ed. Bettina Gräf and Jakob Skovgaard-Peterson (London: Hurst, 2009); Marechal, *Muslim Brothers in Europe*, 147–151.

303. On al-Qaradawi's early role in the Brotherhood, see, for example, Dawh, 25 'aman, 63.

304. Introduction in Gräf and Skovgaard-Peterson, *Global Mufti*, 2–4.

305. Yusuf al-Qaradawi, *The Lawful and the Prohibited in Islam* (New Delhi: Adam, 2011).

306. See, for example, Yusuf al-Qaradawi, *Islamic Awakening between Rejection and Extremism* (New Delhi: Qazi, 1990).

307. Jakob Skovgaard-Peterson, "Yusuf al-Qaradawi and al-Azhar," in Gräf and Skovgaard-Peterson, *Global Mufti*, 40–46, 72; see also Ana Belén Soage, "Yusuf al-Qaradawi: The Muslim Brothers' Favorite Ideological Guide," in Rubin, *Muslim Brotherhood*, 19–37.

308. Skovgaard-Peterson, "Yusuf al-Qaradawi and al-Azhar," 38–39.

309. Ibid., 37.

310. Marechal, *Muslim Brothers in Europe*, 49–52.

311. Sheikh Isam Talima, "Al-kharijun 'an al-ikhwan . . . mata wa kayfa wa limatha?" Ikhwanwiki, n.d., http://bit.ly/2tHqSMu.

312. Alexandre Caeiro and Mahmoud al-Saify, "Qaradawi in Europe, Europe in Qaradawi? The Global Mufti's European Politics," in Gräf and Skovgaard-Peterson, *Global Mufti*, 111–118.

313. Vidino, *New Muslim Brotherhood*, 34. See also Merley, *Muslim Brotherhood*, 25–26; Nada, *Inside the Muslim Brotherhood*, 45.

314. Alyssa A. Lappen, "The Muslim Brotherhood in North America," in Rubin, *Muslim Brotherhood*, 161–179.

315. The authorized Brotherhood website Ikhwanwiki reposted a copy of Zeid al-Noman's report, as well as commentary from Steven Merley and the *Chicago Tribune*, suggesting that they accepted their accuracy. See "Al-Ikhwan al-Muslimin fi al-wilayat al-mutahida al-amrikiyya," Ikhwanwiki, http://bit.ly/2troeV7.

316. Merley, *Muslim Brotherhood*, 5–6; Noreen S. Ahmed-Ullah et al., "A Rare Look at Secretive Brotherhood in America: Muslims Divided on Brotherhood," *Chicago Tribune*, 19 September 2004.

317. Merley, *Muslim Brotherhood*, 9–10.

318. "Al-Ikhwan al-Muslimin fi al-wilayat al-mutahida al-amrikiyya," Ikhwanwiki, http://bit.ly/2troeV7; Merley, *Muslim Brotherhood*, 15; Ahmed-Ullah et al., "Rare Look."

319. "Al-duktur Ahmad al-Qadi . . . wa a'alamiyat al-da'wa," Ikhwanwiki, http://bit.ly/2tSuWJN.

320. "Pangs and Process of Self-Discovery," *Impact International Fortnightly* 13, no. 19 (14–27 October 1983). See also Kalim Siddiqui, "Now that the Conference Is Over," *Impact International Fortnightly* 3, no. 11 (26 October–8 November 1973).

321. Siddiqui, "Now that the Conference Is Over."

322. Merley, *Muslim Brotherhood*, 13.

323. Ibid., 11–22.

324. "Pangs and Process of Self-Discovery."

325. Ibid.

326. Web archive page for "Current News," Muslim Students Association, 23 March 2000, http://web.archive.org/web/20001027023225/www.msa-natl.org/index.html.

327. Husain Haqqani, "The Politicization of American Islam," *Current Trends in Islamist Ideology* 6 (2008), 85–94.

328. A. Ahmad, "Islamizing the Social Sciences," *Impact International Fortnightly* 3, no. 5 (27 July–9 August 1973).

329. Johnson, *Mosque in Munich,* 195–196; Zeyno Baran, "The Muslim Brotherhood's U.S. Network," *Current Trends in Islamist Ideology* 6 (2008), 95–122 (100); Merley, *Muslim Brotherhood,* 25–26.

330. "4th International Conference on Islamization," *Impact International Fortnightly* (8–21 November 1985).

331. Merley, *Muslim Brotherhood,* 23–24, 30–31.

332. Douglas Farah and Ronald Sandee, "The Ikhwan in North America: A Short History," NEFA [Nine Eleven Finding Answers] Foundation, undated; Merley, *Muslim Brotherhood.*

333. It was the subsequent FBI investigation into the Holy Land Foundation (as the Occupied Land Fund was then known), which did much to expose the workings of the Brotherhood network in the United States.

334. Merley, *Muslim Brotherhood,* 35–36.

335. Nada, *Inside the Muslim Brotherhood,* 27, 95, 240.

336. Ibid., 95, 166. On the differences between the Brotherhood in Europe as compared to the Middle East, see also Steven Brooke, "The Muslim Brotherhood in Europe and the Middle East: The Evolution of a Relationship," in Meijer and Bakker, *Muslim Brotherhood in Europe,* 27–49; and in the same volume, Lorenzo Vidino, "European Organisation of the Muslim Brotherhood: Myth or Reality?" 51–69.

337. Vidino, *New Muslim Brotherhood.*

338. Kemal el-Helbawy, interview with the author, London, 4 December 2014.

339. Vidino, *Muslim Brotherhood in the West,* 10–14.

340. Kepel, *Jihad,* 197; Pargeter, *Muslim Brotherhood,* 141; Marechal, *Muslim Brothers in Europe,* 264–265; Vidino, *New Muslim Brotherhood,* 32.

341. Ibrahim Munir, interview with the author, London, 23 February 2016.

342. USNRA, CREST Database, CIA, "The Muslim Brotherhood and Arab Politics: A Research Paper," October 1982.

343. Peter Steinfels, "Many Varieties of Fundamentalism," *New York Times,* 8 March 1993; Timothy D. Sisk, *Islam and Democracy: Religion, Politics, and Power in the Middle East* (Washington, DC: United States Institute for Peace Press, 1992), 6–7. For an example of the output from the project, see Martin E. Marty and R. Scott Appleby, eds., *Fundamentalisms Observed* (London: University of Chicago Press, 1991).

344. On US-Egyptian relations during this period, see Jason Brownlee, *Democracy Prevention: The Politics of the U.S.-Egyptian Alliance* (Cambridge: Cambridge University Press, 2012); Lloyd C. Gardner, *The Road to Tahrir Square: Egypt and the United States from the Rise of Nasser to the Fall of Mubarak* (London: Saqi Books, 2011), 149–161.

8. Blurred Lines and New Agendas, 1989–2010

1. Martin Bright, *When Progressives Treat with Reactionaries: The British State's Flirtation with Radical Islamism* (London: Policy Exchange, 2006).

2. William Ehrman (Director General of Defence-Intelligence, Foreign and Commonwealth Office, FCO) to Sir David Omand (Security and Intelligence Co-ordinator and

Permanent Secretary at Cabinet Office), letter dated 23 April 2004, copy in Bright, *When Progressives Treat,* 68–69.

3. Angus McKee (Middle East North Africa Department, FCO) to Frances Guy (Head of the Engaging with the Islamic World Group, EIWG, FCO), "Engaging with Islamists in the Arab World: Paris Round-table—1 June," letter dated 7 June 2005, copy in Bright, *When Progressives Treat,* 37–40.

4. Richard W. Murphy (former US Assistant Secretary of State for Near Eastern Affairs and former Ambassador to Syria) and Basil Eastwood (former British Ambassador to Syria), "We Must Talk to Political Islamists in the Middle East—and Not Just in Iraq," in Bright, *When Progressives Treat,* 51–52.

5. Angus McKee to Michael Nevin (EIWG, FCO), "Egypt: The Muslim Brotherhood—Terrorists?" memorandum dated 19 July 2005, copy in Bright, *When Progressives Treat,* 44–46.

6. Letter, Sir Derek Plumbly (British Ambassador to Egypt) to John Sawers (Director General, Political, FCO), 23 June 2005, copy in Bright, *When Progressives Treat,* 41–43.

7. Ibid.

8. Julie McGregor, (Arab-Israel North African Group, AINAG, FCO), to N. Banner (FCO), Kim Howells (Middle East Minister) and Jack Straw (Foreign Secretary), letter dated 17 January 2006, copy in Bright, *When Progressives Treat,* 47–49.

9. Eva Bellin, "The Robustness of Authoritarianism in the Middle East: Exceptionalism in Comparative Perspective," *Comparative Politics* 36, no. 2 (2004), 139–157. On the third wave, see Samuel P. Huntington, *The Third Wave: Democratization in the Late Twentieth Century* (Norman: University of Oklahoma Press, 1991).

10. Francis Fukuyama, *The End of History and the Last Man* (London: Free Press, 2006).

11. George H. W. Bush, "Address before a Joint Session of the Congress on the State of the Union," 29 January 1991, http://www.presidency.ucsb.edu/ws/?pid=19253.

12. Samuel P. Huntington, "The Clash of Civilizations?" *Foreign Affairs* 72, no. 3 (Summer 1993).

13. Bernard Lewis, "The Roots of Muslim Rage," *Atlantic Monthly,* September 1990; Judith Miller, "The Challenge of Radical Islam," *Foreign Affairs* 72, no. 2 (Spring 1993).

14. Leon T. Hadar, "What Green Peril?" *Foreign Affairs* 72, no. 2 (Spring 1993).

15. Edward W. Said, *Covering Islam,* 2nd ed. (New York: Vintage Books, 1997). See also Fawaz Gerges, *America and Political Islam: Clash of Cultures or Clash of Interests?* (Cambridge: Cambridge University Press, 1999), 41–73; Maria do Céu Pinto, *Political Islam and the United States* (Reading, UK: Ithaca, 1999), 135–157; Ahmad S. Moussalli, ed., *Islamic Fundamentalism: Myths and Realities* (Reading, UK: Ithaca, 1998), 4–19.

16. See, for example, John L. Esposito and James P. Piscatori, "Democratization and Islam," *Middle East Journal* 45, no. 3 (Summer 1991), 427–440; Laura Guazzone, ed., *The Islamist Dilemma: The Political Role of Islamist Movements in the Contemporary Arab World* (Reading, UK: Ithaca, 1995); Ghassan Salamé, ed., *Democracy without Democrats* (London: I. B. Tauris, 2001).

17. Martin Evans and John Phillips, *Algeria: Anger of the Dispossessed* (London: Yale University Press, 2007).

18. Gerges, *America and Political Islam,* 73–78.

19. "James Baker Looks Back at the Middle East," *Middle East Quarterly* 1, no. 3 (September 1994), 83–86.

20. Cited in Joel Beinin and Joe Stork, "On the Modernity, Historical Specificity, and International Context of Political Islam," in *Political Islam: Essays from Middle East Report,* ed. Joel Beinin and Joe Stork (London: I. B. Tauris, 1997), 3–25 (16).

21. "Symposium: Resurgent Islam in the Middle East," *Middle East Policy* 3, no. 2 (1994), 1–21.

22. William B. Quandt, "US and Algeria: Just Flirting," *Le Monde Diplomatique: English Edition,* July 2002, https://mondediplo.com/2002/07/08algeria.

23. For a good overview of this, see Abdullah Mohammed Al-Ghilani, "America's Perceptions of Political Islam: Roots of Geopolitical Image and Implications for U.S. Middle East Policy" (PhD diss., University of Durham, 2014), 178–188; Gerges, *America and Political Islam,* 144–167.

24. See, for example, the memoirs of the US Ambassador to Algiers, Cameron Hume: Cameron R. Hume, *Mission to Algiers: Diplomacy by Engagement* (Lanham, MD: Lexington Books, 2006), 39. See also Carol Migdalovitz, "Report 98–219, Algeria: Developments and Dilemmas," Congressional Research Service, 18 August 1998, Wikileaks.

25. For use of the term, see "Country Fact Sheet: Egypt," *US State Department Dispatch* 5, no. 35 (29 August 1994), 574–578; and "Symposium: Resurgent Islam in the Middle East." See also Abdullah al-Arian, *Answering the Call: Popular Islamic Activism in Egypt* (New York: Oxford University Press, 2014), 5.

26. Peter W. Rodman, "Co-opt or Confront Fundamentalist Islam?" *Middle East Quarterly* 1, no. 4 (December 1994), 61–64.

27. Martin Kramer, "Fundamentalist Islam at Large: The Drive for Power," *Middle East Quarterly* 3, no. 2 (June 1996), 37–49.

28. "Symposium: Resurgent Islam in the Middle East."

29. Do Céu Pinto, *Political Islam,* 183–197.

30. For a discussion of "accommodationism," see ibid., vii–viii, 172–178; Gerges, *America and Political Islam,* 14–15; Sana Abed-Kotob, "The Accommodationists Speak: Goals and Strategies of the Muslim Brotherhood in Egypt," *International Journal of Middle East Studies* 27, no. 3 (1995), 321–339; Vickie Langohr, "Of Islamists and Ballot Boxes: Rethinking the Relationship between Islamisms and Electoral Politics," *International Journal of Middle East Studies* 33, no. 4 (November 2001), 591–610.

31. "Symposium: Resurgent Islam in the Middle East." See also John L. Esposito, "Islamic Movements, Democratization, and U.S. Foreign Policy," in *Riding the Tiger: The Middle East Challenge after the Cold War,* ed. Phebe Marr and William Lewis (Oxford: Westview, 1993), 187–210; and Esposito's views as recorded in Clifton R. Wharton (Deputy Secretary of State), State Department to Embassy Algiers et al., "Political Islam in Black Africa," 10 June 1993, Wikileaks.

32. Graham E. Fuller and Ian O. Lesser, *A Sense of Siege: The Geopolitics of Islam and the West* (Oxford: Westview, 1995). This was the essence of the "inclusion-moderation hypothesis." For a critical analysis of this concept, see Jillian Schwedler, *Faith in Moderation: Islamist Parties in Jordan and Yemen* (Cambridge: Cambridge University Press, 2006); and Janine A. Clark, "The Conditions of Islamist Moderation: Unpacking Cross-Ideological Cooperation in Jordan," *International Journal of Middle East Studies* 38 (2006), 539–560.

33. Geneive Abdo, *No God but God: Egypt and the Triumph of Islam* (Oxford: Oxford University Press, 2000), 17.

34. Gerges, *America and Political Islam*, 21–36, 103–114; do Céu Pinto, *Political Islam*, 205–213.

35. Edward P. Djerejian, *Danger and Opportunity: An American Ambassador's Journey through the Middle East* (New York: Threshold Editions, 2008), 9–10, 18.

36. Edward P. Djerejian, "The U.S. and the Middle East in a Changing World," *US State Department Dispatch*, 8 June 1992, 444–447. For discussion of this speech, see also Robert Satloff, "Islamism Seen from Washington," in *The Islamism Debate*, ed. Martin Kramer (Tel Aviv: Moshe Dayan Center for Middle Eastern and African Studies, 1997).

37. Edward P. Djerejian, "U.S. Policy on Recent Developments and Other Issues in the Middle East," *US State Department Dispatch*, 4, no. 32 (9 August 1993), 569–573.

38. Robert H. Pelletreau Jr., "Not Every Fundamentalist Is a Terrorist," *Middle East Quarterly* 2, no. 3 (September 1995), 69–76; "Symposium: Resurgent Islam in the Middle East."

39. Gerges, *America and Political Islam*, 90–97.

40. Anthony Lake, "From Containment to Enlargement," *US State Department Dispatch* 4, no. 39 (27 September 1993), 658–664.

41. Edward P. Djerejian, "US Policy in the Middle East," *US State Department Dispatch* 4, no. 11 (15 March 1993), 149–152.

42. Gerges, *America and Political Islam*, 3, 84–103, 227–37. On the importance of the Iranian legacy, see also do Céu Pinto, *Political Islam*, 135–144.

43. Satloff, "Islamism Seen from Washington."

44. Mohammed Zaid and Michael Medley, "Muslim Brotherhood in Egypt and Sudan," *Review of African Political Economy* 33, no. 110 (2006), 693–708. See also James R. Cheek (Ambassador), Embassy Khartoum to State Department, "Bashir and the RCC on the Eve of Their Second Anniversary," 30 May 1991, Wikileaks.

45. O'Neill, Khartoum to State Department, "Islamization of Southern Sudan," 2 September 1998, Wikileaks.

46. Donald Petterson (Ambassador), Embassy Khartoum to State Department, "Turabi Calls for Jihad to Create an Islamic Sudan," 9 June 1994, Wikileaks.

47. Martin Kramer, "Islam in the New World Order," in *Middle East Contemporary Survey*, vol. 15, ed. Ami Ayalon (Oxford: Westview Press, 1993), 172–205 (182–185).

48. USNRA, CREST Database, Bureau of Intelligence and Research, State Department, Weekend Edition, "The Wandering Mujahidin: Armed and Dangerous," 21–22 August 1993.

49. Lawrence Benedict (Deputy Chief of Mission), Embassy Khartoum to State Department, "Sudanese Mischief-Making: Does It Matter?" 14 December 1994, Wikileaks; see also Avis Bohlen (Deputy Chief of Mission), Embassy Paris to State Department, "France on Sudan: Show Us Proof of Terrorist Support," 9 December 1994, Wikileaks.

50. Petterson, Embassy Khartoum to State Department, "Sudan's Turabi on 'Internationalism of Islam,' al-Bashir on a 'Nation of Message,'" 23 September 1992, Wikileaks.

51. Benedict, Embassy Khartoum to State Department, "Sudanese Mischief-Making: Does It Matter?" 14 December 1994, Wikileaks.

52. Linda Adams, "Political Liberalization in Jordan: An Analysis of the State's Relationship with the Muslim Brotherhood," *Journal of Church and State* 507 (1996), 507–528.

53. Marion Boulby, *The Muslim Brotherhood and the Kings of Jordan 1945–1993* (Atlanta, GA: Scholars Press, 1999), 137–157; Gilles Kepel, *Jihad: The Trial of Political Islam*

(London: I. B. Tauris, 2004), 338–341; Shmuel Bar, *The Muslim Brotherhood in Jordan* (Tel Aviv: Moshe Dayan Center for Middle Eastern and African Studies, 1998), 41–50; Jillian Schwedler, "Don't Blink: Jordan's Democratic Opening and Closing," *Middle East Report and Information Project (MERIP)*, July 2002; Sabah El-Said, *Between Pragmatism and Ideology: The Muslim Brotherhood in Jordan, 1989–1994,* policy paper no. 39 (Washington, DC: Washington Institute for Near East Policy, 1995).

54. Quintan Wiktorowicz, *The Management of Islamic Activism: Salafis, the Muslim Brotherhood, and State Power in Jordan* (Albany: State University of New York Press, 2001), 93–101.

55. Wesley W. Egan Jr. (Ambassador), Embassy Amman to State Department, "The Islamic Action Front: Sometimes a Platform Is More Trouble than It's Worth," 5 June 1997, Wikileaks. Some scholars have also drawn this distinction between "radicals" and "hawks," or between "moderates" and "doves" within the Jordanian Brotherhood. See Bar, *Muslim Brotherhood in Jordan,* 47–50. Others point to the fact that the Jordanian Brothers have blended pragmatism on many domestic, especially economic, issues, with a more rigid adherence to ideology on matters relating to foreign policy and the position of women within society. See El-Said, *Between Pragmatism and Ideology.*

56. Egan, Embassy Amman to State Department, "Political Islam in Jordan: Struggling for the Soul of the Muslim Brotherhood," 2 April 1998, Wikileaks.

57. "Muslim Brotherhood Rejects Washington Declaration," *Impact International Fortnightly* (September 1994). On the Jordanian Brotherhood's opposition to the peace process, see also Boulby, *Muslim Brotherhood,* 118; El-Said, *Between Pragmatism and Ideology,* 15–19.

58. Bill Burns (Ambassador), Embassy Amman to State Department, "Jordanian Islamists' Relationship with Hamas," 21 September 1998, Wikileaks.

59. Beverley Milton-Edwards and Stephen Farrell, *Hamas: The Islamic Resistance Movement* (Cambridge, UK: Polity Press, 2010), 77–109.

60. For an overview of this history, see Alison Pargeter, *The Muslim Brotherhood: The Burden of Tradition* (London: Saqi Books, 2010), 87–93; Robert G. Rabil, "The Syrian Muslim Brotherhood" in *The Muslim Brotherhood: The Organization and Policies of a Global Islamist Movement,* ed. Barry Rubin (New York: Palgrave Macmillan, 2010), 73–88 (80–86).

61. Hanna Batatu, "Syria's Muslim Brethren," *MERIP* 110 (November–December 1982).

62. Sa'id Hawwa, *The Muslim Brotherhood,* trans. A. K. Shaikh, 8th ed. (Delhi: Hindustan, 1996), 13, 23–24, 32–47. On the limited nature of the Syrian Brotherhood's reassessment, see also William Eagleton (Ambassador), Embassy Damascus to State Department, "The Syrian Muslim Brotherhood," 26 February 1985, Wikileaks.

63. Hawwa, *Muslim Brotherhood,* 100–102.

64. Liad Porat, "The Syrian Muslim Brotherhood and the Asad Regime," *Middle East Brief: Crown Center for Middle East Studies* 47 (December 2010); Raphaël Lefèvre, *Ashes of Hama: The Muslim Brotherhood in Syria* (London, UK: Hurst, 2013), 170–179.

65. Itzchak Weismann, "Sa'id Hawwa: The Making of a Radical Muslim Thinker in Modern Syria," *Middle Eastern Studies* 29, no. 4 (1993), 601–623. On the evolution of the Syrian Ikhwan, see Roel Meijer, "The Problem of the Political in Islamist Movements," in *Whatever Happened to the Islamists? Salafis, Heavy Metal Muslims and the Lure of Consumerist Islam,* ed. Olivier Roy and Amel Boubekeur (London: Hurst, 2012), 27–60 (53–57).

66. Rashid al-Ghannouchi, *Civil Liberties in the Islamic State* (1993), extract online at MSA News Translation, http://web.archive.org/web/20010209052823/msanews.mynet.net /Scholars/Ghannoushi/liberties.html.

67. HIA, Islamic Fundamentalism Collection, Accession No. 2002C14–16.79–82, Box 98, "The Conflict between the West and Islam: The Tunisian Case: Reality and Prospects—A Lecture Delivered by Sheikh Rachid Ghannouchi (Translated by Azzam Tamimi), Royal Institute of International Affairs," Chatham House, 9 May 1995. For a fuller discussion of al-Ghannouchi's views on modernity and the West, see Ibrahim M. Abu-Rabi', *Contemporary Arab Thought: Studies in Post-1967 Arab Intellectual History* (London: Pluto, 2003), 206–210.

68. HIA, Islamic Fundamentalism Collection, Accession No. 2002C14–16.79–82, Box 98, "Rached Ghannouchi: Interview with Dr. Rached Ghannouchi," by "The Electronic Whip."

69. John L. Esposito, *The Islamic Threat: Myth or Reality?*, 3rd ed. (New York: Oxford University Press, 1999), 161–171; Esposito and Piscatori, "Democratization and Islam." On this view of al-Ghannouchi, see also Lorenzo Vidino, *The New Muslim Brotherhood in the West* (New York: Columbia University Press, 2010), 61.

70. HIA, Islamic Fundamentalism Collection, Accession No. 2002C14–16.79–82, Box 98, "Rached Ghannouchi: Interview with Dr. Rached Ghannouchi," by "The Electronic Whip."

71. Hesham al-Awadi, *In Pursuit of Legitimacy: The Muslim Brothers and Mubarak, 1982–2000* (London: I. B. Tauris, 2004), 161–163.

72. Khalil el-Anani, "A Different Game for the MB," *Al-Ahram Weekly Online* 979 (31 December 2009–6 January 2010); "Khairat al-Shater on 'The Nahda Project,'" *Current Trends in Islamist Ideology* 13 (2012); "The Brotherhood and Mubarak," *Al-Jazeera World* [Television Documentary], 23 May 2012.

73. Cables reflecting on the militant challenge can be seen at: Barbara Schell (Consul-General), Consulate Alexandria to State Department, "Upturn in Fundamentalist Activity in the Delta," 18 March 1993, Wikileaks; and Fishbein, Consulate Alexandria, to Embassy Cairo, "Alexandria: Improving the Neighborhoods and (by) Moving Out the Fundamentalists," 17 May 1993, Wikileaks. For scholarly analysis of this violence, which government repression seemed only to exacerbate, see Kepel, *Jihad*, 282–298; Mohammed M. Hafez and Quintan Wiktorowicz, "Violence as Contention in the Egyptian Islamic Movement," in *Islamic Activism: A Social Movement Theory Approach*, ed. Quintan Wiktorowicz (Bloomington: Indiana University Press, 2003) 61–88; James Toth, "Islamism in Southern Egypt: A Case Study of a Radical Religious Movement," *International Journal of Middle East Studies* 35 (2003), 547–572.

74. For discussion of this period, see Abdo, *No God but God*.

75. On this period, see: Kepel, *Jihad*, 276–298; Mary Anne Weaver, *A Portrait of Egypt: A Journey through the World of Militant Islam* (New York: Farrar, Straus and Giroux, 2000); Mona El-Ghobashy, "The Metamorphosis of the Egyptian Muslim Brothers," *International Journal of Middle East Studies* 37 (2005), 381–382; Abdo, *No God but God*, 99–106; Denis J. Sullivan and Sana Abed-Kotob, *Islam in Contemporary Egypt: Civil Society vs. the State* (Boulder, CO: Lynne Rienner, 1999), 55; Ahmed Abdalla, "Egypt's Islamists and the State," *Middle East Report* 23, no. 183 (July/August 1993).

76. Mohammed Zahid, *The Muslim Brotherhood and Egypt's Succession Crisis: The Politics of Liberalisation and Reform in the Middle East* (London: I. B. Tauris, 2010), 101–102.

77. Mary Anne Weaver, "The Novelist and the Sheikh," *New Yorker,* 30 January 1995. On the shift toward repression, see also Abdo, *No God but God,* 71–106.

78. Abdo, *No God but God,* 77.

79. "Turn Back, Mubarak," *Economist,* 4 February 1995.

80. Mary Anne Weaver, "Revolution by Stealth," *New Yorker,* 8 June 1998. For a fuller discussion of this wider process of Islamization, see Abdo, *No God but God.*

81. *Our Testimony by the Muslim Brotherhood* (London: International Islamic Forum, 1995).

82. Essam al-Erian, cited in Abed-Kotob, "The Accommodationists Speak," 334–335.

83. El-Ghobashy, "Metamorphosis," 382–384.

84. Khalil el-Anani, "A Different Game for the MB," *Al-Ahram Weekly Online* 979 (31 December 2009–6 January 2010).

85. *Our Testimony by the Muslim Brotherhood* (London: International Islamic Forum, 1995).

86. Gudrun Krämer, "Islamist Notions of Democracy," *MERIP* 23, no. 183 (July–August 1993). See also Maha Azzam, "Islamist Attitudes to the Current World Order," *Islam and Christian-Muslim Relations* 4, no. 2 (December 1993), 247–256.

87. *The Role of Muslim Women in Islamic Society according to the Muslim Brotherhood* (London: International Islamic Forum, 1995). On debates about the position of women both generally and within the movement itself, see Omayma Abdel-Latif, *In the Shadow of the Brothers: The Women of the Egyptian Muslim Brotherhood,* Carnegie Papers No. 13 (Washington, DC: Carnegie Endowment for International Peace, 2008).

88. Mariz Tadros, *The Muslim Brotherhood in Contemporary Egypt: Democracy Redefined or Confined?* (London: Routledge, 2012), 124–125.

89. Cited in Abdo, *No God but God,* 57.

90. Ibid., 126.

91. Tadros, *Muslim Brotherhood,* 89–90.

92. See, for example, Mustafa Mashhur, *Tariq al-Da'wa* (Cairo: Dar al-Tawzi' wa-l-Nashr al-Islami, 1995), 14–16, 44–45, 197.

93. Kepel, *Jihad,* 294–296. On the Wasat Party, see Joshua Stacher, "Post-Islamist Rumblings in Egypt: The Emergence of the Wasat Party," *Middle East Journal* 56, no. 3 (2002), 415–433; Carrie R. Wickham, "The Path to Moderation: Strategy and Learning in the Formation of Egypt's Wasat Party," *Comparative Politics* 36, no. 2 (2004), 205–228; Raymond W. Baker, *Islam without Fear: Egypt and the New Islamists* (London: Harvard University Press, 2003), 192–203.

94. Vincent M. Battle (Deputy Chief of Mission), Embassy Cairo to State Department, "Egypt's Muslim Brotherhood—Down but Not Out," 12 November 1997, Wikileaks.

95. Daniel Kurtzer (Ambassador), Embassy Cairo to State Department, "Egypt's Muslim Brotherhood at Low Ebb," 16 March 1999, Wikileaks.

96. Reno Harish (Deputy Chief of Mission), Embassy Cairo to State Department, "Egypt's Muslim Brothers—Part 2: A Popular Political Force," 21 June 2001, Wikileaks.

97. For the elections, see Susan Sachs, "Parliament Elections in Egypt Marred by Scattered Violence," *New York Times,* 9 November 2000; Jason Brownlee, "The Decline of Pluralism in Mubarak's Egypt," *Journal of Democracy* 13, no. 4 (October 2002), 6–14.

98. Wesley W. Egan Jr. (Deputy Chief of Mission), Embassy Cairo to State Department, "The Great Shaykhs: The Muslim Brotherhood and the Radical Fringe," 11 July 1991, Wikileaks.

99. Ibid.

100. Amira Howeidy, "Brotherhood, Divided by Five," *Al-Ahram Weekly* 1054 (30 June–6 July 2011); "Brotherhood Leader Leaves Group to Join Islamist Party," *Egypt Independent,* 13 July 2011; Marc Lynch, "The Next Supreme Guide of the Muslim Brotherhood," *Foreign Policy,* 26 March 2009.

101. Kurtzer, Embassy Cairo to State Department, "Egypt's Muslim Brothers—Part 1: History and Structure," 31 May 2001, Wikileaks.

102. Manal Lutfi, "The Brotherhood and America: Part One," *Asharq Al-Awsat,* 12 March 2007. See also parts 2–6 (13 March–27 March 2007).

103. Battle, Embassy Cairo to State Department, "Egypt's Muslim Brotherhood—Down but Not Out," 12 November 1997, Wikileaks.

104. Kurtzer, Embassy Cairo to State Department, "Egypt's Muslim Brotherhood at Low Ebb," 16 March 1999, Wikileaks.

105. Kurtzer, Embassy Cairo to State Department, "Egypt's Muslim Brothers—Part 1: History and Structure," 31 May 2001, Wikileaks.

106. Jason Brownlee, *Democracy Prevention: The Politics of the U.S.-Egyptian Alliance* (Cambridge: Cambridge University Press, 2012), 45–67.

107. Israel Elad Altman, *Strategies of the Muslim Brotherhood Movement, 1928–2007,* Research Monographs on the Muslim World, Series No. 2, Paper No. 2 (Washington, DC: Hudson Institute, 2009), 16–17.

108. Youssef Nada, with Douglas Thompson, *Inside the Muslim Brotherhood: The Truth about the World's Most Powerful Political Movement* (London: Metro, 2012), 64–68, 82.

109. Hasan Hathut, *Reading the Muslim Mind* (Plainfield, IN: American Trust, 1995), 38–40. For similar, see also Hasan Hathut, *Al-'aqd al-farid, 1942–1952: 'Ashr sanawat ma' al-Imam Hasan al-Bana* (Cairo: Dar al-Shuruq, 2000), 116–117.

110. Nada, *Inside the Muslim Brotherhood,* 122–123.

111. For more on this, see Amr Hamzawy, "Exploring Theoretical and Programmatic Changes in Contemporary Islamist Discourse: The Journal Al-Manar al-Jadid," in *Transnational Political Islam: Religion, Ideology and Power,* ed. Azza Karam (London: Pluto, 2004), 120–146; Roel Meijer, "Authenticity in History: The Concepts Al-Wafid and Al-Mawruth in Tariq al-Bishri's Reinterpretation of Modern Egyptian History," in *Amsterdam Middle Eastern Studies,* ed. Manfred Woidich (Wiesbaden, Germany: Reichert Verlag, 1990), 68–83; Baker, *Islam without Fear,* 212–260; Abu-Rabi', *Contemporary Arab Thought,* 195.

112. Hathut, *Reading,* 90–119.

113. Hathut, *Al-'aqd al-farid,* 116–117.

114. Hasan Dawh, *Sab'a rasa'il min shabab al-ams ila shabab al-yom* (Cairo: Dar al-Fath, 1997), 183–185.

115. Maha Azzam, "The Gulf Crisis: Perceptions in the Muslim World," *International Affairs* 67, no. 3 (July 1991), 473–485; Yvonne Haddad, "Islamist Perceptions of US Policy

in the Middle East," in David W. Lesch, *The Middle East and the United States: A Historical and Political Reassessment,* 3rd ed. (Oxford: Westview, 2003), 504–533 (511–514).

116. Esposito, "Islamic Movements, Democratization"; John L. Esposito, "The Persian Gulf War, Islamic Movements and the New World Order, *Iranian Journal of International Affairs* 5, no. 2 (1993), 340–364; El-Said, *Between Pragmatism and Ideology,* 19–20.

117. Kramer, "Islam in the New World Order," 174–177. On the decision of Mubarak to support the United States, see Galal Amin, *Egypt in the Era of Hosni Mubarak, 1981–2011* (Cairo: American University of Cairo Press, 2011), 58.

118. Kramer, "Islam in the New World Order," 176.

119. Ibid., 178. See also Uri M. Kupferschmidt, "Egypt," in Ayalon, *Middle East Contemporary Survey,* 337–381 (355).

120. Frank Wisner (Ambassador), Embassy Cairo to State Department, "Muslim Brotherhood Calls for Withdrawal of Foreign Forces from the Gulf," 28 March 1991, Wikileaks.

121. Hossam Tammam, "The International Organisation of the Muslim Brotherhood," in *Islamic Movements of Europe: Public Religion and Islamophobia in the Modern World,* ed. Frank Peter and Rafael Ortega (London: I. B. Tauris, 2014), 89–94.

122. Hathut, *Reading,* 90–119. See also Azzam, "Islamist Attitudes," 247–256.

123. ʿAdel al-Ansari, *Al-Ikhwan al-Muslimun: 60 qadiya sakhina: muwajaha maʿ al-mustashar Muhammad al-Maʾmun al-Hudaybi* (Cairo: Dar al-Tabaʿa wa-l-Nashr al-Islami, 1999), 64–66.

124. Kramer, "Islam in the New World Order," 195–198.

125. Kemal el-Helbawy, open letter to Yasser Arafat, 1 May 1996 (copy in author's possession). For other examples of el-Helbawy's uncompromising views, see John Ware, "Time to Wise Up to the Muslim Brotherhood," *Standpoint,* July / August 2013.

126. Al-Ansari, *Al-Ikhwan al-Muslimun,* 64–65.

127. Dawh, *Sabʿa rasaʾil,* 187.

128. Baker, *Islam without Fear,* 212–238.

129. Al-Ansari, *Al-Ikhwan al-Muslimun,* 64–65. See also Zahid, *Muslim Brotherhood,* 116–117; Abdo, *No God but God,* 97–98.

130. Kenan Malik, "Born in Bradford," *Prospect* 115 (October 2005).

131. The crisis began when three girls were excluded from school in Creil for wearing the veil; their case was taken up by both secular antiracist groups such as SOS Racisme and Islamist groups like the Union of French Islamic Organisations (UOIF). In response, the French government formed a discussion group on Islam in France (The Council for Reflecting on Islam in France, or CORIF).

132. For in-depth discussion of this episode, see Paul Weller, *A Mirror for Our Times: "The Rushdie Affair" and the Future of Multiculturalism* (London: Continuum, 2009). See also Gilles Kepel, *Allah in the West: Islamic Movements in America and Europe,* trans. Susan Milner (Stanford: Stanford University Press, 1997), 1–2, 126–132, 152–195; Kepel, *Jihad,* 187; Philip Lewis, *Islamic Britain: Religion, Politics and Identity among British Muslims,* 2nd ed. (London: I. B. Tauris, 2002), 153–160. On the point about the decline of more traditional forms of authority as working to the benefit of newer, often Islamist groups, see Jorgen Nielsen, "Transnational Islam and the Integration of Islam in Europe," in *Muslim Networks and Transnational Communities in and across Europe,* ed. Stefano Allevi and Jorgen Nielsen (Leiden, Netherlands: Brill, 2003), 28–51 (35–36).

133. UK Government, *Muslim Brotherhood Review: Main Findings,* HC 679 (17 December 2015), para. 23.

134. Brigitte Marechal, *The Muslim Brothers in Europe: Roots and Discourse* (Leiden, Netherlands: Brill, 2008), 65. See also David Rich, "The Very Model of a British Muslim Brotherhood," in Rubin, *The Muslim Brotherhood,* 117–136 (120).

135. Kemal el-Helbawy, "The Muslim Brotherhood in Egypt: Historical Evolution and Future Prospects," in Khaled Hroub, *Political Islam: Context versus Ideology* (London: Saqi Books, 2010), 61.

136. Marechal, *Muslim Brothers in Europe,* 71–72.

137. Muhammad Humayda, "Wufat muraqib suriya yujaddid amal ihya' al-tanzim al-dawli li-l-ikwan," elaph.com, 17 March 2009, http://bit.ly/2srs9D9.

138. Mahan Abedin, "How to Deal with Britain's Muslim Extremists? An Interview with Kamal Helbawy," Jamestown Foundation, 8 August 2005, http://bit.ly/2tO5eFv.

139. UK Government, *Muslim Brotherhood Review,* para. 23. On the relationship of MAB with the Brotherhood, see also "Interview with Anas Altikriti," *Cordoba Foundation: MENA Report* 1, no. 11 (November 2013).

140. Dominic Casciani and Sharif Sakr, "The Battle for the Mosque," BBC News Online, 7 February 2006, http://news.bbc.co.uk/1/hi/uk/4639074.stm. Sawalha has been accused of having previously been a Hamas commander. See John Ware, BBC *Panorama,* "Faith, Hate and Charity," 28 July 2006; and United States of America v. Holy Land Foundation et al., United States District Court, for the Northern District of Texas, CR NO. 3:04-CR-240-G.

141. Azzam al-Tamimi, speaking to the Cordoba Foundation National Conference, 12 February 2015 (author present).

142. For the self-description, see Azzam al-Tamimi, "The Legitimacy of Palestinian Resistance: An Islamist's Perspective," *Middle East Affairs Journal* 4, no. 1–2 (Winter / Spring 1998), 93–100. For the further comments cited here, see BBC *Hardtalk,* "Interview with Dr. Azzam al-Tamimi," BBC News 24, 2 November 2004. Transcript available at http://www.geocities.com/martinkramerorg/Documents/TamimiHardtalk.htm.

143. Al-Tamimi, "Legitimacy of Palestinian Resistance."

144. John Ware, BBC *Panorama,* "Faith, Hate and Charity," 28 July 2006.

145. Nick Fielding and Abul Taher, "Hamas Link to London Mosque," *Sunday Times,* 13 February 2009.

146. Abdullah Faliq, interview with the author, London, 19 October 2011.

147. United States of America v. Mousa Mohammed Abu Marzook et al., United States District Court, Northern District of Illinois, Eastern Division, No. 03 CR 978, Second Superseding Indictment (unsealed August 2004).

148. United States of America v. Holy Land Foundation et al., United States District Court, for the Northern District of Texas, CR NO. 3:04-CR-240-G.

149. See "Companies House" documents for Muslim Association of Britain and Land Registry Document for Muslim Welfare House (in possession of the author). See also "New Era for North London Central Mosque," Press Release, February 2005, http://www.salaam.co.uk/mosques/new/finsburypark.html.

150. Screenshot of "Islam Online," n.d., available at, http://www.hurryupharry.org/wp-content/uploads/2008/07/sawalha.JPG.

151. Anas Altkriti, interview with the author, London, 3 May 2017.

152. "Muslim Association of Britain: Historical Roots and Background," *Inspire,* 28 September 2002.

153. Anas Altkriti, interview with the author, London, 3 May 2017.

154. "Muslim Association of Britain: The Organisation," *Inspire,* 28 September 2002.

155. UK Government, *Muslim Brotherhood Review.* On the subject of Jamaat-i-Islami (JI) influence over the Muslim Council of Britain (MCB), see also Bowen, *Medina in Birmingham,* 89–94.

156. "Muslim Association of Britain: The Organisation," *Inspire,* 28 September 2002.

157. *The New Dawn,* Issue 2 (October–November 2000) (copy in author's possession).

158. UK Government, *Muslim Brotherhood Review.*

159. Anas Altkriti, interview with the author, London, 3 May 2017.

160. Muslim Association of Britain, "About Us," Mabonline, http://www.mabonline .net/about-us/(last accessed 4 May 2016).

161. "MAB Responds to Vile Attack," Press Statement, 13 August 2004, available at the Islamic Human Rights Commission website, http://www.ihrc.org.uk/show.php?id=1216.

162. Marechal, *Muslim Brothers in Europe,* 63–64.

163. Steve Merley, "The Federation of Islamic Organizations in Europe," NEFA (Nine Eleven Finding Answers) Foundation, 1 October 2008.

164. "Itihad al-munadhamat al-islamiya fi 'uruba," Ikhwanwiki, http://bit.ly/2tTcfW.

165. Sara Silvestri, "Moderate Islamist Groups in Europe: The Muslim Brothers," in Hroub, *Political Islam,* 265–285 (268).

166. Ian Johnson, "How Islamic Group's Ties Reveal Europe's Challenge," *Wall Street Journal,* 29 December 2005.

167. Merley, "Federation of Islamic Organizations in Europe."

168. Ibid.

169. "Itihad al-munadhamat al-islamiya fi 'uruba," Ikhwanwiki, http://bit.ly/2tTcfW.

170. Ahmad al-Rawi, "Mustaqbal al-'amal al-islami fi 'uruba," in *Risalat al-muslimin fi bilad al-gharb,* ed. Mustafa Tahan (Irbid, Jordan: Dar al-Amal, 1999), 85–123.

171. "Muslims of Europe Charter," http://www.cie.ugent.be/documenten/muslim _charter.pdf.

172. Silvestri, "Moderate Islamist Groups in Europe," 270–273, 276.

173. "Itisal bi-na," EIHS-London, http://www.eihslondon.org.uk/#!Contact/c24vq.

174. Silvestri, "Moderate Islamist Groups in Europe," 279.

175. Merley, "Federation of Islamic Organizations in Europe." A third brother, 'Isam al-Rawi, was one of the leaders of the Brotherhood offshoot, the Association of the Muslim Scholars in Iraq, until his 2007 assassination.

176. Merley, "Federation of Islamic Organizations in Europe."

177. Ian Johnson, "How Islamic Group's Ties Reveal Europe's Challenge," *Wall Street Journal,* 29 December 2005.

178. "History," Forum of European Muslim Youth and Student Organisations (FEMYSO), http://www.femyso.org/about/history; Merley, "The Federation of Islamic Organizations in Europe"; Silvestri, "Moderate Islamist Groups in Europe," 275.

179. Merley, "Federation of Islamic Organizations in Europe"; Silvestri, "Moderate Islamist Groups in Europe," 281.

180. Ehud Rosen, *Mapping the Organizational Sources of the Global Delegitimization Campaign against Israel in the UK* (Jerusalem: Jerusalem Center for Public Affairs, 2010), 12–13.

181. Bettina Gräf and Jakob Skovgaard-Peterson, eds., *Global Mufti: The Phenomenon of Yusuf al-Qaradawi* (London: Hurst, 2009).

182. Steve Merley, *The Muslim Brotherhood in the United States* (Washington, DC: Hudson Institute, 2009), 39.

183. Alexandre Caeiro and Mahmoud al-Saify, "Qaradawi in Europe, Europe in Qaradawi? The Global Mufti's European Politics," in Gräf and Skovgaard-Peterson, *Global Mufti*, 111–118.

184. As Vidino notes, a European equivalent to this memorandum was "The Project" document seized at the home of Himmat in 2001. See Vidino, *New Muslim Brotherhood*, 79–80.

185. "Explanatory Memorandum on the General Strategic Goal for the Group in North America," 22 May 1991, original available (Arabic and English) at https://www.investigativeproject.org/documents/misc/20.pdf. Quotes here are taken from the English.

186. Ibid.

187. Ibid. See also Merley, *Muslim Brotherhood*, 1–2; Douglas Farah and Ronald Sandee, "The Ikhwan in North America: A Short History," NEFA Foundation, undated.

188. Vidino, *New Muslim Brotherhood*, 1–2, 175.

189. John Mintz and Douglas Farah, "In Search of Friends among the Foes," *Washington Post*, 11 September 2004.

190. Ibid.; Merley, *Muslim Brotherhood*, 31–35; Zeyno Baran, "The Muslim Brotherhood's U.S. Network," *Current Trends in Islamist Ideology* 6 (2008), 95–122.

191. Alyssa A. Lappen, "The Muslim Brotherhood in North America," in Rubin, *Muslim Brotherhood*, 161–179.

192. Josh Lefkowitz, "The 1993 Philadelphia Meeting," NEFA Foundation, 15 November 2007; Vidino, *New Muslim Brotherhood*, 178–185.

193. Merley, *Muslim Brotherhood*, 47–48.

194. Ibid.; Noreen S. Ahmed-Ullah et al., "A Rare Look at Secretive Brotherhood in America: Muslims Divided on Brotherhood," *Chicago Tribune*, 19 September 2004.

195. Ahmed-Ullah et al., "Rare Look."

196. Cited in Ware, "Time to Wise Up to the Muslim Brotherhood."

197. Brigitte Marechal, "Mosques, Organisations and Leadership," in *Muslims in the Enlarged Europe: Religion and Society*, ed. Brigitte Marechal et al. (Leiden, Netherlands: Brill, 2003), 136.

198. Pargeter, *Muslim Brotherhood*, 99–132.

199. See, for example, "Current News: Call for Action: Iraq / Chechnya / Kashmir," MSA, n.d., http://archive.li/cQtgP.

200. Marechal, "Mosques, Organisations and Leadership," 100–103; Marechal, *Muslim Brothers in Europe*, 8–9; Jytte Klausen, *The Islamic Challenge: Politics and Religion in Western Europe* (Oxford: Oxford University Press, 2005), 6; Silvestri, "Moderate Islamist Groups in Europe."

201. Runnymede Trust, *Islamophobia: A Challenge for Us All* (London: Runnymede Trust, 1997); Steven Vertovec, "Islamophobia and Muslim Recognition in Britain," in

Yvonne Y. Haddad, *Muslims in the West: From Sojourners to Citizens* (Oxford: Oxford University Press, 2002), 19–35 (24–25).

202. Marechal, *Muslim Brothers in Europe,* 250–256.

203. Yusuf al-Qaradawi, "Al-infitah 'ala al-gharb: muqtadiyatuhu wa shurutahu," in Tahan, *Risalat al-muslimin,* 8–29.

204. Hathut, *Reading,* xxix.

205. Sa'd al-Katatni, "Dialogue Manifisto [*sic*] between Islamists and the West," Ikhwanweb, 27 March 2007, http://www.ikhwanweb.com/article.php?id=934. See also Muhammad Habib, "Muslim Brotherhood Is Not Anti-American," Ikhwanweb, 14 January 2008, http://www.ikhwanweb.net/article.php?id=15359.

206. "A Message from Mr. Muhammad Mahdi 'Akef," Ikhwanweb, 21 February 2006, http://www.ikhwanweb.com/article.php?id=4770.

207. For the best recent book on this phenomenon, see Shiraz Maher, *Salafi-Jihadism: The History of an Idea* (London: Hurst, 2016).

208. For an example of this outlook, see speech by President George W. Bush in November 2001, recorded at, "You Are either with Us or against Us," CNN.com, 6 November 2001, http://edition.cnn.com/2001/US/11/06/gen.attack.on.terror/. For an account of the "war on terror," see Richard Clarke, *Against All Enemies: Inside America's War on Terror* (London: Free Press, 2004); and Peter Bergen, *The Longest War: The Enduring Conflict between America and al-Qaeda* (London: Simon and Schuster, 2011).

209. "Al-Ikhwan al-Muslimun wa nazrathum ila al-gharb," Ikhwanwiki, http://bit .ly/1ylPhn5.

210. Baker, *Islam without Fear,* 252–257.

211. Francis J. Ricciardone Jr. (Ambassador), Embassy Cairo to State Department, "Contact with Muslim Brotherhood Parliamentary Leader," 20 March 2007, Wikileaks.

212. Ricciardone, Embassy Cairo to State Department, "Advancing the Freedom Agenda in Egypt," 17 July 2007, Wikileaks.

213. "Al-Ikhwan al-Muslimun wa nazrathum ila al-gharb," Ikhwanwiki, http://bit .ly/1ylPhn5.

214. Edward W. Gnehm (Ambassador), Embassy Amman to State Department, "Jordan: Engaging Islam," 17 July 2002, Wikileaks; Greg Berry (Deputy Chief of Mission), Embassy Amman to State Department, "IAF Press Release Responds to Press Criticism of Meeting with Ambassador Ross," 31 July 2002, Wikileaks.

215. Gnehm, Embassy Amman to State Department, "Jordanian Islamist Leaders Call for Political Reform; Reject Privatization and Price Hikes," 16 December 2003, Wikileaks; Shadi Hamid and Amanda Kadlec, *Strategies for Engaging Political Islam* (Washington, DC: Brookings Institute, and Friedrich Ebert Stiftung, January 2010).

216. Manal Lutfi, "The Brotherhood and America," *Asharq al-Awsat,* part 1, 12 March 2007, and part 5, 18 March 2007; K. Neimat, "IAF Acknowledges Contacts with Officials 'before 2003,'" *Jordan Times,* 6 September 2011.

217. George W. Bush, *Decision Points* (New York: Crown, 2010), 396–397.

218. Brownlee, *Democracy Prevention.*

219. Jeremy Sharp, *U.S. Democracy Promotion Policy in the Middle East: The Islamist Dilemma,* CRS Report for Congress (Washington, DC, 2006). For an interesting overview of democracy "promotion" and its limits, see Sheila Carapico, "Foreign Aid for Promoting Democracy in the Arab World," *Middle East Journal* 56, no. 3 (Summer 2002), 379–395.

220. Richard Haas, "Toward Greater Democracy in the Muslim World," *Washington Quarterly* 26, no. 3 (Summer 2003), 137–148.

221. Bush, *Decision Points*, 406–407.

222. Manal Lutfi, "The Brotherhood and America," *Asharq al-Awsat*, part 3, 14 March 2007.

223. On the former two, see Zahid, *Muslim Brotherhood*, 23–25.

224. Michele Dunne, "The Baby, the Bathwater, and the Freedom Agenda in the Middle East," *Washington Quarterly* 32, no. 1 (January 2009), 129–141. On al-Islah, see Alex Glennie, *Building Bridges, Not Walls: Engaging with Political Islamists in the Middle East and North Africa* (London: IPPR, 2009), 38; Hamid and Kadlec, *Strategies*.

225. Shadi Hamid and Amanda Kadlec date the break to 2004 (*Strategies*). But the Islamic Action Front (IAF) has claimed that 2003 marked the caesura. See Neimat, "IAF Acknowledges Contacts with Officials."

226. Ahmed S. Hashim, *Insurgency and Counter-Insurgency in Iraq* (London: Hurst, 2006), 23, 50–55, 75–78.

227. Manal Lutfi, "The Brotherhood and America," *Asharq al-Awsat*, part 1, 12 March 2007.

228. Gnehm, Embassy Amman to State Department, "Jordan's Political Parties: Islamists, Leftists, Nationalists and Centrists," 20 May 2003, Wikileaks; Gnehm, Embassy Amman to State Department, "Political Islam in Jordan: Opposition Mostly from within the System," 3 August 2003, Wikileaks; Gnehmn, Embassy Amman to State Department, "Jordanian Islamic Action Front Keeps 'Moderate Leadership,'" 25 February 2004, Wikileaks. The controller general of the Jordanian Ikhwan in this era, 'Abd al-Majid al-Dhunaybat, as well as the secretary general of the IAF, Hamza Mansur, were thought to be "moderates," under pressure from more "extreme" rivals.

229. Gnehm, Embassy Amman to State Department, "Jordanian Islamist Leaders call for Political Reform; Reject Privatization and Price Hikes," 16 December 2003, Wikileaks. On this point, too, see Manal Lutfi, "The Brotherhood and America," *Asharq al-Awsat*, part 1, 12 March 2007, and part 2, 13 March 2007.

230. Altman, *Strategies of the Muslim Brotherhood*, 34–25.

231. David Hale (Ambassador), Embassy Amman to State Department, "Regime Turns Up the Heat on Jordan's Muslim Brothers," 12 July 2006, Wikileaks; Hale, Embassy Amman to State Department, "Jordan's Muslim Brotherhood Plays Election Boycott Card as Rhetorical Clashes Continue," 28 August 2007, Wikileaks; Hale, Embassy Amman to State Department, "Jordan's Islamists Battling over Future of the Movement," 17 January 2008, Wikileaks.

232. Israel Elad Altman, "The Crisis of the Arab Brotherhood," *Current Trends in Islamist Ideology* 6 (2008), 39.

233. Hale, Embassy Amman to State Department, "Pragmatists Lead Muslim Brotherhood's Leadership Race, but Feel Pressure after Hamas' Victory," 16 February 2006, Wikileaks.

234. Hale, Embassy Amman to State Department, "New Islamic Action Front Leader Linked to Hamas?" 22 March 2006, Wikileaks.

235. Hale, Embassy Amman to State Department, "Hawks Reportedly win Jordanian Muslim Brotherhood Shura Council Elections," 19 March 2008, Wikileaks; Hale, Em-

bassy Amman to State Department, "Muslim Brotherhood Shura Council Elects Hawkish New Leader," 8 May 2008, Wikileaks.

236. Hale, Embassy Amman to State Department, "Muslim Brotherhood Shura Council Elects Hawkish New Leader," 8 May 2008, Wikileaks.

237. Rankin, Embassy Khartoum to State Department, "The Changed Face of Political Islam in Sudan," 23 August 2002, Wikileaks.

238. Alberto Fernandez (Charge d'Affaires), Embassy Khartoum to State Department, "The National Congress Party—Sudan's Brutal Pragmatists," 9 March 2008, Wikileaks. For a similar assessment, see also Cameron Hume (Charge d'Affaires), Embassy Khartoum to State Department, "U.S./Sudanese Relations: In a Long War, No Quick Victories," 26 January 2007, Wikileaks.

239. Fernandez, Embassy Khartoum to State Department, "Turabi Decries Lack of Real Political Freedom," 16 December 2007, Wikileaks. On al-Turabi's later repositioning as a champion of "freedom of expression" and "equal rights for women," see William Wallis, "Hassan al-Turabi, Islamist Theologian, 1932–2016," *Financial Times,* 7 March 2016.

240. Altman, *Strategies of the Muslim Brotherhood,* 24–30; Radwan Ziyadeh, "The Damascus Declaration for Democratic Change in Syria," in *Critical Dialogue between Diverse Opposition Groups* (Arab Reform Initiative, 2011), 19–21; Stephen Seche (Charge d'Affaires), Embassy Damascus to State Department, "Mapping Syrian Civil Society: A Wilderness of Conflicting Interests and SARG Pressures," 6 December 2005, Wikileaks.

241. "Regime Change in Syria? Mohammed Walid Explains," *Islamism Digest* 2, no. 4 (April 2007).

242. Pargeter, *Muslim Brotherhood,* 87–93; Rabil, "Syrian Muslim Brotherhood," 80–86. On criticism of the Brotherhood for its alliance with Khaddam, see Seche, Embassy Damascus to State Department, "The Muslim Brothers in Syria, Part One: Could They Win an Election Here?" 8 February 2006, Wikileaks; and Seche, Embassy Damascus to State Department, "C-NE6–00262, Khaddam's and Bayanouni's Faustian Pact," 18 April 2006, Wikileaks. On the Brotherhood's later decision to suspend its anti-regime activity, see Maura Connelly (Charge d'Affaires), Embassy Damascus to State Department, "Movement for Justice and Development Seeking to Expand Role in Syria," 11 March 2009; Porat, "Syrian Muslim Brotherhood."

243. Ibid.

244. Jay Solomon, "To Check Syria, U.S. Explores Bond with Muslim Brothers," *Wall Street Journal,* 25 July 2007.

245. Farah Stockman, "U.S. Building Ties with Syrian Dissidents," *International Herald Tribune,* 26 November 2006.

246. Press Release of National Salvation Front in Syria, "NSF Delegation Meets US Officials, Announces Opening of Washington DC Office," 19 April 2007.

247. Seche, Embassy Damascus to State Department, "The Muslim Brothers in Syria, Part I: Could They Win an Election Here?" 8 February 2006, Wikileaks.

248. Manal Lutfi, "The Brotherhood and America," *Asharq al-Awsat,* part 2, 13 March 2007.

249. International Crisis Group (ICG), *Egypt's Muslim Brothers: Confrontation or Integration?* (Cairo / Brussels: ICG Middle East / North Africa Report No. 76, 18 June 2008).

250. Cited in Israel Elad Altman, "Democracy, Elections and the Egyptian Muslim Brotherhood," in *Current Trends in Islamist Ideology* 3 (2006), 24–37 (28).

251. *Islamism in North Africa II: Egypt's Opportunity* (Cairo / Brussels: ICG Middle East and North Africa Briefing, 20 April 2004), 2. For further analysis of the platform, see Bruce K. Rutherford, "What Do Egypt's Islamists Want? Moderate Islam and the Rise of Islamic Constitutionalism," *Middle East Journal* 60, no. 4 (Autumn 2006), 707–731.

252. El-Ghobashy, "Metamorphosis," 373. For a similar argument, see Abed-Kotob, "Accommodationists Speak."

253. Zaid and Medley, "Muslim Brotherhood in Egypt." For more on the rise of a new generation, see Zahid, *Muslim Brotherhood,* 93–97.

254. Maha Abdelrahman, " 'With the Islamists?—Sometimes. With the State?—Never!' Cooperation between the Left and Islamists in Egypt," *British Journal of Middle Eastern Studies* 36, no. 1 (2009), 37–54.

255. Zahid, *Muslim Brotherhood,* 45–51, 126–128; On Kefaya specifically, see also Manar Shorbagy, "Understanding Kefaya: The New Politics in Egypt," *Arab Studies Quarterly* 29, no. 1 (Winter 2007), 39–60; Ahmed Bahaeddin Shaaban, "The Experience of the Kifaya Movement in Egypt," in *Critical Dialogue,* 16–18.

256. Gordon Gray III (Deputy Chief of Mission), Embassy Cairo to State Department, "Constitutional Reform and the Outlook for Democracy in Egypt," 9 May 2005, Wikileaks; Ricciardone, Embassy Cairo to State Department, "Advancing the Freedom Agenda in Egypt," 17 July 2007, Wikileaks. See also Dunne, "The Baby, the Bathwater."

257. Carrie Rosefsky Wickham, *The Muslim Brotherhood: Evolution of an Islamist Movement* (Oxford: Princeton University Press, 2013), 117–124; Essam al-Erian, "The Coptic Brothers Are Part of the Nation," *al-Hayat,* 30 November 2005.

258. "Women and Copts Named Egypt MPs," BBC News Online, 12 December 2005, http://news.bbc.co.uk/1/hi/world/middle_east/4521392.stm. See also Stuart E. Jones (Deputy Chief of Mission), Embassy Cairo to State Department, "Brotherhood Rising in Alexandria," 26 December 2005, Wikileaks.

259. Al-Arian, *Answering the Call,* 229; Hazem Kandil, *Inside the Brotherhood* (Cambridge, UK: Polity, 2015); Tadros, *Muslim Brotherhood,* 22–23; E. Trager, "Trapped and Untrapped: Mubarak's Opponents on the Eve of His Ouster" (PhD diss., University of Pennsylvania, 2013), 179–184.

260. Ricciardone, Embassy Cairo to State Department, "Increased Assertiveness of the Muslim Brotherhood," 19 November 2006, Wikileaks; Ricciardone, Embassy Cairo, to State Department, "Muslim Brotherhood Deputy Leader: 'I Am Very Optimistic,' " 22 November 2006, Wikileaks.

261. John Esposito, "Islamists and US Foreign Policy," *ISIM Review* 18 (Autumn 2006), 6–7.

262. See, for example, Azza Karam, "Transnational Political Islam and the USA: An Introduction," in *Transnational Political Islam: Religion, Ideology and Power,* ed. Azza Karam (London: Pluto, 2004), 1–27. For other contributions to the debate, see James Traub, "Islamic Democrats?" *New York Times,* 29 April 2007; Toby Archer and Heidi Huuhtanen, eds., *Islamist Opposition Parties and the Potential for EU Engagement* (Helsinki: Finnish Institute for International Affairs, 2007); Joshua Stacher, *Brothers in Arms? Engaging the Muslim Brotherhood in Egypt* (London: Institute for Public Policy Research, 2008); Juan Cole, *Engaging the Muslim World* (Basingstoke, UK: Palgrave Macmillan, 2009), 41–81.

263. Emile A. Nakhleh, *A Necessary Engagement: Reinventing America's Relations with the Muslim World* (Oxford: Princeton University Press, 2009), xi–xix, 2, 30–35, 61–64.

264. Djerejian, *Danger and Opportunity,* 30–62.

265. Ahmad S. Moussalli, *US Foreign Policy and Islamist Politics* (Gainesville: University Press of Florida, 2008).

266. Shadi Hamid, "To Engage or Not to Engage?" *Democracy: A Journal of Ideas,* 7 August 2007.

267. "Assessing the MB 'Firewall,' " Abu Aardvark Blog, 13 May 2008, http://abuaardvark .typepad.com/abuaardvark/2008/05/assessing-the-m.html; Marc Lynch, "Memo to the MB: How to Talk to America?" *Foreign Policy,* September / October 2000.

268. Robert S. Leiken and Steven Brooke, "The Moderate Muslim Brotherhood," *Foreign Affairs* 86, no. 2 (March / April 2007).

269. "First Anniversary—An Interview with Dr. Kemal Helbawy," *Islamism Digest* 2, no. 4 (April 2007); Kemal el-Helbawy, interview with author, London, 29 December 2014.

270. "Habib: MB Adopts Democracy, Rejects Revolutions," Ikhwanweb, 5 May 2007, https://www.ikhwanweb.com/article.php?id=1663.

271. "Inside the Muslim Brotherhood—an Interview with Abdul Moneim Abu el-Foutouh," *Islamism Digest,* August 2006.

272. Quoted in "Dancing with the Devil: Charting the Rise of the Muslim Brotherhood," *Der Spiegel,* 3 July 2007.

273. "Al-Ikhwan al-Muslimun wa nazrathum ila al-gharb," Ikhwanwiki, http: // bit.ly /1ylPhn5.

274. "D. 'Isam al-'Arian: Al-fikr al-islami laa y'arif al-dawla al-diniya; lam yajtama' al-Ikhwan ma' al-gharbiyin siwa mara wahida," *Middle East Transparent,* 14 August 2004, http://www.metransparent.com/old/texts/issam_aryan.htm.

275. Khayrat el-Shater, "No Need to Be Afraid of Us," *Guardian,* 23 November 2005.

276. Ibrahim El-Houdaiby, "Do Not Undermine Moderate Islamists: The Case of Muslim Brotherhood Leader, Khayrat el-Shater," Ikhwanweb, 22 September 2007, http://www.ikhwanweb.net/article.php?id=14133. On this point, see also "Al-Ikhwan al-Muslimun wa nazrathum ila al-gharb," Ikhwanwiki, http://bit.ly/1ylPhn5.

277. "El-Shater: We Do Not Promote an Anti-Western Agenda," Ikhwanweb, 14 March 2006, http://www.ikhwanweb.net/article.php?id=930.

278. "Katatny: Dialogue between Islamists and the West a Necessity," Ikhwanweb, 15 December 2006, http://www.ikhwanweb.com/article.php?id=936; See also Ricciardone, Embassy Cairo to State Department, "Muslim Brotherhood Parliamentary Bloc Leader Calls for Dialogue with USG," Cairo to Washington, 24 January 2007.

279. "Interview with Kemal el-Helbawy," *Al-Sharq al-Awsat* [Arabic], 2 January 2007.

280. See the comments by 'Akef from July 2005 as recorded at "Al-Ikhwan al-Muslimun wa nazrathum ila al-gharb," Ikhwanwiki, http://bit.ly/1ylPhn5.

281. Altman, *Strategies of the Muslim Brotherhood,* 21.

282. "Innuha harb 'ala al-islam: Risala min al-ustadh Muhammad Mahdi 'Akef—al-murshid al-a'am l-il-Ikhwan al-Muslimin," Ikhwanwiki, http://bit.ly/2tjkbyQ.

283. Gray, Embassy Cairo to State Department, "Egypt: Smear Puts Muslim Brothers on the Defensive," 13 April 2005, Wikileaks; Gray, Embassy Cairo to State Department,

"Bogus USG Memo 'Explained' by Al-Sharq Al-Awsat Cairo Bureau Chief," 20 April 2005, Wikileaks.

284. Cited in Altman, "Crisis of the Arab Brotherhood," 42.

285. See, for example, Mahdi 'Akef, "Al-Wilayat al-Mutahida la turidu al-khayr li-l-a'alam al-islami," 12 February 2006, http://www.ikhwanonline.com/new/Article.aspx ?ArtID=17930&SecID=211.

286. Khalil el-Anani, "Is 'Brotherhood' with America Possible?" *Arab Insight* 1, no. 1 (chap. 1), 7–17.

287. "Inside the Muslim Brotherhood—An Interview with Abdul Moneim Abu el-Foutouh," *Islamism Digest,* August 2006.

288. Ibid. See also "Fotoh: West Must Not Pressure Regimes to Curb Islamists," Ikhwanweb, 22 February 2007, https://www.ikhwanweb.com/article.php?id=2354.

289. Helena Cobban, "Interview with Dr. Issam el-Arian," Justworldnews.org, reposted by Ikhwanweb, 18 February 2007, http://www.ikhwanweb.com/~ikhwan/article.php?id =2404.

290. Nour came second to Mubarak at the 2005 presidential election with 7 percent of the vote and was subsequently sentenced to prison on charges of forgery. Ibrahim was an academic who ran a proreform think tank and had been imprisoned between 2000 and 2003.

291. "MB Chairman Confirms Brotherhood's Respect to Americans," Ikhwanweb, 16 May 2007, http://www.ikhwanweb.com/article.php?id=1593&ref=search.php.

292. Muhammad 'Abdallah al-Samman, *Ayam ma' al-shahid Hasan al-Bana* (Cairo: Dar al-Fadila, 2003), 111–112. For similar views again, see Abu al-Futuh 'Afifi, *Rihalati ma' al-Ikhwan al-Muslimin* (Cairo: Dar al-Tawfiq wa-l-Nashr al-Islami, 2003), 81–82.

293. "Opinion of the United States," Pew Research Global Attitudes Project, http://www .pewglobal.org/database/?indicator=1&group=6.

294. Marc Lynch, "Anti-Americanisms in the Arab World," in *Anti-Americanisms in World Politics,* ed. Peter J. Katzenstein and Robert O. Keohane (London: Cornell University Press, 2007), 196–224.

295. Fathi Shihab al-Din, "Mukhatat 'Bernard Lewis' li-taftit al-a'alam al-islami," Ikhwanwiki, http://bit.ly/2uNHRcJ.

296. Muhammad Badi'e, "Wa ma zalat al-mu'amara 'ala al-a'alam al-islami mustamira," Ikhwan Online, 21 October 2010, http://www.ikhwanonline.com/Section/72526/Default .aspx.

297. Al-Din, "Mukhatat 'Bernard Lewis.'"

298. "Mukhatat 'Bernard Lewis' li-taftit al-a'alam al-islami," Ikhwan Online, 16 May 2011, http://bit.ly/2uNZF7j. On conspiracy theories about Sudan, see Altman, "Democracy, Elections and the Egyptian Muslim Brotherhood," 30.

299. Ikhwan al-Daqhaliya, "Ra'is al-Kenisset: Urdun juz' min al-isra'il al-kubra," dakahliaikhwan.com; Ricciardone, Embassy Cairo to State Department, "Election Platform of the Muslim Brotherhood: Political Crisis," 11 July 2007, Wikileaks.

300. Manal Lutfi, "The Brotherhood and America," *Asharq al-Awsat,* part 5, 18 March 2007.

301. Samer 'Eid, *Qisati ma' al-Ikhwan* (Cairo: Al-Mahrusa, 2014), 37.

302. Al-Samman, *Ayam,* 99.

303. Oded Yinon, "The Zionist Plan for the Middle East," trans. and ed. Israel Shahak (Boston: Association of Arab-American University Graduates, 1982), https://archive.org /details/TheZionistPlanForTheMiddleEast.

304. "Arabs Target London for Mideast Terror, Destabilization," *Executive Intelligence Review* 6, no. 30 (31 July 1979).

305. "Muslim Brotherhood: London's Shock Troops for the New Dark Ages," *Executive Intelligence Review* 6, no. 18 (8 May 1979); Edward Spannaus, "U.S. State Department Fingered LaRouche to Muslim Brotherhood," *Executive Intelligence Review* 22, no. 47 (24 November 1995).

306. Mark Burdman, "Balkanization Plan Gains Momentum," *Executive Intelligence Review* 7, no. 35 (9 September 1980); Joseph Brewda, "New Bernard Lewis Plan Will Carve Up the Mideast," *Executive Intelligence Review* 19, no. 43 (30 October 1992).

307. Manal Lutfi, "The Brotherhood and America," *Asharq al-Awsat,* part 5, 18 March 2007.

308. Azzam Hunaydi, head of the IAF, cited in Zahid, *Muslim Brotherhood,* 37.

309. Cited in Marc Lynch, "Young Brothers in Cyberspace," *Middle East Report* 245 (17 March 2007).

310. "Katatny: Dialogue between Islamists and the West a Necessity."

311. Brownlee, *Democracy Prevention,* 103–155; El-Anani, "Is 'Brotherhood' with America Possible?"; Dunne, "The Baby, the Bathwater."

312. *Al-Sharq al-Awsat* (Arabic), 19 November 2001.

313. Baker, *Islam without Fear.*

314. *Al-Sharq al-Awsat* (Arabic), 2 January 2007.

315. Letter, McGregor, AINAG, FCO to Banner et al, 17 January 2006.

316. Ibid.

317. "Engaging the Islamic World, International Priorities," Foreign and Commonwealth Office, archived page, http://bit.ly/2sPf9a1.

318. Since 2006, the Foreign Office has played a key role in Prevent as part of its "strategic priorities."

319. UK Government, Command Paper Cm: 6888, *Countering International Terrorism: The United Kingdom's Strategy* (July 2006).

320. For an analysis of this aspect, see Frank Gregory, "The UK's Domestic Response to Global Terrorism: Strategy, Structure and Implementation with Special Reference to the Role of the Police," *Real Instituto Elcano,* 18 June 2007.

321. UK Home Office, *"Preventing Extremism Together": Working Group Report* (August–October 2005).

322. For more on the Radical Middle Way (RMW), see Department for Communities and Local Government, *Preventing Violent Extremism: Winning Hearts and Minds* (April 2007); Command Paper Cm: 7099, *Foreign and Commonwealth Office, Departmental Report 1, April 2006—31 March 2007* (May 2007). See also Command Paper Cm: 6786, *Government Response to the Intelligence and Security Committee's Report into the London Terrorist Attacks on 7 July 2005* (May 2006).

323. UK Home Office, *"Preventing Extremism Together"*; "Subject: UK NGO Selection for Roadshow Project" (16 August 2005), Document 12 in Bright, *When Progressives Treat,* 74–75. On the Young Muslim Organisation (YMO), see Ed Husain, *The Islamist: Why I*

Joined Radical Islam in Britain, What I Saw Inside and Why I Left (London: Penguin, 2007), 19–66.

324. "Political Islam—REDACTED (Discussion on Projects)" (FCO memorandum in possession of author as result of Freedom of Information Request. The document is undated, but was clearly produced between July 2004 and August 2006).

325. Ibid. See also Command Paper Cm: 6786, *Government Response to the Intelligence and Security Committee's Report into the London Terrorist Attacks on 7 July 2005* (May 2006); and "Who's Who in the Umma: Leading Personalities in the Muslim World" (FCO document in possession of author as result of Freedom of Information Request).

326. See, for example, Anthony Browne, "The Triumph of the East," *Spectator*, 24 July 2004.

327. Letter, Ehrman to Omand, 23 April 2004.

328. Mockbul Ali (Islamic Issues Advisor, FCO) to Sawers, "Shaykh Yusuf al Qaradawi," 14 July 2005, copy in Bright, *When Progressives Treat*, 53–56.

329. Ibid.

330. "Memorandum Annex: Qaradawi Quotes," copy in Bright, *When Progressives Treat*, 57.

331. Robert Lambert, "Empowering Salafis and Islamists against Al-Qaeda: A London Counterterrorism Case Study," *Journal of Political Science and Politics* 41, no. 1 (2008), 31–35. See also Robert Lambert, *Countering Al-Qaeda in London: Police and Muslims in Partnership* (London: Hurst, 2011).

332. "Minutes of Evidence," Select Committee on Home Affairs, 13 September 2005, http://www.publications.parliament.uk/pa/cm200506/cmselect/cmhaff/462/5091309 .htm.

333. Command Paper Cm: 6786, *Government Response to the Intelligence and Security Committee's Report into the London Terrorist Attacks on 7 July 2005* (May 2006).

334. FCO documents in possession of author as result of Freedom of Information Request.

335. Ben Leapman, "£350,000 Trips to Boost the Image of British Muslims," *Daily Telegraph*, 10 December 2006.

336. Letter, McGregor, AINAG, FCO to Banner et al, 17 January 2006.

337. FCO documents in possession of author as result of Freedom of Information Request.

338. Ibid.

339. Ibid.

340. Hansard Online, Kim Howells, *Parliamentary Debates, House of Commons*, 12 May 2006, Column 627W, https://publications.parliament.uk/pa/cm200506/cmhansrd /vo060512/text/60512w0013.htm.

341. "About Conflicts Forum," Conflicts Forum, http://www.conflictsforum.org/about/; Glennie, *Building Bridges, Not Walls*.

342. Alastair Crooke, *Resistance: The Essence of the Islamist Revolution* (London: Pluto, 2009). See also "Should the West Dialogue with Islamists?" *Arches Quarterly* 4 (Winter 2004); James Harkin, "Middleman in the Middle East," *Financial Times*, 2 January 2009.

343. House of Commons Select Committee on Foreign Affairs, *Eighth Report*, 25 July 2007, http://www.publications.parliament.uk/pa/cm200607/cmselect/cmfaff/363 /36308.htm.

344. Abdulrahman Mansour, "Aboul-Fotouh: We Welcome Serious Dialogue for Our National Interests," Ikhwanweb, 15 August 2007, https://www.ikhwanweb.com/article.php ?id=13806.

345. Muslim Welfare House, *Annual Review 2001–2002* (copy in possession of the author); Hansard Online, Beverley Hughes Answer to Written Question from Paul Goodman, 19 September 2002, Column 72W, https://publications.parliament.uk/pa /cm200102/cmhansrd/vo020919/text/20919w18.htm.

346. "The Campaign so Far," *Inspire,* 28 September 2002.

347. Muslim Association of Britain, "Press Release," 13 April 2002 (copy in possession of the author).

348. Richard Phillips, "Standing Together: The Muslim Association of Britain and the Anti-war Movement," *Race and Class* 50, no. 2 (2008), 102–103.

349. "The Campaign so Far."

350. Phillips, "Standing Together," 103–104.

351. "'Million' March against Iraq War," BBC News Online, 16 February 2003, http: //news.bbc.co.uk/1/hi/uk/2765041.stm.

352. Sean O'Neill and Daniel McGrory, *The Suicide Factory: Abu Hamza and the Finsbury Park Mosque* (London: Harper Perennial, 2006), 90–92, 253–264.

353. Dominic Casciani and Sharif Sakr, "The Battle for the Mosque," BBC News Online, 7 February 2006, http://news.bbc.co.uk/1/hi/uk/4639074.stm.

354. "Home," North London Central Mosque Trust, http://www.nlcentralmosque.com /(last accessed 12 January 2014).

355. Peter Bergen and Paul Cruickshank, "The Unraveling," *New Republic,* 11 June 2008.

356. "Dr. Kim Howells visits the Muslim Welfare House (07/04/2006)," Foreign and Commonwealth Office, http://www.fco.gov.uk/resources/en/press-release/2006/04/fco _npr_300306_howellswelfarehse (last accessed 20 April 2014).

357. "New Era for North London Central Mosque," Press Release, 5 February 2005. See also Mahmud El-Shafey, "The New Face of Finsbury Park Mosque," *Asharq al-Awsat,* 12 April 2013.

358. MAB Press Release, Muslim Council of Britain website, http://www.mcb.org.uk /features/feature_print.php?ann_id=800 (last accessed 20 April 2014).

359. On el-Ashaal, see Alexander Meleagrou-Hitchens, "£48,000 Goes to the Muslim Brotherhood," *Standpoint,* 8 September 2009.

360. Lambert, "Empowering Salafis and Islamists"; Robert Lambert, "Salafi and Islamist Londoners: Stigmatised Minority Faith Communities Countering al-Qaida," *Arches Quarterly* 2, no. 1 (Summer 2008).

361. The MAB was granted four seats on the executive board of MINAB. See "Founders," Minab, http://www.minab.org.uk/news/61-about-us-sp-546/founders.html. See also Inayat Bunglawala, "Minab: Community Initiative, or Quango?" *Guardian: Comment is Free,* 15 May 2009, https://www.theguardian.com/commentisfree/belief/2009/may/15/minab -mosques-imams-islam.

362. Dean Godson, "David Cameron and Theresa May Are to Be Congratulated for Their Strategy on Tackling Islamist Extremism," *Conservative Home,* 7 June 2011, http://www.conservativehome.com/platform/2011/06/dean-godson-david-cameron-and -theresa-may-are-to-be-congratulated-for-their-strategy-on-tackling-isl.html.

363. Martin Bright, "Radical Links of UK's 'Moderate' Muslim Group," *Observer*, 14 August 2005; Martin Bright, "Losing the Plot," *New Statesman*, 30 January 2006; BBC *Panorama*, "A Question of Leadership," 21 August 2005—for a transcript, see "Programme transcript," BBC News Online, 21 August 2005, http://news.bbc.co.uk/1/hi/programmes /panorama/4171950.stm.

364. The crisis followed the publication of several cartoons deemed offensive to Islam by the newspaper *Jyllands-Posten*, though the furor only arose after some concerted lobbying by a group of Danish Imams who toured the Middle East to raise support for their cause and, in the process, falsified claims about what actually had been published and added additional offensive material.

365. Introduction to Gräf and Skovgaard-Peterson, *Global Mufti*, 8.

366. James Sturcke, "Police Launch Appeal over Cartoon Protest," *Guardian*, 25 April 2006.

367. Dean Godson, "Do We Have to Treat Muslims as Muslims?" *Times*, 19 July 2007; Vidino, *New Muslim Brotherhood*, 130–131.

368. For more on the evolution of this policy, see Martyn Frampton and Shiraz Maher, "Between 'Engagement' and a 'Values-Led' Approach: Britain and the Muslim Brotherhood from 9/11 to the Arab Spring," in *Western Governments and Political Islam after 2011*, ed. Lorenzo Vidino (Dubai: Al Mesbar, 2013); Vidino, *New Muslim Brotherhood*, 124–133.

369. Anas Altkriti, interview with the author, London, 3 May 2017.

370. Phillips, "Standing Together," 105–109.

371. Bowen, *Medina in Birmingham*, 110.

372. Anas Altkriti, interview with the author, London, 3 May 2017.

373. Phillips, "Standing Together," 105–109.

374. Anas Altikriti, "Live Dialogue," Islam Online, May 5, 2008.

375. Rich, "The Very Model," 125–126.

376. "Muslims for Ken," http://muslimsforken.blogspot.com/2008/04/evening-standard -scare-mongering-report.html (last accessed 12 December 2010).

377. Anas Altkriti, interview with the author, London, 3 May 2017.

378. See "Islam Expo," n.d., http://islamexpo.info/index.php?option=com_content&task =view&id=114&Itemid=163 (last accessed 12 December 2010).

379. "About the Organiser," for "Islam and Democracy: Exploring the Strategies of Political Islam and the Muslim Brotherhood's Contribution," Cordoba Foundation, 12 February 2015 (copy in possession of the author).

380. Anas Altikriti, "In Pursuit of the Common Ground," *Arches Journal* 4 (December 2006).

381. "Schedule" for "Islam and Democracy: Exploring the Strategies of Political Islam and the Muslim Brotherhood's Contribution," Cordoba Foundation, 12 February 2015 (copy in possession of the author).

382. *Cordoba Foundation: The MENA Report: Analysis and Insights from the Arab World* 1, no. 1 (January 2013).

383. Andrew Gilligan, "How the Muslim Brotherhood Fits into a Network of Extremism," *Daily Telegraph*, 8 February 2015.

384. UK Government, *Muslim Brotherhood Review*.

385. *Islamism Digest,* Introductory Issue, August 2006.

386. "Welcome," *Islamism Digest,* Introductory Issue, August 2006; see also *Al-Sharq al-Awsat* [Arabic], 2 January 2007.

387. "First Anniversary—An Interview with Dr. Kemal Helbawy," *Islamism Digest* 2, no. 4 (April 2007).

388. See, for example, A. Costello, " 'British Justice and the New McCarthyism': The Case of the Special Immigration Appeals Commission," *Islamism Digest* 2, no. 4 (April 2007); A. Costello, "The Hidden Agenda behind 'Stop and Quiz' Powers," *Islamism Digest* 2, no. 6 (June 2007); "Critiquing British Counter-Terrorism Policy: Interview with Dr. Farooq Bajwa," *Islamism Digest* 3, no. 2 (February 2008).

389. "Preventing Wagdy Ghoneim and Safwat Hegazy from entering Britain," Ikhwanweb, 6 May 2009, http://www.ikhwanweb.com/article.php?id=20075.

390. United States District Court Southern District of New York in re Terrorist Attacks on Civil Action No.: September 11, 2001, 03 MDL 1570 (RCC), Estate of John P. O'Neill, Sr. et al. v. Al Baraka Investment and Development Corp. et al., Civil Action No.: 04-CV-1923 (RCC); Kimi Yoshino, "To Avoid Visa Fight, Muslim Cleric to Leave," *Los Angeles Times,* 29 December 2004.

391. "Statement by the Brother Wagdi Ghuneim on Current Events," 18 November 2006, www.wagdyghoneim.com.

392. "The Wisdom of Sawalha," Harry's Place, 20 October 2009, http://hurryupharry .org/2009/10/20/the-wisdom-of-sawalha/.

393. B. Lazarus, " 'The Government Wants to Silence Muslims,' says Mohammed Kozbar, Chairman of Finsbury Park Mosque," *Islington Now,* 11 March 2015, http: //islingtonnow.co.uk/2015/03/11/the-government-eants-to-slience-muslims-says -chairman-of-finsbury-park-mosque/[last accessed 12 March 2015].

394. Vidino, *New Muslim Brotherhood,* 108.

395. "Muslims across Europe Unite against Extremism," MAB Press Release, 28 March 2008.

396. See "Tazahira fi Lundun tunaddid bi-qatal al-shirbini," al-jazeera.net, 7 December 2012, http://bit.ly/2uNocGE.

397. See, for example, the data sets collected by "Tell Mama," http://tellmamauk.org/.

398. Fred Halliday, " 'Islamophobia' Reconsidered," *Ethnic and Racial Studies* 22, no. 5 (1999), 892–2002; John Ware, "Inside the World of 'Non-Violent' Islamism," *Standpoint,* March 2015.

399. Jack Lefley, "The Battle of Kensington," *London Evening Standard,* 8 January 2009.

400. "Coalition of British Muslim Organisations Concerned with the Rights of the Palestinian People," MCB News, 6 February 2009, archived version, http: // bit.ly /2tOXNoW.

401. "Clerics Urge New Jihad over Gaza," BBC News Online, 17 February 2009, http: //news.bbc.co.uk/1/hi/world/middle_east/7895485.stm; "Bayan mu'atamar 'ghazat al-nasr' yanus 'ala tahrim i'adat intikhab arkan al-sulta al-filistiniyya," al-Moslim.net, 15 February 2009, http://www.almoslim.net/node/107077.

402. Jamie Doward, "British Muslim Leader Urged to Quit over Gaza," *Observer,* 8 March 2009; Bowen, *Medina in Birmingham,* 93.

403. "Gala in London in Support of the al-Aqsa Calls to Help the Guardians of the Boundaries Protect Jerusalem," Muslim World News, 26 March 2010; "Mahrajan bi-Lundun li-nasrat al-Quds," al-Jazeera.net, 22 March 2010, http://bit.ly/2tkktFS.

404. See, for example, David Cameron, "Speech to the Munich Security Conference," 5 February 2011, https://www.gov.uk/government/speeches/pms-speech-at-munich-secu rity-conference.

405. UK Government, Command Paper Cm: 9148, *Counter-Extremism Strategy* (October 2015), https://www.gov.uk/government/uploads/system/uploads/attachment _data/file/470088/51859_Cm9148_Accessible.pdf.

406. Department of Homeland Security, *Empowering Local Partners to Prevent Violent Extremism in the United States* (August 2011), https://www.dhs.gov/sites/default/files /publications/empowering_local_partners.pdf.

407. Merley, "Federation of Islamic Organizations in Europe."

408. Jason Trahan, "Muslim Brotherhood's Papers Detail Plan to Seize U.S.," *Dallas Morning News,* 17 September 2007.

409. Vidino, *New Muslim Brotherhood,* 196–197.

410. Neil Munro, "Report: Islamist Radicals Find Warm Welcome in Obama White House," *Daily Caller,* 22 October 2012, http://dailycaller.com/2012/10/22/report-islamist -radicals-find-warm-welcome-in-obama-white-house/.

411. Dave Boyer, "Obama Quietly Hands Out Names of Muslim Leaders He Met with Privately," *Washington Times,* 6 February 2015.

412. "Secretary Condoleezza Rice: Question and Answer at the American University in Cairo," US State Department, 20 June 2005, http://2001-2009.state.gov/secretary/rm /2005/48352.htm.

413. Gray, Embassy Cairo to State Department, "The GOE and the Muslim Brother-hood: Anatomy of a Showdown," 17 May 2005, Wikileaks.

414. Sharp, *U.S. Democracy Promotion,* 20–24.

415. Jones, Embassy Cairo to State Department, "Egyptian Muslim Brotherhood: Su-preme Guide and Parliamentary Bloc Dynamics," 19 October 2006, Wikileaks.

416. Ian Johnson, "Washington's Secret History with the Muslim Brotherhood," *New York Review of Books Blog,* 5 February 2011, http://www.nybooks.com/blogs/nyrblog/2011 /feb/05/washingtons-secret-history-muslim-brotherhood/; Ian Johnson, "The CIA's Is-lamist Cover Up," *New York Review of Books Blog,* 30 August 2011, http://www.nybooks .com/blogs/nyrblog/2011/aug/30/cia-islamist-cover-up/. See also Eli Lake, "Administration Weighs Reaching Out to Muslim Brotherhood," *New York Sun,* 20 June 2007.

417. Ricciardone, Embassy Cairo to State Department, "Contact with Muslim Broth-erhood Parliamentary Leader," 20 March 2007, Wikileaks.

418. Al-Saeed al-Abbadi, "MB Is Not Opposed to Dialogue with US despite Reserva-tions," Ikhwanweb, 9 April 2007, http://www.ikhwanweb.com/article.php?id=1880.

419. As referred to in Ricciardone, Embassy Cairo to State Department, 17 July 2007, Wikileaks. See also ICG, *Egypt's Muslim Brothers,* 5.

420. Al-Abbadi, "MB Is Not Opposed."

421. "U.S. Engages Muslim Brotherhood despite Rice; Relations with Mubarak's Gov-ernment Could Be Strained," *Washington Times,* 15 November 2007. For an example of the speculation during this period, see Eli Lake, "Bush Weighs Reaching Out to 'Brothers,'" *New York Sun,* 20 June 2007.

422. Margaret Scobey (Ambassador), Embassy Cairo to State Department, "Dinner with Parliament's Foreign Relations Committee, Including Two Muslim Brotherhood MPs," 23 February 2009, Wikileaks; also Scobey, Embassy Cairo to State Department, "MB Parliamentary Leader on Increased GOE Pre-Election Pressure," Cairo to Washington, 3 August 2009, Wikileaks.

423. "Interview with MB Deputy Chairman in Al Ahrar Daily," Ikhwanweb, 6 June 2008, http://www.ikhwanweb.com/article.php?ID=17267&LevelID=1&SectionID=0.

424. "Muslim Brotherhood Supreme Guide: Bin Laden is a Jihad Fighter," MEMRI Special Dispatch, No. 2001, 25 July 2008, https://www.memri.org/reports/muslim-brother hood-supreme-guide-bin-laden-jihad-fighter. See also Manal Lutfi, "The Brotherhood and America," *Asharq al-Awsat,* part 5, 18 March 2007.

425. Embassy Cairo to State Department, 15 April 2010, Wikileaks.

426. Ricciardone, Embassy Cairo to State Department, "Election Platform of the Muslim Brotherhood: Political Crisis," 11 July 2007, Wikileaks; Ricciardone, Embassy Cairo to State Department, "Muslim Brotherhood: Draft Party Platform Highlights Internal Fissures," 24 October 2007, Wikileaks. For more on the platform, see "Munaqashat al-qira al-ula li-barnamaj hizb al-Ikhwan fi Lundun," Ikhwan Online, 30 October 2007, http://www.ikhwanonline.com/Article.aspx?ArtID=31766&SecID=211.

427. Nathan J. Brown and Amr Hamzawy, *The Draft Party Platform of the Egyptian Muslim Brotherhood: Foray into Political Integration or Retreat into Old Positions?* Carnegie Papers, Middle East Series, No. 89 (Washington, DC.: Carnegie Endowment for International Peace, January 2008). For internal criticism of the platform, see also Lynch, "Young Brothers in Cyberspace"; and Khalil el-Anani, "Brotherhood Bloggers: A New Generation Voices Dissent," *Arab Insight* 2, no. 1 (2008), 29–38.

428. Michael Corbin (Counselor), Embassy Cairo to State Department, "Egypt's Muslim Brotherhood: Internal Coup Reports, Key Leader Disciplined and, Strange Alliance Formed," 10 July 2005, Wikileaks.

429. Attempts to define internal factions within the Brotherhood have also been made by scholars. See, for example, Lynch, "Young Brothers in Cyberspace."

430. Ricciardone, Embassy Cairo to State Department, "The Schizophrenia of the Egyptian Muslim Brotherhood," 20 March 2008, Wikileaks. For more on this "organizational schizophrenia" and the attendant "power struggles," see also Scobey, Embassy Cairo to State Department, "Muslim Brotherhood Elections: Some Internal Reshuffling," 24 June 2008, Wikileaks.

431. See, for example, Scobey, Embassy Cairo to State Department, "Muslim Brotherhood's Party Platform Indefinitely on Hold," 17 February 2009, Wikileaks; Scobey, Embassy Cairo to State Department, "Reports of Divisions within the MB following the Death of a Guidance Bureau Member; Arrests Update," 1 October 2009, Wikileaks; and Scobey, Embassy Cairo to State Department, "Update on Reports of Divisions within the Muslim Brotherhood," 21 October 2009, Wikileaks.

432. Ricciardone, Embassy Cairo to State Department, "The Schizophrenia of the Egyptian Muslim Brotherhood," 20 March 2008, Wikileaks.

433. See, for example, Scobey, Embassy Cairo to State Department, "MB Internal Clashes Continue," 15 December 2009, Wikileaks.

434. Muhammad Hamida, "Ta'yin Muhammad Badi'e Murshidan lil-Ikhwan Al-Muslimin fi Misr," Elaph.com, 16 January 2010, http://www.elaph.com/Web/news/2010

/1/524249.html. See also Marc Lynch, "Conservative Gains in Muslim Brotherhood Elections," *Foreign Policy,* 21 December 2009; El-Anani, "A Different Game for the MB"; Kandil, *Inside the Brotherhood,* 33–34.

435. Scobey, Embassy Cairo to State Department, "Egypt: New MB Supreme Guide Named," 21 January 2010, Wikileaks.

436. Scobey, Embassy Cairo to State Department, "MB Internal Clashes Continue," 15 December 2009, Wikileaks.

437. Fernandez, Embassy Khartoum to State Department, "There Are Neither Moderates nor Hardliners in the NCP," 18 March 2008, Wikileaks.

438. Hale, Embassy Amman to State Department, "Muslim Brotherhood Election Strategy Put to the Test," 19 November 2007, Wikileaks.

439. Hale, Embassy Amman to State Department, "Jordan's Islamists Battling over the Future of the Movement," 17 January 2008, Wikileaks.

440. Al-Arian, *Answering the Call,* 224–226.

441. Yusuf al-Qaradawi, *Al-Ikhwan al-Muslimun: 70 'aman fi al-da'wa wa-l-tarbiya wa-l-jihad,* 2nd ed. (Beirut: Mu'assasat al-Risala, 2001), 256–276.

442. Ibid., 278–280. In making his point on the Christians, al-Qaradawi pointed to the presence of Copts on the political committee of the Brotherhood under al-Banna and the latter's friendship with Coptic leaders, such as Louis Fanus and Makram 'Ubayd (the latter, famously, the only high-profile politician to attend al-Banna's funeral). According to al-Qaradawi, the Brotherhood's creator had dismissed the notion of the jizya as no longer applicable in an age of modern citizenship.

443. Mashhur, *Tariq al-Da'wa,* 384.

444. "Secularism vs. Islam by Dr. Yusuf al-Qaradawi: An extract from *Al-Hulul al-Mustawradah wa Kayfa Jaat 'alaa ummatina,*" Islamicweb.com, http://islamicweb.com /beliefs/cults/Secularism.htm.

445. Matthew H. Tueller (Deputy Chief of Mission), Embassy Kuwait City to State Department, "Islamic Affairs Ministry Campaigns to Spread Islamic Moderation," 18 October 2006, Wikileaks; Powers, Embassy Khartoum to State Department, " 'Now Is the Time,' Turabi tells Williamson," 4 June 2008, Wikileaks.

446. Barack Obama, "Remarks at Cairo University," 4 June 2009, https://www.white house.gov/the-press-office/remarks-president-cairo-university-6-04–09.

447. David Ignatius, "A Cosmic Wager on the Muslim Brotherhood," *Washington Post,* 15 February 2012. See also Steven Brooke, "U.S. Policy and the Muslim Brotherhood," in *The West and the Muslim Brotherhood after the Arab Spring,* ed. Lorenzo Vidino (Philadelphia: Al Mesbar Studies and Research Centre and the Foreign Policy Research Institute, 2013), 25–26.

448. Avi Issacharoff and Zvi Bar'el, "Obama Met Muslim Brotherhood Members in US," *Haaretz,* 4 June 2009.

449. Robert S. Beecroft (Ambassador), Embassy Amman to State Department, "Reengaging with Jordan's Islamists," 10 September 2009, Wikileaks; Beecroft, Embassy Amman to State Department, "Jordan: Political Engagement Furthers Cairo Speech Goals," 18 November 2009, Wikileaks.

450. Beecroft, Embassy Amman to State Department, "Jordan's Islamists Send Congratulatory Letter to President, Call for New Dialogue and Change from Both Sides," 22 January 2009, Wikileaks; Beecroft, Embassy Amman to State Department, "Islamist

Figure Sparks Debate over Engaging the U.S.," 16 March 2009, Wikileaks; Lawrence Mandel (Charge d'Affaires), Embassy Amman to State Department, "Jordan: Dinner Party Results in Unexpected Meeting with Islamist Politicians," 4 August 2009, Wikileaks.

451. Beecroft, Embassy Amman to State Department, "Jordanian Islamists Talk about Cairo Speech, Electoral Politics, Engagement," 19 August 2009, Wikileaks.

452. Beecroft, Embassy Amman to State Department, "Re-engaging with Jordan's Islamists," 10 September 2009, Wikileaks.

453. Mansoor Moaddel, *Islamic Modernism, Nationalism, and Fundamentalism: Episode and Discourse* (Chicago: University of Chicago Press: 2005), 315–319.

454. For an excellent overview of this, see Trager, "Trapped and Untrapped," 184–192.

455. For examples see Gray, Embassy Cairo to State Department, "Arrest of Senior Muslim Brotherhood Official Further Escalates 'Showdown' with GOE," 24 May 2005, Wikileaks; Gray, Embassy Cairo to State Department, "Update on the GOE-Muslim Brotherhood Stand Off," 16 June 2005, Wikileaks; Jones, Embassy Cairo to State Department, "More Arrests: Government-Muslim Brotherhood Tensions Ratcheted Up," 18 December 2006, Wikileaks; Embassy Cairo to State Department, "Muslim Brotherhood Announces Intent to Form Political Party; Arrests Continue," 18 January 2007, Wikileaks; Ricciardone, Embassy Cairo to State Department, "Responding to Egypt's Crackdown on the Muslim Brotherhood," 30 April 2007, Wikileaks. More broadly on the Brotherhood's trajectory in this period, see Samer Shehata and Joshua Stacher, "The Muslim Brothers in Mubarak's Last Decade," in Jeannie Sowers and Chris Toensing, *The Journey to Tahrir: Revolution, Protest, and Social Change in Egypt* (London: Verso, 2012), 160–177.

456. Jason Brownlee, "A New Generation of Autocracy in Egypt," *Brown Journal of World Affairs* 14, no. 1 (Fall / Winter 2007), 73–85; Louay Abdulbaki, "Democracy and the Re-consolidation of Authoritarian Rule in Egypt," *Contemporary Arab Affairs* 1, no. 3 (July 2008), 445–463; Mohammed Zahid, "Egyptian Reforms Post-2005 and the Politics of Succession: Implications and Consequences for the Future Egyptian Reform Process," *Contemporary Arab Affairs* 1, no. 3 (July 2008), 375–389.

457. Ricciardone, Embassy Cairo to State Department, "Muslim Brotherhood: Government Crackdown continues, Party Platform Still in Draft," 30 August 2007, Wikileaks.

458. Ricciardone, Embassy Cairo to State Department, "Muslim Brotherhood Military Tribunal Issues Verdicts," 16 April 2008, Wikileaks. For a good overview, see ICG, *Egypt's Muslim Brothers;* also, Yaroslav Trofimov, "Muslim Brotherhood Falters as Egypt Outflanks Islamists," *Wall Street Journal,* 15 May 2009.

459. Mshari al-Zaydi, "Let's Welcome the Muslim Brotherhood!" *Asharq al-Awsat,* 9 July 2009, http://english.aawsat.com/2009/07/article55254324/lets-welcome-the-muslim -brotherhood; see also Tueller, Embassy Cairo to State Department, "Ramping Up Pressure on the Muslim Brotherhood in Egypt: Recent Arrests," 30 July 2009, Wikileaks; Scobey, Embassy Cairo to State Department, "Reports of Divisions within the MB following the Death of a Guidance Bureau Member; Arrests Update," 1 October 2009, Wikileaks. For more on this case, see extensive coverage in *Al-Masry Al-Yom* (Egypt), 24 April 2010.

460. Scobey, Embassy Cairo to State Department, "MB Parliamentary Leader on Increased GOE Pre-Election Pressure," 3 August 2009, Wikileaks. In the aftermath of the 2011 revolution, all charges associated with this case were dropped.

461. It is this strategy that explains the post-2005 emergence of various efforts by senior Brotherhood figures to court international opinion.

462. Scobey, Embassy Cairo to State Department, "Egyptian Islamist Meets with Staffdel Hogrefe," 3 September 2009, Wikileaks.

463. For reference to discussions with al-Katatni, see, for example: Scobey, Embassy Cairo to State Department, "Update on Reports of Divisions within the Muslim Brotherhood," 21 October 2009, Wikileaks; and Scobey, Embassy Cairo to State Department, "Egypt: New Round of MB Arrests," 11 February 2010, Wikileaks.

464. Gamal Heshmat, "'Islam Online': Al-hiwar ma' jubih 'al-rasmi' la buda an yatim bi-'ilm al-hakuma al-misriyya," al-behira.com, 24 April 2011, http://www.elbehira.net /elbehira/nd_shnws.php?shart=13895.

465. Brownlee, *Democracy Prevention,* 69–97.

466. On Mubarak's moves to secure the succession, see ICG, *Egypt's Muslim Brothers;* Zahid, *Muslim Brotherhood,* 130–145.

467. Brownlee, *Democracy Prevention,* 103–155; el-Anani, "Is 'Brotherhood' with America Possible?"

468. Nada, *Inside the Muslim Brotherhood,* 153.

469. Magdi Abdelhadi, "Muslim Brotherhood Expands Westward," BBC News Online, 22 August 2010, http://www.bbc.co.uk/news/world-middle-east-11060348.

470. Marechal, *Muslim Brothers in Europe,* 4, 70–71, 185, 204–217.

471. Vidino, *New Muslim Brotherhood,* 69–72; Marechal, *Muslim Brothers in Europe,* 186, 226–243, 304–305.

472. For those in the West, see Klausen, *Islamic Challenge,* 6; for the Arab Brotherhood, see Pargeter, *Muslim Brotherhood;* Wickham, *Muslim Brotherhood.*

473. Kepel, *Allah in the West,* 202–203.

474. Marechal, *Muslim Brothers in Europe,* 34, 77.

475. Gerges, *America and Political Islam,* 108–114. See also do Céu Pinto, *Political Islam,* 263–267.

Conclusion

1. For a useful discussion of this phenomenon, contrast the work of Ian Buruma and Avishai Margalit with that of Robbert Woltering. See Ian Buruma and Avishai Margalit, *Occidentalism: A Short History of Anti-Westernism* (London: Atlantic, 2004); Robbert Woltering, *Occidentalisms in the Arab World: Ideology and Images of the West in the Egyptian Media* (London: I. B. Tauris, 2011).

2. Jacques Waardenburg, "Reflections on the West," in Suha Taji-Farouki and Basheer M. Nafi, *Islamic Thought in the Twentieth Century* (London: I. B. Tauris, 2004), 260–295, especially 267–268, 270–272. See also Abdul-Wahab S. Babeair, "Contemporary Islamic Revivalism: A Movement or a Moment?" *Journal of Arab Affairs* 9, no. 2 (1990), 122–146.

3. On this point about authenticity, see Richard P. Mitchell, "The Islamic Movement: Its Current Condition and Future Prospects," in *The Islamic Impulse,* ed. Barbara Freyer Stowasser (Washington, DC: Center for Contemporary Arab Studies, Georgetown University, 1987), 75–86.

4. On this point, see Bruce Lawrence, "Muslim Fundamentalist Movements: Reflections toward a New Approach," in Stowasser, *Islamic Impulse,* 15–36 (32).

5. Mansoor Moaddel, *Islamic Modernism, Nationalism, and Fundamentalism: Episode and Discourse* (Chicago: University of Chicago Press: 2005), 198, 210–214. For more on the modernity of the Brotherhood, see Sami Zubaida, *Islam: The People and State* (London: Routledge, 1988), 38–50; Salwa Ismail, *Rethinking Islamist Politics: Culture, the State and Islamism* (London: I. B. Tauris, 2006), 2–3; Mehdi Mozaffari, "What Is Islamism? History and Definition of a Concept," in *Totalitarian Movements and Political Religions* 8, no. 1 (March 2007), 17–33; Saba Mahmood, *Politics of Piety: the Islamic Revival and the Feminist Subject* (Oxford: Princeton University Press, 2005), 192–194.

6. On the "liminal" character of Egypt during this period, see Lucie Ryzova, *The Age of the Efendiyya: Passages to Modernity in National-Colonial Egypt* (Oxford: Oxford University Press, 2014); Hilary Kalmbach, "Blurring Boundaries: Aesthetics, Performance, and the Transformation of Islamic Leadership," *Culture and Religion* 16, no. 2 (2015), 160–174.

7. Manfred Halpern, *The Politics of Social Change in the Middle East and North Africa* (Princeton, NJ: Princeton University Press, 1963), vii–viii, 25–30, 48, 119–150, 291.

8. Christina Phelps Harris, *Nationalism and Revolution in Egypt: The Role of the Muslim Brotherhood in Egypt* (The Hague, Netherlands: Mouton, 1964); Richard P. Mitchell, *The Society of the Muslim Brothers* (Oxford: Oxford University Press, 1993).

9. See, for example, Muhammad Abdallah al-Samman, *Ayam ma' al-shahid Hasan al-Banna* (Cairo: Dar al-Fadila, 2003), 22.

10. Kepel uses the term "neo-Muslim Brethren"; see Gilles Kepel, *The Roots of Radical Islam* (London: Saqi Books, 2005), 109. On the centrality to the Brotherhood of the idea of a confrontation with the monolithic Western "other," see Salwa Ismail, "Confronting the Other: Identity, Culture, Politics and Conservative Islamism in Egypt," *International Journal of Middle East Studies* 30, no. 2 (1998), 199–225.

11. "Al-Ikhwan al-Muslimun wa nazrathum ila al-gharb," Ikhwanwiki, http://bit.ly/1ylPhn5. Similarly, in an interview, former Brotherhood spokesperson Mona al-Qazzaz confirmed that Palestine was critical to how the Brotherhood viewed the West. Interview with the author, Cambridge, 18 April 2014. It is an analysis with which Kemal el-Helbawy would agree: Interview with the author, Cairo, 4 December 2014.

12. Al-Samman, *Ayam,* 30–31; Mahmud 'Abd al-Halim, *Al-Ikhwan al-Muslimun III: Ahdath sana'at al-tarikh: ru'yah min al-dakhil, al-juz' al-thalith* (Alexandria, Egypt: Dar al-Da'wa, 1981), 167.

13. For a broader discussion of the Brotherhood's ideological continuity, see Hazem Kandil, *Inside the Brotherhood* (Cambridge, UK: Polity Press, 2015); Mariz Tadros, *The Muslim Brotherhood in Contemporary Egypt: Democracy Redefined or Confined?* (London: Routledge, 2012), especially 47–68, 76–82, 98–114.

14. Kandil, *Inside the Brotherhood,* 53–58.

15. Abdullah al-Haddad, interview with the author, London, 6 May 2015. I am grateful to Dr. Robert Saunders, for his thoughts on this issue. He postulates that the myth is rooted in the prime minister's well-known Christianity, as well as his hostility to Turkey. Further, he notes that, in actual fact, Gladstone's views on Islam were likely fairly conventional for the period: he regarded it as a false religion but as preferable to Hinduism, and chiefly of historical interest.

16. Hussein al-Shafi'i, *Shahid 'ala thulathat 'asur,* 2nd ed. (Cairo: Maktabat Madbula al-Shaghir, 2000), 48, 64. More broadly, see Arndt Graf et al., *Orientalism and Conspiracy, Politics and Conspiracy Theory in the Islamic World: Essays in Honour of Sadik J. Al-Azm*

(London: I. B. Tauris, 2011); Daniel Pipes, *The Hidden Hand: Middle East Fears of Conspiracy* (Basingstoke, UK: Macmillan, 1996).

17. Al-Samman, *Ayam,* 19–20.

18. Brigitte Marechal, *The Muslim Brothers in Europe: Roots and Discourse* (Leiden, Netherlands: Brill, 2008), 244.

19. On this issue, see also Waardenburg, "Reflections on the West."

20. Al-Samman, *Ayam,* 100, 116.

21. Yusuf al-Qaradawi, *Al-Ikhwan al-Muslimun: 70 ʿaman fi al-daʿwa wa-l-tarbiya wa-l-jihad,* 2nd ed. (Beirut: Muʾassasat al-Risala, 2001), 256.

22. Robert F. Holland, *The Pursuit of Greatness: Britain and the World Role, 1900–1970* (London: HarperCollins, 1991), 40.

23. John Bew, "Pax Anglo-Saxonica," *American Interest* 10, no. 5 (9 April 2015).

24. On the notion of a "global system of power," see John Darwin, *Britain and Decolonisation: The Retreat from the Empire in the Post-War World* (Basingstoke, UK: Macmillan Education, 1988), 1–33. On the British emphasis on naval, as opposed to land military power, see David Dilks, "The British Foreign Office between the Wars," in *Shadow and Substance in British Foreign Policy, 1895–1939: Memorial Essays Honouring C. J. Lowe,* ed. Brian J. C McKercher and David J. Moss (Edmonton: University of Alberta Press, 1984), 181–202 (184); C. J. Lowe, *The Reluctant Imperialists: British Foreign Policy 1878–1902* (London: Routledge and Kegan Paul, 1967), 5–6.

25. William Roger Louis and Ronald Robinson, "The Imperialism of Decolonization," *Journal of Imperial and Commonwealth History* 22, no. 3 (1994), 462–511 (462–467); Glen Balfour-Paul, "Britain's Informal Empire in the Middle East," in *The Oxford History of the British Empire: Volume IV: The Twentieth Century,* ed. Judith Brown and William Roger Louis (Oxford: Oxford University Press), 490–514; P. J. Cain and A. G. Hopkins, *British Imperialism, 1688–2000,* 2nd ed. (Harlow, UK: Longman, 2001), 26–28.

26. John Darwin, "Britain's Empires," in *The British Empire: Themes and Perspectives,* ed. Sarah Stockwell (Oxford: Oxford University Press, 2008), 17; William Roger Louis, "The Dissolution of the British Empire," in Brown and Louis, *Oxford History of the British Empire,* 329–355. See also Elie Kedourie, "Britain, France, and the Last Phase of the Eastern Question," in *Soviet-American Rivalry in the Middle East,* ed. Jacob Hurewitz (New York: Frederick A. Praeger, 1969), 189–197; Robert F. Holland, *Britain and the Revolt in Cyprus, 1954–9* (Oxford: Clarendon, 1998).

27. Martin Thomas, *Empires of Intelligence: Security Services and Colonial Disorder after 1914* (London: University of California Press, 2008), 9–11, 293–303. See also Chris Bayly, *Empire and Information Intelligence Gathering and Social Communication in India, 1780–1870* (Cambridge: Cambridge University Press, 1996).

28. Melvyn P. Leffler, *A Preponderance of Power: National Security, the Truman Administration, and the Cold War* (Stanford, CA: Stanford University Press, 1992).

29. John Darwin, "The Fear of Falling: British Politics and Imperial Decline since 1900," *Transactions of the Royal Historical Society* 36 (1986), 27–43 (28–29). See also Darwin, *Britain and Decolonisation,* 25–33.

30. Phillip Darby, *Three Faces of Imperialism: British and American Approaches to Asia and Africa, 1870–1970* (London: Yale University Press, 1–6, 213–221. See also John Darwin, "An Undeclared Empire: The British in the Middle East," *Journal of Imperial and Commonwealth History* 27, no. 2 (2008), 159–176 (170).

31. Babeair, "Contemporary Islamic Revivalism."

32. Frédéric Volpi, "Postface: Islamism Is Dead, Long Live Islamism," in *Whatever Happened to the Islamists? Salafis, Heavy Metal Muslims and the Lure of Consumerist Islam,* ed. Olivier Roy and Amel Boubekeur (London: Hurst, 2012), 247–253. See also in the same volume, Amel Boubekeur and Olivier Roy, introduction, 1–13.

33. Joel Beinin and Joe Stork, "On the Modernity, Historical Specificity, and International Context of Political Islam," in *Political Islam: Essays from Middle East Report,* ed. Joel Beinin and Joe Stork (London: I. B. Tauris, 1997), 10–20.

34. Brownlee, *Democracy Prevention,* 10–11.

35. Khaled Fahmy, "The Muslim Brotherhood and the West," *al-Ahram Online,* 3 September 2013, http://english.ahram.org.eg/NewsContentP/4/80655/Opinion/-The-Muslim-Brotherhood-and-the-West.aspx.

Acknowledgments

This book was several years in the writing—and along the way I have been fortunate to benefit from the help and insights of a great many people. I am grateful to the United Kingdom's Arts and Humanities Research Council, which awarded me an Early Career Leadership Fellowship for 2014–2015 and thereby made possible key parts of the research. Similarly, thanks to the John W. Kluge Center at the Library of Congress for hosting me in the spring of 2014 and allowing me to make use of the wealth of material there. My sincere gratitude also to the staff and supporters of the Hoover Institution, Stanford University; the Middle East Centre Archive at St. Antony's College, Oxford (in particular, Debbie Usher); Dar al-Kutub, Cairo; the British Library, London; the United Kingdom National Archives at Kew, London; and the United States National Archives at College Park, Maryland.

My thanks, too, to Professor Julian Jackson and all of my colleagues—both academic and professional services—at the School of History, Queen Mary University of London, for creating an environment so conducive to research. I am fortunate to work in a place that encourages academic innovation, and found both practical and moral support at every stage in embarking on what was, initially at least, new and challenging subject matter.

I would also like to express my appreciation to those individuals who agreed to be interviewed for this project (some more than once), including Kemal el-Helbawy, Abdullah al-Haddad, Anas Altikriti, Dr. Abdullah Faliq, and Mona al-Qazzaz. Likewise, I am most grateful for the support of my editors, Ian Malcolm and Kate Brick, as well as Melody Negron and her first-class production team at Westchester Publishing Services.

I first became interested in the subject that informed this book more than a decade ago, while in the employ of Dr. Dean Godson of Policy Exchange. As anyone who knows him can testify, Dean is a force of nature who never ceases to amaze those of us lucky enough to enter his slipstream with his erudition and originality. I am equally deeply indebted to Udi Rosen—a truly outstanding Arabist who has forgotten more about the Brotherhood than most of us will ever learn. My conversations with him led directly to this project—and I am grateful for his generosity of intellect and spirit. Similar thanks go also to Lily Amior, Hannah Stuart, and Julia Mizen.

I have benefited from two world-class teachers of Arabic: Samir Jabal in London and the inimitable Rif'at Amin in Cairo. It is of lasting regret to me that Rif'at did not live to see the completion of this book. He was a remarkable man; no one who knew him could doubt either his passion for teaching or his love for Nasser! Rif'at was part of an amazing team at the Kalimat Language and Culture Centre of Cairo, which continues to enthuse and instruct students from around the world.

During repeated trips to Egypt, I met, befriended, and learned from a huge number of people who helped me both navigate life there and better understand my subject. My thanks to two outstanding young scholars, Raphael Cormack and Hussein Omar Hussein, as well as to Dr. Hisham Hellyer, Marwa Sabah, Basil el-Dabh, Ghaly Shafik, Amr A. Saleh, and Patricia Kubala.

My thinking on these issues has been enriched further by discussions with many people, among them Dr. Hazem Kandil, Dr. Yossi Rapoport, Sir John Jenkins, Professor Khaled Fahmy, Dr. Eric Trager, Dr. Barbara Zollner, Professor Nathan Brown, Dr. Khalil el-Anani, Professor Yvonne Haddad, Professor Richard Bourke, Dr. James Ellison, Patrick Higgins, Alison Pargeter, Professor Beth Baron, Professor Carrie Wickham, Dr. Aaron Jakes, Dr. James Baldwin, Amna Fairouz, Hany Fairouz, Dr. Julius Dihstelhoff, Aziz el-Kaissouni, Ryan Evans, Gary Schmitt, Iñigo Gurruchaga, Professor Paul Bew, and Justice Sir Stephen Irwin. I am sure there are others who I have forgotten; I hope they will forgive this oversight. But I would say one special word for two good friends who died in the latter stages of the project: Stephen Hayward and the incomparable Sean O'Callaghan. They are both much missed.

I would especially like to thank Dr. Alexander Meleagrou-Hitchens, Dr. Shiraz Maher, and Professor John Bew for their friendship and counsel—not to mention their insights and expertise—throughout the last decade. John is the most gifted historian of his generation, yet wears his genius lightly; it is a privilege to have him as a regular confidant and collaborator.

Last, but by no means least, I must mention my family. I am lucky to have two wonderful parents—Ros and Dennis—whose sacrifices and hard work gave me the opportunities to pursue the career I wanted. Anything I achieve is a testament to their efforts and support; and likewise that of my brilliant sister, Emma. Since 2009, I have been doubly fortunate to have gained a second set of ideal "parents," courtesy of my wife, Rose. The Dougall clan—Neil, Geraldine, Callum, Patrick, and Kate—have not only made me feel at home but also repeatedly sacrificed their front room so I could have an office in which to work! I hope the end result justifies my long hours in solitary confinement.

Finally, to those closest to me, thank you. In July 2014, Rose and I were married; in August, I went to live in Cairo for six months. This fact alone speaks volumes about the extraordinary patience and support I have been afforded by my wife. She has endured my trips away with limitless good humor—so too the countless weekends and evenings where I was locked away in my office. I cannot thank her enough. This book is dedicated to her—in some small measure of recompense—and it is also dedicated to our beautiful son, Dylan, who joined us last year. No one could wish for a more encouraging and loving family.

It remains only to say that if, in spite all of the assistance I have received, any errors linger in the text, the responsibility is mine alone.

Index